P9-ELH-639

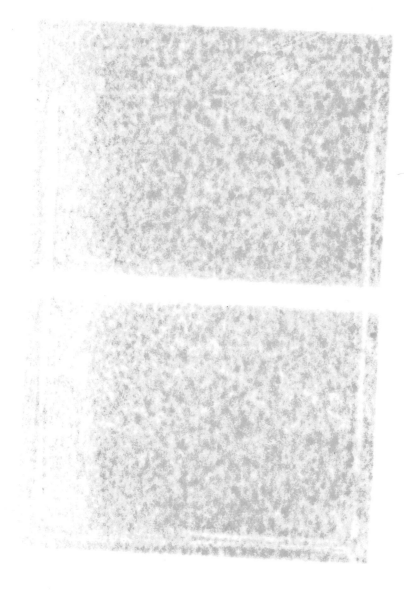

The Westminster
DICTIONARY
of **CHRISTIAN**
EDUCATION

The Westminster
DICTIONARY
of CHRISTIAN
EDUCATION

Edited by
Kendig Brubaker Cully

THE WESTMINSTER PRESS / *Philadelphia*

PUBLISHED BY THE WESTMINSTER PRESS ®

PHILADELPHIA 7, PENNSYLVANIA

PRINTED IN THE UNITED STATES OF AMERICA

PREFACE

Although a number of encyclopedic reference works covering the Biblical, theological, and historical fields have been projected or published in recent years, not until now has a comprehensive work with religious education as its primary focus been published. In this volume there is substantial treatment of most of the subject headings that have a bearing on the educational task of the Christian church.

In order to assure a measure of creative vitality in the presentation of these materials, each writer was invited to develop his assigned subject according to his own understanding. The editor is immeasurably grateful to the large number of persons, each having an authoritative word to speak in his field, who accepted the invitation to write for the DICTIONARY. It will be observed that the writers come from many ecclesiastical backgrounds. Many write out of technical competence in fields other than religious education per se but which have a bearing on it.

Perhaps a word is in order as to how THE WESTMINSTER DICTIONARY OF CHRISTIAN EDUCATION developed. One day when I was looking through a copy of the three-volume *Encyclopedia of Sunday Schools and Religious Education* (Thomas Nelson & Sons, 1915), consigned to one of the dustier and remoter sections of the seminary library, it occurred to me that certainly we needed a new large work setting forth the whole complex of concerns and interests of mid-twentieth-century Christian education. Surely such a work would have a ready audience among scholars, seminary students and professors, directors of Christian education, pastors, lay church school workers, educators in the schools, as well as a place on the reference shelves of every library! After arrangements had been completed with The Westminster Press for the preparation of the DICTIONARY, the first step was to invite a small group of knowledgeable persons to a consultation on the scope and nature of the work. On November 18 and 19, 1960, these colleagues met with me at Mohonk Lake, N.Y., for much brainstorming and considerable conversation, which made the occasion memorable for us all: Iris V. Cully, Margaret A. J. Irvin, Carl Ellis Nelson, Everett M. Stowe, Roland W. Tapp, and Eugene B. Wenger. Although these initial advisers cannot in any sense be held responsible for the eventual categories covered in this work, their gracious help and encouragement spurred the effort magnificently.

I want publicly to acknowledge the faithful, cheerful, and efficient service of our daughter, Melissa Iris Cully, who has been my secretary, in her free time, "for the duration." Indeed, during the last stages of the manuscript preparation, my whole family came to the rescue. There were times when all four of us worked almost in shifts, meanwhile resisting the temptation of sparkling blue Caribbean waters off St. Thomas.

A work of this magnitude represents the accumulated labors of vast numbers of persons. It is to be hoped that its usefulness will reach as widely as its writers themselves are geographically dispersed. For the church is everywhere; and wherever the church is, there must be Christian education. In that work of the church this Dictionary is offered as a tool.

K. B. C.

Evanston, Illinois

A

ADMINISTRATION The function of administration in an educational agency is to provide a bridge between policy and program. Its purpose and character are defined by the nature, objectives, and educational philosophy of the agency. Its efforts are directed to enabling the teachers and program leaders so to function as to enhance the agency's character, maintain its educational philosophy, and achieve its purpose.

Administration is closely related to 2 other functions — organization and supervision. Organization provides the structure within which educational activity can fruitfully function — such as organic relation to the parent agency, departments and classes, time schedules, space assignment, personnel. Administration gives direction and management to assure the smooth running of the organization and to provide the conditions for effective teaching. Supervision is concerned with training, guidance, and support of workers to help them achieve professional growth and effectiveness. Good organization is essential to effective administration; supervision is administration directed to the education of workers for the improvement of both content and process. In practice these 3 are so intermingled in the administrative office that it is neither possible nor

desirable to make a distinction among them.

The church school is created by the church as its agency for Christian education. Hence, it is the nature, message, and mission of the church that determine the spirit, policy, and program of the church school. The administrative function will express this character in its operation and as the goal of its effort. If the church is a people of God indwelt by the Holy Spirit, a redemptive fellowship, a koinonia, nothing less can characterize the basic philosophy of the church school and inform the spirit and method of its administration.

The concept of administration may have a flavor of authoritarian direction, manipulation of persons, push-button control, executive efficiency. Whatever place this type of administration may have when the objective is material accomplishment and output, it does not characterize good administration in Christian education. True, an administrator must have authority to perform his function, appropriate lines and channels of communication, and must strive for efficiency, i.e., economy of preoccupation with administration itself in the interest of maximum educational functioning. But a church school is not an arena in which a big operator may flex his executive muscles. Its primary concern is with persons, both workers and pupils. Procedures in administration will seek the same ends in the development of persons and in the spirit and life of the institution as the program that is administered. Principles of Christian education that apply to teaching and group leadership will also inform procedure in administration.

Administration is not a lower order of service as distinguished from teaching, but merely a way of getting things done, of providing the conditions under which teaching may best proceed. While it serves these purposes, it also partakes of the nature of teaching in the best sense of the word. This is true because (1) administration best achieves its purpose through maximum involvement of workers and concern for their professional growth, utilizing meetings and staff for education as well as business, and (2) it provides for pupil participation in the process of administering, such as service on committees, program leadership, democratic approaches to program planning.

With the foregoing interpretation of the meaning of administration in Christian education, the following principles are suggested to govern its procedures.

The more mechanical aspects of running the organization should be reduced to routine procedures as far as possible so as not to obtrude any more than necessary into the program itself. This includes such matters as maintaining organizational structures according to plan, enrolling new pupils, taking records, maintaining time schedules, ordering and issuing materials and supplies, minor purchases. Within established limits, administrators should be given freedom to deal executively with these.

It will be helpful if such matters are covered in published rules of procedure, the interpretation of which becomes a part of worker orientation. Such a statement might well include also a job description for each of the offices in the table of organization (director of Christian education, superintendent, teacher, etc.), showing duties and relationships. The original establishment of such rules of procedure is more than a routine matter and should have the attention of the policy-making body, but their application is more or less routine. Even so, let administrators not forget that they are dealing with persons in a dynamic process and not mechanically following a blueprint.

One of the chief ends of administration is to increase the interest and further the professional growth of workers through participation. This is best achieved through democratic procedures in direction and management, allowing other workers to share in planning, carrying on, and evaluating at all points where such participation is feasible. So conceived, administration is a dynamic process through which the spirit and life of the church school may be so ordered as to provide the best climate for Christian nurture. It is more than running an institution; it is encouraging persons concerned with nurture to use their own capabilities and skills to best advantage.

Administration is more than overseeing and directing other workers. It is stimulating them to self-discovery of their own creative capabilities, and enabling them to develop the professional skills that for them are most appropriate in achieving the ends of Christian education.

It is not the purpose of this article to give a complete job description for the office of administration. Only a few of the more important tasks will be touched.

1. Establishment and maintenance of Christian education within the main thrust of the church's life. Most of the denominations provide for this in organizational patterns for the local church. It remains for administration to bring it to active functioning. Further, there needs to be a public relations effort to enlist the interest and participation of the people of the church. If the whole church is to be the center and agency of Christian education, and not just a few persons designated for the educational function, this will come to pass only by virtue of constant effort in interpretation and cultivation.

2. Establishment and maintenance of an adequate organization of the church school. Proper grouping of persons is essential for education. The nature of the program determines the size and age span of groups. Certain activities can be carried out in larger groups, with considerable tolerance as to age span. Others, such as teaching, require smaller groups with more homogeneity of age. Since given pupils are likely to be in more than one educational agency of the church, it is recommended that administratively the division (children's, youth, adult) be considered the unit for program planning and leadership coordination, so that each pupil may be seen in the total perspective of his participation in the church school. The department of 2-year or 3-year age span is usually the operational unit for worship and leadership guidance, whereas the class or group within the department constitutes the teaching unit. It is the function of organization, in cooperation with the policy-making body, to devise the best organizational pattern to serve the policy and program of a particular church school — determining ages to be embraced by departments, size of classes, whether coeducational or segregated, etc. — and, once established, to maintain this organization and help it to function as advantageously as possible. Provision for annual promotion is necessary for maintaining the established plan.

3. Enlistment, orientation, training, and supervision of workers. This is the most crucial aspect of administration, for any school will be largely what the workers make it. In turn, the quality of the relationship of the management to the workers is an important factor in their commitment and professional growth.

4. Assignment of available space, provision of equipment, supplies, and other working tools; proper care for servicing building and equipment, and seeing that it is in readiness when needed.

5. Evaluation. Church schools have been notoriously weak in seeking to assess the results of their work. This is primarily a cooperative process, the administration leading the workers in making self-studies and evaluations, not a checking system arbitrarily superimposed on them.

The above has been written from the viewpoint of the total function of administration, not as a job analysis of a particular administrator. The office will be held in varying degree by many persons — pastor, director of Christian education, secretary, division and department heads, and others. — *Paul H. Vieth*

ADOLESCENCE The age boundaries are average and approximate for the flexible and diversified period of transition from childhood to maturity that is known as adolescence. It was formerly limited to the ages from 18 to 25, but extended later to include the full transition from puberty to maturity (about 12 to 25). The recent tendency is to consider that adolescence begins with the prepuberty period at about age 10, and ends around the legal age for maturity — 18 for females and 21 for males. Strong factors for change in estimating the boundary ages of adolescence are the increase in the number of teen-age youth who marry and begin families, and the rising rate of juvenile delinquency. Moreover, youth in the 20th century are showing sober and profound concern with spatial, economic, scientific, philosophical, and theological problems, especially those which pertain to human survival.

The most phenomenal change during adolescence occurs in the emergence of reproductive power. This is the center of a broad group of other changes, and its significance can hardly be overestimated. Biologically, the young person changes from a derivative to a determinative relationship to the continuation of the human species. Sociologically, the young person is endowed with power to become a cocreator of a basic unit of society, the family. Psychologically, the gift of freedom for individual decision carries heavy burdens of responsibility to other human beings. Philosophically, self-realization expands to concern for social self-satisfaction. In a Christian perspective these movements are very important because they include the relations of a person to society, to nature, to God.

One Biblical word picture of the divine-human encounter shows human beings hiding the reproductive organs. Although this gift of God is a means whereby living creatures can with God's help accomplish what God otherwise reserves for himself, that is, the giving of new life, the misunderstanding and taboos that overlie the reproductive function retard and even block youth's vision of the sacredness and blessedness of life. In the adolescent view, similar taboos cover many other aspects of the human predicament.

Growing up during adolescence, the young person must cope with an unlimited number of predicaments. Much emphasis has been laid on youth rebellion but too little stress has been given to the causes of that rebellion. The flexible and variegated changes that occur during adolescence drive many young people into ambivalence. Attracted and repelled simultaneously by objects, persons, and actions, they seem to rely on two authority sources as correctives for ambivalence. One source of authority is the social reference, " Everybody else is doing it." The other is taken from inner and deeply personal efforts to develop a new type of self-organization or personal frame of reference on which to base clear-cut, durable decisions. Neither corrective seems to be completely reliable and the only other alternative to ambivalence and compromise seems to be rebellion.

Part of the motivation to seek authority sources is the urgent need to find an authority that can stand alongside, and even above, the authority that adults seem to derive from an unknown source. Since the world that the adolescent must live in is obviously controlled by adults, and since the boundless energy of the adolescent is impotent to grasp adult authority except by imitation, young people have created a world of their own. The mysterious style of life in this world is marked by symbols of meaning, patterns of behavior, and standards of valuation that are typically and preculiarly youth's own. This style of life or culture helps to render more tolerable the period of waiting for maturity. It also softens some of the secret sorrows that rise out of the ambivalence inherent in the flexibility and diversification of the whole transition period. The youth culture has more material than spiritual characteristics, yet changes that occur within it take place as suddenly and rapidly as some movements of the Holy Spirit. In the youth culture, language and behavioral phenomena change overnight. The subtle standards by which consensus is achieved are not set by a nationwide convention, nor are they universally ratified according to a constitution or bylaws. Nevertheless, when any facet of the youth culture changes, all young people know and demonstrate the change.

Christianity has a mission to the youth culture. It resembles the mission which Christians carry to any other peoples or cultures in that it cannot be effective until those who are under the culture's influence are themselves involved in the mission. It is like the mission to other cultures in that its most effective functions take place via educational channels. The educational function of the mission with youth who are in the church has a difference and

an advantage. It can educe, that is, bring or draw forth, that which has been received through revelation, instruction, and discipline prior to and during the adolescent years. Christian education can assist in opening young minds and hearts to the "wideness in God's mercy" and it can introduce them to the fact that "the love of God is broader than the measure of man's mind."

If young persons are to learn to accept God's love, it is essential that they begin to learn about it or to prepare to accept it during adolescence and not to wait until after they become adult persons. The ever-present, deep need is to learn in relation to and under God the Father, through Jesus Christ, the Son of God and Son of Man, and by the power of the Holy Spirit, while they are adolescents. An understanding of the incarnation as God's self-revelation in the flesh and of God's seeking love in Jesus Christ is mighty enough, if it is shared in the dynamic power of the Holy Spirit, to arouse cordial response.

There are many barriers to this understanding. Sooner or later, young people identify these barriers as Satan, sin, and their sins, which are the damages they do to God's love, to others, and to themselves. The clearest understanding of God's method of dealing with Satan, sin, and sins is available in the concept of justification by faith.

If Christian education were offered to adolescents in and under the proclamation of this good news, what a vast and all-embracing change it would bring! Youth are more aware of the gravity of their sins, more eager to be saved, more ready to accept help, more anxious for a right relationship with the Lord of life, and more burdened with guilt than they can admit. Many of them are well informed as to God's knowledge of their situation. Like the seraphim in Isaiah's vision who hid their faces and their secret parts but could not fly from the awful presence, youth seek to hide the reality of their situation from the ultimate Reality. Is there any way for them to enter personal encounter with him " unto whom all hearts are open, all desires known, and from whom no secrets are hid "? None is possible except that which God offers, for God alone can justify them. God accepts persons, just as they are, by their faith.

Among all the changes throughout the transitory period of adolescence, the greatest change that adolescents long for is to become whole, complete, and justifiable persons. The greatest need for this greatest change is redemption. The price that the person must pay is repentance, but the consequence for the sinner's situation is so radical, glorious, and thankworthy that he cannot be invulnerable to it. Spontaneous response emerges in good works. Liberated from despair, guilty shrinking, and lonely struggle into hope, reconciliation, and glad fellowship, the Christian is set free to fulfill his longing to show gratitude by doing God's will and extending his love to mankind.

— *Richard L. Harbour*

ADULT EDUCATION The education of adults has always been considered important. Almost all the events of Biblical record pertain to adults, and the propagation of the meaning of those events through sermon, story, and chronicle is to adults and through parents to children.

" Adult education," however, is a comparatively new term and movement. The Sunday school movement served chiefly for children and young adolescents. The beginnings of modern adult education in the church are rooted in the same forces that produced the Chautauqua movement, which inspired the establishment of lecture classes for adults in local churches. These were stabilized and reinforced by the development of the International Uniform Lesson Series in 1872 as the standard type of adult education for Protestant churches. In fact, the International Uniform Lesson Series continues as the most widely used curriculum for adults.

Because many organizations were engaging in various types of adult education, the Carnegie Corporation called the first conference on adult education in 1924 to help coordinate the movement. This conference and the subsequent formation in 1926 of the American Association for Adult Education stimulated Christian educators to give serious consideration to the wider potentialities of adult education in the church. During the next decade many books on Christian adult education were written, though as late as 1938 one important book called adult education in the church " new." In 1930 the International Council of Religious Education appointed a staff member to help direct the church's interest in this field: the United Christian Adult Movement was established in 1936. There soon developed a strong young adult movement, partially in reaction to stereotyped adult Bible classes and partly in response to the special needs of young adults.

The traditional 19th-century pattern of Christian education as training for confirmation or as preparation for conversion in adolescents was strongly reinforced during the first quarter of the 20th century by the development of progressive education methods that achieved almost universal acceptance in childhood education. The traditional strategy assumed that if we could educate a child religiously, he would flower into a competent, articulate Christian adult. Now we realize that the child reflects the cultural pattern that is mediated to him by family and community. The Christian faith is in part a judgment on culture and an impulse to reorder society in harmony with God's will; adults must be the starting point of this process or no significant change will ever be brought into being. This shift in strategy does not lessen interest in children or youth but it insists that there cannot be an effective Christian education process for them until adults and parents who have control of the social processes shaping the immature child's mind face their responsibility realistically.

Perhaps the best way to summarize the status of adult education in the churches is to indicate trends since World War II.

Since the publication of Kraemer's *A Theology of the Laity* (1958) there has been a growing concern to reinterpret the place of laymen in the church. The traditional view that the minister was employed to minister for and to the congregation placed the layman in the position of supporting with work and money the institutional program of the church. Now we see that the layman also has a responsibility: he is a minister to other laymen in the church, not just in visitation of the sick but in sharing physical and spiritual burdens. Moreover, it is the layman who is in constant touch with the nonchurch world. This view would formulate the purpose of Christian education of adults as helping them to be ministers to one another and to the world through their work, and would make adult education a coaching for this purpose more than merely for training in churchmanship.

Large, formal lecture classes, often institutionalized with constitution, elected officers, and budget, are a characteristic of the past when adult education was something added to the church's program. Now that we consider adult education as having a prime claim on the church's resources, we are in a position to utilize better methods. Almost all the methods shown to be effective in changing people's attitudes and in helping them to acquire new knowledge are associated with small groups. Usually limited to 15, perhaps more effective if even smaller in size, these groups study, pray, and work together over sufficient time for people to drop their pretenses. They are able under these conditions to develop a concern for, and interest in, one another, thus sharing life experiences at deeper levels.

The leadership role in small groups is redefined. Rather than depend upon the expert or charismatic leader, the small group can function effectively with a leader who has qualities that help a group achieve cohesion. In fact, some functions of leadership can be shared through assignments carried out by individuals or teams within the group. This process expects participation by all or most of the individuals within the group according to their capacity and training.

There is a versatility about small groups. They can be formed by common interest, such as young adult groups or young parent groups; they can cluster about topics such as Bible study or church and state; or they can be formed by occupational concerns. Moreover, many of the small study-work groups are not limited to meeting on Sunday or in the church but rather set a time and place according to their convenience.

For groups who take the theology of the laity seriously there is a renaissance of Bible study and the use of college-level textbooks in religion. Small groups explore all types of materials for parents, books dealing with ethical issues confronting professional persons in their work, and paperback books on the interpretation of Christianity. Many denominations now publish selective units of study in quarterly or book form on a variety of topics. Some of the groups with trained leaders are making a critical examination of the relation of their church to the community in which they live. This latter project requires an understanding of historical, theological, and sociological factors that make up the church's life; and the development of an understanding and utilization of these materials becomes the curriculum for a group who, over an extended period of time, seek to understand the nature of the church in society.

The effectiveness of modern medicine has lengthened life expectancy so that an increasing proportion of the total population is made up of older adults. These adults have special needs, and offer special opportunities because of their experience and available time. Although churches are developing groups for older adults, seldom has enough attention been given to the way the older adult's talents can be used for important tasks in the church.

For at least 25 years Christian educators have been calling attention to the need for more effective ways to help the family. Denominational curricula in the past few decades have been designed to enlist the home in the Christian education of children, reinforcing and elaborating what was taught in the church schools. Without losing interest in that possibility, Christian educators are now proposing that the church center more on efforts and materials that will help the home discharge its unique task as a genuine unit of education. Family camping is an illustration of an activity that has emerged from this newer view. Curriculum materials to be used exclusively in the home are another sign of an important shift in emphasis. — *C. Ellis Nelson*

ADULTS The modern American adult has been the object of concern in innumerable volumes produced by psychologists, sociologists, theologians, and other students of humanity. From this vast plethora of observation and analysis a few basic insights concerning the American adult character are especially worthy of mention because of their implications for Christian educators who would minister to adults in relevant ways.

Pragmatism is deeply ingrained in adult folkways and attitudes. Adult interest in learning generally begins (and all too often ends) with the words "how to . . . ." Adults are far more interested in learning efficient techniques for meeting problems or fulfilling duties or for some other sharply definable purpose than they are in acquiring knowledge whose utility is not immediately evident. Thus almost invariably far more adults will attend training sessions for church school teachers, financial canvassers, evangelistic callers, new members, and parents of children to be baptized than will attend learning groups whose purposes are less utilitarian. The educator in the church must keep in mind that training sessions, for all their obvious limitations, nevertheless command the attention and the energies of a considerably higher proportion of adults than do more generalized study groups.

Conformity as an increasingly salient characteristic of the American adult has been noted by many. Probably no one has described this phenomenon more tellingly than David Riesman in the elaboration of his concept of other-directedness. The trend toward increasing conformism affects not only the externals of life but also opinion and attitude formation. Thus the pressures toward conformity inherent in our culture greatly heighten the leverage that the learning group exerts on the individual adult participant. The power of the group to change people's attitudes, beliefs, and values has been steadily augmented through the years by this social tendency toward other-directedness. Conformity to the cues and expectations of friends is also an increasingly important determinant of group composition and loyalty. Thus conformism can be a powerful ally in the enlistment of adult interest as well as in the effectiveness of the group process itself for learning.

The breakdown of community through the processes of urbanization is one of the most prominent developments in American society. Urban life organizes people tightly together in terms of specialized functions, but it disorganizes them in terms of close human relations. Anonymous or essentially commercial contacts characterize many, if not most, of the associations people have with one another. There has been a marked decline in the strength of social bonds in all phases of urban life. Social anonymity seems to be as great or even greater in the suburbs, especially in those newer and smaller suburbs which do not have the extensive recreational, social, and commercial facilities that in urban areas serve as centers of community life. Furthermore, the uprooting process of frequent relocations plagues suburbanites even more than it does their urban neighbors. No doubt the upsurge in church membership since World War II is partially attributable to an instinctive quest for community through religious identification, a reaction against the depersonalizing tendencies of metropolitan life. This quest for community within the church presents the adult educator with a special challenge and opportunity, since the small learning group is especially well suited for providing the close and redemptive human relationships these people are seeking, whether deliberately or unconsciously. The chief problem that the adult educator faces in this regard is that this quest for community has impelled the great majority of adults into so many other kinds of groups in the community and the church that they feel they have little or no time for a learning group in the church. The great proliferation of voluntary associations, clubs, teams, and special-interest groups of all kinds that has accompanied the gradual increase of leisure time in our society has preempted most of that leisure for a superficial kind of conviviality.

Apathy rooted in a sense of fatalism for the most part characterizes the attitude of the modern adult toward social questions. Indifference or at least passivity typifies his reaction to current events. He feels controlled by the impersonal workings of fate in the area of political decisions, as well as in his business and social life. He feels helpless in the face of social, political, and economic developments, and frequently fails to act responsibly because of this dominant attitude. He is a spectator of the public scene, feeling unable to influence in any significant way the course of events that determine so many aspects of his life. He usually participates in political affairs vicariously or indirectly, through affiliations with special-interest groups such as commercial and professional associations, taxpayers' associations, and the like. He leaves it to these groups to defend his interests and speak for him. His political and economic concerns are generally confined to the effect of these factors on his own family, his neighborhood, and his job.

The Biblical and theological illiteracy of the average adult today constitutes an enormous challenge to educators in the church. What is particularly disheartening about this challenge to the educators is that most adults do not seem to regard it as a challenge. They do not see that such illiteracy matters very much, because their commonsense pragmatism centers on action rather than on ideas. Theirs is essentially a humanistic faith, a system of ethical ideals lacking organic relation to the Christian doctrines from which the ideals originally arose.

Perhaps an even greater challenge than the adult's unspeculative indifference to theology as such is his alienation from the thought world of the Bible. The fact that he shows little interest in reading the Bible by himself does not mean that he is uninterested in its content. It merely means that he is unable to comprehend most of it. One example of the difficulty is that both the formal training and the experience of most of our laymen incline them to interpret all verbal information in a very literal sense. They have trouble grasping poetic and metaphorical meanings in the Bible. Subtle distinctions between fact and truth are often lost upon them. In this and in other ways the modern adult sees little direct relation between his thought patterns, his ways of reacting to things, and the concerns of the Bible. Not only individual Biblical words but also and especially whole concepts and metaphors are in urgent need of receiving relevant translations and interpretations if they are to be meaningfully communicated to the adult.

The aspects of American adult character enumerated above are external symptoms of a central human malady. This underlying malady, viewed theologically, is the alienation of the adult from other persons and from a sense of meaningfulness. The most basic need of the modern adult is help in overcoming his estrangement from other persons and from the sources of ultimate meaning in life. Because the adult's doubt and despair are interrelated with his condition of estrangement, and because the discovery or recovery of ultimate meaning takes place within the context of close personal relationships, educators in the church can help adults simultaneously in their search for meaning and in their quest for redemptive personal relationships through fostering the kind

of small learning groups in which the gospel and the experience of reconciliation reinforce each other.
— *David J. Ernsberger*

ADVENT Advent is the period beginning 4 Sundays before Christmas. The term " Advent," which means " coming," was once applied to Christmas only. Gradually it was expanded to describe the whole season of preparation, which includes 4 Sundays and ends on Christmas Eve. Since the 8th century, Advent has marked the beginning of the Christian year for the Western churches. It has become the prologue to the life of Christ that is portrayed throughout the rest of the year. We celebrate it through worship, prayer, Bible-reading, and hymn singing.

Advent is a particularly significant time for Christians in our day, when the sights and sounds of Christmas appear in the commercial world the day after Thanksgiving. Much is done to tempt us to celebrate Christmas ahead of time, thus robbing the season of its climax of joy. Pastors, parents, and teachers can do a great deal to help avoid this, for a proper keeping of Advent can make our admonitions to the young (" Christmas isn't just presents "; " Christmas does not belong to Santa Claus ") more practical and full of deep meaning. Old and young enjoy anticipation. In Advent we anticipate the wonder of Christ's First Coming upon the earth.

For a thousand years Christians celebrated Advent on a note of pure expectation and joy. By the 12th century the Advent of Christ was interpreted in more than one way: his coming in the past to Bethlehem; his present coming in the hearts of men through grace; and his future coming as Judge at the end of time. It was then that the themes of penitence and resolution crept in, and to this day we think of the threefold coming. Advent continues to be a time of both joy and penance, with the mood of expectation dominant in all hearts.

The Biblical foundations of Advent provide the content for its interpretation in the church and the church school. God's action is summed up in the famous Advent hymn, " O Come, O Come, Emmanuel," which is composed of ancient antiphons (choral responses). The Scriptures point to the need for meditation on the entire past and future of mankind before we welcome the Christ-child. We remember our creation, rebellion, and exile. We read of man's awaiting God in the darkness and of how God delivers him. Always Advent shows the coming of God. Today Christendom continues to prepare the world for the ultimate Advent.

Bible readings, such as the Messianic prophecies, are suitable for private study, for teaching, and for preaching. The references should be given in the parish bulletin or church program so that young and old may think together, and anticipation grow in both generations. This expectation of God is also encouraged by play-readings, the giving of chancel plays, and " hymn sings " when Advent hymns are sung (not Christmas carols, which should be saved for the great time of the Nativity itself).

Pre-Christian peoples celebrated Yule with the burning of lights and fires, and we now use the lighted Advent wreath, brought to America by the Lutherans from eastern Germany. Happily, it has become a cherished custom in many homes, churches, and classes. There are now numerous books and pamphlets that describe how to make simply the wreath of evergreen branches (representing eternal life in Christ) tied to a frame. Four candles are set upright in it, one for each of the Advent Sundays, symbols for the light of Christ. Each Sunday another candle is lighted, and in homes it is relighted at the family table every evening. In homes the wreath is generally placed on a table. In churches it may hang from the ceiling. Used with reverence it can be a splendid help to our worship and a constant reminder of our expectation. We need to be on our guard against turning these customs into " gadgets." They must point to what God has done and is doing, not to our piety. This is true of other symbols such as Advent calendars and Advent houses, with their little paper doors to be opened each day, revealing new Bible verses. Antiphon calenders are also available, excellent for use in homes and classes, each verse depicting one way in which God reveals himself. The value of these customs is lessened if the crèche is set up in the home complete with the baby in the manger. Let the children put a few wisps of straw in the manger as the days go by, then they will have a place in which to put the Christ-child figure on Christmas Eve.

All the preparations for Christmas, especially when families or classes make them together — the buying, making, and wrapping of presents, the cooking and the decorating — may be a part of the spirit of giving for Christ's sake, and contribute to the tiptoe mood of expectation. It is all summarized in the true Advent message, " He came, he comes, he is coming." — *Dora P. Chaplin*

ADVENT CHRISTIAN CHURCH
The Advent Christian Church observed its centennial year in a special program of its General Conference at Aurora, Ill., in June, 1960. It considers itself to be a prophetic people called into being to emphasize the Second Coming and conditional immortality (life only in Christ). In the field of Christian education it has stressed a maturing process that may be described as "gradual."

The Advent Christian congregations embraced Sunday school work slowly in their early years. The earliest stirrings of Sunday school activity occurred in 1845 at the Albany Conference.

The denominational life stems from the organization meeting convened at Providence, R.I., July, 1860. The teaching program was stimulated during the early period by the Advent Christian Sunday-School Union, organized in 1881. Lesson sheets and the *Blessed Hope Quarterly* were first published in 1882. After the turn of the century, a National Board of Christian Education came into being. A representative was appointed to the International Sunday-School Lesson Committee in 1917. Graded lessons were envisioned as early as 1928. From 1928 to 1954, graded series were completed for kindergarten and junior departments. In 1954 a curriculum committee was appointed to pursue this task on all grade levels. By 1958 the Board of Christian Education appointed its first full-time director.

The *Advent Christian Manual* (1961) states: " The Board of Christian Education of the General Conference is composed of eight members, one elected from each of the five regions, one at large, and two representing the Youth Fellowship.

It is the function of this board to have general oversight over the educational program of the denomination. Its more specific functions are to elect, subject to the approval of the Executive Committee, the Director of Christian Education, to direct the Leadership Training Program, and in cooperation with Advent Christian Publications to produce Sunday School lesson material. The planning of the curriculum and selection of lesson writers is largely delegated to the Director and the Curriculum Committee."

— *Elwell M. Drew*

AESTHETICS Aesthetics formally is that branch of philosophy which deals with the beautiful, its nature, apprehension, production, and judgment.

In the classic trilogy, truth was assigned to science, goodness to religion, and beauty to aesthetics. Kant used the term "transcendental aesthetic" to label his critical discussion of space and time as the a priori forms for the apprehension of all objects of sense perception. Hegel used the term *Ästhetik* to label his treatise on the fine arts. Today the tendency is to use the term in the freer fashion so that it may be applied to the history and criticism of works of art, to art appreciation, and to the creative process. Methods of scientific investigation have been applied to artistic experience so that it is possible to speak of "the psychology of art." Though the arts tend to resist measurement, there has been an effort in the direction of experimental aesthetics.

However, partly as a result of the 20th-century revolt against scientism, in which European existentialism has taken the lead, art has been sharply distinguished from science and sometimes championed as its alternative in cultural development. In this mood, science is described as the thrust toward quantification, objectivity, technology, depersonalization; art as the opposite thrust toward appreciation, subjectivity, creativity, individuation. Many artists have taken this theme in their work: Picasso in *Guernica,* Eliot in *The Waste Land,* Camus in *The Fall,* Sartre in *No Exit,* and Martha Graham in contemporary dance ("she abandoned the outer shell and danced the reason why").

Historically, the relation between art as the pursuit of beauty and religion as the pursuit of goodness has been continuous but frequently uneasy. Religion and art began together, perhaps before primitive science, in prehistoric man's celebration of life in worship and dance. Drama became for the Greeks as important in the search for truth as philosophy. The Hebrews rejected painting and sculpture but made use of poetry and music (and sometimes of dance) in worship. The Puritans excised representational art forms from architecture and limited the use of music in worship.

Though John Dewey suggested that the creative experience of the artist be substituted for classical religion, more recent philosophers and theologians have explored both theoretical and practical relations between art and religion, e.g., in the discussions of signs and symbols by Susanne Langer and Paul Tillich. Nicolas Berdyaev equated the creative act of art with the eschatological expectation of Christianity. John Macmurray aligns religion with art as against science in their centralization of the "personal."

Artists in all media seem to be

finding increasing meaning in the symbols and Scriptures of Judeo-Christianity, and some denominational curriculum materials have made use of illustrations in contemporary styles. The National Council of the Churches of Christ in the U.S.A. has formed a Department of Worship and the Arts which is encouraging conversation between artists and churchmen. Courses in religion and the arts and programs in religious drama are offered in theological seminaries.

In the churches there is a marked interest in the meaning of architectural form, and some notable buildings have resulted. Local churches have sponsored religious art festivals combining choral concerts and art exhibits. There has been a revival of interest in drama in the churches, ranging from chancel drama through rhythmic choir and play-reading groups.

The capacity of art forms to communicate feeling, especially at the symbolic and nonverbal levels, interests both aestheticians and educators. In the field of Christian education, both art forms and creative experience are being explored in discussion of symbolism (e.g., Lewis Sherrill) and classroom methods (e.g., role-playing, creative dramatics, " creative " activities). In the field of missionary education, principles of aesthetic communication are being investigated in the effort to bridge intercultural and linguistic barriers (e.g., Frank Laubach, Hendrik Kraemer, Eugene Nida). It must be noted, however, that though many artists tend to think of themselves as communicators, they resist the effort to be used as agents of propaganda, and that a new battle line between religion and art may be drawn. — *Wayne R. Rood*

AFRICA Christian education in Africa is portrayed here according to several regions. The picture to be complete would have to include the new African independent nations in West Africa: Ghana, Nigeria, and Sierra Leone. The French-speaking territories are represented by practices followed in Southern Cameroun; Gaboon, Congo, and Northern Cameroun follow similar practices.

Republic of South Africa. The overall picture is that, apart from the Roman Catholic Church, the theoretical level in most churches is distinctly low. The laity are given little instruction in understanding the Bible. The emphasis is individualistic and moralistic, with strong strains of Pietism and Fundamentalism.

Thorough teaching is given in the many Roman Catholic day schools. Most other church schools have chaplains or specialist teachers for religious instruction. The state schools, which are in the overwhelming majority, are in a very different position. The findings of H. Holmes in a thesis entitled *The Problem of Religious Education in the State School with Special Reference to English-medium Schools in the Transvaal* are as follows: Lip service is being paid to the regulations providing for school worship and periods of religious instruction. The standard of religious knowledge is low, and the methods of instruction are restricted. Too many teachers are willing to teach Scripture but are unqualified to do so, and many more are just unwilling. Too many schools attempt to keep Gentiles and Jews together for the religious instruction period, thus making positive Christian teaching impossible. The difficulties of sectarianism have been highly exaggerated, often merely as an excuse to neglect or water down Christian teaching. Cooperation between home, church, and school is minimal.

These findings could be extended to European English-medium education in all 4 provinces. The position is no doubt better in the Afrikaans-medium European schools, where there is much greater homogeneity, most teachers and pupils belonging to the three Dutch Reformed Churches. The problem of the Jewish minority (5 percent of the white population) does not arise. (There is the right of withdrawal on request from the parents, but it is seldom exercised, because the Jewish community considers the teaching in schools to be innocuous.) The position in African schools is critical, in spite of the zeal of the Department of Bantu Education, which since 1953 has gained control of the vast majority of African schools, previously mission-operated. There is no conscience clause allowing the teachers to withdraw from teaching the subject if it is contrary to their beliefs, as there is for the rest of the population. Many are not Christian in any sense. Many are even aggressively antagonistic, resenting the task of teaching "the white man's religion." Many are frankly ignorant but do their best.

Practically all churches have Sunday schools that meet before or at the same time as morning worship. Many have an arrangement whereby the children are present with the adults for part of the service. Most churches have a course of instruction in preparation for confirmation or church membership. The hiatus between childhood and adult involvement in the activities of the church is being overcome increasingly through youth services, " young people's church." Church youth guilds and clubs abound, but these are not much concerned with systematic teaching of the faith.

In the primary school (for the first 7 years of schooling) religious instruction is accepted as part of the responsibility of the class teacher, along with almost all other subjects. In the high schools the specialist is the general rule for all subjects but religious instruction. It suffers in comparison with other courses through not being an examination subject. Where possible the subject is entrusted to those with some interest in it, provided it can be fitted into their timetables. Under the provinces only teachers employed by the departments of education may teach the subject. No outside body or church may have access to the classroom. The Bantu education system allows the churches to give instruction to their own adherents during schooltime, on condition that this is done in the child's home language. This renders the arrangement practically unworkable, owing to the difficulty of finding qualified persons with the knowledge of the various African tongues. Since vernacular instruction is compulsory for religious instruction, the teacher who teaches Zulu, Sutho, etc., is often found teaching religion as well.

In the churches generally anyone who can be found teaches religion. The minister may conduct a preparation class or even, in some cases, take over the Sunday school entirely. Some Sunday schools have preparation classes and most follow a course of lessons with lesson notes for the teacher. The larger Protestant churches organize voluntary courses, as does also the interdenominational Sunday School Union.

Southern Rhodesia. Religious education in Southern Rhodesia is conducted by the churches through both the churches and schools. On the African side about 90 percent of the primary and secondary schools are under the various church-related organizations. The Government grant-in-aid pays the entire salaries of mission school teachers and also provides generous grants for buildings, equipment, supervision, etc. In the Government schools for the various races, the churches have the right of entry for religious instruction, minimally twice each week. If the churches are unable to take care of their own pupils, the head of each school is required to appoint an acceptable member of the staff to do the teaching. In mission and church schools, adequate provision is made in the curriculum for such instruction.

Religious instruction for adults is conducted through the regular catechumenal classes, Sunday schools, and adult women's and men's organizations.

Ministers of religion are trained in their preparation for ordination, lay church leaders are often ex-teachers, and schoolteachers, usually trained in mission teacher training schools, are given instruction in religious training. Many churches have refresher courses and institutes for the training of those giving religious instruction.

Among African people the average standard of education is approximately grade 5; about half of the primary schoolteachers have taken grade 8 and 2 years of training. A small number have achieved higher training, 2 years of secondary followed by 2 years of teacher training. Among ministers of religion, those who are training at present usually have had 2 or 3 years of secondary schooling, followed by an equal number of years of theological training. The content of the courses is usually Biblical, supplemented by social problems related to home and community. Considerable literature has been produced in English and the vernacular languages of Chishona and Sindebele.

Northern Rhodesia. Schools in Northern Rhodesia are divided into European (including Indian and Eurafrican) and African. These are quite distinct, the former being under the Federal Ministry of Education and the latter under the Territorial Ministry of African Education.

African education was introduced by missionaries. A large proportion of African schools are still under the management of the various missionary societies, and there is a strong missionary influence through the teaching staff in schools managed by the Government.

There is in existence a syllabus of religious instruction approved for use in the 8 years' primary course for African schools, with an alternative syllabus for Roman Catholic schools; a secondary school syllabus is under consideration. Religious instruction is generally given by the school staff.

Of the 5 principal teacher training colleges in Northern Rhodesia, 3 are missionary (1 Roman Catholic, 2 Christian Council). In the mission colleges the teaching of religious instruction forms a prominent part of the training syllabus. Audio-visual aids are extensively used in some districts.

European education has not the same direct contact with the church as African education. The only directly church-sponsored schools are a few Roman Catholic convent schools and some Bible schools conducted for mission employees. There are no church schools. Ministers of various denominations exercise the "right of entry" for a 30- to 40-minute period per week. On other occasions religious instruction is given by the school staff.

Kenya. Religious education in Kenya is usually thought of in terms of the large number of primary and secondary schools and teacher training colleges managed by churches and missions or quasi-independent boards of governors on an essentially Christian foundation. These represent ⅚ of the 6,000 schools and colleges in Kenya, about 3,000 of these institutions under the management of Protestant churches and about 2,000 under the Roman Catholic Chuch. Approximately ¼ of the cost of maintaining these schools comes from fees, the rest from Government grants-in-aid — half from the Central Government and a quarter from local government bodies. Although, therefore, the churches and missions manage very many of the schools and colleges, they make little financial contribution, either recurrent or capital, to their maintenance. The policy of the Kenya Government has been to encourage the churches as their trusted agents in education. Support is also given, particularly in Asian education, to voluntary agencies supported by Muslims, Hindus, Sikhs, etc. Most of the teachers in these schools have had only eight years' primary education followed by two years at teacher training colleges.

The Education Ordinance requires religious instruction and worship to be provided in the schools, but there is full freedom of conscience to withdraw or to request instruction under any other partic-

ular religion. A number of the churches and missions use the material prepared by the Government in cooperation with the Christian Council of Kenya.

Outside the formal system there is some religious education carried out by the churches, but on the whole they have depended upon the day schools. The Sunday school movement is developing slowly, handicapped by the lack of suitable teachers. As of this writing, there is not a single African ordained minister in Kenya who has completed a a secondary course while at school. In recent years there has been a growing interest in youth work in the churches, the Y.M.C.A., Y.W.C.A., and other youth organizations receiving growing support.

The Christian Council of Kenya has a Department of Christian Education and Training in addition to the Christian Churches' Educational Association, its agent in formal education. The Department of Christian Education and Training sponsors activities in lay leadership, industrial relations, youth work, and Sunday school work.

Cameroun and L'Afrique Equatoriale. Religious education in the southern part of Cameroun is given in all the primary and secondary schools of the churches. There are several Bible schools for the training of catechists and 2 theological schools for the training of pastors. A theological faculty on the university level, with an interdenominational and international character, was opened in 1962 at Yaoundé.

In most of the churches there is an hour-long Sunday school for adults and children before the worship service. The teachers and catechists have had some special training in their normal or catechist schools. In some places there are weekly meetings to prepare the Bible lessons. In the secondary schools the history of the church and the great religions of the world are studied in addition to the Bible. Social or political problems are sometimes considered in the higher degrees of the secondary schools, in meetings for the students, and in youth meetings in the churches.

The churches of South Cameroun (Presbyterian Church, Église Évangélique, Églises Baptistes) have developed aids in French for Bible teaching in their schools: copybooks with Bible stories for the pupils, questions to answer, booklets for the teachers and flannelgraphs.

The state of religious education is about the same in the churches of Gaboon and Congo. In the northern parts of Cameroun, in Tchad and some parts of Republique Centrafricaine, the churches are more recent, the schools are still beginning, and a great part of the population is still illiterate. — *Absolom Vilakazi*

AFRICAN METHODIST EPISCOPAL CHURCH The African Methodist Episcopal Church was started in 1787 in Philadelphia by a group of Americans whose forefathers came from Africa. The leader of this group was a 27-year-old " African," Richard Allen. At that time the word " African " was used to designate those persons now called American Negroes.

The movement to organize a separate Negro church was started in response to the "Africans'" need for opportunities for self-expression and fuller involvement in the service of the worship of God and in society as a whole. It was the answer to a cry for social recognition as human beings, and the means through which a group of people started on a program that gave them a growing sense of dignity and self-respect.

To foster this program Richard Allen considered it important to conduct night school classes in which his people could learn how to help themselves. Out of these night school classes has come the church's philosophy of education with a strong emphasis upon self-help that has not been significantly changed to this day. The A.M.E. Church operates 11 institutions of higher education.

Most religious groups had their origin in some theological, doctrinal, or ideological dispute or concern. The organization of the A.M.E. Church was the result of racial discrimination rather than of any theological or doctrinal concern. The A.M.E. Church is a member of the family of Methodist Churches. Allen, its founder and first active bishop, felt that no religious sect or denomination would suit the capacity of his people as well as did Methodism, with its emphasis upon the plain and simple gospel that the unlearned could understand and its orderly system of rules and regulations that the underdeveloped needed. He felt that Methodism had what the " African " needed to encourage him to make progress, to worship God freely, and to fill every office for which he had the capability.

The " Africans " who started the A.M.E. Church were very poor, and most of them could not read or write. Yet, under the leadership of Allen, they managed to buy an old blacksmith shop and to move it to a lot at the corner of Sixth and Lombard Streets in Philadelphia. Bethel A.M.E. Church stands today as one of the historic religious shrines of the city.

Today the A.M.E. Church has 18

active bishops and more than a million members scattered throughout the U.S.A., Canada, South America, West Africa, South Africa, and the West Indies. — *Andrew White*

AFRICAN METHODIST EPISCOPAL ZION CHURCH In the *Minutes* of the General Conference · of the Methodist Episcopal Church of 1780 appears the following: " Ought not the Assistant (Mr. Asbury) to meet with the colored people himself, and appoint as helpers in his absence proper white persons, and not suffer them to stay so late and meet by themselves? Answer: Yes." From this entry, members of the African Methodist Episcopal Zion Church trace their origin as a church, although it was not until 1796 that a separate meeting place was secured. In 1799 the "African" Chapel undertook to build its own house of worship, services meanwhile having been conducted in the John Street Church (New York).

The Methodist Episcopal General Conference of 1800 recognized the existence of the organization by authorizing John McClaskey to make arrangements and effect some articles of agreement with the Chapel for its government. These articles were drawn up Feb. 16, 1801. Earlier, Sept. 8, 1800, a charter had been granted the Chapel by the State of New York. At that time, it is recorded, there were 3 Negro Methodist preachers in the City of New York, 2 of them, along with an exhorter, being identified with the " African " Chapel.

The African Chapel was organized not only for religious purposes but also to advance the welfare of Negroes in the City of New York. In the *Minutes* of the Common Council of the City (July 25, 1804) appears the following: " Returns were received from the following churches of the monies given to them for the use of Schools agreeably to law, to wit, the General Lutheran Church, the Methodist Episcopal Church, the Scotch Presbyterian Church, and the African Church." In 1844 a second step in the development of the church's educational program was taken when the General Conference authorized the establishment of Rush Academy. With the aid of a special convention (York, Pa., 1847) called for the purpose, the selected committee proposed to the General Conference of 1848 that the institution should be established in Essex County, N.Y., where the abolitionist Gerritt Smith had donated a plot of ground for the purpose.

In 1879, Zion Wesley Institute (now Livingstone College, Salisbury, N.C.) was incorporated. It has an affiliated theological seminary, Hood. Other institutions of junior college and college level are located in Arkansas, Mississippi, Alabama, and South Carolina.

Interest in Sunday school work appears to have begun almost with the founding of the denomination. Just when the Sunday school convention became an established practice is not known, but some conferences were holding such sessions by 1888, the year in which the 1st editor of Sunday school literature was elected. The 1st secretary of education was elected in 1892.
— *David H. Bradley*

AGE GROUPS Age groups in the Protestant Sunday school have a prototype in Luther's catechetical instruction classes for children and adults. In both the English Sunday school of the late 18th century and the American Sunday school of the early 19th century there were probably 2 age groups. These were known as the "infant class" and the "senior pupils" class. In the 1830's the New York Sunday School Union provided question lessons for teachers of 3 age-group levels — children, young people, and adults, in which the emphasis was placed upon the varying mental abilities of these age groups for the purposes of teaching. In 1887 the Fifth International Convention of Sunday School Unions gave formal recognition to a fourth age group, the home department.

The present age-group pattern employed in the American church school was developed in the early years of this century. Originally it was merely a children's department containing a 6 to 14 age span. Next, an adult group for those needing elementary religious instruction was added. Finally, a preprimary age group completed the 1st age-grouping design.

The term "age groups" in current Protestant church school terminology refers to the grouping of pupils in classes, departments, divisions, and interest groups for the purpose of religious education and according to a criterion based on chronological age and public day school grading. Broadly classified age groups in the church school correspond to the 3 major phases of the human life cycle — childhood, adolescence, and maturity; or the children's, youth, and adult divisions.

In the children's division there are the infancy, the early, middle, and later childhood age groups. The early childhood age group comprises infants (birth to 2 years), nursery children (2 to 3 years), and kindergarten children (4 to 5 years). The middle childhood age group comprises primary children 6 to 8 years), and the later childhood age group comprises junior children (9 to 11 years).

The youth division is differentiated in terms of physiological maturity according to the classifications of early, middle, and later adolescence. Early adolescence includes the intermediate (12 to 14 years), middle adolescence the senior (15 to 17 years), and later adolescence the older youth (18 to 21 or until adult status is attained). The terms intermediate, senior, and older youth are often designated junior high, senior high, and post high, respectively.

Technically, the adult division is similarly subdivided into periods of early adulthood, middle age, and later maturity. Insofar as age groups are concerned, young adult groups are related to the early adult period, adult groups and classes to the middle-aged period, and older adult groups to the later maturity stage. Actually, however, adults are not rigidly classified. Except for the infirm or otherwise especially disabled, there is relatively little doctrinaire grouping in this area.

The principle for pupil-grouping in the church school is not arbitrary but functional. It is an attempt to construct generally homogeneous groupings for Christian teaching and learning. In the formulation of this principle the research and experimentation of the behavioral sciences have been considered. These data establish several assumptions: (1) persons are dynamic, developing, interactive beings; (2) persons face certain developmental tasks at particular points in the life cycle

(Havighurst); (3) persons develop at different rates; (4) individual pupils bring various learning capacities and abilities to the teaching situation; (5) pupils differ in terms of ability to recognize and negotiate their developmental tasks, and they differ markedly in their motivations to do so. Grouping, then, must consider these findings and provide for the age-grade groupings that will best promote and cultivate the individual growth pattern of each pupil.

In seeking to do this, such factors as chronological age and sex alone are inadequate as criteria for grouping. Factors such as mental capacity, achievement, motivation, social maturity, and special abilities or disabilities are now being recognized as more adequate bases for grouping.

Church school organizational patterns reflect these trends in several ways. First, in the appearance of the 2-year grade-group plan. While it has been customary to group preschool pupils in this way (i.e., nursery 2's with 3's, and kindergarten 4's with 5's), many primary-junior groups are now being reconstructed on the basis of this 2-year plan. Under this arrangement the 6's are grouped with 7's, 8's with 9's, and 10's with 11's. In the youth division this means grouping 12's with 13's, 14's with 15's, and 16's with 17's. Another trend in grouping influenced by public-school grading and developmental psychology is the 1-year age-group or closely graded plan. This arrangement seems most feasible for church schools with sufficient enrollments and balanced sex ratios.

Another approach to the construction of teaching groups is the ungraded group. The principle involved here is that of permissive growth whereby individual pupils progress at their own rate of development without the imposed limitation of grade groups. Administratively this approach structures the church school by departments in both the children's and youth division in a small church. In a large situation there could be ability grouping and/or selective grouping across grade lines and on a departmental basis. Church schools, generally speaking, have not applied this method to their work. In some instances, however, this method is used in churches that have developed a program for exceptional children and youth.

A somewhat different problem confronts the church school administrator in grouping in the older youth area and throughout the adult division. Here it is found that the principle of chronological maturity is least relevant. Older youth or post high school young people should be planned for in terms of functional groupings. Their marital, parental, and vocational status indicate that their groupings should be projected from an interest and *ad hoc* basis.

Several implications for church school administration emerge from this survey of age groups. 1. Age groups should be constituted to provide for pupils individually and groups of pupils collectively an educational experience — situations in which it will be possible for spiritual growth to occur. Grouping is to be implemented in the light of learning purposes, and it is not to be considered as an organizational detail to be expedited.

2. Patterns and practices for organizing age groups for effective learning in the church cannot be prescribed for on a uniform basis. Each situation will have its peculiar cluster of problems.

Generally speaking, church schools with small enrollments will have larger, more heterogeneous age groups and probably only 3 classes, corresponding to the 3 basic age-group divisions in church school administration. Church schools with somewhat larger enrollments will probably have relatively smaller, less heterogeneous and more homogeneous age groupings, with probably 6 to 10 individual classes. In larger church school situations there will be closely graded grouping based on the homogeneous principle and perhaps providing for additional groupings of exceptional pupils.

3. The organization of age groups in local church schools should usually follow the grading pattern and plan of the community public schools. Public-school administrators have developed patterns on the basis of such basic factual data as population trends, birth statistics, age-sex distribution studies, and educational psychology. They are, therefore, in a position to know for their particular communities the size and age-group composition of an effective learning unit.

A 4th implication of age-grade grouping relates to team teaching. It is now generally recognized that persons learn most effectively in and through group-guided experiences. These groups should be large enough to permit a program of activities and experiences that stimulate and yet small enough to encourage individual participation.

Any one of the age-grouping plans discussed in this article is adaptable to this newer teaching technique. Groups for team teaching may be constructed around a single age-grade group, a two age-grade group, or a three age-grade group. The plan to be used would be determined by the recommended group size for team teaching, which varies between 18 to 24 pupils with a ratio of 6 to 8 pupils assigned to a teacher or assistant.

A final implication of age-grade grouping for the church school lies in the area of architecture and design. The small homogeneous grouping approach is probably most effectively implemented in a physical setting where there is adequate space for freedom of movement and creative expression through guided and related activity. This can be accomplished best in commodious single-grade classrooms built as self-contained teaching units adaptable for the integrated learning experience in group teaching.

— *Grant S. Shockley*

ALCUIN   Alcuin (Anglo-Saxon, Ealhwine; Latin, Albinus), Northumbrian nobleman, was born ca. 735 at York (?); died, May 19, 804, at Tours. Egbert, a pupil of Bede's, was his first teacher at York, and then Aelbert, whose associate he soon became as teacher and librarian. In 778 he became headmaster and librarian. In the hierarchy he remained a deacon; that he was a monk is doubtful. On Continental trips he had strongly impressed Charlemagne, who in 781 invited him to Francia as " minister of Christian culture," to use a celebrated phrase. With other Northumbrians he went there in 782, and, save for 790 to 793, spent the rest of his life in Charlemagne's circle, teaching and writing. The king, queen, royal children, courtiers, and select youth from everywhere were his pupils. His lifelong passion for teaching the liberal arts as the basis for Christian virtue had ample opportunity. In 796 he sought to retire to Fulda as a monk. Instead, the king made him abbot of St. Martin of Tours, where he spent his last years.

Wallach states in a recent study: " The unusual versatility of Alcuin made him the foremost figure in Charlemagne's brilliant entourage. His accomplishments as educator, statesman, administrator, poet, writer, and scholar were not paralleled by any of his gifted friends of the palace school fellowship, though the Good Theodulph of Orleans may have been a better poet, the Lombard Paul the Deacon a better historian, and the Patriarch Paulinus of Aquileia a more original theologian " (*Alcuin and Charlemagne,* 1959, p. 3).

Despite Alcuin's love of teaching, his liberal arts manuals are not what educators study now. Charlemagne's great ordinance, *De colendis litteris,* and the allied Carolingian Renaissance, are known to stem from a mandate written by Alcuin in the period 794 to 800. " Alcuin purified the [Bible] text, as well as standardizing it," says Miss Smalley; a modern critical edition of this has appeared (Fischer). Paleographers praise his perfecting and spreading everywhere the newly developed Caroline minuscule, the most perfect book script known (Lowe). More and more historians are convinced that Alcuin's was the guiding hand in the imperial coronation of 800 (Ganshof). The Roman rite being then made obligatory, Alcuin revised the Missal in ways that Rome took over later, perhaps his most lasting monument (Abercrombie). To him, for example, is due the use of the creed at Mass (Capelle).

His other writings cover a wide range. His chief doctrinal treatise, *De fide trinitatis* (PL 101, 9–64), based on Augustine, was written as a *Summa* for priests. Vacandard ascribes to him a decisive influence in the history of confession. His many anti-Adoptionist writings show a growing skill in framing theological argument (Wilmart). A few Scripture commentaries, moral exhortations, lives of saints, poems, and over 250 letters survive.

— *Gerald B. Ellard*

AMERICAN BAPTIST CONVENTION Churches affiliated with the American Baptist Convention exercise a variety of practices within a unity of beliefs that characterize Baptists. As a worshiping group, Baptists are related to the English Puritan movement of the 17th century and share many beliefs and practices in common with churches growing from the Reformation. Along with this common heritage with other Protestant groups, Baptists have emphasized certain aspects of worship and service that made them different from other church groups.

In general, American Baptists may be characterized as believing in: (1) A regenerate church membership, the belief that the church should be made up of those who can give testimony of personal faith in Christ as Savior. (2) Believer's baptism. Only those should be baptized in the likeness of Christ's death and resurrection who have personally accepted him as Savior. (3) Congregational polity in church affairs. Each local church should manifest the qualities of the true church in its work and worship. Each local church has " power " to administer its worship and discipline. Every member should participate in all phases of the church program. (4) Associational interdependency. In order to enhance the spread of the gospel, churches may cooperate in Christian enterprises. Associating with other churches emphasizes the interdependency of the Baptist witness without losing sight of the primacy of the local church. (5) God freedom. In order for God to work through his church, no outside forces should restrict or limit the ministry of the church. Thus Baptists have stressed the separation of church and state.

American Baptists have been characterized by a fervent desire to preach the gospel to every creature. Their strong interest in fulfilling the Great Commission in part determined the early organizational structure of church cooperation. During the 18th century, the associational principle whereby churches cooperated interdependently to worship and serve gained considerable strength. It was envisioned by early American Baptists that local associations would form state or regional associations and these in turn would form a national association. Much planning took place toward that major objective.

During the early 19th century, Baptists were greatly stirred by missionary efforts. In order to support the missionary interests resulting from the work of the Judsons and Luther Rice, to build educational institutions, and to publish materials for study and evangelism, different societies arose. Between 1814 and 1891 eight independent societies came into being to share in the missionary enterprises. In 1907 these societies met in Washington, D.C., and agreed to form the Northern Baptist Convention to unify the denomination and the work of the societies in their missionary efforts. In 1950 the Northern Baptist Convention, with some reorganization, changed its name to the American Baptist Convention.

Subsequent changes in administrative practices to facilitate the spread of the Christian message have been accompanied by extended outreach and increased missionary personnel. At present, American Baptists have over 1,200 missionaries working alongside 15,000 nationals to serve over 5,000 churches and 3,000 mission stations. Some missionaries are called by national leaders to serve indigenous enterprises. The American Baptist witness is shared in at least 16 countries.

On the home front, missionary activities are diversified, seeking to make the Christian message relevant to contemporary problems. Camping programs are carried on in more than 225 camps. Ministries to metropolitan areas are shared by over 85 missionary personnel through 37 Christian centers. Through the Christian Higher Education Challenge, scholarships are provided for students and support is given to 22 American Baptist schools and colleges besides the 9 seminaries. The Home Mission Board also maintains Bacone College for Indians, Mather School, and other schools to develop leadership for particular racial groups and to meet the ever-increasing demand for Christian workers. Emphasis on a Christian witness in the world of work has led to a well-articulated program of vocational evangelism.

Growth and increase characterize the Christian ministry on the contemporary scene. Fifteen new institutions are being added to the home and hospital ministry of the 71 already in operation. Efforts are made to reach Indians and Spanish-speaking people. The love for people everywhere also insists that American youth in trouble should have " a Christian chance." Local churches participate in foreign and home missionary activities through their gifts to the Unified Budget, which totals more than $10,000,000.

One of the distinguishing characteristics of the American Baptist Convention is its emphasis on qualitative Christian education in the local church. This program of Christian education is organized around the curricular materials published by the Board of Education and Publications. In its earlier days the Board performed a distinctive ministry in tract distribution and evangelism through colporteurs. Pioneer work in Sunday school organizations, youth organizations, and daily vacation Bible schools were all significant advances leading toward the comprehensive program in literature and education that is available today.

The development of the educational program and curricular materials have been guided by the theme: " The Great Objective in Christian Education — The New Person in Jesus Christ." The teaching materials and suggested procedures in teachers' quarterlies are means by which God may " enter into the life of growing persons, saving them from sin and empowering them through his Spirit for lives of righteousness and service." To help lead into such a personal relationship with God through Christ, the American Baptist materials emphasize " the tragedy of sin, the grace of God, the redemptive love of God in Jesus, the re-creative power of the Holy Spirit, the coming Kingdom of God, and the promise of the future life."

The American Baptist program in Christian education gives careful consideration to insights from the behavioral sciences by considering patterns of human growth and development, appealing to human interests, and utilizing the better techniques and procedures demonstrated in modern education. In view of the fact that relations with other people are most significant in spiritual relation with God, the curricular materials offer guidance for development in relation with God, Jesus, the Bible, the church, other people, and self. Thus, the materials are both pupil-centered and Christ-centered.

American Baptist churches may choose the International Uniform Lesson Series, which is broadly graded, or the Judson Graded Curriculum. While the difference is primarily one of approach, the Graded Curriculum provides more use of the Bible in fulfilling the objectives of the curriculum planned for closely graded experiences of children and youth. It also uses more external resources to include something to learn about and participate in. In both curricula the materials are designed for comprehensive learning. Thus members from the major denominational agencies work with the age-group curriculum committees to plan the total educational ministry of the churches. The same editors produce the age-group materials for both the Graded and the Uniform lesson plans.

Proper use of the Judson materials assumes training on the part of church school teachers, for " a call to teach is a call to prepare." To help individuals and churches secure proper training, a program of leadership education is sponsored. First and second series courses in leadership, differing in background required and intensity of study, are offered. Conferences are sponsored on the local, regional, and national levels. Leaders from all over the country study in workshop experiences at Green Lake (Wis.) laboratory school, where over 200 conferences are attended by more than 30,000 persons in one summer. Such efforts to promote and sustain trained teaching personnel constitute an outstanding feature of American Baptist church education. — *Cyril D. Garrett*

AMERICAN COUNCIL ON EDUCATION The American Council on Education came into being in 1918 as the answer to an obvious need to coordinate the services that educational institutions and organizations could contribute to the Government in the national crisis brought on by World War I. Since then the Council has become a center of cooperation and coordination for the improvement of education at all levels, with particular emphasis on higher education.

Today, as in the beginning, membership is by organization or institution, not by individuals. This membership consists of approximately 145 national and regional associations and over 1,000 educational institutions.

The Council's functions as set forth in its constitution, membership, and activities reflect the peculiar genius of the American educational system — a system without national control, comprising a large number of autonomous units working together for the establishment and improvement of educational standards, policies, and procedures.

More specifically the Council is a clearinghouse for the exchange of information and opinion. It conducts scientific inquiries and investigations into educational problems and seeks to enlist appropriate agencies for the solution of such problems. It keeps in constant touch with pending legislation affecting education, serves as a liaison agency between the educational institutions and the Federal Government, and has undertaken many significant projects at the request of the Army, Navy, State Department, and other Government agencies. It has pioneered in methodology that has become standard practice in the nation. Publications on college and university business management are representative achievements.

Some Council activities of lasting value to American education are: the psychological examinations for high school students and college freshmen, issued annually by the Council from 1924 through 1947, and the Cooperative Test Service, which functioned under the Council's sole sponsorship from 1930 to January 1, 1948, when both of these projects were merged into the newly created Educational Testing Service; the American Youth Commission, composed of a group of leaders in civic and educational affairs who studied youth problems through a period of years and produced more than 30 volumes of enduring value; and the Commission on Teacher Education, a cooperative, nationwide project in which more than 50 colleges, universities, and public-school systems participated, and which resulted in a series of 20 published reports on a variety of problems. The Council was also active for a long period of years in the development of better and more uniform standards for the accrediting of institutions on the secondary and college levels.

Ongoing Council projects and committees include the Commission on Accreditation of Service Experiences, established 1945; the Inter-

American Schools Service, established 1943; and the Committee on Measurement and Evaluation, established 1949 and continuing in a field in which the Council has long been active. Other areas in which Council committees have been influential in establishing policy in recent years include educational television, college teaching, international cultural relations, and institutional research policy. There are 28 commissions and committees currently operating in various fields. Outstanding leaders in education and public life serve on Council committees and take an active part in educational conferences and studies.

As the end result of its research, special studies, conferences, and surveys, the Council publishes from 15 to 20 books a year. It publishes *The Educational Record,* a quarterly, and *Higher Education and National Affairs,* an occasional bulletin. Two directories inaugurated by the Council are the only directories composed exclusively of accredited institutions of higher education, *American Universities and Colleges* and *American Junior Colleges,* both issued every 4 years. — *Charles C. Dobbins*

AMERICAN LUTHERAN CHURCH

The American Lutheran Church was constituted in 1961 by a merger of the United Evangelical Lutheran Church (Danish in origin), American Lutheran Church (German in origin), and the Evangelical Lutheran Church (Norwegian in origin). It describes itself and its purposes as follows: " The American Lutheran Church, a union of congregations to which the gospel of reconciliation has been given, seeks to focus and coordinate the purposes and resources of these congregations to the end that the Triune God may be more fully known among men through a faithful ministry of Word and Sacrament."

It consists of 4,943 congregations, served by 3,714 pastors, and comprised of 2,306,780 baptized (1,509,174 confirmed) members. Its central offices are located in Minneapolis, Minn. The church is formed into 19 districts, of which 9 are found in the upper Midwestern states of Minnesota, Wisconsin, Iowa, and the Dakotas. Other concentrations of members are found in Ohio, Michigan, and Texas. Scattered congregations are found in most states but only a very few in the South.

The American Lutheran Church is a member of the National Lutheran Council, the Lutheran World Federation, and the World Council of Churches.

More than 80 new congregations are started each year. A world mission outreach is carried on in Brazil, Colombia, Cameroun, Madagascar, Nigeria, South Africa, Ethiopia, Hong Kong, India, Japan, New Guinea, and Taiwan.

The church has a long history of vigorous activity in higher education. Nine of its 10 senior colleges have histories of from 71 to 112 years. California Lutheran College opened its doors for students in the fall of 1961. The church also operates 3 junior colleges and 2 boarding high schools in the U.S.A. and Canada. The church prepares about 236 men for the ministry each year in its seminary, located on 4 campuses in St. Paul, Minn., Dubuque, Iowa, Columbus, Ohio, and Saskatoon, Sask. A growing movement for lay " schools of theology " (a few days to 2 weeks) is discernible throughout the church.

In its parishes the American Lutheran Church has a vigorous program of Sunday, vacation, and weekday church schools, and special education. In one of its 3 curriculum series, it provides also a whole course for parents of elementary and junior high children. A new curriculum prepared in 5 segments (preschool, elementary, junior high, senior high, adult) will be introduced into congregations beginning in 1964.

Training for church school teachers is offered in most congregations, and in a series of 200 ten-hour institutes held each fall in every conference (a group of 20 to 30 congregations) throughout the church. About 40,000 teachers participate in these institutes every year. To operate these institutes the Department of Parish Education trains over 2,000 instructors for the specific course to be taught each year.

A 2d major church-wide teacher training effort is carried on in vacation church school clinics and by means of leaders' training days.

In addition to age-level specialists, the Department of Parish Education provides the full-time services of an audio-visual consultant, a family-life educator, and a research consultant. Nine regional (salaried by synod) or district (salaried by district) directors of parish education spend their whole time in field interpretation and training. Fifty-two congregations operate Christian day schools consisting of at least 1 elementary grade above kindergarten. A part-time consultant for such schools is provided by the Board of Parish Education.

For isolated and housebound families the Department of Parish Education makes available a Sunday series of lessons, with lessons exchanged at regular intervals.

— *C. Richard Evenson*

ANGLICAN CHURCH OF CANADA

Richard Watts is credited with establishing the 1st Sunday school at Annapolis Royal, N.S., in 1727. About 1783 a clergyman named Breynton established the Sunday school at St. Paul's Anglican Church, Halifax, possibly the oldest continuous Sunday school in the world.

The concern for Christian education led to the establishment of the Inter-Diocesan Sunday School Committee. In 1909 the General Synod Sunday School Commission was founded. On May 7, 1919, the General Board of Religious Education was established as a Department of the General Synod.

Under the direction of D. B. Rogers the closely graded *Christian Truth and Life Series* of lessons was developed, continuously revised to meet the changing concepts of Christian education.

The Department has provided materials for Sunday school by post for more than 50 years and narrative manuscripts and dramatized radio tapes of Sunday school lessons for the National Sunday School of the Air for about 15 years.

Plans are now under way to produce a completely new graded curriculum, influenced to some extent by *The Seabury Series* of the Protestant Episcopal Church in the U.S.A.

Beginning about 1908, midweek programs were developed for every age group. The Anglican Young People's Association has spread from Canada to Great Britain and many other Commonwealth countries.

The work of the Department is now divided into 6 divisions — School at Home (correspondence) Curriculum, Leadership Training, College Work, Children's Work, Youth Work, and Adult Work. A major emphasis is being developed in the area of leadership training for clergy and laity. By 1962 there were 9 full-time and 3 part-time national-staff persons engaged in this work across Canada, in close cooperation with diocesan personnel. This program consists of church and group life laboratories, seminars on the liturgy, preaching and pastoral ministry conferences, diocesan consultations on strategy, parish life conferences, and missions. Reading courses are being offered for lay theological study, leading to the Primate's Diploma.

— *Trevor E. Jones*

AQUINAS, THOMAS This man, whom succeeding ages gave the sobriquet of angelic and common (or universal) doctor (teacher), was born to the noble Aquino family sometime in 1225, at the fortress of Roccasecca, near Naples. He received his early training from the Benedictine monks at Monte Cassino, and in 1239 enrolled at the University of Naples. While there he was received into the new Order of Friars Preacher (O.P.), or Dominicans, as they were called after their founder, Dominic. Aquinas' family, who were opposed to his entry into the order, imprisoned him at Roccasecca, but after a time he escaped and went to Paris, where under the famous German Dominican, Albert the Great, he began his clerical studies. There, from 1252 to 1254, he lectured on the Scriptures; from 1254 to 1265 he commented on the *Sentences* of Peter Lombard, the standard theological text of the time; and in 1256, he became one of the two Dominicans occupying chairs of theology on the faculty of the University of Paris. During the period 1259 to 1269, he taught successively at Anagni, Orvieto,

Rome, and Viterbo. In 1269 he was in Paris again, where he taught until summoned in 1272 to organize the Dominican house of theological studies at Naples. It was there, in December, 1273, that he finally put aside his papers and books after experiencing a vision while saying Mass. After it, he said to a friend, his writings seemed " as so much straw." Thomas Aquinas died 3 months later, March 7, 1274, at the Cistercian abbey of Fossanuova, while on his way to the Council of Lyons where Pope Gregory X had summoned him to take part in the proceedings. He was canonized on July 18, 1323.

Thomas Aquinas is indisputably the greatest theologian the Roman Church has produced, and among his theological works the *Summa Theologica* is the most famous and profound. He wrote also a sizable body of philosophical writings, chiefly commentaries on Aristotle.

Certain similarities characterize all his writings. All are noteworthy for simplicity and clarity of style and faithfulness to a fixed purpose. Aquinas had the utmost respect for tradition and the great minds, pagan as well as Christian, who preceded him. It was he who, by means of the translations from the Greek of William of Moerbeke and Henry of Brabant, was primarily responsible for the presentation, amplification, and defense of Aristotelian philosophy in the West, unadulterated by the corruptions of the Arabian philosophers. In his theology, at every opportunity, he makes reference to the Eastern and Western fathers and doctors of the church and to the early Christian apologists. Whenever possible he turns to the authority of the church itself, in the pronouncements of the popes and councils, as a source of corroboration or explanation. But for Thomas Aquinas the authority of sacred Scripture is always absolute. Time and again he applies his own and the accumulated human genius of the past to some theological problem, only to insist simultaneously that " the authority of Scripture is sufficient proof."

In modern times especially, the popes have reiterated approval of the doctrinal and methodological synthesis of Thomism, and have constituted it as normative for judging all other philosophicotheological systems. — *Reginald R. Masterson*

ARISTOTLE   Aristotle (384–322 B.C.), philosopher, psychologist, logician, moralist, political theorist, biologist, founder of literary criticism, and the earliest historian of ideas, has been rivaled in his influence upon European traditions in education, philosophy, and general culture only by his teacher, Plato. Although his influence on classical antiquity was never so deep as Plato's, in the thousand years following the decline of the ancient civilization in the 5th century A.D. it was both strong and widely diffused. In the 13th century Aristotle's authority reached a very high point. With the rise of humanism this authority declined and, in time, was virtually nullified outside the Roman Catholic Church by the rise of modern science, the Cartesian philosophy, and other movements. The efforts of Leo XIII in the latter part of the 19th century brought a sharp rise, within the Roman Church, of the authority of Aquinas — and therefore of Aristotelianism — and the 20th century has seen a widespread revival of the influence of Aristotle in other quarters.

Aristotle was born in Stagira, on the Thracian peninsula. His father was court physician to Alexander's grandfather, and the medical profession is said to have been hereditary in his family. This may have helped him form a taste for accurate detailed inquiry. At 17 he came to join Plato's Academy in Athens, remaining until the master's death 20 years later. By the time of Plato's death Aristotle had already won wide renown for his scholarship, writing, and public lectures. Four years later, in 343, he was called by Philip to undertake the education of Alexander. The details of this relationship are obscure, but its active phase could not have lasted more than 3 years, as Alexander was appointed regent for his father in 340. When the Asian campaign of Alexander began in 335, Aristotle returned to Athens to found his own school, the Lyceum. For the next 12 or 13 years he devoted himself with extraordinary industry to teaching, investigation, and speculation, as well as to the organization of the school. It is to this period that most of his surviving works belong. Political developments following the death of Alexander forced Aristotle to leave Athens. The next year, 322 B.C., Aristotle died in Chalcis in Euboea.

Aristotle's writings fall into 3 groups: (1) literary productions intended for publication, such as his dialogues, which were once an important source of his reputation, but now are entirely lost, save for fragments; (2) set writings of a different character, such as compilations and chronological tables; (3) the treatises. Some of the treatises were begun before his return to Athens, but in the main they were developed in connection with his investigations and teaching at the

Lyceum. As a result, some of them never approached finished literary form. They fall under eight headings: logic, physics, psychology, biology, metaphysics, ethics, politics, and literary criticism.

Aristotle agreed with Plato that real knowledge requires rational mastery of universal principles, but he did not dismiss particular observations. He resisted the dualistic tendency in Platonism and sought to derive universal premises from particular facts. He thus made use of induction.

His "first philosophy" accepted the Platonic rejection of material atomism, but denied the transcendence of the rational order to the world of things. Matter and form are 2 fundamental aspects of things. Matter always exists in relation to form, but pure form is exalted as supreme reality or God — the prime mover and final cause of all things. Thus "first philosophy" culminates in theology. The historic attempts to reconcile this view with the Hebrew conception of God, within Judaism and Christianity, have been fraught with far-flung consequences.

The physical sciences made up the "second philosophy" of Aristotle. He did not develop a satisfactory scientific method, but achieved real stature as a biologist through his keenness as an observer. His psychology leads directly into ethics and politics. Those men who are capable of citizenship (and Aristotle did not assert the dignity of all men) must take an active part in the legislation and administration of the state — but also live an actively individual life. The best order for most states is a constitutional commonwealth in which only the reasonable and virtuous participate.

— *Tyler Thompson*

ART Art provides a most instructive theological paradox. It is an effective form of communicating the gospel, yet the physical medium of art can easily tempt one to an undiscerning idolatry. Theology teaches in words and thought patterns the message of forgiveness and new life in Jesus Christ. Art can do the same thing. Through its various media and forms of color, sound, shape, and rhythm, art conveys the highest hopes and deepest fears of man. These hopes and fears may be in the service of the Lord or of Satan. It is because of its demonic use that art was suspect to both the earliest Christians and to the Puritan Reformers. Nevertheless, throughout Christian history art has been used to convey the Christian message both in subject and in style.

The subjects of Christian art have been determined by the fact that the Christian message is a story and not an idea. Persons and events are involved in meaningful drama. Hence, Christian painters, sculptors, musicians, and artists of all kinds have been preoccupied with the Man on the cross, Madonna and Child, the Master and his disciples at table. There have also been symbolic images such as the sacred heart of Roman Catholic piety and the Good Shepherd of the Protestants, but chiefly the history of sacred art shows a continuing interest in the persons and events of the Passion narrative. The Nativity, the crucifixion, the Last Supper, the Stations of the Cross, Gethsemane, and the resurrection constitute the great bulk of subjects depicted by artists in the Christian tradition.

In contrast to the stylized symbolism of Buddhist art, Christian artists have chosen subjects that tell the story in picture language of God's dramatic action in history to save the world from sin, death, and the devil. The reposeful Buddhas with placid countenance are intended by their craftsmen to represent the ideal of tranquil aloofness from both the good and bad fortunes of this world. The Christian subjects show that we are in this world for good or bad. We cannot escape by our own devices from the evils that torment us, but the God who made us is a compassionate God. He comes and suffers on our behalf so that we and his whole creation can be made new.

Even more important than subject, style is an enlightening factor in the communication of art. In modern times we may say very broadly that 4 major styles have emerged. In the Renaissance a representational style was perfected by such men as Raphael and Michelangelo. Instead of the otherworldly symbols of the medieval artists, the Renaissance painters and sculptors sought to capture in color and stone the natural reality of man. In sharp contrast to this, there has persisted into modern times a minor school of almost surrealistic style which has insisted upon blurring the features of nature in order to reach beyond the empirically given. This kind of mysticism is typified by William Blake and Henri Rousseau in earlier years and by the surrealism of Salvador Dalí in our own time. A more important shift in style, equal to that of the Renaissance, was effected by Cézanne who stopped representing reality and started to reconstruct it. Like Plato, who inscribed over his Academy: " Let no man ignorant of geometry enter here," Cézanne wrote: " God always geometrizes." He wanted to paint the virginity of the world; thus he uncovered its basic, unspoiled shapes and colors.

The result was that Cézanne became the spiritual father of modern art, in both its styles of impressionism and expressionism. The impressionists sought to capture a glimpse or a mood of human experience in all its truth and purity. They discovered that art is more than rules about shapes. It is light and illumination of the spirit through its many colors. The expressionists fractured the world of reality because they were weary of it, and they tried to reconstruct a new world without any of the hallowed rules of the past. Some followed the geometrical faith of Cézanne, as for example the cubism of Braque, but others developed a violent irrationalism, as in the drips and blobs of Jackson Pollock or the piercing, protesting lines of Hans Hartung.

What theological meaning can we find in these various styles lacking as they are in an overt relation to religious subject? The Christian message is the good news of forgiveness and new life for sinners, which comes as a gift of grace from the God who is hidden behind the masks of his creation but who has revealed himself in Jesus Christ. The Christian faith is therefore always involved in the paradox of the God who is both hidden and revealed, indivisible Spirit and visible Word. God speaks in words and shapes and colors and sounds and tastes apprehensible to our human senses, yet always he remains beyond human control.

While realistic style implies that the creation is solid and good and not a chimera, perhaps the surrealists and especially the expressionists register a valid protest in their declaration that reality is more than what can be seen. Certainly Jesus cannot be recognized as the Christ simply by looking at him. Art which expresses a style that is not obvious but is suggestive and disturbing serves the Christian function of declaring that God is not at our fingertips for our idolatrous use. We must wait upon the Spirit before we can confess that Jesus is Lord; likewise, the Spirit communicates to us in strange and difficult art forms.

We must recognize, therefore, that much art with nonreligious subjects nevertheless conveys the Christian message. Christianity rooted in its Hebrew background proclaims a thankful joy in the good creation. The art of Christians must necessarily glorify the Creator. A landscape by Cézanne or an impression of water lilies by Monet can do this as effectively as Michelangelo's painting of the creation of Adam by the finger of God.

Christianity also calls us to repentance for sin. Art often serves as phophetic denunciation. One must be careful here to avoid misunderstanding. Art may truly protest against social evils but it must never be allowed to serve a loveless moralism. When art is used only as a pedagogic device it soon degenerates into a propagandistic tool of the ideology or demagogue happening to be in power. On the other hand, art is not so free and unfettered as to be only for art's sake. Art must serve the Lord and speak his word through its peculiar medium. Picasso has achieved this end in portraying his pathetic clowns and harlequins, and perhaps the most lucid demonstration of repentant self-examination has been executed by Rouault in his series of paintings on man's inhumanity to man.

Finally, the Christian message proclaims joy in redemption with all that this means for both a present new life in Christ and for our eschatological hope. This is more difficult to portray without explicit reference to the Christian story as subject. Rembrandt, Grünewald, and Rouault have told this story effectively with their brushes. Probably because of the nature of the message and the nature of the medium, music is better able to speak of the mystery of a not yet fulfilled salvation. The great mystery that the artist can and must proclaim is not that man and earth can reach to God and heaven by the manipulation of a material medium, but rather that God has come down to earth, that the divine can be declared through the colors of clay. The artistic statement will therefore seek to exhibit the grace of Christ in all its splendor of freedom and renewal. — *Robert Paul Roth*

ASSOCIATE REFORMED PRESBYTERIAN CHURCH (GENERAL SYNOD)

The Associate Reformed Presbyterian Church is of Scottish origin, although it never had an organic existence in Scotland. The Associate Presbytery of Scotland was organized in 1733 by Ebenezer Erskine and 3 other ministers who had seceded from the Church of Scotland. One reason for their withdrawal from the Church of Scotland was the practice of patronage. They maintained that no landowner or patron could place a pastor in a charge. The Reformed Presbytery of Scotland came into existence in 1743. The Reformed Presbyterians were descendants of the Covenanters who had made a "solemn league and covenant" never to compromise their testimony to the crown rights of Christ. Members of both groups migrated to America and by 1782 two Associate Presbyteries and a Reformed Presbytery had been formed in this country. In that year the Associate and Reformed bodies united to form the Associate Reformed Church.

After 20 years the original Synod was divided into 4 Synods. One of these was the Synod of the Carolinas. In 1822 this Synod withdrew from the Associate Reformed Synod and changed its name to the Associate Reformed Synod of the South. The reason for this withdrawal was the great distance to be traveled to meetings of the General Synod, which were usually held in Pennsylvania. In 1858 the Associate churches, which had not gone into the union in 1782, and the Associate Reformed Churches united to form the United Presbyterian Church. At this time the Associate Reformed Synod of the South became the Associate Reformed Presbyterian Church.

The Standards of the church are the Westminster Confession and the Catechisms. The denomination maintains missions in Mexico and Pakistan and supports Erskine College and Erskine Theological Seminary, Due West, S.C. Conferences for all age groups are held each summer at the denomination's assembly grounds, Bonclarken, Flat Rock, N.C. The *Minutes* of the General Synod for 1961 record the total membership at 27,397, with the number of congregations at 147.

— *Florence Craig*

ATTENDANCE Regardless of the concept of Christian education one may hold and of the age of the group with whom he is working, he is and must be concerned about the regularity of the attendance of the learner or student in Christian education classes, schools, and projects. Educational psychologists point out that the frequency or lack of frequency of the repetition of an experience is an important factor in determining the intensity of the learning or growth. If the educational philosophy of the teacher or leader is that of the transmission of knowledge, he is concerned that the knowledge transmitted be retained. And the believer in education as the process and experience through which one comes not only to know the ideas concerning the Spirit, but also how to live by the Spirit, realizes that frequency of association of teacher and learner in meaningful experiences makes for the growth and enrichment of both.

The major objective of all Christian education is the acquiring of the spirit of love so that it becomes the motivating factor and power for guidance in the student-learner. And the most effective means by which this is acquired is seeing it a reality in the teacher or leader's relations with the student-learner. It is equally true that it takes time and many experiences of association with the teacher or leader for the student-learner to be assured that the spirit of love is genuine and not superficial. Regularity in attendance is requisite in order that these many experiences of leader and learner relations may occur.

The plan for organizing the curriculum whereby each unit continues on 1 theme for 3 to 10 sessions also suggests the need for regularity in attendance. Once a unit of study is started, each session makes its contribution to the continuous study and development of the theme. It is desirable, therefore, that no sections of the unit be missed.

The national average of attendance at the Sunday church schools across the country is variously estimated at 35 to 60 percent of the enrollment, 45 percent being the figure most often accepted.

To maintain regular attendance has been one of the most difficult problems of the Christian educator. Yielding to many outside or extra-curricular attractions, the student fails to have sufficient inner discipline or interest to maintain regularity in attendance. The causes for this lack of regularity in attendance are numerous, including: (1) Failure in the curriculum of teacher-leader to relate his teachings to the experience of the learner; hence, a pupil's lack of interest in what goes on in the school. (2) Lack of concern on the part of the parents in the Christian education of their children. Teachers often refer to this as the first and primary cause. (3) Limited follow-up on absentees to ascertain the cause and show a concern for their presence. (4) Many outside attractions, such as Sunday trips, papers, television programs, and community and organizational festivities or celebrations. Because of their dramatic nature, these often hold the fancy of the students. Parents rationalize by saying that " these are valuable experiences for persons too." (5) Failure on the part of the leaders and regular members to give friendly attention to persons of all ages when they come. (6) A feeling on the part of many that Christian education schools are not truly schools but social gatherings, and therefore that neither attendance nor absence is significant. (7) The lack of concern on the part of the total church or community for the moral and spiritual development of their people. This kind of atmosphere reflects the attitude of young and old alike.

Experience has revealed that the solution to these problems lies in one or more of the following direc-

tions: (1) The development of a program of Christian education that involves parents as well as teachers. (2) A plan of persistent follow-up of absentees. Pupils attend when they discover that somebody cares. (3) Providing continuously adequate help to teachers, thus raising the degree of interest on the part of pupils and parents. (4) Developing with the total constituency a realization that a fellowship in which Christian love is a reality is the most important goal. This makes for a " oneness" among the members, who will thus see the values of frequent and regular attendance upon the occasions that promote this relationship.
— *Frank A. Lindhorst*

AUDIO-VISUAL METHODS New tools, like new methods, are difficult to introduce, particularly when the user is given the choice of accepting or rejecting them. Such is the case with the church in its use of audio-visuals.

The public school, the Armed Forces, industry, and others have proved the effectiveness of audio-visuals in communicating ideas more effectively, in speeding up the learning process, and in increasing interest in the subject, whatever it may be — geography, battle techniques, or the selling of automobiles. The church needs these tools even more urgently, since its Sunday teaching program is limited in time. In addition, the responsibility of teaching is left for the most part in the hands of inexperienced and untrained teachers.

Every church that staffs its Sunday school with voluntary lay teachers faces a handicap that audio-visuals can help to overcome, yet the audio-visual method is in no way a substitute for the teacher, who is always the living witness for Christ and his church. This tool for teaching is only an aid to help the teacher arouse interest, stimulate the learning process and present subject matter in a careful manner.

The enthusiasm of the teacher, the attention of the children, and the excellent results of the audio-visual method seem almost too good to be true. Tests have been given in which two groups study the same subject, one in the regular way with only the printed curriculum in the hand of the teacher, and the other using an audio-visual program. Invariably the children using the latter method not only answer more test questions correctly, but the answers themselves reveal a far deeper understanding of the subject.

However, there are limitations to this method, and it is important to know this. At first glance it seems that these audio-visual tools for learning are like instruments of magic: one need only turn them on and wonderful results automatically begin to happen. This is not so. It is only because of the teacher that these wonderful aids actually can produce phenomenal results. Before he turns the switch to set the audio-visuals to work, the teacher must first prepare carefully. This includes reading and studying the material supplied in the printed curriculum or study guide that is always part of every properly produced audio-visual set.

To obtain the desired results the mind must be prepared for what the eye is going to see. This means that the children must be conditioned to receive the visual impressions if they are to be really effective. The producer of an audio-visual device cannot possibly present every conceivable situation related to the subject, he cannot anticipate the many ways in which it will be used in a teaching situation, nor can he arrange to have it begin to answer all the questions that are bound to be raised. It is only an aid to teaching — nothing more. Like any machine, it cannot think for itself. The thinking must come from the teacher, who alone knows the direction the lesson should take, because of time and effort given beforehand in study of the material, which is either integrated with the curriculum or related closely to it.

The audio-visual aid consists of either a 16mm. sound film or a 35mm. sound filmstrip. The latter contains as many as 50 different pictures on a strip of film, accompanied by a 33⅓ LP record. This strip may be run only on a filmstrip projector, not a slide projector. Because of the time element involved, as well as the cost of equipment, the sound filmstrip is rapidly becoming the more useful of the two for classroom teaching. The advent of new compact filmstrip projectors selling from $25 to $35 has made it feasible to think of individual classroom use of audio-visuals. Record players are necessary and may be borrowed or purchased at reasonable prices. For $2 one may buy a small tabletop screen that will be adequate for most classroom situations.

Visualize a teacher seated at a table with 7 to 10 children. Record player, compact projector, and screen are on the table ready for use. The class has just begun, and the teacher has prepared himself the night before by reading the study guide and curriculum material so that a careful presentation may be made before introducing the audio-visual aid. The children readily understand that this is not time for a religious

" show " but an opportunity to learn in an interesting way some great truths of Christianity. Knowing that the audio-visual has been produced for a scholarly presentation of the subject, the teacher is confident that his method will achieve results and he no longer worries whether or not he can get across the ideas that are to be taught.

It is of course necessary for any church school intending to use audio-visuals to have a responsible person who can correlate the curriculum with available A-V aids. The *Audio-Visual Resource Guide,* published by the National Council of the Churches of Christ in the U.S.A., gives the most complete list of all materials produced to date, with ratings and content. Producers are always willing to furnish descriptive catalogues of their available materials. Denominational boards often list relevant audio-visual materials in published curricula.

The 16mm. sound film is without question the finest tool for giving the viewer a " living experience," but it also has its limitations. The average 16mm. religious film is a half-hour subject. This limits its use in most church schools with brief class periods. It is mechanically more exacting to show in the classroom. The 16mm. sound film can best be used in the Sunday-evening group, youth meetings, or week-night Bible-study classes.

— *James K. Friedrich*

AUGUSTINE Augustine Aurelius, (354–430) was born in Tagaste, Numidia, in northern Africa, to Patricius and Monica. Augustine received his first religious training from his mother, a zealous Christian. According to the custom prevalent in northern Africa at that time, he remained a catechumen to be baptized after the pubescent age. When he reached young adulthood Augustine did not want to become a Christian.

He went to elementary school in his own town. Later he studied in Madaura and finally in Carthage, the cultural center of Latin-speaking Africa. Augustine was a brilliant student, excelling in poetry and the oratorical art. At the age of 19 he read Cicero's dialogue *Hortensius,* which kindled in his soul a passionate desire for wisdom. In his search for truth, he turned toward the Manichaean sect for answers to his problems, but the answers they were able to give did not satisfy him. In 383 he went to Rome. In 384, carrying the recommendation of the pagan prefect of Rome, Symmachus, he went to Milan, the episcopal city of Ambrose, at that time the residential town of the emperor, a place sizzling with religious tensions. In Milan, Augustine broke with the Manichaeans and became a Skeptic, but he soon found in the Neoplatonic school a philosophical system that corresponded to his mental structure. The influence of Ambrose helped him through his difficulties concerning the Scriptures. In 386 he became a Christian. He resigned his rhetorical chair in Milan and went back to Africa. He became a priest and lived with his friends in a kind of religious community. In 395 he was acclaimed bishop of Hippo and for the rest of his life he remained in Numidia. He died in Hippo in 430, during the siege of the city by Vandal invaders.

Augustine witnessed an important period of history. The 4th century brought a thorough change in the relation between Christianity and the Empire. The state had been the representative of a pagan civilization, but by the end of the 4th century the Christian religion became the religion of the state. The integration of Christian ways of life into the Empire presented many problems.

Augustine, the bishop of a small and unimportant town in Africa, had a great impact on the centuries to come. Although the larger part of his work is controversial and little read in our day, his *Confessions* belong to the few living classics of world literature. In his *Soliloquies* he established a style of prayer that has influenced Western liturgy. Augustine's great merit consists mainly in the creation of a *Bildungsgut* that furnished teaching material for centuries. His *Confessions* contain valuable observations of children's psychology. He criticizes the teaching methods prevailing in the elementary schools of his time. He condemns the study of rhetoric, which was of the greatest importance in higher education. The low morality of his students in Carthage and Rome brought painful memories to him. Besides his official teaching activity, Augustine had a more informal one. A small group of friends and young men followed him to Rome and Milan. After he resigned his position in Milan they moved to the estate of a friend of his. Their conversations were recorded in shorthand and later rearranged by Augustine. These dialogues show the way of life of the group as an informal educational effort toward the love of the truth. After their return to Africa the friends remained together. Augustine planned a comprehensive work encompassing all studies of higher education of which he wrote only 1 part, *On Music*. When he gave up his plan it was carried out by Martianus Capella whose work became the text for higher studies for about a thousand years.

The leitmotiv of Augustine's life was the quest for wisdom. He lost interest in the secular civilization. Thus education for him is specifically religious education in which the classics have no role. *On Instructing the Unlearned* (*De catechizandis rudibus*) is a long dissertation in letter form to a priest of Carthage who complained about the difficulties he had when instructing adult pagans who wanted to become Christians. Augustine, with the skill of a professional teacher, points to the different didactical and methodical factors of efficient teaching. As illustrations of the theory presented in the 1st part of the book, the 2d part contains 2 model teaching units, a long one and a short one. The other work that shows Augustine's educational ideal is *On Christian Doctrine* (*De doctrina christiana*). As the classical higher education was founded on the reading and interpretation of Homer and Vergil, with Augustine the Bible becomes the center around which the elements of Christian learning crystallize. The teaching of the church originates in the divine revelation that is in the Bible. The methods used by the classical teaching are not rejected but applied to the Scriptures. What is good in the classical tradition must be kept. The wisdom approached by the pagans belongs to the Christians. Henri Marrou thinks that Augustine does not lead toward a new ideal of civilization, but rather sums up the results of the declining Greco-Roman world. On the other hand, Adolf von Harnack calls Augustine the 1st modern man. When we compare the dialogues of Augustine to those of Gregory the Great we can see a striking contrast. Gregory is already medieval. In spite of the often rhetorical style of Augustine, we have in his words the first example of a kind of inner dialogue that through the best Christian authors leads to Kierkegaard. The word "soliloquies" (*soliliquia*) was created by Augustine: the Christian style was his accomplishment. He was to a great extent determinative in the development of Western theology. His works were the common stock of the monastic libraries; his authority remained uncontested up to the rise of the great medieval universities. — *Emod L. Brunner*

AUSTRALIA Religious education in Australia is best understood by examining the influence of the Australian home, school, church, and community.

Australian homes and dispersed families range from those of close involvement with the local church to those of no or only nominal affiliation with the church, and little or no formal religion in the home. Relatively few homes in Australia are antireligious, but a great number are apathetic about religious education either of adults or of children. There is little indication of formal religious education in homes, other than Bible study, with or without aids, but there are signs of church programs overflowing into the homes. This takes place by design. All ages increasingly have take-home material to be acted on for the next session. There seems to be a growing recognition that true religious education cannot take place outside the fellowship and worship of a community.

Australian schools are church or independent private schools and schools conducted by the state governments. The former are day and/or boarding schools, many having chaplains. These schools seek, through programs of religious instruction and genuine attempts to create Christian community, to have religious education of a high order. There are a growing number of parish primary schools and church secondary schools. State education systems increasingly grant permission to have religious instruction in the schools, in some states taught by honorary accredited instructors. The pupils are grouped denominationally, but in Victoria, with an agreed syllabus, the children are left in their school groupings. A few high and technical schools have full-time chaplains, appointed and paid by a state council of Christian education.

The local churches are making progress in religious education, aided and promoted by denominational departments of Christian education and the Australian Council of Christian Education with its state branches. The present accent is in developing adult and parent work to a high level, and incorporating all in the worship, fellowship life, and mission outreach of the congregation. Increasingly, there is depth training in human relationships and group work, and an attempt to motivate people to be conscious not only of the content of the faith but of the purpose and life of the redeemed and redeeming community. There is evidence of growing awareness of the need for denominations to take seriously the effect of their divisions, and to move toward one another in service and witness. Many laymen are asking questions that disturb the conservative *status quo*, and this is uncovering the great need for religious education. The move toward the union of Congregationalists, Methodists, and Presbyterians is being accompanied by religious education programs to meet the situation.

Community life educates. The Australian community both promotes and is apathetic to religious education in its widest sense. Church representatives appear on public platforms; the Services have chaplains; there is statutory time on radio and television for religion; the press gives time and space, and some parliaments often open with prayers. At least one prominent daily newspaper has its Saturday leading article on a religious theme. Universities have no chairs of theology, but it is of interest that at the most recently established university, Monash, Victoria, the secular clause is not in the constitution. Improved theological colleges are influencing religious education as they increase the length and breadth of courses, size of faculty, and standards of entry.

Advances in religious education have come largely through leaders who have visited America, Europe, and Asia. Adaptation to Australian conditions and sharing take place in the ecumenical Australian Council of Christian Education.

— Val K. Brown

AUTHORITY Authority is interpreted as meaning that which forms the basis for belief and action. In religion it pertains to the manner in which one interprets the will of the gods or God. In religious education it provides that which gives purpose, form, and substance to the content and process of teaching.

Some form of authority seems necessary for human existence even though the basis for belief and ac-

tion is often unexamined. Further, whatever one gives his allegiance to as authoritative becomes the basis for his religion. Those who find in Karl Marx the key to human existence have made Marxism a religion. For many today science assumes something of the function of religious authority, just as the process of reasoning did for the men of the Enlightenment. For the "organization man," the organization is authority, while for many teen-agers the latest singer or cinema idol takes on many aspects of authority. One problem of modern man is that there is no clear understanding of what gives meaning and direction to life.

The Jewish-Christian tradition has had 5 major ways of interpreting authority: the living witness, the written record canonized as Scripture, the traditions, the hierarchy of the church, and inner experience. Reason is operative in apprehending and explicating authority but is generally not considered authoritative by itself. Both Judaism and Christianity would generally agree that God is the real authority, and that the prophets were among the living mediators of this authority. For the Christian, Jesus Christ as the living Word is the chief means by which this authority became existential. The question of the priests and elders, "By what authority are you doing these things, and who gave you this authority?" (Matt. 21:23b), is answered in terms of the incarnation. It was the witness of the 1st Evangelist that "he taught them as one who had authority, and not as their scribes" (Matt. 7:29).

The problem remains, however, as to how this authority is mediated. For the Jew, the Torah, or written law, became the source of authority, though later interpretations in the

Talmud ("tradition") were also authoritative. Although Orthodox Judaism still insists that authority lies in these written documents, Reformed Judaism has concluded that present reinterpretation is necessary.

The early church recognized the necessity of keeping the Christian faith pure. Prior to the formation of the canon of the New Testament, church leaders, especially the bishops, assumed an authoritative role in interpretation. The canon arose partly as a means of combating heresy, especially Gnosticism, but the Scriptures required interpretation, and so a body of tradition grew up as various individuals and councils sought to clear up controversial points. Ultimately, the tradition came to bear more weight than the Scripture itself, with the hierarchy of the church as the final arbiter. Thus authority came to center in the church itself, a situation that still prevails in Roman Catholicism.

The Protestant Reformation was based on the return to Scripture as the sole basis of authority. In practice both Calvinism and Lutheranism increasingly set up authoritative interpretations of Scripture, such as Calvin's *Institutes* and Luther's catechisms. In Protestant Scholasticism, post-Biblical statements were held with hardly less rigidity than they were in Roman Catholic Scholasticism, and right doctrine often became the test of faith. Pietism, with its emphasis on feeling, was one reaction against this conception of authority.

Liberal theology, influenced by Kant, Schleiermacher, and others, broke the rigid authority of both Scripture and tradition. Although Schleiermacher's insistence upon the seat of religion as man's feeling of absolute dependence was never intended to deny the importance of the traditional symbols of the faith, increasingly in the 19th and early 20th centuries the tendency was in this direction.

Education within the Roman Church is controlled by the church. Orthodox Protestant Christian education seeks to base its content solely on the Scriptures, though in fact it is the interpretation of a particular church or sect that is taught. Liberal religious education in the early 20th century, influenced by both liberal theology and John Dewey's philosophy of experience, placed the emphasis on present-day experience — "enriched and controlled experience," as Bower described the curriculum. All relevant sources, including the Bible, were utilized to form the nature of education as experience.

Both liberal theology and liberal Christian education were soundly challenged, beginning in Europe in the 1920's and in America in the 1930's, to the point where their conclusions are no longer widely accepted. Although the problem of authority has not been solved, the following line of argument is fairly widely accepted by Protestant Biblical thinkers, theologians, and educators with a postliberal orientation.

We must begin by recognizing God as the sole authority — God as incarnate in and revealed through Jesus Christ. The Old Testament is preparation for, and the New Testament witness to, this living revelation — the "Word made flesh" (John 1:14; see also Heb. 1:1-2). Thus the Scriptures form the nucleus of our perception of the meaning of God's will for two reasons: their proximity to the events of revelation and the fact that they participate in the events of revelation by the coincidence of event, encounter, and witness. The Bible, especially the New Testament, is unique in providing a base and foundation for Christian teaching. Yet it is impossible to deny the traditions that have grown up in the church: creeds, the decisions of the councils through Chalcedon, the interpretations of the Reformers, and more recent developments in Biblical, theological, and ethical thought. The doctrine of the Holy Spirit prevents the holding of any static understanding of God's original revelation in Jesus Christ, though the Holy Spirit does not go counter to that revelation. " If you continue in my word," the Fourth Gospel records Jesus as saying, " you are truly my disciples, and you will know the truth, and the truth will make you free " (John 8:31b-32).

Yet another step is necessary to complete the process: personal reception of revelation within the Christian community. As H. Richard Niebuhr has insisted, revelation is personal but never private. *Our* perception of revelation is in terms of the Biblical witness, 19 centuries of church history, and our participation in the body of Christ today. Because we are finite and fallible as well as sinful, we see through a glass darkly, but the witnesses to revelation help to clarify our sight. Although the Bible is the principal basis for this perception, tradition and the present action of the Spirit within the church must be taken into account.

Christian teaching is thus Biblical, theological, and ecclesiological, but it must also be dynamic, recognizing fully the assertion made by Augustine that God is the real teacher. The individual teacher, while not the authority, seeks to mediate the claims of God upon the lives of his pupils in the light of the written records of the church, especially the Bible, and he must continually examine his own thinking in the light of these documents under the guidance of the Spirit. And he is able to teach only because God is at work among his people today. — *Howard Grimes*

AWARDS The subject of awards brings to mind a great variety of images. These may run the gamut from lapel pins for attendance to class banners for achievement — thus moving from an individual's being available to participate and ranging through the quality of group work actually accomplished. In each case the award is a " bestowing upon," a " prize granted." In looking at the relationship of awards to Christian education, one must examine the meanings of the award to the recipient (individual or group) within the context of the objectives of Christian education.

Among those factors at the base of awards as a rather common ingredient of Christian education two fundamental principles can be discerned. First we recognize that the Christian way of life involves disciplined patterns of living and involvement in the community life of the church. Thus we turn to some method of helping persons establish particular disciplines (regular attendance) and patterns that will stand a person in good stead in the ongoing development of Christian understanding and life (Bible study). In the 2d place, our total culture and educational system lends itself to supporting a positive response to the awards approach, for in much of our society personal worth is measured in terms of production and acceptance granted to those who cooperate. We all know the esteem granted to a good football player and the delight of the teacher with the student who gets good grades. Therefore, awards become a workable method of achieving our purpose. Children and youth can be aided in establishing good habits and helpful disciplines as they respond to their own needs to be valued as worthy and acceptable.

Meanings are elusive and not easily defined. It is difficult to see, however, that the impact of meanings to the person would not relate more to the question of personal worth and acceptance than to the establishment of Christian disciplines. While it is true that lifelong habits may be established, one must discern the impetus for the relevance of the discipline within the image gained of worth and acceptance. As a boy comes to receive an award his feelings tell him that at this moment and in this place " I view myself as having worth and being worthy, and as being accepted and being acceptable because I have satisfactorily met the requirements."

In Christian education, although we may state it in different words, our fundamental objective is to provide conditions that will enable persons to know and respond to God's love in all the responsible relationships involved. It is our objective to communicate a faith in God as a force of understanding, accepting, and forgiving love in such ways that all may discover for themselves, and develop within, this faith. Here, worth and acceptance come to man as a gift from God, moving from his center of love, and not as an award that man either can or must earn.

One cannot escape the conclusion that, in spite of inherent good to be gained in terms of disciplines of life, awards actually communicate meanings that are directly opposed to the Christian gospel. It is entirely possible that the right kinds of disciplines may be established in life for the wrong reasons, and awards contribute to this possibility. One must then stand off and seek to grasp a larger vision within which we would contend that such disciplines are not the right kind but rather when so motivated militate against the essential message of love that Christian education seeks to communicate. Christian education still holds the task of assisting persons in the development of those patterns of discipline in life which will contribute to maturing as Christians. The methods employed, however, to achieve a purpose must always be consistent with and be a part of the communication of the basic joy of God's understanding, accepting, and forgiving love. — *Scott Libbey*

B

BAPTISM Baptism is the ritual act signifying God's forgiveness of sins, renewal through the Holy Spirit, and acceptance into the solidarity of the church.

In the Greek Old Testament the verbal forms of *baptein* and *baptizein* are used to mean "dip" or "wash" and, figuratively, "flood" or "swamp." But the substantives *baptisma* and *baptismos* nowhere appear in the Septuagint or in classical literature. They seem to have been coined especially to refer to the baptism of repentance preached by John and then adopted by Christians.

Baptism as an act of initiation into the Christian life and the New Testament community clearly owes much to the eschatological sacrament preached and practiced by John the Baptist. Following the practice of Judaism in baptizing proselytes into the Jewish community, and perhaps influenced also by the daily ceremonial lustrations employed by priests, the Pharisees, and the Essenes of Qumrân, John proclaimed a baptism of repentance for the forgiveness of sins in the face of the imminent Day of Judgment and the appearance of the King Messiah (Mark 1:4; Acts 10:37). Fleeing from the wrath to come, the crowds who responded to John's wilderness preaching were purified of their sins, moral and ritual, assured of the divine forgiveness, and prepared through moral amendment for the coming of the Heavenly Ruler and Judge whom John predicted would fulfill this initiatory act by "baptizing with the Holy Spirit and with fire" (Luke 3:16 = Matt. 3:11, but cf. Mark 1:8).

Whereas the Lord's Supper in the early church rests back upon certain known acts of Jesus, the sacrament of Baptism as an external form has no such precedent, though sanction was found in the risen Christ's missionary charge (Matt. 28:16-20). The only acknowledgment that Jesus himself baptized is found in John 3:22, but this is corrected in ch. 4:2 and may refer to the period of his association with the Baptist prior to his own public ministry. When Jesus speaks of his baptism, it is significant that he refers to his forthcoming death. "I have a baptism to be baptized with; and how I am constrained until it is accomplished!" (Luke 12:50.) The metaphor of a flood or a storm was frequently used by the psalmists to refer to overwhelming catastrophe, viz., "All thy waves and thy billows have gone over me" (Ps. 42:7). This Messianic suffering and death which he believed a divine necessity was interpreted as a sacrifice "for many," that is to say, of redemptive significance for all people. From the outset of his ministry this mission had been clear. The Voice from heaven at his baptism addressed him in the "servant" language of Isa. 42:1, signifying that his Messianic vocation involved a solidarity with sinners and the promise of their deliverance through his obedience unto death. Into his own suffering ministry Jesus invited his followers. His own death would be a baptism effecting a general forgiveness that could and must be shared by those who would participate in his Messianic victory. "The cup that I drink you will drink; and with the baptism with which I am baptized, you will be baptized." (Mark 10:39.)

Paul gives central importance to baptism as an initiatory act whereby the believer participated in the Messiah's baptism of death and resurrection. The ritual act corresponded to and was expressive of Christ's whole redemptive work. "All of us who have been baptized into Christ Jesus were baptized into his death. We were buried therefore with him by baptism into death, so that as Christ was raised from the dead by the glory of the Father, we too might walk in newness of life." (Rom. 6:3 f.) This death signified God's gracious forgiveness of sins and a freedom to a new life of holiness through the power of the Holy Spirit. (Col. 2:13 f.; Rom. 6:7, 18; 7:4-6.) In this act of divine initiative which is a specific expression of the whole movement of salvation history, the Last Judgment was anticipated and God's deliverance of his people vouchsafed, provided that a life of faith and responsible service ensued. Baptism therefore involved a divine judgment, antici-

pated in the Baptist's prophecy of the "baptism of fire," and vividly represented in the favorite Pauline metaphor of justification. As the sacrament of justification, Baptism represented a submission in advance to the divine judgment and the glad acceptance of a preliminary amnesty that must be made manifest in a new life in and for Jesus Christ, "in order that we may bear fruit for God" (Rom 7:4b; I Peter 3:21). Throughout the New Testament the relation of Christian baptism to the forgiveness of sins based upon the redemptive death of Christ finds repeated mention.

But baptism was regarded as something more than the fulfillment of John's baptism. Indeed, the early church carefully distinguished between the baptism of John, which was a call to repentance before the coming of the Lord, and baptism since Pentecost. (Acts 1:5; 11:16; 18:25; 19:4-6.) Distinctive to Christian baptism was the empowerment of the Holy Spirit and entrance into the life of the new age. (Acts 2:38; John 3:3-5.) Even the difficult passages in Acts 8:14-17 and ch. 10:44-48 still draw into close relationship the baptismal experience and the gift of the Holy Spirit, though these do not necessarily occur simultaneously, since the freedom of the Spirit cannot be bound. There is only one Baptism, not a water baptism followed by a baptism in the Holy Spirit. (Eph. 4:4.) It is essentially one and the same act whereby the believer is purified of his unworthiness, and enabled to begin a new life of grateful praise and obedient service. The seal of the Spirit presently received is evidence that the life of God's new age, still to come, is available as present reality. (II Cor. 1:22; Eph. 1:13;

4:30.) In this sense baptism, while unrepeatable (Heb. 6:4 f.), is nevertheless not a momentary event, complete in itself, but a fresh beginning that must be enlarged and unfolded by the action of divine grace throughout the entire Christian life. In Pauline terms this means a conformity to Christ's dying and rising. (I Cor. 15:30; II Cor. 4:10 ff.; Phil. 3:10 f.) As the starting point in the new life in Christ, baptism is thus expressive of the divine deed whereby men are forgiven, justified, reconciled and sanctified. "You were washed, you were consecrated, you were justified." (I Cor. 6:11.) Growth or sanctification in the Christian life is a continuation and realization of the new righteousness already given by the regenerative Spirit. Since the new life lived toward God is never complete in this world but is set within the eschatological tension of a righteousness now possessed and one that is awaited, baptism points forward to the hope of a perfected life of love and obedience.

Through this event the believer is incorporated into Christ, made a member of his body in the world. As circumcision had been the covenant sign distinguishing the Jew as belonging to the covenant people, so by this " circumcision of Christ " the Christian was believed to be marked for membership in the new fellowship of love, prayer, and service (Col. 2:11; Rom. 4:11; Phil. 3:3 f.). " By one Spirit we were all baptized into one body." (I Cor. 12:13.) From the very beginning, baptism was the universal initiatory rite by which the young missionary church introduced new members into the brotherhood of believers. (Matt. 28:18 f.; Acts 2:41; Rom. 6:3; I Cor. 1:13.) Baptism was " in " or " into " the name of Jesus Christ, that is, an incorporation and participation in Christ, who is united with his people. This was God's own act in setting the convert within the sphere of the Spirit's activity and guidance. The earliest confessions of faith developed in relation to this admission rite and may have taken the form of a simple " I believe " response to the questions that were put by the officiant. It is precarious to read a formal catechumenate preparatory to baptism back into the first two centuries, but it is manifest that preaching and teaching the gospel were intimately related to the sacrament, bringing the hearer to the point of decision and dedication.

Repentance and belief were inseparably related to the baptismal event, conditions that were strongly emphasized in the Reformers' theory of the sacraments. Advocates of " believer's baptism " since Hubmaier have insisted that these are the indispensable preconditions for coming to baptism. While there is no certain evidence of infant baptism in New Testament times, this practice certainly arose very early and finds support in the following observations: (1) the acceptance of whole households together with the convert; (2) the analogy of Jewish proselyte baptism; (3) the use of Mark 10:13-16 in the early church; (4) the nature of the atonement and the meaning of justification as God's saving act in advance of man's decision, awakening and evoking a subsequent faith in response (Rom. 5:8-10; John 15:16). In any event, both adult and infant baptism required an answering response in a " life worthy of the Lord " as a confirmation of the divine decision for man in baptism.

— *Ernest W. Saunders*

BAPTIST FEDERATION OF CANADA Canadian Baptists are organized into 3 corporate groups covering the country geographically: the United Baptist Convention of the Maritime Provinces, the Baptist Convention of Ontario and Quebec, and the Baptist Union of Western Canada. These groups cooperate in matters of common concern through the Baptist Federation of Canada, which was organized in 1943. It has no legislative authority but exists for consultation and coordination only.

There is no national secretary or board of Christian education, but the field secretaries of the 3 conventions cooperate in the Christian Education Committee of the Federation to promote common interests. Program materials for children's, young peoples', and adult groups that meet during the week are provided through this committee. Lesson helps and story papers for the Sunday church schools are published by the Baptist Publications Committee of Canada. Cycle-graded curriculum materials are issued for all departments up to the junior. Lessons based on the International Uniform Outlines are issued for the departments from junior to adult.

Each of the 3 conventions operates its own residential, lay leadership training school. The education of ministers and other full-time workers is provided for at Acadia University, Wolfville, N.S., and McMaster Divinity College, Hamilton, Ont. Among the declared purposes of the Federation are: to foster understanding and goodwill among Baptists across Canada; to sharpen understanding of the nature and mission of Baptist churches and to develop a sense of Baptist solidarity on a national scale; to deepen the awareness of Baptists of their special contribution to Protestant Christianity; to coordinate the effort and resources of Canadian Baptists in those projects they desire to undertake together; to represent all Canadian Baptists in national and international associations and councils, in matters of conviction, concern, and courtesy.

An important function of the Federation is to represent the Canadian Baptist Conventions in the Baptist World Alliance. — *Fred J. Helps*

BELGIUM Belgium is principally a Roman Catholic country with a liberal constitution (1831). Although there are no official statistics on religion, about 1 percent of the 8,800,000 inhabitants are deemed to belong to Protestant churches. The Counter-Reformation and the French Revolution deeply influenced the religious and cultural life, leading to strong opposition between clericalists (primarily in the Flemish regions) and anticlericalists (primarily in the Walloon provinces). There were especially strong educational conflicts, notably from 1878 to 1884 and 1954 to 1958, ending with the "school pact" of Nov. 6, 1958, entered into by the three political parties, stipulating that the Government should pay almost 100 percent of the expenses of the free schools, excepting the costs of construction of school buildings. During the school year 1958–1959, 1,777,596 pupils were enrolled in schools, of whom 723,231 were in state schools and 1,024,365 in private schools, which are 99 percent Roman Catholic schools.

The 1958 "school pact" provided that religious instruction shall be included in the official state schools. During each September every father or guardian may indicate his choice for a child: Roman Catholic, Protestant, Jewish, or ethical instruction. This instruction is given two hours a week by teachers appointed by the Government on nomination by the ecclesiastical bodies. The Roman Catholic program deals with the catechism, inserting also sacred history and the understanding of the liturgy. Since there are only 9 Protestant primary private schools, all in the Dutch-speaking part of the country, and very small at that, the majority of Protestant children are enrolled in the public schools. The number of children in the schools of the state receiving Protestant instruction shows a rapid growth: from 858 in 1949 to 2,821 in 1959 and 3,834 in 1962, to which must be added 1,824 pupils in the schools of the local communities (i.e., in 1962) and 259 pupils in the Europe-school at Brussels, or a total of about 6,914 children from 6 to 18 years of age.

For the primary schools the program consists mainly of sacred history, with some attention also to church history, missions, prayer, hymns, Christian ethics, and the Bible as a book. For the secondary schools the curriculum is as follows: 1st class — Old Testament; 2d class — New Testament; 3d class — church history (ancient and medieval) until Easter, then " Our Neighbors and We "; 4th class — Reformation history in general and Belgian church history in particular until Easter, then " Our Fatherland and the Peoples of the World "; 5th class — modern church history until Easter, then Christian ethics, especially general sociological matters; last class — Christian dogmatics until Easter, then " Outlines of Christian Ethics."

The Roman Catholic Church prefers to have priests, monks, and nuns teach the religion courses in the public schools. Other catechists are instructed at the Higher Institute for Religious Sciences of the University of Louvain. The 300 teachers of the Protestant classes are ministers and evangelists living in the various communities. Other teachers are trained at several local training centers (for the primary schools) and at the Protestant Theological Faculty of Brussels (for the secondary schools). Manuals for the French-speaking classes are edited by the Commission de l'Enseignement. The Dutch-speaking classes mostly use manuals of Dutch origin.

Thus the religious instruction in the public schools forms the nucleus of Protestant religious education. Some Sunday schools, Y.M.C.A.'s and Y.W.C.A.'s exist, but their influence is comparatively small. The confirmation classes of the church communities also build on the school courses. — *Alexandre J. Bronkhorst*

BIBLE CLASS " Bible class " is a term generally used to designate a stereotyped organization for adults that in certain respects is parallel to the local church itself. The stereotype has a number of characteristics that are commonly encountered. Traditionally, Bible classes in a church are taught by lay persons, frequently on the basis of the International Uniform Lessons.

The curriculum for the Bible class may also be derived from the preoccupations of the leader, without regard to any formal or regular course of study; or it may be determined simply by the decision of the group to study a particular part of the Bible, with or without the aid of teaching or discussion materials. Discussion is not necessarily precluded, but it is certainly subordinate to the leader's or lecturer's presentation. Considerable importance is often attached to corporate worship within the group, even though the Bible class may immediately precede the morning service. Such worship has, of course, varying degrees of formality; but in a significant number of instances there is a predilection for so-called " gospel hymns " and very informal prayer, perhaps pointing to the traditional nature of the Bible class as derived from 19th-century evangelism and Pietism.

Strong emphasis on the " fellowship " values of the Bible class is a striking characteristic in modern times. The *esprit de corps* felt by its members has a number of implications for both the congregation in general and the Christian education program of the church in particular. Some degree of autonomy may be cherished, in actual fact if not in the basic assumptions of the large Bible class. The " fellowship " of the group may be more real to the members than participation in congregational life and congregational responsibility. Loyalty to the Bible class as such may sometimes surpass loyalty to the church of which it is a part. Moreover, influences exerted within the Bible class — either by the leader, other particular individuals, combinations of persons, or group opinion as a whole — may be carried over into congregational decisions. Such influences may be good or bad, but the extent to which a Bible class exercises this kind of power challenges the integrity of the congregation as the basic unit and gives the impression that the class is a church within the church.

Concern about " fellowship " is not of necessity opposed to the avowed aim of the conventional Bible class, namely, to be edified by the consideration of the Bible under the guidance of a dynamic leader. It may, however, result in the subordination of responsible Bible study to group consciousness and group unity. The fact that the Bible class meets at all, and perhaps strengthens its position and adds to its numbers, may appear more meaningful than what is actually said by its leader or by speakers brought in from the outside. The size of many Bible classes is such that a feeling of togetherness is more easily achieved than participation in thought, study, or discussion by most of the members. Furthermore, the dependence of the Bible class on the dynamic qualities of its leader not only isolates it from regular congregational life — that is, from the ministry of the word and sacraments, and from the interaction of church members through channels open to everyone — but creates what amounts almost to a second ministry and a second church fellowship alongside the normal structure of the church.

The stereotype under discussion, although possibly an impediment to adult Christian education today, has nevertheless been of service to the church historically. As is well known, the original Sunday school movement begun by Robert Raikes in 1780 was intended to provide elementary education (in religion as well as in other subjects) for underprivileged children. It was not, however, regarded as an enterprise of the church; it was conducted as a venture by laymen without substantial professional guidance from the clergy; and it was directed toward children rather than adults. These conditions did not long continue unmodified. In 1798 working women in Nottingham, England, were brought together for instruction. By 1817 the Sunday school movement, now making headway in the youth and adult fields, brought about the formation of the Philadelphia Sunday and Adult School Union. The adult Bible class developed in the following years.

During the remainder of the 19th century, Sunday schools developed rapidly, and were taken under the wing of the church. By the time of the Civil War, there were a significant number of classes for adults as well as for children. When uniform lessons were established in 1872, churches sought to make sure that all persons in the family, whatever their age, should participate in the Sunday school. This goal was not universally achieved, and adult Christian education has suffered because of the common identification of the Sunday school with the religious instruction of children alone. Moreover, at least 2 other major factors were adverse to the maturing of the idea of adult Christian education. One of these was the association of Sunday schools with evangelism, in the 19th-century sense of the word. This has, of course, strongly affected the character of many Sunday schools to this very day: and the adult Bible class, which developed during the latter part of the 19th century and which is in an especially good position to steer its own course, has in many cases clung to evangelistic, pietistic, and moralistic ideas of a former age. The other adverse factor is the persistent autonomy of the whole Sunday school, which has resisted vigorous attempts to bring it under the control of consistent church policy. Here again, traditionalism has prevailed among many Bible classes, and efforts to persuade adults to adopt more modern and imaginative educational methods have often been in vain. Responsibility for this situation cannot be placed simply with older adults, who may prefer older and less aggressive systems, for there is a multiplicity of large Bible classes for men as such, for women as such, for mixed groups, for couples, in bewildering variety.

When all this is said, however, it must be acknowledged that the traditional Bible class has provided an opportunity for energetic lay leadership and for enthusiastic participation. In times past, more perhaps than is now the case, thoughtful study of the Bible has been stimulated by the Bible class as conventionally conceived. Moreover, in spite of the large number of such Bible classes that still operate along traditional lines, many persons have now begun to " graduate " into smaller groups, where reading, study, and planned discussion are accepted as the normal procedure. The increasing emphasis upon new types of study materials for adults on the part of denominational agencies and local congregations, and the widespread acceptance of these, has obviously not brought every Bible class up to date as to method and approach. But the emergence of numerous groups of a different kind, even while the time-honored Bible class with its large membership and its " inspirational " lecture continues, offers reason for encouragement as to the greater flexibility of adult education in the future.

— *Norman F. Langford*

BIBLE INSTITUTE "An institution for advanced education especially in science or technology" is the definition of "institute." The institute has been incorporated into Christianity, especially in the latter part of the 19th and the 20th centuries. The Bible institute movement has grown rapidly since its beginning in 1882 when Nyack Missionary College was founded, and 1889 when Moody Bible Institute formally opened. At this present time, more than 200 Bible institutes and colleges are in existence.

The Bible institute movement aims at higher education for its pupils, with the main subjects being the Bible and courses related to it. Bible institutes generally have strong doctrinal positions, proclaiming the virgin birth, the deity of Christ, the inspiration of the Bible, redemption through the blood of Christ, the bodily resurrection, and the imminent return of Christ. They also strongly emphasize a direct study of the English Bible. These strong stands were taken by the Bible institutes in reaction to 19th-century rationalism. Thus Bible institutes have attempted to equip their students with the fundamentals of the faith. Large numbers of students have gone forth from these institutes as pastors and missionaries into different parts of the world.

The Bible institute has had many problems in its expansion, however, and has often been criticized. Generally this criticism has been that Bible institutes tend toward anti-intellectualism in their study of the Scriptures and as a result over-simplify their teachings. (This is also seen as a reaction to the intellectualism of the 19th century.) These problems, however, are being faced by Bible institutes today, and efforts are being made to raise their academic standards. In 1947, the Accrediting Association of Bible Colleges came into being for the explicit purpose of raising the standards of Bible institutes. Recommended higher standards pertain to degree levels for instructors, the quality of libraries, and sound administrative principles.

— *Louis A. Barbieri, Jr.*

BIBLE STUDY Bible study, in Christian education, includes all activity in which the meaning and significance of the contents of the Bible are sought after, to the end that the student might be confronted, challenged, and transformed by God's revelation of himself. More specifically, it is (1) the interpretation of Biblical material by literary, historical, and theological techniques, and (2) the examination of the results of Biblical interpretation to discover their significance for our personal involvement in the predicament of mankind, and for the mission of the church. Bible study is a complex process that ranges from the simple reading of the Bible by a single person to a most rigorous examination by teams of scholars using the resources and techniques of many fields of research.

The beginning of Biblical interpretation is inextricably bound up with the formation of the Bible itself. The books of law were a result of the efforts of the Hebrews to interpret the world around them and their relationships with one another in terms of their awareness of God's orderly and righteous working in their midst. In the prophetic writings, this sense of God's righteousness was applied to the particular situation to which the prophet spoke, and became the basis for a penetrating analysis of the history of the Hebrew people. Later Old Testament writings reflect the further refinement and interpretation of the law as it was applied to the problems of postexilic Judaism. Alongside these writings preserved in the Old Testament, there developed a large body of oral interpretation of the law in the postexilic period — the scribal tradition — that eventually was preserved in the Talmudic writings.

Jesus broke sharply with the prevailing method of scribal interpretation as he pierced through the letter of the Old Testament law to its vital center. The Gospel writers and other early Christians searched the Old Testament for references supporting their conviction that Jesus was the Messiah. Paul, on the other hand, used the accepted allegorical methods of the scribes to provide illustrations for his theological interpretations.

During the next 1,500 years, the Christian church perpetuated the literal and allegorical approaches to Bible study, adding a new approach — the anagogical or mystical. The Protestant Reformers challenged the distortion of the meaning of Scripture that often resulted from these approaches, emphasizing instead the need for grasping the basic intent of the Biblical authors, and, with the help of the Holy Spirit, applying the message of the Bible to the basic problems of life. Later, much of Protestant Bible study lapsed into a literalistic approach to the Scriptures that used the testimony of the Holy Spirit as a convenient guarantor of the validity of personal interpretation.

With the Age of Enlightenment, the tenability of literalism began to be challenged, first by rationalism, which concentrated on the ideational content of the Bible, then by historicism, which explored the process by which the Bible came to be. Among those who rejected the idea of the testimony of the Holy Spirit as a practical principle for interpretation were some who concluded that the working of the Holy Spirit had therefore no relevance to Bible study. As a result, there developed the sociological, psychological, and literary approaches to the interpretation of the Bible.

In the last half century, a new approach to Bible study has developed, which has been guided by fresh insights into the nature of God's revelation and the functioning of the Holy Spirit. This approach utilizes the contributions of historical, literary, sociological, and psychological criticism without necessarily compromising the essential character of the Biblical message. In this approach, an effort is made, (1) to determine as accurately as possible the intent of the Biblical writer — what he was trying to communicate, to whom he was directing his message, what the situation was that prompted his concern; (2) to identify the basic human need or problem to which the particular Biblical material is speaking, thus indicating the valid point of contact between the world view of Bible times and the radically different perspective of our present era; and (3) to recognize the specific implications of the Biblical material for one's own personal situation and for the mission of the church. As a result of this process, insights can be deepened, not only concerning the message of the Bible, but concerning the truth about ourselves in relation to God and to our fellowmen.

It is not necessary that these 3 steps be performed exactly in the above order, or that they be performed one after the other. Sometimes they can occur simultaneously. But it is necessary always to be asking the question, What does this mean to me? Only then can genuine confrontation take place, in which one is convicted, restored, and inspired to actions far beyond any he had ever imagined himself capable of. Not that confrontation necessarily takes place, even though fresh insights emerge, for there are many ways for the working of the Holy Spirit to be resisted at every step of the way. But if Bible study is engaged in with expectant hearts, the way is opened for God to speak at ever deeper levels of meaning.

This kind of Bible study is best carried on in a process that involves personal reading and study of the Bible, use of additional resources and tools for Bible study, and group discussion in which individual insights are shared, critically examined, and refined. To the extent that the group becomes a supportive Christian fellowship, the work of the Holy Spirit can be enhanced, thus removing many blocks to significant confrontation at ever deeper levels of meaning and inspiration.

Bible study in its fullest sense is properly an adult enterprise. However, the possibility of confrontation by and response to the Biblical message is present in some sense from the earliest years. At the preschool age, this confrontation is mediated almost completely by concerned Christian adults as they live out the implications of the Biblical message in their relationships with children. Foundations are thus being laid that will enable the children to interpret much more adequately the words of the Bible, without which the message of the Bible cannot become explicit. As the child's facility with words and

meanings grows, he becomes more able to engage in a direct use of the Bible itself, so that by his junior years he can have acquired some acquaintance with the simpler portions of the Bible, together with some skill at finding his way around in the book. Some children are capable of memorizing considerable portions of the Bible, but more important is the emerging sense that the Bible is dealing with issues that go far deeper than the surface meanings of the Bible passages.

By the junior high years, most young people have experienced enough of the basic issues of life that the challenge of the Biblical message can evoke the beginnings of a total lifelong commitment. But this commitment must be strengthened by a continuing exploration of the significance of the Bible, including a comprehension of the overall Biblical story, together with the development of a certain degree of critical interpretative ability, before an adult level of skill in Bible study is reached. — *Robert E. Koenig*

BIBLICAL CRITICISM In its current scientific form, Biblical criticism dates from the 18th century. During that period, secular historians began to develop principles for dealing with documents and literary materials as the sources out of which history is written. When secular historians began to challenge the authority of an infallible Bible by applying to the Biblical documents the same principles they had evolved for dealing with any other literature, Biblical scholars responded by adapting these methods for an inquiry into the history of the tradition of which the Biblical documents are a witness.

Biblical criticism has three more

or less distinct facets determined in accordance with the end in view. Textual criticism is concerned with the actual wording of the Biblical texts; literary criticism inquires into the origin and authorship of the various books of the Bible; and historical or material criticism seeks the original meaning and historical setting of the material that goes to make up the various books of the Bible.

1. *Textual criticism.* Although the methods of textual criticism used in studying the Old and New Testaments have developed in parallel fashion, they have separated into 2 distinct disciplines. Since we possess originals of no book of the Bible, we are dependent upon copies that have been made through the centuries. As soon as we have 2 copies of any book or part of a book of the Bible, textual criticism is born. The text critic works with the ancient manuscripts, which are copies of the Biblical books in the original tongue — Hebrew for the Old Testament and Greek for the New. He also uses the version that has been translated into another tongue — Greek and Latin were early translations for the Old Testament, Latin and Syriac early ones for the New Testament. Finally, the text critic has citations in ancient authors of portions of the Biblical text, a source much richer for New Testament textual criticism than for Old. With these 3 sources or tools he sets about reconstructing insofar as possible the original text of the Bible. In the course of comparing texts and determining which readings are earlier, the textual critic develops principles that assist him in making further similar decisions.

More or less obvious errors in transmission, such as dittography, haplography, changes in spelling, etc., are easy to detect as compared with finding variant readings that have arisen through purposeful alteration of the text by copyists. What is even more difficult for the critic is the fact that an alteration of the text may have been made the accepted text at a given period in history. An example of this is the Masoretic text of the Hebrew Old Testament, which differs considerably from the Greek Old Testament (Septuagint), especially in certain parts. Recent discoveries at Qumrân have produced Hebrew texts that resemble the Septuagint more than the Masoretic text.

Textual criticism of the New Testament began its active period with the discovery in the 19th century of many ancient manuscripts. The progress of textual criticism in the New Testament can be measured by the expansion of the *apparatus criticus* in successive editions of *Novum Testamentum Graecae* (24th ed., Stuttgart, 1960). The most recent edition cites 34 papyrus Greek manuscripts, 47 uncial (large letter) Greek manuscripts, and a large number of minuscule (cursive) texts and lectionary manuscripts. Many of these have shown common ancestry and have been placed in families or text types such as the Egyptian, represented by Vatican 4th-century text, and the Koine that lies behind Luther's Bible and was the 1st Greek text printed. Further, a half dozen Syriac versions and some 7 other language versions are among those cited. This edition also cites quotations from more than 50 ancient authors who employ the New Testament.

Although the chief aim of textual criticism has been to get as close to the original text as possible, more recent textual critics have become interested in the history of textual transmission and the history of dogma as reflected in textual variants.

2. *Literary criticism.* (*a*) *Source criticism.* Recognition that the first 5 books of the Bible (Pentateuch) were not written by Moses, in their present form at least, and that the widely divergent material in the book going under the name " Isaiah " is not from a single hand is the result of source criticism, a branch of literary criticism. This discipline seeks the literary history of the traditions that make up the various books of the Bible. Thus the Graf-Wellhausen hypothesis yielded an analysis of the Pentateuch showing that it was made up of at least 4 layers of tradition, the documents J, E, D, and P. Likewise, in The Book of Isaiah there were separated out at least 2 " Isaiahs " (chs. 1 to 39 and chs. 40 to 66) and some would contend that II Isaiah is made up of 2 strata (chs. 40 to 55 and chs. 56 to 66). The question of sources and the question of authorship are related problems illuminated by the methods of literary criticism.

In the New Testament the literary analysis of books to determine their sources and authorship takes a peculiar turn because of the great similarity among the 1st three Gospels. Laying these Gospels side by side and looking at them together gives rise to the " Synoptic Problem," i.e., how to account for the great similarity. From the latter part of the 19th century, it has been customary to recognize the priority of Mark as a source for Luke and Matthew, thus attributing the triple tradition to Mark. The double tradition, where Luke and Matthew are similar, with nonoccurrence of the material in Mark, has been ac-counted for by postulation of a common source document, Q for German *Quelle* (source). This two-document hypothesis has been expanded by some critics (e.g., B. H. Streeter) who would find documents as the source for tradition peculiar to each of Matthew and Luke, while others would find subsources (e.g., Bussmann) within the 2 documents.

(*b*) *Form history.* The introduction of the method of form historical criticism into Biblical studies is due to H. Gunkel in the Old Testament area and M. Dibelius and R. Bultmann in the New. Its purpose is to trace the preliterary history of the small sections (pericopes) making up the source materials from which the various books of the Bible are eventually constructed. The method of form history is based on a generalization arrived at by critics of folktales and sagas, viz., " So long as a form of literature [preliterature?] leads an independent life, certain content is definitely bound up with certain forms of expression " (A. Alt). Consequently, efforts have been made to trace the history of certain " forms " in the preliterary period of Israel's history. In the New Testament, form history has been of great help in exploring the period before Mark and Q. Sayings, parables, etc., after being classified, can be dealt with as independent parts of tradition, and they reveal the concern of the early church with the preaching situation. The form historian drives one step farther the work of the source critic, but both are still in the realm of literary criticism, although the form historian borders on historical criticism.

3. *Historical criticism.* After textual and literary critics have finished with a piece of tradition, the histori-

cal critic must place it historically. He tries to locate the historical point at which a given story or saying took shape and to trace it to its original relation to an event or a person. In the New Testament this creates the problem of the " historical Jesus " (A. Schweitzer), for the critic must decide the authenticity of an event or a saying. Using the results of textual and literary criticism, the historical critic must go farther, since questions such as the occurrence of miracles cannot be avoided. This is an area where responsible historical judgments must be made, but the critic has available the method of the historian for ascertaining the probable authenticity of specific events and sayings attributed to Jesus as he is portrayed in the tradition of the church.

Biblical criticism is, therefore, the means whereby the Christian gospel is kept relevant to each age as it was once relevant to the age in which it was proclaimed.

— *Jules Laurence Moreau*

BIOGRAPHY The very word " biography " suggests its religious pertinence. Derived from the Greek *bios* (life) plus *graphein* (to write), it refers to " the writing of life." Any life-centered approach must be germane to religious education, since the raw materials of human existence constitute the very groundwork of the Christian gospel's thrust. It is for persons that God acts in Jesus Christ. The whole complex of human life is therefore of the greatest interest and concern to all who are involved in proclaiming the gospel and sharing in redeemed existence through the body of Christ.

The perennial human interest in personalities has manifested itself in concrete representations of particular lives by means of the written or printed word. Prior to the advent of writing, the oral rendition of the exploits of heroes was not uncommon; indeed, the earliest myths centered in persons, whether gods or heroes, would appear to have been compounded of nuclear factual incidents in the lives of certain outstanding members of the tribes, elaborated by imaginative accretions through the years. In the technical sense, however, biography refers to written lives. Early biography tended to be an expression of the " commemorative instinct" (Sir Sidney Lee). This motivation frequently produced eulogies, panegyrics, and the like. The classic example of this approach is Plutarch, who used biography as an opportunity for celebrating certain moral qualities, characters being fitted into the molds of Aristotelian ethics. In contrast to such motivation, modern biography has sought to present a well-rounded portrait, using all available facts and materials in the effort to set forth as authentic a representation of the personality as may be possible from the evidence at hand. It is inevitable in all kinds of biographical writing, of course, that the author's viewpoint will determine to a considerable extent the nature of the portrait. It must be added that biographical writing is a work of art when well done, and this factor will determine also the nature of the portrait achieved by the author.

A word should be said concerning the question as to what extent the Bible contains biographical material. Certainly we do not have in the Biblical writings any full-length biography of any character, in the modern sense of the word. Nevertheless there are innumerable biographical " fragments " in the Bible, and there is every reason to believe that there is an honest portrayal of characters in many instances, which goes far beyond any suggestion of the moralistic " use " of these characters that sometimes formerly was characteristic of some religious education materials. The Bible is truly life centered in that it gives us snapshots out of the depths of the characters it portrays.

The following guiding principles for the use of biography in religious education may be suggested: (1) The subjects selected for study should be related insofar as possible to the needs and interests of those concerned in particular studies. (2) The teacher (or curriculum writer) should seek to give a fair and honest portrayal of the facts regarding any character being studied, without any tendency to gloss over unpleasant elements in the interest of moralizing. (3) Biography will not be used as an end in itself, as if the teacher were presenting a course in literature or history, for example. It will, rather, be viewed as material through which life meanings can be interpreted, providing illustrations of the dynamics by which lives have been lived.

— Kendig Brubaker Cully

BOARD OF CHRISTIAN EDUCATION The board of Christian education, which may also be known as the committee or commission on Christian education, is responsible to the local church for planning and administering its program of Christian education. The membership of the board, its plan of action, its relation to other church committees, and its specific tasks vary with the policies and practices of different denominations.

Elected members are chosen by the voting membership of the local congregation or a group representing the voting membership. These members qualify for office by interest, ability, and active participation in the educational life of the church. The board also has ex officio members who may or may not possess voting power. Among these members are the minister, director of Christian education, minister of music, church school superintendent, and in some churches, departmental superintendents.

A 3d type of members are representatives of other church groups, such as youth fellowship, missions, social action, music, budget and finance committees, and men's and women's organizations.

The chairman of the board may be elected at the time the members are named, appointed by an executive group in the church, or chosen by the board members themselves. Other officers such as the vice-chairman and secretary are customarily named by the board.

The responsibilities of the board may be determined by the denomination or by the local church. If these are established by denominational policy, they are published in the official rules of the church. If the local church defines the responsibilities of its board of Christian education, an authoritative document such as the church constitution usually outlines its duties.

Common responsibilities include the following: determining the purpose of the church's educational program — that is, what it hopes to accomplish in the lives of its members through its educational activities; selecting the curriculum materials that are used in all aspects of the educational work of the church or stating how these shall be chosen;

recruiting and training leadership for the church's educational program; planning for special educational events such as family week, the beginning of the church school year, the celebration of Christian festivals and holy days including Christmas and Easter, vacation-time activities; evaluating the effectiveness of the educational program in the light of the recognized purpose; exploring and implementing new ways of strengthening the educational work of the church; cooperating with other committees and boards in general church programs such as schools of missions, anniversary celebrations, social-action projects, church-building; working for an adequate educational budget and administering its use for the maximum benefit of all age groups and interests; educating the entire congregation on the importance of a sound educational program.

To fulfill these responsibilities, the board of Christian education usually meets monthly at a set time and place. Many boards find it wise to circulate the agenda of the meeting in advance and to ask board members to prepare reports or bring information that will expedite the work of the meeting. Board members may also be asked to report on work that has been completed or is currently in process.

Board members may be encouraged to attend church and community meetings that will help them in their work and to read books, magazines, and other materials that will contribute to their understanding of the educational ministry of the church. — *Grace Storms Tower*

BOOKS, CHILDREN'S Children's books come from many sources, appear in a great variety of formats, and draw on a considerable diversity of subject matter for their content. Basically, however, such children's books are usually designed for the child's personal leisure-time reading or, in the case of preschoolers, to be read to him by an older person, in contrast to textbooks as used in the school classroom under the guidance of a teacher.

One large segment of children's books of value for Christian education is to be found in the pupil's reading books published by several Protestant denominations as integral parts of church school curricula. One or more books may be issued in connection with a particular course of study, and may be intended for use both in class groups and as personal reading at home. In design, these books are usually well illustrated, with good quality artwork appropriate to the reader's age, and are bound in hard or semistiff covers or other relatively permanent forms. These books usually make good reading entirely independent of their use in church school and may appear in more durable binding in trade editions. Such books are to be distinguished from the familiar " quarterly " kind of church school pupil publication, which contains class study and activity suggestions, stories, and other resource material, and is usually bound much less durably.

The content of pupil's curriculum reading books naturally depends upon the subject matter of the courses of study to which they are related. The range, however, often includes the following if the span from preschool through elementary grades is considered: Bible stories; stories based on Bible materials or laid in Bible times; stories drawn from episodes in the church's history or centering about church leaders, past and present; here-and-now stories at various age levels, based on experiences of universal significance to children; biographical stories, usually those of persons with whom children can identify in their life situations; stories of the church at work around the world or of life and people in other countries; stories of the church at work in a variety of situations and locations in our own country. Each book usually concentrates on one of the above content areas unless it is a book of short stories that may either center on one area (as Bible stories or biographies) or may include a cross section of several types of material that are related to some central theme.

A 2d group of children's books useful in Christian education are Bible and other storybooks that are definitely oriented to Christian source material but have no connection with church school curricula. These may be published by denominational publishing houses, interdenominational agencies, or commercial publishing firms. If the latter, the book is usually listed as one of the firm's regular "juveniles." Most familiar is the Bible storybook that gives, in paraphrase or by retelling, either a condensed version or the full sweep of the Bible or selected stories from it. If the book deals with non-Biblical material, the subject is most likely to be church history, Christian biography, or mission stories of the church's activity at home or around the world. Bible storybooks are usually written to be read by children themselves or in company with parents, and a single book may aim to cover an age spread of several years; or books may be graded in reading level and

interest. Great care should be exercised in selecting Bible storybooks, yet perhaps no one type of reading book is more often uncritically chosen for a child or for use in Christian education groups. Among the points to be considered in making a selection are: (1) Is the style of writing good literature or merely an inferior or inept paraphrase of the Bible that obscures the literary power of the original? (2) Is the storybook written in the light of our best understanding of the nature, purpose, and meaning of the Biblical material, or is it unimaginative literalism that glosses over and distorts the religious significance of the Bible? (3) Will readers be led to want to know more of the Bible after reading this book, or will their interests and appetites be dulled? (4) Are the illustrations good art — accurate, in good taste, suitable for the age of the reader, attractive (not garish or gaudy) in color — and do they in themselves convey desirable meanings and understandings of the Biblical material?

In times past, both Biblical and non-Biblical religious storybooks have tended to present idealized versions of people. Christian hero or missionary stories, for example, presented perfectionist portraits, to emulate which, presumably, young readers would strive in their own lives. Biblical heroes such as David were often presented as models without blemish. The newer trend in these reading books is to present persons more realistically, showing their struggles of faith and doubt, their difficulties as well as their accomplishments in living the Christian life. It is hoped that children will identify with such characters and thus find in their own struggles and life situations encouragement in trying to live through their problem in a Christian manner. This mood of existential realism in children's books is in harmony with recent trends in theological thought and Christian education.

A wide range of the better books published, usually by commercial firms, constitutes a third source of books useful with children in Christian education. These well-written and competently illustrated books directly or indirectly promote values, standards, and interests that are Christian in quality and ethical level, although not specifically so in content. At first glance these books might be passed by as good children's books but of no particular value for Christian education, for their range of subject matter is almost as broad as the number of books published. The book may be about a 3-year-old's experience of getting lost or picking daisies in the spring, a 6-year-old's love for his pet, a 9-year-old's enthusiasm for Little League or Indians, a 12-year-old's burgeoning curiosity about space — or any of dozens of other childhood experiences and interests. But such books may forcefully present examples of true love and forgiveness. They may describe sound relationships with parents and warm appreciations for others. They may disclose some of the fears universally present in children and show constructive ways by which these may be worked through. If the book interprets life faithfully and with insight into the meaning of childhood experiences, if it suggests interests that lead to broadened horizons and the development of wonder and enriched living, or if it demonstrates truth and beauty in their many forms, it may be of real value for Christian educational purposes.

Children, in reading such books, may glimpse Christian qualities of life in action that have been talked about in church school, or a new vision of what life can be like may be presented to the young reader. Religious and ethical living of fine quality is often more clearly exemplified in good children's books than in inferior and moralistic books that may bear religious or Biblical labels.

Another group of general children's books useful in Christian education are those which serve as background, resource, or reference books about other countries, scientific findings, peace and brotherhood, natural wonders, and the like. Many books in this area not only supply information but give interpretations, particularly of people and natural wonders, which speak to children's expanding interests and inner motivations.

While the primary use of children's books may be for personal reading at home, all the categories of books often prove useful in other ways. Both curriculum and noncurriculum books serve all ages well when placed on browsing tables in church school classes. They may also serve for reference or research, and may be placed in church libraries for loan to individuals or families. Many denominations issue lists of recommended children's books, especially the specifically religious ones. Book-review sections of newspapers and magazines also provide good sources of recommended listings. But all books, regardless of recommendation, should be carefully examined for content, literary style, quality of artwork, and suitability for the child's age level, before they are purchased.

— *Frances Eastman*

BOOKS, RELIGIOUS By "books" one may mean only printed works, but it is well to remember that publication did not wait for the invention of printing from movable type. Clay tablets inscribed prior to 1800 B.C. were found in the Temple of Bel in Nippur. Egyptian manuscripts on papyrus were much earlier. Vellum and parchment scrolls and codices were widely used until paper was introduced from the Orient, where the Chinese had been printing from engraved blocks since 50 B.C. Religion shared with other fields in the use of these materials of publication.

All the great living religions of the world have produced literature and have continued to live, in part, because they wrote about and taught their faith. Hinduism has its Vedas and Upanishads, Buddhism its Tripitaka, and Confucianism the Classics and Analects. The sacred scripture of Islam is the Koran. Taoism, Shinto, Sikhism, Jainism and Parsism all possess sacred books. Only the primitive cults, some 9 percent of the world's population, still perpetuate their religious beliefs through oral tradition without written sources. As missionaries of the various faiths traveled to new countries, they brought their scriptures and made translations into new tongues, sometimes even creating the 1st written language for a people. And beyond the sacred books of these living faiths are the countless volumes of commentaries, liturgies, histories, and theologies that interpret each religion.

The story of Bible editions from the Masoretic and Septuagint texts of the Old Testament and the earliest codices of the New Testament to contemporary versions in colloquial languages reveals a continuous stream. We think of the more familiar editions: the Latin Vulgate, Luther's German version, the English of Wycliffe and Tyndale and the Geneva Bible, the King James Version (1611), and the more recent American Standard Version (1901) and Revised Standard Version (1946 and 1952). The British and Foreign Bible Society and the American Bible Society, with some 20 cooperating societies, publish English and other language editions. Through the missionary movement books or parts of the Bible have been published in more than 1,000 tongues. Each year sees new dialects added. The Bible has led all other books as a best seller, and its editions often run into millions. The New English Bible (New Testament) sold over 3,000,000 copies in the first 5 months after publication.

In addition to Bible research there is important contemporary writing on the relevance of religion to the world in which we live. Religion is no isolated phenomenon. There is a religious approach to international relations as well as to race problems, a religious criticism of business as well as personal ethics, a religious art and drama along with the secular, and a religious education that ideally challenges all of life. To meet the demand for such religious literature many denominational publishers are active. The largest Protestant presses are Abingdon, Association, Eerdmans, Westminster, and Zondervan, but numerous others produce books of high quality. Many secular presses have successful departments of religion.

Religious books have also had a significant place in libraries. Ancient temples maintained libraries. Monasteries in the Middle Ages preserved and duplicated books and kept the ancient literatures alive. They still perform this function for many religions. The percentage of religious books may have dropped in modern libraries since Harvard reported in 1773 that 30 percent of its collection consisted of religious books, but great university and public libraries have extensive religious holdings. Theological schools offer some of the best collections in America. There are numerous special libraries of religion. For contemporary reading by clergy and laity, postal loan services for special fields are provided by the Missionary Research Library in New York, by the Congregational and General Theological Libraries in Boston, and by the Zion Research Library in Brookline, Mass.

— Jannette E. Newhall

BOY SCOUTS OF AMERICA The Boy Scouts of America was incorporated on Feb. 8, 1910. It received a charter from the Congress of the United States on June 15, 1916. In the charter its purpose is defined in these words: "To promote through organization and cooperation with other agencies the ability of boys to do things for themselves and others, to train them in Scoutcraft, and to teach them patriotism, courage, self-reliance, and kindred virtues, using methods which are now in common use by Boy Scouts, by placing emphasis on the Scout Promise and Law for character development, citizenship training, and physical fitness."

Scouting is a set of principles. These principles are most concisely expressed in the Scout Oath: "On my honor I will do my best: to do my duty to God and my country, and to obey the Scout Law; to help other people at all times; to keep myself physically strong, mentally awake, and morally straight." Four basic duties are defined: duty to God, to country, to others, and to self.

The religious policies of Scouting are defined in the constitution of the Boy Scouts of America: "The recognition of God as the ruling and leading power in the universe and the grateful acknowledgment of his favors and blessings are necessary to the best type of citizenship and are wholesome precepts in the education of the growing boy. . . . The Boy Scouts of America therefore recognizes the religious element in the training of a boy, but it is absolutely nonsectarian in its attitude toward religious training. Its policy is that the organization or institution with which the Boy Scout is connected shall give definite attention to his religious life."

Scouting is a program through which principles and ideals are communicated to boys. Emphasis in this process of communication is on "learning by doing." Wholesome, creative, constructive activities are the medium through which Scout spirit and ideals are implanted in the minds and hearts of boys. The program has three phases: Cub Scouting, Boy Scouting, and Exploring.

Cub Scouting is a home-centered program for boys 9 to 11 years old. The boy's parents take part in his program. The pack is composed of small groups called dens, each of which holds a weekly meeting under the leadership of a Boy Scout known as den chief and a den mother who is the mother of one of the Cub Scouts.

The Boy Scout program for boys 11 years of age and older emphasizes outdoor skills and activities, participation in group life, and personal growth. Recognition is given for the boy's accomplishments. Boys are organized in patrols under boy leaders. One or more patrols make a troop. The scoutmaster and assistant are the troop leaders, selected by the troop committee appointed by the sponsoring institution.

The Explorer program is for all high school age boys. The post carries on a program in the areas of citizenship, personal fitness, social activities, vocational exploration, outdoor events, and service projects. A feature of the Explorer program is the opportunity to pursue special interests in many fields of endeavor that may be related to vocations or hobbies.

Scouting is a partnership through which the program is delivered to boys. The Boy Scouts of America does not operate Scouting units. It charters churches, schools, civic organizations, and service clubs of various kinds to use the Scouting program and to operate their own Scouting units. These chartered institutions are encouraged to gear Scouting into their own administration and program. Half of all Cub packs, Scout troops, and Explorer posts are sponsored by religious institutions. Close to 50,000 Scouting units are in Protestant churches. In these churches Scouting is usually under the direction of the board of Christian education.

The God and Country program relates Boy Scouts and Explorers more specifically to the program of Christian education in local churches. This program was developed by the Protestant Committee on Scouting in cooperation with the Boy Scouts of America. It is a program of study, experience, and service that a boy carries out under the direction of his own minister.

— *Albert E. Iverson*

BOYS' CLUBS OF AMERICA The 1st boys' club of which there is any record was started in 1860 at Hartford, Conn. Thereafter several New England communities started organizations to provide less privileged boys with opportunities for constructive use of leisure time.

In 1906, 50 clubs joined to form a national organization that would not only serve these clubs but assist interested communities in establishing new clubs. With the establishment of the national organization the Boys' Club movement began to grow. Early in the 1940's it gained new impetus, and clubs began to spring up all over the country. In 1956, Boys' Clubs of America was granted a charter by the Congress of the U.S.A., which charges the organization with responsibility for the promotion of the health, and the social, educational, vocational, and character development of boys throughout the nation. By 1961 there were 574 Boys' Clubs, with over 550,000 members.

Although most Boys' Clubs are located in the crowded and poorer areas of towns and cities, there are clubs in small communities that serve all boys who have needs and problems.

A Boys' Club is an all-boy organization. Any boy can afford to belong. Membership dues are kept low enough that the poorest boy can belong on an equal basis with all the other boys. It is nonsectarian in management, leadership, and membership.

The Boys' Club is open every weekday afternoon and evening. It has a varied program so that at all times there are constructive activities for boys with differing inclinations and varying needs. Emphasis is placed on everyday guidance. Every boy is encouraged to develop to his fullest capacity in physical fitness and in mental and manual skills. A professionally trained staff makes possible an individual service and continuous informal guidance.

Each Boys' Club belonging to Boys' Clubs of America is an autonomous organization, managed by public-spirited citizens and supported by the Community Chest, United Fund, or by contributions made directly to the club. Each member club can send delegates to and vote in the National Council, which meets annually, and establishes the policies by which the national organization operates. Boys' Clubs of America establishes standards and methods; develops programs and program materials; plans buildings and equipment; recruits, trains, and places club workers; publishes periodicals, booklets, and bulletins; carries on national interpretation and publicity; and provides guidance plans and materials for the use of the Boys' Clubs themselves.

Eight regional offices have field workers who give guidance and assistance to the Boys' Clubs, and aid communities in organizing and establishing clubs. Organizations must meet certain requirements for membership in Boys' Clubs of America.
— *John M. Gleason*

BUDDHISM To millions of devout Buddhists the founder of their religion, Gautama the Buddha, is preeminently " the great Teacher." He is the great Teacher because he is not only the fully enlightened one (as the title " the Buddha " signifies) but also the compassionate one. As such, when he himself had achieved enlightenment after renouncing the privileges and comforts of the princely life to which he was born in Northern India some 2,500 years ago, he devoted a great part of a long ministry to religious instruction. And he told his monks to do likewise: " Go forth and teach the noble doctrine for the good and welfare of the many." For there is no better gift, it is believed, than sound teaching: " The gift of the Dharma (truth, law, doctrine) excels all other gifts."

Where the Hinayana (or Theravada) version of Buddhism prevails and there is exclusive devotion to Gautama, emphasis on this gift of teaching is especially pronounced. The Buddha taught the way, first, in his doctrine of the Four Noble Truths, attributing human frustration to attachment to what is vain and fleeting; secondly, in his exposition of the Noble Eightfold Path that leads to the goal of that deliverance and release which is Nirvana. In the Mahayana tradition, with its many sects and its development of the concept of other manifest Buddhas besides Gautama, some members of the Pure Land sects do indeed expect more than a pointing of the path. Amida Buddha is regarded as the source of " other help " to follow this path in much the same way as Christians expect divine grace. But here, too, respect for the founders of the different schools or sects means, again, an emphasis on the excellent gift of teaching.

It is therefore not surprising that Buddhists should emphasize religious education. This is particularly evident in a predominantly Buddhist country such as Burma, where for centuries the monasteries established in every town and village have been educational centers. Buddhist boys not only attended the schools conducted by the monks; they also went to live for a time in the monasteries, following a ceremony of initiation in their early teens. Today this pattern has been disturbed by the establishment of other schools where children receive a " modern " education, but arrangements are made for the monks to come to these schools and give religious instruction. There is also a new interest in adult religious education. Some 200 " meditation centers " especially designed for the laity have been set up in Burma within recent years.

In countries where Buddhism is not so firmly established as the national religion as it is in Burma, different measures are taken to ensure religious education. In Ceylon, for example, where the traditional pattern of monastic schools has been interrupted, schools comparable with Christian Sunday schools have been arranged. Similar schools have been established by Buddhists in America. In Ceylon, too, Buddhist printing presses in recent years have been turning out many pamphlets for the better instruction of the laity. One of these pamphlets, *How to Teach Buddhism to Children*, written by a Western convert to Buddhism, enlarges upon the responsibility that Buddhist parents living in Western countries have for teaching their own children. What is said about the important role that " externals " play in childhood reflects general Buddhist practice: " No Buddhist household should therefore be without a *Buddha-rupa* (image) or at least a picture of the Enlightened

One. It is a good idea to let each child have a small *Buddha-rupa* of its own before which it can offer regularly flowers, incense, and lights . . . sometimes candles. But it is vital that we see to it that the child does not come to worship the image itself, but that it pays devotion to the Buddha as the greatest Teacher."

In the case of Mahayana Buddhism, as taught in China and Japan, the situation is again different. Here, Buddhism is one teaching beside others — Taoist, Confucian, and Shinto. In former times some of the temples in Japan were centers of instruction similar to the Theravada monasteries, and today at some of these same temples there are " Sunday schools " after the Western pattern. But a Japanese Buddhist when asked who first instructed him in this faith will generally answer, " My grandmother." On the other hand, in Zen Buddhism the master-pupil relationship is all-important. " To attain the goal of Zen," writes one Zen scholar, " we must begin by receiving guidance from a true master of Zen."

As to methods of instruction, much is committed to memory, with considerable regard for aids to memory. A Buddhist monk will make skillful use of gestures, raising one finger after another to emphasize different points. Many passages in Buddhist scripture take a form that aids recollection. There is a good deal of repetition, with answers to questions repeating the questions in full. At the same time, a good many Buddhist teachers today emphasize that no servile respect for authority is intended. The very nature of the teaching itself, they say, encourages a man to think for himself.

Much of the Theravada instruction is given in the form of story.

Best known of all, perhaps, is the story of the Buddha's great renunciation, for this is not only told but reenacted at every initiation ceremony. The young Buddhist is dressed and paraded in princely finery, sometimes riding through the village on a pony, before he is tonsured and attired in the yellow robe of the *novia*. In the monastery school he will probably learn the verses that tell how the Buddha resisted Mara and other tempters.

There are also stories that refer to virtues demonstrated by the Buddha in previous existences (for Buddhists share with Hindus the doctrine known in the West as "transmigration"). One of the most popular of these *Jataka* tales emphasizes the Buddha's generosity by presenting him as a prince who was willing to give away not only his kingdom and his wealth but was even ready to give away his children and his beloved wife.

In this way the young Buddhist is encouraged to cultivate those virtues which are regarded as essential to any true following of the path. He not only commits to memory the 5 prohibitive precepts: not to kill; not to steal; not to lie; not to commit adultery; not to drink intoxicants. He has before him the positive example of the Buddha's own life, an example that remains vividly in his mind even if he grows up to become a monk, engaged in the subtle analytic meditations prescribed for the members of the order. In a very real sense Buddhism for such a follower is Buddha. The way that he follows is above all else the Buddha's way. To appreciate how this is so is important if we would understand Theravada Buddhism as a living religion manifesting the devotion reflected in, and maintained by, the recital of the threefold Confession: "I take refuge in the Buddha; I take refuge in the Dharma (the truth; the law); I take refuge in the *Samgha* (the monastic order)."

In the greater variety and development of the Mahayana tradition the historic founder may seem at times to be lost to view. To many a Buddhist in this tradition Buddhism is a calling upon the name of Amida Buddha, in grateful response to his vow to save all sentient beings, rather than a remembrance of the founder. But the founder is recollected in the familiar parable of the hesitant traveler to the Pure Land who is not only encouraged by hearing the voice of Amida Buddha saying, "Come," but also by the voice of the historic Buddha saying, "God." If the young Buddhist in this Mahayana tradition is referred to more than one exemplar, what these exemplars all attest is nevertheless the same Buddha character of wisdom joined with compassion. Here, too, religious education means more than the recital of texts and precepts. It means story. It means poetry. — *Robert H. L. Slater*

BUILDINGS   Three major considerations should be uppermost in the minds of those who plan buildings for Christian education, select their furnishings, and provide the necessary teaching tools: (1) a clear understanding of the purpose of Christian education; (2) an intimate knowledge of the people to be served now and in the future by each particular church; (3) a more than superficial acquaintance with the learning procedures considered best in meeting the needs of each age group. To assemble and evaluate these data, each church will need to select, organize, and relate many of its competent people, in terms of their aptitudes, to specific assignments. The result of this comprehensive survey, when completed, should be reduced to a written summary outlining the church's program, the numbers of persons to be ministered to at each age level, and the recommended spaces, furnishings, and teaching tools required to implement effectively the program outlined. This process, if sensibly directed and pursued, will stimulate a lively interest in and an intelligent appraisal of what needs to be done and how it can be done successfully. Furthermore, this summary will enable the designing architect to plan his building fittingly and efficiently to house the parish-wide educational program.

Present-day efforts to heighten the teaching impact of the church stress the need for classrooms large enough to permit the use of the great variety of teaching procedures and tools now available. Such space also prevents overcrowding and overstimulation of pupils. Considerable attention is also being given to the quality of the space provided. Most people, including children, are sensitive to their environment. Pleasant surroundings need not necessarily add appreciably to the cost of the building or unduly pamper the pupils. Rather, such space tends to enhance the learning process by lifting pupil interest, attention, and participation to higher levels of effectiveness than would otherwise obtain.

Factors meriting special attention are: the selection of the right colors for decorating each room to ensure a pleasing but not overstimulating decor; the installation of adequately controlled illumination to afford good visibility and to prevent eye discomfiture; the controlled regulation of temperatures at the right level and the installation of draft-free ventilation in all rooms; the installation of generous window spaces and the incorporation of an inviting openness in all classrooms; good sanitation and rest rooms, particularly in areas where food is stored, prepared, and served; all possible means used to ensure the prevention of accident and fire hazards; good acoustics in controlling objectionable sounds and in assuring good communication in all rooms; well-planned storage spaces in all parts of the building, designed for each situation. Adequate circulation facilities are needed throughout the building so that pupils may safely and readily reach their assigned rooms without passing through or disrupting procedures in other areas. All church-building master plans and church-building sites should anticipate multiple use of space whenever possible, and include a large measure of flexibility, thereby permitting needed adjustments as called for in the future life of the church.

Where attendance is not large enough to warrant a fully graded school or where facilities are deficient, adjustments can be made by the grading and grouping of pupils and by exercising ingenuity in the use of available space in order to assure that the principles of good education are maintained.

The planning, financing, and erecting of an effective church building is an exceedingly complex and important undertaking. It merits most careful thought and the use of such professional skills and the adoption of those standards of procedure which will give each church the largest possible measure of effectiveness in its sacred mission for each dollar invested.

— *C. Harry Atkinson*

BULLETIN BOARD Tools for teaching may be as aesthetic as the stained-glass windows of medieval times, as pointed as the Mother Goose rhymes of the 16th century, or as varied in purpose and design as modern advertising.

The bulletin board can tell a story, teach a lesson, highlight a special topic, praise the pupil, create interest in a subject, dispense information, prompt discussion, or stimulate attitudes and moods. The material displayed has value for every age group and can be used to enhance any subject.

The arrangement of a bulletin board is well worth study and planning. Unity and simplicity are keynotes to be kept in mind. All parts should converge toward a single impression. This center of interest should have balance of color, line, and mass, around which a story or idea can be built. Composition or planned organization of the material used can be further aided by eye-catching titles that can be clearly seen. Precut letters will save time in arrangement. People, places, and things can really live for the observer if properly displayed.

Care should be taken in the length of time displays are left on a bulletin board. This will depend on the purpose. Some might be left a single Sunday, some for a holiday season, others a quarter or for the length of a unit of study. Staleness will destroy the effectiveness of the material used. A conglomeration of materials completely destroys the possibility of usefulness.

Some materials lend themselves especially well to bulletin board use.

Many are inexpensive and easily obtained. Plain brown wrapping paper, burlap, monk's cloth, linoleum, corrugated paper, pegboard, masonite, celotex, soft wood, and cork are all used. Perhaps the best of these is cork, but others will do very well for special projects. The size will depend on the space available in the classroom, on the wall or partition. Churches that must divide classroom space by partitions will find that bulletin boards which can be easily removed and changed often will not only serve as a teaching aid but will dress up the class space and help the children feel that it is their own room.

There are several convenient ways to affix materials on the bulletin board. They can be pinned, secured with colored thumbtacks, or stuck with one of the many adhesives available. Most bulletin board material can be reused if it is easily removed, classified, filed, and preserved. Pictures store more easily and are less likely to be damaged if they are mounted on poster board or heavy paper. Careful planning on the part of the teacher should result in having proper materials when needed. A clear-cut objective should be kept in mind from the installation of the board and the collection and display of materials to the removal at the proper time. After the bulletin board has been arranged with taste, color harmony, and balance, it can be referred to often during a unit of study or a particular lesson. A teaching picture used with a children's class can be of further aid if displayed on the bulletin board as a part of follow-up activity. Thus it can provide a review of the previous Sunday's lesson or be used for the outline of a unit, either to introduce it or to conclude and summarize the topic at the close of the time that is specified.

Children like to see their work displayed or to feel that they have had a part in the arrangement. Each class and department should have some space that it feels free to use. Youth groups soon get accustomed to looking at the bulletin board for meeting times and new events. For adult classes the bulletin board habit soon replaces trite announcements and too much " class business." — *Alice W. Wonders*

BUSHNELL, HORACE Horace Bushnell was born at Bantam, near Litchfield, Conn., in 1802. In New Preston, to which the family moved in 1805, Bushnell's parents joined the Congregational Church, and at the age of 19 Bushnell himself became a member by an orthodox profession of faith. Bushnell had planned to become a farmer like his father, until a decline in the family fortunes made this plan seem imprudent. In 1823 he entered Yale to prepare for the ministry. However, in college he lost his faith, and on graduation taught school, wrote for the New York *Journal of Commerce,* and finally became a tutor at Yale, where he planned to study law. When a revival swept the college in 1831, Bushnell, at first aloof, was converted by resolving to obey the one thing he could not doubt — the moral law. He then entered Yale Divinity School, where he rebelliously studied under the rationalistic Nathaniel Taylor, and discovered in Coleridge's *Aids to Reflection* a " range of realities on a higher tier."

In 1833, Bushnell married Mary Apthorp and accepted a call to the North Church of Hartford. When he entered upon his pastorate, the New England Congregational churches faced many difficulties: the appeal of Episcopalianism and Unitarianism to the upper classes, the division of Congregationalists over Taylor's " heresies," the general neglect of infant baptism. Bushnell's first book grew out of these problems. In *Christian Nurture* (1847) he criticized reliance upon revivals as the major method of expanding the Congregational Churches, and announced that a Christian home and a Christian education could abolish the necessity for the agony of revivalistic conversions. Drawing upon the associationalism of the Scottish commonsense philosophy, Bushnell argued that the child's character was determined by the impressions of his early years, and that children could learn Christian love and virtue through the affectionate discipline of their parents. Under such training, the child would " open upon the world as one spiritually renewed, not remembering the time when he went through a technical experience, but seeming to have loved what is good from his earliest years." Joined in a church, Christian families could manifest Christ to the world. Such a church would not convert by a " slaughter among sinners," but by " her Christlike graces." The Holy Spirit would thus enter history, incorporated in the organic power of the church. *Christian Nurture* integrated contemporary concern over children's moral education with the dominant psychology of the time, and gave a new importance to the Christian home.

God in Christ (1849) was a defense of Trinitarianism against the Unitarian insistence that the essence of Christianity consisted in moral truths. Bushnell argued that religious truth could not be separated from the forms which gave it dramatic expression. Christ made God accessible to the human imagination by expressing the divine love, goodness, and compassionate suffering in finite form. Bushnell thus criticized the rationalism that dominated New England theology, and proposed instead a theology addressed to the sensibility.

In *Nature and the Supernatural* (1858), Bushnell integrated contemporary science with a Christian cosmogony. Man the creator and inventor became the protagonist of the drama. Set apart from nature by his power to act upon things, man had chosen to experience evil, and by that choice had set nature into a disorder that only Christ's descent could redeem.

Though ill-health forced Bushnell to resign from his church in 1859, he continued to meditate and publish. In books of sermons he described the peculiar power of Christ, the unforced goodness that was true virtue, and the nature of Christian faith. In *The Vicarious Sacrifice* (1866) and *Forgiveness and the Law* (1874), he stressed the unique importance of the atonement, and found the peculiar expression of God's love in the sacrificial compassion that led to the cross.

Bushnell died in 1876. Later liberal theologians called upon his portrayal of a God of love, his faith in man, his insistence on the power of Christian training. Recent thinkers have found challenging complexity and insight in his analysis of symbolism and ritual, his Christ-centered theology, and his portrayal of the disorder of man and nature without Christ's redemptive sacrifice.

— *Barbara M. Cross*

BUZZ GROUP The buzz group is a technique of discussion used to increase the participation of group members by dividing large groups into smaller subgroups for a limited period of time. The subgroup of 5 or 6 persons is formed by a quick rearrangement of chairs or by 3 persons turning to talk to 3 persons directly behind them. In smaller groups even 2 persons may form a buzz group for discussion. The time alloted to the buzz group is usually from 6 to 10 minutes. To avoid the danger of using too much of the time in selecting leaders and secretaries, the chairman may suggest a simple procedure for all the buzz groups, such as that the leader of each group is to be the person whose name begins with *A,* or the secretary is to be one who is wearing a certain color.

The chairman of the meeting should designate the task in a simple, direct question and explain the form of report expected. The task may vary from discovering problems related to the topic presented or listing problems in order of importance, to collecting suggestions for solutions to a problem. Buzz groups may also be used to analyze roles of a skit or dramatic sketch presenting a problem for consideration. The large group may be divided into a number of buzz groups needed to consider the individual roles portrayed in the skit. The buzz groups may provide the opportunity to replay or rethink the drama to determine the ending or a solution. The reports from the buzz groups will indicate the variety of solutions and the level of understanding of the roles portrayed.

The leader of the buzz group may use a roll-call device to get a contribution from each person in the group. He should encourage immediate brief responses rather than long discourses on the problem.

Buzz groups are distinguished from work groups by the minimum organization within the group, the limited time for discussion, and the maximum emphasis upon quick, spontaneous response to a problem, idea, or proposal. The distinct value of the buzz group is to encourage involvement of each person in the discussion of an area of thought presented to a large group.

— *Harriet Miller*

C

CALVIN, JOHN Calvin (1509–1564) held educational ideals essentially those of eminent Christian humanist educational theorists such as Rudolphus Agricola, John Colet, Desiderius Erasmus, Juan Luis Vives, Johannes Sturm, and his own admired Latin master at Paris, Mathurin Cordier. The fundamental notion is that of *pietas literata*, a piety enlightened by classical learning. "Without piety," Cordier once wrote, "there is no true progress in learning." Calvin himself taught (1538–1541) in Sturm's gymnasium in Strasbourg, which aimed "to form men who are pious, learned, and able to express themselves well." The need of a Reformed school in Geneva had been felt before Calvin came there, and in May, 1536, Antoine Saunier had been appointed to head such a school, which was to furnish free and compulsory education. Out of this grew the Collège de Rive, in which Saunier, Cordier, and Sebastian Castellio gave periods of service; but poverty and disturbed conditions kept this institution relatively feeble and wholly inadequate to the needs of the community.

In 1537 Calvin and Farel projected a college of a more advanced type, and in the Ecclesiastical Ordinances of 1541, this project became more specific. Here "doctors," or teachers, were placed on an equality with pastors, and a college for languages was approved as a basis for training for ministers and civil magistrates, "to raise up seed for time to come, so as not to leave the church a desert to our children." Dispersed through Geneva were a number of elementary schools in a low condition. These were at length consolidated into 4 only, and came under the instruction of ministers. Several attempts of Calvin to induce teachers of repute to come to the city failed, but he continually planned for a notable advance when conditions would permit this.

In 1556 he was able to revisit Sturm's gymnasium, and the plans he now laid may reflect his fresh observation of that institution. In 1558, taking advantage of a favorable turn of political affairs, he brought the magistrates to action, and having settled with them upon a suitable site for a building, instituted a campaign for a building fund. While Calvin pressed the citizens for gifts and legacies, the structure rose; it was completed in 1563. Meanwhile, classes of the new institution, held elsewhere, came to be thronged with pupils, and the formal opening of the academy took place in an impressive assembly in the cathedral on June 5, 1559. The bylaws of the school, prepared by Calvin, outlining the curriculum, were read and approved, and Théodore de Bèze was installed as rector.

Calvin's rules for the college (the *schola privata*) show a marked resemblance to those of Sturm's gymnasium, and may also have owed something to the Collège de Guyenne in Bordeaux where Cordier had taught. Both these institutions had 10 grades, though Sturm may have reduced these to 8. Calvin compressed an equal or greater range of work into 7 (approximately annual) grades. Latin was begun in the lowest grade (class 7), Greek in the fourth. The upper grades (classes 3 to 1) afforded extensive study of classical authors with grammar, history, and dialectic. Cordier, returning in old age to Geneva, joined the college and published (1564) his celebrated *Colloquiorum Scholas Ticorum,* a guide to Latin teaching. If the boys of Geneva talked, as alleged, "like Sorbonne doctors," Cordier's injunction to have them speak Latin out of school as well as in it may have been responsible. After these studies, pupils were qualified to enter the academy proper, the *schola publica,* for the special study of theology. Courses in law were also given, but the projected medical school languished for lack of funds. The students in the *schola publica* came not only from the college but from many nations, and were to exert an incalculable influence in the spread of Calvinism.

Calvin as educator is not to be separated from Calvin as churchman and Reformer. Scriptural religion was inculcated at all stages. The school owed its curriculum largely to humanism, but took its tone from Calvin's theology. Its creation was possible through the early struggle to success of the Geneva church, and in turn it served to make sure the perpetuation and expansion of Calvinism. Through the academy Calvin imparted to a large group of Protestant churches the principle he stated in a sermon: " No one is a good minister of the Word of God who is not first a scholar."

— *John T. McNeill*

CAMP FIRE GIRLS Founded in 1912 by the recreational innovators, Luther Halsey Gulick and his wife Charlotte Vetter Gulick, with the aid of a group of dedicated men and women prominent in the fields of health, education, character development, and human relations, Camp Fire Girls provides a tested leisure-time program for girls age 7 through high school.

The educational-recreational program of girlhood experience provided by the National Council of Camp Fire Girls seeks to develop the best potentialities of each girl, encouraging in her the application of religious, spiritual, and ethical teachings to her daily living; a love of home and family that grows as she grows; pride in woman's traditional qualities — tenderness, affection, and skill in human relationships; deep love of her country, the practice of democracy, readiness to serve; the capacity for fun, friendship, and happy group relations; the formation of healthful habits; the ability to take care of herself, to do her work skillfully, and to take pleasure in it; interests and hobbies she can enjoy either with others or alone; love of the out-of-doors and skill in outdoor living; a happy heart that will help her find beauty, romance, and adventure in the common things of daily life.

The Blue Bird program is for girls 7 and 8 years old, or in the 2d and 3d grades. After the 3d grade, girls are eligible to go to camp, and the following fall they " fly up " to become Camp Fire Girls.

Camp Fire Girls are the 9- to 12-year-olds in the 4th to the 6th grades of school. Trail Seekers are 9- and 10-year-olds in the 4th grade. Wood Gatherers include the 10- and 11-year-olds. The Fire Makers are the 11- and 12-year-olds in the 6th grade.

Girls may join the program at any time and need not cover ground already covered by the group unless they wish to do so.

At the age of 12, or when she enters the 7th grade, a girl is eligible for the Junior High Camp Fire Girls program. This 2-year program, with special emphasis on working together toward achievement of a group project, offers a variety of activities and provides for individual interests as well.

Horizon Clubs offer the high school girl the opportunity to assume an adult place in her group relationships. Primarily a community volunteer-aid program, Horizon Clubs also offer much club activity, at the same time helping a girl to the realization of her own potentialities.

Camp Fire Girls believe that spiritual development is essential to a healthy, wholesome personality and recognize the importance of the church and of religious experience and teachings in the life of a girl. Each part of the Camp Fire Girls Law is related to ethical living, encouraging an appreciation of God's world, emphasizing the dignity of individual worth and character, and recognizing that service to others is one of the essentials of full living. It reads: " Worship God, Seek Beauty, Give Service, Pursue Knowledge, Be Trustworthy, Hold on to Health, Glorify Work, Be Happy."

Camp Fire Girls welcomes the sponsorship of the program by churches and religious groups, recognizing their right to organize Camp Fire Girls groups under their own leadership. This does not necessarily mean that girls must be in groups sponsored by their own particular church. This is for the particular religious group or the individual church to decide.

Camp Fire Girls seeks the cooperation of leaders of all religious groups in its work with girls, believing that out of the faiths we share, as well as out of our differences in belief, observance, and heritage, we can together make our best contribution toward a more spiritual world in which the concept of the brotherhood of man finds reality and expression in the daily lives of all. — *Elizabeth W. Leslie*

CAMPING   The history of camping is the story of man's sojourn on earth and of his striving to learn ways of woods, winds, waves, and of his fellow creatures. With civilization's march, man continues in withdrawal-return rhythms of relation with his sources and elemental simplicities.

Planned camping goes back at least to 1000 B.C. when Egyptians taught young men health and teamwork in the open. Sparta and Athens used camp life for inculcating their disciplines. Educators down the centuries have affirmed vitalities and values in outdoor settings for developing wisdom for life beyond fact knowledge and personality wholeness. American Indians' skill, lore, and sensitivity to nature continue to challenge emulation. Great teachers such as Agassiz, Muir, Burroughs, Sharp, Seton, and Mills centered their teaching about nature.

In the 1900's camping burgeoned as one of the dramatic and pervasive movements of history. The 1st quarter century in America saw the rapid growth of camps for boys and girls (usually separate) sponsored by Y.M.C.A., Y.W.C.A., Camp Fire Girls, Boy Scouts, Girl Scouts, 4-H, other character-building agencies, community chests, welfare boards, family service and child-care groups, settlements, neighborhood houses, civic organizations, churches, and schools. Private camps also multiplied apace. To give focus to the movement, and to provide aids on site development and counselor training, several coalescing agencies merged in 1924 into the American Camping Association.

The majority of the camps offer a variety of activities indigenous to life in the open; many, including the private camps, have a religious orientation to some degree. Thus indirectly as well as directly camps have furthered religious education. Special-interest camps are set up around art, music, dance, drama, tutoring, ranch living, mountain-climbing, trips, conservation, aquatics, equitation, mass communications, language. Over the world, youth travel to work camps, creating communities of understanding and shared labor through reclamation, rehabilitation, or building across national, racial, cultural, and religious lines.

The pioneer push in America gave rise to camp meetings in brush-arbor chapels, with gathered families living in wagons, tents, or cabins. Fiery evangelism in mass meetings was the custom, expressed in an emotional intensity of fear, repentance, or ecstasy. With the rise of active Protestant youth organizations, summer conferences multiplied, usually in the open with formal worship and classes and but little use of nature settings.

The 2d quarter of the century particularly has seen phenomenal growth of camping as such, as an integral phase of religious education, with thousands of church-operated sites, literature, leader guidance, research, and experimentation. Earlier church camps rented sites from agencies, often copying program methods as well and adding worship and classes. Earlier camps separated boys and girls in different weeks and programs until the values of coeducational camping came to be recognized. Some leaders hold that both types have a place. Gradually camp opportunities have spread under church guidance to junior as well as junior high age levels and through the adult years. With more winterized sites, camping can take its place throughout the calender. At first, camps were on an area basis, with several churches cooperating in finances and leadership; more and more local churches now plan for their own camps as a part of their year-round educational work.

Church leaders came to realize that camping, with its freer, fuller life in the open, its unhurried time plan, and its use of nature offered its own unique values to religious education. In objectives and total pattern, camp plans were sharply differentiated from conference-type programs. More careful age-level planning is being done. Awareness of the significance of small-group life has grown. Sites have been modified accordingly. No movement is without extremists. Overprotest against conference-type programs has led in some cases to omission of planned times for worship or spiritual guidance in any overt way. Some camps have ended up as largely schools in woods cooking. Group techniques have not always produced community, much less Christian community. But effective camping breaks through rigidities of newer as well as older methods.

Family camping, encouraged by secular as well as religious interests, is a fast-growing trend; restored perspectives, activities of discovery, worship, discussion, and playing together not only help families find new ways of life but strengthen their witness in neighborhood and world.

Day camping opens up possibilities for many more thousands each summer, especially among juniors and primaries; they can go to nearby parks or farms for daily camp life, sleeping at home. Retreats, too, are being sought, particularly by laymen of special spiritual concern and professionals needing renewal.

— Clarice M. Bowman

CANA CONFERENCE The Cana Conference is a movement within the Roman Catholic Church in the U.S.A. during the years since World War II. It has as its purpose the instilling of proper human and Christian attitudes toward the various relationships in modern American marriage and family living.

It takes the name Cana from the town in Galilee mentioned in John 2:1-12. This was the scene of the working of the 1st miracle in the public life of Christ, the changing of the water into wine. The occasion was the wedding feast of a young couple. The immediate purpose of the miracle was to relieve the young couple of embarrassment at the possible accusation of inhospitality to their relatives and neighbors. The greater purpose was to indicate the interest of the Son of God in the practicalities of married life.

The Cana Conference movement has its roots in a series of Family Days of Recollection conducted by John P. Delaney, S.J., of New York between 1943–1945. Following 3 such days in August, 1944, a group of laymen and priests laid the foundation of the movement in the Chicago area.

Almost simultaneously the movement began in St. Louis under the inspiration and direction of Edward Dowling, S.J. He gave the name Cana Conference to the movement. In the course of the early postwar years Fr. Dowling led hundreds of Cana Conferences across the country, acting as a sort of clerical Johnny Appleseed to the movement.

The Cana Conference in one form or another is found in the majority of the 142 Catholic archdioceses and dioceses in the U.S.A. at the present time. Besides the Archdioceses of Chicago and St. Louis, early pioneers in the promotion of the Cana Movement were the Archdioceses of Hartford, Milwaukee, and Washington and the Diocese of Peoria, Ill. Extensive programs have also been developed in Boston, Newark, New Orleans, New York, Buffalo, and elsewhere.

The original Cana Conference, and one that has remained basic during the years, is centered around the husband-wife relationship. In the course of time there has been an evolution in content and a deepening of insights, but substantially the theme of "Cana No. 1," as it has been labeled, has been the complementary roles of husband and wife. Emphasis has been placed on an explanation of the physical, psychological, and spiritual differences between the man and woman, unified in marriage by both natural and supernatural love so as to complement and perfect each other and be brought closer to God.

The typical program of a Cana Conference takes 3 to 4 hours. It consists of 2 or 3 talks with intermission, refreshments, and an hour's discussion period. In many instances the modern techniques of group dynamics are used very effectively. These sessions are held in a hall or lounge and are characterized by informality. The Conference is concluded in the church proper with the religious ceremony of Benediction of the Blessed Sacrament and renewal of the marriage vows.

Since the 1st Conference the Cana program has broadened to cover the general areas of premarriage preparation and postmarriage education. In the former area, special programs of a varying nature according to different diocesan emphases have been developed to answer the needs of adolescents and engaged couples. In the area of postmarriage education, special Cana Conferences have been worked out on various phases of husband-wife and parent-child relationships. Generally speaking, the same format prevails: talks, discussion, refreshments, and concluding religious ceremony.

In some dioceses the Cana Conference movement has become an integral part of a wider family-life program. This broader program includes special lecture series, counseling services, public ceremonies, institutes and seminars, and cooperation with secular and civic agencies in the promotion of strong family life. — *John C. Knott*

CANADA Early Christian education in Canada focused in preaching, home instruction, and institutions of learning founded by the pioneer churches. The Sunday school movement, originating in individual Christian concern for neglected children, soon included church children. Parents complained that Sunday schools hindered regular Sunday home instruction.

By 1836 missionary zeal led to a Canadian Sunday School Union in Montreal, Que., with missionaries ranging from western Ontario to the east coast. A national convention movement grew from gatherings at Kingston, Ont., in 1857 and Hamilton, Ont., in 1865, when the Sabbath School Association of Canada was formed. In 1887, the SSA of Canada became the SSA of Ontario. The following year the CSSU became the SSU of the Province of Quebec. Both devoted themselves to promoting conventions and organizing township and county associations. An Ontario association secretary organized the western provinces at Regina, Sask., in 1907. In 3 years each province had a self-sustaining organization.

From the beginning there were close ties with corresponding groups in the U.S.A. These became official at the 1872 gathering of the National Sunday School Convention of the U.S.A., which became international in character and name. In 1875, Canadians were added to the lesson committee and the executive committee. This relationship continues in the present Division of Christian Education, National Council of the Churches of Christ in the U.S.A.

Teacher-training manuals from the U.S.A. became supplemented by a Canadian First Standard Course. In 1906 the 1st summer school for Sunday school teachers was held at Victoria College, Toronto. Secretaries were soon appointed for adult, elementary, and home visitation divisions. Adult Bible classes were prominent. A National Advisory Council for Boys' Work was formed in 1914 by representatives of the provincial associations and the Y.M.C.A. A similar Committee for Girls' Work followed in 1915. Since 1917 Boys' Parliaments have provided workshop training in political and civil responsibility.

National cooperation has been facilitated by the forming of a Canadian Council of Sunday School Associations in 1914. Meanwhile, denominational boards and the independent councils were coming into greater conflict. Tensions increased until in 1917 the CCSSA included denominational representatives and became the Religious Education Council of Canada; in 1947, the Department of Christian Education of the Canadian Council of Churches. Similar changes took place in the provincial organizations.

While big conventions continued for many years, and some county and township conventions still persist, the trend has been toward centralized leadership from denominational offices, with local responsibility in respective church courts. Some local councils of Christian education have developed cooperative leadership training, with varying difficulties due to denominational emphases. Provincial councils have been disappearing. When the Maritime Council disbanded and the Alberta Council was changed to a consultative group in 1961, only the descendants of the original bodies in Quebec and Ontario remained.

The function of the RECC remained ill-defined. As the DCE, it often appears to be more an agency of coexistence than of cooperation. A commission studying the structure, function, and procedures of the department from 1955 to 1961 left many problems unsolved. Growing denominational emphasis has placed a question mark over future cooperative work, while the need for greater unity becomes more urgent.

The DCE was represented at the 1st Canadian Conference on Children in 1960, where a committee comprised of all faiths fashioned a statement on " The Spiritual Needs of Children." A National Conference on Christian Education was planned for 1964. A 3-year project promoting " The Use and Understanding of the Bible " has been fruitful.

Primary concerns in Christian education today are adult work (leadership education, lay training, family-life education, church renewal), and the integration of church school curriculum and youth work with other educational programs (mission, stewardship) into a complete, unified curriculum for the whole church as God's people engaged in his mission in the world. Action in these areas tends to be unilateral. Presbyterians provided helps for Uniform Lessons in 1892 and by 1915 produced departmentally graded lessons for beginners, primary, and junior departments by revising U.S.A. materials. Joined by the Methodists in 1917, Canadian materials were added for intermediates and seniors. By 1930 new outlines for all grades made possible Canadian Graded Bible Lessons, used by the United Church, the Baptist Federation, and the Presbyterian Church. Closely graded materials for beginners through juniors proved impractical in small schools and when revised were graded departmentally.

With the imminent appearance of a new United Church of Canada curriculum, which will be adapted and used by the Baptist Federation, it is expected that the Canadian Graded Bible Lessons will die. Anglicans and Presbyterians are carrying on curriculum studies. The Presbyterian Church in Canada makes extensive use of the *Christian Faith and Life* curriculum of The United Presbyterian Church in the U.S.A., whose 2 editors in chief have been Canadians.

Weekday interdenominational programs have been long established: Explorers for juniors, Sigma-C for intermediate boys, Tuxis for senior boys, Canadian Girls in Training for intermediate and senior girls. Boys' work has languished for lack of leadership and support, while Explorers and especially CGIT have flourished, largely as educational arms of women's missionary societies. Former mission bands are yielding to denominational programs for primary children. Cubs, Boy Scouts, Brownies, and Girl Guides, although popular, have only recently won official recommendation by working out religion requirements acceptable to the churches. In some areas Life Boys and Boys' Brigade are promoted by leaders trained in these church programs in Great Britain.

Christian Endeavor, pioneer coeducational youth movement and training ground for many present church leaders, has largely given way in the last 3 decades to denominational programs focused on older youth aged 18 to 25 years. These programs, in turn, are being critically evaluated and revised in the light of changing conditions and a rapidly decreasing enrollment. New cultural patterns have required the development of coeducational fellowships for high school teen-agers and study groups for young married adults. This has highlighted the specific needs of unmarried older youth facing new experiences in college and employment, usually removed from the home church environment. Although the churches are studying the entire field, the trend is toward more flexible organization, with grouping by interests and needs rather than chronology.

Canada has a long-established tradition of cooperation of church and state in education. Religious exercises are obligatory in 7 provinces, permitted in the other 3. Religious instruction is obligatory in 3, permitted by 3, not permitted by 2, and in British Columbia may be taken extramurally as a high school elective with credits. Manitoba is considering a similar plan. Provision is made for exemption from religious activities upon parental request. Regulations are usually implemented at the discretion of local boards, allowing wide latitude in practice. Agitation is being stirred up against religion in the schools, largely by " ethical culture " groups influenced by the U.S.A. perspective. The DCE has published a study document to clarify the issues.

In Quebec there is a dual school system with both Roman Catholic and Protestant school boards. Three other provinces provide for separate elementary schools for religious minorities. Six have no such provision, but most make some accommodation administratively. No parent supports 2 school systems, being taxed only for the support of that system which educates his children. In Newfoundland all schools are operated by religious bodies and supported by Government grants for salaries and maintenance; tuition and fees are imposed by local boards, and there is no school tax.

Of 15 major universities, 4 are church-related, offering courses in religion. Three offer religion courses in affiliated denominational colleges, but not in the university curriculum. One has a faculty of divinity. Five offer courses within the faculty of arts and science, 2 of these having a department of religion. Two offer no religion courses.

Most universities began with religious impetus, but study of religious subjects now tends to be relegated to denominational colleges preparing students for the ministry. A general need for religion courses on a par with other subjects is slowly being recognized, and some development is taking place in 5 universities. One university sees its most important offerings to be "courses on the frontier where religion meets other disciplines."

Only a beginning has been made with university chaplaincies, impeded by denominationalism. Denominational fellowships have been promoted, usually with indifferent success. The SCM has been active. Although some exciting experiments have been undertaken, the churches are deeply concerned about their relation to higher education. The National University Christian Council is being developed to provide a unified approach and to strengthen the witness of Christian faculty members and students as the church in the university community.

Theological seminaries have treated Christian education as the church has treated the Sunday school. Of 8 major theological institutions only 3 have faculty members with graduate training in Christian education. Two depend upon visiting lecturers. While there is a grow-ing awareness of the importance of Christian education, only a few individuals have recognized its centrality to the total ministry and mission of the church. Studies are proceeding regarding the nature of the ministry and the theological curriculum. These give promise of bringing the place of Christian education in theological training into a better perspective.

— *Albert Ernest Bailey*

CASE METHOD Although the term does not appear in most encyclopedias and textbooks, case method in one form or another is an ancient as well as a modern way of learning and teaching. The method, precisely speaking, has been best known in legal education. There it is a curricular procedure in which the literature on law cases of outstanding importance is read and may be considered in group sessions. Chiefly the student is to discover and master the principles involved in order to gain an insight for further understanding and finally for practice. The plan is said to have been introduced into Harvard nearly a century ago.

More loosely and broadly employed, the term appears most frequently in the vocabulary of workers in psychology or sociology and in education for students in those fields. The more typical expressions are "case study," "case system," or "case work," although case method may be used as a general designation.

In many respects case method is a technique of research. Persons or institutions are cases to be studied. A psychotherapist may make a case study to discover the relevant facts on his client's personality and environing conditions. That study will serve the purposes of diagnosis, prognosis, and treatment. Such procedures are familiar in student or other personnel work, vocational and other forms of guidance, and also are well known in child study. In counseling, which is essentially person-to-person teaching, case studies of the counselees may be made. Similar techniques provide a procedure for social surveys; there can be cases of social disorganization as well as personality disturbance.

Students for work in these areas make studies of the relevant types as means of learning in the fields and preparing for practice in them. Leadership development for Christian education employs case method defined in this manner. In a laboratory school for local church school workers, a student teacher may be assigned a particular pupil or class as a " case " to be observed, studied, and then taught. The trainee thereby learns to do something of the same sort regularly for members of his classes, and to teach according to the findings of such a study.

The method is suggested by practice in courses on Christian education in colleges, seminaries, and universities. Professors may cite real or imaginary cases with the question, " What would you do? " A prospective director or pastor may bring a field-work problem into the classroom for help in solving it. A student may take a particular pupil, class, department, church school, or youth group as a case for his particular study. He may then employ his findings in teaching or in other forms of leadership.

In church school curricula a form of case method is becoming more common. Something of the sort appeared in curricular literature as early as 1925. An example is Maurice Neuberg's *Right Living*, a discussion course for boys and girls, in the *Constructive Studies* of The University of Chicago Press. Each lesson provides for a study of several life situations, presumably true stories of problem experiences such as " The Boys Who Told on Their Friends." Discussion questions are listed and Scripture references cited for light on conclusions to be reached about right living in such circumstances. A similar approach is taken in certain current pupil and teacher guides. Less superficially the pupils would be, and they often are, led to consider their own life situations as the cases for discussion, study, and action. The unit or the session deals with a felt need, a substantial concern of the group; that issue is examined in the light of Biblical teaching and other experience; decisions are reached, with action to follow. The intent is to make the classroom experience as close to learning by doing as possible, hence more effective. — *Ralph Daniel Heim*

CATECHETICAL SCHOOL The catechetical school as it existed in the early centuries of the church was very different from the institution known by that term today. It was never meant for children. On the contrary it provided the first advanced or higher education carried on under the church's auspices. It made its appearance toward the end of the 2d century (ca. A.D. 179) and was occasioned by the widespread influence of Greek thought and culture.

From the beginning, teaching had been one of Christianity's chief preoccupations. This function was carried out by bishops, chiefly, who held the apostolic office of teacher. The basic framework of instruction was the liturgy of the Eucharist and other sacraments. Parents were solely responsible for the Christian education of children, which meant instruction in the dogmas of faith, religious history, and the laws of Christian behavior.

For adult converts the church appointed special teachers. Education was a necessary prelude to faith and baptism, and this was adapted to the background of would-be believers. Jews had to accept Christ as the promised Messiah; Gentiles, to accept the doctrine of one God, the futility of polytheism, and the Christian moral law.

The most primitive kind of adult catechesis took the form of a mission sermon, the kerygma or essential message of faith, i.e., the fact of the death and resurrection of Jesus. As soon as expression was given to faith, baptism was administered. Each new adherent "spread the word" and the church "increased in numbers daily."

The system of individual tutoring was replaced by group instruction when the catechumenate was born during the 2d century. A complete order of this highly developed program is described by Hippolytus of Rome in his work The Apostolic Tradition (ca. A.D. 215). It involved a probationary period of 3 years during which a carefully graded course of instruction was given by a layman. This seems to have been replaced in time by the specialized *didascalia apostolorum* and handed over to the priests, with the bishop himself having the last word. For almost 3 centuries the program of instruction prior to baptism continued to grow. It reached its peak about A.D. 450, after which it gradually diminished in influence, disappearing by the early Middle Ages.

Chief among the works that have come down to us from this developing institution are the Didache, the First Apology of Justin, the Martyr (ca. 155), The Apostolic Tradition already mentioned, Irenaeus' Demonstration of the Apostolic Preaching (late 2d century), Cyril of Jerusalem's course, Instruction for Those to Be Illumined (ca. 348), and Augustine's *De Catechizandis rudibus* (ca. 405), a treatise on religious pedagogy that concludes with 2 sample catecheses.

Cyril's lessons in Christian belief were homilies woven into the fabric of the liturgy. Such instructions were for centuries the sole mode of religious teaching. Forty days of catechetical training were given in 18 lectures. After baptism on Holy Saturday night, 5 instructions followed. These dealt with the sacraments of Baptism, confirmation, the Eucharist, and the new obligations of Christian life as outlined in I Peter 2:1-23.

That Christian education should be influenced by the influx of highly educated converts was inevitable. Their background of Greek philosophy forced Christianity's most learned teachers to consider its implications, and gave rise in the latter half of the 2d century to another educational institution, the catechetical school.

Begun in Alexandria by Pantaenus, it was for a long time the only institution where Christians could receive instruction simultaneously in the Greek sciences and in Christian doctrine. Though it reached a high degree of efficiency under its learned founder, it was Clement (ca. 203) and his pupil Origen (ca. 230) who spread its fame throughout the world.

The most epoch-making result of

these schools, which spread to Antioch, Edessa, and Nisibis in Asia, was their impact on Christian theology. During the 3d, 4th, and 5th centuries both East and West produced a fair share of scholarly theological works, which are still studied carefully by teachers of Christianity. Unfortunately, the more advanced schools of Christian theology did not become deeply rooted in the church and soon faded away.

— *Sister Marie Charles Dolan*

CATECHISM " Catechesis," " catechism," etc., are historic terms used to speak of the church's educative enlightenment and training in the content of the Christian faith. The Greek *katēchein*, from which they ultimately derive, meant "to resound" or "sound through" (Latin: *resonare, personare*) or " to teach" (Latin: *instruere, instituere, docere*). The word is already found in the New Testament with something of this meaning (Rom. 2:18; I Cor. 14:19; Gal. 6:6; Acts 18:25) and soon became a technical term for baptismal instruction (II Chem. 17:1 ff.). Through oral instruction the divine Word is made to sound in the ears of inquirers, enlightening their understanding and informing their life for Christian obedience. It was the later factitive form of the verb, *katēchizein* (Latin, *catechizare*) which gave rise to "catechism."

In the ancient church, catechetical instruction was very closely bound up with the mission of the church in evangelizing the heathen world and was concerned entirely with the training and instructing of adult inquirers and converts and their initiation through baptism into the Eucharistic fellowship of the church. The teaching and training of children was left to their parents, along with whom they were baptized or " enlightened." (Cf. The Apostolic Tradition of Hippolytus, ca. A.D. 215.)

Catechetical instruction in the ancient church moved between apologetic and liturgical concerns. On the one hand it was directed outward as an instrument for propagating the faith and establishing intellectual understanding of its principal tenets; on the other hand, it was directed inward as an instrument for the moral and spiritual formation of Christian lives leading up to full communication of the Christian gospel and solemn participation in the Christian mysteries. The whole course lasted 2 or, more frequently, 3 years. It began with an introductory catechesis designed to give a general account of Christian teaching. This was followed by a fuller account of the history of salvation from creation to final judgment, following the lines laid down in the Old and New Testaments, and then, after reception of the catechumen into the church, by deeper instruction in the incarnation of the Lord, his Passion, resurrection, and ascension, in the teaching of the Gospels, the Apostles' Creed, and the Lord's Prayer. Emphasis was laid throughout upon renunciation of evil and union with Christ, and moral and spiritual progress through faith and hope and love. It was Augustine who seems to have been the first to add the Ten Commandments to catechetical instruction. An excellent summary of the catechesis is to be found in The Apostolic Constitutions VII.39 f. (end of 4th century).

Instruction throughout was largely oral, imparted through homilies and lectures, outstanding examples of which have come down to us (cf.

Cyril of Jerusalem, *Catechesis;* Gregory of Nyssa, *Oratio Catechetica;* John Chrysostom, *Catecheses ad illuminandos;* Augustine, *De Catechizandis rudibus, De Fide et symbolo, Sermo ad catechumenos,* etc.). The course was characterized by a series of scrutinies, usually through abbreviated interrogations, the most important of which took place before baptism. The teaching methods adopted appear to owe much to Palestinian and Alexandrian Judaism, which had already been influenced by Socratic interrogation. After the 5th and 6th centuries catechetical instruction went into a decline.

With the spread of Christianity over the Greco-Roman world the catechumenate disappeared, and instruction, inevitably postbaptismal, changed in character, eventually finding its focal point in the medieval sacrament of penance rather than in initiation into the great mystery of Christ. Under the dominance of the Augustinian tradition the content of the instruction remained largely the same, but it was still directed to adults, mostly clerics and sponsors, and more and more took the form of analyses of liturgical formulas and the commandments. In place of the old catechesis the church relied increasingly upon its formal religious institutions to maintain the life of the faithful. There was no regular instruction of children by the church, but the establishment of parish churches and episcopal schools came to play their part.

It was in connection with confession that something similar to the oral teaching of earlier times was perpetuated, together with scrutinies and interrogations, but these were often directed principally to the sins of the people and dominated by excessive and casuistical use of the Ten Commandments. One of the most notable books of the 12th century was the *Elucidarium,* distinguished for its question and answer form of instruction. In the later Middle Ages there appeared many confessional booklets, largely for the use of priests, and then popular manuals offering teaching in the elements of the faith, with brief explanations of the Creed, the Lord's Prayer, the Ten Commandments, and the sacraments, representing simple codifications of the *Quaestiones* elaborated by the Schoolmen. Notable among the popular handbooks were Gerson's *L'ABC des simples gens* and Kölde's *Christenspiegel.*

But now attention was also directed toward the instruction of children. The need for this was set forth by John Gerson's *Tractatus de parvulis trahendis ad Christum,* and an excellent example of this is to be found in John Colet's *Catechizon,* one of the earliest " catechisms " in the form of questions and answers, which he drew up for the use of the boys of St. Paul's School in London.

It was with the Reformation that catechisms in the modern sense first appeared, concise and clear summaries of Christian doctrine adapted to common people and to children. It was Martin Luther who led the way with the publication of 2 catechisms, a Large Catechism for the use mainly of pastors and teachers and a Small Catechism for children in which his great genius for vivid, direct, and simple exposition is seen at its best. Luther's work had an immeasurable influence both on the evangelical churches and on the Roman Church, awakening them to the need for systematic training of the young in Christian doctrine and to the search for appropriate methods of informing their minds and building them on Christian foundations.

Three other catechisms arising out of the Reformation came to exert widespread influence, Calvin's Genevan Catechism, the Heidelberg Catechism, and the Prayer Book Catechism of the Church of England. Calvin's earliest catechism, Instruction in the Faith, was a brief, straightforward account of the principal doctrines of the gospel, but this was superseded by 2 others in question and answer form: 1 in the new style, the Genevan Catechism, offering systematic instruction in Christian doctrines and ordinances in the traditional framework of creed, the commandments, the Lord's Prayer, and the sacraments, which became a model and a creative source for a host of others in the next 2 centuries; another, with brief interrogations in the ancient style to be used in the admission of young people to Holy Communion. The Heidelberg Catechism became a particular favorite in many countries and is still in regular use in several churches in Europe and the U.S.A. The Prayer Book Catechism was designed for use in preparation for confirmation, and did not include the section on the sacraments until early in the 17th century.

The Reformation catechisms are of signal importance for the history of theological and teaching methods, for they are cast in a form arising out of the essentially dialogical nature of evangelical theology, i.e., the address of the Word of God and the obedient response of faith. Their immense success provoked the Roman Church at the Council of Trent to issue its own catechism, *Catechismus Romanus*. Although it

was more scholastic in nature, it acquired immense prestige and led to the production of a multitude of Roman catechisms in many countries, designed more for the common people than for priests.

In many Presbyterian churches, however, the Reformation catechisms yielded place to the Larger and Shorter Catechisms of the Westminister Assembly (1647), which are more scholastic in form and content, and represent a lapse into the medieval preoccupation with the Decalogue.

In recent decades there has been a considerable revival of interest in catechesis, which is particularly significant after a long decline when romantic and psychological theories dominated religious instruction. New catechisms are being written, and fresh experiments are being carried out under the pressure of a new urgency in educational responsibility, not least in the Roman Church, which has produced much literature on the subject.

Two tendencies appear to be at work everywhere. First, a reassessment of catechetical instruction in the form of question and answer is taking place in the light of modern understanding of scientific inquiry and method. Teaching method must be appropriate to the nature of the subject matter being taught, and teaching must include training in the ability to ask the right questions. Of considerable importance is the fact that in the content of the gospel itself the questioning of Jesus himself has a fundamental place.

Second, in accordance with modern Biblical and theological research, attempts are being made to rethink catechetical instruction within the framework of God's saving action as set forth in the Biblical revelation. Kerygmatic presentation of the mighty acts of God, the dialogical and doxological nature of Christian theology, and above all the focus of attention upon the historical Jesus Christ as incarnate Son of God and Savior of the world, are being allowed to control both the form and method of catechesis.

With the help of modern scientific method, Reformation and early church concepts of catechesis are being brought together in the forging of a new instrument for the evangelical and educative mission of the church. — *Thomas F. Torrance*

CATECHUMENATE The catechumenate was an effort of the early church to provide systematic instruction in the Christian faith for persons seeking initiation into its membership. Although this was undoubtedly the primary intent of the catechumenate, instruction was later adapted to meet the needs of individuals who already had been baptized in infancy or early childhood.

As the church moved through the 2d century into the 3d, the necessity of providing converts as well as inquirers with some definite instruction in what Christianity was became obvious. The challenge presented by the vicious morality of a pagan society in which Christians were only small islands of religious and cultural peculiarity, plus the accumulative pressure of persecution by the state and increasing cases of defection by inadequately instructed and disciplined Christians, provided persuasive arguments for more thorough indoctrination of both the baptized and interested inquirers.

Late 3d-century theological confusion and debate and 4th-century definition of crucial doctrines gave rise to a concern for orthodoxy on the part of the clergy and the faithful while the achievement of peace between church and empire and the conferring upon the church of the status, first, of a licensed religion, next, of a privileged religion, and finally of its recognition as the sole religion of the empire encouraged many new accessions to church membership. Systematic indoctrination was the only adequate response to these successive challenges.

Although the scope of instruction varied in different sections of the church, as did the more detailed regulations that prescribed a catechumen's participation in the life of the church, the course of instruction normally included: (1) Christian ethics, the moral responsibilities of a Christian living in a pagan society; (2) the faith, an expansion of the primitive evangelical affirmations, with pertinent references to current theological controversy; (3) the interpretation of the sacraments of initiation and (after Baptism-confirmation) the Eucharistic liturgy — the mechanics of their administration, and the new Christian's participation in them; (4) periodic examinations (*scrutinia*) of the catechumens, which involved memorization of the Creed and the Lord's Prayer after their solemn delivery (*traditio symboli*), and an explanation of selected portions of the Scriptures. The length of such courses of instruction varied considerably and included periods of probation before and after instruction in the more restricted articles of faith and practice (*disciplina arcana*) and prior to admission into the Holy Mysteries. Some lasted 3 years, according to The Apostolic Tradition of Hippolytus, 2 years according to canon 42 of the Synod of Elvira, 8 months for converts from Judaism, according to the 6th-century Council of Agde, and some the practical minimum of the 40 days of Lent (probably preceded by some weeks or months of probation) set by Gregory. Instruction remained for a long time in the hands of the bishops but in many instances was delegated to priests and deacons, although in some places duties were assigned to deaconesses and a recognized order of teachers.

Catechumens were permitted to attend meetings of a Christian congregation but, in the case of the Eucharist, to remain only through the early prayers, lessons, and instruction (*missa catechumenorum*) before they were dismissed as not yet worthy of participation in the Holy Mystery itself (*missa fidelium*). Such restrictions upon a catechumen's participation in Eucharistic worship often paralleled the handling of persons undergoing penitential discipline, who in effect were reduced to the status of catechumens. Accordingly, there has been considerable confusion as to the various classifications of catechumens and penitents. Recent scholarship distinguishes only: (1) *audientes* ("hearers" or "inquirers"), catechumens who were generally regarded as "Christians" of a sort but who, according to widespread 4th-century custom, were delaying their baptism until just before death or until they felt more sure of their ability to persevere (witness Augustine, the Emperors Constantius and Constantine, etc.); and (2) *competentes, electi* (the "enlightened"), who after interrogation and simple initiation were pursuing instruction with baptism and confirmation as their goal at the next Easter, Pentecost, or (if in the East) Epiphany.

For those resolutely proceeding to baptism, the Lenten fast was a period of solemn discipline and examination. "Scrutinies," which in the Roman Church of the 7th century began with the 3d week of Lent, were climaxed in Holy Week. On Maundy Thursday those who had passed their earlier probation were formally notified, instructed to observe Good Friday in fasting and Saturday in the final exercises of preparation, and then on Easter Eve were solemnly initiated into the Holy Mysteries of Baptism-confirmation and Holy Communion.

Certain of the customary usages of the catechumenate continued in widely scattered parts of the church well into the 10th and 12th centuries, but marked decline in the institution itself occurred during the Middle Ages. For this decline no conclusive evidence and reasons can be adduced. Although infant baptism had been practiced from the earliest days of the church, the accumulation of successive generations of Christian parents and the increasingly widespread admission to baptism of the children of such parents may have created the impression that the thorough instruction required by an earlier age of persecution, apostasy, and adult conversion from paganism was no longer an absolute necessity. Certainly the church's accommodation to vast numbers of "Christians" who, fearing postbaptismal sins, insisted upon delaying their baptism brought about an undoubted shift of emphasis in instruction. Again, it may be that the devastating barbarian invasions of the 5th, 6th, and 7th centuries so disrupted the life of the church that when these barbarian hordes were welcomed into the church, the carefully planned routine of the catechetical system broke down as insufficiently flexible to adapt to the new conditions of church life.

— *Robert H. Whitaker*

CENSORSHIP Censorship is the use of, or threat to use, legal restraints upon the production or distribution of information, reading matter, art objects, or forms of public entertainment. It may be used in the interests of national security, the cold war, or to prevent the corruption of morals. It is in the area of morals that issues frequently arise in respect to the use of censorship.

The use of legal restraints involves legislation and the enforcement of laws by police, courts, and public officials. There are many nonlegal or extralegal attempts at censorship by citizen groups. These take the form of publication of a list of books or plays which are condemned by the citizen group, or the persuasion of a public official to take action against the condemned material that he may not have the legal authority to take. Frequently these groups use economic boycott or other pressures against the producers or distributors. Efforts to influence public opinion through education, example, voluntary discipline, or persuasion are often useful ways of achieving desirable ends, but they are not to be considered as censorship, which seeks to bring some form of force, legal or otherwise, against the offending party.

There are 4 distinguishable types of material that have aroused censorship efforts. The 1st is hard core pornography, defined as morbid craving commercially exploited. It is usually not sold openly or exhibited to the public. There are laws adequate for police action against such pornography, but the problem is one of law enforcement. The 2d type consists of publications that commercially exploit sex or crime and are sold openly and exhibited to the public. According to the United States Supreme Court definition (Roth vs. United States, June 24, 1957) a thing is obscene when, " if considered as a whole, its predominant appeal is to prurient interest, i.e., a shameful or morbid interest in nudity, sex, or excretion, and if it goes substantially beyond customary limits of candor in description or representation of such matters." There are Federal statutes which provide that obscene reading matter may not be published or distributed, sent through the mail, or imported from abroad. The Postmaster General may impound mail for a period of 20 days while seeking an injunction from the court, during which time he demonstrates that a statute with respect to the control of obscene material is being violated.

The 3d type of material consists of novels, movies, plays, and entertainments that treat of sexual matters with greater than normal candor but do not make a predominant appeal to prurient interest. Here issues arise because the attempt to censor materials believed to corrupt morals may encroach upon another person's right to exercise his own critical judgment, accepting the good and rejecting the bad. The censors assume they know what is good or bad for their fellow citizens. This is especially hazardous when censorship leads to the suppression of nonconformist ideas or patterns of conduct and restricts the freedom of others to explore novel and creative solutions, to make changes in social behavior by free choice, and to respond to social tensions with resiliency.

Infringement upon liberties of others is most damaging in the censorship of the 4th type of material — discussions of birth control, psychoanalysis, and extramarital sexual relations. Fortunately, attempts to censor such materials have made little headway. Occasionally some reactionary group seeks to bring pressure upon a school board or library to ban certain texts or books because the book or author is not to their liking, but the courts have consistently frustrated such efforts. Freedom of the press is guaranteed by the First Amendment to the Constitution and cherished by freedom-loving citizens.

A statement of the American Library Association, booksellers, and manufacturers in 1953 summarized the dominant viewpoint in relation to censorship efforts. " The present laws dealing with obscenity should be vigorously enforced. Beyond that, there is no place in our society for extralegal efforts to coerce the taste of others, to confine adults to the reading matter deemed suitable for adolescents, or to inhibit the efforts of writers to achieve artistic expression." This statement on reading matter might be broadened to include entertainment, the arts, philosophy, and religion with undiminished validity. — *Ray Gibbons*

CHALKBOARD Every classroom should have a chalkboard. No longer is this necessarily the rather grim-looking blackboard of a generation ago, for it can have a pleasant pastel-green color, for example.

The best way to describe the use of the chalkboard, perhaps, is to cite some very practical ways in which a teacher can utilize it in class sessions.

First, there are chalk pictures and sketches. Instead of taking a negative attitude toward this use, saying to himself, " I can't draw," a teacher can tell himself firmly that he can do so if he tries. It does not require a great artist to draw modest but recognizable likenesses of trees, flowers, houses, mountains, churches. Stick figures are quite acceptable for the portrayal of people.

Advance preparation before class time is desirable so that while actually teaching one can do something more than point to illustrations in the lesson book or pass around clippings. As an example, if the lesson is about the wise man and the foolish man, the teacher can sketch chalk pictures of the two houses, one on sand, the other on rock, pointing to the sketches as the story is discussed. A discussion on the subject of Christian growth can be enlivened by sketches depicting baptism, Sunday school attendance, prayer and Bible-reading.

The use of colored chalk will compensate for lack of artistic genius. In referring to God's wonderful world, ocean waves may be drawn in blue, marigolds in bright yellow, pine groves in green. The teacher can use his imagination as to what might be done with Joseph's long coat " of many colors."

Children can be encouraged to use the chalkboard too. In addition to asking them questions about the prodigal son, they might be invited to draw some scenes from the story. In the case of younger children, crayons and paper may be given to some children sitting at worktables while others go to the chalkboard in the event the board cannot accommodate the whole class at once.

The chalkboard is also useful with regard to " word ideas." Many teachers confine themselves to writing on the board memory verses, quizzes, and long lists of books of the Bible. For interest and variety, provocative statements, searching questions, and clear, concise outlines and diagrams may be used. For example, in a discussion about science and the Bible, a teacher might write on the chalkboard, " Can a Christian believe the theory of evolution? " A lesson in Christian ethics might be introduced with the chalkboard question, " Exactly what is a Christian supposed to believe? "

Instead of a question, the teacher might write a statement, e.g., on Easter, " Christ is risen! " or when teaching about the doctrine of justification by faith: " Salvation cannot be earned; it can only be accepted." Such statements can be written on the board before the session to announce the subject for the day, or at the end of the period to summarize it.

The purpose of outlines and diagrams is to present information and ideas with clarity and emphasis. For example, Old Testament chronology and genealogy can be confusing. A Biblical " family tree " can be drawn to clarify the fact that Rachel was not Jacob's mother but his wife. In teaching a course on the minor prophets, each book and its theme can be listed on the chalkboard. It can be left unerased for the entire course (or unit) so that the class will be exposed to it as a constant refresher. This is known as visual repetition.

If a teacher wants his pupils to understand that the church of Christ is not confined to the particular building in which they worship, but reaches across space and time to embrace every believer who has confessed that Jesus is Lord, the chalk-board can help. On one side write " NOW "; on the other " PENTE-COST." Between them draw a long arrow, and write above it " 20 centuries of Christians." A circle or globe may be drawn to represent the earth and the present-day brotherhood of believers in every country. No matter how abstract an idea, it can be represented if the teacher thinks long, hard, and imaginatively enough. — *Adah Vosburgh*

CHAMBER THEATER Chamber theater employs a technique for presenting narrative fiction without sacrificing the narrative elements and yet taking full advantage of the dramatic elements. Novels and short stories are presented on the stage in the form in which they are written. The action of the prose fiction is represented much as one would find it in the traditional Western theater — actors play the parts of the characters, performing or describing the action in the text and speaking the dialogue of the story just as they would in a play.

When the action in the story is as simple as " he said " or " she sat down," the directions are deleted from the story and the actors perform the action without accompanying narration. However, sometimes the action is more complex, as in this passage: " He followed her minutely as she moved, direct and intent, like something transmitted rather than stirring in voluntary activity, straight down the field toward the pond." The precise quality of the woman's movement that is here described might be very difficult for an actress to express, so the description is retained in the narration. Since the point of view from which the woman's action is seen is that of the man referred to here as " he," it might be that the actor playing the man's role could speak the narration describing her movement. Perhaps the narrator who is telling this story in the 3d person and in the past tense might speak the narrative description of both his and her action.

The element that distinguishes the novel from the play is the capacity of the narrator to explore the inner condition of the characters at the moment of action. In the passage quoted in the above paragraph, we learn how he responds to her action even as she is acting; we get a double exposure — her action and his view of her action. On the other hand, the element that distinguishes the play from the novel is the capacity the play has for presenting simultaneous action. As in life, the action of the drama allows two people to interact simultaneously. Even as one man thrusts with his sword the other is in the process of executing the appropriate parry. This is not the case in prose fiction, where the action is presented *serially:* " He thrust at his opponent who parried successfully." Here we have the thrust executed *first* and the parry *follows.* We would not be disturbed too much if the author reversed the order: " He successfully parried his opponent's thrust." Here the parry precedes the thrust, a curious condition, indeed, in fencing. But we have accepted the tradition of action being presented serially in the novel even when it happens simultaneously in life.

Chamber theater attempts to preserve the advantage the drama has over the novel in its lifelike illusion, which is maintained through the use of simultaneous action. Chamber theater also attempts to preserve the advantage of the novel over the

drama in its exploration of the inner life and motivations of characters at the moment of action. The chamber theater allows the characters in the novel to perform their action and dialogue in such a way as to give the illusion of a traditional play, but it retains the narration, spoken by a narrator whose actions are integrated with the action of the story or by the characters themselves when the narration represents their own point of view and not that of an objective or omniscient observer.

Narrative stories may be told from the point of view of a major or a minor character inside the story speaking in the 1st person, or they may be told from the point of view of an omniscient narrator or an objective narrator outside the story speaking in the 3d person. Whether the narrator is central or peripheral to the action of the story depends on the point of view. It is the point of view that provides the special dynamics of chamber theater in that the narrator controls and conditions the way the action of the story unfolds. At no time is the narrator to be regarded as ancillary; he is rather to be integrated in a subtle and shifting fashion into the action of the narrative. — *Robert S. Breen*

CHARACTER EDUCATION Educational theory and practice have contributed in this century to the startling rise of character education as a movement, and then to its equally startling decline. Character education has, of course, always been of concern both to education and to religion. There was, however, a very definite rise in interest after World War I. The term is reported to have appeared first in the *Proceedings of the National Education Association* in 1918. Plans for character education were submitted by leading educators. Programs were recommended by state departments of education. Courses for the development of character were introduced into local school systems all over the country. In 1932 the Department of Superintendence of the National Education Association entitled its 10th yearbook *Character Education,* producing a 535-page volume. Religious educators as well as secular educators were thinking along these lines. The periodical *Religious Education* in its 10 issues in 1929, devoted more than 30 articles to the discussion of character development, most of them including the specific words " character education " in the titles. Harold S. Tuttle, writing in the October, 1931, issue of the same periodical, said: " Evidences abound that interest in character education is rapidly gaining ground. Yearbooks and bulletins of educational societies are giving increasing space to the problem. Periodicals are presenting materials on the topic in unprecedented proportions."

In just a few years, however, the term had almost disappeared from indexes and bibliographies. The cause most commonly given for this change was the publication of the findings of the Character Education Inquiry, a research project carried out under the general direction of Hugh Hartshorne and Mark May. Through ingenious tests they investigated traits which churches and schools had sought to develop. They found that such traits as honesty, self-control, and cooperation do not determine conduct as generally as had been supposed. Rather, the behavior of the subjects tested varied considerably from situation to situation. A child might be completely honest on the playing field, yet cheat

in a classroom test. The result was to cast considerable suspicion on the popular character education movement.

Review of the literature of the period shows, however, that not only these researchers but many other thoughtful people had been raising basic questions. Harold Tuttle pointed out 3 limitations of current efforts at character training: its short-range motivation (based on formation of habits), its reliance on mere knowledge that is not dynamic, and its reliance on current ideas of morality. The 10th yearbook (*supra*) pointed out that character education had to deal with " a series of issues which arise in our attempts to explain how character can most effectively be improved." It listed 9 such issues: heredity and environment, conditioned responses, instincts and character, the role of ideas in character, the role of sanctions, specific habits and rules vs. general principles, verbal precept and conduct, the role of reflection on moral issues, and social codes vs. individual analysis. It was clear that character education could not be accomplished by any single form of effort but that it must be " as broad as the entire process of education, informal as well as formal." Editorial comment in *Religious Education* in 1929 pointed out that " even good movements may come to be fads and their popularity may far outrun their wisdom and factual knowledge concerning their best application. . . . The most fundamental need is for research work."

Both public and religious education have moved away from efforts to develop specific character traits and responses. Current public education writings mention few separate courses in character such as were popular in the decade following World War I. Rather, they stress the wholeness of the learning process.

Current literature in Christian education places emphasis not on the development of traits or habits but on the person's response to God. The statement of purpose that has been developed through the Division of Christian Education of the National Council of the Churches of Christ in the U.S.A. and referred for study to the denominations expresses this view. "The supreme purpose of Christian education is to enable persons to become aware of the seeking love of God as revealed in Jesus Christ and to respond in faith to this love in ways that will help them to grow as children of God, live in accordance with the will of God, and sustain a vital relationship to the Christian community." Character, then, is not the direct goal, but rather the indirect outcome in the life of one who responds to the seeking love of God as he becomes aware of that love through his home and the church.

Two research groups have been at work for some years in studies of character. Their findings promise help in realizing the objectives of character education without the pitfalls into which the movement fell some years ago. One that has worked for years is the Character Research Project. The other is a group of researchers who have conducted a continuing study in a selected Midwestern community. The latter, using a wide variety of methods ranging from interviews and objective tests to sociometric and projective tests, made longitudinal studies of selected persons. Their conclusion is that "there does seem to be such a thing as individual char-

acter: a persisting pattern of attitudes and motives which produce a rather predictable kind and quality of moral behavior" (Peck, Havighurst, *et al., The Psychology of Character Development*, p. 164).

This study and numerous other recent ones point consistently to the paramount influence of the family in the development of character. For good or ill, it seems to be the influence of the home that determines the nature of the person who grows up in that home. " Forces outside the family are not negligible or irrelevant in their *indirect* effect on character formation, but it looks as though these forces operate mainly as they shape and guide parents' behavior, and as they reward or otherwise reinforce child behavior that follows the socially approved parts of the parents' behavior." (*Ibid.,* p. 175.) Various findings would suggest that such agencies as the church ought to move in two directions if they would influence the development of character. Their primary effort should be directed at influencing family life. This calls for a strong emphasis on adult education. Their secondary effort should be to develop a program for children and youth in which a persistent and warm personal relationship exists. This calls for great care in recruiting mature and committed persons for leadership in church groups.

Most denominations, in their Christian education programs and guidance materials, have accepted this finding concerning the importance of family life. It remains to build this point of view into the whole range of curriculum materials, and to bring about the required changes in the ministry of local churches to their children, youth, and adults.

— *Lee J. Gable*

CHARACTER RESEARCH PROJECT

The Character Research Project is designed to apply scientific techniques to a study of the problems of the development of character as depicted in a Christian philosophy of life. The central guiding principle in this research is embodied in a concept called the "infinity principle." This principle is a faith that research in any area of universal truth can never be exhaustive; no matter how significant new insights may be, their chief value is the clues they provide for more significant insights.

The development of the project can be divided into 4 periods. The 1st period was preexperimental and covered the years 1920 through 1934. This period culminated in the book *The Psychology of Christian Personality,* which was an attempt to formulate the philosophy of Jesus in modern psychological concepts that in turn could become basic hypotheses for research.

The 2d period, dating from 1935 through 1944, saw the beginning of actual research. During this time the research studies were concerned primarily with exploring the range of individual differences, seldom with groups. This work was an attempt to discover some of the primary principles of the nature of character development, especially with regard to religious education. The book *Their Future Is Now* grew out of this period.

The 3d period, 1944–1951, was characterized by the development of a research curriculum that embodied the project's hypotheses and became the major tool in its experimental design. This curriculum consists of 6 units, with more than 600 lessons, for groups ranging from nursery through high school. These lessons were revised 3 times over a period of 6 years. Churches in various parts of the country (approximately 50), Y.M.C.A.'s, and a boys' school joined in this research. Financial resources became available, primarily from the Lilly Endowment.

The 4th period, beginning in 1951 and still in progress, is characterized by increasing efforts to design more intensive and far-reaching basic research in areas that offer possibilities for fruitful exploration.

One significant concept in terms of psychological theory proposes potential rather than need as the major drive in personality. Some modern psychologists believe that needs constitute the major drive in human motivation. In the project the assumption is made that many actions and achievements arise because man has potential beyond his needs which challenges him to higher levels of nobility and unselfishness.

After the project established 8 general dimensions of character, the next task was to find specific attitude goals that were psychologically appropriate for the various age levels. This made it possible to carry through an age-level calibration in the selection of educational objectives. Evidence from this study supports the hypothesis that there is an optimum age level at which the child can best learn a specific attitude.

One insight that has basic importance in efforts to teach attitudes is: an attitude, as such, has no meaning apart from the individual of whom it is characteristic. It can be said to have been learned only when it becomes an integral part of the total personality. This has been developed extensively in Character Research Project studies by the use of the adaptation procedure.

A major tool that has been developed for several research projects is the dynamics diagram. The diagram includes 10 terms: the S(Situation) — O(Organism) — R(Response) sequence. The PS (Perceived Situation) — the way an individual interprets his environment — was introduced between the S and R instead of the O. The O was then thought of, along with the S, as one of the determiners of the PS. The O was soon divided into Oi(innate organism) and Om(the organism as modified by learning and experience). The Om can be divided into Sk (skills) and Att(attitudes). Finally, Att includes Self (self attitudes) and Nonego (involved attitudes). One more factor included is called T(Tensions) to indicate motivations internal to the individual. The diagram then looks like this:

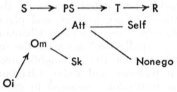

The history of civilization has demonstrated repeatedly that the family must be recognized as the fundamental social institution on which all others must depend. Character Research Project studies have confirmed this fact overwhelmingly. No measurable results have been observed where there has not been home participation. The potential of the home even yet has not been fully explored.

The solution to the youth problem, as the project has approached it, has consisted essentially in challenging young people to seek to achieve their maximum potential. Much research has been done to test the hypothesis that this can best be achieved on the foundation of the Christian philosophy of life.

The Character Research Project camp research was done primarily at the Schenectady Y.M.C.A. boys' camp under the leadership of Richard S. Doty and is described in his book *The Character Dimension of Camping.* — *Ernest M. Ligon*

CHAUTAUQUA INSTITUTION

From all parts of the U.S.A. and many foreign countries thousands of people gather at Chautauqua Institution each summer for inspiration, education, and recreation. Many families make Chautauqua a part or all of their summer vacation location. This pioneer institute of adult education, built on a religious foundation, is situated on the wooded slopes of Lake Chautauqua in the southwestern part of New York State. In 1961 close to 46,000 people visited Chautauqua for varying lengths of time. During its 8 weeks' season a program of variety and interest for all ages is presented.

Courses offered include musical instruction in voice as well as piano and other musical instruments. The faculty includes members of outstanding music schools and the major symphony orchestras. Instruction is also available in painting, ceramics, weaving, sculpturing, and other related subjects. Summer high school courses are also presented, and Syracuse University has operated its Chautauqua extension program since 1953, offering courses for credit.

Major operas in English by the Chautauqua Opera Association and outstanding plays by members of the Chautauqua Repertory Theatre are presented in Norton Hall, which has a seating capacity of 1,367.

The center of program activity is

the amphitheater seating 7,500. On Sunday mornings the large congregations hear outstanding clergymen. A sacred song service is held on Sunday evenings. Concerts are presented on 3 evenings and on Sunday afternoon by the Chautauqua Symphony Orchestra. Guest artists present recitals and concerts at various times during the season. Lecturers speak on varied subjects of worldwide and community interest. Chautauqua's noted amphitheater platform has throughout history been a classic demonstration of free speech and free assembly in American democracy. All questions of vital importance to the people — economic, political, theological, social, and international — have been discussed in an atmosphere of tolerance and understanding by leaders of thought and action, outlining many points of view.

Chautauqua is equipped with its own hotels, cottages, and lodging houses, restaurants, class buildings, and athletic and bathing areas. Its property covers 334 acres.

Chautauqua Institution was originally founded to provide training for Sunday school teachers. In 1874, John Heyl Vincent, editor of the *Sunday School Journal* and later a bishop of the Methodist Episcopal Church, and Lewis Miller, a manufacturer from Akron, Ohio, organized a summer class that met at Fair Point on Lake Chautauqua. The name of the meeting place was soon changed to Chautauqua.

Chautauqua was one of the very first places in the U.S.A. to offer summer study. Beginning in 1879, foreign language and education methods instruction was offered, after which Chautauqua expanded rapidly in many different fields, including the establishment of the Chautauqua Literary and Scientific Circle, which offered a 4-year home-study course directed by the Institution. The Institution chartered a school of theology in 1881 and Chautauqua University in 1883. The university gave instruction both in the summer assembly and by correspondence, and had power to confer degrees. About 1890 university extension work, which had originated in England, was introduced. These areas all flourished for a short time but were eventually abandoned in favor of the original plan of summer assemblies giving cultural and teacher-training courses.

Many people associate the word "Chautauqua" with the circuit or traveling units that visited small towns. They were not connected with Chautauqua Institution, however, and their chief purpose was to provide tent entertainment in the form of music, lectures, and plays. Although these traveling Chautauquas rapidly declined with the introduction of the automobile, motion pictures, and radio, Chautauqua Institution continued to grow. Changes have taken place in its program over the years, but its religious emphasis continues to be the major basis for people's attendance and from which branch out its many other areas of program and educational activity. — *Curtis W. Haug*

CHILD DEVELOPMENT   The area of human knowledge termed "child behavior and development" is the result of research in many sciences over a period of years. During the past 25 years contributions from the sciences of pediatrics, psychology, psychoanalysis, sociology, and cultural anthropology merging with the surge of interest in the scientific movement begun in the early part of the 20th century have enabled us to begin to understand how and why the individual child grows, develops, and behaves in certain ways and under certain conditions. Such understandings are of obvious and great concern to parents, teachers, and ultimately to the entire community.

The above statement must not be construed to mean that we now know how and when or what to do to achieve " desired behavior " in our efforts to "bring up" children. Because research within any given field of science (such as anthropology, pediatrics, and others) usually has been pursued somewhat independently of research in other sciences, child development as an area has not always benefited immediately from the dissemination of such data. In addition, though the implications of many research studies cross boundary lines from one field of science to another, seldom in the past have research workers from various fields engaged in cooperative research. Yet, in spite of this marked lack of coordination in the efforts of various scientists interested in the child, the findings of different groups constitute a vast body of data, suggest numerous hypotheses to be tested, and provide reason for us to change many of our previously held assumptions concerning the child.

One is obliged also to recognize, not only a lack of integration of child development data and of the research methods utilized, both within and among the fields, but also the inadequacy, as yet, of the research directed to facilitate the application of previous data and concepts. An illustration is found readily even in the terminology utilized. For example, words have many meanings to workers within a field as well as among different fields. One might say that the semantic problem is both sizable and confusing. " Growth," " development," and " maturation " frequently are used interchangeably although at the same time they are given distinct connotations to imply mutual exclusiveness.

As a result of the involvement of many disciplines, the uncoordinated and fluid status of various research approaches, the semantic difficulties in terminology, and the relative newness of some of the disciplines involved, the resultant body of data understandably lacks cohesion. However, there is a growing number of clearly structured and generally accepted concepts from which emerge justified attempts to translate findings into practical applications for use in the home, in the school, and in the community.

The question, then, which concerns parents and teachers (and even governments) is, How can the basic similarities found in all children be modified in the individual child through learning? To begin to answer this question the following 3 sets of data must be secured and the underlying principles that interpret the facts must be understood: the ways in which all children are alike; the ways in which children differ; the agents and directions of changes in children (dynamics of human motivation).

All children regardless of their race and culture are alike in some ways because of the physical nature of human beings. We say all children have the same biological needs and that they grow and develop in accordance with known laws which we express as principles: (1) the principle of the developmental direction of growth (growth process from head to foot); (2) the principle of the interrelatedness of the several aspects of development (the reciprocal effects, for example, of physical and mental health); (3) the principle of maturation (behavior that occurs without training).

Children of one culture obviously differ in certain ways from children in other cultures. Such differences we attribute to the variations in goals, to the teaching methods used, and to the differences in age of certain expectancies in socialization (developmental tasks).

Children even within the same culture also differ one from another. There is, of course, a real biological basis for individual differences in growth and development due to hereditary factors and to the difference in the environment in which these constitutional characteristics emerge. Thus, we realize that constitutional and environmental factors are inevitably interwoven in the individual. Here our acceptance of 2 concepts is basic: (1) that behavior is caused; (2) that the causes of behavior are multiple, complex, and interrelated.

Our concern for the agents and directions of changes in children has initiated the most recent research revealing that not only what the child learns but also how he learns it affects him and his behavior. In fact, the emotional well-being, the mental hygiene of the child in each learning situation, is considered an important factor in learning. Thus, research on the dynamics of human motivation, on the child's concept of self, and on levels of aspiration is prominent in current studies.

To these areas are added studies which deal with the child's interaction (1) with the initial social unit, the family, which is of primary importance in terms of its imprint on values and on behavior; and (2) with the child's membership in other groups, where the interrelationships are more shifting and where marked changes may occur in the groupings and within the individual during relatively short periods of time. The importance of the interaction between the individual and the group, of the dynamic interrelations within the groups, and of their implications for society is leading to a substantial and growing body of research and data.

From this complex background of influences and interactions it is apparent that any individual is likely to be subjected to an essentially unique constellation. As a result, each child differs from every other child in feelings, attitudes, values, and purposes.

From research in child behavior and development the following are two of the major implications that concern the organization, methods, and materials of instruction: First, there is need for an insightful approach to the understanding of human development and to the multiple and interrelated influences that shape it: by fostering among teachers and parents awareness of and consistence with regard to the values they themselves hold and stress; by initiating and encouraging the study of human growth and development as an integral part of pre-service and in-service programs for teachers; by developing and transmitting from teacher to teacher developmental data essential in understanding the individual child's growth and development; by evaluating pupils so as to facilitate this continuous and maximum development; and by adapting the curriculum to the developmental tasks of children.

Second, there is need for teachers and parents to recognize, accept, and provide for differences among children: by providing resources and learning materials within the classroom and home that are readily accessible to pupils, appropriately varied in content and in degree of difficulty, and adapted to some extent to the individual child's concerns and needs; by including daily experiences in democratic living and learning; by helping the child to set realistic goals he can attain and to achieve a measure of awareness of his success and growth; by cooperating with the adults in the child's life in such a way that he does not bear the major stress of their differences; by promoting friendships with older and younger children as well as with peers; by fostering both group and individual goals; and by increasing self and mutual understanding and respect among parents, pupils, and teachers. — *Viola Theman*

CHILDREN'S DAY Children's Day has been for many years a widespread observance in the Protestant Sunday school year. Usually held on the 2d Sunday in June, it has been a time of emphasis on the importance of children to the life of the church.

It is not possible to determine how or when the observance of Children's Day originated. From early times many pastors have had special services for children and special emphases on the importance of children.

In 1856, Charles H. Leonard, then pastor of the First Universalist Church of Chelsea, Mass., "set apart a Sunday (the second in June) for the dedication of children to the Christian life, and for the rededication of parents and guardians to the

bringing up of their children in Christian nurture."

In 1867, the Universalist Convention at Baltimore commended " the practice of those churches, in our order, that set apart 1 Sunday in each year as Children's Day, when parents bring to the altar their most precious treasures, and give them to the Lord by appropriate and sacred rites," indicating that such an observance had become common in many churches of that convention.

In 1865 a committee of The Methodist Episcopal Church arranged, in connection with the celebration of the 100th anniversary of Methodism, a children's service, by which a large sum was raised to assist " meritorious Sunday school pupils " to obtain an education. At the next Methodist Conference in 1868, the committee recommended that the 2d Sunday in June be annually observed as Children's Day. This gave the subject wide publicity. The recommendation by this committee of The Methodist Church was continued until, in the year 1881, the Ecumenical Methodist Council at London recommended " that one day in every year be faithfully observed as Children's Day."

In 1883, the Presbyterian General Assembly designated the same Sunday in June as Children's Day. In the same year the National Council of Congregational Churches, and nearly all the state bodies of that denomination in the U.S.A., passed resolutions commending the observance of the day. Many other denominations adopted similar recommendations, and Children's Day became a recognized part of the Sunday school calendar.

The observance of Children's Day began to change from its original purpose of a dedication of children and a rededication of their parents, to a day in which the church expressed its interest in the work being done with children. Often the Sunday morning service was devoted to Children's Day, with a sermon for and about children, and with some participation by the children themselves. In some communities Children's Day was the occasion of an all-day service at the church. Churches were often beautifully decorated with flowers from the fields and woods, and many early observances honoring children were called "Flower Sunday." The second Sunday in June was chosen, almost by common consent, because it was usually one of the most beautiful Sundays in the year. In areas where flowers were at their peak on another Sunday, the suggestion was made that a different date might be selected for Children's Day.

Denominations began to prepare programs for use in individual churches for Children's Day. From the first, the observance of the day was associated with benevolent objects, special offerings being received, often for denominational projects for the extension of Sunday school work in other areas.

Children's Day has continued to the present time to be observed in many local churches and to be a part of many denominational programs, although practices vary widely. In many churches it has been subsumed under the Festival of the Christian Home. Current practices on this day emphasize the place of the child in the total church family, both by contributing to the child's sense of being a part of the church and by increasing the adult congregation's awareness of the importance of the program for children. Special program suggestions are provided by some denominations, and written into regular curriculum materials by others. The service is often a unified sharing of significant experiences from the church school year, either at the church school hour or at the congregational worship service, an emphasis that has caused at least one denomination to rename this observance Church School Day. Since this observance often occurs at the close of the public-school year, it is sometimes used as a service of promotion from one department of the church school to another. Children's Day is still observed on the 2d Sunday of June, although in at least one denomination it has been observed the 1st Sunday in May at the beginning of Family Week. An offering is often taken for a special denominational interest related to children's work or for a special children's project in the local church. — *Elizabeth McCort*

CHINA Protestant education in China followed quickly the introduction of Protestant Christianity in the early 19th century. The 1st primary school was established in Macao (1839). Others were established during the next 30 years at Ningpo, Foochow, Shanghai, Peking, and Tengchowfu (Shantung). Sponsored by American and British mission societies, they were day and boarding schools, and accepted students with little or no previous education. They were small, housed in missionary homes, and sought conversion to Christianity as well as general literacy. By 1920 there were 183,500 pupils in 6,563 primary schools. Thereafter, with the growth of public education, such schools became less essential for a literate church and declined in number and emphasis.

Primary schools prepared the way for and often developed into middle (high) schools. The boys' school established by Calvin and Julia Mateer at Tengchowfu (Shantung) in 1864 had achieved that status by the mid-'70's. A decade later there were "Anglo-Chinese colleges" and "high schools" in such cities as Shanghai, Peking, Foochow, Ningpo, and Wuchang. By 1900 the list included such schools for girls as Bridgman (Peking), St. Mary's (Shanghai), and McTyeire (Shanghai).

During the 1st decades of the 20th century the shortage of public schools encouraged development of many new schools, among them Medhurst College, Shanghai (1904), Yale-in-China, Changsha (1906), Anglo-Chinese College, Foochow (1906), Oberlin-in-Shansi, Taiku (1907), and Gamewell Academy, Peking (1910). In 1915, Protestant middle schools enrolled 170,000 pupils but by 1940 the number had shrunk to some 50,000.

Theological and Bible schools were an integral part of Protestant education. Rooted in the 19th century, with theological colleges and seminaries in Amoy, Canton, and Foochow in the '60's, they developed more extensively in the 20th. In 1935 there were 13 schools (2 for women) requiring graduation from middle school and 41 (3 for men, 5 coeducational) requiring less preparation, with enrollments of 500 and 1,500 respectively. Outstanding among the seminaries were Nanking Theological Seminary (1911) and the Yenching School of Religion (1916).

Institutions of higher learning, one of the most distinctive features of Protestantism in China, appeared well before the end of the 19th century, usually as outgrowths of middle schools. Tengchow College (Presbyterian, later Shantung Christian (Cheeloo) University, offered college-grade work for several years before being recognized as a college in 1882. At about the same time St. John's College (later St. John's University) developed in Shanghai from 2 Episcopal schools. In 1888, Methodists started Nanking University and incorporated Peking University. That same year instruction began in the undenominational Canton Christian College. A year later Congregationalists opened the North China College at Tungchow, near Peking. In 1897 Presbyterians founded a college in Hangchow.

Soochow (Methodist, 1901), Shanghai (Baptist, 1906), and Boone (later Huachung; interdenominational, Wuchang, ca. 1906) universities had their beginnings in the 1st years of the 20th century. The next decade produced 2 interdenominational institutions, West China Union University (Chengtu, 1910) and Fukien Christian University (Foochow, 1916). The same period saw the development of colleges for women with North China Union College for Women (Peking, 1905) and Ginling College (Nanking, 1915), both interdenominational, and Methodist Hwanan College (Foochow, 1916). These were led by such able women as Miss Luella Miner and Mrs. Murray S. Frame (North China), Mrs. Lawrence Thurston (Ginling) and Miss Ida Trimball (Hwanan).

The 2d and 3d decades were a period of consolidation and growing cooperation. In 1917 the scattered units of Shantung Christian University came together in Tsinan. In 1920 the merger of 5 North China units resulted in Yenching University, with J. Leighton Stuart as president. By the outbreak of the Sino-Japanese War in 1937, 15 institutions (including 2 separate medical schools) enrolled over 7,000. At the time of the Communist take-over in 1950 combined enrollments were over 11,000.

Christian medical education began soon after the arrival of Peter Parker at Canton in 1834. For many years it was conducted in hospitals with student apprentices but moved rapidly toward a true medical profession with the establishment of the China Medical Missionary Association in 1890. The 1st medical college was at St. John's University (Shanghai, 1896). It was followed by Hackett Medical College for Women (Canton, 1899); Women's Christian Medical College (Shanghai, 1900); Union Medical College of Peking (1906); Shantung Christian University (Cheeloo) School of Medicine (Tsinan, 1909); Mukden Medical College (Manchuria, 1912); and West China Union University College of Medicine and Dentistry (Chengtu) and Hunan-Yale (Hsiangya) Medical School (Changsha), both in 1914. Union Medical College was replaced in 1921 by the famed Peking Union Medical College, financed by the Rockefeller Foundation; in 1937, Hackett became part of Lingnan University; a few years later Hsiangya was nationalized.

The Sino-Japanese War in 1937 brought most Christian colleges 9 years of refugee existence in uninvaded areas, chiefly West China. In 1946 they returned to campuses that badly needed rehabilitation. This process, financed by funds from abroad, had not been completed when the colleges were taken over by the People's Republic. By 1951 contacts with the West had been cut, almost all the Western staff had withdrawn, and all Christian schools had been absorbed into the communist educational system. Christian education on the China mainland had come to at least a temporary end.

With the closing of the mainland came a rapid development of Protestant education in Taiwan and Hong Kong. Refugee schools added to the institutions already in existence, and new colleges came into being. Chung Chi College (Hong Kong, 1951) and Tunghai University (Taiwan, 1955) became spiritual successors of the old " China Colleges."

Protestant Christian colleges had made a notable record. Including colleges not only of arts and of science but of engineering, agriculture, law, commerce, medicine, and dentistry, they were instrumental in introducing modern education to China, pioneering and setting standards in such areas as medicine, agriculture, science, education for women, and social concern. At their peak, they constituted less than 10 percent of higher education in China, but they contributed leadership for church and nation out of proportion to their numbers.

In their origin, patterns, and support, Protestant schools were predominantly American, with important roles played by the United Kingdom and Canada and a smaller one by continental Europe. Indigenization did not come until well into the 20th century, when official registration hastened Chinese administration.

In the case of the Christian colleges, originally chartered abroad, the 1920's saw the transfer of direct control to boards in China. Chinese presidents also took over administration. However, at the request of the Chinese, considerable numbers of Western teachers remained. In 1937 there were some 157, or approximately 20 percent of the total.

Support also came at first entirely from the churches of North America and Europe. As local support increased for primary and then for secondary schools, Western funds were devoted more and more to higher education, running as high as $1,000,000 a year exclusive of personnel. Plants were valued at some $15,000,000. Mission-board support was supplemented by such organizations as the Rockefeller Foundation, the Harvard-Yenching Institute, the Princeton-Yenching Association, the Yale-in-China Association, and the Oberlin-Shansi Memorial Association, and by widespread promotion among the general public.

During the 1920's increasing coordination of mission board and other support of higher education in China resulted in the Associated Boards for Christian Colleges in China, New York (1932), which became the United Board in 1945. A similar development in Great Britain earlier produced the China Christian Universities Association, London (1931).

Significant in the development of Christian education were such cooperative organizations as the School and Textbook Committee (1877), the China Christian Educational Association (1890) and area associations, and the Association of Christian Colleges and Universities (1919).

Though the Roman Catholic Church was well established in China by the 17th century, schools going beyond mere literacy were largely neglected until after the introduction of Protestant Christianity. Even then, Roman Catholic schools were designed primarily to develop leadership for the church and tended to discourage attendance by non-Catholics. The beginnings of a comprehensive system came after 1900, with great increase in the number of primary schools and the development of secondary schools. By 1935, Roman Catholic schools of all grades numbered some 3,500 with a total of perhaps 250,-000 pupils. Roman Catholic higher education began with the establishment by the Jesuits in 1903 of Aurora University (Shanghai). This was followed in 1922 by L'Institute des Hautes Études (Tientsin), and in 1925 by Fu Jen University (Peking), which soon became the leading Roman Catholic university.

— *William P. Fenn*

CHOIR A choir is "an organized company of singers, especially and originally in church service."

As we know choirs today, they may be groups of adults, youth, or children who rehearse together under a director and sing services in church. Leading the congregation in corporate worship is the first duty of a choir.

In the Roman Catholic and the Protestant Episcopal churches, choirs of men or boys, or combined men and boys, normally are used. In other churches we find mixed adult choirs and high school choirs, or a combination; junior choirs and junior high choirs, or a combination; boys' choirs of 4th grade through 8th grade (unchanged voices) and 2 girls' choirs of the same age level, i.e., a junior girls' choir (4th, 5th and 6th grades) and a junior high girls' choir (7th and 8th grades).

This division at the junior and junior high level is the better one. The 3d grade — boys and girls together — make a fine training choir. Some churches have a primary "choir" of 1st, 2d, and 3d grades. Some have a "choir" of kindergarten children called a "cherub choir," who are too young and certainly not ready to fit into a formal choir program or to understand the responsibility of leading in worship.

A well-trained high school choir is capable of singing a complete service every Sunday. If the church has double Sunday morning services, the high school choir should sing one and the adult choir the other. The high school young people are quite able to sing 2 anthems every Sunday.

Junior and junior high girls' and boys' choirs can sing a complete service and should be prepared to do this 3 or 4 times a year, possibly at the early morning service as part of their training and service to the church.

The 3d-grade choir on occasion will be able to enter into a service and sing at least part of the music — thus "learning through doing" how to be choristers.

There are also special choir services, such as choir dedication, Thanksgiving, Christmas Eve, Christmas Day, Palm Sunday, and Easter Day services.

Easter afternoon is a fitting time for a special baptismal service. The 3d-grade choir, who may have little brothers or sisters being baptized, are a logical group to sing at that service, perhaps a hymn and an Easter carol.

The wearing of vestments by choirs has now become an accepted practice. They give the choir the look and feeling of unity. Earrings, bracelets, hair ornaments, and conspicuous shoes are inappropriate. Instead of "marching" down the aisle, keeping step with the music while singing the processional hymn, choirs ought to walk together normally as they sing, keeping step only with one another.

The growth of appreciation for better music and more significant attitudes toward worship are important goals for church choirs. This growth will be an influence on the whole church for a better understanding and acceptance of fine music and for a deepening experience in worship. — *Helen Hawk Carlisle*

CHOIR SCHOOL Augustine of Canterbury landed in England in 597, bringing singers from Rome who went about the country teaching the ritual melodies of the Gregorian chant. One of the archbishop's first acts was to establish a school in connection with Canterbury Cathedral which survives today as the King's School. In 663 a Song School was founded at York by Paulinus, one of Augustine's disciples who, having baptized King Edwin and founded York Minster, left behind him James the Deacon who "acted as Master to many in church, chanting after the Roman or Canterbury manner." One by one, monasteries were founded, for example, at Wearmouth (647) and Jarrow (682), where daily life included singing in the church. For many years the singing was done by the monks. Later, outside choirboys were brought in to share in this singing, although not all of these entered the monastic life.

The earliest mention of a separate school for choristers is a reference to one at Lincoln in 1236. The real ancestor of the choir school of today, however, is the School of the Almonry. The almoner was an official whose duty was to distribute food and gifts to the poor at the monastery gates. About the beginning of the 14th century, the custom began of appointing definite choristers to sing in the Lady chapels of the monastic churches and provision had to be made for their boarding as well as their education. During the 14th and 15th centuries almonry schools sprang up all over England in connection with the chief ecclesiastical establishments, and it is estimated that at the time of the English Reformation there must have been no less than 1,000 choirboys receiving their lodging and education in them. One of the most famous choir schools was that of the Chapel Royal whose master had the power to conscript boys with good voices into his service, regardless of parental objection. One of the most famous choirboys at the Chapel Royal was Henry Purcell. Practically every English musician of note until the beginning of the 20th century was a choirboy in one of England's choir schools.

At the present time there are some 50 schools in England that give board and a good education at little or no cost to the boys in return for their singing in the cathedral or collegiate chapel.

Choirs of boys were introduced into the Protestant Episcopal Church in the U.S.A. in the middle of the 19th century. On Ascension Day, 1846, music at Trinity Church, New York, was sung by a choir of 14 boys and a double quartet. Women were not dropped from this choir, however, until 1859. An attempt to found choir schools was made in 1870, first at the Cathedral of SS. Peter and Paul in Chicago and later in St. Paul's Parish, Baltimore. Grace Church in New York founded a choir school in 1894 but in 1934 this school was reorganized as an elementary day school. The choir school of the Cathedral of St. John the Divine in New York was founded in 1901 and that of St. Thomas' Church in 1919. At the present time the Cathedral and St. Thomas Schools are the only choir boarding schools in the U.S.A. At the Washington Cathedral the choirboys have scholarships as day students at St. Alban's School, and at St. Paul's Cathedral, Los Angeles, and St. Peter's, Philadelphia, day schools have been founded to educate the choirboys.

The curriculum of a choir school is similar to that of any good independent school except that the work is a little more intensive. The boys must have daily singing rehearsals to prepare for many services; thus the classroom pace is faster than at a comparable nonsinging independent school. However, the small number of boys in a class (9 is the average class) enables work to be covered faster than in a larger class. One important by-product of singing complicated music in a choir is that a high degree of concentration is acquired at an early age. In almost every case a good chorister can learn more quickly than a boy without choir experience. When there is added to this the experience of daily association with the Bible, with the many splendid hymns and the finest music of the church, the experience in a choir school becomes something of great value. — *Alec Wyton*

CHORIC SPEECH Choric speech is a comparatively new art for use in modern services of worship, but it is an ancient art in sacred ritual. It is fairly certain that the first forms of ceremonial worship were communal, and that in them the related arts of communal speech and drama were integrated. The Song of Deborah and the Lament of David for Saul and Jonathan are examples of choric ceremonials.

Choric speech means verbal expression by a group. It is a balanced group of blended voices that speak together or separately. These groups of voices within the larger group will not be so definite in range and quality as we find in a singing choir with its soprano, alto, tenor, and bass sections. However, the voices will be grouped into 2, 3, or 4 sections, with 3 groupings – low, medium, and high voices – the usual minimum.

The range for the speaking voice is remarkable, since it has a span of about 2½ octaves, while the untrained singing voice has a range of about 1 to 1¼ octaves. There are minute gradations of pitch within the span and thus the flexibility and variety give almost endless possibilities for the expression of thought and emotion.

Choric speaking requires that every word be projected clearly and with expression. Blurred words and singsong delivery are 2 imminent dangers against which any choric speech director must guard at all times. Tempo must be controlled or it will tend to grow faster; voices may become loud and the meaning indistinct.

The recurrence of strong beats at definite intervals will be the only concern with meter. Thus if there are 1 or 4 unaccented syllable intervals, the time taken to say the 1 or the 4 will be equal. An ear sensitive to the demands of logical communication of ideas demands a rhythm where stress is actuated by this communication. The speaking choir must be familiar with all patterns of rhythm and cadence from the most free to the most formal.

Choric speech has definite contributions to make to Christian education. Memorization of immortal works of religion and art is done without effort as one takes part in the expression of them. The Bible and other literature of the church are interpreted for the worshipers, both participants and listeners.

Furthermore, the choric speech choir has the distinct advantage of being the only universal medium by which every individual can take an active part without needing any special talent for doing so. There is sheer joy in taking one's part along with others. Better personal adjustments can be expected; the exhibitionist learns to submerge himself as he develops pride in a shared sense of group achievement. Opportunities for leadership can be provided. It helps the timid make a responsible contribution to the group.

A choric speech choir can be assembled if the church can provide a leader and from 4 to 30 people who are willing to participate. Some leaders prefer 15 voices if the group includes both sexes. Thirty is a good number for a mixed group with the ratio of 2 female voices to 1 male voice. Until the choir has achieved good techniques the grouping should be as compact as possible, with different elevations being used.

The speaking choir is never theatrical and thus there should be a dignified restraint in all aspects of its appearance. The costume is usually a robe, cassock, or academic gown. Deportment is always dignified, and the leader should be as inconspicuous as possible at renditions. The attention of the audience should be directed at the group, and distractions of all kinds are to be avoided.

Rehearsals are all-important. Some method should be worked out in order that the 1st word be said in unison if there is no solo passage. Voice and diction exercises should be a part of each rehearsal. Sufficient time should be given to rehearsals. One leader states that a 15-minute presentation requires 3 months of weekly rehearsals to be of value.

Choric speech is an art and as such its techniques must be mastered and the materials must be familiar. The choir assists in the leading of worship, and its high calling is to interpret the immortal message of the Bible and other sacred literature. — *Virginia S. Fisher*

CHRISTIAN METHODIST EPISCOPAL CHURCH
The Christian Methodist Episcopal Church was established Dec. 15, 1870, in Jackson, Tenn. Prior to 1870, this church was a part of the Methodist Episcopal Church South. The act of setting up the Negro constituents of that church as a separate group did not divorce this young denomination from the family of Methodism. The first bishops of this denomination, originally named the Colored Methodist Episcopal Church in America, were consecrated by bishops of the Methodist Episcopal Church South.

From its inception this denomination placed education among its highest aspirations. Organized during the dark reconstruction period in the Deep South, the Christian Methodist Episcopal Church has always sought to promote a vigorous program of education. The founders held in common a burning passion for the enlightenment of all people.

Accordingly, the church was founded on the assumption that religion and education belong together, each being essentially a complement to the other. As early as 1874 a movement was started to purchase land on which to build a school. The church has a plan outlined in its Book of Discipline, by which the entire church organizes itself to administer Christian education. The responsibility for the general program of Christian nurture rests with the General Board of Christian Education. This board plans the program of Christian education for the entire connection. — *C. D. Coleman*

CHRISTIAN REFORMED CHURCH
Formal education, that is, systematic instruction to accomplish well-defined ends in the lives of youth, has been a primary concern of the Christian Reformed Church throughout its history of slightly over 100 years. It inherited this interest in education from its mother church, the Reformed Church of the Netherlands. The baptismal form used by both churches gives evidence of this primary concern when it asks parents to make this pledge at the baptism of an infant: " Do you promise and intend to instruct these children, when come to years of discretion, in the aforesaid doctrine and cause them to be instructed therein, to the utmost of your power? " The church through its properly constituted officers holds the parents responsible for their answer, " We do," by following up their practice through visits to families by church officials at least once a year.

The church looks upon catechetical instruction as the official medium of the church coming to the aid of Christian parents in carrying out their baptismal vow. This instruction begins at about the age of 8 or 10 and continues through the age of about 18 when most young people of the church make public profession of their faith in Christ as their Savior and Lord before the congregation. In the early stages, catechetical instruction consists of Biblical history. At about the age of 12 a simple formulation of Christian doctrine is presented. This is followed by more comprehensive instruction in doctrine based on the Heidelberg Catechism. Instruction in doctrine is actually a teaching of Scriptural doctrine, guided by the confessions of the church. Though the methodology of catechetical instruction is now in many cases being revised to take account of better insights into the learning process, the term " catechetics " continues to be used to designate the official instruction of youth in the Christian faith.

The Sunday school is a later arrival in the instruction of youth. It never has been, nor is it today, regarded as the major agency for religious instruction of the youth of the church. The Christian Reformed Church looks upon the Sunday school as religious instruction on Sunday in which the entire church can participate in a more or less formal way and reach out into the community by bringing in the unchurched youth. The Sunday school has an evangelistic emphasis, though personal commitment to the Lord is purposefully sought in catechetical instruction also. The Sunday school confines its instruction to Bible study, while catechetical instruction becomes specifically doctrinal.

The Christian faith as set forth in the Reformed creeds (for the Christian Reformed Church, specifically the Belgic Confession, the Canons of Dort, and the Heidelberg Cate-

chism) views religion not merely as a phase or aspect of the life of the individual, but as comprising the entire personality in all relations of life. Furthermore, the self-disclosure of God, though infallibly given in his Word, is not limited to the Word written and the Christ as the Word incarnate. God is known also from his work in creation and in the doings of men. The blight of sin on man's capacity to know God is in part corrected by the knowledge of God from Scripture.

This view of religion and the knowledge of God calls for a broader concept of education than merely instruction in Bible history and doctrine. Education comprises a full life and worldview in the framework of Scriptural teaching. The church, therefore, encourages and helps parents and the Christian community at large to erect schools that can provide the education the Reformed faith requires. To provide this education is not the function of the organized church. The school is a community or social institution. How the school is organized to accomplish Christian education is of less concern to the church. Only in extreme cases of urgency would the church directly conduct a Christian school. The church exercises moral and spiritual persuasion to convince parents of their obligation with reference to Christian school education.

The Christian Reformed Church maintains and directs a college and a theological seminary. It gives financial assistance and full moral support to 2 junior colleges. Christian education from kindergarten through university is the goal.

How loyal is the Christian Reformed constituency with reference to the program of education, especially in catechetical instruction and the Christian day school? As to the former, full loyalty is expected and achieved. With reference to the Christian day school a reasonably safe estimate is from 80 to 90 percent. Where no Christian day school is financially possible or when competent Christian teachers are unavailable every effort is put forth to open one as soon as possible.

— *Cornelius Jaarsma*

CHURCH OF THE BRETHREN

Founded in 1708 in Schwarzenau, Germany, the current denominational name, Church of the Brethren, was established in 1908. Although members referred to each other as Brethren from the beginning, their European contemporaries called them Schwarzenau Taufers, Neu-Taufers, or Dompelaars.

The 8 founders came from the Reformed Church, but their ideological break with the old church was almost complete. The determinative forces of the new church flowed from the Pietist and Anabaptist movements. It was not easy to blend these 2 widely different religious approaches. The desire to recover the life and virtue of the early church flowed from Anabaptism, while Pietism contributed zeal, winsomeness, and openness toward truth. The particular emphases of the founders were added to give the church its early character.

Persecution soon struck the new German church. At the same time words of encouragement reached the Brethren from "the new land," and the 1st group headed for Pennsylvania in 1719. Within a decade the migration was almost complete and the organized Brethren movement disappeared from Germany.

As the church moved westward from Philadelphia, it remained primarily within the restrictive influence of German groups, and continued to carry the marks of sectarianism. The identification of the colonial period, German Baptist Brethren Church, lasted until 1908.

The modern era has witnessed a rather rapid movement from sectarianism toward denominationalism. Discernible in the social patterns of its members and in their view of the church, this change appears explicit in the church's involvement in a worldwide ministry, the reception of members from other communions by letter, and the church's wholehearted participation in the ecumenical movement.

Accepting the basic Christian doctrines, Brethren singled out certain ordinances and emphases: believer's baptism, by trine immersion; observance of the love feast and Communion, consisting of foot washing, fellowship meal, and Communion; obedience to Christ, reflected in the faithful practice of simple, spiritual living; freedom of conscience in all matters of faith. The church's witness to society has revolved around brotherhood, nonviolence, reconciliation, and practical service to those in need. Some have designated the Brethren as a "peace church."

God is viewed as the source of truth, and a large place has been ascribed to divine initiative in making known the truth to persons. This truth is described best in Christ, and the Christian finds his basic authority and guidance in Christ. In this connection, the New Testament is conceived as the fulfillment of the Old Testament, and it is anticipated that new light will break forth as believers study it in the fellowship of the church under the guidance of the Holy Spirit.

Genuine respect for human ability, and confidence in the capacity of persons to grow in Christian maturity ran parallel with these foundational concepts about God, truth, and the New Testament. This combination of basic ideas produced a favorable climate for an educational approach touching the whole of life.

The developmental concepts of social science have influenced the church's work in education, but Brethren avoided some pitfalls of humanism because of their deep interest in the Bible, the church, and revelation. Human freedom and confidence were balanced by divine initiative and order.

Among early Brethren, the home was expected to teach the Word of God. Even so, the church joined the Sunday school movement rather early and officially approved such schools in 1857. The first lesson helps were inaugurated in 1876, and a Sunday School Advisory Board was approved in 1896. Additional activities followed in rapid succession, with a vigorous youth camping movement getting under way in 1921.

Today, curriculum is viewed quite broadly, and Brethren have depended heavily upon the cooperative process for their basic church school outlines. In recent years there has been cooperation at other levels with the American Baptists and the Disciples of Christ. Brethren have participated in constituting the new Cooperative Curriculum Project.

The following trends are discernible in the present program: an increased emphasis on the relationship of Christian education to the central mission of the church; a renewed emphasis upon the centrality of the home in Christian nurture; a heightened awareness of the significance of Biblical and theological insights; a broadened concept of curriculum that calls for more inclusive experiences and the use of face-to-face groups; an expanded involvement in the ecumenical movement.

— S. *Loren Bowman*

CHURCH OF CHRIST, SCIENTIST

Church of Christ, Scientist, is the title commonly given to The First Church of Christ, Scientist, in Boston, its approximately 3,300 branch churches, and 240 affiliated Christian Science Organizations at colleges and universities. The church was founded by Mary Baker Eddy, a New England woman, and first received a state charter in Massachusetts in 1879. It now has churches in 48 countries.

The early history of this religion suggests reasons for the unusual importance Christian Science attaches to the continuing religious or spiritual education of its adherents. In 1866, Mrs. Eddy experienced a remarkable physical healing wholly through spiritual inspiration gained while reading the Biblical account of Jesus Christ's healing of the paralyzed man (Matt. 9:1-8). She believed she had glimpsed on this occasion a basic religious truth of immense importance. A 3-year period of Scriptural study and further instances of healing through her own prayers and the prayers of those she instructed confirmed her view that Christian healing was practicable in all ages. Her conclusions were elaborated in *Science and Health with Key to the Scriptures,* first published in 1875. Later, in an article entitled "The New Birth" (*Miscellaneous Writings,* p. 16), she wrote: "Here, then, is the awakening from the dream of life in matter, to the great fact that

God is the only Life; that, therefore, we must entertain a higher sense of both God and man."

As early as 1870, Mrs. Eddy had explained her views in small classes of instruction at Lynn, Mass. Interest in her teachings grew, and in 1879 she and a group of her followers voted to organize a church without creed "designed to commemorate the word and works of our Master, which should reinstate primitive Christianity and its lost element of healing" (*Church Manual*, p. 17). Classes taught by Mrs. Eddy and some who had received previous instruction from her continued to be held. Pupils and teachers formed various chartered associations that played vital roles in furthering the Christian Science movement until several years before the church took its permanent organizational form in 1892. During the 1880's teaching was centered in the Massachusetts Metaphysical College, chartered as an educational institution under the laws of the State.

With the growth of the church structure, a board of education providing for a regular normal class training of teachers in Christian Science was established. Class instruction is not a requirement for church membership, but remains an important step in Christian Scientists' spiritual education.

Further evidence of the emphasis placed upon continuing religious education for church members is seen in the *Christian Science Quarterly* Bible lessons or lesson sermons, used regularly in Sunday church services. Mrs. Eddy wrote, shortly after their inauguration (*Miscellaneous Writings*, p. 114), " The Committee on Sunday School Lessons cannot give too much time and attention to their task, and should

spare no research in the preparation of the *Quarterly* as an educational branch."

Each week Christian Scientists devote daily study to this lesson of correlated selections from the Bible and *Science and Health*. At Sunday services, which are uniform throughout Christian Science churches, this lesson is read by 2 elected lay members and takes the place of a pastoral sermon. Thus on Sunday students of Christian Science join in a worship service that includes the lesson or sermon they have been studying and endeavoring to put into practice in their individual lives during the preceding week. Inspirational individual study of the Bible and *Science and Health* is also encouraged.

Each Christian Science church maintains a Sunday school for pupils up to the age of 20. Children may enter Sunday school in most branch churches as early as the age of 2. Instruction, based on the Bible and *Science and Health*, emphasizes the practical application of Biblical teachings to daily life.

Church periodicals, including *The Christian Science Journal* (monthly), *Christian Science Sentinel* (weekly), *The Herald of Christian Science* (monthly and quarterly in foreign-language editions), and *The Christian Science Monitor*, a daily international newspaper giving analytical coverage to public affairs, are also expected to serve as continuing sources of education for individual Christian Scientists. — *Will B. Davis*

CHURCH OF ENGLAND Every overseas investigator of the English educational system, unless he is unusually well informed in advance, is surprised at the existence and amazed at the complexity of the partnership of church and state in the educational system of the country, especially that part of it usually known as " the dual system." The terms of the relationship have been regulated by successive Acts of Parliament, but its substance is a matter of historical growth.

Education came to England with the Christian gospel. For at least 14 centuries schools were continuously being founded by monasteries and cathedrals, kings and bishops, nobles and commoners, merchant companies and city corporations, and by devout men and women in many parishes. To found a school was an act of Christian piety: the object was most often to provide an education for the poor in Christian faith and practice as taught by their church, and in literacy and useful arts. Many of these old foundations are vigorous schools today. Some are now independent schools, i.e., they derive their income mainly from fees. Among this group are the English " public schools," defined as such by membership of the Governing Bodies' Association. Independent schools, except the few founded on the basis of some other church or none, are Church of England schools; many have chapels or chaplains, give Church of England teaching, and foster church membership. Very few receive finances from or are under direct control by the church. Many other ancient foundations have now become part of the state system of education, but often retain some at least of the tradition and a relationship with a parish church.

The dual system has its origins in the educational history of the 19th century. Briefly, the name refers to the existence within the state system of schools owned by denominational bodies giving denominational religious teaching. One third of the 30,000 " maintained " (i.e., non-fee-raising) schools of England and Wales are denominational schools, and of this third, ⅘ are Church of England (Church in Wales) schools. The 19th century was in many respects the greatest era of school building by the church. Founded in 1811, the National Society aimed at the establishment of a school in every parish. Its method, that of making grants out of private subscriptions to local initiators, enabled it to influence building standards, propose the content and methods of teaching, and recruit and train teachers. By 1831 there were 13,000 " national " schools. Many of the schools were used also for Sunday schools, but the society refused to capitulate to pressures, strong in the days of child labor, to make do with only Sunday instruction; day schools were its avowed aim.

Starting 3 years earlier than the National Society, the British and Foreign Schools Society had the support of dissenting bodies for undenominational religious instruction in schools. Its achievement in school building was far smaller than that of the National Society, but its policies won the ear of the state when in 1870 the state took power by Act of Parliament to set its own hand to building schools. The Cowper Temple Clause in that Act secured nondenominational teaching for the new state schools. Thereafter the free churches advocated a unitary undenominational system of education and the relinquishing of " British and Foreign schools " to the state. The National Society could not accept for the church either a denial of its duty and right to educate, or a religious education for its children shorn of doctrine, of worship in the church, and of preparation for or encouragement in church membership. Following the Act of 1870, the National Society and churchmen in many parishes put forth a renewed effort, providing places for 195,000 extra children by the end of the year and for 935,993 by 1880. The local school boards set up by the state and empowered to raise funds compulsorily through local taxation (" the rates ") did only a little better, providing 1,016,464.

After 1870 two pressures on the church greatly increased — pressure in the name of educational principle for more and better accommodation, equipment, and teaching, and political and denominational pressure against providing or increasing grants for building or maintenance from public funds. Schools in country areas and poor areas in towns suffered acutely. Education became a political issue, with Christians ranged on both sides in a conflict that seemed endlessly unresolvable and was frequently bitter.

The 1944 Education Act preserved and modified the dual system and changed the basis of religious education in church schools. Every church school was given a choice of status — " aided " or " controlled." At an aided school the church would appoint ⅔ of the managers, who would appoint all staff; religious teaching would be denominational (subject to a conscience clause permitting parents to withdraw a child); and the whole school could go to church for services. The church would have to provide half the cost of bringing the school up to, and maintaining it at, a standard required by the Local Education Authorities in their development plans. For the 1944 act was not a meas-

ure to settle the church school question, but a comprehensive overhaul of the whole educational system, carrying with it a new relationship of voluntary schools within the state system. In a controlled school the church would appoint ⅓ of the managers, religious teaching would be in accordance with a syllabus agreed upon between representatives of religious bodies, including the Church of England and the Local Education Authority. The church could appoint only a " reserved teacher " to give Church of England teaching during school hours twice a week if parents asked for it. All rebuilding costs would fall on the state. Church schools would not be allowed to charge fees, and all running costs would be met by the state. Clauses of the Act dealing with religious education in state schools prescribed a daily act of worship in every school, made religious instruction compulsory, and based it on an agreed syllabus.

The effect of the Act has been to close or reduce to " controlled " status nearly half the church's schools. The high and mounting cost of large schemes of reorganization and development led to an appeal to the Government for 75 percent of the cost. This was granted by an Act in 1959 amending the 1944 Act. The total bill that the church has had to pay is about 20 million pounds.

The Church of England is left with a reduced stake in the nation's educational system, more secure, and far better equipped. Through it the church seeks to show what a Christian education can be, not for the rich or privileged, but for ordinary boys and girls in ordinary places, and to give that education to as many children as it can.

The church puts no pressure on parents to send children to church schools rather than state schools. One of its aims in maintaining training colleges is to send teachers not only into church schools (as was envisaged from the foundation of the first college in 1846) but into state schools. The church has 26 such training colleges in England and Wales; together they contain a quarter of all the nation's teachers in training. In the past 3 years the Church Assembly has voted 2 million pounds for capital development, to provide a total of 10,000 student places and 2 new colleges. Every college has a chapel and chaplain: religious education is part of the basic course, and students are encouraged to specialize in it. The church may require that half the students be members of the Church of England; in fact ¾ of them are so. Every church college has a governing body that makes appointments and supervises the conduct of the college.

The National Assembly of the Church of England delegates to its Board of Education the task of advising the Assembly on policy and finance and coordinating the many facets of Christian education in the church. Under the Board a Schools Council and a Training Colleges Council advise schools and colleges on a multitude of matters and negotiate, within the basic policy laid down by the Board, with relevant public authorities. The Youth Council and Children's Council foster Christian education in these constituencies. Each diocese has or aims to have at least one youth chaplain or youth officer and a religious education adviser. Research and publications, training of leaders, and relations with appropriate bodies in other denominations and with the state are their responsibility. The Board's youth work receives grants from the Ministry of Education. The Board of Education administers grants to Anglican chaplaincies in all English universities outside Oxford and Cambridge; it is responsible through its adult committee for assisting schemes for lay training through the dioceses.

— *Kathleen Bliss*

CHURCH OF GOD The religious movement known as the Church of God, with general offices located at Anderson, Ind., began about 1880 under the preaching of D. S. Warner. It witnesses to the essential unity of all Christians. " A united church for a divided world," the identifying banner of the international weekly radio broadcast, *The Christian Brotherhood Hour,* states this movement's central conviction; it is constantly proclaimed in *The Gospel Trumpet,* a weekly journal published continuously since 1881.

Other basic teachings would hold the Bible as the record of God's revelation; salvation through repentance, rebirth, and faith in Jesus Christ; the sanctifying activity of the Holy Spirit in the life of the believers; the divine resources available for holy living and for healing; the Kingdom of God, a contemporary spiritual reality in the church as the redeemed and redeeming community; divine leadership through the Holy Spirit's distribution of gifts.

One is identified with a local church by his Christian faith, worship, and service; formal church membership is thus considered an unnecessary barrier to the free flow of redemptive fellowship.

This movement has never accepted " speaking in tongues " and related esoteric demonstrations that are sometimes characteristic of other groups with similar names. Through the Holy Spirit, God is working in all Christendom to cleanse, purify, and unite his people for a more perfect presentation of his love to the world.

Leadership training, youth work, and church schools are guided by the Board of Christian Education, which works with the Gospel Trumpet Company (Warner Press), publication board of the Church of God, in production of curriculum study materials. Editors and program leaders work cooperatively with others in committees of church councils. Uniform lesson quarterlies and electives for adults and graded lessons for other ages are published for Sunday church schools. The educational philosophy is based on theological and psychological assumptions that have been shared with and strengthened by participants in cooperative lesson outline planning since the early days of the former International Council of Religious Education.

Since the founding of its 1st college, Anderson, and its seminary, both located at Anderson, Ind., the movement has insisted on high educational standards and thoroughly Christian leadership in all its colleges, Bible schools, and institutes in the U.S.A. and other countries.

— *T. Franklin Miller*

CHURCH OF JESUS CHRIST OF LATTER-DAY SAINTS (MORMONS)

From its inception in 1830 the Church of Jesus Christ of Latter-day Saints (Mormons) has sought to educate its members in all the arts and sciences of the day, and in a knowledge of God and of his dealings with men.

The accepted mission of the church "to carry the gospel of Jesus Christ to every nation, kindred, tongue, and people," requires a knowledge of the Scriptures, of languages, customs, and peoples. The philosophy of the church, which centers around the eternal life and the progression of man, glorifies learning. In the words of Joseph Smith, the 1st prophet and leader of the church: "If there is anything virtuous or lovely, or of good report, or praiseworthy, we seek after these things"; "The glory of God is intelligence, or in other words, light and truth"; "Seek ye out of the best books words of wisdom; seek learning even by study and also by faith"; "Man can be saved no faster than he gains knowledge."

In its earlier years the schools of the church provided both secular and religious instruction. With the development of state schools, supported by public taxation and devoted to secular training, the church has largely withdrawn from the secular field on the elementary and secondary level and has concentrated on church colleges, and a unique system of church seminaries and institutes of religion, established adjacent to public schools and offering religious courses to supplement the secular training of the public schools. The exception to the above is found in Mexico, and in the Pacific Islands of Samoa, Tonga, and Vavau, where the church is expanding its school system on the elementary and secondary level because of the lack of state school facilities.

The church has consistently followed the principle of separation of church and state. Although believing that no education is complete without weekday religious instruction, it has always conducted such religious instruction in church-operated schools or in church-owned seminaries and institutes of religion situated off the state school campuses and completely supported by the church on high scholastic standards.

The church pioneered a program of released time from the public schools for religious instruction, starting with the first seminary in 1912. Classes had trained teachers provided by the church. This program grew until by 1961 some 70,-000 high school students in 28 states of the U.S.A. and in Canada and Mexico were receiving daily instruction in religion for a 1-hour period.

Beginning in 1926 the Church Board of Education established an institute of religion near the University of Idaho, offering religion courses to students there. This movement has grown until religion courses are being offered in church-owned or leased premises to students at over 100 universities and colleges in the U.S.A. and Canada, with some 11,000 students being enrolled in daily classes.

Brigham Young University, operated by the church at Provo, Utah, has become the largest church-controlled university in America, comprising 11 colleges and a graduate school offering studies through the doctorate. Other schools include Ricks College, Rexburg, Idaho, Church College of the Pacific, Laie, Oahu, Hawaii, L.D.S. Business College, Salt Lake City, and colleges in New Zealand and Tonga.

Church schools are controlled by a Church Board of Education, consisting of the First Presidency of the Church and the Twelve Apostles. All the church schools in North America were unified in 1953 under 1 administrator. The church schools in the Pacific Islands are under the direction of the Church Board of the Pacific. — *William E. Berrett*

CHURCH OF THE NAZARENE The Church of the Nazarene is characterized by its emphasis upon the doctrine of entire sanctification as a second work of grace, subsequent to regeneration, wrought in the hearts of believers by faith in Christ. It is recognized as a " holiness church," accepting the creed of evangelical Protestantism.

The denomination is of comparatively recent origin, having its official founding date within the 20th century. The roots of the church are in a revival of the doctrine of entire sanctification as taught by John Wesley and preached by Whitefield, Bishop Asbury, and others. This revival occurred in the eastern section of the U.S.A. toward the close of the 19th century. The revival touched various denominations with similar results. Christian men and women sought for a deeper experience with God. They testified to a more satisfying awareness of God's presence, to a consciousness of the fullness of the Spirit. They witnessed to heart-cleansing and to perfection in love.

Some of these persons formed local groups for prayer and mutual encouragement. Where opposition was severe they withdrew from their churches and formed independent groups. Where the groups were large enough local pastors were called to oversee the work. These local groups united in regional or state organizations.

In 1908 three of the stronger organizations, from the Pacific Coast, New England, and the South, united to form the Church of the Nazarene. In 1915 a group of holiness people from Tennessee and the Southeast and a group from the United Kingdom united with the denomination. In 1922 more than 1,000 persons from the Layman's Holiness Association united with the denomination in Minnesota, the Dakotas, and Montana. Most recently 2 groups in the United Kingdom merged with the church — the International Holiness Mission in 1952 and the Calvary Holiness Church in 1955.

From the founding of the church its leaders have been committed to the proposition that a fervent evangelism can and should be combined with a thorough system of education. At the time of the union in 1908 the various uniting bodies were sponsoring Bible schools and colleges in Rhode Island, Illinois, Tennessee, Texas, Oklahoma, and California. In half a century the church has developed 6 liberal arts colleges in the U.S.A., a Bible college in Canada and one in England. Nazarene Theological Seminary in Kansas City, Mo., is a graduate theological school offering a 3 years' course leading to the B.D. degree. Policy guidance for these institutions of higher education is vested in the Department of Education, 1 of the 7 divisions of the denomination's General Board.

Major responsibility for Christian education in the local churches is vested in the General Board's Department of Church Schools. This department, under the direction of an executive secretary, is responsible for guiding the denomination's educational philosophy and its educational programs as they are carried on in the local churches. An executive editor directs the planning of curriculum and the development of curriculum materials.

The church follows a cycle-graded curriculum plan from nurs-

ery through junior high school. Kindergarten and primary lessons are developed from outlines planned by the Committee on the Graded Series of the Division of Christian Education of the National Council of the Churches of Christ in the U.S.A. Nursery, junior, and junior high materials are developed from denominational outlines. Senior high school and adult materials are based on the Uniform Series of the International Sunday School Lessons.

Sunday evening curriculum materials are provided by a separate but closely related division, the Nazarene Young People's Society. Leadership education and certain other specialized elective courses are administered through an interdepartmental division of Christian Service Training. Missionary education materials are planned through an interdepartmental Missionary Study Committee. — *A. F. Harper*

CHURCH YEAR At its heart Christianity is the gospel of the mighty acts of God in Jesus as the Christ. The church that bears his name has a dual role (witness) to play in human history: (1) to celebrate what God has done, once for all, in the man Christ Jesus for the redemption of all mankind from sin, death, and Satan; (2) to participate in the fulfillment of his mission of love and justice to, in, and through each new generation of his people.

The pattern of the Christian year, like the Lord's Day liturgy, is a recapitulation of the whole drama of our salvation. Following the form of the earliest Christian preaching and confessions of faith (Phil. 2:5-11; Acts 2:22 ff.; Acts 10:34-43; and the plot of Luke-Acts taken as a whole), the church relives the whole life of Jesus in the 1st half of each year (from Advent to Ascension) and publicly announces its role as his servant people in the 2d semester (from Pentecost through Trinity). The 2 halves complement each other, in the way indicated by Paul in II Cor. 5:19: God was in Christ (1) reconciling the world to himself; (2) entrusting to us the ministry of reconciliation.

Our Lord's birth (incarnation), healing ministry (identification with sinners), death and resurrection (atonement and reconciliation of mankind with God), continuing presence with his followers (gift of the Spirit), and universal Lordship (exaltation) are at once historical events and theological confessions. The church's celebration is determined by the meanings it confesses and is meaningful to its members because of the events in which it participates.

The earliest Christian celebration was the Lord's Day, that is, the weekly Easter. This observance appears to have begun almost at once in the apostolic church. Since their Hebrew heritage had already structured their life with the keeping of the weekly Sabbath, it was not difficult to develop a weekly Lord's Day. Our Christian observance is different, however, not only because it falls on the 1st day of the week as against the 7th, but more basically because it is primarily a celebration and not a Sabbath. By the same token that the Lord's Day abolishes the Sabbath, however, every day becomes a Sabbath. By virtue of the sacrifice of the Lord Jesus on our behalf, the Christian's whole life is to be hallowed, as a Sabbath is, in the sacrificial service of God.

Our liturgical year, likewise, arose out of the celebration of Easter, that is, around the yearly Easter. Good Friday and Easter, Ascension and Pentecost, Christmas and Epiphany are the 3 centers of interest in the slowly developing Christian calendar. They arose in pairs as indicated and in this order of priority.

Already the Jewish lunar calendar had identified certain historical events as the occasion for the commemoration of the covenant drama of Israel. The Passover recalled the liberation from Egypt, and Pentecost the law-giving on Mt. Sinai. Since, according to the Scriptures, the times of Passover and Pentecost became the occasions of our Lord's death and resurrection and the birth of the Christian church, respectively, the development of a Christian calendar year actually stems in both directions from these 2 focuses.

From the first our Lord's redemptive work was viewed as a single act. The crucifixion and resurrection were one event theologically, seen as the divine triumph in spite of human defeat. Together they become the new exodus and the occasion for the new Paschal celebration. The separation of Good Friday from Easter, the observances of Holy Week and the development of Lent, are parts of the same process — the establishment by the church of periods of fasting, penitent self-examination, and so on, as preparation for the great central event of the resurrection. The later development of the period of preparation into a full Lenten season involved the extension of our Lord's struggle with the powers of evil. In contemporary practice precisely 40 days of fasting and penitence are counted by starting with Ash Wednesday before the 1st Sunday of Lent and excepting the Sundays. Sundays are unalterably days of celebration, no matter where they fall in the yearly pattern.

The celebration of Christmas and Epiphany is also a part of the process of reading the events of our Lord's life backward from its center to the beginning. It appears that here, too, there was at first a single festival of the beginning of the divine manifestation (Epiphany) and that the earliest celebration fell on Jan. 6. Specifically emphasized was the manifestation of the Christ to the world, commemorating at once the birth (Matt., chs. 1 and 2; Luke, chs. 1 and 2), the baptism (Mark, ch. 1), and "the light [that] shines in the darkness" (John, ch. 1).

When, however, the celebration of the coming of the divine Love into our human life is traced back to the most definitive historical event, it comes to rest upon the birth of our Lord (Christmas) as the primary festival of the incarnation. Ultimately this became a separate festival and is celebrated by the Western Church on Dec. 25. The Epiphany remains as a correlative commemoration of our Lord's baptism and is still celebrated on Jan. 6.

The practice of observing Christmas as the festival of the incarnation on Dec. 25 has not been found earlier than the 4th century. Scholars believe that this day was chosen by the church in Rome to strengthen its position in the struggle against pagan sun worship, with its festival at the winter solstice. Thus Christmas became the occasion for proclaiming the birth of the Son of Righteousness as the true Light of the World.

Just as in the case of Easter, the Western Church developed a period of preparation for Christmas. Advent, like Lent, was at one time a 6-week period of anticipation of the fulfillment of the prophetic promises regarding the Savior's coming. Our contemporary practice observes only 4 Sundays. Celebrating the Advent season as our Christian New Year offers an excellent opportunity for preachers and teachers to explain the Biblical doctrine of God's election and his covenant faithfulness. This is the ground of our Christian hope and the framework of the drama that is about to be unfolded once again in the year ahead. This will stand in the sharpest contrast to the weak resolutions and uncertain predictions that abound in our secular celebration on Jan. 1.

Moving forward from Easter, on the other hand, the church was on familiar ground, although living in a new spiritual climate. Pentecost, like Passover, was another traditional Jewish festival that underwent a radical transformation. Pentecost, commonly called Whitsunday in Christian history, is the church's own birthday. It is unlikely that a Christian calendar year would ever have developed had there not been both a Christian Pentecost and a Christian Easter. Easter is "the spiritual transformer" of history, but Pentecost is the event in which the power of God electrified a small group of the followers of Jesus and transformed them from disciples into apostles. This is the point in history where the meaning of our Lord's words in his high-priestly prayer becomes quite clear: "As thou didst send me into the world, so I have sent them into the world" (John 17:18). Reliving Pentecost, year by year, gives the assurance not only that we are sent but that we are empowered by the gift of God's Holy Spirit to carry his mission of hope to the world.

Just as in each of the other cases pairs of festivals arose out of what was at first a single celebration, so Pentecost was originally the commemoration of our Lord's ascension to heaven as well as of his authoritative gift of power to his people. The church's separation of Ascension Day (40 days after Easter) and Pentecost (50 days after Easter) indicates the recognition that the Christian year is really not just one but two overlapping dramas — the second (the life of the church) growing out of the completion of the first (the life of its Lord).

Proclaiming the whole story of the new covenant in the life, death, and resurrection of our Lord Jesus Christ, in accordance with the pattern of the Christian year, is the means whereby the church commemorates his victorious mission to the world. Preaching becomes the occasion for "the nurture and discipline of the Lord" in and through the recapitulation of the gospel, when the "hearer" confesses with Paul: "I have been crucified with Christ; it is no longer I who live, but Christ who lives in me" (Gal. 2:20). Through year-round participation in the life and work of our Lord Jesus, the hearer is helped to grow in grace and in responsible service to the world. — *Allen O. Miller*

CHURCHES OF GOD IN NORTH AMERICA (GENERAL ELDERSHIP)

This group of churches join with other Christians in recognizing the relation of all to the Godhead, looking to Jesus Christ himself as head of the whole church. They stress vital personal experiences of Christ's saving grace, and commitment to follow his teachings and example. Holding the Bible to be the word of God, they accept its authority for faith and practice in individual and church life. Aware of the spiritual unity of all true Christians, they view each local church as the body of Christ visible at that particular place.

The movement started in eastern Pennsylvania during the 1st third of the 19th century. John Winebrenner (1797–1860) began his ministry with the German Reformed churches. His emphasis on the necessity of regeneration and his adoption of "new measures" to foster vital Christian experience provoked hostility on the part of influential officials of churches he served in and around Harrisburg.

Eventually new churches were formed. In Winebrenner's words, they were "spiritual, free, and independent churches, consisting of believers or Christians only, without any human name or creed or ordinances or laws." In 1830 these banded together in the first of the elderships that now make up the General Eldership of the Churches of God in North America.

These churches insist on the necessity of regeneration or the new birth. They teach justification by faith in Christ, and growth in Christlikeness with the help of the indwelling Holy Spirit. They practice 3 ordinances, viewed as means of grace to keep the church in living remembrance of its living Lord: believer's baptism (by immersion), foot washing, and the Lord's Supper. Each of these serves as reminder, sign, and pledge of the life lived in Jesus Christ.

This body operates Central Publishing House at Harrisburg. Findlay College, its liberal arts school, and Winebrenner Theological Seminary are both located at Findlay, Ohio. It supports mission work in India and East Pakistan. — *Fred D. Rayle*

CHURCH-STATE RELATIONS One of the most complex and difficult problems confronting education, both secular and religious, is the relation of church and state.

The separation of church and state has been a firmly established principle since the founding of the Federal Government. The First Amendment to the Constitution provided that " Congress shall make no law respecting the establishment of religion, or prohibiting the free exercise thereof." After the passage of the Fourteenth Amendment (1867) the courts held that the states as well as the Federal Government were bound by this provision. In 1802, Thomas Jefferson originated the inflexible formula of " a wall of separation between church and state." The original issue was accentuated by the exclusion of religion from the public schools by amendments to state constitutions beginning with Wisconsin in 1848, and the requirement of this prohibition in newly admitted states. This exclusion was firmly established throughout the nation by 1875.

The exclusion of religion from the public schools, although measurably solving the then-existing problem, created unforeseen and unintended subsequent problems. For one thing, it resulted in the all but complete secularization of public education, notwithstanding the fact that the nation was founded upon deep religious convictions and that these convictions are a continuing component of American culture basic to democratic ideals. Also, it resulted in the distortion and impoverishment of the cultural heritage which it is the function of education to pass on unimpaired to each coming generation of American youth. Religion is a constituent part of that heritage.

To omit it or neglect it is to rob youth and society of what is rightfully theirs.

There have been numerous approaches to the solution of this problem, mostly by churches: (1) Sunday and vacation church schools; (2) parochial schools; (3) Bible-reading in the schools without comment and prayer; (4) syllabi on the Bible, with or without credit; (5) released time for religious instruction, at the request of parents, by church teachers and on church funds, and generally on church property; (6) teaching religion factually and as a phase of culture as it appears in such subject matters as literature, history, the social sciences, philosophy, and the arts, by school-accredited teachers and as an integral part of the school curriculum; (7) emphasis on moral and spiritual values as indigenous to the relations and activities of the school as a community, the subject matter of the curriculum, sports, interpersonal and intergroup relations, and counseling.

The issues involving such matters as use of school property, school funds, ecclesiastical habit, transportation of pupils, free lunches, free textbooks, and grants and loans to parochial schools by the Federal Government have led to much litigation in Federal and state courts. The Supreme Court has handed down decisions in 3 cases. In the Everson case (1947) the Court approved free bus transportation to parochial schools but ruled that " no tax can be levied to support any religious activities or institutions . . . to teach or practice religion. Neither a state nor the Federal Government can, openly or secretly, participate in the affairs of any religious organization or groups and vice versa."

In 1948, in the McCollum case, the Court reaffirmed the Everson decision and declared the Champaign, Ill., released-time program unconstitutional on the ground of the use of public-school property. In 1952, in the Zorach case, the Court, though it stated that it followed the McCollum decision, upheld the New York program of released time on the ground that religious instruction by the churches was not given on public-school property. The Court also said that it does not follow that " in all and every respect there shall be separation of church and state." In this case the Court seems to have moved from Jefferson's rigid formula to a more flexible application of the principle of the separation of church and state. The state courts have rendered many divergent and sometimes contradictory decisions.

It would appear that the relation of church and state is grounded in the fact that the community is the ultimate social reality, from which each derives its origin and functions. Their relation takes place on two levels: one institutional and the other functional. On the institutional level they are frequently in competition if not in conflict. Historically each has shown totalitarian tendencies in the attempts of one to dominate the other. On the functional level they complement and support each other in serving the needs of the community. Both are answerable to the community. This mutuality of origin and responsibility offers a ground for mutual respect for the integrity and prerogatives of each other and for cooperation in meeting the divergent needs of the community.

In such cooperation there are certain things the schools can do better than the churches and certain things the churches can do better than the

schools without violating the principle of the separation of church and state. The school by its nature as an educational institution can: (1) provide the youth with actual experience of moral and spiritual values through participation in the relations and activities of the school community and curriculum content in which these values inhere; (2) give an understanding and appreciation of the relation of religion to culture; (3) develop respect for different religious beliefs and practices through an understanding of the historical conditions under which they have arisen; (4) give an appreciation of organized religion in the life of the community through observation of its different expressions of organization, beliefs, worship, and activities; (5) avoid as far as possible destructive conflicts between scientific studies and traditional theological beliefs by cultivating objective attitudes and referring theological issues to parents and the clergy. On the other hand, the churches can: (1) make moral and spiritual values explicit through the language of religion — creed, symbols, rituals, ordinances, and corporate worship in terms of the tradition of each given communion; (2) where it is deemed necessary, provide the sanctions of supernatural and ecclesiastical authority; (3) provide a sustained and sustaining fellowship of mutually shared convictions and commitment; (4) provide the stimulus and means for the systematic cultivation of the religious life through prayer, self-examination, rededication, the ordinances, and private and corporate worship; (5) provide opportunities to develop loyalties to religious leaders, a sustaining tradition, and such common causes as missions, social justice, world brotherhood, and peace. — *William Clayton Bower*

CLAY MODELING Pottery-making is an industry with a long historical background and of universal appeal. Varieties of clay are available in different parts of the world, and man has used it since the early ages.

One of the basic native impulses of children is manipulation. Along with other impulses it needs intelligent guidance. Educators are aware of the fact that book learning alone does not adequately serve children's educational needs. Proper opportunities need to be provided for children to express their manipulative needs. Through such experiences children can be motivated and helped to learn.

Young children see the world in a 1-dimensional plane due to their lack of experience. They need to touch and manipulate in order to bring up their development of visual comprehension. Clay is an excellent medium for them. It is simple to use, easy to get, and has great possibilities for manipulative expression. As they work with their fingers, gradually they come to understand the meaning of the 2d and 3d dimensions.

As in the use of other media of art, children go through different stages of development in clay modeling. They need first to explore and experiment before they are able to express themselves in form, rhythm, and movement. Through these initial experiences with clay certain emotional satisfactions are obtained.

A loving relationship between the teacher and the child will foster the child's confidence in himself and deepen his desire to create. A child's sense of confidence and of his own worth is challenged when the object he has created is not accepted by others. Acceptance and appreciation of the child's effort, expressed by adults who are important to him, are essential to his spiritual growth.

Emphasis should be put on the inner meaning of a creating process rather than on the production or reproduction of particular forms. It is the imaginative use of clay that is crucial to the growth of the child.

Encourage children to model with clay freely, to make from their experiences whatever images they may have in their minds. They should be convinced that shapeless forms can be expressive and significant without having to resemble anything. Educators need to remind themselves that mere imitation, repetition, and reproduction will impoverish personal being.

Unselfconscious work seems to last for several years through the first few grades of school. During these first years, it is best to provide the material and a harmonious atmosphere in which children may explore, experiment, and express themselves freely. The understanding of form construction grows with the child's increased mentality. According to experienced artists and teachers of art, by the time children reach 8 years of age they begin to make finished products, and around 11 years of age they are able to model figures in movement. It is from this point on that various techniques of decoration may be introduced. Here must be kept in mind the individual differences in interest and ability.

The most important thing, however, is to help the individual child cultivate his interest and confidence in expressing himself: (1) to enrich his experiences that he may have ideas to express; (2) that he will be comfortable and eager to express those ideas knowing that his contributions are valued and welcome.

Clay, like any other medium, should be viewed only as one of many tools used in Christian education, aiming at the more complete realization of the child in his relation to God and to his fellowmen.
— *Georgiana Wei Sie*

CLERGYMAN'S ROLE IN CHRISTIAN EDUCATION

The 2d half of the 20th century witnesses a shift in the primary focus of Christian education from an emphasis upon perfecting the Sunday church school to an emphasis upon the renewal of the church. Concern for the renewal of the church manifests itself in widespread reexamination of the nature of the ministry and in a search for an adequate theology of the laity. It is reflected in renewed interest and intense activity in adult Christian education as the proper primary educational focus in the church. The spotlight is on the clergy as educators.

Evidence is abundant for 2 propositions: (1) the role of the minister as educator has deep historical roots in the church; (2) this role has been vastly neglected in modern times.

By the very fact of its existence each church is an educational institution of some kind. Lewis J. Sherrill has written: " A church may, indeed, be doing many things and calling them by the name of education, but its authentic education consists in its impact upon people, and that impact grows out of the active body of convictions held." The history of Christianity itself, says Sherrill, attests to the fact " that Christian education did not exist in isolation from a living religion." Therefore, he concludes, it is futile to attempt to remake education " apart from a rebirth of the church itself" (*The Rise of Christian Education*, pp. 1 f.).

The clergy are responsible for the dynamic quality of this churchly context for Christian nurture. They need something of Calvin's view of the church as " a school of doctrine " where persons are instructed in " the ways of the Lord."

The Reformers, following precedent in the early church, clearly gave a central place to the proclamation of the word. For them this meant preaching and teaching. In fact, these words were used interchangeably in the writing of the time. A long line of Reformation leaders could be quoted concerning the necessity for accompanying preaching with teaching, e.g., Bucer in *The Care of Souls*, and Richard Baxter in *The Reformed Pastor*. If Baxter was astounded to discover the ignorance of his parishioners after listening to years of his preaching and how fruitful a few hours of private instruction could be, how much more disillusioned might be the present-day preacher whose neglect of teaching affords him slight opportunity for knowing how little informed or misinformed his people are!

But if teaching has an honored history, it is nonetheless widely neglected by the clergy today. The alarm is being sounded. The growth of secularism, the pressures of militant ideologies, the confusion of countless pseudo-Christian aberrations, all tend to expose the lack of sound Biblical and doctrinal knowledge and understanding.

In the face of wide acknowledgment that the Sunday church school as we have known it is totally inadequate to the task assigned to it, that instrument of the church must be clearly seen as only one of the means of educational relationship and confrontation in a total church experience. It must be undergirded by parental teaching and led by adults carefully selected and properly prepared. Such selection and training are seldom sustained in a parish where the pastor does not motivate the educational standards. Too largely the clergy have either neglected the church school or supported it as administrators and not as educators.

The role of the clergy in Christian education is fulfilled in relation to the traditionally accepted aspects of the ministry of the Word. The worshiping community gives Christian education its relevance. Central to public worship in Protestant tradition is preaching. Preaching and teaching stand or fall together. It is not only that the preacher must teach through his preaching but that through teaching in other ways he must prepare his hearers to accept, understand, and respond to the Biblical and doctrinal content of his preaching. To discharge his responsibility for proclamation the minister must teach. If he is not the chief teacher, he is the teacher of teachers in order that lay teachers may rightly handle their teaching task.

If he is accountable before God by his calling and before the church by ordination for proclamation of the Word, it is incumbent upon him to spare no effort to see that those who teach with him in family and in church are preparing for this demanding part of their discipleship. His relationship to families is significant. For Christian nurture the family is the central unit; the family normally can fulfill this responsibility

only within the church, which recognizes this fact, sustains as a church this concept, and trains parents for their role as teachers. It is as true today as when Richard Baxter wrote in 1850, " You cannot expect general reformation [in the church] until you procure family reformation." As leader of worship, as counselor, teacher, and friend, the pastor must accept a major role in such family reformation.

Everyone agrees that the Christian faith is grounded in the Bible. Few express sufficient alarm not only at the widespread ignorance of the Bible among Christians but at the still more dangerous misuse of the Bible. " Religious " notions quite inimical to the gospel thrive on modern-day Biblicism.

At no time in Christian history has there been greater need for the teaching of sound doctrine and for a right use of the Scriptures. The irrelevance of the church and the impotence of Christians in a world in revolution is due in no small part to the neglect of doctrinal preaching and teaching. Christians either do not know what they believe or are unable to articulate their beliefs. As teacher the minister will need to become skilled in the art of creating and guiding the interactions and relationships of small groups. Much emphasis upon " fellowship " has been spiritually nonproductive. It promotes institutionalism while obscuring both the deep need for, and the difficulty of, achieving koinonia. Trained to speak to large groups in which the individual remains more or less anonymous, and to counsel individuals, the minister is often singularly unskilled in guiding the small group in which persons may come into true communion with one another. If in each particular church there are no opportunities to experience koinonia, the church is likely to be greatly limited in its power to teach.

As administrator the minister is still primarily pastor and teacher. If he accepts his role as teacher, there is almost no administrative task with board or committee or church leaders that does not constitute a learning situation and a teacher-learner relationship. In the Blizzard study of the parish ministry, clergy decried their heavy administrative load and placed teaching at the bottom of the list in the demands upon their time. By accepting their role as Christian educators they could claim administration for the redemptive opportunity that it surely can be.

Christian education is the Christian community's means of imparting its faith by its life, and in the midst of living, explaining what it believes and why it believes it. Effectiveness in Christian education will always depend to a large extent upon the acceptance by the clergy of their responsibility as educators.

— Herman J. Sweet

COE, GEORGE ALBERT Perhaps Coe can be best understood after 2 questions about him and his work are answered. First, what did he perceive to be the problems of men? Second, what sources of knowledge did he use in attempting to solve these problems?

The motif of " the social " governs all of Coe's thought. It is in the realm of man's relation to man, and in the relation of groups of men to one another that the problems of Coe's day had their origin. The new individual and group relations of industrial society, the relation of immigrants individually and collec-

tively to the established groups and their structures and processes, occupied his thinking. The emergence of urban life with its concomitant problems posed a challenge to him as he stood within the church and spoke to the world about him.

What Ails Our Youth?, Education for Citizenship, A Social Theory of Religious Education, and *What Is Christian Education?* are products of the man reflecting upon social problems and processes as a Christian.

There were problems of another order that greatly influenced his thinking. These were the problems created for the church by the explosion of knowledge and theories in the relatively new universities. Academic freedom and devotion to scientific method after the German style of university were developments of the last decades of the 19th century. Darwinism, empirical psychology, experimentalism, and philosophies of society and culture based upon these sources of knowledge confronted the scholar in the church. John Dewey, G. S. Hall, E. L. Thorndike, and many others offered new " grist for the mill " with their theories and data.

One facet of Coe's world that must not be omitted as a significant influence upon him was the prevailing attitude toward education in American society. The mood of the larger social and cultural milieu was one of hope and anticipation for the future because of the power of education. The Progressive Education Association, the Child Study Movement, the labor union movement, the rural Grange, the voluntary associations, and the settlement house movement were penetrated thoroughly by the progressive dream of " salvation by education." Lack of knowledge was the great evil of a rapidly emerging industrial society, a society with dozens of immigrant groups, a need for an expanded middle class, and a genuine need for many kinds of technical and nontechnical knowledge. Most of the structures of American society responded to rid the world of this evil. The church, as one of these social structures, participated with great vigor, particularly the more liberal groups, in ridding the world of ignorance. Coe, as a scholar in the church, threw himself wholeheartedly into solving the problems of society. His answer for the church was "industrial democracy through education." That this was the same answer as was given by those outside the church did not appear to disturb him. The mood of the day decreed that education was to be the chief end of man. It remained for Coe to fit the religious education movement of the church into the mainstream of social and educational philosophy. The theologians, historians, and teachers of ethics did not provide knowledge that would lead him in any other direction. History was of little consequence, since man and the world were evolving. The dialectical philosophy of Hegel had entered theology, and ethics was almost completely under the spell of Rauschenbusch. There were no alternatives within the purview of Coe.

In his social and cultural milieu he sought to unify education and religious education. This unification, he believed, was possible and necessary because the ground, the ultimate reality, the divine Being, was the same for both. He concluded that "religion is life, and life is religion, or neither is anything," because the "dwelling place" of the divine

Being is all reality, all experience. Education, as a major process in society, was one sphere of religion. He consistently maintained that democracy, as an ideal form of government, could not express the will of the people unless it was submitted to its ground, the divine Being. Coe attempted to show what this submission of education to the divine Being might mean for industrial democracy. Since he believed that the ground of education and religious education were the same, and hence were unified by their common ground, their end, industrial democracy submitted to the divine Being, was also the same.

This was a rather remarkable attempt at solving the relation between religion and culture. A thorough reading of Coe's works will give an excellent background for understanding the current efforts to relate "Christ and culture" and religion and culture (education).

— *Robert C. Worley*

COLLEGE, CHURCH-RELATED In general the term "church-related college" is reserved for those 4-year colleges and universities and 2-year junior colleges which were founded by and have retained an organic relation to a national or international church. The term does not encompass the many secondary schools, graduate schools of theology, training schools, or other professional schools associated with a denomination.

The way by which the church relationship is formalized varies from institution to institution and from region to region, but in most cases there exists a charter requirement, an enactment of the board of trustees, or an enactment by the highest organized body of the church within the state or region (synod, board, conference, assembly, etc.) which stipulates that a certain number or proportion of the board of trustees shall be selected from within the denomination. Within this limitation there is great flexibility. The governing boards of the colleges are generally self-perpetuating, and in most cases the agencies of the church accept the actions and recommendations of the boards of trustees without contest. Usually, but not always, the church-related college receives financial support from the state, regional, or national offices of the denomination. The amount of this support varies widely from denomination to denomination and, again, from region to region.

Historically, these colleges reflected the educational and missionary interests of their churches. Soon after a region was well settled in the westward movement of the American people, a denominational college was proposed. Yale College (Congregational) and Princeton College (Presbyterian) were known as " mother colleges," and between them laid claim through their alumni to the organization of 41 new colleges from coast to coast. The Lutherans, Baptists, and Methodists built very rapidly once they accepted the idea of denominational colleges.

Early in their history, reflecting the fact that they were established from religious motives, these colleges concentrated on the education of ministers of the gospel. Their curriculum was traditionally classical, and paid little or no attention to practical or vocational courses. They were avowedly sectarian. In most cases this meant suspicion of science and a conservative (fundamentalist) approach to the Bible.

With rapid proliferation, few qualified faculty, and a confusion of zeal with education, standards quickly deteriorated. There was concurrently a strong negative reaction across the country to the use of educational institutions for purposes of denominational indoctrination. The result was a trend, starting in the early 1800's and running on into the mid-20th century, toward the elimination of many courses in religion, the curtailing of many organized religious activities, and a relaxation of the ties with the church. The impact of the Civil War, recurring economic crises, and the passage in 1862 of the Morrill Act creating the land-grant colleges, when coupled with low standards and anticlericalism, led to the failure of many of the colleges organized in the early years of the 19th century. Of 500 colleges formed by 1860, only 260 still existed when the Civil War started, and only 180 survived in 1962. There are at least 21 institutions, including the University of California and the University of Delaware, that were founded by a church and subsequently became state colleges or universities. Economic pressure is tremendous on small colleges as it is on all small enterprises. In general, only the fittest have survived.

Those church-related colleges of national reputation, measured by their accreditation, the quality of their faculties, and the sense of responsibility manifest in their graduates, find their distinction in the nature of their program. They provide religious instruction and observance. A regular worship service, increasingly voluntary, is a normal part of their program. They are usually small, residential colleges, giving emphasis to close personal relationships as an essential ingredient of higher education. They place primary emphasis on their belief that there is a spirit which derives from religious sources that can and should underlie and motivate the entire life of the institution and its students. — *John R. Howard*

COLLOQUY The term " colloquy " is used to designate 3 things: a literary form for comment upon society; a formal conversation among a group of learned people; a collective inquiry.

The *Colloquies* of Erasmus, published in 1519, was a bitter satire in which good and evil alike were examined under the harsh light of destructive criticism. The book was one of the great humanistic contributions to the literature evoked by the Reformation. It set a standard of inquiry in which honesty was a criterion of judgment more highly regarded than either custom or kindness. The colloquies, as literary comment, became a standard means of inquiry into the usages of society.

As a formal conversation, the colloquy has a place on university campuses and in the societies of professional men and women. A colloquy between high-ranking seniors or graduate students and professors is an exciting event as ideas are explored and wits matched. During the meetings of a professional society a colloquy may be scheduled on some particular inquiry. In this case a paper may be presented by one member and then discussed by a panel and/or the total group.

The colloquy as a form of collective inquiry came into prominence in connection with the 13th annual meeting of the American Association for Adult Education in 1938. In a mood of self-inquiry the leaders of that association selected 7 questions through which an inventory of adult education and its social usefulness might be made. These questions were explored by a process of collective inquiry in advance of the meeting and in a series of discussions at the meeting. In the group sessions the leader, also known as the interlocutor, chose 2 or 3 from the audience to act as his associates in listening to the experts and in raising questions. A panel of staff or other experts spoke to each of the 7 questions, giving information as compiled from the inquiries of the society as a whole. The leader and his associates addressed their questions to both the panel and the audience. In a final session the findings and reactions were summarized.

Thus the colloquy combined research and the presentation and weighing of evidence in a forum-type meeting. Questions were introduced by a panel; and both questions and comments from the audience were encouraged. The technique in this instance assured a thorough presentation of the research material, and discussion that carefully weighed the evidence.

The unique contribution of this form of group discussion is the collective inquiry that precedes and accompanies the presentation of evidence. Taking the cue from Erasmus, it is honest inquiry that may make accepted customs or notions no longer tenable.

A local church school staff may wish to use the colloquy to explore the effectiveness of its work within an accepted framework of the goals of Christian education. Honesty and thoroughness demand that pupils (children, youth, and adults), parents of pupils, and the congregation at large be included in the inquiry.

An instrument of inquiry, such as a questionnaire or interview plan, should be developed so that experience, fact, and opinion can be recorded from the total body and compiled. A committee or panel will then present the results of the inquiry. A chairman with 2 or 3 associates can serve as a listening panel, receiving the report and directing questions to the first panel and to the larger listening group, with the purpose of challenging and weighing the evidence. Finally, the church school staff, its board, or the executive committee can summarize the inquiry in such a way as to make the findings useful in raising the quality of work.

The official body of a church may wish to examine its ministry to the community surrounding the church. Collective inquiry demands the inclusion of that community and others who serve that community in the study. A Bible class may wish to inquire into the current usage of the Bible among church families. Youth groups will find the methods of the colloquy a helpful technique for evaluating social customs and problems.

The procedure is thorough: broad inquiry among those who have the information; compiling, presenting, and weighing the evidence; summarizing the results of this process to make the conclusions available for group usage.

— *Mary Alice Douty Edwards*

COMENIUS, JOHN AMOS John Amos Comenius (1592–1670) is known as an educational pioneer, but otherwise is practically ignored. Nevertheless, his activity was many-sided. As bishop of the Unity of Czech Brethren he cared for his widely dispersed exiled flock; he

was among the first ecumenical leaders; he even strove to secure the inclusion of his homeland in the Peace of Westphalia and thus gain a possibility for the return of the proscribed Protestants. In most of these endeavors he failed. But the project to which he dedicated his life was pansophy — the integration of all scientific, philosophical, social, and religious knowledge into one all-embracing unity. He aimed at nothing less than universal education, unification of Christendom, the ultimate conversion of the world to Christ, and, through these means, universal peace. During his stay in England (1641–1642) he hoped to induce the Long Parliament to implement his schemes; when this project failed, he continued to work for its realization single-handed. He tried to do this by propounding his reforms in a 7-volume work, the *Consultatio*, actually begun in 1645. Only the first 2 volumes were published during his lifetime, and the stupendous work remained unfinished at his death. The incomplete sketches of his grandiose plans were to some degree completed or edited by his two disciples, Nigrin and Hartmann.

The crowning tragedy of Comenius' pansophic lifework was that the remaining 5 volumes were never published and, to all intents and purposes, were lost. It was not until sometime during 1935 to 1940 that Dmitry Chizhevsky found them at a library in Halle. Even so they have not been published except for *Pampaedia* (Universal Education) and *Panorthosia* (Universal Reform) in a Czech translation. Finally, in 1960, Chizhevsky himself published the first-named book in the Latin text with a German translation. It is this work to which alone we can devote our attention because of its importance for Christian education, since it represents Comenius' final theories on the subject. It does not wholly supersede his earlier *Great Didactic* and *The School of Infancy*, because of its incomplete form; nevertheless, it should henceforth be taken as representing the author's mature thinking. It extends his earlier educational system from 4 to 8 stages of training, actually spanning human education from the cradle to the grave. Its aim remains that of integrating all knowledge derived from the observation of nature (science) with the rational ordering of this knowledge by unified principles (philosophy), and combining these with the truths of revelation (Scriptural religion). This is to be accomplished through universal education by means of pansophy. In addition to kindergarten, elementary, secondary, and university education, Comenius now adds a prekindergarten stage and 3 other stages — the school of manhood (adult education), the school of old age, and the preparation for death. This lifetime training aims to make men intelligent for this world as well as for eternity. It is chiefly in his insistence on religion as a necessary component of any educational system worthy of the name that he differs from the Cartesian principles and from modern secular education. From the Christian point of view, it is to be regretted that Comenius' ideas did not prevail.

— *Matthew Spinka*

COMICS Comics trace their origin back to the gay illustrations for such poems as *Max und Moritz*, created by the German artist Wilhelm Busch almost 100 years ago. At the turn of the century they were introduced into American newspapers and were intended to amuse the adult readers and make them laugh. Since children liked them, it was obvious that others would appear, addressed directly to the young readers. The age of mass production gathered the strips and made them into "the comic-magazine industry." Many of today's comics are not funny, and do not pretend to be so. Some of the strips have subtle humor, but most of them are of nonsensical variety. Some comic magazines include bits of humor that are unimaginative or lacking in taste.

These magazines contain adventure, fantasy, magic, humor, and nonsense. Stories are about historical personalities, the West, history, current events, detectives, humanized animals, crime, and horror. A few of the leading publishers of comic books have advisory boards of educators and psychologists who set up standards for guidance as to the suitability of subject matter for different age groups. Some magazines carry seals of approval by alleged "comics code authorities."

In quality the comics differ widely. At the top are some that are justly famous. *Peanuts* contains humor that is both fresh and worldly-wise; *Li'l Abner* satirizes politics and big business; *Terry* fights for social justice; and many of Walt Disney's comics are delightful reading.

A large number of comic books deal with crime or at least with violence of one kind or another, including themes of murder, robbery, sex, lust, death. It is futile to count their number because some titles disappear and new ones come out constantly. Furthermore, some publishing firms function under different names for different books.

The *Superman* group of comic books deal with crime in a special way. Superman often defends the weak and fights juvenile delinquency. He defies the laws of gravity and overcomes the limitations of time and space. He is often accompanied and assisted by weird, alien beings, criminals and submen. The *Batman* and the *Aquaman* comics make aggression too easy and too colorful: they are praised by their advertisements as containing "the world's most famous crime fighters in thrilling action-packed adventures!" There are the female "supermen": *Supergirl, Wonder Woman,* and *Super Woman*. They either fly through the air scantily dressed or are uniformed and share the activities of force and violence of supermen. There are *Superboy* and the *Legion of Super-Heroes* who are able to leave the earth and invade the cosmic world.

In crime comics, violence is depicted for violence' sake. The criminal wins and evil is triumphant, or punishment takes the form of a violent end. In most of the crime comics, including the "harmless" ones, there is the constant motif of power or wealth or a strange combination of the two. A red-haired "dame" does all she can to steal the man from her girl friend; "cops" are despised because they interfere with someone's getting rich; exclusive totalitarian ambition is shown by Lother, who says, after killing Superman: "Only Superman stood between me and my great goal to rule this planet! Soon, I'll be king of the earth!"

A random sampling of plots shows how the imagination of the readers can be stretched to the extent that they are able to think in terms of being able to "shake hands with a shark" or "jitterbug with a mermaid," or to be "charged with the worst crime of overeating," to pick up an Amazon woman for a bride, and to break a lamp in order to be creative!

Average comic books have low artistic and literary standards. Some of the art is mediocre; a great deal of it is not only outrageously bad but sordid and vulgar. Furthermore, they are poor in style and language, and the spelling is often phonetic, for instance, "fer luck," "zat so?", "dis," "dat," "are ya?", "gonna," "oughtta." Some sounds such as "oww," "p-fft," "yiiiieee," "gaa," "eeeek," are not words at all. No doubt such material can harm the basic skills of reading and hinder aesthetic appreciation.

The comic is often difficult to read, for captions are crowded and the dialogue compressed into irregular lines in balloons. Reading comics may slow the development of the reading process and cause eyestrain.

The effects of comics on children is a controversial subject on which more research is needed. Whether or not picture strips can offer possibilities for education as well as pleasure is a subject that needs experimentation by educators.

— *Helen Khoobyar*

COMMUNICATION The word "communication" has become a familiar term in the vocabulary of Christian education only recently. Twenty years ago, a search in a library catalog for such titles as "The Communication of the Christian Faith" would have drawn a blank. The word was, of course, used whenever the "means" of communications received attention. But even the

Encyclopædia Britannica avoids giving the term a content connotation. It merely refers the reader to: railways, signaling, telegraph, telephone, broadcasting, heliograph, television, semaphore, Morse code, fathometer. These are the marvels of the means of communication of our time and deserve to be taken into the service of the church. But they are only " multiplication tools." They do not of themselves create the gospel to be communicated. They must be subjected to the judgment of the " god " they serve. " Shall the ax vaunt itself over him who hews with it, or the saw magnify itself against him who wields it? " (Isa. 10:15.)

If until recently the term " communication " found a niche only on the periphery of Christian education terminology, it may be in danger now of too broad a connotation. It is turning into almost a substitute for the word " evangelism." This shift has, to be sure, certain advantages. Much popular understanding of evangelism equates it with mere verbal proclamation, an evangelist being thought of as the speaker at a revivalist mass meeting. " Communication " has the great advantage of rescuing the church's ministry of winning converts or of nurturing the faithful from imprisonment in mere verbalism.

Indeed, one of the results already emerging in Christian education literature as the word " communication " comes into increasing use is the discovery of the almost limitless avenues that the Christian gospel has of making itself known — means that Christian education must take seriously into account. Communication is not a specialty in our common life. It is " the fundamental human fact " — as Hendrik Krae-

mer's *The Communication of the Christian Faith* reminds us. We communicate the faith or the religion we live by whether we intend this or not. The look in the eye with which we meet a fellow human being reveals whether we accept him as an equal or reject him as an inferior, or treat him as one of " the lesser breeds without the law." The mere endurance of " the other," especially if this includes the grace of listening in place of monopolistic monologue, is communication of love of neighbor. (See Harry A. DeWire, *The Christian as Communicator*, a volume in the Westminster Studies in Christian Communication, for full development of this theme.)

The helpful widening of the dimensions of the evangelizing and educational ministry of the church by way of exploring the limitless avenues of communication between man and man can receive many illustrations. Pioneers of evangelism in France have contributed a valuable triad of symbols which, if taken in order, give a clue to successful communication of the gospel for our time. The 3 terms are: presence, service, communication. Here " communication " still bears the imprint of " verbal proclamation." The full orb of communication, in its wider meaning, however, includes the other 2 — presence and service — which are accorded precedence. Verbal communication must first win the right to be heard. Far more costly steps in the ministry of communication may be presence, especially when this is a love-inspired walking with a neighbor a " second mile," and service, when this asks for no reward, not even that of grateful response.

Another helpful triad of terms

that illustrate the wide dimensions of communication when it is no longer limited to verbal impartation of " truths " or " doctrines " or textbook information (long-accepted as the normal concept of communication in Christian education dogma) is the triple series: proclamation (kerygma), fellowship (koinonia), and service (*diakonia*). Proclamation — what Kraemer calls " communication of " — has, in ultimate valuation, still primary ranking. The gospel is "news" and it must be verbally heralded. (Rom. 10:14-15.) But, as the triad discussed in the previous paragraph warns, verbal witnessing may have to await its turn. It must at least receive authentication in the " life together " (Bonhoeffer) of Christians in the fellowship of the Holy Spirit — what Kraemer calls " communication between." It must also receive witnessing reality in free service to and in the world.

Christian education has long been accorded a somewhat specialized vocation in the life of the church. It can profit from the opening of the wider horizons that the concept of " communication " brings to view. The humble church school teacher, anxious because of inadequate academic qualifications, can relax. She may be communicating the gospel of the incarnation and the cross better than the doctors of the schools. Someone has summarized that gospel in 2 words: " God cares." The ministry of " caring " may prove to be more effective for communicating God's revelation to mankind than textbook or learned lecture.

— *Theodore O. Wedel*

COMMUNITY AGENCIES A study of church history reveals that the church has always been at work to minister to the basic needs of persons. It is true that the church has been more effective at some periods in its history than at others. Charles Kemp has pointed out the stages of the churches' relationship to social service. First, the churches performed almost all the social service work; then there was a period of separation from such activities. Some of the services begun by the churches were taken over by other agencies and some were later dropped altogether. The trend now seems to be toward cooperation between the churches and the social agencies (*The Pastor and Community Resources*, p. 19).

One of the factors in the trend toward more cooperation between the churches and the social agencies is the phenomenal growth in the number and scope of social welfare agencies. The definition of a welfare agency or a community agency may vary from place to place. One authority identifies 3 major types of community agencies: (1) casework, primarily oriented in assistance to individuals; (2) group work, oriented in the understanding of what group experience can mean to the individual member (Boy and Girl Scouts, Y.W.C.A. and Y.M.C.A); (3) community organization for social welfare (Irwin T. Sanders, *The Community*, pp. 308–312). In the past the churches have found their most ready responses to the agencies included in the 2d type, group work. A trend may be noted in the churches' growing interest in the agencies included in the casework type. The emergence of a literature in the area of the education and guidance of exceptional persons may result in the establishment of a more direct relationship between the churches and the agencies that are able to give assistance at this point (the education of the gifted and the retarded, for example). The growth of individual counseling in the churches leads to the referral of persons to agencies best equipped to minister effectively to specific needs. The reorganization of the formal educational plan of the churches to include experiences outside the church itself results in a direct contact between the agencies and the churches (field trips, work camps, day camps, etc.).

There are also indications that the churches are playing an increasingly vital role in a "community organization for social welfare," the 3d major type of community agency listed by Sanders. The interest of the churches in community betterment and their concern for the welfare of all persons has led them to take more direct responsibility in the establishment of such agencies and to contribute leadership to them.

In addition to the 3 types of community agencies (casework, group work, and community organization), there is the division made between public and private agencies. The churches have more often worked cooperatively with privately supported agencies than with the tax-supported agencies. The system of voluntary contributions as the means of support used both by the churches and the privately supported agency provides a more natural basis for cooperation.

Whether the cooperation of the churches with the community agencies means primarily the support of such agencies or goes farther and includes the use of their resources as well as provision of leadership in them, the churches should not lose sight of their unique service in the community of persons. Although the churches seek to carry out their function in part through their educational programs, they will also seek to utilize every resource in the community that can be helpful in that task. (See Charles F. Kemp, *The Pastor and Community Resources,* especially pp. 34 ff., for a "Handbook of Agencies and Resources.")

Some basic principles to follow are these: (1) The churches must know the other agencies serving people in the community. One or more churches may carry out a community survey to ascertain and define the services that are available. (2) The churches must evaluate their educational plan. Are there places in the educational plan where the services of existing community agencies would be beneficial? (3) The churches must be responsible in their relationships with community agencies. The professional ethics of all groups and persons must be respected and followed. (4) The churches must be flexible in their cooperation with community agencies. Constant reevaluation of plan and program, consistent with the aims of community agencies, is necessary and desirable. (5) The churches must maintain their own integrity. When the motives and ends of the agency are not in keeping with those of the churches, other resources should be found.

The fact that we are attempting to provide Christian education for persons in a community leads us to seek to bring to bear all the positive influences in that community upon the task. Although it may seem strange to extend the plan of Christian education to utilize more community services provided by both public and private agencies, such may well be a means of grace heretofore hidden.

— *Marcus D. Bryant*

CONFERENCE The conference has become an important technique in the work of the church. Its rapid rise to prominence in the 20th century roughly parallels the modern Christian education movement.

Coming from the Latin *confero*, the word means " to walk beside " or " bring together " in thought, to compare, consult, confer, deliberate, talk over, and advise with. A conference is a meeting for serious consultation or discussion. Christian educators find these definitions perfectly acceptable, since they aptly describe their use of the term " conference."

In the early 1900's conferences were held at summer conference grounds such as Lake Chautauqua, N.Y., on college campuses, and at camp-meeting sites. Interdenominational summer programs began at Lake Geneva, Wis., in 1914. These early meetings, generally referred to as " camps," were for the most part conferences or institutes held in camping situations. Actually, the primary difference between the conference movement and the related and/or subsequent camping movement lies in the emphasis on training and study for leadership in the church. Learning, information study, serious discussion under the guidance of trained leaders, inspiration, and motivation for service have been characteristic purposes of the conference. Group living, a significant but secondary factor, has added to the enrichment of the lives of those attending. A conference may be held at almost any place and in any season.

The flourishing youth movements in the early years of the 20th century brought conferences into prominence. Although such experiences actually began with interdenominational groups (e.g., United Christian Youth Movement conferences), they were quickly adopted by most of the denominations.

The conference movement for youth has played an important role in Protestantism in our country and has made a tremendous impact upon America's church life. Many young people who participated in this kind of learning process are now rendering conspicuous service in Christian education and in the general work of the church. In the writer's *Study of Directors of Christian Education of the Disciples of Christ in the United States* the conference was 3d in the list of primary factors influencing the persons to choose their vocation, and 6th among secondary factors.

In more recent years the adult conference has become a familiar, popular, and useful procedure in Christian education. Numerous adults are brought together each year by denominations and interdenominational groups. Professional churchmen and lay leaders learn, study, share, and discuss vital areas of the church's concern.

The church should consider conference in whatever form it may be found to be an extension of its own educational program. Care must be taken in the selection of those attending, since they represent the church. Persons must be prepared in advance so that they will understand the program they are attending and identify the kinds of learning they should bring back. Adequate financial backing and provision of proper leadership must be included as a part of the church's responsibility.

The church should also be prepared to utilize the new enthusiasm, knowledge, and skills, as well as the devotion, of the persons who have attended the conference.

— *Gentry A. Shelton*

CONFESSION OF SIN Confession of sin is an act performed by the man of faith as a result of his awareness of his individual humanness and his linkage with the common humanity of the world of persons. This act is directed toward God. It is centered upon God and is made meaningful to the person because of his faith in that God who not only is able to forgive but desires to forgive because of his self-giving love, mercy, and justice.

Confession of sin is implicit in man's recognition of his spiritual sonship with God. This assumption includes the fact that man finds his completion, his selfhood, in God. Man is completed when he emotionally, rationally, and volitionally says, "I believe in God," and recognizes the personal relationship of his spirit to the personal Spirit of God.

The act of man's confession of sin assumes man's feeling of dependence upon God. He realizes that dependence is essential to a continuing relationship. Man realizes also that the very moment the feeling of dependence is not present, assertion of the human self becomes dominant.

Therefore, a meaningful definition of sin that it is the assertion of the human self over against the sovereignty and will of God. Sin is rooted in man's freedom rather than in any inherent natural depravity, since no natural depravity or moral impotence prevents man's response of faith and obedience to God as re-

vealed in Jesus Christ. Original sin may be described as the universal tendency of man's freedom toward self-assertion.

When man performs the act of confession of sin he is acknowledging his human condition as well as affirming his faith in a loving and forgiving God and recognizing his constant dependence upon the personal relationship between man and God.

Confession of sin includes 2 general aspects. The 1st general aspect is man's admission of his sinful nature because he is human and shares the human condition of all men. This is the need of all men; by his nature he is not able to forgive himself. Because of his common humanness, man recognizes his condition as different from that of divine existence and therefore is dependent upon God, the divine Being, for forgiveness.

The 2d general aspect included in confession of sin is man's acknowledgment of his personal humanity. This is intended to describe the fact that every individual is a unique special creation in time. This is readily understood when the observable personality of an individual is considered in the light of personal existence and unique environment. However, because every man is uniquely personal through God's creation of the human spirit in time, he stands in a position of personal responsibility and dependence before God. In other words, no one can manage someone else's personal relationship with God. In the same way, every individual is responsible for his unique human condition before God.

Just as there are 2 general aspects of the confession of sin, there are 2 particular aspects embraced within man's confession of sin.

The 1st particular aspect is man's acknowledgment of those times when self sets itself over against God's sovereignty in personal life: his personal sins, including what he does that he ought not to do as well as what he does not do that he ought to do. These sins may be described in specific terms such as " envy," " greed," " strife," " forgetfulness," "selfishness," "self-centeredness," and " dishonesty." Their observable expression is seen as being committed against man, but their expression is really against God when examined in the context of man's self-assertion against God. Confession of one's sin necessarily includes these specific acts, the ones of which man is aware as well as those actions of which he may be unaware.

Confession of sin includes a 2d particular aspect. Reference is made here to those specific acts of self-assertion which are committed by mankind as a whole. They are often described as social sins and are shared by all persons because of their social and cultural interrelatedness. Among such sins are prejudice, strife, murder, dependence on power, reliance on the domination of a particular political order, and insensitivity. Although individuals may be free personally from these social sins, all share in their nature through their life in an interconnected social order.

Confession of sin is a religious act of man, a manifestation of his faith. It is evidence of man's belief in God, the ultimate Spirit who exists in relation to all men. Redemption for man is made possible by his free response to God's love and mercy. Since redemption is a continuous process, it is sustained and nur-

tured by man's continuous confession of his sins.

Man is enabled to become aware of his sinful condition through knowledge of the life of Jesus Christ. This is God's Son who lived as the God-man among men. Because Jesus Christ did not stand in need of redemption, he is Savior for all men, the Savior of the world. Therefore, confession of sin is acknowledgment and appeal made by man to God through Jesus Christ for his common humanity, his personal self-assertion, his personal malperformed responsibility, and his shared social guilt. — *Lester C. Rampley*

CONFIRMATION Confirmation is the name some Christian groups give to the rite admitting adherents to the full responsibilities and privileges of church membership.

As it developed in the patristic age, Baptism, administered chiefly to adult converts after lengthy instruction as catechumens, was a complex rite. By the mid-3d century in the West, some of the ceremonies connected with Baptism were detached and gradually shaped into a separate rite. One reason was that men (e.g., Tertullian) began to regard the effect of baptism as chiefly negative, the washing away of sin; the anointing with consecrated oil (chrism) conferred the positive gift of the Spirit. Hence, confirmation came to be considered the " completion " of baptism. The West reserved confirmation to the bishop; in the East the priest administered it with oil consecrated by the bishop.

Infant baptism, meanwhile, had become general practice. It was and still is customary in the East to confirm infants directly after Baptism, and to administer Communion immediately thereafter. In the West, infant confirmation persisted into the Reformation Era, but from the 12th century the tendency grew to defer confirmation until "years of discretion," variously set between 7 and 14; since 1931 the Roman Church has fixed the minimum age at 7.

Thomas Aquinas expresses the developed medieval conception: "In this sacrament the Holy Spirit is given for strength in the spiritual combat"; the sign of the cross with chrism and the light blow on the cheek in the confirmation rite correspond to the sign of a soldier's allegiance. The sacrament confers sanctifying grace "for growth and stability in righteousness"; "it imparts an indelible character," viz., fortitude to confess Christ's name, and therefore must not be repeated. Confirmation is not directly tied to instruction in the faith.

As the medieval church and its parish life deteriorated, critics re-examined the church's system. Waldensians (late 12th century) required instruction before confirmation. Wycliffe and Hus censured the mechanical character of current sacramental practice, and questioned the grounding of confirmation upon inferences from Christ's promise of the Spirit (John 16:7; Luke 24:49) and from the connection of unction (I John 2:20, 27), the seal (II Cor. 1:21 f.), and the laying on of hands (Acts 8:14 ff.) with the gift of the Spirit. The Bohemian Brethren (15th century), considering infant baptism salutary only when a personal confession later confirmed it, reoriented confirmation toward full congregational participation and admission to the Eucharist. Emphasizing the subjective factor over the sacramental, the humanist Erasmus advocated instruction to

strengthen the child's will to a personal renewal of his baptismal covenant.

Luther denied that confirmation was a sacrament; it was not unquestionably instituted by Christ. Moreover, Baptism is perfect in itself, as God's adoption of sons — his overcoming of our alienation and his promise to guide his children. All our Christian life is a "return to our Baptism." Hence, confirmation can be no "supplement" or "completion" of Baptism. Luther early commended a congregational rite of confirmation, but he did not promote it. He did insist, however, that without a "minimum of knowledge" one should not be admitted to the Lord's Supper.

Martin Bucer, meanwhile, was the father of Protestant and Anglican confirmation. In his Hessian church orders (1538–1539), confirmation involved: (1) renewal of the baptismal vow after instruction (Erasmian emphasis); (2) the congregation's intercession for God's blessing (Luther's emphasis on God's act); (3) the laying on of hands as the expression of blessing (Bucer was willing to call it a "sacramental ceremony"); (4) admission to the Lord's Supper; (5) acceptance of the congregation's loving discipline. However, little harmony in the interpretation and practice of confirmation prevailed in Germany before the era of Pietism.

Many of the Continental Reformed churches retained confirmation, making instruction, admission to Communion, and acceptance of church discipline the decisive features. Reformed churches of Holland, Switzerland, and France still practice a lengthy instruction and confirmation in middle or late adolescence. Lutheran and Reformed

churches both tended to turn catechization into elaborate theological
courses. Anabaptists, meanwhile,
took up Erasmus' concern for a personal profession of faith, but applied
it to adult baptism, discarding confirmation.

The Roman Catholic Council of
Trent (1545–1563) was reticent
about confirmation, simply insisting
on traditional features and asserting
that Christ instituted all the sacraments. Protestant successes, however, stimulated the Roman Catholics to strong efforts in popular
instruction.

The Anglican Reformers retained
confirmation, not as a dominical
sacrament but as a ratification of the
baptismal vow after suitable instruction in the faith. With the laying on
of hands, "the bishop, in the name
of the church, doth invocate the
Holy Ghost to give strength and
constancy, with other spiritual gifts"
(Cranmer). Thereupon, the person
confirmed was admitted to Communion. The Restoration and especially
the 19th-century Anglo-Catholic
movement revived the emphasis
upon the sacramental character of
confirmation.

English Puritans and Scottish
Presbyterians replaced confirmation
with a ceremony of admission to
church membership. Intensely concerned for personally experiencing
God's grace and understanding
God's will, most Puritans zealously
fostered catechization in home and
church. Pietism similarly arose on
the Continent, in the late 17th century, to revive the emphasis on personal commitment in Christian life.
Under Philipp Spener's inspiration,
confirmation now became normative
throughout Lutheranism, exalted,
however, somewhat at the expense
of baptism as emphasis was laid on

the vow of a pious life, though the
learning of elaborate "orders of
salvation" was meant to provide an
objective foundation. When the
Enlightenment displaced Pietism,
confirmation was commonly viewed
as a ratification of baptismal initiation and a graduation from religious
schooling.

John Wesley generally retained
Anglican doctrinal standards, but
required for church membership
only a personal profession of faith.
Hence, in revising the Prayer Book
for American Methodists he omitted
the order for confirmation. As
Puritanism in America gradually
disintegrated, revivalism arose, especially among Baptists, Methodists,
Disciples, and some Presbyterians, to
generate conversions and a warm
piety. These came to be regarded as
the proper basis for church membership, especially on the American
frontier, and displaced or at least
dominated programs of religious
instruction. The most notable 19th-
century challenge to the revivalist
outlook came from Congregationalist
Horace Bushnell, who suggested a
versatile church program of nurture
continuing from infancy on in order
that young people eventually would
"assume the covenant in their own
choice."

At present few if any communions
profess to be altogether clear about
the relations between baptism, personal conversion, instruction, and
churchly responsibility. Roman Catholicism, especially from Pius X's
time (1905), has intensified its catechetical ("Christian doctrine")
program, and a currently influential
movement exalts confirmation as
active incorporation into the "general priesthood of the faithful" or
"lay apostolate." Anglicans have
recently embarked on a thorough

official review of baptism and confirmation. Presbyterians speak of "confirmation of baptismal vows and admission to the Lord's Supper," though some prefer the expression "reception into full membership." Many revivalist churches increasingly cultivate "preparation for church membership" (or baptism), although retaining the emphasis on individual conversion. In recent mergers crossing denominational lines, such as the United Church of Canada (1925) and the United Church of Christ in America (1957), it seems that the influence of traditions more strongly emphasizing confirmation generally prevails, though in the Church of South India (1947) the Anglican practice has not been required. Perhaps the most urgent current rethinking is being done by German Lutherans, who face a basic rebuilding of church life, especially in East Germany, where communist authorities have promoted "youth dedications" deliberately to supplant Lutheran confirmation. Lutherans there have responded with a flexible "Christian doctrine" program where the old system can no longer survive. A conference in 1957 thoroughly examined this and other problems: whether youth congregations may be a partial answer to the crisis of the geographical parish system; whether a vow of faithfulness is not premature in early adolescence; whether admission to the Lord's Supper should not be granted earlier and the catechization prolonged later than at present — indeed, extended after confirmation. Agreement remained, however, that confirmation is a strengthening of the work God began in baptism rather than a supplement to baptism.

— *Robert H. Fischer*

CONFUCIANISM Confucianism is the name commonly given to one of the three teachings (*chiao*) traditionally reverenced by the Chinese. In a narrow sense Confucianism refers to the ideas and practices of Confucius himself, but in broader usage it pertains to the system of thought, ritual practice, and ethical behavior that grew up in Han times and later, and but little of which, in fact, originated with Confucius.

Confucius, or Master Kung, was born in the tiny state of Lu, situated in the Shantung Peninsula, ca. 551 B.C. Born into the minor nobility, he was a knight or *shih*, trained in the military arts of archery and horseback riding. By his day the feudal system of the early Chou rulers had progressed far in degeneration, and China had become a vast battleground for rival states and petty rulers. Life in this period, for the aristocracy as well as the peasantry, was marked by violence, intrigue, instability, and general difficulty.

Confucius reacted powerfully to the condition of his society, and the whole of his thought and effort was bent to setting it right. His controlling conviction was that men need not live in conflict but can and should live in harmony and peaceful cooperation. The condition requisite for realizing the ideal state of society is virtue in those who rule. Another basic conviction was that virtue is contagious. Confucius believed that if virtue is induced in those responsible for the state, it will reproduce itself in the lower orders of society and so transform social life. Confucius did not claim that his teachings were new conceptions but, rather, saw himself as the transmitter of ancient values, the restorer of a neglected order. Furthermore, Confucius was no mere theoretician, for he actively sought public office where he might put his views into practice, although the fact seems to be that he was never able to attain office except for a brief period.

In the 2 centuries after Confucius' death (approximately 479 B.C.) there emerged a Confucian school, consisting of men who held ideas attributed to Confucius and opposed by schools upholding other principles. For some time, rivalry among these schools was intense, and the Confucians did not triumph and consolidate their position until Han times.

The chief characteristics of the developed Confucian system are as follows: (1) A legend concerning Confucius that represents him as the fabulously learned sage, philosopher, author and editor of the Confucian classics, magician, successful statesman, and even deity. Along with sacrifices to other spirits and deities, the Chinese state cult offers sacrifices to Confucius and his ancestors. (2) The possession of a literature that serves as supreme authority in religion, politics, and morality. The literature consists of the Five Canonical Books (*King*) plus the Four Books of Chinese classics (*Shu*); all are associated with Confucius, who was believed to be the compiler of some and the author of others, while the remainder were written by disciples. Since Han times the literature has formed the basis of traditional education in China, and especially of the education of civil servants. (3) The elaboration of a monistic philosophy, positing as the first principle a Great Ultimate. This principle, the origin of all things, has both a passive and an active aspect, called *Yin* and *Yang* respectively. From the interaction and union of the 2 has proceeded the universe as we know it. (4) A state cultus having one of the most elaborate series of ritual observances ever known. The 2 chief annual ceremonies, devoted to the worship of heaven and earth, were conducted in the capital by the emperor at midwinter and midsummer. (5) An ethical system in which filial piety is the cardinal virtue. Ethically responsible conduct was thought to consist in observing the "five relationships"—between father and son, elder brother and younger brother, ruler and subject, husband and wife, elder and junior.

— *Charles J. Adams*

CONSTRUCTIVE ACTIVITIES In religious education there are 2 general types of constructive activity.

A. The construction or building of a specific item or project as a part of a course of study being used with a specific age group, the planning, research, and execution being carried out together by the students and teacher. The students are first motivated by understanding what they are doing and why, visualizing the results through setting desired goals. The individual is involved in the project through persistence in carrying out a plan of action. Action is followed by an evaluation by all who have been active in any way with the project. This type of constructive activity draws in every member of the group. For example, junior high students who make clay models of the heads of early church fathers, or of Luther, Calvin, and Wesley, as a part of their study of the history of the Christian church, will be able to do so with more understanding after they have studied the life, writings, and historical backgrounds of these persons. The senior high students can plan, plant, and care for a Palestinian garden in the churchyard. This garden then would be a means of helping not only their own class but all the members of the church school, who could then recognize and know the names of flowers and plants mentioned in the Bible.

B. The 2d type of constructive activity common to religious education is the assembling of handwork. It is created and developed by the teacher, the editors of the curriculum, or a commercial company, rather than by the persons who do the work. The purpose of the activity differs from that of the 1st type in that the end product or the finished model is the main interest, not the development of the student through the experience. The finished object is used as a teaching device to illustrate some specific point or make possible an explanation too difficult to understand without its use. As an example of handwork, a teacher can use a picture map of Palestine, with houses to be cut, folded, and pasted. Another type would be a kit of materials to make the items referred to in Ex., ch. 25, the Tabernacle and the Ark of Covenant. Using materials provided, the students set up the inner and outer courts, and place the colored pieces of cloth, as directed, over the Tabernacle. This tabletop model would then be used to study the Exodus passage, not only by the group assembling the model, but by others who would later be making a study of the same passage. The activity or handwork packet also conforms to this type of constructive activity. The patterns are to be filled in with color, cut, and used in a specific way, as directed by the editors or publishers of the activity. The danger of this ready-prepared activity is that it becomes an end in itself and does not require thought or planning on the part of the learner. Using the activity as a crutch results in ineffective learning, for mere busywork does not accomplish the real objectives of the unit of study. A student may have some satisfaction at the completion of a preplanned activity, but it is short-lived, since he has not put much of himself into its construction. The activity contributes little to thinking, to knowledge of the Bible, or to teaching the manner of God's action through his creative Spirit.

Constructive activities are a valuable part of religious education if special consideration is given to the following: A child's development in artistic expression parallels his growing and understanding; activities should therefore be suited to the age of the person involved.

Participation is better in small groups than in large. A group of 4 to 7 members provides opportunity for each person to work at his own rate and to make individual contributions in the way most satisfactory to himself. A small group also gives an opportunity for each one to experience success as he gains a feeling of his own worth. Working as a creative member of a group helps to build an understanding of the Kingdom of God on earth and the church as the body of Christ.

The leader of a constructive activity must realize it is not the completed activity that is most important, but the thinking and religious growth that takes place during the activity itself.

There should be involvement of both pupil and teacher. The best activities are those in which the answers are found together and the thinking is shared. The leader's position is not that of "manipulator of persons." Christian citizenship requires a well-rounded individual who is alert to new ideas, ready to face difficult problems and who can be both a leader and follower.

A teacher or leader knows that a student needs guidance, without which his frustrations may lead to discouragement and resistance to creative effort. It takes time to experience the emotionally satisfying feeling that comes from the completion of something into which a person has put a portion of himself.

Activity often finds its most meaningful expression in the situations where persons learn not only skills and information, but are given an opportunity to learn to meet demands that are unforeseeable and inevitable. This can strengthen the student's faith in himself and in the dependability of others, and create a deep awareness of God, who has planned and understands growth and change. — *Maurine V. Paas*

CONVERSATION To teach religion through the medium of conversation is not without precedent. Buddha, Socrates, and Jesus apparently did some of their most effective teaching as they talked informally with people. Closer to our own times, Bronson Alcott, in his short-lived experimental school, shocked 19th-century Boston by teaching religion to children through "conversation on the Gospels."

The method is not unrelated to the message. Teaching through conversation is peculiarly appropriate to the teacher who has been forced by his own experience to question old ideas and practices and to experiment with new ones. It is a method for the prober, the gadfly, the pioneer. It is a method for the teacher who knows he must himself always be a learner.

The method of conversation demands certain things of the teacher who uses it. He must know something about the persons with whom he wishes to communicate. For example, in order to talk with small children about the miracle of birth, it is important to know whether these children have yet reached a point in their development when they can distinguish between something alive and something not alive. Significant communication depends on rather detailed knowledge of where the learner is developmentally.

Communication is also facilitated by knowing where he is existentially. A conversation about babies will have far more meaning to a child who has a baby at home than it will to a child who has no immediate experience with babies. A conversation about death will strike a man who has just buried his father with far greater impact than it will a man who has not passed through this particular crisis.

The conversational method of teaching makes still another demand on the teacher. He must really care about whatever it is he is seeking to communicate. If there is nothing he cares about very much, there is nothing he can effectively teach. The great teachers have always been those who could not help telling others about those insights which first transformed them.

There are several advantages in using this method. After a sermon, a lecture, or even a storytelling session, a teacher may go away wondering whether anyone present "got anything" out of it all. But the teacher who has carried on a conversation has a kind of built-in check on his own efficacy.

Through an occasional question, invitations for comment, or other give-and-take, an even moderately sensitive person can know with sometimes painful certainty whether he has succeeded in establishing contact and to what extent he was able to maintain it. He can know also when he has been at it long enough.

Another advantage of the method is that learning through conversation almost necessarily moves in 2 directions, enriching both the learner and the teacher. Although the teacher often brings to the conversation new ideas, awareness of relationships among ideas, a longer perspective in time and a wider horizon in space, the learner, especially when he is a child, brings a freshness of perspective, a frankness of response, and an originality of ideas that most adults have lost.

What makes a conversation religious? One element would seem to be the degree of communication among the participants. When we have really helped others see what we see, feel what we feel, know what we know, or when we are able to let others know that we care about something they care about, it is felt to be a religious experience.

The method of conversation can be particularly moving when used with children. They are so spontaneous in their responses that when a moment of real communication is achieved their comments or even their facial expressions afford a sensitive adult an experience of communion.

Another factor that seems to give a conversation its religious quality is the basic and universal character of the vision glimpsed. When, through a conversation, one of the great themes of the human drama — birth, death, joy, or sorrow — is made real to us, we know that we have moved into the level of the religious. Or when some aspect of this miraculous stage on which the human drama is played is spotlighted for us in a sensitively led conversation, we know that we have been involved in religious education. — *Edith F. Hunter*

CONVERSION Conversion means, basically, a turning round, but an adequate definition would include also such ideas as transposition, inversion, transmutation, adaptation, change. By religious conversion is meant the process by which an individual consciously adopts a religious philosophy and commits himself to the way of life demanded by it.

In Biblical thought, in both Old and New Testaments, the emphasis is on man's turning to God in repentance and faith. Prophets and apostles called men to conversion. In later times conversion has come to be associated with the Christian doctrine of regeneration, or the new birth, though there is no uniform opinion as to how the 2 are related. Some consider that conversion is man's response to God's act of regeneration, others that regeneration is God's response to man's turning, whereas still others regard the terms " conversion " and " regeneration " as synonymous, being but different expressions for the one experience of a man's realization of his acceptance by God. Some tend to use mystical language and describe conversion as an individual's " dying and rising again " with Christ. There is no very clearly formulated theology of conversion. Sometimes conversion is thought of in developmental terms that cover any phase or the whole process of the individual's religious growth, and sometimes it is conceived in narrower terms to include but one type of evangelical experience. Generally it is acknowledged that conversion involves a turning from and a turning to — from irreligion to religion, from one religion to another or from one theological position to another, from evil ways to ways of righteousness, or from self to God.

In its broadest sense conversion is not necessarily or essentially a religious experience. Moral transformations sometimes take place without the aid of religious stimuli, and conversions away from religion are not unknown. William Sargent has drawn attention to the similarities between some forms of religious conversion and brainwashing. But one fact is certain: religious conversion as a psychological process is a natural and not an unnatural phenomenon. It may take as many forms as human need dictates. For some it involves the recentering of life's dominant interests. For some it is the acceptance of a new loyalty, as when a person yields and dedicates himself to a life of religious devotion and service. For others it is a rebirth, or the discovery of a way of release, or a form of spiritual enlightenment and deepening religious insight, or a moral transformation, or some other form of self-realization. In psychological language a particular conversion, or a phase or aspect of a particular conversion, may be described in terms of sublimation, transference, and acceptance of a style of life. Thus, according to circumstances, and in keeping with the personality and needs of the subject, a conversion may ap-

pear to be predominantly either (1) intellectual — the acceptance of a new idea or a new understanding of an old idea; or (2) emotional — the birth of a new and dominating affection; or (3) moral — the confession of failure and the reorientation of the will in respect to its dominant aims for life. In all conversions there is a blending of intellectual, emotional, and volitional factors, but these tend to manifest themselves in different ways and degrees in the varying experiences of different individuals.

Most writers on conversion tend to delineate 2 types of conversion experience — the "sudden" and the "gradual." These are useful descriptions but hardly adequate for accurate psychological treatment. Experience shows that there are various forms of sudden and of gradual conversion; indeed, it is not inaccurate to affirm that there are as many forms of the conversion experience as there are converted persons. Conversions occur at all ages, but the experience is characteristically a phenomenon of adolescence. From a comprehensive survey of the findings of various research workers in this field, it seems safe to say that the majority of conversions occur between the years of 15 to 19. This is important, for adolescence is the age of decisions, and it is at this age that most candidates come forward for communicant relationship. This is not to say that conversions do not occur in later life or that they are not so important when they do occur. Indeed, some of the most striking conversions have occurred in adult life; and some observers are of the opinion that conversions in middle life are more frequent now than they used to be, though there is at present no statistical evidence for this. An interesting fact is that in many adult conversions there is a return to childhood experiences, with a revival of childhood memories and the emergence of a child-like faith.

All this has an important bearing upon religious education. It is an acknowledged fact that the influence of early upbringing is the most potent factor in religious development. Experimental studies have shown that the Christian home, the Sunday school, church attendance, and membership in the church youth group are ranked by adult Christians as the most important influences in their religious development. It is also found that the majority of adult Christians continue, not only in the denomination, but in the particular theological school of thought within the denomination in which they were brought up. Furthermore, it has been demonstrated by empirical study that individuals tend to pass through the religious experiences that they have been taught to expect. Thus the incidence of openly professed conversions is higher in those churches where the need for conversion is stressed than in those churches where teaching on conversion is less prominent. And when this is linked with another contemporary empirical finding, namely, that conversions are confined almost entirely to those who are already within the Christian fold or who have, at least in their early days, been nurtured in the faith, the potent influence of upbringing and indoctrination is clearly demonstrated. This is not to discredit conversion or any other religious affection, so as to regard it as nothing but an experience of the expected, but it does emphasize the importance of the role of the Christian educator, whether parent, teacher, or pastor.

The current interest in, and emphasis on, Christian nurture is highly relevant here, for it is evident that religious development follows the pattern of general human development. First, in early childhood, the individual passes through a period of simple credulity, when he believes all that he is taught to believe. Then comes the period of intellection, during which the growing child begins to reflect upon the meaning of what he has been taught. Then follows a process either of acceptance and personal commitment, during which he internalizes the ideas and identifies himself with the ideals that were earlier presented to him; or rejection, when he breaks away from or rejects the ideas he has been taught; or modification, in which he selects from what he has learned, adapts it to his growing personal needs, and thus creates for himself the pattern of a new orientation.

It is here that the importance of religious education becomes apparent, for it is clear that the quality of the religious life of a generation is to a very large degree dependent upon the atmosphere in which it was reared and the kind of teaching to which its members were exposed. If the purpose of instruction is to impart wisdom as distinct from multiplying knowledge, then the religious educator has a unique function to perform. He will see the whole of life as a training school for character. He will not be content merely to impose dogmas and creeds upon the credulous under his care, nor will he try to press them into a stereotyped pattern of experience; he will be concerned, rather, to guide them into the way of wisdom so that they may find their own way to fulfillment. — *Owen Rupert Brandon*

COOPERATIVE PUBLICATION ASSOCIATION

The Cooperative Publication Association, generally referred to in interdenominational circles as CPA, is a voluntary, autonomous association of denominational publishers, editors, and professional age-group educators. The Association came into existence in 1946 as a merger of the Leadership Training Publishing Association (whose purpose was the preparation and publishing of leadership training textbooks for use in interdenominational schools) and the Committee of Nine (organized to develop and publish textbooks for use in interdenominational vacation and weekday schools of religion). Working very closely at first with the International Council of Religious Education, and since the formation of the National Council of the Churches of Christ in the U.S.A. with the Commission on General Christian Education, the Association expanded its charter to include the provision " for the publication and promotion of those curriculum and other materials which may be desired by the denominations cooperating within the structure of the National Council of the Churches of Christ in the U.S.A. . . . The CPA considers that its purpose is to provide the facility for any publication needed to implement (as distinguished from the promoting of) the programs of the several commissions and/or departments of the NCCCUSA."

The Association is composed of 6 publishers, 3 editors, and representatives from the NCCCUSA committees on children's work (vacation and weekday), youth work, adult work, administration and leadership education, and camps and conferences. They are elected for a term of 3 years and may succeed themselves. A nominating committee, composed of persons not members of CPA and representing the different activities of the Division, submits annually the names of 5 persons who are officially employed by a denominational board of Christian education or a publishing house to CPA. The CPA recognizes that participation of staff members of the Commission on General Christian Education is essential to its work, and provides for their active participation.

The Association meets annually in November, delegating to its executive committee the responsibility for carrying on the work of CPA between meetings. The Publishing Committee meets more frequently to determine publishing policies, mechanical specifications of publication, royalty rates, and manuscript fees, contractual arrangements with denominational publishers for printing the manuscripts made available, advertising and promotion, and such other business arrangements as may be necessary for sound operation.

The work of CPA is carried on by 5 standing committees, representing various aspects of the Christian education program. The function of these committees is to receive and examine descriptions originating from committees of the Commission on General Christian Education and other recommendations for publications, secure authors, appoint reviewing denominations and State Councils, and make final recommendations to CPA. The Publishing Committee then assigns the publication to a publisher, whose responsibility it is to carry through on the publication and see that the specifications and recommendations for the particular text are properly carried out.

All promotional materials, which are quite extensive, are offered gratis to all denominational boards of Christian education and publishing houses in quantities needed for their constituencies, and to non-denominational bookstores that would like to handle the publications in conformity with CPA procedures and policies.

CPA publications are identified by an official statement appearing on the flyleaf of each publication: "Published for the Cooperative Publication Association by . . ."
— *Fred E. McQueen*

CORE CURRICULUM The core curriculum is one of the significant attempts to develop a qualitative program of general education. It is usually defined as a program of fused or correlated courses concerned with the problems of youth. The themes or problems studied are most often selected from within a flexible framework of designated course content and are developed by cooperative planning in which pupils play an active role. Pupils are taught to draw upon varied resources as they attempt to develop a solution; skills of problem-solving, research, reporting, and individual and class evaluation are stressed. Most core programs emphasize the development of citizenship in a democratic environment, as well as the interrelation or correlation of compatible subject areas such as English and social studies or, less often, science and mathematics.

Core curriculum classes are more flexible and more pupil-centered than traditional courses. The subject matter to be studied is usually organized into units that include statements regarding objectives, content outline, activities, bibliographical sources, and evaluation procedures. Skills are developed as they are essential to the correctness and competence with which pupils work with certain concepts and functions, though most core programs go beyond functional applications and evident need. Individual and group guidance is an essential aspect of the core class, relating to the personal needs and interest patterns of the pupils; problems may be incorporated into individualized reading, expository and creative writing, individual conferences, group discussion, and evaluation. Scope and sequence considerations emphasize pupil maturity, background, and experience, as well as logical subject-matter sequences.

The core curriculum has been most popular at the junior high level where it is called unified studies, basic education, "block" classes, or common learnings. Such programs are generally regarded as a transitional step between the self-contained elementary classroom and the highly departmentalized senior high schools. Likewise, the core emphasis on behavioral growth is especially appropriate at this age level. Classes usually meet for 2 or more class periods and combine or replace 2 or more required subjects.

The historical origins of core curriculum depend in part upon the aspect being considered. For example, one branch developed from the work of Herbart and of Ziller, who proposed ways of integrating subject matter to remedy the fragmenting that resulted from the division of disciplines into proliferating studies and courses. By concentrating upon one area and relating another (e.g., history and geography), each subject was to be made richer in meaning and more interesting to the learner.

Impetus was given another facet of the core curriculum by the ideas of Froebel, the Gestaltists, and the progressive education movement. In this development, emphasis was placed upon the needs and interests of pupils as the integrating and motivating agency rather than upon the content per se. Subsequently, the Eight-Year (or Thirty Schools) Study indicated that pupils in such experimental programs did as well or better than those in conventional programs.

Recent research and experimentation have contributed to significant data that support certain features of the core curriculum concept. Studies regarding self-concept indicate the importance of each person's being in a group that accepts him. Programmed learning gives promise of freeing the teacher from certain drill functions, making possible more class time devoted to values and to central issues. The recitation method is recognized as a much less productive teaching-learning act than discussions involving reflective or critical thinking. Teachers and students are being encouraged to discover concepts and generalizations regarding certain content areas. Studies indicate the importance of methods that are consistent with and implicit in the structure of the discipline being considered. Interdisciplinary studies are becoming more common as it is recognized that a real problem does not confine itself to a single subject area.

The procedures and objectives identified with the core curriculum concept have applications in many fields. The worthwhile development of each individual is the major goal; units of work are planned cooperatively and are modified by the interests and concerns of the persons involved; perspective, understanding, and a proprietary interest on the part of each individual are anticipated outcomes.

— *Leslee J. Bishop*

CORRELATION, PRINCIPLE OF

The principle of correlation is concerned with the mutual relation between 2 or more things that have intimate and necessary connection with one another. Question and answer, for example, have a reciprocal relation. The existence of an answer implies a question that asks for it; and the question implies that there is an answer.

Paul Tillich (*Systematic Theology*, Vol. I, p. 8) identifies the method of correlation employed in his system as "a way of uniting message and situation. It tries to correlate the questions implied in the situation with the answers implied in the message." After warning that correlation is not a trick or device, he affirms that "it is itself a theological assertion."

The principle of correlation enables the Christian educator to keep a creative tension between the values of content and those of encounter, between knowing about God and living responsibly with God and man, between the doctrine of God and the doctrine of man, between the church and the world. A concern for correlation ensures a polarity between theology and anthropology, a polarity that is essential to a relevant curriculum which affirms both the kerygma and the contemporary human situation to which it is addressed. The task of the Christian educator is to keep in tension the relation between the gospel and life.

The process of correlation calls for dialogue between the participants in the correlation; between the teacher who represents in himself and his teachings the meanings of the Word of God and the pupil who brings to the educational encounter the meanings of his life, which represent the word of man. The teacher, it should be noted, represents also the word of man, and the pupil may not only ask the question out of the human situation but also as an instrument of the word of God. Correlation occurs when the word of God and the word of man are kept in dialogue. The Christian teacher has the responsibility, not only of preparing himself to teach the truth, but also of preparing his students to hear it with the meanings that they bring to it. Although it is true that the proclamation of the gospel has to be faithful to the meaning of the gospel, it is equally true that the hearing of the gospel has to be faithful to the meaning of life.

The loss of dialogical exchange between content and life prevents the mutual relation between answer and question from being realized, so that the purposes of education cannot be accomplished. Sterile transmission of content, on the one hand, leaves life unchallenged and unchanged, so that subject matter becomes idolatrous and sterile. The teacher may become afraid to risk the meeting between his understanding of the truth and the demand of life. He then seeks to accomplish his purposes by hurling his message at his pupils with the hope that the impact will be sufficiently forceful to educate. Exclusive preoccupation with life-encounter, on the other hand, involves the student in a hopeless tangle of relativism. Human experience needs the judgment and guidance of earlier formulations of experience: that is what content is. Encounter thus needs to be in dialogue with content, and content needs to be in dialogue with encounter in order that correlation between them may keep the relation to truth alive and growing.

The employment of the principle of correlation frees the educator for a versatile use of varied methods of teaching. The concepts of " proclamation," " recital," " preaching," which long have been used to describe Christian communication, have lost their stature and meaning, and for many now represent only " monological telling " of one person by another, without the excitement of the renewal of dialogue. Although it is true that the gospel begins with God and his action in history, and is an act which must be proclaimed that all men may hear what has been done for them, it is also true that in an age of religious illiteracy, when the symbols and myths of men's communication come not from the Bible but from their industrial and scientific preoccupations, their minds and hearts have to be prepared to hear the proclamation. More versatile methods of education are needed that are not afraid to move from a concern for answers to a concern for questions, knowing that a true question moves us toward a true answer, and that a true answer leads us to ask a deeper, truer question. The correlation of question and answer, of human need and divine revelation, if undertaken in faith, may lead to astonishing results for both teacher and learner.

— *Reuel L. Howe*

COUNCIL OF CHURCHES A council of churches is an organization through which representatives of cooperating churches can confer with one another, speak with a united voice, and work together at common tasks.

Councils of churches constitute one of the most significant developments in the life of the churches in modern times. Furthermore, the relation between them and Christian education is especially important.

There has been more cooperation across denominational lines in the interest of Christian education than in any other aspect of the Christian church.

Cooperation among Christian education leaders in this country began early in the 19th century as the Sunday school movement got under way. Their common concerns soon found expression in conventions that provided opportunity for exchange of ideas and experience and for inspirational worship and addresses. It has been estimated that by 1910, a half million persons each year attended district, county, state, or " international " (U.S.A. and Canada) Sunday school conventions, all of them interdenominational. Interdenominational training courses for teachers were instituted at an early stage in the movement, and in 1872 there began the cooperative development of lesson materials, a project that grew into great proportions in the following years. Cooperation in youth work also began in the 19th century.

This movement, initiated by individual leaders on their own responsibility, developed into a vast network of Sunday school associations across the U.S.A., and the idea spread to many other parts of the world. Interest generated within the denominations led to the establishment of Sunday school boards (later called boards of Christian education). In 1922 the International Sunday School Association (U.S.A. and Canada) and the Sunday School Council of Evangelical Denominations merged to form the International Council of Religious Education. Then most of the state and local associations changed their names to councils of religious education.

One of the earliest cases, if not the earliest, of local official interchurch cooperation in the United States was in Methuen, Mass., beginning in 1887. Maine was the scene of the 1st state organization of this character, an interdenominational commission being formed in 1891. Other federations of churches followed elsewhere, their formation being stimulated by the establishment of the Federal Council of Churches in 1908 and eventuating in the 1950 formation of the National Council of the Churches of Christ in the U.S.A. In this connection, changes in state and local areas were less marked, but councils of churches in those areas were busy expanding the scope of their programs to include many of the program interests covered by the denominations in their nationwide cooperation. Also, the number of state and local councils of churches grew to nearly 1,000.

Not only do councils of churches owe much of their heritage to one or more aspects of Christian education, but Christian education today is for many of the councils in the United States an important part of their work. In some respects, however, it may seem that the churches of various denominations do less through cooperation in Christian education than they did in the 1920's and 1930's. This appears particularly true in the production of curriculum outlines and materials and in leadership education. One reason is the belief that Christian education in the local church will be most effective if materials and training are closely related to the faith and life of the denomination of which the local church is a part. At the same time, it is true that educational purpose and effort are to be found in many aspects of the total life of a council.

Commonly accepted standards for a council of churches call for accepted representation from cooperating congregations or regional or national denominational bodies. A council is increasingly recognized not as something apart from the churches but as the churches in cooperation for the achievement of common purposes.

— Forrest L. Knapp

COUNSELING While the ministry of counseling is an age-old institution within the church, it has changed considerably within the recent past. From what was previously understood to be primarily a session of advice-giving, counseling is now more closely linked with the ancient practice of confession. Despite its ecclesiastical ancestry, the contemporary practice of counseling is largely the result of the church's integration of the Freudian discoveries in dynamic psychotherapy. Freud's work has been refined and modified for the counseling process by many outstanding therapists. The work of Carl Rogers stands out because his method requires so little knowledge of psychiatry or psychology that it is easily adaptable to the ministry of the church. His nondirective counseling (now called " client-centered ") has been greatly misunderstood as directionless counseling. Actually, it is quite directive in that it has its goals which its methods are directed to achieve. The goal is the growth of the counselee as a self-affirming individual. It is nondirective in that it is based on the premise that such growth is best achieved through the involvement of the counselee in a dialogue in which he must assume responsibility for decisions affecting his own personal life.

Leaders within the institutional church have modified and adapted Rogers to the office of the ministry. Seward Hiltner labels his method eductive counseling — emphasizing the drawing out of the counselee by the counselor. Carroll Wise prefers to modify client-centered therapy to relationship-centered therapy — emphasizing the dynamic of the dialogue between the counselee and counselor. Previously, Rollo May had stressed empathy as the attitude of the counselor which creates the atmosphere for the sharing in counseling.

Counseling within the church can be defined as the unearthing of the counselee's destructive powers of guilt, anxiety, hostility, and despair and resolving them in the gospel of Christianity through a personal relationship with the counselor. The principles upon which this counseling operates are based upon the fundamental needs of the troubled soul. The 1st of these is the need to communicate to another. This means the counselor must listen as an encouragement to sharing. The 2d is the need to confess — to share things that are disturbing, even threatening, to the counselor. This means the counselor must be alert to respond to evidences of guilt, anxiety, resentment, and discouragement. The 3d is the need for the counselee to understand himself and his problem. This needed insight comes after the release of negative emotions that imprison the rational faculties and through the objectification that comes from sharing with another what heretofore was confined to the confusion of the subjective. We see in this achievement of insight a correlation with the educative task of the church. The 4th need is for growth. Problems involve more than the intellect or the emotions; they involve the total person. Solutions therefore depend on a change within the total person — a change in the direction of maturity.

Counseling rests upon the dynamic of a relationship. Dialogue at this depth is difficult to achieve. Not only the counselee but also the counselor may resist it. It is easier to give advice and to offer explanations. We have a tendency to discourage the expression of hostility or despair, or even guilt or anxiety. We feel helpless in an emotionally charged atmosphere. Also, the emotional communication of the counselee threatens to activate the counselor's own inner emotional difficulties as the present moment becomes reminiscent of former traumas. The best defense is to shy away from the uncontrollable momentum of such interpersonal dynamics. However, for the counselee and counselor who dare to enter into such a dialogue, the reward is great. Though the relationship has the necessary limitation on the counselor's sharing, the "I-thou" relationship that ensues is conducive to the growth of both parties.

Like all disciplines, counseling has its methods and techniques. Reflection is the basic technique. The counselor attempts to clarify the feelings expressed verbally or nonverbally by the counselee by responding to them in his own words. Another technique is the focus. It is used when the counselor believes that certain things which the counselee has expressed are significant. He focuses on these things by encouraging the counselee to elaborate further concerning them. The summary is a useful technique when the dialogue seems to be breaking down. If the counselor summarizes what has been expressed up to that point, he may stimulate the counselee to involve himself again. It is also helpful at the close of the interview to tie things together, as well as sometimes at the beginning of a follow-up interview as a stimulus for getting started. Because it has the tendency to be overused, the question is a more difficult tool. Besides being employed sparingly, it should be asked in a casual manner and directed to draw out the counselee's feelings rather than yes and no answers. Upon these basic techniques other methods of more limited application are developed.

Methods give wisdom to the spirit. The spirit of the counselor is one of acceptance, understanding, and respect. These are characteristics of *agapē* love. But *agapē* needs wisdom. Techniques are intelligent ways for the *agapē* of the counselor to achieve its goals. Hence, techniques are inseparable from the personality of the user. Used mechanically or as manipulative tools, they destroy rather than stimulate genuine dialogue. Here is where the religious nature of counseling enters. Religious counseling is not characterized by the use of religious words in the dialogue, although these may be present. Rather, the religious nature of counseling is determined by the attitude of the parties, particularly the counselor. Even though his techniques may be similar in appearance to those of the secular counselor, their role and purpose in his counseling are determined by his own perspective concerning the goals and purposes of the relationship. When his perspective is religious, it encourages the development of a religious character to the relationship.

The usual transfer is involved in religious counseling as well as other forms of psychotherapy. The very nature of counseling within the framework of the church implies that the transfer is from counselor to God. This transfer has its tangible expression in the fellowship of the congregation, which is Christ's body. Even the counselor is involved in this transfer, since within the church he continues to be a part of the counselee's life even after the counseling relationship is terminated. The transfer then is from his role as a counselor to the role of a fellow believer. The transfer to God is also made realizable in the counselee's participation in the worship life of the church, and in his personal devotional life. So the counseling ministry is not apart from the other ministries of the church, but is mutually related to them all.

The correlation of counseling with Christian education is evident in that the basic goal of counseling is the counselee's spiritual growth. The Socratic method of education forms a good point of contact between the 2 disciplines. Even as Socratic questioning attempts to get the individual to search and to think and to find his own answers, so the confrontation brought about by the counseling process moves the counselee to face himself and to find his answers. Reflection means holding up the mirror. Supported by the warm and acceptive relationship of the counselor, the counselee is confronted by the counseling process to face even the dialectic of his own ambivalence — his love for that which he also hates, his desire for that which he also loathes. Socrates said, "Know yourself." Counseling goes one step beyond and, with Kierkegaard, says, "Choose yourself." Decision is imperative for growth. There is no maturity without accepting the responsibility for self-commitment, for which there is also judgment.

In her book on multiple counseling, Driver says the counselor in group counseling enlarges upon or gives an illustration of the idea, attitude, or feeling expressed by one of the group. In this way he emphasizes and clarifies its meaning. This is true also for counseling with individuals. For the religious counselor this may mean tying in the insights and experiences of the counselee with the heritage of the church — its teachings, its Scriptures, and its worship life. In a sense the counselor shifts momentarily to the role of teacher at this point. So we may say that counseling is a way of communicating the gospel when the barriers to the realization of this gospel are too set and formidable for other media of communication to penetrate. It is communication of the gospel at the dialogue level where total sharing of the self not only takes place but is expressed.

— William E. Hulme

COUPLES CLUB Organized groups of married couples, related more or less closely to the program of Christian education in the church, have received special attention in some denominations since George Gleason's study of Church Group Activities for Young Married People (1937) described a number of such groups that had developed almost spontaneously in some parts of the country.

In many cases married couples clubs have grown naturally out of adult Bible classes in the Sunday church school when husbands and wives desired to extend the church life they shared together to include recreation, social and service activities, and types of programs other than those customary in the Sunday class. On the other hand many married couples clubs have been organized primarily to meet the social needs of their members and have little in common with other phases of the Christian education program of their church.

Club meetings are usually held on week nights once a month. In the typical group, husbands and wives hold offices as partners (Mr. and Mrs. President, etc.) and share leadership responsibilities. Programs do not follow any formal syllabus in most cases. They are based on the interests and needs of group members as these are recognized by their own officers or program committees. Subjects related to Christian family life are prominent.

Most denominations do not advocate any particular pattern of club organization for married couples or provide special program materials apart from those available for the adult department in the Sunday church school and for other adult organizations in the church.

In most churches where any special recognition is given to married couples groups they are regarded as part of the total adult (or young adult) program of Christian education. Denominational or national guidance in matters of organization, study, worship, service, and recreation is provided through the Sunday church school leaders' publications, general bulletins on adult Christian education, and through handbooks such as Young Adult Work in the Church and an annual Young Adult Idea Book (United Lutheran); Handbook for Presbyterian Adult Groups (The United Presbyterian Church U.S.A.); Couples Clubs and Young Adults in the Church (United Church of Canada); A Manual for Young Adults (NCCCUSA). A few denominations provide manuals or bulletins directed especially to married couples groups. These include the Southern Baptist Convention (The Work of the Married Young People's Department — for those 17 to 24) and the Reformed Church in America.

Perhaps one third of the married couples clubs in The United Presbyterian Church U.S.A. are associated with National Presbyterian Mariners, a somewhat autonomous organization, though under presbytery, synod, and General Assembly authority. Although they are recognized as part of the total adult program of their denomination, they offer a unique service and fellowship program manual based on a fivefold purpose: To encourage Christian faith and practice in every home; to offer fellowship within the church for couples of similar interests; to serve the church; to develop leadership for the church; to win others to Christ.

Married couples clubs are formed most frequently among younger married people whose needs are recognizably different from those met by the youth organizations of the church. However, many groups that started with " young marrieds " have continued until their members are chiefly middle-aged or older. Some senior adults have formed their own married couples clubs.

In contrast, men's and women's groups in North American church life have little inclination toward regional or national organizations. Their organizational focus is almost entirely within the congregation.

In many cases the enthusiasm for married couples groups seems to express a reaction against the tendency to segregate men from women in the church and to multiply separate groups for study, work, service, and recreation. It is important that husbands and wives be encouraged to grow together in every expression of the church's life. Married couples clubs offer valuable opportunities when their purpose is harmonious with that of the church, when the needs of single adults are not overlooked or neglected, and when this form of organization is integrated into the essential life and mission of the whole congregation and church. — *Frank P. Fidler*

COVENANT How important the concept of covenant is for Christian faith may be accurately gauged by the fact that the Scriptures are called the Old and the New Covenants. They are so entitled because the covenant (Hebrew: *bĕrīth;* Greek: *diathēkē;* Latin: *testamen-*

tum) describes the basic relation between God and man that is the primary concern of the Old and the New Israel.

The Old Testament knows also of covenants between men, e.g., a treaty (Josh. 9:6 ff.), a friendship (I Sam. 18:3), a marriage (Prov. 2:17), a political contract (II Sam. 5:3), etc. In such cases, the covenant bears the features of a legal bond, each party being obligated to certain claims of the other.

The covenant between God and man has a similarly uniting character, insofar as by it God overcomes the estrangement occasioned by man's disobedience, giving himself once more to man (" I will be your God ") and drawing man to himself (" and you shall be my people ") (Jer. 7:23; Ezek. 26:38). God's free giving of himself in the covenant — and it is always God, never man, who institutes the covenant — elevates the covenant out of a merely legal context, and requires that man accept it as a free gift, that is, grace. Unlike the covenant between men, therefore, God's covenant does not provide man with any claim upon him, but, rather, precisely because it is free grace, constitutes God's claim upon man. God's covenant comes to man, then, as grace and as demand.

Nowhere is this more apparent than in the covenant made through Moses at Mt. Sinai (Ex., chs. 19; 20; 24:3-8, 9-11), in which God's demand for obedience (Ex. 19:5; 20:3-17) is consistently placed in the context of his grace, i.e., his deliverance of the people " out of the house of bondage " (Ex. 20:2) and his bringing them " on eagles' wings " to himself (Ex. 19:4). In gathering the people to himself, God really makes of them a people, a community, for the first time; for their acceptance of the covenant (Ex. 19:8; 24:7) is an acquiescence to his claim upon their lives, and indicates their realization of the meaning of the name Israel: " God rules."

Consequently, this event stands in the " center " of Israel's history, and in its light Israel interprets that history: not, however, as a merely past occurrence, but as a present reality. Thus the covenant is " renewed " again and again: in the plains of Moab (Deut. 29:1), under Joshua's leadership at Shechem (Josh. 24:25), in the " Deuteronomic " reforms of the 7th century (II Kings 23:3; cf. II Kings 11:17), and under the priest Ezra after the return from exile (Neh. 8:10; 9:38; 10:29).

Side by side with this, Israel understands the beginnings of her history (Gen. 12:1-3; chs. 15; 17), the establishment of the monarchy (II Sam., ch. 7; Ps. 89; 132; Jer. 33:21) and the constitution of the priesthood (Num. 25:12; Neh. 13:29; Mal. 2:4; Jer. 33:21), in terms of the covenant. In form, these covenants differ from the Mosaic covenant in that (1) they are with individuals instead of the people, and (2) they are not conditional, i.e., they seem to lay no obligations upon those with whom God covenants. Ultimately, however, the differences are only formal, for the individuals in each case represent, indeed embody, the people as a whole, and the demand for obedience is implicit rather than explicit (cf. Gen. 12:1-4; 15:6; 22:1-19, in which great stress is laid upon Abraham's obedience, and II Sam. 12:1-15; Hos. 4:4 ff., 5:1; 8:1 ff., where the prophetic attack on the abuses of the kingship and the priesthood

presupposes disobedience to the claims of the covenant).

Israel, in fact, understands her entire history as one of disobedience to the demands of the covenant, as a continuous rebellion against God. The prophets, especially those who witness the judgment of the Babylonian exile, accordingly look to that future when the covenant between God and man will be completed, i.e., obeyed, and so will be a new covenant (Jer. 31:31-34; 32:38-41; Ezek. 36:23-28). And, finally, the great prophet of the exile, Deutero-Isaiah, understands afresh (cf. Gen. 12:3) that Israel's future as the covenant people of God will not be for her own sake, but for the salvation of the world: she will be " a covenant to the people, a light to the nations " (Isa. 42:6; cf. chs. 49:6-9; 52:13 to 53:12).

From the New Testament point of view, Israel's history, understood from beginning to end as covenantal history, is completed in Jesus Christ (Luke 1:68-79; Acts 3:25 f.). The disobedience of many has been overcome in the obedience of one (Rom. 5:19), viz., the obedience " unto death " (Phil. 2:8), which is interpreted as a convenantal sacrifice (Mark 14:24 = Matt. 26:28 and Luke 22:20). Here, the textual ambiguity respecting the word " new " discloses not only emerging awareness of the thought of Jeremiah, but also an acute sensitivity to a problem that troubled the early church, i.e., what is the relationship between Israel, whose covenant is completed in the death and resurrection of Jesus, and the church that is founded on the same event? Do the modifiers " old " and " new " — they are contrasted as such only by the author of The Letter to the Hebrews (ch. 8:6-13), for whom the " second " is not only different from, but also superior to, the " first " — suggest that there are 2 covenants, 1 for the Old, and 1 for the New Israel?

The answer that Paul gives to the question is less one-sided than that of The Letter to the Hebrews. The covenant, he argues, belongs to Israel (Rom. 9:1-5), and " God has not rejected his people " (Rom. 11:2). Their temporary self-removal from the covenant bond through unbelief — they have stumbled, not fallen (Rom. 11:11) — makes room, so to speak, for the Gentiles (Rom. 11:19-24). As mysterious as it seems, after the " full number of the Gentiles come in . . . all Israel will be saved " (Rom. 11:25 f.), " for the gifts and the call of God are irrevocable " (Rom. 11:29). There is but 1 covenant, 1 " olive tree " of which Israel is the natural branches, and the Gentiles are engrafted, wild shoots.

It is true that Paul, in the letter to the Galatians, refers to two covenants (Gal. 4:24), but both are located in the Old Testament. Moreover, his argument for the priority of the Abrahamic over the Mosaic covenant (Gal. 3:15-22) is, in effect, an argument for the priority of grace over demand (cf. Gal. 2:21; 3:24; 5:4) and has the consequence of emphasizing, rather than weakening, the unity of the covenant: " If you are Christ's, then you are Abraham's offspring " (Gal. 3:29); and he thinks of the church, accordingly, as the " Israel of God " (Gal. 6:16).

We are in the best position to understand Paul's attitude toward the law, i.e., the Mosaic covenant, if we bear in mind that the covenant comprises both grace and demand. For his mixture of positive affirmations of the law (Rom. 3:31; 7:7, 12 f., 22, 25; 8:7) and negative comparisons of law and grace (Rom: 4:16; 6:14), together with assertions that the law serves chiefly to make man aware of his sinfulness (Rom. 5:19; 7:7-13), and that the believer has " died to the law " (Rom. 7:4; Gal. 2:19) can be reconciled only if the " negative " statements refer not to the law itself, but to its improper use. It is not, therefore, obedience to the claim of the covenant that Paul would set aside, but the assumption that man can, by obeying it, establish his righteousness before God (Rom. 9:31 f.). In the face of legalism, Paul's contention is with those who see in the covenant only demand without grace, just as the prophets before him, in the face of complacency and presumption, had to contend with those who found in the covenant only grace without demand.

The " newness " of the covenant, then, consists in this: God's covenant with man has taken on new form, has now appeared in the flesh. Jesus Christ *is* the Covenant, Isaiah's Covenant, to the nations. God's intention, " I will be your God, . . . and you shall be my people," is completed in him. Thus the Christ is at once God's grace to man, and God's claim upon man for obedience.

As the covenant is constitutive of Israel, so it is also of the church. Here, too, God draws man to himself in the closest possible community: the church is the body of Christ (I Cor. 12:27; Eph. 5:23). And this community, above all others, is subject to God's demand: the church is the Kingdom of Christ (I Cor. 15:25; Rev. 11:15).

— Benjamin Charles Milner, Jr.

CRAFTS The usefulness of crafts for learning has varied according to the educational philosophy of the particular time or group. We are only beginning to consider crafts from the standpoint of their place in religious nurture. Unskilled teachers in the church have used a few crafts, hoping for better results in interest and learning, but hardly knowing what results they were seeking or the value of the tools at their disposal. As a means of Christian nurture, crafts present a useful and dynamic medium.

When the person uses media such as paint, clay, mache, metal, wood, his naturally creative spirit may be released through materials that have always challenged the ingenuity of man. As he experiments with ancient materials and ways, he comes to know himself as a creator in the process. Our concern for the development of persons suggests that we find ways for children, youth, and adults to experience this joy of creativity for its own sake. Some churches make practical provision for groups to engage in different types of handicrafts for sheer enjoyment. Increasingly, churches are recognizing the value of creative use of leisure time. As individuals develop new skills with their hands, they play at work that makes life rich and endows it with added meanings.

Especially does the increase in church camping suggest a better understanding of creative use of natural materials. God's world offers a variety of media for satisfying the creative impulse: wood, nuts, clay, stone, plants for native dyes. Crafts may become a powerful teaching aid, as well as a joy, as campers discover and create within the bounds of the " given," and experience the thrill of working " from the ground up."

A knowledge of various crafts also helps us to teach our heritage (Bible, church history); thus older children, youth, and adults may identify with those through whom the story of God's activity comes. The story of prehistoric people told in relics reveals the skill and inspiration with which ancient craftsmen wrought their tools and weapons. The first stories of man are carved in stone and clay. Ancient periods come to life in artifacts — clay lumps, tablets, manuscripts. Knowing the place of crafts in the cultural and religious life of our Christian heritage opens new areas of learning. Work with ivory, metal, precious stones, and leather, and making dyes and weaving fine materials were all important in Hebrew development. A person may genuinely identify with his heritage as he pursues an ancient craft today: making clay tablets or parchments, weaving fabrics, working in leather and metal, carving or printing (block and letter). Constructing a simple panorama, painting a mural, or making puppets can help the workers to identify with those who used these media for many purposes.

Furthermore, crafts offer additional value when the teacher uses them as group activity. Cooperative work to produce an illustrated map or time line (combining historical data with purposeful creativity) brings the long ago and faraway closer, as each member assumes a share of the burden of learning. In the processes required, each can find the place where he may best contribute his gift. The value of crafts for Christian nurture has not been sufficiently exploited to the point where the work of many has been required to produce the finished whole. Group experience through crafts provides a setting where basic principles of our Christian faith become dynamic in human relations: sharing, cooperation, acceptance of both self and others, responsibility, freedom within the structure.

Finally, the need to create beauty has always been felt by young and old. Mental and emotional release accompanies satisfaction of the creative urge; conversely, tension and mounting frustration result from its nonfulfillment. To meet this need the would-be creator must struggle to master himself and to overcome the resistance of the material with which he works. He must strive for harmony and balance, put forth effort to achieve accuracy; he must combine thought and emotion, and project them within the inexorable limits set by form. We may introduce a person to many intriguing ways of expressing ideas through media best suited to his taste and ability. We may give him a new tool with which to enjoy the present, and if kept sharpened, one which may serve him well as long as he lives. — *Helen M. Edick*

CREATIVE ACTIVITIES A creative activity is a person's response in whatever way he is at the moment most capable to the impact of experiences, words, or ideas that are presented to him factually or symbolically. It is a vehicle of communication between persons. It is the response to the question, asked or unasked, What does this mean to you?

Man's deepest need is to belong, to be a necessary, contributing member of his group. Communication is essential to his membership. Herein lies the potentiality for his creative expression. It is through this activity that a person's uniqueness, his "selfness," is revealed. It is his expression, his response, unidentical, new, peculiarly his, that is offered.

Not all persons find conversation a satisfying means of expression. Clay, paint, music, dance, drama, poetry, are often better media.

Symbols are peculiarly necessary to express response to confrontation by the gospel. Words are inadequate. Stereotyped conformities are limiting. When the religious education process is taking place it demands response from the whole person. Many forms of expression are necessary.

Religious educators are concerned with a life-changing process of learning. The learning has not been effective or even taken place until it becomes operative in the learner's life. Each new learning is seen in relation to other learnings, used, tested, refined. It must be expressed by the learner in his unique terms and offered as "This is who I am." Thus communication may be furthered, deeper insights gained, the learning process continued. The creative expression as part of the learning activity cannot take place in a vacuum. Related to man's need to belong is his need to express his gift of creativity.

The recognition of the necessity for creative expression in the religious education process has developed slowly and, as one would expect, in conjunction with education's growing concept of persons and their responses. There are 4 phases distinguishable historically.

1. "Busywork." Teachers' manuals made suggestions for such an activity — coloring printed patterns, stringing beads, weaving raffia mats,

etc. The activity was frankly for the purpose of keeping hands occupied. There was no attempt to relate this activity to the classroom subject matter.

2. "Handwork." This was teacher-directed, step by step, each member of the class proceeding according to specific instructions. The purpose was more markedly that of skill training in the handling of materials, but still without necessary relation to subject matter or individual creative expression.

3. "Purposeful activity." In this stage the form and frequently the procedure was dictated by the teacher but with some opportunity within these limits for individual and group creative expression. The activity was definitely a part of the teaching process, integrated into the lesson plan. Its purpose was that of illustrating, introducing, or summarizing subject matter. This type of activity is a direct predecessor of phase 4 and is frequently mistaken for it.

4. "Creative activity." We are now in the 4th period of development, which has been termed "creative activity," as defined at the beginning of this article.

The key to the developing concept of activity in the educational process is one of motivation. Each of the 4 stages described above had some validity at the time. The last 2 more nearly provide opportunity for aid in the learning process as we have come to understand it.

The aim of the teacher in encouraging creative expression is one of making response to an experience or idea rather than skill in workmanship. However, the ability to exercise the creative gift with which persons are endowed is aided and freed by facility in using the tools of expression. Thus the teacher has the responsibility for introducing new materials and for providing the opportunity to use them and guidance in their use, as well as for allowing the use of such skills learned by the pupil in other situations. Not all materials are equally useful vehicles of expression by all persons. Only by exploring and testing is one able to discover through which means he is best able to express himself. By becoming familiar with several choices, one is able to select what best fits his needs for a particular situation.

The description so far has dealt primarily with individual expression. The learning that takes place in a group is deepened and strengthened through the same encouragement for group expression. Again, the need to communicate is primary. The group's creative expression evolves when in response to a group experience a means of expression is chosen and the group, through discussion, research, and guidance in the technical or skill area, produces a symbol of response to that experience. The resulting creation is the product of all the insights, testings, efforts, and talents, compiled and modified, to express in a creative manner group response — group communication. The resulting effort may be in the form of drama, story, liturgical expression (writing of prayers, for instance), painting, mural, sculpture, model, mobile.

Religious education classes could benefit from increased opportunity for activities in drama, writing, and creative expression through the use of paint, clay, paper-folding, or various types of puppets. Traditionally, crayons and paper, and occasionally scissors and paste, are associated with such classes. They are good tools and useful in many instances. Exercise of freedom and imagination on the part of the teacher helps in the discovery of how versatile the most common materials are. An attitude of confident expectation, appreciation of effort and willingness to accept the learner's offering without the pressure of imposing a standard of workmanship or conformity of style is one of the teacher's contributions to this step in the learning process.

— *Betsy M. Rodenmayer*

CREED A creed is an authorized, concise, liturgical declaration of crucial points of Christian doctrine. As used by the churches of the West, the word was derived from the Latin *credo*, " I believe," and indicated a formally authoritarian statement. Churches in the East, however, designated these declarations by the word " symbol," derived from the Greek *symbolon*, meaning " token " or " sign " — that which stands for or reminds one of something else. Accordingly, the recital of the symbol was an expressive and portentous sign of the participant's identification with the church in the enactments of Christian worship. The nuances expressed by the terms " creed " and " symbol " are manifest, in classical instances, by the Apostles' Creed and the Nicene Creed.

Although the use of creeds has served many purposes, such as settings for catechetical instruction, formal outlines for systematized theology, safeguards against heretical bias, and declaratory proclamations in missionary expansion, it is primarily in the sacramental liturgies for Baptism and Holy Communion that these formulations originated and have been perpetuated. At an early date candidates for baptism responded to ritual queries with a short formula of beliefs that varied in details in different localities. The baptismal confessions were more or less uniform by the 4th century and, following Matt. 28:19, were Trinitarian in structure. Such a confession, from the 2d century, is thought to be the liturgical and historical root of the 8th-century Gallican documents from which originates the Apostles' Creed as the only liturgical baptismal confession of the churches in the West. The Nicene Creed remains the liturgical baptismal confession for the churches in the East. The present practice of using the Nicene Creed in the Eucharistic liturgy began in the 5th century among churches in the East. The use of the Nicene Creed in the service of Holy Communion in some churches of the West is quite probably derived from this prior practice in the East.

The Apostles' Creed is used only by churches in the West whose ritual retains liturgical elements related primarily to the Church of Rome. It falls into 3 sections affirming, respectively: faith in God the Creator-Father; in Jesus Christ; and in the Holy Spirit — to which section are appended statements respecting the church, resurrection, and the life everlasting. The terse clauses are substantiated by, if not grounded in, passages from the New Testament. The legend of its origin as a composition of the Twelve Apostles cannot be earlier than the 4th century, probably ca. 390, which is the earliest mention of the document by this title presently extant. As it is now used, the Apostles' Creed is a text in Latin called the *Textus Receptus* (T) from the Gallican Sacramentary of Gellone (ca.

790). Four other documents (Missals and antiphonaries), dated from ca. 690 to ca. 750, also preserve this text but not in so complete a form. Scholars debate the problem of the point of origination of this text " T." Some favor Rome — and the text in Greek of the old Roman baptismal symbol (R) as the literary core of T. Other more convincing scholars maintain a Latin textual origin somewhere among the monastic establishments or the territorial church of South Gaul. The reason for its formulation was believed to be the Carolingian demand for uniformity and the reverse flow of Gallican influences on Rome during and following the reign of Charlemagne.

Quite apart from its possible genetic relationship to T, the text of the old Roman baptismal confession (R) is traced back to 2 early documents. One, in Greek, is quoted by Irenaeus of Lyons (ca. 180) and was attributed to Rome. The other, in Latin, is quoted by Tertullian of Carthage (ca. 200). Furthermore, the text copied by Irenaeus in Greek is also found in that language, almost word for word, in a creed quoted by Marcellus of Ancyra and recited to Pope Julius in Rome, 336 or 337. There is also a Commentary on the Apostles' Creed written by Rufinus of Aquileia (ca. 400) which, presently extant only in a Latin text, almost exactly parallels the Greek text of Marcellus. By common consent, this old Roman symbol (R), which has so much in common with the *Textus Receptus* — our Apostles' Creed — is believed to have been formulated in Greece sometime after 160 and before 180.

Two creeds in Christendom bear the title " Nicene Creed." They must be distinguished. The 1st, properly so-called, was promulgated in 325 at Nicaea during the First Ecumenical Council of the Church and by scholars is now designated " N." The other, which is the actual text so titled in the liturgies of the church, is, factually, the Niceno-Constantinopolitan Creed set forth in Constantinople (381) by the Second Ecumenical Council, and for purposes of study is designated " C."

The creed of Nicaea (N) is a succinct affirmation of the view that " God was in Christ" and this means that although God existed apart from, and transcendent to, the incarnation, the nature of the deity incarnate in the man Christ Jesus was of the very essence or being of the God existing transcendentally. The non-Biblical word affirming the genuineness of the incarnation was *homoousios*, meaning " of the same being." In this first statement of ecumenical orthodoxy Arianism was anathematized. The Arians had taught that the transcendent God could not, as deity, participate in the processes of history and nature and postulated a tertiary existent — a third form of being lower than God but higher than man — called the Logos. This unique creation became incarnate in Jesus Christ. Four anathemas against Arianism were later erroneously adjudged integral to the text of N. This creed is now thought to be based upon the baptismal confession of the church at Jerusalem in the 4th century as reported to the Council at Nicaea.

The Niceno-Constantinopolitan Creed (C) differs from N in that (1) the section on the Person of Christ is augmented by cumulative phrases of paradox; (2) the locution " from the substance of the Father" is omitted; (3) the statements respecting the person and work of the Holy Spirit are precisely expanded; (4) a section on the catholic church, baptism, forgiveness of sins, resurrection, and the life to come is added wholly; and (5) all anathemas are dropped. This creed was adjudged to have been formulated by the Council of Constantinople, 381, or by the Council of Chalcedon, 451. This judgment, however, scholars now affirm, could not have been based on data available before 449 or 450. Although C — the familiar Nicene Creed — is known *not* to be the work of either the Council of Nicaea or that of Constantinople, the latter Council did promulgate C as a standard of orthodoxy, and its origin, like that of N, quite probably derives ultimately from the baptismal confession of the church in Jerusalem.

A 3d declaration of faith widely used by churches in the West is the so-called Athanasian Creed, also designated, from its opening words, as the Quicunque vult. It is used, liturgically, in the Latin Breviary and by certain non-Roman communions, notably the Church of England and Lutherans, as a replacement for the Apostles' Creed on selected holy days and feasts. The creed expounds, respectively, the doctrines of the Trinity and the Incarnation. It is clear-cut, if not concise, and is prefaced and concluded by the assertion that acceptance of the truths it states is necessary to salvation. The anathemas are explicit. This creed could not have been the work of Athanasius (ca. 296–373) chiefly because it contains precise doctrinal expressions designative of controversies much later in history. Modern scholarship affirms that it was evidently composed in Latin, not Greek, probably by Ambrose (339–397), bishop of Milan. It did not circulate in the

churches of the East until after ca. 1780 and has never been recognized as a standard of faith by them.

The Council of Chalcedon Formula or Definition (451) is not a creed of Christendom, but the crystalline clarity of its determinatively accurate discriminations respecting the Person of Jesus Christ is an abiding ornament of the church. It asserts that in the incarnation Jesus Christ was 1 Person in 2 natures — that is, Son of God and son of Mary, deity nature and human nature — viably one living personality. The deity nature, without prerogatives of coercion, elicits communion and participative at-one-ness from the human nature of Jesus. This Person, therefore, reveals the salvific relationship between God, the Holy Spirit, and the human spirit with whom there is communion. — *David C. Shipley*

CULTURE The concept of culture has, in general, 2 large meanings. It designates the totality of those transformations and refinements which man's mind and spirit work upon the possibilities of nature; and it designates that transmissive and transforming activity of society whereby the gains and values of a people are conveyed to the successive generations.

An epigram that suggests the 1st of these meanings is: "A river is nature; a canal is culture. A plant is nature; a garden is culture." The 2d meaning, "culture as transforming and transmissive," is suggested by the fact that a symphony orchestra is called a cultural institution.

Both these meanings are intended when education is proposed as a cultural activity. For education operates to appreciate, to transmit, to

gain skills for needed transformations of nature, to shape the various
vitalities of man's private and societal existence toward forms ever
fuller and more appropriate to his
endowments and needs.

Christian education is that activity
of the cultus, the people of God,
whereby the events, beliefs, practices, and affirmations of this particular community of faith seek to
actualize their potentialities. Although, to be sure, this broad designation goes far beyond the formal
instructional activity of the cultus,
such a designation seems necessary
if the role of education in the life of
the cultus is not to be superficially
understood and narrowly practiced.
For the particularity of the cultus is
remembered, celebrated, transmitted, within the forms of its own life;
and this activity not only evokes a
specific culture but addresses, enriches, judges, the general life of
culture within which such activity
takes place.

An illustration of this double activity of a specifically Christian culture is the musical form called the
hymn. A great Christian hymn is
both a particular utterance of a particularly constituted community and
may be, and in the history of music
often has been, a musical form of
such strength and integrity as to
shape, even dominate, the emerging
and experimental tonal forms of the
period. The chorales of the German
Christian community, the folk melodies of Scandinavian, Welsh, and
other groups, the English hymn —
all of these have had at one and the
same time a particular life within
their engendering communities, and
have exercised great force upon the
musical culture of the various language and ethnic groups.

The development of operational
concepts in the field of religious education over the past century has
generally, among the non-Roman
churches, been directed to transmission of the life of the cultus
through church school instruction.
This reliance upon schoolroom pedagogy has been effective — but in a
limited and specific sense. It has
been centered upon Biblical content, usually with the intention of
deriving therefrom moral norms for
the practical decisions of the common life. What effort there has been
to ensconce such instruction within
the life of the cultus at worship has
been so determined by the moral intention as to reduce worship to a
mood establishing and enforcing
context for the pedagogical task.

The above understanding of the
task and promise of Christian education is continuous with certain aspects of the history of the Protestant
churches in North America. The
dominant understanding of the
Christian faith on the American
scene has been what Troeltsch has
called the "sect type"; and concepts and procedures in Christian
education have become stylized accordingly. These are generally moralistic, individualistic, aimed at
evoking a personal commitment certified by private experience.

The dominance of this type of
Christian education has had specifi-
able effects upon the general life of
culture in the United States. It accounts, in part, for the moralistic interpretations of national history, for
the quite individualistic, even private, understanding of the relation
of religion and culture, and for a
general reluctance to perceive any
challenge to the Christian faith in
the structures of economic, political,
and social thought. When, indeed,
these relations are perceived, the

general assumption remains that private goodwill and righteousness are adequate resources for dealing with them.

There has been, to be sure, a tradition in American thought more realistic than the above. The political maturity of the fathers of the Constitution, the acknowledgment in the Federalist debates of the complexity of the interaction between self-interest and cultural concern, the powerful influence of the expanding frontier upon the early theocratic assumptions of New England theology and church life — these and other facts received artistic embodiment in certain literary efforts to inquire into the relation of faith and culture. In this connection the work of Nathaniel Hawthorne, Herman Melville, and Henry James is of crucial significance.

Twentieth-century inquiry into the role of religious faith in the life of culture, or the role of religious education in the life of the churches, and of the development of religious institutions has been marked and prolific. The monumental study by Ernst Troeltsch, *The Social Teaching of the Christian Churches,* has been unmatched by any specifically American study, but the theme has been explored by many: Walter Rauschenbusch, Richard and Reinhold Niebuhr, and, more recently, Alexander Miller and John Bennett.

Current studies of the relation between Christian education and culture seem to be preoccupied with the following issues:

1. How is the tradition to be transmitted so as to ensure both changeless substance and flexible interpretation?

2. How is the content of Christian education to be handled so as to administer the personal, corporate dialectic of the Biblical drama in ways constructive for contemporary problems, private and social?

3. How is the pedagogical, transmissive task of Christian education to be so enfolded into the entire worshiping life of the cultus as to release the powers of grace for the hurts of nature — in politics, economics, the new world of natural science?

4. How are the affirmations of Christian education to be made clear and relevant to a culture deepeningly tinctured by secular and scientific methodology and achievement? The reduction of the Christian substance to godly consolation in the midst of general notions within the structure of which the holy has no role is an effort that has exhausted itself. It would seem now to be required of the church that the huge interpretive generality of its basic vocabulary be so reinvested with possible meaning as to provide a holy option to sheer irreligion.

— *Joseph Sittler*

CUMBERLAND PRESBYTERIAN CHURCH The Cumberland Presbyterian Church was organized in Dickson County, Tenn., Feb. 4, 1810, an outgrowth of the Great Revival of 1800. The founders were Finis Ewing, Samuel King, and Samuel McAdow, ministers of the Presbyterian Church who rejected the doctrine of election and reprobation as taught in the Westminster Confession of Faith.

Doctrinally, the church claims a "medium" position between the extremes of Calvinism and Arminianism. It has been unwilling to accept fully either the implications of Calvin's understanding of God's sovereignty or what it alleges to be humanism in the doctrinal system of Arminius.

A constitutional majority approved a plan of union with the Presbyterian Church in the U.S.A. in 1906, but a minority group elected to perpetuate the Cumberland Presbyterian Church.

The educational philosophy of the church from its beginning was oriented to a basically literal interpretation of the Bible, which it accepts as " the word of God, the only infallible rule of faith and practice." Not much specific information is available on the organized work of Christian education during the 19th century, but there is evidence that the young church took its educational ministry seriously and gave strong emphasis to the Sunday school as a means to Christian growth. It was not until the middle 1920's that organized efforts were begun to formulate a denomination-wide ministry of Christian education.

The " modern period " of the Cumberland Presbyterian Church began in the early 1940's, when the church began to show new signs of life and new understanding of its mission. Its educational philosophy during the modern period has been influenced by the liberalism of the 19th century, with its emphasis upon religious education as a person-centered rather than a gospel-centered ministry. However, there are indications now of a rediscovery of Biblical theology and a mood to restore the Bible to a central place in Christian education.

The church makes use of the Uniform Lesson Series and the Cycle Graded Series in its curriculum. However, during the modern period it has found itself increasingly unable to fill all its needs for curriculum materials, especially for children. It has therefore moved in the direction of cooperatively produced curriculum materials, working with other members of the Reformed family of churches.

— *Harold Davis*

CURRICULUM A curriculum is a systematic plan by which Christian education may be carried on by the church, home, or school. A curriculum does not include all of Christian education experience but, rather, that portion of it which is provided by the particular institution.

The term " curriculum " is often used to denote lesson materials or series of lesson plans provided for class or group use. A better term for this purpose is " curriculum materials," to include suggestions, plans, and resource material in printed or other form that may, in actual use in the church, home, or school become a systematic plan for Christian education.

A distinction is sometimes drawn between " curriculum " and " program " in Christian education, the latter term being used to describe the actual teaching situation and educational setting in which the materials and resources are used. This distinction is being rapidly obliterated in Protestant circles as it becomes clear that neither aspect is independent of the other. In some cases the term " curriculum program " is being used to indicate this fusion.

Any program of Christian education is based upon decisions on objective, curriculum, and administration. The objective of Christian education gives direction to the learner and the educator in terms of the purpose of the church and the intention of the Christian faith.

The curriculum is the primary means for implementing the objective. Decisions on the scope, context, process, and design of Christian education determine the character of the curriculum.

The administrative setup, in turn, implements the curriculum by providing for organization, management, supervision, evaluation, and leadership. Context is a key category in administration as well as in curriculum.

Of the utmost importance is the relationship between these 3 elements. A sound situation in Christian education maintains priority for the objective, with the curriculum serving it, and administration serving curriculum. A radically unsound situation exists where curriculum is designed to serve administrative ends or where the objective is cut to fit the assumptions of a particular curriculum.

In America the history of the curriculum embraces the development of colonial education in which religious and other elements were fused, the rise of higher education under church auspices, and the development of theological education.

The Sunday school movement was the center of the growth of various lesson series, first standardized in the Uniform Lessons of the early 1870's, and later developed by the addition of closely graded and group-graded materials.

Since the late 1940's there has been considerable ferment in the preparation of curriculum materials and in rethinking basic approaches to curriculum. Curriculum studies and plans have been developed by such denominations as The United Presbyterian Church in the U.S.A. (*Christian Faith and Life: A Program for Church and Home*), the Protestant Episcopal church (*The Seabury Series*), the United Church of Christ, several Lutheran bodies, and the United Church of Canada; and interdenominationally by the curriculum committees of the National Council of the Churches of Christ in the U.S.A. culminating in the Cooperative Curriculum Project.

The basic principles undergirding the curriculum of Christian education are principles of purpose, scope, context, process, and design.

Objectives have been stated in Christian education in many ways. There is a current trend toward the use of a single objective, or purpose, for curriculum. The function of a single objective is to act as a policy statement governing the whole curriculum enterprise. The objective most frequently used currently is that of the NCCCUSA's study paper *The Objective of Christian Education for Senior High Young People* (1958): "The objective of Christian education is to help persons to be aware of God's self-disclosure and seeking love in Jesus Christ, and to respond in faith and love — to the end that they may know who they are and what their human situation means, grow as sons of God rooted in the Christian community, live in the Spirit of God in every relationship, fulfill their common discipleship in the world, and abide in the Christian hope."

The principle of scope defines the necessary content, substance, and span of experience to be dealt with in the curriculum. To some, this is all of experience; to others, it is a specific key segment of knowledge, such as knowledge of the Bible, or knowledge of the Christian faith theologically understood. A more satisfactory handling of the principle of scope, however, is to see it as the whole field of relationships in the light of the gospel; such a solution preserves the essential pointedness and emphasis of the curriculum in the Christian faith and at the same time maintains its relevance to all life's concerns. The scope of the curriculum as the whole field of relationships in the light of the gospel centers upon the God who reveals himself Biblically as Father, Son, and Holy Spirit, the means of this revelation being the Word of God, and the media being the Bible and the church as it lives its life and does its work. In the light of this self-disclosure of God, life's relationships are seen in new perspectives. Human relationships (self, society, and culture) are interpreted in terms of sin, reconciliation, and redemption. Relationships involving nature are seen in terms of the purpose of God as creator and provider. Historical relationships are seen in terms of the mighty acts of God, the climactic events of the incarnation and atonement, and the perspective of an eternal hope and a destiny to be fulfilled.

The principle of context seeks to point to the definitive locale of Christian education in order to see where Christian education's curriculum may best come into play. Sociologically speaking, there is no one essential locale or context; the curriculum may be put to work in the church school, the home, informal groups, parish day schools, colleges, and other places. But theologically speaking, it is clear that the curriculum cannot take on its necessary and essential meaning outside the worshiping, witnessing, working community of persons in Christ — the church. The church may be represented in this sense by a single teacher or a single parent on occa-

sion, yet the fact remains that in his presence the community of the Holy Spirit is present. Without the church in this sense, the curriculum lacks its essential context.

One of the reasons for establishing the principle of context with care is that the principle of process follows from it. The principle of process attempts to put clearly the essential method of the curriculum. The principle itself may be stated succinctly: The process of the curriculum is participation, engagement, or involvement in the life and work of the community of faith. In terms of this principle the child, youth, or adult makes use of the curriculum significantly only as it becomes a means for his encountering and becoming caught up in the dynamic context of the curriculum.

The community of faith lives its life and does its work through study, worship, action (witness, service, and social action), fellowship (the common life, and outreach), stewardship, and creative expression through music and the other arts. These activities may be interpreted, using the principle of process, as involving learners in undertaking appropriate tasks of participation, engagement, or involvement.

There are 2 basic principles of design: the principle of sequence and the principle of flexibility. The principle of sequence is that there must be a progression within the curriculum by which the learner will be able to move perceptibly toward and into Christian maturity. Sequence is to be psychological, that is, following the progression of the person's developing needs and concerns. At the same time, sequence is to be logical, that is, moving from simple to complex and from initial to climactic elements within the

Christian faith and experience. The learning tasks inherent in the curriculum are both psychological and logical at the same time, preserving the integrity of the faith and following a developmental sequence.

The principle of flexibility calls for flexibility of setting and method, and for flexibility in terms of individual, community, and cultural differences. Flexibility of setting facilitates the interrelation of curriculum and administration; setting for curriculum can be as varied as human need, concern, location, and forms of institutionalization as long as the essential context is operative. Flexibility of method is again potentially as varied as human need and modes of learning. Flexibility in terms of individual, community, and cultural differences calls for constant adaptation of the curriculum to the actually operative learning conditions of the learner and his environment.

The corollary of these principles of design is the concept of " live " curriculum, the system or plan of education embodied in the relationships of person to person in teaching-learning situations, as opposed to the more impersonal " curriculum materials," which at best represent suggestions and raw materials that may be turned into curriculum in the live, interpersonal relationships of learning.

In current practice, these principles are put to practical use as guides to the construction of " units." Stemming from the experimentalist view of the unit as one complete cycle of the problem-solving process, and from the more eclectic " unit of guided experience " used

for many years in Christian education, the current forms of the unit are the resource unit and the teaching-learning unit.

The resource unit is a collection of materials and suggestions from which a particular teacher or learning group can draw the help needed to work in a certain particularized way on a given problem or topic. Resource units are generally built on a topic or problem at one specific age or experience level.

The teaching-learning unit, on the other hand, presents definite lesson plans, usually in one sequence, intended to be followed session by session by the teacher or the learning group. The teaching-learning unit is the predominant form of " curriculum materials," although some (notably *The Seabury Series*) have experimented with the freer form of the resource unit. There is promise that the resource unit may come into more common use in the future.

As an enterprise of systematic planning of Christian education, curriculum construction is presently taking place at many levels: in the parish and home; in the Sunday, weekday, and vacation church schools; in the Christian all-day school; to some extent in relation to the public-school curriculum; in the college and university; at the denominational and interdenominational levels; and in relation to the missionary enterprise. As conceptions of theory and design of Christian education curriculum become of more conscious concern, a trend toward coordination of planning and effort at these various levels is noticeable. — *D. Campbell Wyckoff*

D

DANCE Dance may be defined as a rhythmical and patterned succession of movements; experience shows that dance ranges in character from the secular to the sacred. It is with this latter realm that religious educators are concerned. Whether this medium of expression is called religious dance, sacred dance, expressive dance, rhythmic movement, expressive movement, choric motion, or whether the group that participates in it is a sacred choir, a dance choir, a rhythmic choir, or a motion choir, the concern is with dance.

Expressive movement may be used in the church in many ways — the creative ability of the participants, the quality of the leadership, and the program of the church determining its effectiveness. A rhythmic choir may move toward the altar in a procession on Christmas Eve. Movement may be incorporated into vespers, or a special service may be held in which religious ideas, concepts, and feelings are expressed through rhythmic movement. Through such presentations members of a congregation may identify themselves with the members of a singing or speaking choir. The goal is to assist in providing a channel for the people's worship of God.

Movement may also be used informally in the church school program with all ages from preschool to adult groups. Such activities are often termed " rhythmics " and follow a time structure of music — beats of a percussive nature or the ordered sequence of the rhythmic movements themselves. Locomotor movements that help the participants to move from place to place can be aided by piano accompaniment or other percussive rhythm, as can nonlocomotor movements in which a person remains in one place and kneels or falls or reaches high. Beyond these preliminary introductions to movement possibilities by a leader, the child or the adult may be led to create his own movements or to participate in the creation of movement sequences by the group. Thus, creative ability may be released as movement clarifies religious feelings that may be seeking an outlet for expression.

A further use of rhythmic movement is possible in therapy as one aspect of the psychological help with which the church is becoming increasingly concerned. New insights to spiritual life may be found and new relationships to people may appear as individuals create rhythmic movement patterns together, working in groups with tension-releasing, expressive movements.

" Rhythmics " become " dance "

when the sequence of movements embodies contrast and has a beginning, a middle, and an end; form distinguishes dance from rhythmics. A dance is abstract, whether created by children or adults; if specific gestures become the expressive medium, pantomime takes the place of dance.

Members of the congregation who have had dance experience in college are often interested in assuming the leadership of dance activities in the church. Other lay persons can participate in rhythmic movement emphases at religious education conferences or special workshops. In addition, understanding of creative movement may be sought from professional persons in so-called " modern dance," since many of these dancers are concerned with the communication of those issues of life which are vital to religion.

Assistance from books and magazines is limited in the specific area of religious dance. However, occasional articles will be found in monthly journals of religious groups and in secular dance magazines. Books and journals on physical education may be consulted for aid in understanding rhythms and dances for children; writings concerned with modern dance will assist in developing dance concepts with youth and adults.

Inspiration for creating dances may be found in passages from the Bible, in hymns, chants, poems, music of great composers, drama, prayers, spirituals, or basic religious ideas. But whatever the source of inspiration, the movements should have purpose and should communicate new religious insights to the participants and to the congregation.

Children will make their response in the joy of their faith, young people will communicate their questions about religion and their concerns about the future, while adults will set forth some of the certainties embodied in their concepts of the Creator. There should be a concern that the goals of dance activities are a deepened understanding of religion in all its aspects, an increased awareness of the individual's role in his relations with others, and an expanded response in worship to God as creator. — *Helen M. Laurila*

DEACONESSES History asserts that deaconesses existed as a definite order in the early Christian church. In Rom. 16:1, Paul refers to Phoebe as " a deaconess of the church at Cenchreae." By the 3d and 4th centuries the order was firmly rooted and is mentioned in The Apostolic Constitutions and the Didache.

The functions of the deaconesses were to visit the sick, administer relief to the poor, prepare women catechumens for baptism and then to assist at the service, and to be present at interviews between bishops and women. They also could carry the Sacrament to sick women. In the East in the 4th century constant mention is made of deaconesses, and their scope is widened to include teaching. They were admitted to the diaconate by ordination. Basil mentions 3 deaconesses at Samosata; Chrysostom had 40 deaconesses on the staff of St. Sophia. In the West their ministry was less clearly defined, later being merged into the religious orders. The reason for their decline is somewhat obscure, and may have been due in part to the general diminution of adult baptism. Little mention is made of them after the 11th century.

The early 19th century brought

the revival of the order in the post-Reformation churches, under the inspiration and leadership of Pastor T. Fliedner at Kaiserswerth, Germany, in answer to an acute need occasioned by the degraded condition of ex-prisoners and other destitute people.

Suitable women were given nursing and Biblical training and upon its completion were dedicated as "deaconesses to be faithful and obedient to their calling as long as God will keep them in it." With amazing rapidity the movement spread to Holland, Switzerland, France, and later to England and America but was, and still is, numerically much stronger in the European countries than in the English-speaking world. The main pattern, too, differs. On the Continent the mother-house system is observed. Deaconesses are consecrated as members of the mother house, which then has the full direction of their placement and activities. The majority of these deaconesses, in addition to having theological training, are qualified nurses. The modern trend is for training to be more elastic and versatile, many exercising their ministry as teachers, social and parish workers, and in related avenues.

By the end of the 19th century, deaconesses were reestablished in nearly all the main Christian denominations in England and America. After a period of residential training from 2 to 4 years in a recognized deaconess house, the candidate, following a further term of probation as a church worker, is ordained, consecrated, or dedicated, as the case may be. The deaconesses take no vows at these services, but in the Church of England they are admitted by the Episcopal laying on of hands, conferring lifelong status. The deaconesses do not live together in a community or mother house but in the vicinity of their work. It is usual for them to meet at regular intervals to discuss policy and vocational matters.

In addition to parish work, deaconesses are functioning as Sunday school workers, chaplains or chaplains' assistants, social workers in public hospitals, religious teachers, court workers, missionaries, etc. In some new housing areas deaconesses are in complete charge of parishes, responsible for all ministrations with the exception of solemnizing marriages and administering Holy Communion. The actual status of deaconesses has never been clearly defined or clarified and varies in different countries and communions.

Shortly after World War II a movement, now known as "Diakonia," emerged among European deaconesses for the purpose of welding them into a more comprehensive body. Meetings are now held triennially. English-speaking deaconesses were soon included, and the countries of Australia and New Zealand. — *Kathleen A. N. Sheppard*

DEATH The Christian teaching about death is dominated by 2 apparently contradictory insights, both resulting from the experience of God's people in the encounter with their Lord in the holy history recorded in the Old and New Testaments. Death is known as universal, real, powerful, and an enemy of man. It is also known as defeated and ultimately without any power over God's people.

All men must die. It is the "way of all the earth." (Josh. 23:14; I Kings 2:2; Eccl. 5:18; John 8:52 ff.;

Heb. 9:27.) God "alone has immortality." (I Tim. 6:16.) Nowhere in the Biblical witness is death sentimentalized. It is seen as a real power, the rider on the pale horse followed by Hades (Rev. 6:8), and the fear of death subjects all men to lifelong bondage (Heb. 2:15). Death is the enemy of mankind and of the Christ who became man and met death on the cross; indeed, it is the last enemy to be destroyed (I Cor. 15:26).

The source of the power of death is human sin that has estranged man from God, the source of his life. Death is the result of sin (Rom. 6:20 ff.) and since all men are slaves of sin, they receive death as the wages of sin. As a consequence of the pervasiveness of sin, death dominates human life so completely that even now men living their life in the realm and under the power of sin can be called "dead" (cf. Matt. 8:22; Rom. 7:10).

Although the Christian proclamation takes death seriously, it also knows that death is vanquished and without power over those who are members of the body of Christ. It is through Christ's death and resurrection that he destroyed "him who has the power over death, that is, the devil," and he delivered "all those who through fear of death were subject to lifelong bondage." (Heb. 2:14 ff.) Christ "abolished death and brought life and immortality to light through the gospel" (II Tim. 1:10). He holds the keys of death and Hades. (Rev. 1:18.) Because Jesus the Christ took upon himself all sin that enslaved man to death, he has freed the members of his body from the power of sin (Col. 1:13).

In the teaching of the Christian church concerning death, the 2 elements, complementary in the apostolic witness, must both be retained. In modern society death has been removed from our daily experience and pushed into the obscurity of the hospital or the old folks' home. Thus it has become unreal and obscure. The result is the tendency to ignore it or to sentimentalize it out of existence. But only if the total and all-pervasive power of death is emphasized, does the magnitude of the deed of Christ in overcoming death become apparent. To ignore death or to teach a sentimental immortality inherent in the nature of man runs counter to the Biblical witness and obscures the disastrous dimensions of the human situation. Man is swept away like grass. (Ps. 90:5; I Peter 1:24.) He is dust and returns to dust. (Ps. 103:14; 104:29.) But man's death is not only a biological fact; as a human being he uniquely anticipates death all during his life, and his entire existence is a "being unto death" (Heidegger). For man, and for him alone, death is not merely the final stage of life in a normal biological development but a theological problem that creates in all men the "anxiety of death" (Tillich).

This same Biblical witness demands that Christ's victory over death be proclaimed in all seriousness. Even now death has lost its power. Through Baptism, the Christian baptized into the death of Christ shares already in the resurrection. (Cf. Rom. 6:3 ff.) In the Eucharist, God's people proclaim this life-giving death of Christ to one another and to all the world.

Such proclamation of the death that gives life cannot be merely verbal but must include the daily death of the Christian to his sin and his daily resurrection to the new life in Christ (II Cor. 4:7-12). The new life of the people of God, which has its focuses in Baptism and the Eucharist, is a life in which the old Adam in the Christian, together with all sins and evil lusts, is drowned by daily sorrow and put to death; and the new man is raised daily, cleansed and righteous, to live forever in God's presence (Luther). Only then can the Christian say confidently: " Death be not proud, though some have called thee mighty and dreadful, for thou art not so. . . . Death, thou shalt die "! (Donne). – *George W. Forell*

DEBATE Debate occurs when 2 or more people compete in trying to persuade others to accept or reject a proposal. Debating is an old practice and occurs in everyday living. Debate may be incorporated into Christian education as an effective technique. For example, young people can debate questions related to basic Christian attitudes toward social life, world problems, and other vital topics. Several matters are essential to good debates. The first important area is the topic. It must be timely, important to the listeners, and within the knowledge of the speakers. Once the topic is chosen, the proposition for debate must be worded properly. The proposition should always be simply expressed in the affirmative, embodying one main idea. After the proposition is stated, the speakers should be selected. The speakers must be interested in the proposition, capable of providing a balanced presentation of the topic, and, ideally, equal in ability. One point often overlooked in a debate is the physical arrangement of the room. Equipment such as chairs, a speaker's stand, and a public-address system, if necessary,

should be arranged in advance. Normally, a debate begins with an introduction by a moderator followed by the first affirmative speaker, then the first negative speaker or other speakers, maintaining the positive and negative, in that order. The speeches should be limited in time, closely checked by the moderator. Rebuttal speeches may be allowed if desired and these, too, are limited. In a rebuttal, no new arguments are to be presented. Thus in a debate the audience hears both sides of the proposition, determining for themselves what they feel is correct. Debating as used in Christian education may give a new vitality to lifeless programs, inspire both participants and listeners, and furnish new insights into old problems. – *Louis A. Barbieri, Jr.*

DECISION The word " decision " is derived from the Latin *decisio,* a " cutting short " of a number of alternatives in favor of a definite judgment and/or course of action. To decide is to sum up the case; the decision is the resulting action. The former is a process; the latter is an arresting of the process for the purpose of doing something with oneself about the issue. Decision, however, in this discussion, will embrace both the process and the result, since the 2 cannot be separated.

The Bible refers to the possibility and necessity of making decisions or responses to the initiative of God in his covenant relations with Israel. All life responses are to be made in the light of this master response. Indeed, a responsible orientation to God is one of the major motifs of the Biblical story. Whenever this personal decision of trust and obedience became lukewarm in Israel, it was the role of the prophet, particularly, to call people to the decision or redecision of repentance and faith, lest the judgment of God fall upon the nation for its apostasy. The requirement for continual decisional living toward God was at times displaced in favor of a conformity to the ritualistic, doctrinal, and legal requirements of the law, thus making the existential and immediate relationship with God less exacting. As a result, the security of objectivity was substituted for the dynamism of inward subjectivity. Against this, the prophets called for sincerity in worship and responsible justice in social relations.

This same emphasis upon decisional relations with God himself was stressed by Jesus. He ran afoul of the legalists, institutionalists, and formalists of his day. His emphasis was not primarily upon institutional conformity, moral conduct, or dogmatic proposition, but upon the decision of trust and obedience. He called for personal discipleship, sincerity in worship, and neighborly action toward those in need.

Paul had a strong personal loyalty to Jesus Christ. His decision was initiated by Christ's decision to accept, forgive, and commission him. It was only through his relationship with (in) Christ that he knew the truth about God, himself, and the world. It was through this decision of faith, always the work of the Holy Spirit, that he gained a new self and being.

In recent times the concern for decision has come from a number of sources. Modern science and technology have subordinated persons to a technical and functional order. Powerful and pervasive social processes are circumscribing man's freedom and denaturing his life of personal integrity. Many critics are saying

that man is more than an object; he is a subject who knows and makes decisions. The self stands outside the objective world, and neither history nor nature can tell man what to do. Nicolas Berdyaev and Gabriel Marcel, e.g., regard man's conformity to the objective world as a slavery from which he must be freed. Man must be more than an observer; he must commit himself adventurously.

All schools of existentialism insist that man must take his individual existence seriously, assume responsibility for himself without benefit of illusion, convention, or external authority, make his own decisions, however painful, and create his own values in the deep subjectivity of the self. For the atheistic existentialist, to live is to be caught in a trap, and the only way to victory and selfhood lies in a courageous, defiant assertion of personal freedom. Religious existentialists insist upon the same seriousness about personal life and decision, but they see it within the context of a cosmic meaningfulness in God. For Martin Buber, the emphasis is not only upon the existential I-Thou relation between God and man, but also upon the I-Thou relationship with the neighbor. In short, existentialism emphasizes the necessity of decision as the key to the achievement of selfhood, freedom, personal integrity, truth, and responsible existence.

Several schools of psychology have also felt the influence of concern for decision in their study of personality development and the place of religion in it. Gordon Allport, in *The Individual and His Religion,* speaks of the place of decision in his definition of religion: " A man's religion is the audacious bid he makes to bind himself to creation and the Creator. It is the ultimate attempt to enlarge and to complete his own personality by finding the supreme context in which he rightly belongs."

The concern for decision is manifest in John Dewey's dynamic and pragmatic conception of the educational process. Dewey revolted against rational systems in favor of the process of thinking in the "existential matrix" of society. The human mind is instrumental in meeting problems. Dewey inspired progressive education, with its close relation between thought and action and its concern for the self-expression of pupils in freedom.

Emphasis upon decision is an integral part of depth psychology, its understanding of human nature and the solution of human problems. Man is primarily a dynamic creature of action, but this will-to-action becomes enslaved and makes decision impossible. Only in the premissive atmosphere of acceptance and through insight into the reality of the situation is it possible for the problem-ridden person to develop the ability to act.

Christian education has felt the impact of this emphasis upon decision. It is focused in the relation of evangelism and nurture. The former emphasizes the confrontation of the the estranged individual with the gospel of reconciliation in Jesus Christ, inviting the response of self-giving trust, self-denying repentance, and obedient action. The latter emphasizes the larger nurture of the whole person into a maturity of responsible vocational life and community membership. The former stresses discontinuity; the latter stresses continuity with the context of faith. The 2 are never separated; they are held in unity but always in tension. The Christian life is more than decision, although its decisional nature must always be maintained lest Christian nurture deteriorate into formalism in thought, institution, and practice.

One of the crucial objectives of Christian education is that of nurturing the infant out of the "raw credulity" of cultural religion into which he is born into a self-critical and self-determining person, who by choice learns how to make all his decisions from a Christian stance. Such decision is indeed a painful act, since it means that the adolescent will have to assume full responsibility for his life as it cuts loose from the supports of protecting paternalism, institutional authority, or any other type of escape from freedom that would relieve him from radical decision.

The time when the "age of discretion" is reached is interpreted differently by various Christian traditions. The acknowledgment of such an age is an indication that the Christian decision (whether through confirmation, or confession of faith, or baptismal confession) is regarded as crucial in the life of a growing person. The church has always made much of this decision experience. All other decisions of persons are to be made within the context of this great decision.

However, decision is not to be thought of as a single act. All "life is meeting," and all meeting involves decision or response. The Christian educator is concerned about the decisional orientation of the growing person all through life.
— *Elmer G. Homrighausen*

DE LA SALLE, JEAN BAPTISTE
Jean Baptiste de la Salle, priest and educator, was born at Reims, France,

on April 30, 1651. His family were members of the new aristocracy, the *noblesse de robe*. In 1668, de la Salle was attracted to the priesthood, and was made a canon of Reims Cathedral. Philosophical and theological studies soon followed at St. Sulpice Seminary, the Sorbonne, and the University of Reims, where he received his Th.D. degree. He was ordained in 1678.

His great love for Holy Scripture, particularly the Gospels and the Pauline epistles, his training at the seminary of St. Sulpice, his work with Canon Nicholas Roland, and, later, his conferences with Père Nicholas Barre profoundly influenced his thoughts concerning Christian life and education. However, he said that his work in Christian education began in earnest when he helped Adrian Nyel, an energetic secular teacher, obtain official permission to open a charity school in Reims. Since he saw that no lasting results could be accomplished in schools without capable and efficient personnel, he personally trained Nyel's teachers. Before 4 years had elapsed he resigned his canonry, gave away his fortune during a time of famine, and founded a teaching order of dedicated religious who, in 1684, took the name Brothers of the Christian Schools (*Fratres Scholarum Christianarum*). This order was given an official Bull of Approbation by the Roman Catholic Church in 1725, and continues to flourish throughout the world.

Since the Brothers taught chiefly in cities, de la Salle attempted to provide for educational needs in rural areas by founding 3 training colleges — prototypes of the modern normal school — exclusively for secular teachers. The first of these was in existence in Reims between 1687 and 1690. The others followed from 1699 to 1705 at Paris in the parish of St. Hippolytus, and between 1709 and 1712 at St. Denis.

De la Salle was characterized by exceptional energy and determination, and a practical common sense in adapting the most efficient educational method to particular concrete situations. For example, when his teachers were faced with classrooms of 50 to 100 pupils, he chose the simultaneous method of instruction; but at the same time he required his teachers to keep detailed records and to make special efforts to understand the temperament and needs of each pupil. Knowing that many of his students would not remain more than 2 or 3 years in primary school before they were sent out to work by their parents, he insisted that they learn to read from books written in the vernacular rather than in the customary Latin. His schools were characterized by quietness and order. By eliminating disorder valuable time was saved for the teaching process.

De la Salle also opened secondary and technical schools for the youth of the rising middle class. Courses were given in draftsmanship, architecture, agriculture, commerce, industry, geometry, etc. These schools filled the gap existing in 17th-century France between the primary school and the classical college. Other educational establishments founded by de la Salle included a Sunday school for adolescents and young adults, a training school for seamen and their sons at Calais, boarding and reform schools at St. Yon, a school for the sons of the Irish nobility who were followers of James II of England, living in exile in Paris.

His ideas on education are found chiefly in his *Conduct of Schools, Meditations for the Time of Retreat,* and in parts of the Common Rules and Constitutions of the Brothers of the Christian Schools. The teaching profession is an exalted one: " They who teach youth are co-workers with Christ in saving souls " (Third Meditation). Christian teachers exist not only to prevent disorder and to build up society by giving pupils an education suitable to their talents and social station, but most of all they are to teach youth the truths of the Christian faith and inspire them to think and live as Christians. Both secular and sacred knowledge are important; but the latter must never be sacrificed for the former. Faith and zeal for the Christian instruction of youth are indispensable prerequisites for the Christian teacher.

De la Salle died at St. Yon, April 7, 1719. He was canonized in 1900; and in 1950, Pius XII proclaimed him " Patron of All Teachers."

— *Paul Claudius Laberge*

DEMOCRACY It is almost a commonplace to say that by democracy we mean more than certain political forms. Democracy is essentially a process, a way of life. Democracy is in no singular fashion a child of the church, nor is the task of the church that of the promotion and maintenance of democracy. Yet the local congregation is a primary institution where the democratic way may be seen in operation in a comparatively simple form, but at the same time reflecting the many complexities of our intricately interrelated society.

Democracy recognizes the real worth of the individual. It is a society based on the belief that human life (personality) is an end in itself, to be measured in no material terms. All social institutions are always tools in the service of persons, and never do persons merely serve the ends of institutions. Founded on the Hebraic-Christian ethic, democracy is a faith not only in the worth but in the potentialities of the individual man.

Democracy includes belief in the equality of all men. This is not a belief in equality of natural endowments, but maintenance of the right to equal treatment and consideration. Each individual is entitled to the opportunity to develop his own capacities, and each has needs that are equally as important as any other person's.

Democracy is a society of free men. People are the best judges of their own interests, can be trusted with liberty and power, and can rule themselves. Historically, liberty has been one of the most emphasized of the characteristics of democracy, but it must always be balanced with equality, and from it must proceed a sense of responsibility. Liberty involves more than freedom of action. Democracy maintains also freedom of thought and conscience. This means freedom of learning and teaching, the practical justification for which is the fact that democratic government is self-government. People cannot make momentous decisions to the best advantage unless the majority are intelligent and informed.

Democratic government is only by consent of the governed. It is founded on the belief that no set of men is entitled to rule others without their consent. Those who must abide by laws and policies ought to have a voice in the formation of those laws and policies. There is a necessity for the participation of all mature human beings in the formation of the values that regulate their living together.

Democracy is rule by the majority, with protection of the rights of minorities. It rests on the assumption that men have or may acquire sufficient intelligence and integrity to govern themselves better than any one or any few can do it for them. But while democracy is the rule of the many, it rejects completely the principle of absolute conformity and acquiescence. It realizes that human values are destroyed by the passions aroused in the persecution and suppression of minorities. It sees in the minority, in the dissident individual or group, a major creative force in society.

Shared interest is a necessary characteristic of any functioning democracy. If government is to be by consent of the governed, with those who abide by laws and policies having a share in their formation, and with the majority will prevailing, unless there is a sufficient community of interest to permit wide agreement there will be not government but stalemate.

Tolerance means sympathetic acceptance of ways of living and behaving and of modes of thinking and believing different from one's own or different from those of the community at large. This is not, however, unlimited tolerance, for within the democratic way there is also a high degree of intolerance for any philosophy or behavior that seeks to limit the rights and liberties of individuals or attempts by subterfuge or force to destroy the democratic way.

Shared power and respect are irrevocably wedded together. Whenever power becomes concentrated in the hands of a few individuals or a single group, others may at best be treated benevolently, but never with the respect that comes from a recognition of equal worth and dignity. Conversely, whenever the respect is lacking, stronger individuals and groups will employ any strategy available to exercise power over others.

Public enlightenment is the necessary condition for any democratic operation. True freedom of action, mind, and conscience can be exercised only as the facts of any situation are known by those who are to exercise their will and formulate policies.

Democracy is the way of interaction, of gradual change by social process rather than by revolution. This is the rejection of government by brute force, the affirmation of a belief that cultural change should be accomplished through deliberative action rather than by methods of uncontrolled violence. It is founded on faith in the capacities of human nature and intelligence.

Democratic government is government under law rather than primarily by men; it is constitutionalism in contrast to absolutism. Shared power, respect, and interest when ideally balanced should result in the conditions necessary for an ideal society. But the vast majority of democracy's proponents have been realists, recognizing imbalances and imperfections present, and, as far as the Puritan strain in democracy is concerned, the sinful nature of man. Thus has developed the necessity for the social contract, the agreement of law under which men can be protected against those who amass too much power or would exercise arbitrary authority over the community. — *Joseph W. Baus*

DEMONSTRATION Demonstration is a basic method of instruction, practiced by ancient as well as modern man, by children as well as adults, by animals as well as human beings. It is based on the individual's ability to observe and the desire to imitate. Among primitive people, hunting and warfare are taught through demonstration from one generation to another. The modern child observes and strives to imitate other children, parents, teachers, and adults in general. The little girl who dresses up in her mother's hat and shoes has observed and consciously imitates. The boy learns through observation how to operate the family car long before he is old enough to obtain a driver's license. The small child learns his family's tongue, his table manners, and even his acts of worship through observation and imitation.

Demonstration is the most direct type of instruction. In the so-called trial and error method of problem-solving, the successful solution may be altogether a matter of chance. A rat running a laboratory maze will eventually discover the right route to the goal but usually after a number of errors. With practice these errors will be gradually eliminated. If the hunger drive is strong enough, the rat will continue through trials and errors until the goal, the food, is reached. At best it is a roundabout way of learning.

In the insight type of learning, there is often a long delay with unsuccessful attempts to solve the problem before the learner, through insight, gets an idea of how it may be done. Köhler and other psychologists, in their laboratory experiments with apes, have demonstrated that insight in solving a problem requires a type of reasoning. Human adults with their mature mentality and accumulation of past experiences are able to *see* more readily than a child with its immature mind and lack of experience. In both trial and error and insight learning there are elements of nonproductive experimentation and delays. The demonstration technique attacks the learning problem directly: " This is how it is done! " It may be used to teach an individual, a group, or a class.

In demonstration an ideal pattern of action is presented for the learner to observe and to imitate. The demonstrator-instructor must himself have mastered the skill he demonstrates. It must not be some clever sleight of hand performance to exhibit his own skill, but a deliberate effort to help the learner observe how it is done. Both instructor and learner must be motivated: the instructor must have a deep desire to show the learner; the learner must be eager to observe and reproduce.

Soon after the presentation the learner should be given an opportunity to duplicate what he has observed. Although the first attempt may be far from perfect, errors may be pointed out by the instructor or by fellow members of the class. What was wrong? Practice without a critical evaluation tends to fix rather than to eliminate errors.

A film may be used in demonstration. The learners should be briefed beforehand about important details to be observed lest they devote attention to interesting trivialities rather than matters of primary importance. After the demonstration, opportunity should be provided for a discussion of what was observed. If impressions seem vague or confused, a second demonstration may be indicated.

Religious education presents many opportunities for the use of the demonstration method. It is usable in classes, laboratory schools, workshops and training institutes. Leading a worship service, conducting a business meeting, teaching a class, and personal counseling are a few examples of skills that may be taught effectively through demonstration.
— *Peter P. Person*

DENMARK The inspiration to gather children into Sunday schools came to Denmark from England. Attempts to start Sunday schools were made as early as 1830, but they were not firmly established until 1875. Today every parish in the country has one. The church bodies chiefly promoting Sunday school work are the State Church Union for Inner Mission, the Lutheran Mission, the Baptist Union, the Salvation Army, and The Methodist Church. Each body has its own committee, but all work cooperatively.

The numbers enrolled and the types of meeting place vary considerably. Some classes are held in private homes, some in public school buildings, and many in church buildings. Although there is close or departmental grading in many instances, many smaller schools have only two departments, one for very small children and another for those who can read.

Training programs for workers have been set up in the form of courses, conferences, and evening schools. New methods of teaching and visual aids are being introduced. Each worker is trained to study his Biblical text for the lesson, making a careful analysis of its content before planning the best way to present it to the children. Weekly meet-ings for Sunday school teachers are regarded as indispensable, providing text exposition and study through group discussion.

Bible camps in the summer period have been developed to undergird the yearly Sunday school program. In these camps the teachers have opportunities to know each child intimately. Parental visits establish fine home contacts.

The religious education work is supported financially through collections in the churches and among the parents. No government aid is available.

A boys' brigade (the FDF) and a similar girls' organization (the FPF) have an extensive program. These are uniformed groups, providing camps, musical activities, and sports. The FDF, organized in 1902, has as its motto: "With God for the youth of Denmark." The FPF's goal is: "Working to prepare the way for the Kingdom of God among girls."

The Y.M.C.A. movement is strong in Denmark, also. The boy and girl Scouting programs are related to the Y.M.C.A. program. The "youth schools," offering free courses for adolescents aged 14 through 18, have contributed toward helping young people achieve a Christian orientation during a period when these adolescents are often rebellious against authority and are psychologically disharmonious.

Danish Sunday school work is carried on in close cooperation with Norway, Sweden, and Finland. A Scandinavian committee plans and coordinates curriculum materials. A Scandinavian Sunday school congress is held annually. Leaders in all the countries regard this cooperative effort as productive of mutual inspiration and a valuable exchange of experiences and ideas. All denominational schools in Denmark are related to the World Council of Christian Education through a committee that has been under the leadership of Bishop Fuglsang Damgaard.

The statistical picture is as follows: 115,000 pupils are enrolled in Sunday schools, 111,000 in other Christian education agencies.

— *Ejnar Jensen*

DEVELOPMENTAL TASKS " A developmental task is a task which arises at or about a certain period in the life of the individual, successful achievement of which leads to his happiness and to success with later tasks, while failure leads to unhappiness in the individual, disapproval by society, and difficulty with later tasks." Thus the present writer defined the concept in *Developmental Tasks and Education*.

The concept grew out of the research on child and adolescent development that flourished in the 1930's and resulted in a science of human development cutting across disciplines in the biological and the social sciences. More recently the concept has been developed on the basis of psychological and sociological research on attitudes and social roles. Recent research on adulthood and old age has elaborated the developmental task concept and applied it to the entire life cycle.

The developmental tasks of a particular group of people arise from 3 sources: physical maturation, cultural pressure (the expectations of society), and individual aspirations or values. Research in these areas tells what the developmental tasks are and where they are located by age, e.g., it was research on physical development in adolescence

that led to the definition of one of the tasks of adolescence as " accepting one's body."

More light has been thrown on the nature and influence of the concept by the attention paid to the concept of social role in the past decade. A social role is a pattern of behavior defined and expected of a group of people who occupy a certain position in society. If a given social role is expected of people generally when they reach a given age period, this role will constitute a developmental task, e.g., since the role of husband is generally expected of young men, it is proper to consider " getting married " to be a developmental task.

Another source of clarification of the concept has been Erikson's use of the concept of psychosocial task. He sees the life cycle as a matter of meeting and mastering a sequence of 7 psychosocial tasks. Each task must be met and mastered during a certain period of life. If any is not well achieved, there will be difficulty with the later ones. Thus one might say that Erikson has described a series of basic major developmental tasks. These are psychosocial, not biological. Each is broader than a developmental task as defined by the present writer and by others. For example, Erikson's task of " achieving identity," the central task of adolescence, contains the following developmental tasks: learning a masculine or feminine social role; accepting one's body; achieving emotional independence of parents and other adults; selecting and preparing for an occupation; achieving a scale of values and an ethical system to live by.

There are 3 conceivable procedures for discovering and defining developmental tasks. One is to observe people and infer what their principal developmental concerns are at any given age — to discover in this way what they are " working at." Another is to ask people what their chief concerns and interests are, assuming that they are conscious of their developmental needs and willing to talk about them. A 3d procedure is for the social scientist to think about his own career, past and present, and to define his principal developmental motives. In all 3 cases one looks at people and asks them, directly or indirectly, what their developmental tasks are.

The basic hypotheses about developmental tasks are that performance on them is positively interrelated at any given age and that performance in a given task area at one age is positively related to subsequent performance in that area. To test these hypotheses, data on developmental task performance are needed for a group of people over a period of years. Such data were available in the " Prairie City Study of Moral Character Development." Schoeppe and Havighurst made a study of the interrelations of developmental task performance among a group of boys and girls at the ages of 10, 13, and 16, and of the relationships between performance on a given task at those 3 ages. Their results confirmed the basic hypotheses and indicated that there is not much compensation of low performance on one task by high performance on another task, although this does occasionally occur.

The concept has found a number of applications in the field of general education. One is the formulation of educational objectives around developmental tasks in the areas of personal development and social maturation. Although the schools cannot take responsibility for helping children accomplish all their developmental tasks (the home, the church, and other social institutions have major responsibilities in this connection), there are certain tasks where the schools should be the central agency — such as selecting and preparing for an occupation, and learning to get along with age mates in middle childhood. The " nonacademic " teachers in the secondary schools find the concept especially helpful, because it calls attention to the importance of other kinds of experience and learning as well as the achievement of mental skills in mathematics, language, and science.

Another application is the doctrine of the " teachable moment." According to the theory of developmental tasks there is a time or a period of time when a person learns a certain developmental task most quickly and successfully because his body is ready, his personal aspiration calls for it, and society expects it at about that time. Thus there is a best time to learn to talk, another to learn to associate with the opposite sex, and another to become a communicant church member. This doctrine is useful in the placement of courses and subjects at certain age levels. In adult education, and in the informal education of such agencies as the Y.M.C.A. and the Scouts, the developmental task concept is useful in the selection of educational matter and objectives.

In the field of religious education one use of the concept has been illustrated by the Joint Curriculum Committee of the United Church of Christ. In effect this group has said that religious education should help the individual achieve his developmental tasks in an ethically superior way. There are Christian performance goals for many of the ordinary developmental tasks that are somewhat different in quality from the performance goals set by the general community. Thus, at the high school age the religious education program should help young people select their lifework (a developmental task) in a way that takes account of religious and ethical values. Again, in the task of achieving emotional independence of parents the church may be able to help young people do this in a way that emphasizes the religious virtues of love and compassion. Or, at the age of middle childhood, the church may help boys and girls with their task of forming attitudes toward other races, nations, religions, and economic groups so that their attitudes reflect religious values as well as the scientific and historical knowledge that the public school imparts.

Another way of using the developmental task concept is to discover and define certain specifically religious developmental tasks, such as "becoming a communicant church member," and "achieving responsiveness to God." Then the religious education program might be organized around the important religious developmental tasks of the various age levels. This is especially useful when a church regards itself as also a society, with a culture of its own and with members strongly committed to that culture. In such a situation, the church will have the force of society behind it in setting developmental tasks for its members. Thus, the task of making the *bar mitzvah* in early adolescence for a boy in an orthodox Jewish community is a real developmental task, whereas the analogous task of

"joining the church" in a "liberal" Protestant denomination may not have much importance in the eyes of boys and girls.

Workers in the field of religious education who stress the "spiritual" as different from the "ethical" purposes of religion are likely to utilize the idea of a set of specifically religious developmental tasks. To define such a series of tasks there is need for research and intensive analysis of what the Christian life is.
— *Robert J. Havighurst*

DEVOTIONAL LITERATURE The word "devotion" comes from a Latin word meaning "to dedicate" or "consecrate." Devotional literature, therefore, is something written to help people to dedicate themselves to God, to worship him. One writer defines it as any religious book other than doctrinal and technical that is intended mainly for meditation and prayer in the home as differentiated from formal liturgies used in public worship. Yet often the same materials are used both in public worship and in home or individual devotions.

Certainly this is true of the Bible. Like all other true devotional literature, the Scriptures, from a human standpoint, grew out of men's experiences with God and a desire to share them. Inspired by the Holy Spirit, the record reveals these experiences as rooted in God's outreach to man, His revelation of himself.

Not all the Biblical writings can be considered equally useful as devotional material. Much of Leviticus, e.g., has to do with rules and regulations for everyday health, safety, and honesty. The Psalms, on the other hand, contain records of, and invitations to, worship and personal devotion.

There is no distinct or complete separation between doctrinal or theological books and books that lead to the worship of God, for dedication to God grows out of what a person believes about God.

The beginnings of devotional literature cannot be dated. Private prayers, along with those for public worship, appeared in the Jewish prayer book as early as A.D. 866. These included prayers to be said at midnight, on Friday night, on Saturday, both day and night, and prayers for children to use. Vernacular prayers in Aramaic began to be published in the 9th century.

Prayer books and books of meditation were well known during the Middle Ages (roughly 476 to 1492) and became popular during the Protestant Reformation.

In the 14th century came John Wycliffe's translation of the Bible into English, and in the 15th the invention of printing from movable type. More people learned to read. These factors, along with the Protestant emphasis on every man's responsibility before God, stimulated devotional books.

The 16th century was marked by the publication of religious diaries and writings like John Foxe's *Book of Martyrs*. Confessions of faith, tracts, and pious novels appeared. Funeral orations were published as biographical memorials. By the latter part of the 17th century devotional books with as many as 2,000 pages became common. These included story parables such as *The Pilgrim's Progress*.

Special devotional materials for children began to be developed, though many children read adult books, especially collections of the then vivid sermons. *A Token for Children* (1671) may be considered typical of a child's devotional book, since it was most widely used next to the Bible itself. It featured 13 model children who delighted in pious books and speech, wept over their sins at the age of 8 or 9 years, and died with "spiritual" words on their lips. This book was popular both in England and America well into the 18th and 19th centuries. The same tone of emotional indulgence is evident in various publications for children. *The Child's Magazine and Sunday Scholar's Companion* regularly carried a section devoted to the "happy" deaths of children.

The New England Primer adopted the tone of the 17th century, and, some say, was based on John Cotton's *Spiritual Milk for Boston Babes in Either England*. Later came the development of Sunday school literature and various magazines for both children and adults.

The devotional literature of the 20th century suggests evidences of an older influence, especially in its emotional content. It also reflects an approach to devotional life based on the marvels of God's world, sensitivity to human need, and the avenues of appreciation. There is a return to the use of some older books and an increasing reliance on the Bible in various versions.

— *Robbie Trent*

DEWEY, JOHN The philosopher John Dewey thought and lived within the evolutionary vision. The world is on the move, with everything permeable to everything else. The universe and its species of life were not created at one particular time into set patterns but are continuously being created and reconstructed. We live in a universe of possibilities. The participation of man from within such a universe of life is crucial. And such participation, interfused with memory, thought, and valuing, is what education essentially is.

In order to get in touch with the " go " of things, man must experience, i.e., risk transaction with the other vitalities of the world. Only thus can he really come to know them and exist in the rushing process of life. A passive spectator can have only impotent " knowledge about," and this is neither creative nor saving.

An experience is a transaction with some otherness in the world; it is not a self-contained emotional feeling. The individual must sense that " this situation has to do with me." Experiencing is basic; then thought, moral valuing, and memory transform the experiencing into an enriched and shaped experience. An experience is a punctuated length of the flow of consciousness, desirably coming to a culminating climax. Over the long haul, man puts together various experiences into a dramatic story that is the thread of meaning for his life, and whatever specifics do not fit this frame tend to be rejected or become occasions of radical learning. Not all experiences are of equal value, so that the function of a school is to select the potentially most enriching experiences for its curriculum. Some experiences recur so commonly, affecting the weal and woe of the whole community, that they eventually become basic content of the society.

Man is incurably societal; the epidermis is not the boundary of a person. Conjunct communicated experience is both democracy and personal existence. Participation, communication, and the significant symbol are the processes of life, and therefore of learning.

For in a universe " on the go," education is not learning but development — the continuing emergence of enriched man-in-society — or perhaps society-in-man. A child is not a miniature adult; his experiencing at his own level is significant — only it must have a " leading on " potential from which the next developmental stage can come. The scholarly man of action is the goal of education — not merely for the elite but for every son and daughter of democracy. Knowing and doing must not be torn apart.

The popular opinion of what Dewey meant by " learning by doing " is therefore grossly absurd, for his fight was against the " empirical " (action without control of insight and moral values, usually repeating what had been done in the past). He was for the " experimental " (life directed by an understanding of conditions and their consequences as discovered by risking experience with it). A school is a laboratory of the Department of Philosophy — for pupils as well as teachers.

What, then, is the truth about anything? Its truth is our total net of knowledge and imaginative vision regarding the total consequences of our continuing transactions with it. The truth about a clock is not whether the picture in our mind corresponds to a photograph (copy) of the clock's face. A " copy theory " of truth leads to a dull, repetitious life. Truth is the potentiality we see in the present and what it has become down the road of history. Man is a historical existence, and to be " in truth," means to journey with truth through a wilderness. The world is precarious; society can disintegrate unless held together by man's structure of meanings and resolute action.

Dewey was convinced about the finiteness of man. Along with men of science, he was clear that any formulation or institution is only an approximation — always an expression of the power structure of the society and the goals of the person thinking. He therefore rejected every principle or idea as an absolute. It was merely a present working document in need of future reconstruction, a perch upon which man could rest for a while until a new flight into the vastness of the universe could be made. Yet ideas-rooted-in-experiencing were mankind's distinctive possession and the hope of continuing society. Without the method of intelligence, man was condemned to a bestial life of irrational passion.

For a number of years, Dewey was known in educational circles for his analysis of how man thinks. True to his evolutionary theory, man thinks when he becomes disconnected from that which has supported him and when his old habits no longer bring off desired consequences. To survive, he must effect a new relationship; he must solve the problem he is in. Not in any fashion but in accord with the sequence of the moral act, and with satisfaction of the demands of the situation, not just his own pleasure. In his later years Dewey came to the conclusion that life is not all problem-solving. In *Art as Experience* he enlarged his description of man's consciousness to include consummatory experiences — experiences in which one is enjoying an immediacy of pattern or relationship. Art experience is not the sole possession of "the artist"; every man in some degree is busy clarifying his experience, intensifying its vivid points, putting it into compelling design. Education should sustain and train him in this process, and the educational community engage in discriminating celebration of experience. Such action is not contrary to thinking, for thinking comes from things deeply felt.

In *A Common Faith,* Dewey made clearer his concern for the religious in life. True to his hatred of all dualisms (the tearing apart of things that belong together in an evolutionary universe) he rejected the view that some experiences are religious and constitute religion. For him all experiences worthy of that term potentially have a religious quality. He believed that only such religiousness could rescue educated man from his rejection of dogmatic special religion. God is the connecting of the actual and the visioned good; the religious is man's similar action, at whatever cost to himself. Such action begins with reverent imagination — the projecting of a desirable future out of potentiality seen in the present moment and in the flow of history. The religious is therefore not concerned with rootless, abstract ideals but with possibility rooted in the concreteness of life. Dewey's "religious" also involves a high awareness of oneself as the link between the past generations and those yet to come. Our destiny as men is to pass on the culture without which man would be animal, and to pass it on in richer and more generally available form.

John Dewey had wide influence upon Christian education. George Albert Coe was the principal instrument of his influence, but it is wide enough to include people who reject his philosophy but use his learning-teaching theory. The latter would cause consternation, if not disgust, in a Dewey who believed intensely that there must be no gulf between means and ends, or between content and method. At many points Dewey's thinking is Hebraic. And he opened up views that existentialist thought affirms — such as the idea that the "world" is organized by the human mind.

Criticisms of Dewey's position have included the following: He never really developed a doctrine of the person (Kilpatrick, his principal interpreter to the teachers of America, was much clearer about the self, its choices and decisions). Dewey always seemed to evade answering where the teacher would get his criteria for "leading on to further growth," although he did offer such generalizations as participation, communication, openness to humane potentiality, fidelity to thoughtful experience and the history of man. In educational practice, schools have seemed to underrate the importance of ideas, perhaps due to Dewey's lack of enthusiasm for making statements about the structure of an entity. He perhaps left truth too much a matter of our own creation, instead of believing with Peirce in a "real" that had character whether we knew it or not. He has contributed to religion in an age of science as one who brought religion down out of a 2-storied universe by insisting that whatever truth we have is to be at work changing the world into its own embodiment; and if God is, then he is here — involved in the concreteness of life on the move.

He was against the doctrines of special revelation and set his face like a flint against many traditional ways of maintaining belief. He was deeply concerned with how procrea-

tive ideas and originating truth come to birth in the human situation.

— *Ross Snyder*

DIDACHĒ *Didachē* is that part of the gospel dealing with exhortation and "teaching" as relatively distinct from *kērygma*, or "proclamation." In the preaching of Paul the 2 cannot have been held separate, for in speaking to the Thessalonians (I Thess. 1:9-10) about their conversion he reminds them that they are now awaiting the coming of Jesus, "who delivers us from the wrath to come" — and some explanation of the reason for this wrath must have been given (cf. Rom. 1:18-32). Exhortatory passages are fairly common in his letters, as in Jewish literature both Hellenistic and Rabbinic (also at Qumrân). One situation in which such teaching was given was obviously before baptism, when it was necessary to explain to converts what the Christian "way" was. Proof that such teaching was provided at this point is to be found in Pliny's letter to Trajan concerning the Christians (*Ep.* x. 96), in Justin's First Apology (ch. 61), and in the late 1st-century manual known as the Didache. Pliny relates that Christians took an oath, apparently based on the Decalogue; Justin says that those baptized promised that they could live in accordance with Christian teaching; and the Didache begins by describing the 2 ways (a theme both Jewish and Greek in origin) of life and death, then proceeds to more general ethical admonitions before describing the rite of Baptism.

The lists of virtues and vices to be found in the New Testament were largely taken over from Hellenistic Judaism (ultimately from the Stoics, apparently); other examples occur in the Dead Sea scrolls. In addition, the New Testament letters contain descriptions of household duties that are Greek in origin.

It need not be supposed that moral teaching was confined to the time of baptism; among Philo's writings there are homilies on ethical themes, and the so-called letter of James is largely a collection of moral teachings on various subjects. Some of the themes common to such letters as James, I Peter, Colossians, and Ephesians can be fairly easily explained, however, as reflections of a prebaptismal "catechism," primarily moral in content.

The pastoral letters (I and II Timothy, Titus) consist almost entirely of *didachē*, and the word itself occurs more often than in the (other?) Pauline writings. Timothy is to "put . . . instructions before the brethren" (I Tim. 4:6); he is to "attend to the public reading of scripture, to preaching, to teaching" (v. 13); he is to "take heed" to himself and to his teaching, and by so doing he will save both himself and his hearers (v. 16). Sometimes this kind of emphasis is viewed as evidence that Paul did not write the pastorals, and that they come from a later, more decadent time than the Apostolic Age. Such a view neglects the emphasis upon teaching that is to be found in both Jesus and Paul. Jesus was sometimes called "Rabbi" — "which means Teacher" (John 1:38), and his sayings, both in form and, to a considerable extent, in content, resemble those of his Jewish contemporaries. Paul mentions teachers only after apostles and prophets (I Cor. 12:28), but he himself taught his "ways in Christ" in every church (ch. 4:17). He spoke of "the standard of teaching to which you were committed"

(Rom. 6:17), and urged those who had the gift of teaching to use it (ch. 12:6-7).

What they taught was largely, but not exclusively, based on the Old Testament: "whatever was written in former days was written for our instruction" (Rom. 15:4; cf. I Cor. 10:11). It was also based on more strictly Christian considerations: "You learned from us how you ought to live and to please God"; "You know what instructions we gave you through the Lord Jesus" (I Thess. 4:1-2); more often he used his own words, for what he wrote was assisted by the Spirit (Rom. 7:40) and could be regarded as containing "a command of the Lord" (Rom. 14:37).

The emphasis on moral teaching characteristic of the apologists of the 2d century is due in part to the prevalent accusations of Christian immorality, in part to the apologists' own understanding of Christianity not only as a kerygmatic theology but also as a way of life with rather definite rules of conduct — as in the letter of Polycarp to the Philippians and in The Shepherd of Hermas. This understanding reaches a climax toward the end of the century in the writings of Clement of Alexandria: the *Protrepticus* (*Exhortation*) to pagans; the *Paedagogus* (*Instructor*) of Christian beginners; and the *Stromateis* (*Miscellanies*) of teaching for those who were spiritually more perfect. A similar view of the Christian life as an educational process is reflected in the writings of Origen. In Clement's time a collection of brief " sentences " was drawn up, largely from Pythagorean sources, and later ascribed to a bishop of Rome.

Gnostics, on the other hand, rejected this kind of teaching and derived their ethical ideas partly from Paul, partly from the Cynics. Among them there was no place for *didachē*. The Gospel of Thomas, for example, opposes prayer, fasting, and almsgiving.

The element of *didachē* in Christian instruction reaches a high point among the early Latin fathers in the moral writings of Tertullian and Cyprian; among the Greeks we should give special mention to Cyril of Jerusalem, who in the mid-4th century delivered important catechetical orations. To some extent *didachē* was also employed in sermons and commentaries on the Old Testament, in which the creation story, for example, was often given a moral-allegorical treatment.

During this whole period the old manual known as the Didache was undergoing revision and supplementation; in 3d-century Syria it formed the base of the *Didascalia apostolorum*, and in the 4th century it was similarly employed in the Apostolic Constitutions. Since these documents were generally regarded as authentically apostolic, Christians could view the apostles as having provided moral instruction for their converts. As we have already seen, this notion was correct in general if not in specific details.

In modern New Testament criticism quite a few attempts have been made to free the "authentic" gospel from the element of *didachē*, on the ground that this element is late, not apostolic, and inferior to the Pauline ideas of grace and of justification by faith. In these attempts, of course, emphasis is often laid upon the relative lateness and/ or uniqueness of the catechetical materials provided in Matthew (not to mention Luke), upon the inade-

quacies of James and the pastorals, upon the lack of brilliance manifested by Polycarp and Hermas, and upon a one-sided interpretation of Paul's thought. Such attempts can be justified neither historically nor theologically. The New Testament materials are what they are, whether or not they appeal to later historians and theologians. Paul himself devoted considerable attention to teaching, as is evident from all his letters. In Gal. 5:22 he spoke (explicitly) about the fruit of the Spirit; but first he repeated to the Galatians what he had told them of the works of the flesh. He certainly set forth "the indicative" (what Christ has done, what the consequences are), but he never hesitated to continue with "the imperative." At the end of his great discussion of freedom and responsibility (I Cor., chs. 8 to 10) he gave explicit teaching about the practical problem of idol meats, setting forth first a general principle (ch. 10:25-26), then instructions for 2 kinds of circumstances (vs. 27-29a). In Galatians he proclaims freedom from the Jewish law but ends by speaking of "the law of Christ" (Gal. 6:2). In other words, *didachē* is an essential element of the Pauline gospel, as it is of the gospel in general. — *Robert M. Grant*

DIDACHE, THE   The subtitle of the Didache is "The Lord's Teaching to the Gentiles by the Twelve Apostles." In addition to the books that found a place in the New Testament, there remain other works produced during the 1st century or so of the church's existence which either never were seriously considered or lingered for a time on the fringe of the canon before finally being excluded. Among these the most important is the group collected under the designation "Apostolic Fathers," the Didache being one of the most prominent.

The early church compiled this treatise for the purpose of instructing and preparing Gentile Christians for church membership. It contains a short early-Christian manual on morals and ecclesiastical practice. Before the churches had reached agreement as to what books should be read in church and before Christian practice in prayer and worship had been fixed, Christian leaders felt the need for a brief handbook that would regulate church rites and practice. The early church, in its organic function, produced 2 important methods in carrying its mission into the world: one being the *kērygma* (preaching) and the other *didachē* (teaching). Although the original nature of the kerygma may be reconstructed only from the writings of the New Testament, *didachē* was preserved in written form in this manual.

Its 16 brief chapters fall into 3 parts. Chapters 1 to 5 describe the "Two Ways" — the "Way of Life" and the "Way of Death" — and are used as a manual of instruction for nurturing Christian character in the church. Each of the "Two Ways" is explained: what one must do to have life and what leads to death and therefore must be avoided. They include many quotations from the Sermon on the Mount and have close affinities with chs. 18 to 20 of the Letter of Barnabas. The problem therefore arises whether Barnabas used the Didache or the Didache used Barnabas, or whether both used a common source. It is perhaps best explained by the theory that both the Didache and the Letter of Barnabas made use of an earlier Jewish-Christian (perhaps originally Jewish) document used for catechetical purposes.

Chapters 6 to 16 contain a manual of church order such as baptism, fasting, prayer, the Eucharist, the observance of the Lord's Day, itinerant prophets, and the local ministry of bishops and deacons. The earliest formulated liturgy of the Lord's Supper is presented here, holding to the Lucan order of the cup's preceding the bread. Here the cup has been displaced from the end of the meal to the very beginning, showing perhaps the marked recognition of the importance of the Messianic banquet. The Lord's Prayer is given in full in the words of Matthew, with slight alterations and with the addition of the closing Doxology. Baptism is by immersion if possible; otherwise by threefold affusion. Fasting on Wednesdays and Fridays is offered in contrast to the Jewish practice of fasting on Mondays and Thursdays. In addition to bishops and deacons, the traveling prophets fill a role of great importance ("They are your high priests," ch. 13:3) and may celebrate the Eucharist.

Chapter 16 closes the book with reference to the Antichrist, the coming of Christ on the clouds, and the exhortation to be faithful to the end. The joyful expectation for the eschatological hope serves as a basis for the preceding discipline.

The book perpetuates what were originally Jewish-Christian forms in a Gentile document, which is fully catholic in the sense of visualizing Christianity as a world religion. The Gospel of Matthew is referred to as "the Gospel." The Didache may be regarded as a supplement to Matthew, taking its title and inspiration from the last verses of that Gospel in which the apostles are commissioned to go out and "make disciples" of the Gentiles, baptizing them and teaching them to observe what the Lord had commanded; that is to say, what he had commanded in that particular Gospel. Thus what appears to be at the outset a peculiarly Jewish legalistic expression in this book is actually the outcome of the gospel principles. It is significant to note that the moral ideal put forward for realization is not made up of commandments from the law but from the sayings of Jesus. The author is strongly attached to the traditional teaching of the church and feels no need to prove or even to affirm that the teaching is true, holding that what contradicts it is only error or vanity. To give any kind of instruction which differs from that of the church is to teach "without God" (ch. 6:1). The author seems to have dreaded the influence of Jews upon the church and makes every effort to distinguish the 2 groups (chs. 8:1-2; 14:1).

The book as a whole presents many still unsolved problems both of textual and literary criticism, of date and provenance. The author prefers to remain in the background, and he is content to let his work stand on its own merits: it is "The Lord's Teaching . . . by the Twelve Apostles." It is clear that the Didache is itself a compiled document, and the author avows his dependence upon other sources. There are 8 express quotations: 2 (chs. 14:3; 16:7) are from the Old Testament (Mal. 1:11, 14; Zech. 14:5); 5 from the Gospels introduced by certain formulas (chs. 8:2; 9:5; 11:3; 15:3-4), and 1 (ch. 1:6) from some unknown "Sacred Scripture." The author did not hesitate to enrich his inherited code of Christian morals with a block of sentences from Matthew, Luke-Acts, I Peter, and The Shepherd of Hermas (Commands 2:4-6) which was written about A.D. 100.

The chronology of this complex document is very obscure. Some scholars considered the Didache to be very ancient, as early as A.D. 70 or 90. Recent study, however, has shown conclusively that in the present form it belongs to the 1st half of the 2d century. The place of origin may be located in the East, with some balance of probability in favor of Syria. The book had an influence upon later liturgical documents, especially the Apostolic Constitutions, the Apostolic Church Order and the *Life of Schnudi*. It was apparently known to Clement of Alexandria, Eusebius, Athanasius, and other church fathers.

Lost for centuries, the Didache was discovered by P. Bryennios in a Greek manuscript called the Jerusalem Codex at Constantinople in 1873, and published by him 10 years later. Two small papyrus fragments of the Didache in Greek have since been published from 2 leaves of a parchment manuscript found at Oxyrhynchus. The 3d-century Latin translation of the "Two Ways" and a 5th-century Coptic fragment of chs. 10:36 to 12:2a are also available in the British Museum. Two extracts in Ethiopic also have come to light, as well as a Georgian version.

— *Tadashi Akaishi*

DIORAMA "Diorama" is derived from the Greek *dia,* meaning "through," and the verb form *horan,* meaning "to see." The diorama is a lifelike, graphic reconstruction in 3 dimensions of a scene. Essentially, the diorama is a form of model and belongs to a family of 3-dimensional materials including objects, mock-ups, globes, and relief maps. A diorama, then, is a collection of objects or models arranged against a painted background.

Originally, perhaps, the diorama was used as an exhibit in museums and was later because of cost and difficulty of construction reduced to miniature. It is often thought of as the miniature representation of the museum habitat group. In its most highly developed form, however, it is a sort of stage enclosed in a box. Some writers point out that dramatics students have used dioramas for years.

The diorama usually consists of a boxlike case with a curved background. To achieve real-life impression, depth is exaggerated by making the objects in the background smaller than those in the foreground. This forced perspective makes the figures and accessories in the foreground appear to merge into the background. The combination of curved background and forced perspective is what gives the diorama vividness and realism.

In education the diorama is usually constructed to illustrate some aspect of a topic under study. Usually it is a portable, miniature scene built into a box; however, it can be large or small, simple or elaborate, depending upon the age and ability of the one making the scene. School-made dioramas (peep boxes) are most often produced in miniature and are of temporary interest and value. Their principal use is to aid in the development of accurate concepts by bringing a small section of the world to the classroom.

As a rule, a teacher may use 3 techniques with the diorama. He can use a ready-made scene, he can plan with his students and construct a 3-dimension picture, or he can plan a field trip to see a diorama. Although ready-made scenes can be used very effectively in the classroom and take much less time than class-made models, usually their educational value is also limited. (Commercially made cardboard cutouts called dioramas serve even fewer educational purposes.) A ready-made diorama placed in the classroom may create interest in a topic, but as soon as it ceases to be appropriate or fails to create interest it should be stored away out of sight. In addition, such dioramas may help to stimulate questioning, channel discussion, sharpen observation, provide a review, and motivate other learning experiences. Although custom-made dioramas assist the teacher and pupils in reaching some goals, the actual making of a diorama offers a wider range of educational possibilities.

The making of a diorama usually enlivens a classroom, for it presents a challenge to student ingenuity. However, it requires considerable time, and this creates a difficulty for the teacher who has a short class period. Making a diorama also involves the teacher in many small-group activities. The construction of a diorama during the class session offers educational opportunities when time and experience in group work are available.

As previously noted, a class-made scene requires time but can be very rewarding. It requires time for planning, research, and actual construction. Also, time is required to use the diorama and evaluate the process. Since the principal values of making a 3-dimensional picture come from the group experiences it provides, there should be time in which to experience these. Where dioramas are made during the class period the students have opportunities to work in committees, to participate in decision-making, to engage in individual and group research, to contribute according to their abilities, to receive individual recognition, to have satisfaction in accomplishment. Where there is adequate time for planning, study, work, use, and evaluation in a thoughtful, challenging, yet permissive atmosphere, these group activities may outweigh the values of the actual information acquired.

A visit to and study of a diorama in another place may be valuable. Churches, museums, commercial firms, and communities often produce dioramas which are life-size, carefully housed, and permanent. It remains for the teacher to learn to make use of community resources. To visit a diorama involves the teacher and students in all the steps of a school journey or field trip.

— *Ruth Lister*

DIRECTOR OF CHRISTIAN EDUCATION The office of minister of Christian education, better known as director of Christian education, has largely evolved in 20th-century America. Several circumstances led to its development.

In the U.S.A. there has never been a nationally administered religion as in several European countries. Here, careful provision has been made for the churches to operate in freedom, with the result that there are many denominations with varied creedal emphases and programs. Religion is administered by the several denominations according to their own separate responsibility without interference by the state. Some of them make wide use of parochial schools.

These are growing in size and number.

For many Protestant denominations the program of Christian education is largely the responsibility of the local church, with a certain amount of help from regional and national offices. Early in this century it became evident to leaders in general education as well as in theological education that Protestant people were in great need of better moral and character education.

The Protestant Church has not generally depended on special orders for the education of the laity. The average church has had a single minister, often overworked and generally unprepared for the Christian education of all age levels in his parish.

For a long period the chief attention given to the education of the laity was in Sunday schools administered by them and frequently carried on by people with little or no suitable education. This school expanded in American Protestant churches, largely as an adjunct to the church, and so it rarely received any guidance or supervision from the educated ministry.

Such are some of the many circumstances that led to the creation of the office of minister of Christian education early in this century. Schools for their preparation were established in several universities such as Boston, Northwestern, Teachers College at Columbia, and in a few special independent schools such as the Hartford School of Religious Education, the oldest (established 1885). Later, many of these programs were abandoned or absorbed by the theological seminaries.

The local church minister of education differs greatly from the public-school administrator whose teachers are generally chosen because they have already been trained to teach. The church religious educator is entrusted with the task of setting up plans, aided by the other ministers and the laity, for the education of his own teachers, the continuous education and growth of adults of all ages, and the development of Christian homes.

Besides this basic adult program for the whole parish, the minister of education, through a board of Christian education, works to provide adequate teaching for all the children and young people of the parish. This may involve a weekday preschool program, and also a more extended program of teaching for older children and young people than the limited " old-fashioned Sunday school" hour. His work involves thorough understanding of the teaching of all age levels as well as knowledge of the best materials and books for use in class and home, and how to coach and guide the laymen who teach.

When churches are backward, as many are, in their educational program, the minister of education has a prophetic role that involves great vision and understanding of all kinds of people as well as a personal dedication that inspires confidence. His task will require years of effort in the strategic preparation of the adult parish for its work.

The church is as strong as the dedication and vision of its laity. People are the church. Thus the church must become a peculiar kind of community. The religious educator should understand this and help to prepare laymen for their Christian vocation.

The educator in the church is not a mere organizer or promoter of national programs and publications. He must be sensitive to the meaning of God's will in every area of life. The faith taught must be relevant to the age level that is being taught and to the conditions under which the group are now living. Each program should be worked out to suit a particular parish and its problems. It should never be a mechanical program or process. It requires people of special dedication.

Such a comprehensive task as that assigned to the director of Christian education may seem impossible. It can only be done as laymen are educated in their vocation as Christians and as they receive help that is specific, continuous, and significant for their particular work. Gradually the abilities of people in a parish can be employed for God's service in the church and in the world around it. The work of the director of education is vast and continuous. This leader is an interpreter of the Christian faith in one realm after another. He is involved in continuous study and prayerful searching into the needs of people in these times. He must be alert to the questions and confusion of children, young people, and adults, and know how to deal with them.

The church with a vision of the vocation of its laity and the meaning of Christian fellowship has power to work with God far beyond its present practice and comprehension. The Christian church is unique in providing opportunity for Christian education and growth for all ages and kinds of people. A dedicated director, well-prepared for his work, performs a unique service to the people of the church as well as to those in related institutions and beyond. The significance of this office needs to be better understood by the church. — *Edna M. Baxter*

DISCIPLES OF CHRIST The Christian Churches (Disciples of Christ) constitute one of the largest religious bodies originating on American soil. The communion began in the early years of the 19th century, largely on the frontier in western Pennsylvania and Kentucky. At that time, though only a small percentage of the population were church members, there was bitter competition between the denominations, as they perpetuated the differences that had arisen in their home countries of Europe. Several ardent churchmen in widely separated places came to 2 strong convictions: (1) it was imperative that churches should unite; (2) there could be Christian unity if primitive Christianity were restored as exemplified in the New Testament and man-made creeds, names, and organizational practices were discarded.

Some of these reformers who rallied fellow church members to their cause were Barton W. Stone among the Presbyterians in Kentucky, Thomas and Alexander Campbell among the Presbyterians and later the Baptists in Pennsylvania, James O'Kelly among the Methodists in Maryland, Virginia, and North Carolina, and Abner Jones among the Baptists in Vermont. These reforming groups were unsuccessful in staying within their respective denominations. Having pleaded for churches to unite, they reluctantly found themselves in the position of having to form a new communion. However, throughout their history the Disciples' central plea has been the cause of Christian unity, based on simplicity and freedom, and aptly expressed in these oft-repeated slogans:

"The church of Christ upon earth is essentially, intentionally, and constitutionally one"; "Where the Scriptures speak, we speak; where the Scriptures are silent, we are silent"; "In faith, unity; in opinions, liberty; in all things, charity."

Walter Scott, a resourceful and aggressive evangelist, presented a message to the pioneer settlers that appealed to them as simple and rational. Thousands responded. In 1832 there were about 20,000 Disciples; by 1840, about 40,000; and by 1850, 118,000. The movement grew and spread with the westward migration of the 19th century. As a result the major concentration of churches is in the Midwest, South, Southwest, and West.

Some of the early leaders of the communion took the movement to Great Britain, establishing churches in England and Scotland. From there it spread to Australia, New Zealand, and South Africa. These churches, as well as the American churches, have conducted missionary work and established churches in Africa, Asia, South Pacific, and Latin America.

There are now approximately 8,000 congregations with a total of 1,800,000 members in the U.S.A. and Canada. An additional 1,000 congregations with 200,000 members are in 14 other countries, making a world total of 9,000 congregations and 2,000,000 members, not counting the congregations in Japan, the Philippines, and Thailand that in recent years have entered into the united churches of those countries.

Throughout the more than 150 years of its history, the Disciples have established colleges, seminaries, state, regional, and national agencies of missions, benevolence, education, evangelism, pensions, finance, promotion, church extension, social action, men's work, women's work, and a historical society. There is also a Council of Christian Unity. The overall body through which the agencies are created, through which they report to the churches, and the church members in turn voice their convictions, is the International Convention of Christian Churches (Disciples of Christ), which meets annually.

The Disciples of Christ do not have a set of formal beliefs or doctrines. In general, however, the following statements would meet the approval of most members:

Jesus is the Christ, the Son of God, and the personal Savior of every individual who accepts him as the Lord of life.

The New Testament, particularly the life and teachings of Jesus, forms the basis for Christian thought and action.

The church, which is the body of Christ, is a holy fellowship, through which God seeks to work his will in every age, including all who profess their faith in him and his Son, Jesus Christ.

The unity of all Christians, which today finds expression in the support of the ecumenical movement, continues to be one of the major concerns.

The Christian Churches have no creed except the person, life, teachings, and mission of Jesus Christ.

Baptism is a symbol of the burial of the old self and the birth of the new life that comes to one who accepts Jesus Christ as his Lord and Savior and agrees to unite his life with Christ.

The clergy, recognized as part of the laity, have specific responsibilities within the Christian fellowship and are expected to maintain high standards of education, conduct, and worship.

Each person is sacred in the eyes of God and has a responsibility to serve and teach wherever there is opportunity.

Each individual has access to God without the benefit of a priest or minister to serve as intermediary. Each person can approach God directly, expressing praise and adoration and seeking forgiveness.

The Fatherhood of God, the Saviorhood of Jesus Christ, and the brotherhood of man offer a basis for common worship, placing a responsibility for worship and service on the part of every Christian.

Characteristic practices of the Disciples include the following: recognition of the freedom of thought and opinion of each individual member and congregation; recognition of the principle of self-government for each local congregation, state and national bodies serving in advisory capacities only; recognition that the church is universal as well as congregational, ecumenical as well as local; recognition of the clergy's freedom of the pulpit and the local congregation's right to select whichever minister it may choose; observance of the Lord's Supper or Holy Communion every Sunday and a welcome to Christians of all communions to participate without restriction; reception of new members on the basis of their expression of faith in Jesus Christ as Lord and Savior, such expression usually made at a public service of worship, being followed by baptism; baptism by immersion, a New Testament practice recognized as the most adequate symbol of complete surrender and of the reenactment of the resurrection; participation in interdenominational fellowship in worship, study, mission, and service.

A functional type of organization is predominantly used among the churches of Disciples of Christ in which the Christian education function is coordinated with other functions: worship, evangelism, Christian action and community service, membership, property, stewardship and finance, and world outreach. Program services and materials are provided by national and state agencies along parallel lines for these 8 functional program phases, including program-planning manuals and annual listings of national emphases and current resources. In this way Christian education has its appropriate and responsible place in a balanced church program.

Plans and principles for the program and the curriculum materials for Christian education are reviewed and officially approved by the Curriculum and Program Council, a body of some 90 persons representing national and state staffs and local church workers. The council meets annually.

— George Oliver Taylor

DISCIPLINE The word " discipline " still carries implicitly and properly in it the idea of control. Through discipline a child develops the kind of control that is based on self-awareness. For this enables him to become more aware of others, more spiritually attuned.

We want to prevent his being unconsciously so preoccupied with holding himself in check that emotional isolation occurs. We want him to grow up as unhampered by envy, jealousy, greed, and hostility as he can realistically be.

To be able to control himself when such feelings arise, he must be able to recognize their presence. He must be able to face them as part of his heritage of being human. Discipline must help him learn what to do with them when they crop up.

A child copies many things from us. Our giving him models is part of our guiding him. But discipline is not this simple. As he grows he needs to give up many of his impulsive desires, e.g., his desire to have his mother all to himself. When he fails to get what he wants, he normally feels hostile. This happens even though in his wants he is pursuing his dreams rather than what is actually possible for him. Normally, too, when he is fearful or in pain or discomfort he gets angry. In the way of small children, he blames his parents — his mother mainly — for whatever misery befalls him, just as he relies on her as the primary source of his comforts and joys. His anger often increases when he sees that she and his father are the authoritarian figures who, in helping him become " civilized," must many times take away his primitive pleasures. Then, if the anger is left unhandled inside him, it accumulates. Reverberations take place in the nervous system, making inner tension mount. Some release must be found. When a child is left to his own devices, this often takes socially undesirable forms that lead him into trouble. It begets counter-anger from the adults around him, which makes him all the more uneasy. The release he sought fails to come; instead, tension mounts farther. Disciplinary problems accrue.

Essentially, every disciplinary problem has at its base a child's protest against his parents. Yet he is taught to shut in most tightly the component of his resentment toward them. Consequently, he displaces his anger at them onto siblings, companions, teachers. In later life he still carries resentment in him, enlarged through years of being stored up. He continues to displace it: onto mate or scapegoats; in prejudice, bigotry, and in the embracing of war.

A sounder solution lies in finding more tolerable forms of discharge for hostility. "You may not hit the real baby. You may pummel this baby doll instead." Or with an older child: "You may not act out your feelings by being destructive. You can talk them out instead. You can communicate them frankly — with courage and faith in the honest approach. This way is legitimate. It is tolerable, socially and morally, and true to the inner self that is you."

This is a 1st principle in discipline. We can call it "channel identification." It helps the child find a tolerable channel through which his feelings can flow. We cannot, however, help a child see that frankness is tolerable unless to us the whole range of human feelings is tolerable. Otherwise, we condemn and give him cues to hide the negative feelings, and again they pile up.

By itself, identifying channels of action will not lead to self-control. One problem is that the same feelings may take different outlets. Hostile protest may, for example, be expressed by refusing food in early childhood or by stealing cars in adolescence. As long as the underlying feelings go untouched, one disciplinary problem may be cured only to have another take its place. Discipline must not stop, therefore, with attempting to cure the noneating, the stealing, the truancy, or whatnot. Discipline must go farther. If self-control is to come about, the child must have self-knowledge of the underlying feelings that are pushing him.

This takes us to a 2d principle — that of "affect identification." The adult identifies the affect, or feelings, for the child ("You feel angry . . . mean . . . resentful") without censoring his feelings. For if an adult whom he respects blames him, he will blame himself. He loses his sense of human worth and dignity. Whereas if the adult accepts him with all the feelings in him, he gains in courage to communicate with honesty what he feels.

Besides these 2 principles of channel and affect identification, a 3d principle of discipline is called for in a world where man's universal brotherhood needs to be perceived with unprejudiced eyes. This is the principle of "object identification." Children need to face frankly the knowledge of whom they are angry with, not to shunt anger off onto a substitute object or scapegoat. Yet there is such extreme prohibition against feeling anger toward parents that a child often develops a pattern of shunting his anger off onto a scapegoat or substitute. The child who picks on friends indiscriminately or revolts against a teacher disproportionately, the delinquent who revolts against society, or the child who turns anger against himself into a psychosomatic disease or into habitual failure is usually the child whose hostility is being displaced. The present-tense object — friend, teacher, society, self — has become a substitute for the historical object — parent. Grievances against a present object may, of course, also exist. The point is that a child needs help in identifying both present and historical objects. "You feel angry at Tim now. Just as you sometimes also feel angry at people at home — at Mother, at Father. It's only natural for children to get angry at moments at their parents. And when they do it's best to talk it out. If you can talk to your parents directly, all the better. If you can talk more readily to me, all right for now. Perhaps I can help your father and mother to be better listeners as time goes on."

The importance of getting at the original, historical objects of hostility in a child's world is often difficult to comprehend. But unless it is done, the release of energy to live and love successfully is only partial. Too much tension from unconscious and often unnecessary pressure remains. The child is in the tragic predicament of believing that his normal feelings make him abnormal. He fears the hostility in himself because of his anxiety that it may get out of control.

In contrast, a child's confidence in the ability to discipline himself increases when someone who is mature and confident can say: "I understand. You feel this way. And I'm here to listen. But I'm here also to see that you learn to control what you do."

Discipline needs constantly to consider feelings as well as acts. On the feeling side, it helps to encourage the child to tell what he would like to do: to listen, accept, not censor; and on the action side, to state simply what he should do — how he should act or behave.

Children sometimes find it easier to talk to a teacher, a doctor, a clergyman. Parents sometimes find it easier to have them do so: for a while at least, until they can learn that a child's anger need not deny his love. In fact, parents often find that under this regimen their own acceptance increases. For when the child finds that his hostile feelings can come out safely in a way that is tolerable to his ego, he is not only easier to discipline but his way is cleared to show

more uncluttered stretches of love.

How about punishment? Most punishment will not be necessary when feelings are considered as well as acts; when they are differentiated clearly from acts; when feelings are accepted in unlimited fashion in contrast to acts that must be limited and often cannot be countenanced. The adult's firmer, sterner voice, naturally angry at moments, will ordinarily be proclamation enough of the last. But if an adult feels he must punish to be effective, then generally his being natural is best, as long as there are times — as antidote — when he can accept feelings with real sincerity. How about rewards? They are unnecessary. The warmth that comes to a child when his feelings are appreciated is reward enough.

As indicated, all children are hostile some of the time. But some children are hostile too much of the time. There may be so many hostility-provoking circumstances in their environment that hostility is fed in faster than it can be got out. Then discipline of any sort fails. To counteract this a child needs much down-to-earth, solid loving — not spoiling, not being given his own way. A child needs sincerity of feelings in those about him: adults who dare face their own anger but who are not forever angry. A child needs a regimen of requirements fitting to his mind and muscles, to the age and stage of his development, not requirements that are out of his range. And last, but not least, a child needs someone to have faith in him so that he can have faith.

— *Dorothy W. Baruch*

DISCUSSION No single definition can be linked unchallenged to the word "discussion." Three reasons for this diversity stand out. First, the word defines one of mankind's most stubbornly and long pursued activities. Human conversation about a problem or interest predates civilization. In one sense, all language is an attempt to store information for future use and exchange. Second, discussion is probably just as necessary as it is ancient. More often than not, human problems defy the resources of a single mind. (Here, Carl Sandburg's dictum, " Everybody is smarter than anybody," is in point.) Besides, the price men often put on their agreement to a decision is some chance to help make it. Third, discussion has always held a special fascination for people. One vantage point for the definition of literature would be to understand it as a sharing of experience undertaken for its own sake. Because, then, discussion is necessary, of long standing, and interesting, the settings in which it has been defined and the assumptions that have gone to make up its definition are many.

The root meaning for " discussion" may be of general help. The Latin *discussionum* might be translated by such expressions as a " shaking" or " breaking open," an "agitating" or " dispelling." From such expressions it is a short step to define discussion as " a freeing," or " an examining," as of issues.

There is little use to push beyond the word's Latin ancestry for a more ultimate parentage. The terms that the Bible offers for " discussion," for instance, are not its forebears or exact modern synonyms. One can link the Hebrew *dabar* (speak) with our word " discussion" in only the most general way. The New Testament has words to offer that veer more directly toward or even into more modern definitions. *Dialegomai*

can mean to forward a point of view in the sense of lecturing or arguing (Acts 17:2, 17; 18:4, 19; 19:8, 9; 20:7, 9). *Dialaleō* seems to imply comparison of ideas for collective problem solution (Luke 6:11). *Dialogizomai* is the genuine ancestor of our word " dialogue." We have here the idea of mutual or reciprocal reasoning, but with the sense of individual consideration too (Mark 8:16, 17; 11:31). *Homileō* is the springhead for our word " homily." It points to a talking over among people, a conversation (Luke 24:14, 15).

One cannot go directly from thought forms of ancient times to modern ideas about " discussion" if one is to understand even the major meanings that the word has collected around itself. The English-speaking world has attached several significations to " discussion." Most of them are still with us.

Certainly a really old idea survives in this description: " Miss Brown discussed her understanding of the parable of the good Samaritan with us." There is no great mystery about what Miss Brown was doing — obviously, lecturing or briefing. A lecture, of course, has social elements. One cannot give a lecture to oneself without being deemed quite queer. Besides, a good lecture makes the hearer think along with or argue against the speaker, even if he does it in silence. Still, in this early idea of discussion, hearers were expected to do just that.

But proclamation and monologue have seldom carried the day by themselves. People have a way of making up their own minds and clinging to their own ideas. History is far more the record of struggles between men of differing views than it is the record of proclamation by one and passive reception by many. Very early, men had to get used to the jostle and rivalry of other men's determinations. Enter a 2d idea about discussion: discussion could be a technique for compromise.

How did discussion come to be popularized in the Western world? Because of its help to politics. It had 2 kinds of help to give: (1) Sometimes it could prevent war. When rival groups shouted their differences to each other, they were not always courteous or pleasant. But this bandying of ideas was early seen to be less expensive than the bandying of blows. (2) Discussion was a help to democracy. In time, it developed from a hotheaded wrangle to a really civilized art. Even opponents and minorities came to have some recognized rights. The history of English-speaking parliaments is, in part, the record of just such a change. But whether wrangle or considered debate, the point to this kind of discussion was working agreement between rival factions — compromise.

The 3d understanding of discussion is built upon the 2d, but is to be distinguished from it. In the early 19th century, some of the most gifted thinkers turned to the human mind, experimented for data, drew conclusions. Problem-solving came into vogue as a way to understand human thought. From here it was a short, easy step to think of discussion as group problem-solving. People were to be listened to as well as talked to. (This had been learned from political life.) But they were to be listened to for a different reason. Not because their faction was powerful, but because they could make a contribution to the solution of the common problem.

When thinkers began to define discussion as problem-solving, not factional compromise, they had already turned from politicians to social thinkers for help. Behavioral scientists turned out to be helpful. They had become interested in the human group. They in turn began to think about discussion. They took insights from psychology and even the physical sciences. They added some ideas from their own research. How would these social psychologists define discussion? Perhaps something like this: discussion is a way for group members to develop their points of view, their personalities, and their insight about group forces. Group members were no longer just the means to an end. They were ends in their own right. Hence, groups began to use discussion with member development as their product goal.

As they have thought about discussion, social scientists have helped us to take a sharper, more knowledgeable view of group forces that affect it: the social status of the various speakers, the power structure of cliques, the pressures pushing group members from outside the group, the " hidden agenda " or private (sometimes even unrealized) goals of individuals in the group, the emotional needs of a given member. The list is incomplete, but it can show us how inadequate it is to think of discussion as a purely rational affair.

Social scientists did not end their contributions to discussion as the group-dynamics movement developed from their insight. Language scientists have probably not made a clean-cut school of thought about discussion. Yet they have attracted attention for one of its chief components: the transmission of notions, facts, and feelings from one person to another. They have reminded us that what A thinks he is saying and what B hears A as saying may be 2 different things. Why is this? Here are some possible answers that double as considerations for the discussion leaders: (1) Words cannot stand for objects with 100 percent efficiency. (2) Words are not individual enough to catch one man's special point of view. (3) Our families and general culture have a say in how we react to words. (4) Our experience can make us welcome certain words and put us off from others. In short, for the language scientists, discussion is the setting for an attempt at communication.

Finally, in the course of their speculation and insight, religious thinkers have touched on discussion. Conversations between God and man are set into the earliest part of the Old Testament as a part of the report on Adam's sin (Gen. 3:9-10). In The Book of Job, one is treated to considerable interchange between the Divinity and his creature. Interchange between God and man is a perennial item in religious literature.

Martin Buber seems a fit representative of those concerned about theology and interchange. Some would choose him as the most profound and influential thinker about relationship in all its forms as seen from a religious vantage point. Buber holds that relationship and exchange (of which discussion might presumably be one form) is a setting for God's special revelation. The exchange in living relationship (between 2 mutually respecting entities) is the arena for divine disclosure. Thus in *I and Thou*, Buber can say: "And the theophany becomes ever *nearer*, increasingly near to the sphere that lies *between be-*

ings, to the Kingdom that is hidden in our midst, between us " (p. 120). Buber would not equate "the sphere that lies between" with what often passes for conventional discussion.

To summarize, then: the word "discussion" is a reservoir of historical and current meanings. In the most distant past, men probably looked at it as a way to proclaim to, teach, or win a group. Later the word became associated with politicians and was linked with the idea of parliamentary compromise. From here the educators took the word into their camp. For them it was problem-solving. The social psychologists added their understanding of discussion as a setting for the mutual development of persons. It was a laboratory for the operation and analysis of interpersonal forces too. Language scientists underscored problems of communication. Finally, religious thinkers suggested that discussion could be a process by which God entrusted profound and ultimate disclosures to men about themselves, one another, and himself.

— *Max M. Pearse, Jr.*

DISPUTATION The Christian believer, answering the Word of God that addresses him, becomes spontaneously a seeker of understanding. Yet the order of truth to which he is now admitted, concealed beneath image, symbol, and event, wholly enveloped in mystery, does not yield itself readily to rational investigation. This is a sacred Word, not to be touched, not to be added to or subtracted from. Here is a paradox that at once anguishes and stimulates.

This tension began to make itself felt acutely in the early Middle Ages. The attempt at resolution resulted in the genesis of a completely new methodology respecting the assimilation of the Christian message. This new approach, called the *quaestio*, consisted of "calling into question" the intelligible content of revelation. In earlier ages the process of learning had centered upon the *lectio*, an exercise upon the sacred text comprising 3 distinct phases: the reading of the text; the commentary upon it (in turn literal, grammatical, and logical); and lastly the formulation of the meaning and sense (the *sententia*). The order was historical rather than systematic; doctrinal and moral issues were treated of as the gospel narrative provided occasion. In this, the epistemological demands of a learning process native to human intelligence were largely ignored. With the transition of the centers of learning from the monasteries to the universities and the emergence of Aristotelianism with its highly defined notion of speculative, theoretical science, this inadequacy was quickly felt.

The *quaestio* is a whole new learning process, more indigenous to the human mind, wherein the content of revelation is opened to the challenge coming from every source. Arguments are examined pro and con, contrary authorities cited, and the objections of alien systems of thought allowed to play their role in the determination of the question. The technique that lay at the heart of this process was the *disputatio,* a school exercise, highly formalized along officially recognized lines to prevent deterioration into mere clash of opinion. Its movement was provisionary; its tools, dialectic and logic; its tone, that of inquiry and methodological doubt. Differing from the Socratic dialogue, the Cartesian doubt, the Hegelian dialectic, it is

nonetheless in some wise comparable to these. The scope of the disputation tended to be large; no subject, no partner to the debate, was barred. For this reason it became the special province of the "master," who, on certain specified days, ordinarily before the entire university body and in spoken controversy, would seek to uncover the root reasons of things to the inquiring mind. Its guiding principle was not so much to overwhelm opponents through dialectical adroitness as to explore a question mutually in a spirit of free inquiry. The formality was to aid the process of arriving at the truth, not to impede it. The disputations of Thomas Aquinas at the University of Paris, published as *Quaestiones disputatae* are perhaps the finest fruit of this academic exercise.

The disputation no longer occupies a position of honor in the contemporary university. Outside realistic systems of thought — in idealistic philosophies, in the world of logical positivism and symbolic logic (where exposition is by way of some symbolistic scheme other than discursive language), in existentialism (with its preference for a purely literary style) — its effectiveness lessens considerably. Even in the Middle Ages, however, the disputation left room for other techniques, other methods. Still it is contemporary. Orderly, rational discussion can never entirely be set aside in human learning. Disputation, freed of its narrowing, archaic conditions, can prove a valuable discipline, especially for the mind at work upon the mystery of God, for that penetration into the nature of and innermost reasons for transcendent matters. Dealing with living issues, its spirit can initiate a rethinking of accepted solutions

within the context of contemporary thought, replace the mere transmission of information with a genuine solicitude for understanding, and function as a selective instrument in the assimilation of alien religious and cultural heritages. In a day when there is much encroachment (sectarian, economic, political) upon academic autonomy, such debate as this does create a "free realm" within which truth can survive. For the guiding spirit of the disputation is not submission to authority (this is rather the province of faith and obedience) but that illumination from within which marks the vital act of encounter, of personal, intelligent commitment. There is, lastly, its efficacy in the conjoining of faith and reason in the continuing dialogue between divided Christians.
— *William J. Hill*

DOCTRINE — DOGMA The word "doctrine" is derived from the Latin *doctrina,* with which the Vulgate invariably translated *didachē* and *didaskalia,* each of which bore the twofold meaning of the act or activity of teaching and of what is taught. In ecclesiastical usage "doctrine" has retained these 2 meanings. On the one hand, it means teaching, instruction, and edification; on the other, the teachings of God's Word or of the church. The term is applied to the articles of faith contained in creeds, confessions, and catechisms, as well as more broadly to all theological themes. According to the Reformers, "pure doctrine," together with the "right administration of the sacraments," was a mark of the true church of Jesus Christ. Although Christian education and instruction may be formally distinguished from kerygma and the sermon, doctrine

and the problem of its purity are involved in both.

Speaking generally for the moment, "dogma" differs from "doctrine" in that it denotes a doctrine that bears greater divine or ecclesiastical authority. However, the 2 words are often used interchangeably, as in dogmatic or systematic theology and in the history of dogma or of doctrine. The Greek word *dogma,* from *dokein,* "seem, seem good, think," signified either a philosophical principle (axiom) or a published decree (edict). It is used in the latter sense in Luke 2:1; Acts 17:7; Heb. 11:23. In Acts 16:4 it is used in reference to the "decision" of the apostles reached at the conference in Jerusalem. In Eph. 2:15 and Col. 2:14, 21, it also refers to the commandments and ordinances of the Mosaic law which have been abolished in Christ.

During the period of the apostolic fathers, "dogma" was first employed to denote the commandments of Jesus and the apostles. Tatian and the Alexandrians were the first to employ the term with reference to Christian teachings or to the body of Christian doctrine. Very early in the church's history, creeds appeared to serve liturgical and catechetical purposes, culminating in the Apostles' Creed. This came to be regarded as the "rule of faith." Gradually it was made the standard not only for orthodoxy but for the interpretation of Scripture and derived its authority not from Scripture but from tradition sanctioned by the church. The acknowledgment of the "rule of faith" became the condition for saving faith. It found its classic formulation in the so-called Athanasian Creed: "Whosoever will be saved: before all things it is necessary that he hold the catholic faith; which faith except everyone do keep whole and undefiled: without doubt he shall perish everlastingly." Eventually in Roman Catholic usage "dogma" came to have a twofold source in Scripture and tradition. It was defined by the Vatican Council of 1870 as follows: "Further, by divine and catholic faith, all those things must be believed which are contained in the written word of God and in tradition, and those which are proposed by the church, either in a solemn pronouncement or in her ordinary and universal power, to be believed as divinely revealed" (Denzinger, 1792). Moreover, when the Roman pontiff speaks ex cathedra he operates infallibly and his definitions are unalterable (Denzinger, 1839). Dogmas as *veritates a Deo formaliter revelatae* are thus equated with God's Word. Whenever possible, the Roman Catholic Church bases its dogmas upon Scripture but, as in the case of the dogma of the bodily assumption of Mary, it can dispense with Scripture and be satisfied with an appeal to tradition. Once a dogma has been officially defined by the church, its denial is rejected as heresy and heretics are anathematized.

The Reformers protested against the arbitrary definition of dogma by the papacy and restored to Scripture its unique authority. For them, to elevate dogma to the status of revelation or to make it the law of the church's preaching was to equate the church with revelation. The Reformers held that dogma, such as the dogma of the Trinity, as well as a creed or confession of faith in which dogmas are contained, possess genuine church authority only as a word of the fathers and brethren, and that their au-thority is strictly spiritual. That is, their authority depends upon their character as correct exposition of Scripture and upon the present attestation by the Holy Spirit. Moreover, dogmas are not lifted out of Scripture but are the church's response to God's Word in its act of confession in the face of a heresy that threatens the unity and faith of the church.

Although a tendency to systematize and to distinguish between essential and unessential dogmas appears in Protestant orthodoxy following the Reformation, the Reformation understanding of dogma was preserved and – in spite of the influence of rationalism and Pietism – persisted until the end of the 18th century. Friedrich Schleiermacher initiated the modern Protestant interpretation of dogma as exposition of the faith of men united in the church when he defined Christian doctrines as "accounts of the Christian religious affections set forth in speech" (*The Christian Faith*, Sec. 15). He taught that "there is only one source from which all Christian doctrine is derived, namely, the self-proclamation of Christ," yet "it all arises out of the religious consciousness itself and is its direct expression" (Sec. 19, postscript). Ritschl interpreted Christian doctrines in terms of moral value judgments; Troeltsch and the *religionsgeschichtliche* school relativized them. The establishment of the individual's subjective experience of faith as a criterion of doctrine resulted in the words "dogma" and "dogmatics" being discredited.

The theological revival of the 20th century represents an effort to recover and deepen the Reformation conception of dogma. Barth distinguishes between dogma and dogmas. The latter are "the doctrinal propositions acknowledged and confessed by the church, which are deposited in the church symbols with their relative authority" (*Church Dogmatics,* I. i, p. 305). "Dogma is the agreement of church proclamation with the revelation attested in Holy Scripture." (P. 304.) "The inner meaning of all possible propositions of the kind, the thing all dogmas mean to express when they strive toward the truth of revelation, is the dogma after which dogmatics inquires. . . . It is what is intended in all possible propositions of the kind; it is the dogma for the sake of which the church proclaims dogmas." (P. 307.) Harking back to the New Testament meaning of dogma as "behest" or "command," Barth teaches that dogma is a "concept of revelation," (1) between church proclamation and the Word of God, and (2) between the commanding God and the man who hearkens to his command. Dogmas as such are impersonal, rational propositions; dogma involves a personal encounter between God's revelation and man. "A theology which would assert its knowledge and possession of dogma (that is, agreement with God's Word) would be *theologia gloriae.*" In contrast to Barth's reserve at this point, Lutheran theologians, although maintaining the subordination of dogma to Scripture, tend to regard dogma as containing objective truth. "Dogma is the sum of the church's faith-knowledge disclosed in God's revelation." (Althaus.) "God's truth desires to be acknowledged not only existentially but also to be 'objectively' known and expressly transmitted in doctrinal proposition." (Gloege.) In Bultmann and Tillich and their followers there is today a

movement to interpret Christian doctrines in terms of existential faith.
— *Arthur C. Cochrane*

DOUBT Skepticism, in its most creative sense (as distinguished from sheer psychological negativity), is an instrument of civilized man. Primitive man lacked the unifying principles against which he could protest. Facing a world characterized by arbitrariness, he relied on forms of magic to influence the powers with which he needed to contend. Civilized man, on the other hand, conceived of life as having a responsible center. For Hebrew culture the center was the God of Abraham, Isaac, and Jacob; for the Greek culture the center was nature, "an ideal order lurking behind the manifold appearances of things" (Bowra).

Yet neither nature nor God is ever decisively provable. Each represents a kind of hypothesis that is necessary for rational and spiritual fertility. Once accepted, each hypothesis creates an interlocking panorama of art, morals, and logic. The emerging intellectual structure loses its precariousness and, therefore, its vitality, unless doubt saves it from becoming an enclosed system.

The Old Testament bound the positive and skeptical principles together. Chaos was the auxiliary of cosmos, trust the partner of anxiety, faith the corollary of doubt. The radical skepticism of Ecclesiastes stood side by side with the Deuteronomist's bold faith in a just history. Jeremiah both trusted in the redemptive power of God and called him a liar. (Jer. 15:18.)

The New Testament, on the other hand, was too close to its sacred event, the resurrection, to create either a dialectical spirit or good literature. The New Testament lacked the critical principle of Ecclesiastes and the magnificent skepticism of Job. As a result, its affirmations tended to become heroic and to transcend the human dimension. As an example, one recalls that Sarah, upon being told that she would conceive, laughed (Gen. 18:12), whereas the restatement in Heb. 11:11 makes Sarah into a puppet by saying, " By faith Sarah herself received power to conceive, even when she was past the age, since she considered him faithful who had promised."

In spite of the grandeur of New Testament vision, and in spite of occasional examples of lyric power, the atmosphere in the New Testament borders on a protective pietism as it ignores humor, radical searching, etc.

There can be little doubt, however, that had the New Testament community survived as an integrated culture, it would have developed a literature as graceful and as dialectical as that of the classical Hebrew community.

The post-Biblical church was unable to develop a critical principle for 2 reasons. In the 1st place, the church faced the task of creating a foundation that would save it from being fragmented by the multiplicity of cultures that characterized pre-European civilization. Skepticism, the critical principle, was not and never is a useful weapon with which to tame chaos. In the 2d place, the church was engaged in the energy-consuming task of establishing a coalition with the best elements in classical culture. Tertullian, who would have isolated Jerusalem from Athens, was, happily, repudiated, and Justin Martyr and Athanasius, for instance, laid the foun-

dations for an amalgam of the positive Biblical principle — faith — with the positive Hellenic principle — knowledge. The great unifying realities — God and nature — were brought into harmony. A false synthesis was created by Augustine that was, because of its Platonic bias, semi-Docetic. Man was precipitated into an eternity divorced from time, a knowledge that was a priori rather than spiritual-material. Under Augustinian terms the emergence of the critical principle was postponed.

It was in the 13th century that the positive principle was defined so perfectly, so classically, that the negative principle — radical doubt — was required, and because of this demand, the modern world was born.

The classical formulation of the positive principle was found in the monolithic *Summa Theologica* of Thomas Aquinas. Here, faith and reason, the natural and supernatural, philosophy and theology, were harmoniously married. Here, furthermore, matter and spirit, God and man, were related in a magnificent intuition of *being*. Only one thing was lacking in this all-but-perfect system — a critical and skeptical principle.

The modern man, from the perspectives of his radical skepticism, looks back upon the medieval (and classical) man as naïve. What the modern man forgets is that his skepticism is possible because it was called into existence by the creative audacity of the metaphysical principle. Without the premise of either nature or God, skepticism is impossible.

The Reformation was only in part a reformation of theology, morals, and ecclesiology. It was also a protest against the obliteration of the skeptical principle by the positive principle. By eliminating the possibility of doubt, the religious answer transcended human existence. It was Martin Luther's contribution, through his doctrine of justification, that demolished the medieval principle by marrying radical doubt and radical faith. The elimination of the self-evidences of natural theology created the possibility of a union between religious insight and an existence that was authentically human. The positive principle — God's grace — was linked to the critical principle — the inability of man through his reason to storm the gates of heaven. By its union of the 2 principles, the Lutheran theology was able to escape the sterile classicism which defined medieval theology. Unfortunately, Lutheranism could not escape the enervating Pietism that ultimately made a positive principle of the "yes" and the "no" of Martin Luther.

Calvin, stimulated by Luther, succeeded in incorporating a part of the content of Luther's dialectic in his theology. Unfortunately, Calvin's Latin temperament and classical training forced him to build a comprehensive theological system and to restore, in part, the natural theology that Luther had destroyed. Theoretically Calvinism declared the positive principle to be the sovereignty of God, election, and predestination. The skeptical principle — the ground of authentic human existence — became increasingly devitalized as, more and more, the principle of certitude acquired semidogmatic authority.

If medievalism represents the triumph of the positive principle, the modern world represents the triumph of the skeptical principle. Unlike the medieval man, the modern man does not begin with a knowledge of such universals as causality and substance. Instead, the modern man, with Descartes, begins with doubt. Shaped by Locke and Hume, he is forced to recognize that such knowledge as he has is reduced to sensations and the judgments that he makes about them.

It was Immanuel Kant who decisively demonstrated that thinking must concern itself with phenomena (appearances) rather than with the things in themselves. Kant's *Critique of Pure Reason* buried the positive principle of medievalism. Kant, in spite of his magnification of the critical principle, was reluctant to relinquish the world of universals. Reason being discredited, Kant turned to the will as the ground of universals. The idea of the categorical imperative placed knowledge within moral responsibility.

The jettisoning of reason, and the emphasis on will, guaranteed that the modern man would live with more nerve than knowledge. Thus existentialism, a strange compound of trust and anxiety, emerged. Existentialism, by embracing the critical principle, has sought to create a sense of responsibility within a world that had been unable to attain metaphysical knowledge.

This, then, is an age of doubt. To be true to its own rhythm it must be skeptical. But it can also remember and hope. It can remember when men combined functional creativity with knowledge, and it can look forward to that day when a doctor of philosophy profounder than even Aquinas or Kant will bring together the indispensable conditions of human understanding, the "yes" of knowledge and the "no" of doubt. — *Fred Denbeaux*

DRAMA The climate of Christian culture, in its earliest phases, was generally hostile to the institution of the theater and to the dramatic arts. In the writings of Tertullian, Cyprian, and Chrysostom, we can detect various characteristic expressions of the antagonism toward the drama that consistently runs throughout the tradition of the fathers. The reason for this strain lay in the fact that the theater which Christianity first encountered was that of the late Roman decadence, whose *spectacula* exhibited a moral dubiousness intolerable to a rigorous Christian conscience. So it is not surprising that, once the church became the controlling center of the Roman Empire, its influence was heavily brought to bear against all theatrical enterprise, of whatever sort.

Thereafter, discounting the various semitheatrical traditions of medieval minstrelsy, the stage ceased to count for anything as an autonomous cultural force for more than 800 years. Yet throughout this period there remained in the liturgy of the church itself the seeds of a rich dramatic development, and very probably by the 9th or 10th century, and perhaps even earlier, the offices of the church were being interpolated on special occasions by chants and stylized actions that were intended to illustrate the great moments in the history of redemption, as these were commemorated by the church's worship. This was, of course, a kind of ceremonial that was originally in the hands of the clergy; but, as it gradually took on greater elaborateness and complication, it began to move outside the churches and into the adjacent churchyards. By the 13th century, various lay guilds of players were beginning to perform mysteries, miracle plays, and moralities in their own establishments. Once historical personages began to be introduced into the morality play, the chronicle history was being foreshadowed. Hence, there was already under way the 1st stage in the process of secularization to which all the great transformations of the Renaissance were to lend enormous impetus.

Since the 16th century, apart from occasional towering presences such as Calderón, or Corneille, or Racine, the Western theater has been a predominantly secular theater, owing very little of its dynamic to Christian inspiration. Yet it is one of the remarkable incongruities of 20th-century cultural life that at a time when many specialists in *Zeitgeist* are telling us that ours is a "post-Christian" epoch, there should be evidence indicating a profound renewal of interest among some of the most gifted dramatists of our period in the great themes of Christian tradition and experience.

Of one major impulse and line of development, T. S. Eliot's work in the theater is perhaps the most important expression, and this is a development that is very largely British and Anglican, stemming originally from Canterbury Cathedral, where, after successful productions of John Masefield's *The Coming of Christ* in 1928 and of Tennyson's *Becket* in 1933, new plays began to be commissioned for performance in connection with the annual Canterbury Festival. Eliot's *Murder in the Cathedral* was the first of these, receiving its premiere production in the chapter house in the spring of 1935 and being performed later in the same year in the Mercury Theatre in London. Like the play of Tennyson that had aroused so much interest in its revival 2 years earlier, the protagonist of *Murder in the Cathedral* is the great hero of Canterbury, the martyred Thomas of the 12th century, and Eliot's play makes him the vehicle for exploring our "last temptation" — which is "to do the right deed for the wrong reason." But, though brilliant and moving, it is essentially a piece of liturgical drama whose idiom and appeal are too special to disclose any viable new stratagem for the Christian dramatist working within the terms of the general modern theater. Thus in his subsequent work, *The Family Reunion, The Cocktail Party, The Confidential Clerk,* and *The Elder Statesman,* Eliot has been attempting to discover devices of indirection that would serve a Christian ordering of the human story and, at the same time, permit the achievement of a dramatic structure free of didacticism.

Since the early 1930's, Canterbury Festival commissions have resulted in many other notable contributions to the development of a contemporary Christian theater. Charles Williams' *Cranmer* came in the spring of 1936. Dorothy Sayers, Laurie Lee, Christopher Fry, and Hugh Ross Williamson are among others who have done distinguished work for the festival. Since the close of World War II other great cathedral churches in England have followed Canterbury in commissioning new plays, and a lively movement has been set afoot, with which such able writers as Ronald Duncan and Christopher Hassall have cooperated. Nor has this group been in sole possession of the field, for, un-

elicited by cathedral patronage, many other playwrights have been using their stage to explore the complex relations between nature and grace. Foremost among these is the distinguished Roman Catholic, Graham Greene, whose plays, *The Living Room* and *The Potting Shed,* have enjoyed a very considerable success in the West End.

There has been no insurgency on the American scene comparable to this English development. But, ever since Paul Claudel's *L'Annonce faite à Marie* was first produced in Paris in 1912, the French theater has been confronted, again in Claudel's *Le Soulier de Satin* and *Partage de Midi* and in the plays of Henri Ghéon, François Mauriac and Julien Green, with formidable examples of a dramatic art that is drenched in a profoundly Christian ethos.

The recognition has been growing, however, in recent years that what is religiously vital and significant in contemporary drama is by no means confined to the work of those writers whose art is controlled by Christian presuppositions. In the plays of Bertolt Brecht, Jean-Paul Sartre, Samuel Beckett, Eugène Ionesco, and the late Albert Camus we often encounter, it is true, some of the bleakest expressions in recent literature of the deep hopelessness that takes possession of the mind when it is seduced by the malaise of unbelief. Here, indeed, are the great cartographers in the modern theater of the dark, wintry universe of " post-Christian " man. Yet the most sensitive interpreters of this material find it possible to descry, even in Sartre's *Huis Clos* or Beckett's *En Attendant Godot* or Camus's *Le Malentendu,* a kind of " negative witness " to the gospel, at least insofar as here the world is shown to be what it would be like were it as utterly abandoned as these modern artists believe it to be. So this too is a body of literature that in its own way is rich with religious resonance and deserving of the closest attention from the Christian community. — *Nathan A. Scott, Jr.*

DRAMATICS In its general use the term " dramatics " refers to any activity by amateurs in the field of drama, especially by children or youth. Dramatics as a teaching medium in Christian education implies the use of dramatic techniques in teaching the Christian religion.

Drama was first used as a teaching medium in Christian education when the priests and choirboys of the medieval church began dramatizing the Easter service in the *Quem quaeritis* trope. When the church realized the tremendous power of dramatic representation, other Biblical dramas were developed. This practice proved to be so effective a way of teaching that the miracle and morality plays growing out of the first simple dramatizations flourished for fully 5 centuries.

What the early Christian church discovered about dramatic techniques is being rediscovered in today's Christian education: that ideas and events can be made so vivid in drama that both players and audience have the feeling of sharing the experience of the characters in the play. Since dramatic material involves conflict situations in which decisions must be made between right and wrong, this experience concerns patterns of behavior — some admirable, others weak or unprincipled. Though it is vicarious rather than actual experience, the drama's emotional impact causes it to become part of persons' thinking, feeling, and consequently their actions.

Because the purpose of any art is primarily the joy and enrichment of living, drama, when used as a teaching medium, must first of all be enjoyable. An indirect use of it, such as teaching religious truths through dramatization, is effective only when it is first an enjoyable experience. The fact that almost everyone has a strong natural interest in dramatics, whether as player or audience, makes it a good teaching medium, provided the leader is fully capable of guiding it.

In modern Christian education both formal and informal drama are used. Children participate in many forms of creative dramatics, while young people of high school and college age have a part in both informal and formal drama.

" Creative drama " is the term used for any type of drama created by children and played with spontaneous action and dialogue. It begins with dramatic " play living " in which little children play out experiences they have had, " try on " the characters of people, of animals, and even of objects around them, and interpret their small world in terms they can understand. Such creative play, always without an audience, is the type of drama most natural to little children.

With the guidance, though not the direction, of an adult teacher, older children plan and create plays, puppet shows, shadow plays, creative rhythmic movements, and dramatic worship services based on ideas, experiences, poems, hymns, and stories from the Bible and other literature, leaving the specific dialogue and action to the individual players. Since this informal drama is not written, it changes and develops with every playing.

The purpose of this type of dramatics is not entertainment for an audience as formal children's theater is, but rather a valuable experience for the players. Although children's theater has much value for a child audience, it is not used as a teaching medium in Christian education but, rather, as a joyful and artistic experience for the children of a community. The casts of formal children's theater are most often partially or entirely adult.

Creative dramatics under qualified leadership gives children much opportunity for creative thinking, a controlled emotional outlet, a strong incentive for adjusting to the group, a basis for understanding people, appreciation of content material, and leadership training resulting from the responsibility of developing their own drama. Junior and junior high pupils occasionally share with other boys and girls a play that they have created if it has been developed to the point where it has value for an audience.

Informal drama for youth and adults may take the form of improvisation similar to the creative dramatics of children but with more mature content, role-playing, original worship services, or choral speaking of a dramatic nature.

Though plays are written to be acted, groups of young adults often find that the reading of great plays can launch interesting and challenging discussions of social and ethical issues. Another form of discussion takes place in what is known as "situation drama." After actors read up to the point of crisis in a play, the members of the audience divide into groups to discuss the problem and possible solutions. After each group has shared its conclusions with the others, they hear the actors read the rest of the play. This process stimulates thinking about the solution of problems in human relations.

A "walking rehearsal," in which the reading of parts in a play is accompanied by action but not the memorization of lines, is often the form of reading used in "situation drama." Players rehearse at least once before doing a walking rehearsal for an audience, but seldom use costumes and scenery. Scenes from plays such as *The Crucible*, by Arthur Miller, *The Sign of Jonah*, by Guenter Rutenborn, and other plays too difficult for the group to produce are sometimes presented as walking rehearsals.

Formal drama for youth and adults is the production in the church of formal plays for audience or congregation. Drama suitable for the chancel is usually presented there, and in such cases, costumes and properties are used but no set scenery. Other plays are given in the auditorium of the parish house, with scenery, costumes, and special lighting. In any case, this is carefully produced rather than experimental dramatics, with lines memorized from a playscript, and action directed by a trained leader. The production of such plays in the church can be a deeply religious experience for both actors and audience. Three plays that have often been effectively produced are *Christ in the Concrete City*, *Noah*, and *Our Town*. — *Winifred Ward*

E

EASTER Easter is the principal festival of all Christian people, observed in the universal church since the days of the apostles. The first Christians celebrated Easter conjointly with the Jewish Feast of Passover, which was the historic occasion and context in which Christ fulfilled in suffering, death, and resurrection his redemptive mission. After the church's membership became predominantly Gentile, most churches transferred the observance of Easter to the Sunday following the Passover (in Greek called *pascha*). So it was decreed by the 1st Ecumenical Council of the church, held in Nicaea in 325 that Easter should always be celebrated on the Sunday next after the 1st full moon following the spring equinox. Thus Easter is a "movable" feast, occurring anytime between March 22 and April 25, since it depends, as does the Jewish Passover, upon the spring full moon. But Easter Day is always a Sunday, for it recalls the resurrection of the Lord on the 1st day of the week.

Every Sunday of the year commemorates the resurrection and is in consequence a "little Easter." Like Easter Day, it has been observed since apostolic times as the regular day for Christian corporate worship, especially in the celebration of the Eucharist, for the risen Lord was made known to his disciples "in the breaking of bread" (cf. Luke 24:35; I Cor. 16:2). Sunday is "the Lord's day" (Rev. 1:10). For Christian believers it replaced the Jewish Sabbath as the appointed time for worship and refreshment. The Sabbath looked backward in commemoration of God's rest from his work in creation, just as the Passover looked backward in remembrance of God's historic redemption of his people from bondage in Egypt. But the Christian Sunday, including Easter, looks forward to the promised age to come, the re-creative work of God in final redemption of his people from sin and death, of which Christ in his resurrection is the firstfruits. The Sabbath concluded the old "week" of creation; Sunday and Easter begin the new "week" of the renewal of the world until the glorious fulfillment of the Kingdom of God in the triumphal coming of the Lord at the end of time.

In the ancient church, the Easter observance began with an all-night vigil on the eve, which concluded toward dawn with the initiation of new members in baptism and confirmation and in the celebration of the Eucharist. In preparation for this occasion, the season of Lent was developed later as a time of testing and instruction of the cat-echumens, the candidates for initia-tion. The festival continued for 50 days — until Pentecost (Whitsunday) — during which time all the mighty acts of the Lord for our redemption were held together in undifferenti-ated commemoration: Passion, re-surrection, ascension, and gift of the Holy Spirit. Beginning in the 4th century, however, this ancient unity of the festival began to be elaborated in a chronological se-quence of commemorations, starting with the dramatic ceremonies of Holy Week, and distinguishing in Eastertide the resurrection appear-ances on Easter Day and through Easter Week, the ascension 40 days later, and the gift of the Spirit on the concluding day of Pentecost. More-over, the rapid growth of infant bap-tisms, the separation of confirmation from baptism and their administra-tion at the convenience of the min-ister, removed from the Easter lit-urgy the uniqueness of its initiatory ceremonies.

The ancient structures, however, survive in the liturgies of the Roman Catholic and Eastern Orthodox, and to a lesser degree of the Anglican and Lutheran Churches. In non-liturgical Protestant churches, there are survivals of the custom of admin-istering Baptism at Easter, and the celebration of the resurrection at sunrise services on Easter Day. Even the new clothes generally worn by Christians at the Easter services derive from the ancient custom of giving the newly baptized a special white garment to wear during Easter Week.

Unlike Christmas, Easter has not suffered from secular or pagan asso-ciations to any great extent, although its conjunction with the older spring fertility rites has contributed to popular observance of such fertility symbols as eggs and rabbits. But the eggs, no less than the special pastries of Easter feasting, also have asso-ciations with the breaking of the Lenten fast. The English word "Easter" — like the German *Ostern* — has been thought to be derived from a Teutonic spring goddess; but it probably refers to the place of the sun's rising in the east, symbol of new life and new birth.

— *Massey H. Shepherd, Jr.*

ECUMENICAL INSTITUTE Accord-ing to the resolution of the General Assembly of the World Council of Churches in Evanston, 1954, the Ecumenical Institute (at Château de Bossey, Celigny, near Geneva, Switzerland) has the following func-tion: " It provides an opportunity for leaders, clerical and lay, from many churches and nations to live together, to worship and study to-gether. It is an essential instrument of the Division of Studies, and for consultations and conferences essen-tial to the work of other divisions and departments. It is an exploratory and creative center for all our shared concerns for the renewal and mis-sion of the church. The closely re-lated Graduate School of Ecumenical Studies gives promise of offering the opportunity for the training of highly competent leadership in ecu-menical thought and action, which can have wide influence in the years ahead."

In existence since 1946, the Insti-tute has had from the beginning much in common with similar in-stitutions such as evangelical acade-mies and lay centers all over the world, except that Bossey is inter-national and ecumenical in character. To a certain extent the work of the

Institute reflects the variety of activities of the different divisions and departments of the World Council of Churches. It is especially closely related to the department of the laity and deals with themes referring to the role of laymen in the church and in everyday life. The Institute is interested in entering as far as possible into the realm of public and professional life with representatives of different professions as well as in helping the churches to find new perspectives as stimulus in their work.

Problems of education in an ecumenical setting have also been studied. The Institute not only attempts to promote an exchange of views but also to examine the relationships, e.g., between church and mission, Christian life in society, sociology, science, philosophy, theology, etc. But Bossey has also a general educational task: to foster studies related to the history and present situation of the ecumenical movement and to initiate the participants at conferences and courses into the processes of ecumenical thinking and action. The results of ecumenical study are discussed; practical experiences in ecumenical cooperation are shared. Thus arises among the participants an ecumenical cooperation that prepares them for their own future work in the ecumenical field.

The Institute regards personal contact between men of different denominations and nations of great importance. Going back to the Biblical foundations, they may rediscover what they have in common and find new ways of overcoming differences. In common worship as well, there is a similar experience of discovering common ground, which creates a link between the participants of such conferences when they realize the differences that exist. Ecumenical work is not interested in achieving synthesis and uniformity at the cost of truth. The representatives of the churches who come together at Bossey do not ignore or efface the differences among the churches, but discuss them openly, thus coming to new relationships.

Since 1952 a Graduate School of Ecumenical Studies has been operated in connection with the theological faculty of the University of Geneva. Academic studies are offered to those who have already had a 3 years' academic (not necessarily theological) training. In a semester of 4½ months (Oct. 1 to Feb. 15) professors — theologians and non-theologians — and about 50 students from all over the world live together and are given the opportunity of studying problems of the ecumenical movement that cannot be sufficiently treated during the short conferences and courses. In living closely together, students are confronted with critical questions by churchmen of various traditions. In some cases this leads to deeper confessional consciousness, perhaps a necessary stage in the ecumenical process of theological thinking and acting if one is not to be contented with easy solutions of the problems. It is essential to face all such problems realistically and to bear in mind the aim of all ecumenical work, which is the realization of the unity of all Christians and a common witness and service in the world. — *H. H. Wolf*

ECUMENICAL MOVEMENT "Ecumenical" (from Greek *oikoumenē*) means "the whole inhabited earth." In current usage it refers to the worldwide extent of the church, its mission, unity, and the wholeness of its faith and worship. The ecumenical movement received impetus from the 19th-century missionary awakening. The Student Volunteer Movement (1886) and the World's Student Christian Federation (1895), both led by John R. Mott, a Methodist layman, were among the first organizations embracing Christians of many communions for the purpose of mission and unity.

In Asia and Africa missionaries from the West experienced frustrating hindrances due to denominational divisions; they sensed the need for cooperation, at least, if not yet unity. Many conferences were held during the 50 years before 1910. In that year, the 1st World Missionary Conference was convened in Edinburgh with 1,170 persons present. Mott was chairman and J. H. Oldham, secretary. The 1st meeting of its kind in history, it marked the formal beginning of the modern ecumenical movement.

A continuing organization after Edinburgh became in 1921 the International Missionary Council. Not a council of churches, but of mission societies and national Christian councils, it has ever since been the chief means of cooperation in missionary study and planning. Its conferences have been milestones in missions: Jerusalem, 1928; Madras, 1938; Whitby, 1947; Willingen, 1952; and Ghana, 1957–1958.

Ever since New Testament times, Christians have sensed the wrongness of divisions in the church. The church is one, but churches are divided. Efforts to make unity a reality have been attempted repeatedly.

No specific discussions of church unity were permitted at Edinburgh in 1910. The time seemed unripe to all but a few. Among the few

was Bishop Charles H. Brent, American Episcopalian. He envisaged a succession of world conferences on the causes of division and the ways to unity. He was chiefly responsible for convening the 1st World Conference on Faith and Order at Lausanne, 1927. Questions of doctrinal clarity, ministry, sacraments, and ecclesiastical unity were treated by delegates from most Protestant and Eastern Orthodox churches. It was a study conference, not a convention for planning church unions. (Only the churches themselves have authority to enter into unions.) But the Conference on Faith and Order continued in the form of a large committee for another 25 years.

The next gathering was at Edinburgh, 1937. Here were studied questions of authority, grace, the church, the communion of saints, and again the ministry and sacraments. The conference authorized further studies on the church, worship, and intercommunion. Leadership was mainly in the hands of William Temple, Archbishop of Canterbury.

Faith and Order became in 1948 the Commission on Faith and Order of the World Council of Churches. In 1952 at Lund it held its 3d world conference. Here it broke the former pattern of comparative studies of various church teachings and began more intensive theological inquiry, seeking common ground for the unity of the church beneath denominational traditions. It laid greater stress on the social and cultural factors affecting division and unity.

Parallel with and related to these ecumenical studies on faith and order were numerous negotiations of the churches in many lands for intercommunion or full union. These have been consummated in this century on an average of one a year. Most notable have been the forming of the United Church of Canada, 1925, from Congregational, Methodist, and Presbyterian churches; the United Church of Northern India, 1924, from Congregational and Presbyterian churches; the Church of Christ in Japan, 1941, from the above-mentioned and others; the Church of South India, 1947, from Anglican, Methodist, Presbyterian, and Congregational churches; and the United Church of Christ, 1957, from the Congregational Christian Churches and the Evangelical and Reformed Church. In addition, many reunions of churches of the same tradition have taken place. Still pending at present are comprehensive union plans in Ceylon, North India, Australia, New Zealand, the United States, etc. It may confidently be expected that this unitive trend will continue in the future with increasing strength as the theological bases for unity become better understood and the complexities of the church's task require the elimination of useless conflicts and schisms.

Apart from these movements among Protestant churches, there has been a remarkable drawing together of Protestant and Eastern Orthodox Christians in common work and conference. A new openness among Protestants, Orthodox, and Roman Catholics has appeared, not for approaches to union but for uninhibited conversation.

Despite limited collaboration between representatives of the conservative Evangelical churches (including the Lutheran Church, Missouri Synod, and the Southern Baptist Convention) and those which take part in the newer ecumenical councils, the avenues of communication remain largely unexplored or else blocked by theological conflict.

The concerns for mission and unity have been complemented by ecumenical programs advancing the ethical and pastoral work of the church. During World War I, the World Alliance for International Friendship Through the Churches was formed. Following the armistice, Archbishop Nathan Söderblom of Sweden took the initiative to convene a world conference of churches on questions pertaining to peace, economic justice, racial tension, alcoholism, education, etc. This met at Stockholm in 1925 with great effect upon the churches' sense of ethical obligation and their common task in the world. After Stockholm the Universal Christian Council on Life and Work continued its studies, pointing toward the next world conference at Oxford, 1937, on the theme of " Church, Community, and State." The leaders were Mott, Temple, and Oldham. The rising threat of totalitarianism in Germany and Italy gave the conference special urgency.

American participation was fostered effectively through the Federal Council of Churches, which had been formed in 1908 with emphasis upon the churches' cooperation in social witness and service. Related concerns were being dealt with through the world alliances of the Y.M.C.A. and the Y.W.C.A. and the World's Sunday School Association (since 1947 the World Council of Christian Education).

In 1937 the responsible leaders of the ecumenical movement decided that the time had arrived to form a permanent organization. At both Oxford and Edinburgh they voted favorably on the proposed World

Council of Churches. In 1938 at Utrecht a provisional committee laid the groundwork. Appointed as the 1st general secretary was W. A. Visser 't Hooft of the Netherlands. Plans to constitute the council in 1941 were delayed by World War II. But in Amsterdam in 1948 the council became a reality at the inaugural assembly. More than 150 church bodies of more than 50 countries covenanted to stay together in this new body, unique in church history.

The main tasks of the World Council of Churches were those of faith and order and life and work, but these were enlarged with the new needs of the postwar world. At the 2d assembly in Evanston in 1954 a working structure of divisions and departments was provided to carry on the following program: (1) studies in faith and order, evangelism, church and society, and missionary trends; (2) interchurch aid and service to refugees; (3) stimulating renewal among the laity, women, and youth; (4) promoting peace through the Commission of the Churches on International Affairs. The Council is governed by 6 presidents; the assembly meets every 6 years or so, and the central committee has 90 members. Although drawing the churches together in common study and service, the Council has no authority over any member church.

The International Missionary Council and the World Council had long maintained an associated relationship. In 1961 at the 3d assembly in New Delhi (India), they merged into 1 body, thus consolidating the 3 main streams of the modern ecumenical movement.

In the U.S.A. the National Council of the Churches of Christ was constituted at Cleveland in 1950. It continued the former Federal Council but included as well 7 previous organizations: the International Council of Religious Education, the Foreign Missions Conference, the Home Missions Council, the Missionary Education Movement, the National Protestant Council of Higher Education, the United Stewardship Council, and the United Council of Church Women. The National Council has enabled the member churches to do together a great many significant things that they could scarcely accomplish in isolation from one another.

The emphases of the world and national councils are brought to bear on localized interests of churches through more than 100 city and state councils of churches.

There are comparable national councils in many countries of Europe, Africa, and Asia. Of unique importance is the East Asia Christian Conference, inaugurated in 1959 to facilitate a united mission in that most populous quarter of the earth.

In addition to all the ecumenical councils of churches are the denominational or confessional bodies, each with its own emphasis, structure, and program: Methodist, Anglican, Presbyterian, Baptist, Congregational, Lutheran, Friends, and Disciples of Christ.

— *J. Robert Nelson*

ENGLAND — WALES For centuries it was the church that carried out the work of education, in its religious orders and in the universities and schools that it founded. Education in England and Wales, in common with the whole of civilization, is founded upon the Christian faith and still bears the mark of that in-heritage, despite the increasing secularism of modern life.

When the state in 1870 first took over responsibility for providing elementary education, there was only a small minority pressing the view that it should be secular. Under the Education Act of 1870 and succeeding acts, the controlling authorities were empowered to provide religious instruction in the schools, as long as it was not given on a denominational basis. Although in theory religious instruction might be omitted from the curriculum, in practice this did not occur, and the general assumption was that Christian teaching should be given. Moreover, the provision of state-maintained schools (equivalent to the public schools of the U.S.A.) did not mean that voluntary schools provided by the Roman Catholic, Church of England, or Free Churches were closed down; but these continued side by side with the maintained schools, being aided by state grants.

Under the Education Act of 1944, religious instruction and school worship became a statutory obligation in maintained schools. The liberty of the individual is preserved by the right of parents to withdraw their children and of teachers not to undertake obligations in the field of religious teaching. Comparatively few parents exercise this right; those who do are chiefly Jews, Roman Catholics, and a few atheists or agnostics. Despite a lack of religious practice and church membership in many homes, the majority of parents wish their children to have religious teaching; others are so indifferent to the whole subject that positive objection is ruled out. Teachers in some cases are not willing to undertake religious instruc-

tion, the reason frequently being their own feeling of inadequacy for the task rather than any objection as unbelievers to it. Heads of schools on the whole are conscientious in carrying out the regulations concerning Christian teaching and worship; even some who lack personal conviction regard it as a professional duty to make the necessary provision. Most of them conduct the daily corporate assembly for worship themselves, though some delegate it to religious instruction specialists or other members of staff.

The content of religious teaching is regulated by an agreed syllabus compiled for, or adopted by, each county or other administrative area — "agreed" in the sense that it must be authorized by a syllabus conference consisting of representatives appointed by teachers, the Church of England, other main Christian denominations in the area concerned, and the Local Education Authority. Each of these groups has 1 vote, and the 4 must unanimously recommend the proposed syllabus. Provision is made that in case of failure to agree, the matter should be referred to the Minister of Education, but this has in fact never yet occurred. No agreed syllabus may contain teaching that is distinctively denominational. This rules out teaching based on a particular church catechism, or views on the sacraments or church order, but leaves a wide field of Biblical and doctrinal teaching that is common to the churches. School worship also must be broadly based and must not follow the particular order of any one church.

Baldly stated, such provisions may suggest very restricted limits within which the instruction and worship may be carried out, but this is far from being the case. The agreed syllabi leave room for a comprehensive study of the Christian faith and give adequate freedom of interpretation to the teacher, while the daily worship, given sincere and thoughtful preparation, may provide the one truly religious experience encountered by a number of pupils.

Denominational schools have complete control over their religious instruction and worship. Church of England diocesan syllabi are provided, but in many cases these take the local agreed syllabus as a basis, adding Prayer Book and sacramental teaching. Independent, self-governing schools are free to do what they wish in the matter of religious education.

Some main problems of the present time are these: the need for more teachers with specialist knowledge and training for the work of Christian education; the difficulty of communicating the faith to young people to whom not only the language of the Bible but the ideas that it sets forth are foreign, due to our materialistic civilization; the constant tension between the Christian standard of values as taught in school and church and those observed at home and in modern society at large.

The task of teachers concerned in religious education is greatly assisted by the work of such voluntary bodies as the Institute of Christian Education and the Student Christian Movement in Schools. The former, founded in 1935, exists to offer practical help and encouragement to teachers and others who give religious instruction or are in any way concerned with the promotion of Christian education. It is recognized by the Ministry of Education as a body specializing in this field,

from which reliable information about the needs and views of teachers of religious education can be obtained. They have sought its collaboration in such matters as the organization of refresher courses and the compilation of bibliographies. The Syllabus of Religious Instruction prepared by the Welsh Society of the Institute was adopted by nearly all Local Education Authorities in Wales. The SCM in Schools is engaged in organizing 6th-form conferences in grammar schools and is extending this work, with official aid from a number of LEA's, to the secondary modern (vocationally oriented) school field, having established groups in many schools and published a variety of study outlines and pamphlets for pupils of secondary school age.

The British Broadcasting Corporation's 6th-form courses provided by distinguished Biblical scholars and experienced teachers are followed in many grammar schools, and another series for secondary modern schools has recently been launched. Weekly services for schools, broadcast for many years, are of high standard and widely appreciated.

Within the past 20 years there has been a notable increase in help provided by the Ministry of Education and the LEA's to teachers of religious knowledge. Residential courses in the subject are provided annually by the Ministry; weekend and day conferences are held under the auspices of the Authorities; handbooks, bibliographies, libraries of textbooks and of filmstrips, are available in some areas, while general supervision and help is given by religious advisory councils, inspectors, and in some cases special advisers in religious education.

Although Christian education in

schools maintained by the state is in the hands of the teachers, the clergy are invited by many heads of schools to provide special services and to cooperate in other ways.

— *Juliet E. Sladden*

EPIPHANY This term comes from the Greek word *epiphaneia* and means "manifestation" or "appearance." In the New Testament the word is used several times, especially in I Tim. 6:14 ("until the appearing of our Lord Jesus Christ") and in II Tim. 1:10 ("through the appearing of our Savior Christ Jesus").

The appearing or manifestation of the Lord entered into the consciousness of the church at an early time. By the end of the 4th century the festival of the Epiphany was well established in the Eastern churches.

In the Eastern Church the Epiphany included the manifestation of Christ as shown 1st in his birth (the manifestation in the flesh) and 2d in his baptism (the manifestation of the Holy Trinity). To the present time the Eastern Epiphany festival emphasizes the story of Christ's baptism by John the Baptist.

In the Western Church the emphases were different. Here the Epiphany was focused upon the visit of the Wise Men to the child Jesus in Bethlehem (Matt. 2:1-12). The Western Christians had in their calendar a double festival: at Christmas they observed the birth of the Lord and the visit of the shepherds and the human birth of the Savior, whereas at the Epiphany festival they recognized the divine aspects of the Nativity and the tribute paid by the Eastern visitors to the Lord of all the nations. The bringing of gifts by the Wise Men became the occasion for the giving of gifts by the followers of Jesus. In many countries of Europe, Epiphany, rather than Christmas, is still the time when people exchange gifts.

With the development of the "Christmas season" in the Western Church in later centuries, the Epiphany festival on Jan. 6 became "the last day of Christmas" and was frequently called "Twelfth Day."

The overtones of the Epiphany celebration have brought additional themes into the church's calendar of celebration. Since the Wise Men were considered representatives of the non-Jewish, Gentile world, the manifestation of the Christ-child to the non-Christian peoples was a complementary theme, hence the church's subject for teaching during this season.

The weeks following the Epiphany festival varied in number according to the date of Easter; there might be as many as 6. The traditional Gospel lessons for Epiphany develop more fully the idea of the manifestation of the Savior in different areas of human life, centered about the appearances of Christ and the areas of his power.

In some Western churches the Christmas decorations include a *crèche* (crib), which is changed in details for Dec. 25 and for Jan. 6. For the Christmas *crèche* there is a setting that represents the Christ-child in the manger, Mary and Joseph, the shepherds and the cattle. The Epiphany *crèche* presents a different scene, in which the Wise Men with their gifts appear before the Holy Family.

At the Eastern Epiphany there is a different kind of observance. Either "the Great Blessing of the Waters" is performed at the font in the church or, especially among the

Greeks, there is a ceremony at a river or other body of water. There, men of the congregation enter the water to recover a cross that has been cast in by a priest during the ceremony.

In the midst of all the observances, customs, and teaching at the Epiphany, the central theme remains the appearance or manifestation of Christ in his power and love for the salvation of the human race, in every time and in every land: the manifestation of the universal Savior. – *George R. Seltzer*

EQUIPMENT Adequate space, conveniently and attractively arranged, is the primary physical provision for Christian education, and only equipment that serves the purpose of a group should be introduced into a room. The amount of space per person recommended for children has been increased as group activities have been used in the curriculum. In recent years the space recommended for young people and adults has been increased as informal teaching procedures have been employed. Certain items of equipment are essential. Others are desirable and useful. Nevertheless, it is best to avoid overcrowding and restricting the use of effective procedures, even if it means that 2 or 3 sessions of the church school must be held in order that enough space can be provided.

Nursery children need play equipment and open floor space where they can play or gather in a cluster for a story, singing, and conversation. A table or 2 and a few chairs are needed, but it is not necessary to provide a chair and table space for every child. The tables should be 18" to 20" high with tops about 18" x 36". Chairs should be 8" to 10" high, with 8" to 10" between

the chair seat and the tabletop for leg room. Some large hollow blocks (4" x 8" x 8"; 4" x 8" x 16"; 8" x 8" x 8"; and some smaller ones), a few boards (¾" x 6" x 48") to use with the blocks, wooden transportation toys, a small jungle gym, a painting easel or two, a nature-study center, and housekeeping toys are some of the first items of equipment to be provided. Open shelves will be needed for the toys and some cabinet space for other supplies. A record player and recordings will be greatly appreciated. A piano is not necessary but can be useful at times.

Kindergarten children are ready to do some artwork and other handwork at tables, but the tables should be small (about 24" x 36") and easily moved out of the way to free the floor space for activities. Chairs should be 10" high and tables 20" to 22" high. A piano is not necessary but is useful. An autoharp is used in some kindergartens instead of a piano. Toys such as those suggested for nursery children are needed, with more housekeeping toys, more large blocks, and clothing for dramatic play. A few well-selected books will be appreciated at a book table.

Primary and junior tables should be not over 30" x 48" and easily moved. Chairs will range from 12" in height for lower primary to 14" for upper primary and lower junior, and 16" for upper junior. Tabletops should be at least 10" above the chair seats.

If possible, children through the junior departments should have solid, rather than folding, chairs and tables. Chairs and tables for all ages are now available that can be stacked for storing when not in use. Their quality and usability vary radically, making careful selection necessary. Excellent folding chairs and tables with tubular legs are available for young people and adults.

A piano, a leader's table, an easel for display of pictures, and possibly offering plates are needed in each room in which worship is held by primary and junior children and by young people and adults.

A church needs to think carefully about whether to have stationary or movable coat and hat racks. Since shifts in room assignments often become necessary, as the number of persons of various ages changes, either portable racks or those built to set in but movable add to the adaptability of a building. Excellent portable racks (some of them collapsible) are now available. Some churches prefer to have theirs designed to blend with the interior finish of the building, but resting on table gliders for easy movement as needed. For the children's rooms the racks should be the right height for the children using them. It is important to have plenty of hat space. Rods and hangers rather than hooks are recommended for coats.

Multiple use of many rooms in churches is becoming common. This makes necessary the movement of children's equipment into closets or a storeroom while adults use the room, and the reverse while children use the room. Stacking and folding features facilitate such changes. Movement of furnishings is made easy by use of dollies on low wheels, made to accommodate the tables, chairs, and other furnishings.

The needs of evening and weekday groups must be considered along with those of Sunday morning classes. Since the Sunday church school is usually the largest organization of the church and often uses all the rooms, churches sometimes make the mistake of planning primarily for the school on the assumption that other groups can fit into the church school rooms. Yet, Sunday evening youth groups, weekday club groups (such as Scouts), couples clubs, and many adult groups may use the rooms many more hours each week than do the church school classes. Adaptability of rooms is, therefore, important.

It is well to give careful thought to the selection of tack boards and chalkboards. If the rooms are to be used primarily by groups that need them, it is well to have the boards permanently installed. If the rooms are to be used by other groups also, there are ways to make the rooms adaptable. Some churches use portable boards that can be moved into a nearby storeroom when not in use. One advantage is that these can be placed in the room wherever they are needed. Other churches place the boards behind panels that can be rolled aside or opened like doors when the equipment is needed. Some churches use tack strips, about 2 inches wide, colored to blend with the wall. They are relatively inconspicuous when not in use. In rooms used only by children they should be placed low enough to serve the children at eye level. If the strips are to be used by both children and adults, 2 can be installed, 1 higher than the other. Many churches are now using turnover charts (tablets or pads of newsprint about 18" x 30" to 24" x 36" mounted on an easel) instead of, or along with, chalkboards.

A work counter and sink in each room used by children will be found useful, since water is used in some activities as well as for washing.

Most church groups need some cabinet or closet space for storing songbooks, reference books, toys, charts, maps, and other equipment and supplies. It may not be possible to provide a closet for every group, but cabinets can be installed for groups not needing closets. Some of the cabinets can be built in; others can be built to set in and can be moved from one room to another if changes in room assignments are necessary. Two- or 3-decker cabinets will accommodate more groups.

The use of audio-visual materials is made easier if electric outlets are placed in each room, conveniently near the place a projector is most likely to be used and on a circuit separate from the room lights. A church is likely to need more than 1 slide and filmstrip projector, 1 screen, 1 record player, and 1 tape recorder, since more than 1 group may want to use equipment at a given time. One motion-picture projector may be adequate. It should have 1,000-watts power if it is to be used in a large room. Some churches build in screens that roll into the ceiling or into a recess in the wall, or wall screens that are concealed behind panels or tack boards when not in use.

There should be a separate power line in any room in which motion pictures are to be used at night. Otherwise, house lights in other rooms or nearby buildings may use so much power that there will be faulty projection of sound with the picture. This question should be carefully checked with the power company.

Storage is needed for portable audio-visual equipment, preferably in a small room with a workbench and an electric outlet, where equipment and films can be cleaned and repaired. Shelves and racks for storing equipment are needed. The rooms should be fitted with a lock, for audio-visual equipment is expensive.

Club groups such as Scout troops do not ask for rooms designed especially for them, since they can meet in the dining or fellowship hall or in a clubroom, but they do need cabinets or closets for storing their equipment between meetings. They, too, have use for audio-visual equipment, chalkboards, tables, and chairs. They also need recreation equipment and can share these items with other groups.

A good church library is a much-needed facility. There should be enough shelves for an expanding library, a place to display new books and magazines, reading tables and lamps, and a checkout desk with card files.

Some church libraries also include religious recordings, pictures for lending to classes and families, and audio-visual materials for use in classes and other groups.

Religious art is one of the important resources for Christian education. Reproductions of some of the best paintings can well be mounted and framed for hanging on walls of rooms. Others can be mounted and filed for use as needed by classes and other groups.

An illuminated display case in a central area can be a helpful educational tool for the exhibiting of items made by the children, for jackets of new books and objects of missions interest. It can be used for announcing major emphases in the church and church school.

Many equipment items can be homemade if a church is unable to buy them. In many churches, cabinets, housekeeping toys, chalkboards, tack boards, book carts, blocks, jungle gyms, screens, easels, and other items have been built by persons who were determined that the children and young people should have the advantage of good equipment even though money was not available for buying it. In any case, understanding of the educational purpose to be served and careful planning are the keys to equipping a church for Christian education. — *Virgil E. Foster*

ETHICAL CULTURE Ethical culture is fostered by the Ethical Culture Movement embodied in Ethical (Culture) Societies. These groups in the U.S.A. are members of a national body — the American Ethical Union, with headquarters in New York. This body is a constituent member of the International Humanist and Ethical Union, which was founded in 1952 and now embraces organizations in more than 20 countries. World congresses are scheduled every 5 years. A similar international union had been formed in 1908, but its work was disrupted by the 2 world wars.

The 1st Ethical Society was established and the movement inaugurated in 1876 at New York, largely under the leadership of Felix Adler, then a lecturer at Cornell University and later a professor of social and political science at Columbia. By 1878 the society had established "the first free kindergarten east of the Mississippi River," known as the Workingmen's School. This has developed into what is now known as the Ethical Culture School System, which includes the 12-grade Fieldston School in New York City.

Other interests of the movement have included the establishment of settlements and similar agencies for social betterment. It claims a significant part, through its leaders and members as well as societies, in building the Child Study Association of America, the National Child Labor Committee, Visiting Nurse Society in New York, and Legal Aid in Chicago. Many of its activities are similar to those of churches in the social action and educational fields, such as encampments, forums, conferences, a women's auxiliary, tours, and others.

The movement's relation to religion is of special significance here. Its literature states: "The Ethical Society occupies the place of a church or synagogue in the lives of most of its members. It differs from traditional religious bodies in that ethical concerns rather than theological doctrines constitute the basis of fellowship." Ethical culture is, in fact, designated as "a religion which seeks, through education, service, and community action to increase man's knowledge, practice, and love of right living."

A statement on "This We Believe" includes such emphases as these: "We believe in religious freedom, the freedom of the mind and the spirit of the individual. . . . Without theological creed or metaphysical doctrine, we affirm that the highest spiritual values are to be found in man's relation to man. . . . We believe in the spiritual equality of all men, . . . in the uniqueness of every human being. . . . In the name of this vision, we find meaning and purpose in life, a sacredness in our own lives and the lives of our children. . . . In the name of this vision we marry, we find consolation at death, we name our children, and undertake to educate and serve mankind. . . . We believe in the creation of an ethical culture, a civilization which gives support to the goodness in man and through which mankind can evoke the vast untapped powers that are still to be found in human personality."

Ethical Culture Societies have Sunday meetings and Sunday schools. A Sunday meeting consists of readings, music, and an address "of a general philosophical nature" or on "subjects of a more specialized and concrete content, such as human relations, political ethics, civic and global affairs."

The Ethical Society Sunday school is said to seek, through a variety of "shared activities," to guide the child in his constant struggle for understanding and to assist him in formulating his pattern for a worthwhile life. However, the schools are for youth and adults as well as children. The curriculum centers upon the problems met by the pupil in his everyday living. It is expected that "ethical religious experience" will be developed in the school's processes.

Ethical Culture Societies, such as a representative one in St. Louis, may have a building for headquarters. The Union publishes a monthly bulletin, *Ideals at Work*, and a bimonthly journal, *The Ethical Outlook*, besides leaflets and booklets. The organization involves the usual administrative staff with leaders and leadership education for overhead or local groups and for fieldwork. — *Ralph Daniel Heim*

ETHICS Ethics is a discipline that studies judgments of good and evil as they bear upon the actions of individuals and groups in relation to each other. Christian ethics is a branch of theology that attempts to relate judgments of right and wrong

motivation and behavior to the teachings of Jesus and his gospel.

Whether it be philosophical or theological, ethics customarily has followed 1 of 2 directions: (1) description of what is held to be the good in common practice, as in the case of anthropological, sociological, or phenomenological research; (2) classification of goods in a normative fashion, as in the case of moral philosophy and casuistry. Recently a 3d approach, known as contextual or situational ethics, has been developed on the thesis that personal authenticity holds priority over descriptive and normative ethics.

The study of ethics as an independent discipline developed from the Greek split between philosophy and religion. Eastern cultures were not originally conducive to the development of ethics because philosophy itself was so closely tied to the religious belief and practice that behavior could not be dealt with independently of the quest for salvation. Thus the Way (Tao) in Chinese culture was to be pursued by the proper orienting of oneself to the natural order, as in Taoism, or by the precise reduplication of age-old, fixed civil relationships, as in Confucianism. For the dominant Indian philosophies the good was identified with the predestined path or rule (*dharma*) one should follow in working out release from the cycle of births and deaths.

Philosophical ethics arose in the discussions of the Greek Sophists, who rejected the scientific inquiries of their predecessors in favor of an investigation of the nature of justice, order, and goodness. Socrates tells how he turned from the study of nature to the study of concepts in order that he might discover the nature of reality. It was his theory that goodness can be taught, and that no one knowingly chooses evil, for so to do would be to go against one's self-interest. What constitutes goodness is a question Socrates was unable to determine, though it is clear from Plato's dialogues that Socrates did not doubt the reality of goodness. Plato is believed to have delivered a famous lecture on the subject, the content of which has not been preserved. The 2 dialogues dealing most extensively with the Socratic-Platonic conceptions of ethics are the *Republic* and *Laws*. Opinion differs as to whether the *Republic* represents Plato's or Socrates' position.

Arthur W. H. Adkins (*Merit and Responsibility: A Study in Greek Values*) has suggested that the Greeks, including Plato and Aristotle, were unable to develop compelling ethical theories because Greek culture did not consider such quiet virtues as justice, temperance, and mercy on a par with others. Thus the most highly valued life for the Homeric Greek was that of the aristocratic warrior for whom honor was the highest good. " What will others think? " took precedence over " What is the righteous thing to do? " In later times personal success and happiness epitomized by the question, What is good for me? were the marks of virtue. Socrates embodies the chief departure from this pattern because he recognized the authority of an inner voice that never told him what to do, but prevented him from taking certain actions. Plato's ethics placed the well-being of the city above all else, and he maintained that justice was to be determined by a philosophical elite (in the *Republic*) or by a Council of Elders (in the *Laws*) who repre-

sented only the interests of the leisure class.

No study similar to Adkins' has been attempted for the Old and New Testaments, but if it were, it would point to fundamental differences between the Greek and the Judeo-Christian ideas of the good society. The most important distinction between them would be the belief of the Hebrews that their nation had been constituted by the very personal God of the Bible. The most highly valued life for the people of the Old Testament, therefore, was that of the patriarch blessed by many offspring, who achieves well-being in reward for obedience to God. The Holy God requires him to behave justly toward rich and poor, neighbor and stranger, alike, and his worship and social behavior are inseparable from each other. It is clear that ethics as a philosophical discipline, like philosophy itself, is undreamed of in such a society.

In the New Testament the most highly valued life is not that of the prosperous patriarch, but rather that of the disciple who renounces every worldly possession in obedience to the call to serve the Messiah. He observes ethical rules in keeping with the highest standards of the day (slavery is not considered a contradiction to the will of God), but these rules are binding only for the interim between Christ's ascension and his return to earth.

H. Richard Niebuhr has enumerated 5 typical ways in which Christians have interpreted the relationship between the church and society. His analysis, which has profoundly influenced contemporary American theological thought, holds that the most satisfactory relationship between Christ and culture is the transforming one, as suggested by

Maurice. Reinhold Niebuhr's ethic, which has exerted a greater influence upon secular thought than that of any other theologian, has emphasized the pragmatic way in which absolute norms are modified in actual situations without thereby ceasing to be more adequate to the needs of the situation than no norms whatever. John Bennett has refined this approach into a methodology which uses "middle axioms" between absolute principles and completely relativistic choices. By this means Niebuhr and Bennett are enabled to distinguish between the relatively more Christian use of power in democracy than in communism.

The ancient question of Socrates, "Can goodness be taught?" has played a significant role in contemporary theories of education. The liberal reaction against rigid categories of right and wrong led in recent decades to various forms of ethical relativism. Some doubted that there were any moral absolutes; some held intellectually that there were, but behaved as if there were not. Almost alone among modern schools of philosophy, Thomism maintains that the distinction between right and wrong is to be ascertained by the natural light of reason, and that a hierarchy of values can be discerned by a study of natural law. The extreme reaction against ethical norms that characterized the middle decades of this century has been followed by recent studies which show that certain moral values are held by every known human society, and that there are discernible differences between authentic and inauthentic ethical principles.

Contextual, or situational, ethics takes several forms. The emphasis is upon man's obligation to act responsibly in every situation; the decisions have as much to do with his personal integrity as with the social effects of his choices. A choice ending in social failure may therefore be more ethical than one with effects that seem superficially to be for the common good. Atheistic existentialism represents 1 aspect of this philosophy. Barth weaves his ethics into his exposition of the doctrines of creation and redemption, with the old covenant that binds every man to his neighbor and the new covenant that reconstitutes every relationship in the new humanity. Bonhoeffer speaks of the 4 "mandates," rather than orders, which thrust the Christian responsibly into the world: the mandates of labor, marriage, government, and the church in the world. Men are called upon to act in obedience to Christ without knowing what the ultimate effects of their decisions will be. It is the decision to act – to choose between alternatives of action – that characterizes man as ethical.
— *William L. Bradley*

EVALUATION Evaluation is the process of identifying the major goals of Christian education and determining the extent to which these goals are achieved in the church's program. It establishes goals, collects evidence of growth or lack of growth toward these goals, and makes judgments about this evidence. Evaluation should be used to revise procedures and even curriculum in the light of the appraisal. Evaluation is a continuous, cooperative experience involving the teachers, pupils, parents, and church school staff.

The concept of evaluation today has developed gradually as a result of the changing philosophy of education that involves the growth of the whole person in relation to his attitudes, appreciations, interests, ability to think, and personal-social adaptability. The distinction between modern techniques of evaluation and the older forms of appraisal are that the former evaluate in light of the comprehensive objectives of the total program of the church rather than by measuring factual content. Through the use of a variety of evaluative procedures, it is possible to integrate and interpret various indications of behavior into a total picture of the individual's reaction to life. Thus evaluation provides a basis for improving the curriculum, analyzing learning experiences, and guiding desirable changes in human behavior.

What are the trends? In 1928, Hartshorne and May published a detailed evaluation, *Studies in Deceit,* which indicated that the church had limited influence on the patterns of honest behavior. The methods used in this study were very complex but alerted the thoughtful educator to the importance of discovering usable techniques for lay and professional leaders in the church. The Character Research Project has guided churches in the use of open-end material, the method of characteristic differences, and simple statistical methods of evaluation. Daniel Prescott has directed a child-study program for many years that acquaints teachers with the scientific process of collecting information about children's growth and methods of analysis and interpretation. Recently, he has served as a consultant to denominational groups and church councils to develop an evaluation technique for analyzing the effectiveness of the

church's program of Christian education.

In the past 10 years, there has been active study and research in the committees of the National Council of the Churches of Christ in the U.S.A. and denominational staffs on the objectives of Christian education. The Presbyterian Church in the U.S.A. (now The United Presbyterian Church in the U.S.A.) was the first to formulate a new approach to curriculum in their *Christian Faith and Life: A Program for Church and Home.* A recent evaluation of this program as it relates to the home is reported by Roy Fairchild and J. C. Wynn in *Families in the Church.* This depth research analyzes what the families value most in their church affiliation, what are their biggest problems and needs, and the areas in which they desire more help from the church.

Following a long period of experimentation, the Protestant Episcopal Church has developed *The Seabury Series* for each age group. This curriculum focuses on the experiences of everyday life where God's action is taking place and shares the heritage of God's people. Continuous evaluation is established through the use of the team of teacher and observer who develop insights, choose resources, and select teaching techniques.

Many denominations have revised their curriculum in the light of developmental tasks of learning as developed by Robert J. Havighurst, with planned involvement of the home in the Christian nurture process.

In guiding the growth of individual students, analyzing their strengths and weaknesses, and discovering areas where improvement can be made in the church's program of Christian education, these steps may be followed: (1) Formulate a clear-cut statement of the purpose and meaning of Christian education. (2) Collect the evidence of how individuals develop at various age levels as well as any other background information providing understanding of the individual. (3) Analyze the evidence by using a reliable technique of evaluation such as *The International Standard for the Sunday Church School,* 1 type of rating scale for use in the local church. (4) Interpret this information in order to formulate a judgment of the value of the program as it is being presented. (5) Determine what course of action will be followed and allocate responsibility for the work that needs to be accomplished.

A committee on Christian education in the local church could simplify the preceding process in evaluating their program by asking such questions as: (1) What did the pupils learn from a particular unit of study? What were their reactions? Did they participate with interest? Did their questions reveal what they were learning? What changes were evident in the students' behavior or attitudes? (2) Was the presentation related to their developmental needs? Did the methods encourage group learning and acknowledge the structure and dynamics of the group as it influenced the behavior of each member? (3) As teachers, what could we have done to make the learning situation more effective? Was our preparation adequate to challenge the students?

Teachers and group leaders can evaluate the group and individual experiences of learning by using the following techniques:

1. Observe and record individual and group reaction on a weekly analysis chart that indicates students' attendance, type of contribution made to group discussion or project, types of questions asked, responsibility assumed in the group, and whether contribution to the support of the church program is regular.

2. Keep an anecdotal record that gives the date, place, and situation in which each action occurred. Such a record describes the actions of the student and reactions of other persons involved. It provides cues to the student's feelings, but does not interpret his feelings.

3. Use an autobiographical report for the student to relate his feelings about his learning. An introductory statement to start thinking could be used: " Changes that I would like to see take place in my church school class." Or, " When we were studying about the prophets, I wondered about . . ."

4. Present an incomplete sentence or story to bring out the feelings of the student. If the story is used, questions should be asked that will bring out the student's self-concepts or his attitude toward the particular problem situation enacted in the story. Children enjoy role-playing the ending of a story. This characterization reveals ways in which they are beginning to look at life.

5. Make use of self-rating scales with older children, youth, and adults. Denominations are including these in curricula and preparing them for teacher education purposes.

6. Keep a file of the individual and group projects that interpret what the students gain from each unit of study. Weaknesses are revealed in the expression of inadequate concepts, hazy information, or lack of background facts.

7. Analyze the local church program through audio-visuals. Filmstrips that can be used to diagnose a local program of Christian education are *Together We Grow,* and *The Church Plans for Children.* The latter has a rating scale at the end that provides a good basis of evaluation. The recordings by Helen Parkhurst on prayer, ideas of God, and ideas of death can be used to stimulate group analysis.

The teacher's concern in evaluation is whether the students develop their religious concepts, whether they show evidence of growth in Christian attitudes, and how adequately they apply these learnings to everyday experience and decisions.

In reviewing the adequacy of the program of evaluation in the church, it must be recognized that it includes the major objectives that the church proposes to achieve for each individual in his Christian development. The final proof in the Christian education program of the church will be in the changed attitudes and behavior of boys and girls, youth and adults.

— *Dorothea K. Wolcott*

EVANGELICAL ACADEMY The evangelical academy expression grew out of the rubble and spiritual revolution following World War II. It was cradled in Europe, specifically in Germany. There was a twofold shock of awareness. First, there came the realization that nazism and communism grew up in the heart of Christian Europe. Secondly, it became obvious that the church in its structured, institutional form was irrelevant to and remote from the crises of society. The church, preoccupied with its institutional preservation, was unable and unwilling to face the hostile, secular institutions of society in which its members were living and working.

The Protestant evangelical academies took their pattern from the ancient Greek centers where conversation and a common search for an answer to the fundamental questions of life took place. In the 20th-century expression, there is the climate of freedom for the spirit of man to discover God as he converses with the Bible and the world.

These academies and centers vary in approach and purpose. Some of the earliest European centers include the evangelical academies of Germany, started by Eberhard Müller at Bad Boll; the laymen's training institutes of the Church of Finland; the Christian colleges for English laymen, such as William Temple College; lay institutes in the Netherlands; Iona (Scotland); Agape (Italy). These have been followed by numerous centers and institutes in Europe. An association of directors of these centers, called the Association of Lay Colleges in Europe, meets annually.

These academies and institutes have been driven to reconsider the task, mission, and role of the laity in the church. The Greek word *laos,* which came to mean " the whole people of God," is being used to express the corporate nature of ministry. Undergirding this concept is the affirmation that the ministry of Christ belongs to the whole people of God. All are given the opportunity to share in this ministry of reconciliation in the world and therefore all need to be equipped. This discovery places the laity on the front lines of ministry in the world.

The questions that arise from these affirmations are: (1) What does one need to have or know to be equipped for ministry in the world? (2) Where should this equipping of the laity take place? (3) Can the local congregation restructure itself to be a supportive and enabling fellowship?

Whereas the European centers grew out of the crises and chaos of the war, the American expressions emerged from the deep unrest with the nature and role of the clergy and, therefore, the nature and task of the church. Early manifestation of this unrest and concern developed at Kirkridge in Bangor, Pa.; Parishfield in Brighton, Mich.; and Five Oaks in Canada. Later the Faith and Life Community of Austin, Tex., attempted a corporate witness within the university community. More recently, Packard Manse in Stoughton, Mass., adhering most closely to the German approach, has brought a unique style of academy life to the American scene.

A further development on the American scene has been the experimentation with the academy approach in local parishes. The 1st of these was at the First Presbyterian Church, of Rahway, N.J. This was followed by the Middleburgh Experiment in the Reformed Church of Middleburgh, N.Y.; the Indianola Presbyterian Church, Columbus, Ohio; the Laymen's Seminary sponsored by the Reformed Churches of Somerville, N.J.; and the Faith and Life Academy of the Winnetka Presbyterian Church, Winnetka, Ill. These represent a diversity of attempts and still are too new to be adequately evaluated.

The many diverse American expressions are joined together in a North American association called the Columbus Group. This group combines lay centers and lay programs emphasizing business and in-dustrial vocational groups, and local churches with special academy programs. It meets annually for discussion and sharing of mutual concerns.

These European and American centers are dynamic judgments on the present form of the institutional church. They are discovering new and mobile approaches to Christian witness and life in the secular society. In the midst of analysis and discussion, these centers desire to rediscover by the guidance of the Holy Spirit how life should be lived together and structured in the economic, social, and political realm. The primary challenge is how to take seriously the fact that " Christ is present in these structures " and at the same time is " Lord and Judge over them."

— William H. Cohea, Jr.

EVANGELICAL UNITED BRETHREN CHURCH, THE One could not speak about the development of Christian education in The Evangelical United Brethren Church without taking a quick look at the historical development of this denomination. The Evangelical United Brethren Church formally came into being on Nov. 16, 1946, through the organic union of the Evangelical Church and the Church of the United Brethren in Christ. Both of these groups originated in eastern Pennsylvania about 1800 out of a deep sense of mission to the German-speaking people.

Theologically, The Evangelical United Brethren Church is rooted in 16th-century Reformation thought. The rise of Pietism under the leadership of Philipp J. Spener (1635– 1705) produced voices within the church that were labeled " sectarian " but that were nonetheless influential in proclaiming a " theology of the heart" as opposed to orthodox creedalism. This is the religious milieu within which the 2 streams of The Evangelical United Brethren Church started by Philip William Otterbein (1726–1813) and Jacob Albright (1759–1808) had their beginning.

The highest tribunal of the denomination is the General Conference. The authority of the denomination resides in this body of an equal number of ministers and laymen elected by their respective conferences. These geographically determined conferences meet annually. The bishops, elected by the General Conference for a term of 4 years, act for and by the authority of the General Conference, implementing and directing the program of the denomination.

In the early part of the denomination's history the Sunday school was the main educational thrust of the church. The Sunday school movement in the United Brethren Church was started as early as 1820 by John G. Pfrimmer at Corydon, Ind. In 1827 a German Sunday school was organized in the Old Otterbein Church, Baltimore. By 1857 the denomination had recognized the educational values of the Sunday school so that the General Conference Committee on Sabbath Schools could submit the following preamble to a recommendation: "That the Sabbath School is the great nursery of the church and hope of the rising generation, appears to us no longer problematic, but a truth that comes upon us with resistless power." The Sabbath School Association was authorized by the General Conference in 1865.

In similar manner Christian education was introduced among the Evangelicals. The 1st Sunday school was organized in 1832 at Lebanon, Pa. The governing body of this denomination urged local churches to establish such schools for the training of the young. One of the inherent problems was the lack of leadership.

The emphasis of the 19th century for The Evangelical United Brethren Church was on the education of children within the church. At the close of the century the church was turning its attention toward the organization of "young people's work." In 1890, the delegates from 14 conferences meeting at the 1st youth convention in Dayton, Ohio, adopted the name "Young People's Christian Union of the United Brethren Church." The motto for this organization was "For the glory of God and the salvation of men." The name was changed in 1908 to "Young People's Christian Endeavor Union of the United Brethren Church."

During this same period of time the Evangelical Church moved in the direction of developing youth work. The 1st young people's society was organized in Dayton in 1880 by C. F. Hansing. In 1922, the Evangelical League of Christian Endeavor came into being.

Early in the 19th century the denomination came to a real appreciation of the place of Christian education in the church in relation to children and young people. However, there was a deep fear that advanced education and a genuine Christian experience could not be compatible partners. Education meant spiritual death and lifeless formalism. Training for the Christian ministry was particularly frowned upon. There was little sympathy for "preacher factories."

The rapid growth of urban centers and the changing culture accompanying the move of people from the country to the city forced the church to look more seriously at higher education. Young people were beginning to move into colleges of other denominations. If these persons were to be conserved for the denomination and other potential leadership developed, the church would necessarily have to encourage schools of higher education.

The initial move in this direction was led by W. W. Orwig for the Evangelicals and Lewis Davis for the United Brethren. In 1843 and 1845, respectively, action was taken by both churches to establish institutions of learning. Today, out of the almost 70 colleges and theological schools started by the 2 denominations, 7 colleges and 2 seminaries are in existence and supported by the denomination. The oldest college is Otterbein (1847); the most recent, Indiana Central College (1905).

Until the adoption of the International Uniform Lesson Series by the National Sunday School Convention in 1872, the Bible was essentially the only curricular material available in most of the churches. This was partially due to a lack of financial strength to produce materials. The borrowing or buying of materials was also difficult, since, at least for the Evangelicals, the church was ministering to German-speaking people. *Der christliche Botschafter*, a periodical established in 1836 by the Evangelical Church, was the 1st literary medium to carry information about the organized Sunday schools. In 1855 the church started a publication, *Christliche Kinderfreund*, strictly for children. In 1860 an English-reading paper appeared, entitled *The Evangelical Sunday School Messenger*. In 1875 the Evangelical Church authorized the use of the Uniform Lesson Series.

The United Brethren Church also made a few attempts at curricular materials prior to 1872. The *Sabbath School Songster* was published in 1842 for specific use in the Sunday school. In 1854, the *Children's Friend* and in 1865 the *Missionary Visitor* were established as Sunday school papers, the latter also being used for adults. In 1872 that denomination adopted the Uniform Lessons, which were the chief source for curricular materials until recent years. The United Brethren Church used the closely graded curriculum of The Methodist Church, and the Evangelicals made use of the cycle-graded outlines produced by the International Council of Religious Education. Since the merger in 1946, The Evangelical United Brethren Church has used the cycle-graded outlines of the National Council of the Churches of Christ in the U.S.A. and the International Uniform Lessons. — *Eugene B. Wenger*

EVANGELISM The English word "evangelism" derives from a Greek root *euangelizesthai*, meaning "to proclaim good tidings," and is usually translated in the New Testament by "gospel," which comes from the Anglo-Saxon words *gōd* (good) and *spell* (tale, or tidings), and was later interpreted as "the story about God," i.e., Christ. Evangelism has historically meant the process of proclaiming the gospel, being applied primarily to the extension or outreach of the church.

In the case of the ministry of Jesus, as described in the New Testament, no distinction is made between preaching and evangelizing. The content of his preaching is the glad tidings that the Kingdom of God is at hand for those who will repent and enter. For those who are willing to cast off the yoke of the world and take up the yoke of God, there is a new birth and a new life. These "new men" are free to serve God by loving their neighbors as themselves. It is quite clear in the New Testament that Jesus' preaching ministry was accompanied, or followed, by teaching, and it is of some note that the characteristic word used to address him was "teacher," whereas he is never referred to as a preacher.

The history of evangelism is the history of the expansion of Christianity from the apostles to the present time. It is clear that evangelism cannot be identified with any particular method or procedure. It may be observed, nonetheless, that more often than not there has been a kind of unity between evangelism and what is today called Christian education. Clement of Alexandria, for example, wrote that "the Word, once he begins to call men to salvation, takes to himself the name of persuasion . . . but the Word also heals and counsels, all at the same time. In fact, he follows up his own activity by encouraging the one he has already persuaded, and particularly by offering a cure for his passions." It is to be noted here that evangelism does not end with the conversion of a person, that is, his persuasion, but continues beyond that. Cyril of Jerusalem in the Introductory Lecture to his Catechetical Lectures, which were delivered to prepare people for baptism, makes it clear that the purpose of this particular teaching is that the people become truly Christian, dying to

sin in order to live unto righteousness.

Jerome and John Chrysostom see the evangelistic work of Christian education more as a kind of character-training. In this they are akin to those much later theorists of Christian education (e.g., Horace Bushnell) who emphasized the thought of proper childhood training as a moral pathway into Christianity over against those who emphasized a sense of sin and some almost traumatic conversion experience.

Evidently the teaching of children with an evangelistic purpose fell into disrepute in the late medieval period, for we find Jean Gerson, chancellor of the University of Paris at the end of the 14th century, defending himself vigorously for engaging in this particular activity. In his work *On Leading Children to Christ* he states that he was accused of wasting his time, of misusing his place in the church, and of breaking precedent by his actions to win children (and he admits the last charge). Apparently, he was expected to be more academic and less religious. With Luther and Calvin the evangelistic task of education, as education by and for the Christian community, was so taken for granted as to be scarcely noted in any specific fashion. The primary purpose of education for them was that God be properly served in the world, and certainly this could hardly be done apart from faith.

In American Protestantism in the 18th and 19th centuries, evangelism was mainly associated with the revival movement. More often than not, perhaps, emphasis was placed on the experience of conversion, and the process of becoming a Christian was believed to require an emotional experience. Horace Bushnell and those who followed his teachings saw religious education as a successor and superior replacement to revivalism with its demand for conversion. Emotionalism, however, continued to be emphasized by the more radical sects and was identified with evangelistic procedures. This pattern, unfortunately, is still partially true even today.

Evangelism, in almost any sense, was strong in America in the 19th and early 20th centuries but suffered a sharp decline after World War I. Many factors appear to have been involved in this decline, such as (1) the growing effects of the historicocritical study of the Bible on a naïve church population; (2) the secular binge of the "roaring twenties" with its emphasis upon material pleasures and its skepticism toward anything old-fashioned; (3) the crass and irresponsible methods of many mass evangelists whose appeal was almost entirely emotional and whose converts were left adrift and prejudiced against the usual pattern of church life.

The years during and after World War II saw in America a return to evangelism by the churches. Membership rose rapidly and visitation evangelism, in which laymen went out 2 by 2 to win new members for the church, became prevalent. Certain dangers arose as a result of this process. There was too often an overemphasis on getting members, with an accompanying neglect of the spiritual and educational needs of those who had become members.

Soon after the midpoint of the century, readjustment and rethinking began to appear and are still in process. The church is not viewed as an institution, but as the fellowship of reconciliation and evangelism. Sweazy, for example, in *Effective Evangelism* (1953) remarked that "education without evangelism makes Pharisees; evangelism without education makes fanatics."

It seems clear from the above survey that evangelism is a necessary activity of the church, indeed its primary activity, and further, that Christian education has an important part to play in that activity. In the view of some, if evangelism is understood to mean something more than simply the process of getting a person to become a member of the church, then Christian education may be the most important evangelistic activity of the church. Certainly, whatever one calls it, whether "growth in grace" or "growth in understanding," the church is concerned with every member's continuing development in the understanding of Christianity and the problems of being a Christian in the world. In the present form of the church, the task of developing Christian understanding is ordinarily carried out primarily by the educational activities of the local church. Further, for the long-range solution of the critical problems facing the church in its relation to the world, faithful intelligence is the most effective implement given into our hands. Evangelism is the great mission of the church, but it needs to be understood in a broad sense. It seems now that the future influence of the church upon the world will be that exerted by its people and not primarily by its institutional aspects. If this is correct, then one can see the wisdom of those who wrote of evangelism at Evanston in the 2d assembly of the World Council of Churches:

"The people of God are in this world as the church, and they are never alone with their Lord in isolation from the world; it is the world which he came to save. . . . Evangelism is no separable or periodic activity, but is rather a dimension of the total activity of the church. Everything the church does is of evangelizing significance."

— Gerald H. Slusser

EXCEPTIONAL CHILDREN The term " exceptional children " is used to refer to children or young people who deviate from the " normal " or " average " group. This deviation may be intellectual, physical, social, or emotional.

" Intellectually exceptional " includes both those who have great potential and those who have great limitations. " Gifted " refers to those who are in the top 1 to 3 percent of the population. It also includes rapid learners who, while not so superior as some, are different enough to need and deserve special attention.

" Retarded " refers to the mentally deficient who cannot benefit from education and training. A bit above them in mental capacity are the trainable retarded children who need special instruction adapted to their level of learning. We should also include the slow learners, a rather large group, who can participate in school but cannot be expected to learn at the same rate or to the same extent as the average.

The physically handicapped include a diversity of distinct groups: the crippled or orthopedically handicapped; those with spastic paralysis or cerebral palsy; the visually handicapped and blind; those who are deaf or have impaired hearing; also, children who have a speech handicap, although this could be a functional rather than a physical difficulty.

Emotionally disturbed children who have problems of social and personal adjustment range from those with mild emotional involvements to the psychotic. The epileptics are usually included here, although epilepsy is physical rather than emotional. But it is true that all physical handicaps have emotional factors.

Other groups presenting their own problems include those with disorders of growth, the extremely tall and the extremely short, or those with lowered vitality. Some would include albinos and those with birthmarks or other conditions that make them aware of being "different."

Historically, the plight of the handicapped has not been a pleasant one. They were often the subject of ridicule and abuse and commonly misunderstood. Society in general was not aware of their needs or possibilities.

In the 19th century, medical science began to give attention to the problem, primarily in terms of correcting physical difficulties. In the 20th century, educators developed programs of education for those who needed special attention, equipment, and help. More recently social work has been giving attention to their needs.

The result is that specialists now work with exceptional children — teachers in special education, psychologists and social workers in child-guidance clinics, speech and occupational therapists, vocational guidance counselors, etc.

The church thus far has done very little work with the exceptional, yet their religious experience is as important a part of their total life response and adjustment as any other factor; in fact, it would seem to be more important than any other factor.

The church must be aware of, and work in cooperation with, specialists and agencies. Many times the family of an exceptional child is not aware of the possibilities for correction, guidance, education, and training that exist. The pastor or religious educator can render a real service in helping them find and accept the best help available.

The church should have a program of its own as well. Sometimes this requires the establishment of special classes or programs, e.g., many churches offer church school classes for retarded children. In some cases it may mean developing a home-study program by appointing a visiting teacher for the homebound. In other cases it may mean providing special guidance and training for a teacher or leader so that the exceptional child can be related to an already existing group. It may mean providing extra projects, such as reading activities for the gifted child who can proceed at a faster pace and is both interested in and capable of covering more material than the group.

Any program for exceptional children must include ample opportunity for counseling and guidance. No group approach alone is adequate. Their problems are personal problems that can be solved only on a 1-to-1 or face-to-face relationship. Counseling and guidance must include parents, who need to understand and accept their children and to understand their own feelings and attitudes.

From the standpoint of the program of the church, there are 4 groups: (1) Those with minor devia-tions and handicaps are in the church schools and in the youth programs. Their handicaps may cause real emotional problems, but the children are active in community and church programs. (2) Those whose disability is more severe require the care of a specialist. They need special education, special vocational guidance, perhaps special treatment or equipment. But they are still in the public schools and in the church activities. (3) Those whose handicaps are such that they are confined to their homes are in the community, but if they receive any religious training or guidance, the church must go to them. (4) There are those whose condition is such that they must be cared for in institutions. When this is the case, any religious guidance they receive depends upon whether the institution includes a chaplain on its staff or at least provides for some program on a volunteer basis.

Any work with exceptional children should keep 2 paradoxical thoughts in mind: they are different, yet essentially like everybody else. Both facts are important. The retarded child cannot understand abstract ideas; the visually handicapped cannot read a church school quarterly; the crippled child cannot take part in some forms of recreation. At the same time full recognition should be given to their basic similarities to others. They all have the same emotional needs, the same desires for love, attention, and achievement.

They should never be subsumed under groups. Each person is unique. Some gifted children are poorly adjusted socially, but most of them are not. Some handicapped children are overly sensitive and shy, but some are not. We should see each as an individual rather than in terms of stereotypes.

The limitation, the difference, the handicap, is important and must be considered. It may require special planning, special equipment, special groups — yet equally important is the child's personal reaction to it. What does it mean to him? This should be the religious worker's concern.

The emphasis should always be on what a person can do, not on what he cannot do. Every effort should be made to help these children accept responsibilities. The handicapped and the retarded also need to feel that they have an important part to play.

They have spiritual needs. The exceptional child, because of his very differences, needs resources of courage and strength. He also needs challenge and a sense of commitment.

This means that in its programs of religious education the church needs to experiment with all possibilities. It needs to learn from special education. It must be aware of the research that has been done. It needs to develop new programs and materials for those with special needs, to recruit people who will minister to the homebound and the institutionalized so that none will be overlooked. — *Charles F. Kemp*

EXHIBITS An exhibit is an arrangement of 3-dimensional objects designed to motivate or inform the observer concerning a specific theme. It may include objects, specimens, dioramas, models, slides, a viewer, charts, pictures, and signs to explain objects or their purpose. Teachers use exhibits to give concreteness and meaning to words and concepts.

In motivational exhibits the teacher may collect a majority of the objects. In a work research exhibit the children add their articles, findings, or products of work. The culminative exhibit brings together the classwork and serves as a summary.

In planning an exhibit a teacher should set a purpose, then arrange the articles and captions to make it immediately apparent. It should be in a conspicuous place, contain only one main idea, make use of color and of lettering, be well-lighted, and give opportunity for pupil participation. Children should be allowed to handle, feel, taste, or smell the objects. When an exhibit has served its purpose it should be dismantled immediately, for objects seen constantly and without purpose lose interest value. Exhibits are most effective when used in conjunction with other forms of learning.

Exhibits in kindergarten might include collections of small pets, nature objects, and fruits to be felt and tasted to help children appreciate God's provision and the helpers involved in bringing it to them. Primary exhibits might include a menorah or prayer shawl such as Jesus would have used or foods he might have eaten. Dolls or toys of other countries enhance a mission unit. Juniors and young people are interested in culture objects of other countries or of Bible times, such as clothing, Bibles in various languages and translations, specimens of early scrolls, and exhibits of church vestments or worship equipment. They are capable of quality artwork that can be included in exhibits.

Parents become involved as permission is needed for bringing objects or as they visit to view the exhibit. This is a means of their finding out what is being taught.

Whether an exhibit be motivational or pupil-constructed, the teacher must continually evaluate its effectiveness as a part of the learning experience for the particular unit. — *Bonnie Miller*

EXISTENTIALISM Existentialism is not strictly a philosophic school but, rather, an intellectual revolt against the systematization of man by science, philosophy, and religion. Inspired by the works of 2 great dissenting thinkers of the 19th century, Søren Kierkegaard and Friedrich Nietzsche, it declares that philosophy should express the concrete and total life experience of the individual rather than the abstract view of universal reason.

Existentialists are both secular and religious. However different their conclusions, they have arrived at their commitment out of a common interest in certain themes. All affirm the freedom and uniqueness of the individual. All emphasize the ambiguousness of existence and the omnipresence of death. All insist on the need of a free being continually to choose his own future, and agree on the "anxiety" this choice arouses. All raise the question, What is the authentic life for man to lead?

Secular existentialism would be impossible without Friedrich Nietzsche. A master of language, he struck many expressions that have become common currency, such as "superman," "will to power," "beyond good and evil," and "eternal recurrence." A psychologist before his time, he saw in the will to power the ultimate driving force of all human behavior. A ruthless critic of hypocrisy and convention, he divided morality into 2 types, that of the "slave," springing from resentment, and that of the "master," originating

in self-affirmation. Above all, without despairing, he faced the dilemma of nihilism. If "God is dead" and the world lacks all purpose, can man justify living? Nietzsche's answer is the superman, who is "Caesar with the heart of Christ," and he joyfully affirms this life as an end in itself. The superman is his own judge, for he creates his own values and his own destiny. He is man as he can be, provided he accepts the stark challenge of a meaningless universe.

Two contemporary thinkers, Karl Jaspers and Martin Heidegger, are both indebted to Nietzsche. In his unfinished work, *Sein und Zeit* (*Being and Time*), Heidegger examines the nature of human existence as a preliminary to the study of Being in general. Man, he concludes, is cast into the world, doomed to die, and yet utterly free. To live "authentically" he must consciously embrace the human condition, accepting freedom and death every minute of his life, while refusing to submerge his identity in the anonymity of the crowd. Since the war, Heidegger has become more elusive, turning to such matters as the analysis of the pre-Socratics and the poems of Hölderlin, which he believes come closer than Western rationalism to the undiscovered secret of Being.

In contrast to Heidegger's monumental compression, Jaspers writes discursively. Less provocative than Heidegger, he began by studying psychology and only later became a philosopher. He insists that the sciences, both natural and behavioral, can only partially explain man, since they consider him as a natural object and not as a free being. Certain "border situations," such as old age, sickness, and death, remind us of human limits. Though limited, we nevertheless remain free and capable of transcending ourselves to encounter Being, the mysterious ground of all things, which we may experience but never explain.

Existentialism is often popularly, though mistakenly, equated with the work of the French philosopher and man of letters, Jean-Paul Sartre. Where Heidegger urges the individual to seek his fulfillment in the company of a select few, Sartre replies that all human intercourse is ultimately futile, for in any relationship one must either dominate or be dominated. Distinguishing 2 basic types of existence, that of physical objects which are determined (being-in-itself) and that of human beings who are free (being-for-itself), he points out that when 2 people are in contact they cannot both continue to exist in a distinctively human way. One treats the other like an object, while the other surrenders his freedom in order to become an object to his partner. Sartre concludes that each of us is alone and anguished in an alien universe. Each of us must fulfill himself in utter freedom by creating his own values and accepting full responsibility for all his actions. Another French writer, Albert Camus, expressed his belief in the ultimate "absurdity" of existence by comparing the apparent meaninglessness of the natural order with our equally natural instinct to find order in it. Less pessimistic and less profound than Sartre, he saw a hope for the individual in accepting life as it is and dedicating oneself to the service of his fellowmen.

Although none of these writers has applied his philosophy to educational issues, the implications are there. In education, secular existentialism stands for an intense, in some cases, an extreme, individualism. It rejects the current preference for group methods on the grounds that they diminish individual responsibility and encourage conformity. The school's purpose is not to adjust the young to nature or society but to launch the student on his way to absolute responsibility for himself. Instead of group feeling, the school should encourage self-examination; instead of "adjustment," it should nurture independence. Each child is a person to be formed, and each should create himself afresh rather than fit himself to patterns imposed from without. Neither knowledge nor mental discipline is an end in itself but a means to the fulfillment of freedom. What we call "objective" knowledge is never in itself decisive, but must be used by the student to meet his own needs and purposes. The existentialist school will emphasize individual study, personal interpretation, and creative work rather than group activity, factual study, and absorption of specified subject matter.

Under existentialism the child must learn to create his own standards. Right and wrong, beauty and ugliness, exist within the individual, who should never allow them to be fixed for him in religion, ideology, or outward moral code. He should also be acquainted with the inevitability of suffering and the finality of death, not in any morbid sense but so as to understand that freedom in this life with all its possibilities is an end in itself.

In contrast to Nietzsche's attack on organized religion, Kierkegaard declared that Christianity must be revolutionized from within. In a series of anonymous works, written with great force and urgency, he dismissed the claims of rationalized religion and in particular the philosophy of Hegel. Christianity, he said, must cease to be an abstract system and become once more a personal challenge to each individual, who must choose what kind of life he will lead, whether hedonistic, negatively " ethical," or positively " religious." Man does not find God by argument alone, for no amount of reasoning can bridge the gap between the human and the divine. To attain salvation he must make the " leap " of faith, trusting even to what the intellect finds " absurd."

In this century, Paul Tillich, Gabriel Marcel, Nikolas Berdyaev, and Martin Buber have all sought to develop the insights of existentialism within a theological framework. In contrast to the secular existentialists they extol courage and love. According to Marcel (like his fellow Frenchmen, Sartre and Camus, a creative writer as well as a philosopher), man achieves true freedom through intercourse with others and by surrendering himself to God.

Buber is best known for his influential philosophy of " I and Thou." There are, he says, 2 fundamental relationships, those between persons (" I-thou ") and those between persons and things (" I-it "). This view recalls Sartre's distinction between the " for-itself " and the " in-itself," but where Sartre sees the destructiveness of human relations, Buber insists that it is only through interpersonal communion that we genuinely realize ourselves.

In the field of education, religious existentialism has advanced a highly fruitful conception of the teacher-pupil relationship and its implications for learning. Since individual growth is possible only

through intercourse with others, education must become a meeting of persons through the medium of knowledge. The teacher must regard the educative process from both his own point of view and that of the pupil. In so doing, he increases his own sympathy and understanding and enriches the experience of his students. They in turn encounter, not a mass of impersonal facts and concepts, but a world of knowledge embodied in the person of the teacher. Thus subject matter is no longer data that the student absorbs willy-nilly but something in which he finds a truly personal significance.

This brief résumé can only hint at the range and intensity of existentialist thought. In this country an existentialist philosophy of education has yet to be attempted, though it offers a new approach which bypasses many of the tired categories of traditional theory. Where secular existentialism is concerned, the educator's chief problem will be to reconcile the deep pessimism of the movement and its uncompromising individualism with the demands of an educational system that is pragmatic, socially conscious, and suspicious of brilliance and eccentricity. The Christian educator, on the other hand, will have to strike a balance between the existentialist's hostility to doctrinal systems and the claims of a more orthodox theology.

— George F. Kneller

EXPERIENCE That experience is the best teacher is common knowledge. In an experience one is involved in a situation; one is a participator. Something does not merely happen to one; one reacts and thereby interacts with the external process. Reaction and interaction change one both structurally and functionally. Subsequent situations are dealt with in the context of a changed personality. Only experience accomplishes this change. Hence it is the best teacher, for by teaching we try to change people in the right way.

Experience may be concrete, that is, firsthand. One is directly involved in an automobile accident, for example. Or, it may be vicarious, that is, one may see a picture of an accident or read a very realistic description of it. The degree of involvement is considerably greater in the former, to be sure, and therefore affects one more. The latter may be very effective, and from the standpoint of total adverse effect much more desirable. A 3d kind of experience is more abstract, that is, detached in the form of symbols, as in the case of words. A symbolic experience changes a person only when it can accomplish a degree of involvement.

To all of this must be added that experience (personal involvement in a situation) accomplishes desired results most generally and most effectively when it is valued in a total structure of meaning. The richer the structure of meaning and value judgment, the greater the benefits that accrue.

It would seem that on the basis of current knowledge in psychology the above is clearly evident from research studies. We have no native, inborn, latent ideas at birth. Nor are ideas abstractly communicated. They are born of experience. The older debates of realism versus nominalism, idealism versus realism, and empiricism versus creationism have lost some of their pertinence by our better insight into experience.

However, the debates have not lost all their validity. One must still ask, Whose experience? When asking this question, the whole field of philosophy and of theology opens up. The question, then, is: What is man? Does cumulative experience describe him? Or is he in experience realizing a unique power of a creative, self-initiating nature? Or do we see in man a bringing together into functional interrelationship the spiritual and natural realms of a living creation? If man is image of God in the structural and functional relationships of his being, what we have said about experience has further light shed upon it in its full significance. It is then viewed as the experience of a person who in and through experience on the horizontal level experiences the vertical or spiritual. — *Cornelius Jaarsma*

F

FAITH No word in the Christian vocabulary is richer in meaning and more vague in specific content than " faith." It is frequently used in the objective sense as "the Christian faith" and also in the popular sense as blind confidence in what cannot be proved. It is not only what is believed but also the capacity to believe in it. It is intellectual assent and it is trust. Now one, now the other, is stressed, but the characteristic meaning is belief-ful trust in God's mercy and grace for man's salvation; it is man's response to the promised acts of God.

Although the word is used only twice in the Old Testament (KJV) — Deut. 32:20 and Hab. 2:4 — and even there is better translated as " faithfulness," as in RSV, it is implied many times as trust and belief in the truth of every word that comes from God and in his activity in history. Abraham (Gen., ch. 15) becomes the prime example of perfect trust within the framework of the covenant relationship and is referred to in the New Testament (Hebrews) as a witness to personal faith prior to law. In many of the psalms (see especially Ps. 22, 25, 34, 37, 40, 71), Christians have similarly found expression for their own trustful reliance on God, who is himself faithful. The man who

thus believes in God is in turn made steadfast and reliable.

Within this general Biblical understanding of faith as trust, the New Testament moves to a deeper dimension as it relates the believer to God's acts in the Christ event. Jesus Christ is the object of faith, and the relationship of the believer to the one believed in is a personal one. The object is not a law to be obeyed, a dogma to be accepted, or a code to be copied, but a person to be trusted. In the Synoptic Gospels, Jesus makes faith as belief in the gospel the condition for entrance into the Kingdom of God (Mark 1:15); as confidence in what he is able and willing to do, the prerequisite for healing (Matt. 8:5-11); and as humble trust in a Heavenly Father, the essential in prayer. Faith in these references is a combination of both belief and trust: belief as the intellectual confidence that God through his chosen Messiah is doing what he promised through the prophets, and trust as personal submission to the person and message of Jesus. In John, the element of belief is predominant, as belief in God (ch. 5:24), in the name of Christ (v. 12), in his words, in his deeds, and in Christ himself (chs. 2:11; 3:16), but never does it imply mere credence. To believe is to be related to God through the historical events that cluster around Christ.

Paul employs the word in several ways: as the gospel which teaches that faith is essential in man's relation to God (Phil. 1:27); as assent to right teaching (Eph. 4:13); as adventure or conviction issuing in action (Gal. 5:6); or as the capacity to receive the righteousness of God in distinction from mere fulfillment of the law (Gal. 3:11). But these uses all derive from the simpler but profound concept of faith as trust and personal response to the grace of God that Jesus proclaimed and manifested in his life, death, and resurrection. It is therefore not a human attitude or work but a gift of God. The initiative is God's; the decision to respond is Paul's. Although faith stands in direct opposition to works as a basis for a right relation with God, it is never in isolation from works. Faith implies faithfulness. The faith of the Christian makes him trustworthy. Faith acts in ethical relationships as motivated by the love of God or as Luther stated it, "Faith is a most vivid, active, and busy thing, which cannot help doing good deeds all the time."

Augustine follows Paul's thinking in his stress on the inability of man to achieve faith. The twisted, self-centered will of man finds that to trust God is of all things the most impossible. In the later development of Roman Catholic thought the intellectual character of faith is more prominent. By the time of Thomas Aquinas, faith is understood as assent to revealed truth and as volitional response to the revelation. Although natural reason is not adequate to man's spiritual requirements, there is no conflict here, as

we detect at times in Paul, between knowledge and guidance that revelation provides through faith. A modern Roman Catholic, Gustave Weigle, summarizes this position: "In Roman Catholic theology faith is an active intelligence."

Luther builds on Paul's position. Insofar as faith is a human act at all, it is a voluntary act whose chief element is trust. In a deeper sense, however, it is personal trust in the saving work of Christ and does not arise out of a human power. It is more like the turning of the flower toward the sun: the total redirection of a man's powers to act, think, and affirm in obedience to God. It is the awakening of love in man toward God. Faith is therefore justification, for the one who has thus been redirected to God is made righteous in the eyes of God. The righteousness of God is the righteousness of personal and absolute trust.

John Calvin defined faith as a knowing "revealed to our minds and confirmed to our hearts by the Holy Spirit," and in subsequent Protestant thought, as in the long history that preceded it, the 2 elements, trust and belief, are always in creative tension. In Protestantism generally, the justifying element is trust, but knowledge is never absent.

Contemporary theology, as in H. Richard Niebuhr (*Radical Monotheism and Western Culture*), assuming that the intellectual character of faith is no longer open to question and that faith demands reasoning, lays greater stress on the element of commitment and decision. Faith is defined as confidence in and loyalty to sources and centers of value. It is the basic trust and allegiance without which men do not live. It manifests itself in the total human life as well as in religion. " Not only the just but also the unjust, in so far as they live, live by faith" (p. 117). Man cannot live without some center of value, without a cause; so " to have faith and to have a god is one and the same thing." It is in his encounter with the revelatory event of Jesus Christ that he discovers the inadequacy of all his gods and transfers his faith to the one God beyond all gods. Now the One in whom he has confidence and to whom he is loyal is found to be faithful. As a person-to-person relationship, faith in the ultimate source of all being is not a human possession but is given in this encounter with Jesus Christ.

Within the context of Christian education, as understood by Iris V. Cully, Randolph Crump Miller, and others, faith is a key word describing a personal relationship. Sometimes it refers to the teaching situation itself where faith is created through the encounter of person with person and the trust one has in another. In its theological meaning, however, it refers to a faith-grace relationship in which God acts toward man in love before faith is present, and man decides to trust in God's gracious favor toward him. The Christian home and the church can provide the environment in which grace is known and experienced and in which faith in the God of Jesus Christ is the source of meaning. The relationship, however, is not the product of education; it is still an act of God. Faith arises from the encounter.

— *Wesley M. Westerberg*

FAMILY LIFE EDUCATION Although the role of the family is viewed differently by various church bodies, the task of family education is generally seen to include 3 aspects: education *about* family living, education *of* the families themselves, and education *through* the families to individuals. Each aspect has roots reaching deeply into the history of the church; quantities of material from the early church, the church fathers, the Middle Ages, the Reformation, and subsequent periods deal with family life, its duty and its faith. Currently a widespread interest in the family, sometimes characterized as " neofamilism," has reached new intensity throughout the world church.

Education *about* the family has generally been sociologically oriented, assisting churchmen to understand the relationships of the family constellation, its social history, its interpersonal relationships and patterns. Much of this body of material is taught in mothers clubs, parent-teachers organizations connected with the Sunday church school, parents classes, and within units in the adult curriculum. On a more technical and intensive level, it is handled in theological seminary course work and in special courses for pastors either in short-term institutes or correspondence studies and reading programs.

Education *of* the families themselves understandably overlaps that about family life. But it has a different focus; in this they are not learning about families in general but about their own family relationships. Churches now offer an impressive amount of guidance in child-rearing, not only through learning groups but also in the kind of literature to be found in Christian family magazines with their numerous pertinent articles and columns of specific advice to the parents who write in asking questions. The pulpit, too, offers guidance not only in discipline of children but also about the place of religion in the home, the relationships among family members, and information about marriage relations. Not insignificantly, a notable amount of practical post-nuptial education for married couples comes about informally in the numerous couples clubs to be found throughout the churches of North America.

Education *through* families is traditionally seen as a nurturing process from parent to child, the task of bringing up the child " in the nurture and admonition of the Lord." However much this is the case, and however much it is the assumption of most home-related publications in Protestant streams of curriculum material, the education that takes place through family life is also from child to parent and from adult to adult. In one sense, families are gospel bearers not only to one another but also to the world beyond their homes. Evangelism from neighbor to neighbor, rare though it is, and Christian educational materials beamed at the home, few though these remain, are examples of the educational movement *through* families.

The family is seen in differing light by various church traditions: as an object of parish program, as a unique institution with untransferable functions, or even as an extension of the church body itself. The way the home is regarded largely determines the methods used in Christian family education.

In the U.S.A., it was the Federal Council of Churches through its Commission on Marriage and the Home that sparked significant developments in the family field, beginning in 1932 with the appoint-

ment of Leland Foster Wood as the Commission's staff executive. Cooperative Christianity has continued and stepped up this concern through the National Council of the Churches of Christ in the U.S.A., whose Committee on Family Life brings together responsible representatives from scores of church denominations, educational and social agencies. In recent years, denominations and agencies have devised definitive statements regarding family living, dealing with such variegated subjects as the practice of Christianity in the home or the uses of contraception in Christian marriage. As a result, a large body of material now exists on the subject.

Church family education of all types owes much to its interdisciplinary support. Borrowing heavily from the mental health movement, it is shot through with findings of psychology, sociology, theology, and the philosophy of education. Components of family education in the churches include a network of interrelated subjects: parent education, preparation for marriage, sex and reproduction education, family worship, camping, recreation, church school curriculum for the home, budgeting, counseling of many types, training in family ministry for seminary students, in-service training of the clergy for family education, etc. An emphasis on the educational opportunities connected with developmental stages in family life has been seized by some churches as the natural connection with certain rites and sacraments: baptism with infancy, reception into communicant membership with puberty, marriage with young adulthood, funerals with death in the family, etc., to utilize inherent educational opportunities.

The media of communication used

by churches in family education are not different from those of church education in general: the pulpit, church school curriculum, literature of numerous types (books, magazine articles, pamphlets, leaflets), films and recordings, small-group discussions, conferences, and counseling interviews. Taking account of the changes within family living since the turn of the century, churches (especially American suburban parishes) are mindful of the often-expressed desire of families to maintain their integrity as a group. Family church services, church family night suppers and programs, family vacation church schools, classes for the entire family cutting across age departments, and publications designed for the whole family are some expressions of this concern.

Recently, denominational conventions and assemblies have paid fuller attention to topics in the sex and family areas. Whereas they previously published resolutions and statements about marriage and divorce, mixed marriage, and family faith, some now also offer specific information concerning the issues of contraception, artificial insemination, homosexuality, abortion, and similar personal and social issues. These statements, recent surveys show, are couched less as directives than as studies to aid pastoral counseling and to relate needed light from Biblical theology and the behavioral sciences. Currently several denominations have been engaging in depth research in family living among their constituencies.

Theological consideration about the family gets it aegis from the Bible, every book of which contains some reference to family living either in direct reference or in allusion. In Old Testament thought, the family is the basic unit of society, whereas New Testament teaching presents a challenge to the unity of family life (Matt. 10:21 f.; Mark 3:34 f.; John 7:5) and the gospel is seen as bringing a division among family members (Matt. 10:34 ff.; Luke 12:51 f.). Fatherhood is accorded peculiar honor not only in the patriarchal period, but also in latter days when sonship is interpreted in terms of a father's characteristics (see " son of encouragement," " sons of obedience," " sons of peace "; also, Acts 4:36; I Peter 1:14; Luke 10:6). So sonship in the New Testament is seen to be a gift to those who have faith in Jesus Christ as Lord. Likewise brotherhood is interpreted both empirically and theologically; Christians are enjoined to treat each other in brotherly love even beyond the degree practiced in many households, accepting one another in Christ, practicing forgiveness and sacrifice where these are needed. Marriage in Scripture has a God-given sanctity, analagous to the union between Christ and his church. (Eph. 5:25 ff.). The church is also understood in family terms as the household of God; Paul alludes to "the church in their house" (I Cor. 16:19). Family stability, the love of one for another in family life, authority in the home, and the sexual relationship itself are all subordinated under the rule of God. As a necessary part of the tension of Christian living, even the strongest of human ties and earthly loyalties must be subsumed under the demands of the Kingdom (Matt. 10:37; Luke 14:26). — *John Charles Wynn*

FAMILY PLAN IN SUNDAY SCHOOL Still in the experimental stage, the Family Plan in Sunday

School has elicited considerable interest. First organized in Holy Trinity Lutheran Church, Dubuque, Iowa, in Oct., 1952, by the writer, pilot classes have been conducted in various denominations and areas.

The Family Plan brings entire families to the same class in Sunday school. Two, 3, or 4 families of similar background and abilities can put the plan into action. The Family Plan class is held like a regular Sunday school class and is not ancillary to it.

Those experimenting with the Family Plan deem it to possess a number of advantages. Such a study plan involves both home and church on an almost equal basis. The educative process flows back and forth between the two. It may be that one of the emphases most vital in this arrangement is that both parents are involved.

Education becomes nurture in that Sunday school efforts become a 7-day-a-week process. Since each child not only studies the same material but also participates in the same discussion, further discussion at home becomes more natural.

The plan seems to be evangelistically fruitful in that whole families and not only the children are invited to Sunday school.

The plan is socially desirable, bringing whole families into contact with one another. This has been of greatest value in large congregations. Solidaristic families (holding tightly together) are brought into contact with other family units, while atomistic families (having a tendency to fly apart) are brought together at least for the Sunday school period on Sunday morning.

The plan permits grading according to background rather than a mechanical grading according to age.

Families well established in the faith can engage in more profound discussion during the Sunday school hour and at home, whereas families needing assistance in elementary matters of the faith can engage in study on their own level.

One of the discoveries of those who have assisted in this experiment is the eagerness with which many parents participate. The novelty of the situation at first prompts parents to serve as policemen in the classroom. Once the situation has become natural, discipline problems seem to disappear completely.

Questions not yet solved are: Shall an outsider or one of the parents serve as teacher? What materials are best suited for such a class? Where can room be found if all parents come to Sunday school? Shall the children of " prodigal " parents form a separate class or be absorbed in regular family classes? Adult classes for those who have no children at home can, of course, be continued. — *William D. Streng*

FIELD TRIP   A field trip may be defined as a planned and purposeful visit to some place outside the regular classroom. However, a field trip worthy to be included in an educational program must meet certain conditions.

A field trip must be closely related to the planned curriculum and integrated into the program. To be used it should be the best way to accomplish a specific purpose or provide a needed experience. It should be timed to fit most purposefully into the unit of study.

The field trip should stimulate a vital learning experience. It should provide useful opportunities that could not have been presented by ordinary classroom methods. The class journey should not duplicate what can be and is being done more meaningfully by the family or by small informal groups.

A field trip should be more than informative. New insights and viewpoints, often not even thought about by the teacher, frequently come as a result of a journey. There are also opportunities to develop responsibility, initiative, self-discipline, courtesy, and practice in good public relations on a well-conducted field trip. Pupils often develop appreciations and understandings that could not have been gained by classroom "telling."

Where can a church school group go on a visit but to a synagogue or a church? The answer is that the church is interested in the community it is attempting to serve. It cares about where its people live and work; it is concerned with the sick, the handicapped, the criminals, the orphans, and the underprivileged. The world of nature also opens doors for field experiences. Art museums, historical places, theaters, and concerts offer many possibilities for meaningful experiences. However, what happens to the pupils and not the destination is the chief criterion for evaluating a field trip.

In carrying out a field trip, the following practical questions may be helpful: What will be the destination? Is this the best choice for the teaching purpose? Consider economy of time, money, and energy. Is it a typical and most desirable example? Does it give a generally truthful picture? Does it fit the age level and experience of the members of the class? Determine what the trip will mean in the way of goodwill and better understanding. What might this experience mean to the pupils?

Are there physical hazards? What can we hope to gain in information, understanding, personal enrichment?

Make careful preparations. Make a preliminary trip to the place; communicate with those involved. Integrate the trip into the program. Make sure pupils know the purpose and have necessary background information for the journey. Provide directions, such as standards for safety, conduct, what to bring, where to meet. If a guide is used, be sure all can see and hear him. Give opportunity for questions, drawing, taking notes and photographs where appropriate. If there are small children, see that there are enough adults to assist.

Evaluation should be made by pupils and teacher. Did the trip serve its purpose? What about attitudes and conduct? Were there problems? What information and insights were gained? What further study is needed? What changes in emphasis and interests may result from the journey? Record your evaluations, making helpful notes and recommendations for other times or groups. — *Ruby Peregrine*

FINANCE Functionally speaking, financing Christian education often begins with concerns about payment of bills incurred in the operation of a program. Experience with these concerns points to the advisability of building a budget to facilitate distribution of available funds in the most useful way. These items may well be representative of a list of needs that must be met by the budget of the Christian education program: printed curriculum materials; other classroom supplies; rooms and equipment of permanent nature (cost of rooms might well be carried for bookkeeping purposes under the congregation's property budget rather than the education budget, as might the items of permanent equipment; nonetheless, authorized persons from the education program should make available the findings from systematic study of needs); audio-visual materials (rental and/or purchase); library books and supplies; leadership training within the congregation and in joint denominational and/or interdenominational settings; vacation church school; summer camping program; Scouting program; recreational or athletic programs; any remuneration for paid supervisory or teaching personnel (exclusive of minister or director of Christian education, whose remuneration might properly be listed as a cost item of general church administration); scholarships or other grants for Christian higher education (e.g., ministerial candidates); missionary and benevolent concerns; promotional materials, postage, etc. (these, also, might be preferably figured in the general administrative cost of the church program; the education administration should again make available the findings from a systematic study of its needs); beyond-Sunday-morning age-level programs (e.g., youth fellowships, etc.)

Even a cursory survey of the range of program needs can lead to the building of a preferred budget in full recognition of the fact that a compromise budget may become an economic necessity. Realism suggests that the compromise budget be prepared as an alternative proposal readied for the arising of that necessity. Facing this possibility may prompt a study of a number of different ways of looking at Christian education budgets.

Should Christian education be financed by separate offerings in its various program units or as part of a unified church-wide budget? Whatever the counsels of expediency, a unified budget testifies to the integrity of Christian education as one of the central ministries of the church rather than as a parallel program somehow separate from the life of the church. This consideration alone is sufficient to weight discussion in favor of the unified budget. Offerings from program units should be regarded as receipts to the total church budget. The assumption here is that such scrupulous regard for the interests and needs of education program units is expressed in total church financing as to render designation of the purpose of a given offering an unnecessary safeguard for realization of the intention of the donors.

Distinction should be made between funds needed for current operation of the program and capital investments required to undergird the teaching task. Each of these, in turn, ought to be viewed in terms of immediate needs and of long-range goals. Steps should be planned for reaching the long-range goals. These will vary with local conditions, but they should be spelled out by administrators of the education program in consultation with other authorized church officers. There may be the possibility of endowments for the education program. However, endowments, like memorial gifts, must remain responsive and responsible to the living witness of the church's ministry through education. As mere expedients or as monuments frozen to some particular way of expressing that witness, either the endowment or the memorial gift may entomb the hope for vital churchmanship; this makes either one too expensive a gift to be accepted.

Finance, like everything else in church life, teaches. Financing Christian education is properly a learning task shared by the entire congregation. The quality of concern manifested at this juncture must reflect a high interest in the nurture of the individual's life in Christ through his church. This is the crucial question in financial decisions as much as in classroom procedures or other processes overtly labeled as educational. Decisions here and the way they are reached may either support or negate what the church seeks to teach.

There is implied here that a sense of dialogue in the light of the gospel and in the spirit of redemptive community will mark all levels of financial decisions. In reaching these decisions, administrators and authorized program unit representatives ought to follow a clearly stated and understood pattern of operation that is responsive to the program unit, representative of the entire education program, and acceptable to the total church. In formulating budget askings, the requests of each program unit should be set in the perspective of total education budget, total church needs, and available funds.

At all steps in the process, the relative importance of items may be decided by pooled ranking in terms of contribution to past program achievements, present needs, and/or opportunities of the future. The pooled ranking might also be done in terms of what a given program unit has contributed or should contribute to Christian nurture of in-

dividuals within the church. There may be a need to balance the per capita cost of each program unit against total needs and resources.

Care in the process receives added importance from the fact that functional responsibility for final decision and action will become a task for those to whom this authority must be delegated in the name of efficient operation. These are the persons who must represent Christian education in the planning of the entire church budget and financial program. The process of dialogue within the education department must be followed by representation at the total church level.

When decisions have been reached within the education department, communicated to and accepted by total church officiary, those in charge of Christian education must recognize and act upon their responsibilities, implicit or assigned, to assist in interpreting the financial program to the congregation and in underwriting it.

Administration of education finances must be compatible with the total church program. Within its own operations Christian education must set up and follow with integrity procedures that are clearly understood, flexibly responsible to needs of program units, responsive to periodic review (e.g., annually), and subject to audit along with other church finances. There should be a statement of policies for requisitioning of funds and payment of bills; and a system of bookkeeping. Whereas forms for implementing these policies should be as simple as possible, probability favors the formulation of some instrument for authorization of expenditures and delegation of authority to a designated person or persons to draw on budgeted funds in a regulated manner.

The financing of Christian education ought to be a laboratory experience for learning sensitive, responsible Christian stewardship.

— *W. Clinton Henderson*

FINGER PAINTING Finger painting as a modern art form began a little more than 30 years ago in Rome where Ruth Faison Shaw was conducting a school for English-speaking children. Finger painting was brought to the U.S.A. by Miss Shaw in the early 1930's. It is now used widely as a children's art medium and as a therapeutic measure with both adults and children.

It had its origin in a very natural way when a little boy in Miss Shaw's school smeared the bathroom wall with iodine. Since "smearing" is a basic impulse on the part of nearly all children, the teacher, inspired by her young pupil, set out to develop a way in which children could indulge their propensity for smearing in a satisfying way that would be emotionally healthful to themselves and not damaging to the physical surroundings. It was named "finger painting" by a small boy "because we don't use brushes."

Finger painting involves the use of the fingers, palms, heel or side of the hand, the thumb or the forearm, in free and rhythmic movements. Great bodily freedom is allowed in the manipulation of the paints. It is done standing so as to allow for the freedom of movement necessary. Sometimes music is played during painting so as to increase the possibility of rhythmic movement of hands and body.

Children from 3 to about 8 years old are those who usually achieve greatest satisfaction from this activity because it does not require fine muscle coordination and makes use of the big muscles. A teacher who understands this medium can use it with children in a number of ways that will help them release stored-up emotional tensions that need outlet in acceptable ways. Young children sometimes have a legitimate and psychological need to be messy. Sometimes a child has intensely strong personal feelings that he can release creatively by responding to the stimulation of finger painting.

These same therapeutic values are also possible for older children and adults through this easy medium. They begin to find or add to their sense of worth and value as they create in ways that are truly their own, because finger painting requires a minimum of rigidity and does not demand artistic ability for satisfactory achievement.

The materials for finger painting are easy to acquire, and no skill is needed on the part of the group or the leader of the group in the use of them. Commercially prepared paints, water-soluble and nonpoisonous, may be purchased. Or the paints may be prepared at home. One recipe is as follows:

1 cup cornstarch or laundry starch mixed with enough cold water to make paste
1 cup soap flakes
½ cup salt
1 cup talcum powder (not necessary, but gives smoother texture)

Cook in double boiler in one quart of water until thick. Increase amount of water if necessary. Add 1 teaspoon glycerine. Beat with egg-beater. Pour into small jars, such as baby-food jars. Add powder paint of a different color to each jar for a variety of colors.

A wet, glazed surface is needed for painting. If the paintings are to be kept, the paper may be commercially prepared finger-painting paper or glazed shelf paper. If the painting is not to be permanent, it may be done on a piece of oilcloth, a piece of masonite wood, or any other glazed surface that can be sponged off for future use. The paper or painting surface should be at least 18″ x 24″ so as to make possible sweeping, rhythmic movements. The paper is wet with a sponge or by dipping it into a pan of water. About a teaspoonful of paint is put on the paper. As hands, arms, and body are moved freely, interesting and unexpected effects begin to appear. No skill is required and if the results do not suit the "artist," they may be erased with a sweep of the hand and a new effect attempted. Younger children and beginners should try one color. As experience is acquired, other colors may be added. Too many colors given to young children mix into a muddy brown.

Finger painting is used with all age groups, but it is more commonly used with preschool children. In the preschool its purpose may be the same as any other free-play material (such as clay and tempera paints or the use of music for creative rhythms) designed for emotional release and the satisfaction of the creative impulse.

In the primary group there may be a conscious purpose in addition to the values mentioned for preschool children. The finger painting may be used to make book covers, murals, borders, posters, or even to illustrate stories.

Junior and junior high groups can do more conscious representation with finger painting, using several colors in a more complicated, previously planned drawing.

The principal limitation in the use of this medium comes from the unwillingness of a leader to allow a group to be "messy" to its full measure of satisfaction.

— *Mary Elizabeth Mason*

FINLAND Since about 95 percent of the population of Finland belong to the Evangelical Lutheran Church of Finland, the pupils in the elementary schools on principle receive instruction from teachers belonging to this church. Generally there are 2 lessons in religion a week. However, there has been full religious freedom since 1923, which means that pupils whose parents do not wish to have the children receive this instruction may be excused from it. Wherever possible, other confessional teaching (e.g., by teachers belonging to the Greek Orthodox Church, the other folk church of Finland) is arranged. Children not belonging to any religious community receive no religious instruction, these persons amounting to no more than 3 percent of the population.

The fact is, however, that not all elementary school teachers give satisfactory religious instruction if this matter is regarded from a Christian ecclesiastical point of view. Some are void of personal interest or of direct church involvement. However, there are Christian teachers' associations, members of which are recruited from teachers and training-college students active in Christian work, which promote this aspect of the teacher's work.

Officially, the school teaching of religion is subject to the school's supervisory board and the minister of education of the state. In theory a remnant of an older system remains, permitting rectors of local parishes and bishops to have the right of visitation to the divinity teaching in the elementary schools. In practice this is seldom done. Nevertheless, the cooperation between school and church is excellent; ministers and teachers come together for consultations, courses in Christian education are held with many participants, and solid programs in support of the teaching are arranged by ecclesiastical organizations.

In recent years the Center for Religious Education was officially founded by the church. This Center was charged by action of the bishops to work out a total program for the church's educational activity. Although this program has not yet been approved by the ecclesiastical organization, the performed research has produced a noteworthy document that in principle is grounded on the thought of a total catechumenate of the church, growing out of the baptism of children. It insists that baptized members of the congregation must be taught the meaning of their baptism from cradle to grave.

Hitherto the obligation to teach has been considered to have been fulfilled through the preparation for confirmation after young people entered their 16th year. Besides the formal school instruction in religion, the children usually attend Sunday school, 25,000 voluntary teachers acting among 300,000 children. There also have been clubs for young people (ages 12 to 15), Scouting, youth circles, adult Bible classes, etc. Voluntary associations usually have guided such activities. The current change taking place in

this connection is that instead of being regarded as a lay activity parallel to the life of the church, Christian activity of all kinds is being viewed as a total ecclesiastical catechumenate. The voluntary organizations should exist only to serve the local parishes in their endeavor to fulfill the obligations of their baptism to teach. On the whole, there is developing a fruitful cooperation between the ecclesiastical direction and the laymen's movements within the church. A corollary of this is a new accent on the need for more intimate contact between the local parishes and the homes of the people. The house-congregation is the 1st class of the catechumenate; parents ought to be the 1st divinity teachers, trained to their task by the support of the church.

— *Arne Rosenqvist*

FIVE YEARS MEETING OF FRIENDS

The deep concern of Friends for a guided education for their children was evident even in the early days of the 17th century. George Fox urged the setting up of coeducational schools as early as 1668, saying they were to "teach whatsoever things are civil and useful in creation." The inclusion of girls on equal standing with boys was an important emphasis of Friends.

Although religion was not listed as a subject in these schools, all education was religiously motivated and interpreted in terms of religious values. John Bellers expressed the concern of Friends: "Next to the care of our souls a right education of our children is greatest."

From earliest times this passion for the right education of children caused Friends to build their schoolhouses adjacent to their meetinghouses, and to see to it that those who presided over the schools were persons whose lives were worthy examples of the convictions held by Friends. In America, in those states where Friends had great influence, elementary schools flourished and led the way for public schools that later replaced them. Later, secondary schools and colleges were founded and supported until gradually the secondary schools, known as academies, were replaced by the public high school.

When the Five Years Meeting of Friends was officially organized in 1902, committees were appointed to be responsible for education.

In 1922 a Board of Religious Education replaced the former Bible School Board, indicating the broadening interest in this area of concern. The decline of Friends' elementary and secondary schools gave importance to the need of their Meetings for material for the use of Meeting schools. The new Board was charged with the responsibility for " promotion of Bible-school material," and the encouragement of the use of Friends' literature.

The present activities of the educational board are in 3 areas: the development of curriculum for all ages in the Meeting schools, the encouragement of better preparation for leadership through laboratory schools, and the provision of better resource materials for the use of Meetings. — *Russell E. Rees*

FLANNELGRAPH The flannelgraph is a medium of illustration originally employed in some churches for the purpose of teaching Bible stories in a manner that would make them real and dramatic for boys and girls. It provides more action than flat pictures; it does not require the expense and equipment of projected visual aids. The characters can be placed on the scene when their part comes in the narrative and can be moved to different positions or removed as the story requires. Flannel background scenes also aid comprehension of the Bible setting, whether it be the Sea of Galilee, the barren desert, a Palestinian town, or the Temple.

Flannelgraph figures are usually colored, often die-cut to save work for teachers, and come in book form with pockets in which to keep the figures when not in use. In the book are also the author's suggestions for their use, and sometimes adaptations for various age levels. The artwork often leaves something to be desired, yet is usually not distracting to the action. The figures are printed on sturdy paper backed with suede or flocking that adheres to the flannel backgrounds. Sometimes a piece of flannel or suede-paper is pasted on the front of a figure so that it may come and go with either side adhering to the background. Sometimes a figure has moving parts that may be raised and lowered by a small brad fastener hinging the arm or head. Though elaborate backgrounds are available, simple scenes that teachers themselves can crayon on flannel are often as effective, especially with younger children. Care should be taken that the perspective of the scene is not distorted; that figures are kept the proper size when in the foreground and background; that objects and buildings are in proportion.

Bible stories with clear-cut action were first selected for illustration by flannelgraph. It can very effectively show Naaman dipping 7 times into the Jordan River through a slit in the blue river of the background. Baby Moses can be clearly shown;

his mother makes a reed basket, takes it down to the river; sister Miriam hides in the rushes; the princess comes to the water with her maids, finds the baby; Miriam asks if she wouldn't like a nurse for the baby and runs home to bring the baby's mother.

Conduct stories demonstrate Biblical principles in action today. Stories of missionary adventures help people visualize the problems in foreign lands. Objects that are easily pictured make an illustration more forceful. Adults appreciate scenes such as the structure and arrangement of the Tabernacle in the wilderness, or analogies such as the fruit of the Spirit, depicting both the vine of John, ch. 15, and the corresponding Christian virtues.

Flannelgraph is probably most helpful at the primary level. Most juniors should be able to visualize Biblical scenes and should be ready to use their own Bibles. Beginners need models as well as pictures; they need to use their large muscles to play out the actions of the Bible characters whom they can understand.

Since good storytellers do not want anything to come between their eyes and the eyes of the children as they tell a Bible story, a flannelgraph is often used as a review. After that the boys and girls can show the action themselves. Therefore, flannelgraph is not confined to teacher activity. Though the children may not make their arrangement as pleasing as the teacher's, they can show the essential action using the Bible's own words when possible, thus motivating Bible memorization. They enjoy repeating a story frequently. Children also enjoy making their own simple illustrations from flannel or paper backed with flannel.

A few words of caution are in order for the use of the flannelgraph. Some teachers become so fascinated with this method that they overuse it at the expense of other good methods. It is only 1 of many good ways of illustration. Moreover, this method requires careful preparation. The materials need to be laid out in the order of use where the teacher can readily pick them up and lay them down. Practice is required until the action is very clearly in mind. The easel that holds the flannelboard must be set up solidly so that it does not collapse when a child inadvertently hits one of its legs. If more than 1 flannel background is to be used for a single story, they may all be placed on the board ahead of time, with the 1st one to be used on top. The figures must be kept flat so that some do not fall off while others are being moved. — *Lois E. Lebar*

FLASH CARDS The use of flash cards is a technique for mastery of tool facts or skills. The public school uses flash cards for word and phrase recognition, number combinations, or any skill that asks for rapid automatic recall. The number combinations or a key word for a memorized portion are printed on cards that are then " flashed " before the child or group, calling for instantaneous recognition, or sum, or related fact. Thus the name of a state may be flashed for the response of the state capital, or the numbers 9 and 6 may call for immediate addition or multiplication.

Educators recommend flash cards for limited use only, cautioning against sacrificing meaningful context or overdoing the method till it becomes a monotonous exercise.

In Christian education there are

few tool skills or facts. Indeed, the constant danger is that the individual is learning cliché responses that will bring approval as right answers, without thought or conviction. The problem is to achieve life-related thought that will result in a change in the person's behavior pattern.

Nonetheless, there are a few possible uses of flash cards. As soon as a child is able to read the Bible for himself, he should know the books so that location is automatic. Flash cards may call for a group of books, such as the law; or an individual title may be flashed for the child to give the name of the following or the preceding book. Flash cards also have a place in memorization of Scripture. After the meaning of the verse or passage has been carefully taught, drill games may stimulate recall through key phrases or words on flash cards that help carry the individual or group through the memorized portion. References on flash cards may call forth the correct verse, or key words of the verses on cards may call forth the references.

An extended use of the term refers to large cards on which stories may be shown in pictured parts, or songs shown by word sections. These may be adaptations from the Japanese street *kamishibai*. The emphasis here is not on speed, however, but on clarity and attention-holding, a purpose similar to the showing of slides.
— *Mary E. Lebar*

FORUM The forum is a method in which material is presented, following which members of the audience participate by asking questions and giving their points of view.

The main purpose of a forum is to help persons in a small or large group to secure information and in-sight into significant issues and then through active participation by questions and sharing to enable them to gain a broader perspective through which they can come to a conclusion on the items discussed.

There are many different types of forums. The simplest one is to have someone introduce facts and/or an interpretation of an idea by a lecture and then have the audience ask questions and give their opinions. A moderator is in charge.

Additional types of forums have made this method meaningful in Christian education in recent years. In film forum a movie is shown, followed by questions and comments from the audience. The symposium is another variation. In this type a group of persons give differing points of view on an issue. A debate is still another type of forum. Here 2 sides of an issue are given. There is the possibility for audience involvement in each of these, as in the other types.

The panel is still another option. One can either have the members of a panel submit material to open a forum, or the forum can begin with persons in the audience referring questions to the members of the panel.

Still another technique that has become popular more recently is the dialogue forum as a method to present and discuss a topic. In this method 2 persons have a conversation and an encounter on a topic both before and after the audience becomes involved.

A number of items should be considered in planning a forum. The issue should be a real one and should be clearly stated. The audience should be prepared both on the nature of the question and on the nature of the methodology to be used. A good moderator is one who knows and can handle this particular technique.

In some cases, particularly if the forum is a long one, it is valuable if all the questions are raised by the audience before any of them is discussed. Following this, a small group can arrange the questions in an orderly manner. This takes away a little of the spontaneity of the method; however, it provides for the possibility of handling the questions in a systematic way. Many times in shorter meetings the audience becomes involved immediately following the presentation, both in raising questions and in discussing the issues.

The forum is used primarily from the high school through the adult ages. However, even a simple story told by a teacher to children when followed by questions and comments can be called a forum if one thinks of the term in a broad sense.

The forum as a method in Christian education has some specific values. It brings new material to persons so that they can react to it and clarify the issues. It is one of the best methods in Christian education for persons in a large group to become involved in a topic in a concrete way.

Possibly the major value is inherent in the method itself in that it is in keeping with Christian education at its best, in which persons do not simply accept material handed to them ready-made but are always urged to react and to arrive at their own conclusions.

The forum also has some dangers. If a lecture is used to introduce a point of view at the beginning of a forum, there is the possibility of the group's securing only one side of a question. If the group approach is used, there is the danger of relativism when a number of persons give their statements and then abide by their points of view rigidly. Or if the group presenting the material is made up of like-minded persons, those in an audience find it difficult to enter into the period of involvement in a meaningful way when the group defends its position. These items are not always dangers; the possible dangers themselves can be seen also as strengths of the system. — *Paul R. Shelly*

FRANCE When the crumbling of the Roman Empire brought about the disappearance of centers of education in French towns, all the spiritual and intellectual life took refuge in the monasteries. Monastic schools were opened for the children of the nobility and the future churchmen. From the 13th century on, universities also began to appear in France, always led by men of religion. Christian education among the common folk depended on the community life of the parish. Festivals and pilgrimages were a means of initiating children and adults into the story of the Bible and the lives of the saints. Moreover, these stories were reproduced in the church edifices. The whole of society was based on a hieratic order, cemented together by religion, while all human thought was bound up in theology and the supreme end of every soul was preparation for the Last Judgment.

In the 14th and 15th centuries this sociologically Christian society was upset by a combination of factors: the development of individual conscience, troubled by certain abuses within the church; the awakening of a new confidence in man's reasoning powers; a return to the sources of heathen antiquity. In addition to the traditional Roman Catholic view of life, other conceptions of man arose, hence possible other forms of education: man, an end in himself, who must be brought up with his own dignity and maximum development in view; man, a cog in a collectivity he must serve for the welfare of the whole, etc. In the face of these conceptions the Reformers found again the significance of man according to the Bible, i.e., man responsible solely to God but submitting in love to the order of the world and his fellow beings. In this view, all human situations were regarded as a calling from God, including a family life in which father and mother should be the 1st educators, a nurturing cell within every church. This rediscovery by the church of the adults' responsibility for the care of the child was not put into practice, however, because of events in France.

After 50 years of persecutions and religious wars the church of the Reformation was able to blossom for a short period (Edict of Nantes, 1598). Then family education flourished, along with Bible and catechism teaching; elementary schools opened in each parish, as well as secondary schools, colleges, and academies.

Yet at the end of the 17th century, thousands of Protestant children were taken from their parents to be brought up in convents. The flight of many Protestant families from the country left only those in the remoter country regions where family worship could be safely practiced. It was during this period that scorn of the ancient order of things, both political and religious, deepened, and aspirations to liberty and progress arose throughout Europe. It

was mostly atheists, interestingly, who asked and obtained the recognition of Protestantism in France (1787), and it was Napoleon who granted the Protestant churches the right to exist. In the face of anticlerical rationalism, which swept away the authority of the Bible along with that of the Roman Catholic Church, the Protestants of France sought help and inspiration in German Pietism and Anglo-Saxon Methodism. At the end of the 18th century, Jean Frédéric Oberlin showed admirable fervor and Christian love, undertaking the systematic education of his whole parish, including all ages.

Within 50 years the Reformed and Lutheran Churches of France produced a rich variety of missionary and educative societies. Practically every parish instituted a primary school. When the state decreed that primary education should be severed from religion and be obligatory and free for all, " *laïque, gratuit et obligatoire* " (Law of 1881), the Protestant schools came into the state school system. Since that date, numerous Protestant teachers have been completely at ease in teaching positions within the primary and secondary schools, although no explicit religious teaching is permitted. Alsace remained under a special concordat, which permitted primary schools to remain confessional, as they are to this day, religious teaching being permitted in the schools, as in Belgium and Switzerland.

Except for Alsace, the Sunday school (and, in certain places, an additional Thursday school) has been the principal medium through which children can obtain a knowledge of the Bible and an initiation into the life of the church. Youth movements and children's clubs supplement the Sunday schools. In-struction in the catechism (*instruction religieuse*) is offered by the pastors to young people of 13 to 16 years of age prior to confirmation and First Communion.

The curriculum is divided into that for the primary school (6 to 9 years); junior and middle school (9 to 13); and seniors (13 to 15). The Bible and church history are basic ingredients.

The Sunday Schools Society is made up of representatives of the various Protestant churches. It de-vises curriculum materials adapted to age groups and publishes period-icals and courses related to both children's and adult work. The director makes extensive visiting tours among the churches. Because of the modest number of Protes-tant children in France (roughly, 70,000), the society concentrates on booklets and leaflets rather than on general materials such as flannel-graphs, posters, etc.

There is at present great interest in Biblical studies in France, often taking a cooperative form. Swiss publications are used widely.

— *Denise Hourticq*

FRANCKE, AUGUST HERMANN

Francke (1663–1727) was born in Lübeck. As a young man he attended the Universities of Erfurt, Leipzig, and Kiel, where he studied mainly theology and languages. At this time he wanted to make a great name for himself as a scholar. In Luneburg, in 1687, Francke expe-rienced a conversion, as a result of which he renounced his worldly am-bitions and dedicated himself to God. The next year he returned to Leipzig, full of zeal to help his students to feel deeply the message of the Bible. He was enormously

popular, but his colleagues distrusted him, partly because he taught in Ger-man instead of Latin, partly because they considered his theology un-orthodox, partly because he became one of the founders of Pietism — one of the many return-to-the-Bible movements that have appeared in the course of history.

Francke became so uncomfortable at Leipzig that he moved to Erfurt, where he both taught and preached, but again he was so hounded by criticism that he asked to have a church committee investigate him and clear him of the charge of un-orthodoxy. Finding that even this clearance could not protect him, he returned home for several years and then accepted a position at the newly opened University of Halle.

At the same time he became pastor of the tiny nearby village of Glau-chau. Here his real life began. He first opened a school for the children of the poorest families in Glauchau (1695). Three years later he built an orphanage. His teaching was so good that boys of well-to-do families were soon sent to him for training. Since the lines of social demarcation between classes were rigid, Francke could not simply add these children to the village group but had to found a separate school for them, called the Paedagogium. As the years went by he discovered that some of the boys from the charity and village schools could profit by secondary education, so he founded a Latin school for them. At about the same time he opened a boarding school for girls. He had already established a normal school (1695) for ele-mentary teachers, and now (1712) he founded one for secondary teach-ers. The course took 5 years, of which 3 were devoted to practice teaching under supervision. In 1712 he opened still one more institution — a home for old men, into which he gathered the many beggars that came through Glauchau.

His schools were supported partly by private donations and partly by 2 business enterprises that he fostered: a drugstore and a printing press. In the former, various patent medicines were sold. The press turned out thousands of inexpensive Bibles. Since it was a basic tenet of Pietism that the individual should go directly to the Bible for help and inspiration, it was necessary to have Bibles that were within the financial reach of everyone. Through this work Francke exerted a great influence upon German religion, and through his normal school graduates, who were in demand everywhere, and through his writings he exerted a profound influence upon German education.

Francke wrote mainly upon either theology or education. In his theological writings he discussed the basic attitudes of Pietism. In his educational writing, he presented his thoughts about the proper conduct of schools and the best methods of teaching. His schools were so good that they are still in existence, as is the publishing house, after 250 years. The entire group of institutions is called Die Franckeschen Stiftungen, located in Halle an der Salle. — *Luella Cole Lowie*

FREEDOM The reality of freedom is the most concrete and personal characteristic of human existence, yet in the history of thought it often has been discussed in abstract and impersonal terms. This has been due in part to the fact that the defense of freedom has been shaped historically by climates of opinion, theological or philosophical, whose basic

inspirations and concerns were derived from subhuman or transhuman dimensions. Thus the tendency has been to use models in the resolution of the problem that were singularly inappropriate to the human reality under discussion. This can be seen on the theological side in the extreme strictures placed on freedom by the Reformers, and especially in the subsequent Reformed tradition where the conception of divine sovereignty was imaged frequently as divine power or force that negated man's freedom through the irresistible pressures of grace or wrath.

A comparable process of development occurred in the dialogue between the exponents of freedom and the expositors of a scientific world view, whose primary model was the law of cause and effect operative in the subhuman mechanism of the natural order. As applied to human freedom this meant that all human action must be explained by using a model derived from the physical sciences. Man is an object and like all other objects in nature he is determined by the whole complex of external forces that contour his existence. This image of man as the passive effect of causal forces has perpetuated itself in divergent patterns ranging from man determined by economic forces to man as the pawn of sociological or psychological powers over which he has no control.

Reactions to these deterministic conceptions have been expressed by both theologians and philosophers. The most cogent defenders of freedom during the 19th century took their stand in terms of metaphysical idealism. Man's creative and autonomous freedom is the prior ground of the phenomenal and causal order of objects. Others followed the more moderate suggestions of Lotze, who demanded more respect for the scientific model than Fichte had granted. They interpreted freedom as the creative power of the self to utilize the mechanisms of cause and effect in the service of human or divine purposes and values. As Tillich and Fromm have observed, this idealistic defense of freedom has had ironic consequences. The attempt to vindicate freedom as essentially exempt from determining forces led to an understanding of freedom as autonomy. Such autonomy is too free, that is, it leaves man exposed in his individuality, estranged from nature, cut off from community. This places such a burden on man's self-consciousness that it leads to neurotic fracture and to the attempt to escape from freedom into the anonymous collective or into the sheer vitalities of nature. This ironic conclusion makes necessary a reformulation of the question of freedom in which freedom from determining forces becomes at best a helpful preliminary to a more adequate conception.

In the reformulation of the question of freedom it should be emphasized that the issue cannot be stated in terms of an isolated faculty called free will which chooses between alternatives and is somehow independent of or indifferent to external solicitations and pressures. Freedom implicates the whole man in his engagement in the world and in his relationship to God.

With this in mind the Sartrian formula of freedom in facticity may be helpful in restating the issue. Each human life inhabits what may be called a facticity situation, that is, each man inherits a certain geography or space, exists in a particular time, and comes equipped with a physiology. In addition to this exterior facticity, each has an interior facticity summarized by Erich Fromm as the inner need to satisfy physiologically conditioned drives and to overcome isolation and moral aloneness. These facticities give form or structure to freedom. But the crucial issue for freedom is that man is aware of these facticities and of his power to relate to them, to give them the stamp of his own personal uniqueness. This capacity is not absolute, but its presence in man enables him to choose himself, that is to choose *how* he will be related to the facticity that is his fate.

When freedom is understood in this relational context the modern identification of freedom and autonomy collapses. There is no abstract will that is independent of the world of personal or subpersonal realities. Freedom is always engaged; it is the self-in-relationship or, as Brunner says, it is freedom-in-responsibility. Man knows himself as free only when he is involved in the world. Freedom, like nature, abhors a vacuum, but comes to itself precisely through those interrelationships and dependencies that establish the limits of autonomy. It is the false pretension that man can live out of himself, can be independent of other persons, or, from a theological perspective, of the grace of God. Thus what many moderns view as autonomous freedom is referred to in the New Testament as sin, as the delusion of self-sufficiency. In contrast, Marcel has observed, a relational view of freedom establishes an indissoluble correlation between freedom and love, since both can be understood only in terms of responsiveness.

On the theological level, this relationship view of freedom has a certain cogency with reference to the traditional problem of freedom and grace. In the sense that freedom has reality only within a context of relationships and dependencies it follows that such freedom is always in part the gift of grace. That is, it can come into being only through the presence of the other, the human or divine other. Hence, God's presence which is his grace is not controlled by man's freedom, but is the very ground of the possibility of its response. Moreover, this grace comes, not as an irresistible power to which man reacts by necessity, but as a gracious call inviting freedom's " yes " or " no." Thus neither nature's supposed causal forces nor divine power determines man's freedom-in-relationship. True relationship can only be solicited or invoked. And because freedom is always the *how* in a relationship, it will always be embattled, exposed perennially to the possibility of fidelity or betrayal. — *J. William Lee*

FRIENDS GENERAL CONFERENCE

Friends' concern for Christian education began in 1859 to 1861 with the establishment of several classes for the teaching of the Scriptures to the young. As the movement spread, Friends from the Yearly Meetings of Philadelphia, Baltimore, New York, and Indiana met in 1868 to organize the Friends General Conference to Promote an Interest in First-day Schools. This organization, faced with the need of publications to interpret the Friends' viewpoint, issued in 1885 the 1st number of *First-day School Lessons,* containing Bible lessons for adults.

Adult classes, led by one of their own members, and meeting simultaneously with the children's classes, have been a real strength in the Society of Friends, developing leadership, ability to gain new insights, and, through discussion, tolerance of divergent views.

Since 1904 the courses for children have been graded. These have presented Biblical subjects and applications of Jesus' teachings to everyday living. Since needs and size of First-day schools have varied greatly, the Religious Education Committees of both the Friends General Conference and the Philadelphia Yearly Meeting of Friends have issued objectives and given guidance in curriculum-making, with lists of recommended books and lesson material. A quarterly, *Religious Education Bulletin,* was started in 1916 by Jane P. Rushmore. A small collection of hymns, printed in 1919, was developed into the *Hymnal for Friends* in 1955.

However, the Meeting for Worship continues on the basis of silence. The preparation of children for this type of worship has been a responsibility shared by parents and teachers, whom the committees frequently assist with studies and suggestions. They seek to find in worship the consciousness of God as a reality and to know " the Christ within as an immediate, ever-present guide to the will of God."

In 1947 there was held the 1st Family Institute where parents with children between the ages of 3 and 12 gathered for religious guidance while living, playing, and worshiping together.

— *Marguerite Hallowell*

FROEBEL, FRIEDRICH WILHELM AUGUST

Friedrich Froebel (1782–1852), known today as the father of the kindergarten movement, was one of the educational leaders of Europe, who in the 18th and 19th centuries sought to reform European society through the establishment of enlightened and humane programs of education. These educational reformers thereby contributed directly to the Liberal movement of the 1840's. Froebel in particular rejected the authoritarian basis of the theological and social doctrines current in his time and taught that man may learn to know God and the life that is good for men through close communion with the natural order itself. His educational theories and methods reflect this belief.

Froebel was born April 21, 1782, in Oberweissbach, Thuringia (Germany), where his father was the Lutheran minister. His mother died before the end of his 1st year, and when his father remarried, the young child found himself excluded from his father's house by the unsympathetic stepmother. This caused him to wander through the streets and surrounding countryside hours on end, to neglect his formal elementary studies, and to look for security and comfort in the natural beauty of his surroundings. This early trend was strengthened by an apprenticeship to a forester at the age of 17, and subsequent studies in the natural sciences at Frankfurt am Main, Göttingen, and Berlin.

Although Froebel gave promise as a scientist, he soon recognized teaching as his true calling. While at Frankfurt he met Anton Gruner, a disciple of Pestalozzi's and director of a *Mutterschule*. Gruner offered Froebel a position in his school, and thus he was persuaded to spend several years in Pestalozzi's Institute at Yverdon. Finally, in 1816, following a variety of study and teaching experiences, Froebel established his own school at Greisheim. Two years later, with the help of his 3 closest associates, Langethal, Middendorff,

and Barop, he established the school at Keilhau that became the center for the Froebelian movement. Although Froebel established other schools, notably at Wartensee, Willisau, and Burgdorf, all in Switzerland, Froebel's life ended in Germany, where he was engaged for a number of years defending his ideas against the bitter attacks waged against him by some ecclesiastical and civil authorities.

In the opening paragraphs of *The Education of Man*, Froebel wrote: " In all things there lives and reigns an eternal law. . . . This all-controlling law is necessarily based on an all-pervading, energetic, living, self-conscious, and hence eternal unity. . . . This Unity is God." On this conviction Froebel founded his system of education. While Froebel believed that the physical senses provide the data from which knowledge of this inner Unity might be discovered, he believed that such knowledge is not given directly, but must be comprehended through the activity of the individual intellect. Froebel went on to write, " A quietly observant human mind, a thoughtful, clear human intellect, has never failed, and will never fail, to recognize this Unity." To Froebel it followed that education must lead the child to observe carefully the wonders of nature, to cultivate a reflective attitude, and thereby to stimulate the child to discover through his own intellectual activity the true nature of God. " Education," he wrote, " consists in leading man, as a thinking, intelligent being, growing in self-consciousness, to a pure and unsullied, conscious and free representation of the inner law of Divine Unity, and in teaching him ways and means thereto." The *Kindergarten* (garden for children) was to him the ideal environment within which to foster this development; and his formal use of objects, symbols, songs, and games was a deliberate effort to engage the child in this developmental process.

— *I. N. Thut*

FUNDAMENTALISM A "fundamentalist" has been defined simply as "one who believes in the basic truths of the Bible; distinguished from modernist." However, a neat classification of fundamentalism is almost impossible, since it has assumed various moods in its history and is usually classified according to the theological persuasion of the interpreter. Many who hold to the basic truths of the Bible dislike the fundamentalist label, since they do not want to be identified with some of its rather extreme positions. Fundamentalism is both a doctrinal system and a movement in history, and an understanding of the latter will help to clarify the real spirit of fundamentalism.

At the beginning of the 20th century, secularism was already making an impact upon Protestantism. At the same time, the employment of the scientific method of inquiry, higher criticism in the study of the Scriptures, and the popularization of the evolutionary hypothesis, brought dismay to some Protestants because they felt that their faith was being undermined. Orthodox scholars became devoted to the refutation of liberalism.

The term "fundamentalism" seems first to have emerged out of the controversy that arose over the publication of 12 paperback books, under the series title *The Fundamentals*. These books began to appear in 1909 and were written by outstanding churchmen and scholars such as James Orr, professor in United Free Church College, Glasgow; Benjamin B. Warfield, professor in Princeton Theological Seminary; Robert E. Speer, secretary of the Board of Foreign Missions of the Presbyterian Church U.S.A.; and E. Y. Mullins, President of Southern Baptist Theological Seminary, Louisville. Lyman and Milton Stewart, wealthy California laymen, supplied the financial backing for the printing of this series, which was distributed free to pastors, evangelists, missionaries, seminary professors and students, Y.M.C.A. and Y.W.C.A. secretaries, college professors, Sunday school superintendents, and religious editors throughout the English-speaking world.

Also contributing to the rise of fundamentalism was the Bible Conference movement, with a strong "prophetic" element included in the program. In 1919 a World Conference in Christian Fundamentals was held in Philadelphia. Most of this phase of fundamentalism was of an undenominational character.

Fundamentalist action within denominations began as seminaries, literature, and missionary agencies began to feel the influence of liberalism. In 1913 the Northern Baptist Theological Seminary was established in Chicago as a protest to liberalism in the Divinity School of the University of Chicago. The Presbyterians were also affected by the rise of liberalism, and under the leadership of John Gresham Machen, Westminster Seminary was founded in Philadelphia as a protest against the encroaching menace in existing seminaries.

In 1920 conservative delegates to the Northern Baptist Convention, who desired that the convention reaffirm the fundamentals of the New Testament, were mentioned in an editorial of a New York newspaper as "fundamentalists." It was not long before a Fundamentalist Fellowship was formed within the Northern Baptist Convention. This group, like similar groups in other denominations, attempted to preserve allegiance to the basic truths of Scripture, but failing in that attempt withdrew from the denomination and formed their own organization. In many cases, churches became independent of any denomination. The fundamentalist movement gained strength as many of these groups joined informally to oppose liberalism. However, by 1930, the movement came to a stalemate and lost much of its influence in Protestantism. While some of the groups preferred to be known as "conservative," others have retained the term "fundamentalist."

Many of those who continued to hold the "basic truths of Scripture" began to identify themselves as "evangelicals" and in 1942 the National Association of Evangelicals came into being. These people were seeking to cooperate across denominational lines in 8 fields, one of which was Christian education. Following is a summary list of the articles of faith of the National Association of Evangelicals: authority and infallibility of the Bible; the Trinity; the deity, virgin birth, substitutionary death, bodily resurrection, ascension, and return of Jesus Christ; regeneration by the Holy Spirit; indwelling of the Holy Spirit in the believer; resurrection of all men — the saved unto life eternal, the lost unto eternal damnation; spiritual unity of believers.

Adherence to doctrinal statements sometimes becomes a test of fellowship and in some groups there are strict standards of conduct. Salvation has sometimes been characterized by deliverance from such alleged evils as dancing, card-playing, attending the theater, smoking, and gambling.

In the early days of the fundamentalist movement, the infiltration of liberalism into theological seminaries and colleges caused many to become suspicious of higher education. An answer to that was the establishment of Bible schools, wherein the student was subjected to an intensive study of the Bible. Emphasis was placed upon Scripture memorization and a literal interpretation of the Bible. Although the fundamentalist movement has declined, the Bible Institute movement has continued to gain strength.

One of the results of the NAE's cooperative effort in Christian education was the formation of the National Sunday School Association in 1944. This association helped to revive interest in the Sunday school. National enrollment had been declining prior to that time, but through national and local conventions church people were awakened to a new enthusiasm for the Sunday school. In the years 1950 to 1954 the national Sunday school enrollment increased about 26 percent but the enrollment of the eight largest groups affiliated with the NAE increased about 67 percent.

With this increase in Sunday school activity has come a demand for literature. This demand has been met largely by independent publishing houses who advertise their Sunday school materials as "covering the entire Bible" or as "true to the Bible."

Extreme Biblical literalism is

much less prominent in the latest materials and in some instances memorization is de-emphasized. There appears to be more concern that Sunday school students engage in a systematic study of the Bible, with definite application to life's problems. — *Paul R. Finlay*

G

GERMANY For centuries there has been a people's church (*Volks-kirche*) in Germany. Except for the Jewish faith and a number of sects, most Germans belonged to either the Protestant or Roman Catholic Churches, which predominated over the free churches even after 1918, when the close association between church and state was dissolved. From the time of the Reformation there were several established churches that combined after 1945 to form the Union of the Evangelical Church in Germany. In this union there are 3 large confessional groups: the Evangelical Church of the Union, the United Evangelical Lutheran Church in Germany, and the Reformed Church. These ecclesiastical distinctions in no way affect Christian education, since national characteristics play a more important part in that function.

Since 1945 the national character of the church has been different in the Western and Eastern regions. The Western occupation powers strengthened Christianity and the people's church after the oppression suffered during the Third Reich. A strong political party, the Christian Democratic Union (*Christliche demokratische Union*) was made possible only by the tradition of a people's church, and the other political parties, almost without exception, regarded the people's church favorably. The situation is quite different in the Soviet zone. The political situation there is more or less inimical to the church. In the West, Christian education, separated according to the confessions, is a regular element in all state schools, the churches having the right to determine the subjects for inclusion. In the Eastern zone there is no Christian education in the schools, though the churches may give religious instruction outside the school curriculum and the school buildings. However, atheistic propaganda makes it difficult to carry out such instruction.

In Western Germany practically every child comes in contact with the gospel through classes in the schools. Parents, it is true, may withdraw their children from religious instruction. Since few parents use that privilege, almost every child learns Bible stories, hymns, and the catechism. When children enter the confirmation class held by the pastor, they possess the knowledge already acquired in school religion classes. In some parts of Germany pastors teach the school classes; in other parts, school teachers do so.

Whether this participation of the schools in religious instruction can be considered true Christian education depends on a variety of conditions. Not every teacher is an active member of the Christian community. Many give religious instruction just like any other subject, merely to impart information of the course of study in question. If a teacher does this impartially, no harm is done. During the Nazi regime many teachers willfully did harm by agitating against the " Jewish Book " and by propagating political ideology against the Bible. Both the Roman Catholic and Protestant Churches learned from this experience. In the Roman Catholic Church there always was the *missio canonica,* the authorization by the church to impart religious instruction to the young. Since 1945 the Protestant churches also have agreed with the state for a corresponding authorization. This provision requires that a teacher, desiring to have such authorization, has positive religious views, and no teacher can be forced to give religious instruction. It is recognized, however, that even the best religious instruction can count only partly in Christian education. It is important whether the children belong to families ruled by the Word, and whether parents and children are united in a Christian relationship. Indifferent homes fail to help the school instruction bear fruit. On the other hand, youth societies can play a helpful part.

Up to now we have used the old terms " religious instruction " and " religious teaching." At this point we must mention a theologically incisive change in the meaning of such expressions. It concerns the distinction, recognized during the church's battle in the Third Reich, between " religious " and " evangelical." What follows concerns in particular the consciousness of the evangelical church, even if it has not completely succeeded in restoring the tradition of the people's church in the West. " Religious " is the general term used for the human need to keep in contact with the divine power on which man recognizes his dependence. Such " religiosity " is not of necessity Christian or Biblical. All religiosity is affected by the sin of man, wishing to be as God but wishing to determine for himself just what God must be for mankind. There is this ingredient also in the Christian form of religiosity. But Jesus Christ and his gospel disturb all religiosity. Education not judged and changed by this gospel and rendered completely different is not true Christian education in the sole sovereignty of the Word of God, as certified for us in the Bible, in law and gospel, in the cross and resurrection of Christ.

Thus we must speak of education by the gospel. Evangelical instruction is related to the religious community, living the gospel in promised forgiveness, in the imitation of Christ, in the hope of God's eternity. Thus Christian education will be freed from any general religiosity for service in this ephemeral world and will require no segregation of Christians and non-Christians. The aim is that the Christian, free in this scientific and technical world, may love his neighbor for the good of all. So the gospel will be honored within as well as outside the tradition of the people's church, giving a testament to the future world concerning the relevance of Christianity to man's total existence.

We are thus concerned with 2 different types of "religious" education. Education under the gospel has no part in power or desire for power. In Eastern Germany the "religious" education of atheism is ousting the church. This is most clearly seen in the "youth consecration" (*Jugendweihe*) which the Communists hold in place of confirmation or First Communion. Under such pressure belief in Christ is purified among the little flock that remains faithful to the gospel, as in the days of the Confessional Church during the Third Reich. It must not be forgotten, however, in Western Germany that in its more favorable situation the church there, too, owes the world an education because of what it has received from the cross and the resurrection.

The churches also promote Christian education through children's services (*Kindergottesdienst*), the German equivalent of Sunday schools elsewhere. "Religious school weeks" are held for the upper classes of the high schools from time to time. Roman Catholic school chaplains and Protestant pastors gather pupils together during those weeks for Bible study and free discussions about the church and Christianity. In church homes "leisure-time periods" of 2 to 3 days or even for several weeks are held for young people. Parishes conduct young mother circles and discussion evenings for married couples. Periodicals are published to help parents, teachers, and pastors. Ecumenical meetings are promoted during holidays abroad with Christian youth of other churches. A "daily Bible reading" is published annually for young people, taking them through the Biblical writings and concentrating each year on one of the Gospels. In all church councils youth pastors advise young people and hold divine services especially for them.

— *Oskar Hammelsbeck*

GIFTED CHILDREN Who are the gifted? In his famous study, Louis Terman included children whose IQ's on the Binet Intelligence Test were 140 or higher. Leta S. Hollingsworth and Paul Witty studied groups whose qualifications were similar. More recently, the range has been extended down to 120 IQ. The concept of giftedness has been further broadened to include children who are specially talented in mathematics, art, music, and other fields; the socially and the mechanically gifted; and, most recently, those who score high on tests of creativity. Witty's concise general definition has been widely accepted; we designate as gifted those who show exceptional performance in any line of socially useful endeavor.

Some would go farther and seek giftedness in every individual; one teacher, when asked to list the gifted children in her class, said, "All my children are gifted." Although we subscribe to the democratic ideal of helping every person to develop his potentialities, whether he has 1 talent or 5, we still find it valuable to reserve the term "gifted" for an exceptionally able group.

At the top of this group are the geniuses, persons whose achievement is outstanding. They combine the qualities of "ability, zeal, and readiness to work." Character traits are important in all persons of exceptional ability, especially from the standpoint of their contribution to society. A "gifted heart" and a keen mind comprise a combination greatly needed for leadership today. Untempered by loving-kindness, the analytical, logical mind may arrive at solutions that negate humanity. Unperceptive sentimentality may bog down in futility or even hasten the advent of disaster. The enlightened heart combines powers of both analysis and synthesis in the service of humanity.

What are the components of giftedness? Some psychologists, especially the British, put a great deal of weight on a general factor of intelligence that pervades all aspects of the individual's achievement. Others recognize only specific factors, which range in number from Thurstone's 7 primary mental abilities to Guilford's 55 factors. P. E. Vernon unites these 2 points of view into a hierarchical schema that includes: (1) a general overall factor; (2) 2 major divisions — verbal-numerical-educational and practical-mechanical-spatial-physical. Under each of these latter 2 main categories would be found innumerable specific factors.

How may gifted children be identified early? Parents can observe whether a child shows the common characteristics of giftedness: alertness and interest in the environment, ability to see relationships, quickness in learning to walk and talk and do other things, an unusual memory, interest in words and reading, ability to concentrate on a task that is interesting and suitable, social sensitivity, and insatiable curiosity. Teachers may also note these signs of giftedness, and not confuse docility with ability.

An individual intelligence test given at 6 or 7 years of age will identify many bright children, including some whose previous environment has not developed their native ability. A group intelligence test given after a child has had 6 or 7 years of schooling will predict quite well his ability to succeed in high school or college — provided personality and character traits do not interfere with his academic achievement. Many tests of special talent and creativity are also available. All test results should always be interpreted in the light of knowledge of the child's background and observation of his actual functioning under favorable conditions.

Is giftedness inherited? It is certain that babies are born different. At birth some are more alert, more sensitive to their environment, than others. They differ in their nervous systems as well as in other bodily structures. In this sense, intelligence is inherited. Special talents seem to depend much more on opportunities to develop interests and to win approval and rewards than does the general ability that underlies exceptional achievement in any line.

Heredity sets an upper limit to each child's attainments. Whether he does or does not develop his innate capacities within his given scope depends upon his environment. Geneticists and psychologists tend to emphasize the importance of heredity; sociologists give much more weight to environment; educators say, "Let us provide the best possible conditions for learning and see how the child develops, regardless of his measured intelligence."

What conditions are favorable for developing a child's gifts? In infancy close contact with a loving mother helps to build a basic sense of trust. As the child grows older he needs things to handle, to look at and listen to, to babble about. When he begins to talk he needs someone to listen to him, to talk with him, and to read aloud to him; he also needs many opportunities to explore and satisfy his curiosity. The gifted preschool child needs a "lush" environment. He needs encouragement to work things out for himself, to experiment, and to wonder; he should develop habits of concentration and persistence, and should know the satisfaction of many tasks well done. He is best disciplined by the demands of the given situation. In addition to love, gifted children need the constructive personality-building experience of work.

The gifted child usually enters school with an eagerness to learn. About half the gifted children who have been studied knew how to read before they came to school. They do not need to go through a reading readiness program, nor do they need all the detailed instruction in reading that less able children require. They are bored by the usual primers and preprimers. Fortunately, there are now many interesting beginners' books, both stories and factual material, that bright children can read with pleasure and profit. Parents can supply similar reading materials at home, and should continue to encourage the curiosity and creativity of their gifted children.

During the elementary school years, gifted children are often 2 or more years above their grade placement. For these able learners, the teacher should provide suitable supplementary books. He should also encourage them to undertake projects through which they can be of service to the group, as for example, in planning an assembly program or serving as editors of a class newspaper.

In high school the gifted child may take an extra subject and engage in extracurricular activities such as industrial arts, home economics, typing, music, art, and dramatic or science clubs. Gifted children need guidance in making and carrying out suitable educational and vocational plans. This is especially important in the case of those who come from homes where education is not highly valued and where the children are discouraged, rather than encouraged, to develop their potential ability.

Gifted high school students also need some special provisions. Those who are physically, emotionally, and socially mature will profit by doing 2 years' work in 3, and by participating in advanced college placement or other accelerated programs. Special interest groups and extra library discussion periods afford stimulation for gifted children, usually without any adverse effects on their social relations with their classmates.

The 2 main reasons why gifted high school students do not go to college or do not remain there to graduate are lack of financial assistance and insufficient motivation. The 1st deficiency is being rapidly remedied by the colleges themselves, by government loans and scholarships, and by scholarship funds raised by local communities.

The 2d cause of underachievement by gifted students of college age is much more complex and difficult to handle. The tendency to underachievement may be inherent in the personality as a whole. The same underlying motivation may manifest itself in different levels and different kinds of performance. Although a gifted child may in the beginning have a strong basic drive toward self-fulfillment and an eager curiosity to learn, his life experiences and associations may give rise to a value system and a self-concept that induce indolence instead of industry, pleasure-seeking rather than social responsibility, apathy in place of willingness to put forth effort.

Underachievement can be forestalled only by a developmental program beginning with the earliest years. Children catch their parents' attitudes toward education and life. They build work habits and a sense of responsibility only if adults make appropriate responses to their day-by-day behavior. Parents and teachers should make reasonable demands on the child and help him to set appropriate standards of excellence for himself. The most pervasive influence is a system of values, a philosophy of life, a sense of responsibility for one's gifts. As Albert Schweitzer put it: "Whatever you have received more than others in health, in talents, in ability, in success, in a pleasant childhood, in harmonious conditions of home life, all this you must not take to yourself as a matter of course. You must pay a price for it. You must render in return an unusually great sacrifice of your life for other life."

— *Ruth Strang*

GIRL SCOUTS Girl Scouts of the United States of America is a national organization with an informal education and recreation program open to all girls. Girls and adult advisers are united by the Girl Scout Promise: "On my honor, I will try to do my duty to God and my country, to help other people at all times and to obey the Girl Scout Laws."

The purpose of the organization is to help girls develop as happy, resourceful individuals, willing to share their abilities as citizens in their homes, their communities, their country, and the world. It is the spiritual force behind Girl Scouting that gives life and meaning to its program. Belief in God and acknowledgment of one's responsibility to God are recognized by the Girl Scout organization as basic to the development of good character and sound citizenship.

The founder of Girl Scouting in the U.S.A., Juliette Gordon Low, organized the 1st troop of 12 girls on March 12, 1912, in Savannah, Ga. Mrs. Low's interest in Scouting was the result of a stay in England during which she became inspired by the ideals and work of Sir Robert (later Lord) Baden-Powell, the founder of the Scouting movement in Britain.

The Girl Scout organization is affiliated with the World Association of Girl Guides and Girl Scouts. Building international friendship and understanding between girls of all nations is an important part of the Girl Scout program. Each year more and more girls from the U.S.A. have the opportunity, both at home and abroad, to meet and share programs with Girl Guides and Girl Scouts from different countries through an international exchange program.

In the Girl Scout program, girls in each troop have the democratic prerogative of choosing their own activities from 11 areas of program interest: agriculture, arts and crafts, community life, health and safety, homemaking, international friendship, literature and dramatics, music and dancing, nature, the out-of-doors, and sports and games. Adaptations of a single, continuous program are made to suit the capabilities and needs of the different age groups — Brownies (7 through 9), Intermediate Scouts (10 through 13), and Senior Scouts (14 through 17).

Girl Scout troops are frequently sponsored by religious groups or other community organizations that share the ideals of the Girl Scout movement. Sponsorship is a voluntary association based on mutual agreement.

Life in the out-of-doors is a vital part of Girl Scouting. The organization provides a variety of camping opportunities for girls — troop, day, and established (resident) camps. The out-of-door program is geared to help girls develop resourcefulness, initiative, self-reliance, and recognition of individual worth and dignity; it should contribute to physical, mental, and spiritual wellbeing.

Living up to the Girl Scout Promise to try to do her duty to God is an essential part of a girl's Scouting experience. Through this emphasis on spiritual values, the Girl Scout organization encourages each girl to become a better member of her own religious group. At the same time it recognizes that religious instruction is the responsibility of parents and religious authorities. Girl Scouting also seeks to help the individual member to respect and appreciate the religious convictions and practices of others.

At the national headquarters of Girl Scouts of the U.S.A. there are professional staff members who serve as liaison with each of the 3 major groups in this country. In addition, clergymen appointed by several national religious bodies — the National Council of the Churches of Christ in the U.S.A., the National Catholic Welfare Council, and the Synagogue Council of America — serve as advisers on 2 Girl Scout national committees, the Religious Policy Committee and the Advisory Committee on Relations with Religious Organizations.

The Girl Scout organization, on both a national and a local level, frequently calls on the churches to provide religious programs for Scouting events. Each year in celebrating Girl Scout Week (the week that includes March 12), girls across the country begin by observing Girl Scout Sunday or Sabbath as a special day of rededication to the ideals and principles of Girl Scouting. — *Helen C. Pidgeon*

GOD, UNDERSTANDING OF The Christian understanding of God centers in God's own self-disclosure in Jesus Christ as holy love. With special references to education, this affirmation involves 3 areas of knowledge: orientation, motivation, and fulfillment.

God's self-disclosure in Jesus Christ as holy love involves God's being the presupposition and central perspective for all knowledge. God is the supreme being upon whom all else depends as its source, condition for being, and power for operation. Therefore, he is the central reality for knowledge in terms of which alone it can be adequately organized, interpreted, evaluated, and directed. As Supreme Being, God is personal Spirit, not spiritual personality, for although the personal category is the highest in the scale of love, there are areas of creation in nature and history where God is impersonally present and at work. As Spirit, God is capable of such impersonal presence and participation.

In himself God is love, and all other aspects of his being are to be understood in terms of love. These other aspects have their own kind of reality and function but are centrally dependent upon and work within God's love. Thus the power of God is the control exercised by

God's love, whether in creating or in directing, in judging or in fulfilling. Similarly, the holiness of God is the perfect purity of God, in himself, and with reference to all his relations in the world, for his creatures and creation, and against all sin and imperfections. The justice of God is likewise the creative work of God's love inclusively, and only in this sense impartially, for the rehabilitation and fulfillment of each and all. The freedom of God, again, is his sovereign capacity for creative initiative and the liberty of his love finally to fulfill his creation with the consent and understanding willingness of his creatures. The " wrath " of God is the love of God punishing, not vindictively, but to frustrate man's fear and to fulfill his freedom.

God's nature and work are thus to be understood throughout in terms of the holy love that he himself has disclosed in the life and teachings of Jesus Christ. When God limits his freedom and power for pedagogical purposes, to ensure the reality of love, God's revelation of himself accordingly provides for education the final presupposition and the central perspective of all knowledge. The meaning of all reality and of every life ultimately becomes clear through a deeper and fuller understanding of God as holy love.

Not only does the doctrine of God provide orientation for education but it also furnishes its motivation. Man knows what is right and what to do more than he does it or is even willing to do it. He lacks motivation. Mere meaning never moves man, for man lives, thinks, and acts as a whole being. God is the power for being and the drive for the fulfillment of being. Therefore proper and effective motivation depends upon man's right relation to God, in understanding, and in the participation of his life. Such understanding of God's love and participation in it is possible only through God's own gift of his Spirit. The nature of God is willingness to share his Spirit. God is not self-sufficient being, but self-sufficient love. Such self-sufficiency involves no deficiency but perfection of nature. God needs no one in the sense of lack, but on account of the perfection of his love for his creatures he needs them all to be in right relation to himself.

God thus creates the world, his children, and all the needed conditions for his creatures to obtain their intended end. To share with God, through his free gift, the creative joy and the responsible concern of his spirit is to find the needed motivation for discovering truth in all areas of life and to live such truth with increasing effectiveness. Especially are the vision and the experience of the life and work of God, as understood through Jesus Christ at its center, the best and most enabling incentive to communicate the truth in ever more genuine and helpful manner to all God's children. The nature of God is therefore the truest and most forceful motivation for education.

Thus the nature and work of God, disclosed in Jesus Christ as holy love, underlie both orientation and communication of knowledge, both as presupposition and perspective and also as motivation. Similarly, the Christian understanding of God provides meaning and motivation for man's fulfillment. The chief end of man is to become rightly related to God according to his purposes for man in creation, education, and transformation. God has made man to find fulfillment in the kind of life Jesus lived and in the kind of community he founded. Because God is love and man is made in his image, man is constantly driven and drawn by the demands of love in duty and in the lure of love for community. God is the perfect pedagogue who works mostly indirectly through the processes of nature and history in order to preserve inviolate the freedom of man. God works in nature to provide man with the setting of predictability and precariousness within which man can plan and provide and yet be ever dependent upon God indirectly, especially because of destruction and death. Nature is the proper setting within which man can both develop responsible initiative and learn that he finally cannot himself control the conditions of life. God thus uses nature to help man both to grow in self-reliance and to develop interdependence.

God also works in man's history, driving him on by his needs in order that he may learn to utilize the resources in nature and to develop an ever more complex and interdependent kind of community. Man's community, because of God's work in creation as the spring of history, has been steadily expanding throughout man's life on earth; but God has also been drawing man on by means of the love he experiences, which came to its culmination in God's self-declared purpose in the universal, unconditional love of Jesus Christ. Thus God, as the perfect pedagogue, works indirectly in nature and history, through the push of process from behind and the pull of purpose from before, to frustrate man's fear and to fulfill his faith. Earthly history is only the beginning of God's pedagogy with

man. God's fulfillment of his total purpose comes only within the incomprehensible depths of his eternity. The clear implication of the Christian faith, however, is that God remains educator in eternity and knows enough eventually to complete his teaching. Sin and suffering are real and serious as by-products of God's working with man's freedom, but they are not the central realities either of God's relation to the world or of man's relation to God. They are to be understood through the cross of Christ and in relation to God's means of redemption, and not as the end of God's purpose in creation, which must be seen in the resurrection of Christ over sin and over all other enemies of man. God's nature and purpose cannot be understood apart from creation, but creation itself must be seen in the light of God's own self-disclosure in Jesus Christ as holy love.

The Christian understanding of God, whether of his nature or of his work, is thus to be grasped through the central reality of God's revelation in Jesus Christ as holy love. All other aspects of his nature and all God's work in creation and redemption are to be understood in terms of God as the personal Spirit who is holy love. Education in the light of God consequently makes central to its aim, communication, and concrete methods, the fostering of the kind of community of open, inclusive, and creative concern that receives its pattern of orientation, its power for motivation, and its measure of fulfillment in the life and teachings of Jesus Christ.

— *Nels F. S. Ferré*

GOSPEL The word " gospel " (Anglo-Saxon: " godspel ") is used in the English versions of the New

Testament to translate the Greek *euangelion* (cf. " evangel " and its derivatives), meaning " good news," " glad tidings." There is also a verb, *euangelizesthai*, " to announce glad tidings."

The verb is derived from the Septuagint where it translates the Hebrew *BSR*, a verb that originally denoted the bringing of good news of any kind, though particularly of victory in battle (I Sam. 31:9). Later it acquired a specifically religious connotation (Ps. 40:9a; 68:11), meaning the good news of God's acts. Most important, however, for New Testament usage is its use in Deutero-Isaiah (chs. 40:9; 52:7; cf. ch. 61:1): not just of any act of Yahweh, but of his one mighty act of redemption in bringing Israel back from exile, in which he is decisively establishing his kingly reign. Also, the prophet's announcement is itself part of that act, for it is the word of Yahweh himself (Isa. 51:16) that accomplishes what it announces (ch. 55:11).

The return from exile proved a disappointment: the final reign of Yahweh was not established. The hope of it was shelved to the end time (Kingdom of God — Messiah). This hope included the expectation of a messenger whose proclamation would mark the inauguration of God's kingly reign.

Although Jesus did not use the noun " gospel " (the Marcan passages where it occurs are clearly secondary), he undoubtedly described his own proclamation in Deutero-Isaiah's term *BSR* (Matt. 11:5; Luke 7:22). The hoped-for age of salvation is dawning: God was acting to establish his kingly reign in the words and works of Jesus, which are signs of its in-breaking (cf. Luke 4:18, 43; 16:16). The content of

Jesus' message is the reign of God, not explicitly himself, though it implies a Christological self-understanding: God is acting redemptively in him.

The cross called Jesus' proclamation radically into question (Luke 24:21a). But God vindicated Jesus' message by raising him from the dead. The earliest church therefore not only continued Jesus' own proclamation of the reign of God, but transformed it into an explicitly Christological preaching of Jesus himself: Jesus became the content of the good tidings.

The earliest church probably continued Jesus' use of the verb *BSR* to denote its own activity, despite the fact that Acts 5:42; 8:4, 12, 35, 40, come from the author of Acts. The noun *euangelion* (thought by some to have played an important role in the imperial cultus) was adopted to denote the actual message. Since *euangelion* does not occur in Q but is firmly established by the time of Paul, it is probable that its use originated in the Hellenistic mission — hence, Mark's fondness for it (Mark 13:10; 14:9). It means both the act of preaching the good news and the content of the news. It may be used with a qualifying genitive (" of God," " of the kingdom," " of Christ ") or, as frequently in Paul, absolutely.

Paul indicates the content of his gospel in I Cor. 15:1 ff. and Rom. 1:1 ff.: it was the Christ event, especially his death and resurrection, interpreted as the saving act of God. Paul sometimes speaks of " *my* gospel ": this does not mean that the content of the Pauline gospel differed from that of the original apostles (see I Cor. 15:11), but that the person of the apostle was totally engaged in his proclamation. As in

Deutero-Isaiah the proclamation of the good news is part of the redemptive act of God itself (I Cor. 15:2); the preaching of the gospel makes the Christ event present. Paul's specific contribution was to distinguish clearly between law and gospel as ways of salvation (Galatians, Romans). Salvation is not to be achieved by the works of the law, but by the gift of God proclaimed in the gospel.

In the subapostolic age both noun and verb become less frequent. The verb is absent from the Johannine writings, the pastorals and some of the catholic epistles (James, II Peter, Jude); the noun is absent from these writings (except the pastorals) and also from Hebrews. The reason for this is that dogma is replacing kerygma: the typical terms of this age are "tradition," "sound doctrine." Gradually the noun, which had in apostolic times always meant oral proclamation, is used for written documents. The Didache speaks of the gospel as if it had a fixed written content (e.g., it contains the Lord's Prayer). Irenaeus uses it as the name for the 4 written Gospels of what came to be the New Testament canon. Still, the original usage is traceable in the formula "according to" Mark, etc. The written Gospels are versions of the one good news, which is Christ himself, not merely the literary forms.

Since the church was brought into being by the redemptive act of God in Christ which the gospel announces, the church depends for its continued existence on the constant re-presentation (making present) of that act through the gospel. The gospel is thus fundamental to the continuing life of the church.

Preaching is not merely religious speech of any kind, but it is the means by which the gospel is heard anew in the church today. It is therefore true preaching only if it is based upon a true exegesis of Scripture as the authoritative witness to the gospel. All preaching, whether it be evangelistic (*kērygma*) or pastoral (*paraklēsis*) is a preaching of the gospel, a making present of the redemptive act of God in Christ to which the gospel testifies.

The sacraments of Baptism and the Lord's Supper are complementary to the preaching of the word as the means by which the gospel is made a present reality, and derive their whole meaning from the gospel. In Baptism the candidate participates in the death and resurrection of Jesus (Rom. 6:5-11). In the Lord's Supper the church proclaims the Lord's death until he comes (I Cor. 11:26) and participates in his sacrifice as a present reality (I Cor. 10:16).

The ministry of the church is the means by which word and sacraments are performed, and thus (cf. Paul's understanding of his apostolate in II Corinthians) derive their whole meaning from the gospel.

The creeds are summaries of the New Testament witness to the gospel, indicating by their inclusions what is important in that witness and by their omissions what is peripheral. The dogmas of the church (e.g., the incarnation and the Trinity) are designed to safeguard the gospel against later perversions and corruptions of the New Testament witness.

The liturgy and the church year are means by which the gospel is presented and relived in all its fullness in the life of the church. They are intended to ensure that the total gospel, and not just those parts of it which appear to have contemporary appeal, is heard.

It is the task of Christian action in the world to bring the insights of the gospel to bear on all aspects of man's common life, and thus to further the redemption of that life by the gospel.

Thus gospel and church are inseparable: there is no gospel without the church, for without the gospel the church would be merely a human religious institution, and without the church the gospel would be an abstract idea. But both gospel and church derive from the redemptive act of God in Christ.

— Reginald H. Fuller

GRACE "Grace," a technical theological word, refers to the undeserved mercy and love of God in Jesus Christ.

"Grace" is primarily a New Testament term, but the New Testament concept of grace has antecedents in the Old Testament. In the Old Testament (RSV) the word "grace" occurs only 6 times; but it is close in meaning to "mercy" and "steadfast love." God is characterized in the Old Testament as showing "steadfast love" to his elect people or to a remnant of them; but his "favor" or "loving-kindness" is entirely undeserved and unearned. In early times it was bestowed upon the patriarchs, and it was by God's "grace" that Israel was redeemed from Egypt (cf. Ex. 15:13). Israel did not deliver herself (Deut. 8:17 f.); but the Lord delivered her because he "loved" her (Deut. 7:7 f.), and not because of anything Israel was or had done to earn deliverance.

The grace of God in the Old Testament is also closely related to the ideas of the covenant and the law. God's favor is bestowed upon

the covenant community, and it is incumbent upon this community to obey God's law.

It is in The Psalms and in Second Isaiah that the idea of grace reaches its culmination in the Old Testament, assuming an eschatological significance after the exile (cf. Isa. 54:8; Ps. 89:4).

In the New Testament the word "grace" is of frequent occurrence (appearing 119 times in the RSV), and it is here that the full meaning of the term is revealed; grace is inseparable from Jesus Christ. The word "grace" does not occur in the Synoptic Gospels (RSV), and is used only 3 times in John (ch. 1:14, 16, 17). It is primarily a Pauline word in the New Testament, and refers essentially to God's gracious act in Jesus Christ whereby in love, salvation is offered to those who have faith (or believe).

For Paul, grace is a gift (cf. Rom. 3:24). The *grace* of God does not refer to a disposition or quality of God, but to an *act* of God, a gift, an offering in Jesus Christ for the salvation of men. This act, or gift, or offering of God centers in Christ, but more particularly in his crucifixion: God put Christ "forward as an expiation" (Rom. 3:25); he "gave him up for us all" (Rom. 8:32). "Putting forward" and "giving up" both refer to hanging upon the cross. Hence the grace or gift of God is also at the same time the "grace of our Lord Jesus Christ" (Rom. 16:24; II Cor. 8:9; Gal. 6:18; I Thess. 5:28; II Thess. 3:18; etc.). God "put Christ forward," but the Son of God also "gave himself" (Gal. 2:20) and "died for all" (II Cor. 5:15). The grace of God and the grace of Christ are the same grace, and refer to the same act — God's offering of the Son, and the

Son's offering of himself on Calvary. Being a gift, grace results solely from God's initiative. Man cannot initiate it; he can only receive it.

On occasion Paul also thinks of grace as a *power* that increases to counteract sin as sin increases (cf. Rom. 5:20 f.). As a power, grace is similar to Spirit when conceived as a power: both are manifestations of God's love.

In the Western church, particularly, a conflict arose on the subject of grace versus freedom. Tertullian, in the 2d century, laid stress on man's sin, speaking of it as " original vice." Correspondingly, he also stressed God's grace, which, like Spirit, he conceived of as a fine substance, infused in the believer. Following Tertullian, a dispute developed between those who emphasized grace and its irresistibility and those who emphasized the freedom of the human will to determine its own destiny. The question was put in this way: Is salvation dependent ultimately on God's grace alone or is it ultimately dependent on the free decision of man?

This debate culminated in the Pelagian controversy of the 5th century. Pelagius maintained that man's will had remained free and had never been completely enslaved by sin. He argued that grace does no more than help man achieve his natural potentiality. Augustine, on the other hand, taught that when Adam fell his will became evil, and that Adam's sin had involved the whole human race. Thus salvation was possible only through grace; it was not obtainable by any acts of the human will, even though they were aided by grace. Augustine also taught that grace first becomes operative at baptism when the guilt of original sin is removed. For him,

grace is the gift of a supernatural divine power, and being irresistible, is closely related to predestination. In Augustine's thought everything related to salvation has its origin in divine grace.

Thomas Aquinas' view of grace was basically Augustinian. Aquinas also believed that grace (or love) was infused into the soul, and that it was only by grace that salvation was possible. But Aquinas tried to hold free will in balance with grace, teaching that conversion occurred by a combination of the 2, and also that acts are meritorious, but only when grace cooperates in their performance.

Luther broke with the view that grace is infused, becoming a quality of the soul. He identified grace, rather, with the mercy of God in Jesus Christ, received by faith, and experienced primarily not as moral transformation but as forgiveness of sin. Thus, in Luther's mind, grace and Jesus Christ were once again made inseparable as they had been in the thought of Paul. God's grace, for Luther, is made known and available in the gift of the Holy Spirit, who works in and through the Word or gospel and the sacraments.

For Calvin, also, grace and faith are correlative, with the emphasis being, perhaps, on grace, because of Calvin's particular view of predestination. But in both Reformers salvation is by grace only and cannot by any means be merited.

—*Burton H. Throckmorton, Jr.*

GRADING Grading in Christian education must, of necessity, be based on academic considerations. It is a way of grouping *for study* those whose general knowledge and ability to grasp ideas or concepts is somewhere near the same level. To grade on a basis of spiritual perception or practice — intangibles almost impossible of measurement — is an obvious impossibility. Experiences of fellowship and service must, in the nurture of the church community, frequently cut across all academic and age lines. So grading becomes primarily the concern of study groups whose purpose is the attainment of certain kinds of knowledge and an understanding of the meaning of that knowledge.

With this purpose in mind, the reasonable approach seems to be to parallel the grading of the public schools in the area of a particular church, or those (near or far, public or private) which are attended by most of its children and young people. Even here, there are choices to make, for schools differ in their entrance schedules and times of promotion. The traditional grading pattern has been a grade for each year of age. But many school systems are moving toward group or cycle grading, and in some parts of the country the broad grading of a 1-room school is still in effect. Since, however, church school curricula are based on a rough correlation with public school achievement, and since children and young people usually like to be with their day-school mates in other groups, local public-school grading should be taken into account.

Close grading, a grade for each year of age, allows for a clear-cut plan of progress in curriculum. The groups are closely integrated by age. Problems of preparation by the teacher are less complex, and training can be more concentrated. But close grading fails to take into account the wide differences in experience, cultural background, edu-

cational level, and general development that are found within an age group, and therefore tends to become somewhat rigid in its assumptions.

Cycle grading in most church schools using it has meant grouping pupils in 2- or 3-year combinations of public-school grades. In some areas a high school department includes 4 years; in most places nursery and care groups include only 1. Cycle grading is increasingly the practice in elementary public schools. It allows for more flexibility in placing pupils, and in the movement of teachers when necessary. But it requires a high degree of skillful administration, and the creation and use of a curriculum with logical movement is more difficult.

Broad grading (across 5 to 8 years) also presents difficulties in using a standard curriculum and in administration. However, a skillful and creative teacher can take advantage of the opportunities this type of grading offers for peer-group teaching, for directed study, and for much more natural family situations. It can be a privilege as well as a necessity in the very small church. A recent development in broad grading is study of the same subject matter in family units, working through projects and the arts.

In each of these types of grading, the group can study and work together as a whole or share certain experiences and separate into smaller units for others. The terms " group teaching " and " team teaching " have been used interchangeably, but there is a very real difference between them. Any type of cooperative teaching allows, however, for better supervision and orientation of new teachers, hence greater satisfaction on their part.

Each of the types of grading or teacher relationships mentioned can operate successfully if the advantages and disadvantages of a chosen method are carefully considered, and if staff planning, consultation, and training of a high order are carried on almost continuously.

Why go to all this trouble? Because wherever large groups of people are concerned — even in a church — one must choose between order and chaos. If, in a church school, everyone were free to enter at any point and move about at will, no one (pupil or teacher) would be satisfied, and little or nothing would be accomplished. Therefore, much time and thought must be given to the best basic plan for registration, grading, and promotion in a given situation. Once determined, it should be carefully explained to all concerned and adhered to. Exceptions should be neither casual nor frequent. For instance, if annual registrations are held (and they are a necessity in multiple-session schools, and a help in others) everyone must register, and movement from one session to another should not be permitted without "due cause and consideration."

But people are human and have human needs, so no plan should exclude considered exceptions. Problems of transportation, changes in school grade, physical and mental handicaps, the gifted pupil, must all be thoughtfully reviewed by the proper persons. Changing and creative patterns of Christian education must be taken into account. Every effort must be made to provide experiences that cut across age and group lines. The school of the church must operate more as a good family than as a good school, with all adults in a parental relationship to all growing persons, sharing their learning experiences, whether in worship, study, or service.

— *Dorothy B. Fritz*

GRADUATE STUDY IN RELIGIOUS EDUCATION

Graduate study in religious education is required or desirable in many church vocations. These include: the parish minister, often required to direct the total program of his church; directors of Christian education, devoting full time to the oversight of the educational program of the parish, who have developed into a professional group of more than 10,000; missionaries to other lands or those assigned to service in this country, who are required to take graduate training in religious education as preparation either for general church service or for specific assignments in mission schools, or for administrative responsibilities in religious education; teachers in parochial schools and professors in church-related colleges, universities, and seminaries; the various regional and national staffs of denominational boards and publication houses; religious education specialists on the staffs of local, state, national, and world councils; teachers and supervisors of weekday released-time programs of religious education; directors of student religious activities on college campuses, and certain personnel of related agencies such as the Y.M.C.A. and the Y.W.C.A. The denominations are just beginning to assume their responsibility for defining this comparatively new profession. Many are now developing professional standards with certain requirements or recommendations for graduate study. The total number of persons engaged in all the professions outlined above is not sufficiently large to warrant separate programs of graduate education for each. Further, the professional standards are still confused, so that there is little agreement as to just what the training should be. Some training programs place great emphasis on educational theory and methods. Others give major attention to the content of the Christian faith. Still others try to combine these emphases, since professional competence seems to include both areas.

For the person combining religious education supervision with the pastoral ministry, obviously the specific courses in religious education must be a minor in his graduate education. A teacher in a parochial school or in a weekday released-time system should meet state educational requirements as well as have an adequate understanding of the Christian faith. For each of the other careers, religious education courses must be balanced with other requirements for the particular situation in which the student will serve.

Most of the professional leadership in religious education secures training in seminaries, especially since several denominations encourage their students to finish a regular B.D. course. However, a number of students are trained in state-supported or private universities, and there are several graduate schools of religious education.

Considerable work has been done by the directors of Christian education, working in the Directors' Section of the National Council of the Churches of Christ in the U.S.A., on standards and educational qualifications for their profession. Denominational boards of Christian education have also studied it. A consultation of these groups, under National Council sponsorship, in 1960 considered professional standards, job description, and training, and recommended that the title "Director of Christian Education" should apply to any person with an A.B. or B.S. degree plus a master's degree in Christian education from an accredited educational institution (whose requirements include basic study in Bible, theology, church history, etc.) or a B.D. from an accredited seminary, provided his work for a B.D. included a major in Christian education, and who is employed by a local church for the primary purpose of guiding an educational work.

The American Association of Theological Schools in 1959 surveyed degree programs in Christian education in its member seminaries. In 49 institutions replying, 1,601 students were enrolled. The M.R.E. degree was granted by 35 schools, the M.A. by 13; both of these degrees by 4, and other degrees by 6. In 42 schools, 2 years of study were required beyond the A.B. Nineteen schools had a working relationship with a university. Schools were asked to report the ratio of practical to content courses in the prescribed program: 13 schools reported it to be 50–50; 12 reported a 40–60 ratio, and 10 reported a 30–70 ratio. Forty-three schools required supervised fieldwork, with 22 of them requiring 2 years of fieldwork.

The results of the survey raised many questions. Should both the M.R.E. and M.A. degrees be given, and if so, what should distinguish each? What emphasis can be made by the Association regarding the inadequacy of educational opportunities for students in schools with a high faculty-student ratio? The Association is currently seeking reactions from its members on a tentative statement of standards for the master's degree in Christian education, including: purpose, curriculum, educational field service, admissions, faculty size, length of program, library, and graduate professional school.

The religious education curriculum of one seminary, although not to be considered typical, may be outlined as representative of schools making a serious effort to provide training in this field. The M.R.E. degree in this school requires 60 hours of work, 42 being within the B.D. "core" curriculum, on the theory that religious education specialists need the same basic training in theology as ministers. Fifteen hours of religious education courses are required, leaving very little opportunity for elective courses. They include basic courses in theory and philosophy of religious education, age-level courses, a course in curriculum, and a heavy concentration of courses in administration and supervision. Each year this school enrolls 20 to 30 students with a religious educational vocational preference. The faculty for the specific religious education courses consists of one full-time professor of religious education, a full-time professor of psychology of religion and pastoral psychology, and courses by a professor of administration and a professor of communications. There is a definite pattern for the use of staff of the denominational education board, who come to the seminary for 3 to 4 weeks each year and provide laboratory training, especially in the age-level courses.

Graduate training for religious education is a worldwide concern, as evidenced by the Seminar on Training Ministers for a Teaching Ministry held in Tokyo, Japan, in 1958, sponsored by the World Council of Christian Education and Sunday School Association. Thirty-six seminaries in 19 countries were represented. The emphasis was on the importance of the seminary's demonstrating that Christian learning takes place within the fellowship of a Christian community and that the sense of fragmentation in theological studies should be overcome by interdepartmental courses and a willingness by faculty to see their courses in the light of the whole curriculum. The seminar stressed that a seminary is hardly complete unless it has personnel whose specific responsibility is Christian education, although a survey showed many seminaries making little or no provision for such personnel. Minimum preparation for the teaching ministry was considered to be: courses in principles of Christian education, the role of the minister in the Christian education work of the church, the understanding of specific age-group programs; at least 2 semesters and 2 summer recess fieldwork experiences where different aspects of the teaching ministry are met; practicum seminars as occasion requires.

Additional courses in Christian education were outlined, including organization, administration and leadership training, age-group electives, training for special needs, Christian education through worship, Christian education and church music, and guided reading. Although in many countries the limited number of persons with graduate training for church leadership has precluded the development of specialized ministries, this seminar did look to the future in considering training for the specific ministry of

Christian education, postseminary assistance to ministers in the educational task, and opportunities for seminaries to train laymen for a role in Christian education.

— *Helen F. Spaulding*

GREECE Greece is one of the few countries where a single church incorporates almost the entire population; 97 percent are baptized in the Orthodox Church. From the Middle Ages to modern times that church has played a great role in the sphere of national independence and in maintaining freedom. It is on this basis that the so-called system of " friendly relations " between state and church has been maintained. It is thus possible for religious education to be included in the state school program. Financial and other forms of assistance are available from the state to prepare religious teachers and priests.

Elementary religious education based on simple Biblical narratives is given to children aged 8 through 12. In the secondary school (gymnasium), ages 13 to 18, such instruction takes a more systematic form; state and private schools are required to offer 2 weekly periods of 1 hour each of strictly religious education. In the lower classes of the gymnasium a history of the divine economy is taught, starting with the Creation, the Fall, and redemption in Christ. In the 3d year, pupils are given Biblical texts and are introduced through a simple exegesis to the Biblical message. In the 4th, 5th, and 6th years they are taught, respectively, church history, divine liturgy and worship, culminating in ethics and the elements of Christian apologetics. The teachers are mostly lay theologians who are graduated from 1 of the 2 state theological faculties, Athens or Salonica. The faculty at Athens was established in 1835 with the foundation of the university. The Salonica faculty was founded in 1942. Both comprise a full curriculum of theological academic studies, including the 4 branches: historical, exegetical, practical, and systematic. These faculties prepare priests as well as teachers of religion for the state schools, approximately 10 percent of the students entering the Orthodox clergy.

Apart from these state schools the church itself has set up special institutions in order to give ecclesiastical education in the more specialized sense. Eight ecclesiastical schools receive pupils after the 2d year of the gymnasium. Pupils are required to take an entrance examination and to promise to join the clergy after completing their courses. These schools follow a full state school education, but religious teaching constitutes the basis and the greater part of the program. The students also follow a " Christian brotherhood " discipline. Seven superior ecclesiastical seminaries receive students 22 to 30 years old possessing school certificates and wishing to follow a 2-year pastoral preparatory course in the fundamentals of theology, with the specific purpose of serving as priests and preachers under particular diocesan appointment. In many cases these students are scholarship students of their dioceses.

Refresher courses on pastoral activity are organized in various parts of the country. Priests having had some practical experience are invited to enroll in these 2 to 4 months' courses. These have been found indispensable in view of the need to readapt pastoral care in the period since World War II.

The non-Orthodox minorities come under a different category from the examples given above. Non-Orthodox boys and girls of school age are exempted from Orthodox religious education upon request. Two private Roman Catholic schools are acknowledged by the state; since their students are mostly Orthodox, they offer optional Orthodox instead of Roman Catholic teaching. The same condition applies to evangelical secondary schools. Non-Orthodox theological students usually study abroad.

Another kind of religious education has taken place, either by the evangelizing body of the church (*apostoloki diakonia*) or the pioneering lay movements that early in this century took up evangelistic efforts independently but within the church. This education starts with Sunday school work, covering ages 6 to 17. In view of the fact that religious instruction has been given in the state schools for many years, the Sunday school curriculum has developed with the primary purpose of being a center of Christian life, preparing conscious membership in the Orthodox Church and training future leaders for the lay movement. The large number of lay theological students and theologians as well as the flourishing lay movement within the church at present are due in large measure to the Sunday school movement. — *Nikos A. Nissiotis*

GREEK EDUCATION Since the intellectual life of ancient Greece has never been surpassed, the process of education by which that life was brought into being, ordered, and passed on to succeeding generations is of special importance. Curiously enough, the 5th century B.C., generally considered the century when the glory that was Greece shone most brightly, was not distinguished by its schools or by its pedagogic theory. The 4th century B.C. was the age of the great teachers, but by that time the lowering of the cultural tone was widely observed, as though the ironic role of the schools was not to participate in the creative genius of their time but, rather, to draw upon that genius and perhaps in the end to dissipate it in the interest of a higher commonalty.

The idea of education — the formal transfer of a culture — was not always so obvious a notion as it seems to us. There was no formal education in Homeric Greece, the young learning what they needed to know artlessly in the very act of living. The Sophists (the Wise Men) conducted private schools in the 5th century for a small number of boys. Girls, of course, acquired such education as they could at home, Euripides expressing the received notion when he said that intellect was a handicap to a woman. The archetypal idea of the ancient schools was to train the *pais* (child), and the *ephēbos* (youth) so that he might become a worthy *anēr* (adult), a useful citizen of the state in peace and in war.

The 2 rival cities, Sparta and Athens, were both aware that wisdom need not be discovered afresh in each generation, but could in some degree be passed on. The Spartan schoolmasters thought that the transfer could be effected only if discipline was strict. Their pupils were barely literate and were not distinguished by intellectual graces, but they were trained in morality and were expected to be paragons of martial courage. " There is little difference between man and man,"

Thucydides quotes King Archidamus as saying, " but the superiority lies with him who is reared in the severest school." Athenian youth had a broader and more humane education. They studied writing (which included reading and mathematics), music, and gymnastics. It may be some measure of the military relevance of the 2 methods that Sparta triumphed over Athens after 27 years of fighting in the Peloponnesian War.

All schools in ancient Greece intended to cultivate a quality called *sōphrosynē,* a word for which no English rendering is adequate. One can translate it " self-control " and be partly right; but it means also what is implied in the Delphic sayings: " Nothing in excess " and " Know thyself." The difficulty of defining the word lies in the fact that it is not so much a concept with a fixed content as a style of life. An *ephēbos* was ready to become an *anēr* when he had learned to value above all else harmony and proportion. Aristocratic, unhurried, and ceremonious, he was the prototype of Aristotle's magnanimous man." Without a trace of the shyness that the early Christians admired, he " thought himself worthy, being worthy."

It is as instruments for the nurture of *sōphrosynē* that the great schools of the 4th century B.C. are to be understood. Isocrates' school of rhetoric was the most popular. He described the *anēr* he had in mind: he must be " first, capable of usually hitting upon the right course. Second, he will meet any company, however disagreeable, with easy good temper and show to all men fairness and gentleness. Third, he will be master of himself in misfortune and pain. Fourth and most

important, his head will not be turned by success. Those whose soul is well tuned to play its part in all these ways I regard as educated." The graduate of Isocrates' school was ready when the presiding officer in the assembly asked his great question, "Does anyone wish to speak? "

The ideals of Plato's Academy were quite different. Following the Socratic mode, what was sought for here was not at all cleverness in persuading but profundity in understanding. " The particular learning," said Plato, " which leads you throughout life to hate what should be hated and love what should be loved will rightly be called education." When a student had mastered this learning he might still be a poor speaker, but he would know mathematics and metaphysics, and would have had some sort of vision of the Good. Motivated by this exalted sense of rational mission, the Academy was the intellectual center of Greece for 900 years.

On the other hand, Aristotle's Lyceum was much more concerned with the understanding of the everyday world. He criticized his predecessors for having confused concepts with the palpable universe, and he dealt with each separately and with great brilliance. Concepts were ordered in the 1st and most influential system of logic; things were to be studied carefully and impersonally, yielding their categories to the fastidious researcher. Impatient with Plato's visionary ideals, he encouraged his students to work out practical principles of dramatic criticism, compare 158 Greek constitutions, and watch patiently the reproduction of eels.

The roads to *sōphrosynē* varied, but no one quarreled with Plato

when he said, "Education is the fairest thing that the best of men can have." Not before or since has the work of educating the young been given such dignity and importance. When someone asked Aristippus why he thought education worthwhile, he replied for all the excellent schoolmasters of Greece, "If the pupil derives no other good, he will not, when he attends the theater, be one stone upon another."
— *Paul H. Elmen*

GROUP DYNAMICS Since 1935, social psychologists have given much thought to the nature of the group, to the dynamic forces within the group, and to the forces outside the group that impinge upon it. At present, some social scientists are specializing in the study of group dynamics. The word "dynamics" is derived from the Greek *dynamis,* "power." Group dynamics is a branch or aspect of social psychology and the term "group dynamics" is sometimes used to stand for the accepted body of knowledge about the dynamics of groups. Group dynamics also stands for the indubitable fact that all groups have dynamics — forces and powers growing out of the interpersonal relationships that exist in the particular group. Sometimes the term is used loosely to designate any of the many new techniques of group work. In addition to the social psychologists, both churchmen and educators have recently given much consideration to how people function in groups, and psychiatrists and psychiatric social workers have made rich use of group therapy. Perhaps the most significant name back of the group dynamics approach is that of Kurt Lewin, though there were pioneers before him and many able follow-

ers. In general, the basic research in group dynamics has been done at several American universities, such as Michigan, Harvard, Chicago, Ohio State, and Boston. Under the auspices of the National Education Association, a national training laboratory for group development has been held annually for a number of years. Since 1956, under the auspices of the National Council of the Churches of Christ in the U.S.A., a Protestant Church Leadership Laboratory, with leaders from the National Training Laboratory at Bethel, has been held at Green Lake, Wis.

The researchers in this field of study have worked on such questions as the nature of the group process, how people relate in a group, how the power flows in the process of interpersonal relations within the group, how groups can function effectively, how groups can mature, and the nature of group leadership.

Strictly speaking, the findings of group dynamics relate to the forces at work within a group, to the ebb and flow of psychological forces, the influences of likes and dislikes, the effect of varying types of leadership, the depth of acceptance of all as members, and the optimum size. Growing out of the scientific study of these forces, some dependable techniques have been discovered for increasing the meaningfulness and effectiveness of the small group. A whole new vocabulary has arisen — group observer, group recorder, hidden agenda, feedback, postevaluation session, role-playing, sociogram, and similar terms. Many of the research findings are just common knowledge or even common sense validated by careful experimentation. Despite the banality of much of the material, we now have scientific evidence that the democratic leader is more effective than the authoritarian leader and that both are more effective than the laissez-faire leader; a group has something like a "group personality" ("syntality," Raymond Cattell calls it); groups may and should mature; a group on a given occasion has a distinct emotional climate; the emotional climate may be changed by certain attitudes. Group dynamics has taught us that everybody in a group has a contribution to make and in a sense is exercising leadership functions at times. We know that by careful self-evaluation of its processes a group can improve those processes and become healthier and more productive.

The relevance of such findings for the church is reasonably clear. The church has always known that the individual is central and is to be treated with utmost respect as a person for whom Christ died; it has always known also that "no man is an island," that the individual is a member of a community. In and through that community he has been brought face to face with his Maker, and in that community he becomes part of the body of Christ, a servant of his God and his fellowmen. The priesthood of believers signifies the worth of every man, the value of the contributions of every man to the life of the whole body (I Cor., ch. 12, and Rom., ch. 12), and the necessity of the whole body to be a ministering, serving, nurturing, redemptive fellowship, alive by virtue of the power of the Holy Spirit at work within it. Since the time when Jesus "appointed twelve, to be with him," the Christian church has rightly placed great emphasis upon the small group. It has never denied the worth and need of the total congregation or of the larger concept of the church universal, but it has rightly stressed in many ways the value of small groups.

Practically, group dynamics as a science gives the church more facts on which to function through its groups, and certainly the success of the study of the group process in business, education, and therapy has had its effect in strengthening the church's program of small-group work. The circles in the women's organizations have always had tremendous values that only now are being fully appreciated and developed; the youth fellowships through their work groups and commissions follow the principles of group dynamics more deliberately nowadays; significantly, a determined effort is being made to break up huge adult lecture classes in the church school and make of them vital, functioning small study groups; cell groups and prayer groups have revivified many churches in recent years; and today many pastors make use of insights derived from the study of groups to work more effectively with church boards and committees. One large denomination is projecting its new curriculum upon the principle that no adult class will be larger than 15. Further, some churches have had success with small groups that meet for mutual strengthening and that have a healing effect. A therapy group normally assumes the presence of a professional person, but genuine mutual support and growth toward emotional maturity may take place in informal church groups.

The dangers of group dynamics are those of democracy itself. Some persons, including some educators, have confused democracy and Christianity. The Christian view of man as sinner in all aspects of his being must be kept in tension with the naïve, humanitarian, democratic view. Some enthusiasts for group dynamics have come close to equating this approach with the ultimate in Christian living, and this may be nonsense. The small group and its dynamics are of enormous significance to the church, especially large city churches, but the Kingdom will not come by way of group dynamics alone. The group process is no substitute for individual responsibility, thought, and preparation; the group is no better than what its members put into it. There is still a place for the lecture as well as group discussion; there is always a need for able, consecrated, charismatic, and official leadership as well as for recognition of the fact that everybody has leadership functions in a group; the priesthood of believers is a rewarding Christian doctrine, but it can be so taught as to denigrate the doctrine of the ordained ministry of word and sacrament; some groups have become so enamored of the self-evaluation of their group processes that they have ceased to eventuate in Christian action; and, not least, wrongly motivated persons using keen knowledge of group dynamics can manipulate groups and persons; and some have even hinted that this will be necessary for mankind's welfare, thus rounding the circle from totalitarianism to manipulation through democratic processes.

Although the claim that the Holy Spirit works best through small-group processes is questionable, that he may and often does so work is undeniable. The values of group dynamics for the church are many and great. Wise understanding of the findings of the science, with careful study of the dynamics of one's own group, can lead to far more effective and more Christian group life in the church. The worth of the small group has been notably demonstrated. The value of the small group for the teaching-learning process is unquestioned. It has promoted the renewal of respect for persons. The emphasis upon understanding and acceptance that become in the church love and forgiveness, and the likelihood that in the climate of the small group the Holy Spirit will work powerfully, lead to this conclusion: the church can gain much from a wise use of group dynamics.

— *Harry G. Goodykoontz*

GROUP LIFE LABORATORY A group life laboratory is an intensive training experience of 12 days' to 3 weeks' duration in which the major method of learning is through the observation and analysis of one's own firsthand, face-to-face experiences in groups. Similar training methods are used in shorter programs, sometimes called group leadership institutes.

Because of the many facets of a laboratory, different people find in the training experience such different values as: a way of learning how to conduct church committee meetings more efficiently; a means of improving human relations through greater acceptance of persons, clearer communication, etc.; a way to bring about change in individuals, groups, organizations, and communities; a way to see oneself as others see one and thus gain self-insight; a springboard to continuing education or a way to keep on learning through the analysis of our interaction with others; a form of evangelism and spiritual renewal of the church, since God often seems to confront people when they meet one another in honesty; an experience of the redemptive fellowship in which people really care about and genuinely trust one another and so become ministers to one another in Christ's name.

The word " group " implies a focus upon a small number — about 15 — of persons, although the program also includes reading, conversations between individuals, and some attention to intergroup, organizational, and community problems.

The word " life " connotes the vital, dynamic process of human interaction that is the center of attention and the means of learning. This process is the way people are relating to and feeling toward one another as they talk about some topic, subject, or matter of content.

The word " laboratory " suggests a situation deliberately controlled for the purposes of learning or research. Therefore, it is not intended that back-home committees should operate without structure as do some of the groups in a laboratory.

A typical day at a laboratory includes the following kinds of experiences: a 1-hour theory session where the relevant principles and research findings about groups are presented to the entire membership of the laboratory by means of lectures, newsprint diagrams, films, and live demonstrations; a 2-hour training group (known as T-group) in which about 15 people sit around a table with 1 or 2 trainers but with no designated discussion leader, no imposed agenda, and no group standards regarding how decisions are to be made; a skill practice group of about 15 people who learn through structured exercises, such

as role-plays, how to deal with typical problem situations in groups. In church laboratories, a typical day includes worship, recreation, free time, and perhaps a general evening session on how to apply the laboratory learnings to the back-home church job.

In addition to this factual and objective description each participant will have his own unique experience and hence a subjective description. However, most people testify that they have gained some of the following values: increased ability to endure and even utilize situations filled with ambiguity, frustration, hostility, and conflict; more competence in observing a group and diagnosing the many forces at work; greater skill in dealing with group difficulties such as decision-making; a concept of leadership as the functions that a group needs to have performed, rather than the personality traits possessed by the chairman; more skill at performing these leadership functions at the appropriate time and in the appropriate way, when serving either as a group member or a group leader; greater concern for others and hence greater ability to listen to them attentively and with sensitivity to their nonverbal communication; increased capacity to take criticism and absorb hostility without becoming anxious, tense, or defensive; more courage to express negative feelings openly and to give criticism frankly but lovingly; greater insight into their own mixed motives and greater acceptance of other people as they really are; more ability to predict the effect of their words and actions upon others; a keener realization that all people are alike in having the same kinds of feelings and problems as well as having the uni-

versal yearning to love and to be loved; more awareness of the way God is working in, among, and through people, and hence of the nature and mission of the church.
— *W. Randolph Thornton*

GROWTH In its broadest meaning, growth for an organism involves any change that occurs with time. The term " development " is perhaps its closest synonym. Two factors contribute to the process we call growth: maturation, the change resulting from internal or innate generation; and nurture, that coming from the total impact of the environment.

Growth is universal among living organisms. Usually, but not always, it means positive progression toward some goal, with an increment rather than a detriment involved. Where used specifically for a human being, growth includes all the ways he develops over a period of time.

Human growth includes learning. This aspect occurs at a high level, involving symbolization and communication between persons. The end or goal of human growth therefore extends indefinitely into the complexities of personal maturity and relationships. Although in some areas of man's life, development slows and can even turn backward, in other areas the future beckons him on with the promise of higher levels of meaning and deeper degrees of relationships with other persons and the world.

Although man's growth is complicated by the complexities of his nature, it is possible to chart his development with some satisfaction. One of the major contributions of psychological sciences in the past half century has been the increasing understanding of the different areas of man's development that can be measured, and the growing usefulness of this understanding.

The 1st major measurement project, and the simplest, dealt with the physical growth of human beings. Careful studies of enough persons to get a valid average picture, over a period of time long enough to cover the complete life cycle, have resulted in helpful data by which individuals can be compared and helped. For instance, the newborn baby grows more rapidly during his first 2 weeks of life than in any later period. Thereafter, with the exception of a spurt in late childhood, the rate of his physical growth decelerates. Certain factors have been identified that have great causative effect on physical growth. The general rise in consumption of healthful foods helped produce men for World War II whose average height and weight were greater than those in World War I. However, it is impossible to cite exact causes for particular growth phenomena, for growth comes both from within and from without, and from multiple influences. Also, there are mysterious problems like the rapid growth of fatal cancer cells that are not yet understood or brought under control.

Great advances, too, have been made regarding mental or intellectual growth. The early work of Binet in the 1st decade of this century launched a widespread movement of measurement of " intelligence." Later studies have refined and modified earlier claims, but the ability to measure something of the relative mental ability of persons has contributed greatly to the efficiency of educational practices. In addition to testing for a person's " intelligence quotient," behavioral sciences have devised means for measuring his interests and abilities on a much wider base. Vocational counseling and other services depend heavily upon such indices to a person's development.

More recently still has come significant study of the social growth of human beings. Data from these studies and their instruments help teachers and others discover a person's relative development in his relationships with others, so that they can concentrate upon each pupil's particular needs. Social psychology also has produced helpful data regarding the growth of groups of persons together. Although the development of a " corporate being," a work group, a family, or any group of persons bound to one another in significant fashion cannot be plotted and aided as simply as can the growth of a single person, what has been learned in this area has been quite useful.

Another dimension of human growth is a person's emotional development. After Freud the expansion of psychoanalytic and psychiatric research has brought great gains in the understanding of how human beings grow emotionally. The various factors that are important here, particularly those arising from interpersonal relationships, have been widely discussed and have influenced the understanding of human nature in our culture.

Man grows, however, as he lives: as a whole, and not in pieces. He cannot be sliced up in actuality as he must be for some of these studies of various aspects of his growth. The increasing cooperation between the various fields that study human behavior, each with its own methods, data, and perspective, indicates growing awareness of the wholeness of human personality and the inter-relationships of the parts. Each person has his own unique " style," development of which as a whole characterizes his growth. Awareness and measurement of the various dimensions of that growth contribute to understanding the person, but their sum does not equal his totality.

Much of the research into human growth has concentrated upon abnormal persons and aberrant behavior, so the construction of a picture of the " growth of the healthy personality " has been slow. Recently, however, the " man sciences " have sought to complete that task, e.g., the concept of " developmental tasks " by Havighurst and others; Erikson's study suggesting the one major problem at each crucial period of life for the person as he grows up in his physical and social environment. From these comes a ladder of developmental stages of human growth upon which learning and other activities can be regulated. These studies describe human growth in rather general terms, for persons vary greatly, as do their environments. Although their " averages " and charts are indicative and quite useful, the authors recognize the fact of individual differences.

There are religious dimensions to these areas of human growth, so that it is possible to speak of Christian personality, and of fostering the growth of Christian personality. One can measure outward responses related to a person's attitudes and habits regarding his religious experience, such as attendance at and service for the church. From other observable behavior and the person's shared self-understanding it is possible to note development of personal qualities of Christian response. Recent studies of man's growth as they have become more sophisticated have explored his inner nature, emotions, motives, attitudes, and other aspects related to his spiritual growth.

However, man is more than an object of statistical study. As the concern moves from outward and easily observable characteristics to more inward and hidden parts of personality, scientific inquiry becomes less adequate. In charting religious growth, satisfactory measurement is quite difficult. The continuing inquiry in Christian education over objectives and evaluation bears witness to the difficulty of identifying and measuring growth in these areas of human life.

The Biblical witness affirms that " Jesus increased in wisdom and stature, and in favor with God and man " (Luke 2:52). Stimulated by that ideal of human development, Christian educators through the centuries have sought to help persons grow up in their own being after that fashion. Today, although they recognize the difficulty and ultimate impossibility of adequate measurement of the deeper dimensions of human development, Christian educators nevertheless are seeking greater understanding of human growth. Believing that God created man in his own image, and that in some way that image has been marred by sin, Christian educators affirm the mysterious work of God's Spirit, who will not be confined to human efforts to foster man's growth. But they also recognize that the Spirit uses human wisdom and operations to nurture persons in their relationships with God, man, and the world. In this perspective, studies of human growth bring increasing aid to those engaged in Christian education. — *William B. Kennedy*

GUIDANCE Guidance is one of the helping professions that aids a person to discover his capacity, aptitudes, and skills in order that he can function effectively, using his full potential and living in good adjustment with his environment. This assumes that there is a wide range of individual differences in personality characteristics, physical endowment, and cultural background. Each person is of value and deserves individual attention. Understanding of this individual is of greatest usefulness when it is based on objective data and measurement where possible. There is inherent in guidance an optimism about the possibility of change, growth, and adjustment on the part of the client. Problems usually have multiple causation and, therefore, require a comprehensive study of the whole person as well as of his social setting.

Frank Parsons was one of the pioneers who organized the Vocational Bureau of Boston in 1908. Others had seen the need for industrial and commercial education, but he recognized the need for guidance of youth in vocational choice, special training, and job placement. His book, *Choosing a Vocation*, had wide influence. Local businessmen, the public schools, and social agencies such as the Y.M.C.A. supported the idea. Guidance services spread throughout the country, especially in school systems. In 1913 the National Vocational Guidance Association was organized, indicating that the effort had become a permanent movement.

An increasingly complex technology required specialized skills and the accurate selection of workers with certain characteristics. World War I required the screening and placement of recruits according to their aptitudes and skills. Psychological testing was initiated on a large scale and continued to be part of the guidance program after the war. The rehabilitation of servicemen through the Veterans' Administration after World War II also emphasized the need for guidance and counseling services, and created a large demand for trained specialists. The United States Employment Service has also emphasized guidance services on the assumption that the nation must conserve and utilize its manpower effectively. The educational philosophy of John Dewey and the subsequent movement called "progressive education" focused attention upon the development of the total personality and the individual's adjustment to life situations as the goal of education. This naturally directed much attention to getting to know the student as a person, to helping him with his problems and life adjustment. Because of the increasing complexity and anxiety of society in the space age, the adjustments required of automation, population mobility, etc., it appears that there will be an increasing demand for guidance services.

Intelligence tests, measurements of mechanical aptitude or spatial perception, vocational interest checklists, and other personality tests have become a standard part of the guidance process. Rating scales, temperament surveys, and personal interviews are also used. These may constitute an inventory or diagnostic work-up of the client. Counseling may be indicated to help him think through his feelings and conflicts concerning self-perception, motivation, and goals. Information is made available, especially in vocational or educational guidance. This could range from the educational requirements the client would need to reach his objective to actual job opportunities and referral to employment agencies. Placement in a job and, sometimes, follow-up to check on the adjustment of the worker complete the cycle. Naturally, the methods used will depend upon the type of guidance service involved.

Guidance services in schools and colleges comprise perhaps the largest segment of the profession. Educational guidance relies heavily on the student's "cumulative record," which should be a comprehensive history of the pupil's development, the results of psychological and academic testing, his behavior, his social and physical growth, his academic record, extracurricular activities, problems, achievements, etc. Large school systems have many staff members engaged full time in guidance and counseling. Small schools rely on the teaching staff to perform guidance functions. Although modern school systems believe that guidance is for everyone, special attention is often required for such cases as the physically handicapped, the gifted, the mentally retarded, and the emotionally disturbed. At the college level, guidance includes special orientation for new students, "how to study" helps, a counseling service, a system of academic advisers, and a placement bureau for graduates. In business and industry, guidance falls under the title of personnel department. It is credited with improving worker morale and cutting down unnecessary turnover due to unsuitable placement. Child-guidance clinics have grown up as a result of the mental-health movement. This type involves the developmental psychology of the child. These clinics specialize in counseling and psychotherapy for the problem child and his parents. Guidance services are being recognized as applicable to all age levels, not least for the adjustments involved in retirement and aging. Both public and private social agencies are involved in guidance. Relief departments use vocational guidance to try to assist the indigent to become self-supporting again.

Although the ramifications of guidance reach out in many directions, the field of guidance is developing into an increasingly self-conscious profession. Like social work or counseling, it draws from many disciplines, yet like them it has its own standards for accreditation and admission to the profession. The national professional organization is the American Personnel and Guidance Association. The official publication in the field is *The Personnel and Guidance Journal.* Most teachers' colleges and universities offer specific professional training leading to certification in various fields of guidance. A growing body of literature, research, and specialized terminology is evident.

The influence of the guidance movement can be seen in the newer curricula for Christian education developed by the denominations in recent years. There is much emphasis on personality and character development and much awareness of the "whole person," not merely the subject matter of the lesson. Youth workers are alert to bring the sense of Christian stewardship and commitment to the attention of young people involved in making their vocational decisions. Frequently, the church supplements the public school's "career day" program by adding its own interpretation of vocation. The churches use guidance methods in presenting the cause of church vocations. In theological schools it is common to find psychological testing, counseling, and other guidance procedures used with students. Pastoral care and counseling as well as all efforts to aid parishioners live the abundant life and use all their God-given potentials could be classified as religious guidance. — *David Belgum*

H

HABITS A habit may be defined as an established pattern of behavior (in the narrow sense as a specific act), usually learned as a result of a series of experiences, and which operates rather automatically in the life of the individual. A habit is thus a long-range, more or less permanent adaptation to a stimulus or to a type of situation. Psychologists usually make a fairly sharp distinction between habits and traits of character, viewing a habit as a specific response to a limited range of stimuli or situations, and a character trait as a more general pattern of response to a wide range of circumstances. Thus one might develop the habit of daily Bible-reading, of saying grace at meals, or of weekly attendance at Sunday morning worship services, while he might manifest such general religious traits of character as deep gratitude, reverence, and loving service. It should be noted that not all psychologists accept the hypothesis of a generalized character trait, such as neatness, thriftiness, courtesy, and the like but, rather, maintain that personality is made up of thousands of independent and specific habits, with no organization at higher levels. This point of view is less commonly held today than it was a few decades ago.

Very little is known about how habituation, or habit formation, takes place, although the phenomenon itself is extensively documented. We observe that behavior can be modified quite specifically through training; we know some of the elements that seem most essential to produce such adaptation; we know that habits once established tend to persist through the passage of time; the training that produces habits adds a certain consistency to the individual's pattern of behavior (on repeated occasions of a specific kind the person tends to respond in ways that can be called "the same"); and we learn something of how habits die out or can be broken deliberately as other habits are substituted for ones previously learned. Yet habits cannot be directly observed and measured. Therefore, the idea of habits has the scientific status of a hypothetical construct. We can infer that some *theoretically* measurable modifications have taken place in the nervous system when a habit has been formed, but what these modifications are or how they take place is largely unknown.

Although in both lay and psychological discourse the concept of habit is more generally applied to specific *acts*, which must be understood in terms of a particular stimulus and a particular response, this would seem to be too narrow a use of the term. Habits also appear as a type of mind-set or predisposition to view one's world in certain ways. Not only does one receive certain stimuli and block out others, but one learns as well (forms the habit) to " see " what one does receive in predetermined ways. For example, a child may develop the habit of " seeing " adults either as persons to be trusted or to be feared, depending upon his experience with adults. His perception of adults is thus colored by his fears and his hopes regarding adults, i.e., he projects his feelings about adults in general onto particular adults, and " sees " what he hopes to see or fears to see. In like manner the individual may learn to see or perceive persons of other races or nations through stereotypes, which are habitual intellectual shortcuts that may seem to serve his needs at the moment. Although specific habitual *acts* are a fairly passive form of adaptation that must be energized by relevant motives, the habits of perception are more autonomous and dynamic predispositions that, once established, would seem to be far more difficult to change. Further, it would seem to be these mind-set habits which are of greater importance to the religious educator and others interested in character formation.

Many habits need to be learned if the individual is to live effectively and efficiently. The child needs to learn good work habits in school; members of the family need to reduce many of the activities of the home to habitual patterns; indeed, the growing person will need to master hundreds of specific tasks of living until their performance is habitual. Habituation is most likely to occur if: (1) the appropriate stim-

ulus is repeated at short intervals; (2) the stimulus is barely above threshold, i.e., just strong enough to produce the desired behavior; (3) the desired behavior is immediately followed by a sense of satisfaction in the task accomplished or other appropriate reward; (4) the learning situation is similar to the living situation where we want the habit to function; and (5) the causes of failure are identified, understood, and corrected immediately so that poor habits will not be perpetuated or the motivation for learning decreased. — *Walter L. Holcomb*

HERBART, JOHANN FRIEDRICH

Herbart was born in 1776 at Oldenburg, Germany. His early academic interests lay in philosophy, and he studied under Fichte at Jena. A visit to Pestalozzi's school at Burgdorf developed in him a lasting interest in education. Henceforth, he was to combine philosophical and educational concerns. He was appointed when still very young to the chair of philosophy at Königsberg, which had earlier been occupied by Immanuel Kant.

At Königsberg, Herbart opened a pedagogical seminary, a sort of demonstration school in which university students of education worked directly with pupils under the close supervision of the professor. This has been called the precursor of later schools of teacher training and education as they came to flourish in Europe and North America.

Herbart was a pioneer in psychology. He was especially interested in the way in which consciousness and unconsciousness were related, and the manner in which ideas arose within the human psyche. He developed a doctrine of apperception — the manner in which new ideas develop out of material already mastered. He argued that a system needed to be developed to assist the child in learning new things. And he proceeded to develop the system, which has been influential in Western education as the "Herbartian method." Knowledge should be presented to the child in a clear fashion so that the new knowledge will be related to what has already been learned, and associated with the pupil's whole experience. The knowledge then needs to be applied to new facts. The result was a formal system of schoolteaching, elaborated by Ziller and McMurry, consisting of 5 steps: preparation, presentation, comparison, generalization, and application.

Herbart's method of teaching was introduced into early Sunday school curriculum materials in the U.S.A. He was attractive to church educational theorists because of his concern with the moral ends of education. He argued that no true learning takes place without concern for "virtue," defined as "the idea of inner freedom which has developed into an abiding actuality in an individual." He was personally a Christian and urged the churches to be concerned for a pedagogy that transcended merely denominational goals.

Herbart wrote voluminously until his death in 1841.

— *Kendig Brubaker Cully*

HERMENEUTICS   Hermeneutics (from the Greek *hermēneutikē,* from the verb *hermēneuein,* "to interpret") is the discipline of exegesis or interpretation, usually of sacred writings, particularly the Old and New Testaments. As the exegesis of sacred writings generally presupposes that their message or teaching has permanent validity, its aim is thus not mere formal correctness but also a degree of contemporary relevance.

Since in the Hellenistic world the Homeric poems enjoyed a quasi-scriptural status, scholars were concerned with their interpretation, and, especially in the case of the Stoics, sought to harmonize them with philosophy. The system of allegorical interpretation thus developed was later utilized by Hellenistic Jewish apologists, especially Philo (1st century A.D.), who aimed at building a bridge between Greek philosophy and the Old Testament. The main stream of Jewish hermeneutics, however, was more literal, and sought to apply the precepts of the law to current needs.

The New Testament writings themselves show how the Christian church entered into this hermeneutic inheritance. The early fathers, particularly of the Alexandrian school, found in the Scriptures a complex system of imagery over and above the inevitable figures of speech. If a passage lacked a satisfactory literal sense, this was held to indicate the presence of a higher "spiritual" or mystical sense. Some writers, e.g., Origen, went as far as to reject the literal truth of narratives such as those in Genesis in favor of their mystical sense. The excesses of mystical interpretation on the part of Gnostics and other heretics, however, led to stress on the primacy of the literal sense of the text and the establishment of "the rule of faith," the church's living tradition of doctrine and worship, as a governing principle of hermeneutics.

Following the precedent of Augustine, the medieval Latin church greatly favored mystical exegesis. In the "spiritual" sense of Scripture a threefold distinction was made — "insofar as the contents of the old law indicate the contents of the new, the sense is allegorical. Insofar as the deeds of Christ or the things which signify Christ are signs of what we ought to do, the sense is moral, and insofar as they signify what belongs to eternal glory, the sense is anagogical" (Thomas Aquinas, *Summa Theologica* I.i.10).

In the early church, literal exegesis of Scripture was championed by the school of Antioch, of which John Chrysostom was typical. In Latin Christendom it was cultivated by the great 12th-century Victorines, Hugh, Richard, and Andrew, and by Nicholas of Lyra in the 14th century, all influenced by the great Jewish scholar Rashi. Thomas Aquinas, while asserting the legitimacy of mystical exegesis, insisted on the primacy of the literal and grammatical sense, and in the *Summa Theologica* faithfully adhered to it.

Renaissance humanism, coupled with the Reformation, led to a complete dominance of literal exegesis. Its development led, on the one hand, to the extremes of fundamentalism; on the other, to the rise of Biblical criticism. The application, particularly in the 19th century, of literary and historical techniques to the Scriptures opened new perspectives and achieved great triumphs in ascertaining the exact meaning of texts. Yet its presuppositions were often questionable, while exegesis tended to become purely antiquarian and archaeological and thus religiously sterile.

More recently this failure has led to a revival of theological exegesis. As against the exclusive stress on their immediate historical setting,

passages are viewed in their total context in the Biblical revelation. In various ways the Bible is being interpreted in terms of *Heilsgeschichte*, the history of salvation, the Old Testament being continued in the New, and both in the life of the redeemed community, the church.

Some writers, e.g., Wilhelm Vischer, have in effect revived the old allegorism. Of this the demythologizing of Rudolf Bultmann and his school, who seek for a relevant existentialist message beneath the allegedly mythical forms of the Gospels, may be considered a specialized form. More characteristic of current trends is the method of typology (from the Greek *typos*, "pattern"), which seeks to discern recurring patterns within the Scriptures and to determine their mutual relations. Thus the redemptive act of God incarnate in the Passion and resurrection is interpreted as analogous both to the redemptive act of the exodus and to the sacramental impartation of redemption in holy baptism. Such exegesis appears amply justified by the New Testament; it is far from clear, however, that its present exponents have wholly freed themselves from either subjectivism or the excesses of the older allegorism.

— *Carmino J. de Catanzaro*

HIGH SCHOOL DEPARTMENT
"High school department" taken quite literally designates the personnel, curriculum, and procedures that comprise the Sunday morning session of church school for high school young people. From this point of view, grading conforms to the public-school pattern, and study, formally earmarked for this particular period, is teacher initiated and teacher led. In contrast the evening youth meet-

ing is more informal and largely youth led.

This stereotype of the high school department has been exploded by reports of youth directors and an examination of approaches and curriculum materials from the major denominations. The emerging "youth work — new style" actually puts little stress on the department as such, nor does it segment the youth program into periods of time.

Both reports and descriptive materials refer merely to persons of senior high school age called to be the church, and who come together to partake of, reflect upon, and participate in its life and mission in the world.

Without exception the current focus is on persons and not programs; on genuine meeting and not on organization; on unity and not on compartmentalization by content, procedure, time, or function. These young people are further identified as persons who with their adult leaders are called to bear a particular relationship to God, to one another, and to self, at the very radical level at which life is lived and decisions are made, rather than, as one put it, "doing little jobs with little or no support or guidance, and putting on little programs."

It becomes apparent, then, that this new understanding of "the church's ministry with high school young people" has taken on a changed character from that of a decade or so ago. In the 1st place the broadened perspective compels the church to view young people as an integral part of its life and ministry rather than as a department, an arm, or an object for evangelization. No longer does one speak of the church's ministry *to* its youth, or of the church's ministry *by* its youth. The term "with" reflects a concept of ministry as God's activity in the contemporary world in which members (including young people) participate but never completely encompass or perform.

Not a few churches report that when this context is recognized, the youth themselves initiate the question of what the church is and what it is about. Quite properly when the church has not been inclined to take seriously the varied and sundry ways in which the young people verbalize such questions, resistance and even scorn are directed against the church. The disturbance created by this shifting emphasis is of no small consequence. A new kind of anxiety has arisen in the church's attitude toward young people. It may be voiced as being "nonplussed" or "not understanding young people today" or "Young people are totally different from last generation," but it often expresses itself in anger. This anger can only be explained because adults see in young people exaggerated tendencies and frustrations that they as adults face all the time: living with rapid change; knowing separateness and dividedness at the core of their existence; evading and even rebelling against a serious consideration of vocation and destiny; being puzzled by a contemporary culture that exploits sex (and other aspects of living) by isolating it from the total personality; feeling pressures to conform to values that may be challenged by the faith, on one hand, or by lack of finances, on the other; wanting privileges yet resenting the responsibilities that accompany them; openly declaring independence yet awkwardly handling it with limited social skills; being unable to come to terms with the meaning of authority; seeking desperately a sense of intimacy and selfhood or evading both in subtle or unconscious ways.

When adults of the Christian church look at their young people they are reminded afresh of all the unfinished business in their own lives and of how cleverly but surely they have evaded the meaning and implication of the Christian message. The chasm widens until it becomes at times almost unbridgeable when adults withdraw from making contact with the world of young people, and society isolates youth until they have developed a culture of their own in order to live within the kind of culture that is around them. A further tragedy is that although the culture and the language created by young people bulwarks them from the adults, it has, to their own horror, shut them away from one another. In the light of this, the role of the teacher of high school youth has correspondingly shifted from the "personality guy" to the individual who can meet a young person in spite of the threat to himself.

The importance of person-to-person confrontation in the community of faith must not be construed as "togetherness" or a seeking to lift oneself up by one's own recreational program. It is described more accurately by the New Testament word *koinōnia* in which excessive activities are bypassed, pretensions and self-justifications are laid aside. In meeting, one person makes contact with the world of another, accepting the threat of the presence of the other as he really is and in turn being present to the other. The paramount developmental task of the high school young person —

achieving identity and intimacy cast realistically in the context of Christian community — has as its starting point divine grace and mercy.

As genuine meeting rarely occurs in large, overactivated groups, the structure of the new senior department allows for small, intimate groupings (not called classes, please, say some), where discussion in depth can take place between adults and youth and between youth and youth. For depth discussion and study lie near the heart of the Christian faith and become powerful instruments of the church. In such groups the real questions can be heard, and support provided for the intolerable moment of facing and accepting oneself and owning one's own predicament. In such groups surface thinking can be punctured and pushed to a level where the Biblical situation illumines the present and God's breakthrough is recognized, whether in the wilderness in camel's hair or on the sidewalks of New York in blue denim.

Adults accept vigorous responsibilities along with the young people and do not leave so serious a matter as study and program for young people to bear alone and unguided. Nor is the council allowed to become straddled with the brunt of the world. In a truly shared leadership it is commonly recognized that no one person or even a handful of persons can perform all its functions. Nor can the functions themselves be defined in a vacuum, but only after the group is informed by study, investigation, and worship.

The young people themselves have challenged so sufficiently the artificiality of compartmentalizing them by such predetermined labels as "now we pray, now we study, now we raise the question, now we discuss, and now we recreate," that all national educators and administrators now stress a unified program.

Small, intimate groups are discovering the Bible as a book relevant to life. Young people who have protested Bible lectures and dull teaching are voluntarily turning to the Bible to explore anew its meaning, to listen to it faithfully until it begins to question them and speak to them. Curriculum materials seem to be shying away from the "use" of the Bible in the sense that it may support a certain position or undergird an ethical decision. Therefore, 2 types of approach are emerging. One deals directly with large blocks of Biblical text without apology, believing that in its own right it has a story to tell. The 2d approach begins with an actual situation or with contemporary expressions of culture, such as art, music, drama, novel, and story, seeking to examine them for their Biblical dimension. Thus curriculum materials are often drawn from the common life of seniors. A course may deal with the Christian faith and jazz while another probes modern literature for its theological implications. Thus participation in the church rightly pushes the young people to a deeper participation in the world itself at the point they live in it.

This clear-cut refusal to compartmentalize religion into a spiritual as over against a secular sphere has given new importance in curriculum to the calling of a Christian and the exploration of the meaning of Christian vocation.

Perhaps the senior high young people themselves, so intolerant of sham, may yet be one means of helping the church examine the nature of its own faith. Although curriculum materials are more person-centered and deal with situations crucial to young people, they have become by the same token and at the same time more theological and Biblical and emphasize the radical nature of worship and the mission of the church in the world.
— *Nelle K. Morton*

HIGHER EDUCATION, RELIGION IN

The phrase includes, generally, a wide and diversified type of interest in the proper and adequate inclusion of the role of religion in college and university education, given the history, nature, and traditions of higher learning, the nature of religion, and the mission of the church. It refers to an academic discipline that has been growing in importance since World War I in theological seminaries. In this discipline there is both theoretical and practical examination of the ministry in colleges and universities, of church-university relationships, and theological inquiry related to higher education. The training of campus religious workers, college pastors and chaplains, teachers of religion to undergraduates, and the development of a theology of education take their place within it. The life and mission of the church in higher learning, the relation of theology to culture as represented in the liberal arts and sciences, and the appreciative understanding of academic approaches to human knowledge form the central part of this field of inquiry in the curricula of increasing numbers of seminaries and graduate schools.

Historically, the basis for concern regarding religion and higher education belongs to the earliest Western university traditions. Medieval institutions of advanced and professional learning were frequently founded by the church and designed to train the Christian ministry as well as other Christians for the learned professions. A world view informed by the religious heritage provided the context for the various basic academic disciplines. The Renaissance made its humanistic contributions, often within the same context, and the Age of the Reformation, which had its beginnings and gained its impetus in university circles, gave a renewed impact to the role of the religious heritage in Western higher education. Most universities and colleges founded in Europe and the New World in the wake of the Reformation were established by the churches upon these same Christian (and classical culture) foundations and for the same purposes of training the ministry and professional leaders in society.

During the same period (ca. 1400–1850), heads of local, state, or national governments, as well as parliaments, also saw in the advancement of higher education a way of enhancing their prestige and increasing the nations' development. Other institutions, founded under Christian and classical auspices, had often built up endowments and reputations adequate to a status of relative independence from both church and state. Despite the counterinfluences of some classical and early modern learning to religion, nevertheless most of the independent institutions were conscious of Christian objectives and included divinity studies or engaged in worship as a normal part of their academic life. In Europe, indeed, theological faculties and the traditions of the medieval universities continued even in government-established institutions. Thus, various types of university

polity were developed and a diversity of new intellectual developments made their influence felt at the same time that a basic Christian heritage continued to provide the foundations of modern higher education.

An emphasis upon the place of religion in higher education was in evidence in the 19th century in the great expansion of colleges in the U.S.A. and in areas of the world reached through the century's missionary endeavor. Churches founded institutions for higher learning along the moving frontier and as an integral or preparatory part of the Christian mission. As governments, state and local, as well as Western-supported governments in mission lands, expanded the range of public services, higher educational institutions under tax-supported auspices were also being established alongside those of the church and others of the independent type. Regardless of the auspices, academic traditions had already assigned a role to religion, both as a subject matter for instruction and study and as the basis for a climate among students and teachers determining their values and concerns.

With the tensions between the rapidly developing sciences and religion, the advancement of secularization throughout modern life and thought, and difficulties posed by sectarianism in pluralistic societies, the broad historical involvement between religion and higher education was disrupted during the latter third of the 19th century and the 1st third of the 20th century, both in Europe and in America. Many of the causes of conflict between religion and science are now seen to have been neither strictly scientific nor theological, but philosophical. Secularization was taking place amid the society and in intellectual fields generally, but a vigorous Christian movement among students, represented by the Y.M.C.A. and Y.W.C.A., the Student Volunteer Movement, and the World's Student Christian Federation, was gaining ground at the same time. After World War I the churches reentered the higher educational field with new vision and enthusiasm on these student-led bases, establishing campus ministries, student movements, and interdenominational work. Moreover, colleges and universities, having suffered academic disruption, reestablished or established new departments or schools of religion and chaplaincies. Cooperation between higher educational institutions and religious organizations since the 1930's has reopened the doors of relationship.

Recent theological scholarship has provided many new insights and vigorous encouragement of religion's place in higher education. The treatment of the subject in curricula (even in fields such as history, literature, philosophy, and increasingly in the social and natural sciences) and the role of the church (as a community of faith) in the university (as a community of learning) are now the primary areas of impact. Improvements in graduate faculties of religion have strengthened the quality of graduates entering the field of teaching of religion.

The mutual strengthening of the work of the churches and of the institutions of higher learning in relation to religion is both quantitatively and qualitatively in abundant evidence today. A number of organizations, some professional, others established more broadly by churches, suggest the degree of vitality in the field. Among such organizations are these: National Association of Biblical Instructors, National Council on Religion in Higher Education, Commission on Higher Education of the National Council of the Churches of Christ in the U.S.A., National Association of College and University Chaplains, National Student Christian Federation, and others. Some philanthropic educational foundations have also found this field of special importance, among them the Edward W. Hazen Foundation, the Danforth Foundation, and the Lilly Endowment. Many churches have prepared official or semi-official reports and statements about their concerns with higher education, their relationships to it, and their involvements within it. The production of books, pamphlets, journals, and published reports bearing upon this concern has also been impressive, especially since the end of World War II, stimulated in large part by the recognition of " the crisis in the university" and the stake of Christianity in it. The demand for a Christian philosophy of education is being voiced among educators and churchmen alike. The field promises much further development and expansion in the future with the anticipated increases in college enrollments, the further impact of the theological renaissance, the renewed concern of the laity, and the further growth of the many initiatives already present. — *John Edward Dirks*

HINDUISM Hinduism is the religion of 300,000,000 inhabitants of India. There is no " church," no official dogma, and customs and beliefs differ not only from sect to sect but from area to area. However, the Vedanta philosophy, which is rooted in the Upanishads (ca. 500 B.C.), integrates what seem to be contradictions and thus provides a system for understanding Hinduism. According to this philosophy, Brahman is the Absolute, the Ultimate, the "really Real," apart from which, existence has no meaning. I am aware of myself, but the "I" is illusory because the soul that is within me is the same Soul, or Atman, that is within all creatures, and the Atman is a part of the Brahman. In fact, the Ultimate is Brahma-Atman — the 2 cannot be separated. The Brahma-Atman or Brahman has no attributes, is beyond personality, and therefore cannot be referred to as "He," is beyond good and evil, life or death, and what happens in the world. Brahman can be realized intuitively only as the individual dispels any self-awareness and is absorbed into Brahman in a state of bliss or Nirvana. Since this is the ultimate goal, history has no positive meaning. It merely repeats itself, providing continually a snare of illusions to keep man from realizing his oneness with Brahman. Deliverance (moksha) cannot be achieved in one life by most persons; thus they are born again and again until karma (defined as wrong thoughts, words, and deeds) is removed.

The highest way to achieve deliverance is through knowledge. As this road is difficult for those of lower caste, there are other ways for them. One way is through bhakti, or devotion to a deity. The Brahman (neuter) can be approached through a triad, 1 called Brahma (personal) the creator, a 2d, Vishnu the preserver, and a 3d, Shiva the destroyer. Brahma is deeply respected, represented in art as a kingly personage riding a white goose symbolic of his aloofness. Shiva is "the great God" to his followers. He stands for life itself, for force and energy, and is identified with reproduction. His most popular representation, especially for worship, is the male sexual organ, the linga. He is often represented as Nataraja, the Lord of the dance, with 4 arms, 3 eyes, and the Ganges river symbolized as flowing from his head, and poised on a dwarf, symbolizing the ego that must be crushed if the Lord is to dance. He is sometimes represented as a naked man smeared with ashes and with hair braided like an ascetic's, for he is a favorite patron of ascetics and holy men who impose ashes in 3 horizontal lines on arms, chest, and forehead to indicate their renunciation of the body to free the soul. Shiva has many consorts, among them Parbati, gracious and kind; Durga, unapproachable and the patron of the robber caste called Thugs; Chandi, who is wild; and Kali, the black, who is terrible. Also associated with Shiva are Ganesha, the elephant-headed boy, and Nandi, the white bull. Although most worship related to Shiva and his consorts is concerned with renunciation of the world and is strongly ascetic, an offshoot of the worship of Durga and Kali, called Shaktism or Tantrism, is orgiastic with ritualistic sex rites.

The other great god is Vishnu, who is always benevolent and comes to earth whenever values are threatened. He has been incarnated as a dwarf, as Rama and Krishna, as a fish, tortoise, boar, and man-lion, as a Brahmin, as Gautama, the founder of Buddhism, and, according to some Vedantists, as Moses and Jesus. He will be incarnated in the future, for, according to the Hindu interpretation of history, if an incarnation occurred once, it is bound to occur again. This tolerance and philosophy make it easy for the

Hindu to accept the divinity of Christ but difficult for him to accept Christ as unique.

The stories of Rama and Krishna are found primarily in the epics, the *Ramayana* and the *Mahabharata.* Rama is the ideal man who preserves his integrity through every adversity, and Sita is his ever loyal and faithful wife. When Sita is abducted by a wicked king, Rama enlists the aid of Hanuman, the monkey king, and the wicked king is found and slain. Rama and Hanuman are worshiped as deities in their own right, but Rama and Sita are also worshiped as incarnations of Vishnu and his consort, Lakshmi. Turning to the *Mahabharata,* Krishna is presented as a chubby, mischievous little boy and as an adolescent seducer of milkmaids in some of the tales. In one section, the *Bhagavad Gita,* he is the charioteer who counsels Arjuna, who has questioned whether it is right to fight his own relatives, that man is not responsible for his actions if he has no personal or individual concern with the results. Krishna and Radha, his consort, are worshiped as deities, claiming absolute devotion, or as incarnations of Vishnu. The epics abound with countless other figures to whom one can give his devotion. Some Hindus have claimed that they have 330,000,000 deities, which suggests the polytheism that seems everywhere apparent.

The 3d way to achieve release is by means of dharma, or duty, especially in relation to caste. The castes are the Brahmins, priests and teachers; the Kshatriyas, rulers or administrators; the Vaisyas, artisans, traders, and merchants; and the Sudras, the ordinary workers. There are also about 2,000 subcastes, and until recently there were outcastes

or untouchables who could claim no prerogatives. To achieve release through dharma, a person is to follow his caste rules pertaining to occupation, social intermingling, marriage, and food taboos. He must know the appropriate prayers for various occasions, including the proper gestures, and must know and observe the proper ceremonies pertaining to birth, name-giving, marriage, sickness, and death. Those pertaining to death are important because without them, it is believed, the soul would have to be reborn at once. The rules for women are as prolific and as binding, the chief obligation being to serve their men meekly.

Philosophically, the various deities do not exist — they are merely ways in which man can approach Brahman, the Ultimate. The common man is no philosopher but worships the main god of his community, sees to it that his household shrine with its god is properly tended, visits other shrines to invoke the blessings of gods who have special functions, such as giving health, and observes the duties of his caste and cult. Hinduism has so saturated the culture that most of the beliefs and practices are absorbed unselfconsciously. There are no services of corporate worship and no sermons for instruction. The average temple is dedicated to one deity whose image is enshrined in a dark inner room. The priests chant the Vedas in Sanskrit, which many of them do not understand, and the devotee cannot comprehend. Approaching the shrine alone and at no prescribed hour, the devotee says the proper prayers and then departs. There are ashramas where those more philosophically or spiritually inclined can sit at the feet of great teachers who teach as much by example as by word.

In spite of the diversity of belief and practice in Hinduism, the Vedanta school has given a philosophic unity. There are other schools of philosophy that are dualistic or express other concepts of reality and deny that Hinduism can be defined and placed into an integrated thought structure. A rejuvenation of Hinduism has accompanied the development of nationalism, but changes have affected many of the traditional mores. The Republic of India has outlawed untouchability, and there is now great fluidity in the caste structure. Various movements, such as the Ramakrishna mission, have been concerned with social service and social reform. Vedanta centers are now located in many cities in the Western world, proclaiming Hindu spirituality while secularism challenges many of the religious presuppositions in India.

— *Lee A. Belford*

HISTORY OF CHRISTIAN EDUCATION The history of Christian education consists of the story of the teaching of the Christian faith.

Arnold B. Come has written that from the standpoint of the Reformers the Christian faith " included the whole providential revelation of God in history, including the Law and the Prophets of the old covenant . . ., the whole of the incarnation, atonement, and resurrection in Jesus Christ . . . and the whole continuing presence and working of God as Holy Spirit through the means of grace in the body of Christ, the church " (*Human Spirit and Holy Spirit*, pp. 173 f.).

Such a description of Christian faith keeps in view the historical context ranging from the revelation of the divine plan to the continued " working of God " in communicating the faith through the church. These 2 facets are always necessarily involved. The roots of Christian education are traceable deep in the instructional history of mankind, and its branches and fruit are intimately related to every aspect of contemporary life.

The Pagan-Christian Period (400 B.C. to A.D. 529). The continuity of the history of Christian education with pre-Christian educational history and the complementary position it holds with the continuing educational problems of mankind finds illustration in the lives and contributions of early Christian teachers. The men who inherited the gospel from the life, work, and teaching of Jesus also inherited an education rooted in the Old Testament and, indeed, they were encouraged by the Master to cherish that heritage. Also, 2d- and 3d-generation teachers who played such an important part in the formation of Christian education recognized the affinity a relevant Christianity had with universal human culture.

Augustine (354–430) expressed it thus: " If those who are called philosophers, especially the Platonists, have said aught that is true and in harmony with our faith, we are to claim it for our own." Both Augustine and Ambrose (ca. 340–397) employed Cicero's 4 cardinal virtues in their ethics — prudence, justice, fortitude, and temperance. Cyprian (ca. 200–258), on the other hand, rejected his early training. He determined to read nothing but the Bible and Christian writers. Tertullian (ca. 160–220) likewise wrote, " Away with all attempts to produce a mottled Christianity of Stoic, Platonic, and dialectical composition. . . . We want no curious disputation after possessing Christ Jesus, no inquisition after enjoying the gospel." Nevertheless his *De anima,* which has been called the 1st Christian work on psychology, accords with the views of the Stoics.

The formation of the earliest schools for the training of Christian leaders started at Alexandria in A.D. 190 in the midst of the intellectual currents of that time. The catechetical school at Alexandria was founded by Pantaenus, a converted Stoic philosopher, and his successors were Clement (ca. 150–220) and Origen (ca. 185–ca. 254). It is probable that the famous Greek schools of higher learning, such as Plato's Academy, Aristotle's Lyceum, Epicurus' School of the Garden, and Zeno's School of the Stoics, stimulated the early Christian scholars into meeting their intellectual challenge. It is significant that such pressure is still levied on Christian teachers, inasmuch as the major modern schools of philosophy trace their lineage to these pre-Christian schools. In any event, we know that the first Christian teachers met the world with fearless and informed scholarship after the pattern of Alexandria, followed in the middle of the 3d century at Rome, Antioch, Caesarea, and Edessa.

Early in the 2d century the catechumenate was established as a means for preparing adult candidates for church membership. This consisted of courses of lectures in the Scriptures, creeds, worship, ethical conduct, and all other things a church member ought to know prior to his baptism. Persecution drove such instructions underground intermittently from the time of the reign of Domitian (51–96) to Constantine's edict of toleration in 313. The catechumenate continued in some places as long as the 5th and even the 6th century, but the decline of adult conversions from paganism after Christianity became the accepted religion tended to produce a situation in which postbaptismal rather than prebaptismal instruction was the general practice.

The fact of persecution and the stubbornness of Christians in defying it is important because it brings into focus the inseparable tension history records between education to become a Christian and the prevailing education to which the Christian is exposed in any culture. The attitude of the Roman authorities affecting Christian teaching was reflected in laws of the Empire against the worship of foreign gods and against the formation of societies. The Christians had no choice but to worship and witness, but the fundamental aim of Christian training, involving the goal of the gospel itself, always lurked behind the social issues.

The real issue was drawn when persecution ceased, rulers became nominal Christians, and contemporary life maintained its pagan mores and customs while espousing Christian conviction. It was Pelagius (ca. 360–ca. 420), England's 1st Christian scholar, who precipitated a crisis. He thought the prevailing low tone of Christian morality was due to a lack of a vivid sense of personal responsibility. He believed that the doctrine of original sin and Augustine's teaching of the sovereignty of God undermined human freedom and responsibility.

The controversy was settled in the 2d Council of Orange (529), 1 of the series of councils in which the church decided what was to be regarded as Christian teaching. Although it rejected Pelagianism, the church was not happy over irresponsibility among Christians. The period closes, therefore, with Christianity as a subject of instruction dogmatically defined but with the education of the Christian in an alien society in an unsettled condition.

The Period of Conflict (529–1100). Plato's Academy and the teaching of philosophy in Athens were suppressed in 529. In the same year Benedict formulated his rules. Pope Gregory I (the Great) revived the papacy and reaffirmed Augustinian theology. But Christianity was faced with serious conflict. Barbarian invasions had already overrun much of the Western world, the Vikings were yet to come, surrounding the institutions of civilization with ignorance and superstition, and Mohammed (570–632) brought into being a competitive religion in the East that eventually threatened the West via the Iberian Peninsula.

In these days, which history sometimes calls "dark," assistance came from an unexpected quarter — from Irish monastery schools that had been developed by the strongest church outside the Roman Empire. The work of conservation in the monasteries of the Continent must not be overlooked or that of the great scholars such as Cassiodorus, Isidore of Seville, and Alcuin, who had been imported from Britain to become head of Charlemagne's famous Palace School. Meanwhile, philosophy in the Christian tradition began in this period with John Scotus Erigena (ca. 815–ca. 877), and inconspicuous scholars were translating the classics, procurable in Arabic from Muslim scholars. Many Christians studied with Avicenna (980–1037) and Averroës (1126–

1198), as well as with Maimonides (1135–1204), a great Jewish scholar.

Having access to the classics only through Latin, Western scholars had been limited to Roman literature until they studied at Cordova and Toledo in the Muslim schools. Christian initiative applied the new knowledge to a vast area of fields. Kenneth Scott Latourette has suggested that there is something inherent in Christianity that seems to take up the functions of society when the latter has faltered. In the "dark ages" the church assumed society's teaching function, with the result that the seeds of survival on which civilization depends were conserved, fertilized, and made ready for more favorable circumstances.

The Period of Revival (1100–1500). The Schoolmen ushered in the period of revival. Scholasticism, however, cannot be confined to a period of years but overlaps the centuries. Boethius, e.g., can be called "last of the Romans, first of the Schoolmen." Anselm lived from 1033 to 1109. It is agreed that Scholasticism reached its highest accomplishment in Thomas Aquinas. After him came Duns Scotus (d. 1308) and William of Ockham (d. 1349), reckoned as transitional to modern scholarship. Ockham denied papal infallibility, accepting only Scriptural authority. He argued against the support of faith by reason on the ground that divine freedom precludes the necessity of God's acting within the limits of human understanding. Ockham thus opened the door to continued speculation on grounds familiar to modern students.

Scholarly considerations alone, however, without the aid conjured by social realities, would not have kept the door open. The gradations of modern educational systems were emerging, but in reverse order from the way they appear today: first the universities, then the secondary schools for youth, and finally the elementary schools for children. Social circumstances at work during the 11th to the 13th centuries were destined to lay the foundation for radical changes in education, particularly at the vocational and common-school levels.

These circumstances centered in the Crusades, which occurred intermittently from 1096 to 1270. They resulted in the breakdown of the feudal system that sustained them. Power was decentralized. A new class of merchantmen, artisans, and the trade guilds arose, and society moved from an agrarian to an increasingly industrial character, making towns and cities points of life as contrasted to the lord's castle. Under chivalry, education, although on the surface Christian in its idealism, was little more than training in arms and equitation, and the system was one of caste.

The changes now demanded utilitarian knowledge and skill — training in the vernacular, arithmetic, geography, navigation, bookkeeping. Roger Bacon (ca. 1214–1294) was the intellectual forerunner of a new education, centered in science. In the midst of the Crusades he declared that the non-Christian would not be won by arms but by "knowledge integrated with divine truth as seen in the Christian revelation" (H. G. Good, *A History of Western Education,* p. 125). Meanwhile, cities, guilds, and individuals were setting up schools in competition with the Latin schools of the church, teaching in the vernacular, with a practical aim. It is significant that the universities, which were an out-

growth of the cathedral schools, became independent, their academic freedom being championed by guilds of scholars. Secularization of education, a dream in Charlemagne's time, was now emerging under social compulsion. However, at this time instruction of the Christian for participation in practical life was not differentiated from instruction of the individual to be a Christian. The well-rounded life was assumed to be the Christian ideal.

The 1st great writer on education to recommend the new learning was Pier Pablo Vergius (Vergerio), b. 1349. His definition of liberal education might well be construed to criticize overemphasis in either direction: "We call those studies liberal which are worthy of a free man; those studies by which we attain and practice those highest gifts of body and mind which ennoble men and which are rightly judged to rank next in dignity to virtue only." The influence of classical humanism is here apparent, linkage with Aristotle's ideal for free men in a free state, and reaction against the medieval emphasis on preparation for the future life in favor of present life. But it carries a criticism of the Latin schools of the church and the utilitarian overemphasis of other schools at the expense of character training.

The Period of Orientation (1500–1800). The next 3 centuries contain the story of orientation to new concepts affecting the education of the Christian, in theology, philosophy, educational practice, and social life. The Protestant Reformation occupies a central place. It was a twofold series of events, involving changing thought processes, on the one hand, and their practical implications, on the other; of changes in Biblical theology and practical theology. The 1st was made possible by Roger Bacon, Ockham, Wycliffe, Hus, and others; the 2d by contemporary realities such as the invention of printing, increasing literacy in the vernacular, the decadence within the life of the church, and a rising spirit of nationalism. Luther (1483–1546) and his Theses (1517) and Calvin (1509–1564) and his *Institutes* appeared in a world scene ready for vast change.

Because of its doctrine placing responsibility on the individual believer to take the Scriptures as the prime authority, the Reformation was a stimulant to literacy. At first, however, education fell off because so much of it had been directed toward training for the priesthood. As a consequence Luther was among the first moderns to favor compulsory education, albeit with the church as the teaching institution. Calvin supported universal education, which, however, was not really to be achieved for several centuries.

Orientation to the growing influence and power of Protestantism was inevitable on the part of the Roman Catholic Church. A Counter-Reformation was begun by Ignatius Loyola through the organization of the Society of Jesus, composed of preachers, missionaries, teachers, and founders of schools. Recognized by Rome in 1540, it became a militant, zealous, and uncompromising supporter of the Roman Church. Educationally, its curriculum was formalized humanism; its method was autocratic, designed to teach what to think and how to defend it.

Orientation in this period took another form, namely, a reaction against humanism. Humanism itself had been a reaction against Scholastic asceticism and the contempt for the world that had characterized much of the Middle Ages. But the humanist, in his effort to reclaim the importance and beauty of life, paid only lip service to the Christian faith and tended to rule out the need for redemption. Francis Bacon's inductive method is usually credited with the transition alluded to. Montaigne (1533–1592) provides insight on the contemporary education: "We toil and labor to stuff the memory, and in the meantime leave the conscience and the understanding unfurnished and void." The trend away from humanism was an attempt to make education realistic, and produced attempts to suggest not only what worthy citizenship should include but a commonwealth as well. A number of treatises along this line were produced (e.g., Thomas More's *Utopia*, Thomas Elyot's *Boke Called the Governour*, even Machiavelli's *The Prince*). These writings manifest the practical responsibilities inherent in the task of instruction and reveal a deep optimism in the power of education to accomplish desirable personal and social changes.

The 17th century reflects the effects of the Reformation in the breakup of the Empire, the disunity within Christendom, and the rise of nationalism in 30 years of fratricidal war. Nevertheless, the Christian instinct to teach and learn persisted. Something of its unquenchable spirit is seen in John Amos Comenius (1592–1670), who desired to have instruction dedicated to knowledge, morality, and piety. He advocated universal education in the vernacular, grading according to ability, visual aids, preschool preparation, and a realistic relation of all learning, including religion, to life.

The 18th century, sometimes called "the age of reason," brought the orientation engaged in by men of these centuries to a plane issuing eventually on the modern philosophical, educational, and social scene. John Locke had laid down the principle (in the 2d of his *Two Treatises of Government*): " All men are free and equal; no man is by nature sovereign over other men. . . . The law of nature governs the state of nature; reason reveals the law of nature, which is derived from God." His successors in the 18th century wrought out the implications for society's institutions — Rousseau (1712–1778) in his *Social Contract* and *Émile,* followed by others scarcely less important.

A new orientation was necessary, however, to the new freedom from dogmatic authoritarianism that scholarship enjoyed. The issue was struck by David Hume (1711–1776), who projected Descartes's thesis of doubt to an agnostic conclusion. Reason, he contended, did not lead to certainty but to doubt. The directions from which answers immediately came are important to the succeeding history of philosophy and education as well as to religion. The 1st was from the Continent in Immanuel Kant's *Critique of Pure Reason,* in which he proposed a moral " ought " that reason must accept to predicate a desirable world. This resulted in new foundations in philosophy away from an agnostic position toward a renewed confidence in faith. A 2d source of criticism came from Thomas Reid, of Edinburgh (1710–1796). Committed to a Calvinistic point of view, he argued that Hume's use of reason to discredit reason was absurd. It was Reid's " Common Sense " school of philosophy that Puritan scholars brought into the young American colleges.

The Modern Period (1800–   ).

The rise of the democratic system in America and France and the advance of the common man as a participant in his own government are the signs of the emergence of what might safely be called a " modern " period. Educational philosophy and method had reached a high point. Liberal and humanitarian reformers became everywhere evident, although at the same time opponents of education available for all argued that such would make the poor dissatisfied with their lot in life. Two religious movements, having philanthropic motivations as well, performed signal service in emancipating man from ignorance: the Protestant missionary movement and the Sunday school.

Education's close association with the Christian church for almost 2,000 years came under fire in the Western world as a result of the very freedoms religious men sought in emigrating to the New World — freedom of worship, conscience, assembly, thought, expression, and equality of opportunity. Education assumed an increasingly important role as a preserver of the freedoms gained, but it also was apparent that it was likely to fail if dependent on voluntary response. A problem that the Greeks and Hebrews had been forced to face now presented itself in the modern world: the importance and desirability of state support and control of education. History affords no evidence of an easy solution of that problem.

Even after the principle of separation of church and state had been established in the U.S.A., allusion to religion in the classroom proved impossible to escape. The attempt to treat it with objective neutrality often resulted in its consideration as a philosophical phenomenon and in the debunking of spiritual entities in favor of naturalistic processes of one form or another. Time revealed that Horace Mann's confidence in education as an instrument of reform, either personal or social, was not justified without motivation operative beyond the limits of mere knowledge. John Dewey's influence had permeated the school system with its lofty ideal of democracy. A sympathetic but critical evaluation of American education in the heyday of the Progressive Education Movement noted the lack of motivation.

This lack of motivation did not go unnoticed or unheeded. Herman Harrell Horne (1874–1946) sought motivation in a Creator theology in which democratic processes and behavior became an expression of creative living in a free society. George Albert Coe (1862–1951) attacked the same problem from the standpoint of the educational function of the church in a democratic setting. Other trends since the days of Mann seem to agree that religious motivation is not only desirable but necessary as a part of the preparation of the individual for participation in free society. Parochial schools at all levels have increased; religion has been recognized as a legitimate part of liberal education in some states as well as church-related schools; released time has been made legally possible.

The thesis that all of this is a part of the history of Christian education may be authenticated in the crisis the modern world faces as a result of science's epoch-making strides since the formulation of Einstein's theory of relativity. Man, the created being, can now destroy himself, his civilization, and all that has been created. He can disrupt the results of the Creator's act. But he cannot replace it. Gnosis is his; genesis evades him. Only obedience to the Creator's law can give man the hope of remaining alive, let alone living creatively as the divine image within him prepares him. It is in such a climate that existentialism has arisen, a philosophy with religious connotations. Its educational implication is a constant interplay between man and God, man and man, man with institutions, institutions with institutions, and all with society, the whole in constant adjustment to the unfolding plan of the Creator, the blueprint of which is in Scripture. Authority is defined in the nature of freedom and the educational processes operative in its framework, wherein there can be no dominating individual or institution with " all the answers," and wherein the learner is respected and his creative potential released. Christian education as a phenomenon of history exists, then, not as a body of doctrine transmitted by the church at any given point or age, but as those convictions, beliefs, attitudes, behavior patterns, and faith responses adopted by the learner as a result of his contact with Christians and permeating and conditioning all of life, motivating man in the fulfillment of his Creator's will.

— *Donald G. Stewart*

HOLIDAYS The program of Christian education is certainly not dependent on secular cues. However, since the people of the church live also in the larger community of the nation, it is important that the church recognize the pivotal significance of many secular events for the lives of its people as they live in the world. To that end careful programming in the church school will take into consideration the more important secular holidays. In many instances this can mean the giving of a religious dimension to events that otherwise would be limited to considerations of patriotism. This article will encompass a few salient points of emphasis in some of the distinctively American holidays, including 1 important Canadian holiday.

New Year's Day. This can be an indication of the significance of time in human existence. It can be a season of faith rather than fear, a time to conjure and reflect, a day of expectation and anticipation. The observance of Watch Night by many churches is a well-ingrained custom to make their members suitably conscious of their dependence on God, who is timeless, even as others may revel and carouse at the New Year's coming.

Presidents' Birthdays. The spiritual strength of the lives and characters of several of the recognizedly great Presidents of the U.S.A. causes passing time to add to the greatness of both George Washington and Abraham Lincoln. Washington's courage and honor arose from Christian sources. Lincoln epitomizes for the nation the qualities of unselfishness and humility. Churches of all denominations, as well as people of all faiths, do well to lift up the examples of these 2 men who guided the nation in perilous times.

Memorial Day. This observance has definite religious overtones, expressing themselves in sermons, prayers, hymns, and services. The fervent prayer of all men of goodwill is "that there shall be no more war, but that righteousness and just peace shall be known by all mankind." This day should be kept as a day of remembrance of lives ventured and lost for the cause of great ideas and ideals that led men to deny themselves and endure all things, even death. The idea of "memory" is deeply instilled in the observances of all religion, particularly in Christianity. In remembering those who died for their country's purposes, we show that we are grateful for what they did, we prove ourselves desirous of being worthy of their sacrifices, and we join in prayer that "peace with justice" may prevail.

Dominion Day and Independence Day. It is significant that the near neighbors Canada and the U.S.A. should observe the commemorations of their national origins in similar vein. The spiritual undergirding given to Canada's July 1 Dominion Day arouses a national enthusiasm that is an important factor in the life of a nation. Independence Day, July 4, is a birthday occasion for the U.S.A., but also a remembrance of moral and spiritual forces that were involved in the founding fathers' purposes, especially as reflected in the writing of the Declaration of Independence.

Labor Day. Workingmen's holidays are not new, but this one has a special meaning. Coming on the 1st Monday of September, it affords the churches an opportunity to emphasize their concern for sharing in labor's tasks, burdens, and achievements. It is an opportunity to demonstrate that the church affirms a moral basis for the just dues earned by all who share in the world's work.

Thanksgiving Day. In 1863, President Lincoln said in his Thanksgiving Proclamation that "no human counsel has devised nor any mortal hand worked out the great purposes of thanks-giving. These gifts are the gracious gifts of the most high God, who, while dealing with us in anger for our sins, has nevertheless remembered mercy." Beginning with the colonies in 1621, there was much feasting. But the people were also given to psalm singing and prayers, valid ways through which the concerns of the thankful spirit are evidenced. Spiritual ideals must be brought to the forefront, and thanks for personal mercies in the spiritual realm emphasized over the many material blessings we receive.

By noting the secular holidays and giving them spiritual interpretation according to traditions shared by nation and church alike, the church can do much to redeem such holidays from the constant tendency they have to become merely patriotic or materialistic manifestations.
— *Paul Price*

HOLY SPIRIT Holy Spirit, Spirit of God, Spirit of the Lord, Spirit of Christ — these are Biblical terms that all denote the same reality. The rarity of the words "Holy Spirit" in the Old Testament and their frequency in the New Testament reflect a tendency in later times to avoid direct use of the name of God for fear of profaning it. "Holy Spirit" means "God's Spirit," for holiness is the peculiar and distinctive characteristic of God, who can himself be called quite simply "the Holy One." In the New Testament, Jesus Christ is called "the Holy One of God," and with him the Holy Spirit is inseparably connected.

The Bible speaks also of other spirits, notably those that are unholy or "unclean" (demons, Satan). There is less about these in the Old Testament than in the New Testament. because in Old Testament

times opposition to God and his Spirit was seen chiefly in terms of the human enemies of his people, the heathen neighbors of Israel. It came to be realized, however, that spiritual forces lay behind heathenism, and behind the waywardnesses of Israel too. Hence, in the New Testament we find a whole kingdom of evil spiritual powers arrayed against the Kingdom of God, and the Christian life is seen as a warfare, "not contending against flesh and blood, but against . . . spiritual hosts of wickedness" (Eph. 6:12).

The fact is that unholy spirits have laid hold of all mankind. They have invaded human nature ("the flesh") like a deadly virus, and man's plight is hopeless unless they are driven out and replaced by the life-giving Spirit of God. In the Bible we see the unfolding of the divine plan to this end.

God's Spirit was first known in Israel as the source of extraordinary gifts and achievements in men. Later he was recognized as operative in the creation and conservation of the world, and as the source of life in man and beast. But his most important activity had to do with prophetic inspiration. Through the spoken words of the prophets, and through the "inspired" Scriptures that were a fruit of their work, God put his holy Spirit in the midst of Israel "to instruct them" (Isa. 63:11; Neh. 9:20).

But Israel "rebelled and grieved his holy spirit" (Isa. 63:10; Acts 7:51) by disobeying his instruction. Hence, disasters like the exile and the Dispersion overtook them. Yet there was always a remnant that was faithful, taking to heart the prophetic teaching and looking to God for salvation. For through the prophets God had promised that he would one day infuse new life into the dry bones of Israel by his Spirit (Ezek. 37:1-14); he would send Messiah to them, anointed with the abiding fullness of the Spirit (Isa. 11:1 ff.); he would, indeed, pour out his Spirit "on all flesh" (Joel 2:28 ff.).

In the New Testament the promises of God are fulfilled in Jesus Christ, in whose story the Holy Spirit plays a part from the beginning (the Nativity). At his baptism, Jesus is anointed "with the Holy Spirit and with power" (Acts 10:38), and thus equipped for his mission as the Messiah, the Beloved Son, and the Suffering Servant of the Lord. Then at once he is led (Matthew, Luke) or driven (Mark) by the Spirit into the wilderness to be tempted of the devil. That is to say, as the bearer of the Holy Spirit he engages in a trial of strength with the prince of all unholy spirits. Here the Second Adam meets the tempter in the wilderness as the first had met him in the garden, and, unlike the first, he prevails.

But that is not the end of the matter. Satan returns to the attack — through the enemies of Jesus and even through his friends — until the climax is reached in the treason of Judas and the pain and shame of the cross. But Jesus' acceptance of the cross is itself a refusal to yield to the tempter, so that even here he prevails. Therefore, having now fulfilled the role of the Servant, he is "designated Son of God in power according to the Spirit of holiness by his resurrection from the dead" (Rom. 1:4).

Then follows Pentecost and the promised outpouring of the Spirit, which is likewise accomplished through Jesus (Acts 2:33). Its immediate result is a powerful preaching of the Word, by which multitudes are added to the church and joined together in a quite idyllic fellowship. The glory of that day, it is true, did not last; it gave only a momentary revelation of the destined character of the church, a brief anticipation of things yet to come. But as a living reminder of it there has always remained that "earnest" and "firstfruits" of the Spirit which is also promise and assurance that God will complete the work he has begun.

Because of this abiding gift of the Spirit, the church with all its imperfections can be called "the temple of the Holy Spirit," "a habitation for God in the Spirit," "a spiritual house." Into it Christians are built as "living stones," and within it they serve as a holy and royal priesthood, offering spiritual sacrifices to God and proclaiming his wonderful deeds (I Peter, ch. 2), all in the measure in which they participate in the Spirit.

And how do men come to participate in the Spirit? The answer is: By hearing and believing the gospel of Christ, the Word of God (cf. Gal. 3:2; Rom. 10:17). It is just as the spirit of fascism or communism is received by hearing or reading fascist or communist propaganda and believing it. Only believers receive the spirit, whether of fascism, communism, or Christ; and the more firmly they believe, the more the spirit (or Spirit) possesses and controls them.

It is important to note the connection between the Spirit and the Word of God. The Word is the expression and vehicle of the Spirit. But the Word must not be equated simply with words. Visual symbols and dramatic actions as well as words are used by preachers and teachers, and sometimes these speak louder than words. No less than words, they can give expression to a spirit, and even to God's Spirit. God's Spirit is in fact conveyed through the Word both as proclaimed in words and as dramatized in the gospel sacraments. These are the chief means by which God now puts his Holy Spirit in the midst of men, and as men believe his Word, so they become possessed of his Spirit.

But how can we tell whether a man is possessed of the Spirit? How can we "test the spirits to see whether they are of God" (I John 4:1)? Some groups demand evidence of the more spectacular working of the Spirit — speaking with tongues, the gift of healing, etc. — but the New Testament itself shows clearly that these are not meant for everyone (cf. I Cor. 12:1-14). Some spiritual gifts are more, some less, significant; some are intended for all men, whereas others are not.

The character of the Spirit himself furnishes a threefold test that is universally applicable. (1) As the Spirit of truth (John 16:13 ff.) he bears witness to the truth as it is in Jesus, the truth once preached by the apostles and now available to us in the New Testament. Therefore, nothing at variance with this truth is Christian truth and an utterance of the Holy Spirit. (2) As the Spirit of adoption or sonship he bears witness with our spirit that we are children of God (Rom. 8.15 ff.). He enables us to cry "Abba, Father," i.e., to approach God with the same childlike confidence that Jesus did. (3) As the Spirit of love, he pours God's own love into our hearts (Rom. 5:8). Love is the first of the fruits of the Spirit (Gal. 5:22), love for God and for our fellowmen; and it is perhaps the chief test of the Spirit's effectual working in us.

But the Spirit meets with resistance in our human nature, the resistance of the unholy spirits that have laid hold of it, and this is not overcome in a moment. Hence, the New Testament speaks of a conflict between "the flesh" (human nature) and the Spirit (Gal. 5:17). Where a man feels this conflict, he can be assured that the Holy Spirit is at work in his life. He may also take heart, knowing that his struggle is simply a continuation of the warfare in which Christ won the decisive battle on the cross, and of which the final outcome is therefore in no doubt. — *Philip S. Watson*

HUMANISM The word itself is relatively new. F. C. S. Schiller is the authority for the statement that it was used for the first time in 1897 by A. Seth Pringle-Pattison in his *Man's Place in the Cosmos* (p. 61), where it had an anthropocentric meaning. Schiller used it in 1907 in a more technical way to describe the pragmatic position held by himself and William James. The movement for which the word stands, however, traces back to the Renaissance of the 14th and 15th centuries and was primarily a literary effort to free thought from the Scholastic mold. The humanists of this period were concerned with antiquity or, more especially, with Grecian and Roman classical culture. Dante illustrates this interest, for his guide through Hell in the *Divine Comedy* is Vergil, the embodiment of human reason, who guides him as far as reason can go. Although Dante and others of humanistic interest, including Pope Nicholas V and the celebrated Erasmus, stayed within the church tradition, many of the leaders of the movement were either religiously indifferent or in opposition to traditional dogma. Duns Scotus (ca. 1265–1308) can be credited with the beginnings of the separation of philosophy from theology; with this wedge driven into the Middle Ages, a new way of looking at the world began to develop, the anthropocentric view of things, as over against the Scholastic approach, which was that of piety and dogma. Bit by bit, Scholasticism with its dialectical method, its supernatural metaphysic, its transmitted doctrines, and its abstract discussions began to crumble before a nominalistic, this-worldly concern. Humanism must be seen as a rebellion of spirit against medieval ecclesiasticism and mood; but more than that, it was a new-found interest in man, derived not only from the ancient classics but also from an emerging cosmopolitan point of view.

Humanism wears many faces but it has some defining characteristics by which it is known. J. A. C. Fagginger Auer describes it as "a system of thought which assigns predominant interest to the affairs of man as compared with the superhuman, and which believes man to be capable of controlling those affairs." (*Humanism vs. Theism,* p. 3). Protagoras' doctrine, "Man is the measure of all things," is the nuclear thought of humanism. Immediately this ranges humanism against supernaturalism, absolutism in any form, and at least the older forms of naturalism. Embracing relativism, humanism sees truth as having little or no meaning apart from human consciousness. Human thought is competent to deal with human needs and to achieve human values. Because man is essentially good, he can respond in sympathy and understanding to create those values which he is striving to attain. Since humanism is evolutionary in spirit, it is optimistic about the winning of these values, and this despite the fact that most humanists see man as being alone; yet they see him when he faces frankly and courageously the fact of his aloneness as freed from metaphysical trappings and able to get on with the production of value. There is a strong social concern among humanists to eradicate all that impedes the growth and fulfillment of human good. Since man is the center of things, humanism is often as antinaturalistic as it is antisupernaturalistic, for in much naturalism, man is not the center of things but simply one of innumerable natural phenomena; nature, being greater than man whom it produces, is the primary datum. However, E. S. Ames and John Dewey have been classified as humanists, and theirs is a neonaturalistic metaphysic that would hold the natural world to interact with man for the achievement of value. Some humanists accept a naturalistic metaphysic in which the world is judged to be neutral to man's good and man's role is to subdue nature to his own good. In method, humanism is empirical and looks to the scientific method for the fulfillment of human ends.

Humanism is as much a faith and a spirit as a theory of knowledge or reality. As a consequence it has become an expression of religion. Locating the meaning of religion in man's search for satisfying human living, religious humanism is concerned for values that man can realistically hope for, unhampered by traditional loyalties. God is redefined, generally in terms of "humanity considered in its noblest aspirations and capacities, together with nature so far as expressed in and serviceable to humanity" (Charles Hartshorne, *Beyond Humanism*, p. 2). August Comte (1798–1857) tried to establish "the religion of humanity," with humanity as God, to be worshiped through an elaborate liturgy, in a church founded to revere humanity's saints and to fulfill humanity's good. Although Comte's attempt met with little success, religious humanism received its impetus from him. Much of the leadership of religious humanism in America can be credited to the more radical Unitarian clergy who rejected "supernatural guarantees" and embraced the philosophical tenets of humanism as exposited above. Perhaps the most forthright statement of religious humanism is contained in the *Humanist Manifesto,* issued in 1933, which after denying supernaturalism and affirming for religion both the scientific spirit and method, gives content to its faith in these words: "Religion consists of those actions, purposes, and experiences which are humanly significant. Nothing human is alien to the religious. It includes labor, art, science, philosophy, love, friendship, recreation — all that is in its degree expressive of intelligently satisfying human living. The distinction between the sacred and the secular can no longer be maintained."

With this much the theist would agree as he would also be in accordance with some of John Dewey's *A Common Faith,* Julian Huxley's *Religion Without Revelation,* and Lewis Mumford's *The Condition of*

Man, which are 3 serious attempts to delineate a religious humanism. Yet these expressions beg the question which all religious humanism begs, namely, that man can achieve his highest good and fulfill his deepest needs by himself, that is, without God as he is known in the Judaic-Christian sense. Therefore, to speak of themselves as Christian humanists, as some religious humanists do, is to employ a contradiction in terms if any serious usage of words is intended.

Humanism invaded the churches in the first 4 decades of the 20th century through the religious education movement, the use of the term "religious" instead of "Christian" being itself of fundamental significance. Although religious education was not antisupernatural, it was essentially anthropocentric. George Albert Coe, perhaps the outstanding leader of the movement, defined religion as the "discovery of persons" (*Psychology of Religion,* 1916, p. 240). William C. Bower, another leader, viewed religion as a functional process leading to integration both of the self and of the self with its world (*Religion and the Good Life,* 1933). The issues of *Religious Education* during the 1920's and 1930's reflect this anthropocentric slant. During this period, religious education was influenced largely by the educational theory of John Dewey, progressive public education, and sociological and psychological findings. These influences merged into a controlling secular point of view through which many of the philosophical tenets of humanism became implicit, if not explicit, in religious education. The liberal theology of the period, with its romantic view of man, its interpretation of Jesus primarily as teacher and example, its ameliorative understanding of history, and its ethical idealism, not merely allowed for but encouraged humanistic religious education. Confronted with the critical theological self-analysis and reconstruction beginning in the 1930's, religious education not only continued with its humanistic point of view but also reacted negatively and defensively against the theological reconstruction. Harrison S. Elliot's *Can Religious Education Be Christian?* (1940) is illustrative, as are numerous articles in *Religious Education* and the *International Journal of Religious Education* by such leaders as Coe, Bower, and Stewart G. Cole. It cannot be said that the practice of Christian education has as yet emerged from its humanistic plight, although the signs of emergence are visible in its newer theoretical formulations in which theological categories are becoming primary.

— *Gordon E. Jackson*

HYMNS Christian hymnody is second only to the Bible in its contribution to the life and worship of the church. Uniting the inspired songs of men of all centuries, our hymnals contain the power to lift men's souls into meaningful communication with God. They are potent educational and evangelical agents that must not be regarded lightly in the program of the church. That the use of hymns in church schools and churches is not always on this high level, however, is evident.

The origin of Christian hymnody lies in the church of the 1st century. Their rich heritage of psalms provided them with an immediate and familiar medium for expression of praise. It also served as a pattern for songs of their own creation. Exuberant joy predominated in the hearts of these people, and their songs were outpourings of praise to God and to their risen Lord. Among the earliest Christian psalms are the Magnificat, the Nunc Dimittis, and the Benedictus, recorded in The Gospel According to Luke. Some Biblical scholars believe that portions of primitive hymns are embedded elsewhere in the New Testament, e.g., Eph. 5:14, which *The New English Bible* translates, " And so the hymn says: ' Awake, sleeper,/ Rise from the dead,/ And Christ will shine upon you.' "

In Col. 3:16, Paul directs, " Teaching and admonishing one another in psalms and hymns and spiritual songs, singing with grace in your hearts to the Lord " (KJV). Three things are evident about Paul's view: (1) song is an effective Christian educational medium; (2) all spiritual songs are not hymns; (3) psalms are to be distinguished from hymns and spiritual songs.

All great movements within the church have been accompanied by a surge of new hymns and a revival of zeal in singing. Hymnals of the major denominations are compilations of hymns of all periods of the history of the church.

Not all the songs born of spiritual revival are worthy of perpetuation, and many cannot rightfully be classified as hymns. What makes a song a hymn? This question has been asked for centuries and has been answered in a variety of definitions. Eminent authorities from the time of Augustine to the present day have expressed their opinions. Early definitions included only songs of praise. A superficial glance at any hymnal will show the inadequacy of this definition. Lewis F. Benson in *The Hymnody of the Christian Church* (pp. 24 f.) states: " A Christian hymn therefore is a form of words appropriate to be sung or chanted in public devotions."

A hymn is a lyrical poem, sung to appropriate music, devotional in character, spiritually uplifting, expressive of the worshiper's attitude toward God or God's purposes in human life, suitable to be used as a spiritual expression by the entire congregation. A hymn should be simple and emotionally genuine. To this should be added Paul's idea of edifying through the use of hymns.

For some people hymn singing is perfunctory, with little if any effect upon them. The church school should teach persons to understand and appreciate the heritage of church hymnody. Until we give hymns a rightful position of prominence and respect in the teaching program of the church, they are not apt to reach deeply into the hearts and minds of men, women, and children. It is the responsibility of the minister, the director of music, and those who administer the church school program to plan for growing experiences with hymn literature. These people should study and confer together to provide such experiences.

A basic hymn list for the entire church and a plan for implementing hymn study should be produced cooperatively, based on recognizable standards: a theology consistent with the church school curriculum, worthwhile poetry, music suitable to the words, a lofty and reverent style.

Hymns must communicate meaning to the age groups who will learn and sing them. Heavy symbolism and exaggerated subjectivism should be avoided in hymns for children. Graded hymnals are a boon to church school teachers because the hymns have been carefully edited for their suitability to children, theologically, poetically, and musically. However, children also need to learn hymns sung in the whole congregation's worship. Many hymns may be learned, either completely or in part, by children of primary age. Hymn tunes may be used for listening experiences with younger children. The educational approach to hymns should be extended to the adults of the congregation. Excellent available books will help in the selection of appropriate hymns and suggest ways of teaching the congregation to appreciate and sing an increasing number of the great hymns of the faith.

— *Vivian Sharp Morsch*

IDEALISM Idealism is not so much a consistent body of conclusions as a starting point for speculative thought. It is characterized by the tendency to understand reality in terms of mind or spirit. From this common position there have been developed philosophies wholly divergent in their conclusions. Idealism will be treated here as of 3 distinct though overlapping types.

Metaphysical Idealism. Although there are idealistic elements in the religions and philosophies of the ancient East, the history of idealism in Western thought begins with Plato. He believed that ultimate reality consisted of eternal or timeless Ideas, disembodied essences. These were hierarchically ordered and at their highest were subsumed under the Good. They operated both as archetypes for thought and as dynamic causes of existent things. Their realization and appreciation were thought of as the goal of the good life. Knowledge consisted of the recollection of these universal and eternal Ideas which had been known in a previous existence. Education was educing (drawing out or bringing to consciousness) the forgotten Ideas.

Christianity's emergence in the Greco-Roman world was accompanied by the utilization of Platonic and Neoplatonic categories; the Alexandrian School (Clement and Origen — 3d century) was dependent on Philo Judaeus (ca. 20 B.C. — ca. A.D. 50) who had transformed by allegory the historical events and persons recorded in Scripture into abstract ideas and virtues. In general, the Christian Neoplatonists held that universal Ideas are ultimately existent in the mind of God.

Augustine of Hippo (4th century) underwent a double conversion: to Neoplatonism intellectually and to Christianity spiritually and morally. His was the creative mind from which stemmed the culture and religion of the Middle Ages. Platonism was also mediated by Boethius and Dionysius the Areopagite. Anselm of Canterbury (12th century), one of the first of the Scholastics, was typical of many in the medieval period who agreed with Augustine that Platonic Idealism witnessed to the truth of Christianity. His famous " ontological argument " for the existence of God is derived from the Platonic view that the most universal idea is the most real: the Idea of a supreme or perfect Being implies his existence.

Epistemological Idealism. The Platonic tradition was swamped in the 13th and 14th centuries by the popularity of the semirealism of Thomas Aquinas, whose philosophical approach was Aristotelian. The idealistic tradition continued in only an attenuated form through the teaching of a few thinkers, e.g., Duns Scotus and Ockham, who, in an effort to combat radical nominalism (the theory that abstract terms, or universals, have no real existence but are merely words or names applied to things), maintained that universals may have real status in the *mind.*

The main founder of modern idealism was George Berkeley (1685–1753) who stated that the world as it is experienced is dependent for its existence on minds that perceive it. *Esse est percipi* — "Being is to be perceived." There is a necessary substratum for the objective world, and that is found in the infinite mind of God. Accordingly, a tree falling in an uninhabited forest, therefore unheard by man, would make no noise except for the fact that God is everywhere present, creating the qualities we perceive and himself perceiving them. Berkeley argued that knowledge of both God and self is inferential, not from direct experience.

Berkeley was followed by David Hume (1711–1776), who dispensed with the concept of God, being left, therefore, with only the experience of ideas or mental states.

Challenged by the radical skepticism of Hume, Immanuel Kant (1724–1804) undertook his reconstruction of philosophy in the form of what he termed "transcendental," or critical, idealism. Awakened from his "dogmatic slumbers," as Kant confessed, he argued that the crude, formless stuff of the world, things-in-themselves (the noumenal world), or matter, may exist but it cannot be directly known. There are certain a priori "forms of intuition," i.e., space and time, which convert this stuff into knowledgeable form. It is like looking at the world through colored spectacles; to be seen at all, the world is seen as colored by the glass. Nothing can be known except as it is known spatially and temporally. A 2d set of psychologically built-in factors are also operative. These are called "categories" or "principles of understanding," quality, quantity, substance, and causality. Thus the world is experienced as corresponding to the principles that the mind prescribes. Kant's role as a mediator between rationalism and empiricism stresses the activity of the experiencing subject. Human beings are not passive recipients of stimuli but active knowers.

George Wilhelm Friedrich Hegel (1770–1831) was linked to Kant by Johann Gottlieb Fichte (1762–1814). It was Fichte's view that Kant was wrong in thinking of the world as unknowable and as a thing-in-itself. It could be better described as an "ego-in-itself" or a purposeful will who was responsible for the phenomenal world as a school for the training of man's will and character. Taking this hint, Hegel transformed the critical, subjective, and pluralistic idealism of Kant into an objective and monistic idealism.

Hegel's thought is discursive and complex. His "dialectical" method is basic. Hegel analyzes the processes of thinking by the pattern of *thesis* (any idea in general), which reveals on examination its *antithesis* (contradictions and opposites). The two opposing ideas are irreconcilable but are held together in a higher concept (*synthesis*) that does justice to the truths in both of the earlier notions.

The synthesis in turn becomes the thesis for a new movement of thought, and so on to the final Absolute Idea. Hegel believed this to be a description of the thought process as well as the world process, history. Also, he rejected the distinction between the knowing subject and the known object; they are 2 aspects of a single "knowing."

The "concrete universal" is the ground and goal of the world process; it is Mind, Spirit, or God. Religiously, the Hegelian view verges on pantheism, perhaps due to Hegel's strong interest in Oriental philosophy and mysticism.

The influence of Hegel has been mediated to the English-speaking world by Edward Caird (1835–1908), T. H. Green (1836–1882), Bernard Bosanquet (1848–1923), and F. H. Bradley (1846–1924). In America, Ralph Waldo Emerson, whose viewpoint was post-Kantian idealism, espoused transcendentalism. Influenced by Coleridge, Schelling, and Orientalism, he asserted the existence of an oversoul, in effect the immanence of the divine in finite existence.

Josiah Royce (1855–1916), a neo-Hegelian, believed that in the experience of the Absolute, thought of as a closed whole, can be discovered the ultimate explanation and meaning of finite experience. William Ernest Hocking, of this century, has carried on the idealistic tradition — with, however, some concessions to the pragmatism of William James and to naturalism.

Alfred North Whitehead (1861–1947), whose organismic philosophy is best described as neonaturalism with Platonic (idealistic) overtones, distinguishes between the spatio-temporal flux of events, a creative and changing process, and what he calls "eternal objects." This parallels Plato's distinction between the world of becoming and the world of Ideal Forms.

Moral Idealism. As both metaphysical and epistemological idealism were found in Platonic thought, so also moral idealism can be traced to the Platonic view that knowledge is virtue and virtue depends on right knowledge. This position was not especially prominent in early Christian thought, with the possible exception of Augustine, whose concepts of good and evil, right and wrong, were generally in the Platonic tradition. Kant is responsible for the 1st definitive formulation of moral idealism: the theory that there is a scale of values or moral principles, which may be known to man, wherein universals excel particulars, and spiritual or mental values are higher than the sensuous or material, and that man has a degree of moral freedom rather than is wholly bound by necessity.

In his *Metaphysics of Morals* and *Critique of Practical Reason,* Kant postulates a doctrine of persons who are never to be regarded or treated as means but as ends. He holds, secondly, a view of an indwelling sense of the right, a moral imperative. This "categorical imperative" is innate and a priori, but reason confirms such as being universally binding.

The "formalistic" ethic of Kant bypasses what in fact is good in favor of the proper motivation or attitude of the moral person. This has led to widespread criticism by ethicists of other schools of thought. Moreover, ethical idealism, although favored by many Christians, is weakened by an inadequate doctrine of sin. Sin is thought of, even by Augustine, as failure, "missing the mark," or falling short of perfection, rather than in Biblical terms as disobedience and rebellion.

The effort from time to time to make a religion out of idealism or to make idealism a precondition for religion has never been successful because it requires, as in the case of any other philosophy, the introduction into idealism of elements from religious life and thought that are not part of the philosophical enterprise. Nevertheless, the significance of idealism for religion and education cannot be overestimated, because, as Whitehead said, "The European philosophical tradition is a series of footnotes to Plato."

— *Alden D. Kelley*

INDIA The beginnings of education in India are lost in antiquity. Even though Hindu education was limited to the 3 twice-born castes, all education has associated religion with life.

Education along modern lines was started by mission schools. Two important areas in which they have worked — areas that had been ignored by the Government — were the education of women and of backward classes. The emphasis by mission schools on religious training was accepted naturally by the people of India because of their own background of the understanding of the place of religion in life.

Christian boarding schools and colleges are located in centers where missionary work has been strongest. Schools also have been developed in village areas surrounding these larger centers, giving children a few years of formal education before they are brought from their homes to a boarding situation.

With independence (1947), the Government started to work on plans for the education of youth, envisaging a primary school within a mile of the home of every child. Great strides have been made. As a secular nation, India placed emphasis on the freedom of all religions to worship. At the same time it was necessary to train the children of each separate religious group. Therefore, regulations were passed stating that all religious instruction must be outside school hours and that permission to participate in this must be given by the guardians of the children. Because of India's spiritual heritage, a time of opening worship for schools was maintained, but care was taken that this did not favor any religious group.

The changed situation following independence has caused problems for those in charge of Christian institutions. This has resulted in serious reevaluating of the work being done by Christian educators. It is rather generally accepted by these leaders that the Christian school has a unique contribution to make. If it is not making this contribution, it would be preferable for the students and staff to become a part of the Government schools rather than to remain an isolated, mediocre institution.

The Government's policy of providing education for all children has led to the opening of many new schools in rural areas. This has meant the closing of Christian village schools so that the teachers and students would become a part of the larger Government school. Educational gains have resulted because of the larger student body and more adequate teaching staff in many instances. From a Christian viewpoint there have been losses unless the church has been ready to provide the Bible-teaching that was formerly an integral part of the Christian village school.

Because of the large number of non-Christian students in high schools and colleges, religion courses have had to be rethought. Bible courses could still be offered for Christians and non-Christians whose parents so requested. Courses in ethics were developed for others. Greater stress is being placed on hostel life in boarding institutions, and some study is being made of the provision of hostels for young people coming to a city to study in the Government high school or college.

The Christian institution needs to have dynamic Christian leadership both on its staff and in its student body. In various parts of the country Government regulations are causing problems such as the following. The principal of a college must be selected from a list of candidates secured by advertising the post for a certain period of time and voted upon by a committee made up of representatives from the university as well as the local institutions. This committee may not place the same value on a Christian institution's having a Christian in a responsible position as the church does. Teacher training schools must select their students on the basis of grades rather than the fuller consideration of grades and character heretofore deemed so important in the development of real teachers. When a teaching post falls open in a school or college, it is sometimes difficult to find a qualified Christian to fill the position. Vocational counseling is beginning to be stressed in the schools, but few people are qualified for this.

The India Sunday School Union has for many years been the source of supply for teaching materials for Sunday schools. Much of this material was translated or adapted from Western materials. However, in 1953, the Union sponsored the preparation of a new curriculum prepared by Christian educators in India. In the development of plans it was discovered that 3 things were needed: graded lessons with illustrative materials for churches with well-qualified teachers; ungraded lessons for small churches and villages where leadership is limited; a coordinated program for the Sunday and day schools to provide an understanding of the Bible and the Christian faith.

Largely because of the fact that the child going to the mission boarding school was the only literate person in the village, the church in the past has been dependent on the school for all Christian education. However, the church is beginning to see its own responsibility. Parents have looked to mission-school teachers as those who would carry the Sunday school. The training program for the new curriculum materials has led to the enlistment of more lay people as Sunday school teachers, youth leaders, and counselors. — *Gertrude S. Nyce*

INDOCTRINATION In the simplest sense, indoctrination is definite teaching, as in Mark 4:2: Jesus "said unto them in his doctrine" (RSV, "teaching"). An authoritarian teacher is presumed, who drills his pupils in subject matter that has been taught to him and that he believes to be true. The process is by means that convey specific truths to the learner in carefully selected words for his permanent direction. The process is thought to be complete when the pupil shows that he understands by repeating the formulas. In this sense he has arrived at the state of "indoctrination."

The content of such teaching usually consists of exact statements, formulated by some church authority for convenience in teaching. This is intended to assure that the learner receives the official belief correctly for his own edification, and to prevent the teacher from deviating from the form by substituting his own opinion or questionable restatement. Texts from the Bible are frequently used to prove the statements, and the formulas are claimed to be "Bible doctrine."

At its best, this emphasis in Christian education has prevented heresy from being taught and has tended to keep all teachers in close touch with the Scriptures and the early church. By means of it the apostles clearly intended that the original deposit should be preserved without change for the future. This is the ideal shown in the pastoral letters. "A bishop . . . must hold firm to the sure word as taught, so that he may be able to give instruction in sound doctrine and also to confute those who contradict it." (Titus 1:7-9.) This method emphasizes the importance of tradition as it had been received from such apostles as Paul himself. "Follow the pattern of the sound words which you have heard from me . . . ; guard the truth that has been entrusted to you." (II Tim. 1:13-14.)

The method is transmission through official teachers. The New Testament writings are the effort of the 1st generation in the church to preserve in permanent form their recollection of the Lord's words, acts, and instructions. It may be noted that the books of the New Testament were edited for, or addressed directly to, those already within the Christian community, and were preserved and used for edification and permanent guidance. They were not to be broadcast to unbelievers, but were used for the teaching of children and converts and in corporate worship.

The Reformers appealed to the Scriptures against the authority of the medieval church. Various groups produced confessions, articles, and catechisms, worded in terms of the controversies of the times. Catechisms were prepared to aid teachers in lodging exact truths and to assure orthodoxy. Today, teaching by some form of catechism is held, in some Christian circles, to be sound discipline (i.e., discipline-ing) for teacher and pupil, with accomplishment easily measured. The language of catechisms tends to reflect the diction and outlook of a generation (of elderly, authoritative theologians already out of touch with childhood) that is past.

Indoctrination in a broad sense is accomplished by current methods in another way. In contrast to the lodging of exact verbal formulas for future use, the aim is to guide the pupil to find redemption now by helping him to understand his situation, and to discover under guidance applicable resources in the Christian tradition. The growing pupil learns the Christian religion by living it within the active fellowship of the church. He is thus indoctrinated in the historic faith. — *Victor Hoag*

INNER MISSION "Inner Mission," a term used in Germany, Scandinavia, and until recently in the U.S.A., refers to social welfare activities carried on under the sponsorship or encouragement of the church. In 1848, Johann Hinrich Wichern (1808–1881) proposed the term in his address to the Wittenberg *Kirchentag,* assembled to federate the Evangelical Churches of Germany. Dramatized by the Revolution of 1848, his plea for the church's involvement in contemporary society resulted in the formation of the Central Committee for the Inner Mission of the German Evangelical Church, ultimately a kind of Council of Social Agencies. His *Denkschrift* of 1849 became the program for Inner Mission.

Inner Mission expresses the following principles: (1) The church has an evangelistic task within its own geographic borders (hence, " inner " mission). (2) The church's task is the winning of men to Jesus Christ as Savior. Hence, Inner Mission does not content itself with social service, not even when offered in the name of Christ. Rather, it sees any adverse social condition as an opportunity to remove " inward as well as outward poverty," an opportunity to restore to Christ those alienated by external circumstances. (3) The restoration through sharing love is a task laid on the church by its Lord. Hence, Inner Mission is church-related, though not officially church-sponsored. In the U.S.A., however, Inner Mission work is often church-sponsored, and since 1957, *Hilfswerk*, the social work agency of the Evangelical churches of Germany, has been closely coordinated with Inner Mission.

Inner Mission has taken direction from its leaders' experiences. Wichern became the principal teacher of the 1st Sunday school in Germany. To help his pupils, he organized *Das rauhe Haus* for destitute boys. Anticipating contemporary findings with institutionalized children, he organized a " family system " for groups of 10 or 12 boys, whose life together was presided over by a " house father." To secure these men, Wichern trained a male diaconate in a *Brüderhaus*.

Theodor Fliedner (1800–1864), pastor in Kaiserswerth, became interested in prison work, and, impressed by the unfulfilled opportunities for Christian women to minister in love, organized the 1st Deaconess Motherhouse, in 1836. Here, Florence Nightingale found her inspiration for the nursing profession.

Wilhelm Loehe (1808–1872), pastor in Neuendettelsau, at first extremely skeptical of Inner Mission because of its extrachurch orientation, turned its way to implement the social responsibility of the church when, in the Revolution of 1848, he was alarmed to see " the godless even more godless than he feared." Due to his sensitivity to the centrality of the koinonia in Christian life, the church-relatedness of Inner Mission was thereafter emphasized.

Friedrich von Bodelschwingh (1831–1910) founded the famed " colony of mercy " at Bielefeld where several thousand psychologically crippled are cared for. When his son successfully resisted the Nazi attempt to liquidate the colony members as an unnecessary drain on the Reich's economy, the incident dramatized the Inner Mission characteristic that the church has the mandate to help wherever men are in need. This, not the state's support, is its charter for social service.

Finally, Inner Mission became integral to American Lutheran Church life when William Passavant (1821–1894) founded the 1st American Protestant hospital, the Pittsburgh Infirmary. His extensive work from Nova Scotia to Texas impressed

the congregations that though they were " missions " themselves in many cases, they were to share in social responsibility. Inner Mission was seen as the whole church's work, not the privilege of an interested few.
— *George H. Muedeking*

INSTRUCTION Instruction is the art of helping persons to learn. Traditional practice, generally speaking, has focused upon the transmission of information by way of lecture, reading assignments, and recitation, and testing for content retention and conceptual comprehension. Although subject matter and cognitive learning remain important in education, contemporary theology and the behavioral sciences have radically modified this concept of instruction.

Within the context of the Christian faith, instruction or teaching becomes a ministry of love. It is to stand within the fellowship of the church to bear witness to its concern for persons in their relationship to God and to one another. It is to approach learners with an understanding of man's dignity and his misery. It is to be sensitive to fundamental human needs, especially the need for recovery from oppressive guilt, meaninglessness, and alienation and the concomitant acts of sin. Instruction that is Christian in purpose is to guide a process of communication in which teachers and pupils alike become involved in a personal " I-Thou encounter " and in faith respond to the confrontation of God in Christ.

The teacher represents the worshiping community. He stands in relation to the members of his class, to borrow from Erik Erikson, as an " adult guarantor," bringing into the fellowship something of spiritual maturity and authenticity. By his very bearing he communicates an assurance that what is verbalized can be concretized in character and a way of life. This is not to place oneself on exhibit. Rather, it is with empathy to enter into the life of the pupil, to listen, to understand, to affirm, to counsel.

A teacher is a resource person. His 1st responsibility in this regard is to bring systematized knowledge to bear upon the learning experience. On occasion his approach is didactic — he tells. He relates a historical event, a narrative, or a parable; he treats some passage of Scripture exegetically or interprets a doctrine; he may talk out of his personal experience. At other times he utilizes such materials and skills as he may have in drama, music, and art or calls upon other persons of talent to work with the class.

To teach is also to be a group leader. This is a skill to evoke within the members of the class a sense of responsibility for their own learning destiny. Such leadership offers an accepting emotional climate that reduces anxieties and defenses and fosters affirmative attitudes toward self and others. Exploration and planning are involved. Communication issues in community.

Here emerging is the spiritual fellowship, " members one of another." But the people of a true koinonia are a historical people. What is distinctively Christian and makes the difference in this learning, is when the group is confronted by its religious heritage in the events and personalities that tell how " our " God spoke to " us " in other days and places. Such " remembering" places the pupil's existence within the context of the history of redemption.

Although a wide range of materials

may be used for the purpose of enrichment and remembering, including church history, biography, theological and ethical treatises, art, music, poetry, drama, and fiction, the Bible remains the primary source. Much teaching has begun by helping a group explore their needs and the major issues of their expanding world of experience, and turn then to the Bible for assistance in solving their problems. The trend today is to commence with portions of the Scripture, as implied in the concept of "remembering," and encourage a vicarious participation in the recorded events and their meanings.

In the use of the Bible the teacher must take seriously the work of historical and textual criticism and the findings of archaeology. Instruction that enables pupils to lay hold of the knowledge of Biblical scholarship is in no sense to be minimized in importance. But in its dynamic and truly religious dimension, Biblical remembering and learning are existential. Knowledge about one's religion remains important, but instruction that seeks for the learner a personal encounter is centrally redemptive in purpose.

Persistently throughout the lifespan God takes the initiative in entering into the experience of the growing person, desiring to meet him as I-Thou. Instruction serves to evoke and prepare the way for the encounter. — *Paul B. Irwin*

INTEREST The concept of interest (intrinsic motivation) has been propounded for many centuries, especially by writers like Rousseau, Pestalozzi, Herbart, and Dewey. In recent years, however, the doctrine of interest has been somewhat the victim of a changing mood that emphasizes firmer discipline in the classroom, and of motivational research that stresses external manipulation.

Briefly stated, the doctrine of interest refers to the ability or willingness of the individual to give attention to or think about things and experiences that seem to have value for him.

The word "interest" itself is the substantive form of the Latin "to be between"; in other words, that which establishes a relationship between things otherwise unrelated, as, for example, a pupil and a subject to be learned.

The doctrine of interest works on the assumption that where a pupil manifests a preoccupation with a subject or a preference for a certain activity there is no necessity for external compulsion, for he already will have a spirit of enthusiasm and joy in learning, will be engrossed in the learning activity, and will exhibit singleness of purpose.

How can it be determined whether students are interested in a certain activity? They may profess an interest; they may manifest an interest by some observable behavior; they may be tested to see if they have any interest in a certain enterprise; or by means of an inventory it may be gathered that they have a greater preference for one phase of study or activity as over against other areas.

In order to secure initial interest in a study the teacher may have to use the strongest and most fascinating teaching methods and materials at the beginning of the enterprise. If curiosity is high at the onset but is likely to wane rapidly, he may find it expedient to keep the most interesting materials to use later. One may secure immediate attention by any number of devices, but motivation is useful in education only if it sustains interest to the very conclusion of the process.

Among the factors determining how much interest a pupil brings to a learning situation are his native intelligence, the richness of his previous environment, his earlier experiences, the amount of encouragement he receives to study or explore, his whole emotional relationship with teachers and peers, and the life goals of his family and community.

Interest is one of the associative factors of the learning process that may have moderate relationship to the success of an educative enterprise. Studies on the subject discount inherited or inherent preferences and incline toward experience, age, personality development, socioeconomic status — in other words, factors conditioned more by environment. Often what people expect a pupil to do, what he can do well, and what he feels he needs and values may give good indications as to his interests. Certainly pupil interests should be considered in determining both the content and the methods of instruction. — *Howard A. Worth*

INTERNATIONAL MISSIONARY COUNCIL On the opening day of the New Delhi Assembly of the World Council of Churches, Nov., 1961, the International Missionary Council became the Division of World Mission and Evangelism, an integral part of the World Council.

Although the International Missionary Council was established in 1921, its roots go back to 1910. Indeed, it would be more accurate to say that in essence it is as old as the modern missionary movement dating back to William Carey. Not long after Carey went to India in 1793 and gave the modern impetus to missions, he was thinking of cooperation among missionaries and proposed a conference to be held at Cape Town in 1810. The climax of various cooperative efforts came in 1910 when representatives of missionary societies working in non-Christian countries came together in a worldwide conference at Edinburgh.

Directly out of Edinburgh flowed the 3 streams that all finally came together at New Delhi in 1961: Faith and Order (unity), Life and Work (service), and the International Missionary Council (witness).

At Edinburgh was expressed a willingness to respect and recognize differences within the non-Roman and non-Orthodox groups. Also indicated was a desire to work together as Christians in interdenominational and international cooperation. To carry on this work a continuation committee was established with John R. Mott as chairman, and J. A. Oldham as secretary.

Although some conferences were held in America, Europe, and Asia, and National Councils were founded, World War I prevented other action. Soon after this break in international relations, however, at Crans, Switzerland, there came together in 1920 representatives from world missionary bodies. This was another step toward the founding of the International Missionary Council at Lake Mohonk, N.Y., in 1921.

The Council was constituted by the national missionary organizations of a number of countries — the largest being the Foreign Missions Conference of North America. Following the Council's founding, Mott and Oldham carried the worldwide vision to Asia, Africa, Europe, Australia, and New Zealand. *The International Review of Missions,* established at Edinburgh, grew to greater importance. New leadership — Paton, Warnshuis — came in; leaders of the younger churches gave additional support.

The Jerusalem gathering (1928) was concerned with the Christian message in modern secular society and gave a new impetus to the whole field of religious education. The decade from 1928 to 1938, a time of world turmoil — economic depression, war threats, and theological upheaval — was reflected at Madras (Tambaram), 1938, in 2 major thrusts: a concern for the faith and a new awareness of the church.

At Madras the younger churches came into their own, inasmuch as more than half of the delegates were from the former " mission " lands, and they took the lead in many discussions. A wider concern was evidenced by the activities of departmental agencies — social and industrial research, rural surveys, Christian literature and educational commissions, and the Christian approach to the Jews.

By the time of Whitby, 1947, a new day had dawned. New leadership — Mackay, Neill, Van Dusen, Niles, Warren — was taking over, and the new concerns were evangelism and unity under the Lordship of Christ. " Partners in obedience " emphasized the determination to see the worldwide task as one.

Between Whitby and Ghana (1958) came the establishment of the World Council of Churches at Amsterdam in 1948 and the enlarged meeting of the Council at Willingen in 1952. The meeting in Ghana was important as preparation for the future: the Theological Education Fund to lift the training of leaders was established; the integration of the International Missionary Council with the World Council of Churches was approved and referred to national or regional councils for ratification. — *Don W. Holter*

INTER-VARSITY CHRISTIAN FELLOWSHIP

The 1st student chapter of the Inter-Varsity Christian Fellowship in the United States came into existence at the University of Michigan in 1940. The IVCF has grown over the past 2 decades to include chapters and groups in more than 300 colleges and universities. Its organizational lineage goes back to the formation of the Cambridge Intercollegiate Christian Union in 1877. The movement spread to other British universities and became the Inter-Varsity Fellowship of Evangelical Unions in 1923. Five years later, Inter-Varsity Christian Fellowship was organized in Canada, subsequently spreading to the U.S.A.

In ethos, Inter-Varsity also has its roots in the evangelical student societies that have been active in American college and university life for over 250 years. Students at Harvard first banded together for Bible study, prayer, and discussion in 1706 under Cotton Mather's influence. A similar group functioned at Yale in the 1740's, and hundreds of such student-initiated fellowships came into existence in the 19th century. These groups, thoroughly indigenous to the campus, were characterized by student initiative, leadership, and responsibility, and were independent of outside control.

A similar independence is seen in the nature of IVCF chapters today. IVCF chapters generally are a recognized student activity on campus. The responsibility for planning and executing campus programs rests with the students. The Inter-Varsity staff representative, who visits 10 to 15 chapters, serves only in an advisory capacity at such times.

The IVCF is nondenominational, with membership from a wide variety of denominations. Supplementing the ministry of the local church, it is an evangelistic wing of the church on the campus. Chapter and national leaders of IVCF accept the Bible in its entirety as the Word of God written, and the formulations of Biblical doctrine represented by the large areas of agreement in such historic declarations as the Apostles' and Nicene Creeds, the Augsburg, Westminster, and New Hampshire Confessions, and The Thirty-nine Articles of religion.

IVCF has included the Nurses' Christian Fellowship since 1947. Chapters and informal groups carry on a program of evangelism, spiritual growth, and foreign missionary recruitment in 300 colleges and universities, and 160 schools of nursing. Chapters affiliated with the Student Foreign Missions Fellowship are found in 85 Christian colleges, seminaries, and Bible institutes. Inter-Varsity is a member of the International Fellowship of Evangelical Students, organized in 1947.

The ultimate objective of the IVCF is to recruit and train students for the life and work of the church. To that end it has a threefold purpose: evangelism — to communicate the gospel of Jesus Christ through personal witness, group discussions, and mass meetings, in terms relevant to students in a secular culture; Christian maturity — to work out the implications of the Lordship of Jesus Christ in all areas of thought and life during these crucial years; missionary concern — to discover God's purpose for vocation and service in the worldwide mission of the church.

Inter-Varsity also has a concern for the welfare of students from overseas. It conducts an extensive hospitality program for these visitors, both on campus and in conferences.

The Inter-Varsity Press has a publications program offering books and booklets on the Christian witness, Bible study discussions, Christian living, theology, and world missions. *HIS*, the "magazine of campus Christian living," has been published monthly during the academic year since 1941.

An intensive summer training program is carried out through a number of camps across the country. Sessions range from 1 to 4 weeks and are designed to train leaders for the college and university chapters. Special attention is given to personal evangelism and the leading of inductive Bible-study groups. Qualified scholars present messages on the elements of Biblical and systematic theology, contemporary thought, and the overseas extension of the Christian mission. The camps also help students develop a personal devotional life and counsel them on vocational possibilities. These camps are supplemented throughout the year by weekend and holiday conferences. Every 3 years since 1948 a student missionary convention has been held at the University of Illinois to present the implications of the Great Commission in today's world. Several thousand students have attended each of these conferences at Urbana.

— *Charles E. Hummel*

ISLAM Education in Islam made religion include and dominate all life's interests and activities. The religion it promoted is that of Muhammad and the Koran, the Muslim religion. Muslims dislike the name

Muhammadan. "Islam" means "submission," "surrender." Its adjective, "Muslim," applied to the religion, implies relationship to Islam; applied to adherents, it means surrendered to Allah. "Allah" is used by Arabic-speaking Jews, Christians, and Muslims for "God."

The pre-Islamic Arabs had no formal educational institutions. Theirs was a tribal society, chiefly nomadic, each tribe moving its tents and flocks within its own accustomed range. They developed self-reliant personalities, regulated by customs and taught by family experience how to survive under hardship and scarcity, and yet to practice hospitality. Even those who settled in villages and towns jealously retained their tribal identity. Mecca in Muhammad's time listed 10 clans. The youth of each generation was taught his own genealogy and his tribe's heroes and enemies.

Early Arabian culture was not expressed in splendid architecture or artistic handicrafts. The basic materials for these were not available. Rather, it is enshrined in its language and expressed, not in the prose of fable, philosophy, or science, but in poetry. Pre-Islamic Arabic poetry, all Arabs have always declared, is the best in the language. It was, and still is, preserved in the memories of illiterate as well as literate Arabs. Some prized poems received written form even before Muhammad's time.

Besides poetry, the Arabs had produced much practical philosophy in finely expressed proverbs. This early language, although 1500 years old, because of the Koran, is not alien to today's literary Arabic. Both the proverbs and the poetry survive because of their intrinsic excellence. Even in translation the poetry has powerfully impressed Western people, especially those endowed with poetic appreciation and facility, such as Tennyson and Browning in England and Emerson and Whittier in America.

Muhammad himself was illiterate. Islam teaches that Muhammad's recited pronouncements were divinely composed and therefore both inimitable as literature and supreme for religion. Muhammed's other words and acts were considered to be God-directed and therefore also authoritative. Muslims obey the Koran and traditions acceptably ascribed to Muhammad. Only Allah is worshiped. As Christianity progressed from Judaism, so Islam as founded by Muhammad, 610–632, has paganism, Judaism, and Christianity as background. Later, non-Arabic systems of thought influenced its development.

Formal education in Islam was begun by Muhammad. After the victorious battle of Badr (A.D. 624), Meccan prisoners of war earned their ransoms by teaching children in al-Madīnah to read and write, using portions of the Koran that Muhammad had recited and his followers had written. Thus the Koran became Islam's 1st primer and so has continued for nearly 50 generations of literate Muslims.

The various subjects of early Muslim education were Koran-inspired. Its vocabulary led to the production of anthologies of poetry, dictionaries, grammars, and philology. Facing Mecca in worship gave importance to geometry and astronomy. Pilgrimage and travel for traditions involved geography. The demand for a written Koran promoted calligraphy, Arabic Islam's only artistic handicraft, which was not destroyed by Muhammad 'Ali's introduction of the 1st

Koran text printed with separate type. The call to worship led to minaret-building, Islam's chief gift to architecture. Loudspeakers are now making minarets unnecessary, just as lithography is making the handwritten Koran uneconomical.

After Muhammad's first 4 successors (khalīfahs) the Umayyad regime of 14 ruled Islam from Damascus (661–750). This period brought the Arabs into contact with Greek, Persian, Indian, and other cultures, older than and different from their own.

Outside Arabia, medicine, philosophy, and the mathematical, political, and social sciences had flourished. Books on all subjects in the original languages were numerous in Mediterranean Europe and Western Asia. Some Arabs learned these languages. Others married the daughters of foreign families. Non-Arab teachers and scholars and the new generations of the conquered peoples became Muslims. Arabian energy produced a culture new to Islam. Jews, Christians, and others, whether they became Muslim or not, became translators and authors, writing in Arabic, which became the lingua franca of the Islamdom of the premedieval period of European history.

During the Umayyad period education was not under government control but rather remained a voluntary or family activity. However, the central government provided Koran manuscripts, making for easier reading and understanding. Government fiscal accounts were written in Arabic, instead of Greek and Persian. The best cultural monument is the Dome of the Rock in Jerusalem, built in 691.

The Arabs as Muslims in 100 years extended their empire to the Atlantic Ocean, to Central Asia and the Indian subcontinent. That revealed their military and political prowess. But in religion divisions multiplied. Kharijite, Shiʻa, Muʻtazila and other sects separated themselves from Sunni orthodoxy. Each group claimed exclusively correct adherence to the Koran and its 2 clauses that had become the universal Muslim creed: There is no god at all but Allah (37:34 and 47:21), and Muhammad is the apostle of Allah (48:29).

When Islam's geographical expanse westward ceased at Tours in 732, Muslim cultural superiority began and continued until 1100. That was Islam's golden age of religious and secular culture. Intensive educational activity by Jews, Christians, Sabaeans (Mandaeans) and Muslims put the learning of the known world into Arabic in quantity and quality hitherto unequaled.

Islam's greatest contribution to its flowering during the early Abbasid dynasty (750–1258) was its strong belief in one supreme God, the creator of the universe and the immediate cause of all that ever occurs, along with his complete guidance for the life of mankind through his messenger, Muhammad. Education, although sometimes sectarian, as in Fatimid Egypt, was everywhere available to all boys and frequently, within limits, to girls. It was never compulsory. The poorest of boys could become the Chief Justice of the Empire at Baghdad, and one did.

In Spain, orthodox Islam did its best to make its culture attractive. Muslims promoted the translation into Latin of the ancient Greek learning that had been put into Arabic in the East. This occurred 3 centuries before the fall of Constantinople in 1453 spread Christian refugees all over central Europe with their books in the original Greek.

When the unchristian crusaders from Europe invaded Western Asia in the 12th century and the Mongols of Central Asia moved westward in the 13th, education and its consequent culture were smothered. The Ottoman Empire officials later fostered their own ideals of political power and exploitation. Liberal education in arts and sciences for all was not promoted. Dervish orders for religious satisfaction flourished. The lack of material welfare prevented their educational and cultural improvement.

Islam has always included both beliefs and practices. Many officials and other leaders remained within the bounds of Islam by their conformity in observances while intellectually they adopted non-Muslim ideas. Muslim belief held that Allah's will immediately and directly causes all occurrences. Another Muslim belief is that the early religious leaders had made new judgments and new ways unnecessary. Practically everywhere Islam became static, backward, decadent.

Napoleon's invasion of Egypt in 1798 marks the first turning of the tide. The Arab awakening followed. A new spirit arose, with new ideas of political freedom, social justice, and education for social betterment through the natural sciences and technology.

In this century thousands of Muslims, largely through Western educational institutions in the East and Muslim students in Europe and America, have been preparing a new era based on mutual understanding through association and education.
— *Edwin E. Calverley*

ITALY Christian education in Italy always has been predominantly Roman Catholic. However, due to secular trends prevailing at the time, the Coppino Laws caused religious teaching to be suppressed in the state schools in 1877. Fascist educational reforms restored religious teaching in primary schools in 1923. The Concordat of 1929 states: " Italy considers the teaching of Christian doctrine according to the Catholic tradition the beginning and end of public instruction " (Article 36). One hour weekly of religious instruction given by priests, monks, or laymen approved by the ecclesiastical authorities was introduced into the secondary schools also, comprising 5 years of Roman Catholic doctrine and 2 years of Bible-teaching, without examinations. The catechism is taught by the clergy, and children are confirmed at 6 or 7 years of age.

Secular, even Marxist, influences are possible in schools today because of liberties allowed to teachers; sometimes this neutralizes the Roman Catholic doctrine. Most pupils attend the state schools. Of 6,420,100 pupils in 1958–1959, only 429,104 attended church schools. Through the Christian Democratic Party the Vatican advances its thesis that " education is primarily the concern of the church and the family, because of the indelibility of both natural and divine rights (*Divini Illius Magistri,* 1929, confirmed by Pope John XXIII, 1959). The state ought to protect the rights of the family and the church; it cannot, therefore, compel attendance at its schools, but rather, must favor the development of confessional schools and give them equal support, leaving to families freedom of choice between them, in accordance with Article 30 of the Italian Constitution. Italian Catholic schools have developed considerably since 1942 and are federated in the Federazione Instituti Dipendenti dall'-Autorità Ecclesiastica. Among religious orders the Jesuits, Scolopi, Brothers of the Christian Schools, and especially the Salesians are very active in Christian education. Catholic Action also works among youth and older persons, training them for the lay apostolate in the modern world.

Theological faculties at state universities were suppressed by the Correnti Law (1872). But there are numerous theological faculties and papal universities in Rome today, e.g., the Gregoriana (Jesuit, founded 1552) with the Bible Institute, and a number of athenaea, viz., Lateranense (1824), Urbanum "De Propaganda Fide" (1624), Angelicum (1580), St. Anselmo (1687), Antonianum (1933), Salesianum (1940). These have an international character, preparing teachers for many countries. There are also many ecclesiastical colleges of non-university status. Elsewhere in Italy there are 5 theological faculties and numerous seminaries. The University of the Sacred Heart, founded in 1920 at Milan, has 14,000 students and has branches in Piacenza and Rome.

Among Italy's 50 million inhabitants there are about 100,000 scattered Protestants, who enjoy religious liberty. Their children may claim exemption from Catholic teaching in schools, according to the Law of the Recognized Religions (1929) and receive their own education in Sunday schools and catechism classes. Confirmation is between 14 and 17 years. In the Waldensian villages (Piedmont) the Waldensian Church supports 2 secondary schools and 3 colleges. In Piedmont, too, the state schools often have a Protestant character due to the fact that Protestants are in the majority of the population. In several parts of the peninsula and in Sicily, Protestant congregations support kindergartens and schools. The Methodist Casa Materna does important evangelical relief and educational work among the poorest children of Naples. Foreign Protestant congregations often have schools for their nationals.

Besides periodicals and books, another means of Protestant education is the youth centers (all founded since World War II), e.g., Agape (Waldensian); Ecumene (Methodist), in Velletri, near Rome; Santa Severa (Baptist), near Civitavecchia; and Carro (Lutheran), near Varese. The Y.M.C.A. (since 1851), Y.W.C.A, and Salvation Army join in religious education. Pentecostals, Adventists, and Jehovah's Witnesses have active programs featuring correspondence courses in Biblical material. The Waldensians have a theological seminary in Rome (founded 1855 in Torre Pellice) and the Baptists a Bible school in Rivoli (Turin), thus influencing theological education for the ministry.

— T. Valdo Vinay

J

JAPAN In late 1587 the then military government of Japan looked adversely upon Christianity, which had been brought into the country by Francis Xavier, a Roman Catholic priest, in 1549 and had flourished in the western part of the country. It was banned with the penalty of capital punishment. The entire population were required to register at one of the local Buddhist temples.

In 1859, after the country had been opened to foreign trade, both Roman Catholic and Protestant missionaries came to Japan. Signboards on the streets prohibiting the citizenry from having anything to do with Christianity remained for 14 years, and the 1st official announcement of freedom of religion was not made until the national Constitution was adopted in February, 1889.

At first, Christianity was taught in private Bible-study groups to youth who came to missionaries for English-language study. This eventuated in Christian mission schools for boys and girls. Many future leaders of the country were trained in these schools, including some who became leaders among the intelligentsia. There are now 6 universities, 12 junior colleges for women, 89 high schools, and 51 primary schools under the Roman Catholic Church, and 18 universities with 7 postgraduate schools, 34 junior colleges, 142 high schools, and 17 primary schools under the Protestant Churches, some of the latter not related to mission boards. About ⅔ of the congregations in Japan have kindergartens and day nurseries. The curriculum outline for the higher schools is set up by the Government, whereas the preschool curricula are largely free for the churches to organize as they see fit.

The earliest attempts at Sunday schools among Protestants seem to have been made in the fall of 1873 by a Methodist missionary's wife in Tokyo and by a missionary in Kobe. By 1878 it was possible to have the 1st students' Sunday school rally in Tokyo at Shin-Sakae Church, when 200 girls from 7 mission schools and 200 adults assembled. The organized Sunday school movement in Japan was begun in 1898 under the support of the World Sunday School Association. A national convention of Sunday school workers was held at Shiba Church, Tokyo, in May, 1907, at which time the Japan National Sunday School Association was formally organized. For 11 years the association developed closely graded lesson materials, conducted teacher training, and published journals. The 10th world Sunday school convention, held in Tokyo in 1920, stimulated an interest in children's religious education and even inspired the Buddhists to open Sunday schools (for their own faith) in their temples, adapting some features of the Christian Sunday school program. The association was eventually merged into the United Church of Christ as the Department of Sunday Schools in 1940.

Air raids destroyed about 75 percent of the church buildings in the country during World War II and greatly reduced (due to fatalities) the Christian population, which had been about 300,000. Since the war, the church has had to undergo a process of rebuilding its entire life. The church, which had been unified by Government action in 1940, faced the withdrawal of some denominations and the importation of new denominations by missionary efforts from abroad. The National Christian Council was formed, with the Church School Activity Department as a constituent part. In recent years, religious education was much influenced by the theology of Karl Barth.

Although the 1st modern Christian missionary arrived in Japan over 100 years ago, the entire Christian population of the country is only .7 percent, or 7 Christians to 1,000 non-Christians. Thus every phase of church activity, including its religious education, must possess an evangelistic challenge. A unified Sunday school curriculum was published in 1957 on the basis of 3-year cycles on the themes of Jesus Christ, the Bible, and the church, covering the preschool ages to post high school in 8 courses. An audio-visual aids commission is providing new materials for the use of the churches.
—*Sabrow Yasumura*

JEHOVAH'S WITNESSES Jehovah's Witnesses are a society of persons from all walks of life who have dedicated their lives to Jehovah God, the supreme Sovereign, and who recognize as a primary reason for their existence as a united world organization the fulfilling of Jesus' words: "This good news of the kingdom will be preached in all the inhabited earth" before the foretold end of the present system of things comes (Matt. 24:14).

Convinced through a study of the Bible that this world has reached the prophesied time of the Lord's return, they have directed all their efforts from the early 1870's to advertising this event to all peoples of the world. This has resulted in the printing of over a billion pieces of Bible literature in over 140 languages, most of which has been distributed to people in their homes. They follow the primitive pattern of teaching set by Jesus and his apostles, using as pulpits the doorsteps, living rooms, store counters, ball parks, stadiums, and civic auditoriums of all lands. This method of Bible instruction has produced 1,000 new active ministers, not mere members, each week since 1950 and has resulted in the organizing of 1 new congregation somewhere in the world every day of the year.

The name Jehovah's Witnesses is taken from the Bible at Isa. 43:10 (ASV), which says: "Ye are my witnesses, saith Jehovah, and my servant whom I have chosen." In modern times the organized work of Jehovah's Witnesses began about 1872. Charles Taze Russell was 1st president of the Watch Tower Bible and Tract Society from the time of its incorporation in 1884. This society is one of many corporations chartered by Jehovah's Witnesses to aid them in their worldwide activity. When C. T. Russell died in 1916, he was succeeded by Joseph Franklin Rutherford, who was president until his death in 1942. Nathan H. Knorr became president in 1942.

Jehovah's Witnesses have no creed but the Bible, which they accept as the inspired Word of God and hold as setting forth the only true revelation of God's name, his will for his creatures, and his own purpose to sanctify his name in the earth through the complete restoration of the Paradise that he created and which Adam, the 1st man, forfeited. Jehovah's Witnesses believe that man's present dying condition is the result of Adam's sin of disobedience of God's law, which brought death to him and condemnation to all his offspring (Rom. 5:12). God's justice required the forfeiture of Adam's right to life, but God's mercy toward those of Adam's children who desire a return to God's favor makes possible a provision for their reconciliation and eventual restoration to the right of everlasting life. That provision is the ransom sacrifice of Jesus Christ, who left his prehuman existence in Heaven as a Spirit Son of God and became flesh and blood as an exact corresponding price for the life forfeited by Adam (Matt. 20:28; I Tim. 2:5-6). His voluntary sacrifice of his perfect human life has not only resulted in a way of redemption for obedient mankind, but has brought Jesus himself a reward of a resurrection to heaven, this time at the right hand of God as an immortal Spirit, now in position to rule as God's rightful King of all the world (I Peter 3:18-22). Since 1914, God's government has been ruling in Heaven and within this generation will move against all governments of men on earth, replacing them after the final war of Armageddon with a rule of righteousness that will never end. Those now warned who find God's way of escape will survive Armageddon into that endless paradise that will then be restored (Rev. 16:13-16; 21:1-5).

Their sense of urgency regarding the message they bear is what has stimulated the activity and subsequent growth of the organization. Each of Jehovah's Witnesses spends, on the average, about 10 hours monthly preaching the gospel to others and conducting Bible studies in homes. In addition, he spends another 30 to 40 hours in studying the Scriptures privately and in connection with the 5 weekly Bible studies provided by each congregation through the facilities of its central meeting place, the local Kingdom Hall of Jehovah's Witnesses. Personal training and Bible instruction are vital parts of the educational program being conducted in this way. As a result, those who become interested in the message through the preaching work, themselves become teachers of the Word as they appreciate and accept its significance, dedicating their lives to Jehovah God and taking up his service in the interest of the world of mankind not yet reached by the good news. — *Nathan H. Knorr*

JESUS CHRIST In a unique sense, Jesus Christ *is* the Christian religion. Unlike the founders of other faiths, he is not basically a religious " hero " or a spiritual teacher and guide, nor is he a pattern and example to be imitated or a mythological embodiment of man's spiritual yearnings. According to the New Testament, he is a historical character who conceived of his life and death as the unique event whereby the Kingdom of God was to be established. Into this Kingdom all men were to be summoned to enter by faith in order to know forgiveness of sins, to overcome their alienation from God, and to receive from God as sheer grace the gift of eternal life. Christianity is the conviction that this purpose which Jesus attached to his life and death was indeed the action of God.

As presented in the New Testament, neither Jesus' teachings, whether by sayings or parables, nor his mighty works, nor the course of his life which moved inexorably toward his death on the cross, can be understood apart from the conviction that these were all parts of God's decisive, redeeming act in behalf of man. Jesus did not merely speak words about God; he was a Word from God. He was not a mere man with a uniquely keen sense of mystical communion with God or a mere human teacher of an ethic of uncommonly exalted nature, nor was he a mere human embodiment of the highest spiritual and religious values. The directional focus of the New Testament with regard to Jesus is not a climb from the human to the divine but, rather, a condescension of God to man in gracious action for man's salvation.

This is confirmed by the relationship which the apostolic church saw between Jesus and the Old Testament. The Old Testament is not a mythology or a collection of spiritually edifying stories or meditations. It is a history of the people of God, with whom and through whom God was acting in a unique way for the redemption of the world. The Old Testament is a record of " the saving acts of the Lord " (Micah 6:5). Jesus saw himself as the one who was to inaugurate the final act in this divine drama of history. " The time [of which the prophets spoke] is fulfilled, and the kingdom of God is at hand; repent, and believe in the gospel [the " good news " that the Kingdom is now being inaugurated]." (Mark 1:15.) The New Testament writers likewise saw Jesus as the climax of the Old Testament history, the final and decisive " saving act of the Lord." At Pentecost, Peter proclaimed: " This is what was spoken by the prophet Joel " (Acts 2:16; cf. 10:43). Paul reiterated: " We bring you the good news that what God promised to the fathers, this he has fulfilled . . . [in] Jesus " (Acts 13:32 f.). The apostolic witnesses are unanimous in seeing in Jesus one " whom God put forward " (Rom. 3:25). Jesus is God's supreme saving act in the history of salvation and as such is the very essence of Christianity.

This conviction is embedded in the Gospels as a sort of substructure on which every pillar of the whole story rests. It is dramatically apparent in the miracle stories. Only a superficial reading of these can see in them artificial efforts to exalt Jesus' significance by presenting him as a wonder-worker. The miracles are, rather, presented in connection with the teaching of Jesus as Messianic claims. In them Jesus is engaged in God's battle against evil and is manifested as God's instrument by which that battle is to be won. Through the miracles, Jesus is doing what the prophets pictured would happen in the Messianic Age (see Matt. 8:17). The mighty works, then, were done not to excite mere wonder but as signs that the drama of the Old Testament was reaching its climax, that the one who does the wonders is the Messiah in the midst of God's people, challenging evil at every level and inaugurating God's final act of redemption.

The same is true of Jesus' teachings. Both Jesus' sayings and his parables have beneath them an undercurrent of meaning that transforms them from mere ethical maxims and spiritual counsel into Messianic claims. The sayings in the Sermon on the Mount have their Christian significance in the claim that the one who spoke them was inaugurating God's Kingdom, of which these were the new law. The parable of the prodigal son has its meaning not only in a new idea about God — that God is kind to prodigals. It is not likely that those who disagreed with this idea of God's would have sent Jesus to the cross for holding it. The parable is told in connection with the fact that "tax collectors and sinners were all drawing near to hear him" (Luke 15:1). The anger of Jesus' enemies was stirred by this: "This man receives sinners and eats with them" (Luke 15:2). Jesus' parable about God's receiving prodigals has its full meaning only in connection with the fact that Jesus was receiving prodigals. By his behavior, coupled with his story, he was implying: *I stand in the place of God to men!* And for this — not for the story — he died. His teachings, as his mighty works, draw their significance from his Person.

The unique relationship that Jesus bore to God, however, as well as the unique mission he came to perform as God's final redeeming deed, can be seen only by faith.

Jesus came in great humiliation, despised and rejected by men, a man of sorrows whose destiny was a cross. There was no outward display that could be interpreted apart from faith. The resurrection was God's authentication of Jesus' mission to those who believed. It indicated that his humiliation was prelude to glory, and that in him God's final action for men was one of victory over the last and worst resource of evil — death. But the resurrection was witnessed by no one. It is certain, however, that those who believed in him bore witness that he met with them after his death in ways not open to historical investigation but which were nonetheless real — sufficiently real to convince them that Jesus was God's victorious act over death, to annihilate their own fear of death, to make Jesus' presence with them the ultimate reality in their lives, to mold them by the coming of the Holy Spirit at Pentecost into a unified community created and sustained by their certainty of the living presence of this crucified and living Lord, and to send them into the world with the passionate proclamation that Jesus who died was alive as the final good news that every man must hear and be summoned to believe. This conviction cannot be proved. It can only be heard and believed — or disbelieved. But there can be no question that the apostolic church believed that the Jesus who had died was very much alive and that it was he who created, and sustained, and was at work in their individual and corporate lives. The dynamic by which the early church survived persecution was their conviction that by the resurrection God had given to him "all authority in heaven and on earth" (Matt. 28:18). He therefore "reigns" both as "the ruler of kings on earth" (Rev. 1:5) and of the "invisible . . . authorities" of the cosmos (Col. 1:16).

As his earthly humiliation concealed his identity, so his present Lordship is hidden, seen only by faith. But the final "end" will come, when "every eye will see him" (Rev. 1:7) and "every tongue confess that Jesus Christ is Lord" (Phil. 2:11). In the meantime, the church exists to bear witness both by word and by life to his hidden Lordship in the power and joy of his promise: "Lo, I am with you always, to the close of the age" (Matt. 28:20).

— *Donald G. Miller*

JOURNALS In the field of Christian education there is no dearth of printed materials. Among the many publications there are 4 representative journals cutting across denominational lines and designed to serve different purposes.

Religious Education is a bimonthly publication of the Religious Education Association, whose membership includes Protestant, Roman Catholic, Orthodox, and Jewish constituents. It is a magazine primarily for the professional and the scholar. Its readers are among those concerned with the improvement of religious education at every level. Within its pages will be found articles, symposia, and research reports on leadership training, curriculum development, private and parochial education, intercultural relations, theology and religious education, and problems of religion and higher education.

The *International Journal of Religious Education* is a monthly publication (except for August) of the Commission on General Christian Education of the National Council of the Churches of Christ in the U.S.A. It is written especially for laymen who serve as teachers and leaders of the Sunday church school. Its pages provide a means of giving general information in the total area of Christian education. Each issue includes "Worship Resources" for leaders and teachers in the primary, junior, junior high, and senior high departments as well as evaluations of projected audio-visual materials. Occasionally a special issue is devoted to a particular theme, such as "Teacher and Administrator Work Together," "Drama in Christian Education," "Families in the Church," "Church Vocations," "How to Use Audio-Visuals in Christian Education," "Church and College," "Art in Christian Education," "Building and Equipment," "The Christian Education of Adults," or "What Is Christian Education?"

World Christian Education, a quarterly published by the World Council of Christian Education and Sunday School Association, provides a means through which leaders in Christian education around the world are able to share and exchange experiences, information, and ideas of common concern. Most issues contain contributions from over 15 countries. The publishers claim a distribution that reaches into almost 100 countries.

The Christian Scholar is a quarterly publication of the Commission on Higher Education of the National Council of the Churches of Christ in the U.S.A. It is addressed to professors, administrators, and students. It reflects the ecumenical life and work of the church in relation to higher education. Some of its characteristic emphases include the relation of Christian faith to the vocation of the scholar, the role of the Christian college, and the nature and task of higher education in relation to both the cultural crisis and theological concerns.

While the major publications in the field until the late 1930's or early 1940's were *Religious Education* and the *International Journal*, the depression years brought a decline in their circulation. The new interest in worship, Biblical studies, the revival of the various historic Christian traditions, as well as the new ecumenical concern, led to the appearance of a great number of journals published by individual denominations, each designed to provide practical help and guidance to the leaders of the local church in the whole area of Christian education. These became channels through which the official position and faith of a denomination could be shared with local church leaders. Greater emphasis was placed on the teachings of the church and matters of faith compared with the former stress on administration, teaching techniques, and "building Christian character."

During this same period there appeared a new urgency on the part of the denominations to rethink, experiment, and restructure curriculum materials. Along with this restructuring came new denominational journals or a new type of editorial policy for those already in existence. They were tied very closely to the "stream" of curriculum materials and designed for leaders in the local church educational program. These denominational publications include, among others, *The Church School* (Methodist), *The Christian Educator* (United Presbyterian U.S.A.), *The Baptist Leader* (American Baptist) *Presbyterian Ac-*

tion (Presbyterian U.S.), *Bethany Church School Guide* (Disciples of Christ), *Findings* (Protestant Episcopal), *Church School Worker* (United Church of Christ), *Resource* (Lutheran), and *Leader* (Church of the Brethren).

Some journals are devoted mainly to special areas of concern. Each issue can be devoted to providing more complete information, guidance, and resources than could be included in a general publication. Among such journals are *Children's Religion* (United Church of Christ), *The Church Librarian* and *Church Recreation* (both Southern Baptist).

— *Donald L. Leonard*

JUDAISM Judaism is generally defined as the religion of the Jewish people. In recent years, philosophers such as Mordecai M. Kaplan have used the term "Judaism" to refer to the "evolving religious civilization" of the Jewish people, reserving the term "Jewish religion" for that aspect of the civilization which deals with the beliefs and practices directly related to God, rituals, and other sacred activities.

The Jewish people is that chain of generations which traces its origins to Abraham of the Bible. Although the line of descent has not always been direct from the patriarch because throughout the centuries men and women have been converted to Judaism, those whose biological ancestry derives from other families of the earth have, nevertheless, adopted Abraham as their ancestor and the entire tradition as their own tradition. Hence, conversion to Judaism involves not only the acceptance of basic beliefs and responsibilities but also absorption into the "household of Israel."

Thus the religion of the Jews has always been confined to those who regard themselves as members of the Jewish people. In this respect, Judaism does not separate religion from peoplehood. During certain periods in Jewish history, the hope was expressed that the nations would acknowledge the God of Israel as the God of the entire world; but it was also assumed that in doing so they would become Jews. At other times, particularly after the 1st century of the Christian era, when the center of gravity shifted to the world to come, the rabbis taught that Gentiles, too, were qualified for salvation in the hereafter, provided they lived in accordance with the so-called Seven Commandments of the Sons of Noah, which dealt with justice between man and man, the prohibition of idol worship, blasphemy, incest, murder, theft, and the prohibition of eating parts cut from living animals. At no time, however, did the Jews conceive of anyone's adopting the Jewish religion without at the same time identifying himself with the Jewish people.

This indissoluble relation between religion and peoplehood accounts for the continuity of Judaism throughout a long history, despite the far-reaching changes that the Jewish people experienced. This history may be divided into 3 major periods. The 1st begins with the earliest memories of the people reaching back to Abraham (ca. 2000 B.C.) and continuing down to the period of the 1st captivity (586 B.C.). The events of that period are recorded in the Pentateuch, the books of Joshua, Judges, Samuel, and Kings. The books of the prophets (Isaiah, Jeremiah, Ezekiel, Amos, Hosea, etc.) also throw light upon the life of the Jewish people in that era. The era is characterized mainly by the following: the occupation of the land of Israel; the establishment of a self-governing nation with a king at the head (during the divided Kingdom, each nation had its own sovereign); the worship of YHWH as the God of Israel, at first at altars in many places, later at 1 central Temple in Jerusalem; the absence of any clear ideas concerning life after death; the stress upon righteousness as the true way of living; the belief that obedience to God's law spelled wealth and security, and disobedience, destruction and exile from the land.

The 2d period dates from the destruction of the Temple by the Babylonians in 586 B.C. until, roughly, the destruction of the 2d Temple by the Romans in A.D. 70. This period may be described as having the following outstanding characteristics: the status of Judea as a province of a larger empire, first Persia, then Syria, then Rome; the creation and development of the synagogue as an institution of worship and study; the adoption of the Torah as the "constitution" of the Jewish people; the replacement of the king by the priests as the source of authority; the importation of foreign ideas such as angelology and life after death into accepted Jewish thought; the development of an oral law running parallel to the written law, expounding and expanding the written law; the coexistence of the Jews living on the land with those communities of Jews who remained living outside the land but maintaining close bonds with the land through periodic pilgrimages to the Temple and the payment of the annual half-shekel tax. (It should be mentioned parenthetically that for a brief time, an independent sovereign state was established after the Maccabean rebellion [168 B.C.] against the Syrian Greeks; but with the advent of the Romans, Judea became a province of Rome.)

The 3d period, lasting from A.D. 70 until approximately the 18th century, is frequently referred to as the Rabbinic period, because authority was shifted from the priest to the rabbi. During this era, Jews were scattered throughout a broad Diaspora (Dispersion), living in religiously and culturally autonomous communities (ghettos). Jews attributed their "exile" to disobedience of the Torah, and prayed 3 times a day for God's forgiveness and their own return to the land. They believed that in God's own time they would be redeemed by the coming of the Messiah, a descendant of the royal house of David, who would summon them back home and reestablish the sovereign state. Those who would have died before his coming would be resurrected, brought to the land of Israel, and together with those living at the time would be subjected to a Final Judgment. Those who qualified would then be privileged to inhabit the world to come; the others would be destroyed forever.

To be worthy of the world to come, the Jews sought to live in obedience to the entire corpus of Jewish laws, which they reckoned to include 613 commandments (the sum of the written and oral laws combined). This included ritual as well as ethical commands; the observance of the Sabbath and festivals, daily prayers, donning the phylacteries each weekday ("as a sign on your hand or frontlets between your eyes"); and the giving of char-

ity, redeeming the captives, offering hospitality to the stranger, visiting the sick, etc.

The end of the 18th century and the beginning of the 19th marked a radical turning point in the history of the Jews, and hence of Judaism. With the breakdown of the ghetto, Jews were admitted to full citizenship in the new democratic nations of the West, and were exposed to the Enlightenment. For the 1st time they were able to identify themselves with other nations without having to surrender their Jewish religion. However, basic changes had to be introduced in order to adjust Judaism to the new conditions of emancipation. Thus they had to modify their ideas of "exile." They could no longer regard themselves as Judeans awaiting their redemption. Some, however, with the advent of modern anti-Semitism, did indeed leave the countries of the Dispersion and reestablish a sovereign state in Israel.

This state, however, created by Zionists, was itself a revolutionary departure from tradition, since its founders did not regard themselves as bound to wait passively for the supernatural Redeemer. How the traditionalists in Israel will reconcile themselves to the modern, secular state of Israel remains to be seen. In the meantime, various interpretations of Judaism for the Diaspora have sprung up, each seeking to adapt Judaism to the new conditions of life. The Reform movement stresses the uniqueness of the Jewish idea of God and the Jews' mission to disseminate it to the world. The Orthodox stress continued obedience to the *Shulhan Arukh* (the code of Jewish practice widely recognized) as a means of attaining spiritual perfection. The Conservative movement is a more liberal interpretation of Orthodoxy. The Reconstructionist movement, of recent origin, stresses Judaism as a spiritual civilization with Israel as the center.

— *Ira Eisenstein*

JUNIOR CHURCH " Junior church " was a term familiar in the Boston area in the 1930's and 1940's for an experiment started by a Unitarian minister, Dan Huntington Fenn, who achieved a distinguished level of teaching his church children almost single-handedly. Because of the response of children and the appreciation of their parents, the plan was copied by other churches. Such was the vitality of 1 junior church led by a suburban minister's wife — herself an ordained minister — that a diminutive colonial church was built on the exact model of the parent church. But today little is heard of what seemed destined for success.

The plan is for a number of grades to meet in 1 group — grades 5 through 9, or a junior high department, or even the senior highs, with the leadership taken by the top grade. The worship service is held in the church nave, those attending being seated by ushers as in any church. If adults come, they, too, are there to worship, not to supervise. The order of worship is like that in the adult church, except that the reading of the Scripture is followed by commentary and interpretation, while the congregation consult the Bible. The sermon continues and applies the subject of the lesson, the 2 periods using about 35 minutes of the hour. Informality is permitted in these periods; sometimes there are questions, with a show of hands indicating those ready to answer. The entire service, except for Scripture, sermon, and pastoral prayer, is conducted by 1 of the elected officers.

As in many churches a junior church depends upon a choir, a board of deacons (or other officers), and a number of active committees — finance, membership, ushers, library, social action, bell ringers. Committees require frequent meetings and are chaired by members of the top grade under some adult supervision. In congregational meetings, elections are held and such important matters as the objects of offerings are decided upon. A small library is needed for background books, along with maps, charts, a globe, copies of great religious art. Weekday activities are a possibility, such as religious drama groups, expeditions, parties.

As for subject matter taught, in one junior church the 1st year was given to the Old Testament, the 2d to the life of Jesus, the 3d to Jesus' teachings and the life of Paul, the 4th to church history.

Obviously, this method is not suited to a church whose minister is not gifted in preaching to young people or who does not choose this time-devouring project. As the membership of a junior church had best not exceed 75 so that no one will be lost in the crowd, or number less than 25, very large and very small churches are ruled out. Critics point to the fact that this method goes against every psychological truth about teaching. The denominations do not promote or approve the method. And the fact that committed church school teachers are deprived of their classes is another criticism.

But there are advantages. First, it is not in the least like day school, of which most children have enough during the week. It usually increases enrollment and attendance, because they like it and want to come. There are few disciplinary problems and what there are can be dealt with in no uncertain terms by ushers, or even by the whole governing body. Though the minister needs some adult helpers, such as choir director and librarian, he is spared the often impossible task of supplying qualified teachers for all grades in the church school. It is evident that young people consider a junior church their own, are proud of it, look forward to holding office, and recommend it to their friends, sometimes from unchurched families. In the course of several years they learn churchmanship and enter naturally into adult church membership.

It should be added that the term "junior church" also had been loosely used to designate the opening worship prior to the class session in church school.

— *Margaret M. Morton*

JUNIOR DEPARTMENT The "junior department," as the term is used generally, is that part of the church which includes boys and girls in the 4th, 5th, and 6th grades of school. Included also are the adults whom the church has designated as the leaders in the junior department.

The juniors themselves are neither children nor adolescents. Boys tend to be noisy and girls giggly. They often disregard adults' standards of good behavior. They have a tremendous desire to be accepted by a group of their own age and sex. They are defining their own sex roles. Though this period of later childhood is a time for asserting independence, juniors continue to have a need for understanding

adults upon whom they can rely. At this age, boys and girls want to be useful and find satisfaction in making others happy. They can share responsibly in planning and work, and can fulfill leadership tasks. Justice and fair play are extremely important to them. Curiosity pushes them to question sometimes, and on occasion to do profound thinking.

To meet some of the specific needs of the junior, the church must provide for him a group in which he feels accepted and important. Thus, the supportive fellowship with his peers and with adults in the church helps him come to a greater understanding of God's steadfast love, and he can experience on his own level the reality of God's guidance and strengthening power.

Places of leadership and service give opportunity for maturing and developing skills. As juniors reach out to others in service they gain understandings of others' needs, and confidence in their own ability to be useful in helping to fulfill God's purposes in the world. Jesus' life and teachings have special appeal for juniors.

Recognizing the many needs that boys and girls have at the junior level, church leaders need to provide a rich and varied program. It should include worship, study, service, fun, and fellowship. Each type of program activity provides for specific kinds of learning and growth.

In most churches there is a Sunday church school session of 1 hour, although an increasing number of churches are lengthening their sessions to 2 or 3 hours. It is a classroom situation. In some instances, classes are expected to meet together for worship. However, groups that meet in their own rooms for the entire session are able to use the available time to greater advantage. Study, planning, work, worship, and other activities can be woven flexibly into a unified program. On occasion, and as there is reason, 1 group may join another group for some activity.

During the summer months daily vacation church school sessions of 2 to 3 hours may be provided for a period of 1, 2, or more weeks. This is usually a classroom situation with opportunity for study, worship, and work activities. The day-to-day schedule of longer sessions makes possible a greater variety of activities, a more relaxed experience, and deepening personal relationships. In some instances vacation church schools are interdenominational, conducted cooperatively by 2 or more churches.

Camping uses outdoor resources and relationships within the small group in the development of program. Each camper is a part of a small group for the entire camp period, and each group is responsible for planning its own program activities. The distinctive values of camping include: firsthand experiences with the natural world; close relationships with peers and adult leaders in a small group; leisure for exploring, thinking, and talking with others in the small group about things that are important to juniors.

Day camp is a camp that is in session 6 to 8 hours a day on consecutive days. It is recommended that a day camp continue for at least 2 weeks, Sundays and probably Saturdays excluded. It is especially appropriate for younger juniors who may not be ready for an away-from-home experience.

A resident camp is held away from home, and campers engage in a 24-hour-a-day program. A minimum of a week is recommended for the camp period.

A junior choir program, educationally conceived, affords opportunity for boys and girls to become familiar with the music of the church and to grow in their appreciation of it. Important to boys and girls of this age is the additional opportunity to contribute on occasion to the worship of the entire church family. Care must be taken lest the juniors be exploited for the sake of the personal satisfactions of a choir director or adults in the congregation, and be expected to render weekly an anthem in the Sunday morning worship service. Many choir leaders make excellent use of music found in the church school teaching materials and hymnals.

Provision is made in most denominations for other group meetings of juniors, in some instances termed " additional sessions." Some denominational plans include a club or " society," with specific name, curriculum, and organization plan. Such a group may function independently of the rest of the junior department.

Teaching procedures appropriate for use with juniors include the following: reading and study — to find answers to questions, for personal help and enrichment; sharing in planning and organizing work; studying maps, charts; taking trips — to learn about situations not already familiar to them, churches other than their own, service that their church renders to others; interviews — for information; dramatizing — stories, situations; writing — poems, stories, dramatizations, hymns; reporting — orally on interviews, reading, trips, work of a committee; participating in discussion; exploring, investigating, experimenting; painting, drawing, poster-making; making gifts for shut-ins, other groups in the church, hospital patients; carrying out service projects for the church; selecting materials and planning a service of worship; making dioramas, paper movies, peep shows; memorizing Scripture passages, hymns, and other meaningful material; making and using information cards.

Patterns of organization are influenced primarily by denominational polity in regard to Christian nurture and the way it shall be administered, the size of an individual church, and the number of juniors in its constituency.

The increase of 2-grade departments has raised the question about terminology. Shall the junior department include 4 grades, the 3d through the 6th? Shall there be lower and upper junior departments? Junior 1 and junior 2? Or shall the 3d-4th grade department be the upper primary? Various terms are used, but none has had general use as yet.

There is some variance in the types of curriculum materials provided by denominations, but among them may be found: closely graded courses for single-grade situations, as well as materials for 2-grade and 3-grade groups. Both dated and undated resources are used.

— *LaDonna Bogardus*

JUNIOR HIGH DEPARTMENT The Sunday morning program for junior high young people is a particularly crucial part of the task of Christian nurture in the church. First, these young adolescents and preadolescents are torn by ambivalent feelings. On the one hand, they wish to achieve independence from their parents and establish self-identity as individuals. On the other hand,

they identify with their parents or with surrogate parents and seek to emulate them. Throughout childhood there was no serious question about Sunday school attendance. Now, however, there is. Early adolescent rebellion is reinforced by their feeling that Sunday school is "for children." Few churches have strong adult education programs on Sunday morning. The junior high youngster may perceive giving up Sunday school as a movement toward adulthood.

A 2d reason for the importance of the morning church school stems from the fact that 65 percent of those who drop out of Sunday school do so during the ages from 12 to 15. An effective church school program is a vital necessity if these young people are to be retained in the life of the church.

The 3d factor is the necessary preparation a strong junior high program can give for the self-leadership that will be enjoyed by the youth in the senior high program. The church that develops and maintains a good, well-attended Sunday morning junior high department has taken a major step toward the assurance of continuing participation by high school youth.

The junior high department that meets Sunday morning is an integral part of the total youth fellowship of the early adolescent. Young teenagers need to sense the interrelationship of all segments of their program in the church. Difficulties do arise due to different leadership for the various parts of the program. Frequently communication breaks down. Care will need to be taken in order that adequate coordination of the total program may be achieved.

The essential objective of Christian education for junior highs, as for all age groups, is "to enable persons to become aware of the seeking love of God as revealed in Jesus Christ and to respond in faith to this love in ways that will help them to grow as children of God, live in accordance with the will of God, and sustain a vital relationship in the Christian community." The implications of the objective are outlined in detail for each of the 7th, 8th, and 9th grades in *Junior High Objectives* of the National Council of the Churches of Christ in the U.S.A. The distinctive character of the Sunday morning junior high department is seen in relation to this objective. It is the major opportunity for a formal teaching situation through which young people can come to understand the meaning of the Christian faith and its significance for their lives. As the primary place in which Christian nurture may take place, the morning junior high department deserves careful planning and thoughtful execution.

Four major problems need to be considered in planning for the Sunday morning junior high department. These are the place of worship, an adequate schedule, necessary leadership, and the teaching situation.

One of the most important and distinctive functions of the church is that of worship. The church is frequently defined as the worshiping community. Most junior high young people are mature enough to take their place in the regular worship service of the church. In some congregations it is customary for these young people to accompany their families. In others they may attend the service with their youth group. In any case, they should take their places in the church on Sunday morning. If this be the case, immediately the question of departmental worship arises.

In many situations 20 to 30 minutes of the Sunday school hour are given to departmental worship. This practice is self-defeating. It reduces the effective teaching time that is the primary function of the department. It may provide a substitute for the service of the congregation. Finally, all too often it is a travesty upon worship due to the extraneous elements that are included.

Departmental worship has a significant place if it is brief, closely integrated with the study material, and if the young people are encouraged through the departmental worship to participate in the congregational worship.

The question of the place of worship contains implications for the morning Sunday school schedule. The latter needs to be considered within the context of the teaching function of the morning program. In many churches class time is limited to 20 or 30 minutes at most. The average Protestant child spends only approximately 24 hours per year in a classroom teaching situation. How much more effective could a program be that would double the time for the class to meet? The following schedule is suggested to provide a greater measure of teaching opportunity: Fifteen minutes before the starting hour the teacher arrives to prepare the room, secure resources, and meet early-comers. Forty to 50 minutes are given to class time. The young people arrive and go immediately to their individual classes. Ten to 15 minutes at the close are spent in brief departmental worship, preceded or followed by necessary announcements.

Customarily a department super-intendent will be appointed in a church that has enough young people of 7th and 8th, or 7th, 8th, and 9th, grades to form more than a single class. This person has the responsibility for supervising the entire morning activity. In the smaller group he may be the head teacher or worship resource leader. In every situation he is responsible for supervision and administration in the department.

Ideally, 1 teacher should be provided for every 7 to 10 young people. The use of team teaching, in which several teachers work together and share responsibilities, has proved to be effective in many situations.

The major task of the junior high department is to teach. But teaching is not "telling." Teaching is guiding the learning activities of young people. The effective teacher must keep in mind 3 things: (1) the basic objective of Christian nurture and the specific goals of the particular unit of learning; (2) the needs, interests, and developmental tasks of the junior highs; (3) the cardinal fact of learning, namely, that persons learn to the degree that they participate in determining learning goals and in being actively involved in their accomplishment.

Junior highs think and act in concrete terms. A specific project with a tangible goal will facilitate their learning. Paul may be only a name they read in a quarterly, or his life may be etched in theirs through a dramatization of the crises of his ministry. With increased class time it is not only feasible but desirable to plan and execute such projects. Such activities, jointly selected through discussion of pupils and teacher, must of course, be relevant to the unit of study. When these conditions are met, motivation is high, and the junior high department becomes an effective educational agency for God and his church.

— *Richard S. Ford*

JUSTIFICATION The meaning that the word "justified" has in the current phrase, "I feel justified in doing this or that," is far from the Hebrew, Greek, and Biblical understanding of justification. The genuine meaning of "to justify" is "to set right," "to deem right," "to give a fair trial," "to do justice," "to pronounce judgment," "to punish," or "to pronounce and treat as righteous." Based on Old Testament precedents, the New Testament uses the term in a threefold sense:

1. The caught and condemned criminal confesses that God, his judge, is right (Ps. 51:4; Rom. 3:4; Luke 7:29), i.e., he gives God the glory (Josh. 7:19).

2. God vindicates an elect servant by hearing his cry, by restoring or extolling him after he has suffered from enemies or interceded for evil-doers (Isa. 53:11-12; I Tim. 3:16; Luke 18:14).

3. God accepts Jesus Christ's plea for sinners (his sacrifice, his "crying" blood, Heb. 12:24) and declares, treats, and makes them free from the power and fear of sin, accusation, guilt, and punishment. God gives peace by graciously acquitting guilty men, for Jesus Christ's sake (Rom., chs. 3 to 5; Gal., chs. 2 to 5), as it was foreshadowed by the ritual of the Day of Atonement (Lev., ch. 16) and by Isa., ch. 53.

The 3d meaning of justification has been specifically elaborated by Paul — perhaps in dependence upon concepts found also in the Qumrân literature. Among the New Testament writers, Luke comes nearest to Paul, e.g., in the parables of the prodigal, the Pharisees and the publican, and the unrighteous judge. The act and mode of justification by grace stands opposite to justification by law, by works, or by man himself. When it is called justification from faith or by faith (e.g., Rom. 3:30), then "faith" means the faithfulness of God, the obedience of Christ and/or the dependence and reliance of man upon God who accepts Christ's intercession (Rom. 3:3, 22-25; Phil. 3:9; cf. Gal. 2:20). This verdict, based upon what has happened before God's tribunal and what was "accounted" by him, has the same declaratory and effective power that forgiveness has; "justification" is a synonym for "forgiveness" (Rom. 3:24-25; 4:5-8; Eph. 1:7; Col. 1:14; Acts 13:38-39). It is restoration by grace of the right relation between God and man, and it conveys the certainty that nobody — nothing — can separate man from God (Rom. 8:1, 32-39).

Justification is not one among many stages of Christian experience or developments, but it is the basic deed of God performed on Calvary and Easter Day, and guaranteed by Christ's continued intercession at God's right hand. Through the gospel man learns of it; by faith he grasps it. So it is the presupposition of gospel and faith rather than only a part of Christian life. It cannot be achieved or left behind like a step on a ladder.

The concept of justification of the sinner (used in Rom. 4:5 only) appears predominantly in Augustine's and the Reformers' writings, and again in so-called orthodox Lutheran or recent neoorthodox literature. When justification by grace is taught or preached, silly obstacles such as the following are to be met:

(1) The juridical or Old Testamental origin and nature of the term "justification" seems to lack the warmth and brightness of the talk about the Father's *agapē*. (2) The doctrine that sinners only, by grace only, are saved, seems to betray a pessimistic notion of man that ignores freedom, will, and the capacity to be or to do good. (3) The message that all life depends on sheer forgiveness seems to quench challenge and urgency to do good works or to hope for reward. It appears to invite indulgence in laziness (as I and II Thessalonians show) or ethical libertinism (I Cor.), and to produce quips such as, "Let us do sin that grace increase" (cf. Rom. 3:8; 6:1, 15). (4) The emphasis put upon faith appears to lay religion on a psychological, emotional, or intellectual foundation upon which necessarily the Protestant extremes of subjectivism, individualism, and existentialism must develop and flourish.

Indeed, justification of the sinner by grace contradicts man-made images of a divine judge, father, or educator, humanistic ideas of man, and the notion of an institutional church that can spend or withhold absolution. The message of justification is the permanent revolution of the church, of all theology, and of personal piety. It is also the rock on which both the pride and despair — of organized religion and of people's not knowing God — have shattered and will crumble.

For it manifests God's freedom to be father and judge at the same time, even by making right what is wrong with man. It discloses God's pleasure to create and provoke works of gratitude and praise rather than of a slavish drudgery. It reveals God's will to be voluntarily and heartily loved and trusted precisely by sinners. Although in the Pauline epistles justification is the core and theme of the gospel of Christ (Rom. 1:16-17), other parts of the New Testament use other terminology to proclaim the same mighty act of God.

Acquaintance with the distinctly Biblical meaning of the term "righteousness," a study of the task given in the Old Testament to elect, representative servants for redeeming the community, and willingness to learn from original Biblical stories and passages rather than from generalizing secondary sources, are a necessary presupposition to learning and teaching about the miracle of justification. — *Markus Barth*

JUVENILE DELINQUENCY A juvenile delinquent is a child or youth who has committed an offense against the law, has been apprehended, and has been found guilty by a court of law. Such a person is in most states between 10 and 17 years of age. The offense is either one for which an adult would be punished by fine or imprisonment or an act in violation of one of the numerous regulations, such as those against truancy and incorrigibility, which would apply specifically to juveniles.

This is to say that juvenile delinquency is a legal status for law violators under the age that the community chooses to designate as the legal minimum for full criminal responsibility. The philosophy undergirding such provision of a special legal status for young offenders is a reflection of growing humanitarianism and of developing social science insights into the dynamics of human behavior. Only a few centuries ago children and adults were treated alike before the law.

Statistical measures of juvenile delinquency in the U.S.A. indicate a persistent and alarming rate of increase. Arrests of juveniles more than doubled between 1950 and 1960, while the juvenile-age population increased by less than one half. Some 2,000,000 or more children and youth "come to the attention of the police" each year. About 3 out of every 100 individuals between 10 and 17 years of age in our population are adjudged delinquent each year, and about 1 in every 9 between these ages has a delinquency record.

A major disquieting consideration has to do with the fact that a legal definition of juvenile delinquency is far from adequate. All children tend to have some difficulty in learning to conform to social expectations, and there is a qualitative difference between "normal adjustive behavior" and serious maladjustment that points toward a chronic, "antisocial grudge." This difference may not always be apparent in a single isolated act, but a careful assessment of it should be reflected in treatment. Failure to make the distinction can turn normal learning processes into patterns of delinquency.

The philosophy of the juvenile court and of most of the legislation that supports its work with juveniles is that rather than follow a strictly punitive course in dealing with young offenders, everything possible should be done in behalf of the juvenile delinquent to correct his errant tendencies and save him from a life of crime. Considerable confusion still exists, however, in laws, courts, and public thinking because of persistent conflict between punitive and rehabilitative attitudes.

The causes of juvenile delinquency are difficult to assess for the reason that they are many and varied. Although no really comprehensive research has ever been conducted on a national scale to ascertain facts related to causation, such fragmentary research as has been done has shown quite clearly that no single cause or particular set of causes can be identified. A dynamic combination of influences figures in every case, though similarities are often apparent, and a clinical rather than a categorical approach is best.

The old notion that physical maturation automatically brings about an "age of accountability" beyond which the individual enjoys complete freedom of will and is wholly responsible for his behavior has been seriously challenged and somewhat discredited by discoveries in the psychological and social sciences. It is now obvious that a large measure of responsibility for what the individual is and does is widely dispersed in the whole society of which he is a part.

Treatment that is redemptive must recognize unmet needs and try to make amends for them. Juveniles whose physical, social, emotional, spiritual, and other needs have been met with reasonable adequacy are not likely to become delinquent. Maximum therapy is often required to repair the damage done delinquents by deprivation.

Official (legal) treatment, involving courts, police, and law, is probably more handicapped in providing therapy than is unofficial (nonlegal) treatment, which makes use of clinics, social work, and social agencies.

In the latter treatment process, the child or youth is dealt with as a person with problems that need correcting, and is never labeled a juvenile delinquent. Unfortunately, however, it is still necessary to place greatest reliance on official (legal) treatment processes because there are not enough unofficial (nonlegal) services available to handle more than a small fraction of the total case load.

Juvenile courts, which were designed to try to blend social-work therapeutic practices with administration of the law, are seriously handicapped by inadequate financial support, insufficient trained personnel, lack of a well-integrated system of specialized referral and treatment resources, and negative attitudes on the part of those segments of public opinion that are impatient with nonpunitive procedures. Even so, juvenile courts are performing an important function. The tragedy is that there are not more of them and that they are not more generously supported.

An uncoordinated hodgepodge of institutions and agencies for the official care and treatment of delinquents exists in many states. Having little relationship to one another, and often operating without significant state supervision, these institutions and agencies tend to lack uniformity of standards, to duplicate unspecialized services, and to compete with one another for political prestige. Their impact on the children and youth who fall into their hands is usually of little remedial value, and is frequently seriously damaging. California has done a pioneering job of developing a statewide system of specialized treatment facilities.

According to the National Council

on Crime and Delinquency, community standards for good care of children and youth who become involved in delinquency or who are especially exposed to delinquency risks should include provision of a special police youth bureau, a full-time juvenile court judge, a good probation staff, psychiatric and psychological services for the juvenile court, a detention home — not a jail — for children, shelter care for dependent and neglected children, foster homes for delinquent and neglected children, family service agencies, special facilities for mentally defective and disturbed children, and training schools that really reeducate.

It is easy to oversimplify approaches to delinquency protection. Appealing panaceas are, therefore, very prevalent. It must be recognized, however, that the causes of juvenile delinquency are deeply rooted in the total culture — including the institutional arrangements, value systems, patterns of behavior, and other influences that prevail in community life. Nothing short of a broad program of social reform may be expected to accomplish much in the way of prevention.

Churches have a great responsibility in connection with the problems related to juvenile delinquency. Their 1st obligation is, of course, to be diligent in sharing with all persons the Christian gospel of love. Embraced in this obligation is the responsibility to keep themselves sensitive to fundamental problems of human need in the unredeemed social order around them, to keep clearly in the focus of their concern " even the least " persons in their parishes, to maintain love for and nonjudgmental attitudes toward offenders, to keep the church fellowship broadly inclusive and open to all, to maintain an effective ministry in demoralized areas of their communities, to cooperate wholeheartedly with all persons and agencies in community life that have a concern for the welfare of children and youth, and to accept fully the imperative to encourage social action toward needed reform.

—Haskell M. Miller

K

KERYGMA Symptomatic of the shift in theological emphasis from the liberal era of the early 20th century to the neoorthodox period of midcentury is the emergence into prominence of the term *kērygma*. The primary meaning of this term refers to the concrete content of the apostolic preaching of Jesus as the act of God (cf. Acts 2:14-39; 3:13-26; etc.). Derived from the Greek verb *kēryssein* (" to proclaim," then " to preach "), it is from a noun denoting the result of the action of the verb (hence "what is proclaimed," "proclamation"). In modern theological parlance, it is frequently used in New Testament studies and systematic theology.

The term occurs only 8 times in the New Testament, or 9 if we count the shorter ending of Mark. In the Gospels, it appears twice (Matt. 12:41; Luke 11:32) to designate the preaching of Jonah. The other occurrences refer to preaching the gospel of which Jesus is the content. Outside its use in the shorter ending of Mark, which may be influenced by Pauline usage, the word is confined to the Pauline and post-Pauline tradition. Within this tradition, 3 related, though distinct, meanings are to be found. (1) In the genuine Pauline uses of the term, the predominant notion is *the content of the preaching* (Rom. 16:25; I Cor. 1:21; 2:4; 15:14). This particular use of the term gave rise to the distinction worked out by C. H. Dodd, in *The Apostolic Preaching and Its Developments* (1936), between *kērygma* and *didachē* (teaching), the former being roughly the equivalent of what Paul calls " my gospel" (Rom. 2:16), the saving acts of God effected in and through Jesus the Christ, and the latter comprising ethical instructions and similar catechesis. In this sense, *kērygma* is what the apostolic church proclaimed to the rest of the world about Jesus. (2) *The act of preaching* (Titus 1:3), whereby the divine Logos comes to the hearers, is an action entrusted to the apostles and their followers so that God's power to save might reach the age anew. (3) *The office of preaching* (II Tim. 4:17) is a usage that comes from the postapostolic age when the apostolate had given place to a more developed and formalized ministry.

In recent years the imported word " kerygma " has found wider use as a theological term. The adoption of this term untranslated from the New Testament corresponds with the erosion of such terms as " gospel " and the recognition that something

unique is involved in the preaching of the Christian church. Certain fundamental features are thus kept in the foreground: (1) The use of the term specifies that the Christian proclamation is not knowledge about religion in general and ethical truth but is, rather, the heralding or proclamation of an *event* — the crucifixion (and resurrection) of Jesus and the concomitant divine victory over sin and death. (2) It further asserts that, more than a simple report about this event, *kēygma* constitutes a real claim, since by way of the *kērygma* the event of redemption occurs in the hearer with power and seizes him into that power. (3) Moreover, *kērygma* is the continuation of the word and act of God himself, which is reported in the *kērygma*. What took place concretely in the Christ event becomes present for the hearers, providing the link between the "thenness" of God's act and the "nowness" of acceptance or rejection of that act. The word also implies that there are 3 factors in the preaching: announcement of sin and judgment (man's situation before God); proclamation of God's saving act in Christ; and the appeal to accept God's gracious act of forgiveness and to live as becomes those who have been forgiven of all sin by God who alone has been wronged and who alone can forgive.
— *Jules Laurence Moreau*

KINDERGARTEN Kindergarten is that segment of formal education provided for children 4 and 5 years of age, which consists of enriching experiences in school and community carried out in cooperation with parents.

The term *Kindergarten,* "children's garden," was originally used by Froebel in 1837 for the school in Germany where he developed his principles of education. His *Kindergarten* was a society of children — equals living and learning through natural play activities under the guidance of a trained adult. A student of Froebel's opened the 1st kindergarten in the U.S.A. in 1855. The 1st English-speaking kindergarten was started in 1860 in Boston by Elizabeth Peabody, who promoted the kindergarten movement zealously and in 8 years had organized a training school for teachers. The 1st public kindergarten opened in St. Louis in 1873. By 1961 approximately 50 percent of the 5-year-old population of the U.S.A. was enrolled in kindergartens.

American educators are convinced of the value of kindergarten for the young child in the areas of self-understanding, physical and emotional health, creative expression, social relationships with peers, social relationships with adults outside of the family, mental stimulation, preparation for formal learning in the primary grades, and improved relationships with more understanding parents. A 4-year-old kindergarten is more simplified in schedule and content than one for 5-year-olds and in many places it is called nursery school. In a kindergarten for 5-year-olds there is preparation for reading, writing, and arithmetic through "readiness" programs using numbers, clocks, calendars, letters, labels, games, and other materials and activities.

Inasmuch as the growth of children in their early years is of utmost importance for the rest of their lives, a kindergarten teacher is selected for more than academic qualities. Emotional and social maturity is required, because children learn through the kinds of relationships they have with people. The teacher must be able to establish a relationship of loving concern, understanding, security, justice, and freedom within bounds, that permits healthy growth to take place for each and every child. She provides an environment conducive to learning and initiates a program of experiences in physical activities, social science, creative arts, language arts, and natural science. In ample space, both indoors and outdoors, with safe and colorful furnishings, she arranges centers for varied activities such as: using big-muscle play equipment; housekeeping with dress-up clothing and a family of dolls; block-building that includes play with toy people and animals, trains, cars, trucks, airplanes; listening to and making music; dancing and all kinds of rhythmic games; creating with the use of papers, paste, scissors, crayons, paints, chalk, clay, foods, wood, and carpentry tools; enjoying pictures and picture books; caring for pets and plants; experimenting with water, batteries and bells, magnets, magnifying glasses. The teacher develops "units" of learning or guided learning experiences on the basis of the needs, interests, and capabilities of her children. She has a schedule or routine within which there is freedom for the individual to choose pursuits. She leads the children in assuming responsibility for the care of materials and equipment. Along with the kindergarten room, the teacher uses the school building and neighborhood as suitable environments for certain learning experiences. She maintains relationships with parents in order better to understand and help the children at home as well as at school. There are also "traditional" kindergartens wherein the teacher thinks more about subject matter than about the child as she plans a formal circle time, highly organized games, patterns for handwork, precise dramatizations, and rehearsed programs or exhibitions.

The trend in kindergarten education today is toward more and better educational programs for the young child, coordination of the kindergarten with the primary grades, more publicly supported kindergartens, and better training for teachers. In 1962 a qualified teacher of kindergarten in the U.S.A. was required to be a graduate of an accredited 4-year college with a major in early childhood education (or said major may be completed in graduate school). Some states require that teachers in both public and independent kindergartens be certified by the state education department. The professional organization for teachers of young children in America is the Association for Childhood Education International, Washington, D.C.

— *Kathrene McLandress Tobey*

KINDERGARTEN DEPARTMENT

The 4- and 5-year-old children skipped down the hall to the door marked "Kindergarten." A hum of happy sounds greeted them as they entered. In the room were other children of their age and friendly teachers ready to give help when needed. In a medium-sized church 22 fours and fives met together in 1 room. The room is well-planned with adequate light and ventilation. The chairs are durable and just the right height, 10 to 12 inches, and light in weight so that the children can move them about easily. A pretty rug is placed near the "beauty center" for the children to sit on. There is ample floor space (30 to 35 square feet per child) to allow for free movement for group living and activity. Although there are not many tables, there are enough to provide space for 5 or 6 children to model with clay, 5 more to draw or cut and paste pictures, and room for a few more to look at books or do puzzles. At an easel in a well-lighted corner 2 children can paint.

Everything about the room is inviting to the children. There is a place to hang up wraps near the entrance. Walls are painted an attractive pastel color that looks well with the woodwork. There are many clear glass windows low enough to make the outdoors seem a real part of the room. There is direct access to the toilet facilities and to a drinking fountain.

There are supplies in adequate quantities — large sheets of drawing paper, large-sized crayons, scissors, paste, and clay. These work materials are placed on shelves low enough to enable all the children to help themselves.

The room has ample play equipment. The housekeeping corner has a child-sized stove, sink, cupboards, and other necessary toys for playing house. The blocks are large and well-sanded. They are arranged in another corner with ample space for building. To stimulate dramatic play, there are sturdy trucks, cars, and wooden toy community helpers.

These activity centers encourage the friendly, cooperative play so essential to Christian nurture and help the children develop ethical attitudes — sharing, taking turns, respecting the rights of others, cooperating, being thoughtful and courteous. The children are encouraged to have many experiences that they may develop personal responsibility and be able to express the thrilling satisfaction that accompanies a task well done.

The children like to look at the large, colorful pictures, hung at eye level. One of their favorite spots is the music center where they can experiment with drum, triangle, xylophone, cymbals, or record player. A well-tuned piano is available.

The "surprise center" has nature objects to arouse the children's interest and curiosity. The children often look through a magnifying glass at the shells, nuts, seedpods, a cocoon, and an empty bird's nest displayed on a low table with a formica top.

On another low table there are a Bible, a picture, and flowers arranged attractively in a colorful bowl to make a "beauty center" where the children sit for conversation, story, singing, sharing, and worship moments. All the children are part of a group, yet are also individuals treated with respect. They feel secure because there is a schedule — not rigid, but flexible — calling for times for informal work and play, sharing and conversation, cleaning up the room, music and story, and worship.

The kindergarten department has a smoothly running organization due to the superintendent (sometimes called a coordinator). She knows the ongoing work of the department and its relationship to the program of the entire church school. She is a good organizer, a friend, and a guide to her teaching staff. It is her responsibility to be the leading teacher and to help select additional workers, 1 for every 5 children. She calls regular staff meetings for planning units of work. She sees that the teachers have the correct curriculum materials well in advance and helps them understand and achieve the purposes of Christian education. She also is responsible for organizing parents' groups to bring about a closer working relationship with the home.

The kindergarten department is for all the children within 2 years of entering 1st grade, or from age 4 to entrance into grade 1. The grouping together in one room of 4's and 5's and young 6's who have not entered 1st grade seems best when the enrollment is not over 25 children.

In a church where the enrollment is from 25 to 40 or more children of kindergarten age, the department would consist of separate groups. There should be at least 1 room for every 20 to 22 children approximately 4 years old, and at least 1 room for every 20 to 22 children 5 years old, including older children who have not entered 1st grade. Each group would be a complete unit for the entire session, with a leading teacher and helpers for every 5 or 6 children. The kindergarten superintendent would supervise the work of both rooms.

In some very large churches there might be such a big enrollment of children that they would have to be divided into separate classes on a 6 months' grading: 1 room each, with a complete staff, for children from 4 to 4½, 5½ to 6, and those who have not entered 1st grade. Each group would also be a complete unit for the entire session, with a leading teacher and helpers for every 5 or 6 children.

In every case, the size of the room, the space available, and the number of children enrolled will affect the number of kindergarten classes a church provides. If there is a room shortage, the church should investigate the advisability of having multiple sessions in the kindergarten.

Where the number of children do not make more than 1 session necessary, an expanded session (longer than the regular session) may be held. It may begin at the opening hour of church school and extend through the hour of the church service, with the same teaching staff remaining for the entire period.

The kindergarten department may also include a through-the-week session where children come to the church 5 mornings a week for a 2-, 2½-, or 3-hour session. The Sunday session and the weekday session should be regarded as closely related parts of the total program of the church for this age group. The superintendent of the Sunday morning sessions may be the director of the through-the-week school. This helps coordinate the Christian growth of 4's and 5's. In some cases several of the helping teachers also work in the weekday sessions. The vacation church school kindergarten is also a part of the total program of the church for kindergarten children. — *Rosemary K. Roorbach*

KIRCHENTAG *Kirchentag* is, literally, " church day "; as applied to the great post World War II lay assemblies of German Protestantism, it meant " rally of the church." *Kirchentag* was the name given to the congresses sponsored by leaders of the German Pietist revival in the mid-19th century, out of which grew the philanthropic Inner Mission program. Some roots of the modern *Kirchentag* lie in those congresses; others in the Evangelical Weeks, the rallies at which German churchmen who refused to go along with the Nazi regime's efforts to mold the church in its own image met together to find inspiration and courage in prayer, Bible study, and fellowship; still others, in the little Bible-study and prayer groups formed across confessional lines by Germans in Russian prison and labor camps.

Kirchentag owes its modern inception and much of its impetus to the efforts of a layman, Reinold von Thadden-Trieglaff, who in his student days had been active in international projects of the World Student Christian Federation, had joined in the resistance offered by a number of churchmen to the Nazis' " German Christian " program, and had spent a period of time in a Siberian slave-labor camp. His experiences convinced him that lay Christians must be aroused to the need to interpret their faith in all sectors of public life — a radical step for a people for whom church membership had traditionally been as automatic as citizenship, and who had long considered the church's role to be properly confined to purely "spiritual" affairs. Other churchmen agreed; looking back over the excesses of the Nazi period they had concluded that that debacle could be traced in part to the church's failure to be a vital force outside its own walls. At a meeting in Hanover in 1949 they responded to von Thadden's appeal for increased assumption by the laity of responsibility for the spiritual fate of the nation.

Since 1949 the *Kirchentag* has become a dramatic focus for the wider movement for renewal throughout the German churches. To each rally, thousands of Protestants come to listen to lectures and participate in Bible study and group discussion on matters of public and private con-

cern. Each is the occasion for musical and dramatic presentations and art exhibits, many of which implement creative experiments in those media for religious purposes. The *Kirchentage* have had tremendous impact on the populace of the areas in which they are held, particularly through the final public assembly in which thousands participate in song and liturgy and listen to stirring addresses. A valued feature of the earlier *Kirchentage* was the rare opportunity they offered for Protestants from the 2 Germanys to meet and worship together; however, in recent years restrictions imposed by Soviet zone authorities have made it impossible for all but a few East Germans to attend rallies held in the West. The 1st *Kirchentag*, held at Essen in the industrial Ruhr in 1950, drew 25,300 participants, with 200,000 people attending the final assembly. Subsequent years brought sessions in East and West Berlin, Stuttgart, and Hamburg. In 1954, Leipzig, in the Soviet zone, was host to 60,000 Germans from both East and West, while no fewer than 650,000 gathered for a closing service of worship that is still hailed as a high-water mark in moving fellowship and sincere dedication. Since 1954 the *Kirchentage* have been held less frequently (Frankfurt, 1956; München, 1959; Berlin, 1961). Since 1956, provision has been made for participation in special discussion groups by ecumenical visitors from abroad. The *Kirchentag* does not aspire to become a " church " in any sense of the word, or even a separate movement. Its purpose is simply to gather up the various elements that strive for renewal within the church and for the construction of bridges between church and world, and to dramatize those efforts. A headquarters is maintained at Fulda.

— *Margaret Frakes*

KNOWLEDGE, THEORIES OF The theories of knowledge advanced through the centuries can best be examined from the viewpoint that the knowing enterprise is an event occurring within the whole range of events. Epistemology (the knowledge of "knowing") is, in other words, a part of ontology (the knowledge of "being"). This position is consistent with the predominant view of classical tradition. The basic consideration, then, becomes the relation between subject and object in the knowing event. On this issue, the severe objectivism of Greek and Scholastic philosophy received its most shattering blow in the rise of German idealism, under the leadership of Kant. Criticism was aimed at naïve realism, which claimed the essential identification of the objective world and absolute being. The resulting phenomenology shifted the center of philosophical gravity from the *object* to the *subject*, relegating to secondary place the world of objective realities and objects. This mistakenly rendered the object itself outside the range of experience and knowledge. The consequence was to depersonalize philosophy, for it took from man his prerogative as the "knowing subject," making knowledge the primary function of universal reason (sometimes referred to as the "universal spirit").

This position left without adequate consideration, however, the problem of the nature and function of man (the ego), as the "knowing subject," in relation to the pure subject of cognition. This "problem of man" became the primary concern of existentialist philosophy in facing the epistemological issue. To this movement, so influential in philosophical and theological discussion today, must go much credit for the rediscovery and rehabilitation of man as a being in his own right instead of a bit of flotsam on the sea of the objective world. In correcting the severe humanistic tendencies of existentialism, theologians of the classical tradition have dealt with the basic issue under consideration in terms of the relation between reason and revelation. Reason, as the structure of the mind enabling it to lay hold on and to transform reality, is conceived in ontological terms. Distinction is made between reason, in the sense of *logos,* and reasoning (technical reason), which is used to meet the essential demands of reason.

Since the middle of the 19th century, the chief error and greatest threat to culture, inherent in many theories of knowledge, centers in the attempt to separate technical reason from ontological reason. The philosophical system that refuses to recognize anything transcending technical reason ends in impoverishing its own life and work, and ultimately in dehumanizing the man who supposedly is the chief master of technical reason. The threat inherent in such systems of thought throws us back to the age-old problem of the relation between subject and object, between subjective and objective reason.

Since the time of Parmenides, philosophers have agreed (in varying degrees and ways) that "the *logos,* the word which grasps and shapes reality, can do so only because reality itself has a *logos* character" (Tillich). The necessity of dealing with the *subject-object* relationship has been commonly acknowledged. The relation between the rational structure of mind and the rational structure of reality has received consideration in 4 outstanding types of philosophies: *realism* — which sees subjective reason as an effect of the totality of reality on the mind, which is a part of reality; *idealism* — which sees objective reason as being derived from subjective reason, actualizing itself in what would otherwise be simply unstructured matter; *dualism or pluralism* — which sees subjective and objective reason as being ontologically independent, though functionally interdependent, finding mutual fulfillment, the one in the other; *monism* — which sees subjective and objective reason having an underlying identity, expressing itself in and through the rational structure of reality (cf. Tillich). Classical theology has always assumed a critical position with respect to all these philosophies and their epistemological assertions. However, their common presuppositions have been helpful to theology in its attempt to give meaningful explanation to many of its symbolic expressions such as creation, Spirit, man as the image of God in his rational structure, etc.

The essential relation of reason and revelation now becomes clear. As Being itself, the Power in all that is, God is in every way the answer to all that man inquires concerning the situation of his life and the nature and meaning of his being. Only thus can reason, the essential structure of man's mind, and reality (the world relative to it) be truly affirmed. Under the conditions of existence, man's reason is seen as ambiguous; it needs revelation for its completion and fulfillment. Revelation does not negate it, but rather breaks through it and lays hold upon it in order to fulfill it. Experience, as we know it, is thus the medium through which genuine and authentic truth comes to answer the questions asked by the human self through reason. Genuine knowledge comes to answer the questions asked by the human self through reason. Genuine knowledge is received, collected, and interpreted through the medium of experience, but it is not created by experience. To view man's reason in this manner is to give it both structural and functional character. It affirms that man can understand reality only because reality is itself understandable. The correlation in structure of both makes this grasping and shaping of reality possible. Reception and revelation are understood as 2 movements always operative in the knowing process, penetrating into the very depths of essential nature and giving it a structure. In every act of reasonable reception and reaction, we transform reality according to the way we see it, and we see it because we receive it and react to it.

Knowing is thus seen to be an " act." In John 3:21 this understanding is made clear in suggesting that we know the truth only by doing the truth. Berdyaev has clarified this understanding of knowledge still further in suggesting that it is " essentially active because man is active." Knowledge (as truth) is essentially " personal." The basic considerations involved in the setting forth of any adequate theory of knowledge must begin with the affirmation clearly set forth by Kierkegaard and others of the existentialist persuasion, that truth and reality coexist in a subjective state. The problem of the relationship of the subject and the object in the knowing enterprise is placed in proper perspective only in this way. The object has no criterion of truth, except in relation to an ego that supplies intellectual and moral consciousness. We must conclude with Berdyaev that " communication with truth invariably helps the ego to escape from its self-confinement. Knowledge attained is a symbol of victory over egocentricity." Thus, knowledge is finally and essentially personal and active, and only secondarily a theoretical object. Understanding implies involvement and participation in the very being of the one or the thing which is the object of our knowledge. Any other view of the cognitive function tends toward the ultimate dehumanization of man and his world by the very exercise of his cognitive and rational powers. — *Charles H. Johnson*

KOINONIA *Koinōnia* is a Greek noun that occurs 19 times in the New Testament to express such ideas as " fellowship," " sharing " or " participation." Because of the significance of these concepts in the life of the Christian community *koinōnia* has been taken over into English as a technical theological term — although the same concepts were also expressed in Greek through other words or phrases related to *koinōnia* or partially synonymous with it. *Koinōnia* remains the central term in this group, and it has even been argued, though probably incorrectly, that the early Christian community identified itself as " the *koinōnia* of Jesus."

The significance of koinonia should be seen against the background of a major problem confronting every society, namely, the problem of the relation between the needs or aspirations of individuals and those of the group as a whole. " No man is an island, entire of itself." (Donne.) A human being can neither come into existence nor live in total isolation, but neither can his life achieve its individuality unless it has some area of freedom over against the group. The Greeks, who were conscious of the problem, dealt with it at length, e.g., Plato's *Republic*. Among the Pythagoreans the term *koinōnia* was used to describe the sense of community that should unite gods, men, and even irrational animals because of their common participation in spirit or life. The Stoics confined this communal feeling to gods and men, since, they said, it grew out of a common participation in reason (*logos*). " The Good, then, for a rational creature, is *koinōnia* with others. . . . We were constituted for *koinōnia*." (Marcus Aurelius.)

Although the Hebrews were not given to abstract speculation, they dealt practically with this problem through their concept of themselves as the people of God united in a common obligation to him and to one another. It is characteristic of their sense of the gulf between God and man that they did not use *koinōnia* to describe the relation between God and man, although Jewish Greeks used the term occasionally in other contexts. However, Philo, who combined Greek and Jewish thought at the beginning of the Christian Era, in referring to Moses, spoke of " the joy of his *koinōnia* with the Father and Maker of all."

The New Testament community regarded itself as the new or renewed people of God bound together by a unity from God in Christ. It was chiefly, though not exclusively, Paul who described this aspect of the Christian community as "koinonia." The term identified the God-given sense of fellowship within the community as well as particular acts and forms of behavior that reflected or undergirded that unity.

The 19 occurrences of "koinonia" in the New Testament may be divided into 3 groups. First, those passages in which it is related to the divine, i.e., to God, Christ, or the Spirit. See II Cor. 13:14 ("The grace of the Lord Jesus Christ and the love of God and the fellowship of the Holy Spirit be with you all"); or I John 1:3b ("and our fellowship is with the father and with his son Jesus Christ"). See also, I Cor. 1:9; 10:16; Phil. 2:1; 3:10; I John 1:6. Second, those passages in which koinonia is primarily a spirit within the community. See I John 1:7 ("If we walk in the light, as he is in the light, we have fellowship with one another.") See also, II Cor. 6:14; Gal. 2:9; Phil. 1:5; I John 1:3a; and probably Acts 2:42. Third, those passages in which koinonia finds active, external expression. Thus Paul 3 times used the term for the relief offering that he collected on the Third Missionary Journey for the Jerusalem Christians (cf. II Cor. 8:4; 9:13; Rom. 15:26). A more general use is Heb. 13:16. Acts 2:42 belongs in this group if koinonia there refers to the sharing of possessions (cf. Acts 2:44 and 4:32).

The above classification leaves unsolved numerous problems of interpretation associated with specific passages. Does "the fellowship of the Holy Spirit" refer to the relation that Christians have with the Holy Spirit or does it refer to a fellowship given by the Holy Spirit and experienced among Chris-

tians? Or what is the structure of thought behind the Eucharistic passage II Cor. 10:16? The classification also ignores the occurrence of related terms as in Rom. 12:13; 15:27; Heb. 2:14; I Peter 4:13; 5:1; etc. But it does underline the central truths that Christian koinonia is rooted in the relation of the believing community to the God who manifests himself through Christ and the Spirit, that it stands at the center of the church's life, and that when present it is expressed in practical concern and sharing.

Every thoughtful participant in the life of the church is disturbed by the contrast between the New Testament ideal of koinonia and the spirit that actually prevails in a local congregation. Yet the observant reader of the New Testament will note that this contrast existed from the beginning. For example, the Corinthian correspondence deals almost entirely with problems created by the absence of koinonia. Christian koinonia is not mere "togetherness" but arises dynamically out of a common participation in the Christian faith. Therefore, the task of the church leader is to exalt the realities of the faith that the members of the congregation may, by their response, be drawn into a new fellowship — a fellowship transcending the conventional barriers of race, class, or personality. This may never be perfectly realized, but insofar as it does occur it witnesses to the continuing power of the message of reconciliation.

But the denial of koinonia is not only at the local level. The divisions of the church have multiplied since the days at Corinth, and the passing of centuries has given to each division a jealously guarded heritage. Even the Lord's Table, which should strengthen unity, has served to divide Christians. Yet the 20th century has seen the revival of the vision of a universal church united in fellowship through the power of the Spirit to which men have responded. Living in the midst of these events it is impossible to know what the outcome will be. But it is the task of responsible leaders to proclaim the renewed vision without the self-righteousness or rancor that would prevent its fulfillment.

Will the entire world finally be united in Christian koinonia? This is part of the Christian hope. Yet it must be recognized that the very intensity of koinonia in one group places it in conflict with others. Tertullian was only restating II Cor. 6:14 f. when he exclaimed, " What has Athens to do with Jerusalem? What concord is there between the academy and the church? What between heretics and Christians? " It is a paradox that the vision which has the potential of uniting the world also creates a deep divide between those who do and those who do not share that vision. This difficulty is not resolved by lessening the exclusiveness of Christianity, since this would also lessen its power to unite mankind. Although the tension cannot be eliminated, it can be mitigated if the believing community abandons arrogance and self-righteousness and accepts the outside world with the love of him who came to seek and to save that which was lost. Then in the fullness of time (that is, in the fullness of God's time) all may be gathered together in the grace of the Lord Jesus Christ and the love of God and the koinonia of the Holy Spirit.

— *Harvey K. McArthur*

L

LABORATORY SCHOOL A laboratory school provides an intensive experience in which church workers study together with a special opportunity to observe boys and girls who are a part of the school. It enables teachers to grow in insight and understanding as they relate to the age group for whom they have responsibility and to other teachers who also are on a similar quest.

The basic plan in a laboratory school is to provide adequate time for teachers to observe a particular age group engaged in a significant unit of study, to allow them to help plan the work from session to session, and then to participate in the actual teaching under careful supervision. After the dismissal of the children the period of observation and practice teaching is followed by an evaluation session engaged in by all those related to the work — the teacher of the children, the teacher of the adult class, and the adults enrolled for the work. This is highly important, for it is in this session that the strengths and weaknesses of the teaching with the children are discussed. The evaluation deals with the responses of the boys and girls, the ways in which the content and activities were introduced and used, the anticipated growth as an outcome, and the relation between the teachers and children. The session to follow with the children is planned in the light of the evaluation as the lead teacher works out with her class the next steps in teaching. This daily plan is followed for the duration of the school.

In the total experience of the laboratory school, provision is made for guided study, worship, class discussion, research, and an exchange of experiences. Because of the advanced type of work and the demanding schedule, such schools are usually open to those above the high school age, and some limit the lower age to 21 years. The laboratory method can best be appreciated and utilized by those who previously have had other types of leadership education.

Several plans are in use in various schools regarding staff and time schedule. In some a double teaching staff is used, with a teacher who has been successful in working with children of a given age being responsible for that phase of the work. A 2d teacher who is especially skilled in working with adults is responsible for guiding the work of those who enroll in the school. It is of utmost importance that when this plan is used the 2 leaders are able to work together harmoniously, have a common approach to effective ways of learning, and show sympathetic understanding of the interpretation of the content to be used in the demonstration. The purpose in thus using 2 teachers is to provide for the specialized work of the laboratory school and to lighten the teaching load in order that the necessary time be given to each part of the total experience. It is essential, in order to avoid confusion in this dual approach, that there be close cooperation in planning the daily work, in directing the practice teaching, and in evaluating the class sessions with the children.

In other situations, 1 teacher is used both as a teacher of the children's class and as a teacher of the adult learners. This teacher is observed as the work progresses with the children, directing those who assist in practice teaching, guiding the evaluation, making plans with the group for the following periods, and guiding the class discussions and study.

Laboratory schools often meet in summer sessions for a week or longer. There are also local laboratory schools set up in an intensive 5-day plan. In any type of laboratory school the home church situation of the teachers attending the school is kept in mind, realizing that the new insights and understandings resulting from the observation, study, and practice should enable the enrolled adults to interpret and use effective methods after returning.

The laboratory plan of leadership education provides an encounter with an actual teaching situation in which the learner has been guided in determining helpful approaches to children, has been supervised in this practice, and has been led in an evaluation of weaknesses and strengths to the end that the most valuable and effective ways of learning may be recognized and utilized in other teaching-learning situations.

— *Edith Frances Welker*

LAITY, THEOLOGY OF THE The term "theology of the laity" came into prominence in the U.S.A. with the publication in English of Hendrik Kraemer's *A Theology of the Laity* (1958), although groundwork had been laid in the historic report on the laity at the Evanston Assembly of the World Council of Churches (1954). Kraemer's thesis is that the essential nature and work of the church is ministry (*diakonia,* "service") and that this ministry is "incumbent on the church as a whole and not only on a special and specialized body of people 'set apart' for the ministry. . . . All members of the *ekklēsia* have in principle the same calling, responsibility, and dignity, have their part in the apostolic and ministerial nature and calling of the church." This thesis was developed by Arnold B. Come in *Agents of Reconciliation* (1960) and has been operative in various experiments toward the renewal of the church in our day.

A major problem lies in the terminology being employed. Words such as "laity" and "ministry" are commonly associated with 2 separate and distinct groups of people in the church: the unordained, nonprofessional volunteer churchman and the clergy. The theology of the laity attempts to use both terms to describe the whole church: all the people are the *laos,* or laity; all the people have a ministry. So great is the ambiguity here that Kraemer prefers the term *diakonia* for "ministry" and Come substitutes "agent."

The Biblical concept *laos theou*

(people of God) means that God's people are his by his choice and call and that he chose a people for mission, to make his name and his Word known. The term was applied to Israel and then to the inclusive church. The phrase carries none of the distinction between clergy and laity known today; it is often asserted that such is a non-Biblical distinction.

The clergy-laity distinction was solidified between Biblical times and the Reformation. The leaders of the Reformation sought to recover the laymen for the church with the doctrine of the priesthood of all believers while still maintaining the clergy-laity distinction along either functional (Calvin) or sacerdotal lines. Luther developed a " high " doctrine of the congregation to replace a " high " doctrine of the ministry and abolished the former distinction between " rulers " and " subjects." Calvin did not abolish the need for clergy, as the sectarians were doing. He simply sought to restore the clergy to their proper function as ministers of the word and sacraments. It remained for the present century, however, to develop a full parity of the whole people in mission, although the theological issues involved in this are by no means settled.

Two factors brought about the present rediscovery of the *laos theou* concept: the failure and weakness of the institutional church; the theological awakening to the role of God in history and his activity outside the confines of the organized church. The World Council of Churches through its Department of the Laity has greatly facilitated this rediscovery.

The weakness of the church was most apparent on the Continent of Europe and in Great Britain before, during, and after World War II. Iona Community in Scotland sought to strengthen the church's witness through a program of discipline, study, and work uniting laymen and ministers in a common calling. The evangelical academies of Germany grew out of massive resistance to Hitler and were an attempt to bring the gospel into the common life of Christians and non-Christians alike. The Agape Community in Italy provided a common meeting ground for people to discuss the rebuilding of their lives and their homelands after the devastation of the war. In North America, particularly the U.S.A., the weakness was less apparent; hence, the experiments for renewal have been less spectacular. Nevertheless, we can point to places like Five Oaks (Canada), Parishfield (Michigan) and the Faith and Life Community (The Austin Experiment, Texas) that are dedicated to the renewal of the church through a rediscovery of the ministry of the laity in the world. It is significant that these are experiments which, while committed to the church as the instrument of God's mercy, are operating outside the structures of ordinary parish life. The institutional church is seen as inhibiting the mission of the church.

The present thinking in theology makes much of the world as the arena of God's action. God is at work here, under some circumstances, more than he is at work in the security-ridden church. Christians go into the world to bear witness to God's being at work there and to learn from it what God is saying to the church. They go not to convert, because this is the Holy Spirit's business. They bear witness, then let God give the increase.

Obviously, if God is at work in the world and if the church's mission is to witness there, the laymen have primary responsibility for the mission, since they are perforce more in the world in their daily work than the clergy are. By and large the clergy must work within the life of the local congregation. It is the function of the local church to prepare or equip the laymen for their mission in the world. Some are willing to say that the church is mission, and that all other church activities and functions are to be subsumed under this purpose of being the church in the world.

Christian education, preaching, and worship carry the burden of preparing the whole people of God for mission. This means that the church will give much greater attention to the Christian education of adults and young people than it has done in the past. Young people are not second-rate Christians or churchmen but are responsible along with adults for the Christian mission. The theology of the laity also requires a reexamination of present practices in evangelism, social action, and mission. For one thing, these 3 aspects of church program are more interrelated than has been apparent in practice. Social action is evangelism; a possible trend in evangelism away from "preaching for decision" toward witness in the community illustrates this interrelatedness. Further, mission is as much *being* as *doing;* here the stress is on witnessing through a Christian "style of life" where verbal witness is impossible or inappropriate. At the present time, however, these implications are being explored more thoroughly outside the local congregation than within particular parishes, which may indicate that there is strong resistance when a theology of the laity is taken seriously. — *George Laird Hunt*

LATIN AMERICA Latin America is a short-cut name for the vast area of more than a score of countries extending from Mexico in the north to Cape Horn in the south. More than 188 million people, of whom over 15 percent are Indians or Negroes, about half white, and the rest of mixed ancestry, live in these countries.

Although Latin America is often thought of as Roman Catholic in faith, competent authorities (Roman Catholic and Protestant) agree that only about 13 percent of the total population are actively Roman Catholic. Another 3½ percent are Evangelical (the Latin-American word for Protestant). The other 83½ percent have no active affiliation with any Christian church.

Latin-American countries vary greatly in language, culture, racial makeup, literacy, degree of democracy, and stage of social and economic development. Although Spanish is the dominant language, Brazil's 65 millions speak Portuguese; and other areas, French, English, and Dutch. Such variation means difficulty in generalizing about the area.

Theologically, Latin America's Protestants are largely "conservative" and represent nearly all the North American denominations. Cooperative Protestantism is giving ever more attention to Christian education, as evidenced by area-wide consultations in cooperation with the World Council of Christian Education in 1949 and again in 1961.

Generally, the program of Christian education in Latin America has been weak. Sunday schools are found in nearly every denomination throughout the area, but the equipment and planning of Christian education have left much to be desired. Six million children, young people, and adults are enrolled in these Sunday schools. Many of the churches began as Sunday schools, but a pentecostal emphasis has played down religious education.

Some 30 to 40 persons, missionaries and nationals, are giving full time to the work of Christian education, training leaders for regional and local educational responsibility. The Christian youth movement is developing rapidly among Protestants. Four countries have Protestant national youth organizations and an area-wide organization, ULAJE (Latin-American Evangelical Youth Union), now has a full-time secretary training youth leaders. The Y.M.C.A. is found in nearly all these lands, as is the World Student Christian Federation in the universities.

A highly successful venture has been the interdenominational church school curriculum *Curso Evangelica Hispano Americano*, produced over a period of a decade and used by 10 denominations in all the Spanish-speaking lands. Thoroughly prepared in Spanish by nationals, this curriculum has provided lessons (some 198 texts) in a graded series around 4 themes: Jesus Christ, the Bible, the reign of God, the Christian life. Differences in backgrounds have made this series too difficult for some, and a simplified series has been called for. This curriculum has also had distribution and promotion problems. At present it is being revised.

Unfortunately, no Portuguese curriculum of equal proportions has been produced, but several denominations publish their own curricula in Portuguese.

Vacation church schools are proving popular in all lands, but again no adequate curriculum materials have been produced in Latin America. The need for better teaching pictures and training in audio-visuals is great. Radio has been used somewhat for teaching church school lessons.

Consultations have pointed out the need for more leadership training. A scarcity of trained Sunday school teachers and youth leaders handicaps the work of Christian education in the churches. Brazil has developed a short basic course for Sunday school teachers, but the Spanish-speaking lands need one. Some laboratory schools have been conducted in 1 or 2 lands. Only gradually are the theological seminaries introducing courses in Christian education. Family life education is not well developed, and the consultations reported a need in this area.

Some of the earliest efforts of Protestant missionaries involved the conducting of day schools in areas where Government was not doing so. Even today only half the school-age population of Latin America are actually in school. Crowded Protestant schools are able to take only a portion of those seeking admission. Graduates of such mission schools are found among the leaders in government, business, and professions. Lack of popular education has been a large factor in the development of Latin-American despotisms. Roman Catholic controlled education in the colonial period was reserved largely for the ruling families. When the 1st Protestant missionaries were not allowed to preach they opened schools. Such private schools continue to be superior in quality of education to the public schools.

The Spanish and Portuguese brought with them a dislike for work with their hands. Therefore they developed no technical schools and paid little attention to training for better agriculture. This defect the Protestants have sought to overcome.

In 1962, Protestants conducted about 1,157 primary and secondary schools in Latin America. Of these about 1,000 are primary, about 125 secondary, and some 25 or more are technical and commercial schools.

Protestants have 3 major universities: Inter-American University, San Germán, Puerto Rico; Mackenzie University, in São Paulo, Brazil; and Candler University, in Havana.

All these schools and universities have courses in Christian education and its many facets. In addition the churches are permitted in some lands to conduct religion courses in public schools.

Many local churches also conduct nursery or kindergarten schools, and sometimes full primary schools in countries where these are permitted.

Closely related to the educational work of the churches are the campaigns against illiteracy and the effort to supply simple literature for new literates. Writing conferences seek to prepare writers for such simple literature on a whole range of social and personal problems.

Latin-American churches are seeking to train a ministry, but lack of resources and the limited pretheological preparation of candidates are constant handicaps. Scores of denominational theological seminaries and Bible institutes are found in Latin America. Major union theological seminaries, involving from 3 to 6 denominations each, are located in Matanzas (Cuba), Buenos Aires, Mexico City, and San Juan. Brazil has a half dozen denominational seminaries enrolling some 500 students. Brazil reports a shortage of good books on Christian education in the Portuguese language; yet this land has nearly half the Protestants of South America.

Factors encouraging ministerial candidates to cut short their training include the desperate shortage of ministers, lack of educational background, and the limited offerings of many of the seminaries and institutes.

The 1961 consultation on Christian education called for a Latin-American Commission on Christian Education to be set up by the Evangelical Councils of the area.

Protestant Christianity with its stress on individual dignity and responsibility and at the same time on social concern has much to contribute to the life of Latin America. This it can do more effectively and efficiently by full cooperation in the area of Christian education.

— William C. Walzer

LAY APOSTOLATE The words "lay apostolate" are derived from the Greek *laos*, "the (chosen) people," and *apostolos*, "someone sent." "The lay apostolate consists in this, that laymen undertake tasks deriving from the mission Christ entrusted to his church." (Pope Pius XII, Allocution *Six ans*, Oct. 5, 1957, *Acta Apostolicae Sedis*, XLIX, 1957, 922-939.) The apostolate is the sacred activity continuing the Messianic offices in the church and world to restore all things in Christ. Subsidiary and complementary to the hierarchy's, the laymen's apostolate is specified by their rightful and vocational involvement in temporal affairs to orient them to comply with the will of the Creator.

Based on sacramental and extra-sacramental gifts, the lay apostolate in its widest sense pledges all to bear the witness of Christian life and to lead others to Christ. In the stricter sense it is organized lay activity bringing Christian principles to penetrate institutions, milieus, and professions. This 2d form is sometimes called "action of Catholics" or "Catholic Action in the wider sense," and is characterized by lay competence and initiative, with only doctrinal and spiritual dependence on the hierarchy. Lay apostolate in the strictest sense includes the added basis of a particular hierarchical mandate and direct dependence on the hierarchy. This 3d form, mandated Catholic Action, confines itself to integral Christian formation for the general aim of active collaboration in the apostolate of the church, leaving to each member to enter into involvements that appear most likely to succeed in establishing the order willed by Christ the King.

Although the hierarchy was never without collaborators, the Council of Trent marks the time when the laity took rank and progressed in apostolic activity. Women's groups and Marian congregations of men formed then an elite of laity to defend the faith against socially accepted unbelief. The Enlightenment, rising industrialism, and revolutions in the 18th century led to complete church-state separation and widespread unbelief, leaving to the 19th century radically changing and unsympathetic social structures dechristianizing and demoralizing the masses. Political and apologetical-literary defense of the church described the lay apostolate until Leo XIII and Pius X began to elaborate the role of the laity in the church, calling for the practical solution of the social question according to Christian principles. Pius XI created Catholic Action, participation of the laity in the apostolate of the church's hierarchy, giving to lay apostolic activity a new and more effective institutional form and organization.

General movements of ideas and of the world influenced its form, but historically the lay apostolate received most impetus from factors internal to the 19th-century church, namely, renewed consciousness of the mystery of the church and the ecclesiastical character of the laity, renewed interest in holiness lived in the world, mysticism, and Bible study.

Today the lay apostolate follows the general principle of adaptation, evangelization of like by like. It seeks to be universal in extension and to be rooted in sanctity. It includes a humanistic perspective especially for discovering ways to incarnate Christ in the economic, professional, civic, and political fields. The Young Christian Workers, e.g., seek the humanization of all levels and personal witness through apostolic presence in the individual's milieu.

Respecting the autonomy of each association, activities common to all apostolic groups are coordinated by structuring them into a central office — in the U.S.A., the Secretariat of the Catholic Bishops, the total organization being the National Catholic Welfare Conference. The apostolate's unity is thereby rooted and based in the hierarchy. The structure includes national, diocesan, deanery, and parish levels, pursuing the public defense of Christian principles, rights of the church, Christian family, and opposition to fundamental errors through activity in some or all of the following fields: religious activities, family life, youth, civics, and social action (apostolate par excellence), legislation, and communications.

Pius XII wrote 2 parts of an incomplete trilogy giving warp and woof to the lay apostolate — *Mediator Dei* and *Mystici Corporis*. The agenda of the 2d Vatican Council included further articulation of the lay role in the apostolate.

— *Francis J. Abbass*

LEADERSHIP EDUCATION In a broad sense " leadership education " refers to the processes by which the church trains its people for responsible participation in the Christian community. In a narrower sense the term usually has been interpreted as referring to the training of lay persons for the tasks normally discharged by them, in contrast to the more technical education provided for those who enter into professional religious leadership.

The rise of the modern religious education movement led to many agencies designed to improve leadership, especially among Sunday school teachers. " Schools of methods," summer conferences, and teacher training institutes arose in response to a felt need to improve the quality of lay teaching.

In recent decades leadership education has been interpreted as a preparation in depth on the part of members of the Christian community who see their tasks as the exercise of a vocation under God. It is a continuing process rather than exposure to isolated training experiences, and includes participation in the total life of the church as well as study per se. Most denominations have leader-

ship education departments, as does the National Council of the Churches of Christ in the U.S.A. The rise of new curricula has elicited fresh, imaginative approaches: observation-practice schools, parish life conferences, group life laboratories, in-service training, team teaching, depth counseling by ministers and directors. Instead of " package " arrangements that might be perennially valid, the search has been for forms of training that combine versatility of methodology with thorough grounding in the abiding realities of the faith.

Leadership training materials include age-level manuals, audio-visual aids, and discussion guides. Having themselves pioneered in producing paperbacks with an admittedly limited audience in mind (e.g., course outlines for teacher training), the churches now evidence an awareness of the rich resources available in the total paperback production of the publishers. Basic Biblical and theological works, formerly available only in expensive editions and used primarily by professionals, are now purchased and read by innumerable laymen and referred to in denominational literature.

— *Kendig Brubaker Cully*

LEARNING, THEORIES OF Within the discipline of educational psychology, most of the numerous theories of learning seem to cluster around 1 or the other of 2 poles. The 1st, centered in stimulus-response theories, has also been called the molecular or atomistic view of learning, and stands within the Lockean tradition. The 2nd, designated as cognitive theories, with emphasis on a molar view of learning, stands within the Leibnizian tradition.

Although generalizations about

either group of theories are likely to be misleading, it may be tentatively stated that in the stimulus-oriented psychologies, the intellect is viewed as passive; the important matter is what happens as the organism is stimulated from the outside. As the organism is conditioned to respond to effective stimuli, it moves from simple reflex action to more complex patterns of behavior. Because attention can be focused on details of action or reaction and on external conditions giving rise to observable response, theorists often claim to follow the only true scientific approach to analysis of learning. Much is made of the physiological basis for learning, and thus of laboratory study of animals. Within this general area are to be found various specific interpretations. Thorndike's connectionism, holding that connections formed between situations and responses are physiologically rooted in neural bonds or circuits, has eventuated in a series of laws of learning descriptive of those factors most conducive to the forming of these "connections." Conditioning is built on the recognition that an organism learns what it does in response to stimuli. A substitute stimulus can be made to produce the same response as the original stimulus with which it was associated. This suggests the possibilities of human control of learning, although few theorists have expressed as much confidence in this respect as John Watson did in his behaviorism.

In contrast, cognitive theories of learning, sometimes called field theories, assume the existence of an active intellect, capable of selecting out of a total situation those stimuli to which it will respond and also capable of perceiving the relations among factors in a dynamic "field." Moreover, the organism, which is changed by the complex of forces impinging upon it, is itself a factor in the change, and in fact is operative as a power in changing the situation of which it is a part. Insight, closure, tension reduction, are among the terms heard in connection with the classical Gestalt school, Lewin, field theories, or other approaches holding to the Leibnizian tradition that the person initiates action and that cognitive structures both result from and are a determining factor in learning.

Many other theories cannot be clearly placed in either general grouping. Edward Tolman's purposive learning theory draws from both. It emphasizes the role of purpose in learning and sees the learner's goal as providing an inner stimulus. Functionalism emphasizes the fact that mind is a latecomer in the evolutionary process and is active in enabling man to adjust to his environment; it includes such views as those of Dewey, James, and Woodworth.

In general, these theories are based on a view of learning as change of a more or less permanent nature that takes place within the individual. What Freud contributed to the picture, although not directed to the area of learning theory per se, has great significance. Therapy actually involves learning. Thus academic learning theories have benefited from the contributions of medical psychiatry. They have also benefited from the work of social scientists. A person learns as a member of a group. He learns through the process of acculturation. Some scholars even hold, as does George Herbert Mead, that the self arises out of social interaction, so that participation in a group is essential even to the existence of the self. The work of cultural anthropologists and sociologists is of special significance for the education that takes place in home and church.

Of what significance are these learning theories for Christian education? It may be said that many of them are valuable at the point of describing the process by which persons acquire ideas or attitudes often considered to be manifestations of the Christian faith. A person may be conditioned to certain orders of worship, certain symbols. He may be strengthened or destroyed by his relations within a group. Other isolated illustrations might be given. But no one theory is adequate to explain how a person becomes a Christian. Even such points as are applicable in explaining or inducing factual or experiential learning must be tested by the theological discipline which is normative for Christian education.

What may be happening is that Christian education is in process of formulating its own theories of learning, drawing upon various foundation disciplines against a theological norm. There is need for a terminology consistent with a view of learning as changes in the depths of the self. The question of learning thus becomes one of how persons receive the new life offered by God through the disclosure of himself or of how persons appropriate revelation.

Systematic theories cannot be elucidated, but several directions may be suggested. One approach is to say that learning is more dependent on the content of revelation than on anything else. That is, the Biblical message has inherent within it the dynamic activity of the Word of God, bearing the power to effect transformation of persons. To the degree that the educator can help

this message to stand forth clearly for the learner, he has played his role in preparing the way for the Holy Spirit to bring his gift of new life. Such terms as remembrance and identification are helpful here in indicating the way through which the learner receives the message. Reason and will are important as a person articulates his faith, thus possessing it more firmly, and works out in suitable conduct the expression of what he believes to be true. Both knowing and doing are thus means of "becoming." This view is more congenial with the cognitive theories of learning than with the behavioristic, but does not depend upon or even draw largely from any 1 school.

Another approach is to say that learning occurs as a person participates in the drama of redemption witnessed to in the Bible and continuing in the church. Learning is viewed as a social process; participation in the redemptive fellowship of persons among whom the Holy Spirit is present is the way in which a person becomes a Christian. It is as a person experiences truth that he appropriates it. Participation, experience, and interpretation of experience are clues here. In giving attention to the language of relationships as well as to the language of words, the educator hopes that verbal and nonverbal learning will reinforce each other within a climate conducive to experiencing the reality of the gospel message. This view draws from the social sciences, and from those cognitive and functional views of learning emphasizing the fact that change is rooted in social process and experience.

There are views in between the 2 described here, drawing upon both of them. Lewis J. Sherrill, for example, views learning as the process by which the "being" of a person is reborn in a "becoming" as it encounters God within the Christian community. Conscious use is made of Gestalt theory and of depth psychology.

Many theological problems remain to be worked out before it can be determined what the exact relation is to be between a scientific understanding of learning and the Christian view that revelation is the basis for all religious knowledge.

— *Sara Little*

LECTURE The lecture is a formal discourse delivered for instruction. Generically, the term signifies that the lecturer has selected from available choices the material to be presented, and arranged it in some formal fashion for delivery to a class. In use the term often refers to the practice of simply presenting verbally to a class information of the sort not otherwise readily available to them. In either case, the lecture is a system of language actions directed to a class for their instruction. The language in the lecture is described as action, since this is the medium employed in the act of instructing, and the language used is a dimension of the lecturer's total performance in teaching.

The lecture procedure is initiated and carried out by the teacher. The lecture as a technique in the teaching-learning process is best understood when teaching is considered a task word rather than an achievement word, i.e., to teach by lecturing is to engage in an activity that can be pursued independently of the desired outcome. The lecture, like an art form, makes its own demands on those who employ it. This means the lecture, as a method, may be employed successfully without learning's taking place at the same time. Since a teacher ordinarily, however, is concerned that instruction result in learning, the action in the language of the lecture should be adequate and appropriate for the desired learning to take place.

The lecture's instruction potential in the teaching-learning process is a primary consideration for its use. Advocates of pupil-centered methods, which have been so popular in this century, have criticized the lecture method for its emphasis on the teacher and for its seeming lack of provision for the learner as a "whole person." The lecture has been condemned as a poor means of inducing learning in pupils. Studies of the various teaching methods reveal no warrant for this accusation. While a sufficient number of studies exercising proper controls and covering a wide sample of subject matter have yet to be made, studies reported thus far suggest that any method which is adaptable to the demands of the teaching situation, which takes into consideration the pupil's capabilities and interests, and which is carried out with zeal and enthusiasm, appears likely to be successful in the inducement of learning. No method is supported on the argument that it ensures success in learning.

The lecture method as a teacher-centered technique has received less criticism in recent years. By mid-century, the swing of the educational pendulum from extremes in pupil-centered techniques focused attention on the lecture as a valuable means of confronting the class with a specific stimulus. Criticisms leveled in the past, however, have prompted advocates of the lecture method to a serious study of its uses and limitations. The concept of language as action has its importance at this point. The basic question is, Can the action possible in the lecture perform the desired task? This question requires that at least 2 items — language usage and teaching aims — receive thoughtful consideration.

The necessity of participation, at least to the degree of attentiveness, for learning of the kind expected in classwork to occur, demands that language action be appropriate for pupils to respond psychologically and logically. The lecture must deal with areas within the range of the pupils' experience and with concepts that are meaningful to them. Successful lecturing built on these principles does not imply that learning takes place; but for learning to occur through the lecture method appropriate language usage must be possible.

The aims to be achieved through the lecture method are another consideration. Teaching aims frequently involve the development of specific ways of behaving. A lecture can describe qualities of the desired behavior and can prescribe its appropriateness for specific situations, but the class may learn these things without learning so to behave. In the area of character formation, lectures need to be supplemented by other methods, or aims must be limited to what can be accomplished with this method.

The effectiveness of the lecture in the teaching-learning process depends upon allowance for the inherent limitations of the method and upon the skill of the lecturer in both preparation and delivery. The lecture continues to be an honored teaching technique when used with discretion. — *J. Don Reeves*

LEISURE "Leisure" traditionally has been defined negatively as "time that is free from 'the more obvious and formal duties which a paid job or other obligatory occupation imposes upon us'" (Lundberg, Komarovsky, and McInerny, 1934). But it has recently come to be defined more positively as consisting of several elements: an antithesis to work as an economic function; a pleasant expectation and recollection; a minimum of involuntary social-role obligations; a psychological perception of freedom; a close relation to values of the culture; and often, but not necessarily, an activity characterized by the element of play (Kaplan, 1960). In a sense, the shift in thinking about leisure has been away from the remedial function of providing recuperation from work to the developmental function of providing "time for living." This shift is reflected in the modern definition of recreation as "an activity or experience that a person engages in during his free time because he wishes to do so and with no outside compulsion of any type. He recreates to meet inner desires and urges for enjoyable, creative activity, self-expression, and relaxation; to achieve immediate and direct satisfactions. Recreation is an activity engaged in for its own sake and not for any reward beyond itself" (Williams, 1960).

Several attempts have been made to develop categories of uses of leisure. One such classification includes: physical play, crafts, reverie, intellectual play — or knowledge for its own sake, and artistic play (Foote and Cottrell, 1956). Another classification assigns all meaningful use of time: to meet bodily needs; for production of useful goods and services; for private production of products that are not bought or sold but compose the "small things of life," such as hobbies; for service to friends, family, church, and community; and for enjoyment and new experience (Havighurst, 1959). Kaplan identifies 6 types of leisure: sociability, association, games, art, exploration, and immobility.

The amount of leisure time enjoyed by American citizens has increased markedly in this century as a result of 2 forces. The 1st is the reduction in the work week — from 51 hours in 1909 to 39.7 hours in 1960. The 2d is the steady rise in life expectancy — from 47.3 years in 1900 to 69.6 years in 1956, with the corollary, increase in years in retirement. In 1900 some 3.1 people, or slightly more than 4 percent, were aged 65 or over; by 1950 the proportion had doubled to more than 8 percent and the number had quadrupled to 12.3 millions. Concrete evidence that leisure-time activity has increasingly become a leading occupation of the American people is provided by the fact that personal expenditures for recreational goods and services rose from 860 millions in 1909 to 15.9 billions in 1957, as compared with a rise for religious and welfare activities from 819 millions to only 3.6 billions in the same period. Reliable projections indicate that the work week will continue to shorten, increasing numbers of Americans will enjoy lengthening years of retirement, and leisure will continue to grow as a social problem and challenge.

Perhaps the central implication of the expanding role of leisure in American life is the issue of social policy that it poses: shall we "waste" or "use" this enormous national resource? We can choose as the Romans chose, and use leisure for the degradation of human values — with the predictable consequence of the decline of civilization. Or we can choose as the Greeks of the Golden Age chose, and use leisure for the advancement of human values — with the predictable consequence of the flowering of culture. The choice depends on which value system prevails in our society.

Since religious institutions carry a special responsibility for the cultivation of values in our society, the promotion of the value of the constructive use of leisure time would seem to be an appropriate element in the curriculum of religious education. The development of human beings to their full God-given potential is a religious as well as a civic imperative. Even such mundane activities as weekday crafts classes are justified as means to this end, especially if they are tied into a larger program of lifelong development of the total human potential. But perhaps the root objective of religious education in regard to leisure should be to help every individual to discover for himself the "ideal image" of what he can become, and then guide him in the use of his leisure for the achievement of this goal.

— *Malcolm S. Knowles*

LENT The season of preparation for Easter, which in English is called Lent, derives its name from the Anglo-Saxon word *lencten* which, referring to the lengthening of the days, had come to mean "spring." In Latin the name is *quadragesimum*, which means "40." The French is *carême;* the Germans call it "fasting-time" — *Fastenzeit*. Actually, in the early church there was no common agreement as to the number of days (or even the number of hours) during which the faithful should fast. Commonly the fast lasted 1 or 2 days at most. It was not until the 4th century that a fast of 40 days was being urged, and even after that the Lenten period of 6 weeks was not made up totally of fast days. The Eastern Church started Lent with a very simple fast for the first 5 weeks and only imposed severe fasting in Holy Week. In Rome, only the 1st, 4th, and 6th weeks were made up of fast days. The Western Church, with its passion for numerical accuracy, by the 7th century added 4 more days, so that the total number of fast days (Sundays being excluded) was exactly 40. This number was so dear to Christians because of their Lord's 40-day fast in the wilderness that it never occurred to them that there was no basic analogy between Christ's postbaptismal fast and the prebaptismal fast required of catechumens. This confusion, together with the Lenten discipline laid on penitents, resulted in changing a season of joyful meditation upon the mighty and redeeming acts of God into a season of sorrow and soul-searching penitence.

It was inevitable that the fast and preparation of the catechumens should become general, for the early Christians were most community-minded. If a man preparing for Christian initiation was required to fast (and he was!), then his sponsors fasted with him. An experience thus shared is not easily forgotten; its healing qualities would eventually bring about a general demand for a like privilege.

Faith, hope, and charity cannot exist in the vacuum of 1 single personality; they must result in fasting, prayer, and almsgiving. Christ's calm assumption that religious people would normally and inevitably do all 3 is reflected in the phrases: "When you fast," "when you pray," "when you give alms." His only concern was that these should be done without ostentation. The practice of Lent makes them possible for the ordinary person; the discipline of Lent gives them meaning.

— *Edward N. West*

LESSON PLANNING A lesson plan is a teacher's road map. Like any traveler setting out into new territory, he locates where he is, where he hopes to arrive, and some of the places he will pass through on the way. Since he will be traveling with the members of his class, he should consider their present location too.

The opening session of the church school year is usually given to getting acquainted. Plan games and activities through which everyone will learn everyone else's name. Arrange to exchange information about past experiences and present interests. Such information will help the children and the teachers to recognize each class member as a person worth knowing better.

After the opening session, the 1st step in formulating any class plan is to recall and evaluate the previous session: Who were present? In what was each most interested? What significant remarks were made? What questions were raised? And left unanswered? Did the teacher or a member of the class offer to look up any needed information?

Such a thoughtful recollection of the previous sessions should sift out a question, or theme, to focus on for the following Sunday. The teacher will state this theme in terms of a purpose — not a goal to achieve, but a direction to take, e.g., to explore the meaning of forgiveness, to deepen our understanding of the meaning of the church, or to consider Moses' reluctance to do what God asked.

Next, the teacher should clearly state the understanding he is working toward, e.g., forgiveness is _____; the church in its deepest sense means _____; Moses felt unready to take responsibility, but _____.

The teacher now has a direction to take (his purpose) and a distant objective (the understanding to work toward). He is ready, therefore, to plan what steps he will take.

At this point he needs to decide on his 1st step: a challenging question, a startling statement, a pertinent picture, or a story to illustrate a problem. Sometimes he may need to open the session with a review of what was said or done the previous Sunday. Such a review should make clear how the problem or question for the day has grown out of that earlier class meeting.

When a teacher knows where he will start, he then plans 3 or 4 steps in development. Like the starting step, any 1 may be a question, a picture, an activity, a story, or a Bible passage. Each should move the thinking of the class forward and prepare the members for the next stage of the journey. These developing steps are the milestones along the way. Each should be worth the time spent on it. It should be "discussable" or productive of new insights.

The time of the journey can seldom be accurately estimated. There will be delays and detours. There should be sudden opportunities to explore a side road or to collect valuable bits along the highway.

Children (and adults) learn in so many different ways, and the Holy Spirit acts through so many channels, that we dare not schedule the course we want to take lest we crowd out the most important moment of the class session. We must go to class with several clearly planned steps that are directed toward some new understanding of the faith. But we must be ready to turn from that plan when a new and vital direction is indicated by the class. We can come back; we are not being irresponsible. We are just being ready to explore and learn to live with our class.

The last step is a practical one. The teacher should make a list of what he will need in class. To what books will he turn? What supplies does he need? Pictures? Newsprint? Chalk? Paper? Pencils? Crayons? Paints? Clay? What does he need to do to get ready?

When he has planned his journey and gathered his baggage he is ready to set out on Sunday morning.

An outline for a lesson plan might look like this:

I. Significant data from last week
II. Purpose for today's session
III. An understanding to work toward
IV. A starting point
V. Steps in development
   A.
   B.
   C.
   D.
VI. Materials needed for class
       — *Eleanor E. Sandt*

LIBERALISM "Liberalism" is a term used along with "liberal" to describe 2 differing schools or trends within Protestant Christianity. The name may denote, as self-styled liberals insist it always must, a particular spirit or attitude toward both old traditions and new understanding. On the other hand, the name is also employed in referring to a particular body of doctrine giving a distinctive exposition of the basic beliefs of Christians.

As applied to the 1st instance, the term refers to receptivity to that which is new, to freedom from prior commitments (save those to the liberal spirit), and to the willingness to break through present structures of thought or practice in order to formulate new patterns. Usually, the liberal spirit includes acceptance of a particular method by which the old is challenged and new insights, practices, and visions are gained. The method acceptable to the liberal spirit is that of science: the empirical, inductive process by which anything — any law, any common belief, any human experience — may be explored in the quest for knowledge or in the exposing of old falsehoods. The liberal spirit informs anyone who is dissatisfied with things as they are and who is willing to challenge the *status quo*. This attitude of openness and inquiry informed a large and influential segment of the Christian church in the late 19th century. Christian liberalism was founded in part by the movement of secular liberalism that swept into Western culture in the wake of the broad success of naturalistic humanism in such diverse fields as science, literature, art, and political life. It was founded also in the reaction of some churchmen to the aridity and sterility of the rigid orthodoxy that occupied itself almost entirely with the deductive spinning out of the dogmas of Calvinism. The liberal spirit began to make itself heard in the church as men like

Schleiermacher became increasingly convinced that the church had to engage in conversation with the world if it was to be effective. The apologetic task undertaken with such high motivation led theologians not only to listen to what secular thinkers were saying but also to attach to themselves some of their assumptions and conclusions. Christian theology gradually, therefore, assumed the cast of a naturalistic humanism of the time. As this process continued, a body of doctrine developed that set forth in systematic form the concepts characteristic of liberalism as it is understood in the 2d sense of the term.

In America the liberal school followed the basic archetypes of the great European thinkers, developing nevertheless certain of its own particular ideas. Schleiermacher's subjectivism, which described religion's foundation as the "feeling of absolute dependence," and the ethical emphasis of Ritschl and Harnack informed the work of men like William Adams Brown, William Newton Clarke, and Lewis French Stearns. The ethical thrust of the liberal movement found its most vociferous exponents in Washington Gladden, Walter Rauschenbush, and George Albert Coe. The activity of these men served not only to express the social thrust of liberalism but also to help shape some of the characteristic doctrines. It is an indication of the importance of the methodology of liberalism that it was unhesitantly put into practice; all suppositions and premises were corrected, not by logic, but by experience.

Among the distinctive tenets that have come to characterize liberalism are the following:

1. Man: Anthropology is the heart

of the system, for the infinite dignity and value of man as man is the cardinal affirmation of liberalism. Further, man is believed to have almost unlimited potential for growth toward a more ethical way of life. Closely allied to the evolutionary theory, this view has led to constant reference to the as yet unrealized possibilities for both society and the church as men develop, through increasing practice, their inherent capacities for love and justice.

2. God: The continuity of the divine Being with his creation marked the stress on God's immanence. In addition, the picture the liberals drew of God was copied to the greatest extent from the Gospels' portrait of Jesus. The liberals used a process Stearns called " Christologizing," thereby gradually losing sight of God as judge or king and reducing him simply to the kind Father.

3. Jesus Christ: The Son of God came to be described more in terms of his humanity than his divinity. In some minds he was not the incarnate Lord but the prototype of man at his highest and best — having fully realized the potential within. Attaining " Christlikeness " became the goal of much liberal practice and training.

4. Ethics: Christianity tended to be defined as an ethical religion or at least primarily of such a nature. The basis of the Christian religion was the commandment to love. The whole Christian life was caught up in the declaration: " The brotherhood of man under the Fatherhood of God." Love was to be expressed in the struggle for social justice through reconstruction of the forms of social organization.

5. The church: Liberals lost sight of any truly unique dimension in the church, coming to see it largely as an institution of society (1 among many) devoted to character development and social action. The main function of the church was to assist in the maturation of individual spirituality and to serve the community at large.

6. Revelation: Men secured knowledge of God more by introspection and the application of scientific inquiry than by the study of Scripture or the proclamation of the Word from the pulpit. What was learned was not so much the nature of the divine as his will for people in their everyday lives and actions. In some areas the collection of data and resultant conclusions embraced perforce the entire range of possible and relevant knowledge of divine things. Revelation was seen as primarily progressive, the result of men's building up a body of knowledge — increasingly precise — and truth by which society and men might be transformed.

7. Scripture: The Bible stood as a book among books of religion, full of wisdom and guidance for men in the living of their lives. Also, it demonstrated the progressive development of men's religious consciousness and perception as they came to know more and more of God and his purposes by reflecting upon their experiences. The Bible was definitely separated into Old and New Testaments; the former was regarded as an antique representation of primitive spiritual experiences. Within the New Testament, the Gospels stood forth in bold relief as the pure " religion of Jesus " that later authors had perverted with too much theologizing.

8. Salvation: Men were saved, not by radical conversion following

upon conviction of sin, but by gradual growth in knowledge and self-control. The educated and disciplined person who practiced love in his relationships and helped his neighbor gained the victory. In general, salvation has never had anything to do with right relationship to God but, rather, with concern for following the way of Jesus.

During the first 40 years of this century, the creative and influential leaders in Christian education were by and large inspired and instructed by both the liberal spirit and these liberal doctrines. But at the same time that liberalism was crystallizing its doctrinal system and reshaping Christian education, the events of world history, new discoveries by Biblical scholars, and the reaffirmation of the power of the past were altering the theological perspective. Gradually the so-called theological revival affected the philosophy and practice of Christian education, so that by 1950 individuals and groups were hard at work recasting the foundations of the church's educational work. Although Christian educators never fully accepted the new theology, some of the most important and viable of liberal ideals, i.e., the refusal to consign men to insignificance and a recognition of the consequential role that action must always have in Christian life, run like stout threads through current thought on education in the church. Christian education, therefore, has a common ground with a still newer trend in theology that is called neoliberalism and can be expected to make contributions to it in the future. — *David W. Jewell*

LIBRARY, CHURCH A simple plan is presented here as a guide to any church realizing the importance of a church library and wanting to start one.

A church library serves the whole church and is usually directed by a library board or committee with full representation from various age and interest groups in the church. Each church will decide upon the best procedure for selecting this committee — by official board, board of education, or the pastor. The board should appoint the librarian and assistants.

The librarian will determine in a large measure the success of the library. With few exceptions, church librarians are volunteer spare-time workers without previous library experience. Proper training is essential. Such training is fostered by methods like the following: a leadership education class on the church library, offered in denominational and inter-denominational schools; staff members assigned to work with local church library committees and librarians; manuals of instruction and handbooks, giving a step-by-step plan of organizing and operating the church library, including a simplified system of classification and cataloguing; bulletins and newsletters giving additional information on library procedures, recent books, and general news about church libraries; classified and annotated book lists. Many of these aids are provided by denominational publishing houses.

The library, as part of the church program, should be included in the church or church school budget. Here are ways to supplement the budget: a memorial fund for books in memory of loved ones; books (chosen from recommended lists) given in honor and appreciation of service; contributions from friends of the library, classes, and other groups to a fund for new books;

book fairs; church library discounts and free book offers given by denominational publishing houses. Use bookplates to indicate the source of book: " in honor of," " in memory of," " presented by."

Some churches have sufficient space to allow a room for the library. Others use a makeshift arrangement until a room is available: a corner in the sanctuary is fitted with shelves or a folding bookcase; a folding bookcase, rolled into a hallway, or narthex, serves as the library; a book truck carries selected books to a class or group.

A good plan for equipment is to start with the minimum needed for the library to function. Add additional units as the library grows and funds increase. Consult denominational handbooks and manuals for a checklist of library furniture and equipment.

Know the purpose of the library and evaluate all library materials in the light of this purpose to provide: enrichment materials, both printed and audio-visual, needed in all phases of the church program; additional materials to guide teachers and group leaders in their work; materials for all ages for personal enrichment as voluntary leisure reading. These book selection tools are available: church school curriculum; supplementary book lists and resource manuals issued by denominational headquarters and publishing houses; church library bulletins, newsletters, and church periodicals.

The church library is fast becoming a place where the teacher can find anything he needs in the way of instructional materials — printed materials (books, pamphlets, periodicals) and audio-visuals (pictures, maps, filmstrips, slides).

The library board should set certain policies concerning the operation of the church library and assume the responsibility of letting these policies be known: hours scheduled for service, gift books, fines, rules for circulation.

The best way to encourage the use of books is through the teaching program of the church school. Teachers need additional resource materials. Learning experiences are enriched by a variety of carefully selected materials. The church can encourage its members to read good books and other materials by letting them know that what they need to read is just around the corner in the church library. — *Mildred Eagan*

LITURGICAL MOVEMENT The liturgical renaissance is one of the most significant movements in the life of the church in the 20th century. It is characterized by a pastoral renewal growing out of a Biblical, doctrinal, and catechetical revival, and seeks to provide wholeness to corporate worship through the restoration and enrichment of tradition. The primary emphasis is not the restoration of ancient forms or anachronistic ceremonials but a return to church tradition in order to overcome the weaknesses and correct the defects of the present. The main objective is the restoration of vitality to the liturgical expression of the church through full participation of the people in the central Eucharistic action, and through an explicit witness of the people to their faith in daily life. The middle of the 20th century is marked by a liturgical consciousness that perhaps has never been equaled before in Christendom and that can be traced in the various communions of the Western church.

The earliest expression of the movement is found in the work of the French Benedictine, Prosper Louis Pascal Guéranger, founder and 1st abbot of Solesmes (1837). His work was strongly ultramontane and centered about the restoration of the Gregorian chant and pure Benedictine practices. Because this expression was monastic and removed from parish life, it has been strongly criticized as idealistic and romantic and remote from the ordinary practical concerns of the Christian community. The contribution of Guéranger and others in this early period was in scholarly studies of form leading to a doctrinal and devotional appreciation of the liturgy as the prayer of the faithful and as a foundation of personal piety.

The encyclical *Motu proprio* (Pius X, 1903) was the 1st papal sanction for the modern liturgical movement. It restored Gregorian chant to the liturgy and emphasized the active participation of the congregation in the liturgy of the church. The main impetus for the liturgical renaissance as we know it today came from the program outlined at the Catholic Congress of Malines (1909) by Dom Lambert Beaudoin, of Belgium. The stress upon dialogue Masses and the use of vernacular Missals sought the renewal of Christian life through the fuller participation of the laity in the liturgy. The most widely known center of the liturgical renewal has been the Benedictine Abbey of Maria Laach in Germany under the leadership of Dom Idefons Herwegen and Dom Odo Casel. In America the movement has found its fullest expression in the work of the Benedictines at St. John's Abbey, Collegeville, Minn. Romano Guardini's *The Spirit of the Liturgy* (1918) and Gerald Ellard's *Christian Life and Worship* (1933) gave ex-

pression and definition to the full scope of the movement. Pius Parsch, of the Abbey of Klosterneuburg in Austria, through his writings popularized the new emphasis for both the clergy and the laity.

The movement for liturgical reform and renewal that began at Solesmes and grew in depth and definition in Belgium, Germany, and Austria during the 1st half of the 20th century received the official sanction of the church in the encyclicals and decrees of Pius XII. *Mediator Dei* (1947) has been called the "great charter of the liturgy." Pius XII brought reality and vitality to the movement by providing for full participation of the people in the Eucharistic sacrifice, wider use of the vernacular, evening Masses, and greatly simplified rubrics in the Holy Week rites and the Easter Vigil.

A listing of the primary emphases in the Roman Church would include the following: the concept of the church as the mystical body of Christ and the community of believers; the centrality of the Eucharist and the self-oblation of the worshiper in the sacrifice of the Mass; emphasis upon the universal priesthood of the laity and the participation of the congregation in the liturgy; the urging of more frequent Communions; the primacy of the Word of God in the liturgy and restoration of the balance of Word and sacrament; revival of Biblical preaching and role of the priest as minister of the Word as well as the sacrament; official encouragement for reading and studying the vernacular Bible by the laity; wider use of vernacular Missals, dialogue Masses, and the discouragement of extraliturgical devotions at Mass; the correlation of liturgical worship and private devotion; a simplification of rubrics, fasts, and ceremonials; fuller appreciation of the church year, with stress upon the great historical events in the life of Christ and less emphasis upon the cult of saints; simplification in church architecture, with focus on free-standing table altars facing the people and the removal of excessive ornamentation; new expressions in liturgical music and art; the continuation of liturgical celebration in the daily life and work of the faithful as the activity of the body of Christ in the world.

The liturgical movement has not found widespread expression in Roman parish life, and the new emphasis has not been without opposition. The conservative hierarchy of the church has been quick to check extremes of the *avant-garde*. The omission of the *confiteor*, the reading of the Epistle and Gospel in the vernacular without the recitation of the Latin text, the audible praying of the canon, the position of standing rather than kneeling for reception of the Sacrament, and other practices have been abandoned in places under episcopal direction. However, the liturgical movement in its present expression in the Roman Church does represent a renewal in the Biblical and ecumenical faith and practice of the church.

The liturgical movement in the non-Roman Western churches cannot be described in any comprehensive manner. Each communion reflects in varying degrees the movement to regain the wholeness of catholic and ecumenical tradition lost in reaction against medieval practices.

Renewal in the Anglican communion is traced to the Oxford Movement (1833) under J. H. Newman, E. B. Pusey, and J. Keble.

The Oxonians were primarily concerned with academic study of ritual (text of the liturgy) and with the historic doctrine of the church. They reflected the 19th-century interest in the Middle Ages and their interest resulted in the ceremonial revival of the Anglo-Catholic movement. G. Hebert's *Liturgy and Society* (1935) marked the modern renewal in England with the emphasis on the church as the mystical body of Christ to check religious individualism; on a Biblical-theological renewal to overcome liberalism; on the social responsibility of the church to the world to correct irrelevance.

In the Lutheran Church the works of Rudolf Otto, *The Idea of the Holy* (1923), Friedrich Heiler, *Spirit of Worship* (1926), Yngve Brilioth, *Eucharistic Faith and Practice* (1930), resulted in a renewed interest in corporate worship and the sacramental life. In Europe the Lutheran revival has been strongly theological, finding little outward expression in the worship life of the congregation; in America it has been thoroughly indigenous, influenced by the Protestant Episcopal tradition.

In the Reformed churches the movement has been marked by a strong reaction to sterile intellectualism, emotional subjectivism, and pietistic individualism. The renewal in Europe has grown out of Biblical theology with a new understanding of the church and a revaluation of tradition, stressing corporate worship as the divine-human encounter.

In the Protestant churches the liturgical movement is not an organization but an emphasis. In some places it has been charged with substituting archaic ceremonials for evangelical preaching and aesthetics for faith, and with adoption of liturgical symbols and actions without regard to the doctrines implicit in their use. In its fullest expression the contemporary revival is deeply rooted in a recovery of the Biblical and ecumenical tradition of the church as the redemptive community in Christ. Its focus is upon the corporate action of the community in Word and sacraments rather than on the externals of worship. The Eucharistic action of the liturgy is expressed in the social concerns of the body of Christ in the world. — *J. Stephen Bremer*

LOGICAL ANALYSIS " Logical analysis " is the term applied to the popular philosophical school that is also referred to by names such as " linguistic analysis," " analytical philosophy," " conceptual analysis," and " language philosophy." It is often identified as " logical positivism," but this overlooks the fact that logical positivism is only 1 school, now rather discredited, within the total movement.

The movement is rooted in British empiricism, Kantianism, and modern science. Its contemporary form began with the thought of G. E. Moore and the logical atomism of Bertrand Russell and Ludwig Wittgenstein. It received its most spectacular expression in the work of the Vienna circle and " logical positivism " or " logical empiricism." As these movements waned, the later thought of Wittgenstein became most decisive for developments in men like Gilbert Ryle, A. G. N. Flew, and John Wisdom.

This philosophy cannot be identified in terms of any system, and its exponents are widely separated on many important conclusions. What makes it a school is its adherence to a method. It believes that the main

purpose (and sometimes the sole purpose) of philosophy is to analyze the way in which language operates. The philosopher comes to every statement asking: " What does it mean? " " To what family of statements does it belong? " " What is it meant to do? " " What is its logic? " " How would it be verified? " By this method the philosopher hopes to provide a " therapy " for language. Language, which is man's means of communication, all too often becomes a cause of confusion. Before any answer can be obtained, we have to clarify what questions we are really asking.

This language therapy, it is argued, reveals that many of the classic questions of philosophy have remained unanswered because the questions themselves are improper logically. Such questions have to be analyzed in terms of what would answer them. Analysis may prove that the question is meaningless, unanswerable in principle because it does not ask a real question. But analysis may so clarify the question that it can be answered by the appropriate science or discipline.

One of the chief causes of language confusion is found in " category mistakes." In normal speech there are several " language games," as Wittgenstein calls them, which have differing logic. Man all too easily moves from one game to another without realizing that he has done so. To use one of Wittgenstein's simple analogies, time on earth is counted in terms of the relationship of the sun to the earth. But if someone asks what time it is on the sun, he has asked a question that cannot be answered within the logic of the time " game "; the category has been shifted in the middle of the question. In the same way we may commit the blunder of trying to answer ethical questions by the rules of empirical science, questions of fact by the logic of mathematics, or metaphysical questions as though they were logical extensions of factual questions.

Negatively, this method has meant that the philosopher no longer considers himself the custodian of a superior wisdom. The philosopher has no monopoly on discovering the meaning of life, the ultimate nature of reality, or the truly good life. Instead, he offers assistance to all thinkers in clarifying their thought. This has given rise to the charge that this philosophy ignores all of the " important " questions of life. To this the analyst replies that it is not given to the philosopher to be a superman with an answer to all the ultimate questions. Being a man, the philosopher also wrestles with these questions, but being a philosopher does not give him superior answers; it only helps him and others to think about such problems with more rigorous logic.

Logical positivism was hostile to religion, terming all theological and ethical statements " meaningless " or " emotive." More recent logical analysis has recognized that there is a meaning and logic to religious and ethical statements. They belong to their own " language game." The conversation between these philosophers and theologians is still in its beginning, and time alone can tell what fruits it may bear.

— *William Hordern*

LORD'S SUPPER, THE The Lord's Supper is the central sacrament of Christian worship. The rite is known by many different names in different churches, e.g., Eucharist, Holy Communion, Mass, Divine Liturgy.

In the New Testament the Lord's Supper was derived directly from the Last Supper of Jesus with his disciples, which was probably a pre-Passover kiddush or *chaburah* (fellowship meal). The Pauline (the earliest) and Lucan versions of the institution of the Supper (I Cor. 11:23 ff.; Luke 22:19 ff.) include our Lord's injunction that the disciples should " do this " in remembrance of him. Other versions (e.g., Matt. 26:20 ff.; Mark 14:22 ff.) omit it. It is clear, however, that whether or not the command was uttered in these words by Christ, the early church had no hesitation in understanding Jesus' intention that the Supper should be continued by the church in this way.

It appears that early Christians celebrated an agape (love feast) and that this was held often in conjunction with the more formal Lord's Supper or Eucharist, and it was on account of the irregularities that had entered the conduct of this common meal that Paul had to remind converts of the significance of what they were doing (I Cor. 11:20-34; cf. ch. 10:16). In considering the theological significance of the Lord's Supper to the New Testament writers, I Cor. 10:16 and John, ch. 6 (and John 4:1-26), are crucial.

Although there was speculation on the meaning of the Supper that foreshadowed the Eucharistic debates of the medieval and Reformation periods, the patristic writers did not define too precisely how Christ was mediated. They rested content in the faith that they received the body and blood of Christ in the Eucharist without defining " how " in such a way that it became a test of orthodoxy.

Another emphasis that was to become important later is that of the Lord's Supper as a sacrifice. From the beginning it was believed that the sacrament represented the sacrifice of Jesus on the cross (I Cor. 11:26), and with the prospect of martyrdom some of the early writers certainly saw their own suffering as proleptically offered to God in the sacrament. The idea of the Eucharist as Christ's sacrifice offered *by* the faithful for their sins became more pronounced, until during the Middle Ages it became the dominant element in popular devotion.

The differences between the idea of a change in the elements and a symbolic understanding of the Supper were continued in the 9th-century writings of Paschasius Radbertus and Ratramnus, but within 2 centuries it was the conversion theory of the former that had won acceptance: by consecration the bread and wine became physically transformed. The way was open for the theory of transubstantiation, and by the Lateran Council of 1215 the dogma was formulated: the consecrated bread and wine gives place to and becomes 1 substance with the body and blood of Christ. The dogma was developed by Thomas Aquinas and incorporated into his authoritative system. Transubstantiation is thus the official doctrine of the Roman Catholic Church, reaffirmed by the Council of Trent.

Perhaps it was inevitable that in reaction to magical elements in medieval piety the influence of the Reformation was to rationalize the Lord's Supper. Luther himself was conservative, and taught a theory of consubstantiation — the view that although remaining bread and wine, the elements became also the body and blood of Christ through the ubiquity of Christ's risen body. Zwingli denied any Real Presence of Christ in that sense, and explained the Supper as a memorial of Christ's Passion and resurrection.

Calvin seems to have stood midway between Luther and Zwingli. He rejected the literalism in Luther's doctrine, but equally rejected the limitations of Zwingli's rationalism. In his view the communicant by faith receives from Christ the saving power of his body and his blood (receptionism). This position became dominant in the English Reformation. Starting from a very conservative position under Henry VIII, the English Church veered to virtually a Zwinglian position under Cranmer (Edward VI), but ended in very much the same position as Calvin in the Thirty-nine Articles (Nos. XXVIII and XXIX) and in such writers as Jewel and Richard Hooker. The Anglican Communion, however, did not lack those among the Caroline divines who tried to get back to the more " catholic " patristic position. Through Puritanism the Eucharistic view of the churches in England and Scotland affected the doctrine of most churches that trace their origin to an Anglo-Saxon environment. It is worthy of note that against the irregularity with which the ordinary church member partook of the Eucharist during the Middle Ages, Calvin (and his Puritan followers in England) pressed unsuccessfully for a more regular (weekly) celebration of the Lord's Supper as the central act of Christian worship.

Within modern Protestantism, Eucharistic practice covers the whole range between the comparatively " high church " position of Lutherans to those who, like the Society of Friends (Quakers) and the

Salvation Army, do not celebrate the Sacrament. Some Protestant churches, notably Baptists in America, retain the rite, but regard it as an "ordinance" rather than as a sacrament. In the main stream of Protestantism, however, the Lord's Supper is celebrated regularly as 1 of the 2 sacraments instituted by our Lord.

As our understanding deepens, and as liturgical reform in "catholic" circles begins to echo some of the great pleas of the Reformers, ecumenical conversation on the meaning of the Sacrament becomes more possible. On the other hand, great difficulties of interpretation still remain, and perhaps the greatest is that which exists between the "catholic" approach which sees the Real Presence in the Eucharist in terms of incarnation (the saving presence of God in Christ) and the "protestant" approach which interprets it in terms of atonement (the saving action of God in Christ). But Christians are beginning to speak unanimously at least at this point — that when they take bread and wine in the Lord's Supper they are in the presence of a saving Christ.

— *Robert S. Paul*

LUTHER, MARTIN That Martin Luther was mightily concerned for education is a matter of common knowledge. Besides many casual remarks on the subject, he devoted 2 tracts to the theme: *To the Councilmen of All the Cities of Germany That They Should Maintain Christian Schools* (1524) and *A Sermon on Keeping Children in School* (1530). His fellow Germans, he charged, were ready to let their land degenerate into a pigsty. Since monasticism had been abandoned, they were saying, "If our boys are not to become monks, what point is there in educating them?" "Belly-minded, you are," retorted Luther, while he rallied stoutly to the defense of the schoolteacher whose work was often deemed soft and despicable.

When Luther thus upbraided the utilitarians who decried education because the monastic profession toward which it had been primarily directed no longer existed, it might be inferred that he espoused the ideal of education for its own sake; in other words, that he was one of the humanists. He was at one with them in so many respects and yet so fundamentally at variance with them that a prior word is in order as to their educational ideal. It was basically what the Greeks called *paideia* and the Latins *humanitas*. The purpose of education was to form the cultivated man, to round out his personality by exciting his interests and perfecting his skills. He should be trained in body and in mind, able to ride, run, dance, swim, woo, and warble. He should be adept in poetry, music, the graphic arts, the natural sciences, theology, and sermons. Of necessity, humanism had to be aristocratic, since not many could afford the wealth or leisure for such pursuits, and it had to be individualistic, because each individual was called upon to develop his own potentialities. But it was not, therefore, antisocial. Humanism included *humanitas*, an attitude of civility and courtesy to one's fellowmen.

Luther was very different. His ideal of education was not that of the cultivated man, but of the civic man, set in society to serve his fellows. His scheme of education, therefore, closely followed his concept of the callings. They are not primarily professions by which to earn a living, though man does have to earn a living. They are, rather, areas in which each, as he is placed, undertakes to contribute to his fellows. There are 3 main areas: *Lehrstand,* including the preacher and the teacher; *Wehrstand,* including the magistrate, the lawyer, and the soldier; and *Nährstand,* including the domestic and the economic.

Luther began with the *Lehrstand.* He would train the teacher in order to get the preacher. Boys must be trained for the ministry if the church is not to fall. There must be learned ministers, and their training must be in many of the humanist disciplines, particularly the philological. The program of the humanists was thus taken over, but with a different emphasis. Luther's all-absorbing concern was to interpret the Word of God. Since the Bible was given by the Spirit in Greek and Hebrew, these languages are essential to its understanding. If the very gospel is not to die, if God's supreme gift to mankind is not to perish from the earth, someone must know Greek, and since the New Testament is the fulfillment of the Old Testament, someone must know Hebrew. The very salvation of mankind depends on the ancient languages. Luther gave himself to the acquisition of these tools, seeking faithfully to achieve accuracy. When the New Testament of Erasmus came out in Greek (1516), Luther was lecturing on the 9th chapter of Romans. He brought the great work to the classroom, and from then on it became the basis of his exegesis. The next edition of 1519 served for Luther's own translation. Throughout his life he continued to revise his early work in the direction of greater precision, even

at the expense of piquancy and of his own theological penchants. To be sure, Luther recognized that the gospel might be preached by those who do not know the ancient tongues, but he felt that their preaching would be insipid.

After his plea for an educated ministry, Luther turned to the preparation of servants for the civil state. Rulers require secretaries and assistants in administration. They also must have legal advisers; the state entails legal machinery. At this point the canon law was to be dropped, with the Roman law to replace it. The jurist thus has a calling, and for this he must be trained. Luther recognized that the soldier also has a calling, but apparently assumed that no formal education in the schools was necessary in his case.

As for the economic order, under which Luther included the domestic, he was not much interested in training merchants, but stressed the education of mothers because they are the educators of their children. It was the mother's rather than the father's responsibility to give this training. Luther's concern was not to produce cultivated women such as those of the Italian aristocracy in the Renaissance, but intelligent women. He would teach them Latin. Here we must remember that Latin was the lingua franca of Europe. Luther at this point shared the humanist ideal of a universal culture. He desired that as many as possible in Germany should be bilingual.

As for the other disciplines, Luther had not too much to say. He did love music, and he proposed that it be taught in school. He made provision for the training of both adults and children in congregational song. Luther did not despise the subjects that intrigued the humanists. He regretted that he had not been taught more poetry and belles lettres. Especially he esteemed history because there could be seen the dealings of God with man. Luther had little to say in some areas that did enlist his interest, for example, the graphic arts. He supervised some of the illustrations for his works, but there was no need to enter a plea for education in the schools for woodcutters, draftsmen, or architects, for these skills, like many others, were acquired through the apprenticeship system.

One thus sees that Luther achieved a certain synthesis of the ideal of the cultivated man and the civic man. His point of departure was not man's self-development but his place of responsibility in society.

Luther committed education to the state, that is, to local municipal authorities. Heads of families, he said, were not in a position to educate their families. The church had not the resources. The municipal governments should then set up schools and require attendance of boys and girls, though perchance the girls could not be spared for a full day. Here was compulsory state education, but not to the exclusion of religion. The church should inculcate obedience; the state should patronize piety.

Luther did not regard the state, as such, as a Christian institution. The state was ordained by God as the creation for all peoples. The church goes back to the incarnation of God in Christ and applies only to his followers. The state implements the sub-Christian ethic of natural law. The church lives according to the ethic that is above law, flowing spontaneously from gratitude and love. Much of the instruction, then, which Luther enjoined was not to be considered Christian — not anti-Christian, to be sure, but sub-Christian. Yet Christian instruction was also to be given to all and not simply to those who would become ministers. This scheme of education represented the sort of synthesis which medieval Christianity had attained and which Luther did not disrupt, a synthesis of the classical and the Christian worlds. That was why, even for Luther, Aristotle and Cicero had a place in the curriculum. — *Roland H. Bainton*

LUTHERAN CHURCH IN AMERICA

The Lutheran Church in America, with nearly 3,200,000 members, is the largest of the 3 major Lutheran bodies in America. It was constituted in June, 1962, by the merger of 4 groups: the American Evangelical Lutheran Church (Danish, 24,000 members), the Augustana Lutheran Church (Swedish, 605,-000), the Lutheran Church — Suomi Synod (Finnish, 36,000), and the United Lutheran Church in America (predominantly German, 2,477,000).

Although the new church did not begin to function fully as a merged body until January, 1963, its curriculum for Christian education had been under development since 1955. At that time the Board of Parish Education of the ULCA launched what it called its "Long-Range Program of Parish Education," which was designed to look a decade into the future to anticipate the church's educational needs. In 1957 the Boards of Parish Education of the other 3 bodies began working cooperatively on the project. A joint staff was established, with the assignment of readying the curriculum for the merged church.

From the outset the new program

of parish education was based on 4 principles. It was to be frankly Lutheran, growing out of the theological position of the Lutheran Church and relating to it the insights of the educational sciences. It was to be comprehensive, providing the curriculum for all age levels and all educational agencies of the parish. It was to be fully coordinated. This meant building a single, overarching curriculum that related the educational work of the family, Sunday church school, weekday church school, vacation church school, catechetics, school of religion (a weekday program for senior highs and adults), church camps, and leadership education. It was to be long-range in the sense that it sought to envision the kind of educational program the church would require in the late 1960's and early 1970's.

Development of the program was divided into 4 phases. Phase 1 dealt with the statement of general and age-group objectives for Christian education. In this study the position was taken that the new curriculum should at all times be concerned with 1 central purpose:

"Inasmuch as the church, as the body of Christ, seeks to become more effectively that community of believers in which the Holy Spirit calls, gathers, enlightens, and sanctifies individuals in their relationships with God and their fellowmen, the church's central education objective, therefore, shall be — To assist the individual in his response and witness to the eternal and incarnate Word of God as he grows within this community of the church toward greater maturity in his Christian life through ever-deepening understandings, more wholesome attitudes, and more responsible patterns of action."

It was conceived that this growth toward Christian maturity is a never-ending process that occurs in 6 basic relationships of life. These are the learner's relationship to God, the church, fellowmen, the Scriptures, the physical world, and himself. The general objectives governing the program were stated, therefore, in terms of changes in understandings, attitudes, and patterns of action developed in these relationships.

Once the general objectives were drafted, the next step was to calibrate them in terms of various age levels. In this process, growth objectives in these same relationships were stated for each year of life from birth through age 17 and for older youth, young adults, middle adults, and older adults.

Phase 2 was concerned with curriculum design. Since learning was conceived of as changes in a personality occurring within certain relationships, curriculum was viewed as the organizing of experiences within which such changes might take place. The key to arranging such experiences, it was felt, lay not simply in the structure of content or subject matter but more importantly in the learning process itself whereby the pupil relates new experiences to the existing structure of his own person. On the assumption that a person learns most effectively when he is met at the level of some deep need or involvement, the curriculum planners set up a scheme of "continual life involvements" that are characteristic of persons living in our culture and that provide the context of common learning experience. Matching these involvements, they outlined a series of "continual Christian learnings" anticipated when a person is confronted at the point of his life involvements by the Word of God. Specific age-group objectives are related to, or are aspects of, these continual Christian learnings.

Armed with a thread of continuity for both context and content of learning, the Lutherans then set about assigning functional curriculum responsibilities to the educational agencies of the parish. This involved extensive research as to the potential and limitations of the existing agencies in the merging bodies. On the basis of these data it was determined what function each educating arm could serve best. For example, the Sunday church school is regarded as the "nuclear school" because it reaches the largest number of persons over the greatest span of years. It has the function of dealing with the most significant learnings at a given age and helping the pupil relate to them the experiences he has elsewhere in the educational program.

Phase 3 of the program deals with the production of instructional materials to implement the curriculum design. These include several hundred reading books, workbooks, activity kits, teacher's guides, parents' manuals, and correlated teaching aids, such as audio-visuals. Almost all the new materials are field-tested in an elaborate research program in some 60 pilot parishes.

Phase 4, introduction of the curriculum, began in 1961 with a year of readying the churches for launching a new leadership educational curriculum in 1962. Major emphasis in the program is given to leadership classes in every congregation and thousands of coaching conferences conducted by national and regional staff.

Examination of the basic documents undergirding the new Lutheran curriculum and the instructional materials being produced reveals several significant developments. (1) There is clear evidence of the resurgent interest in theology in educational circles. (2) The curriculum shows an earnest effort to utilize the insights of the educational sciences regarding the teaching-learning process. (3) Many practical changes are being made in the educational program of the parish, such as lengthening the traditional Sunday school "hour" to 75 minutes, abandoning departmental grading in favor of close grading, introducing team teaching, providing administrative structure to coordinate the work of all schools and agencies, increasing confirmation instruction to 3 years and making it a part of weekday church school, creating a "school of religion" for youth and adults, relating the family much more closely to the congregational program of education, replacing much of the worship in church schools with education in worship, and making leadership education the key to using the new curriculum. (4) The Lutherans have been giving new weight to research in Christian education, the whole curriculum being built around a framework of research, experimentation, and evaluation. — *W. Kent Gilbert*

LUTHERAN CHURCH — MISSOURI SYNOD The Lutheran Church — Missouri Synod is basically an association of congregations banded together to accomplish certain purposes that the congregations cannot achieve individually. One of the purposes of the organization is the promotion of Christian education. This is reflected from the beginning of the Synod in 1847 by the inclusion of such objectives in its constitution as the training of teachers, the publishing of schoolbooks, and the furtherance of parochial schools and confirmation instruction.

Since the promotion of Christian education is one of the primary purposes of the synodical organization, all synodical officers give some leadership for this aspect of the church program. Demands for increased unification and supervision of the program and for more service to the congregations in parish education led to the creation of special boards or committees on parish education in the Synod and in the districts of the Synod.

The development of the synodical program of special leadership in parish education began with the establishment of a General School Board in 1914. In 1920 a General Sunday School Board was created to serve the growing number of Sunday schools in the Synod. These 2 boards were merged into a Board of Christian Education in 1932. This board gave attention to all aspects of elementary education, and in the Sunday school area included attention to the high school level. In 1944 the Synod assigned the area of adult education and the promotion of Lutheran high schools to this board and renamed it the Board of Parish Education.

The Synod is presently divided into 32 districts, each of which has a District Board of Parish Education. The district boards cooperate with the synodical Board of Parish Education and assist and advise local congregations in the organization and maintenance of parish schools and offer suggestions for furthering the work of parish education. The districts in turn are divided into smaller units called circuits, many of which have a circuit educational representative.

Among the basic concerns of the Missouri Synod in the area of parish education have been the following: elementary schools (promotion, recruitment, training of teachers; publication of textbooks and curriculum guides); Sunday schools, vacation Bible school, weekday classes, Saturday school (publication of lesson material and manuals for teachers; encouragement of teacher training; development of Sunday school associations, workshops, and conventions, encouragement of vacation Bible school workshops); catechetical instruction for confirmation; high schools (promotion, service publications, curriculum studies); adult education (Bible study; family-life education); church-state relations (resisting antiparochial school legislation; studies on state aid for parochial schools and Federal aid for education; study of religion in the public school); leadership training (a comprehensive program of Sunday school teacher training in the local congregation, with 14 courses; a program of lay leadership training in 90 evening Bible institutes); professional training of teachers for elementary schools and high schools (teachers colleges are maintained at River Forest, Ill., and Seward, Nebr.; in addition, many students study at one of the 9 junior colleges of the Synod; a graduate program is maintained at River Forest); training of pastors in Christian education (the program of ministerial education at Concordia Seminary, St. Louis, and Concordia Seminary, Springfield, Ill., include a broad emphasis on Christian education); in-service training of pastors, teachers, Sunday school teachers.

— Arthur L. Miller

M

MANN, HORACE Horace Mann was born at Franklin, Mass., May 4, 1796, and died at Yellow Springs, Ohio, Aug. 2, 1859. His youth was spent working on his ancestral farm in a rural New England community. The death of his father and older brother while he was young required that he remain at home until he was 20 years old. He was admitted to Brown University with full sophomore standing despite a most limited formal schooling and just 6 months' intensive preparation with an itinerant schoolmaster.

After graduating with honors from Brown and the Litchfield Law School, he was admitted to the Norfolk County Bar in Dedham, Mass., in 1823. He was a successful lawyer and politician and was elected to the General Court in 1827. There his efforts centered on the founding of the state hospital for the insane at Worcester, the revision of the laws of the Commonwealth, a spirited defense of religious freedom, and a stricter enforcement of laws controlling the sale of liquor and lottery tickets. All these reflected an intense interest in legislation that might improve the conditions of those about him. The fact that he was later called the "father of American public education" has detracted from his impressive record as a legislator.

He was elected to the State Senate in 1833, becoming its president in 1836. This was a time of bitter partisan strife, and Mann found a diminishing satisfaction from his political endeavors. In 1837 he accepted the newly created position of Secretary to the Massachusetts State Board of Education. Although he had little legal authority over the schools in his new post, he used all his powers of persuasion to awaken a lethargic public to the low estate of public education. Through the *Common School Journal,* which he established, and especially in his 12 annual reports, he evolved a comprehensive rationale for the public schools as an essential part of republican government. He argued that since men could not be free and ignorant at the same time, the public needed to finance and direct a system of education for all children, regardless of their religious, ethnic, or social origins.

Mann viewed education basically as a moral endeavor, but because of the diversity of pupils in the Commonwealth, he insisted that all such training be nonsectarian. A state law had prohibited the use of any textbooks in the schools that contained sectarian teachings. Mann therefore prevented the use of several obviously Calvinistic publications in the school libraries. This was quickly attacked as the 1st step of a concerted attempt to create " godless schools." In the ensuing pamphlet wars, Mann maintained that while sectarian teachings had no rightful place in the schools, there were still some universal principles, basic to moral training and accepted by all religious groups. Many of these principles, he felt, could be found in the Bible, and he vigorously supported its use in the classroom, provided each child was allowed to make his own interpretations of the readings. To the more orthodox this " least common denominator approach " appeared to be a thin disguise for Mann's own liberal Unitarian beliefs, but Mann's views gradually prevailed.

In 1848, Mann resigned the secretaryship and took the seat of John Quincy Adams in the United States House of Representatives. As an antislavery Whig, his adamant opposition to the Compromise of 1850 gained him the animosity of Daniel Webster. In 1852 Mann received the gubernatorial nomination on the Free Soil ticket in Massachusetts, as well as an offer to become the 1st President of Antioch College, a coeducational and nonsectarian school being founded by the Christian denomination. Disillusioned by the apparent success of the coalition of Webster supporters and Southern slaveholders, Mann decided to reenter educational work. At Antioch his efforts were plagued by religious and financial troubles, but he managed to weather the many vicissitudes. Mental anguish and overwork finally caused his collapse 2 months after the school's commencement in 1859. His speech to the graduating class proved to be his own valedictory. In it he ably expressed the driving motif in his own life, as well as that in the lives of other humanitarian reformers: " I beseech you to treasure up in your hearts these my parting words: Be ashamed to die until you have won some victory for humanity." — *Jonathan Messerli*

MAPS A map is a graphic representation of the relationship of places in space and (through a historical series) in time. Since religious history, like man's life in general, unfolds in space and time, the use of maps is important in the process of Christian education.

The oldest known map in the world was found in the excavation of the Old Akkadian city of Gasur (later Nuzi; now Yorgan Tepa) in Mesopotamia. It was inscribed on a clay tablet, probably around 2500 B.C. Apparently intended to show the location of some estate, it clearly indicates mountain ranges, rivers, and cities. The oldest known city plan was also found on a clay tablet in the excavation of the Mesopotamian city of Nippur. It dates from around 1500 B.C., was carefully drawn to scale, and shows rivers, gates, and buildings. It was so accurate that the excavators used it as a guide for their further work. In Egypt the earliest equivalent of a map was carved on a temple wall at Karnak shortly before 1300 B.C., and shows forts and lakes on the coast road between Egypt and Palestine. Two maps on papyrus, of slightly later date, now in the Turin Museum, show mining regions near Coptos east of the Nile. Of the Greek map makers the most famous were Eratosthenes (3d century B.C.), whose work is known from fragments preserved by Strabo; and

Ptolemy (2d century A.D.), whose work became known in western Europe through a Latin translation made in the 15th century. A Roman drawing of the 3d century A.D., preserved only in a 13th-century copy, the so-called *Tabula peutingeriana,* provides a sort of strip map, 25 feet long, extending from Rome to Jerusalem. In the Palestine area the oldest map is the badly damaged floor mosaic of a now destroyed 6th-century Christian church at Madeba in Transjordan. With deep green for the sea, light brown for the plains, dark brown for the mountains, and place names in Greek letters, this originally gave a panoramic view of the Holy Land. Best preserved is the portion showing Jerusalem, where walls, towers, streets, and many buildings, including the Church of the Holy Sepulchre, are plainly recognizable.

For modern study, a base map of the entire Near East has been prepared by the Oriental Institute of the University of Chicago. The Bible lands and the classical lands of the ancient world appear in maps of the National Geographic Society. Detailed maps of Palestine were compiled by the British Survey of Palestine; and a new survey is being made by the State of Israel.

Detailed geographies of Palestine have been written by George A. Smith, F. M. Abel, and Denis Baly. Modern Bible atlases often combine accurate maps, beautiful photographs, and descriptive text. Such volumes have been prepared by George E. Wright and Floyd V. Filson (The Westminster Press), L. H. Grollenberg (Thomas Nelson & Sons), Emil G. Kraeling (Rand McNally & Company), Samuel Terrien (Golden Press, Inc.), and Herbert G. May (Oxford University Press).

There is also an atlas of the early Christian world by F. van der Meer and Christian Mohrmann (Thomas Nelson & Sons) which follows the history of the church into the 7th century.

By the use of such maps and related materials the events of Biblical and early Christian history can be placed in their setting in space and time. Indeed, space and time can also to an extent be transcended as stimulated imagination and instructed thought so reach across the miles and the years that the events upon which Christian faith rests become again present and contemporary. — *Jack Finegan*

MARRIAGE EDUCATION Education for marriage in a formal sense has developed during the 1st half of the 20th century. Such an approach has come about as a result of the disruption of our society and its family life by the impact of total revolution. Prior to that time growing up in the home was considered adequate preparation for marriage.

Before the turn of the century the family form universal throughout the country was patriarchal. Father was head of the house, made major decisions, handled all the money, and supplied a great deal of the discipline. Woman's work was in the home. Images of husband, wife, father, and mother were clear, and the young could imitate and later participate in the kind of activities that moved them from childhood into adulthood and prepared them for these roles. Most of the experiences of life, including work, social life, recreational activities, education, and worship, were experiences within the family or with the family. Individuals to a great extent existed for the family.

The industrial revolution developed into a technological explosion. The population of our country was moved from ¾ on the farm to ⅘ in towns and cities. Father's work used to be with members of the family, and he operated as boss on the job. He was there to make decisions, handle funds, and supply the discipline. Today, fathers for the most part work away from home and much of the responsibility for what goes on around the home is placed upon the wife and mother. In her discharge of these responsibilities, she has been accused of usurping the man's authority within the family.

Most of the experiences formerly enjoyed with the family are now sought outside the family in institutionalized or commercialized form by individual members separately. Today the family exists for the individuals, and among the things that hold it together are affection and what little companionship may be had. Not much of life is experienced as a family.

The idea of democracy has filtered down from government through the culture into the home and affected the ideas and expectations of the people in it. A strong emphasis upon the worth and rights of the individual is defense against increasing demands for conformity. Developments in education resulting from scientific research concerning child care and guidance through the developmental processes of youth have radically affected parent-child relationships.

All families have not moved at the same rate or to the same degree away from the benevolent autocracy of the patriarchal family toward emerging forms of equalitarianism or democracy in family life. Young people coming from these families frequently intermarry and discover a radical difference in their background responsible for conflicting ideas of husband, wife, father, and mother, and many other things about the home.

Other influences add to the need for understanding marriage and the family in our modern world, e.g., the changing attitudes of society and the church toward divorce, new legislation providing more grounds for it, and the rising tide of irresponsible sex behavior both prior to and after the wedding.

Some of the more thoughtful college students began to demand help from educators as far back as 1928. The readiness of college young people for help in their approach to marriage was demonstrated by the attendance of thousands of students at a series of lectures upon the subject given by specialists in the field at Stanford University in the decade preceding World War II. At the University of North Carolina, a men's school at the time, a group of students interviewed the president with a direct request that someone be found who could help them get ready for the experience of marriage. The 1st credit course in education for marriage was offered there by Ernest Groves in 1928. A few years later, Henry Bowman began to develop a course in preparation for marriage at Stephens College, Columbia, Mo.

With the exception of these 2 courses, the pattern of development on the college level has been from the lecture by specialists in a noncredit series to a credit course, with a symposium composed of authorities from the various fields of knowledge involved. Students were left to themselves to integrate the material.

Experience demonstrated the need for a teacher to aid in the integrative process, and professors in various departments at different universities were asked to assume responsibility for the course. This resulted in an inevitable slanting of materials in the direction of the teacher's specialization.

Teacher training emerged at Florida State University and in the graduate schools of several others. Interdivisional and interdepartmental experience involving sociology, psychology, philosophy, religion, economics, biology, law, medicine, and such other areas as were indicated by the experience of marriage was provided. Today there are approximately 800 liberal arts colleges and universities offering functional courses in preparation for marriage and the family, as differentiated from the traditional course in sociology entitled " Family."

The education for marriage movement spread into the high schools, so that today thousands of high schools have some such course in the curriculum. Its adequacy is directly related to the preparation of the teacher and the attitude of the school board and the parents in the community. In some of the larger cities the entire school system has a plan for the education of senior high school students for marriage and family life.

At first, research was grounded in the trouble area of sex relationships. Later, psychologists and sociologists began to investigate interpersonal relations in marriage and family life. The early textbooks show a blend of material borrowed from the traditional areas of subject matter and the findings from direct research into the marriage and family experience.

Churches, especially through the Federal Council of Churches' Commission on Marriage and the Family, began to develop materials and programs intended to be helpful to young people in their dating experiences and as they moved into the courtship and engagement process. The Department of Family Life of the National Council of the Churches of Christ in the U.S.A. has continued this cross-fertilization among denominations in behalf of the Christian home. Catholic, Jewish, and Protestant leaders interested in better preparation for marriage have been in communication with persons in all professions having a similar concern.

The Groves Conference for the Conservation of Marriage and the Family was established in the early 1930's, and the National Council on Family Relations was organized not long thereafter. Both organizations have memberships of an interprofessional nature and are functioning with a common concern: better education for marriage and better-trained counselors for people in trouble in their marriage.

Agencies such as the Family Service Association became involved and moved in the direction of educational effort through their experiences of counseling with families in difficulty. The American Social Hygiene Association, at first primarily concerned with the prevention of the spread of venereal disease, broadened its interest to include the family and has recently developed an emphasis upon education for marriage. The Planned Parenthood movement, starting with concern about the timing and spacing of children, realized the involvement of their concern with the total life of the family and included materials and classes in education for marriage. Public agencies, notably the Court of Domestic Relations in Cincinnati, and the Court of Domestic Relations in Lucas County, Toledo, Ohio, have begun to attempt reconciliation prior to the granting of divorce.

The American Association of Marriage Counselors was established in 1942 for the purpose of setting up standards and making an effort to protect the public from exploitation by those ill-equipped and untrained to counsel. Theological seminaries now include training for both premarital and marriage counseling.

— *W. Clark Ellzey*

MASS MEDIA Mass media of communication are technical means by which ideas, words, and images can be propagated in readily accessible forms to large and largely unselective masses of people. Among these means several are literary: newspapers, magazines, and books oriented toward wide readerships. Others are audio-visual: radio, motion pictures, television.

Not all technical modes of communicating qualify as mass media. If a select portion of a large population is chosen, the mass assumption is absent, e.g., a technical book or a film produced for salesmen of a specific firm. The technology that produces material for the appetites of a mass market, and, to complete the circle, also produces the mass market, is thus involved only superficially. What is decisive in this category is the intention and the relative degree of success in the distributing of ideas, words, and images.

With this in mind, the communicator is necessarily forced to carry assumptions about his potential audience in mind. His assessment of those unitary factors that underlie modern pluralistic societies will be determinative. His communications will operate within the broad contexts of least common denomination. He may on occasion raise or sophisticate the expectations of an audience or a market. He may on occasion lower or vulgarize them. Basically, he thrives to the extent with which he moves within the established contexts of mass communication. Thus his industry is closely related to the whole endeavor of determining and polling public opinion.

Motives for communication are manifold. They include 1st, in a market-oriented society, the commercial. The communicator sells a product or uses the advertising of products to subsidize the propagation of other ideas, words, and images. A 2d motive is the desire to influence the ideas of large numbers of people because the communicator believes in them and desires to see them prevail by the free choice of the audience. If the 1st motive involves the communicator in the advertising industry, the 2d provides him with an opportunity to engage in acts of public service or social reform. A 3d motive, evident particularly in the sociopolitical and economic fields, is the exploitation and manipulation of masses of people through biased communication (propaganda), with intention to control them.

If these are varied motives of the communications industry, the audience is also attracted for a variety of motives and reasons. It is attracted, for one, by the efficiency and effectiveness of the media and by their pervasiveness and accessibility. Measurements of response can be objectively deduced through statistics of public acceptance (television ratings or newspaper circulation figures are cases in point). It is, however, more difficult to measure the depth of response and the psychic effects on the people who are engrossed in the media. Without question, the mass media do alter opinions and shape attitudes, but it may be safe to generalize that other shaping forces in life (the family, other associations, personal anxieties, etc.) are partial counterforces to the impact of mass media. Even the pervasiveness and accessibility of the media militate against their effectiveness: the public, bombarded with so many " signals " and claims, tend to build inner defenses in either casual or conscious manners.

Historically, the mass media are related to the industrial and technological revolution of the modern secular period. The invention of movable type late in the 15th century and the development of vacuum tubes and electronic devices some four centuries later made technically possible the development of modern communication. Developments in transportation that brought men physically nearer each other; developments of mass production that made numbers of products available to large masses of people; the spread of ideologies: all these created new possibilities and new needs for more rapid communication.

Because mass media are involved in changing the basic relations of men to other men; because they represent competing value systems; because they bear a potential for shaping attitudes, they have always represented threats and opportunities to Christian churches and particularly to Christian educators. They can be threats because the sheltered

communities of Christian nurture are interrupted by attractive, efficient, competitive systems of value. Here is 1 illustration: the typical American child who spends 1 or 2 hours per week in the circle of Christian nurture may watch television 20 hours per week and have dramatic portrayals of a way of life often contrary to the Christian way brought to his attention. But the media can also represent opportunities because Christian truth and action can also be represented on these media.

Illustrations of such uses can be summarized in a fourfold way. First, the development of mass media has technically profited the Christian churches. It has provided new languages, new forms of communication. It has produced means (motion pictures, filmstrips, religious magazines) by which the religious community nurtures itself. Second, churches may use the media in a limited way to reach a limited portion of a potential audience or market. This could be termed " hitchhiking " — sharing space on vehicles that have other destinations in mind. The church page segregated in a metropolitan newspaper is an illustration. It is usually read by the church-minded and serves as a bulletin board; it does not seek to enter into the broader consciousness of the mass market.

Third, a particular emphasis may be directed to a mass audience within still definable forms of community other than those which modern urbanism represents. Low-wattage radio stations and small-town newspapers use the technical aspects of mass communications to saturate relatively homogeneous public communities.

Fourth, Christian education can be advanced by adapting modes of representation used for reaching a mass audience. This may be done by representing Christianity as 1 particular voice within a pluralistic society. It may be done by Christian participation in a dialogue with other elements of the society. It is perhaps done most effectively when the Christian story is made dramatic in news events or in easily portrayable lives and actions.

Educators within Christian spheres are given the task of relating Christianity to audiences shaped in no small measure by mass means of communication. They must interpret the other signals that people receive, and they must translate Christian expression in the light of secular and religious assumptions.

— Martin E. Marty

MATURITY Maturity as applied to human beings or animals means that they have reached their limit of development in a particular area. This is not the result of learning but is due to changes that come naturally. As bodily structures develop there is also the unfolding of bodily, mental, and emotional qualities. Simple examples of certain kinds of maturity are the ability of a young child to walk and the usual change in voices of boys at puberty. The glands as well as the nervous system, which is composed of literally billions of cells, each one capable of making hundreds of contacts, must mature in order to bring about adult behavior.

Learning depends on the development of the individual. It is, for example, impossible to teach persons to walk or talk or make love until their powers to do so develop. Maturity and learning go together, as a child develops in age and intelligence. Thus, education depends on maturing as well as on learning.

Maturity is clearly distinguished from childhood, for it involves vocation, marriage, parenthood, middle and old age. Parents and educators should recognize that maturity is achieved where conditions are right for that end. The younger in years may sometimes be more mature than the older in some ways. The older, though more mature in years, may be childish in certain aspects of life. Good behavior as well as skills marks the mature.

The child must feel that he belongs. He then relates himself to the other members of the group, gradually extending his contacts to neighbors and to members of the school. If he is not happy in his home, all life may be, and probably is, disrupted. If love is there, it easily extends to God, the giver of all good. If parents are careless and indifferent to God and the good, the child is apt to develop similar attitudes. If the parents are devout and attend church, it is natural for the child to do the same.

Adolescence is a trying time for most young persons and for most homes. It is easy for the parents to misunderstand the youth and equally easy for the youth to be intolerant of all restraints. If parents and youth are good friends, these problems and difficulties may be met by consultation and friendly give-and-take. But if mother or father is intolerant and gets angry at any expression of change from the child to the adult — such as in the youth's contact with other boys and girls, his use of the family car, his value of school, or in any of the hundreds of problems that every youth meets — then there is nothing but trouble and perhaps tragedy in that family. But if the boy or girl is sure of friendly counsel, he will likely come for counsel, and the love of the home will be maintained. This is what matters. But if it is otherwise, then the parents, not to mention the child or children, are in for serious trouble. Adolescence is a time of difficulty, but it is as trying for the youth as for the parents. If there is deep faith in God on the part of parents and youth, even the worst trials are overcome and family love and loyalty are maintained. This is more important than any other consideration.

Adolescence passes into what is here called youth. Many of the problems of this age have been touched on already. The most important now are marriage, lifework, and the individual's attitude to others. If good family relations have been maintained, they are a wonderful blessing both to the young people and to their parents. But if home life has broken under the strain, the results are serious both for the youth and perhaps especially for the parents, who, as they grow older, will feel the loss tremendously. Excessive drinking and other evils wreck many homes and lives. The older theologians pictured the tragic results, especially in the next world, but the results here are bad beyond description.

The last stage in life is what Shakespeare's melancholy Jacques described as

" Second childishness and mere oblivion,
    Sans teeth, sans eyes, sans taste, sans everything."

But Jacques was a pessimist. Although it is true that physical powers decline, it is also true that often intellect remains and spiritual powers multiply. This is more apt to be true where the powers of mind and heart are kept active. Interest in everything that is going on is a wonderful stimulus to continued intelligence. But a person who is not alert or who lets his mind die, " vulgar, smug, deadened," is already past living. One who has memories of having deliberately done wrong to others and gained by their loss must be an intolerable burden to himself and to others. On the other hand, thoughts of having helped others constitute a wonderful blessing. Every older person should try to ally himself with some good cause and keep alive and alert. Old age is a stage in life where one is relieved from earning his living and can devote himself to longed-for pursuits. All shortcomings and sins blacken the moments, but the sense of having tried to do God's will is a continuous comfort and blessing.

Everyone has a " philosophy," though many might be surprised to know that their attitudes constitute a philosophy. Love, kindness, consideration, and forgetfulness of wrongs done to oneself are real enliveners of later life — of all of life. If one believes in God and seeks to know and do his will, that is a " philosophy of life" which is the mark of true maturity.

— A. J. William Myers

MEASUREMENT Measurement assumes that there is orderly, lawful behavior in certain aspects of the process of growth in religion. Counterbalancing this is the recognition that the total pattern is not now known, and that the irrational has a place in religious experience.

A theory of measurement also assumes that it is possible to define that which is measured. Although it may be impossible to measure an individual's growth in relation to

God, measurement assumes that it is possible to measure the "fruits" of that relationship. The element of disinterestedness in the process of measurement makes researchers seek to eliminate unconscious personal bias. Various checks are employed to eliminate the bias in the measurer or the instrument so that the measured results will be "public," i.e., available to others who will accept the same assumptions and follow the same procedures. Although complete objectivity is humanly impossible, the measurer seeks to state clearly his own presuppositions and his relationship to the persons being measured. Findings of "participant observers" may vary from those of "onlookers," but both may be valuable in the attempt to attain a true measure of the situation.

The individual aspect of religious growth means that measurement must often be concerned with idiographic (individual case) rather than nomothetic (general laws applicable to human beings as a class) aspects of research. Only when nomothetic measures are sought is it meaningful to rank or compare one individual's measure with that of another.

A clear statement of the goals that are to be measured is essential for good measurement. Experts in theology, Christian education, and science should be consulted to assure that the statement truly represents what is to be measured. Another problem is the translation of these goals into terms relevant to the persons being measured (e.g., a preschool child or adolescent, in a Chinese or American culture). The more precise the statement of the goal, the more likely that it can be measured, though the nature of the goal must not be sacrificed to a false

precision. Necessary also is the establishment of criteria, to which a qualified group of judges agree, indicating that the persons concerned have achieved the goals. Measurement in Christian education is a very young discipline. Stimulated by the development of experimental psychology in the 19th century, its major work has been done in the 20th.

In all measurement, validity and reliability are essential concepts. Validity is concerned with whether a process or instrument measures the goals it is designed to measure. If the goal is repetition of the books of the Bible, measures may be devised to test the achievement of this goal. Growth in Christian relationships with God and one's fellows may not now be directly measured. Indications of growth will probably best be achieved through the use of a variety of measures, each of whose limited validity is clearly recognized. Judgment as to the validity of an instrument should be made in consultation with a number of qualified experts in the areas being measured.

Reliability is concerned with whether the instrument, which measures only a sample of the person's or group's behavior, is measuring a reliable (that is, a representative) sample of the total universe of knowledge that is being tested. A test of a person's knowledge of the names of Old Testament books that required no mention of those in the Pentateuch would not be a reliable instrument. A 2d test, in which the Pentateuch was included, might yield a totally different score from the 1st test. Statistical means are available for estimating the degree of reliability of a test based on probability theory.

The representatives of the sample

studied must also be considered. The performance on a test of a group of bright, educationally privileged children will not be a representative sample of the performance of all children on the same test. Statistical devices, based on probability theory, are available for estimating the degree to which the performance of a particular small sample is representative of the total universe from which it is drawn.

The limitations of measurement in Christian education follow from the nature of "measurement." Christian education measurement (by definition) is concerned with the limited, therefore it cannot fully measure man's growth in relation to the Infinite. The deepest motivations of human beings and their Christian growth is known only to God. As in many other fields (e.g., one does not measure intelligence; one measures only its products), only indirect measures are possible. We may not measure growth in Christian relationship to God, but we measure its fruits in behavior, and explore some of the motivations that led to the behavior. In order to prevent the abuse of measurement, we must recognize that we are dealing with an estimate rather than an absolute. We are as blind men, each feeling different parts of an elephant, who attempt to describe the elephant. We need all the reports we can get in order to form any estimate of the nature of the elephant.

Christian education is concerned with persons. Each person's religious response is unique. For this reason measures that compare one individual with another may not be applicable. We may rank a person in knowledge of the Bible's content or in relation to his fellows or in his verbal or behavioral responses to his neighbors, but we cannot rank what this response means to the person himself. The uniqueness suggests the need for flexibility rather than rigidity in measurement in Christian education. A variety of measures must be devised to evaluate a variety of educational experiences instead of trying to fit one standardized measure to all persons or situations.

The nature of the objectives being measured determine the instruments that must be used. Statistical refinement is not justified where original measures are not themselves precise.

The degree to which quantification of a particular quality is possible must be remembered through the whole process of measurement and interpretation. Great care must be taken to avoid drawing unlimited conclusions from a limited set of measurements. The complexity of the network of interrelationships of various factors must be recognized before sweeping claims are made for any one factor.

The combination of many types of measurement offers our present best technique for estimating the effectiveness of particular educational procedures or printed materials in contributing to stated goals in Christian education. Although final evaluation is beyond human judgment, class records, interviews, case studies, objective tests, and essays, gathered by researchers trained to objectivity and yet also aware of the subjective issues involved, do give a true enough estimate of the situation to enable educators to use them in planning future programs.

Class reports (either written or taped oral records) and anecdotal records are invaluable in picturing the development of a class and indicating its strengths and weaknesses, and the degree of pupil participation. The younger the child, the more reliance must be placed on observation of situational and verbal rather than written behavior. This descriptive research furnishes an essential base for later, more refined measurement.

The sheer mass of data gathered by such a process as well as dissatisfaction with the interpretive bias of any one investigator has forced researchers to devise means to analyze and quantify the data gathered, while at the same time the complex subjective interrelationships are recognized.

Rating scales, semistructured interviews, value analysis of essays or class reports, and projective techniques that use pictures are all structured sufficiently to permit some objective scoring, but leave considerable freedom for individual response.

The recognition of the influence of the group on the individual has led to the development of a number of techniques (1st set forth by Moreno) for rating the dynamics of group interaction as measured by trained participants and observers; and by postmeeting reaction of participants on rating sheets and directed essay reports. Children's evaluation of their peers has been measured extensively by the use of sociograms.

Cross-sectional research may combine the use of many techniques in surveying a large number of persons of the same age at one time.

Longitudinal studies describe the development of individuals in relation to a group over a period of years. Although costly, slow, and limited by the preconceptions of the researchers planning the studies, this method still gives the most promise of measuring some aspects of a person's growth in religion. Under relatively controlled conditions a variety of measures are used, and attempts are made to analyze and synthesize findings. The individual is studied as a unique person and in relation to the groups that influence him.

Measurement in Christian education will serve to promote effective Christian education when its limited area is recognized, and when experts in theology, education, and science cooperate to assure that clear statements of goals are enunciated, appropriate procedures are used, and justifiable interpretations of gathered data are made.

— *Frances E. Bailey*

MEMORIZATION Perhaps no aspect of the teaching-learning process in Christian education has been discussed so vehemently as memorization or " memory work." A few generations ago no child went to Sunday school without his " memory verse " ready for recitation, and his progress was frequently judged by the number of such verses he was able to repeat. Even curriculum materials were evaluated by the amount of memory work they contained. Then the pendulum swung. In " progressive " Christian education programs, rote memorization was something only to be criticized. Persons " learn by doing," leaders said, and it is experience that counts. If words were memorized, it was almost by accident. Neither extreme is beneficial to Christian education; either practice misunderstands in some measure just what memorization implies.

Long before written words were used to communicate, man shared his knowledge and ideals through memorized words, passed faithfully from generation to generation. We know the early Hebrews passed their religious heritage from one generation to another via the so-called oral tradition. Memorization was not only a part of learning, it was essential to preserving and communicating knowledge.

With the development of written words, and, in modern times, the abundance and availability of them, memorization is needed less for the preservation of knowledge, but the function of memory itself is no less central to the learning process.

One dictionary defines memory as " the power or function of reproducing and identifying what has been learned or experienced; the faculty of remembering. This function includes learning, retention, recall, and recognition." One learns by retaining past ideas and concepts for later association and application, and without this process of retention there is no learning, no matter how dull or creative the methods.

Historically, man was aware of memory as an activity of the mind very early in human experience. Impairment of the process is so obvious and distressing that the existence and nature of memory has aroused the curiosity of thoughtful men from the very beginning. References to memory in learning are found in the earliest civilizations, but the Greeks (between 550 and 350 B.C.) considered the puzzle of memory with such effectiveness that until this century very little additional information had been gathered (cf. Feindel, *Memory, Learning and Language,* 1960).

The discovery of the particular part of the brain responsible for memory (the temporal lobes just inside the temple) has been identified only recently, but this discovery has added little to the central fact that memory is an integral part of the whole thinking process.

Memory is essential to all learning, but it has special significance where words are involved. Granted that learning takes place by doing (experience), seeing (example), and hearing (precept), these methods are not always possible, and much learning comes secondhand, through words. Because words are so valuable in interpreting and recalling experiences, it is important to understand the experiences preserved in great words and then to associate them with our own experiences.

This heritage of words is especially important in Christian education, for the central truths of Christian faith have been carried through the centuries in large measure by words: 1st, from those who knew Jesus Christ, and then from those who witnessed the action of his Holy Spirit through the church and in the world. Great words in the Bible, in the creeds, rituals, and hymns of the church, and in the writings of men of deep Christian conviction throughout the ages, have made Christian faith alive and real today. To know and understand these cherished and precious words is to be a literate Christian, which is a joy and an obligation.

What, then, are the practical implications for those who are concerned with teaching the Christian faith? Purpose and motivation come first. Why should these great words of faith be memorized? Certainly not because memory work is good discipline and mental exercise, or because these words might be useful later in life; never because one can " earn " a Bible or a trip to camp. Rather, these words should be memorized because through knowing them and understanding the experiences they portray out of the past, God speaks today. It is then that these experiences, known through the medium of words, take on special significance for each individual as he appropriates them into his life and God speaks to him.

The sole motive is that of understanding what of God's truth and his will for men's lives these words impart, and how this truth can be applied — not a gold star on a chart or a promotion, or even learning for learning's sake. The motive for learning the words is that they help us grow in faith and our knowledge of God.

Keeping these purposes in mind, how does one select material for memorization? Here are some suggestions:

1. It should be worth memorizing. The material should contain concepts and values essential to Christian faith, and not be just a collection of words. Even some Biblical passages, such as certain genealogies, have little value for memorization.

2. It should be selected with a particular age group in mind. The Bible and most other Christian writings were intended for adults. Therefore great care should be taken in choosing material appropriate for each age level. For example, preschool children could use "Let us love one another, for God is love" or "He has made all things beautiful." Simple songs and poems are also suitable for kindergartners. Primary boys and girls can appreciate the Lord's Prayer and selected psalms (e.g., Ps. 23; 100; 150), adding short prayers, simple litanies, and more songs. Juniors are able to struggle with Scripture such as the Beatitudes and the Ten Commandments, plus extra-Biblical materials

such as the creeds, many classical prayers, great hymns of the church, and much factual data about the Bible itself.

3. It should be understood and appreciated. Memorization has no value if a person does not know the meaning of the words. Careful discussion and explanation should be a part of the process, allowing time for questions and clarification. The 5-year-old who utters, "Lead us not into Penn Station" memorized words beyond his capacity, without the benefit of guidance and explanation.

4. It should be relevant to the learner. "What does this mean to me and how can I apply it to my life?" is a wise question to ask concerning all passages to be memorized. With younger children, the question is not verbalized, but the application should be made with the help of teachers just the same.

Memorization should be carefully planned and selected in a continuous process from childhood through youth and adulthood. There are some generally applicable rules:

1. Give persons an opportunity to see the words used appreciatively and with understanding by capable adult leaders who will stress their importance through personal use and significance in their own lives.

2. Try to avoid mechanical drill as a means of memorizing. Be creative and use a variety of methods in teaching the material. For example, a psalm might first be used as a call to worship, then as a choral reading; pictures might be used to illustrate it, and then a group might dramatize it. This kind of creative repetition through study and use will accomplish the goal as surely as drill, and with much deeper understanding.

3. Make the material so much a part of the study program that there is no need for individual or class competition. Memorization should never be used as a basis for awards, earning merits, or gaining promotions. The " rewards " of memorization should be in the intrinsic value of the words themselves as they add meaning to a person's life, and not in some token prize.

4. Repeat the materials after they have been memorized, in study, conversation, and worship. If the words are not worth using many times over, with increasing significance from every use, they are not worth memorizing at all.

A final comment about a possible danger in rote memorization: although memory itself is part of the learning process, it is only a part of it. It is not a substitute for understanding and comprehension. Real learning has results in the utilization of experiences and changes in attitudes and behavior, and is not just a transference of words. When words are memorized, they must be absorbed, assimilated, appropriated. Merely saying words, no matter how sacred they are or how accurately repeated, is not the ultimate goal. Rather, it is that the words are understood, convey new meaning for faith, and thereby make a difference in living. — *Christine P. Stockley*

MENNONITE CHURCH, GENERAL CONFERENCE Mennonites trace their origin to the 16th-century Anabaptist movement in Holland, Germany, and Switzerland. Since that time Mennonites have migrated to France, Russia, Canada, Mexico, Paraguay, Brazil, Uruguay, Argentina, and the U.S.A.

The General Conference Mennonite Church, now the 2d largest Mennonite body, was organized May 28, 1860, at West Point, Iowa, later joined by Mennonites coming from Russia, Poland, and Germany. The Conference is divided into 6 districts. The denomination has a congregational type of church polity. The Board of Education and Publication is 1 of 4 major boards.

Among the more distinctive doctrinal characteristics of the group are adult baptism, acceptance of the doctrine of nonresistance, refusal to swear oaths, emphasis on Christianity as a way of life, and discipleship.

Because the Sunday school was an institution of English-language churches, it was slow in winning acceptance among German-speaking Mennonites, but by 1860 when the General Conference was organized the Sunday school movement began to make an impact. The Conference began the publication of a Sunday school quarterly in 1889.

A brief description of the educational philosophy of the church would need to include the following: education for the perpetuation of the Christian faith from 1 generation to the next; education to know what it means to be Christian. The training of leaders for the church, culminated in the establishment of 2 senior colleges, Bethel College, North Newton, Kans.; Bluffton College, Bluffton, Ohio; a seminary at Elkhart, Ind., and 2 junior colleges — Canadian Mennonite Bible College, Winnipeg, Man., and Freeman Junior College, Freeman, S.D.

The General Conference Mennonite Church publishes Sunday school materials under the name *Living Faith Series*. On the adult and youth levels it publishes a quarterly based on the Uniform Outlines; it publishes jointly with the

(Old) Mennonite Church a Christian education magazine, *The Builder*. It has completed the publication of the *Living Faith Graded Sunday School Curriculum* for the primary, junior, and intermediate age groups in a cooperative publishing venture with the (Old) Mennonite Church.

Presently this denomination is studying its church polity, is reformulating a statement of its position on the Scriptures, and is restudying the church's relationship to higher Christian education.

— *Willard K. Claassen*

MEN'S GROUPS Men's work as a part of the parish program has yet to come into its own in the Protestant Church in America. Unlike women's organizations, youth activities, and children's work, it has crystallized into no common image in the mind of the average church member. From parish to parish its pattern varies according to denominational differences, variations in church polity, and even the temperaments of local parishes. As a real force in the church it has been neglected, misunderstood, and underrated. Its chief failure lies in not having tapped the hidden sources of manpower within the church and put them to work.

However, evidences of a real breakthrough are showing on the horizon. Stirrings at the ecumenical level are focusing increasing attention on the function of the laity in the activity of the church as a whole. The men of the church are being increasingly recognized as an important factor in helping the church to find its wholeness. More and more man as layman is being given the responsibility of his own essential calling in the body of Christ, and in the American church he is coming to be seen as something more than an assistant to the clergy.

Basic to the contemporary stress on the laity is the importance of giving careful attention to setting up the local parish program so as to give a proper place to men's groups. Men's groups do not succeed if conceived as the counterpart to the usual women's program. Creative thinking calls for programming and structuring that are peculiar to the purpose of man's place in the parish program. New forms may be in order for a new day. Discovering the uniqueness of man's task in the church is the only solution for the problem of finding the place of men's work in the church.

The organizational form of a local men's group will be set up closely in conformity with the pattern of its parent organization in the national and denominational body. Frequently it may be loosely constructed in relation to the parent organization, depending on the degree of rigidity in denominational polity and control. In any case the local group will assume its own peculiar character. In the American church, local men's groups have been quite independent.

Organization at the local level is a direct reflection of the greater church within which the parish operates. The men's group may be structured as an integral part of the total program, whether that program is educational, worship-oriented, or evangelistic in outreach. It may be independent of the parish structure, serving only as an auxiliary body according to the peculiarities of the local situation or according to the whims of its members. That the men's group should be a part of the total church program is much to be preferred if the purpose is basically to provide an agency for helping the men to assume an effective place in the church.

There should be no order of priority or importance given to the areas of programming for men's groups. Each has its own peculiarity in establishing its place and in contributing to a whole program.

It is of basic importance to recognize how men's work fits into the church's total educational program. The curriculum should be arranged to suit the needs of men as men, geared to the male mentality, touching those questions that occupy the forefront of the male's position in the church and the world. Bible study, the history and life of the church, Christian doctrine, worship, and the total involvement of the Christian man with the world are proper areas for study. Denominational headquarters usually provide guidance and materials for such study. The method and procedure of the program must vary according to need, with the stress placed most frequently on discussion, dialogue, and cell groups.

Each group has needs peculiar to its own nature, in addition to the needs related to the common worship life of the church. A church without a special worship and devotional emphasis for its men lacks fullness. The men themselves will be given opportunity for and practice in leading a devotional period, publicly reading Scripture, and offering prayer. Singing of hymns takes on new meaning when done in a men's group. Special services of public worship may be arranged, for which the men themselves are the leaders. In an effort to strengthen the devotional side of the men's program, many churches are arranging retreats in various forms to give the setting for deeper impressions on the inner life.

A Christian man must be in fellowship with other Christian men. The average men's group in the church has readily found many forms for sociability, which often have tended to become the whole program. However, the fellowship must be a meeting of Christians in which each can help the others, and in turn be helped, to understand more fully the meaning of the Christian community.

The church is primarily mission. Some hold that the church exists only for those who are outside of itself, and that Christians exist only for others than themselves. A self-centered group, even in the church, can hardly remain Christian. Men's groups may be said to exist in order to lead men to get to work as Christians, in the church and in the community of the world. There is an unlimited field open for the Christian man, most of it as yet touched upon only superficially in the parish program: community concerns, missions to industry and government, work with senior citizens, boys' work, and projects on behalf of the men in the Armed Forces.

History may record that one of the significant discoveries of the church of the 20th century is the emerging awareness of man's place in the church. — *Paul M. Lindberg*

METHODIST CHURCH, THE The Methodist Church(es) grew out of the pietistic-evangelical movement of the 18th century under the leadership of an Anglican churchman, John Wesley (1703–1791). The early movement was aimed at making religion vital to the masses of common folk who were not reached by the established church. Wesley had no intention of leading a movement against or away from the Church of England.

Wesley's approach to religion combined the warm heart of personal religious assurance, the clear mind of an Oxford don, and a zeal for doing things methodically — " decently and in order," this latter element accounting for the name " Methodist."

Albert C. Outler points out that Wesley created a unique fusion of many theological elements, based on the principle of evangelical catholicism: " He believed in faith and good works, Scripture and tradition, revelation and reason, sovereign grace and human freedom, particularism and universal redemption, the witness of the Spirit and an ordered polity, repentance and the expectation of perfection, the priesthood of all believers and an authorized representative ministry."

The historic doctrines of Christendom are summarized in the denomination's Twenty-six Articles of Religion, adapted by Wesley from the Articles of the Church of England. The church's polity, ritual, and doctrines are systematized in an official book, *Doctrines and Discipline of The Methodist Church.* There is an official *Methodist Hymnal.*

The church's structure is basically connectional, rather than congregational, patterned somewhat on the order of the U.S.A.'s Federal Government. It is governed at all levels by elected representatives, half lay and half ministerial (except in the local church). Bishops provide administrative and religious leadership, preside at annual, jurisdictional, and general conferences, and appoint pastors to local churches. Bap-

tism is usually by sprinkling, but any mode is permissible. The church practices infant baptism and " open " Communion.

Although Wesley was, for his day, a well-educated man, most of the early Methodist preachers — either in England or in America — were not. Yet they soon began to establish Sunday schools and colleges. With nearly 125 institutions of higher learning in the nation, there is justification for the phrase, " Methodism's obsession with higher education." Early in the history of Methodism in America, Sunday schools became a concern of pastor and people, although they were not always considered a part of the basic structure of the church.

The Methodist pastor is charged repeatedly to see to the Christian nurture of his congregation. He is to " instruct candidates for membership in the church in the doctrines, rules, and regulations of the church. . . . To form classes for the children, youth, and adults for instruction in the Word of God, and to perform the duties prescribed for the training of children. . . . To organize and maintain church schools. . . . To preach on the subject of Christian education. . . . To see that the people . . . are supplied with our church literature, including books, church school literature. . . . To lead the children of the church to an understanding of the Christian faith, to an appreciation of the privileges and obligations of church membership, and to a personal commitment to Jesus Christ as Lord and Savior, and to guide them in the use of the means of grace in living the Christian life." However, this is not considered simply the pastor's task, or that of a small group of professional leaders.

It is conceived as a task for the whole church, essential to the church's vitality and progress.

The Methodist Church, through its official Curriculum Committee and its General Board of Education, has declared what it means by Christian education:

" Christian education . . . is concerned with the Christian faith which comes to us out of the past, is based especially on the Biblical revelations, and is subject to the continuing activity of God through the Holy Spirit. It finds its focus in Jesus Christ — God as revealed at a particular time in history through Jesus of Nazareth, the Christ, and God as revealed in the continuing Spirit of Christ or the Holy Spirit.

" Christian education is also concerned with people, with people as they are but also as they may become under God. The process of Christian teaching and nurture is an attempt to bring persons into relationship with the gospel, not with the gospel as a dead tradition out of the past but rather with it as God's continued activity in the world today. . . .

" The distinctive element in Christian education is that it views man in relationship to God and is carried forward in the light of the gospel. . . . Christian education is focused on the meeting between God and man in Christ. . . .

" Methodism has long held that the only genuine religion is experienced religion. Doctrine did not first produce Christianity. Doctrine emerged out of the transforming life of Christianity. Thus, Methodism, standing in the tradition of evangelical Protestantism, has never regarded doctrine as an end in itself, and has found room for variation in theological thought among its members. It has long insisted that there is no conflict between mature faith and unfolding knowledge, and has encouraged the search for new truth. The unity of Methodism is found not so much in doctrinal conformity, as in the shared quest for the new life and hope God makes available through Jesus Christ. . . .

" The mainstream of Methodist thought has held to the doctrine that God's grace and man's responsibility go hand in hand. On the one hand, we reject the view that God does everything and man does nothing in the saving process. On the other hand, we reject the view which holds that man must work out his own salvation independently of divine resources. Methodism holds to the doctrine of divine grace and initiative at the same time that it insists on the importance of human works and responsibility.

" It is the point of view of The Methodist Church that in the Bible we are confronted by God's claim upon us, his judgment of us, his promises to us, the reality of his healing, reconciling love, the commission to witness for him, and to minister to the needs of all men in his name."

Methodist curriculum is committed to an ecumenical approach in its basic planning. The denomination shares with other bodies in the National Council of the Churches of Christ in the U.S.A. in carrying on as much planning as possible through cooperative committee work.

Methodist curriculum materials are frequently revised and issued in a variety of patterns because of a varied and widespread constituency. There are no static forms and structures that must be maintained.

As plans for new curriculum materials go forward, an effort is being made to follow several principles: (1) Universality. In a mobile society it is important that a student moving from one state to another shall be able to continue in the same basic curriculum. (2) Contemporaneity. In a day of rapid change a curriculum must be fashioned that will not become frozen and out of date for long periods of time. (3) Flexibility. In a time when new patterns of grouping, grading, and promotion are emerging, it is important to provide a curriculum plan that is flexible and adaptable to varying situations.

In the Methodist program of Christian education the following trends seem to be emerging: (1) A new and deeper understanding of the meaning and significance of the Christian church, which has implications for the view of the nature of the ministry of the clergy and of the laity, values in the traditional Christian year, sacraments and historical worship forms, the nature and function of the church as a worshiping, evangelizing, nurturing, redemptive fellowship. (2) An attempt to incorporate into the program of Christian teaching the significant new appreciations for Biblical and theological understandings. (3) An effort to utilize new understanding of the ways persons learn — through the influence of group relationships, developmental tasks, and deeper self-understanding. (4) A concern for ministering to certain groups that call for special attention and that tend to be neglected in our traditional program, such as older youth, young adults, young parents, older adults, exceptional persons — gifted or with handicaps; those committed to institutions, hospitals, jails; those who have no natural social grouping in the community in which they live; those who lack a sense of belonging to a community because of frequent moving. (5) An effort to utilize properly the wide range of instructional materials, old and new, available for teaching today, that recent technological advances have made more potent than ever before.
— *Walter N. Vernon*

METHODOLOGY The means by which communication is attempted is called methodology. This is the bridge between teacher and pupil. Usually initiated by the teacher (whether this be a person, community, school, neighborhood group, or church), it is a means for disseminating knowledge, learning skills, changing attitudes, or accepting experiences. In a group-centered approach to learning, it is possible that the learners themselves will initiate the means by which their learning will take place. Regardless of who chooses the method, its acceptance by the learner is imperative if learning is to be accomplished.

The media for communication must be considered before a theory of methodology can be outlined. The basic medium for religious learning is the religious community itself, church or synagogue. The home is a medium, especially in such specific areas as the ceremonial surrounding holidays, grace before meals, the child's first involvement in prayer, and the witness of religious life in the family. The school is a medium in some countries (in the U.S.A. chiefly in the private school) where specific course material may include Biblical teaching, church history, or doctrine. The religious community is a medium for teaching, through its common worship in which the growing child participates and through which the adult is strengthened in his understanding of the faith; it becomes a medium for specific teaching through the teacher, chosen from the group for specific tasks with children, young people, or adults.

A theory of methodology must include the point that learning is a person-to-person action. The categories "I-Thou" as over against "I-It" (Buber) may be employed here. The learner is not an object; he cannot be acted upon without his personal and voluntary response. If he revolts against the method, no positive learning takes place. Certain methods may be more useful than others in evoking a free response. Such methods will invite the learner to use his own powers of intellect and emotion and to achieve patterns of insight, synthesis, and change at his own level of acceptance.

Since religious learning is primarily concerned with relationship to God and knowledge about him, this necessitates a consideration of the categories of revelation and response. If revelation be defined as God's self-disclosure, then this is surely involved in learning. Methodology must be aimed at so preparing the learner that this self-disclosure of God may be more easily apprehended. In this context, learning involves the total response of the whole person. The learning of facts may be a part, a change of attitudes may be a necessity; but these are a response to God. The first initiative does not lie with the teacher or with the learner. The methodological bridge involves 3 persons. Faith, as response to God's action in both the teacher and in the learner, is a prerequisite.

Methodology has been categorized in several ways. Some speak of methods through seeing (filmstrips, etc.), hearing (music), acting (construction, dramatics). Methods may be broken into "passive" (hearing stories) and "active" (painting) or into teacher-centered and pupil-centered methods. For the purposes of this essay we shall look at methods of participation through which the learner becomes involved in the saving events of religious history and witness: the acts of decision by which he recognizes the necessity for personal response and the methods of communication by which the learner makes his newfound faith and knowledge available to others.

Methods of participation are found primarily in the arts. As the learner studies a great hymn or cantata, looks at an inspired religious painting, reads religious poetry, or takes part in religious drama, he becomes involved in the historical and Biblical events through which God's work has been made known among his people. Those who listen to a story become participants in the story and understand it from within. By historical remembrance, they know themselves to be part of these events, for the history of the people of God is their own personal history. The words become their own; they sing the music with meaning; they grasp the significance of sculpture; they feel the poetry; they become involved in the dramatic roles they read aloud. It may happen that art simply enunciates significant questions or sets forth a situation calling for attention. This faces the learner with the necessity for asking how religious faith answers this need.

Participation may also take place through present events. This happens when learners struggle with a discussion question, listen to a speaker's presentation of an immediate situation, or take part in a field trip. Involvement in the actual life of the religious community is a way of learning. One learns how to understand others, to respond to them, and so to act that life is a witness to the work of the Holy Spirit in the person and through the community. This can happen as kindergarten children "play family" or adults plan a financial canvass.

The purpose of methods of participation is that involvement may bring insight. Through this process the learner comes into a recognition of religious knowledge. His faith is not a simple acceptance of that which he has been told or has seen in others. It becomes the response of his own life to God. This is commitment. Decision is involved, but this may be a repeated event. Every facing of knowledge requires the decision to accept or reject it. Each situation that calls for a change of attitude involves making the change or remaining the same. Response to Biblical faith inevitably includes the facing of decision. This is indicated many times in the stories of encounters between God and men. Life is not an inevitable pathway before which the individual is passive, but a call to decision in which one answers yes or no. Even the one who thinks he has ignored or evaded the question thereby has made a response. Although the child is brought up within the religious community of church or synagogue, there comes a year at which he must personally accept this name to be his own name. The Jewish boy becomes *bar-mitzvah*, a son of the law. The Christian child becomes "confirmed," taking upon himself the promises made for him in infancy. Thereafter he is ex-pected to witness for his faith under any circumstance.

The learner who has become so involved in religious learning through participation that he has arrived at decisions is ready to communicate his faith to others. At this point the methods of communication become useful. Under this heading come the various constructive and "creative" methods used with the children and the types of discussion used with young people and adults. When these seem weak (pictures without content and discussion without depth), it is because the earlier steps have not been carefully taken. One can only make clear to others that which has meaning to the self. If the child who has listened breathlessly to a Biblical story can draw a picture of the story, he probably will be in the picture. The young person who has read a part in a great religious play is ready to discuss with meaning the question raised by the play as it impinges on contemporary life. The adult who has taken part in Biblical study can explain to others through a panel or colloquium.

Methods of communication require the formulation of ideas and attitudes into one's own words. The learner has understood sufficiently, so that he is free from the explanations of those who were his teachers. He can explain the faith to others, within and outside the religious community, in such a way as to convey some measure of clarity and understanding. Here is the final aim of method. The learner who has understood himself in relationship to God's action is now able to transcend himself in an attempt to explain God's action to others. He has become a witness. His whole life is an expression of his relationship to God, and his deeds undergird his words. — *Iris V. Cully*

MIDDLE EAST The Christian church was founded and had its early development largely in the area long known as the Near East, and now increasingly as the Middle East. The early church soon realized the importance of education, and particularly religious education. Origen, who lived in Egypt in the 3d century, had a passion for enriching Christianity with the best of Greek thought. It was said of him that " he wanted his students to grow into an intelligent Christianity." The Eastern branches of the church, however, were soon rent by theological controversy and henceforth there was little communication between them and the church in the West. Sterile orthodoxy became the rule, and religious education was largely restricted to the clergy. The ancient languages continued to be used for the Scriptures and liturgies, even after Arabic, Turkish, and Persian became the languages used in the area. In the 7th century, these churches came under Muslim rule. Although Christians, as " people of the Book," usually had a recognized minority status, the Eastern churches largely spent their energies in self-preservation. Christian learning was confined for the most part to the monasteries, and in general, teaching the faith to youth and the laity declined to a minimum. Thus, as the centuries passed, isolation, tradition, and Islamic pressures brought stagnation to the churches. Lay Christians had little education of any kind and the intellectual curiosity of the clergy of Origen's day disappeared.

Protestant missionaries from the U.S.A. came to the Middle East in 1820. By 1840 missionaries were at work in Syria (now divided into Lebanon and Syria), Turkey, Palestine (now Israel and Jordan), and Persia (now Iran). A little later they came to Egypt. All but Persia were then part of the Turkish Empire.

The establishing of schools in all the countries concerned was a primary task of the missions. The 1st school for girls in the Turkish Empire was opened at Beirut in 1836 and its successor is still rendering outstanding service. Schools for boys were founded in various centers. In 1836, also, the 1st boys' school was opened in Persia and a girls' school 2 years later. In these early schools and in the many others founded later all over the area, the aim was Christian education through Christian teachers and Bible courses, as well as in the spirit of the schools. As a rule, only children of the Eastern churches were first enrolled, but Muslims soon began to send their children, and when Protestant churches were established, the schools served them as well. Many of the original primary schools grew into secondary schools and, in a few cases, became colleges and universities. Some of the latter are no longer related to mission or church. Nothing has so changed the Middle East as the impact of this wide program of education under Christian auspices.

Protestant Christian schools still function in the Middle East. In Turkey only 5 secondary schools remain. All have good enrollments, but no specific religious instruction is possible. In Iran the mission schools were nationalized in 1940, but in their stead several thriving Protestant parochial schools continue religious instruction, though Muslim pupils do not take the Bible courses. In Lebanon, the United Arab Republic (Egypt and Syria), Sudan, Jordan, Iraq, and the Persian Gulf — all Arabic-speaking areas — Christian schools enroll thousands of pupils. Sponsoring agencies in Europe and the U.S.A. share in their support by both personnel and funds. One of these is related to 6 boys' schools, 20 girls' schools, 4 junior colleges, and a girls' college granting the A.B. degree. These institutions, located in 6 of the Middle Eastern countries, are typical of the scores that have provided a Christian education for many of the leaders of these nations and continue to do so.

Long ago the missions conducting these schools prepared texts in Arabic and Persian for use in Bible courses. From time to time revisions were made in these. A series, *Graded Lessons in Christian Nurture,* was published in Beirut in 1924 for schools in Syria and Palestine. There were 9 grades in Arabic, followed by 3 in English. Publication was begun of a complete revision in 1958, prepared by an interdenominational committee. The series contains lessons for kindergarten, 6 primary and 2 secondary grades in Arabic, and for grades 9 to 12 in English, under the general title *Evangelical Religious Lessons for Day Schools.* The materials are used by the schools of the Evangelical Synod of Syria and Lebanon, and by some schools under Anglican, Friends, Baptist, and Nazarene auspices. In general, these Bible courses have been given to all pupils, regardless of religious faith, but Middle Eastern Governments are beginning to press for their restriction to Christians.

In Egypt the large Coptic Evangelical Church developed its own Arabic curriculum for use in the many schools conducted by the church and the related American (United Presbyterian) Mission. Since the formation of the United Arab Republic, new laws have been enacted requiring Bible instruction for all Christian pupils as well as provision for Islamic instruction for Muslim pupils in Christian schools. As a result, a unique series of religious textbooks has been issued for Christian pupils of the various communions, including those in Government schools as well as in church-related schools. The committee that prepared this course was composed of 1 member each from the Coptic Orthodox, Roman Catholic, and Evangelical churches. The material covers 4 levels from primary to junior high school in a 3-year cycle, dealing with the life of Christ and the apostles, and the history of the church. The course has been printed in large quantities by the Government for use in all schools in Egypt and Syria.

Christian education through Sunday schools has been emphasized in the Middle East from the beginning of Protestant missionary effort. The Sunday School Union of Egypt and the Sudan was organized many years ago, and the Uniform Lessons were made available in a 7-year cycle. The Union also has conducted workshops for teachers and rallies for pupils, and published a number of teacher-training books. The effectiveness of this organization has had much to do with the awakening of the Coptic Orthodox Church to its need for religious education, and a gratifying church school movement is under way in that communion. Its leader has an American degree in Christian education and currently holds a key post in his church.

A similar program in the northern Arabic-speaking area was developed by the Bible Lands Union for Christian Education. Since 1925 this organization, in which 12 denominations share, has pursued its aim of "developing and making available better programs and methods in Christian religious education." It promotes Sunday schools, youth societies, work camps, summer conferences for youth, institutes for teachers, and daily vacation Bible schools. In cooperation with local committees, it also stimulates the use of audio-visual materials. In much of this the Greek Orthodox Church, now keenly aware of the needs of its youth, cooperates with the Evangelical churches, and a priest of that church is a member of the executive committee of BLUCE. Separately, Sunday schools are being organized also by Armenian Orthodox and some Syrian Orthodox Churches in the area.

BLUCE first prepared a series of Sunday school lessons in 1925. Although these materials and those of the Sunday School Union in the South were revised from time to time, the need for fresh material became urgent. Therefore, under the auspices of the Near East Christian Council, representatives of both Unions and other groups attended a "Near East Curriculum Conference" in 1957. The conference was supported by the World Council of Christian Education, and an American leader in this field took part. An editorial board, representing the countries and churches concerned, has since prepared and published an Arabic and Armenian curriculum in 2- and 3-year cycles, using current religious education techniques. Sunday schools from Sudan to Iraq and the Persian Gulf are gradu-

ally making use of these courses. In Iran another interchurch committee is producing a graded Persian curriculum for the church schools in that country.

— *William N. Wysham*

MISSION, THE CHRISTIAN The origin, authority, definition, and scope of the Christian mission are given in Jesus' words to his 1st disciples, "As the Father sent me, even so I send you" (John 20:21). The Christian mission is an extension of the 1st mission, God's mission in Jesus as the Christ of Scriptural tradition. In truth there is no other mission except God's mission in Jesus as the Christ, for in that mission all previous missions are recapitulated and all subsequent missions are anticipated.

As the mission of Jesus is the source, so the authority of Jesus is the authority of the Christian mission. As the Son sent by the Father, Jesus says to the Twelve minus one: "All authority in heaven and on earth has been given to me. Go therefore and make disciples . . . , baptizing them in the name . . . , teaching them to observe all that I have commanded you" (Matt. 28:18-20). This Great Commission has behind it all the authority of heaven and earth, the authority of the Great Commissioner. God, the creator of all things in heaven and on earth, has given to the man Jesus all authority, i.e., all "right and power," in the 2 realms that comprise the whole of creation. The man Jesus — not some invisible spirit or nonincarnate being — is Lord of creation. All the compassion and noble sentiments of the whole succession of disciples and apostles and the full spectrum of human need, physical and spiritual, do not provide a mandate comparable to that which Jesus gave.

The mission of God in Jesus as the Christ initiates and authorizes the Christian mission and it also defines that mission. Jesus as the one sent from God (i.e., as the Christ of Scriptural tradition) is God with us; the Christian mission is therefore the prolongation of God's intention to be with us as Jesus Christ.

That God has presented himself elsewhere and in other manners than in Christ is acknowledged in the proclamation of Jesus as the Christ, the Presence of God. Prior to being with us in Jesus Christ, and still today in a manner apart from Jesus Christ, God presents himself in such a way as to leave everyone "without excuse" either for worshiping him falsely or for worshiping a false creaturely god (Rom., ch. 1). To all people God makes his eternal power and right to be God evident in the order and life of his creation and in the human conscience.

God further presented himself in a covenant with the people Israel who were "nobodies" until God made them his people and bound himself to them with the promise that he would be with them as he was with their fathers. That is what the covenant with Israel means, God's binding himself by a promise to be present with Israel and her posterity.

Whereas God gave to all peoples for all times knowledge about himself through cosmos and conscience, he gave to the Jews direct acquaintance with himself through a covenant of promise that he makes good at every moment of their existence. Because God keeps this promise to be present, the Jew knows God to be holy, one, and living. On the part of the Jew, unbelief cannot be a denial that there is a God; it can only be disobedience, refusal to be present with God as God wills to be present with the Jew.

In Jesus as the Christ of Scriptural tradition, God presents himself to all men without any exception whatsoever and here he presents himself as one of us. Only by the most violent travesty upon the testimony of the New Testament can Jesus as the Christ be made out to be anything other than God's mission to be present with every man, Jew and Gentile alike, and to be present as one of us, namely, as Jesus Christ.

The mission that Jesus fulfilled was the making of disciples who would be the 1st in a chain of disciple makers who would encompass the whole of creation. The end or purpose of Jesus' disciple-calling was that they might "be with him" (Mark 3:14) who is God with us. And "to be with him" is to be a maker of disciples for him. Jesus, with all authority in heaven and on earth, creates the apostolic church by his command, "Go therefore and make disciples." The creation of this body of Christ, existing not for itself but for Christ, is the decisive event of Jesus' mission. The reality of the apostolic church consists not only in the apostles' preaching and an audience's listening. Significantly, Jesus' charge is not, "Go therefore and preach" but "Go therefore and make disciples."

"To be with him" is to be an apostle, to be sent by him even as he was sent by the Father to make disciples of all men. The apostle's mission, the making of disciples, is accomplished by baptism and teaching. Jesus gave to the Twelve minus one his apostolic authority to make disciples and he also gave them his priestly authority to baptize. In his command to baptize in the name of the Triune God, Jesus transfers to the apostolic church his power as the priest of all men to hold and use "the keys of the kingdom of heaven."

Jesus further transferred to the 11 apostles his authority and function as prophet and teacher. To be his apostle is to be sent to be priest, prophet, and teacher to others. As baptism "in the name" gives existence to disciples, so teaching through preaching and instruction constitutes the work of the disciples. However, the original Twelve minus one are cautioned by Jesus to teach others to observe only what the original Twelve had been commanded, which was "to be with him." There is no other apostolic teaching and there can be no teaching in the church of Jesus Christ except apostolic teaching.

In its mission the Christian church is not left to go forth alone. As God was with us in Jesus Christ "under Pontius Pilate," so he will continue to be God with us until the *eschaton* ushered in by his appearance in Jesus shall have run its course. That is how we are to understand Jesus' promise to those to whom he first gave the Great Commission, "And lo, I am with you always, to the close of the age" (Matt. 28:20). The Christian imagination has only begun to survey the range of possibilities in "being with" Christ between now and "closing time" when the distinct reign of Christ will come to an end and he will deliver the Kingdom and every authority and power over to God the Father (I Cor. 15:24 ff.). It is becoming increasingly apparent that the Christian mission includes "being with" the natural world as well as with one another, for the natural world is Christ's and he has been and is present with it. What is the distinctive Christian responsibility for understanding and caring for creation is a horizon of the Christian mission only recently acknowledged. With this, Christians are not surprised, nor will they be surprised if other horizons appear.

— *Edmund Perry*

MISSIONARY EDUCATION Missionary education in the churches since the Reformation may be said to have started with the beginning of the modern missionary enterprise. Bartholomaus Ziegenbalg (1684–1719), who reached India in 1706 and remained there until his death, and William Carey (1761–1834), who was in India from 1793 until his death, used certain means to awaken and sustain the interest of church people in missions. Some of their efforts became the accepted educational procedures of later years. Ziegenbalg was a prolific letter writer, making vivid the situation in which he found himself; and he made 1 lengthy visit to Europe from India during which he spoke to groups and to individuals about his work, seeking to gain support from his hearers. Carey was responsible directly for the formation of the Baptist Missionary Society, and did much to inform its members of the task he had undertaken. In addition, by his letters he was indirectly the cause of a widening interest in missions in church groups other than his own out of which came at least 1 and possibly 2 missionary societies.

The missionary societies organized early in the 19th century were made up of people who were interested in sending the gospel to other lands. At their beginning those societies saw little need to undertake educational efforts, for their members were already committed to the support of missions. Soon, however, these societies realized that all Christian people should be aware, as they were, of the God-given missionary obligation, and that they would require more funds than they could command if they were to meet the opportunities opening in lands across the world. Thus the societies came to plan programs that would educate the churches and result in a substantial increase in available funds. Various methods were used: missionary deputations, often a number of Christian laymen, traveled from place to place, describing in public addresses the lands in which missionaries were stationed and the work they were doing; local societies were organized in churches, becoming centers of missionary education; leaflets for general distribution were published. For example, the Society for the Propagation of the Gospel organized its 1st Parochial Association in 1819, and 20 years later had nearly 2,000 such groups meeting in churches with some degree of regularity. The Church Missionary Association in 1813 started printing *The Missionary Register,* a monthly report of missionary activities that was continued until 1855 and was the pattern for other similar journals. The London Missionary Society, formed in 1795, early made use of traveling teams of men to inform the churches of the missionary undertakings of its representatives.

During the latter half of the 19th century a series of conferences were held, attended by the directors, secretaries, and missionaries of various missionary societies, for the purpose of sharing their experiences and examining the work of their agencies. At each of those conferences the subject of missionary education was prominent. In the addresses and discussions the various methods used by the societies to teach church people about missions were reported and their effectiveness assessed. The conference held at Liverpool, England, in 1860 agreed that "whoever desires to maintain the missionary spirit must seek to have an intelligent knowledge of the mission field." To those attending that conference the chief person in missionary education was the pastor of a church. He needed to be educated about missions and inspired to lead his people in their understanding and response. The conference discussed various ways in which this could be done, and suggested among other things that an approach should be made to the theological schools, urging them to include appropriate courses in their curricula. From the report of that conference one learns that the mission societies were doing their educational work through publications, deputations, and juvenile organizations.

At subsequent conferences, London (1880) and New York (1900), the methods being used by societies were much more clearly defined. Women's boards of missions, formed in a number of denominations, had undertaken the publication of missionary material, planned courses of study for their members, and taken in hand the sponsorship of societies for children. Missionary associations had been formed in churches that through regular meetings sought to inform members about work overseas. The annual Missionary Sunday, when the sermon of the day was given by a missionary or a society representative, had become rather widely established; missionary festivals and concerts, designed to introduce church members to life in other parts of the world, were frequent events. A good deal of dependence was placed on literature; the conference of 1900 listed over 100 publications being issued regularly by the societies in Europe and America; there were weekly newssheets, popular monthly reports, and a few quarterlies designed to appeal to the thoughtful and well-educated. Efforts were being made to include the study of missions in the program of the church schools. Juvenile and youth societies were being conducted, though with no great degree of success. The Student Volunteer Movement had established an educational department that published textbooks on missionary subjects. Some of the societies had appointed an officer whose responsibility was made clear in his title of " Educational Secretary."

Up to this point in Protestant history the missionary enterprise had been in the hands of the missionary societies. They had conceived of their educational task as involving 3 fairly distinct lines: the informing of their own members of mission activities; the continuing effort to enroll other people as members of the societies and thus bring them within the sphere of the educational program; and the attempt to instruct the entire church membership about the work of the societies. With those 3 aims in view, organizations were formed and materials provided. Gradually a change took place in the attitude of the churches toward missions. Denominations began to absorb the societies into their total organization, thus making missionary work a matter of interest for the entire church instead of for a group within the church. The society became the mission board, and the board set up an educational department as one of its subsidiaries.

The 20th century has witnessed a determined effort on the part of the churches to carry on missionary education in as united and as efficient a way as possible. Churches have realized the futility and waste of duplicating efforts and have sought to combine work wherever possible. In 1900 the Central Committee for the Study of Foreign Missions was formed by the women's boards of 5 denominations. In 1903 the Young People's Missionary Movement became the Missionary Education Movement, which was given the responsibility for the preparation of materials to be used by all the churches in their educational work. Themes are chosen years in advance, thus giving ample time for effective writing and publishing. The actual work of publishing is done by The Friendship Press. The distribution of materials is done through the denominational houses. To this material the denominations add literature dealing with their own enterprises and countries in which they are especially interested.

The responsibility for education in missions has been shifted, in the main, from the mission boards of the denominations to the departments of education. This change has been made so that missions can become an integral part of church education. The mission boards have not given up all responsibility for education or dropped educational secretaries from their staffs, but churches have placed educational tasks in the hands of their educators. Through this study, missions has become a part of the church school curriculum and special classes in mission subjects a recognized part of church programs.

Some of the earlier methods used in missionary education have been dropped or altered. New methods have been introduced. Denominations have made use of what is called "the project." Churches are encouraged to learn all they can about their "project," thus developing a tie between themselves and a particular mission enterprise based on knowledge and personal contact. Programs, though directed at lay people in the churches who have responsibility for the missions program, are open to all interested. Students coming from foreign lands to the educational institutions of the West have increased in number. Churches have invited such students to talk about their countries and have found the experience beneficial in helping local people to understand the present-day situations in which mission operates.

— *J. Leslie Dunstan*

MORAVIAN CHURCH The Moravian Church traces its origin to the Hussite rebellion in Bohemia-Moravia following the martyrdom of John Hus in 1415. In 1457 the Unity of the Brethren was established as a separate group, obtaining the episcopacy from a Waldensian bishop 10 years later. During the 16th century the church grew rapidly in spite of periodic persecution, but when the Counter-Reformation gained control of Bohemia-Moravia the Brethren were given the choice of acknowledging the authority of Rome or leaving the country. Most of them, some under the leadership of Bishop John Amos Comenius, did leave and were absorbed into the Lutheran and Reformed state churches of surrounding countries. Others remained, outwardly conforming to Roman practice but secretly practicing their Protestant faith and handing it down to their children.

In 1722 this "hidden seed" (to use a phrase of Comenius') had the opportunity to grow again when one of the group, while traveling in Germany, discovered a young German nobleman who, strongly influenced by Pietism, was willing to grant them a large measure of religious liberty if they would settle on his estate. The nobleman was Count Zinzendorf. When the refugees slipped across the border they were dubbed "those Moravians" by the Germans, and the nickname stuck. Thus was born the Renewed Moravian Church, which in Europe has functioned more as a spiritual life society and foreign mission agency within the state church than as a separate denomination, in keeping with Zinzendorf's desire to provide spiritual nurture for all but to keep denominational competition at a minimum.

The Moravians began mission work among the slaves of the West Indies in 1732 and came to continental North America in 1735 to establish mission work among the Indians. They founded Bethlehem, Pa., in 1742, and Salem, N.C., 20 years later.

The Moravian Church in America presently carries on an educational program similar to that of most other Protestant churches and since 1948 has cooperated with the Presbyterian Church U.S. in the production of church school curriculum materials. — *John S. Groenfeldt*

MOTION PICTURES The motion picture, even in the form of drama, progresses by the projection of a series of symbols, each of which has a unique function in the communication of meanings. These symbols express the meanings that situations and ideas have for the film producer. If the picture is well done, it will transmit meanings with a clarity and vividness that is seldom exceeded by other forms of classroom presentation. However, for the audience member the pictorial symbolism will be apperceived as a congeries of cues that will arouse meanings he already holds about the ideas and situations being treated. The symbols become media of communication when there is an approximate or overlapping identity between the meanings expressed by the communicator and those aroused in the audience member. Since there is no possibility of interpersonal give-and-take in a filmed presentation, it is necessary for the producer and the audience to think in the same frame of reference and to appreciate each other's viewpoints if the audience members are expected to accept information or to change beliefs as a result of seeing the picture.

Obviously, this intimate identification is seldom possible between producer and audience if only because motion pictures are so often used to present the new and the strange, which the audience members cannot experience in person. But in almost every instance where a film is pertinent to his course of instruction the teacher can make it meaningful. He should prepare himself to use a motion picture in the same way he prepares for the use of the textbook or any other curriculum aid. He should 1st thoroughly familiarize himself with the content of the picture. Next he should prepare any necessary explanation to relate the film to the experience of the audience members and to his objectives for the course. Finally, he should show the picture — over and over if necessary — making sure his pupils are as familiar with it as they are with any other important textual material. There are few, if any, limitations on the use of a film for teaching purposes if it is properly and carefully integrated into the curriculum.

Studies have shown that church schools use motion pictures more than do other groups in the local church. Youth groups, men's clubs, and adult classes, in that order, follow in frequency of use of films. All these bodies look upon motion pictures (1) as a source of information, (2) as a means of evoking emotional response to Christian teaching and example, and (3) as a basis for discussion.

Unfortunately, purposeful relationship between production objectives and the needs of consumers in local churches seldom occurs in the making of religious films. Denominational and interdenominational sponsors of films often have only their own objectives in mind. Typically, they are stimulation of support for programs or budgets. Commercial producers of religious films design their product to reach the widest possible market so as to reap maximum profit. Their pictures, especially Biblical films for church school use, are, therefore, almost uniformly theologically obscure and artistically sterile.

Both such classes of motion pictures fail to fulfill the requirements of instructional films — that they be designed to attain concrete objectives with specific audiences. As a consequence, these pictures are generally shown primarily as entertainment features and fail to achieve educational objectives.

The use of motion pictures is now routine in all forms of education. Films are expected by both children and adults. Although churches invest heavily in films, they have fallen behind secular educational groups in film utilization. The alternative to sporadic and nonobjective use of motion pictures in churches is the widespread production of adequate instructional films by responsible agencies of Christian education. Course units need to be planned with motion pictures as an integral part. Sometimes existing pictures, like existing textbooks, can be used if they are properly interpreted. (This may be true even for the commercial films on Biblical subjects.) The criteria for judging a movie are the same as those that apply to any other textual material. It must meet rigid standards of accuracy in content, possess artistic integrity, and be related to the level of understanding of the student group.

— *Everett C. Parker*

MOTIVATION Popularly, motivation is thought of as that which causes (moves) a person to do what he does, to behave in one way and not another, to act at one time and not another. Explanations of why a person does what he does too often have been confused with description. Such statements as: " He acts this way because he is lazy " or " He did this because he was frightened," merely describe rather than fully explain behavior. Behavior here is broadly understood as synonymous with activity or reaction of any kind, whether external or internal, whether of the whole person or part.

On a more sophisticated level many theories have been devised to explain behavior. Each has had its period of popularity. Concepts of " soul," " will," " instinct," and " drive " have been used to explain and help predict behavior. Currently, few problems dealt with by psychology are less understood and few terms are more confused. Motives are defined in many different ways in many different psychological systems. There is as yet no large area of agreement among psychologists on motivation theory. In the final analysis motivational theory practically involves the whole of personality theory. The problem grows out of the fact that what we know about motivation has to be inferred from the observation of a person's behavior within a particular environment on the basis of an understanding of the internal structures of the neural and endocrine systems and in relation to social systems and cultural patterns.

Each theory, understood within its own frame of reference, may be helpful. No one theory may be entirely adequate. It is possible that we need to call upon several theories to guide us. In the meantime psychologists try to gather more data and develop more satisfactory theories. While this is going on, it is easiest to adopt a particular frame of reference and to make it central, calling upon others when the theory we are using does not seem applicable.

In recent decades the most widely influential theory of motivation has been the psychoanalytic theory of drive that was first elaborated by Sigmund Freud to account for deviant, abnormal, psychotic behavior and then enlarged to take in the whole of human development and behavior. The force field theory of

Kurt Lewin and his disciples, which has been adopted mainly by the social psychologists, probably comes next in influence. Variations of both these theories are profuse. Although the following propositions are greatly oversimplified and perhaps overgeneralized, they point to some areas of consensus.

It is the nature of living organisms to be active and constantly in motion. Even when asleep a person is never still. Life is energy and energy is motion. Energy is expended in transforming matter, maintaining and repairing the organism, reproducing more organisms, and restructuring the environment.

This motion or activity may be observed as being in a particular direction or as having more or less intensity and range. Motivation may be said to have come into the picture when the level of activity or agitation markedly increases or when the rather random character of the activity takes a consistent direction or when the direction of the movement with reference to a particular object or goal changes. Sometimes the organism moves toward an object or goal (adience) and sometimes definitely away from it (avoidance).

It may be observed also that these activities tend to take on certain definite patterns that are repeated. The formation of the pattern as well as the activity itself may be said to be motivated.

The church school teacher may visualize the restless child who is constantly active, often in almost random, aimless fashion — wiggling, running, touching, tasting, feeling, testing, talking — sometimes engaged in a well-organized project, whether breaking stones to see what may be inside or building a play house. Some of his activities, such as looking for something to eat, occur much more regularly than others. Much of education and social organization consists of shaping activity into patterns and sequences of movement in relation to particular objects and goals — directing activity already motivated.

Affect or feeling is related to activity inasmuch as it is the awareness of the heightened activity and the change of functioning of the visceral system. Emotion is not the cause but the manifestation or the accompaniment on the visceral level of strongly motivated behavior. Emotion accompanies all levels of activity, although on the less intense levels it does not force itself upon the attention. Heightened activity is accompanied by heightened emotion, which may be perceived as either pleasant or unpleasant, and valued as either good or bad.

Some psychologists would abandon the concept of motivation altogether as being of little use to the student of behavior. Others make a distinction between " caused " and " motivated " behavior, limiting the term " motivation " to those activities which are responses to the internal, physiological needs, or " appetitive drives." Some would distinguish between motivated, or " coping," behavior and that which is merely " expressive." Falling downstairs because one has slipped or has been pushed, or jumping when a door is slammed is caused behavior. The attempt to catch oneself or to cushion the shock of landing at the bottom of the stairs, or investigating the door-slamming is motivated activity. The grace, vigor, quickness, and style with which one copes with the problem of falling or jumps when startled is expressive of the structure, temperament, and motility of the person, which is to a large extent given as his constitutional endowment.

Behavior is motivated when it arises in response to internal needs. There is considerable agreement upon the basic organismic needs, such as the need for nutrition, rest, activity, excretion, sexual outlet, and avoidance of that in the environment which is injurious. There is less agreement elsewhere toward the importance of such factors as the need to be positively related to others or the knowledge and meaning that might lead to exploration and mastery. It is agreed that certain needs are basic or primary, and others are derived or secondary. Secondary needs are particular, learned ways of satisfying basic needs that have in themselves taken on some of the value and strength of the basic needs because they are so closely associated.

It is generally agreed that behavior is overdetermined, that is, the forces and motives are complex and multiple, with more than enough in any situation to lead to a particular activity. Simple explanations and solutions miss the baffling richness, complexity, and depth of the forces operating upon and in our behavior. Psychologists attempt to measure the presence and the strength of motivation by depriving subjects of satisfiers, by applying persistent stimulation of various intensities, and by structuring situations in such a way that the presence or absence of ego involvement, success, frustration, anxiety, or failure is built in. Data are collected by the use of self-rating scales, observer judgments, and physical apparatus to indicate various response levels.

It is generally agreed that the motivation for much of behavior operates beneath the level of our awareness, so that the actor himself is not able to report on the forces that move him in certain ways or directions. If we ask the child why he is misbehaving, he is doubtless quite honest and accurate in saying he does not know why. It might be more constructive to point out that his behavior is disrupting the group, alienating his friends, or irritating his teachers, and to help him find more adequate ways of coping with his needs. Or it might be helpful to attempt to restructure the situation so as to eliminate some of the causes or stimuli of undesirable activity.

In summary, pupils do not need to be motivated to learn, for they are already motivated to learn, and are already active in learning that which might meet their needs and fulfill their nature. It is the teacher's responsibility to structure the situation in such a way that deleterious influences are eliminated or neutralized, opportunities for satisfying responses are present, and the environment is rich and exciting. The teacher then directs and organizes learning by presenting models and images and by helping the pupil see how particular learnings (patterns of behavior) or ways of responding will meet his needs and satisfy the urge to exploration and mastery. Motivated learning is more likely to be authentic, autonomous, and lasting than caused learning. Caused learning tends to be conformist, conventional, and superficial, leaving the self undeveloped.

— *Paul B. Maves*

MOVIE FORUM A movie forum is a session in which a feature motion picture is viewed and/or discussed from a Christian perspective. We are not dealing here with films produced for in-church use, but with the "entertainment" movies ordinarily distributed through commercial channels. The film forum may occur after the participants have attended a theater either individually or in a group, or the discussion may follow a special showing scheduled for a church auditorium or public hall. Many older feature films can now be rented in 16mm. form from distributors, a current listing being included in the biennial edition of the *Audio-Visual Resource Guide*, published by the Department of Audio-Visual and Broadcast Education of the Division of Christian Education, National Council of the Churches of Christ in the U.S.A. The same department is developing a study program with printed materials to assist local groups in the conduct of film forums.

Many types of films lend themselves to this purpose. Some evoke healthy responses and sound ideas that are clarified, expanded, and intensified through dialogue. Others arouse questionable responses and ideas that can be ventilated and evaluated through conversational exchange.

Some films or scenes from films portray life with such vividness and reality that they focus attention on fundamental questions of existence. They may even make a more penetrating and prophetic judgment than most preachers on the shallowness, irresponsibility, and deceit of much of society. Such films may prepare viewers to give serious consideration to the claims of the Christian faith. A forum can demonstrate or at least suggest the relevance of the gospel to real-life situations.

There are also films or elements within films that are false, contrived, unreal. Many cinematic themes are based upon unchristian, or at least sub-Christian, presuppositions, but these, too, are useful resources for forums. Thoughtful discussion can lead to the development of more discriminating viewers who will be better prepared for general exposure to the mass media. A person who can distinguish between the phony and the authentic will be less likely to become addicted to the predominantly escapist fare of the American media. What films do to viewers depends, to a great extent, on what viewers do with films. Educators concerned with the possibly harmful effects of motion pictures (and television) on children can attack the problem at one point by means of film forums for both children and parents.

Forums can deal profitably with many issues that can be exposed by such questions as the following: Is the film a fantasy or a portrayal of reality? How authentic and believable are the characters and situations in the film? How is the basic conflict resolved? Does the conclusion proceed naturally from the preceding situations and character development or is there an incongruous "happy ending," suggesting too-easy answers to life's problems? Is evil punished and good rewarded in an artificial way that contradicts the nature of life in this world? Does the conclusion put a moral stamp of lofty disapproval on what has otherwise been a clandestine and delicious orgy for viewers in a darkened theater? What are possible alternate endings? Why do you suppose the producer chose this one? What are the standards and values behind the motives and actions of people in the story? Is there an undercurrent of naïve optimism or hopeless despair? To what extent is this due to the scenario, the acting, or the direction? How did you, as a viewer, respond to various scenes in the film — with laughter, agony, envy, desire, sympathy, cynicism? With which characters did you identify? What does this reveal about yourself?

The moderator should have both artistic sensitivity and theological awareness, but he should not impose his own judgments on the group. He must exercise leadership primarily through sharply focused questions. He must recognize the dangers of straining symbolism and allegory, or of laboring diagnoses. In some cases the emotional impact of a film may make it wiser to allow time for reflection than to enter immediate discussion. An informal coffeehouse atmosphere will often contribute to full participation.

In France, Germany, Holland, and other European countries many Christian groups are active in the promotion of film forums. Ideas are exchanged through an international organization, *Interfilm*, Hilversum, Holland. — *John W. Bachman*

MUSIC Music is the ordered progression of time, given significance by sound arranged in considered pitches and sonorities. Music rescues time from meaningless and endless duration in silence. Like speech, it articulates and defines time through distinction and form of sound endowing even colorless and formless silence with attributes of repose, stillness, and potentiality. For silence is the ground out of which music springs. Music struggles through suspension and resolution in time to return to silence. Silence is not known as eternal until de-

fined by the temporal event, by the word, by the articulate.

Space is defined by matter; time by event. The wholly and specifically human, intentional, and conscious definition of either or both of them we call art: spatial, visual, graphic art, on the one hand; temporal, verbal, lyric, aural, on the other. David joined the 2 together when he danced before the Ark of the Lord. Then and there, movement in space and time defined dance, dancer, and him who was praised. Man defines himself (thereby limiting himself) in space and time. Through articulate life, the deathly silence is itself changed. Music, like painting or poetry, is a particular articulation in time (though not in space) for the ear (not the eye), proceeding from the creative, structuring mind and intentive will of the composer and performer to the discerning ear and willing understanding of the listener, employing as symbol and language the particular conventions of sound in time that not only constitute the musical idiom itself but recapitulate 16 centuries of musical history.

Music at large and in the worldwide sense is not specifically Christian. Historians and anthropologists trace 2 roots: the 1st in the dance, the linked spatial-temporal art that generally gave rise to music of regularly recurring, metrically patterned, insistent rhythm; the 2d in speed, creating the lyric patterns of melody and the irregular rhythms of recitative and chant. There is no culture, ancient or modern, primitive or advanced, that has not found music to dance or chant to, to make love with or with which to invoke the gods. Yet music in the highly developed form we know it — music with a history, with a past made present and accessible by accurate and commonly understood notation, music with a written literature enriching the fragile and shifting remembrances of improvised forms — music per se and independent of dance, song, and liturgy — such music is confined to Western Christian and post-Christian civilization. Some kinds of non-Western music have exploited particular areas of musical sensitivity more thoroughly — the African his complex polyrhythms, the Far Easterner, subtly microtonal melody; but no non-Western musical tradition has produced music comparable to that of Palestrina, Bach, Beethoven, Brahms.

Christianity may claim music as its peculiar art in a way it can no other. The years from A.D. 400 to 1000 saw the development and flowering of the tremendous repertory of single-voiced liturgical melody that we call the Gregorian chant, begotten of Jew and Hellene, spread throughout the West in the grave sobriety of the Roman rite, and perfected in the Carolingian Empire. About A.D. 1000 musicians began singing 2 or more melodies simultaneously, which in the first days of experiment became more and more independent of each other and in later centuries more and more suited to each other and euphonious in their independence. Thus musicians addressed themselves to an entirely new dimension in musical art — "polyphony" or "harmony," the science and art of sounding different pitches at the same time as well as in succession only, as heretofore in the pure melody of the Gregorian chant. The same medieval century saw the evolution of a simple and accurate system of written musical notation, just in time to pre-

serve at least the melodic forms of the great repertory of Gregorian chants before decay set in, and in time to record, spread, and invite further experiments in harmonized many-voiced singing. This vocal polyphony probably reached its greatest and most polished heights in the 16th century. From 1600 onward we see the development of opera and independent instrumental music, both increasingly divorced from Christian and liturgical context.

What relation the unprecedented growth of musical art in Christian and Christianity-influenced culture bears to Christianity itself is problematical. Certainly the crucial invention of an accurate and commonly understood musical notation did for music what alphabet and written language have done for every literature. But it is tempting to think that the Christian religion, to which time is central, which constantly recalls a certain year in its creeds and in its chief act of worship, a certain night, which regards history as meaningful and the end as consummation, nourishes and welcomes an art whose very substance is time, whose every example has beginning, middle, and ending. Painting, sculpture, literature, and eventually drama were all impressed into Christian service, liturgical or apologetic, acquiring "Christian" tone and style, and dealing with Christian subject matter. Only music, of all the arts, grew from childhood to maturity in a Christian environment.

We ask, "How can we use music in Christian education?" and especially, "What hymns should children sing and how can we integrate this music into courses for Christian nurture?" We do well to ask, but we also need to ask, " How can Christian education produce Christians who are (among other things) good musicians and who make good music? " The Hebrew-Christian tradition at various times and in various ways has employed all the arts as well as music as vehicles of its expression and of its catechetical, worshiping, and prophetic purpose. It has sometimes appropriated them as it found them; it has developed them and at times claimed them wholly as its own. Sometimes it has rejected some or one of them as for that age and place unsuited to its purpose. At best it has redeemed them, exactly as it tries to do with the men and cultures which it touches — not by the conversion of the church to the values of the world but by the taking up of the world into the church and at last to God.

The question is often asked, " Is it right to use secular music in church? " The composer knows how minor are the distinctions separating the " secular " music of one age from the " church " music of the same age when compared with stylistic differences separating various ages and with that great elastic chasm separating good music from bad in any age. It is far more important to ask, " What is the relation between the redeemed society and the total culture of the world that surrounds it? " There have been times when the church has so permeated the world, so informed its thinking and being, that the church could freely and safely use the culture of the world in its rites and worship and be the richer for it. There have been other times when the church felt itself as an ark separated from society and redeemed from worldly values. For the church then to have borrowed indiscriminately from the culture of the world would have meant the conversion of the church to the values of the world. In the 2d and 3d centuries instrumental music was forbidden in Christian worship, more by common agreement than by legislation or ruling, for instrumental music was strongly associated with the pagan theater and arena, the archetype of all in ancient society that Christianity opposed. What is the nature of our post-Christian age? What is or shall be or ought to be the relation of the church to our society? Answers to these questions, if we find them, must underlie answers to narrower questions about " secular " music in church.

The question of what is musically and artistically suitable and apt for a given purpose and what is not apt can be dealt with. An anthem written for the resources of a trained choir is obviously not suitable as a hymn tune. But the vexed question of what is good and bad in music and specifically in church music is resolved only by the firm and sifting hand of passing time. The individualist says, " The good is what I like." The aristocratic traditionalist says, " The good is what most people of taste, such as myself, like." The moralist says, " The artistically good is what tends to produce the ethically good in human action and affection." The communist says, " The artistically good is what promotes the social goals and goods of the state." The theologian says, " The artistically good is what tends to bring men ultimately to God." All these views speak of art in terms of " instrumental " values, and ask, " Is this music good for a particular purpose? " The question is valid. The church, for instance, must ask not only, " Is this music good? " but also, " Is it good for the worship and education of these particular people? "

A song is good or bad in itself as well as for something. Known in fullness only to God who will come to be the Judge not only of songs but of men, always partly hidden to imperfect and selfish human judgment, worth is still partially revealed to us: the worth of terminal artistic value, the worth of corporate or national achievement and character, the worth of personal, self-emptying holiness. Worth in art is often revealed in terms of a Scriptural idea — the idea of the new (cf. Erik Routley, Massey H. Shepherd, Jr.). " O sing to the Lord a new song " (Ps. 98:1) — namely, the song that says something that has not been said before or that says old things in a different way; the song that must use the old scales and words but so combines them that we recognize a fresh song and a song worth singing. Bad art is usually plagiarism. Why is the exact copy of a great painting worth so little? Because it is not new!

The new life is the risen, the redeemed, and the transfigured life — the life in which the old things, the ancient situation, the repetitive circumstance, are made new. " Behold, I make all things new! " The Christian man is the new man; the Christian order is the true new order of the ages, the New Jerusalem. The Christian song, the good song, is the new song. Here aesthetics and theology meet. — *John M. Boe*

MYTHOLOGY Myths are stories that account primarily for the origins of beings, things, situations, or events. Many myths are prehistorical in origin; others were created in subsequent historical periods.

Myths may be classified according to the subjects with which they deal, the major questions centering on the following: the origin of the world, the gods, and men — all often closely related; the origin of families, tribes, and nations, often traced to heroes; the origin of animals; the origin of various developments in civilization; the dead and the places they inhabit; the transformation of men into other forms (e.g., animals, trees, bushes); beings (e.g., nymphs, demons, monsters of various kinds) that inhabit special places on the earth (e.g., rivers, pools, deserts, woods, mountains); changes and recurrences in the natural world: day and night, winter and summer, seedtime and harvest, birth and death; odd or violent aspects of nature: earthquakes, storms, floods, eclipses, etc.

Most (but not all) mythology is traditional, is in narrative form, and is etiological — that is, accounts for origins. But myths also vary considerably, one from another; hence, the study of mythology is difficult and often obscure, and should be pursued with caution and discretion.

In the 2d half of the 19th century, many scholars, principally philologists, undertook the study of comparative mythology, accounting for the origin of myths by assuming a lapse of memory among the peoples who originated them. The following development was postulated: 1st, a descriptive name (or several names) was given to a natural phenomenon in a story told about it; subsequently, the original meaning of the story was forgotten, and a myth ensued. For example, it was said that the myth about Hercules' death by the shirt poisoned with Nessus' blood developed from an earlier story about the sun's setting behind red clouds. According to this view, mythology resulted from the failure of memory caused chiefly by the migration of tribes from their ancient homes. Words that originally had characterized various natural phenomena came to designate human forms; hence, mythology was born. Mythology, according to this theory, came into being accidentally and unconsciously; and the myths are held, accordingly, to hold no truth value: they are illusions stemming from forgetfulness.

The origin and significance of myths, however, may be understood from a very different point of view. The interpretation of them outlined above is untenable. It is noteworthy that while lapse of memory is said to account for the origin of myths, an extraordinary memory must be assumed to account for their perpetuation, once they came into being.

Biblical myths are dramatic stories in symbolic language about God and his relation to men and the world, which demand of man a decision and a commitment. Mythology appropriates symbolic language. The believer who uses mythological language knows that it is symbolic, that it does not denote exactly, that it does not describe (as, e.g., scientific language does) but points beyond itself to truth apprehensible in faith.

Furthermore, Biblical mythology deals with God in relation to men and world. It does not paint pictures of divine beings to be gazed and marveled at, but it speaks of God only as he relates himself to his created world. Therefore, the mythology of the Bible demands of its hearers both a decision and a commitment. It places its hearers in the position of having to accept or reject it, of having to affirm the God of whom it speaks and whose actions it declares, committing themselves to him, or of having to deny him. Biblical myths do not portray wonderful panoramas; they ask men questions of ultimate significance regarding life and destiny.

It would appear that the full gospel can be communicated only in mythological language, for only such language speaks in terms of universal perspectives. To relate Christ to universal history, as the gospel does, is necessarily to speak mythologically. Myth is the only language in which the vision of heaven and hell, of the beginning and the end, and of the Savior of all in the center of the whole can be expressed. The language of science or of logical propositions is unable to communicate the truth to which only mythological language can point.

A myth, then, is not a fantasy, or an illusion of primitive mentality; it is a unique way of communicating what is created and perceived by the imagination. Myths are believed in faith; though they cannot be proved to be true by reason, they are accepted by reason as pointing to truth.

The following New Testament data may be said to have, in one degree or another, mythological aspects or characteristics: references to creation, heaven and hell, angels, Jesus' preexistence; to the incarnation and the virgin birth, miracles, the crucifixion, the descent into Hades, the resurrection; to the Antichrist, the Second Coming, and the Holy Spirit; to the millennium and the Last Judgment.

— *Burton H. Throckmorton, Jr.*

N

NATIONAL ASSOCIATION OF EVANGELICALS The National Association of Evangelicals is a Protestant interdenominational movement founded in 1942 to promote interchurch fellowship and cooperation on an evangelical (as opposed to an inclusive) theological basis. Its membership includes 38 denominations and many individual churches and agencies with a combined membership numbering more than 2,000,000 persons, its affiliated commissions and agencies serving some 10,000,000 American Protestants.

The NAE grew out of an all-night prayer meeting held by 150 churchmen in St. Louis in 1942 because of a common dissatisfaction with liberal theological and social trends in the Federal Council of the Churches of Christ in America. They disputed the Federal Council's right to speak for all Protestants, noting that several major denominations were unaffiliated, and that Council pronouncements frequently misrepresented the conviction of a large segment of its own membership.

The organization adopted this doctrinal statement in 1943 at Chicago: "We believe the Bible to be the inspired, the only infallible, authoritative Word of God. We believe that there is 1 God, eternally existent in 3 Persons, Father, Son, and Holy Ghost. We believe in the deity of our Lord Jesus Christ, in his virgin birth, in his sinless life, in his miracles, in his vicarious and atoning death through his shed blood, in his bodily resurrection, in his ascension to the right hand of the Father, and in his personal return in power and glory. We believe that for the salvation of lost and sinful man regeneration by the Holy Spirit is absolutely essential. We believe in the present ministry of the Holy Spirit by whose indwelling the Christian is enabled to live a godly life. We believe in the resurrection of both the saved and the lost; they that are saved unto the resurrection of life and they that are lost unto the resurrection of damnation. We believe in the spiritual unity of believers in our Lord Jesus Christ."

The movement now has its national headquarters office in Wheaton, Ill. Its official magazine is *United Evangelical Action*. A public affairs office in Washington, D.C., provides liaison with government.

NAE sponsors commissions in the areas of world relief, international relations, stewardship, spiritual life, social action, evangelical action, chaplaincy, educational institutions, radio, and television. Interest has increased in corporate theological study by related denominations. The Commission on a Christian Philosophy of Education sponsored the volume *Christian Education in a Democracy.*

In 1947, NAE sponsored the organization of the National Association of Christian Schools to promote Christian day schools in the U.S.A. and in mission outposts, maintain a teachers' agency, sponsor courses in the Christian philosophy of education, and publish *The Christian Teacher.*

The admission of the Assemblies of God, largest segment of American Pentecostalism, marked the identification of a large and virile segment of the so-called 3d force with NAE. NAE's official membership includes also the following: Anchor Bay Evangelistic Association, Association of Fundamental Ministers and Churches, Bible Meditation League, Brethren in Christ, Christian Church of North America, Church by the Side of the Road, Church of God (Cleveland, Tenn.), Church of the United Brethren in Christ, Churches of Christ in Christian Union, Conservative Congregational Christian Conference, Elim Missionary Assemblies, Evangelical Free Church, Evangelical Mennonite Brethren Church, Evangelical Mennonite Church, Evangelical Methodist Church, Evangel Church, Inc., Free Methodist Church, Full Gospel Church Association, Inc., Gospel Association for the Blind, Grace Gospel Evangelistic Association, Holiness Methodist Church, International Church of the Foursquare Gospel, International Pentecostal Assemblies, Mennonite Brethren Church, Missionary Church Association, National Association of Free

Will Baptists, National Holiness Association, New England Evangelical Baptist Fellowship, New England Fellowship of Evangelicals, Ohio Yearly Meeting of Friends, Open Bible Standard Churches, Oregon Yearly Meeting of Friends, Pentecostal Church of Christ, Pentecostal Church of God, Pentecostal Holiness Church, Primitive Methodist Church, Reformed Presbyterian Church in North America, Rocky Mountain Yearly Meeting of Friends, United Fundamentalist Church, United Missionary Church, and Wesleyan Methodist Church.

— *Carl F. H. Henry*

NATIONAL BAPTIST CONVENTION, U.S.A. The 2d largest body of Baptists in America, the National Baptist Convention, U.S.A., Inc., has a constituency of more than 5,000,-000 members. Its members are predominantly Negro, drawn from every section of continental U.S.A. and from the Bahamas, B.W.I.

A free association of Baptist churches, district associations, and state conventions, it advocates no single theological concept to which it has made formal commitment in any deliberative session and which it holds to be binding upon its constituent members. The theological tradition exerting dominant influence upon the member churches may be broadly called "evangelicalism," although every shade of theological thought and opinion is expressed by individual members without jeopardizing their membership in the Convention.

To maintain membership in the Convention, member churches, district associations, and state conventions must be known to be in harmony with its purpose: "To promote home and foreign missions; to encourage and support Christian education; to publish and distribute Sunday school and other religious literature; and to engage in whatever other Christian endeavor is required to advance the Redeemer's Kingdom throughout the world."

The denomination is the result of the merger in 1895 of 3 separate national Negro Baptist organizations, one of which had been founded as early as 1880. The Convention's history included internal conflict and dissension, which erupted in 1915 into a major split. This split was unique in that it was caused by no doctrinal dispute but was an issue arising out of the ownership of a publishing house at Nashville, Tenn. A seceding group of churches formed themselves into the National Baptist Convention of America, Unincorporated, and it continues to this day with considerable strength and a constituency of more than 2,500,000 members.

The Convention embraces 3 subsidiary bodies – the Sunday School and Baptist Training Union Congress (founded in 1899), the Women's Convention (1900), and the Baptist Laymen's Movement (1924), and carries on its work through 6 boards and a number of *ad hoc* committees and commissions. The Foreign Mission Board and the Sunday School Publishing Board represent its largest operations.

Through its Sunday School Publishing Board, the Convention maintains and operates a publishing enterprise dating back to 1896. In 1960 it established the Townsend Press and under this imprint prepares and produces a variety of Sunday school lessons and materials in both the Uniform and cycle-graded series curricula of the Division of Christian Education of the National Council of the Churches of Christ in the U.S.A. – *Jesse Jai McNeil*

NATIONAL COUNCIL OF THE CHURCHES OF CHRIST IN THE U.S.A., DIVISION OF CHRISTIAN EDUCATION The Division of Christian Education is 1 of the 4 program divisions in the National Council of the Churches of Christ in the U.S.A. The cooperative church work that the Council (and the Division) carries forward goes back many decades, to the early years of the 19th century.

Although denominations, by action of their highest plenary bodies, officially constitute the Council, the membership and accordingly the outreach of the Division of Christian Education is substantially larger than the membership of the Council. Council legislation makes possible board membership in units independent of denominational affiliation at the higher levels. Mutually productive associations with Canadian denominational boards have been perpetuated. A very old pattern of membership of state councils of churches has continued. Because of such historic and productive relationships, the Division of Christian Education in the triennium 1960 to 1963 numbered in its membership 47 denominational boards of Christian education and 39 state councils of churches.

The educational work of the Division is carried on chiefly through 3 administrative and program units: the Commission on General Christian Education, the Commission on Missionary Education, and the Commission on Higher Education, each of which corresponds roughly with 1 of the 12 merging agencies which in November, 1950, at Cleveland came together to form the Council.

The focus of concern for the Commission on General Christian Education is the educational work of the church in the local congregation, the family, and the community. The Commission on Higher Education holds within its concern not only the programs of the more than 450 Protestant church-related colleges and universities in the U.S.A. but also the churches' ministry to state and independent universities as well. The Commission on Missionary Education works as an interpretive agency to hold before the U.S.A. and Canadian churches the geographical and spiritual proportions of the missionary task of the Christian church. The Standard Bible Committee, translators and custodians of the Revised Standard Version of the Bible, is administratively related to the office of the executive secretary.

A helpful, though oversimplified, summary of the Division's program might be put into 4 key words, corresponding roughly to these 4 program units: nurture, learning, mission, and communication.

The administrative separation of the program of the Council is confusing to the outsider. The careful observer will soon notice, however, that the Divisions are in constant touch with one another on program matters. *Ad hoc* committees for special purposes are formed and dissolved, more permanent committees are established for programs of longer duration, and in the case of the Commission on Missionary Education and the Commission on World Mission (one of the units of the National Student Christian Federation) the 2 Missions Divisions hold as direct a program involvement and relationship as does the Division of Education. Joint spon-

sorship of documents and programs for approval of the Council's General Board is a frequent procedure.

The Division of Christian Education is deeply involved in the world mission of the church and seeks to play its role in all contemporary efforts for the renewal and reunion of the churches. It is a member of the World Council of Christian Education and Sunday School Association, and its leaders have accepted responsibilities on that Council's Assembly, on its board of managers, and at its world conventions.

Youth leaders and their advisers in the United Christian Youth Movement play a responsible role in the Youth Department, jointly sponsored by the WCCESSA and the World Council of Churches. The National Student Christian Federation serves as the U.S.A. office of the World Student Christian Federation and through its Committee on Voluntary Service Projects makes important contributions of understanding, manual labor, and common living in an average of 36 countries every year. The Commission on Missionary Education is recognized as the foremost agency of its kind in the world; it publishes approximately 47 titles a year, on every aspect of the mission program of the churches.

The Division of Christian Education, as is true of the other units of the Council, is the creation of its member boards and councils. They brought it into being. They determine and modify its policies, educational program, and basic operational procedures.

The Division, therefore, is not an organizational toy, manufactured by ingenious individuals and responsible to them. It is not the possession of a headquarters staff that has become both an operator and a policy maker. The Division is the agency of the churches, fully responsible to them. Its elected officers have only delegated powers. Its employed staff work under policy directions and in democratically determined areas of responsibility.

The official and responsible educational program of the Division is administered by 42 committees carrying responsibilities for program outreach. In many instances there is a great deal of program coordination and a large amount of interunit adjustment.

The Commission on General Christian Education and the Commission on Missionary Education act as single educational units much more than does the Commission on Higher Education, where departmental lines are more operative. In the case of the Higher Education work the specialized nature of the several approaches to institutions, trustees, faculties, administrative heads, students, and others, many of which approaches were enshrined in quite independent organizations before 1953, has not yet allowed the Commission on Higher Education to act as a reviewing and coordinating body in the manner and to the extent accepted in the other 2 commissions. Whether any particular resulting program has been carefully coordinated with related efforts or not, it is, when adopted, a Division program and the Division accepts administrative responsibility for it.

A significant exception to this principle of program responsibility has to do with the Associated Sections. These bodies are autonomous units composed of individuals holding purely personal memberships brought and held together by common professional interests. In 1961

these sections were as follows: Administration and Leadership, Adult Work, Children's Work, City Executives, Directors of Christian Education, Editors, Family Life, Missionary Education, National Denominational Executives, Pastors, Professors and Research, Publishers, Regional Denominational Executives, State Executives, Weekday Religious Education, Youth Work. The programs of the annual meetings of these sections are largely arranged by the officers of the sections themselves, and the membership of individuals involves no commitments to the Division itself or its official programs on the part of any agency or institution that may employ these professional workers.

Under such a loose fraternal association there come together every February, in what is known as the Annual Meeting of the Division, persons from a great variety of educational, professional, and religious backgrounds. Many of the section members come from Christian bodies that cooperate in the Council's program or in the Division's work. Others do not; some belong to denominations that are not eligible for Council membership. About 2,400 persons hold such section membership and in February, 1960, e.g., 2,000 persons attended sessions of the sections. — *Gerald E. Knoff*

NATIONAL EDUCATION ASSOCIATION OF THE U.S. The Association was organized in 1857 by 43 " practical teachers " who had answered a call sent out by the presidents of 10 state teachers associations. The organizers represented state and local associations in a dozen states and the District of Columbia. The purpose of the Association, embodied in the 1st constitution and still the official view, was stated: "To elevate the character and advance the interests of the profession of teaching, and to promote the cause of popular education in the United States." Although there were other "educational" groups in 1857, the NEA was the 1st truly national organization of teachers.

The 1st name of the Association was the "National Teachers' Association." Under a plan of reorganization in 1870 the name was changed to the "National Educational Association." When granted a charter by Congress in 1907 the present name came into use.

The NEA is an independent, voluntary membership group. Although it has no official structural relationship with the Federal Government, the Association has a long record of cooperation with and assistance to governmental officials and agencies. The absence of basic, structural connections with organizations in other occupational fields has not prevented the Association from extensive, cooperative efforts when designed to improve the educational opportunities of children and youth and to raise the quality level of education. Thus today it has joint committees with the National Congress of Parents and Teachers, the American Library Association, the American Medical Association, and other groups.

Affiliated are about 7,000 local associations of teachers and state education associations in all states. These are independent groups with their own officers, funds, and programs. The NEA members in the affiliated associations choose delegates to the Association's annual convention, held during the last few days of June and the 1st days of July. These delegates constitute the Representative Assembly, which elects the officers, adopts official resolutions, approves the general program and goals of the Association, adopts the annual budget, and considers any question the delegates wish to raise. Between meetings of the Representative Assembly the governing body is the Board of Directors of 90 members.

Operating in the NEA's general framework are 32 national organizations serving the specialized interests of the profession. These "departments" include the American Association of School Administrators, the Department of Classroom Teachers, the American Educational Research Association, the Department of Elementary School Principals, and others. Each department elects its own officers, manages its funds, adopts policies, issues publications, and otherwise deals with matters of interest to its membership.

The Association has 27 committees, councils, and commissions. Among these are the convention committees (e.g., Auditing), the joint committees (e.g., with the American Library Association), and the bodies concerned with special questions (e.g., tenure, ethics, financial support of education, safety education). Periodically, usually for brief periods, the NEA organizes specialized committees and staffs to deal with current questions (e.g., juvenile delinquency, education of the academically talented, and the curriculum).

During the more than 100 years of its existence the Association and its affiliated state and local associations have exerted a constructive influence upon American education. These achievements have been accomplished by discussion, research, demonstration, and persuasion. Through its meetings, conferences, publications, and other activities the NEA informs teachers of educational, social, economic, and other trends. It seeks the counsel of non-educators and interprets education and the profession to the general public.

The Association's interests extend to the world. Hundreds of NEA members are serving abroad in schools operated by the Armed Forces. The NEA had a leading part in organizing the World Confederation of Organizations of the Teaching Profession, an organization that is building international goodwill and sharing educational methods. A number of NEA departments have committees on international relations. The Association cooperates closely with the agencies of Governments and the private groups that arrange exchanges of students and teachers. — *Frank W. Hubbard*

NATIONAL SUNDAY SCHOOL AS-SOCIATION The National Sunday School Association is an interdenominational, Protestant organization for the promotion of Sunday school work, committed to a conservative theological position. The Association originated out of the concern of evangelical leaders for the American Sunday school. The founders attributed the decrease of the Sunday school in members and its alleged ineffectiveness in good part to the liberal theological influences then prominent in the religious education movement. Dissenting from the doctrinal position reflected in the International Sunday School Lessons, they felt the need to develop a new uniform Bible lesson series along distinctly evangelical lines.

Preliminary meetings devoted to this project led to the establishment of the NSSA on May 1, 1945. The initial series of Uniform Bible Lessons was prepared in 1946.

From its beginning, NSSA has had for its declared purpose the vitalization of the Sunday school and a return to the evangelical message and Biblical methods. Its doctrinal statement is that of the National Association of Evangelicals, with which it became affiliated in 1946. The means used for the accomplishment of its purpose are fourfold: new uniform lesson outlines; promotion of Sunday school conventions, including regional as well as annual national conventions; the production of literature (books, pamphlets, periodicals) to help the evangelical Sunday school; research and service commissions.

National conventions have been held annually since 1946. The 1961 convention, meeting in Detroit, had a registration of 10,000, with an attendance of over 20,000. Fifty Sunday school associations, which hold their own conventions, are affiliated with NSSA. The uniform Sunday school lessons have an estimated circulation of 3,000,000, and 10 publishers are authorized to use them. The constituency of the Association covers some 70 denominations, classified as follows: denominations having members on the General Council of NSSA; denominations with an unofficial representative appointed by NSSA; those having no representative but cooperating with NSSA; denominations representing varied and lesser degrees of cooperation. Among the member groups are the larger Assemblies of God, the Free Will Baptists, the Free Methodists, and the Wesleyan Methodists.

The Association publishes an annual *Sunday School Encyclopedia* and a monthly periodical, *Link*. It maintains 4 commissions: Research (composed of Christian education professors), Youth, Camp, Denomination Sunday School Secretaries. NSSA also sponsors a National Association of Directors of Christian Education, and promotes Youth Week, National Family Week, National Sunday School Week, and a special month-long observance called "March to Sunday School in March."

The Association is operated by a General Council of representative denominations, Sunday school associations, and Sunday school publishing houses. It is financed by voluntary membership fees from individuals, families, Sunday schools, local churches, denominations, and publishing houses. — *Frank E. Gaebelein*

NATURALISM The term "naturalism" encompasses a variety of views in philosophy which, doctrinally viewed, largely share the belief that nature is everything, that all that is, is a part of nature, and that nature is self-existent, requiring reference to nothing beyond it. Many naturalisms tacitly employ a distinction between appearance and reality, holding that what is fundamentally real is what exists in space and time, and that anything that is not spatiotemporal enjoys only a derivative status, whether that of an aspect, appearance, epiphenomenon, or emergent. Thus naturalism denies a transcendent God or Creator; at most it permits a god or gods who are within nature. A few naturalists do affirm an immanent conception of deity, in which case naturalism tends to coalesce with either pantheism or panentheism.

In recent times definite doctrine, except as a matter of adherence to scientific method, has become quite secondary, partly because of the rapid development of science. Accordingly there is a strong tendency to identify naturalism with scientific empiricism, and to manifest a fitting intellectual restraint with respect to what the future of science will discover. Still more loosely, there are tendencies to identify naturalism with certain tempers of mind, e.g., intellectually curious, nonmystical, nontranscendental, this-worldly, but not necessarily devoid of aesthetic attitudes or natural piety.

1. *Greek atomism.* It is customary to signalize the Greek atomists Leucippus and Democritus as the ancestors of modern naturalism, for their mode of explanation was found to be useful by John Dalton and the pioneers of modern physics and chemistry. The Greek thinkers were providing a theoretic scheme to account for change: nothing exists but the atoms and space, although there is motion in space; the atoms, which are external, enter into combinations that come into being and dissolve, thus explaining change. There were practical as well as theoretical motives toward the adoption of the view, epitomized in its appropriation by Epicurus: removal of the fear of interference by gods in this life and removal of fear of another life. The existence of gods was not denied, but they were somewhere within the universe, remote from the world, and unconcerned with man. Immortality was categorically denied, for each man was thought to be a composite of atoms that dispersed at death.

Epicurean atomism is most accessible in the great literary work *De rerum natura* (*On the Nature of Things*), by the Roman poet Lucretius (ca. 96–55 B.C.). In dignified verse, Lucretius argued for the existence of space and of "first bodies" (atoms) that are eternal, various in shape, infinite in number, solid, indivisible, and devoid of color, taste, odor, and heat.

Aristotle was not an atomist, and under no strict doctrinal definition of naturalism is he properly to be called a "naturalist," for he held to the universality of teleological explanation, and had recourse in his multileveled world to fundamental realities that are nonspatial, nontemporal, and discontinuous with events in nature. However, his temper of mind was that of a scientist-philosopher; he objected to the transcendent Platonic Forms; and he had many prime movers as well as the Prime Mover. Thus a number of our contemporaries regard him as a naturalist. Similar remarks, *mutatis mutandis,* could be made for such thinkers as Averroës, Cusanus, Bruno, and Spinoza.

2. *Modern mechanistic materialism.* Metaphysical materialism is a species of naturalism; all adherents of such materialism are naturalists; but not all naturalists are materialists. Although Thomas Hobbes was a precursor in his reliance upon the explanatory power of the category of "motion," modern mechanistic materialism may be viewed as a development of the material side of Descartes's dualism into an exclusive account of everything. Presumably such an impressive development would never have taken place had it not been aided by the great physical synthesis of Isaac Newton, who was himself a man of intense religious faith. Universal gravitation and universal mechanics were further supplemented by the atomic theory of matter, the kinetic theory

of gases, and comparable theories of liquids and solids; the conservation of matter was partially evidenced and became a principle; likewise (in accord with the mechanical equivalent of heat) the conservation of energy. The term "mechanistic" has covered a spectrum of meanings, seldom carefully formulated, beginning with the applicability of the laws of classical mechanics, stretching across the incorporation of the principles of chemistry, and even reaching the generalized notion that all phenomena are strictly law-abiding. At this extreme, the doctrine of thoroughgoing mechanism has sometimes simply meant determinism, although usually it has at least carried further restrictions as to the kinds of entities that are allowed to carry the determinations, e.g., sometimes alleged emergent vital forces, psyches, etc., are ruled out, as well as free wills, God's will, and objective chance.

Again, if one considers a list of thinkers who were called "materialists," he may find less close unity among them in their positive doctrines extrapolated boldly from natural science than in such practical attitudes as antiauthoritarianism, anticlericalism, antiotherworldliness. Those whose behaviorism is not simply methodological (for the sake of the public character of science) but metaphysical can be counted as continuing the materialistic tradition. And there are some who would urge that cybernetics, as based upon the solid performances of digital computers and elaborate feedback systems, has given a new evidential thrust to mechanistic materialism.

3. *Dialectical materialism.* The dialectical materialism of Marx, Engels, and their successors purports to be a theory of the total cosmic

development. The inorganic realm is most briefly treated, but it is occupied on behalf of "materialism" in order to preclude religious and idealistic interpretations. Apparently Marx anticipated certain features of what was later called "emergence," although it is doubtful whether he should proleptically be labeled an "emergent evolutionist." Changes that have been gradual and quantitative become, at certain critical points, qualitative and novel. Such critical points are apparently associated with crises, as delineated in Hegel's dialectical method (conceived to be at once both logical and real). Thus, Marx was opposed to mechanistic materialism, and where he refers to "science" he usually means, as does Hegel, a grasp of the supposed necessary dialectical movement and not knowledge achieved by the natural sciences. The latter is not so much false as inferior, seeking static formulations of certain abstracted relations of things at a given stage of their development, without recognizing that these represent forms that have emerged and that theoretically are or may be caught up in further qualitative transformations. Marx admired Charles Darwin and (unsuccessfully) desired to dedicate *Das Kapital* to him, perhaps wishing at once to honor the discoverer of the mode of evolution of living forms and to associate therewith his own name as the discoverer of the principle of the succession of institutional formations in the history of human societies.

In its application in the realm of human history, dialectical materialism is usually called "economic determinism" or "the economic interpretation of history" or the "materialistic theory of history." Marx did not absurdly deny consciousness; rather, he maintained that it is not consciousness that determines the forms by which men live but that the modes of production and the consequent class division determine the persuasions of consciousness. Nor did he deny that there appear to be legal, religious, and artistic activities; these, however, are designated as being in the superstructure, the foundation of which is the economic. Engels, late in life, reformulated the earlier teaching to state (apparently) that the economic is the source and necessary condition of other human activities, but that when the noneconomic formations have emerged they do exercise distinctive causal influences of their own, albeit weaker than that of the economic. This thesis is one that is probably held by a number of non-Marxians.

4. *Emergent evolutionism and nonreductive naturalism.* In its narrower forms mechanistic materialism may still find numerous adherents in the popular mind, but as a seriously delineated theory it has almost vanished, a consequence that probably owes less to the refutations of philosophers than to the revolutionary changes in physics and to the intellectual pressure of indigenous biological conceptions. (A few metaphysical behaviorists and a few confident cyberneticists may constitute exceptions to this generalization.) Apparently persons with inclinations toward the more elastic forms of materialism have, after self-criticism, gone over to a nonreductive naturalism. If one was hopeful that chemical processes could ultimately be explained in terms of particle physics, one found difficulty maintaining the same confidence in confronting the animated portions of

nature, including the conscious imaginings and inventings of men. In the main such thinkers feel that the conception of the activities of organisms and of men should not be forced into accordance with preconceived notions and that possibly the idealists possessed certain insights that should be incorporated into naturalism. Some thinkers found themselves dropping any notion of "mechanism" borrowed from physics but retaining some kind of testimony on behalf of unspecified matter as general matrix. Others found themselves dropping materialism and broadening the meaning of "mechanism" to where it required little more than lawfulness. With the compounding of these and kindred tendencies, mechanistic materialism largely disappeared, and naturalism took its place.

No sane man wants to deny existence to anything that does exist. Growth, reproduction, breathing, thinking, intending, deciding, framing of ideals, all exist in the world. No alleged teleology outside nature is to be admitted; but if teleologies are found within nature, they are to be readily acknowledged rather than denied out of deference to categories found useful in a more abstract science. Some things that have emerged in cosmic time cannot be reduced to the characteristics of their constituents or antecedents; they are "emergents."

The naturalism resulting from these trends is often called "nonreductive," "critical," and "emergent." It is patently multiform. Perhaps the largest contrast manifest among the species lies between those who essay a large speculative scheme of cosmic development — e.g., C. Lloyd Morgan, Samuel Alexander, Jan Christian Smuts, etc. —

and those who feel that the lesson of the shaking of the foundations in metaphysics and physics is to embrace only a method and not a doctrine. Especially among the latter, an earlier monism of substance has thus sometimes been transformed into a monism of method: scientific method. This commitment has in turn raised questions as to the unity and definition of scientific method. As a previous generation learned not to tie naturalism to the extant categories of the natural sciences, should one not now be careful not to tie it to extant method? One wishes to define "scientific method" so as to exhibit its unity in concrete diversity and yet leave it open for the incorporation of new successful techniques.

5. *Naturalistic theism.* This label has only recently come into use. However, a large portion of the core of its meaning has long been familiar in Western thought, namely, in the idea of "natural theology." "Natural theology" stood for that portion of theology which could be attained by the unaided reason of man, as distinct from "revealed theology," the essential disclosures of which lay beyond the reach of the natural force of man's reason. In looking at contemporary naturalistic theism, it is convenient to note 2 markedly distinguishable sorts of views, which actually are only 2 conspicuous groupings within a theoretical spectrum of standpoints. One group places its emphasis upon ostensible respect for scientific method, with (in the actual procedure) a consequence that the activity of God is identified with certain denotable processes in the world. Various religious pragmatists illustrate this standpoint; Edward Scribner Ames is an excellent exam-

ple; in a very restricted way, even John Dewey could be counted in identifying "God" with what, as an active relation between ideal and actual, unifies forces in nature and society that create and support purposes. Doubtless the best contemporary protagonist is Henry Nelson Wieman, for whom God is certain creative processes that increase good and make for mutuality; these creative events work in human life but may be called "suprahuman" in the sense that they create good in a way that man cannot deliberately do. Traditional theists urge that this procedure is utterly weak toward establishing the transcendent aspect of God; some would declare it to be a purchasing of the actuality of God by a shifting of definitions.

With the previous viewpoint, the emphasis was upon "fact" with a minimum of theory; with the 2d major group of naturalistic theists there is manifest confidence in an extensive construction of theory held to be justified by the facts. These theists — however unorthodox in outcome — are thus in procedure closer to traditional natural theology; they are building their doctrine of God as part of the theory of accounting for the world in all its complexity and in its value tendencies found in the higher phases of animal and human experience. The conception of God is primarily an immanent one, however, for — with the careful avoidance of dualism — God's activity is in and continuous with so-called natural processes. Outstanding examples of philosophers who have recently constructed such a naturalistic theology are Alfred North Whitehead and Charles Hartshorne. Hartshorne labels the view, illustrated in Peirce, Whitehead, and himself, "panentheism,"

as distinct from both plain theism and pantheism. Panentheism holds that God, as well as being conscious and possessed of knowledge of the world, is inclusive of the world, affected by the world, and thus in some aspects capable of change. There is no question in theory of the unity and actuality of Hartshorne's or Whitehead's God. God is not the one Creator. In the classical sense he is not transcendent, but in a partial and technical sense he is; all other actual entities also transcend the past in their respective processes of coming to be. The power of God is described by Whitehead as that of persuasion — toward richness of value — and that of conservation in his own experience of what can be saved.

The predominant forms of naturalism today can be placed in the last 3 groupings, wide as these are. In communist countries dialectical materialism (3) is of course strong, and is fostered by the Governments. Religion is held to be the opiate of exploited people, and it is supposed to disappear when the new social order attains a flourishing status. Ideological debates take place, however, between those who feel that an aggressive campaign of militant atheism must be continuously waged until, say, a generation after the achievement of communism and those who are relatively willing to allow religion to wither and die. Outside observers would note that communism, like respective nationalisms, exhibits psychological features of historic religions, in dogma proclaimed, in cultus maintained, in dedication elicited, and in apocalypticism manifested.

In Anglo-Saxon and Western European countries, nonreductive varieties are probably now dominant among naturalisms. The more speculative of these thinkers had better not be labeled "humanists," because of the deference they (like Samuel Alexander) would give to "natural piety." Probably most contemporary philosophical naturalists, being men of humane or humanitarian sentiments, could be called "humanists," to indicate that they recognize that man possesses certain distinctive capacities among the animals and that the flowering of these capacities is the locus of their chief concerns. A rather small minority of these actively support humanist associations or extremely liberal churches, feeling that religious celebrative functions (purged of supernaturalism) are appropriate and that service activities of an organization are practically important. Many would deem themselves antisectarian, and some would view themselves as in principle opposed to organized religion, holding it to be either an anachronism or a contradiction in terms. A few would be antireligious in addition, either making criticisms akin to the Marxist or offering their own reasons from depth psychology for attacking what they would maintain is the neurosis of religion.

In contrast with this extreme, some naturalists would affirm that the religious quality of living is the natural culmination of the healthy individual; they would be disposed to satirize the desperate efforts of professional sectarian religious educators who fear that religion will perish unless children are being indoctrinated in reverential habitudes toward 1 particular set of holy scriptures; or, correlatively, they would be alarmed at the restrictive effect of the selection exercised on behalf of a provincial view. John Dewey used to remark that there was more

religious education to be found in having children from all groups cooperative in life together in the public schools than in the separations of released time or of parochial schools. A few pragmatists looked to the future to develop new religious forms not continuous with those of the past; some did suggest that labor unions and professional associations might generate the collective expressions of future religion (an anticipation that thus far manifests scanty realization, albeit revolutionary social and political movements do sometimes exhibit in marked degree the features of personal religious dedication and of collective cultus). More "conservative" naturalists, perhaps feeling that the phenomena of nazism do not allow one to take an optimistic view of human nature, and opining that a vague "religion in general" is hardly religion, are disposed to look with sympathy and hope upon the slow internal transformation of the religious bodies. Thus an unknown number of contemporary naturalists are probably supporting existing liberal churches, justifying their adherence with the notion that theological conceptions are of very minor importance as compared with the multiform social roles performed by the living church, ministering to sundry religious, moral-educational, and pastoral needs — needs both known and as yet unformulated. Dewey himself came to hold that economic obscurantism is a throttling power more serious in our society than religious obscurantism.

Ernest Nagel and Sidney Hook have at last brought out explicitly the latent side of Dewey's thought, recognizing that human intelligence is not omnipotent and that there are irremediable evils as well as remediable ones. They look upon the existentialists, however, as romanticizing loneliness and death. Certain other pragmatists have made overtures toward Buddhism, whether that of the founder or that of Zen.

Naturalistic theism (5) in turn exhibits considerable variety, but the implications of the positions for ethics and for religion are rather clear, owing to the plain lineaments of the respective theologies or of the value orientations that have generated them. A common consequence of the generic viewpoint may be noted: the tendency to reject the number of sharp dualities of historic faiths, e.g., the sacred as against the secular, the one true religion as against all other false religions. Correlatively, as opposed to the strong current movement toward Biblical theology and a Biblical world view, naturalistic theists — although showing much respect for the evolution of the Hebrew community and for the richness of the Christian church — are likely to suggest that the primary fields of religious tutelage lie in the firsthand achievement of human and cosmic relatedness, requiring the development of social sensitivities and personal valuational commitment.

— *Robert W. Browning*

NATURE STUDY From earliest history, man has been profoundly interested in the kind of universe in which he lives. Early Egyptian and Mesopotamian man confronted nature as a "thou." There was no created nature that stood over against the gods who created it; nature was the gods in action. Nature had its own characteristics, moods, and will.

Prephilosophical Greek thought was in many respects similar to this type of cosmology. Here, man encountered a daimon or numen in the sun, moon, winds, and other natural phenomena. He made sacrifices and offered prayers to these spirits, seeking their help and the avoidance of punishment.

Greek speculative thought inquired into the nature of things, but abstracted the numen from nature. This thought took several forms, but the main line of reasoning was to present the world as an intelligible whole that reflected a philosophical absolute which was the ground of all existence.

The Hebrew held to a personal Creator God who was other than nature but did not hold himself aloof from it. Nature is not divine; it is created by God. "The heavens are telling the glory of God; and the firmament proclaims his handiwork." (Ps. 19:1.) God has given nature many voices and they chant of the glory *above* the heavens. Man is the crowning achievement of this creation and is crowned with a "glory and honor" above all other created beings (Ps. 8:5).

In this same spirit the early followers of Christ saw in nature the "invisible" Presence. Nature proclaims God's eternal power which those who have eyes to see may clearly perceive "in the things that have been made" (Rom. 1:20).

This attitude sees God as actively involved in the natural processes, although not identifying him with nature itself. Here, God is not some "metaphysical argument" imposed upon the universe to account for it; rather, he is the ground of its existence, its Creator and Sustainer. Neither is he a "god of the gaps" called in to account for that which science is unable to explain. The whole is the handiwork of God, proclaiming his glory, testifying to his power, and calling upon man to worship the Creator rather than the creature. It is from this point of view that many in Christian education turn to the study of nature and natural phenomena in order to illustrate and exemplify the nature and glory of God.

Aside from the tenets of natural theology there is also a psychological aspect of human nature upon which such a concept as this may be built. In his *The Construction of Reality in the Child*, Jean Piaget develops the thesis that the growing child, in his " perception and representation of the world," makes a " transition from chaos to cosmos." Self-perception and perception of the world develop hand in hand, so that inadequate development in one weakens adequate development of the other. Further, in relation to the world about him, the child moves from that earlier stage of development " in which objects are centered about a self which believes it directs them " to that stage where he must make adjustments to the permanent and orderly changes in the patterns of the external world.

Some of the conclusions to be drawn from this are evident. If the child's conception of the external world is to proceed beyond the level of magical manipulation by wish-thinking, he must come to see himself " as an element in a totality which is coherent and independent of himself " (Piaget, else he will carry this magical idea into later stages of development with others, with nature, and even with prayer.

In his encounter with the external world the growing child " discovers " a world that, although it is independent of himself, is enduring and not subject to whimsical disappear-

ing; organized and not untrustworthy, ordered and not chaotic. If both his social and natural worlds have these elements, the child adapts himself to his world in confidence and trust because here is a world that will not betray him. These attitudes or " feelings " of confidence and trust then become the cornerstone on which Christian parents and teachers lead the child to join with nature in " telling the glory of God."

Such teaching must be done here, as in every area of learning, with care and wisdom, keeping in mind the age and needs of children and youth lest wrong views of God be planted in their minds. But just as the ant may inform the sluggard, so nature may " teach " us something of the God of nature who is also our Father and Redeemer.

— *Burt E. Coody*

NEOLIBERALISM The term "neoliberalism " seems to have been launched into theological discussion by Walter Marshall Horton, in his Eugene William Lyman Lecture at Sweet Briar College, on Nov. 14, 1952. Speaking under the title " Liberalism Old and New," Horton pleaded, not for a resurgence of the liberal theology dominant in the early years of the century, but for a new liberalism. The new theology would recover certain themes prominent in the older liberalism, but with corrections learned from the historical disasters and the neo-orthodox teachings of the intervening years.

Both in that lecture and in his later book *Christian Theology: An Ecumenical Approach* (1953; rev. ed., 1958), Horton especially identifies L. Harold DeWolf's thinking with neoliberalism. Since he pleads for the new movement, it is evident that Horton, too, is to be regarded as a liberal. Representing another wing of the same movement, rising from a more naturalistic type of thought, is another contemporary theologian, Daniel Day Williams. Examples of new liberal thinking could be drawn from many other writers, but these 3 names will identify some principal types of thought within the movement.

Some readers may question whether neoliberalism is a movement at all. There has been no cooperative planning of such a trend and no attempt to discover agreed definitions of position. The term " neoliberalism " is not widely used. Nevertheless, it is true that among the various tides and eddies of theological opinion there is a considerable current moving toward some such modified renewal of liberal emphases as Horton has described.

Certain characteristic neoliberal ideas may be pointed out under 4 topical headings, the first 3 indicated by Horton and a 4th added here.

Søren Kierkegaard and, less consistently, Karl Barth, have so stressed the unique, revealed character of the Christian faith as to depreciate the place of reason in determining the substance of Christian belief. The new liberals regard these neoorthodox teachings as needed correctives of such liberal rationalism as tended to reduce Christianity to a system of philosophy or an ethical mood. However, they insist that it is a mistake to limit so severely the place of reason in Christian theology. Reason must be relied upon to receive revelation, to distinguish between true and false revelation claims, to interpret the implications of revelation for living, and to establish bridges of understanding for communication of the revealed truth to many kinds of people.

Some recent theologies rigidly restrict revelation to the Biblical tradition. The new liberals, although stressing more than many of the older liberals the unique message and essential importance of the Bible, still insist that God has also disclosed himself and much truth among men of other traditions. They believe, moreover, that the Bible itself supports this view. (See, e.g., Rom., chs. 1 and 2, and Acts 14:16-17.)

The new liberals freely grant that some theology of the last century, especially under the influence of Schleiermacher, so stressed the immanence of God as to lose sight of his mysterious and awesome transcendence. They agree with the neo-Reformation writers that God is transcendent beyond all human imagination. Yet they insist that he is immanent also. He is radically other than man, but also deeply concerned with man and continuously active in the world.

Some liberal preaching has come close to identifying the Kingdom of God with human movements of reform or certain social institutions. The neoliberals join other recent theologians in emphatically denying such identification. Yet they insist that the Kingdom of God is God's reigning in human hearts, wills, and relationships. Its coming depends on God, but also upon the faithful obedience of men in subjecting all human existence, institutions, and relationships to his rule.

In recent theology there has been much stress on the depravity of man, as contrasted with the overoptimistic appraisals that preceded the World

Wars. Karl Barth was especially influential in bringing about this changed estimate of man. It is the more significant, then, that Barth himself now believes that the negative emphasis has gone too far. In Christ, God has said yes to man and we ought not to regard as depraved one whom God has accepted. New liberals stress, not an inherent natural goodness of man, but God's high purpose for him and the God-given grace by which that purpose can still be won. Daniel Day Williams especially well captures the positive but God-centered estimate of man in neoliberalism by his book title *God's Grace and Man's Hope* (1949). — *L. Harold DeWolf*

NEOORTHODOXY Neoorthodoxy is one of those vague but perhaps inevitable words that dominate theological conversation in a particular period. It stands less for a set of doctrines than for a broad movement of thought — the chief movement of the 2d quarter of the 20th century. This movement reformulated in striking contemporary terms some of the content of traditional Christian theology. It was often dramatically new in impact yet orthodox in many of its doctrines, hence the name. The term, in this meaning, belongs almost entirely to the North American vocabulary, but it designates a worldwide force.

Neoorthodoxy is one phase of the continuous Christian attempt to relate the gospel to the human world. On the one hand, the Christian must maintain the distinctiveness of this gospel, lest it be diluted and corrupted by the various cultures in which it lives. Hence, orthodoxy seeks, for the sake of fidelity to Christ, to maintain the purity of faith as against the world's idolatries.

It is suspicious of tempting middle grounds, remembering Jesus' warning, "He who is not with me is against me" (Luke 11:23).

On the other hand, the Christian, believing that the gospel is good news for mankind, seeks to relate it to human culture. The missionary task prompts a search for receptivity in creation to the Creator. The apologetic and educational task requires bridges between Christian faith and the best of human expectations. Therefore, the liberal Christian spirit seeks to cultivate the middle ground that orthodoxy distrusts. It recalls Jesus' saying, "He that is not against you is for you" (Luke 9:50).

Modern Christianity, seeking an honest relation between the gospel and the world, has faced an unprecedented set of problems. Following the Protestant Reformation the physical sciences produced a new picture of the universe, radically different from the traditional Christian picture. Biological sciences challenged the Biblical account of the creation of man. Historical and literary sciences led to new awareness of non-Biblical religions and to the analysis of Biblical documents and their sources. From technology and economic enterprise arose the "bourgeois mind," contemptuous of traditional authority and confident of its ability to control the future.

The Christian church responded with a divided mind. One impulse was to accept all the knowledge and much of the mood of the modern world. The resultant "liberal theologies" rejected old views of authority, building their doctrines on religious experience and on rational-empirical grounds. The opposing impulse was to cling to the ancient faith, rejecting the alluring temptations from the modern world. This impulse produced fundamentalism and the various conservative theologies that insisted on the verbal inspiration and literal truth of Scripture.

In this situation the neoorthodox movement offered new possibilities. It was quite open to all scientific findings, including Biblical criticism, but it made a sharp distinction between Christian faith and the prevailing spirit of modern culture. Neoorthodoxy, however, was more than a way out of the intellectual impasse between liberalism and orthodoxy (or fundamentalism). It addressed Christian faith to the shattering experiences of the 20th century.

The demands of the parish led Karl Barth, the dominant figure in the movement, to launch the theological revolution during World War I. Going into his pulpit on Sundays, he later wrote, " it required only a little imagination for me to hear the sound of the guns booming away in the north." He began to question his own preaching and the liberal theology he had been taught. In Bible study he discovered the message of Paul and decided that Luther and Calvin were better interpreters of Scripture than later generations. His commentary, *The Epistle to the Romans,* published in 1918, heralded the new direction in theology.

Barth's theology was often called the " theology of crisis " — with a double reference to the historical crisis of the 20th century and the continual crisis in man's relation to God. Another designation, " dialectical theology," emphasized the discontinuity between man and God. The phrase " neo-Reformation theology " marked the powerful influence of Luther and Calvin.

The response to Barth's work in Europe was so great that the phrase " Continental theology " became a virtual synonym for neoorthodoxy. However, many diversities emerged within the general movement. Emil Brunner in Switzerland, Gustaf Aulén and Anders Nygren in Sweden, and prominent Lutherans in Germany felt the influence of Barth but developed their own theologies. The impact of Søren Kierkegaard, the 19th-century Danish layman, became far greater than in his own time and inspired theologies of Christian existentialism.

The events surrounding World War II offered neoorthodoxy a challenging mission. Barth's sharp distinction between the Word of God and the word of man struck directly at Hitler's attempt to control the German Church, and the Barthian theology achieved an intensified social relevance. The sin of man and the tragic quality of history found obvious confirmation in events, and the declaration of God's grace became increasingly significant.

In North America, where society did not persecute the church but almost absorbed it, neoorthodoxy came later and in less radical form than in Europe. In 1936, Reinhold Niebuhr, a son of the social gospel, wrote of the need for " a more radical political orientation and more conservative religious convictions." His Gifford Lectures of 1939, *The Nature and Destiny of Man,* quickly became a landmark of American theology. Despite Niebuhr's stinging polemics against liberal theology, he has always maintained much of the liberal spirit, e.g., in his concern for social problems and his lack of interest in any doctrine without experiential relevance.

Obviously the limits of neo-orthodoxy cannot be defined with precision. But any appraisal of contemporary theology must note the renewed interest in traditional doctrines once widely regarded as passé. Thus theology appeals often to Biblical revelation, to the transcendence of God, to the awareness of human sin, to justification by grace through faith, to Jesus Christ as the revelation and deed of God, to recognition of tragedy in history, to an eschatological hope. These discussions echo the themes of the Bible, of Augustine, of the Protestant Reformers.

But current theology likewise owes much to the "liberal" elements within neoorthodoxy. It looks to science rather than Scripture for the description of cosmic processes. It often takes Biblical doctrines (e.g., of the Fall of man and the resurrection of the body) "seriously but not literally," in Niebuhr's well-known phrase. It recognizes the relativism of all human thinking, including creeds and theologies. Especially in the U.S.A., it appeals not to the formal authority of the Bible but to a Biblical interpretation of experience.

By the present time the usefulness of the term "neoorthodoxy" has ended, except as a description of history of the recent past. The new debates center on a different set of issues. Thus Paul Tillich, once widely regarded as neoorthodox, has built a theological system attacked more often from the right than from the left. Rudolf Bultmann combines orthodox elements with a radically modern existentialism. To classify Dietrich Bonhoeffer as "liberal" or "neoorthodox" would be completely futile. The liberal elements in Reinhold Niebuhr and H. Richard Niebuhr are more evident than in past years. And Karl Barth, the most forceful voice of neoorthodoxy, has turned from his stress on the gulf between God and man to an unprecedented emphasis on the identity of God and man in Christ (cf. *The Humanity of God*).

Yet neoorthodoxy, if past, has changed the climate of the present. It has educated the present generation of theologians, in Asia and Africa as truly as in Europe and America. Discussions in the World Council of Churches and the increasing Protestant–Roman Catholic dialogues show its influence. Future generations will have to decide whether it has marked a basic reversal of liberal theology or a redirection within the ongoing liberal movement. — *Roger L. Shinn*

NETHERLANDS In the Netherlands there are the following types of schools: (1) primary schools (6–12 years), offering a nondifferentiated basic teaching; (2) secondary (high) schools (12–18 years), offering education oriented to the practical fields (e.g., commerce, domestic economy, technology, agriculture) or to the university (lyceum, atheneum, gymnasium); (3) universities, of which 4 are state-operated (Leiden, Groningen, Utrecht, Amsterdam) and 2 are confessional (a Free Reformed university at Amsterdam and a Roman Catholic university at Nijmegen), along with specialized high schools and seminaries. Both state and confessional schools are completely underwritten financially by the Government, but the state schools are governed by state authorities. The confessional schools are free to develop their own curricula and to appoint their own staffs. The proportions of the schools according to type in the primary group are as follows: state, 27.2 percent; Protestant, 26.8 percent; Roman Catholic, 44.2 percent. Of the secondary (high) schools, 42.5 percent are state schools; 22.1 percent Protestant; 35.3 percent Roman Catholic.

In the state schools there is no obligatory religious instruction. The churches have the opportunity to offer one hour a week of such instruction. About 70 percent of the children who leave the state schools have had 1 or 2 years of religious instruction. Since the Roman Catholic and Free Reformed Churches are not interested in this privilege, it is mostly Dutch Reformed Church children who receive the instruction. There is no form of worship in the state schools.

In the confessional schools 2 hours are usually devoted to religious instruction each week in the primary schools, 1 hour a week in the secondary (high) schools. Daily worship takes place. Primary religious instruction is Biblical. In the secondary (high) schools the 1st and 2nd forms have Bible; in the other forms, church history, world religions, and ethical and moral problems.

All Protestant churches have preconfirmation instruction in the catechism, and a great deal of emphasis is placed on this. Catechesis takes place 1 hour a week from October to Easter. Young people are confirmed at the age of 18 or older. Since confirmation involves personal decision, the percentage of young members is not high.

The Sunday schools are open to children from ages 5 through 12, after which they attend the youth church. Sunday school work in the Netherlands has been deeply influenced by the Westhill Training College, Selly Oak, Birmingham, England.

Since life in families in the Netherlands is more solidly established than in many Western countries, a religious education in the home is of great importance. It is a tradition in most Protestant homes to read the Bible with children daily. Many well-illustrated children's Bibles have been made available.

Laymen teach in the Sunday schools. In primary schools the regular teachers teach religion; in the secondary and high schools, clergymen and theologically trained laymen. Teachers are trained in training colleges, both state and confessional training colleges offering religious education. Clergymen receive theological education in the universities or, in the case of the Free Reformed Church, in theological seminaries.

Several problems exist in Dutch religious education: (1) the relation between school religious instruction and church catechesis; (2) the relation between state schools and confessional schools, the Dutch Reformed Church favoring the former, the Free Reformed Church the latter; (3) the coordination among school religious instruction, Sunday school, and catechesis, some pupils receiving a great deal, others receiving too little, religious instruction. — *O. V. Henkel*

NEW ZEALAND New Zealand is one of the most British of all the member countries of the British Commonwealth.

Almost all the European population are of British origin. All the major churches began as offshoots of British churches and since independence have retained close association with their parent denominations.

Sunday schools followed colonization in the 1st half of the 19th century. They were of the British pattern. Children of confirmed members and adherents and other children of the neighborhood were gathered weekly for formal Biblical instruction. A minority (estimated at 25 percent) attended the service of worship and a larger number, still a minority, went on to be confirmed.

In the 1st decade of the 20th century denominational youth movements were established, catering to young people from the beginning of their teen years. This Bible Class Movement sponsored Sunday Bible study groups, camping, leadership training, and social and recreational activities. The BC Movement is largely self-governing and until comparatively recently was single sexed. Each denomination has a Young Men's and Young Women's BC Union, with national and district councils and officers. Cooperation between the denominations has been encouraged by the BC Movement. National ecumenical youth conferences arranged by the Youth Committee of the National Council of Churches have been held in recent years.

The BC Movement helped to develop leadership for the New Zealand churches at a time when self-governing youth movements were rather novel. For clubwork or through-the-week activities, most of the churches have encouraged their congregations to work through Boy Scouts, Girl Guides, Boys Brigade, or Girls Life Brigade.

Y.M.C.A., Y.W.C.A., Student Christian Movement, and the Inter-Varsity Fellowship organizations have significant places in this country's Christian education activities.

All denominations have been evaluating their Christian education programs. Changing patterns are now emerging. There is a marked tendency for leaders to be guided more by the philosophy and programs of the North American churches than by those of the British.

The following principles are giving direction to these changes: (1) The realization that the church's teaching ministry belongs to the very nature and mission of the church. (2) The need for the coordination of all Christian education activities. The Sunday school as a separatist organization is disappearing. (3) The worshiping congregation as the focal point of the church's program and the desire to make the worship service more of a family activity. (4) The provision of a planned program of education for all ages.

Lesson materials for most denominations are produced in cooperation with Australia and sometimes interdenominationally. The Australia and New Zealand Joint Board of Graded Lessons, a partnership of Presbyterian, Methodist, and Congregational churches of the 2 nations, produces group-graded curriculum.

These changes are reflected at the national level by the replacement of Youth Departments with Departments of Christian Education.

The Roman Catholic Church (3d in size after Anglican and Presbyterian) has a complete system of schools. Some other denominations have a few public schools, but the great majority of children are educated in the state schools, which are "free, compulsory, and secular." Nondenominational religious instruction is given by voluntary teachers in these state schools on a basis of released time. The instruction is based on an agreed syllabus with a complete range of lesson materials.

Universities are state supported and have very meager provision for Biblical or theological studies. Denominations provide their own institutions for training ministers.

— *Wilfred F. Ford*

NORWAY The population of Norway in 1961 was 3,596,211, of which 4 percent do not belong to the Episcopal Lutheran Church of Norway. Of these 123,314, a total of 22,035 have stated that they do not belong to any religious community. Next to the state church, the largest religious communities are The Methodist Church with 11,570 members; the Baptists with 8,964; the Episcopal Lutheran Free Church with 17,319; the Missionary Association with 3,138; and Pentecostal congregations with 30,036. In other words, about 96 percent of the population of Norway are nominally members of the state church and according to the Constitution are obliged to bring up their children according to the Episcopal Lutheran doctrine. All these children are taught (by law) in the public primary school (7 to 14 years — soon gradually to be increased to 15 years); children whose parents belong to other religious communities are given similar teaching in Christianity within their own congregations.

In 1739 an enactment required that all children over 7 should be taught the Christian religion. Various subsequent enactments eventuated in the Act of 1959 for all schools. The pattern in the successive acts shows a declining graphic curve, religious instruction gradually being reduced over the past century to a minimum amount of time in relation to other old or new subjects in the curriculum. Article 1 of the Act of 1959 states: " The school shall work together with the home in order to make the children good citizens. It shall give the pupils instruction in Christian and moral ethics."

Most primary schools now have a minimum of 2 periods of religious knowledge a week; the secondary schools (realgymnasiums and gymnasiums) 1 period a week. Religious knowledge is an examination subject in both primary and secondary schools.

In addition to the school classes considerable voluntary work is done among children and youth. Sunday school work has existed in Norway since 1844. Even before that there were children's meetings held by Hans Nielsen Hauge's followers and others. Today there are 4,341 Sunday schools with 259,670 children and 9,390 teachers. More than 57 percent of the teachers are men. About half the children of Norway attend Sunday school, though in some sections of the country the percentage attending is as high as 90 percent (elsewhere, only about 25 percent).

The total Christian education picture includes thousands of Norwegian homes where family prayers are still the practice. There are many Christian school clubs. In addition, there are more than 30 Christian youth schools, which gather thousands of young people between the ages of 16 and 17 annually. There are 2 Christian schools of agriculture, 1 Christian school of horticulture, 4 Bible schools. — *Sverre Seim*

NURSERY DEPARTMENT The nursery department of the church school covers more than the Sunday class for 3-year-olds. It operates also in church offices when parents come to confer with ministers, directors, and teachers; it operates in homes and hospitals when church workers go out to visit parents and children. Church nursery work goes on late at night around discussion tables as parents and teachers compare observations and insights, as they study the needs and abilities of the ever-changing, growing child and possible ways to stimulate and guide his Christian growth.

The whole church fellowship participates in the work of the nursery department as it invites, accepts, understands, and helps parents of young children. The birth of a child, especially the 1st child, almost inevitably bestirs parents to examine and develop their religious life. Feelings of guilt and inadequacy must be faced, and human frailties strengthened with divine love. The parents recognize as never before the need to deepen or begin their own relationship with God if they are to introduce their child to him and endure the new dimensions of joy and sorrow that come with this new, close human relationship. In recent years churches have been challenged to provide a more meaningful and comprehensive nursery program than one consisting merely of a dusty string of paper cradles with names written on them or a baby-sitting service during the church hour.

Weekday church nurseries with closely coordinated parent programs contribute most adequately to the Christian development of both children and parents. However, the Sunday morning program backed by parent meetings, teacher-parent conferences, and active, interested home visitors can provide a framework in which the redemptive work of the church can operate.

However earnest may be the dedication to the Christian enterprise, a good degree of emotional maturity must have been achieved before a person takes up church nursery work. The ability to overlook some annoyances (in parents as well as in children), the grace to forgive, the willingness to work at the task of loving those for whom love does not come readily, are prime requisites for the nursery worker of whatever age or sex. People whose own emotional needs are satisfied by family and friends are able to relate to nursery children and parents in a wholesome way and to offer them the growth-producing love which, through the working of the Holy Spirit, becomes redemptive.

Experiences of being loved, accepted, forgiven, understood, trusted, respected, wanted, and needed by other human beings are now being counted as valuable religious experiences for young children. Nursery teachers plan for such experiences. Together with many spontaneous, worshipful moments, occasional participation in formal worship (as in a family church service), and some exposure to the terms and language of Christianity, this is the nursery curriculum.

At the age of 3, verbal communication may not get through to the child. Belonging to a group that meets for only 1 hour a week may not develop as many close, warm relationships with other members of the Christian fellowship as are formed in a 5-day, all-morning church nursery, but any young child who comes to church regularly with his parents learns something about the Christian religion. "Bible," "God," and "Jesus" become at least familiar words to him. In the course of the church year he has a firsthand experience of the festivals of Easter and Christmas, worship, prayer, and praise. His concepts may be vague and undeveloped, but the experiences now will aid later development and clarification.

In crowded churches, however, in churches where the nature and needs of the young child are not fully understood, or where ceremonies and rituals are empty of feeling, these early learning experiences can be negative ones, and can delay rather than encourage the young child's Christian growth. After a year a child might know the church as a place of confusion. Fears could develop and misinterpretations arise. But in congregations where a warm feeling of fellowship prevails, where worship and prayer are entered into in spirit and in truth, where the Bible is read reverently and meaningfully, where the name of Jesus is voiced by people who know of whom they speak — in a word, when the child is surrounded by the reality of the Christian fellowship, his first experience of the church can be a valuable part of his total Christian education.

Person-to-person relationships, however, are the biggest factor in aiding Christian growth in the nursery years. As the child relates to teachers and friends in the fellowship, as they and he respond to each other in love and forgiveness, as he feels the never-failing love of his parents (themselves nourished by the church in order to be able to give such love), attitudes of trust and security develop that lead to an unshakable faith in God.

In churches where Christian education is planned in a framework of total development — physical, emotional, social, and mental — places are prepared for the children on Sunday and care is taken to maintain standards in the nursery programs. Two-, 3-, and sometimes 4-year-old children (4's are usually included in kindergarten programs) meet in clean, spacious rooms in groups of not more than 15 children with not less than 2 teachers for each group. Play equipment suitable for the age (such as big blocks and trucks that exercise and develop large muscles), dolls and housekeeping equipment for dramatic play, puzzles, books, and pictures, musical instruments, manipulative material (such as dough or clay), and paints that can be applied with full arm movements to large sheets of paper today take the place of the few small crayons and outline pictures that used to cramp the development and try the emotions of both teachers and children. Educational experiences as outlined above take place in normal play situations under the guidance of the teachers.

Older nursery children, after they have become accustomed to the environment, their companions, and the teachers, sometimes come together in small groups for stories, songs, prayers, and brief worship experiences. Sometimes they share toys and begin to be aware of each other's needs and desires.

Toddlers, who have not yet grown out of the long and highly dependent period that develops sensitive human qualities as distinguished from animalistic behavior, must have their needs and wants supplied readily and cheerfully. Warm, outgoing mother-figures ready at hand in every situation that may seem threatening to the children help them face life with the characteristic Christian qualities of courage and trust rather than fear and belligerence.

Infants need expert individual care, a separate room, and utmost cleanliness. Some churches, unable to maintain standards for infant care in the church, send nursery-roll workers and nursery volunteers to the homes of parents who cannot afford sitters during the church hour. Young parents sometimes cooperate in offering sitting services to one another.

Parent programs grow naturally out of needs that become known as teachers relate to children and parents. New parents can be helped to see that children grow and learn gradually and at different rates of speed. Study programs, lectures, films, discussions, and individual conferences with teachers, directors, and ministers are programmed throughout the year.

Nursery-roll visits are begun within a few months after the child is born. Some churches send welcome letters directly to the hospital with an invitation to confer with the pastor or a deacon about the meaning of baptism. Periodic meetings of parents of babies help them see their children as part of the church fellowship even in infancy and to understand their role as Christian parents. — *Florence Schulz*

NURSERY SCHOOL Increasing numbers of churches in the U.S.A. have a weekday nursery school meeting in one or more of the preschool rooms of the church. In some cases these nursery schools are sponsored by the church and are the responsibility of the board of Christian education or a similar committee. In other cases, the church provides no oversight for the nursery school. The school may be a commercial one — that is, it is a business that provides an income for the owners (most likely the teachers), who rent space from the church. Or the school may be one that serves the community. The children will come from families of different religious backgrounds. The church provides the space for the school rent free or at cost as a service to the community.

Churches that sponsor a weekday nursery school as an aspect of the total Christian education enterprise often carry on an adult program for the parents of the nursery school children and frequent activities for all the families together. Thus the whole family has important experiences in the life and fellowship of the church.

It has often been asserted that the home is the primary religious institution. It is in his home that a child learns to love, trust, accept, and forgive. These verbs partly describe the nature of the relationship between persons that we call Christian. A child grows into Christian adulthood through living with persons who love one another (even when the other is unlovable), who trust and accept one another (just as the other is — small, awkward, slow, boisterous, whatever), who forgive and seek forgiveness. Of course, in many homes children do not have these experiences, and in no home, even the best on earth, does a child experience complete love, acceptance, and forgiveness, for parents are finite and imperfect. Because this is true, one goal for the nursery school–family program is to provide parents opportunities to learn about themselves, their children, and the Christian faith.

This learning can take place in a variety of ways: through conferences between the nursery school teacher and the parents, through visitation and observation of the nursery school by the parents, through parents study groups. These latter groups might be 2 six weeks' courses held during the school term or a regular monthly session on whatever topic seems needful at the time.

As parents come to see and know themselves, to understand their children, and to experience some trust and acceptance in relation to the other parents, they do, in fact, become "new" persons. The climate of their homes changes, and their children are increasingly able to love, give, and trust. That the educational mission of the church must be designed to include the teaching of adults, specifically parents — if the Christian faith is to mean anything to children — is the conviction that underlies this kind of nursery school program.

Churches operating weekday nursery schools must inform themselves concerning the standards and regulations for nursery schools established by the state in which they are located. In many states the schools must qualify for a license in order to operate.

Although standards vary in detail, specifications such as these usually prevail:

Location: The 1st floor of a building is preferred for the nursery school. Basements and 2d floors are often permitted if other standards of adequate heat, light, cleanliness, floor coverings, and fire exits prevail. In some places fire doors and sprinkler systems must be installed throughout the building that is used to house a nursery school.

Space; toilet facilities: Specifications often require 50 square feet of indoor play space, 75 to 100 square feet of outdoor play space, per child. There should be 1 washbowl and 1 toilet, preferably child-sized, for every 8 to 10 children, as well as adequate facilities for the teachers. These facilities should be convenient to both indoor and outdoor play space.

Equipment: Equipment must provide for small-muscle and large-muscle activity, for individual and group play. A climbing gym, wheel toys, tree house or playhouse, and a sandbox are usual outdoor equipment. Blocks, cars, trains, dolls, buggies, puzzles, a rocking boat, and a movable gym are good indoor equipment.

Program: The program includes free play indoors and outdoors, a light snack, and a rest period. The child chooses to do whatever appeals to him. Activity centers set up in the nursery school rooms provide for block play, housekeeping and doll play, "creative" art activities, music, looking at books, working puzzles.

Hours of school: Nursery schools usually run 2½ hours, most often in the mornings. Some churches have 1 group of children 5 days a week. Others have 2 different groups, 1 coming 3 days, the other 2 days per week. In these programs, consecutive days have been found to be better than alternating days.

Health regulations: States usually require that provisions be made for isolation of a child who is sick, for health inspection of each child upon arrival at school, for physician's approval for readmission to school after several days' illness.

Staff qualifications: At least the head teacher of the school should be a fully qualified teacher. Assisting teachers can be mothers working on a cooperative basis, apprentice teachers from a nearby college fulfilling student teaching requirements, or sensitive, dedicated, skilled women from the congregation itself. The ratio of teachers to children is 1 teacher to every 8 children; never should there be fewer than 2 teachers for any group.

Churches finance nursery school programs in various ways. The church budget for maintenance of the building — heat, light, janitor service, repairs — often includes the space used by the nursery school so that the nursery school budget does not have to designate funds for maintenance. The other major costs of operating a school are for repair and replacement of equipment, supplies, and teachers' salaries. Tuitions pay part of these costs but usually only a part. The deficit can be made up by monies raised by events sponsored by the board of Christian education or by the nursery school committee. Many churches write the amount of the deficit into the year's budget for Christian education.

In states such as Pennsylvania in which the public school system does not include kindergarten children many churches have weekday schools for 5-year-olds. The standards regarding location of the school, space, equipment, health and safety regulations, and staff qualifications are similar to the standards for nursery schools. A kindergarten program, however, is considerably different from a nursery school program. — *Phoebe Anderson*

NURTURE Nurture means providing the conditions and resources that facilitate and promote the growth of any creature endowed with the capacity and tendency to grow. As a verb, the word denotes the process of nurturing a growing creature; as a noun, it means the provisions for nurturing. Growth may take place under unfavorable conditions and with inadequate resources, in which case the outcomes would be a poor or inadequate fulfillment of the growth potential of the individual. The more adequate the nurture, the more fully and wholesomely the available capacities or potentialities are enabled to mature.

The term " nurture " applied to the religious life usually implies a theological interpretation of human nature. This carries us immediately into prevalent and persistent doctrinal controversies as well as conflicts between scientific and theological views of human nature and personality formation. Is the capacity for religious growth inherent in original human nature? Is human nature favorably disposed toward religious growth or is it antagonistic? Is religious nurture a human process like any teaching, or is God involved in a peculiar sense? How are nurture and conversion related? There are 3 principal viewpoints from which such questions are answered.

The orthodox point of view is that of a corrupted human nature which must be miraculously regenerated before nurture can begin. The neo-orthodox point of view, though somewhat softened, is in substantial agreement. Even if the Garden of Eden story is interpreted symbolically as a description of the " fall " of each individual, the implications for nurture are the same. Nurture begins only after " fallen " human nature has been miraculously reconditioned for it. The Biblical background of this doctrine is Pauline, and it has been the prevalent doctrine throughout Christendom.

At the opposite extreme is the humanistic doctrine that human nature, fresh from the hand of the Creator, is good. The child is naturally religious. Nurture begins at birth and, if adequate, can prevent the development of evil tendencies and sinful behavior.

The 3d viewpoint may be called the "Christian nurture" concept. Its practical implications were 1st worked out by Horace Bushnell. His thesis was that "the child is to grow up a Christian, and never know himself as otherwise," if those responsible for his nurture, chiefly his parents, fulfill their nurturing function.

The scientific view of human nature and personality formation is reticent about moral values and such terms as "sin" and "virtue." Nor is original nature regarded as a *tabula rasa* upon which environment and experience may inscribe at will. Rather, the infant is possessed of many "drives" or impulses that are varied and inconsistent, some being egocentric, or autonomous, and some social, or "homonomous." They have both demonic and angelic potentialities if viewed theologically. Personality is a product of the interaction of the organism with its environment, and this interaction is determined both by the relative strength of the respective drives and by what the environment (or nurture) offers in the way of rewards and punishments. The trend is toward regarding the personality or character outcomes as more a product of the environing culture than of the individual biological heritage. Science sees both our original human ancestors and each newborn child, not as virtuous creatures who will "fall" into sin, but as amoral creatures who will rise into moral

character by making forced choices among values.

Although theology regards evil as transmitted biologically from generation to generation, having its residence wholly in the individual, science regards such phenomena as largely embodied in the culture and social institutions and as transmitted to the individual as a part of his cultural heritage along with the good. Theology assumes that moral gains are made only by converting individuals and that therefore they cannot be transmitted to the next generation. Science asserts that cultural changes can be embodied in the cultural heritage and so passed on to succeeding generations. Science grants that the individual may acquire a "second nature" which is evil, or at least antisocial, but its source is in his cultural heritage.

The practical or functional implications of the Christian nurture view and the scientific view are identical. Character or personality is a product of nurture. It properly begins when life begins and should be carried on continuously throughout life. Its operation is most momentous in the earliest years. Consequently, the primary responsibility rests upon the home and family. At best, the church and the school are supplementary to the family, and a major task of the church is to help the family do its primary job of personality production well.

In this view it is the function of Christian nurture not to prepare the individual for a radical conversion but to prevent its necessity. This does not mean that the religious life is one continuous inclined plane upward. No kind of learning or growth is exactly that. Even physical growth has its fast and slow stages. Plateaus of learning are normal. So in the spiritual life there are times of great refreshment and achievement and times of dryness. " Conversion " as a right-about-face with respect to God and the Christian life is in order only when nurture has failed. After it takes place and retrieves the misfortune, nurture still has the major job of conservation and continuous growth.

Among the periods or experiences of deepened religious life that nurture expects and fosters, it is normal that " the encounter " will stand out. This is a part of the achievement of individual self-realization and internalized authority which usually constitutes early adolescence. This is a vivid and firsthand encounter with God in which the individual supplants the faith of his fathers with a faith of his own. It might be called religious awakening or even rebirth or 2d birth, but if nurture has done its work, it will not be literally a conversion. It will be a forward step within the Christian life, not a step into the Christian life from outside. For this reason the pattern of radical adult conversion should not be imposed upon children and young people who are receiving proper Christian nurture. Gradual growth with high seasons of refreshment constitute the ideal nurture pattern of Luke 2:39-52. – *Harry C. Munro*

O

OBEDIENCE Obedience is the submission of one's will to that of another, be it that of a deity or another man or the combined will of a group or society laid down in rules or laws.

In the Judeo-Christian religion, obedience is considered the basic attitude of man toward God. In the Old Testament, God gave his law and he demands implicit obedience. Man's rebellion against God's will constitutes his "fall"; sin is disobedience. "To obey is better than sacrifice." (I Sam. 15:22.) This obedience was spelled out later in Judaism as strict observance of the 613 laws in the Torah and of the innumerable detailed injunctions that were constructed by the theologians as a fence around the law.

Jesus gave the law a spiritual interpretation (Matt. 5:17 ff.) but retained obedience to the will of God as man's purpose in life. "My food is to do the will of him who sent me" (John 4:34); "Not my will, but thine, be done" (Luke 22:42). The apostles saw in Jesus the example of complete obedience, even to the death on the cross (Phil. 2:8). The same obedience to the will of God and of Christ as Lord was expected of all Christians. Paul speaks of himself as the servant ("slave")

of Christ. Later this obedience was transferred to those who represented Christ and his church, the clergy, who in turn were bound by obedience to their superiors and ultimately to the pope. Complete surrender of one's own will to a religious superior was considered of such benefit that obedience, with poverty and chastity, became 1 of the 3 monastic vows. The Reformation freed men from the bondage of obedience to a hierarchy and put it on the Scriptural plane of obedience to God's Word and will. Faith itself is obedient acceptance of God's revelation in Christ (Emil Brunner's *Glaubensgehorsam*).

In Christian education, obedience has long played an important part, beginning with the obedience of children to their parents, as enjoined in the commandment "Honor your father and your mother" (Ex. 20:12). This obedience was absolute, and not dependent on the wisdom of the parents' commands, because the parents were regarded as God's representatives to the child (Eph. 6:1-2). This was extended also to "all those in authority," guardians, teachers, magistrates, etc. Schleiermacher stated: "For children there is no other ethic (*Sittlichkeit*) than obedience." In school strict obedience was the basis of discipline and was enforced with corporal and other punishments.

With the advent of modern education the emphasis shifted from obedience to self-development. The teacher is no longer the dictator, but the counselor and friend. The child, instead of being forced into submission, should be free to develop in his own way and at his own pace. In the family the old patriarchal system where the father's will was law was replaced by the democratic system of the family council in which the children, too, are given a voice and vote. However, it is clear that complete freedom of the individual in this world is not only impracticable but would lead to utter chaos. Society requires rules that man is expected to obey, voluntarily if he is mature, involuntarily if he is not. The child, at an age when he cannot yet understand the reason behind the rules, needs parental authority that insists on obedience. The transition from enforced to voluntary obedience is made mainly during the period of adolescence. The growing child, on the other hand, rebels against authority in his striving for independence and longs for an authority that will offer guidance and security. The wise educator will provide both: an increasing measure of freedom and responsibility and also authority that recommends rather than commands.

In religious education we must 1st undergird parental authority as the will and order of God. With growing understanding, the child's obedience should become a conscious submission to the will of God in all things, out of love and gratitude for his love to us. In case of a conflict between the laws of society and the will of God this may mean

that one must "obey God rather than men" (Acts 5:29) and bear the consequences. In complete surrender to God alone we attain to the "glorious liberty of the children of God" (Rom. 8:21).

— Erich T. Voehringer

OBJECTIVES A history of Christian education could probably be functionally organized around a search for and an examination of objectives down through church history from apostolic catechetical instruction, through Robert Raikes, Horace Bushnell, the rise of the religious education movement and culminating, perhaps, with 2 such militant books representing opposite viewpoints as Harrison S. Elliott's *Can Religious Education Be Christian?* (1940) and H. Shelton Smith's *Faith and Nurture* (1941), which rang the curtain down on an era.

However, an examination of some representative "main line" Protestant writing on Christian education since World War II such as *The Church and Christian Education* (Paul H. Vieth, ed., 1946), *Man's Need and God's Action* (Reuel L. Howe, 1953), *The Teaching Ministry of the Church* (James D. Smart, 1954), *The Dynamics of Christian Education* (Iris V. Cully, 1958), and *Church Education for Tomorrow* (Wesner Fallaw, 1960) reveals that neither in the tables of contents nor in the topical indexes does the word "objectives" appear. This may be because (1) it is a word tinged with secular overtones from another era, since these books reflect the new "ecumenical theology" resulting from the revival of Biblical and Reformation studies in America during and following World War II, or (2) it is associated more with the projection and development of curriculum and age-group studies. Yet, on closer scrutiny, these authors do use words such as "aims," "purpose," "goals," "program," "tasks," "assumptions," which are obviously related to the word "objectives," making it therefore seem to be a kind of "omnibus" word. It will also be further observed that no longer is there a clear dividing line between objectives for the church, the Christian life, Christian education, the church school or curriculum, since Christian education is variously defined but "as being fundamentally the Christian community sharing its life with its members, young and older — its traditions, its experiences, its hopes, its faith, its mission" (Paul H. Vieth, ed., *The Church and Christian Education*, p. 193).

Thus for current writers, Christian theology underlies in varying degrees all that the church is and does, and Christian education is one form of Christian communication; revelation and education are interrelated and inseparable. James D. Smart's phrase "the teaching ministry," Iris V. Cully's emphasis on kerygma-didache communication, Wesner Fallaw's watchword "church education," point to the inclusive understanding of the centrality of the preaching-teaching ministry of the church reflected in today's writing on objectives, by whatever name they are called. There are those who "would question the expression 'Christian *education*' [italics added] on the ground that it implies an assimilation of Christian nurture to general education." (See "Christian Education and the Seminary," by Norman Langford in *The Hartford Quarterly*, 1960, p. 29.)

Most current writers are at pains, then, to clarify what seems to be their chief quarrel with the recent past regarding objectives, namely: "The purposes of community education grow out of affirmations about man, democracy, and moral values. The purposes of Christian education grow out of affirmations about God made known through Christ in the Bible. The work of Christian nurture is to explain this good news of God's love in Christ in such a way that those who were born into the faith will know this in their own lives, and those who have responded in faith may understand. The purpose of Christian nurture is to help people through their growing relationship to God in Christ so to live that they may glorify him and effectively serve others, in the assurance that they partake of eternal life now and forever" (Iris V. Cully, *The Dynamics of Christian Education*, pp. 29 f.).

Randolph Crump Miller in *Education for Christian Living* sums it up: "Christian education involves a point of view, for it is a particular kind of education. It is not secular education with a halo, although the Christian can ignore secular insights only at his peril. Christian education is concerned with the relevance of revealed Christian truth. Theology, which is the 'truth about God in relation to man,' is the determining factor in the development of a philosophy of education, of techniques to be used, of goals to be attained, and of the nature of the learners to be taught" (p. 5).

Thus a theory of objectives or of arriving at objectives is a process within a specific context rather than a superimposing or integrating of aims and approaches from educational psychology, as was so apparent when the field of education within the church was developing and emerging. The attempt to close the wide gap of the past between education and Christian theology goes on at a great rate with the theory of and/or approach to objectives being continuously overhauled and subjected to the same criteria as that of the mission of the church with which it has become inseparable, if not identical. "The church has no choice in the matter; its commission is not to teach anything and everything that it may find interesting or valuable in human life, but specifically to teach the gospel. All Christian teaching must be measured by the standard: Is there to be heard in it the same message of God which is the center and heart of the Scriptures? On the other hand, everything that is said and done by the church in teaching must proceed from a sympathetic understanding of the particular situation and needs of those who are to be taught" (*Basic Principles — Christian Faith and Life Curriculum*, p. 9).

D. Campbell Wyckoff, in a more textbooklike approach in *The Task of Christian Education*, comments directly: "Any program should be founded upon inclusive and representative general objectives. But the general objectives of Christian education need translation into specific form in every situation" (p. 25). Then, "on the basis of its general objectives, the study of the nature and needs of the pupil, and the statement of carefully developed objectives of a specific character, the process of Christian education moves into another area, the area of planning for curriculum, content, and methods" (p. 31). In his later, more technical book, *The Gospel and Christian Education*, Wyckoff treats at length the development of

a theory of Christian education, including the arrival at objectives. (See Part II, Ch. 8, p. 113.)

Randolph Crump Miller, in his lengthy textbook, *Education for Christian Living*, probably deals more thoroughly with the subject of objectives, historically, theologically, and educationally, than any other author cited. (Smart, Iris Cully, and Fallaw have historical sketches but with more interest in interpretation than in detail of development.) Miller's first 3 chapters are basic reading for anyone involved in a study of objectives. Starting with a synagogue school in Nazareth, he brings us to the 20th century with comment on the persons and books that matter. At the other end of his book, he discusses fully the relationship of the local church and its board of Christian education to the use of objectives, including their relationship to the subject of evaluation.

In this article it has been pointed out that in mid-20th-century Christian education there is no longer a divorce between theology and education in the church, and that most objectives in use appear to have assumptions applicable to the mission of the local church, Christian education, and curriculum. This can also be clearly seen in the manuals that accompany Protestant curriculum.

In conclusion, 2 other representative sets of objectives are recommended for examination: those listed under the "Purpose of the Curriculum" in *Christian Faith and Life at a Glance*, a pamphlet for parents, teachers, and others, explaining the structure of the curriculum of The United Presbyterian Church in the U.S.A., and those included in the volumes of *The Seabury Series* of the Protestant Episcopal Church. These 2 bodies of study materials represent the most notable post World War II curriculum experiments in the integration of Protestant theology and educational psychology. — *Carol C. Rose*

OBJECT LESSONS Object lessons are a type of instruction in which objects such as pictures, charts, and maps are used to concretize ideas to be conveyed. It is a method of showing.

The use of object lessons is probably as old as the human race; in fact, primitive peoples may have been limited to this approach. As long as most people in any culture cannot read or write, the use of objects in teaching is the only major method available. This is particularly true in the area of religion, though object lessons are used in all major subjects to make presentation of subject matter more concrete.

Supporters of this method maintain that since a student proceeds from concrete to abstract, the recognition of this principle is essential for effective communication. It takes advantage of the fact that nature has endowed us with the ability to learn through seeing, touching, feeling. The Chinese proverb, "One picture is worth a thousand words" has become a popular motto in this emphasis.

Object lesson teaching is never used exclusively but serves to augment other methods. When a society becomes more complex and printed materials are readily available the use of object lessons may become "the lost dimension."

However, whenever educators forget the value of object teaching, men seem to arise to remind them of its value in effective instruction. Among the leaders of this emphasis was John Amos Comenius, the 17th-century bishop-educator. At a time when most of the church's teaching was a matter of "book learning," he advocated universal education. In order to facilitate this effort he stressed the principle, "Nature prepares matter before giving it a form. . . . Since the beginning of knowledge must be with the senses, the beginning of teaching should be made by dealing with actual things. The object must be capable of making an impression on the senses." The charts that Comenius used have been refined, but the principle he enunciated has stood the test of time in education. Through the discovery of projected visual aids this method has gained real impetus and complexity. The use of object lessons in teaching is sometimes referred to as the "natural method" of teaching, a phrase already employed by Comenius.

Jean Jacques Rousseau (1712–1778), author of *Émile*, advocated the "natural" approach in education, and maintained: "Never substitute the sign for the thing itself unless it is impossible to show the object, for the sign absorbs the attention of the child and causes him to forget the thing represented."

Johann Heinrich Pestalozzi (1746–1827) made the principle of intuition or sense impression (*Ansohauung*) fundamental for the whole process of education. Sense impression refers to the image formed, like a miniature painting, in one's consciousness. He maintained it to be the "only true foundation of human instruction, since it is the only true basis of human knowledge. All the rest results from this sense impression and the process of abstraction that is made through it."

Support for the use of object lessons is found in Scripture. The Old Testament is rich in the use of this method, e.g., the serpent or the tree or the flaming sword in the Garden of Eden, the Flood, the potter's flask in Jer., ch. 19, the brick in Ezek., ch. 4, the valley of dead bones. This is even truer of the New Testament. The star in the Nativity story, the devil's use of objects when tempting Christ in the wilderness, make these events more real than if they had been expressed in purely philosophic terms.

Jesus, however, excelled all others in making his teaching concrete. When he was confronted with a catch question, " Is it lawful to pay taxes to Caesar, or not? " he did not respond with a dogmatic principle but used an object lesson: " Show me a coin. Whose likeness and inscription has it? " To the Samaritan woman who came to draw water, he put the request, " Give me a drink." Using water as his object lesson, he gave a profound interpretation of " living water." Similarly, he used flowers, birds, fish, nets, bread, all of which were readily at hand, to share truths with those who were willing to listen. Children were possibly his " masterpiece " when it came to object lessons, for their qualities became symbolic as requirements for entrance into the Kingdom. His washing of the disciples' feet has remained ever since an object lesson in humility. While his cross is more than a symbol, it does concretize for his followers his suffering and death. He himself referred to it as a symbol when he bade his followers take up their cross and follow him.

In classic Christianity, object lessons have served the cause of Christ well. The danger is that they could so become the center of interest and devotion that the other need — that we are to worship God " in spirit and in truth " — might be overlooked. — *William D. Streng*

OBSERVER The observer is a member of the teaching team (of teacher and observer) in the classroom. His main responsibility lies in helping the class to understand what is happening in its group. He watches what is happening in the class: Who is talking? Who is silent? Why are they participating as they are? How does the class deal with this problem or that? How could the problem-solving process be improved? These are some of the questions that run through an alert observer's mind.

This means that he becomes involved in the discussion only for very specific reasons, as when the teacher and/or group request a report on the process of the group or when the observer feels that a comment from him would facilitate the group's work. Whenever asked, or impelled by his own insight, he should be free to make comments. The observer is definitely not intended to be a silent, mysterious adult who sits writing away on a clipboard while the class is in session. As the class members become more and more aware of the role that the observer holds in the teaching team, they will find many opportunities to use him as a resource to good class operation.

Usually the observer's report will include just a few words to help the class know where they are, what they have been doing, what they have accomplished so far, and where they may be going at the moment. The observer is to give his attention to how things are said and done in the group. This is termed group process.

Observer's (or process) reports can be used by the " teaching team " to serve many purposes. Among these are the following: (1) To isolate and reflect to the class the needs that seem to be important to the whole group. This would include what is happening to the group and to group members as they work together, the identification of common concerns, etc. (2) To locate problems (and identify their cause) that serve as obstacles to the progress of the group. A great deal of the growth of the " teaching team " comes from reviewing things that have happened in the class which seem to facilitate or to block the progress of the group or of individual class members. (3) From time to time it may also be important to identify events in the group that give clues to the difficulties which one or more members may have in saying what they think. (These may be family problems, school involvements, community relationships, etc.) Such observations may lead to helpful conferences outside class with particular members and/or a profitable discussion between the teacher and observer as to ways in which they can be more helpful to that particular member in future class sessions. (4) To chart the progress of the group as they grow together in religious concepts. It will also help the teaching team to keep track of the ways in which the group is growing closer together in their concern for one another.

There are several relationship areas that the observer should keep in mind and comment upon, either to the class as a whole or to the teacher: pupil to pupil, teacher to pupil, teacher to observer, and relationships to outside resources and resource persons. It is within these areas of class relationships that group process bears its fruit. Since the way in which we treat one another actually reflects our basic feelings toward one another as children of God, the answer to the question, Does this discussion have a religious meaning? is often found in group process. — *Donald E. Bodley*

ORTHODOX CHURCH The Orthodox Church is a majority faith in Russia, Greece, Bulgaria, Yugoslavia, Romania, and some of the Near Eastern countries. In Poland, Finland, Estonia, Latvia, Albania, Japan, there are large, old local Orthodox communities. In addition, several million Orthodox people are scattered in Western Europe, the U.S.A., Canada, South America, Australia, and the Far East. Their communities are administratively tied in with the different Orthodox jurisdictions stemming from their countries of origin and they use different languages for their liturgical services, but they are all part of the one Orthodox Catholic Apostolic Church, sometimes called Eastern Orthodox Church or Greek Orthodox Church.

The Christian education situation, under such a variety of conditions, can be briefly described in general terms only.

The teaching tradition of the Orthodox Church is rooted in the earliest age of Christianity, with no such break occurring in later centuries as that caused by the Reformation in the West. The instruction of catechumens was carried on during the 1st half of the Divine Liturgy. This part of the Communion service is still called the Liturgy of the Catechumens, finishing with a special prayer for them and the exclamation: "All that are learners go forth; ye learners go forth!" Uninterrupted tradition is very characteristic. New teaching methods must be organically bound with the fullness of church life, going back to the roots of the church's liturgical, spiritual, and doctrinal experience. This determines a certain conservatism in the Orthodox approach to religious education. New ideas, new interpretations, or new methods are almost instinctively checked against the wisdom and the inspiration of the great church teachers of the past.

For long centuries the manner of preservation of faith among the younger generation and the teaching techniques were affected by the position of the church under non-Christian rule or persecution: the Arabian conquest of the Near East, the Mongolian invasion of Russia, the conquest of Byzantium by the Turks, and in modern times the persecution of the church in Soviet Russia and its precarious existence in all the countries behind the Iron Curtain have laid their imprint on the teaching techniques of the church. Liturgical services of worship were often, and for long periods of time, the only vehicle for spiritual growth and for acquiring knowledge of the Bible, doctrine, and ethics. According to Orthodox tradition, the language of the services is always the spoken language of the people. The colorful Orthodox ritual introduced audio-visual and "learning by doing" methods of education centuries before the terms began to be used. The abundant use of Biblical material throughout the services made them true "schools of religion" in the life of the people.

Formal religious instruction given as part of the public school curriculum in Orthodox countries where there was no separation between church and state seems to have been far less fruitful. Home piety, the influence of monasteries, and liturgical services were the true educators of the Orthodox people in the Old World.

Today religious education in the Orthodox Church has been adjusting to a great variety of conditions.

In the U.S.S.R. all formal religious instruction for minors is forbidden. Church attendance is discouraged but remains theoretically free. The church uses the vehicle of sermons not only on Sunday morning but on all occasions: at christening, instruction of the parents in their duties, at marriages (on the Christian meaning of family life), at burials, memorials, and at all the numerous special services of the calendar. Pastoral visitations, as long as they are informal and officially unplanned, are permitted and are used to instruct the young. Individual spiritual guidance is given through the sacrament of confession. A strong sense of community ties, e.g., assistance to those in need of help, and a carefully camouflaged yet strong missionary spirit add much to the teaching function of the church. A tragic handicap is the total lack of religious literature, except for a very limited reprinting of the Bible. Religious education suffers from the almost complete isolation of the church from the rest of the world. There is little understanding or knowledge of the problems that stir the rest of the Christian world. Theological training of future priests is permitted and there are approximately 6 theological schools in the U.S.S.R.

In Europe and in the Near East

the period after the 2 world wars was one of Orthodox revival and of awakening interest of young people in their church. The Zoe Brotherhood in Greece, a teaching order, monastic in character, produced a network of schools and a vast amount of literature, and trained a great number of lay preachers. An Orthodox youth movement came to life in Syria and Lebanon. The Russian Student Christian Movement among the Russian *émigrés* in France, enriched by the elite of Russian *émigré* religious philosophers and theologians, became a veritable laboratory for Orthodox educational work among children and youth. Though necessarily small in numbers, this group influenced Orthodox religious educational work all over the world. The St. Sergius Institute, a graduate school of theology founded some 35 years ago in Paris, produced a number of eminent theologians and enlightened hierarchs. Syndesmos, a pan-Orthodox youth movement, maintains contact between the Orthodox youth movements of the various countries.

In the U.S.A. the Orthodox Church became established in hundreds of communities toward the end of the 19th and in the beginning of the 20th century. The 1st religious education effort was identified with language schools started in most parishes. The newly arrived immigrants felt that speaking Russian or Greek or Serbian was essential to the maintenance of faith and loyalty to the church. Generally speaking, the parish language schools were not a success and taught neither religion nor language. As the American-born generation of Orthodox grew into adulthood in the 1930's many of them became concerned about their own and their children's lack of religious instruction. A Sunday school movement was started, with instruction given in the English language. At first there were no textbooks, no trained teachers, no guidance of any kind. Gradually the dioceses of the various Orthodox jurisdictions began publishing sets of lessons of uneven quality and with much duplication of effort. Yet the enthusiastic cooperation of many hundreds of young Orthodox Sunday school teachers became a vital power in the life of the church. No reliable statistics on the number of schools and pupils are available, but probably the total number of Orthodox Sunday schools approximates 700 to 800, varying from small groups meeting in church basements to large schools with enrollments of over 500 occupying well-equipped, modern school buildings. A few parochial elementary schools are maintained by the Greek Archdiocese. A Russian church-sponsored private school for grades 8 to 12 exists in New York. Teacher training courses, conferences, and summer schools have been organized in most dioceses, sometimes as a pan-Orthodox project. The most ambitious one is the Eastern Orthodox Catechetical Conference held at Michigan State University, East Lansing, every summer, with an attendance exceeding 200.

In 1956 an Orthodox Christian Education Commission was founded to promote study and research and to coordinate the work of the 9 participating jurisdictions. The work is carried on under the guidance of Orthodox theologians, and its challenging approach to the task of religious education has attracted a number of college-educated young Orthodox. A new and deeper understanding of the specifically Orthodox character of religious education is promoted by the Commission, namely, an emphasis on the fullest participation by the child in the liturgical life of the church, even before there can be any explanation of its meaning. There is also an emphasis on the meaning of doctrine at every age level.

Theological education of future priests is carried on in a number of seminaries founded by the national Orthodox jurisdictions. St. Vladimir's in New York is the only graduate school of theology where all studies are carried on in English with students of various jurisdictions attending. — *Sophie Kolumzin*

P

PAGEANTRY A pageant is a show with a purpose. The purpose may be a beautiful display or a rendition of history. Whatever its subject matter — historical, religious, civic, or social — its form is achieved through a theme that binds together the episodes used. The design of the pageant and its cohesion are secured by prologues, allegorical figures, choruses that bridge the episodes and hold the theme of the pageant before the audience. It is usually on a large scale, using mass effects. Its acting, therefore, cannot be characterized by detailed character analysis. It seeks to impress by large effects through music, movement, and color.

Wycliffe mentions pageants in England in 1380. The medieval world called its mystery cycles pageants, and the wagons on which the series of plays were presented were known as "pageant wagons," fitted out at a place designated as the "pageant green."

The church has used the form to celebrate Christmas, Easter, Corpus Christi, and other feast days. Because detailed dramatic values did not need to be perfected, the pageants became a rather easy and often slipshod method of presenting Christian history or of celebrating major events in the Christian year.

The revival of the medieval pageant in contemporary England and the use of pageant techniques to celebrate historic events has brought the form into good repute. Louis N. Perkin's *Sherborne Pageant* and Percy MacKaye's triumphant success with the Augustus Saint-Gaudens pageant at Cornish, N.H., *Caliban* for the Shakespeare Tercentenary, and the *St. Louis Masque* marked the beginning of a revival that has produced some distinguished work. George Pierce Baker's *The Pilgrim Spirit* given at Plymouth, Mass., and the *Lexington Pageant*, written by Sidney Howard, stimulated a revival of outdoor pageants in the middle Southern states also. *The Lost Colony*, written by Paul Green, given at Manteo, N.C., *The Common Glory*, produced annually in Williamsburg, Va., *Home in the West* at Boone, N.C., and *Wilderness Road* at Berea College, Ky., are outstanding examples of some of the pageants that have celebrated the pioneering aspects of American history.

The advent of the spectacular motion picture has threatened to make real-life pageants obsolete, but the cinema cannot be used for local history or for significant events in religious history that allow participation of the local producing group. The motion picture has produced some outstanding pageants of the early West and some biographical pageants such as *Monsieur Vivant* and *The Life of St. Francis.*

— *Harold Ehrensperger*

PAINTING Painting, when used in religious education, is not taught as a fine art, nor is its purpose to produce artists. It is a method of teaching, one of the more important creative activities through which some of the aims may be accomplished. Painting in the church school is not an independent and unrelated activity; it is an integral part of the curriculum.

Children in a lower grade, for example, may decide to make a mural for their room. They choose a story that has been a part of their class program. Each child paints his own interpretation of a part of the story, and when these are put together, they have their mural. A junior class may decide to make posters describing an excursion. Again, a junior high group may paint illustrations for their class books as a record of the year's work. In every case, painting is an integral part of the curriculum.

Children of the kindergarten and lower grades paint directly on large sheets of newsprint (or brown paper) with long brushes and poster paint. No pencils are used. The paper is often spread on a table or on the floor and the child dips his brush into the jar of color he wants, painting freely. He should be taught to wash the brush in a container of water before dipping into another color. Most children have already learned how to manage paints and brushes at day school. Some churches own regular kindergarten easels, and there is also a place to put their jars of paint. Little children, especially, need to wear smocks or aprons; sometimes they make their own from their fathers' old shirts. In these younger groups, painting is usually connected with stories and experiences of the class session. Finger painting is sometimes done in the nursery or kindergarten, but rarely in older groups.

In the upper grades, painting projects are more varied and reflect skills gained in day school. There may be class-book illustrations, painting "reels" for a "movie," posters, charts, settings for dioramas, murals, friezes, special designs — all related to the study theme and class program. Pupils may use transparent watercolors (semimoist) as well as poster (or tempera) paints. There are times when certain technical problems will need to be explained, but the good teacher remembers that painting in Christian education is not intended to exhibit a child's technical skill but is a means of self-expression and a way of showing his imaginativeness and initiative.

The special contribution of painting to the creative approach in teaching has long been recognized by progressive leaders in both religious and secular education. It calls for personal and creative interpretation. It is not only the means of recording fact but a way of showing how the pupil feels about it. This involves emotion, expressive of what is within. The individual's choice of color depends on which colors he enjoys. The use of warm or cool colors has both a psychological and a physiological effect. Strong reds and oranges and quiet blues and violets become emotional outlets as well as indications of an inner mood.

Through painting, the child expresses the mystical, the imaginative, and the idealistic — all vital in religious growth. It is needless to say that the teacher who recognizes these values and uses painting as a way of promoting them makes sure that a child's painting expresses his idea in his own original way, and that decisions as to color and arrangement are his — not the teacher's.

The good teacher does not have children " copy "; neither does she " touch up " a child's painting. To do either would defeat her purpose. Many untrained teachers have no interest in teaching creatively because they do not know how and because they do not want to bother with the needed paraphernalia.

For many years, however, in both general and religious education, painting has been included as a teaching method. There has been an increasing emphasis on the expressive approach and, in this, painting has had an important place. For some years religious education summer conferences, laboratory schools, and training institutes have featured creative activities in their program, including painting and its use in teaching. It is also significant that the newer curriculum materials of the various denominations suggest painting projects along with other activities.

— *Elizabeth Miller Lobingier*

PANEL The panel is an educational technique designed to give from 3 to 6 persons with special knowledge of a particular area and demonstrated ability to speak well an opportunity to present to an audience in an orderly fashion their views on an assigned topic.

The members of the panel sit at a table in full view of the audience and carry on an informal, orderly discussion among themselves under the direction of a moderator on a specific topic.

The panel is one of many specialized techniques that, under certain conditions, can be effectively used in Christian education. Like any other educational procedure, the productiveness of the panel as a technique for the transmission of ideas is closely related to the diagnostic skill of those responsible for the planning of the educational venture.

The panel is selected as an appropriate technique by a program-planning group or person when the educational design indicates a need for a technique to accomplish a task such as the following: to inform a group of a particular project or plan where accurate and diverse evidence or testimony is desirable. For example, a congregation is considering expanding church facilities or building a new structure. Should it be expanded on the present site or moved to the edge of town? There are advantages and limitations to both locations that should be explained to the congregation by persons who have studied the problem carefully. A panel for this project might be composed of an architect, the minister, the chairman of the planning committee, the finance chairman, a city traffic officer or student of traffic problems, and the Sunday church school superintendent. These persons, after having carefully studied all sides of the problem, would sit before the members of the congregation and discuss among themselves its various facets. The panel members do not make prepared speeches to the audience. (This is done when a symposium is selected as the educational technique.) Neither do they debate the problem. This, again, would be another technique. Each clearly and succinctly presents his point of view as accurately as possible, and the members then discuss each point informally among themselves under the direction of the moderator, who refrains from participating in the discussion itself.

The above illustrates one of the many ways in which the panel can be productive. It can serve to treat a subject by including the following phases either individually or in combination: identifying and explaining the problems involved; exposing the advantages and disadvantages of a specific course of action; promoting understanding of the possible solutions; transmitting information regarding an issue; creating congregational interest; making use of a range of informed opinion.

While bound by certain rules of effective operation, a panel discussion is an informal procedure. The panel members do not discuss the issues at stake directly with the congregation, which forms the audience, but the congregation listens to their discussion. If questions and discussion with the congregation are desired, this occurs after the panel members complete their discussion. The moderator secures questions and statements from the audience and directs them to those panel members he thinks best equipped to answer. It is desirable that the panel members and the audience work through the moderator, if a discussion period follows the panel, in order to help assure a more orderly and productive meeting. The total time of the meeting should not exceed 2 hours.

Among the limitations of the panel are the following factors: panel members may not have enough time to present their full views adequately; panel members are sometimes poorly selected, which often results in a series of speeches and defensive arguments being given rather than in an informal discussion; the moderator sometimes is unable to keep panel members on the subject, and he also may neglect to make a complete and accurate summary; the meeting is restricted to a relatively short educational experience. — *Paul E. Bergevin*

PARENTS CLASS Parents classes are organized study groups within the church for adults with children. Although there have been adult classes for many years in Protestant churches, the parents class per se is of recent origin.

There are 2 basic approaches to parents classes. The 1st is that fathers and mothers study data on the emotional, physical, and religious development of their children and the environmental stimuli, particularly the home, which influence the growth and maturing of their offspring. The primary purpose of such study is that parents may understand children and cooperate as effectively as possible in their education. Parents are in such classes primarily because they are parents and the parental role is stressed. This is the approach used by the Character Research Project and some parish churches.

The 2d approach is based on the presupposition that parents are primarily persons who function in parental roles. Therefore it is necessary for them, first of all, to face the religious issues in their own lives. It is then, and only then, that they will be able to understand

Christianity, and with such insights they will be persons conscious of a new faith-grace relationship. Thus they will be more proficient Christians and more effective parents. This particular theory is based on the fact that all people, regardless of age, face the same basic religious issues and have the same fundamental religious problems manifested in various ways at different age levels. It is highly important that parents understand that many of the problems they face are the same ones faced by their children, although the manifestations of them may be radically different. Children and parents are essentially the same in their human condition; the gospel speaks to them and demands a response regardless of age. This is the approach used in *The Seabury Series* of the Protestant Episcopal Church.

The place of the teacher is different in the 2 approaches. In the 1st, the teacher is an expert who transmits information. In the 2d, the teacher or leader is one who guides a group of parents into an exploration of religious issues, how these manifest themselves at various age levels, and how the gospel speaks to the person in such a situation. Such classes usually are under the direction of a committee of parents. What is happening in the development of parents as Christians and their response to God, their families, and their fellows are as important as the factual data they may be receiving about children. The 1st approach by necessity has parents organized according to the age levels of children. The 2d approach does not necessarily use this grouping.

The development of parents classes has had several results: (1) Usually when these are combined with family worship, such a service tends to become *the* service in the average parish. (2) Parents will respond in the degree of the demand made upon them to cooperate in the religious nurture of their children. Left on their own, they show little overt interest. When the demand comes to participate, they respond in surprisingly large numbers. (3) Attendance of children in the church school is usually in direct ratio to attendance of parents in classes. If children are in church school, parents are not necessarily present, and the child's attendance is often influenced by the Sunday activities of parents. However, when parents are in worship and classes, invariably their children tend to be also. (4) The relationship of the home and church is on an entirely different basis. The parent sees correctly his important role in the Christian nurture of the child. In addition, the parent experiences in a new way the corporateness of the church as encompassing persons of all ages, and is able to see the family as a new means for the operation of God's grace. — *Charles E. Batten*

PARENT–TEACHER RELATIONS
Education carried on by the Christian church fosters growth of persons in the grace and knowledge of our Lord. This growth requires the ministrations of parents in the home and teachers in the church. Before formal education begins, throughout the years of schooling and thereafter, the influence of parents figures largely in what kind of person the child becomes. What he believes and what his characteristic behavior is derive mainly from interaction with his parents. Thus it may be said that his character depends no less on interpersonal relations experienced in childhood than phys-

ical structure depends on birth by human parents.

A valid theory of human development, however, takes into account the freedom of the individual to be selective in his responses to the human environment. By nature highly adaptive, a person is endowed with purposes of his own that preclude his being wholly subject to the influences of those associated with him in daily living. Plato and countless others have perceived that virtue is not guaranteed to sons of virtuous fathers, yet Roman, Hebrew, Christian, and modern secular educators in Western society agree on the importance of parental influence for giving direction to human growth. It is widely recognized that both character and learning – the 2 major concerns of all education – depend on a healthy relation of the child with parents or parent substitutes. Particularly the child psychologist, the schoolteacher, and lately the church teacher see direct connection between parental acceptance and affection for the child and his learning to relate to persons in a trusting and loving manner. The quality of the child's emotional life directly affects his spiritual development. If he is to love God whom no one sees, he must first love his fellows whom he does see. And before he can give them love, it is necessary that he shall receive love. In more instances than not, learning to love God depends on whether consistent and dependable human love is experienced in childhood; hence, the assertion that " parents are the first and foremost teachers of religion."

Like the teacher in public or private school, the church school teacher is familiar with the arguments in favor of establishing a work-

ing relationship with one or both parents of the child. Although much remains to be done in this area, 1 fruitful aspect calls for parent-teacher conferences about the child's particular needs and responses within the learning process. During the past generation united Protestantism, acting through established councils of churches, has emphasized anew the merits of forming parent and teacher partnerships in Christian nurture.

There is some misunderstanding as to what sort of partnership is desirable and how the parent and teacher alliance is to handle the Christian nurture of children. Because the values, faith, attitudes, and practices of parents put an indelible imprint on the growing person, there are those who advocate the church's giving major attention to educating young parents so that they, in turn, may enter more fully into a planned program of Christian nurture in the home and serve as senior partners in the teaching work of the parent-teacher combination. This viewpoint reverses the usual assumption that it is the business of the church school to carry the main responsibility for Christian nurture, aided by the family. Accordingly, in recent years, several denominations have held that the family should carry the main responsibility for Christian nurture, aided by the church. But Fairchild and Wynn's research leads them to observe that denominational curricula are not edited that way. However great Protestant concern is that parents shall be equipped to guide their children in Christian growth, a realistic view of church families permits no relaxing of the teaching of children in the church. As the parent and church teacher think together about their respective Christian education tasks, the former may be expected to see clearly the importance of the example he sets and the latter may gain a deepened conviction that his primary responsibility is that of teaching by precept. Yet each shares the function of the other. This basis of understanding fosters mutuality in parent-teacher relations.

Certain specific steps mark the cooperative work of parents and teachers. For instance, teachers' manuals recommend visits to pupils' homes. If educationally proficient, the teacher might better spend his time conferring with individual parents in the church school office, where, desirably, records of the pupil's progress are available. Granted that few churches are ready for this practice, it is a goal toward which to move as churches decide to become first-rate educational enterprises. While the 1st objective of the teacher is to gain a fuller understanding of the child, the 2d is to aid the parent in the measure that he or she proves willing to receive help in guiding his child's spiritual development. Obviously a teacher capable of guiding parent as well as child must be professionally competent, therefore serve as the senior partner in the instructional phase of the parent-teacher partnership. Presently, in the average church school, it is wiser to confine parent-teacher contacts to group meetings of less personal nature than individual guidance conferences connote.

Whether a church is staffed by professional or amateur teachers, more mothers than fathers are likely to be active in the parent-teacher partnership. Those who regret the absence of fathers can take comfort from a study made by the Committee on Human Development of the University of Chicago, entitled *The Psychology of Character Development*. The authors report that although the mothers they worked with were more involved than fathers in the tasks of character development, the fathers were likely to be cooperating in formulating and enforcing family policy. There are indirect means of enlisting fathers for sharing in Christian nurture, among them being family and teacher worship services in the church, parents classes, and family nights. Whatever the significance of these efforts, it seems fair to say that there has been a diminution of the notion that religion is a woman's affair. Perhaps increased democracy in the family and companionship of the marriage partners facilitates male participation in Christian nurture. One of the best ways to bring fathers into partnership with teachers is through the nursery school. Extension of the nursery-parent education idea to older pupils and their fathers and mothers offers a means of drawing parents and church teachers into a continuing cooperative venture.

In summary, it can be said that at the center of Protestant thinking about parent responsibility for Christian nurture is the belief that fathers and mothers have the greatest influence in the spiritual growth of their children. Whether they intend to or not, they are teaching some sort of faith. The daily influence of adult personality on the emerging personality of the young is of utmost concern to the church. Parents whose church establishes a working arrangement with them for the guidance of the young know that they are not alone in the nurture task but are linked with the larger family of God experienced in the life of the local church.

Two brief notes of caution should be sounded. Despite the numerical increase in adult education of all kinds in America, a minority of church-related parents wish to engage in formal or informal instruction offered for their improvement as fathers and mothers and for the purpose of causing them to be co-teachers with church school teachers. Even those leaders who have presided over successful parents classes testify that interest and participation are difficult to maintain. Resistance to reading matter designed for family life is demonstrated in Fairchild and Wynn's *Families in the Church*. Furthermore, it is the exceptional teacher — amateur or professional — who has the time, patience, and tact to confer regularly and helpfully with parents or whose approach overcomes the rivalry if not hostility which a parent and teacher more or less feel toward each other. Hence, it must be pointed out that however sound the principle of parent-teacher partnership is, something less than whole-hearted response attends any given program along this line. Yet it remains true that churches which provide a variety of approaches to family life education and succeed in uniting parents and teachers for guiding the individual child are likely to be the ones enjoying effective Christian nurture.

— *Wesner Fallaw*

PARISH LIFE CONFERENCE Christian education requires leaders who are trained in more than the knowledge of subject matter and the use of methods. The church's leaders and teachers, whether clergy or lay, periodically need to submit themselves to a retreat or other activity that is in the nature of a faith experience. The parish life conference has become a valuable and reliable means of providing such an experience. It is the purpose of the parish life conference, which 1st developed in the Protestant Episcopal Church, to communicate the faith in such way that the communication will use both the language of relationship and the language of words in accomplishing its end. It is an experience of the faith as well as a verbal encounter with the meaning of the faith.

The typical parish life conference takes place as 5 or 6 persons from each of 5 or 6 parishes, with a team of specially trained leaders, gather in a place apart for the evening meal on Friday and remain together until the midday meal on Sunday. Through participation in a variety of activities they become involved in discovering what their faith really is, in sharp contrast to an experience of defining the faith or hearing it defined.

The place of the leader is crucial to the effectiveness of the conference. His role calls for initiating, stimulating, and expediting the discussion. His purpose is to aid the members to discover for themselves, by the power of the Holy Spirit, a deeper understanding of the meaning and place of the church in their lives. He does not, therefore, supply answers, ask leading questions, or "fish" for his own answers. He allows the group to have its own definition of the purpose of the church and the needs of persons, for instance. But he will help them to test these understandings through real situations (their own within the conference or ones contrived). He serves the group in such a way as to guide and encourage them in their search, keeping their problems and needs rather than his own at the center of the discussion. He might help the members use such methods as: taking roles both of persons in deep need and of typical parishioners trying to minister to them; small-group Bible study on an existential level, in contrast to historical or theological levels; personal and corporate meditation. Integral to the life of the conference are corporate worship, the sacrament of Holy Communion, and the life of the members in dormitories, corridors, and dining room as well as the conference room.

As the conference proceeds, the leader relies almost entirely on reflective questions, holding the group to the problem at hand and, by reflecting what has been said, helping them to a deeper understanding. Members usually discover that they are often communicators of bad news, the very opposite of gospel. This painful discovery is possible because the conference employs the language of words and symbols. When they discover their predicament they cry out in their own way, " Who will deliver us from this body of death? " Whereupon the leaders do what they can to assist the group to recognize the power of the Holy Spirit amongst them in their predicament and to test it against the records of the Bible. Often there emerges a genuine answer for each person where he is and thus the beginning of an answer for his parish.

During the latter part of the conference, especially Sunday morning, the leader begins to assume the role of resource person, applying the church's terminology to the experiences the group has passed through and the insights gained. It is imperative that persons who have participated in such conferences shall follow up its life-changing effect with further orientation and training for the specific ministeries. Moreover, as understandings grow, even the parish life conference is changing in both design and procedures. — *George L. Peabody* (with the assistance of *William J. Coulter*)

PAROCHIAL SCHOOL " Parochial school " is a term applied to schools offering a general education sponsored or supervised by a religious organization. More precisely, it is limited to educational efforts stemming from the life of the church on a parish level in contrast to diocesan or monastic schools, and, technically, refers only to the elementary school. In the U.S.A. the usually accepted connotations of the term imply Roman Catholic or Lutheran schools due to the preponderance of them. The concept and reality is present in other denominations. Episcopalians, Society of Friends, Seventh-day Adventists, some Jewish congregations, and others operate parochial schools. The same description underlies the contemporary use of the term " parish day school."

As distinguished from public schools, parochial schools are private in that the support for the schools comes primarily from the families of the children educated and from the sponsoring religious groups and not from public funds. As distinguished from private schools, they normally admit children from the parish regardless of intellectual ability, believing that the school offers a unique opportunity to instruct in the context of the faith of the sponsoring group. Most parochial schools will admit children of any faith as well as their own children.

Parochial schools set up standards for teaching and curriculum, equal to public school standards, but are free to modify and enlarge and to experiment as their particular system requires. State and provincial standards, however, must be maintained, and many states require the public licensing of the schools.

Historically, the role of the church in general education is not new, but can be traced from pre-Christian Judaism.

In the Jewish household, the father stood as both priest and teacher. The responsibility assumed by the father to train the young males of his household was supplemented by the instruction offered in the synagogue. Over a period of time the basic responsibility for education appeared to shift from the home to the synagogue; thus the institutional features of schooling were well developed by the time of the birth of Jesus.

It is reasonable to suppose that Jesus benefited from formal instruction on the content of the Law and the Prophets, which was to become the canonical Old Testament. This would be implied as a prerequisite to his taking part in the routine of the synagogue and his mastery of the history of his people. Jesus was prepared for his earthly ministry in a tradition that held teaching to be a compelling imperative. This is illustrated in the account of his natural rapport with the rabbis in the Temple when he was 12 years old.

Teaching was an integral part of Jesus' own ministry and a part of his command to the disciples, hence, to the apostolic church. The continuance of synagogue-type training into the early Christian era influenced the later catechetical schools for adult converts. The Christian was taught within the community of the church that which was necessary to prepare him to confront the pagan world with confidence and security.

Through the early centuries of the Christian era education was limited primarily to preparation for the ministry.

From the Scholastic period through the Renaissance nearly all scholarship and learning was allowed and authorized under the patronage of the church's parishes, cathedrals, and monasteries. The guilds, also sponsored by the church, sought to train and aid men and boys in the learning of trades necessary for their livelihood. Although the church continued its concern for education and scholarship, it became less the exclusive function of the church by Reformation times due to the independent nature of the " new learning " and the revolt from the corruptions in the pre-Reformation church.

In the American colonies prior to the Revolution, the state considered whatever education there was to be the distinct function of the church. The traditional interdependence of the functions of the church and state, unimpaired through the Reformation, gave the church the natural responsibility to exercise its educational role even more strongly on the new frontier. Not only did the church control the schools but it determined the curriculum. In some areas where the churches were too poor to support themselves, the state provided the necessary funds and lands.

Schools were organized for 2 primary purposes. First, the upper classes, unwilling or unable to send their sons back to the Continent for an education, placed the burden on the local " parson," usually a scholarly man, to establish the Latin grammar schools or academies. These were often called the " parson's school." Instruction in reading, writing, language, manners, morals, and a form of religion was given. The 2d type of school resulted from the need to care for the children of the working people, and often was called the " charity school." Both these types of school met a need in the society, and the church accepted its challenge.

Following the Revolutionary War, the political and social changes brought about new ideas of education, building upon the ideas of democracy and freedom of speech and religion. No longer did people look to England and Europe for direction. A new nation was to be built. Changes came rapidly. The industrial revolution was creating new demands in knowledge and skill. Within 75 years after independence a public-school system was in formation. At the same time the Roman Catholic Church, held more or less in subjection until freedom was allowed, showed a sudden surge in educational institutions of every kind, not least, the local parish school. As the public school developed, many churches relinquished their control of education in favor of the new system. Although not objecting in principle to a great public educational program, the Roman Catholics were unwilling to lose control over the daily education of their children in the principles of Christian living and faith. Therefore, the Roman Catholic parochial school made continuing advances through the 19th century up until the present day, now sponsoring the largest nonpublic school system in the world.

During the industrial revolution a new development took place in England. Working conditions were such that much too frequently the young children in the lower classes were forced to labor daily. In an effort to aid these young people, the church began a period of general education similar to the charity schools mentioned earlier, on Sundays. As working conditions changed for the children and other opportunities for education were evident, there emerged a Sunday school with the specific task of educating the young in the teachings and life of the church.

In recent years, following World War II, there has been a resurgence of interest in the development of the parochial school in the U.S.A. In some instances the schools were prompted by a general dissatisfaction with what progressive education was doing to the children. But also, the technological age with its attendant economic growth, diversity of concerns, and mobility of population has created a demand for nonpublic education in smaller classes more easily adaptable to changing conditions.

The church, true to its commission to teach, is accepting the challenge, motivated by the desire to meet a real need. The changing conditions have also caused many to believe that the Sunday school is not enough to ensure a strong conviction as to the nature of God and man's purpose. No doubt there are also other causes and motives behind the present growth in the number of parochial schools. — *Clarence W. Brickman*

PERSONALITY, THEORIES OF

Theories of personality are attempts to explain the fact that individual human beings exist, and are aware of their existence as individuals in a variety of relations with other individuals and with the environing milieu. These explanations can be grouped into families, schools of thought, or classes, according to the similarities in their approach or in their intellectual ancestry.

The term "personality" is usually applied to the simplest distinguishable unit of human existence that can be regarded as aware of its individuality. There is no general agreement as to what this unit includes. The range of views is extensive. At one extreme is the suggestion that personality is the organization of certain processes in the brain. At the opposite extreme is the view that personality is the complex of relationships and interactions of a human organism with its environment.

The usage of the plural term "theories" is intended to call attention to the fact that no one of the explanations has been able either to win a universal acceptance by scholars in this area of study or to establish the superior adequacy of its predictive and explanatory power over alternative views in relation to all the data regarded as legitimately within the scope of its responsibility.

In addition to the formal theories based on scholarly investigations, there are innumerable private conjectures currently in circulation. Persons have tended to speculate about their own existence since the results of human thought have been recorded and preserved.

The major topics receiving attention in contemporary theories of personality include: (1) the structure of personality; (2) the dynamics of personality; and (3) the development of personality. This threefold classification of the data from personality research was recognized in 1950 by R. R. Sears. Later summarizers of personality studies have treated these categories as normative for their purpose. Within the 3 major topics are many subtopics, defined to a large extent by the interests and date of the formulators and developers of the specific theories.

A definitive summary of the major contemporary theories of personality was provided in 1957 by Calvin S. Hall and Gardner Lindzey. The 12 approaches that they described and summarized as the major alternatives available in current personality theory included: (1) the psychoanalytic theory of Sigmund Freud; (2) the analytic theory of Carl Jung; (3) the social psychological theories of Alfred Adler, Erich Fromm, Karen Horney, and Harry Stack Sullivan; (4) the personology theory of Henry A. Murray; (5) the field theory of Kurt Lewin; (6) Gordon Allport's psychology of the individual; (7) the organismic theory of Kurt Goldstein, Andras Angyal, Abraham Maslow, and Prescott Lecky; (8) William H. Sheldon's theory of constitutional psychology; (9) the factor theories of H. J. Eysenck and Raymond B. Cattell; (10) the stimulus-response theories of Clark L. Hull, John Dollard and Neal E. Miller, Robert R. Sears, and O. Hobart Mowrer; (11) the self theory of Carl Rogers; and (12) the biosocial theory of Gardner Murphy.

The major works in personality theory that have appeared since the Hall and Lindzey survey have been primarily either developments in one or another of these 12 major approaches or attempts to integrate various aspects of 2 or more existing approaches into a more comprehensive synthesis.

One of the most interesting facts about contemporary theories of personality is the relatively small amount of hostility and conflict evident in the relations among the holders of these divergent views. To be sure, it is almost impossible to find a book in the field of personality theory that has not been viciously attacked and clawed by the scholars who have reviewed it. But it is equally rare to find 2 personality theories pitted against each other in an open battle for the survival of 1 at the expense of the other.

This relatively high degree of tolerance displayed by personality theorists toward viewpoints that are different from their own indicates a major characteristic of contemporary theories. The several personality theories tend to concentrate upon specific aspects of personality. As a result the theories do not overlap to any great extent in the areas of their central concern and emphasis. Thus, with significant qualifications, it can be noted that each approach has almost exclusive possession of a research area and emphasis in which the results of alternative approaches can be largely ignored or minimized.

Insofar as trends are discernible in the relatively brief period since the Hall and Lindzey volume, it appears that the major directions being taken by the personality theorists are those toward overcoming the compartmentalizations of the field by attempts at synthesis, and toward working out the implications of existing understandings of personality for precisely defined individual or social processes. Thus, one is able to observe a tendency for the majority of recently published books in this area to carry the words "personality" and "and" in their titles, e.g., *Personality and Social Encounter, Social Structure and Personality, Emotion and Personality,* etc.

A whole new complex of developments in mathematical theory, statistics, and data-processing by means of electronic computers has provided methodological tools for the tasks that personality theorists are presently attempting. Multivariate analysis is becoming an increasingly common means of managing the overwhelming complexity of levels and dimensions of personality data.

These considerations would seem to suggest that the field of personality theory is moving beyond the initial stage of theory creation toward the stages of (1) testing existing hypotheses in a variety of situations, (2) congealing partial theories into more comprehensive master theories, and (3) making applications of the growing body of factual knowledge to the problems and processes of individual and social concern that have been somewhat neglected by previous research.

One of the most significant *rapprochements* discernible within recent years has been a largely voluntary and nonorganized confluence of compatible approaches. This can be seen in the increasing evidences that those who view personality primarily in terms of interactions, transactions, and relationships are becoming aware of, and making positive valuations of, the insights of those who are concerned primarily with the dynamic, noncognitive processes that influence the development and functioning of individuals and groups. Another major confluence of initially separate streams of thought is that of the incorporation of the insights from European and American existential philosophy into personality theory, and, in comparable fashion, the assimilation of psychological insights into the general thought patterns of both technical and popular philosophy in America and some parts of Europe.

Two developments in recent personality research that will be of special interest to educators may be noted. The 1st of these is the beginning of a significant literature on the cross-cultural study of personality. By observing the specific dynamic effects of varying environmental conditions upon an individual or a group, it is possible to have much more precise and reliable information as to the conditions under which certain changes or learnings can be expected, and those in which other results will obtain. A 2d development holding promise of special significance for educators is the beginning of a body of literature reporting the results of longitudinal studies of personality development and functioning. A particularly encouraging aspect of this development is the fact that only the barest beginnings have been made in reporting the tremendous accumulation of data from these longitudinal studies. Some of these longitudinal studies which are just beginning to be reported have massive quantities of precise data on their subjects over a period of 2 and sometimes 3 generations. With the aid of electronic data processing equipment, which is becoming increasingly available, the results of these longitudinal studies can be expected to become a major source of our most dependable and reliable information during the next several years.

In general, personality theories seem to be moving in the direction of viewing personality structure as a dynamic organization rather than as a static or substantial entity. Personality dynamics seem to be increasingly viewed as both conscious and unconscious, and as both driving and attracting forces. There is increasing attention being given to needs, stimuli, attention, and motivation in the study of personality dynamics. Personality dynamics are increasingly seen to have a significant role in personality development. Personality development seems to be regarded increasingly as an experienced and perceived continuity within a diversity of processes having a functional organization and focused upon a series of tasks, situations, and problems of living in a social and physical environment. Despite the overwhelming convergence of professional psychologists in the area of clinical psychology, there has seemed to be a decline in the frequency of major breakthroughs in either the diagnosis or treatment of personality disorders. This may reflect either the adequacy of early studies or the probability that major advances can be expected in this area sometime in the near future.

Religious educators as well as general educators can profit immeasurably from a serious study of contemporary theories of personality. The implications of presently available insights have received only the barest minimum of attention by those whose efforts, perhaps, would profit most from such understandings.

— Howard Miller Ham

PESTALOZZI, JOHANN HEINRICH
Johann Heinrich Pestalozzi (1746–1827), a native of Zurich, Switzerland, was the 1st to introduce elementary education for all the people. He was passionately concerned about the state of society, especially of the lower classes, and he endeavored to bring about more humane conditions. This, he held, could be done in 2 ways: by improving external circumstances and by educating children, for in an industrial age a sound education was the precondition of a higher living standard. He exhorted governments to reform social legislation, and he devised means for elementary education applicable to all. As a personal contribution he founded on his estate a school for poor children in which the teaching of rudimentary knowledge was combined with character training and with manual work. Although this and similar later enterprises failed materially for lack of business acumen, they yielded valuable pedagogic results that Pestalozzi laid down in substantial writings and handed on to innumerable pupils. In 1805–1825 his institute in Yverdon, Canton of Vaux, was a renowned educational center. From there his ideas spread all over Europe and into the U.S.A.

Pestalozzi's theory is that education should be "according to nature." Nature, being God's creation, is good, and man, being God's child, has the "divine spark" within him. Therefore, every child, even the lowest, has the ability and thus the right to be educated. Education must develop the faculties lying dormant in the child, not impose anything alien upon him from without. It must cultivate his own powers, encourage his self-activity, strengthen his whole personality. It must be applied equally to the mind, the body, and the heart in order to achieve a balanced personality, a useful citizen, and through him and others thus educated a stable and prosperous world.

Pestalozzi laid down a number of fundamental principles on which education should be founded. The 1st is that education begins at birth and in the early stages should be conducted in the home. The mother plays a most important role in the child's development. Her love and devotion create his responsive love from which stem all other qualities such as confidence, sense of security, reliability, as well as obedience and a sense of duty. An undisturbed family life with mother and father as 1st educators is the basis of a successful upbringing. A contented heart is the necessary accompaniment of a healthy body and the prerequisite of a sane mind.

Education should progress slowly and gradually. No advance should be made before the previous stage is fully comprehended, and nothing should be taught that is above the child's capacity. Thus completion and perfection would be reached at every stage and bring reliability, satisfaction, and happiness.

The educational material should in the 1st place be taken from the child's nearest surroundings: family pets, house, neighborhood. Nothing should be taught by mere words; everything, if possible, should be shown in its natural shape. Only after the object has been perceived with the senses should it be expressed in words. Not the content but the form of learning is the more important; children should be taught how to think and act for themselves.

Pestalozzi did not regard school subjects as being the primary units in teaching. He conceived of more elementary categories which, in the intellectual field, are form, number, and language. Especially his arithmetical exercises became the foundation of mathematical teaching.

Education according to Pestalozzi is threefold: intellectual, physical, and moral. The same principles formulated for 1 branch also govern the others. Physical education comprises the exercise of the body, preparation for the future occupation, and education for citizenship. Moral education is the development of character, which accompanies, deliberately or unconsciously, the training of the other faculties, and embraces religious education. The love of God and men is the supreme quality that underlies and unites them all. The good life in the service of others is the final aim.

Pestalozzi was a loving and lovable personality. He exerted himself far beyond his means in the struggles for his ideal. His influence on a great number of disciples was profound. His 1st American follower was William Maclure, a geologist. With the help of Joseph Neef, who was trained by Pestalozzi, Maclure founded the 1st Pestalozzian school in Philadelphia (1807). Since then Pestalozzi's ideas have permeated elementary education generally, but outside Switzerland and Germany often anonymously and unacknowledged. — *Kate Silber*

PHILOSOPHY OF EDUCATION

Philosophy of education defies satisfactory definition because philosophers practice philosophy and education in different ways depending on their philosophies and cultural backgrounds. Historically, philosophy (*philos,* "fond of," and *sophos,* "wise") has varied considerably both in meaning and in scope. Plato used the term in the most general way in his *Republic,* applying it to "those who see the absolute and eternal and immutable, . . . those who love the truth in each thing." Thus all knowledge was fused together by him into a semireligious synthesis. It remained for Aristotle, with his methodic intellect, to separate the vast field of philosophy into the disciplines we recognize today as logic, psychology, ethics, aesthetics, metaphysics, etc.

Philosophy, however, has not remained the grand subject it was in ancient times, for it has been rocked to its very foundations by the advance of knowledge and by science in particular. Much of what was once epistemology has become the chief concern of the physiologist and psychologist. Cosmology has yielded to the researches in astronomy and physics, while logic has been greatly modified by the work of mathematical logicians. Meanwhile metaphysics and ethics have not gone unscathed. Today there are those philosophers who would completely reject all metaphysical statements as nonsense, for they believe them not to be verifiable, at least as the term commonly is used. These same philosophers are likely to think of ethical statements as imperative sentences that express the attitudes of the persons uttering them.

Even though, as we shall see presently, not all philosophers are as skeptical as some of the comments above would indicate, it is true, nevertheless, that philosophy is no longer the pretentious and all-inclusive subject it was in the days of Plato. Much of its subject matter as well as the absolute, the eternal, and the immutable have been eroded away, even for those who are not skeptics.

The philosophy of education likewise has undergone, and is now undergoing, some very profound changes. Whereas a score of years ago one who formulated a definition of the philosophy of education had only to please realists, idealists, and pragmatists, an almost impossible task in itself, the writer now has to define philosophy of education in such a way as to encompass the thinking of the existentialists and the critical analysts too. But press the problem of defining philosophy of education far enough and one finds even the analyst agreeing that the traditional problems of philosophy are still apparent. He only disagrees as to the nature of these problems or as to the kinds of answers one is likely to have for these problems. Thus it would be defensible to define the philosophy of education as an attempt to find answers to questions that some would call ultimate. The philosopher in education desires to learn what can be known and what this has to do with education. He is interested in the nature of reality, sources of value, and what these may mean for education: aims, curriculum, and method. He may or may not believe that values are discovered by intuition or revelation. He may or may not reduce all knowledge to observation and experimentation. But whatever his views on metaphysics, epistemology, and axiology, he is concerned with the implications of his views for education.

This very general definition perhaps will become more meaningful if some illustrations are given. There are differences of opinion among philosophers, who, for the most part, are interested in the same problems but each of whom tends to take a different view toward them.

J. Donald Butler divides knowledge into 2 kinds: specific discoveries that are tentative descriptions produced by the sciences; truth, a kind of knowledge that seems to go beyond discoveries. Perhaps his ultimate values fall into this category of truth. Butler believes that the cosmos partakes of the nature of selfhood and that God speaks to man through " a cosmic movement which is equivalent to the coming of God to man." God is existence and man has a personality that is more than what is seen by the psychologist or the sociologist. His personality includes a spiritual element. God intends goodness for man but man can achieve this goodness only when he brings himself close to God.

Butler thinks that his metaphysics, and most especially his value theory, have a direct bearing on the kind of education he recommends. He feels that the school should be conceived as a value-realizing institution next in importance to the church. At the same time he doubts that the common school in America can give us the kind of education that he seeks. Instead of limiting all education to the public schools, a " composite of institutions " will be needed to achieve the ends he seeks. Butler is an excellent example of a philosopher who still holds steadfastly to the ultimate and immutable. He is in the grand tradition that has descended to us from Plato.

Sidney Hook, on the other hand, represents the pragmatic school of thought that has held sway in America for most of this century. Hook rejects the religious and metaphysical approach of men like Butler, for he believes that such an approach seeks to deduce what men should be from what men are thought to be. In other words this approach is sheer tautology. Hook would discover the nature of men in the developing careers of men in time and in relation to the world. The nature of man is nothing more or less than a set of conditions that limits the possible educational aims, allowing us to select from among the many aims those which are most desirable. Hook couples this cultural relativity with the method of intelligence. This method of intelligence becomes the center of his " liberal philosophy " because it undercuts the absolutes that stand in the way of the development of new knowledge and insights. " Method should be central in educational activity because it not only evaluates the funded tradition of the past but enhances the capacity to enrich it." Hook appears to reject most, if not all, metaphysical considerations, reduces values to hypotheses, and conceives of knowledge as that which is produced as a result of human experience. Education is a human endeavor, with human purposes, procedures, subject matter; the process of education is subject to human error and correction of this error by the exercise of the method of intelligence.

More recently the analytic philosopher has emerged on the scene. Since analytic philosophy is devoted to the clarification of language, one philosophizes about almost anything. This being the case, the analytic philosopher has on occasion turned his attention to education. He hopes to develop some defensible statements about education. He plans to do this by analyzing the language used by educators, i.e., " needs," " real experi-

ence," " lifelike situations," etc. Finally, he hopes to provide some models and to state criteria for establishing meaning and verification. The analytic position is an even further departure from conventional philosophy.

These illustrations should serve to warn those who try to understand philosophy of education that it would be wise to proceed with caution. Except in the most general way what is philosophy of education to one philosopher is not likely to be philosophy of education to another. The safest thing to do when studying philosophy of education is to seek to understand what each writer means when he philosophizes on matters educational. — *Joe E. Park*

PHILOSOPHY OF RELIGIOUS EDUCATION It is customary to find listed among the course offerings in theological schools one that usually bears the label " The Philosophy of Religious Education." It is usually assumed or required that such a subject will have been studied by all candidates for degrees in the field of religious education or by majors in that field who take the B.D. degree. Normally, such courses probe into the underlying ideological bases for the educational task, with special reference to the presuppositions that issue in educational institutions and procedures.

In a sense the usage here is parallel to what one might find in similar terminology in other fields, e.g., " the philosophy of science " or " the philosophy of law." Pure philosophy probably would prefer to avoid such " professionalized " employment of the term. In a technical sense there is only philosophy — the examination of the nature of reality on the basis of man's use of his intellective apprehensions. As soon as one says "philosophy *of* " one is getting into a far different area of investigation. The " of " implies use, practical ends and means, etc., that instead of being " pure " analysis, turn out to be colored by the particularized vocational interests of the " philosopher." At the same time, it must be recognized that the pragmatic philosophy — which claims a secure place in the philosophical universe — recognizes these practical considerations as themselves essential to the understanding of reality itself. In the case of religious education philosophy the question becomes even more complicated by 2 factors: (1) " Religious " education is an aspect of the broad field of education as a whole, so that one has to ask, " What can we say about the philosophy of education? " and then, as a further refinement or dissection of the question, " What can we say about the philosophy of religious education? " (2) The inclusion within the area of investigation of " religious " introduces the large question as to the theological understandings that religion inevitably involves, so that theology, itself a " science " with its own presuppositions and methods of procedure, must be taken into consideration along with the theoretical matters pertaining to " philosophy " proper and " education " proper.

It is then obvious that to speak of " philosophy of religious education " is no simple task. This is also to suggest that it is altogether proper that those who desire to become professionally competent in religious education should struggle with the whole complex represented by this field of inquiry. It is good that some persons deliberately essay the interrelations of philosophical, theological, and educational thought.

This serves to keep the intellectual quality of religious education on a high level, and assists the total process of interpenetration of fields of inquiry, which is itself a philosophical interest of greatest importance.

Perhaps a simpler way to state a definition of " philosophy of religious education " would be to say that it is " the analysis of the underlying principles or presuppositions implied in the religious community's effort to teach its faith."

At various times in history the educational activities of the church have reflected prevailing philosophical interests and views; sometimes theological considerations have taken definitely 2d place to philosophical ones. As many observers have pointed out, this tended to be characteristic of the " religious education movement " of the early decades of the 20th century. When some leaders in the so-called liberal period urged that religious educators ought to be involved in remaking the theology of the church, what they really were saying, often, was that as philosophers they considered it their task to bring the church's education into line with the prevalent interests of humanistic, pragmatic views. Similarly, it could be demonstrated that rationalism in various forms, which came to dominate educational thought in the late 19th century, tended to supplant the traditional Biblical bases of Christian nurture, e.g., the view of evolutionary progress, which well nigh eliminated eschatological considerations from Christian education thinking in the earlier decades of this century.

Another way to regard " philosophy of religious education " is to view it in terms of the thoughtful setting forth of the various foundations for Christian education: theological, philosophical, psychological. Such a view would make no claim for technical philosophical systematization as the goal of the discipline. Rather, questions of the relation of the "what" and the "how" are grouped together in such a manner as to portray the total educational task of the church in any given period. This assumes that the task is never completed, and that restatement is legitimate and proper as understandings change and as new factors arise which must enter the thoughtful consideration of religious education theorists. For example, the renaissance in Biblical theology, the rise of the ecumenical movement, the impact of existentialist philosophies — characteristic phenomena of mid-20th-century life and thought — need to be taken into consideration as the church examines its tasks of nurture.

The literature of recent decades that has had principal influence in what might be called, broadly, the ecumenical theological climate of our time seems to proceed along the lines last indicated above. The seminary courses in "philosophy of religious education" do not content themselves, usually, with purely philosophical analyses of the educational implications of the traditional "schools" of philosophy so much as they take into their purview all such ideas and experiences and phenomena of the total culture as will shed light on the fundamental task of the church.

One further matter may be indicated, also: there is arising a more clearly discernible trend for religious education theorists to take the historical dimension more seriously. Whereas some years ago some writers may have been inclined to proceed as if it had been possible to create a "philosophy of religious education" *de novo,* increasing evidence gathers that there is an intellectual honesty compelling writers to see themselves as creatures in a time-bound situation. In this they are at one with many philosophers, who, seeking to view things *sub specie aeternitatis,* realize that they are called to a task in the present situation that their predecessors also had to face. In this respect, belatedly, religious education is catching up in its area of concern with the historical views that have come to play such an important role in Biblical studies, technical theology, and pastoral theology in general in recent decades. — *Kendig Brubaker Cully*

PLAY Play may well be called a child's preparation for life. To a child, play is natural, spontaneous, and absorbing. It is his way of learning.

Watch a small girl at play, imitating her mother in her household tasks and in the care she gives the baby. Watch a small boy pretending to be his father coming home from the office. As you watch, you are observing the learning process at work. The little girl is learning to be a woman, the little boy to be a man.

The play patterns of older children widen out to include more interests and more playfellows. The children play in 2's and 3's and groups. They play singing and folk games; racing, tag, and competitive games; games requiring skill. As they play, they are not only helping their bodies to become strong, they are learning important lessons in how to get along with others; they accept defeat gracefully, deal with success, work for the team rather than for the self. For these older ones also, play is preparation for living.

The leader and the parent are wise who recognize the central importance of play in the life of the child, who accept it, adapt it to the learning processes, and use it to deepen the child's experience and widen his understanding.

The leader or parent who understands play can use it in the religious training of the children in his charge. Play can be directed so that the children will gain new learnings. With a group of kindergarten children, the leader may say: " Let us play that we are picking flowers or gathering fruit. What are you picking? What color is it? Has it a nice smell? Do you like it? God sent us these flowers (or fruits) to enjoy. Shall we thank him for the good gifts he has given us? "

Such play as this not only gives the growing bodies of the children the activity they crave but gives their minds new ideas and touches their awakening spirits.

Little children and older ones, too, enjoy the experience of acting out stories they have heard, particularly Bible stories. As they dramatize the events of a story, they participate in its action. For the time being, they feel the emotions of the characters they represent. Their experience is broadened and deepened by such dramatic play. In this way children can learn ideals of honesty, truthfulness, generosity, nobility, and uprightness.

With groups in the home or church school, play directed by a parent or leader not only gives enjoyment but relieves tension, releases pent-up energy, and prepares the children to receive other types of teaching that may follow. A quiet game will often bring calm and restfulness to a riotous group of children.

Teaching children to play games enjoyed by boys and girls in other parts of the world is one way of broadening their experience. Play is almost universal among children. Only those who are sick and weak or who have adult duties thrust upon them at an early age do not play freely.

Similar games are found in many parts of the world. The play patterns of " Fox and Geese " and " London Bridge " are found under different names, and with some variations, in many countries of the world.

As they play the games of boys and girls in other parts of the world, the children will have a feeling of respect and fellowship for those boys and girls, who also enjoy good games. Such an enjoyment of the games of others may be one of their 1st steps toward the understanding and appreciation of people different from themselves.

Children are going to play, wherever they are. They play with a passion and singleheartedness that makes them forget time, space, and even hunger, for play is their way of life. — *Nina L. Millen*

POETRY Everyone knows that poetry and dancing are among the earliest expressions of the artistic impulse. As far back as the mind can penetrate, men and women have danced to the poetic chanting of a chorus. For untold centuries this simple poetry, which sprang from earth and heart, was celebrated by long-balanced cadences with no thought of meter, rhyme, or stanza form. Something of its rhythmic nature may be found in the folk poems of the Old Testament and in some of the psalms.

It is easier to recognize poetry today than to define it. This is because poetry is a form of literature, and literature is manifold in its forms. Furthermore, poetry is the most civilized and complex of all the arts — certainly the most difficult to teach, and perhaps the last one that ought to be taught. This consideration is of profound relevance to all who are engaged in Christian education.

All the arts are simpler than poetry. Painting long has been the attempt to give visual form to the ebullience of the unconscious. Dancing is the simplest of the arts, for the physical posture and the facial expression indicate both emotion and cerebration. Architecture began with the simple post and lintel construction and, as engineering developed, moved into its various forms. These arts and others are obvious, easily understood and used by all.

Poetry is more difficult, however. Not many people read it in spite of the fact that substantial units of poetry are taught, even though they may not be understood, in both the public and the church schools.

The truth is that children, and even high school young people, not to mention adults who are arrested psychologically on an adolescent basis, are not mature or sophisticated enough to understand poetry. The really great poetry is too profound for their limited experience. How can one read and understand the poetry of life and death, of war and hard work, of deep sorrow and bereavement, or prophetic vision and hope for the future, until one has matured psychologically? That is why so many young people leave

high school hating poetry. They have been subjected to an experience that they do not understand.

Poetic appreciation does not seem to develop until later adolescence. It is then that death is sometimes dimly revealed; it is then that love comes in overwhelming splendor; it is then that one enters into the mystery of birth, pain, purposeful work, and social responsibility. Most of the great poetry celebrates these activities. One has only to think of the poetry of the Romantic movement to know how true this is. A high school student, unless he is a most extraordinary individual, cannot understand Wordsworth's " Lines Written Above Tintern Abbey," or his " Ode on Intimations of Immortality." Nor can he understand the immediately contemporary poetry of cerebration as written by such poets as T. S. Eliot and contained in anthologies such as those edited by John Ciardi, *Mid-Century American Poets*, and Oscar Williams, *A Little Treasury of Modern Poetry*.

Christian education, therefore, must keep the level of intelligibility in mind in choosing poems for worship and classroom use. Thinking of the church school by and large, one might say that one could safely choose the poetry of nature and social responsibility, some of the seasonal poetry related to the liturgical year, and an occasional poem about God that does not make too many demands on the understanding, e.g., " Wind in the Pines," by Lew Sarett.
— *Clarence Seidenspinner*

POSTER A poster is a placard posted in a public place, designed to be understood at a glance. It must combine immediate visual effectiveness with the concise communication of a single important idea. The poster is a visual combination of bold design, color, and a brief message, which is to catch and hold the attention of the passer-by just long enough to implant a significant idea in his mind. The poster has become a unique communication medium.

Modern research traces continuity in the use of the poster from about the year 1600. The 1st posters that have been preserved carried notices of royal proclamations, fairs, and newly published books. In 1796, a new method of printing from stone — lithography — produced brilliantly colored posters easily and cheaply. In 1860, Jules Chéret, a French lithographer known as the " father of the poster," was commissioned by Sarah Bernhardt to prepare large-scale advertising illustrations for her forthcoming stage appearance in Paris. It was there that the poster as we know it today was born and became a notable success. Since then the poster has played an important role in industrial and commercial enterprise. It has also proved effective in government projects, such as recruitment, Savings Bonds, etc. The use of posters in educational and religious work is a medium with great possibilities but as yet is used only to a limited degree.

The poster as a teaching medium can be used in connection with many types of classroom and school activities. It encourages creativity and participation on the part of the pupils. The poster may be a culminating and application-type of activity arising from a unit of work. Pupil-made posters represent the fruition of social concepts and measure the effectiveness of teaching. Since posters may be made in a variety of ways, from the simplest to the most involved, this teaching

medium is usable with a wide range of age groups.

Composition, color, and technique are the principal elements in effective poster preparation. A good poster requires a strong and commanding center of interest. This may be a drawing, a picture cut from a magazine, or a photograph. Occasionally wool, cotton, or swatches of other materials are pasted on poster board, forming a collage effect that greatly vitalizes a poster. Three-dimensional, free-standing designs selected for their interest and combined into an original composition also add appeal to poster-making. The final arrangement of letters and decorative unit within the poster area must be pleasing and in good taste. This involves wide margins and good spacing of all elements. Color adds greatly to the effectiveness of the poster. Whatever colors are used should be few, strong, and contrasting. Colored construction paper offers many fine combinations for cut-out letters and designs. Poster paint and India ink add color and contrast.

Whatever materials and techniques are used, it is essential that the pupils feel and recognize a genuine need for the poster. The process of planning, making, and using the poster should be an integral part of the teaching unit.

A poster can be used to create a learning atmosphere. Teachers of geography, social studies, and religion will use posters made by students to bring the reality, charm, and attractiveness of distant lands and places into the classroom. The poster can give terse, attention-getting information on health, vocational choices, missionary education, etc., for classroom and assembly room use. The poster can also be used to exhort, emphasizing the importance of a certain action: " Cross Crossings Cautiously," " Be on Time Next Sunday," etc.

The poster may also be used to announce and advertise an event such as a party or basketball game. The use of the poster to produce action will have to be preceded in the classroom by reasons as to why the suggested action is important. The poster itself does not convince, but it can remind in a convincing way. — *Alethea S. Kose*

PRAGMATISM Pragmatism is a movement in philosophy which in America received its basic directions from such men as William James (1842–1910) and John Dewey (1859–1952). According to James, who was influential in refining and popularizing the pragmatic method and theory of truth, Charles Peirce (1839–1914) gave early impetus and expression to the central ideas that became the core of pragmatism. Peirce influenced James through their mutual sharing in the Metaphysical Club in Cambridge, Mass., and through his writings. Peirce published an article entitled " How to Make Our Ideas Clear," which appeared in *Popular Science Monthly*, January, 1878. Here he coined the term " pragmatism." He stressed that beliefs are " rules for action " and encouraged the practice of anticipating practical consequences as the criterion for determining the meaningfulness of ideas. In an address before a philosophical group in 1898, James observed that Peirce's suggestions largely had been ignored until then, and proceeded to follow up the leads given to him by his friend and mentor.

Pragmatism flourished during the early decades of this century. Yet it was not without still earlier antecedents. Francis Bacon (1561–1626) emphasized the inductive approach to knowledge, giving central place to the observation of particulars rather than deductive argumentation based on a priori generalizations. He viewed science as a social enterprise designed to push back the frontiers of knowledge in social and moral areas no less than the technological. John Dewey recognized in Bacon such a kindred spirit that in *Reconstruction in Philosophy*, he referred to him as the " prophet of a pragmatic conception of knowledge."

Auguste Comte (1798–1857) made much of the close connection between ideas and their social context and significance. He encouraged man to live at the " positive " stage of human development, i.e., oriented scientifically in relation to laws and relations in the universe. In the more primitive " theological " stage man had been guided by the assumption that supernatural powers grounded existence. At the " metaphysical " level man advanced to the point where supernatural sanctions were no longer regarded as necessary to ground substantial realities. Comte was convinced that the " positive " or scientific stage represents the most significant advance yet made by man. At that level man seeks especially to discover the laws governing social and political relations and to live in harmony with them.

Immanuel Kant (1724–1804) also deserves mention as part of the historical background. Kant introduced a note of caution regarding our ability to know reality as such.

We know only the "phenomenal" side of the "noumenal," i.e., the thing-in-itself. The deepest grasp of reality comes not abstractly but morally, not theoretically but practically. Man as a moral agent is himself the best clue to the nature of reality. In and with the apprehension of "duty" are given the presuppositions of "practical reason": God, freedom, immortality. Although these "regulative" ideas lack theoretical objectivity, they are adequately grounded in moral experience. Kant's agnosticism regarding truth in itself, his suspicion of speculative metaphysics, his emphasis upon truth in action (particularly the action of the self as responsible agent) represent significant points of contact with pragmatism.

Nor is pragmatism without contemporary heirs. With the decline of idealism in America, tendencies associated with "logical positivism" or "linguistic empiricism" have come to represent a dominant direction in contemporary philosophy. Representatives of this movement (A. J. Ayer) acknowledge basic indebtedness to the Vienna positivists (Moritz Schlick, Rudolf Carnap). Particularly at the point of the search for a criterion of meaningfulness and the orientation toward empirical experience as the basis for verification, the connection with the pragmatic temper is clear. "Existentialism" represents another major option in philosophy today. Pragmatism's stress upon truth in process, upon the lack of fixed "essences" and relations, and upon man's challenge to be a free agent who appropriates truth inwardly rather than simply objectively and dispassionately suggests analogies with this contemporary orientation as well.

In his essay "What Pragmatism Means," James stated that there is basically nothing new in the pragmatic method. He mentioned Socrates, Aristotle, Locke, Berkeley, and Hume as among its forerunners. James saw his own era, however, as the time when pragmatism was becoming conscious of its universal mission. His many essays, published under such collective titles as *Pragmatism, The Meaning of Truth, The Will to Believe,* and *Essays in Radical Empiricism,* witness to his confidence in its "conquering destiny."

Pragmatism involves the basic attitude of "looking away from first things, principles, 'categories,' supposed necessities." It advocates "looking toward last things, fruits, consequences, facts." It recommends turning away from "abstraction and insufficiency, from verbal solutions, from bad a priori reasons, from fixed principles, closed systems, and pretended absolutes and origins." It proceeds empirically, aiming toward concreteness, adequacy, action, and power.

James contended that this method has far-reaching possibilities for settling metaphysical disputes that traditionally have disturbed men. He cites the illustration of a man who circles a tree around whose trunk a squirrel keeps moving. Does the man really go round the squirrel? It all depends on what is practically meant by "going round" the squirrel. The man obviously does if you mean that he successively is north, east, south, and then west of the squirrel. He does not if the meaning is that the man is respectively behind, to the right, in front of, and then to the left of the animal. By the simple expedient of focusing upon the practical issue involved, many of the ancient metaphysical puzzles (i.e., problems about substance, design in nature, freedom of will, materialism or spiritualism, monism or pluralism) can be restated and dealt with productively.

James felt that pragmatism represents the empiricist attitude both in a more radical and less objectionable form than had previously been true. The method involved is likened to a corridor in a hotel whose doors typify a variety of intellectual pursuits: metaphysical, religious, or scientific. No particular results are presupposed. Nor is the empiricism reductionistic in temper. Pragmatism makes room for logic and the senses, for religion and science. Indeed, James went out of his way to allow room for freedom of will, for theological ideas and beliefs. But the basic focus upon practical fruits, consequences, and facts is the setting for this openness even to mystical experiences.

Pragmatism refers in a still broader sense to a theory of truth. Both James and Dewey stress the instrumental character of ideas and beliefs. Truth is not a static property or relation. It is something that "happens" to an idea. The stress is upon verification and validation as an ongoing process. A true idea enables us to attain satisfactory relations with other parts of our experience. It is an idea "upon which we can ride." It carries us competently "from any one part of our experience to any other part, linking things satisfactorily, working securely, simplifying, saving labor."

Critics repeatedly have charged this theory of truth with subjectivism. Throughout his essays James tries to show that "workability" and "expediency" are related to the "real" world of experience. It is not a matter simply of private whim or subjective feeling. Truth is what facilitates harmonious and satisfactory relations between experiences. True ideas must prove consistent with other ideas. That only is true which can be assimilated, validated, corroborated, and verified.

John Dewey went farther than William James in applying pragmatism to education. The classic statement in this regard is his book *Democracy and Education.* In terms of educational theory many of the basic insights of pragmatism gained their most pointed application. Education is not a matter of communicating static materials to timeless minds and souls. Movement and activity are presupposed both from the side of the learner and that of the teacher. To be sure, the pupil is a creative center of experience, but he is vitally caught up in the life process with its biological, psychological, and sociological aspects. The student is a total organism who participates in distinctively human meanings and values. Education is an experimental process aiming at enlarged experiences and social efficiency. Learning arises in connection with indeterminate situations. Effective teaching relates to the tension situations where familiar habit patterns and beliefs no longer suffice. Tentative solutions, in the form of imagined patterns of action, are aroused and put to test.

Education is open-ended, seeking in the broadest sense to facilitate ongoing growth and creativity. Although subject matter as such is secondary to this process, it is nevertheless important and necessary. The pragmatist orientation in education is opposed to rigid formalization and stereotyped patterns of dealing with content. However, the assembling and assimilating of facts are encouraged, especially insofar as the materials help mark out tensions and uncertainties in human growth, speak relevantly to problem situations, and contribute constructively to the ongoing development of the learner.

The contemporary Christian education movement has been deeply influenced by pragmatism in terms of both basic philosophy and program. In recent decades, however, new directions have appeared, particularly stimulated by neoorthodox theology. Karl Barth, a key spokesman in this regard, has challenged the Christian church to reaffirm its deeper Biblical and theological grounding. The "truth" revealed in Jesus Christ is normative in relation to the "truth" that may be apprehended and tested pragmatically. The starting point for Christian education is not general experience, but the specific experience of the learner in relation to God's revelation in Christ. Without necessarily repudiating pragmatism in all respects, those who have followed Barth's lead increasingly have brought to Christian education a more specifically Biblical orientation.

— *Warren F. Groff*

PRAYER   Prayer is one of the oldest of all human forms of expression. From the very beginning man has felt a need to placate, court, or communicate with the divinities that he has assumed to be present about him. Out of this pristine deference before the face of mystery there has developed, in the long course of time, a multitude of religious ceremonies, sacrifices, liturgies, arts, and acts of personal devotion.

In a preliminary way, prayer may be defined as man's response to any of God's infinitely varied revelations of himself. It would not be necessary to specify precisely what is meant by the word "God," or even to accept a systematic creed in order to give such response. But to pray it is essential that one believe in the existence of the Divine, be aware of his presence and activity, and give him some sort of free-willed assent. Prayer is therefore at once faith, perception, and reaction. It may clothe itself in prescribed formulas, spontaneous utterance, wordless outpourings of love, or the offering even of life itself.

All historic civilizations seem to have cultivated prayer. From the obscure days of early Hinduism, as long ago as 1500 B.C., has come a collection of exalted Vedic hymns. In Egypt, not long after this, the Aten psalms were composed, forming an eloquent expression of devotion to the living Lord. The Old Testament, even in its most venerable sections, abounds in references to prayer. Socrates prayed, and talked frequently of his companionship with God. Romans, Germanic tribes, dwellers in the isles of the sea and depths of inland jungles have included praying people.

Although in recent times a considerable segment of men have renounced prayer as superstition, the majority — including Christians, Muslims, Hebrews, Hindus, and other groups — still practice it gladly. Even Buddhism, which in its purity does not clearly acknowledge any god, seems at times to approximate deistic devotions. Most Buddhists seek to lose themselves, through meditation, in the timeless, nonassertive all-inclusiveness of Nirvana, while Hebrew and Christian prayer put the worshiper into intimate intercourse with a very present Father, with whom one may speak "as a man speaks to his friend."

To Christians and others who postulate a single and personal God, prayer is the very soul of religion. For followers of Jesus, God is known not only in his creative acts in nature and in the inner stillness of their own spirits, but also in the life, character, teachings, consciousness, sufferings, death, resurrection, and redemptive work of Jesus Christ, and in the history, sacraments, and services of his body, the church. Christian prayer is directed — to use a classic phrase — " to the Father, by the Spirit, through the Son." Jesus himself prayed often and gave us his own prayer as our model. Among his teachings are many words dealing with prayer, the chief stress being upon the necessity for sincerity, simplicity, and complete faith. " Pray without ceasing," said Paul; and by that he must have meant that anything felt, thought, said, or done in conscious companionship with God through Christ is prayer.

Christian prayer may be either individual or social in form. Although it is difficult to disconnect the 2, we are here primarily concerned with its private aspects. There are as many settings and attitudes of individual worship as there are individuals. One may pray alone in church or chapel, or while walking, standing upon a solitary beach, riding in a jet plane, working in a shop or kitchen, or behind the shut doors of one's " closet." One may stand, sit, kneel, lie in bed, close or open the eyes, clasp the hands, lower or raise head and arms, smile or shed tears.

At times a season of preparation may seem helpful or even necessary, reminding the worshiper that he is standing before the all-splendored Presence. Among aids here, Bible study may be mentioned, as well as recourse to the hymnal, Creed, inspired music or poetry, or the contemplation of a painting or sculpture by some spiritually perceptive artist.

In the prayer itself, a great variety of helps and procedures is available. The use of words from the Bible (particularly the psalms), the hymnal, or one of the several historic prayerbooks, an anthology of contemporary prayers and collects, or a devotional manual may be counted on to stimulate worship. (By " collect " is meant a brief topical prayer, generally in 1 sentence of 5 parts: " O . . . God, — who . . . , — grant us . . . , — in order that . . . , — through Jesus Christ our Lord.")

To many persons set schedules and devices are helpful. The sanctifying of daily and weekly times goes back through the earliest Eastern churches to ancient Hebrew tradition. Eight periods of devotion a day are called for by the Roman Catholic breviary. Though nonmonastic priests have a degree of liberty in adjusting these " hours," their methodical repetition is obligatory upon all Roman clergy. In praying, it is undoubtedly beneficial to arrange one's thoughts in logical categories, perhaps corresponding to liturgical formulations such as: adoration, confession, thanksgiving, meditation, petition (for self), intercession (for others), and dedication. (The terms " petition," " intercession," and " supplication " are partially interchangeable.) Often a list of objects or persons to be prayed for is kept. Such contrivances avail as reminders, to hold attention, and to provide a healthy balance of thought.

Many of the saints recommend ejaculatory prayers — snatches of adoration or praise, phrases of the Lord's Prayer or verses of psalms — uttered or silently repeated between items of business, or upon seeing some unusual sight, or hearing a child's laughter. A modern mystic suggests that we articulate brief prayers for those whom we pass on the street, and this idea is suggestive also for other relationships or encounters.

But whether upon regular or upon variable occasions, a Christian may ignore all form and speak joyfully to God at any time, using any words, in unpremeditated freedom. Or one may altogether banish desires, relax both mentally and bodily tensions, place one's self completely in God's hands, enter into the inmost sanctuary of silence, and wait, as the Friends do, in serene expectancy for God's surging influx. Many methods of prayer open themselves before a trusting soul; nor need he confine himself to any one but may freely give proof to all.

Most contemporary students of prayer warn us that it should never be used to attempt to manipulate God for our own ends. Humble in our approach, we must keep on repeating, "Not my will, but thine, be done." Yet surely God desires that we should at all times be eager to share with him not only our joys, sins, and sorrows, but also our hopes for ourselves and others. Anything that can be sincerely requested through Jesus Christ (that is, through the sieve of his acts and purposes) is a legitimate object of Christian prayer. We may rest in complete confidence that God will be found on the side of justice, peace, happiness, and health. He is never neutral and always our Father.

Nor may we look upon prayer as an exercise in pedagogy or personality enlargement. Though we should teach our children how to pray, we may not " use " prayer as a method of teaching. Prayer does, to be sure, have its inevitable results upon the pray-er. Even adoration, which asks for nothing but only exalts God, ministers to the author's religious development. It raises sights and sets ideals. " The fruit of the Spirit is love, joy, peace, patience, kindness, goodness, faithfulness, gentleness, self-control." It also steeps us in Biblical thought and language, draws us into fellowship with all men, and unquestionably teaches us many truths. But these effects are indirect and incidental. True prayer is friendship with God, and friendship is never a means to an end. The knowledge of God is life itself. Man can have no higher joy than this.

— *Richard H. Ritter*

PREACHING Preaching is the forthtelling of the Word of God, in the church or in the world, by one who has accepted that Word and has been renewed by it. What is the word of God? It is the saving activity of God through which, of his own free will, he seeks to bring man into right relations with Himself and thus into right relations with his fellows. This was always God's effective purpose in both the Old Testament and the New. For the Christian, such saving activity is uniquely demonstrated in the life, death, and resurrection of his Son, Jesus Christ. It is continued within the church by the working of the Holy Spirit. This Word is the eternal good news which the sermon, preached and heard, makes contemporary. For the sermon is the joint enterprise of speaker and listener. As a baseball pitcher requires a catcher to be effective, so the pitcher in the pulpit needs the catcher in the pew.

There are 3 aspects to this preaching. The 1st is "kerygma," a word that has been sadly abused by many of its users. It is popularly conceived as the preaching of the gospel at a normal diet of corporate worship. If C. H. Dodd is to be believed, this is not the New Testament usage. Kerygma is, for him "the public proclamation of Christianity to the non-Christian world" (*The Apostolic Preaching and Its Developments*, p. 2). It may be true that many church members are not Christian in any complete sense of the term. But if they have confessed with their lips that Jesus is Lord, believing in their hearts that God raised him from the dead (Rom. 10:9), if they have been baptized, and if they receive the sacrament of the Lord's Supper, then they are not prime representatives of the non-Christian world ready for the kerygma. The gospel (*euangelion*) has still to be preached to them. But *kērygma* is certainly not the New Testament word to describe the sermon, within a sanctuary, at 11 A.M. or 7:30 P.M. on the Lord's Day. The place for the kerygma is the street corner, the marketplace, in pool halls, saloons, civic clubs, and all of life. Yet it is important for the church to remember that the whole service of corporate worship — not the sermon, but the liturgical gamut from adoration to benediction — may be kerygma to some non-Christian who drops in on the service.

The 2d aspect is preaching whose specific intent is to revitalize the faith of the believer, the reviving of those once "vived." C. H. Dodd refers to this as *paraklēsis* or *homilia:* "Much of our preaching in church at the present day would not have been recognized by the early Christians as *kērygma*. It is teaching, or exhortation (*paraklēsis*), or it is what they called *homilia*, that is, the more or less informal discussion of various aspects of Christian life and thought, addressed to a congregation already established in the faith" (*ibid.*). This is valid preaching, provided one knows when to use it. It is appropriate on the "high" days of the Christian year, when the occasion is to recall the great moments in the life of our Lord. *Paraklēsis* may well be the type of homiletical emphasis at an evening service when the more saintly saints gather to worship. It is surely the distinctive feature of the meditation at the Lord's Supper. It is right and good for the minister to voice the beliefs of the congregation that longs for words to express itself. He makes patent from the pulpit what is latent in the pew. He reminds his flock of something loved long since and, maybe, lost awhile.

The 3d aspect — a most important one, too often absent in contemporary preaching — is teaching: the sermon to explain, to instruct, to give lessons for the faith professed. It may be unscholarly to apply the word *didachē* to this kind of sermon, for Dodd has quite rigorously distinguished preaching from teaching in the New Testament. He does not minimize the latter; he merely raises doubts as to subsuming it under preaching (*op. cit.*, pp. 1–3). Inasmuch as "preaching" is not limited to kerygma in this article, the instructional sermon, the purpose of which is not to remind the listener of something already accepted but to explicate the gospel with specificity in the areas of belief and action, is accepted as one valid way of preaching. The history of the pulpit would back such a conclusion. Jesus came "teaching and preaching," and it is not always easy to separate one activity from the other. Moreover, the verse "And he opened his mouth and taught them, saying" is the preface to what the church calls The Sermon on the Mount! The gospel requires explanation and application because it is neither easily grasped nor obviously implemented in our culture. Doctrine has to be imparted, for *doctrina* is "teaching." Doctrinal preaching is teaching-preaching. Lasting inspiration is usually the result of good pedagogy. There is still virtue in the designation of the minister as the "teaching and preaching elder," and there is no law that the pulpit should not be the place of both or, better, that the 2 should not be interwoven, on occasion, in the sermon. The New Testament insists that those brought into the church by kerygma, and encouraged by *paraklēsis,* had better be instructed in the meaning of the faith and in the ethical obligations of the new life. The Bible class, the minister's study course, and the like are normal places for *didachē.* But if it is localized there, many members will never be taught. They will be proclaimed to or exhorted or admonished (or scolded!) from the pulpit.

Preaching, for all involved, is dependent on 3 interrelated and cooperating branches of homiletical study: exegesis, exposition, and application. Exegesis is the critical analysis of an expression of the Word of God in its geographical, political, and cultural setting. It rigorously endeavors to discover what that particular Word meant to the person who heard it — to Abraham, Moses, David, Isaiah, Jesus, Paul, Augustine, Calvin, Luther, Wesley, Barth, Bultmann. This requires the continued and continual use of the discipline of theological training — linguistic, literary, historical — so that one may understand the religious mind-set of the hearer and interpreter in his own time and place. The 2d step is exposition: the endeavor to elucidate the eternal message set in this historical Word in an effort to find its repeated validity down the centuries. Is it a Word regularly returned to by later generations? Is it a Word that is modified by deeper insights or changing environment? What is at the very heart of it for all time? Some preachers do good work on exegesis and exposition, but their sermons seldom come home to the hearer. Why? Because they forget the essential 3d step: application. This is the conscious, contemporary setting of the Word discovered by exegesis and refined by exposition in the immediate here-and-now situation of the preacher and the hearer. It is the eternal Word made embarrassingly or winsomely, but obviously, relevant for our day and generation. This is the homiletical corollary of the doctrine of the incarnation. The everlasting Word becomes pertinent in these times, for these times, as the Word once became flesh in a Galilean Jew in the early years of the Christian era. God is given a chance to effect this if the minister in his study will honestly wrestle with these 3 ways of discovering and elucidating the Word of God. Exegesis analyzes the "then"; exposition makes clear the "always"; application asks about the "now."

Preaching is one channel for the continuing of the Word, the making current of what was once, and again, and again, an effective Word of

God, to the end that man may be saved, made healthy, by hearing and absorbing and living it now. Such preaching is the Word of God.

— *James T. Cleland*

PRESBYTERIAN CHURCH IN CANADA The life and history of the Presbyterian Church in Canada have been formed by the strong forces of Reformed theology and government. The dominant streams flowed from the Reformation in Switzerland, France, and Scotland. The 1st Presbyterians in Canada were French Huguenots. They were followed by Scottish and Irish Presbyterians who brought with them the vigorous faith of their churches. Enrichment and strength came from people and leaders of other Reformed churches at various periods in history.

In matters of doctrine the Presbyterian Church in Canada believes the Scriptures of the Old and New Testaments to be the Word of God written, and constituting the canon of all doctrine by which Jesus Christ rules the faith and life of the church. The work of God's grace is recognized and accepted in the subordinate Standards, which include the Westminster Confession of Faith and the ecumenical and Reformed creeds and confessions.

Christian education occupies a central place in the fellowship of Christians. It is the teaching ministry by which they are prepared and equipped to fulfill the Christ-given mission of the church.

Christian education is rooted in the Reformed doctrines of the Word of God, the nature and mission of the church, man, and the world. It accepts advanced educational principles consistent with the church's doctrine of man and the doctrine of the nature of Biblical witness. It uses educational methods which take into account the whole person at each stage of his growth and which assist persons to be open to the work of the Holy Spirit.

By action of the General Assembly the *Christian Faith and Life* curriculum of The United Presbyterian Church in the U.S.A. is approved for use in the home, nursery, and kindergarten and primary departments of the church school. The Assembly's Board of Christian Education produces curriculum for use in all other departments and study programs for weekday groups for all ages.

The Boards of the General Assembly and the theological seminaries are now engaged in the study of a new curriculum, not for the church school only, but for the total membership of the church.

— *James S. Clarke*

PRESBYTERIAN CHURCH IN THE U.S. The Presbyterian Church in the United States (in this article to be called the Presbyterian Church) was organized Dec. 4, 1861, at Augusta, Georgia. Its history goes back to the earliest records of Presbyterianism in the 13 colonies, and is inseparably related to the mainstream of Presbyterianism in the U.S.A.

The Presbyterian Church is a confessional church. Its doctrines are stated in the Westminster Confession of Faith, and the Larger and Shorter Catechisms. Its Form of Government, Rules of Discipline, and Directory for Worship are set forth in the *Book of Church Order,* revised and approved by the 1961 General Assembly. These doctrines have their historic roots in the Protestant Reformation.

The General Assembly of the Presbyterian Church elects a board of 24 members, consisting of ministers, lay men and women to direct, develop, and promote Christian education. The Board elects a staff to carry out its policies, develop a program, edit material, and recommend procedures for its program of work.

A new curriculum is now being created by the Board and will be offered the church on Oct. 1, 1964. A group of theologians, educators, and churchmen was asked by the Board to undertake a study *de novo* in 1955 and define what Christian education ought to be in churches holding to the Reformed faith. Their findings were summarized in a paper entitled " Christian Education Within the Covenant Community — the Church." This paper was approved in 1959. The new curriculum, entitled *The Covenant Life Curriculum,* will be based upon that study and reflect the principles it sets forth. The central theme of the curriculum will be the Biblical doctrine of the covenant in which God calls man to a life of fellowship with him, a fellowship to be marked by faith in and loving obedience to God. A strong emphasis will be placed upon the study of the Bible as a witness and instrument of revelation.

The new curriculum is based on the fact that Christian education takes place in the home, the church, and the church school. Materials are being prepared to assist these 3 groups to perform the role expected of them.

Materials for use in the church school will be organized around 3 annual themes: " The Drama of Redemption (The One Story of the Bible)"; " The Covenant People (The Church)"; and " Christian Life (Life Under the Lordship of Christ)." The educational philosophy of *The Covenant Life Curriculum* is that the contents of Scripture and the message of the church are to be studied as dynamic truth given by God to lead men into the deepest relationship of faith in God and into a responsible relationship with man.

The Covenant Life Curriculum will also feature the education of adults. Only when adults have a greater knowledge of divine truth, a deeper Christian experience, and are more thoroughly committed to the mission Christ has entrusted to the church in the world, can there be any improvement in Christian education in the family or for children and youth in the church school.

Christian higher education, also under the direction of the Board, is a vital phase of Christian education. The church college is regarded as the church on mission through higher education. The Board assists colleges in developing their programs so they may offer excellent academic instruction and provide adequate facilities for students in the field of liberal arts. A program of study in Christian truth and doctrine is provided faculty and students in state colleges.

— *Marshall C. Dendy*

PRIMARY DEPARTMENT The primary department of the church school is the organization through which the church endeavors to serve those children within the fellowship who are 6, 7, and 8 years of age and attending 1st, 2d, and 3d grade in day school. Its purpose is to provide for the Christian education of children of these ages or grades, guiding them into the fullest and most meaningful relationship to God, Jesus, the Bible, the church, and others, as well as helping them to achieve the greatest degree of personal Christian growth of which they are capable.

In the years between their 6th and 9th birthdays children grow steadily but unevenly. They are becoming independent and want to do things for themselves. They like to work and play with other children. They are active physically and their social life expands rapidly. Their enthusiasm and interest often lead them into more than they can accomplish and they tire easily. No 2 children are quite alike. In addition to food, clothing, and shelter, all children need to feel loved, secure, recognized, and approved. They need to feel that they belong, and to have self-respect as individuals. They need opportunities to achieve something for themselves. These needs motivate their actions. They greatly influence our teaching, which must take them into account realistically if it is to be effective.

The organization of the primary department varies with the size of the church, the number of children, and the space and leadership available. The superintendent is the executive in the primary department regardless of the details of grouping followed within the department. It is he who represents the department in the church's committee on children's work, and who coordinates the work of the various classes or groups within the department.

In larger churches a variety of groupings may be found:

1. The department plan is the traditional plan for primary departments. It appears in 2 forms, the group plan and the class plan. The group plan is more often followed where the entire primary group is less than 12 children. Then the group often meets as 1 class taught by the superintendent, who sometimes has 1 or 2 helpers for guiding pupil committees or smaller interest groups. The class plan is usually found where the number of children makes it possible to have 1 class for each grade or age, boys and girls together. The major time is spent in classwork, each class with its own regular teacher, with the whole department meeting for some activities such as worship, but not necessarily every Sunday.

2. The single-grade plan is desirable when the church can provide adequate space and leadership and when the attendance in each grade is as high as 25 to 30 children. Under this plan each grade has its own superintendent or leading teacher with 1 or more helpers who work with him as a team to guide interest groups or committees and to carry out projects in line with their special abilities and interests. The department meets in its own room for its full program each Sunday, but occasionally shares in some activities with the total primary department.

3. The 2-grade plan in which only 1st and 2d grades (ages 6 and 7) are grouped in the primary department is growing in popularity, especially where the group plan of teaching is used. The advantage over the more traditional plan of 3 grades cannot be missed by those who recognize the difficulty of meeting the needs of the 1st-grader and the 3d-grader with any one program.

In smaller churches the superintendent of the primary department may be the teacher of the only primary class. To determine who will be in this class requires study of the number of children and the possible ways of grouping them to avoid wide age ranges within any 1 group.

It may include grades 1 to 3 if there are only a few children of these ages or only grades 1 and 2 if there are enough to follow the 2-grade plan. Or there may be no primary class as such but, rather, a class for younger children and 1 for older children.

Basic to the teaching-learning experience are the ways in which children learn: (1) through their senses — smelling, tasting, hearing, seeing, touching; (2) through imitation of ways of living observed; (3) through experience — learning by doing involves the most thorough kind of learning; (4) through relationships — learning through living with other people.

The room in which children meet does its share of teaching, good or bad. A room that is attractive, light, and well-ventilated, furnished with good sturdy furniture and work equipment of the proper size to fit the children tells them that what goes on at church is important and worthy of the best. It therefore challenges their best efforts and interest in return. Such a room does much to help create a climate in which children can grow naturally.

Mature, friendly, thoroughly dedicated Christian teachers who are relaxed and have time to answer questions and listen to what each child wants to say do much to assure that a good teaching-learning experience will be under way as soon as the 1st child arrives.

Good curriculum materials, carefully planned and prepared to meet the special needs and abilities of primary children, are necessary tools for the teaching-learning experience. The wise teacher uses them as tools, and plans for the special needs of his own group of children.

The traditional plan whereby 1 teacher has a class within the primary department that he teaches every Sunday is still common in many churches. Another plan in which the department has a group of teachers who work as a team from week to week, each one guiding the children in a special type of activity, is developing in a variety of patterns. In team teaching, the teachers plan together, agree on their purpose and procedures, and divide the responsibilities. They may rotate among the smaller groups or classes to guide them in special projects such as music, painting, constructive activities, or creative writing.

The variety of activities and teaching techniques used in the primary department is limited only by the imagination and skill of the teachers. Among the most basic and commonly found are conversation and discussion, storytelling (once the major method but now only 1 of many), creative dramatics (including pantomime, role-playing, play-making, and often the use of puppets), the creative arts (such as writing, painting, music, and rhythmic expression), research, interviews, trips and excursions, sharing enterprises. The test of whether any procedure should be used in the primary department always must be the question, Will it help to achieve the purpose for our teaching today? Activity that is merely busywork has no place.

Through the early years the 1 hour of Sunday school was usually the entire educational program of the church. Long ago, however, the need for more time was recognized by leaders of children. The expanded session of the Sunday church school, 2 to 3 hours in length, instead of the traditional hour, provides a far better opportunity for effective teaching. This is 1 session with 1 purpose. It has the distinct advantage of more time for leisurely work on a variety of activities that provide for an enriched program of learning.

— *Elizabeth Tibbals McDowell*

PRIVATE SCHOOLS AND RELIGION

The private secondary school today accounts for over 77,000 students in attendance at more than 590 institutions. These statistics, obtained from the Council for Religion in Independent Schools, do not take into account the very sizable number of students involved in Roman Catholic secondary schools. Although accurate figures are not available, it is estimated by the Information Service of the Bureau of Research and Survey of the National Council of the Churches of Christ in the U.S.A. that more than 5,000,000 children attend some private educational institution at the secondary level.

The sizable enrollment of students in the private schools (most of which are denominationally related) is of significance for the religious educator. Because of the historic concern for the separation of church and state, the public school is severely limited, religiously speaking, in both its offering and its observance. The contemporary fetish of absolute separatism appears to tend more toward abolition than distinction. The private school, on the other hand, within the limitations of its charter, has the freedom to incorporate into both its curriculum and its corporate life as much or as little religion as it chooses. For the most part, curriculum offerings of religion in the private school are limited only by the overall academic requirements and the availability of qualified teachers.

Depending on the nature of the institution, denominational, nondenominational, or affiliate, the nature and extent of formal religious observance is affected in both content and schedule. Some institutions adhere strictly to the particular denominational form of worship that is most familiar, whereas others are of a more eclectic nature, with a consequent breadth of both scope and approach. An examination of the denominational affiliations of those enrolled in private schools indicates that the ecumenical movement is experienced and at work at the secondary school level just as well if not more practically than at the level of the international conference table.

The denominational school enrolls many students from "outside" the ecclesiastical family. The religious backgrounds of these individuals and the contribution they can make to the welfare and growth of the whole cannot be disregarded. The nondenominational institution, on the other hand, cannot settle merely for the lowest common denominator. Its understanding of itself will be in direct ratio to the depth of the understanding and appreciation of each member of that community for the denominational group out of which he or she has come and the relation of that specific group to the others. There is, then, both a horizontal and a vertical dimension to effective religious communication at the level of the private secondary school. The community of interest and sharing is informed and empowered by the depth of denominational understanding. Each contributes to the other. Denominational understanding is benefited by community expression even as community expression is given substance by denominational depth.

The teaching of religion in the private schools involves a wide variety both of methodology and of materials. A representative sampling is provided by an examination of 26 representative institutions. Published by the Council for Religion in Independent Schools in August, 1958, the sample was edited by William A. Opel and is entitled *A Bibliography for Teachers of Religion in Private Schools*. The variety of course offerings is comprehensive and indicates the usual basic requirement of 1 required course in religion, with the subsequent possibility of a great range of elective choices. Particularly helpful in this bibliography are the notation of the academic year in which the particular course is offered and the primary resource material used for instruction.

This sampling of the religious curriculum may be considered as indicative of the philosophy of religion at the level of the private secondary school. This philosophy can be described as a concern to impart basic information that will complement and complete the foundation laid in the home and/or the Sunday school. The elective courses and the wide range of voluntary religious activities provide an excellent opportunity for the exercise of individual religious development and responsibility. The framework of the private secondary school thus provides a comprehensive religious program in which the student is invited and encouraged to explore and experiment under guidance and with a measure of control. The minimal compulsory requirements, the opportunity for free choice of both academic electives and individual service, have obvious merits. If during this formative period of life the individual is encouraged to examine and evaluate at his own level and on his own terms the significant relevance of religious truth, he cannot help developing a sense of responsible concern. This can and will remain with him through the questing years of college and graduate school, providing a firm foundation both for them and the hectic years of initial establishment in his chosen field of vocational endeavor. Thus, by exposure and encouragement the individual is helped to an awareness and an assumption of personal religious responsibility.

Any program of religious education at the adolescent level must take into account 2 prime factors: the pride of the individual in his or her individuality and the need of the individual for companionship and guidance. The fact that the years of adolescence are years of exploration and experimentation is as important religiously as it is intellectually and emotionally. The student must be permitted to reach and to seek. The student must be encouraged to question and to criticize. The student must be inspired to receive and to respond. Only thus can there be discovered the particularity of reference and the specific point of contact that will result in and resolve the need for personal commitment.

As the individual begins to assume the responsibility for and consequences of his or her individuality, however, there is a genuine need for companionship and communication. Truth in the broadest sense, sufficient to inspire and contain the high idealism of youth, must be revealed. There must be a recognizable framework in which religious truth is communicated in such faithfulness that it is permissive enough to allow individual exploration, yet sufficiently interpretive to maintain relevance and to hold open channels of communication from the past to the present for the benefit of the future.

Recognition and acceptance of these facts lay upon those who teach and preach at the level of the secondary school 2 prime responsibilities. The 1st of these is to be so sensitive to the seeking of individuals and so alert to the ground on which they stand that such communication as takes place will be perpetually relevant to the individual and to the age in which he or she lives. This requires on the part of the adult an involvement in the total life of not only the existing community but the prior community as well. That is to say, there must be an awareness of the various communities represented in the society of the school from which the students have come and to which they prepare to return. The existential situation is of grave concern to the adolescent. The interest of the young person in the immediate present is matched, perhaps, only by a heroic idealism. The demand by the student for specific application in terms of both principle and profession requires on the part of both teacher and preacher a comprehension of the contemporary cultural and community situation that is possible only through an active involvement in and a sensitive awareness to mood and the underlying dynamic.

The 2d responsibility is the ability and the patience to illustrate and reveal the general from and through the specific. The fundamental purpose of the secondary school is preparation in the broadest sense of the term. This implies a concern for a firm foundation upon which can be constructed a dwelling adaptable to the needs and opportunities of the particular individual. Both the foundation and the dwelling, however, must be capable of withstanding the tensions and pressures of time and temptation. In a sense, the secondary school teacher of religion plays a role similar to that of the consulting architect. He or she must anticipate and prepare the "client" to cope with a wide variety of physical, intellectual, emotional, and spiritual dangers. In view of the fact that "now we see through a glass, darkly," the responsibility of religious education in the private school is exceeded only by the opportunity and the challenge with which it is confronted.

— Allen F. Bray, III

PROBLEM–SOLVING Problem-solving as a central concept and method in religious education received its impulse from the educational philosophy of John Dewey. In contrast to the prevailing emphasis upon subject matter and teaching methods, Dewey and his school focused upon the experience of the learner and the learning process. Experience is roughly defined as the interaction of the learner with his environment. The task that life sets for every man is to make satisfactory adjustments to the physical and social world and to become in the process a mature person competent to go on meeting issues as they arise without recourse to authoritarian answers. Education, in this setting, is not primarily concerned with transmitting knowledge of the past to the present as an end in itself or of adding more data to what has already been learned. The wisdom of the past lies in its instrumental character to aid the learner in making creative adjustments and responses to present situations. However, the aim of education is not simply solving problems. It is also person-centered in that it aims at a free and democratic society made possible through the development of persons who have learned to meet the problems of life with intelligence and self-reliance.

In this view there is no need for educators to contrive problems. Life itself is the curriculum. The task of formal education is to select from the problems that arise at each state of human development pertinent issues to be resolved, and to guide the learner through the process of achieving a satisfactory solution. The emerging problems are the basis for instruction. Chapman and Counts wrote (1924) in their *Principles of Education* (p. 554): "Problems, problems, and again problems should be the basis of instruction. All the orthodox subject matter of the school should be examined to see the manner in which its essential elements can be taught around problems which grow wider and wider in their scope."

The process by which solutions are achieved is called the "scientific method," or the "project method." The problem is identified and analyzed, information is collected that bears upon the solution, action is taken toward resolving the problem, and the results are tested, evaluated, and generalized. Inasmuch as the matter at hand is something in which the learner is personally involved, it is reasonably assumed that motivation will be heightened. Equally important is the contention that thinking takes place only when automatic responses fail, i.e., when we face problems. Consequently, it is argued, education should concentrate upon those situations where thinking goes on and where it may be guided.

Leaders of the liberal religious education movement of the 1920's accepted in principle the emphasis upon experience and problem-solving that characterized progressive education. There is general agreement in the writing of George Albert Coe, William C. Bower, Harrison S. Elliott, and Ernest J. Chave that religious education should concern itself primarily with the experiences of the child, and that appreciation for Biblical literature, theology, and history should derive from their utility in guiding the learner to the solution of present problems. Insofar as many of the issues in life are of a religious character, religious education has its place alongside secular education. Bower, who defines the central approach to the learning process as "the intelligent and purposive resolution of the basic issues involved in living" (*Religious Education in the Modern Church*, p. 138), points to the continuity between secular and religious education by saying, "Secular education seeks the development of the physical, intellectual, emotional, social, aesthetic, and moral personalities; religious education would complete the process by the development of spiritual personality" (*The Educational Task of the Local Church*, p. 24).

Problem-solving as a method of education reached beyond the church school and, through the popularity of Harry Emerson Fosdick, set the pattern for preaching in many pulpits. No single piece of writing in the field of homiletics has been more influential within the last quarter century than Fosdick's article, " What Is the Matter with Preaching? " (*Harper's Magazine,* July, 1928) in which he attributes the dullness of the pulpit to wrong methodology and suggests that it may be corrected by applying the " project method " of progressive education. More recently problem-solving has become an important aspect of pastoral counseling. Although the growth of this discipline has somewhat different roots, it shares the emphasis upon learning through the resolution of personal problems and the concern for personal growth through the insight gained in the experience.

Problem-solving as an educational method was originally joined with liberalism in theology, and the question of a divorce has been a much debated issue. Although some are inclined to think that the method cannot be fully employed when claims to supernatural revelation are held, it is fair to say that the problem-solving method has affected the methodology of most religious educators, though in recent years the philosophical and theological presuppositions have undergone searching scrutiny. — *Wayne K. Clymer*

PROJECT A project may be defined as a plan, a design, or a pattern. When a person connects himself with a project, he plans or designs a course of action and carries it through. Interest and feeling of worthwhileness in the undertaking ensures effort. As the work is carried on there is constant evaluation of the progress and the outcome.

A project is never to be confused with busywork. The teacher in a 1-room school while working with 1 age group had to be sure that the rest of her charges were occupied, but unless these children felt a sense of worth in the activity provided for them, it did not keep them out of mischief.

A project is not a project unless it provides opportunity for the learner to purpose, plan, execute, or do the work, and to evaluate both the process and the result.

The name of John Dewey will ever be connected with education through the activity of the learner. In his *School and Society,* which went into 6 printings between 1899 and 1907, he says: " Out of doing things that are to produce results, and out of doing these in a social and cooperative way, there is born a discipline of its own kind and type." There followed such provocative books as *How We Think* (1909), *Interest and Effort in Education* (1917), and *Schools of Tomorrow* (1915). In the last volume he says, " Learning is a necessary incident of dealing with real situations."

William Heard Kilpatrick followed John Dewey and became the exponent of the project method while he taught philosophy of education at Teachers College, Columbia University. He defines the project method as a " learning enterprise " in his book *Remaking the Curriculum,* claiming that " it is the process itself, especially as socially conditioned, that educates," and "the principle of leading on to finer and better activities is the principle of life itself."

These theories produced " child-centered schools " in some places, although other schools clung to the teacher-dominated and subject-matter-dominated methods, thinking that learning is represented in the rote recital of words formulated by older and wiser minds. The child-centered schools encouraged a child to be a distinct personality and to believe in his own ability; they set up situations that provided constant practice in cooperative living; they encouraged activities in which each could make a contribution to group enterprises; the social experiences were graded to fit each child's level of social development; and each child was encouraged to regard himself as an accepted and respected member of a society of which he approved.

The project method influenced religious education more slowly. *The Project Principle in Religious Education*, by Erwin L. Shaver was published in 1924. " Experience is educative," says Dr. Shaver, " only in proportion to the degree in which it is entered into purposefully; only to the extent to which it is psychologically complete, giving opportunity for the learner's purposing, planning, executing, and judging; it is most educative when it is true to life; and valuable in proportion as it is social and shared."

Advocates of the project method argue that if projects are to be valuable in a program of Christian education, the purposing must be done in harmony with Christian ideals, and the Christian purpose must be completely carried out. Ideas about morality, honesty, or kindliness are not automatically transmuted into good character and conduct. A project must make a useful and needed contribution to the furthering of the Christian enterprise, and the sharing of experience must be on a Christian basis.

As children and those who are older learn together, competition between individuals or classes tends to result in unchristian habits and attitudes. Thus the Christian educator must help pupils to select enterprises that are constructive, in which pupils are set to thinking, rather than rehearsing the ideas of others, unless these ideas promote individual thinking and give opportunities for personal touch with others. The rewards for good work done should not be temporal things such as individual prizes, but the achievement of spiritual values to be shared with the working group or with some other person or group.

— *Jessie Eleanor Moore*

PROTESTANT EPISCOPAL CHURCH, THE Although Episcopalians are far from being noted for illiteracy or lack of education, the Protestant Episcopal Church has not until recent years placed very much program emphasis on church-sponsored education. Compared with other denominations, the Episcopal Church has founded and maintained very few institutions of higher learning and only since 1947 has it moved decisively to strengthen the educational program of the local parish. This apparent lack of concern for the educational function of religion has not been entirely unrelated to the fundamental nature of the Episcopal Church. Because of its Anglican heritage, it has always been a liturgy-centered communion rather than one which makes central the proclamation of the Word. Its educational life has been prone to develop around the altar and in the liturgical life of the church.

The middle decades of the 20th century have seen 3 powerful factors awaken and change the educational life of the Episcopal Church: the emergence of a revitalized Biblical theology, an intensified search for a deeper understanding of the nature of the church, and a new emphasis on the ministry of the laity. Under the impact of these forces the church, although becoming no less liturgical in its orientation, has sharpened and pushed forward its horizons both in college work and in parish education.

New developments in higher education have taken the form chiefly of strengthening existing institutions rather than creating new ones. In company with other Christian bodies Episcopalians have developed an extensive outreach to college communities designed to carry the Christian witness to both faculty and students. Some pioneer work has been done, particularly with faculty members who are communicants of the Episcopal Church.

In parish education 2 singular developments have characterized the Episcopal Church at mid-century. One has been a heavy increase in parish day schools in the decade immediately following World War II. More than 400 were founded, making this church 2d only to the Lutherans among non-Roman bodies in the U.S.A. with regard to parish schools. This is still a marginal movement affecting less than 6 percent of all Episcopal parishes, but it is noteworthy for the brief period of time in which it has taken place. It should also be noted that most of these schools were started before the Supreme Court's action on segregation and are not a reaction to this decision.

The other development in the field of parish education has been the rapid emergence of an approach to Christian education that has taken sharp issue with inherited educational objectives and procedures. Whereas education is traditionally thought of as predominantly a proc-ess of culture transmission and preparation for future experience, the new official program of the Episcopal Church gave priority to nurturing people in relation to their immediate encounter with the Triune God. In doing so, this program revealed the effect of a liturgy-centered heritage, to which its educational process was now dynamically related, while also showing the impact of Biblical theology, the doctrine of the church, and the ministry of the laity.

After more than a decade of development the purpose of this program for children, youth, and adults is now stated in twofold form, referring both to the life of the church gathered and the church scattered. It aims to help people to respond now to what God is doing in their lives and in the lives of their fellows. Further, it would do so in such a way as to enable them to become engaged now in his mission on earth. The emphasis is strongly on the " now."

The new program has manifested itself in many ways. It has probably had its most pronounced effect on the place and function of the total parish in the life of the church. Beginning with the publication of 6 basic volumes, *The Church's Teaching*, a growing emphasis was placed on adult education. Two conference designs, known as parish life conferences and parish life missions, were used by a great majority of congregations and have had a wide use in other communions both here and abroad. The effect of each was to enable an adult to find his place in the redemptive life and task of his parish church.

These same conferences were the beginning of a training methodology that was new to the churches. This was a methodology which used the findings of the social sciences, particularly those growing out of the study of small group life. Laboratories on the church and group life, modeled after the Bethel, Maine, social science laboratories, 1st appeared in 1953 in the Episcopal Church and then spread to other bodies under the aegis of the National Council of the Churches of Christ in the U.S.A. There was a broad application in all training operations of the in-service or involvement principle of learning. There was wide acceptance of the adage that maximum learning takes place via the data of one's own experience.

Perhaps the most unique characteristic of the entire program is the organizing principle employed in its teaching materials, particularly those designed for Sunday school and youth work.

The organizing principle of most curriculum materials is subject matter. The work of a given year is organized around a certain body of material such as church history or the Bible. The official curriculum materials of the Episcopal Church differ from other materials by employing an organizing principle providing the structure for the year's work but without timetable, schedule, or any predetermined sequence of activity. This organizing principle uses the religious issues that arise out of the action of God in people's lives — the demands he makes upon men and the offering of his reconciling love, followed by man's response, either positive or negative. Within the dialectic of this divine-human encounter are found the religious issues that provide the sequence and structure of this new curriculum. Although these issues are essentially the same for all per-

sons, they present themselves under various guises, depending upon the age, characteristics, and circumstances of the individual. Each graded course in the curriculum seeks to provide the teaching team with resources that have meaning in relation to the religious issues most common to the age group with which the team is working.

As the new program goes into its 2d decade it is preoccupied with enlarging and expanding its conception of training. Like other Christian bodies, most of its leadership development work has been in relation to the life of the church gathered. It has been directed toward enriching the life of response within the holy fellowship. Yet this response when full is always in significant part a response to God's demand that we carry out his will in the world beyond the warmth and security of the gathered church. Hence, the new thrust in the Episcopal Church has become training for mission in the world where the church is scattered.

It is already clear that this new training program will use some of the same methodological procedures employed in the in-church training program. There must be initial motivation for engaging in mission in daily work, the community, and the larger world. There must be a process of orientation that will enable people to discover their real situation as Christians in an unchristian culture. There must be strategy planning for coping with this situation. Finally, there must be the in-service phase of the total educational experience where Christians engaging together in tactical encounter with the situation can be helped to grow and improve their mission. To recite these 4 types of training is to restate the approach which had already characterized the leadership training program of the Episcopal Church. Yet it has never been used on any scale in the task of training for mission.

— *David R. Hunter*

PSYCHODRAMA Psychodrama is a 3-dimensional enactment of the private world of an individual. If the enactment involves an entire group and collective problems, it is a group psychodrama. In either individual or group context the underlying structure is that of the sociometric theory of interpersonal relations, and the key to the success of the drama is spontaneity. It is from spontaneous production that a clarification of problems and a change of behavior is expected.

The psychodrama employs 5 instruments: the stage space, the patient, the director, the auxiliary egos, and the audience. It focuses upon present time and immediate contacts as vehicles for demonstrating not only pathology of behavior but spontaneous, alternative possibilities as well. These possibilities are worked out in an action synthesis of emotional and cognitive responses to life situations.

The psychodrama concentrates on the content of a given production for clues as to its utilization, production in the present, expansion of free association to acting out and interacting, and translation of the therapeutic experience throughout a given volume of space.

Jacob Levy Moreno, originator of psychodrama, sociometry, and group psychotherapy, achieved perception of the group as an entity. The psychodramatic goal is the achievement of catharsis by the patient in interaction with the group. The group (i.e., the psychodrama cast and audience) share in the therapeutic potential of the patient's relationship, and share, thereby, in the cathartic experience. Psychodramatic catharsis is not only release of and from crippling emotions, it is also the achieving of perceptual and operational adequacy through dramatic test. The movement of the drama rises from reflection to action and back to reflection in an attempt to integrate the cathartic levels at a more spontaneous point than that on which the drama began.

The drama revolves about the triad of the therapist-director, the patient-protagonist, and an intermediate, supporting figure, the auxiliary ego. In the 1st phase of the drama, called the warm-up, the director must seek the emotional level of the protagonist. If dealing with a group, the focus must be on themes that will increase the sense of group entity to a point desiring group action upon representative problems of individuals, potential protagonists. At this point the action moves from audience to stage and into the task of setting the scene and the roles in sufficient detail to allow the auxiliaries and protagonist to assume them, but not so specifically as to inhibit their spontaneity.

In actual production the director employs many techniques to shape the drama. Characteristic of these are the aside, the soliloquy, role reversal, and the double. The aside and the soliloquy offer means of rationalizing resistance to a role. The aside is a commentary on the feelings of a role as it is performed. The soliloquy drops to the lower level of the stage and moves away in reflection from completed action or toward action that is anticipated. Again the concern is with the difficulty of the experience. The role reversal also deals with resistance to roles, but it goes farther, opening the unconscious content of relations by forcing an exchange of identity between auxiliaries and protagonist and multiple viewings of the experience.

The role of the double represents the overcoming of resistance interpersonally — the central drive of the production phase of the psychodrama. When the protagonist experiences difficulty with a role, auxiliaries may be sent in to help him play himself. The effectiveness of the technique depends upon the training and skill of the auxiliary. An empathetic double will register the feeling of the protagonist by assuming his bodily state and verbalizing the empathetic state he discovers. At best, however, this is a parallel warm-up to a problem. In the true double, the warm-ups merge. The auxiliary and the protagonist act as 1 person in the grip of a single, almost completely emotional experience. But they cannot remain at this level. It is the director's task to bring them and the drama as a whole from this point to an integrating and rationalizing of the impact that retains the interpersonal gains.

The degree to which the director can achieve integration is the measure of the range and effect of psychodrama. As a therapeutic education and, secondarily, as an aesthetic experience, it is an exceptionally flexible instrument, requiring great skill of its users. The classic, 3-level, circular stage and theater effects are most valuable, but the essence lies in the deep investment of 2 people in overt activity and a 3d who joins them that they may as a unit interpret and integrate the spontaneous catharsis of the interpersonal experience.

— *Dale Anton Anderson*

PSYCHOLOGICAL TESTING Psychological tests can be helpful tools in guidance and counseling. What the tests do is to take samples of an individual's behavior (depending on what one wishes to learn) — a series of candid camera shots, if you will, which, when put together, give a composite picture of the individual. Typical behavior sampled might be the ability to work with mathematical detail, reading speed and comprehension, driver reaction time, understanding mechanical relationships, attitudes toward foreigners, vocational interests, space relations ability, personality integration, etc.

The psychologist does several things with his results: diagnoses, predicts, controls. A very common example of these 3 objectives at work can be found in almost any classroom today. For example, so-called intelligence and scholastic aptitude tests might be used to diagnose an individual's educational strengths and weaknesses. Let us assume the tests diagnose superior behavior in areas of scholastic performance. The psychologist might then predict superior performance in the classroom. To control or help ensure superior performance, the individual might then be placed in a group of his peers.

Generally, when one talks about measurement, he thinks in terms of constant units of measurement. A foot, for example, is always 12 inches. Psychological measurement is not this exact. Not all the tests in psychology are quantitative. Some very useful guidance tests give only verbal descriptions of subjects — not numerical scores. Lee J. Cronbach gives us an acceptable definition: A test is a "systematic procedure for comparing the behavior of two or more individuals" (*Essentials of Psychological Testing*, p. 11). On the other hand, Noll says, "Not all methods of appraisal or evaluation in education are quantitative, but those which are not cannot properly be classified as measurement" (*Introduction to Educational Measurement*, p. 9). Thorndike once said, "If a thing exists, it exists in some amount, and if it exists in some amount, it can be measured." The hard reality is that psychology is in its infancy, and it is attempting to measure human intangibles, some of which elude exact measurement. When we use test results, therefore, they should be considered as straws in the wind — objective checks of subjective opinion. Tests are not infallible, and the more complex the behavior measured, the more difficult to get precise measures of response.

In the light of the foregoing, the reader may question, "Just how dependable are psychological tests anyway?" In an effort to refine measuring instruments the psychologist subjects his findings to statistical analyses in order to determine how reliable and how valid his tests are. A test is reliable when it is consistent with itself. For example if an individual receives an IQ score of 100 on a test today, can we be sure a similar alternate form of the test tomorrow will produce approximately the same 100 score? If the test is reliable it will not produce a 100 IQ today and a 130 IQ tomorrow. It will be consistent.

If a test measures what it is supposed to measure, we say it is valid. For example, high scores on scholastic aptitude tests such as

the College Boards should equate with strong scholastic achievement. It is the responsibility of any test maker to conduct sufficient research in the selection of his test items and in the standardization of his test to assure a reasonable degree of validity. Here again it must be kept in mind that it is relatively easy to establish the validity of, say, a mathematics aptitude test, but extremely difficult to validate a test of personality or attitude.

Psychological tests are classified in a variety of ways. The following classification is functional so that the reader may know the purposes for which tests are designed:

1. *Achievement tests.* Such tests seek to measure the individual's acquired knowledge in specific subject-matter areas such as arithmetic, language usage, history, etc. Since the individual either knows or does not know the answers (i.e., there are either right or wrong answers), achievement tests are the most reliable and valid tests we have. Typical achievement test batteries (groups of tests) are the Stanford Achievement Tests, the Metropolitan Achievement Tests, the Iowa Every-Pupils Tests of Basic Skills, Iowa Tests of Educational Development, California Achievement Tests, Cooperative General Achievement Tests.

2. *Aptitude tests.* Since we can never get inside a person we can never really know his ultimate capacity or his maximum potential in any area. We can only measure aptitude — those characteristics which develop in an individual independently of training. H. C. Warren, in his *Dictionary of Psychology*, defines aptitude as a "condition or a set of characteristics indicative of ability to learn." Aptitude tests are given,

therefore, to try to measure untrained potential with a view to predicting what might happen if training followed. There are tests of scholastic aptitude (among which are the so-called intelligence tests), mechanical aptitude, space relations aptitude, clerical aptitude, musical aptitude, art aptitude — to mention a few. Some of the better-known tests in these areas are the Stanford-Binet Test of Intelligence, the Bellevue-Wechsler Scales of Mental Ability, the American Council on Education Psychological Examinations, the Army General Classification Test, the Otis Self-administering Tests of Mental Ability, the California Short Form Test of Mental Maturity; these are all measures of so-called intelligence or scholastic aptitude. Well-known tests in other areas of special ability are the Minnesota Paper Form Board (space relations), the Bennett Test of Mechanical Comprehension (mechanical relationships), Minnesota Clerical Aptitude (speed and accuracy in handling clerical detail), the Seashore Measure of Musical Talents (pitch, rhythm, tonal memory, etc.), Meier Art Judgment Test (aesthetic judgment), the Purdue Pegboard and the O-Connor Finger and Tweezer Dexterity Tests (manual dexterity).

3. *Interest measures.* Interest inventories serve a relatively simple purpose: to measure a person's likes and dislikes in a variety of situations. What interest tests do is to compare the interests of the individual being tested with various vocational group interest patterns already established through research. The primary use of the interest inventory is to aid in the selection of courses of study and in vocational choice. Among the well-known measures of vocational interest are the Kuder Preference Record, the Strong Vocational Interest Blank, the Cleeton Vocational Interest Inventory.

4. *Personality and attitude tests.* The area of personality measurement is one of the most chaotic in all the fields of measurement; it is an area in which tests are least well-refined, yet where claims at interpretation are most boastful. Many tests currently in use are neither reliable nor valid. Hence, there is need for considerable discretion in this area of measurement. What the measures of personality attempt is to diagnose and describe the individual in terms of his personal traits — how well he relates both to himself and society. Among the better tests are the Bernreuter Personality Inventory, the Rorschach Inkblot Test, the Minnesota Multiphasic Personality Inventory, and the Murray Thematic Apperception Test. Related to the measurement of personality traits are attitude-testing and opinion surveys. These attempt to measure feelings ranging all the way from attitudes toward communism, Negroes, labor unions, peace and war, to those toward birth control, the Democratic and Republican Parties, and whether a person is in the frame of mind to make major purchases of goods such as autos, refrigerators, etc. Here again we are on shaky ground as some of the pollsters will readily confess.

Thousands of psychological tests are available. Very few of these relate directly to religion, yet for the alert clergyman and director of religious education many different kinds of tests can be aids in counseling.

Unless the church worker has had specific course work in general psychology, tests and measurements, and psychology of personality, he should refrain from the administration and attempted interpretation of psychological tests. There are willing helpers in the community: the local high school guidance counselor, the nearby college department of counseling services, and various testing bureaus approved by the Ethical Practices Committee of the National Vocational Guidance Association.

Again let it be said that psychological tests are not infallible; judgments must not be made on the basis of test results alone. However, when interpretations of tests are made in the light of other pertinent personal, educational, and vocational data, they become a valuable counseling tool.

— *Everett W. Stephens*

PSYCHOLOGY, DEPTH This term had a great vogue in the early decades of the 20th century, only to give way terminologically to the preferred term, "dynamic psychology."

The concept of a *depth* versus a superficial dimension in human behavior and experience is not new in the history of man's understanding of himself. However, what previously was sensed and expressed by poets, artists, dramatists, seers, and philosophers, came generally to be recognized by clinicians and ultimately accepted by a large number of nontechnically trained laymen. The turning point was Freud's disclosure of the unconscious, a reach of the mind inaccessible to man except indirectly through dreams, slips of the tongue, and symptoms. Through the method of psychoanalysis and subsequently derived projective psychological tests, the characteristics of the unconscious came to be familiar to experimenters and therapists, to patients, and to people who read about dynamic psychology and psychiatry.

Viewing man in depth means being aware that what appears in surface behavior may or may not correspond to what is going on at another level of his personality. It means that instead of ignoring or minimizing the apparently accidental or irrational slips of tongue or pen, unaccounted-for ideas, hallucinations, delusions, etc., the depth psychologist recognizes in them signs of unconscious mental activity that must be taken seriously. It means that an act may have more than one meaning; that what appears on the surface to be loving may be, at a deeper level, spiteful; that an overt act may fulfill a covert function, unknown to the person himself.

The question of depth may be viewed from several perspectives. One may think of depth in terms of the extent to which a given theme is archaic. The assumption is often made that the older a motif, the deeper and more basic it is in man's nature; also, the more inaccessible to consciousness and the more resistant to conscious volitional efforts to change. Whether the primeval be viewed in terms of the really archaic (phylogenetic) or in terms of the individually archaic (ontogenetic) also makes a difference in our understanding of what we mean by depth psychology. Another dimension of depth that is sometimes meant by this term is that of the repressed. Whether experimentally repressed through the use of hypnotism or spontaneously repressed through the impact of traumatic experience, the power of repression to drive memories underground is well known. Depth may also refer to the extent of regression or the movement backward on the time scale to certain aspects of ego and id stages.

Depth psychology by definition and in practice includes all the foregoing to a lesser or greater extent. Some workers would put more emphasis on genesis or origin as a factor in the psychosis, character disorder, or neurosis. Others would stress the depth of interpretation used by the therapist or analyst in reaching or modifying the state of the psyche. Still others would claim that the extent to which the psychic processes approach the somatic (perhaps even influence them, as in the case of psychosomatic illness, or constitute their direct derivative, as in the case of somatopsychic conditions) is the touchstone of depth.

Finally, some workers would view the religious dimension as the ultimate dimension of depth that they conceive as existing at the boundaries of being and nonbeing, of meaning and meaninglessness, of ultimate trust versus existential anxiety, of self-acceptance versus existential guilt.

It is interesting at this point in the 20th century that the term " depth psychology " seems to be dropping out of conventional usage. It is given scant space in dictionaries and glossaries on psychiatry and psychology. It seems to have come to mean simply a psychic level that is out of awareness, whether this be the Freudian unconscious (including the unconscious aspects of the superego and ego as well as the id) or the Jungian personal and collective unconscious or the Sullivanian selective inattention. Perhaps the term " depth " is more likely to appear by itself as modifying psychotherapy of a type that

interests itself more in the unknown than in the known, the covert than the manifest, the obscure than the clear.

Whatever the meaning of " depth " in our concepts of depth psychology, it is clear that when man is viewed in depth, he is viewed multidimensionally. This means that no single cross-section of his behavior is self-explanatory but that everything is influenced by and influences everything else. It means that man is a complex being and that what passes for evil as well as good is part of his reality that cannot be ignored but must somehow be incorporated into his complete self-discovery and self-fulfillment. It means moreover, that if human beings are to find resonance with other creatures of depth — amphibiously, to use Aldous Huxley's term — human groups and society must have access to depth perception, depth communication, and depth resistance. By the latter is meant that those who face the depths in themselves and others face a dramatic threat, one, indeed, that is even more than dramatic: it is also potentially lethal. To survive this invasion from below and within, demands neither isolation nor merger but a dynamic interrelatedness within which growth can happen. It is to this adventure that depth psychology dedicates itself. It is from this adventure that depth psychology draws its strength.

— *Earl A. Loomis, Jr.*

PSYCHOLOGY, GESTALT The term *Gestalt* is the German word meaning "form" or "pattern." In psychology it refers to the movement usually considered to have started in Europe with the work of Max Wertheimer about 1912. Influential in bringing the movement to America were Kurt Koffka, Wolfgang Köhler, and Kurt Lewin. It started as a protest against the various attempts to reduce mental experience to a collection of elements, as of stimulus-response bonds, for example, in the conceptions of the behaviorists and E. L. Thorndike. The principle may be very simply illustrated by asking the reader to imagine a collection of 4 sticks. In a pile these can readily be thought of as an aggregate of sticks, each one a stimulus to which the mental response to "stick" might be conceived to be made. But let the 4 sticks be arranged in a certain pattern, and the mental perception is that of the letter *E*. The Gestaltist would point out that the determining aspect in the perception is that of the pattern.

Prominent in the Gestalt system are certain concepts, of which the following are among the more important: (1) Figure and ground. This is simply the distinction, not unfamiliar to other schools of psychology, between what is central in the individual's mind and what is peripheral, for example, the central figures in Leonardo da Vinci's *Last Supper* as opposed to the room detail, or the action of a church liturgy as opposed to the incidental organ music. (2) Pregnance (*Prägnanz*) is the principle of form or equilibrium that is held to be inherent in every mind and disposes it to perceive stimuli this way. Closed geometric forms such as circles or squares are seen as units, whereas balanced or symmetrical figures are more likely to be perceived as unitary than unbalanced or poorly made figures. (3) Closure is a special case of the principle of pregnance. This is the tendency of the mind to correct or finish a poor gestalt so that

it demonstrates pregnance as closely as possible. Thus the gap in an unclosed ring is ignored, so that the whole is perceived as a perfect circle; the unfinished task weighs on one's mind until it is done. Probably the Gestaltist would look on the longing of the religious man to find meaning in his world through the worship of God as an illustration of this law.

To prove their theories, Gestalt psychologists have devised many experiments. Köhler trained hens to find grain spread on the darker of 2 papers. Thus the hens would approach a paper of a certain shade when it was darker than another but would avoid the same piece of paper when it was lighter than a neighboring piece. From these results Köhler argued that it was the configuration of the total situation that determined the perception of the hens. If stimulus-response psychology is right, the hens should have pecked at the same piece of paper regardless of the shade of the neighboring sheets. Again, in experiments with chimpanzees, a stick was placed inside an animal's cage and a banana outside the cage just beyond reach. At first there would be futile attempts to get the banana. Eventually the situation would be perceived correctly, sometimes after a period of seeming inactivity. The chimpanzee appeared to "put the various elements together" suddenly, then reached out with the stick to push the banana within reach.

Kurt Lewin demonstrated Gestalt principles with human subjects. In one he showed that children were more apt to remember tasks they had left unfinished than those that had been completed. This was explained as demonstrating the principle of pregnance. Since to finish a task is to relax tension and therefore to complete closure, the uncompleted task is more apt to be remembered through the stresses set up by pressure toward closure.

Though insight is not a term invented by Gestalt psychology, nevertheless this school has brought it into prominence, sometimes as a descriptive term and sometimes as an explanatory principle. As has been said, in many of the experiments with chimpanzees the animal seemed suddenly to comprehend the situation and solve its problem with no false moves. In the same way, say Gestaltists, human beings solve more complex problems. While non-Gestaltists have no objection to the term "insight" as a descriptive term, they tend to balk at it as an explanatory principle. It smacks of mysticism or intuition, they say, and their scientific gorges rise at the thought that psychology may be accused of being vague and fuzzy.

Nevertheless, Gestalt psychology has been a creative force in Western psychology. It has called psychological preconceptions into question in such a way as to refine and sharpen psychological theory, and it has led to much fruitful experimentation. For example, a number of Thorndike's experiments were devised in such a way as to test and take into consideration Gestalt principles and criticism. His early, naïve formulation of the law of exercise, which simply stated in effect that repetition improves learning, was revised to include the idea of meaning. Repetition, he concluded, improves learning only in conjunction with meaning or insight. We see, then, that Gestalt psychology has tended toward enriching psychology by calling attention to more complex mental processes.

Such enrichment has its implications for the psychological study of religion, for religion is a complex process. This is not to say that Gestalt psychology has paid any more attention to religion proper than most other psychological schools. Nevertheless, in studying the larger masses of mental processes and behavior it has opened the way for a more hospitable treatment of religion by psychology, particularly religion's more inward and essential aspects.

Then, through its influence on general education, it has indirectly influenced religious education. In general education Gestalt's effect has been to diminish emphasis on mechanical drill and to draw teachers' attention to broader principles in learning. Many experiments have demonstrated the superiority of memorizing with understanding over mere rote. Also, it has been clearly proved that tasks that are learned with insight can much more readily be generalized so that the skills gained can be transferred to other and different situations. In another field the researches of Kurt Lewin have demonstrated that personality changes in the child are affected not so much by forces acting singly but rather by a complex of forces acting together and on one another.

In the field of religious education these findings have led to the decline of the old-fashioned practice of requiring the child simply to rote memorize such things as the books of the Bible, Bible verses, and catechetical responses. Even when such practices survive, there has been an increase in the attaching of meaning to the exercise and its contents. At the same time there has come an increase in the emphasis on discussion in church schools, increasing thereby the chances for transfer to life situations. Also, more attention has been paid to meaningful goals as opposed to artificial motivating devices such as medals and honor rolls.

The work of Lewin and those in his tradition has led to the insistence by religious educators that the church school treat the child as a whole person. Among the many factors operating on his personality are the influences of his home, school, peers, and community. Learning must be not only conceptual and factual in nature but also emotional and attitudinal. Thus it has been realized that relationships are important: the personality of the teacher may be more important than what he teaches; theological pietisms are hollow without the practical demonstration of Christian love in groups and between persons.

It would be too much to ascribe all such changes in religious education practice to the influence of Gestalt psychology, for such principles have been known by keen educational theorists through the centuries. But there is no doubt that the vigorous Gestalt tradition has left its mark on the teaching ministry of the church.

— *Walter Houston Clark*

PSYCHOLOGY OF RELIGION The psychology of religion appeared as a field of special study just before the present century began. One of its founders, G. Stanley Hall, was concerned with development in adolescents; another, Edwin D. Starbuck, studied sudden conversion experiences in teen-agers. The classic early work, mainly responsible for lifting the psychology of religion to fame, was William James's *Varieties of Religious Experience*, published early in this century. Part of James's intent is suggested by his title. He gave some attention to conversion and adolescent religious development, but also attempted to mark out a potential psychological section of a "science of religions," a term then widely used in Europe. A remarkable feature of James's book was his use of cases. Even though these were taken from publications and manuscripts, they brought concrete life to the entire inquiry, and made his theory exciting.

Another pioneer was J. H. Leuba, in whose writings there was often a debunking tone toward religion, but whose scholarship commanded respect. Then came a considerable group of persons, including E. S. Ames, Irving King, and G. M. Stratton, who took the psychology of their day and examined such religious topics as conversion, worship, prayer, mysticism, and belief. They and most of the subsequent writers were more sympathetic to religion than Leuba had been.

The last of the pioneers in this field in America were George Albert Coe and J. B. Pratt. Coe's special concerns involved both the psychology of religion and religious education; he did more to consider the relation between them than anyone else. His book *The Psychology of Religion* (1916) is still worth reading. Pratt's work *The Religious Consciousness* (1920) was oriented in a more philosophical direction. At a minimum, the modern religious educator will want to be familiar with James and Coe.

During the 1920's a large number of general books on the psychology of religion was published, of which the best were probably by R. H. Thouless (1923) and E. S. Conklin (1929). None, however, broke much new ground. With the large amount of attention given to psychological analysis of religion, a new kind of approach was given by Sigmund Freud, especially during the 1920's. Although Freud attacked religion as the principal enemy of science, he brought a wealth of specific insights to phenomena such as religious ritual. Still more important, his dynamic psychology, which has made all modern psychologies dynamic even if they disagree with him, made possible a new kind of psychological inquiry about religion in which the significance of unconscious as well as conscious factors could be recognized. Carl G. Jung's psychology includes very far-reaching religious dimensions, but for many complex reasons has not become widely understood either by psychologists or by religionists. Indeed, definitive works interpreting the contributions of both Freud and Jung to the psychological understanding of religion are yet to be written, although they are much needed.

A genuinely new field for research was set forth by Anton T. Boisen in *The Exploration of the Inner World* (1936). Boisen held that some forms of religious experience were akin to some forms of mental illness, and presented many cases of both to demonstrate his thesis. He also did much to foster direct case study as a method in the psychological study of religion. H. N. and R. W. Wieman, about the same time, set forth what they called a "normative" psychology of religion. This was the precursor of some modern work that attempts to discover the proper relationships between psychology and theology, as was an early work by Walter M. Horton (1931).

The best recent works on the psychology of religion are by Gordon W. Allport (1950), Walter Houston Clark (1958), Paul E. Johnson (1959), and Orlo Strunk, Jr. (1959). However, much of the best work that has been done to elucidate the ways in which psychological data and methods may illuminate the understanding of religion tends now to appear under other headings than " psychology of religion." " Pastoral psychology " has become a much used term to indicate study of the ways in which psychology can illumine pastoral and church practice and the theory underlying it. The relation between religion and personality, religion and psychiatry, theology and psychology, are but some of the ways in which exploration is now proceeding. The largest amount of current study is being done either clinically (through case studies and the like) or developmentally (such as the excellent work of the late Lewis J. Sherrill). Despite some good early leads given to potential experimental work by persons such as Ernest J. Chave and Hugh Hartshorne, very little actual work of this kind is now going on. Much more is needed, and a group of able young psychologists is beginning to set its hand to this promising field that now has more potential tools than in the pioneer days.

The early pioneers in the psychology of religion were, for the most part, psychologists with a concern for religious phenomena rather than clergymen, theologians, or professional religious workers. As the potential and widely ranging significance of psychological data and methods have become clearer in recent years, much of the work in the general area has been carried out by religious professionals. During the same period there was a decreasing tendency for professional psychologists to concern themselves with the study of religion. Fortunately, there is now a new beginning at making the study of religion respectable among psychologists. Both groups are needed. Research and inquiry are needed on various levels and from various points of view. As this takes place, a new and more comprehensive kind of psychological understanding of religion should emerge. — *Seward Hiltner*

PUBLIC RELATIONS Millions of people of all ages are involved in the Protestant church schools of America on an almost entirely voluntary basis. No one is compelled to attend or teach. The immediate rewards are scant. Such an institution is dependent upon goodwill. Satisfactory public relations are essential to its continued life.

Once it was assumed that the assembling of multitudes of children and adults to study the Bible could not help but do good. This attitude persists in the South and in many rural regions, but skepticism as to the automatic blessings conferred by the church school increases as we go from the South and West to the East and North, from the country to the city. Most people are now at least somewhat disillusioned as to the effectiveness of the formal religious training offered by our churches on Sunday morning.

Little has been done to improve the popular conception of the teaching methods used by Protestantism. No one has dared tackle this problem on a national basis. The change of name from Sunday school to church school was promoted in the hope of dissipating some of the less fortunate associations with the former. The increasing stature of the church has reflected a certain luster on the church school. The old jokes about the Sunday school seem to be dying out. Yet it can fairly be said that the general public is quite indifferent to the church school. Many intelligent people are oblivious to its existence.

Much of this attitude carries over into the church itself. There are denominations in which the Sunday school is central and the church service incidental and almost an afterthought, but they are not the ones that set the tone of American church life. In most congregations the church school is the concern of the few rather than of the many.

The growing number of children and expanding ideas as to the conditions under which they can best be taught have compelled those who work in the church school to turn to their fellow church members for the financial means with which to provide better facilities. Usually the people with many children have little money, whereas those who are rich in this world's goods are past the child-bearing stage of life. To get the dollars that it needs, the church school commonly has to prove its case. This is often done through special programs in which the children participate and through exhibitions of the handwork which they may have done. Brochures produced in connection with money-raising campaigns are another means of communicating with the congregation as to the nature of the church school. Overcrowding can usually be portrayed through pictures, but there is need for an equally vivid presentation of the newer ways of working with children.

The most difficult problem connected with the church school is the recruiting of teachers. The need for both more and better teachers is often desperate. Essentially it is a matter of public relations. The more intelligent persons are often reluctant to enlist in what looks like a random effort. People of real capacity do not respond to a call for volunteers. They need to be convinced that the proposed task is worth doing, and that they have the ability to do it.

If a school is to have pupils, it must enlist the cooperation of parents. This involves more effort than in the good old days with their large attendance, of which we hear wistful memories. Before the advent of the automobile all that was required of the parents on Sunday morning was that they get their children dressed and shoved out the door; today it is necessary that at least one adult member of the family be properly attired to be seen in public and that the family car be in running order. Parents must be convinced that the church school is worth the trouble of getting the children there and back.

Parents are increasingly sensitive to whatever affects their children. This works 2 ways for the church school. If it appears to be achieving little or nothing, families will not insist on their children's attending. On the other hand, if the youngsters come home with glowing reports of what goes on in the church school, father and mother will make every effort to get them there.

From the point of view of public relations the facilities and services provided for the smallest children are of the utmost importance, as it is through them that new families are most likely to be recruited. The arrangements provided for baby care should be hygienic and safe. Investing in light, airy, spacious rooms for 2-, 3-, and 4-year-olds pays off both for the church school and the church — as many congregations have discovered. Next to the service of worship, such facilities are the most potent attraction for newcomers in a community.

How can a church school best commend itself to its immediate constituency, the pupils who attend it?

From the point of view of the church the younger children are more important than the older ones. There are more of them, they are prospective attendants for a longer period, more can be done to shape their characters, and their parents are more likely to be drawn into the church through them.

A crying child in a church school may indicate a spiritual tragedy. If a small soul has been unhappy in the house of God, this early experience may color the attitudes of a lifetime. The cause should be investigated and, if possible, eliminated. With children the urge to go to the toilet or the demand for a drink of water is more likely to spring from boredom than from any physical need. Disorder is frequently evidence that the school is failing to hold the interest of lively boys and girls. These may not be primarily problems in discipline so much as indications that the school is not doing its job. From the point of view of public relations, they are danger signals. The best recommendation any school can have is interested pupils.

The older a child, the greater both his freedom of choice and his influence with his fellows. As a young person progresses toward high school, he can either drop out of the church school or become a recruiting agent to bring in others. He is likely either to yield to indifference or to develop enthusiasm. With young people and adults the most effective publicity is that which travels by word of mouth. The successful church school — or church — is one that inspires pride in those who belong to it. How is this achieved? A multitude of factors enters the situation, of which 2 are of prime importance. The 1st is the radiance that comes with success. We are happy to be associated with any institution that seems to be making headway. This usually means that it is different from the ordinary, and that there is some element of adventure associated with it. The 2d root of enthusiasm is our sense of participation. If we are convinced that we have had a share in making a class, a school, or a church move forward to higher ground, we shall be disposed to talk about it to others. The more this happens, the more people will be drawn to the class, school, or church. The high art of public relations in the church school is to encourage those who will do the most talking to think of themselves as having helped bring into being the situation about which their tongues are wagging. It pays to be overgenerous in the distribution of credit. — *John R. Scotford*

PUBLIC SCHOOLS AND RELIGION

Two great contributions to Western civilization made by the U.S.A. through its founding fathers are the concept of the separation of church and state and the secular public-school system. True, the integrity of these principles is often compromised while their virtues are being extolled, and they are frequently honored more in breach than in fulfillment. But they still stand as major planks in the platform of American political philosophy.

Those who oppose the theory of separation of church and state have traditionally centered their attack on the public schools. Such attacks have been largely directed at 2 fundamental propositions basic to our public-school system. These are: (1) public funds shall not be granted to sectarian schools; (2) sectarian instruction shall not be given in the public schools. Although most Americans agree with these principles in theory, they cannot agree as to how they shall be practiced.

Since those who believe in the separation principle frequently disagree over what specific practices violate this doctrine, those who oppose the principle have frequently been able to take advantage of the resulting confusion. As a result they have been able, in some states, to syphon off public funds to parochial schools, and to introduce into the public schools Bible-reading, prayers, and other exercises that many people regard as sectarian education.

Although the debate over whether it would be constitutional to grant Federal funds to sectarian schools has captured the contemporary limelight, the matter of what practices constitute sectarian instruction in the public schools has been a more nettlesome problem throughout American history.

A brief historical survey reveals that during the heyday of the Puritan Commonwealth and its single established church, the primary purpose behind public education was to enable the student to read and understand the Bible. Bible-reading in the public schools was universal during this period. In the early days after independence, it became apparent to thoughtful persons that the multiplicity of sects arising in the U.S.A. required some form of divorce between church and state, for the good of both.

This theory became national policy with the inauguration of the First Amendment. Jefferson and Madison, 2 of the leaders in the fight to achieve religious liberty, were both critical of religious exercises in public-supported schools. Jefferson in particular objected to programs of Bible study in these schools.

Despite the attitudes of such leaders, Bible-reading was quite common during the antebellum period. This era saw increased attacks upon sectarianism in the public schools by newly arrived Roman Catholic and Jewish immigrants, and they included Bible-reading and prayers in their list of sectarian influences. Horace Mann, who played such an important part in the development of public schools, felt, however, that it was possible to study the Bible in such a way that it would not be sectarian. He believed the Bible read without comment in order to study the common elements of Christianity could not possibly injure the religious sensibilities of anyone.

Following the Civil War the debate over sectarian instruction and Bible-reading in the public schools grew especially heated and took on national scope. It became a lively issue in the political campaigns of the day. During the process of the dispute the Roman Catholics and Jews who had consistently opposed such exercises found themselves joined by " liberal intellectuals " and some important Protestant clergymen who objected to any type of religious service. Thus the attitudes regarding such programs were no longer crystallized along denominational lines, and this has become

increasingly true in present-day America.

By the end of the 19th century several state courts had declared Bible-reading and related practices in the public schools to be illegal. But from a legal standpoint the problem of sectarian instruction in the public schools does not submit to generalities and even attempts at summarization must be made with a great deal of caution.

At the present time, the constitutions and statutes of the various states reflect an abiding desire to keep public funds from supporting sectarian institutions of any type. All states but Vermont have constitutional provisions prohibiting the expenditure of public funds for sectarian purposes. In addition, 24 states have statutes prohibiting sectarian instruction in the public schools. But these enactments do not stipulate what practices constitute sectarian instruction. As a result Bible-reading and religious exercises of various types, which some consider as falling under these bans, are not regarded as sectarian in many states.

Thirty-seven states permit Bible-reading in their public schools today. Mississippi is the only state having a constitutional provision that permits such an exercise. (No state constitution specifically prohibits programs of this type.) Twelve states have statutes that require Bible-reading in the public schools. Five other states have statutes that permit but do not require Bible-reading. Five states, in addition to the above, have court decisions in the absence of statutory provisions that permit Bible-reading, and these are equally binding. Furthermore, 14 states permit Bible-reading in the absence of any provision whatsoever, and this practice has not been challenged in the courts.

In only 10 states is Bible-reading considered sectarian instruction. In 7 of these states this conclusion has resulted from judicial decisions. In the remaining 3 states educational policy formulators have looked at the state constitutions and statutes and have concluded that Bible-reading in the public schools is illegal. Montana, Hawaii, and Alaska have not been included in any of the foregoing categories because of an absence of evidence regarding their policies.

The high courts of 20 states plus a Federal district court in Pennsylvania have ruled on the legality of Bible-reading and related exercises in the public schools. In 1952 and again in 1959, the Supreme Court of the United States was faced with this problem. It refused, in both cases, however, to rule on the merits of the problem because of jurisdictional reasons. In June, 1962, the Supreme Court ruled adversely regarding prayers in public schools.

In 13 states the high courts have specifically upheld Bible-reading in the public schools. Their major conclusion is that the Bible is not a sectarian book. They deny that the King James Version of the Protestants is sufficiently different from the Douai Version of the Roman Catholics to require its being classed as sectarian. Furthermore, they refuse to accept the contention that such exercises constitute a public expenditure for sectarian purposes on the grounds that the Bible is not sectarian. They also contend that Bible-reading is important for an understanding of literature and history. Most of these courts, however, stressed that such reading must be done without comment and at-

tendance must not be made compulsory.

The high courts of 7 states and a Federal district court in Pennsylvania have concluded that Bible-reading and related practices in the public schools are illegal. They concluded that the Bible is a sectarian book and that exercises of this sort clearly violated the religious sensibility of non-Christians and unbelievers. They note that these practices violate the American principle of church-state separation, since they constitute Governmental preference of one religion over another. These courts stress the importance of keeping the public schools open to children of all religions; the only way this can be accomplished is to prevent the teachings of the schools from injuring students' religious sensibilities. Permitting a student to be excused from such programs does not mitigate the problem, they conclude, since such exclusion stigmatizes the student in the eyes of his fellows, for he is leaving because of apparent hostility to a book which those remaining revere. Some of the courts noted, moreover, that the free enjoyment of religious worship includes the right not to worship.

Apart from the controversy over Bible-reading and prayers in public schools, a host of other controversies have arisen over various practices alleged to be sectarian relating to public-school programs. Although a number of the court cases arose in states where the Supreme Courts had previously ruled on the question of Bible-reading, the rationale and general rule of related cases was not always consistent with the conclusions reached by the state's high court in a Bible-reading case.

In Wisconsin, for example, the courts have held Bible-reading illegal. But public high school baccalaureate exercises in which various clergymen give nonsectarian prayers and invocations were upheld by the courts of that state. In Illinois the courts have prohibited Bible-reading in the public schools, but they have taken a favorable view of religious instruction at the state university. The Illinois court also approved a program involving the payment of public funds to Roman Catholic institutions for the education of delinquent children. The Wisconsin Supreme Court held that the state Educational Bonus Act of 1919, under which Wisconsin veterans received $30 while attending school, was not invalid if the veterans should attend nonpublic religious institutions.

In a number of instances where a church exercised some control over a school, the courts of 8 states have ruled that a denominational school does not become a public school simply by calling it one. These courts have decided that such schools are not entitled to state financial aid. Moreover, there is little agreement among the courts of the various states regarding the legality of public-school teachers' wearing distinctive religious garments, such as those worn by nuns. Three states permit such practices, and 5 states prohibit them. The New York Supreme Court, in 1957, upheld a state regulation recommending that public-school students recite the Pledge of Allegiance including the words "under God."

"Released time" programs of religious instruction held in school buildings, which have been common in various state-supported schools, have been banned by the United States Supreme Court in the McCollum case. This Court has added to the confused status of religious exercises in the public schools, however, by upholding (in the Zorach case) "dismissed time" programs where students received religious instruction off school property during the school day.

From this it is clear it would take an educator with the wisdom of Solomon and with substantial legal training to forecast the potential legality of any proposed program of religious education in the U.S.A. Only the Supreme Court can clarify the picture, but that body has been reluctant to enter the fray.

—Donald E. Boles

PUPPETS A puppet (from the Latin *pupa*, "girl" or "doll") is a manipulative doll scaled to life size. The puppet may be made from any of a large number of materials such as wood, paper, cloth, boxes, grasses, twigs, cornhusks, peanut shells, or any others that may be shaped into the semblance of a figure. The puppet is manipulated by rods, sticks, or pencils from either the top, bottom, or side of the figure. Hand puppets are made in the shape of a mitten and are operated by the thumb and fingers. String-operated puppets are called marionettes (little Marys) after the supporting characters in the religious plays of medieval times with the Virgin Mary as the main character.

In this way and many others puppets were used centuries ago to tell people about the Bible. Printing had not been invented, and Bibles were not available to people. Today puppets may be used in many aspects of Christian education — to motivate, to instruct, to aid in retention of learning, to stimulate the imagination, to help understand the past or present, to satisfy the need to use muscles, and to bring about group goals.

To make a simple puppet use 7 half sheets of tissue paper 20″ × 30″. Crumple 1 of the half sheets into a ball to be used later for the head. Fold 1 sheet crosswise; roll tightly to form arms. Fold remaining 5 sheets as 1 unit. The size is now 10″ × 15″. Have ready 6 pieces of string. Place head in center under the fold and tie at the neck. Shape tissue at shoulder to figure size. Place the armpiece below the neck and tie at the waist. Starting at the bottom of the lengthwise sheets, split them in half toward the waist. Twist each half to form legs. Tie at the angle; tie arms at the wrists. Discourage painting the face. Insert rods or substitutes either in the back or side of the figure.

This same process may be used in making puppets from other materials including those found outdoors. Grasses are easily manipulated when slightly damp. Cornhusks because of their natural variety make for highly individualized puppets.

The stage may be made from a cardboard or wooden box. Cut away either the bottom or back of the box depending on the placement of the actors. Place the stage on a table or in a doorway. Hang a curtain where it is needed in order to hide the performers.

The end purpose of puppetry is not, however, the making of the puppet or the stage. The use of puppets in all phases of Christian education is a means to an end, the end being better to accomplish the purpose of the group whether it be a class, a committee, or a vacation school or camp group. The group purpose may be to learn what Amos had to say to people long ago and says today, or who the Lollards were and why they felt it important to carry the Bible to their neighbors. They may set out to understand a church fellowship in Thailand or to convey thoughts on stewardship. Or they may use a procession of puppets to show the onward march of Christianity. A teacher may use a puppet to arouse curiosity.

After the goal is determined the group will use books, maps, and other materials to gather information about the historical setting, suitable clothing, events, attitudes, conflicts, character, etc. The teacher will direct the research, asking some leading questions, such as why, how, when, what happened next, who was he? While hands are busy questions may come naturally from the group as they project themselves into the situation. One member can take notes of thoughts and feelings and then block out on a chalkboard the sequence of events for the actual play. From the directed research the group will be ready to put into dialogue their knowledge, thoughts, and feelings. If the purpose is to present the play before an audience, more time may be necessary to perfect the play.

From the initial establishment of purpose through the presentation, puppets are helpful as a means of establishing an effective group; in achieving the common goal under direction, many thoughts, individual responses, and talents are used. The teacher, too, has time to gain insights into the minds and thoughts of the pupils. Imagination and curiosity are stimulated, and learning is put to use in a concrete way. As a review technique puppets can help in recall and in placing people of remote times in chronological sequence. — *Mildred Toogood*

Q

QUESTION AND ANSWER METH-OD The question and answer method performs several functions in teaching: (1) It gives the teacher information as to where the class is in learning at the moment. At the beginning of any study this is useful, for it prevents repetition (both boring and time-wasting) and it gives teacher and class the opportunity of discovering unknown areas and planning the study ahead. (2) It is an avenue for review and for testing. Carefully chosen questions will help a class to recall previous learning and thereby build up the spiral of learning to give a base for continuing learning. Testing is a form of review, the purpose being to help pupils and teachers evaluate both the extent and depth of work accomplished. (3) It is a primary method for arousing thought. "Why" is the basic word for accomplishing the purpose. The pupil is thus forced to go beyond facts in order to find meanings. "How" is the word that urges the pupil to explore the process that produced a fact. Thus facts become interpreted in the light of background understandings. Another form of thought question invites the pupil to ask what meaning the material has for himself.

The use of questions may be illustrated by looking at the story of Elijah. A fact question could be asked: "How would you describe the event on Mt. Carmel?" Such a question reviews and reinforces learning as the class goes forward into a study of the prophets, forming a basis for staking out areas of research (geographical, political, Biblical) if the study is at its beginning. Further questions follow, such as, "What was the significance of the contest on Mt. Carmel?" This helps the pupils to look for the meaning in the Biblical story and in the background material. It asks what *really* happened and guides the pupils into the habit of looking beyond the word itself to the implications. A 3d type of question brings another dimension, that of the relation arising from the story: "What is the relation between this event and other struggles with idolatry narrated in the Old Testament? Who would you be in this story?"

Notice that the 3d area of question has two focuses. First it tries to set the story of Elijah in the whole context of the Old Testament up to that point. Then it tries to find out whether the listener thinks of himself as Elijah or if he is able to see that idolatry is a constant temptation, though in differing forms.

Question and answer may be carried on in 2 basic forms — written or oral — and in 2 basic settings — addressed to the class or to the individual.

The written question gives each individual an opportunity to think or remember. It helps the teacher to evaluate the learning and thinking of each; it helps the pupil to make decisions in learning and to offer concrete answers. A question addressed to the group gives an opportunity for interplay of ideas. It may be 1 question addressed to each in turn, "What would you say?" so that the answer is built up from many angles. It can be thrown out to the class or it may be 1st addressed to 1 personally and then to others (always the name 1st: "Jane, what do you think . . . ?" followed by "What would you like to add?"). Skill and courtesy are requisites for the use of the question. The purpose is to encourage the learner to express what he knows or thinks. It should not make him feel fearful of the question or inadequate because of his answer.

The question may also be used to help the individuals or the group into self-understanding. Here the teacher, having asked an initial question, becomes a listener, encouraging further expression by low-keyed questions such as: "You thought this was what happened?" "You wondered about that?" "Would you tell us what you were hoping for?" This form of question hopes to evoke that which disturbs the individual or the class, in order that discussion may turn into religious insights as to how to solve problem situations.

One caution in all questions: the teacher must not expect a certain answer or a certain expression of an answer. Since pupils want to please the teacher, they will bend every effort not to give their answers but to fathom what answers the teacher wants. This is not learning. The object of questioning is not to receive back the teacher's answer, but to encourage pupil and teacher to explore answers together.

— *Iris V. Cully*

QUESTIONNAIRE Some form of questionnaire seems to have been in use as early as 1541, when a form of " questionary " or series of questions was sent out. The term " questionnaire " itself is French in origin. In 1847, Horace Mann sent a 10-page circular asking questions of teachers. It began, " I desire to obtain the opinion of teachers who are both scientific and practical on a subject of great importance to the cause of popular education." In 1899 a questionnaire investigating the characteristics of more than 10,000 children was used.

The use of the questionnaire is a highly popular way of gathering evidence. It is a " research instrument " used " (1) To ascertain the state of practice in some field of activity. (2) To secure basic data to be used in ways more fundamental than to afford mere studies of practice. (3) To secure opinions, judgments, and preferences on the expressions of attitude of respondents along a variety of lines " (Leonard V. Koos, *The Questionnaire in Education*, p. 52). Again, " a questionnaire consists typically of a series of written questions similar to those which an interviewer might ask, but perhaps even more carefully formulated (because the interviewer will not be on hand to explain what each question means). (Tyrus Hillway, *Introduction to Research,* p. 193.)

There are basically 3 types of questionnaires. The 1st and the most common is the mail questionnaire, an inexpensive method of gathering data. Its limitations lie in the poor structure often used, and in the unwillingness on the part of many to answer. The 2d type is the person-to-person interview involving the use of a written questionnaire. This method is limited, in that data-gathering on a large scale would be prohibitive. Its advantage is found in the fact that the respondent can be questioned directly. The 3d type is the questionnaire administered to persons while they are gathered in a group. Its cost prohibits any large-scale sampling; however, it retains some personal elements considered valuable.

The questionnaire may be of either open or closed form. In the 1st the respondent is permitted to answer the questions as he will. The 2d form limits the answer by having the respondent answer yes or no or circle a provided answer. Pictures are sometimes used to clarify questions. Since the closed form provides easy tabulation of results, it is the more useful.

Structuring is important. Principles of good structure are: (1) The questionnaire should deal with matters of fact. (2) It should ask only for data the respondent will give. (3) It should require a minimum of writing. (4) Responses should lend themselves to tabulation. (5) The questionnaire should be given a preliminary tryout. (6) It should meet certain standards of mechanical form. (7) Its purpose should be stated. (Cf. *Research Bulletin of the N.E.A.,* p. 8.) Struc-

turing must also take into account the willingness and the ability of the respondent to answer. Since the questionnaire is an extremely delicate research instrument, it must be made up with care.

Only recently have religious education personnel used the questionnaire. It has been used primarily by social scientists, psychologists, and secular educators. Now ministers are using it to note trends. In interdenominational work it is used for problem-solving of a group nature, as well as for determining trends and developments. Of 174 research efforts in religious education reported in a 1959 magazine, about 45 percent had used some form of questionnaire. Despite its limitations, the questionnaire is a valuable instrument of research for the religious educator.

— Charles R. Munson

QUIZ The word " quiz " designates especially a relatively short test. In education it is a form of pupil evaluation based on brevity and frequency of administration.

In day schools the quiz is usually thought of as being given on a daily basis. This procedure emphasizes recently acquired materials that have been presented in the classroom. It operates on the basic assumption that since tests increase effort on the part of the pupils, more frequent testing will yield greater total effort. It attempts to measure the performance of the students particularly in regard to the degree of the retention of facts or subject matter dealt with in a specified amount of time. This approach is used usually not to investigate what the person can do but what he is doing, particularly within a specific time limit. However, this kind of test is often looked upon as a sample of behavior (which is true of all testing procedure) through which the teacher makes an inference about what the student's performance would be if he had been given a complete and thorough examination.

The use of the quiz not only serves as an energizing function in that it endeavors to increase the general level of activity and effort on the part of the students, but directs the variable and persistent activity of the students into desirable channels. Consequently, it can stimulate the achievement of the most acceptable objectives. There is also a selective function in this testing technique, since it helps to determine correct and desirable study behavior and to eliminate undesirable study responses. This selective function becomes especially evident if a discussion on the results of the quiz transpires and remedial work follows immediately. It can furnish the teacher with up-to-date information regarding the growth record and status of each pupil, at least in the field of subject matter under consideration.

The quiz as used in the teaching-learning process presents the following advantages: (1) Significant aspects of subject matter or a unit are noted in this means of evaluation, enabling exclusion of insignificant areas. (2) It helps to determine the extent of knowledge mastered and can aid in identifying concepts that have not been understood. (3) It develops good study habits and stimulates pupils to study, thus contributing to the effectiveness of the instructional program. (4) The student is encouraged to self-awareness of his comprehension of subject matter. (5) Goals and objectives are clarified by the tangible, viz., the extent of acquired factual knowledge. (6) Evaluation is emphasized as a continuous process rather than a single, static event. (7) The teacher develops fair and honest evaluation of his pupils, which becomes evident to them in terms of appreciation. (8) Situations are identified in which students can be expected to display progress toward objectives. (9) The concept that evaluation is a cooperative affair, involving students, teachers, and even parents is encouraged.

There are also some obvious disadvantages: (1) This procedure does not evaluate student growth on a sufficiently broad basis. (2) The differences among students are not taken into consideration. (3) Education is presented as merely an emphasis on the amount of retention or mastery of facts or knowledge. (4) It interprets the role of the teacher autocratically. (5) As it is essential to present quizzes frequently in order that there may be validity in the evaluative procedure, it becomes educationally time-consuming. (6) Extrinsic motivation can be encouraged in this testing technique. (7) It encourages a kind of rote learning, thus discouraging perceptual learning. (8) Memorization, cramming, regimentation, are given an impetus in this approach. (9) Research indicates that the validity of the quiz is questionable because of its brevity; also, that it does not necessarily have a more energizing effect than daily assignments. — *Clarence J. Sahlin*

R

RADIO Though dismissed by some as a moribund medium of effective communication, radio remains an active channel today for any number of secular messages. More to our point here, radio retains many of its highly helpful roles for the educational tasks of the church. Local leaders and teachers need only exercise a moderate amount of creative ingenuity to obtain a variety of teaching aids from the medium.

Its unique contributions apply potentially whether some or all of the program types discussed below are utilized at the moment of their broadcast or are tape-recorded for later use. As long as the recordings are employed solely within a context of some curriculum activity and not for any commercial or money-raising reason, no legal or ethical questions should arise.

Another general comment relates to the possible sources of radio programming related to Christian education objectives. Numerous and varied values can be found in both other-produced and self-produced broadcasts, although a host of justifiable cautions and conditions surround the latter. Excellent nationally produced programs are available easily and without cost to local stations through the Broadcasting and Film Commission of the National Council of the Churches of Christ in the U.S.A., for example. Nonetheless, if persons in a community are able and willing to use talents and skills in this field, a significant share of radio resources can be prepared for that community by or through the local council of churches, ministerial association, Christian education directors' fellowship, or similar cooperative bodies. A calculated combination of sources for these resources should offer maximum enrichment possibilities.

There are 5 major uses for radio in Christian education. Many program examples will possess multiple use opportunities, to be sure, but some cataloging is in order.

1. Devotional. To the numerous shut-ins who are members of churches, moments of meaningful devotion may be brought by radio. The airwaves seem to be clogged at times with a jam of pseudoinspirational programs — especially on Sunday — but at least 1 half-hour preaching service of high integrity is available to any NBC station. The *National Radio Pulpit* presents responsible Protestant messages enhanced by music from leading church, college, and seminary choirs.

Locally produced programming

certainly is possible in this regard, provided the speakers are familiar with the special requirements of broadcast sermons and do not merely condense one previously given from a pulpit. Provision of incisive and helpful devotional programming may not be a central part of Christian education as such, but it should be included in comprehensive planning.

2. Instructional. Dozens of councils and associations already are providing 15- and 30-minute Bible-study programs to community stations. Such 1-man lectures often can impede or distort learning, but competent clergymen, aware of these dangers and knowledgeable in broadcasting techniques, are tapping the growing lay interest in solid study of the Scriptures with just such programming.

With or without "reactors" (sample students) in the studio to ask questions and debate among themselves, thus including as much on-the-air "involvement" as possible, these radio teachers assign and grade homework and tests. Although millions of American families have few periods when they might participate in such study as a family, at least thousands of others could be enrolled by a well-promoted and carefully conceived study series running from 3 to 13 weeks. A local sponsoring council or association would want to distribute whatever home-study materials were desirable for use in conjunction with the oral presentation.

3. Discussional. Fruitful topics for public debate surround every Christian community. Whether those selected for broadcast are explicitly religious or indirectly related to the total gospel, provocative programming is more than possible.

In cooperation with the Amer-ican Broadcasting Company, the NCCCUSA presents a weekly half hour named *Pilgrimage*. Over the months it shares a spectrum of church-related topics ranging from contemporary theological thought, to domestic social and economic concerns, to the impact of international developments on the world-wide mission of the church.

Usually featuring a panel of competent spokesmen for varying positions on each theme, *Pilgrimage* in its actual 28 minutes of air time can stimulate extensive follow-through discussion within a group of older youth through adults. A tape recording of any program easily could be held over until a group's regular meeting time.

Potentialities for local production abound here. A West Coast station refused to accept any religious programming until the local council's radio-TV director came up with the idea of an *Ask the Clergy* broadcast. Manned by articulate clergymen, the program caught the station's imagination, was placed tentatively on the air, and today ranks as one of the most popular in the community.

The several opportunities for reinforcing the Christian education effort within church walls by preparing appropriate and professional broadcast (and other materials) for home "use" must not be underestimated. Panel programs probing responsibly some of the problems of Christian faith and life may be most effective if they can reach a person in the relative solitude of a living room or bedroom. All learning need not take place in the midst of a group.

4. Informational or promotional. How many persons in a parish have even a passing knowledge of what is happening in religious circles day

by day? Much of this "news" is quite exciting and inspirational. *Church World News* should be relevant. Produced as an interdenominational, international view of the religious world and its impingements on secular life by the Lutheran Church in America, the taped program is distributed by the BFC.

An increasing number of local councils and ministerial groups are developing this type of broadcast beamed at local manifestations of the church at work. As a matter of fact, the *Church World News* format provides for a local segment between the opening and closing nationally prepared sections. Produced to professional specifications, such a program can command rather good air time if a community demonstrates its ongoing tuning-in.

5. Motivational. Good drama probably is the most effective type of motivational programming. Very little drama remains on radio, but a pair of recorded series produced for religious use are still available. One, *Let There Be Light*, was produced by the BFC; the other, *All Aboard for Adventure*, was produced by the United Church of Christ. Both dramatize biographical accounts of Biblical characters and other major historical figures as well as fictionalized stories of current Christian activity in some part of the world.

The secret in the educational use of such dramatic resources lies in the provision for the listener to hear them in the "theater of the mind." A relatively simple radio drama can conjure up all kinds of imaginary, fill-in details without any literal visual stimulus. The purely audial channel, ideally used in subdued light so as to minimize distractions, can be helpful as a change from motion pictures, and as a resource when a leader or teacher wants each pupil or group member to "imagine" something of a drama's setting.

A trio of production and utilization agencies may be of interest for further study of radio as a Christian education tool. First, the NCCCUSA offers 2 units working in the field: the already mentioned Broadcasting and Film Commission, majoring in production and station placement, and the Department of Audio-Visual and Broadcast Education, majoring in utilization ideas.

Second, there are 2 stations owned by religious groups which feature some imaginative programming and seek a degree of educational effect from it. From the more liberal segment of the church, WRVR of New York City's Riverside Church airs a rich variety of religious and semi-religious material in addition to purely secular or cultural broadcasts. Within the more evangelical circles, WMBI of Chicago's Moody Bible Institute has demonstrated a continuing ability to produce programs of many types that evidence professional skill.

— Donald J. Kliphardt

RAIKES, ROBERT Robert Raikes, the originator of the Sunday school, was born in Gloucester, England, Sept. 14, 1735, and baptized in the church of St. Mary de Crypt 10 days later. He was the eldest of the 6 children of his father's 3d wife. His father, likewise Robert Raikes, a printer, had come to Gloucester from York and in 1722 was 1 of 2 partners who founded the *Gloucester Journal*, a weekly newspaper of which he soon became sole owner. Raikes's formal education was apparently limited to that available in his home city. He was enrolled in the Cathedral College School in

1750 and may previously have been a pupil in the St. Mary de Crypt Grammar School. He evidently mastered the printer's trade, for his composing stick has been preserved in the museum at Gloucester. On the death of his father in 1757, Raikes, then 21 years old, succeeded as publisher of the newspaper. Ten years later he married Anne Trigge, of Gloucester County.

Raikes's contemporaries described him as being very pompous in manner, fastidious to an extreme, and accustomed to dress in the expensive garments that characterized the dandies of his time. Nevertheless, from earliest manhood he manifested a concern for human well-being, to the promotion of which he dedicated himself and the pages of the *Journal*.

Raikes early interested himself in the prisoners confined in the county and city jails, which were crowded and unsanitary as were most English prisons of that time. He supported the cause of prison reform, raised money to buy food for imprisoned debtors for whom no other provision was made, and tried to effect the rehabilitation of individual prisoners by promoting educational activities in the jails and by assisting them after their release. He won the commendation of John Howard, whose campaign for reform resulted in prison legislation by Parliament in 1774, and he witnessed the construction of a new and better county jail.

Raikes never lost his concern for those confined in the local prisons. However, the experience of a quarter of a century convinced him that imprisonment seldom led to moral reformation and that his efforts for the rehabilitation of criminals needed to be supplemented by a preventive program. He believed that much

vice and crime was the result of ignorance and that the most effective way to prevent their incidence would be to educate the children of the working classes. Most of these were illiterates for whom there was no free schooling. They worked 6 days a week. Their Sundays were spent in aimless play and offensive and riotous conduct punctuated with vulgar and profane language.

The 1st step taken by Raikes to alter this was to get a group of these underprivileged children to accompany him to the early Sunday morning service at the cathedral. His generosity in bestowing rewards of coins and other gifts no doubt contributed to the success of this undertaking, but it seems likewise evident that he won their respect and affection. Then, in order that they might be profitably occupied the rest of the day, he began his Sunday schools.

The procedure that Raikes followed was to find a skilled woman and to induce her to open a school in her home on Sundays to teach reading and the catechism. The teacher was to receive a shilling for the day's work. Then he visited parents to persuade them to take advantage of this opportunity for their children. He was fortunate in securing the cooperation of Thomas Stock, headmaster of the Cathedral School and vicar of the Church of St. John the Baptist.

At least a half dozen Sunday schools were organized in Gloucester between 1780 and 1783. The one that Raikes regarded as peculiarly his own and in whose pupils he showed a lifelong interest was held in a house opposite his parish church, St. Mary de Crypt, and only a short distance from his home.

After 3 years of experience Raikes

was convinced of the validity of what he was doing. In the Nov. 3, 1783, issue of his journal he described the Sunday schools of Gloucester and recommended the establishment of similar schools elsewhere. His achievements and recommendations received further publicity in the *Gentleman's Magazine,* a periodical of general circulation.

In spite of considerable opposition the movement initiated by Raikes spread widely and rapidly. A London Society for the Establishment and Support of Sunday Schools throughout the Kingdom of Great Britain was founded in 1785. Two years later it was estimated that the Sunday school enrollment amounted to 250,000.

Raikes later paid his Sunday school teachers to meet their pupils for supplementary instruction during the week and also took an active part in the establishment of free industrial day schools. He was thus one of the pioneers whose ventures led to universal free education in England.

Raikes gave up the editorship of the *Gloucester Journal* at the age of 66. He died 9 years later, April 5, 1811, survived by his wife, 6 daughters, and 2 sons. The Sunday school children who sang at his funeral each received a shilling and a plum cake. — *William C. Seitz*

REALISM Realism was the school of scholastic thought that stood over against the nominalists in discussing the nature of universals. Medieval realists, after Plato's Idealism, maintained that abstractions (e.g., justice, love, the good) have a real existence prior to and independent of their specific actualization.

The modern term "realism" is more akin to medieval nominalism than to medieval realism. Realism maintains that reality exists independently of any knower who may come to a knowledge of it; reality exists independent of, and antecedent to, the act of knowing. That which is known is disclosed by the knowing process but is not created in the knowing process. Thus, the nature and property of reality is not affected by being known, but in order to be known it must be experienced. The primary characteristic of modern realism is its epistemology, and in this it is opposed to the idealist emphasis on metaphysics.

Realism in education arose as a reaction to the verbal classicism of the Renaissance. Realists maintained that education must concern itself with realities, not just words. We may note several groups: (1) Humanistic realists such as Erasmus (ca. 1466–1536) and Milton (1608–1674) urged the study of ancient language and literature solely for its value in real life, rather than for literary style or eloquence. (2) Social realists, e.g., Montaigne (1533–1592), emphasized contemporary life, language, and culture to the exclusion of the ancient. (3) Sense realists such as Comenius (1592–1670) and Bacon (1561–1626) centered education around empirically verifiable knowledge and directed study to concrete objects within the physical environment.

A philosophy of education based on realism rests on the hypothesis that things are, and continue to be, as we experience them. The universe consists of entities that exist in and of themselves and in extramental relation. These independent entities which are dependable referents for human knowledge include not only material objects but also nonquantitative data such as love, knowledge, justice, and other abstractions.

Each individual must experience these entities in the process of knowing them, and in the knowing process these entities as they are in themselves become related to the human mind. This relation involves a union or identification of the knowing process with the existent entity and eventuates in thoughts or concepts about that which is experienced. In terms of objective entities, that which is external is apprehended in sensation. The neorealists say that in this apprehension the object is presented immediately to the mind of the knowers. Knowledge is derived at the point of convergence between the knower and the known. Critical realists hold a refined concept of the inner nature of the mind, rejecting the immediate presentation in favor of a mediate representation of objects to the knower through their sensed qualities. The emphasis in either case is on cognition as a human function of the knower in the apprehension of that which is external to him.

The entities of realism can be symbolically represented in expression and can thus be communicated. It is this communication and the presentation of the entities of experience which the realist educator seeks to achieve. The teacher is the guide who leads or directs the student into reality. The teacher mediates between the free mind of the student and the independent being of reality, and thus leads him into an experience of reality through the knowing process.

Realism places a high value on content, but this content is always allied with experience. Content is not equated with the printed curriculum, although the curriculum is the basic guide to the content. In the last analysis, content is the reality itself to which the curriculum points. This reality is selected and organized by the educating society and provides the substance and framework for the educative process.

Content never reverts to the non-utilitarian verbalism or the memorization and mastery of verbal facts against which realism arose as a reaction, although in some systems verbal content and reality are almost identical. In such cases, reality is interpreted as verbally expressed norms by which society lives, and the epistemology of realism insists that the student go beyond memorization of those norms to a personal appropriation or experience of the content. Realism's insistence on experiential commitment is evident whether the educating society embraces Russian dialectical materialism, Roman Catholic Thomism, American democracy, or American Protestantism.

As a philosophy, realism may be theistic or nontheistic, its distinctive feature lying in its epistemology rather than its metaphysics. Much educational practice utilizes realism's understanding of the knowing process without basing it on a conscious philosophy of realism. In religious education, elements of realism are seen wherever the content of a faith is viewed as an interpretation of reality to be shared from generation to generation.

1. Protestant Christian education, as recently developed, arose from the theology identified with Barth, Brunner, and Niebuhr, and has found exponents in D. Campbell Wyckoff, Iris V. Cully, Randolph Crump Miller, Lewis J. Sherrill, James D. Smart, and Howard

Grimes. The theories of Christian education held by these and other writers evidence indebtedness to realist philosophy when they assert (a) that the reality of the Christian faith can be discerned through experience and (b) that the experience of God is prior in value to a conceptualized understanding of God. Further relationship is seen in the abundance of content, especially historical, which is the interpretation of reality, and through which the student is led to the experience and knowledge of reality.

In this view Christian education takes place in the firsthand experience of the learner. Learning experience is within the context of the Christian community and of the world as interpreted by that community. In this context the goal of education is a face-to-face meeting with, or awareness of, a God who has revealed himself in love. Through the content, which is the historical foundation of the community, this experience is identified with the Spirit of Jesus who was declared to be the Christ and the Lord of life by the resurrection. Through the appropriation of this historical content, specifically as it is found in the Bible, the student is brought into a knowing relation with God.

This view guards against the reduction of reality to verbal symbolization of reality. It fears that ideas of God (theistic proofs) may be accepted as equal to God, thus standing in the way of a confrontation with God. The verbal content either of the Bible or of doctrine may in itself become impersonal reality and stand as a barrier to the experience of God. The place of such Biblical and doctrinal content is to give substance and identity to the experience that may be secondary in terms of chronology, but is primary and indispensable in terms of value.

Man (the student) is viewed realistically as a sinner and as a creature of God who is responsible to God and to society. In this view God is found not so much in contemplation or mystic withdrawal as in the turmoil of human interaction.

Realism that holds a representative epistemology recognizes the possibility of disparity between the consciousness of the knower and the nature of ultimate reality which is known. This disparity, attributed to the finitude of man, may manifest itself in stressing unduly or reverencing the symbols or representations of reality.

2. Roman Catholic education (Neoscholasticism) and certain groups within Protestantism follow the tenets of realism without holding that the experience of God is prior to a rational understanding of that experience. According to these groups, experience of God in Christ is found in the organized doctrine of the church, the sacraments, or the word of God as it is in the Bible. These entities constitute reality as it is interpreted by the church, and the goal of Christian education is the presentation and appropriation of them. — *Arlo D. Duba*

RECITATION Basically, recitation means the act of repeating, telling over, rehearsing, or the content of such an act. It usually has referred to the delivery before one or more hearers of something memorized or of content mastered. In education recitation has traditionally designated an oral repetition or explanation of material learned under the teacher's direction. It may be in the form of simple drill. Often it is elicited by the teacher's question and takes the form of a student answer based on the preparation of material previously assigned. Recitation may also take written form in answers to tests, quizzes, and examinations.

In the church school the term has often referred to the repetition of memory work. The student recites catechism answers and Bible verses. After a partial eclipse, this method of teaching is receiving new emphasis. The teacher now is usually more inclined to inquire after the pupil's understanding of meaning as well as knowledge of words because this is sounder teaching and is more in accord with the original purpose and usage of both catechisms and Scripture. The selection of memory work gives more consideration to that which is meaningful in relation to the student's experience, to that which he can recite in his expression of worship and in his daily living for Christ.

In more recent years educational circles have used recitation to designate the whole planned procedure of a class under the teacher's direction. There has been some tendency toward disuse of the term because of its formal and mechanical connotations. Where it continues to be used it has often taken on this broader meaning. Thus the recitation may refer to a whole lesson or to a series of lessons that together form a unit.

With the de-emphasis of simple content learning, the recitation is more often made up of various types of experiences that provide both the content and method of the recitation. The student can then report on what has happened to him or what he has done. He reports or recites by relating various types of experience for his fellow students. The student might recite what he has learned of the geography of Palestine by making a map. He might recite the Beatitudes by helping others to experience the meaning of "poor in spirit" (Matt. 5:3) through his own evidencing of humility. He might recite the joy of his salvation in song or his learning of the new creation in evangelism.

What is sometimes referred to as socialized recitation emphasizes pupil participation in the teaching-learning process. The learners may recite by participation in various types of discussions, panels, forums, role-playing, and other group activity. A class may report on Job by producing it or an adaptation in the form of a drama. They may recite what they have learned of the Council at Jerusalem (Acts, ch. 15) by debating the issue of admitting Gentiles to the church or a contemporary version of a similar problem. In such recitation the students plan and carry out units of experience making use, as the body of Christ, of different individual gifts to minister to the whole organism. They recite their learning of the Spirit by bearing the fruit of love, joy, peace, and patience (Gal. 5:22) in their group relations; their learning of the 2 great commandments (Matt. 22:37-39) is exhibited by their common service of God's purpose in their common life of love. Such recitation is defined by action. It makes use of the insights of group dynamics but is used by the dynamic of the Christian church who is the Holy Spirit. It uses group leadership and certain democratic procedures because they are sound educationally and because of the recognition of the corporate quality of created man and of the priesthood of all believers.

The Christian educator understands recitation also in terms of what G. Ernest Wright has called Biblical theology as recital (cf. *God Who Acts*). This shows that education in the Old and New Testaments includes the recital in words, worship, and ceremony of the mighty, saving acts of God in and through the history of his people and especially in Jesus Christ. Such recitation is both a remembering of the past and a witness to the present. It makes the past present in the recitation of word and life.

— *C. Don Coffey*

RECONSTRUCTIONISM The term " reconstructionism " is most commonly identified with a philosophy of education that regards the informal as well as formal experience of learning and teaching as an inclusive process that both transmits culture and innovates culture toward the achievement of compelling life goals. The term is also recognized in religious education to characterize a theory associated with an extreme liberal wing of Judaism. As yet, reconstructionism is much more largely a theory than a tested form of educational practice, although aspects have been practiced with or without that term in many schools and colleges both in the U.S.A. and in other countries.

As a secular theory, reconstructionism is located in the mainstream of naturalism. Therefore, its ontology emerges from the empirical and realist traditions in the history of philosophy more than from the rationalist and idealist traditions. At the same time it acknowledges and tries to incorporate in its outlook strains from virtually all the important philosophic movements of the West — so much so that undoubtedly it reveals eclectic elements in its overall formulation.

More specifically, the theory acknowledges the special influence of the pragmatic, experimentalist position in American philosophy, and is regarded by some interpreters as an extension of, more than a departure from, that position. In common with experimentalism, for example, it considers experience as the key to reality, and it interprets mind as one important kind of experience — that is, as the functional capacity by means of which man is able to inquire into problems and to act reflectively in solving them. Education, for both the pragmatic experimentalist and the reconstructionist philosophies of education, is the central instrument through which human beings organized in societies both perpetuate and continually modify nature, including human nature.

But reconstructionists are strongly influenced by several strains of theory that are much less congenial to experimentalism or to other contemporary theories of education. One such strain is Marxism: reconstructionism rejects important aspects of the Marxian world view, particularly what it considers to be an outmoded ontology and epistemology, but it also insists that some aspects of Marxism have important lessons to teach both philosophy and education. Perhaps most fruitful is the theory of class power and class conflict: this theory, modified and updated by such 20th-century thinkers as Karl Mannheim, enables teachers, for example, to develop more sophisticated awareness of their own roles — to help them discover whether they are functioning chiefly as perpetuators of an economic-political power structure that proves in many ways to be undemocratic, and whether also they should resolve the question of where their own allegiances belong if education is to serve as the ally of widening economic-political democracy. Reconstructionists, of course, hold that teachers should "take sides" with "the forces of expansion" toward such a democracy both in America and on a world scale. They oppose the Sino-Soviet power bloc for its dictatorial system, but they also oppose industrial monopoly and other types of economic minority control in the U.S.A. and elsewhere. They align themselves with the "radical democratic forces" that constitute a 3d, although as yet less organized and less powerful, economic-political movement, and maintain that education's central energies should be channeled in support of this movement.

The contention that education neither is nor should be neutral in the wider cultural struggles of our time derives from a crucial assumption of reconstructionist theory, namely, that the period of history through which mankind is passing is fraught with unprecedented crisis. Traditional institutions and values are everywhere subject to severe strain; some have already collapsed; others have replaced them. The crisis extends, moreover, not only to political and social organization; it infects human personality, generates anxiety and other emotional ills, and produces the widely recognized phenomena of alienation and anomie. Education, therefore, must assume responsibilities that might not be equally pressing in a more stable period of human evolution. For example, the contributions of Freud and his followers should be incorporated much more fully in the professional training of teachers. Thereby the latter in turn may more competently recognize and cope with the emotional disturbances chronic among children, who are directly or indirectly often the victims of the wider crisis in political and moral affairs as these impinge upon families and occupations.

Here the contention of reconstructionism that education should serve as the agent of cultural innovation toward powerful and realizable human goals is paramount. Indeed, in this contention probably more than any other the theory departs from progressivism and from other prevailing views of education. From the psychiatric viewpoint, reconstructionism holds with Erich Fromm and other neo-Freudians that mental health and personal happiness require orientation toward constructive, realizable, magnetic life purposes. From the social viewpoint, the Marxian influence may once more be detected in its utopian goal of a "classic society" — a society redefined by reconstructionists in terms of "cultural designs" for planet-wide democracies in which major physical and spiritual resources are made available to, and come under the control of, the vast majority of the earth's peoples. Only such democracies, reconstructionism holds, can prevent man from destroying himself through nuclear war, overpopulation, or moral deterioration. And education is derelict, in turn, unless it throws its vast intellectual and aesthetic resources in behalf of the creation of a world civilization, directed by a democratic world government and empowered to enforce its policies of peace and abundance.

This philosophy of education does not overlook the gigantic obstacles that stand in the way of implementing its far-reaching proposals. It contends, however, that many of these are due more largely to inertia and misunderstanding than to deep-seated public opposition. Granting that some powerful groups bitterly oppose its program because it threatens their own authority, it also believes that large numbers of typical parents, teachers, and children in America and abroad would support it if given opportunity. It suggests that beginnings can be made by means of "pilot projects" — experiments in curriculum, teacher organization and training, adult education, and in other ways.

One example is a suggested design for the 2d curriculum. Assuming that increasingly young people will remain in school until 20 years of age, reconstructionism would test out a program of general education for the final 4 years in which the entire course of study is integrated around one question: What kind of world do we want and how can we achieve it? The focus thus becomes normative and goal-centered. Each of the 4 years would be devoted to 1 great area of reconstruction, such as economics-politics, human relations, the arts, and the natural sciences. Students would work constantly in teams as well as individually, learning all they can about the present status of knowledge in these areas while bringing such knowledge to bear on the pressing questions of world conflict, survival, and renewal. Subject-matter courses in the conventional sense would be provided also, but even these would not be treated separately from the common theme. Thus a student could major in physics, say, but he would never graduate oblivious to the social and moral dimensions of his field. The same principle would operate in the languages, arts, social

studies, and vocational education. The aim would be to develop sound citizens not only well informed about the most urgent problems of the 20th century, but equipped with at least the groundwork of a life purpose and a mature sense of responsibility to share concertedly and aggressively with others in moving toward such a purpose.

In one sense, reconstructionism thus emerges not merely as a philosophy of education but a philosophy of life. Education is viewed as the core of a much wider human sphere of life. Indeed, for some of its exponents, reconstructionism is a philosophy of religion as well as a philosophy of culture or of education. That is, it is infused with commitment to magnetic ideals and it conceives of the personality in terms of its relations to a wider and more encompassing whole than itself — an "ideal superego" which, while not defined in sectarian, supernatural, or transcendental terms, enables the human being to act cooperatively with others as well as with consistency, conviction, and a sense of dedication. The school, so conceived, thus becomes likewise a religious institution.

— *Theodore Brameld*

RECORDS, CHURCH SCHOOL An adequate and accurate record system is essential for an effective church school. A system conforming to its needs should be adopted by each school. Some denominations request use of their specific plans of record-keeping.

At the center of administrative records is membership and attendance information. Basic enrollment information will include name, address, telephone number, and church relationship; and, for children, grade in public school, the age and names and church membership status of their parents. A practical type of permanent record is a centrally located alphabetical card file (preferably visibly indexed) of the entire constituency from birth through home department, including teachers and officers. Cross-reference files by families and classes, with duplicate class cards for each teacher or department superintendent, are helpful. Service records on teachers, including in-service training, are also needed, as well as names of prospective teachers. Accurate reporting of attendance is important, although a plan that will not disturb classes should be worked out for checking attendance.

Denominational publishing houses prepare printed supplies of many kinds. Various types of individual permanent record cards, providing for a wide range of information, are available. One such card, for example, makes provision for registering a pupil's progress from nursery through the high school department, with a summary of attendance not only in Sunday church school but also in weekday and vacation church schools. Some cards furnish space for a progressive record of courses studied. Other types of available supplies are roll books for classes of various sizes, quarterly or annual class roll cards, and a variety of record books for use by the church school secretary.

A church school may find printed supplies that exactly serve its needs, or it may prefer to design its own forms for printing or mimeographing. In *The Church School Superintendent*, Philip C. Jones reproduces the various forms prepared by one school. The enrollment forms are of special interest, providing for nota-

tions as to who brought the new pupil and where he had previously been enrolled.

Teacher's records may include many items about each pupil to supplement the administrative records. A useful device is a notebook with a few pages designated for each member of the class. Teachers of children and youth may list such data as names and ages of brothers and sisters, while teachers of adults will be concerned with other facts. Interests, hobbies, responses to situations and people, and other information discovered by observation, conversation, and class discussion will be added from week to week. A good illustration of the teacher's notebook is in Hazel Lewis' *Knowing Children Better*, which quotes one teacher's records regarding a boy in her class. For a full treatment on recording and using information about children, see Daniel Prescott's *The Child in the Educative Process*, much of which is applicable to the church school, although written from a public-school viewpoint.

To be of value church school records must be used and must be kept up to date. They not only furnish information for quarterly and annual reports but assist in evaluating progress, helping to determine whether purposes are being achieved. Attendance records may throw some light on the effectiveness of the teaching and of the course of study. Follow-up of absentees is facilitated by accurate records. Consistent membership and attendance records can provide information useful for historical summaries or for building committees. In small schools that must consider regrouping of children and young people each year complete records of the course studied and the age and public-school grade of each pupil are essential.

The teacher's records not only help him to understand and relate to his pupils but can also assist in evaluating class sessions and give encouragement when pupil growth is evidenced. In some schools the teacher's notebook is shared with the new teacher at promotion time, whereas other schools, fearing that the new teacher's attitude may be affected by subjective opinions, recommend transmittal of only objective information.

— *Meta Ruth Ferguson*

RECREATION Recreation in Christian education may be said to come to the person through experiences of re-creation that involve him in meaningful relationships to God, his fellowman, and the natural order. Re-creation begins when persons become aware of who they are and what their human situation means; when they become aware of God's self-revealing love through Jesus Christ and respond to it in faith and love. This is truly re-creation — the new person in Christ. Recreation, however, is usually associated with play, sports, games, and leisure-time pursuits. Recreation provides opportunities for renewal. It alternates with strain and stress to bring release and refreshment. It affords opportunities for communication between persons that are not found through other types of activity.

After 25 years the persons attending a nationally known recreation laboratory developed a statement of philosophy of the use of leisure time which said, in part: " By definition, leisure is time free from the compulsion of work. For our purpose, let us say that it is time unrelated to the paycheck. Increasingly, our world chains us to a place and a clock. Leisure frees us from these chains of clock and place. It is time when there is no external compulsion to give up what ' I ' want to do. Leisure is time to think, to dream, to see life in its perspective. Leisure is time to enjoy the riches of life, to associate with persons, to be alone, to occupy oneself in the pursuits which will add richness and enjoyment to the present and the future. Leisure is time to explore new vistas, to learn new skills, to discover the beauty of a freshly cut stone, to create a bracelet out of silver, to carve a face out of beautiful wood; a time to make and to feel a part of the great spirit of creation pulsing through one's soul and one's hands. Leisure is time to enjoy the dance and re-create its movement and expression. Leisure is time to recover the height and depth of feeling through great music, to rediscover the joy and thrill of linking one's life with the lives of people in other places, other lands, other cultures, and other ages through the folk songs which have been passed on to us. Leisure is a time to sit by the campfire at night and reflect upon the day and upon life, upon our relationship to God and to our fellowmen. Leisure is time — precious time, recovery time, productive time " (*Northland Creation Laboratory: Notebook, 1959*).

Christian educators are coming to recognize the opportunity that increased leisure provides for the church, by way of working with people through the resources of recreation. Experiences found in play and use of the arts provide added dimensions to relationships among persons and groups.

Many groups have discovered a

new dimension of fellowship through singing together some of the great music of the church, for their own enjoyment rather than for public presentation. This experience can contribute to the deepening of Christian faith. There is increasing interest in the use of " folk " music by church groups. Some groups have dusted off their musical instruments, and the members have discovered one another anew through instrumental music. Drama offers a great variety of opportunities for fellowship. Many groups are turning to play-reading, walking rehearsals, and even to formal presentation of plays as a way of exploring and presenting the message of the Christian faith.

There are much greater possibilities in the use of games to increase fellowship than most groups understand. Abundant resources of games are available, with many games going back to ancient origins and relating participants to cultures of the past. Games selected according to the following criteria contribute to the deeper needs for fellowship: (1) those selected from among games long in existence; (2) those requiring some skill; (3) those calling for creative participation; (4) those including all persons in the group, so that they unite rather than divide the group. Folk games usually have the advantage of combining music with action and using a variety of patterns and numbers of persons. Since they come from many countries, they relate the persons using them in any one country to the persons in the country where the game originated.

Hobbies and crafts offer many ways of meeting needs for fellowship. Since they call for creative initiative and the use of the hands,

they relieve tensions, release creative talents, and restore nervous energy. This helps to create a climate in which persons can come to know one another on the level of their deeper needs and interests.

– Maurice D. Bone

REFORMATION DAY Reformation Day, in the calendar of the Christian year followed by many Protestants, occurs annually on Oct. 31. This is traditionally the anniversary of the day in 1517 when Martin Luther nailed his Ninety-five Theses to the door of the Wittenberg church, an action generally thought of as initiating the Protestant Reformation. (Hans Volz has published evidence supporting Nov. 1 as the day Luther nailed his statements to the church door.) When Oct. 31 does not fall on Sunday, various denominations have designated either the Sunday immediately before or after as the occasion for the festival of the Reformation. In more recent years there has been a pronounced trend toward stabilizing the date of Reformation Sunday as the Lord's Day on or immediately before Oct. 31. The chief purpose was to make possible a more widespread emphasis of All Saints' Day on the 1st Sunday in November. The latter festival, an ancient and important occasion of the ecumenical church, was thus accorded an equal observance with the newer and more sectarian celebration of Reformation Day.

There is a long history of the commemoration of Reformation Sunday among several denominations, especially the Lutheran, Evangelical, Presbyterian, and Reformed Churches. The yearly celebration of the posting of Luther's Theses was introduced into Germany as early as 1667 by John George II, Elector of Saxony. Other German provinces followed his example, and the observance spread eventually throughout the world.

In 1948, when Oct. 31 fell on a Sunday, the Executive Committee of the Federal Council of Churches (predecessor of the NCCCUSA) recommended that "Reformation Day, Oct. 31, 1948, be made the occasion for an emphasis upon our heritage in the Reformation and that as many key communities as possible bear a united witness to the positive principles of the Reformation and their significance for our life today." That year, through the promotion of the Department of Evangelism and the Commission on Worship of the Federal Council, Protestants in 66 American communities united for special observances. In succeeding years the practice has continued and grown with several hundred communities holding interdenominational services. Now Reformation Sunday has become one of Protestantism's great celebrations. Churches in many of the larger cities have staged ceremonies involving considerable pageantry, with processions, massed choirs, and colorful displays. — *Peter N. Vandenberge*

REFORMED CHURCH IN AMERICA

The Reformed Church in America is the oldest Protestant Church in America with an uninterrupted history. It began in 1628 when a congregation of 50 members called Jonas Michaëlius from the Netherlands and established his leadership over the church in the fort in New Amsterdam (now New York City). At first called the Reformed Protestant Dutch Church, with its ecclesiastical relationships in Holland, it played an honorable part in the struggle for independence and be-

came independent with the nation. It changed its name to the Reformed Dutch Church in 1819. Again, in 1867, when the Dutch background had faded almost entirely the name was changed to the Reformed Church in America. Though proud of its Dutch heritage, the church today knows no barriers of national origin or race; its table of Holy Communion is open to all Christians.

The final authority in the Reformed faith is the Reformation principle of Holy Scripture, the living Word of God, spoken to every man through the Holy Spirit of God. The wellspring of this faith is God's Spirit making his Word real and actual in everyday life.

The Standards of the Reformed faith are 3: (1) The oldest is the Belgic Confession written in 1561 by Guido de Brès, a Reformed Church minister. Forbidden to preach openly, he did so preach, in the fields and on the dikes. The Spanish authorities hanged him in 1567. The Confession, a document of 37 chapters, was prepared as a personal message to Spanish King Philip that he ought to cease persecuting the Reformed people of his dominions. Philip probably never saw the document, but others did and it soon became the confession of the church. In his statement De Brès sought to maintain the unity of the church on the foundation of the marks of the true church; the pure service of the word and of the sacraments according to the Word. (2) The most familiar is the Heidelberg Catechism. This was written in 1562 in Heidelberg, Germany, by 2 young ministers named Ursinus and Olevian at the request of Elector Frederick III. Its fame sped quickly and in 1574 it was adopted by the Dutch Church as its official catechism. The statement was an effort on the part of the elector to bring religious peace to his people. The catechism, dealing in its 3 parts with man's misery, man's redemption, and thankfulness for redemption, avoids all arguments. It is a personal confession of faith born out of Christian experience. The 2d part of the catechism is largely an exposition of the Apostles' Creed, including the meaning of the sacraments. The 3d part contains explanations of the Decalogue and the Lord's Prayer. (3) The Canons of Dort. An international synod of the Reformed faith met in Dordrecht, Holland, in 1618–1619, largely to resolve a dispute in the church itself between Arminians and Gomarists. After long discussion the synod adopted certain decisions known as " canons." The 1st of these was a reaffirmation of the Belgic Confession as an adequate statement of the Reformed Church. Further statements dealing with highly technical theological points of view were added to the Confession.

The Reformed Church together with other churches of Christendom accepts the historic catholic Creeds as the heart of its faith: the Apostles', the Nicene, and the Athanasian. Thus the Reformed Church joins in the great central affirmations of the Christian faith.

The Reformed Church believes in an educated ministry and a well-informed laity. For the training of its leadership it maintains accredited colleges and theological seminaries. Its prospective ministers and missionaries must have college degrees before admission to theological education. It has a program of graded catechetical instruction for children and youth, as well as a graded curriculum for the church school.

The Board of Christian Education has set forth these objectives: (1) to present Biblical religious instruction; (2) to secure commitment to Jesus Christ and his way of life; (3) to encourage intelligent union with and active service in the church; and (4) to project the worldwide program of the Christian way.

— *Bernard J. Mulder*

RELATIONSHIP THEOLOGY " Relationship theology " is a term used to describe both the sources of theological truth and the means of communicating it. It begins with a definition of theology as " the truth about God in relation to man." It recognizes the living God at work in man's world as the source of religious living. It derives this in part from Horace Bushnell's concept of the organic relations of man and God as spelled out in *Christian Nurture* and from Martin Buber's interpretation in *I and Thou*. It recognizes that nurture takes place in the community and that the church, among other things, is to be described as the community of the Holy Spirit. It puts the primary emphasis on personal relations on both the human and the divine levels, Reuel L. Howe makes the distinction that God created persons to be loved and things to be used and that any reversal of this leads to a breaking of human and divine relationships.

The source of our knowledge about God is to be found in revelation. Revelation, as seen from this position, is derived from a definition by William Temple: it consists " in a coincidence of divinely guided events with minds divinely illuminated to apprehend those events, so that there [are] no revealed truths, but there [are] truths of revelation "

(*Nature, Man and God,* pp. 315, 499). Revelation is always something that happens and something that is apprehended; it is event plus meaning. This dynamic view of man in relation to God means that the "truths of revelation" are descriptions of relationships, not propositions. Faith is a description of a personal relationship, an attitude of trust in the living God. Love is relational and exists between persons. The process of reconciliation and forgiveness, offered to us by the free grace of God, is a description of a new relationship, experienced in the community of the Holy Spirit.

These illustrations of how the key words of the Christian faith describe relationships can be spelled out specifically in terms of the process of redemption. We live in community and experience loneliness, anxiety, and sin. Loneliness and anxiety may or may not be the result of responsible moral action in relation to persons, but sin is seen as a free choice that separates us from God and from our fellows. But the result of sin is such that we remain in this broken relationship unless, by the grace of God, we are empowered by God, working either directly or through others, to heal this broken relationship. The good news of the gospel, therefore, is the gift of the new relationship as God acts through persons in the community of the Holy Spirit to make this gift available to us. The life of the church is basically oriented to being a channel of God's grace, whereby broken relationships are healed, we are sustained, and we live out the implications of this new relationship as Christians in the world.

This tells us much about the life of the church. We enter the church through baptism. Oliver Quick writes that in baptism God acts to declare and seal his relationship to the child; he acts through the community, primarily through the ministry, to make possible the implications of baptism in the ongoing life of the child. The Lord's Supper, which Howe calls "the sacrament of the common food and the uncommon love," is seen in terms of its table fellowship as well as in terms of the relation to the living Christ who is present. An understanding of the relationships between persons in the congregation is essential for seeing the meaning of the Lord's Supper, yet the supernatural works in and through the believing congregation. The corporate nature of relationships leads to a reevaluation of the nature of the church as the people of the new covenant, the body of Christ, the followers of the way, those who have been called out, and the fellowship, or communion, or community, of the Holy Spirit. The church is seen as an event of revelation, for God has acted in history through Jesus Christ to form this new kind of community. The redemptive love of God is at work in the members through the power of the Holy Spirit, and they become the channels of God's redemption. But the church still stands under judgment.

Education is a reflection of the life of the community in which the learner participates. The specifically Christian element in the community life is the redemptive and sustaining love of God as it is mediated through the personal relations of the community. Growth in grace occurs as the learner is enabled to respond in faith to the free gift of God's love.

This places an almost impossible demand on the life of the modern congregation because it is a fellowship of sinners in need of repentance. It is not able to be the kind of community in which Christian nurture will take place. Therefore, in order to understand the true function of a parish, a reevaluation in terms of interpersonal relations is the starting point. Education through relationships may use the insights of group dynamics at this point. The emphasis is on the quality of life of the group in which the grace of God is communicated.

Lewis J. Sherrill, following Paul Tillich, has shown how the themes of the Biblical faith are correlated with man's predicament. Within the community the saving truth of the gospel is communicated. Marjorie Reeves suggests that such a community should include consistency, recognition of all members as persons, a significant part for each member, a variety of interests, and the service of God.

The goals of such an educational process are in terms of discernment and commitment. Teaching begins with the genuine concerns of the learner and the content of Christian teaching becomes a guide to living as a Christian in the world. The learners are enabled to discern the work of God in their midst, and the community sustains them as they are faced with the reality of decision. This decision cannot be manipulated, but once it is made (subject to renewal from time to time), the process continues in terms of their being sustained in relation to God and their fellows.

The language of relationships is a primary means of communication whereby through living together we find the personal meanings for the words we hear and use. It is effective with the young before they can use language. The language of words deals with characteristically personal situations and provides a new dimension in which the understanding of God's relation to man may break through. It builds on relationships, it uses words to express relationships with God and man, and often finds that things are a means of discourse. Symbols other than words participate in the reality of personal relationships.

The gospel speaks to those who know they are separated from the Lord and need to be redeemed. It speaks to those who know that God has redeemed them even when they do not deserve it. The whole gospel is relevant to the needs of everyone, and through what we call the language of relationships it is possible for God to work in human community, especially through the home and church, to alter our lives, and to help us face our essential problems, and be the church in the world.

— Randolph Crump Miller

RELIGIOUS EDUCATION ASSOCIATION At the turn of the century a number of far-seeing leaders in religion and education were beginning to perceive the relative inadequacy of the institutional provisions for religious education in the American culture. The Sunday school was bearing the brunt of the burden, and doing its job for the church with only moderate effectiveness. Meanwhile, elsewhere in the American scene no great attention was being paid to the necessity for strong moral and religious foundations if the society were to remain strong.

To the end of exploring these matters a group of persons determined to issue a call for the formation of a Religious Education Association. Among the laymen and clergymen involved in the movement were many distinguished persons, such as Nicholas Murray Butler, S. Parkes Cadman, George Albert Coe, Charles Cuthbert Hall, Francis G. Peabody, James E. Russell, Henry van Dyke, Booker T. Washington, and Mary E. Woolley, all of whom served in some official capacity in the new organization.

The Proceedings of the First Annual Convention of the Association (Chicago, 1903) refer to the concerns of the founders: " That the religious and moral instruction of the young is at present inadequate, and imperfectly correlated with other instruction in history, literature, and the sciences; . . . that the Sunday school, as the primary institution for the religious and moral education of the young, should be conformed to a higher ideal; . . . that the home, the day school, and all other agencies should be developed to assist." The intention was to provide a clearinghouse and forum of information, ideas, and proposals. From the beginning it was intended to be interfaith, and although Protestants have constituted its largest membership group, there have always been Jewish and Roman Catholic members as well.

The " broad objectives " of the Association are stated in an undated pamphlet of the Association as follows: " To inspire the religious forces of our country with the educational ideal; to inspire the educational forces with the religious ideal; to keep before the public the ideal of religious education and the sense of its need and value."

Local chapters are conducted in some cities. The Association publishes a journal, *Religious Education,* regarded as a most influential professional journal of interest to thoughtful religious and secular educators. Seminars and national conventions are held from time to time. Special projects are undertaken, such as the administering of a foundation grant to encourage the development of research designs in religious and character education.

— *Kendig Brubaker Cully*

REPORT CARD Available evidence indicates that report cards are not widely used in Christian education. Several decades ago religious educators gave much attention to developing tests for analyzing Christian growth. (See G. W. Watson, *Experimentation and Measurement in Religious Education* [1927] or W. S. Athearn, *The Indiana Survey of Religious Education* [1923].) The Character Research Project has stressed this kind of approach more recently.

Church schools employing progress reports include a variety of items. Some forms concentrate on objective data such as attendance, punctuality, offerings, and behavior. Others wrestle with more intangible features such as showing reverence in worship, growing in Christian faith, and developing Christian character.

Whenever using report cards, the church school involved must consider carefully its purpose in doing so. Most churches supporting such a program justify it in terms of both guidance and measurement. Chief values center in home-church cooperation. Parents need to know what and how children do in church school.

Dangers include difficulties in measuring Christian development and possibilities of discouraging pupils. The decision of what grading system to use is important. Few churches use letter marks or a percentage method. More prevalent is a rating system of "usually," "frequently," or "seldom" as applied to items such as "pupil participates in a group discussion." Personal notes and comments from the teacher can enhance the value of reports. Particularly helpful are interviews of teachers with pupils and/or parents to explain markings and elicit reactions.

The age level for which reports are intended suggests areas to include. Thus, younger children would not be checked on Bible knowledge. Preschool departments often prefer anecdotal records.

No single form can be applied to all churches. For greatest effectiveness each church school should consider its particular goals and then devise its own report cards. If parents and teachers share in developing a reporting system, the venture may be more meaningful. In some situations class members themselves can help determine purposes and areas for grading. For sample report cards, see John Leslie Lobingier, *The Better Church School*, p. 4; Wesner Fallaw, *The Modern Parent and the Teaching Church*, p. 224, and *Church Education for Tomorrow*, pp. 158 f. — *M. Dosia Carlson*

RESEARCH The term "research" means many things to many people. It includes historical and philosophical investigation as well as experimental study. Research in Christian education is one specific aspect of the more general field of educational research and includes many methodologies. In developing a curriculum, for example, philosophical

and theological study help to establish the foundations and objectives of the curriculum. Experimental research suggests effective teaching methods and is used in curriculum evaluation.

Christian education research may be defined as systematic investigation of the processes and results of Christian education through the collection and analysis of objective evidence. Its purpose is usually to provide a more adequate understanding of the processes and results of Christian education, in the hope that this understanding will provide a basis for more effective educational efforts. Research procedures usually include precise formulation and definition of the problem to be studied; collection of relevant data from as wide as possible a range of sources; objective analysis and study of these data, often including statistical tests; and statement of findings, including careful evaluation of their probable limitations and sources of error. The purpose of these rigorous procedures is to move as far as possible from armchair opinion toward dependable knowledge about processes and results.

Program research is designed to answer specific questions or to help in solving specific problems in the development of program or curriculum. This may include descriptive research, designed to provide accurate information about the conditions under which the program is used, the backgrounds, experience, and opinions of persons involved in the program, etc. Program research may also include evaluation, studies designed to test the extent to which a program or curriculum achieves its objectives. Program research is designed to answer specific, immediate, practical questions. It provides a basis for making objective judgments about the program and improving it on the basis of those judgments.

Basic research is designed to provide understanding of complex phenomena related to the more basic processes and results of Christian education. (For example: What is the relation between theological beliefs and moral or ethical behavior? What are the dimensions of religious growth? the developmental stages in religious and character formation?) Findings of such research have implications for all aspects of Christian education; their significance is not limited to any specific program or curriculum. Since the findings of basic research are to have such wide application, research methods are usually more complex and rigorous than the methods used in program research.

These types of research are not, of course, mutually exclusive. Basic research findings can have immediate practical implications. Program research can be designed so that its findings contribute to basic understandings as well as to the solution of immediate problems.

The foundations of educational research were laid well before 1900. In the early 19th century Pestalozzi proposed the scientific study of teaching and began a practice school. The period from 1900 to 1925 was marked by widespread interest in objective tests and measurements, the study of individual differences, and varied efforts at educational evaluation. The 2d quarter of the 20th century was a period of refinement of research techniques and their extension to such new fields as group dynamics and learning theory. During this period little basic research was carried on in the field of Christian education. Important contributions to the theory and practice of Christian education came from educational research in such areas as developmental psychology and individual differences; the nature, organization, and integration of personality; the nature of group processes; teaching methods, such as audio-visuals. Many of the research methods developed for these studies were also applicable to the study of Christian education. Useful summaries of educational research can be found in *The Encyclopedia of Educational Research*.

It is not always possible to use the techniques and findings of general educational research in Christian education. The basic presuppositions, settings, and objectives of Christian education differ widely from those of general education. These research findings do, however, point to fruitful areas for research in Christian education.

Philosophical, theological, and historical research have always been a part of the development of Christian education. Experimental research in Christian education received its first major impetus with the publication in 1927 of Watson's *Experimentation and Measurement in Religious Education*. At this time, however, research methods were cumbersome and few trained persons were available for research in Christian education. As a result, although general education made steady advance in the fields of research and evaluation, there was a slackening of interest in Christian education research. Activity in this field began to grow again in the early 1950's.

Several organizations have developed and maintained interest in Christian education research. The

National Council of the Churches of Christ in the U.S.A. maintains a Bureau of Research and Survey that conducts its own studies, sponsors workshops and conferences on research and evaluation, and provides liaison among those doing research in Christian education.

The Religious Education Association, an interfaith group, also maintains a steady interest in research. Its journal, *Religious Education,* provides a channel for the publication of Christian education research findings and publishes annual abstracts of doctoral disserations related to religious and character education. In 1958 the Association conducted and published a survey of research related to religious and character education, and in 1961 it sponsored a research planning workshop that resulted in the production of 50 designs for basic research in religious education.

The Character Research Project of Union College was organized in 1935 for the purpose of basic research in Christian character education. It conducts research in such areas as individual differences, the home and family, youth work, learning, and experimental design.

During the 1950's denominational boards began to make specific staff provision for research in Christian education. At the end of the decade, most of the major denominations had departments or staff persons primarily responsible for Christian education research. At this time, however, most denominational effort was still being invested in program research. Basic research was still being done, for the most part, by individuals, especially members of the faculties of colleges and seminaries.

One may wonder why such slow progress was made in Christian education research at a time when rapid progress was being made in general educational research. A number of factors are probably involved:

1. Cost: Educational research is complex, time-consuming, and expensive. Denominational leaders sometimes find it difficult to estimate the potential values of research and to find the funds and staff to support it. However, denominations that have made such investments in research have usually found their investment justified in terms of more acceptable, usable, and effective programs of Christian education.

2. Need for a theological foundation: Scientific research techniques have not always been an integral part of Christian education. Efforts to do research in this field have been met by the objection that religious experience is an ineffable inward event that is beyond the reach of measurement and observation. In addition, there is the theological objection that God is at work in Christian education, and we cannot evaluate God's activity.

Theological questions have not been adequately answered, but answers have begun to emerge as Christian educators themselves have become more deeply involved in research and evaluation. Starting points for theological thinking have been that God is at work in all of life; therefore, if we cannot evaluate activities in which God is at work, we cannot evaluate anything. Man, as sinner, is always wrong to some degree; therefore, man stands in constant need of taking a measure of his imperfection, seeking guidance for redirection and change.

3. Need for competent personnel: Christian education research must be an interdisciplinary effort. The

researcher must be at home in theological, philosophical, and ethical frames of thought; he must also be aware of the findings of psychology and sociology; he must be competent in the use of empirical methods of research. One of the major problems of Christian education research has been that of finding or developing individuals with this broad background of training and experience.

Social scientists are becoming more interested in and sympathetic to Christian education and religion as fields for research. Denominational interest in and support of research are growing. If these trends continue, many problems can be solved and research can become an integral and productive part of Christian education. — *Leonard A. Sibley, Jr.*

RESOURCE PERSON A resource person is one who is engaged to contribute to a learning experience by reason of his particular skill, experience, or knowledge of a subject. The resource person usually serves a learning group by presenting facts, personal experiences, observations, objects, or opinions that are related to their study. In the same way that visual resources are utilized a resource person is sought in order that he may make a contribution to the learning process.

A teacher should guide the group's use of a resource person just as he should guide their use of books, maps, or a field trip. He should make it easy for the resource person to make the best contribution to the group and relate it to their ongoing experience. The resource person, though skilled in his own field, may not be acquainted with teaching or with the age group he is asked to help. This need not deter his being invited as a resource person. The

teacher should talk with him in advance (or guide group members to do this), discussing with him his special field, showing him where his contribution is needed by the group, and planning with him how it can be made.

One of the best means of utilizing a resource person is an interview, with the teacher or a member of the group questioning the resource person. The interview should be characterized by leading questions that provide the resource person a means of sharing with the learners his special knowledge of a subject. An informal, friendly atmosphere encourages such sharing.

Another effective way a resource person may be used is for a panel of students to prepare to interview him. The whole group may list in advance questions they want to ask, or a few representatives may be chosen to visit the resource person and make a report. A tape recording of their interview with him, or parts of it, may be a good way to bring the personality of the resource person to the group if his schedule does not permit his presence at their meeting. It is well to have the resource person know in advance of an interview the questions likely to be discussed. A less formal approach is to have him available as a source of authority only in case the learners in their discussion become aware of the need for additional help.

Another use of a resource person is with teachers. A person skilled in a craft or well versed in nature may be best used as a resource person for the teachers and leaders before they meet their class or camp groups. Thus the teachers may gain skills themselves and can develop ways of using skills according to the needs and interests of the group.

The resource person differs from the leader in that the leader is charged with the responsibility of helping to plan and guide the learning session, whereas the resource person is charged only with making a specific contribution to the session or of being present to furnish information if the need should arise.

Many resource persons often are available to groups, e.g., when a group is studying the meaning of church membership, the pastor of the church may be a resource person; when young people are discussing vocations, the high school guidance counselor may be called in; an amateur photographer with photographs or colored slides — of another country, of beauty spots or a striking sunset — can enrich units of study for children. A person who has visited another country and knows the land, manners, and customs of the people can greatly enrich a study for children. He might be willing to share examples of their arts and crafts. One caution, however: the teacher should ascertain the attitude this person has toward people of other countries, for children should be led to think of them as persons like themselves, not as curiosities, or as having less value or ability than themselves.

In a sense every learner is a resource person to his group, for he brings to a session his particular fund of experience and knowledge. Groups should not fail to use the resources of their own members, and should usually turn to outside resource persons only after making full use of the abilities within their membership. On the other hand, groups should not fail to gain the enrichment that can come through well-planned use of outside resource persons. — *Mabel Metze*

REVELATION The word "revelation" comes from the Latin *revelatio,* which means an unveiling, uncovering, or disclosing. The hidden is disclosed. The secret is opened. The concealed is revealed. The Greek word *apokalypsis* occurs several times in the New Testament with the same cluster of meanings. For example, "Nothing is covered up that will not be revealed, or hidden that will not be known" (Luke 12:2). Notice that the last book of the Bible, usually called The Revelation to John, is sometimes titled "The Apocalypse."

Revelation, simply as a word, is neutral. In itself it lacks specific content. The word, consequently, permits such a wide variety of usage as to be almost meaningless. Is every opened secret a revelation? Christian thinkers have generally agreed that the word must properly be restricted to disclosures of God; and here they are at one with the thinkers of many religions who would also claim that their prophets, their visions, their sacred books, also offer genuine disclosures of God.

The word "revelation" has a general and unrestricted meaning as the opening of any secret. It has a more specifically religious meaning as a disclosure of God. Is there a specifically Christian meaning? What does the Christian properly mean when he uses the term?

Revelation means an unveiling, but it offers no clues as to who unveils, where the unveiling takes place, what is unveiled, or the purpose of the unveiling. Who reveals? Where? What? Why? These are distinctive questions in a Christian understanding of revelation. They are asked and answered in the conviction that a genuine disclosure of God has taken place. The Christian thinker does not try to fit the facts to a definition; he tries to frame his definition from the facts. If God has in fact revealed himself, then a Christian definition of revelation is based on what God has done rather than on a general and unsupported notion of what he might or could do.

Such a definition might be: Revelation is God's activity in Jesus Christ, by whom God discloses himself for man and man for him, that man may be restored to God, his neighbor, and himself. An analysis of this definition shows some of the issues involved in a Christian understanding of revelation.

Revelation is God's activity. A neutral definition of revelation could say that all human knowledge is a result of some sort of revelation. In this sense there would be no real distinction between disclosure and discovery. Do we " discover " God in the same way that we discover a new medicine, atomic fission, a shortcut to the office, or a long-lost friend? Most Christian thinkers have agreed that revelation is more properly seen as God's disclosure than as man's discovery. God is the initiator of the search; he opens himself to man. If man " discovers " God, it is because God has disclosed himself so that he can be discovered.

It is also God's act. Neutral definitions of revelation often tend to overlook its active character. It is an unveiling, a disclosing, an uncovering. It is something that happens. It is not static but dynamic. It is a process. It is a story to be told, not facts to be memorized and recited. It is the story of God's activity with Israel. It is the story of Abraham, Isaac, Jacob, Moses, the prophets, and Jesus Christ and his church.

Revelation is in Jesus Christ.

This is the precise point where a genuinely Christian understanding of revelation breaks company with all general, neutral, and abstract definitions. Such definitions have often distinguished between " general " and " special " revelation. The gist of this distinction is whether God is somehow open to discovery generally in the beauty and orderliness of nature, the workings of conscience, and the religious spirit of mankind; or is he available only where and when he chooses to reveal himself? Or is this question unfairly put? Perhaps the helpful question that should be introduced into this discussion is, Where do we know God significantly?

The answer to this question is, for the Christian, that God is known significantly when he is known as the Father Almighty of our Lord Jesus Christ. Hence, many Christian thinkers no longer talk about general revelation as if it were a doorway to special revelation. Jesus Christ is the clue, the focus, the fulcrum of revelation. In this way, it is not asserted that God's activities of self-disclosure are confined to Jesus Christ; it is asserted that they are defined in Jesus Christ.

An analogy may be helpful. When you meet a person you almost immediately become conscious of a host of facts: height, weight, facial contours, dress, color of eyes, etc. Yet you do not know this person as a person until he chooses to disclose himself as a person to you. The details of size and shape are quite irrelevant apart from their relation to someone who has disclosed himself to you as a person. In this sense such things as are claimed for " general " revelation are of no value except when they fill out one's understanding of the God who has addressed us in Jesus Christ.

Another aspect of this same issue relates to the place of the Bible and the church in revelation. Are they revelation in the same sense in which Jesus Christ is? Do they share his authority? Are they equal to him or to each other? These questions have puzzled Christian thinkers for centuries. There is still no general agreement among Christians. What has been suggested, however, by several thinkers of our time is a distinction between revelation and witness. In this sense, both Bible and church stand under Jesus Christ as witnesses to him. They possess authority only insofar as they are faithful witnesses to him. In such an understanding, Jesus Christ is the only true and proper revelation. The written word of the Bible and the preached word of the church are only dependently revelation. Only Jesus Christ is truly, primarily and properly the Word of God.

So long as the Bible is thought of as being in itself revelation in a primary sense, there is real confusion. Such a notion of revelation becomes static, fixed, dead. Revelation is no longer an activity; it becomes a collection of rules for thought and practice. The confusion is compounded by the question whether such revelation is God's activity. If it is not, then it is trivial; if it is, then the Bible loses its focus, it becomes blurred, and the Christian is caught in an endless battle of proof texts.

God discloses himself for man, and man for God. So long as revelation is defined apart from Jesus Christ, it is possible to distinguish between the act of disclosing, the thing disclosed, and the vehicle of the disclosure. However, a Christian understanding of revelation sees these 3 aspects bound together in him, and only in him. The act, the content, and the means of revelation coincide only in Jesus Christ.

In Jesus Christ, God discloses himself for man. What is offered is not information about God, the world, or man. What is offered is a new relationship. Jesus Christ is God's offer of himself to man. Jesus Christ is also man's true offer of himself for God. Hence, the content of the Christian revelation is nothing other than the true and proper relationship between God and man. This is its center, its focus, its content. The witness of Bible and church surround this center, pointing to it, guarding it, proclaiming it. Revelation, therefore, has its content in the offer of a relationship, not an offer of information.

If the act, content, and means of revelation are Jesus Christ, then the purpose of revelation is not that we may be granted information, but that we may be restored. It is in our conversations with the Bible and the church that we are confronted by God's activity in Jesus Christ. It is in him that we are proffered God's grace. He is God's act of restoration of man to God, his neighbor, and himself. Revelation cannot be separated from salvation. It is never a matter of indifference. It is a matter of life or death. Hence, the Word of God is witnessed to in the Bible and the church where matters of life and death are involved. — *John E. Burkhart*

ROLE–PLAYING Role-playing is an educational tool in which group or class members portray, through acting out, the roles, functions, or emotional stances that persons employ, either knowingly or unknowingly, in interpersonal relationships. Sometimes the word "sociodrama" is used to describe the same technique.

The differences between role-playing and psychodrama should be carefully delineated. In psychodrama, a somewhat specialized form of group therapy, the scene to be enacted is specifically constructed to heighten the emotional or interpersonal problems of a group member or members. In many instances the person with the problem portrays himself. Generally speaking, psychodrama focuses on the problematic individual, his relation to the group, and theirs to him. Psychodrama should be employed only by trained therapists. Role-playing, on the other hand, focuses on the more normal social and interpersonal situations. In the casting of a role-playing scene, a participant is never given a role that is known to be an emotional problem to him. In both instances, the substance of the drama is from everyday life rather than from fiction, but psychodrama focuses primarily on the individual whereas role-playing utilizes interpersonal relations in the day-to-day world.

Role-playing also is differentiated from creative dramatics in that the latter takes the material to be portrayed from literature or from some block of heritage. The literature or the heritage may be pertinent or relevant to present problems. Nonetheless, the material has not been generated by the group or class itself. It is in the area of the source of the material to be played that the definition of difference resides. This does not mean that creative dramatics cannot accomplish some of the same aims as role-playing.

Role-playing is the acting out of normal (even though possibly problematic) human relations situations.

The material upon which the role-playing is built comes from the group or class, either directly or through the leader's sensitivity to what is characteristic of his group. From his sensitivity the leader may fashion or suggest the scenes.

A role-play seeks to portray real life, and in pursuit of this aim the characters are encouraged to play the role as it comes to them. Briefing may be given to persons acting so that they will understand the roles to be presented. Scripts, however, are never used. Role-playing is not a problem-solving device; rather, it is a technique that sets forth situations dramatically. The scenes are "situation presenters" or "problem presenters" and they do not go beyond the setting forth of the situation to the resolution of the situation.

Role-playing divorced from subsequent discussion should never be tried. After seeing enough of the situation to grasp the problem, the group should proceed to probe the scene, then should discuss its import. Role-playing is part of a continuum that begins with constructing a scene and then goes on to playing the scene, probing or interrogating the characters to bring out how they felt in the particular interaction, quizzing the group to see if all minimal as well as maximal interaction was noted by the observers and, finally, discussing the import of the role-play. This last stage may suggest to the group another scene that it would like to see done (perhaps changing the behavior of 1 or 2 characters), but the same continuum should be employed again. Role-playing should move the group to deeper insight or deeper levels of discussion.

There are certain times in the life of a group when role-playing can be helpful. When the group is about to embark on consideration of a problem, role-playing can be a provocative initiating device. The whole group sees the problem set forth dramatically. Much valuable time is saved, since the need for intricate verbal description is eliminated. Role-playing also can help carry a problem to deeper or broader levels. A group may reach a certain level of discussion and then find it cannot communicate successfully to all its members unless it stops and sees portrayed what was hard to communicate. An example of this would be a group impasse concerning what form of behavior would be most appropriate in a given situation. The group would be helped by seeing alternate forms of behavior enacted so that members might reach more realistic conclusions. Role-playing can help a group "reality test" conclusions or decisions that it reaches. Role-playing enlarges the sensitivity of the group regarding the feelings of others. "Putting on another's shoes" can be illuminating, and this added sensitivity can carry the group to new levels of consideration. Good role-playing always objectifies a situation, and such objectivity is itself always helpful to group life.

Role-playing has been used with groups as young as nursery age. However, in instances where it has been employed with young children the leader always has been fully trained not only in the use of this tool but in child development as well. The ordinary group leader would do well to restrict the use of this technique to late juniors through adults; even with late juniors the leader should be especially sensitive to the children. Role-playing should not be suggested until the leader and the group have an established rapport or "trust relationship." Before a leader encourages group members to role-play, he himself should have had the experience of role-playing and also a level of training that would be given at a good church school teachers training institute. If leaders in a parish feel that role-playing should be introduced to their groups but feel uneasy about launching it, the film *Role-playing in Human Relations Training* issued by the National Education Association can be shown at a leaders meeting.

A procedure for the use of role-playing might be suggested:

1. Choose the scene to be portrayed. Isolate the scene either through group discussion or by the leader's knowledge of the group. One problem, and not a multiplicity of problems, should be enacted.

2. Choose the characters and brief them regarding their roles, if necessary. Here, again, this can be a group procedure or a leadership function.

3. Role-play. Short scenes are usually best, lasting no longer than 5 to 7 minutes. Play only enough to communicate the problem; do not try to push to its resolution. The leader cuts the role-play when he feels the group has caught the situation.

4. Interrogate the characters as to how they felt in the interaction, how they felt about the roles others portrayed, and how they wish it might have been different.

5. Interrogate the observers as to what they noticed in the role-play, how the characters responded to one another, what facial or bodily clues were manifested. Do not let the observers comment on the quality of acting, however.

6. Launch into group discussion regarding the importance of what they have seen or what could be done to help relieve the problem.

After role-playing has been cut by the leader, he should take care that he helps the characters " de-role." They should be brought back to the reality of their own personhood, abandoning continuation in role. This is easily accomplished by using the person's given name rather than the character name at the time of interrogation.

— Francis W. Voelcker

ROMAN CATHOLIC EDUCATION IN THE U.S.A. Religious formation by Roman Catholics began in what is now the U.S.A. with Dom Bernardo Buil, O.S.B., who accompanied Columbus on his 2d voyage (1493). Ponce de León brought priests to Florida (1521); Dominican friars with Vásquez de Ayllón 1st brought the Mass to the banks of the James River in Virginia (1526). The Italian Franciscan Padre Marco reached New Mexico in 1539; a shrine was built at Pensacola by Tristán de Luna in 1559, and the 1st parish was erected in St. Augustine, Fla., in 1565. Franciscan friars had an estimated 75,000 under instruction in 21 missions in what is now California in the period 1768–1822. When Mexico revolted against Spain (1825), the friars were expelled. As to French influence, 2 Jesuits settled on Mt. Desert Island off the coast of Maine in 1612; in 1646, the year of the martyrdom of Isaac Jogues, the Abnaki tribe of Maine was sending to Quebec for the " black robes " they had formerly had and rejected.

Regarding English influence, the 1st Roman Catholics landed at St. Clement's Isle in Chesapeake Bay on March 25, 1634, accompanied by a Jesuit priest, Andrew White. Two Capuchins from England joined them in 1643. Through a series of political mischances the Roman Catholics were deprived of their civil rights in this colony in 1654. Twenty Jesuits were at work there when the Maryland Declaration of Rights restored their liberties in 1776. In 1784, Pope Pius VI named John Carroll prefect apostolic of the English-speaking colonies and on Nov. 6, 1789, his appointment as the 1st bishop of Baltimore was ratified. Carroll was Maryland-born but trained at St. Omer's in France and in England. Although he was a professed father of the Society of Jesus, his entire American apostolate took place during the suppression of that society by the papacy.

The oldest native published work in the U.S.A. is thought to be the translation of Pareja's *Doctrina Christiana* into Timucua, an Indian language spoken around Mobile.

The 1st Roman Catholic school in the U.S.A. was a classical school founded by Spanish Franciscans in St. Augustine in 1606, which died out shortly. There was a French Capuchin foundation for boys in New Orleans in 1722 and another made there for girls by Ursuline nuns in 1727. The English and Dutch schools of 17th-century America are properly termed " children of the church," whether New England Congregational or Church of England as in Virginia, Carolina, and Georgia. Moravians, Quakers, Lutherans, Presbyterians, and Baptists likewise conducted schools with public colonial funds both before and after 1776.

A Roman Catholic synod, held at Baltimore, Nov. 7–10, 1791, with 20 priests in attendance, stipulated that confirmation should not be administered before the age of reason; it also discussed the conditions for the reception of First Communion and penance. The 1st Provincial Council was held at Baltimore, Oct. 4–18, 1829. It decreed among other things that bishops should promote the reading of the Douai-Reims version of the Bible; that sponsors at baptism should know the rudiments of faith; and that "schools should be established, where youth might imbibe the principles of faith and morality along with human knowledge" (Decr. 34). Another canon recommended that good books be diffused throughout society.

The country's 2d Provincial Council met in the same city Oct. 20–27, 1833. It called for a seminary in each diocese, and charged the presidents of St. Mary's Seminary, Baltimore, Mount St. Mary's Seminary, Emmitsburg, Md., and Georgetown College near Washington with revising and expurgating the books intended for Roman Catholic schools, since "the entire system of education is tinged . . . [and] history itself has been distorted to our serious injury" (Decr. 9).

Meantime, the institutions of learning founded in the colonial period included Bohemia Manor, Md. (1744–1765), and Georgetown College (1791), founded 1 year before the nearby Federal city of Washington. Members of the Baltimore clergy, many of them Jesuits by religious profession, staffed Georgetown. A Sulpician priest, Louis Dubourg (afterward bishop of New Orleans), became its president in 1796. St. Mary's College, Baltimore, was opened under another Sulpician, François Nagot, in 1791, but it afterward became a seminary exclusively. Bishop Neale

in 1805 turned a property of French Poor Clares (Franciscan-rule contemplatives) over to the Visitation nuns, who opened a school there (now Georgetown Visitation Junior College). Carmelite nuns did the same in Baltimore in 1831 after a false start (out of Belgium) in Port Tobacco, Md. The now Venerable Mother Elizabeth Ann (Bayley) Seton, with 4 companions, took the habit of the Sisters of Charity at Emmitsburg in 1809; foundations were made in Philadelphia in 1814 and New York 3 years later. In 1809 the Abbé Dubois (later bishop of New York) became a Sulpician and founded Mount St. Mary's College and Seminary in Emmitsburg. When the Society of St. Sulpice abandoned it in 1819, the diocesan clergy took it over. Loyola College, Baltimore, was founded by the Jesuits in 1852. The Brothers of the Christian Schools made foundations in Baltimore in 1846 and New York in 1848. Important to the story of U.S. Roman Catholicity was the poverty of the liturgy and Gregorian chant except in the parishes conducted by the German Redemptorists in Baltimore, Philadelphia, and New York.

The forerunners of catechetical instruction in the U.S.A. were the counter-Reformation theologians, Peter Canisius and Robert Bellarmine, both S.J. More proximate influences were Bishop Richard Challoner, of London (whose catechism appeared in 1737), and 2 authors of catechisms in Ireland and Germany respectively, Bishop James Butler, of Cashel (1775), and Josef Deharbe, S.J. (1847). The Napoleonic catechism of 1806 (the work of Bossuet) was doubtless in partial use in the Louisiana territory. Bishop John England, of Charleston, S.C.

(1821), Coadjutor Bishop Jean-Baptiste David, of Bardstown, Ky. (1825), and a Jesuit active earlier in Pennsylvania and Maryland, Robert Molyneux (1785), all produced catechisms. American editions of European works — frequently unacknowledged as to authorship — predominated: Butler (1788) and Bishop George Hay, of Edinburgh (*Abridgement of Christian Doctrine*, 1800), chiefly. The Douai Catechism of Henry Turberville (1649) made its appearance in the States in a New York reprint of 1833 in its archaic form, but also in Philadelphia in the modernized form in which it was prepared for the Irish dioceses of Kildare and Leighlin. Josef Deharbe's work began to appear in America in English translation in 1869. The 2d Provincial Council of 1829 decreed on this subject: " A catechism shall be written which is better adapted to the circumstances of this province; it shall give the Christine doctrine as explained in Cardinal Bellarmine's catechism, and when approved by the Holy See, it shall be published for the common use of Catholics." (Decr. 33.) The prescription about Bellarmine's catechism was included at the suggestion of the Congregation " De Propaganda Fide." An Italian-English version of this work of 1597 appeared in Boston in 1853. Nothing came of the decree, however, except that it was repeated in the 1st and 2d Plenary Councils of Baltimore in 1852 and 1866. At the 3d Plenary Council (1884) many bishops favored a revised edition of Butler, but the production of a " catechism perfect in every respect " was asked for by the council and referred to a committee of bishops. It was produced in 6 months' time, the work of Bishop J. L. Spalding,

of Peoria, and Jannario de Concilio, pastor of St. Michael's Church, Jersey City, who had been a theologian at the council. It did not represent any radical departure from medieval patterns. Theologians and teachers began to criticize it immediately, but nothing was done until 1941, when, after 6 years of labor, there appeared under the patronage of the Episcopal Committee of the Confraternity of Christian Doctrine a revision of the catechism of 1885. It is characterized by greater theological precisions of a post-Tridentine character.

The attention of Roman Catholics in the U.S.A. to the problems of excellence, specifically in religious formation, has been deferred, paradoxically, by the success of their religious schools. These schools were established for 2 reasons chiefly: to protect the Roman Catholic faith of children in that period when militant religious groups attempted to turn the public schools to their own purposes (1825–1850), and to preserve the religion, language, and culture of immigrants, chiefly Germans but later Poles and others. Attempts to gain public funds for Catholic schools such as those disbursed for Protestant schools succeeded briefly in Faribault, Minn., and Poughkeepsie, N.Y., but the ultimate solution of the individual states and the Federal Government was to give no public funds to any religious school.

There can be no doubt that the strength of Roman Catholic faith in the U.S.A., respect for the clergy, and vigor of apostolic movements is due in good part to the system of religious schools.

In the 144 dioceses in 50 states, 10,278 of the nearly 16,500 parishes with resident pastors conducted elementary schools in 1960. Another

407 private and 200 institutional elementary schools (enrolling 92,933 students) give a total enrollment of 4,262,100. This is estimated to be about ½ the country's Roman Catholic children of elementary school age. At the secondary level, 1,567 parochial or diocesan schools (some 400 of the latter type) enroll 520,128 pupils, while 866 high schools administered by religious communities teach 324,171 pupils. Among the almost 845,000 secondary school children are included those in protective institutions. The total represents about 16 percent of all American Roman Catholic children of school age. This figure of over 5,000,000 is expected to rise to 6,500,000 by 1965.

There are about 108,000 teaching sisters in the U.S.A. Lay teachers employed in elementary schools number 25,450 and in secondary schools 9,428. These represent increases over 1946 of about 900 percent and 170 percent respectively. Priests, religious brothers, and sisters who teach in high schools number 31,280. It has been estimated that the sister teachers will have risen to some 121,000 in 1971, and the lay teachers to 137,000. The rate of increase as between religious and lay teachers in the years 1946–1956 was, respectively, 22.5 percent and 156 percent.

A sociological study of 1 elementary school (Joseph H. Fichter, S.J., *Parochial School*) yields the information that of the 1,500 minutes spent by 8th-grade pupils in school each week, 10 percent of the time is spent in religion study. Of the remainder 37.3 percent is devoted to English language and literature, 15 percent to arithmetic, 16 percent to social studies, 6.7 percent to music, 5.3 percent to science and health,

4 percent to art, and 5.7 percent to out-of-school activities: lunch, play, and miscellaneous. An attempt is made to have these schools fully Christian in their complexion without thwarting the proper ends of the subject matter dealt with. The Commission on American Citizenship was established at the Catholic University of America in 1939, on the 50th anniversary of that institution's founding, to inculcate Christian social thought in Catholic schools. This it does through developing curricula and textbooks, in conjunction with the university's department of education.

The estimated number of Catholic students not enrolled in Catholic elementary schools in 1961 was 2,458,-673; in secondary schools, 855,180. These figures have doubtful value because they correspond more to the expectation of bishops that all children of school age will be under religious instruction than to anything else. The totals probably represent all those who have received some instruction during the year, whether in regular classes, religious vacation schools, or preparing for Communion or confirmation.

In many parishes the sisters on the school staff instruct the children who do not attend the parish school. The great bulk of instruction is attended to, however, by an army of devoted lay people enrolled as members of the Confraternity of Christian Doctrine. These act as teachers, " fishers " (i.e., home visitors), and " helpers " who see to such matters as pupil transportation and materials for instruction.

In numerous dioceses where the CCD works according to national office plans, teachers receive a minimum of 60 hours of instruction before being certified, of which 30 are in doctrine and 30 in methods of teaching. This modest preparation hopes to build on more than ordinary familiarity with Catholic faith. In the better organized dioceses it is supplemented by considerable in-service training. Each diocese and parish within a diocese has a board of lay directors working under priestly supervision. Some efforts are made to integrate the children of a parish into 1 body where there is a parochial school and a CCD unit, but the children of the latter group have a history of 2d-class citizenship that clergy and teachers do not easily put behind them.

Young Roman Catholics have courses of study and aid books without number written for them for use with the Revised Baltimore Catechism. This fact constitutes an undeniable challenge for any teacher familiar with sacred history as it is recorded in Scripture and the life of the church and celebrated in the liturgy — who is familiar, in a word, with the renewals in sacred studies and pastoral care of the last 60 or 70 years. Some catechists solve the problem by using newer, better catechetical textbooks. Most are not free to do so because of externally administered examinations or the question period that precedes the administration of confirmation. An occasional bishop prescribes departure from the older pattern on the basis of the needs of his people. Interestingly, this is much likelier to happen to students outside the Roman Catholic schools than within.

Some of the best work in American catechetics is being done by The Grail (an international company of apostolic women whose U.S.A. headquarters is at Loveland, Ohio) and by certain institutes of sisters whose exclusive work is cate-chizing. Motherhouses of teaching brothers and sisters are facing the problem with varying awareness and concern. In 1962 it remains relatively rare for a priest, sister, brother, or layman to be prepared at a higher catechetical faculty, e.g., the Catholic University of America, Lumen Vitae Centre (Brussels), Institute Supérieur Catéchétique (Paris), or a theological faculty that has a sequence in pastoral theology such as Rome's Gregorian University, or the Universities of Innsbruck or Tübingen. Summer study in catechetically oriented programs in theology becomes increasingly more common, e.g., at the University of Notre Dame, Marquette University, or Mundelein College, Chicago.

Individual superintendents of diocesan school systems and diocesan CCD directors, invariably autodidacts in this critical area, join publishers in the production of those books and materials responsible for the considerable progress that is being made. Until now, however, the very success of the Roman Catholic school system has worked against eminence in the field of catechetics. Lately the progress of pastoral liturgy, specialized apostolic movements, and thinking in teaching congregations of men and women with respect to theological preparedness has given reason for hope that the U.S.A. is on the brink of a resurgence in religious instruction. The production of the German national catechism in 1955 (*Katholischer Katechismus für Bistumer Deutschlands*) remotely prepared for since the 1930's by the Innsbruck school of *Verkündigungstheologie*, has contributed to this revival in large measure. The English-language writings of Johannes Hofinger, S.J., of Manila and his frequent lecture series in the U.S.A. have apprised thousands of the notable catechetical contribution of Josef A. Jungmann, S.J., who might otherwise be recognized for his contribution to the field of liturgiology only. Good work in preparation for this catechetical renewal has been done by Thomas Edward Shields, George Johnson, John M. Cooper, and William H. Russell, all of the Catholic University of America. J. A. Baierl, Rudolph G. Bandas, Anthony N. Fuerst, and Joseph B. Collins, S.S., are others who have been especially active in this field. Fructified by the liturgical spirit of Virgil Michel, O.S.B., Michael Mathis, C.S.C., Gerald Ellard, S.J., and H. A. Reinhold, and rallying their forces around the journal *Worship* (edited by Dom Godfrey Diekmann, O.S.B.), the catechists of the contemporary period are seeking new ways to make religion both a doctrine and a life.

Some outstanding contributions would include the *On Our Way Series* by Sisters Maria de la Cruz and Richard, H.H.S., for the first 6 elementary grades (William H. Sadlier, Inc., New York); *We Are Children of the Church*, by the Sisters, Servants of the Immaculate Heart of Mary, Monroe, Mich. (Liturgical Press, Collegeville, Minn.); and the pre- and post-First Communion catechisms of Sisters Mary Charles and Germaine, O.S.B. (Herder & Herder, New York). As this volume goes to press, no less than 4 series of secondary school pupil textbooks of high quality are in preparation, as well as an outstanding set of lessons for the preparation of secondary school teachers emanating from the Confraternity of Christian Doctrine Office of the Archdiocese of Chicago. — *Gerard S. Sloyan*

ROMAN EDUCATION Aristotle laid it down that any man or institution must be judged by his or its highest and best manifestation. Quite certainly the ideal of Roman education was very high. As T. C. Tucker writes, for the Roman, the ideal education was " a training which should fit a man for his duty to the gods, the state, and family." " The greatest reverence is due to the boy," said Juvenal (*Satires* 14.47), and in its earliest days Roman life very definitely set the child in the midst.

1. In the years prior to about the middle of the 3d century B.C., the school hardly entered into education at all. At this time the family was basic. The home was also the school. The great dominating factor in education was *mos maiorum,* the customs of our ancestors. Education was the handing on of tradition and a way of life. The education of the boy fell into 3 parts:

(*a*) Up to the age of 7 his mother was the supreme influence in his life. As Tacitus writes: " In the good old days every man's son . . . was brought up . . . in his mother's lap and at her knee." (*Dialogue on Oratory* 28.) It is of this time that we read of Cornelia, the mother of the Gracchi (Plutarch, *Tiberius Gracchus I*), and Julia Procilla, the mother of Agricola, " a woman of rare virtue . . . from whose fond bosom Agricola imbibed his education " (Tacitus, *Agricola* 4). The Roman mother is one of the great figures of history.

(*b*) At the age of 7 the boy became the responsibility of his father. Gwynn writes: " A companionship began between father and son for which it is hard to find a parallel outside Roman society." " The father of every youth," says Pliny, " served

as his instructor" (*Letters* 8.14.6).
The father became the teacher of
the boy, and the boy went everywhere with his father. Plutarch gives
us a picture of how Cato dedicated
his whole life to the education and
the training of his son (*Cato Major*
20). It was then that the boy learned
the Twelve Tables and the simple
austerity of the Roman way of life.

(*c*) Sometime between the ages
of 14 and 17 the 3d stage of the
boy's education began. It was known
as the *tirocinium fori*. At this stage
for a year or more the boy was attached to some famous man and
accompanied him everywhere. Young
men, said Cicero, "must attach
themselves to men who are wise
and renowned, men who are famous
for their patriotism, if possible men
of consular rank, men who have
played and are playing their part
in public affairs." (*De officiis* 2.46.)
So the boy became, as it were, a
disciple of greatness.

2. It is quite clear that in this
education little was formal; it was
education in character; it was a
growing into *gravitas*, that high seriousness which was Roman life at
its best. It is equally clear that this
kind of education could not continue. It was characteristically the
education of a peasant community;
once Rome became a great power,
another and a different kind of education had to begin. The Roman
tradition is that the 1st man to open
a school of letters was Spuriur
Carvilius, about the year 230 B.C.
(Plutarch, *Roman Questions* 50). We
may take it that it was about this
time that Roman education began
its 2d stage with formal schools and
professional schoolteachers. This
kind of education had 3 stages, each
of which had its special teacher.

(*a*) The *litterator* was the elementary schoolteacher. It is quite
true that in the *Institutes of Oratory*
Quintilian outlines a method and
curriculum of elementary education
which can hardly be surpassed; but
in point of fact, as Carcopino writes,
at this time "popular education in
Rome was a failure." The boy
learned his reading, his writing, and
his arithmetic. He had certain pro-
verbial sayings drilled into him:
"The miser is the cause of his own
wretchedness"; "Man's life is lent,
not given, to him"; "You will make
fewer mistakes if you know what
you do not know."

The conditions for teaching were
impossible. Schools met in an open
shop looking onto the street. They
met very early in the morning. The
schoolmaster was himself an ill-
educated, badly paid drudge. He
savagely sought to beat knowledge
of letters into his boys. Horace's
master, *plagosus Orbilius* (Orbilius
the flogger) goes down in history
(*Epistles* 2.I.70). There can have
been few Roman boys who enjoyed
their school days, and they emerged
from them with the minimum of
knowledge inserted into them in the
unhappiest of ways.

(*b*) There followed the *grammaticus*. He was the teacher of literature, and in the early days, since
Rome had no literature of her own,
the literature he taught was Greek.
He taught grammar and diction. He
took a passage of some poet and
expounded it. His lecturing was a
kind of exegesis of the poets. He
dealt with the most unlikely questions: Who was Hecuba's mother?
What was the name of Achilles
among the maidens? What was the
song the sirens sang? (Suetonius,
Tiberius 70). He taught music, but
only for the practical purpose of
rhythm and melody in speech. He

taught geometry, but only for the practical purposes of the farm and the estate. He taught gymnastics, but only for physical fitness. Quintilian warned against those "who kill the mind by overattention to the body" (*Institutes of Oratory* I. II. 15). Slowly, Rome built up her own literature, but the teaching of the *grammaticus* was always a sadly artificial thing.

(*c*) There followed the *rhetor*. For a man to be an orator was the goal. But too often oratory was a training in making the worse appear the better reason; and in the days when freedom of speech had died oratory consisted in making artificial speeches about the most unlikely subjects; the orator's stock-in-trade was ingenuity to provoke applause.

In actual practice Roman education was a failure. Yet at the back of it there still remained dimly alive the old ideals. Quintilian still insisted that character was greater than knowledge, and that nothing was good enough for the boy, whose very nurse must be a philosopher (*Institutes of Oratory* I, preface 9–12; I. I. 4). The old ideal of *gravitas* never was wholly lost; the old tradition never wholly died. And to the end of its day Roman education still succeeded in producing some men who were Romans in the finest sense of the word.

— *William Barclay*

RURAL CHURCH The term "rural" is a census term, usually defined negatively. In the U.S.A. Census the current definition of "urban" includes all persons living in population divisions of 2,500 or more plus those living in divisions of lesser population adjacent to a city of 50,000 or more. "Rural" includes all the rest. In Canada "urban" involves the process of incorporation, and the Canadian Census carries tables of "urban centers having less than 1,000 population." Persons not included in an "urban" center are "rural." Other nations have different criteria. To complicate the picture the American and Canadian churches customarily use the term "town and country." In their definitions they do not agree, but the majority would set a dividing line between "urban" and "town and country" at 10,000 population.

In general, rural churches are in areas of low population density while urban churches are in areas of high population density. Commonly, but inaccurately, rural churches are identified with churches made up of farmers. In the U.S.A., while 30 percent of the population in 1960 was classified as rural, not more than 10 percent was rural farm. Two thirds of rural Americans are rural nonfarm, that is, they live in areas of low population density but have an occupation other than farming.

Rural churches in the U.S.A. are dominantly Protestant. The U.S.A. Census sample study of religious confessions made in 1957 indicates that while only 59 percent of our urban people identify themselves as Protestants, 78 percent of rural nonfarm persons and 83 percent of rural farm people call themselves Protestant. Rural churches are relatively small institutions, e.g., town and country Methodist churches average 177 members against 656 for urban churches. Figures for the American Baptist Convention are similar: an average membership of 152 in town and country churches and 409 in urban churches. To put the matter in another way: 84 per-

cent of Methodist churches but only
59 percent of Methodist members
are in the town and country category.

Rural churches reflect and express the class structures of their
community; some denominations
characteristically serve upper- or
middle-class persons, others serve
lower-class persons, and the lowest
class is neglected by all. Studies
show that a person's place in the
local social hierarchy is best indicated by his church membership.
Upwardly mobile persons often
change churches to symbolize their
new status.

Because of their small membership and modest financial resources,
rural churches are served frequently
by the marginal or inadequately prepared minister. They almost always
receive a part-time ministry, either
sharing their pastor with one or
more other churches or accepting
the services of a minister who devotes a part of his time to some other
gainful employment. Whenever
clergy are in short supply, rural
churches tend to be left without
leadership. Prominent in their activities are the Sunday school and
the woman's society, largely lay activities, which can and do flourish
in numbers and activities whether
the church has a pastor or not.

Modern leaders in the town and
country church field suggest that
such churches be grouped so that all
those lying within a common social
area, the town-country community,
are served by a single staff of ministers operating throughout all the
churches. This arrangement is variously called the " larger parish " or
the " group ministry." It maintains
the small local church organization
but relates it and its people to the
other religious organizations within

their area of social interaction. The
parish is governed in matters common to all the churches by a lay
council. It may involve churches of
several denominations or of one.

Rural churches chosen as successful by administrators in a denomination are generally inferior in the
commonly accepted standards of
church efficiency that are the average of their denominations. They
find themselves at a disadvantage
in attempting to reproduce the organization and structure the denomination suggests, a form often derived from the successful practice of
the larger urban churches. Though
most denominations have town and
country church departments, no denomination has taken seriously the
establishment of standards and patterns appropriate to the town and
country scene. — *Rockwell C. Smith*

RUSSIA A regular school system
was established in Russia only by
the end of the 18th century. In the
earlier period instruction was given
in an informal and personal manner. It was the task and duty of
clergy, secular and monastic. Certain schools were organized, according to the *Primary Russian Chronicle*,
immediately after the Christening of
Russia, under St. Vladimir (the end
of the 10th century), but our information about them is scarce and
occasional. The study of Scripture,
beginning with the Psalter, was in
the center of the program, and it
was closely related to worship. The
main emphasis was on practical
issues: formation of Christian character, training in humility, obedience,
and virtue, development of devotional habits. No specific textbooks
were used, apart from Scripture and
liturgical books. The whole structure of Russian society was at that

time theocratic and religious.

The change came with Peter the Great, in the 1st decades of the 18th century. He could not tolerate any independent authority of the church, even in matters spiritual. Yet he was compelled to use the church in education, because the church alone was able to develop at that time a consistent system of general schools and to supply competent teachers. The state itself could create but very few regular schools in the course of the 18th century. All these schools were primarily professional. The whole philosophy of education was strictly utilitarian, adjusted to the needs of the civil and military service. Only at the end of the century the theme of general education was raised, in the spirit of a vague humanitarianism of the epoch, and 1st in the field of feminine education. The duty of the clergy to give religious instruction to youth in their parishes was formally acknowledged, but no provision was made for any regular religious instruction in the school.

In the 1st decades of the 19th century the whole educational system was revised, and a great number of new schools were started. The secondary school was the center of attention. Elementary schools were opened in all minor cities; secondary schools — gymnasiums, according to the German and Austrian use of the word — in major cities. The teaching of religion was included in the program of all schools, and entrusted to the local clergy. In the course of time, however, special chaplains were appointed, especially if the school had a boarding hostel. In many schools there were chapels with regular services on Sundays and major feast days. All instructors on the secondary level had to have university degrees, and this requirement was extended to chaplains: they were selected from among the graduates of theological academies, which were training students not so much for pastoral duties, as for various educational jobs. It took some time before the new system began to function and an adequate teaching personnel could be secured.

The organization of the schools and their programs was changed several times in the course of the 19th century, but the basic pattern remained the same until the Revolution in 1917. The program of religious instruction in the secondary schools was comprehensive. There were normally 7 or 8 forms, and in each, 2 hours were assigned per week for religious instruction, under a rather archaic name: "The Law of God." Accordingly, chaplains were denoted as "Teachers of the Law." The program included: the story of the Old Testament; New Testament; liturgics; the catechism — on the basis of the book published by the Holy Synod; church history, general and Russian; an outline of Christian doctrine; Christian ethics. In the beginning, no suitable textbooks were available in any of these fields, and instructors were compelled to dictate their lessons. In the course of time standard manuals were compiled and approved for use by ecclesiastical authorities. Local bishops or their suffragans had general supervision of religious instruction. Indeed, the main emphasis was precisely on religious instruction, not so much on religious education in a deeper sense. Religious instruction itself was never properly integrated into the general system of the schools. There was often no more than conventional formalism.

It is not easy to say to what extent this religious instruction was really effective, especially in the upper forms. The efficiency of any educational system depends very much on the ability and dedication of the teaching personnel. But it also depends upon the general climate of opinion and culture in the country. The general climate in Russia in the 19th century was not in favor of any religious influence, especially through the channels of the established church. Moreover, all controversial issues were deliberately avoided in the religious program, except in the form of blunt repudiation. Religious instruction ignored the possibility of doubt or unbelief.

On the other hand, it was also in the spirit of the time to shift attention from doctrine to morals, and thus the distinctive features of the Christian faith were never adequately presented. Only in the last years before the Revolution were these problems raised and discussed at special conferences of chaplains, convened on the national level. The character of textbooks was changing, and new methods of instruction were introduced. Much more important, however, was the deficiency in the field of elementary education. The schools were intended when they were 1st organized in the early decades of the 19th century for the free population of the country, that is, with the exception of the peasants. Indeed, parish priests were expected to teach also the peasant children in their village parishes. Not always could it be properly done. Upon the emancipation of the peasants in 1861 the problem of the village schools was faced as an impending duty. Again, the clergy were invited to continue their ed-

ucational work, but no formal status was given to the parochial schools and no funds were assigned. On the other hand, general educational responsibility in every district was entrusted to the offices of local self-government, the so-called Zemstvos, and to the municipalities. Indeed, religion had to be taught in all schools, but general supervision of the total program was in the hands of secular officials who often were quite indifferent to the interests of religion. It was the time of increasing secularism in Russian society, and there was no desire to center the educational program around religion. This led to profound tension between the society and the church in the field of education.

Finally, in the early 1880's the Holy Synod initiated its own system of elementary schools, under the authority of local clergy and the supervision of a special educational board of the diocese. There was a central office on national education at the Holy Synod. Thus an unhealthy duality was introduced into the work, implying rivalry and competition. The general tension between the intelligentsia and the church was vigorously reflected in the field of education. After the bill of obligatory education was passed by the Duma in 1912, it was ruled that there should be but one school in each locality, and it was decided to include quite a number of parochial schools in the general net of education. But this was just on the eve of the general collapse. The Provisional Government was inclined toward total separation of the state from the church, but its policy was of no great importance, as it was overthrown by the Communists after only 8 months of existence.

The basic concern of the Communists was to exclude the church, and any religion, from the new society; separation of the schools from the church was specifically emphasized. No organized teaching of religion was permitted by the constitutional law. Instead, antireligious propaganda in various forms was officially included in the program of all Soviet schools, beginning with the younger children. Even at present, when a certain freedom of worship is granted in the Soviet Union, no change in the educational law has been made.

Only among Russian emigrants are the problems of religious education still discussed and new experiments made. In this connection one has to mention the Office on Religious Education in Paris, founded and directed since 1928 by Basil Zenkovsky, formerly professor of philosophy at Kiev University, and later professor of religious education and philosophy at the Orthodox Theological Institute, Paris. A research center in the field, it has been in close touch and cooperation with similar organizations in other Orthodox countries, especially in Bulgaria and Greece. — *Georges Florovsky*

S

SACRAMENT A sacrament, an outward seal of the inward grace in Christ, has been called "visible word" (Augustine). In the relation between the Word and the visibility lies the mystery of the Christian sacrament. A sacrament exists by the fact that God spoke to the world and that God acted through the Word he spoke. Israel was captive in Egypt, and through the Word addressed to Moses, God led the Hebrew slaves to freedom. In Christ, God proclaims and enacts freedom for a humanity that has become enslaved in its estrangement from God. At the root of the sacrament lies the incomprehensible mercy of God toward a cosmos of hate (John 3:16), the love which came to man in the One who contained the fullness of God (Col. 3:16).

Since this Word becomes event and reaches man through the event, the Word itself can be called sacramental in a broad sense. It uses physical means in order to enclothe us in the reality of grace. An outward act, through which the Word speaks, lets us share in Christ and the new life that he brought in his death and resurrection and that he will fulfill in the coming of the Kingdom. The Word can become sacrament in numerous physical events and seals in which man is concretely and immediately confronted with the grace of Christ.

However, there is a specific meaning of sacrament that lies in the liturgical life of the church. In the corporate worship of the primitive church, the Word of grace reached the congregation in the visible acts of Baptism and the Lord's Supper. In the course of consecutive centuries, 5 more sacraments were added by the Roman Catholic Church (ordination, confirmation, marriage, penance, and extreme unction), with a definite trend toward a juridical understanding of them as accepted by the Fourth Lateran Council of 1214. The Protestant churches reverted to the 2 liturgical sacraments that appear in the earliest Christian church. However, they should not forget that alongside the specific sacrament of the worshiping community the Word itself has a broader sacramental range. The Roman Catholic tradition has understood this, but Protestant understanding of the sacrament could never accept its juridical limitation of 7 sacraments.

When Moses led his people out of their captivity in Egypt, he gave them the meal of the Passover. God gives to man the outward, the visible. How could there be life without the outward? Jesus stands at the banks of the Jordan River and accepts John's use of water in the act of baptism. At his own Last Supper he does not only speak of broken bread but he breaks such bread and eats it with his disciples. God knows the earthiness in which he has created man, and when God's grace reaches man it does so in and with the elements of this earth, water and wine. Such is the visibility of grace.

This Word of grace that becomes visible is called a sign. We are not merely cleansing a body in Baptism, nor are we merely feeding hungry people in the Lord's Supper. The sign refers to something other than that which appears in the action. Baptism as such could have a host of other, non-Christian meanings; what makes it Christian are the words spoken at Baptism. Thus neither is the sacrament self-existent, nor is it a symbol of nature; in order to understand its meaning we need the Christian faith. Only in faith do we grasp what is meant by "Take, eat." The sacrament betrays itself when it ceases to proclaim and convey "nothing among you except Jesus Christ" (I Cor. 2:2); it can be understood only "in Christ."

The seal of faith, the sacrament in the narrow meaning of the term, exists in the body of Christ, the worshiping community. The sacrament is not merely an individualistic experience but a corporate act. As God's word of deliverance created the freedom of Israel, and as Christ ate with his disciples, the sacrament takes place within the visible congregation of faith. The child is baptized into the community of faith which is present at Baptism and into which the child will grow. The Lord's Supper takes place, not as an uplift of an individual, but in the household of God where forgiveness and new life receive meaning. In the community of faith the sacramental seal both precedes and follows faith.

The history of the Christian church teaches us that it has been difficult to speak about Word and sign simultaneously. Here lies one of the deep cleavages among the Christian churches, and the roots of it go back to the early church. As we trace the history of theology we find a constantly growing tendency to spell out the meaning of the visible, beginning with Ignatius' "drug of immortality," until finally magical concepts totally reversed the Biblical sacrament. There followed a rationalistic criticism of this tendency which led to a spiritualism in which the sacrament became merely rational and parabolic. Between these 2 extremes, both Biblically unacceptable, all intermediary solutions are often equally unsatisfactory.

For an understanding and teaching of the sacrament, it is vital to remember that the juristic Latin word *sacramentum* is a translation of the Greek *mystērion* (mystery), a word that connotes something quite different. For the New Testament the mystery is not primarily the supernatural transmutation of substance or nature, but the hidden dimension of the self-disclosure of God. The history of Christian thought has been dominated by categories in which there is a Greek distinction between substance and phenomenon, form and accident, intellect and matter. Once such a metaphysical frame is accepted, the only alternatives are rational symbol or transubstantiation. The Biblical concept of life, however, has an awareness of a unity of life, on one hand (man is one, creation is one), and of the alienness of God, on the other (God is not man; God is the creator). Having both in mind we can say: the sacrament is the mysterious act of grace, using and accepting elements and products of nature for the proclamation and conveyance of new life.

There is a double consequence that results from such Biblical thinking. First, the outward sign and the inward grace belong together. We may not understand how and why. But has science or philosophy ever totally revealed to us the complex relation between "inward" and "outward"? Our world has not even begun to solve the riddle of the complexity of man, of the relation between his body and mind, between the "thing" and its "shape." What happens between the Word and its sign is indeed the great mystery of God's grace. We may not be able to spell it out; as a matter of fact, we may destroy the mystery by attempting to do so. Our children growing up in the riddle of the modern universe may well be much more capable of grasping the unity of Word and seal than many theologians, twisted by high-church or low-church arguments.

Second, the Biblical realism of life knows of an alien and sovereign God. No faith, no church, no act, and therefore also no sacrament can stand over against this God. Here lies the threat in any sacramental emphasis. Man tries to master God by setting up an *opus operatum* as a secure means of salvation. Yet the juridical emphasis cannot become a substitute for the intangible; the sacrament cannot replace the Christ. We must say: The grace of God comes to man in the sacrament; but we cannot say: In the sacrament, God is unfailingly present. The seal is Christ's, but the seal shall not master Christ. The 2d-century *logion* of Mark 16:16 has well understood the promise and limitation of all sacramental language: "He who believes and is baptized will be saved; but he who does not believe will be condemned." Word and seal constitute the promise of Christian faith, but the denial does not include the seal. The sacrament, vital as it is for the life of the church, shall never manipulate the reality of the living Christ. — *Samuel Laeuchli*

SANCTIFICATION Sanctification is the process or condition of being made "holy." In the New Testament sanctification is not sharply distinguished from justification, regeneration, righteousness, redemption, etc. All the believers are called saints (though collectively, never individually). The term suggests particularly that quality of existence whereby the believer is set apart from the "world," is participant in the new age of life and obedience to God rather than the old era of sin and estrangement, and by participation in Christ shares in a holiness that includes but is not restricted to the "moral" (cf. Rudolf Otto, *The Idea of the Holy*). The separation from the world has the negative aspect of renunciation (cf. Paul's catalogs of vices), which has often been developed in a dualistic-ascetic direction; but the positive sense is more characteristic of the New Testament, as seen in the preponderance and greater variety of terms and injunctions designating Christian "virtues" in relation to God and neighbor.

Sanctification is described in the New Testament as an accomplished fact, as a process and as a future reality (cf. I Cor. 6:11; Heb. 10:10; I Thess. 3:13; 5:23). In all respects, however, the New Testament emphasis falls unequivocally on the divine activity. The primary fact is the salvation deed in Christ and the work of the Holy Spirit, whereby the believer has been set in a new context of existence (Heb. 10:10: "We have been sanctified through the offering of the body of Jesus Christ once for all"; I Cor. 1:30: "Christ Jesus, whom God made our wisdom, our righteousness and sanctification and redemption"; cf. also Rom. 6:22; I Cor. 1:2; 6:11; Eph. 5:25 f.; Heb. 2:11; 10:29; 13:12; I Peter 1:2). The basis and source of all human hallowing is God's holiness (cf. John 17:11, 17; I Peter 1:15). But the indicative involves inseparably an imperative, an obligation to active holiness: "As you once yielded your members to impurity and to greater and greater iniquity, so now yield your members to righteousness for sanctification" (Rom. 6:19; cf. II Cor. 7:1; I Thess. 4:3; Heb. 12:14).

In the light of the New Testament, then, sanctification is not a property or accomplishment of man but an aspect of his being called into a new relationship with God, which is to be expressed in an appropriate form of life. As a growth in new life, it rests in God's sanctifying activity in Christ and the Spirit.

In Protestant development, 2 different tendencies have acted to obscure and distort the proper meaning of sanctification. In Protestant scholasticism, sanctification came to be sharply distinguished from justification (and even from regeneration) in an artificial and sterile way. The primary motive was doubtless fear of the concept of merit in justification, but the sharp distinction tended falsely to separate the forgiving and transforming activity of God and to suggest an overly simple, almost chronological, pattern of Christian existence. On the other hand, sanctification has often been interpreted in a highly moralistic way, either in the left-wing Reformation and Pietist conception of the "true" church, or in the "holiness" movements' restriction of the term to a finally achieved state of "entire sanctification," often described in legalistic terms. Hence the concept of sanctification has often come to have misleading connotations and has not played an important role in recent discussion.

Yet both these distortions involve the exaggeration of valid elements in the Biblical conception, elements that are of importance in a time of recovery of the Reformation doctrine of justification. The distinction of sanctification from justification has the heuristic value of indicating that the salvation event is not only forensic, or pronouncement of forgiveness, but also involves the transforming of human existence into a form expressive of holiness; justification issues in sanctification. The concept of sanctification as a culmination of the divine work in human life (cf. Rom. 6:19; II Cor. 7:1; I Thess. 5:23) indicates that the Christian life is not adequately described as a continual series of beginnings, but involves growth in (not into) the "holiness" wrought by Christ and the Spirit. The need for forgiveness is not left behind, but the gracious and free gift of God forms both the possibility of and the obligation to a quality of life expressing fullness and stability of obedience to Christ.
— *Claude Welch*

SCIENTIFIC METHOD Science is an inquiry into the nature of things, of man and of his place in the universe. It is the accurate observation and classification of inorganic, organic, psychological, and social data for the purpose of understanding, prediction, and control. Science is a body of organized and exact knowledge. The scientific method is the means employed by scientists to obtain such knowledge. Today, scientists object to the phrase " the scientific method." They know that there are as many scientific methods as there are scientific problems. Whenever, herein, the phrase " the scientific method " is used, it is to be understood to mean what is common to all scientific methods — objectivity, the testing of hypotheses, cooperation, " the search for truth." Scientific methods have arisen from man's desire to explore, to understand, to learn the fundamental nature of things and to use this knowledge for human purposes.

Although scientific methods were anticipated by the 5th-century pre-Socratic Greek world, they are usually equated with the extraordinary intellectual activity that arose in Italy in the 16th century and spread to the rest of Europe in the 17th. The experimental observations of Galileo, Gilbert, Bacon, and others brought about a revolutionary change in point of view among learned men.

While the impact of the scientific method on Western culture has been apparent since the Renaissance, what is really new in the world is not so much science as the prestige that is given to scientists. Men have not always and everywhere been free to use their scientific methods. Their use has varied greatly from culture to culture and from age to age. Today more and more scientists are playing an important role in Western culture. In the U.S.A. they have become advisers to Presidents, to Congress, and to various departments of the government. Their assumptions, procedures, and methods are having an important impact on contemporary life.

A scientific method presupposes objectivity — observing facts as they are, insofar as this is humanly possible, regardless of the interests or preferences of the observer. When the scientist is faced with a fact he must accept it, no matter what havoc it may wreak on his carefully thought out theories. He notes welcome as well as unwelcome data; he is not influenced by prejudice or bias; he attempts to see things as a whole.

The scientific method is concerned with facts, hypotheses, theories, and laws. It assumes that a knowledge of facts is imperative, nothing happens without cause, and, given the causal antecedents, prediction and control are possible. In the early modern period, Sir Francis Bacon sought inductively, i.e., by direct studies of experience, to formulate scientific laws. Scientific methods are still primarily concerned with facts, but since it is impossible to obtain them all inductively, they also rely on the trained imagination as well. Knowing that facts without hypotheses are of limited value, the scientist tries to formulate imaginatively, on the basis of admittedly insufficient data, a general statement, or hypothesis, for the purpose of establishing some degree of order in a particular set of facts.

Scientists are concerned with testing hypotheses by means of factual evidence. In the 18th century, Kant and Laplace hypothesized about the origin of the solar system in the light of their information and formulated a " shrewd guess " that in the beginning a gigantic nebula spun faster and faster until it finally flung off planets. Later Chamberlain and Moulton presented another hypothesis that was more in harmony with the contemporary evidence, namely that a wandering star entered our heavens and pulled from the sun the stuff out of which the planets were condensed. More recently another hypothesis was suggested as other facts became known — that the sun was once a nova that blew up and threw off rings from which the planets were formed. All these hypotheses present the imaginings of scientifically oriented minds — the result of the thoughtful analysis of the known facts.

A given hypothesis stands or falls in the face of the concrete evidence. When the explanation of a given problem is supported by a reasonably large amount of data, and data otherwise unrelated are brought into meaningful relations, it is called a theory. A scientific " law " replaces a theory when the relationship among phenomena under specified conditions is explained by an even greater number of facts. The scientific method is actually a fruitful interplay of fact and imagination in the process of systematizing human knowledge into hypotheses, theories, and laws. The progress of a given science is measured by the historic process of rising above the ruins of discarded hypotheses.

By its nature a scientific method is based on cooperation. The appeal of science gets its impetus from the drive to explore the unknown. Since this appeal is universal, science from its beginnings has transcended the limitations of the particular countries in which the scientists lived. Ideally, science has never known national boundaries, is devoted to the principle of the free exchange of knowledge, and has welcomed the cross-fertilization of ideas. Typified by the Dutch microscopist, who as early as 1692 shared his observations with members of the Royal Society in England, scientists from different countries when uninhibited by political restraints have always communicated freely and engaged in joint efforts for the advancement of human knowledge. Such cooperation not only reveals the power of the human spirit to transcend artificial barriers but provides one of the best examples of human brotherhood. Today science is one of the basic disciplines on which men of understanding are agreed.

The methods of scientists are synonymous with " the search for truth." The scientist, as such, is a devoted thinker dedicated wholly to the advancement of knowledge. Popular resistance has frequently been strong against men of science as it has against religious reformers. But social criticism usually has not been a deterrent to either. They have much in common — above all, their other-worldliness. To the saint, the quest is for sanctity. To the scientist, the goal is truth.

Two implications of the scientific method are pertinent. First, the use of a scientific method is most fruitful when the scientist is " free." For a man to become a scientist he has to learn to doubt dogma. He must at all times be ready to question, to reexamine, and to discard hypotheses or theories in the light of new facts. The scientist who is burdened by ideologies that restrict his thinking, whether religious or political, is not free to examine the world objectively. Scientific creativity flourishes where there is a high degree of independence and individual freedom.

Second, the use of the scientific method in a given society is a reflection of its basic values. Science in evil hands can make men slaves; it can produce lethal bombs, poisonous gases, or brainwashed personalities. On the other hand, men can use science to further human freedom, accelerate social progress, develop a more perfect world. The statement is often made that as far as value judgments are concerned, science is neutral. That statement has the dangerous characteristics of a half-truth. Consider the medical sciences today. Those scientists who are concerned with the problem of human disease unconsciously have accepted a set of values. Only in a culture where human life is a supreme value would funds be available for the study of disease or would medical scientists take the Hippocratic Oath. Medical science today is based on a long series of value judgments. Similarly, there is increasing evidence among physical scientists of a positive value orientation. The existence of the Society for Social Responsibility in Science, an international association of physical scientists concerned with the social impact of atomic energy in war, is a case in point.

The scientific method when viewed historically appears as one of the great adventures of the human mind. Science emerged from the same intellectual ferment that created literature, music, sculpture, and architecture. Its goals of objectivity, truth, and freedom of observation are lofty. But in the last analysis, the use of science depends upon the human and religious values of the social order. How the findings of scientific methods are ultimately employed is determined by what people themselves hold to be intrinsically dear. — *G. Norman Eddy*

SCOTLAND A national system of compulsory education came into existence in Scotland with the passing of the Education (Scotland) Act of 1872. Before that date the schools of Scotland could be divided roughly into 4 categories of comparable size but of varying quality and importance. These were parish, church, undenominational, and private schools. The first 2 groups included within them the great majority of Scottish children of the period who were attending school.

First in importance were the parish schools, of which there were about 1,100. These schools were provided and maintained by local landowners in accordance with the law, but the parish minister was responsible for supervising the work of the schoolmaster. The 2 great Presbyterian churches of the period owned and controlled about 500 to 600 schools each. About 180 schools owned and managed by smaller Presbyterian churches, by the Scottish Episcopal Church, and by the Roman Catholic Church brought the total of church schools to about 1,300. In addition to the undenominational schools belonging to religious or charitable bodies and to the schools run for private profit there was a small but important group of about 80 to 90 burgh or grammar schools, provided and controlled by town councils.

Directly or indirectly, the influence of the church, especially the influence of the national church, dominated the educational scene. Since the great majority of Scottish school children were attending parish or church schools, the national church could regard the day school as an agent of the church in its concern for Christian education. Since the training of teachers was controlled, in the main, by the 2 larger Presbyterian Churches, the Presbyterian influence was powerful and pervasive in Scottish education.

The Act of 1872 made no appreciable difference in the situation at first. Responsibility for religious worship and teaching in the public school was laid on the local school boards set up under the Act. The voluntary schools were given the option of transferring to public control and those not wishing to do so became entitled to Government grants on evidence of efficiency. Nearly all the Roman Catholic and Episcopal schools remained under church control. The Episcopal schools have steadily diminished in number, but the Roman Catholic schools have increased substantially with the growth of the Roman Catholic population. Barely 300 of the Presbyterian schools were transferred to public control, but the Presbyterian schools gradually have passed out of existence. Presbyterian ministers and elders were prominent in the composition of the school boards, the traditional system of religious teaching was maintained, and the custom of religious supervision by the local parish minister was widely practiced. The resultant situation was succinctly described by one of Her Majesty's Inspectors of Schools in a report for 1878: "The public schools are to all intents and purposes denominational schools. Public and Presbyterian are practically interchangeable terms."

The Education (Scotland) Act of 1918 brought the main body of existing church schools within the national system by sale or lease to the local county or burgh education authorities that had replaced the parish school boards. These public authorities accepted responsibility for maintenance and control of the schools and were empowered to regulate the curriculum and appoint the teachers. It was stipulated, however, that (1) teachers so appointed must be approved, as regards religious belief and character, by the appropriate church authority; (2) time set apart for religious instruction in these schools should not be reduced; (3) a church supervisor should have right of entry during periods of religious instruction. As a result of this Act the Roman Catholic Church has a substantial measure of religious control in schools maintained and controlled, in all other respects, by local education authorities. Such schools are to be found wherever there is a substantial Roman Catholic population. Since 1918 the number of these schools has increased but the number of Episcopal schools has diminished to negligible proportions. An Episcopal training college established in 1855 was closed some years after the passing of this act, but there are still 2 colleges for the training of women teachers in which the Roman Catholic Church has a measure of control over the appointment of staff and the provision of religious teaching.

The prevailing climate of opinion in Scotland has altered radically since 1872, and it could not be said now that "the public schools are to all intents and purposes denominational schools." The direct influence of the national church on education has diminished substantially. Control of the schools passed out of its hands in 1872. The Presbyterian training colleges were transferred to the state in 1907. Educational administration reflects the changing outlook of the age, and teachers are not immune from secular and materialistic influences. In such circumstances it would be unrealistic to claim that Scotland's public schools provide a Christian education, yet the Christian influence within them is still strong and religious teaching is faithfully given by the great majority of teachers in primary schools and by a substantial proportion of teachers in secondary schools.

Two developments are of special interest and importance. Since 1927 a new relationship between the churches and the teaching profession has been built up and has found expression in the work of the Scottish Joint Committee for Religious Education. This committee is responsible for the preparation of syllabi and teachers' aids used in primary and secondary schools. Through a standing subcommittee it organizes an annual conference for teachers and promotes day conferences through which local interest in religious education may be focused and strengthened. A policy of local cooperation between ministers and teachers promoted by this committee has gained wide support throughout the country. Many local education authorities now appoint a minister to be an honorary member of staff in each school as its religious adviser and chaplain. These chaplains visit the school and conduct services or assist in other ways at the invitation of the head teacher. This development has provided, in many cases, a most valuable local link between school and church and it has brought many children into touch, for the 1st time, with the life and worship of the Christian church.

The 2d hopeful development concerns the training of teachers and the use of specialist teachers of religious knowledge in secondary schools. When the Presbyterian training colleges were transferred to the state in 1907, special provision was made for the continuation of religious instruction in them by representatives of the churches. In 1947 the state itself accepted responsibility for such instruction through the National Committee for the Training of Teachers. Since then the subject of religious education has had a place in the regular curriculum parallel to that of other academic subjects, and additional staff has been provided to meet expanding needs. The Scottish universities have also provided courses in religious studies that enable students to acquire some knowledge in this field before they begin their professional teacher training. A growing number of teachers with special qualifications in religious knowledge are becoming available, and education authorities are beginning to use them as specialist teachers in secondary schools. The existing statutory position prevents the full recognition of such teachers by the Scottish Education Department. Provision for religious instruction is still the responsibility of the local education authority. There is therefore no uniformity in the special qualifications required of such teachers and no system of Government inspection or external examination as in other subjects. The position of such teachers thus remains anomalous and insecure, but their increasing numbers is a hopeful augury for the future.

The Church of Scotland and the other churches have their own schemes for the Christian nurture of children and young people. These are supplemented by the work of such organizations as the Boys' Brigade, the Girls' Guildry, the Scout and Guide movements and clubs under voluntary or local Government auspices. Although the church no longer controls education and cannot regard the day schools as its agents in Christian education, it can still count on the sympathy and cooperation of many valuable allies in the public system of education and in the numerous auxiliary agencies. The school in particular still has a vital contribution to make to Christian education in Scotland, although that contribution must lie chiefly in the field of knowledge and understanding rather than in the direct training of Christian disciples.

— *James W. D. Smith*

SECULARISM Originally the secular way of life was understood to mean the revolt against moral and spiritual laws in favor of a way of life characterized by worldliness and ease. It is not, therefore, a condition of modern society alone, although its elevation to the status of a systematic philosophy has occurred only in the last century. The Old and New Testaments, the Greek tragedies, and the Latin moralists all were aware that prosperity brought with it the disabling effects of confidence in material things.

The early church was a clear-cut separation from the secular mind of its period, and Christians lived with their mind set on things above. At the beginning of the 4th century, after the church had become a victorious element in the Roman Empire, its doors were opened to the secular spirit. From that time until the present the church has been subject to a dual struggle — that of waging war against the secular spirit outside its ranks and, at the same time, struggling against that spirit from within.

Secularism became 1 of the central intellectual problems of the Middle Ages. The concept of a universal kingdom controlled as a Christian commonwealth was always endangered by the secular interests of feudalism, national sovereignty, and by developing concepts of political and personal independence. In devoting its full energy to the combat with the enemies from without, the church was not always alert to the spirit developing within itself. The only serious attempt to withdraw completely from the world was found in the monastic movement.

By the beginning of the Renaissance and, later, the Reformation, secularism began to develop something akin to a spirit or philosophy. The rise of nominalistic thought, the appearance of literature in the vernacular, growing scientific interests, the founding of the classics as the basic educational curriculum, and the belief that education existed to prepare men for life as nobles and merchants were factors that gradually were to pry educational supremacy out of the hands of the church.

By the 17th century, under the leadership of Francis Bacon, a new secularism in science began to develop. In philosophy, Thomas Hobbes squarely challenged prevailing theological dogmas of the church by maintaining that man by nature is competitive and not social, that all there is to know about life can be traced through man's experiences, and all that needs to be described can be so described within the framework of an understanding of the natural phenomena of men's lives. Hobbes and Bacon, being the intellectual giants that they were, not only startled the church by these revolutionary interpretations of life, but, as well, drew to themselves a considerable following willing to give some attention to these developments. Although the philosophy of Thomas Hobbes failed to gain universal recognition, the scientific notions of Francis Bacon were readily gathered up and turned into a movement that coincided with the trend of the age, which was toward scientific and geographical discovery. In some regards this led to a denial of God, which Bacon had no intention of doing, although his religious thought leaned in the direction of deism.

Religion was able to recoup some of its losses in the rise of Pietist, Puritan, and other separatist movements, which advocated new concepts of devotion to private and public search for divine power, and reached a wide public through works of piety and labors of preaching.

By the 18th century the world was feeling the effects of the 17th century's insistence upon the material needs of man. On the whole, religion was being pushed aside. Large masses of people were in need of religious enlightenment. What remained of the pietistic movement was soon obscured by the image of the businessman and merchant, who were completely engrossed in their business all week and generally uninvolved in any form of worship on the Lord's Day.

However, it was not until the middle of the 19th century that George Jacob Holyoake codified in *The Principles of Secularism* (1859) the concept of secular philosophy. He made a gallant attempt to develop a theory that would be nontheistic without being antitheistic. The essential principle of his thought was to seek for human improvement by material means alone. His work came hard upon the Reform Bill of 1832, which was directed toward the alleviation of suffering among the poor classes and directed negatively toward the selfishness of the wealthy and influential people. For Holyoake, material means were more proximate, and therefore more logical than the dogma of the church, to bring about victory in this struggle against wealth. He maintained that science and religion were not hostile to each other, although they were certainly mutually exclusive. Science could fulfill man's needs, since its method proceeds by experiment and observation. Whatever comes as a result of dealing with the "unknown" world is not practical for the known world, and cannot offer it anything by way of a solution to its problems. It is only a strong social movement that can eliminate poverty and teach people the laws of happiness. Reason must not be tested or fettered by dogma. It depends wholly on experience.

Holyoake made no attempt to attack theological dogma or minimize its efforts. He simply disregarded it, unless it actively interfered with human progress and happiness. Secularism, as it was developed in the 19th century, therefore, was irreligion. Indeed, it made a great moral protest against the intolerance in humanity and poverty that the church had ignored. Some scholars, such as E. E. Aubrey, have defended the secular movement as not only having validity in its own right but also being historically inevitable as a source of creative advance within the faith itself. He views it as a corrective both for the ills of the faith and for the tendency that organized religion has shown to ignore the blight of human life and the ills of society. Whereas the church has attempted to solve earthly problems with "otherworldly" answers, secularism has endeavored to find the answers to society from within society itself. It is only the more unreasoning and unreasonable segments of the secular movement that have made serious attempt to cast aside all moral presuppositions.

The secular movement in the 20th century is difficult to define. It is no longer a strong and important countermovement to religion. The church and religious education have invited into their ranks many concepts and practices that have had their origin in secular thought. They have been affected by industrialism, urbanization, and intellectual trends growing out of the theory of evolution. Large churches were built, often for the benefit of exclusive and aristocratic congregations. Administrative and organizational practices are taken over from the secular world without change. The pragmatic movement, which places emphasis upon natural process and tests hypotheses by experiment, began to find expression in religious education. These trends have continued, albeit in modified form.

Science and technology, which are conspicuous and easily understood in our culture, have become the norms for much of our concept of faith and education. While the church looks to God for its standard of authority, others look to science. But as these 2 areas develop their own philosophies of life, the line that separates them becomes less obvious.

Secularism as an independent thought system has all but disappeared from the culture. What remains of its philosophy has been taken in by ethical culture and other rationalistic movements. The church has tended to make peace with the secular mind, both within and without its fold. Gone is the strong denunciation of the "atheist"; and as long as the church maintains dialogue with the secular spirit, secularism as a separate movement is not apt to reappear.

Secularism is no longer simply an intellectual revolt against theological domination; rather, it is a dominant aspect of our culture and extends into all phases of its life. Where it persists, whether in business, politics, or religion, it carries with it a notion that man can achieve personal and social growth by means of loyalties other than to God.

It is likely that for some time to come there will continue to be a strong interplay of the secular and religious in both church and society. The interdependence of the natural sciences and religious education upon each other tends to develop mutual insights. The tendency of science to ask questions concerning 1st causes, and the unanswered questions growing out of the inadequacies of scientific investigation make inevitable a coexistence that is bound to be in evidence for some time to come.

By its very nature, secularism will always be a live option to the people in periods that feel confident in material strength. However, serious lacks in its basic hypotheses — failure to deal with the reality beyond fact, limiting man's knowledge to the world of "facts," and attempting to establish an ethical system without faith — will ever prevent it from becoming a substantial system of thought. It will always be a protest movement; as such it may provide a much-needed corrective for uncritical and inflexible dogma. Danger arises when the secular protest begins to prevail and mold men's minds over patterns that disregard the reality of God and men's need of him. — *Harry A. DeWire*

SERMONS, CHILDREN'S A sermon has been defined as a "discourse delivered in public, usually by a clergyman, for the purpose of religious instruction, and grounded on some text or passage of Scripture." The same dictionary identifies a child as a "young person of either sex, especially one between infancy and youth." The 1st definition invites modification, but the 2 statements are sufficiently precise to establish the principal boundaries of children's sermons.

A sermon is not less a sermon because addressed to children. Christian in its context, it is Christian in its content. Its origin is in the Christian Scriptures, which bear witness to the saving work of God in Jesus Christ. Its burden is the Christian gospel, whose particularity in Christ claims a universal relevance both to the one God and to every person. Its purpose is religious instruction for the initiation and nurture of Christian discipleship.

Thus conceived, a children's sermon is not simply a story, nor even simply a story with a moral. Neither is it simply a moral lesson with or without a story. A sermon meant for children is not meant for their amusement or even — ultimately — for their education. No less a sermon because the persons to whom it is addressed are children, it is subject to the standards properly applied to other forms of preaching.

A children's sermon is solidly grounded in a theological substructure consistent with the historic Christian proclamation. It is constructed in accordance with the homiletical principles that govern the ministry of the pulpit wherever it is undertaken. Its reason for being is neither exclusively eternal truth nor exclusively human life, but the claim of the former on the latter and the dependence of the latter on the former. Commonly delivered in a service of worship, the children's sermon is itself an offering that the preacher makes to God. It is prepared with the care due its context and presented with the dignity required by its purpose. Being concerned with the totality of the gospel, it does not deal lightly with the meaningful progression of the ecclesiastical year. Understanding the varied needs of its congregation, it ministers to its hearers sometimes through a priestly celebration of the ancient verities, sometimes through a prophetic declaration of the Christian revelation, sometimes through a pastoral provision of necessary sustenance, and sometimes through an administrator's counsel to the ministering community. Like other sermons, a sermon to children derives its power from a variety of sources, among them the authority of the historical gospel, the context of the witnessing church, the personal experience of the preacher, and the relevance to the listening congregation. Like other sermons, too, a sermon to children is an act in its own right, and although some of its meaning must be sought in the subsequent attitudes and behavior of its hearers, much of its significance lies in the success with which the preacher makes his sermon the means of actual religious experience during its delivery. It is part of the sermon's function to encourage obedience of God in the world, but it is no less part of its function to provide encounter with God in the church. In this sense, it is the task of the children's sermon to introduce the children to God and to interpret God to the children.

But if it must not be forgotten that a sermon for children is fully a sermon and hence that its preparation and delivery are to be undertaken within the proper limits of that category, it is equally essential that the peculiarities of the congregation not be neglected. A young person " between infancy and youth " has more similarities with his parents than his parents often assume, and there is no place in a children's sermon for the oily condescension that often claims it. But there are important differences between a congregation of children and a congregation of adults, and effectiveness in preaching to the young is much rarer than comparable skill in preaching to the old.

The justification for a sermon specifically to children is that the gospel is intended for all people, that children are persons, and that many sermons addressed to adults are no more intelligible to children than a sermon in Greek to a congregation of Chinese. One of the most common reasons for a minister's failure in preaching to children is the contradiction between the asserted and actual relevance of the sermon. The preacher faces children, but he speaks to adults. To the latter he presents mature religion as if it were childish; with the former he leaves the impression that all religion is incomprehensible; and from the children's sermon he removes the warrant for its use.

The children's sermon is not a cute device for communicating information to adults. Indeed, the best sermons for children will often be so pertinent to their intended congregations that none but the more imaginative adults will understand or be impressed by them.

For one thing, both the language and concepts of the sermon will be children's language and concepts. This is not to say that the verbiage will be infantile or that the concepts will be related only to children. But the words will be words in common usage among children; the ideas will be manageable by children's minds; and the illustrations will be susceptible to children's reconstruction and participation. The world in which the sermon moves will be peopled by adults as well as by children, but it will be a world seen through children's eyes, described in children's terms, and entered on children's levels.

Moreover, a sermon for children will be concerned with children's needs. Here 2 dangers are frequently faced: on the one hand, the preacher peoples his adult world with children and preaches to children as if they were adults, and, on the other hand, he fills the child's world with adults and preaches to adults as if they were children. But a good children's sermon handles children's needs as they are felt by the children themselves in a world inhabited by both children and adults. Insecurity, loneliness, and fear; frustration, bafflement, and misunderstanding; hatred and love; despair and hope; greed and generosity — all this and more will have a place in children's sermons, but always in the context of the child's actual situation and achieved understanding.

Further, a sermon for children will be relevant to the children's opportunities. When the service of worship is over, the child returns to a world where the avenues of Christian discipleship are more extensive than either he or his elders may suppose, but his inescapable immaturity makes it inevitable that his opportunities to act as a Christian will be different from those of his parents. Neither implicitly nor explicitly will the children's sermon impose upon its hearers burdens that they cannot carry, problems that they cannot solve, or responsibilities that they cannot discharge. Remembering that children are persons, the minister will belittle neither their present stature nor their potential strength; but remembering that children are very young persons, he will match his commands to their capacity.

It is a commonly accepted precept that abstractions are largely ineffective in preaching to children and hence that stories will be used more frequently with children than with adults. But the desirable concreteness has an even more important aspect. Children are not simply creatures engaged in the process of becoming persons: they are also creatures who are already persons — already capable of participating meaningfully in the worship service of which the children's sermon is a part and already competent to manifest the Christian life in their own environment. Hence, a good children's sermon is addressed only in part to persons in abeyance and is concerned only in part with what the child will do when he has reached maturity: in even larger part, it is addressed to persons in fact and is concerned with what the child does in his childhood. — *Roy Pearson*

SEVENTH–DAY ADVENTISTS The *Seventh-day Adventists* was officially organized in 1863 following a formative period of approximately 18 years. The name was chosen because it sets forth clearly 2 Biblical teachings — in addition to the Christian beliefs common to all Protestant denominations — concerning which the denomination wished to bear a special witness. In the early 1870's, with the young denomination well under way, the Adventist leaders perceived that in the public schools their children were exposed to influences tending to lessen their commitment for the Christian faith; they also felt the lack of adequate means for training church workers for which there was an ever-growing demand. By their need they were compelled to add yet another activity to the church program, that of Christian education on all levels.

In 1874, Battle Creek College was founded (it now operates at Berrien Springs, Mich., under the name of Andrews University). In the U.S.A. the denomination now operates 9 senior colleges and 1 junior college, plus numerous secondary and elementary schools. Its largest school enrollment is outside the U.S.A. In 1960, Seventh-day Adventists operated 4,460 elementary schools having 228,345 pupils enrolled. This is said to be the largest Protestant elementary school system in the world outside the U.S.A. and the 2d largest in the U.S.A.

The basic philosophy and objectives of the Seventh-day Adventist school system are based on the belief that the ultimate purpose of man is to love and serve God and his fellowmen and that all instruction and learning in the school must be directed toward helping achieve that end. Seventh-day Adventists endeavor to operate their schools in such a way that the curriculum, the extracurriculum, and every school experience contribute to reaching the following goals: (1) In each school there will be a spiritual climate in which prayer, worship, and doing the will of God is, in the eyes of the majority of the students, the ideal and accepted pattern of living. (2) The Bible and Biblical world view will be central in all the study and teaching. (3) Learning in subject matter will be of high quality, with emphasis on independent thinking and the highest achievement possible for each individual. (4) A total school program will promote the highest development of the physical powers and balance study with useful exercise. (5) A total school program will prepare for, and is, life; and prominent in life is the problem of establishing a successful Christian home and the fulfilling of civic responsibility and leadership. (6) The youth will develop personal commitment of their capacities and strength to the service of God and of mankind. — *Richard Hammill*

SEX Primarily "sex" denotes "either of the two divisions of organic beings distinguished as male and female respectively." Its original purpose was evolutionary. Binary fission, the earliest form of reproduction, propagated only more or less identical organisms, but variation became possible when sexual specialization required the cooperation of dissimilar yet complementary individuals, whose characteristics were transmitted to and combined in their offspring. Thus sex made possible the progressive development of ever higher and more complex forms of life, and the establishment and elaboration of distinct species. It also caused within each species the marked differentiation of male and female. With the emergence of man a new factor, personality, sharpened and deepened this differentiation, creating between man and woman a profound metaphysical antithesis,

over and above the biological distinction between them.

In humanity the metaphysical significance of sex is uniquely important. Nevertheless, Western conceptions of sexuality have been colored more by the biological, and particularly the venereal, associations of sex. Today this tendency has culminated in a virtual restriction of the word "sex" to generative and venereal contexts. "Sex" has also acquired limiting overtones and emotional content; it conveys a subtle hint of sensuality or salacity — it can offend or disturb; it can excite disgust or prurient interest. Often it refers solely to coition, a common synonym for which is "sex." Thus the metaphysical and personal dimensions of human sexuality have become obscured and neglected, and one of Christianity's most urgent educational tasks is to redress this lack of balance.

Man cannot be considered apart from his sexuality — that is, his existence as male and female — and to define sex is in part to define man. The Biblical accounts of man's creation offer a convenient starting point for an elucidation of sex. The later (P) narrative describes man as created male and female in the image of God (Gen. 1:27), and states that God "called their name Adam" (Gen. 5:2, KJV) — i.e., *'Ādhām*, the Hebrew term for man in the generic sense. The earlier (J) myth is simple and primitive. God makes an "adam," or human prototype, conceived of as male in form, from which he takes a rib and fashions it into a woman — resolving, as it were, the original being, or "adam," into its sexual components, and endowing them with separate personal existence as man and woman. Brought together, they recognize their common origin, and cleaving together as husband and wife, they become one flesh, thus restoring in some sense the original unity of man.

The rabbis tried to reconcile and explain these narratives by supposing that the "adam" was androgenous (a notion possibly borrowed from Plato); but this hypothesis is scientifically and theologically objectionable, and a more satisfactory interpretation is suggested by the idea of man as an image of God. We cannot say precisely what this expression meant, but clearly the writer regarded the "adam" as in some significant way a reflection of the divine nature. In the past, theologians have sought the image chiefly in man's possession of spirit, freedom, reason, and moral consciousness, but recently attention has been directed to its relational implication. Christianity conceives God as a coinherence of 3 divine entities or "persons," and man, the finite image of God, reflects the structure of the Godhead; he is a "being in relation," and one in whose constitution the basic element is a personal sexual polarity.

Thus sex in man is not simply a reproductive device. He was created a "dual being," comprising 2 distinct, correlative personal components, man and woman, each individual fully and independently human, yet both naturally oriented toward each other, and existing in a mutual belongingness that they are continually impelled to realize in manifold kinds of relation. In man the reproductive purpose of sex is 1 element only in a factor of great complexity that divides humanity radically into 2 opposite yet complementary parts, and permeates the individual's being to its depths, conditioning every facet of his life and personality. Human sex is the personalization of an ontological distinction in man. Creation in the image of God means that from the moment of his emergence out of the prehuman condition, man was something new and unique — a "twofold being," a sexual duality having man and woman as its individual and personal poles.

Man's sexual structure creates certain obligations for men and women in their personal lives and relationships. First, they must preserve their sexual integrity by repudiating false conceptions of sex and seeking to conform to true patterns of manliness and womanliness. This entails a critical appraisal of cultural stereotypes of sexual roles and characteristics. Manliness and womanliness are relative, not absolute, qualities, and do not consist in conformity with contemporary sexual stereotypes but in being true to the principles implied in the creation of man as a sexual duality. In this connection it is important to recognize that we have no intuitive comprehension of the meaning of manhood or womanhood; awareness of sexual distinction conveys no metaphysical understanding of sex — that can only be learned through relation itself. When God created sex he cast the "adam" into a deep sleep; consequently man is aware of the fact of sex, but not intuitively of the inner significance of that fact. Hence, God's act in bringing the man and woman together; sexual knowledge is always empirical.

Sexual relation of every kind, on every level of intimacy, means moving into a new dimension of experience in which, through personal encounter, sex becomes meaningful in personal terms. As one is most human when one forgets self, so one is most manly or womanly when one loses false or artificial sex consciousness (of the kind stimulated by many influences in our culture) in relations of sincerity and integrity with the complementary half of humanity. Then one discerns that manhood and womanhood are more than maleness or femaleness — which are simply impersonal sex. The significance of sex consists, not in what one is for oneself, but in what one is for another — this particular one, encountered in this particular relation.

Second, there is the duty of sexual partnership. The 2 sexes are naturally oriented toward each other; being complementary and mutually dependent, they need each other for everything in life, and not merely for procreation and domesticity. Sexual partnership means the free and equal association of man and woman in all the manifold interests and enterprises of social, political, and ecclesiastical life, thus liberating the creative dynamic of sex for the furtherance of the common good and the enrichment and elevation of human life.

Unfortunately there are obstacles to partnership. Our cultural obsession with the venereal element in sex creates a barrier between men and women, and gives an unwholesome twist to a natural and normal feature of human life. The persistence, often in subtle forms, of androcentric theories of sexual status and function inhibits creative cooperation between the sexes and buttresses false stereotypes of their social roles and status. There are no evolutionary, scientific, or empirical grounds for holding that woman is in some sense subordinate to man. But it is difficult to speak of sexual order more positively for, like sex itself, it is essentially mysterious — something of which we have no a priori or intuitive knowledge. As with manhood and womanhood, its meaning can be discovered only in and through responsible relation — the experience of man and woman as they live and work together in real partnership. It cannot be defined precisely, if only because it is as variable as sexual relation itself; but this at least can be affirmed: sexual order is always basically one of complementation. Headship and subordination are really irrelevant issues; what matters is that each sex should complement the other by playing the role appropriate in the particular relation of the moment.

— Derrick Sherwin Bailey

SHINTO " Shinto " is the term most commonly used for the indigenous religion of the Japanese people and for certain later developments growing out of the earlier religious practices. Due to the influence of Chinese on written Japanese, " Shinto " came to be used as a variant of the purely Japanese phrase *kami no michi* ("way of the *kami*"). The *kami* include a wide variety of beings such as trees, mountains, animals, outstanding ancestors, heroes, emperors, and a pantheon of celestial gods of whom the sun goddess has come to be the most important. As the great 18th-century Japanese scholar Motoori observed, *kami* may refer to the actual tree, mountain, etc., or to the spirit of the entity in question.

Attention to the *kami* — from magical control or simple respect through reverence to worship — is focused particularly in the shrine. A Shinto shrine may vary from a small wayside structure that is hardly more than a box to elaborate buildings and grounds such as the famous Ise shrine. The *kami* are approached principally in connection with the needs of everyday life. The prevalent attitudes expressed spontaneously or ritualistically are love, gratitude, a desire to please, and a great concern with ritual purity.

In its basic form Shinto is inseparable from the traditional culture of Japan. It has been, and in certain areas still is to some extent, a way of life that is on the prior side of reflective objectification. At this level, Shinto has not developed a systematized philosophy or theology, and its perpetuation has not been so much through formal education as through transmission of a whole cultural tradition.

After the Meiji Restoration in 1868 the Government took over Shrine Shinto, declared it to be nonreligious, emphasized the cult of the sun goddess and emperor worship as symbols of patriotic, nationalistic identity, and, taking control of the shrines out of the hands of hereditary priests whose families had served the shrines for centuries, put in Government officials as priests. Only about 10 percent of these Government appointees received any specialized training in Shinto literature and ritual. The centers for such training were Kokugakuin University, Tokyo, and Kogakkan University, Ise. Today only Kokugakuin continues to offer specialized training in Shinto. It has received considerable aid from the Rockefeller Foundation to help broaden the work of its students. Since 1945 control of the shrines has reverted to the hereditary priests, most of whom do not have formal training at Kokugakuin but learn what they do know about their special functions from family tradition.

In the modern period before 1945 mythical accounts of the origins of Japan were included as history in the curriculum of the public schools. A code of behavior and loyalty toward the emperor and state based on these traditions was also a part of general public education. All of this ended with defeat in 1945. Today there is, generally, no formal instruction in Shinto for the layman. With the abolition of the Government's program of nationalistic Shinto the shrines have remained as centers of religious devotion dependent on the devotees for their only support. In a few local cases individual priests have begun instruction or discussion classes in an endeavor to have people reflect on and develop consciously in their lives the meaning of Shinto as a religion.

When the Meiji Government established its "nonreligious" program of nationalistic Shinto it recognized a number of heterogeneous movements as "Shinto sects." Some of these groups were strongly influenced by Shinto traditions as well as by other religious streams such as Buddhism, Confucianism, and Taoism. Some had very little in common with Shinto. One of the fastest-growing religious groups in postwar Japan, Tenrikyo, was classified as "Sectarian Shinto," but its adherents disclaim any connection with Shinto. Originating in the revealed teachings of its inspired female founder, Miki Nakayama (1798–1887), Tenrikyo has grown through the cooperative efforts of the many common people who are its followers until it has become one of the most influential religious groups in Japan. At Jiba, the headquarters of the sect in Tenri City, Nara Prefecture, are 6 schools including a kindergarten, elementary, middle, and high schools, a junior college for women, and a university specializing in literature and foreign languages. The stated objectives of all schools are better education for the children and propagation of the faith. The Women's Junior College and Tenri University have the additional aim of training overseas missionaries. Backing up the schools are a central library of over 600,000 books, a very fine museum with special collections representing foreign and ancient cultures, and the Oya-sato Institute, devoted to the study of the religions of many peoples.

— *G. Ray Jordan*

SLIDES " A slide is an individually mounted transparent picture or image which is projected by passing a strong light through it." (Walter Arno Wittich and Charles Francis Schuller, *Audio-Visual Materials: Their Nature and Use*, p. 344.) Slides come in 2 general sizes: 2" x 2" and 3½" x 4". The major advantage of the smaller slide is that teachers or leaders can make their own slides with a 35mm. or Polaroid camera. The color of these slides is usually more natural and authentic. The larger slide has the advantage of usually being better protected between pieces of glass, and also has a projected surface 5 times larger than the small slide.

As an aspect of visual aids, slides provide an effective teaching tool. Among the many advantages of this type of still picture projection, these could be mentioned as of special significance: slides can be shown in any desired order; they provide for a variety of material (almost anything that can be photographed can be put on a slide) and are suitable for color or black and white; they can be made by groups for their own use; they are easy to project and inexpensive; they are magnified for clear viewing; an entire group can see and respond to the picture; attention of a group is focused in one direction.

The equipment required for using slides is relatively inexpensive and simple to operate. A 35mm. projector, with an adapter for showing both slides and filmstrips, depending on the intended use, can usually be purchased from $50 up. A beaded screen on which to project the slide is desirable, but substitutions can be made using a blank, light-colored wall or a white window shade attached to a wall. Slides can be used by groups of all ages. They can help to make the lesson material more alive and meaningful for small children. They can be used creatively by groups of children in a worthwhile learning experience as the children develop their own slides. Young people and adult groups can use them effectively in helping to create a climate of worship or make reports, to show the results of a study or outline a proposed study.

Certain basic principles need to be considered in the use of slides so that they do not become just " time fillers." It is important to plan carefully for the use of slides, keeping in mind these things: selection — must be made with care and thought; preview — all slides should be previewed before use; preparation — both on the part of the leader and with the group — is important; follow-up — discussion on the use of slides is helpful.

An excellent source for the listing of slides of a variety of religious topics is the annual *Audio-Visual Resource Guide*, published by the Division of Christian Education of the NCCCUSA. For directions as to making slides, see *How to Make Handsome Lantern Slides* (Keystone View Co., Meadville, Pa.).

— *Vera Largen*

SOCIAL ACTION "Christian social action is the effort of the church to fulfill its mission by seeking God's will for human relationships as revealed in Jesus Christ; by studying the social situation in the community, state, nation, and world; by evaluating social practices from the perspective of this understanding; and by working with others to change economic, racial, political, and international relationships in the light of the Christian faith." This statement, taken from *A Manual for Christian Social Action* used in the United Church of Christ, is a working definition of Christian social action that would be recognized by most Protestant denominations.

The Christian church, when it has been vital, has inevitably affected society both indirectly and directly. Some of the opposition to chattel slavery can be attributed to religious and ethical concerns rooted in the Christian heritage. During the latter part of the 19th century, however, the "social gospel" movement crystallized certain convictions: that there are serious problems embedded in modern industrial society; that the Christian gospel has a bearing on these problems; and that these problems will not be resolved merely by preaching or by the conversion of individuals. Representatives of this movement, such as Washington Gladden, Henry Codman Potter, and Walter Rauschenbusch, were disturbed by the plight of modern industrial workers — the squalor of their surroundings, the drudgery of their work, and their estrangement from the church; were challenged by the difficulty of an effective evangelistic approach to these and other social groups; were outraged by the impersonal forces that debased men and the society that tol-erated economic injustice as economic "law"; and yet were encouraged by new views of theology and of human nature to hope for the possibility of change. (The last-named influence also affected the development of Christian education.)

One result of these discoveries was the development of the settlement house, the institutional church, and various social services. The other response included efforts at cooperation with labor leaders, economists, socialists, and others in the interest of mutual acquaintance, reform, and social change. This ferment led to the writing of tracts and books, to the publication of various journals, and to the founding of voluntary organizations both within denominations and across denominational lines, such as the Church Association for the Advancement of the Interests of Labor (Episcopal, 1887) and the Brotherhood of the Kingdom (originally but not exclusively Baptist, 1892). This new awareness of what exists in the social situation and what resources inhere in the gospel made for a conscious effort to understand and influence social institutions and structures.

With the turn of the century, social Christianity received new and increased attention from the organs of the major Protestant denominations. In 1901 both the Protestant Episcopal and the Congregational denominations set up commissions on the relations of capital and labor. In 1903 the Board of Home Missions of the Presbyterian Church in the U.S.A. added Charles Stelzle to its staff as secretary for its Department of Church and Labor. These agencies may be regarded as the predecessors of the present-day Department of Christian Social Relations (Episcopal), Council for Christian Social Action (United Church of Christ), and Office of Church and Society (United Presbyterian).

During the next few years social welfare committees were established by the Disciples of Christ (1911), the Evangelical Synod of North America (1913), the Reformed Church in the U.S. (1914), the United Lutheran Church (1920), and others. These agencies, reorganized under various names or replaced by more inclusive boards, were at various times assigned broader responsibilities, and provided with increased resources. Especially during the 1930's and 1940's a number of denominational social action agencies were established, staffed, or given new status. The (unofficial) Methodist Federation for Social Service, founded in 1907, exerted a considerable influence for nearly 4 decades; but, except for its Boards of Temperance (1916) and World Peace (1924), The Methodist Church did not until 1952 establish an official Board of Social and Economic Relations, which in 1960 combined with the others to form a General Board of Christian Social Concern. During this period, denominations such as the Brethren and the Friends, with a historic interest in peace, developed also a concern for race relations, citizenship, and other social areas.

There has been a parallel development of concern for the social order, particularly in the areas of labor and social justice, on the part of the Roman Catholic Church, which has a strong department of social action lodged in the National Catholic Welfare Conference. Thus today, except for the Orthodox churches and certain theologically conservative Protestant bodies, most Christian denominations in the U.S.A. have official social action agencies.

The other major advance dating from the beginning of this century was the formation of the Federal Council of the Churches of Christ in America, through which the denominations furthered their common interests in evangelism, social action, and interchurch cooperation. Its initial meeting in 1908 adopted the " Social Creed of the Churches " based on a similar document approved by the General Conference of The Methodist Episcopal Church. The Federal Council became a major force in concerting the thought and life of American Protestantism in relation to the social order. These interests have been continued and extended in the Division of Christian Life and Work of the National Council of the Churches of Christ in the U.S.A. The Council's General Department of United Church Women has been instrumental in making the women of the churches especially well informed on social issues. The formation of the World Council of Churches and the Commission of the Churches on International Affairs in turn reflected an intensification of social thought on the part of Christian churches everywhere, and stimulated the member churches in the U.S.A. in their social outreach.

The methods used in carrying out the church's responsibility in society vary with the area of concern, the specific matter in question, and the particular group or agency attempting to deal with it. Denominational and interdenominational agencies commonly issue pronouncements or resolutions to interpret their Christian understanding of a problem or their response to it. They make large use of publications, study conferences or consultations, seminars, study tours, and other educational devices. Occasionally, they offer public testimony on issues before Governmental bodies or intervene directly in social conflicts. Synods, presbyteries, and state or local councils of churches, may use similar measures in dealing with local or state issues. Congregations, in turn, through councils or committees may deal directly with social tensions, economic disputes, community problems, or civic enterprises — while utilizing the various organizational and educational channels of the congregation to provide information and stimulate action.

During the 1st decade of the present century, as during the preceding period, the social action movement was very largely occupied with the urban and industrial problem. World War I compelled many of its representatives to face the reality and seriousness of international problems. War and its prevention became a major concern during the 1920's until the depression compelled fresh attention to our economic maladjustments. During the late 1930's, the issues of racial discrimination, anti-Semitism, and fascism became objects of more intense concern. Although some exponents of social Christianity accepted pacifism as the answer to war, nazi aggression led many to rethink this position. The emergence of Soviet Russia as a world power during and after World War II led to a more critical appraisal not only of political communism and its Marxist foundations but also of the anticommunist and antilibertarian reactions to the communist danger. The development of nuclear weapons and power, the acceleration of automation, pressure to conformity,

mass communications, and mass culture have called for increasing attention. The evolution of the Department of Worship and the Arts in the NCCCUSA reflects a fresh awareness of the importance of the arts for the understanding of modern culture and for the communication of Christian insights in this society.

As compared with the earlier social action movement, Christian social action today tends to be more theological — more articulate in its interpretation of the Christian revelation as determinative for Christian action; more church-related — not only in that it is responsible to the denominational households from which its leadership comes, but in that it is enriched by the broad ecumenical conversations that serve as correctives to partial and sub-Christian points of view; more astute in its awareness of technical complexities and in its search for expert knowledge regarding the specific issues on which ethical judgments are based; and more pragmatic — in the sense that it emphasizes not easy solutions but a responsible search for the best answers to the concrete situation in the light of our total Christian commitment.

— *Huber F. Klemme*

SOCIAL GOSPEL Concern for the application of the gospel to the corporate life of man is as old as the Bible. The term " social gospel " developed in the late 19th century for the particular movement that arose concurrently with liberal theology and the general shock of urbanization and industrialization. Stimulated by George D. Herron, of Grinnell College, a group of socially concerned Protestants launched in 1896 a utopian society in Georgia whose publication was called, *The Social Gospel, A Magazine of Obedience to the Law of Love*. In 1910, Shailer Mathews, of Chicago, used the term as the title of a book on the teachings of Jesus and, in 1917, Walter Rauschenbusch delivered the Taylor lectures at Yale, published under the title *A Theology for the Social Gospel*. Roughly speaking, the social gospel covers the theological and ethical outlook of Protestant social concern from the post Civil War days until the rise of Hitler, when a sharp reaction against it was articulated by Reinhold Niebuhr in America and the crisis theologians on the Continent.

It is a mistake to assume that the reaction against the theological foundations of the social gospel destroyed appreciation for the enduring contribution of the movement itself. In the *Festschrift* for Reinhold Niebuhr, *Christian Faith and Social Action*, the editor praised the social gospel for recapturing the social nature of the Christian faith from its bondage to individualism and otherworldliness. Moreover, it also broke the alliance between Protestantism and the American business class.

The master motif of the social gospel was the coming of the Kingdom of God, understood as the Reign of God, through the progressive growth of love in society. The function of the Kingdom was the Christianizing of the social order through the abolition of unjust privilege. Basically, it was a reaction against pietistic subjectivism and a false apocalypticism. The attack on the latter took place at the very moment Albert Schweitzer raised serious questions about a simple, mustard-seed gradualism as the context for Jesus' understanding of the Kingdom. The mold had set on the

writings of Rauschenbusch before this new insight could be considered.

The sociology of the social gospel was its most permanent contribution. Life was seen in a solidaristic, socio-organic context. Sin expresses itself in superpersonal social institutions binding us together in the kingdom of evil, a common yoke of suffering. Economic exploitation, usually referred to as " Mammonism," was the major devil in the kingdom of evil. The Kingdom of God, expressed through social movements of reform and far-reaching change, comes to challenge the kingdom of evil.

The ecclesiology of the social gospel was, in the main, radically " free church " in form. The true church was viewed as a disciplined, democratic voluntary association rejecting sacramentalism and ceremonialism, hierarchical priesthoods, Hellenized theology, and alliances with the state. When the church is a democratic, voluntary association it becomes a channel for the Kingdom and a stimulus to social change. When it is autocratic it spawns autocratic social institutions and frustrates the Kingdom. At this point God works through dynamic social movements regardless of the explicit denial of the Christian faith in these movements. Indeed, the social gospel movement was quick to label the church as anti-Christian when it was not heralding this socially defined Kingdom of God.

The philosophy of history of the social gospel was also vulnerable to attack with its gradualistic, evolutionary outlook. Its bold social hopes stimulated motivation but it was baffled when history brought forth stubborn, demonic elements impervious to a simple discipleship and a willful commitment. Yet there was the exciting feeling of periodization before World War I in which the leaders felt they were living in one of the greatest moments of history since the Reformation and Renaissance.

Meanwhile, more profound source analyses of the origins have raised questions about an oversimplified view of its foundations as uncritically liberal in relation to Ritschl and Harnack. The present writer's unpublished dissertation, *The Origins of Rauschenbusch's Social Ethics* (University of Chicago, 1957), reveals a complex formulation based on pietism, sectarianism, liberalism, and the Anglican transformationism of Maurice and Kingsley. As Rauschenbusch was dying of cancer in the midst of the tragic world of 1918, he talked more like Dostoevsky than Emerson. Given more than his 57 years of life, he would have presented social concern in a more chastened form while preserving its basic validity.

— Donovan E. Smucker

SOCIAL WORK The term "social welfare" is generally all-inclusive. It is used to designate the totality of efforts and programs aimed at helping individuals, groups, and communities to meet their needs, solve their problems, and enjoy the benefits of well-adjusted, creative lives. It is deeply rooted in society and culture. The latter could not have evolved without the contributions of social welfare theory and practice.

Social welfare and social work have often been used synonymously in the past. More recently social work has come to denote the more professionalized services in social welfare. In the process of the growth and development of modern social work, a number of areas, each with its appropriate body of knowledge and skills, have come to be identified. They include, among others, social casework, social group work, community organization, social agency administration, social welfare research, and social action.

Of these methods, perhaps the highest degree of professionalization has been achieved at present by social casework. This method is used to extend services to individuals and families in difficulty. The assistance offered is primarily on a person-to-person basis and may involve manipulation of the environment, supportive help, clarification and interpretation of the nature of the problem faced by the individual or the family. Leading examples of social casework are at present found in the fields of family and child welfare, medical and psychiatric social work.

Social group work is also concerned with individuals but as members of certain groups. It includes leisure-time educational and recreational activities under competent leadership. One of its chief objectives is the creative use of group experience in the development of character and personality. Neighborhood houses, community centers, settlement houses, and institutional churches are major users and developers of social group work as a method in social work.

Community organization is the social work method most directly concerned with the coordinating, planning, and financing of the community welfare programs. It endeavors to identify areas of chronic or emerging needs, promoting and interpreting welfare services, eliminating or preventing duplication of service, establishing order in the complex of many and varied existing services, determining priorities among projected programs, sharing in the development of future plans, and jointly financing welfare agencies. United funds, community chests, welfare councils, and councils of social agencies constitute some of the more important agencies functioning in the area of community organization.

Social agency administration involves a network of functions related to the efficient operation of the services offered by welfare institutions and agencies. Chief among its many functions are: determination of objectives and policies; development of organizational structure, procedure, and programs of service; finding the needed resources in personnel, funds, buildings, and equipment; establishing desirable interagency and public relations. Among the factors that often influence social agency administration favorably or unfavorably are the purposes of the organization, the auspices under which it operates, the area — geographic or social — it serves, and its size and setting.

Social welfare research is in many ways related not only to all the other methods of social work but also to research taking place in other professional areas such as public health, public welfare, the social and psychological sciences, etc. Within the profession of social work, research is generally limited to the investigation of problems, practices, policies, and trends of special importance to the field of social work. In recent years research has been used increasingly to provide a basis for sound planning and financing. Beginnings have also been made to examine and study theoretical positions. Such research programs are carried on, often, under the auspices of united funds, welfare councils, schools of social work, and agencies of the several Governments.

Social action comprises the activities and plans directed to the mobilizing of public opinion, the influencing of legislation, the modifying of public administration. Many of the problems with which the profession of social work is concerned are inextricably related to larger social and cultural conditions that cannot be dealt with effectively through the application of other methods of social work.

Education for social work may be said to have had its official beginnings when, in 1898, a summer training course was offered by the Charity Organization Society of New York. Six years later a 1-year sequence of courses was given by the New York School of Philanthropy, which eventually became the New York School of Social Work, affiliated with Columbia University since 1940. Chicago's experience has been somewhat similar; a program 1st initiated in 1899 evolved into the School of Social Service Administration of the University of Chicago — the 1st school fully integrated within a university.

In 1961 there were in operation 57 accredited schools of social work in the U.S.A. and 7 in Canada.

Currently, social work education is a 2-year graduate course of classroom study with supervised field instruction under educational auspices leading to a master's degree. The aims of the course of study are threefold: (1) to transmit knowledge derived from social work practice, from the sciences, and from the practice of allied professions; (2) to develop sensitivity and skill in the use of the methods of social work; (3) to communicate values related to the improvement of conditions, the dynamics of human behavior and motivation. Eighteen of the schools also offer post master programs.

For the 7th consecutive year full-time enrollment in the accredited schools increased, reaching a total of 6,028 in 1961. That same year the largest number of students in the history of social work, 2,310, completed their training. The number of full-time faculty members was 879. In 1961 there were 97 undergraduate departments that offered courses in keeping with the standards of the Council on Social Work Education. They had an enrollment of 3,150 juniors and seniors, of whom 1,216 received their bachelor's degree during that academic year.

American social work is currently promoted under 3 major auspices: Governmental programs at the local, state, Federal, and international levels; voluntary nonsectarian plans; and the services offered by a great variety of religious bodies. These 3 categories are seldom found in complete isolation from one another. Their interrelations are deep and extensive.

Although Governmental programs have increased phenomenally since the 1930's, there has been no corresponding decrease in religious or secular social work effort. On the contrary, voluntary social work has kept growing and has continued to provide top-level professional leadership to the entire field. Notwithstanding the presence of powerful secular influences in American culture, social work under Jewish, Roman Catholic, and Protestant auspices has tended to expand. It is deeply rooted in their organizational structures, their folkways and mores, their histories and theologies. One Jewish and 9 Roman Catholic schools of social work were in operation in 1961. Protestant groups play important roles in recruitment of students and workers. Several denominations actively support the training and recruitment programs of the Council on Social Work Education. Substantial scholarship assistance is available, among others, through United Presbyterian, Lutheran, and Protestant Episcopal sources. Joint programs of study are offered by McCormick Theological Seminary and the schools of social work at the Universities of Chicago and Illinois.

National organizations that play important roles in advancing the interests of the profession include the Council on Social Work Education and the National Association of Social Workers. The latter founded, in 1961, the Academy of Certified Social Workers in order to safeguard standards of professional practice. Early in 1962 the number of certified social workers totalled more than 18,000.

— *Charles G. Chakerian*

SOCIETY OF JESUS The Society of Jesus, whose members are commonly called Jesuits, was founded by Ignatius Loyola (1491–1556) and constituted an order of clerks regular by approval of Pope Paul III in 1540. Its history has 2 phases: from 1540 to the Society's suppression by Clement XIV in 1773 and from its restoration by Pius VII in 1814 until the present. In both periods, works of scholarship and teaching have been the chief, though not the sole, ministries of the order.

At first it had only a general dedication to teaching in the broad sense of evangelization but during Ignatius' lifetime it passed from conducting seminaries for young Jesuits to establishing *collegia* or secondary schools for lay students. These provided a classical curriculum or faculty of letters having 5 divisions: 3 of grammar, 1 of humanities (poetry), and 1 of rhetoric. To this was sometimes added a faculty of arts (philosophy, together with some science and mathematics) and a faculty of theology. At Ignatius' death there were over 1,000 Jesuits, whose activities included maintenance of 33 *collegia*. In 1749, the year of the last complete census before the suppression, there were 22,589 Jesuits, half priests and the rest scholastics (seminarians) or coadjutor brothers, and 845 educational institutions of which more than 600 were *collegia*. The restored Society began this work anew, for most of its resources had been confiscated during the suppression. By 1960 there were 34,687 Jesuits in some 78 provinces and vice-provinces in Europe, the Americas, and the Far East, and in mission territories of Africa, Asia, and Oceania. A third of these men, assisted by over 31,000 non-Jesuit teachers, conducted some 707 educational complexes embracing 2,939 schools with nearly 800,000 students. Over ⅕ of all Jesuits worked in the U.S.A. and maintained there, in 1960, 43 high schools and 28 colleges and universities, including graduate departments and schools of medicine, dentistry, nursing, law, education, music, social work, and business. The professional and graduate schools and some colleges are coeducational; the high schools are for boys only.

Since these schools believe in the viability of a Christian humanism, they aim to develop both the secular and religious dimensions of education. Their curricula include the physical and social sciences as well as languages, philosophy, and theology. The educational philosophy here is substantially determined by the nature of man, particularly as he is the subject of schooling, and by the specific requirements of the Catholic world view. To this the Jesuit tradition adds a family nuance. The spirit of that tradition is preserved in the Ignatian documents, the *Spiritual Exercises* and the 4th Part of the Society's *Constitutions*, and in the plan for curricula and methods that appeared in 1599 under the title *Ratio atque institutio studiorum societatis Iesu*. The *Exercises* were not written for schools but are a means of Christian character education, since they provide materials and directions for a series of coordinated meditations upon such themes as the finality of life, sin, and redemption through fidelity to the person and teachings of Christ. All Jesuits spend 8 days every year making a " retreat " based upon the *Exercises*, and the Catholic students in their schools make an annual retreat of at least 3 days.

The *Ratio studiorum* consists of 30 sets of rules for administrators and teachers and resembles other Renaissance plans dedicated to the cultivation of Ciceronian eloquence and Aristotelian wisdom. Its methodology is derived from Quintilian's precepts and the procedures of Paris. The early Jesuit schools gained their ascendancy not only because of their orderly sequence of studies but also because their teachers were dedicated, enthusiastic, and well prepared academically and professionally. The schools, moreover, charged no tuition, though today fees are necessary for maintenance.

Beneath the letter of these documents, principles can be discerned which together constitute the Jesuit accent: an optimistic belief in the possibility of synthesizing the best of secular culture with Christian life; an instrumental approach to curriculum and methods, which are considered means to the broad objectives; a willingness to adapt procedures to circumstances; an emphasis upon the teacher whose vocation ideally includes both an academic and a guidance function; insistence upon student self-activity for learning; and an esteem for order, humane discipline, and tested teaching techniques.

— *John W. Donohue, S.J.*

SOCIODRAMA Sociodrama is a comparatively new group technique that reveals the cause and effect of a situation or problem in dramatic form. The term " sociodrama " is sometimes confused with the term " psychodrama." Psychodrama focuses the attention on the individual's problems, tensions, and feelings; it is used to help an individual release his tensions, overcome his personal handicaps, and express his needs. The focus on sociodrama is on group rather than individual concerns.

Sociodrama is used primarily for the purpose of working out effective ways of dealing with normal situations and problems of life within the group structure. The technique helps the group to become aware of its problem, look at the problem from many aspects, and discover that there are many ways to a solution of the problem. It causes the individuals to think for themselves and helps individuals within the group to solve many personal problems in relation to others. Individuals discover that many of the problems which they felt were only their concern are actually quite common in the lives of others; also, that ideas which individuals believed to be universal and common are really out of line with reality.

Sociodrama is an entirely spontaneous and unrehearsed technique. It requires no dramatic talent either on the part of the leader or of the players. Props, scenery, or costumes are not needed. It requires only a few minutes to produce quickly real-life situations or problems, stimulating active discussion and personal involvement.

After a group discussion, individuals within the group suggest life situations that they would like to enact. Then they decide on the problem that is the most challenging to the majority. The group decides upon the characters necessary to act out the real-life situation. The group then selects the characters who will portray the different parts or types chosen. Through discussion guided by the leader, the group helps brief the players so that each one knows the type of person he is to portray.

Two players come to the front, discuss the scene to be enacted, clarifying questions regarding the character traits to be presented. Players portray types, not particular individuals. The audience is then briefed by a member of the acting group or leader as to the background or any other information necessary for the enactment. The leader keeps the action moving, but does not dominate the thinking or the direction to be taken by the group.

The players enter spontaneously into a logical conversation, expressing their feelings and thoughts as they become involved in the situation or problem. The discussion continues until the leader ends the scene at a point when a good opportunity for total group discussion and involvement appears. The group discussion that follows is an important factor. Various aspects of the situation are considered, and different solutions are discovered. The players will discuss why they acted as they did and how they felt as they were involved in the discussion. Self-expression is encouraged on the part of both players and audience. If a permissive atmosphere exists, all involved in the experience can express themselves freely, discover different solutions to the problem, and achieve self-integration. The focus is not on gaining information, but on the awareness and growth of the participants. As solutions are found, the participants learn to work cooperatively rather than on an individual basis.

New insights are given to the same problem by reversing the roles of the players. Other emotions come into the play, new attitudes are developed, and other motivations are recognized. Players begin to experience the viewpoint of the other person.

Christian education can utilize sociodrama in many ways. Many opportunities are available in areas involving Christian social relations and human behavior. It affords a means of practical application of what is being taught in home and family situations, church school class areas of concern, youth group work, vocational guidance, and leadership development. Sociodrama gives opportunities to try out skills, for the group is working in the area of reality. Emerging concepts can be put into practice. Sociodrama is a moti-

vating technique by which individuals can solve many personal problems, thus better understanding their relations with other individuals.

— *Margaret E. Lobb*

SOCIOGRAM A sociogram is a sociometric device used to objectify the informal social structure of a group. It is useful as a means of diagraming and analyzing patterns of interpersonal friendship and repulsion or potential patterns of acceptance and rejection. For this reason, the device has practical significance for teacher-leaders and for group members interested in the quality of their group life. Essentially the sociometric method refers to the procedure of (1) asking the persons in a given group with whom they would like to work, go on a picnic, or carry on some other activity that requires interpersonal interaction; and (2) plotting those personal preferences on paper by drawing lines linking the symbols of persons who indicated similar preferences, the resulting diagram being known as a sociogram.

This essentially simple procedure can be varied in many ways. For example, the participants may be asked to indicate 1st, 2d, and 3d choices. These may be plotted by using different types of lines. A common practice, however, is to plot all the choices, making no distinctions between 1st, 2d, and 3d because the number of choices received tends to be a reliable index of sociometric status.

To some extent social development of individuals in a group can be studied by the use of devices that measure either actual or symbolic social participation. The sociometric device was developed by Jacob L. Moreno, a Viennese psychiatrist who emigrated to the U.S.A.

There are 4 well-defined steps in the use of this sociometric device. The 1st step is to prepare an appropriate question. In formulating the "choice" question the practitioner must consider the age group involved and the purpose of the group, e.g., "play with" preferences and "work with" preferences will differ.

Step 2 is to apply the questionnaire. In young children's groups the questionnaires may have to be posed informally to each child and the group diagramed over a period of time. If a group is composed of older youths or adults of any age, they will wish to be told the practical purpose of the questionnaire and how its results may be used. Instructions to participants should be the request that they sign their names to the questionnaire and the assurance that no one except the leader or teacher will see the signed slips.

Step 3 is to record the preferences on paper. Small circles, squares, or triangles may be used to symbolize the participants (or squares for males, circles for females, and so on). For convenience plot 1st, 2d, and 3d choices as equal choices, linking each appropriate person-symbol and adding a small arrow to indicate which preferred the other. The symbols of those who choose each other should be placed fairly close together, and other preferences (although not mutual) should be placed near the chooser. It is also advantageous to place the symbols of those chosen by many near the center of the symbol cluster.

The 4th step is that of using the resulting sociogram to the best advantage. With groups of younger children, the teacher-leader will probably find it useful to use the data privately as means of identifying clique patterns, potential social rejects, and growth in socialization. For the last-named purpose sociograms for the group should be constructed periodically so that data will be available for different points in time.

In using the results with older youths and adults, it is important that an enlarged copy of the sociogram be constructed and that all names be omitted. The teacher-leader should interpret the data in terms of general tendencies in the group and not dwell on "isolates" or high-status persons, which would encourage speculation and name-calling. It is the possible significance of all the data that should be stressed, not the data themselves.

Certain possible dangers are involved in using sociometric data. It is important to remember, for example, that the social relationships reflected on a sociogram are valid only within that specific group and at that particular time. They are not reliable evidence for predicting an individual's relationships in other groups. A sociogram reveals some facts, but does not reveal causes of behavior. For this reason, the facts that appear graphically on a sociogram must be interpreted, e.g., what we might consider as a negative trait in a person whom the sociogram reveals as a social "isolate" may be an effect (not a cause) of his rejection by fellow group members.

— *John McKinley*

SOCIOLOGY OF RELIGION Sociology of religion (or religions) embodies within it the scholarly concerns and methods, as well as the ambiguities, of its parental disciplines, the study of society and the study of religions.

Sociology as a discipline developed only in the 19th century, although its heritage can be traced to antiquity. For many centuries the study of the nature of human society and group living was considered the task of philosophers, theologians, and jurists. Even Auguste Comte (1798–1857), who first used the term "sociology," was in fact a social philosopher. Other pioneers of sociology, such as Émile Durkheim, Georg Simmel, Max Weber, Herbert Spencer, Lester F. Ward, William Graham Sumner, and Charles Horton Colley, combined social philosophy with social scientific concerns. With the gradual emancipation of sociology from social thought and social philosophy, the distinction between the terms "social" and "political" came to be taken for granted. Undoubtedly the development of the discipline of economics during the last century, in its concern with the division of labor and the relation of social structure to process, greatly aided the growth of sociology. Biology, which then was preoccupied with the theories of evolution and of organism, exerted significant influences on the theory and method of sociology. Subsequently, psychology and other disciplines helped sociology in defining itself as one of the specialized social sciences.

Sociology has advanced greatly since the turn of the century, especially in the U.S.A. Scholars have published numerous works on social organization and disorganization, social stratification, social change, collective behavior, social psychology, population and ecology — utilizing the methods of qualitative, quantitative, and content analysis. A growing emphasis on specialization has resulted in the emergence of many "fields" within sociology, such as rural sociology, urban sociology, minority groups, industrial sociology, political sociology, sociology of law, sociology of education, and sociology of religion. Parenthetically, it might be added that sociological research in some of these fields has been utilized by administrators, educators, religious leaders, and other "social engineers," for the purpose of analysis, modification, or promotion of their respective programs. This type of "applied sociology," however, should not be confused with sociology per se.

General science of religion (*Allgemeine Religionswissenschaft*), known in the English-speaking world as comparative religion or history of religions, developed as an autonomous discipline during the 19th century through the efforts of Friedrich Max Müller (1823–1900) and others. The emancipation of the scientific study of religions from philosophy and theology was a slow process, and the pioneers of the discipline, such as Müller, Cornelius Petrus Tiele, P. D. Chantepie de la Saussaye, Robertson Smith, Nathan Söderblom, and Rudolf Otto, combined religious and scientific concerns with philosophical and theological interests. Even today some scholars regard the task of the discipline of history of religions as the understanding of religion as such, while others consider it to be that of understanding religious phenomena, especially those of the historical religions. Nevertheless, there is general agreement that the scientific study of religions lies between the normative disciplines, such as philosophy and theology, on the one hand, and the descriptive sciences, on the other. Thus the scientific study of religions, although having its own methods and principles, has been greatly influenced by, and has been sensitive to, the contributions of other disciplines. For example, an attempt to study the reciprocal relationship that exists between religion and society requires the cooperation of sociology, and such a concern has fostered the development of a sociology of religion as a specialized " field " within the general science of religion.

Sociology of religion, therefore, has been developed both by general sociology and by general science of religion as a " field " of their respective disciplines. Moreover, scholars of specific religions or denominations have developed sociological studies of their own religious groups and institutions. Much confusion can be avoided if we recognize that there are at least 3 kinds of studies, commonly designated by the term "sociology of religion," with a certain amount of overlapping among them, to be sure.

1. In the discipline of sociology there have been many scholars who have taken a strong interest in the relation between society and religion. For instance, Émile Durkheim (1858–1917), as evidenced by his work, *The Elementary Forms of the Religious Life,* regarded religion as one of the important forces that hold a society together. Max Weber (1864–1920), on the other hand, stressed the importance of the " understanding " of social behavior, and contributed a useful methodological tool in his concept of the " ideal type." He wrote not only on the impact of Protestantism upon the capitalistic socioeconomic order but also on the influence of Judaism,

the religions of India, and those of China on economic development. His *Gesammelte Aufsätze zur Religionssociologie* was one of the 1st attempts to systematize sociology of religion. Understandably, sociologists in their study of religious phenomena — religious institutions, their structure, processes, and relationships to other institutions and society at large — tend to regard these as products of group life, since their type of scientific concern is for the understanding of the nature of society and group living.

2. Those who are engaged in the study of religious groups, on the other hand, aim at their own specifically religious type of analysis and understanding even though they employ sociological concepts and methods. The classic example of this approach is seen in *The Social Teaching of the Christian Churches,* by Ernst Troeltsch (1865–1923). H. Richard Niebuhr's *Social Sources of Denominationalism,* Samuel Kincheloe's *The American City and Its Church,* Reuben Levy's *The Social Structure of Islam,* Pandhari-Nath Prabhu's *Hindu Social Organization,* and Joseph H. Fichter's *Social Relations in the Urban Parish* and *Southern Parish,* as well as a host of other recent publications, belong to this category. Today we find many religious groups engaged in " sociological survey," employing sociological categories and methods, in order to assess and improve policies and programs.

3. Sociology of religion as a field of the general science of religion is not, contrary to the impression of many, a sum total of various sociological studies of specific religious groups and institutions. The scientific study of religion, even in its so-

ciological dimension, attempts to analyze the common elements of the different religions and seeks to depict the general patterns of their evolution by studying religious phenomena sociologically. This aim is clearly demonstrated in the works of Joachim Wach (1898–1955), especially in his *Sociology of Religion, Types of Religious Experience,* and *The Comparative Study of Religions.* Some of the French scholars who belong to the *Groupe de Sociologie des Religions,* founded by Henri Desroche, also reflect this concern (cf. *Archives de sociologie des religions*).

Whatever the nature of sociology of religion, as interpreted by the 3 schools we have mentioned, it is invariably concerned with the investigation and analysis of the reciprocal relations that exist between religions and societies. Every religion grows out of a certain sociological milieu and is conditioned by its influence. For example, the influence of society is often observable in the religious attitudes of those in a definite social group in their divisions into ethnic and cultural ranks, classes, and castes, and in the characteristics of a particular religion arising from the sociological background of its leaders and adherents. Conversely, a religion exerts influence directly or indirectly upon the shaping of the social structure and/or develops specific kinds of religious fellowship within society. Certain kinds of social organizations, such as families, clans, vocational guilds, and nations, as well as the types of social relations that develop within them, are often colored by religious influences, to say nothing of the institutions and groups created directly by religions, e.g., the Christian *ecclesia,*

the Buddhist *samgha,* and the Islamic *ummah.* It must be kept in mind, in this connection, that the mutual relation between religion and society is never static because both religion and society are in continuous movement and development, such that the points of contact and impact between the 2 shift, depending upon time and place. Thus a study of cross sections of both society and of religious groups must be analyzed in reference to the study of the historical development of both society and religions.

As stated earlier, there are at least 3 kinds of sociology of religion, motivated by 3 different, though related, aims. Each has implications for education — especially Christian education. An educator certainly can benefit from a sociological analysis of religious groups and institutions — their growth, development, structure, and processes, as well as their relationship to society — because the Christian church, as long as it is an institution within society, can be analyzed by general sociological concepts and methods. An educator can also gain important insight from a sociological study of a particular religious group, denomination, or parish. Fichter's classification of the urban white Roman Catholics as nuclear, modal, marginal, and dormant, for example, can be applied to other religious groups as well. An educator can obtain from the sociology of religion and from the general science of religion a comprehensive knowledge of the typology of religious thoughts and feelings, religious ideas and institutions, and religious theories and practices that have influenced the human race throughout the ages.

— *Joseph M. Kitagawa*

SOCRATIC METHOD The Socratic method (developed by Socrates in the 5th century B.C.) is a method of moving from an unconsidered opinion to a carefully considered statement of truth by means of skillful questioning. It is not, strictly speaking, a method of teaching, as we use the term today, i.e., it was not intended for teaching a body of subject matter or a skill. It was rather the way Socrates penetrated and ultimately destroyed the arrogance of the Sophists, who regarded man as the measure of all things, by his procedure of asking questions until he 1st revealed their ignorance and then led them to a consideration of truth.

The Socratic method was a method of dialogue, but is not to be confused with the simple question and answer method or with our modern method of discussion. Rather, the teacher (Socrates) regarded himself as a midwife, whose function it was to enable the student to get rid of unfounded opinion and bring forth valid knowledge that could be accepted by teacher and learner alike.

There were 2 steps in his procedure — a negative one and a positive one. The negative step is often spoken of as " Socratic irony." Pretending to be ignorant of a subject, the teacher asks questions of the learner, who may at the outset believe himself to know the truth about the subject. Very often the learner expresses an opinion with some confidence, whereupon the teacher plies him with further questions in such a way that the one questioned is forced to acknowledge his ignorance on the subject. At this point he is ready to learn.

Then follows the positive step, which we may call the maieutic method, or the method of midwif-ery. Now by skillful questions the teacher is able to elicit from the student thoughts of which he had previously been unaware. The teacher does this by induction. Beginning with a concrete instance he asks questions until the accidental and contingent aspects of the situation are separated from the essential. Then appear the universal characteristics that the teacher assists the pupil to summarize in a logical definition that both can accept as true. The conceptual knowledge, or knowledge by definition that was the outcome of the dialogue, was for Socrates the only true knowledge and the basis of conduct.

The value of the Socratic method in Christian education is obvious. The method calls for a somewhat dramatic participation of both teacher and pupil in the search for truth. The teacher's role is to elicit activity on the part of the learner, acknowledging that learning takes place only as the learner becomes involved in responsible thought. It requires the learner to go beneath accepted ideas to test their validity before establishing his life on them.

The Socratic method, however, has a limited usefulness in Christian education. The view of truth upon which it rests — that truth is to be found in man — is not held in the Judeo-Christian tradition. Therefore, the view that ultimate truth can be uncovered or discovered by questioning is not valid for the Christian teacher. The Christian gospel, which is the truth to be communicated in Christian education, was made known to man by revelation. It came to man from without. Moreover, the recognition of man's sinful nature is at the same time a recognition that our judgments are likely to be perverted even when we have examined them most closely. With these precautions in mind, the Christian teacher can use the Socratic method with good effect.

—*Rachel Henderlite*

SOUTHERN BAPTIST CONVENTION

Southern Baptist churches had started some small program of religious education when the Southern Baptist Convention was organized in 1845 with 4,126 churches and a membership of 351,951.

Curriculum materials and guidance during the early days were furnished by the International Sunday School Association and the American Baptist Publication Society, but delegates from Virginia, South Carolina, Georgia, and Alabama met at Savannah on May 13, 1847, to form the Southern Baptist Publication Society. This society was short-lived; another effort was made in 1857 to organize the Southern Baptist Sunday School Union. The present Sunday School Board, which has responsibility for the promotion of Sunday school work as well as Training Union, music, student work, etc., was organized in 1891.

The Training Union, which grew out of the older Christian Endeavor and Baptist Young People's Union of America, is now provided through the Baptist Sunday School Board. It is found in most Southern Baptist churches, and has a total membership of approximately 2,375,000.

The Sunday School Board's *Curriculum Guide* states: "The overarching objective is to help persons become aware of God as revealed in Jesus Christ, respond to him in a personal commitment of faith, strive to follow him in the full meaning of Christian discipleship, live in conscious recognition of the guidance and power of the Holy Spirit, and grow toward the goal of Christian maturity."

The Woman's Missionary Union, auxiliary to the Southern Baptist Convention, was organized in 1888 and promoted a graded system of missionary education in the churches. The meetings usually are held on some day during the week rather than on Sunday. The Union also promotes special offerings for foreign and home missions, related to a week of study and prayer.

The Baptist Brotherhood, organized 1907, promotes the Royal Ambassadors, a missionary organization for boys that meets during the week, and also the work of the laymen of the churches.

One distinctive phase of Southern Baptist religious education has been in the area of professional training. A department of religious education was established at Southwestern Baptist Theological Seminary, Fort Worth, Tex., in 1915, and became a school of religious education in 1952. The trustees of the Southern Baptist Theological Seminary, Louisville, in 1953 authorized the establishment of a school of religious education, extending a department that had been offering courses in this area since 1920. Similarly, the department of religious education at New Orleans Baptist Theological Seminary became a school in 1952. Courses are also offered at Midwestern Baptist Theological Seminary, Golden Gate Baptist Theological Seminary, and Southeastern Baptist Theological Seminary. Doctor of religious education degrees are offered by the seminaries at Louisville, Fort Worth, and New Orleans, as well as masters' degrees in the field. Many Southern Baptist colleges now offer religious education as a part of their curriculum in the fields of Bible or religion.

Problems dealing with the administration of religious education programs in the churches are usually worked out through the church council, while problems in Southern Baptist Convention administration are worked out through the interagency council. — *Porter Routh*

STAFF RELATIONSHIPS Staff relationships exist within the total structure of the institutional life of the church. It is crucial to recognize that these organizational structures exist only to facilitate the achievement of the purpose of the Christian community. Any cooperative activity must have organization. However, the organization always has its reason for being in the purpose to which the activity is directed.

The purpose of Christian education in the life of the church has been stated by the Commission on General Christian Education of the National Council of the Churches of Christ in the U.S.A. as follows: " To enable persons to become aware of the seeking love of God as revealed in Jesus Christ and to respond in faith to this love in ways that will help them to grow as children of God, live in accordance with the will of God, and sustain a vital relationship to the Christian community." The church (and all its structure and organization) exists to serve its Lord in whatever ways it may to achieve this purpose.

In achieving this purpose the entire Christian community — the church — is involved. It is not accomplished by the preaching of the minister or the formalized teaching in classes, but by the life the church lives. Just as the total civic community is a more powerful educator than the public schools, so the church is a more powerful educator than the church school.

Consequently, staff relationships must be guided by a theory of administration that is related to the purpose of the church. If relations in the staff are characterized by autocratic use of authority, violation of individual worth and dignity, constant bickering and feuding, the staff cannot really serve the purpose of the church. Rather, the theory and practice of administration must exemplify the nature of the community the church is called to be.

In this light, efficiency of organization and administration in the church is evaluated from a different perspective. Any operation is evaluated finally in terms of how effectively it has served its purpose. The church can never be evaluated in terms of the number of letters mailed, the number of calls made, or even the number of persons who attend its activities. Rather, it is efficient only if it has been true to its mission to witness to the Lordship of Jesus Christ and to save men for his Kingdom.

The 1st relationship that every member of a staff has is to the larger Christian community. It is this community which has called him to this ministry. It is this community which determines the nature of the task to which he has been called. It is this community that nourishes and sustains him as he carries on his work.

Two major concerns to staff members serving the church are how decisions are made and what the lines of responsibility are. Certainly in the Christian community decisions should be made with as full involvement as possible of all who are affected by the decisions. Harrison S. Elliott defined democratic process as "that arrangement of life by which the members of a group, small or large, have opportunity to participate, in proportion to their maturity and ability, in deciding, planning, executing, and evaluating all matters in which the group is concerned, matters both within the life of the group and also in the group's relationship to other groups and the common life of which the group is a part." It is clear that there are levels of participation in terms of age, maturity, and experience, but what these levels are and how they are to be applied must be determined. Surely those who are in staff positions will be sufficiently matured and experienced that they will be involved in all decisions affecting them or their areas of work. Decision-making is a major task of administrative and organizational structure and needs to be planned for in the most careful manner. Each staff person needs to understand fully how decisions are made and what his relation to these decisions is to be.

Another area of major staff concern pertains to the lines of responsibility. How is each staff member related to the structure of the church? To what group is each responsible? What relationship of responsibility is there among the staff members? Who finally resolves conflicts about responsibility? All these questions need to be faced and settled in order to avoid friction and to free the staff for their most effective work.

Another area is the way staff members are related to one another and to all who have been set apart to fulfill certain tasks within the structure of the church. Certain of these staff relationships will involve professional with professional; others will involve professional with volunteer. These relationships will vary from church to church, but in each instance they need to be clearly defined and understood.

In almost every church situation there will be a clergyman who has been called or appointed as the responsible leader of that church. He is held responsible for the well-being of the total life of that congregation. He will be concerned with and involved in all major policy decisions. If he is true to his responsibility, he cannot adopt a "hands off" policy in relation to any of the church's life. If there are other professional staff people involved in the church, they will need to understand this. On the other hand, the pastor in charge will need to recognize that each other professional on the staff also has a responsibility to which he must be true. He has special skill, training, and experience that caused the church to set him apart for these special responsibilities. He should be free to fulfill this task in responsible relationship to the total mission and ministry of the church. Each staff person should see his relationships, however, in light of all the other tasks and roles the church has to fulfill. Each should find mutual strength and support from other members of the staff.

Besides the area of relationships within the professional staff, there are also relationships with the lay staff. Each professional staff person will find that he has relationships with certain lay persons who are concerned in his special area of responsibility. In these relationships each must understand that the other is not trying to replace him but only to supplement and make more effective the total work to which each is committed. Neither should be threatened by the other, for they are not in competition. Each is working for the effectiveness of the church as it tries to fulfill its mission. The professional staff member is a resource person who has had wider training and experience. The lay person may look to him for help in whatever area his need lies. He has the right to expect whatever resources he needs in order to do effectively the job to which he has been assigned. The lay person is no threat to the professional; rather, he is a devoted churchman attempting to fulfill a necessary role.

In all areas of staff relationships the primary instrument for providing harmonious working together is communication. Usually when friction develops, it is because of lack of real communication. True communication is a 2-way process. To whatever is communicated there must be response. This means that an openness must exist on the part of all persons involved in the process. A staff member has the right to feel that he has been heard and that his ideas have been given a thoughtful evaluation when he speaks to another person on the staff, even the senior minister. No matter how often the staff is together, if channels are open in only 1 direction, if all movement is from the upper levels of the line organization down to the lower, true communication cannot take place. There must be real willingness to listen, honest participation in the process, and real involvement with one another if true communication is to take place.

Further, there must be adequate opportunity for communication to take place. This means that regular channels are provided for talking back and forth. Staff meetings will be held at frequent and regular in-

tervals. These will not be just an opportunity for the senior staff member to announce decisions. Rather, these will provide opportunities for frank and open evaluation of the present and projected program. Relationships within the staff will be faced in a sensitive and honest way. Each person will feel that he has a right to participate freely and openly. Only then can real relationships develop.

The working relations within a staff provide the opportunity for warm personal relations. On the other hand, the very closeness of these relations can make for friction. The Christian community can be a witness to all the world only if it has achieved within its own life qualities of the fellowship it is called to be. — *William F. Case*

STEWARDSHIP Stewardship has come to prominence in recent American church life with regard to directing man's attitude toward his possessions and his use of them. As commonly understood, Christian stewardship has 2 related meanings: (1) the responsibility man has for the proper care of all resources inherent in his own person and in the persons and earth around him; (2) the responsibility of the Christian to support religious institutions with a portion of these resources.

The steward, in secular use, is one entrusted with the care of property or business affairs that are not his own. He acts in behalf of the owner and under his direction. In religious use, being a steward is every man's condition under God.

The 1st meaning of Christian stewardship is the application of the doctrine of creation to man's life in the world. Stewardship is a principle of behavior, an attitude of life, a posture from which man views himself and the world, arising from the Christian's understanding of God's creating activity and man's situation as a dependent creature. " In the beginning God created the heavens and the earth." (Gen. 1:1.) " So God created man in his own image. . . . And God blessed them, and God said to them, ' Be fruitful and multiply, and fill the earth and subdue it; and have dominion over the fish of the sea and over the birds of the air and over every living thing that moves upon the earth.' " (Gen. 1:27-28.)

The 2d related meaning of stewardship rests more directly on God's covenant with his people and the response of man to God's redeeming love. Out of gratitude to God and in recognition of God's purpose for his people, the Christian practices the faithful use of his possessions and talents as a witness to God's law and love. Christians are to regard themselves " as servants of Christ and stewards of the mysteries of God " (I Cor. 4:1). These words of Paul's imply the obligation which a church member has to support with his talents, possessions, and prayers the program of the church.

Christian education expresses its concern for stewardship in its objectives and curriculum. The purpose of Christian education is to develop persons who in all the relationships of life are guided by an awareness of their particular relation to and dependence upon God as revealed in Jesus Christ. Stewardship is thus listed as a subject-matter item to be included in the curriculum of Christian education.

Christian education is concerned with stewardship as motive, as doctrine, and as a guiding principle of behavior. Christian behavior springs from both obedience and gratitude. There are law and grace in God's reach toward man, and the Christian person responds to both. Law often gives guidance to the response of gratitude. Men in creation have certain duties to God and to one another laid upon them. The Christian knows that a man's life is created and nurtured in community, that his continued existence depends upon the contribution of countless creatures. Christian education teaches men their duty to God and his creation as a motive for stewardship. The added consciousness of God's searching and redeeming love that sparks the response of gratitude is also the work of Christian education. Christ's sacrifice transforms the Christian's duties into offerings of a loving and willingly committed soul. Man's right use of his possessions becomes his glad worship of the One whose reconciling love is made known to him in Jesus Christ. By laying the bases of Christian motivation, Christian education provides the bases also for stewardship. The Christian learns that he lives under obligation and grace, both motivations issuing in the use of life and possessions as stewards, as creatures responsible to God.

Christian education, furthermore, has the responsibility to teach the doctrines of creation and of man in God's Kingdom upon which an intelligible statement of stewardship may rest. The Christian educator's task is to demonstrate that these doctrines make sense in a scientific age as in all periods of history. The teacher opens the message of Genesis and of the Creeds to contemporary man where he thinks and lives. So-called secular society has removed from men the sense of God's presence in the creative processes of life. An industrialized and mass-produced culture has no rituals by which it can easily be related to religious reality. Each segment of life, including politics, economics, family, and education, appears to go its own way, to serve its own aims as an autonomous entity, unrelated to the others, with no overarching purpose and subject to no life beyond its own. Nontheistic philosophies blur modern man's image of God and of himself. Man knows neither his source nor his purpose. He cannot grasp the meaning of stewardship of life until he is taught to know what God has done in creation.

Christian education begins with the children, to teach them that God is the Creator of all existence and that they are bound to him as to their parents. Youths learn from the church that God is Lord over his creatures and even their bodies are temples of his Holy Spirit. Adults are led to acknowledge the creative power of God in the life processes in which they share, in marriage and parenthood, in earning a living, in citizenship, and in all other areas of their participation in society. Much of stewardship education in the churches is directed toward the interpretation of those doctrines upon which men rest their understanding of the Christian as steward.

Finally, Christian education teaches men the principles of behavior that are consistent with the practice of stewardship. Christians are led to discover the application of stewardship to their daily decisions. An attitude of humility and respect is becoming to the Christian when he stands before the created universe. He will behave responsibly in the use of the possessions over which he has control. He practices

conservation of all natural resources that are essential to the continuation of life on the earth. He cultivates his own talents and dedicates them to enlarge and enrich life where he lives, works, and worships.

It is in relation to the support of the church and its mission that much contemporary concern is expressed in the application of stewardship. Most denominations agree that " Christian stewardship is the practice of systematic and proportionate giving of time, abilities, and material possessions based on the conviction that these are a trust from God, to be used in his service for the benefit of all mankind in grateful acknowledgment of Christ's redeeming love " (NCCCUSA, Department of Stewardship).

Many denominations teach that the tithe, $\frac{1}{10}$ of a person's income, is the proper proportion to be given to the church, and a few require tithing as a condition of membership. The tithe has a Biblical foundation and is referred to in both the Old and New Testaments as the practice of the people of God for the support of the religious community. While assuming the tithe as a legitimate proportion, Jesus did not give much emphasis to it, but was more concerned with the total costs of citizenship in the Kingdom of God. Churches that have a strong tithing emphasis today appear to have more resources for their missionary and benevolent work in proportion to their size than those which do not.

Many denominations also have a department of stewardship within their national organizations, as does NCCCUSA. These departments often have responsibility to provide stewardship education and guidance for the financial program in their congregations. They vary in their specific programs, but all emphasize some principles of church support as a part of stewardship.

Stewardship education is implemented in the life of the church through various procedures. Curriculum materials for regular church school classes provide for sessions specifically on stewardship and undergird it indirectly in many courses on other subjects. Elective courses on stewardship have been prepared for youth and adults and are introduced into the programs of the regular organizations for men, women, and young people. Some denominations recommend "schools of stewardship" in local churches and provide material for them. Leadership education courses are available to assist lay leaders in teaching stewardship. — *Edwin L. Becker*

STORYTELLING It is agreed among Christian educators that the art of storytelling has great value as a medium for happy group cooperation in thinking, feeling, and enjoying. No art surpasses it in its power to give constant, genuine joy as it imparts knowledge or in its ability to arouse and stimulate the imagination. No art can better guide the listener into aesthetic and constructive channels, or better give an awareness and appreciation of the power, beauty, and color of the spoken word. The art of storytelling not only conveys the moral truths of our culture but cultivates moral standards and keeps alive the wonder without which adults and children cannot live. Storytelling is an art that can be enjoyed by the great and the humble, the old and the young, the learned and the unlettered.

If this is so, why then is story-telling sometimes the weakest part of the church school program? Perhaps it is because much of the success lies with the storyteller, and too many teachers are convinced that they are not "born storytellers." They forget that very few people are, that storytelling is an art that can be cultivated by anyone who will simply learn to use all the means of telling a story well and have an adequate reserve fund of wisely selected stories available to tell.

The choice of a story is most important. The various periods in the listeners' lives should not only determine their interest but also the selection of the story. The choice of stories is as wide as life itself.

What are the generally accepted criteria for choosing a good story? A story is made up of 4 parts: (1) a brief, compelling beginning that gains the listeners' interest, states the setting, introduces the characters, and gets the chain of events started; (2) the narration of events, sometimes called the "rising action"; (3) the climax that solves the plot or answers the question; (4) a brief conclusion. The plot should be clear enough for the storyteller and the audience to recognize easily. The characters must be true ones — so real that the listeners actually care whether the lonely woman gets the child she longs for; whether David will have the strength to kill Goliath; whether the father regains the love of his prodigal son. The setting of any story should give true pictures of the time or place in which the story is laid. The story must develop a mood in the listeners that immediately sets the stage. Perhaps the most important criterion in choosing a story is an appropriate literary style. For those who do not feel competent enough to judge style, the following are invaluable: *Your Child's Reading Today*, by Josette Frank; *Storytelling*, by Ruth Tooze; *Children and Books*, by May Hill Arbuthnot, and *Horn Book* (a bimonthly magazine devoted to children's books).

Even the " right " story may fail if the storyteller has not given it proper preparation. This simply means knowing the story so thoroughly and feeling it so deeply that the storyteller can " be the story." It is only when he is as comfortable with a story as he is in old walking shoes that he is free to interpret it through attitude, voice, and give-and-take with the audience. When a story is sad, the teller is sad. When it is gay, he is gay. When it loves, he loves. This freedom, through knowing the story well, is the magic that sweeps away the rigid body, the strained expression, the flat, monotonous voice pitched high and " breathy," the embarrassed, stilted gestures.

There are many ways to learn a story. Most storytellers read and re-read a story new to them. They realize that the teller must understand the purpose of the story. As Edna Dean Baker once wrote, " To tell a story without understanding the purpose of your story is like starting a journey with no idea of the destination." Tell the story. Re-read it. Tell it again and again and again, using all the imagination, perception, insight, enthusiasm, spontaneity, concentration, sensitivity, warmth, and joy necessary to get across to the listeners all the pictures the author has painted in the choice of words. Rehearse the story with an imaginary audience. Then be pliable enough to adapt the story, if necessary, when the listeners are faced.

The storyteller should let his face show how he feels, using expressions of joy, sorrow, or anger. His body can take care of itself; it should be free and wholly at ease as he expresses himself naturally in any gesture he finds necessary. Because storytelling is a shared, vital experience in which words are the means of communication, the storyteller must watch his choice of them. They must be appropriate not only to the character but to the mood, the setting, the place of action. The storyteller should practice saying various words in the story clearly, distinctly, softly, loudly, quickly, slowly, in anger, in sorrow, in despair. This is important because there is usually more than one character in a story, and thus the voice must change its tone, the face mirror emotion. Someone has suggested that a story is to the curriculum what windows are to a house — the necessary objects that let the light enter.

Marie Shedlock, an English storyteller, was once complimented on her telling of a particular story. " I'm glad you enjoyed it," she answered. " I spent six months of work on that story." " Born " storytellers recognize that a well-told story has numerous advantages over the " read " story. Once the children realize the storyteller is not dependent upon a book for a prop, there is no need to scramble for choice seats up front. As the eyes go from child to child (or adult to adult) each listener becomes a living part of the experience, and re-creates the picture of the story in his own imagination. There is a " unity of listening " as the storyteller and listener share experiences together. Tools of suspense, repetition, action, and pause will help make the story really live.

The storyteller must resist any urge to violate the art of storytelling by trying to drive home a moral. The storyteller must not or cannot force the audience to partake. The listener is self-selective. Perhaps the greatest reward in storytelling is remembering that tomorrow or the day after that, or even in years to come, because of one's story, some child may find his inner desire to feel, think, work, give, or love extended far beyond his dream.

— *Dorothy Westlake Andrews*

STUDENT CHRISTIAN MOVEMENT

Informally, the term " Student Christian Movement " (abbreviated SCM) connotes any program or association of Christian students; formally, it is the "official" delegated non-Roman student Christian organization in any of some 40 countries or (in the U.S.A.) only in New England or New York State. In the U.S.A. the National Student Christian Federation (NSCF) has been since 1959 the delegated council, correlative with SCM's in other countries, and the U.S.A. member unit of the World's Student Christian Federation (WSCF).

Before the mid-1800's religion in colleges (almost all church-related) was curricular and administratively sponsored. The 1st student Y.M.C.A. began at the University of Virginia in 1857. By 1877, Luther Wishard could gather at Louisville delegates from 40 colleges to form the national student Y.M.C.A., a similar Y.W.C.A. following in 1886. When evangelist Dwight L. Moody held in 1888 a month-long conference of college men at Northfield, Mass., 100 volunteered for overseas missions; thus began the Student Volunteer Movement (SVM). Over 250 campus Y chapters in 1890 repre-

sented 12,000 members, having buildings, vitality, and prestige. Global extension of this spirit, especially by a young Cornell graduate, John R. Mott, brought forth in 1895 the WSCF; in the 2 following years 22 new national SCM's were formed abroad.

In America student enrollments burgeoned after 1900. Campus Y's were more attracted to doctrinal and social Christian liberalism than were the churches. The Inter-Varsity Christian Fellowship had already begun abroad as a conservative campus group specifically critical of the SCM in various countries. But U.S.A. denominations were also soon impelled to set up their own campus programs, the 1st in 1907 at the University of Illinois. These grew rapidly, though only Y.M.C.A.–Y.W.C.A. and SVM represented this country in WSCF until 1938. Then the 1st of a series of delegated groups gathered to coordinate national programs, becoming in 1944 the United Student Christian Council (USCC) and in 1959, with other elements, the NSCF. SVM became NSCF's Commission on World Mission. The Interseminary Movement (ISM) founded in 1898 and related to the Y.M.C.A., also became part of NSCF. A parallel Y.M.C.A. affiliate for a younger student group, the National Preparatory School Movement, had already become an independent agency now known as the Council for Religion in Independent Schools.

The historic major shifts have obviously been from church-related college to campus Y.M.C.A.–Y.W.C.A.–SVM and then to denomination-staffed student movements, which now vastly dominate the movement in numbers and activity. Student initiative and adult leadership have always been in conflict. Early associations employed secretaries to help with their student-conceived programs. Later these men and women found themselves asked more and more to inspire and administer such activity, as was the case still later with hundreds of denominational campus chaplains or "foundation directors." (In a few cases tax-supported universities still employ Y secretaries.) Thus what has been known as "student Christian opinion" has sometimes been more actually that of staff or of informed postgraduate students who are also part of the movement. When NSCF became related through staff to the NCCCUSA, this traditional issue of "student movement independence" was carefully studied and safeguards were spelled out. At this juncture, however, the history of student Christian groups did tend to merge with that of the denominations themselves.

Member groups of NSCF were these in 1961: Baptist Student Movement (BSM), Westminster Fellowship (Presbyterian, Southern), Lutheran Student Association of America (LSAA), Methodist Student Movement (MSM), National Canterbury Association (Protestant Episcopal), National Student Council of Y.M.C.A.–Y.W.C.A. (NSCY), United Campus Christian Fellowship (UCCF — student groups, merged in 1960, of Disciples of Christ, Evangelical United Brethren, United Church of Christ, and United Presbyterian), together with delegates of these denominations' boards of higher education and missions. Related agencies: SCM's of New England and New York State; Committee on Friendly Relations Among Foreign Students (CFR)

founded 1911, and World University Service (WUS), an interfaith agency begun in 1916.

Main factors in the continuing life of the movement have been local campus voluntary groups and leadership, regional and national conferences, multigroup study programs and publications, nationally correlated work projects for summers or weekends, and shared giving for international student needs. Ecumenical activity among the various communions has drawn much of its impetus and leadership from the Student Christian Movement.

— *John Oliver Nelson*

SUBURBAN CHURCH Urban expansion has taken place increasingly on the suburban fringes of the major cities since 1920. This type of growth produces a new kind of city; it also creates new problems in religious and communal life. The net result is the metropolitan agglomeration: linking communities through superhighways and integrating residential suburbs around great central cities. From one half to two thirds of the population of the U.S.A. probably will be concentrated in these huge aggregations by the end of the century. Political and religious communities face a pressing task of integrating the suburban and central city sectors of these agglomerations; however, in the present article we shall focus attention on the suburban region as a separate context for religious education.

One feature of the suburban development is the insulation of residence from place of work. The tasks and joys of parental life are not only separated by great distance from factories and business offices but the interests of the family community are radically segregated from the concerns of occupational activity. The common denominator is money income earned in one place and expended in another. Changes in technology of transportation have made possible this rapid decentralization of the population of metropolitan areas, and yet one need not assume that suburban growth is simply a result of technological development. Improvements in technology could conceivably have transformed central city areas so that transportation would be entirely by means of conveyors and the streets would be transformed into parks. Residence might have been concentrated and more adequately planned; in fact, visitors from other countries are often struck by our prodigal destruction of green space.

Technology is now being applied to extensive suburban growth instead of urban concentration; in general, the cause for this movement seems to be the American middle-class aspiration for a private residence in an insulated community. The suburban home and the opportunity to associate with people of one's own kind fulfill some aspects of the American dream. It is this dream that shapes the suburban context and provides the setting for the church's task of proclamation and education. The key word for understanding the suburban religious situation is " segregation ": the suburb is a context in which homogeneous groups segregate themselves from the larger population, the consuming community of parents and children is segregated from the productive community of factory and office, and residence is segregated from the bustle of urban activity.

The suburban transformation of residential life has been crucial in reshaping the culture of the American churches. The Christian church has maintained an institutional center of gravity in the residential community for many centuries. To be sure, the vitality of Christian life shifted at times to other centers such as the monastery, or the parish, or the guild. Nevertheless, the residential locale has formed the nucleus of parish and congregation throughout most of Christian history. The suburban church gives an impression of outward continuity with this tradition, since the ministrations of the churches continue to revolve around familial events such as baptism and marriage; moreover, churches continue to prosper where stable family life can be sustained. This appearance of historical continuity is deceptive, however, since the residential locale has ceased to be an intersection of political, social, familial, economic, and religious interests. Residence no longer provides a point of nucleation for the diverse activities and interests of human life, particularly because kinship has ceased to be a pivotal structure of society. The church once stood at the center of society as it stood with the family in its residential context. The church now stands on the periphery of life as it stands with the middle-class family in its suburban context. The suburban church is no longer a parish or congregation in any sense that these terms acquired in the history of Christianity. It is a new form of Christianity with certain evident strengths and some serious weaknesses.

A notable strength of the suburban church issues from the fact that the residential setting continues to be the primary context for socialization, by which is meant the process of incorporation of the young into the culture and community of a society. To be sure, socialization has usually occurred in the residential environment, but in most societies this task is closely bound to a community of kinship. In the suburb the age group of so-called peers serves as the basic unit of socialization after the very earliest years. The suburban church enters into this task when the children are very young, playing a much more significant role in socialization than heretofore. The location of the field of socialization in the play yard and peer groups accounts for the increasing other-directedness of American character; similarly, the externalization of suburban religion in activity is linked with this new religious role in socialization.

Certain obvious problems arise with the concentration of so much of the process of socialization in age groups. The family, for one thing, becomes much more anxious about the neighborhood as a field of association for small children. Threats to the stability or composition of a residential area become threats to the children and are met with a fierce kind of violence that is rather uncharacteristic of middle-class people. Moreover, the suburban church as a religious style becomes dependent upon peer-group activities for all age levels. The moment this type of peer-group community is undermined by high mobility, as in areas of population change, this style of religious life collapses. The suburban church is the creature of peer-group association rather than a center of authentic communal life within the society. This characteristic weakness of the suburban style of religious life has made it utterly useless in confronting the problems of social disorganization in central city areas.

Another aspect of suburban segregation is its insulation from the productive community of work. The suburb is withdrawn from the whirring activity of the productive apparatus. There is, indeed, a great deal of activity in suburban communities and churches, and even a considerable amount of actual labor on home and garden, but this activity and labor have rather the character of occupational therapy. The suburb is one great therapy session in which men, women, and children attempt to regain the emotional equilibrium that is so seriously threatened by the impersonal, competitive struggle of contemporary society. The suburb is, to put the idea rather extremely, a psychiatric couch rather than a field of active life. One withdraws from the arena of struggle to the insulated environment of the suburban matriarchy. Here the deepest conflicts of contemporary life are generated, for the women carry the serious work of the household in this setting for occupational therapy, working in an atmosphere that no one considers a setting for serious struggle, but, what is perhaps even more serious, bearing the full burden of responsibility for the life of the family while the husband engages in occupational therapy. One can perhaps interpret the deep resentment of home and housework among middle-class women — a resentment that is often covert and displayed only indirectly through psychosomatic symptoms — in terms of a suburban setting where work should be therapy and where they find themselves seeking therapy while playing the role of chief therapist.

The suburbanite is preoccupied

with his emotional problems; hence, the suburban milieu presents a special setting for the educational task of the suburban church. For one thing, the excessive concentration of middle-class people on preserving the illusion that they enjoy an " ideal " marriage makes it difficult for the pastor to deal with the real marriage until it has already collapsed. The search for emotional balance through the mutual fulfillments of marital life has transformed marriage from a community looking forward into an adolescent couple looking at each other. Pastors encounter the greatest difficulties in cutting through this world of illusion into the daily bread of marital life, although they hold some of the most needed resources for suburban marriage. Premarital training and marital counseling have become infinitely more difficult tasks of ministry in the emerging suburban society.

The ministry to the community of socialization and the pastoral care of partners in marriage are, after all, traditional tasks of the pastorate. There is, however, another type of suburban segregation that radically limits the role of the Christian church: the tendency for people of a similar social and economic level to cluster in particular suburbs. This trend is partially promoted by housing developers who hope for profits by catering to supposed desires for monoclass and monochrome neighborhoods. Nevertheless, the trend to a homogenized community has deeper roots in familial values than the cupidity of speculators. The homogenized community is most profoundly rooted in the middle-class search for a stable social identity. The neighborhood becomes a way of assuring oneself of the particular position that has been achieved on the economic ladder; that is, one *is* what one *does* in the productive apparatus, and yet one only knows this identity through its confirmation in the presence and acceptance of others who have achieved a comparable position on the ladder. Thus the suburb becomes a segregated enclave of those who are precariously perched on comparable rungs of the economic ladder.

The Christian church confronts serious problems in proclaiming and mediating a universal identity in Christ through suburban communities whose principles of exclusiveness are matters of social and economic position rather than religious commitment. The net effect of the suburban context is to impoverish the Christian message, even as great words are emptied when they are mouthed by vile men and rich symbols are impoverished when they are repeatedly used in trivial contexts. The scope of relevance of the Christian message is restricted by circumscribing its concern with preoccupation for emotional equilibrium, even as the command to love is trivialized by limiting its applicability to a segregated enclave.

The suburban churches can work to overcome their segregated context by moving from local autonomy to a form of ministry designed to express the universal identity of the Christian proclamation. Such new forms undoubtedly require long years of work in training pastors and laymen through centers in which people from all walks of life can share their concerns and problems. Such centers already exist in many parts of Europe and several have developed in the U.S.A. The final stage of segregation has reached the suburb, for a kind of narcosis has dimmed the awareness of the social reality outside the enclave. The proclamation of the Christian message and the educational task thus require most immediately an enrichment of context for reflection on the gift and task of life in Christ. At this point, the suburban church with all its strength in ministering to the growth of the young and the emotional stability of adults needs the help of the great church yet to be born in the metropolis. — *Gibson Winter*

SUMMER CONFERENCE Just as Europe has given the youth hostel idea to the Western world, so the summer youth camp and conference is a unique contribution from America to the Christian world. As to its exact place and date of origin there is considerable doubt, but as to its tremendous value there is general agreement and this is testified to by its phenomenal growth among all Protestant groups. More recently Roman Catholics and Jews also have entered this exciting field.

As early as 1880 churches were engaged in camping for children, but not until the early 1900's were young people involved. Almost from the very beginning their conferences were coeducational, much to the startled amazement of European visitors unaccustomed to the spectacle of boys and girls living from 6 to 14 days in the same camp or on the same school campus for a summer conference. Such conferences early became interdenominational in nature and sponsorship. By 1914 the International Sunday School Association was conducting a summer youth conference at Lake Winnipesaukee, N.H. However, the leadership in the summer youth camp and conference field has now passed from interdenominational agencies to the denominations. Today every major denomination employs a staff at national, regional, and state levels to plan programs and train leaders. Virtually every state can boast at least 1 attractive and excellently equipped camp and summer conference center, sometimes representing investments in excess of $500,-000. A new architectural profession has developed for long-range development of camp and conference sites. So effectively have these activities captured the attention of young people that even though more than 650,000 were enrolled in the 1960 program, many more thousands were turned away for lack of space.

Initially the summer youth conference was planned by adults for youth, with a minimum of youth participation in the rather routine aspect of the conference once it was under way, through a camp or conference council. Major matters of the program profile, curriculum, and the day's schedule were determined by adults in accordance with purposes determined by them for youth.

A typical day in these earlier conferences would begin with morning watch, followed by breakfast and housekeeping. The rest of the morning was given over to rather formal classes or discussion groups on such subjects as Bible, Christian beliefs, church history, missions, and Christian social action for about half the time, with another sizable portion given to rather more subjective matters such as the Christian's personal devotional life, boy-girl relations, and personality development. Sometime during the morning a rather formal chapel service would be held. Afternoons would consist largely of interest groups, handicrafts, and recreation, both organized and free.

Evenings were used for listening to or talking with visiting missionaries or foreign nationals plus a " campfire program " or games and fun.

Each group of from 6 to 10 youths would be under the direct supervision of a counselor with whom the closing hours just before sleep would be spent in discussing the day's events or other matters of concern, followed by evening devotions.

Highlights in such a conference period would usually include ball games between leaders and conferees, stunt nights, treasure hunts, water-front regattas, a rather formal dance or banquet, and, most frequently of all, a closing Communion service. The intimacy of friendships formed during the week and the close association of attractive leaders with impressionable young people, plus the magic of the setting itself, frequently raised this closing service to such emotional pitch as to cause deep concern among responsible adults. However, many conferees testified to a depth of personal experience with Jesus Christ as could hardly occur under less favorable circumstances.

Although some camps or conferences still follow this older and more traditional pattern, most of these summer activities, now frequently and properly called youth camps, offer striking contrast to their forerunners. Counselors have become group leaders employing the latest group work techniques, and young people participate freely in both the planning and the conducting of the camps and conferences. At the close of the conference period, the young people engage in evaluating the camp or conference itself in the light of aims and purposes they have helped to establish. Informality and an emphasis on developing a Chris-

tian community composed of adult and youth campers engaged in a mutual quest for deeper understanding of and devotion to the Christian faith are increasingly characteristic. Although study, worship, and play are still very much the order of the day, rarely is there a set schedule of unrelated " classes " following one another. Still very much in evidence is the guest leader, perhaps a foreign national in his native garb or a rabbi from a nearby synagogue, but such guests, too, become a part of the family and make their influence felt throughout the program rather than in formal lectures.

Frequently these newer camps and conferences include work projects and participation in special service " caravans " or deputation teams. Although much of the artificial and rather rigid scheduling of classes and activities has disappeared, results indicate even greater knowledge of so-called " content " matter, a growing disposition to consider vocational choice on a Christian basis, more frequent declaration for full-time church-related vocations, and a generally stronger emphasis on other Christian values. In addition, these camps and conferences draw into their leadership rolls a rapidly increasing number of adults both attractive to and effective with teenagers who thus increase the leadership pool for year-round church service. Both clergy and lay leaders who have served in summer camps and conferences tell of the values that have come to them through the development of new leadership skills, new understandings of young people, and greater enthusiasm for such service as a result of the summer's working, playing, and living with their teen-age co-workers.

Family camping is rapidly coming

into prominence with its own particular kind of housing, program, and leadership. Although this movement is growing more slowly, it is showing real strength and a disposition to hold ground gained even while it expands. Special conferences for rather formal adult study and all kinds of leadership training conferences and schools have continued to thrive. In the area of leadership education for church school teachers and administrators, interdenominational agencies continue to hold the lead with state councils of churches and the NCCCUSA, by far most vigorous in this field. Several such conferences under state and national council leadership boast more than 40 years of continuous service. During this time they, too, have undergone marked change. From earlier conferences, which were largely teaching by lecture and study in a usual classroom atmosphere, they have developed the " observation-practice school " technique. More recently they have gone into the true " laboratory school " situation in which student teachers under expert guidance engage in actual teaching under near-normal church school conditions.

A recent development in the summer conference field is the gathering together of vocational groups such as physicians, teachers, lawyers, business people, leaders of organized labor, and others in their respective vocational groups at a conference center to consider the implications of Christian witness through their respective vocations.

In these varied summer conference activities certain common values stand out. All provide excellent opportunities for developing a sense of Christian community. Each provides an unexcelled opportunity for group experience and learning through doing. All provide an intensive period of time for learning and consistent and consecutive attacks on problems. These summer experiences offer opportunities for exploring and understanding the outdoors, and allow for creative and experimental activities with opportunity for almost immediate evaluation. Each, by emphasizing both the nature and life of the church and the needs of individuals, provides exceptional opportunities for individual growth and the strengthening of the church.

— Carl A. Hansen

SUNDAY CHURCH SCHOOL Sunday school patterns are quite numerous, and their complexity is usually correlated with size. In the smallest churches only a few classes prevail — 1 for preschool children, another for 6 to 12 years, a 3d for youth, and 1 for adults. Refinements occur as available space and number of pupils increase. The most widespread pattern includes a nursery (1 to 3 years), kindergarten or beginners (4 to 5 years), primary (grades 1 to 3), junior (grades 4 to 6), junior high (grades 7 to 9), senior high — sometimes called " young people " — (grades 10 to 12), and the adult department. Further growth in enrollment occasionally produces a 2-year grading in the children's departments (grades 1 to 2, 3 to 4, 5 to 6). The largest Sunday church schools are completely closely graded with each age group in a separate department and usually in a separate room. Adult departments are ordinarily comprised of several classes occasionally separated by sex but more frequently in recent years for couples or single persons of both sexes and separated by age differentiation.

Churches vary considerably in

their patterns of control for the Sunday church school, but certain positions are found rather uniformly. The chief officer is ordinarily called the superintendent. It is his function to carry out the policy that the committee on Christian education — or other similar body — has established. Depending primarily on the size of the congregation, there may be 1 or more assistants assigned to such areas as literature and supplies, budget, membership, and personnel. Age-group or divisional superintendents are often selected for the children's, youth, and adult segments of the school. Each separate department is also headed by a superintendent, thus making 3 levels of administrative responsibility bearing the title of superintendent. Additional administrative officers — often called " directors " or " secretaries " — may be assigned to such duties as audio-visual materials, equipment, leadership development.

The great majority of Sunday church schools use printed materials purchased from the denominational publishing house and produced by their national boards of education. There are several varieties of organization of these materials, based primarily upon the size of the church being served. Broadly graded materials are designed for the smallest church school, having only a few classes with an age span of several years in each. Group-graded or cycle-graded lessons are usually arranged in a 2-year cycle for the kindergarten and a 3-year cycle for primary, junior, junior high, and senior high departments. Closely graded materials are produced for the large church having separate classes for each grade of public-school age. The outlines for these materials used by many denomina-

tions are prepared cooperatively by the Division of Christian Education of the National Council of the Churches of Christ in the U.S.A. It maintains 2 large committees — 1 for graded series, the other for uniform series — for this purpose, committees composed of representatives of the participating denominations. Uniform lessons provide materials using the same theme in all departments from primary upward.

A small minority of local Sunday church schools use 1 of 2 other types of lesson materials. Several private publishing houses market full sets of curriculum usually written from a theologically conservative point of view and stressing especially a thorough use of the Bible. This emphasis proves attractive to occasional individual congregations. Other local churches produce their own materials, usually prepared under the guidance of a skilled director of Christian education.

The curriculum of Christian education also includes worship experiences. A present trend toward family worship is evident in a few denominations, and this often replaces worship as an integral function of the Sunday church school. But for other churches, worship remains a standard element in the curriculum. Current emphasis favors departmentally organized worship services located in a self-contained classroom especially for children. Corporate worship for youth and adults is still a common practice, though usually held separately for each age group.

The Sunday school began as a laymen's venture often operating against the active opposition of the clergy. Throughout the 19th century it continued to receive its primary inspiration and leadership at every level from devoted lay persons. Something of this same spirit still prevails in American Protestantism. Although churches have employed directors of Christian education in increasing numbers since the early 1920's, these professional leaders have not replaced the lay teacher in classrooms. Classes are still almost entirely taught by volunteer instructors who receive no financial compensation for this service. Good character and previous skill or training are ordinarily the factors operative in their selection. Continued training during their tenure of office is universally considered to be vital for the improvement of their effectiveness.

The Sunday church school is an integral part of a total Sunday-morning experience, and scheduling reflects this. Older patterns placed the school in the 1-hour time block preceding the morning worship service, often 9:30 or 9:45 A.M. or 11.00 A.M. respectively. In some instances this order was reversed. Newer trends, especially since World War II, have emphasized multiple worship services primarily because of inadequate seating in church naves. Church schools have adjusted accordingly. Many churches, especially in suburbia, now have 2 and even 3 completely separate sessions. Often each is fully staffed independently of the others, and each has its own pupils. These multiple Sunday school sessions are usually confined to children's classes, with a few youth classes and an occasional adult class included, operating on the same time schedule as the worship services.

Sunday church schools have traditionally been confined to a single hour. However, with the recognition that this is quite inadequate for the ends desired, plus the considerable agreement that worship services have not primarily been structured for the young, many churches now carry on 2-hour Sunday church schools for children through the 4th or 5th grades. This extra hour, which coincides with adult-oriented worship, is not merely " child care." It is an extension of the educational experience of the 1st hour, often with emphasis upon projects and activities. The same staff is usually retained for the full 2-hour session. Other local churches accomplish this expansion through additional sessions held on Saturday mornings or other weekdays.

Several recent trends have altered the profile of the Sunday church school. Adult classes are moving steadily away from the large, lecture-oriented session toward the small-group, discussion-centered procedure. This diversification has resulted in the abandoning by some groups of the traditional Sunday-morning time in favor of other Sunday hours or weekday periods. There is an increasing trend toward family worship and a corresponding reduction in worship activities in the Sunday school. This is altering the character of the class session by adding to the time available for instruction. Sunday school youth programs are increasingly being caught up in the youth fellowship concept and integrated with all other youth activities. Local church-sponsored weekday education is growing, and adjustments in the Sunday school are necessary to avoid duplication.

— *Marvin J. Taylor*

SUNDAY SCHOOL MOVEMENT

Although the religious education of children and adults has been a matter of concern to Christians throughout church history, the modern Sunday school movement arose in the late 18th century under evangelical auspices. By the end of the 1st quarter of the present century, there were an estimated 30,000,000 participants in the Sunday school movement, 21,000,000 in North America.

The movement is usually considered to have begun with the work of Robert Raikes (1735–1811), a layman of the Church of England, who in 1780 in Gloucester gathered poorer children of the community for Sunday instruction in reading, writing, and the elementary truths of religion. His work was extensively publicized, given ecclesiastical and royal approval and widely copied. Applauded especially by evangelical leaders, the movement was spread by the network of missionary, Bible, and tract societies that burgeoned into prominence in the early 19th century. In 1803 there was formed a nondenominational National Sunday School Society with headquarters in London. It gave conspicuous leadership to the planting, growth, and improvement of Sunday schools in Britain and, through missionary work, abroad. In the last half of the 19th century, the society cooperated with the International Uniform Lesson Committee in the U.S.A. In the 20th century it did notable work in developing graded materials, and continues as a center of Christian education affairs in Britain.

The 1st American Sunday schools of the Raikes type were apparently begun in Virginia in the 1780's under Methodist auspices. In 1790 a Sunday school society was founded in Philadelphia; Episcopal Bishop William White (1748–1836) was elected president. These early schools were largely for underprivileged children between 6 and 14. They met for long periods as illiteracy had to be overcome before much catechetical instruction could be imparted.

A transformation of the Sunday school in the U.S.A. began about 1815, as the movement became a part of the crusade of evangelical Protestantism to Christianize the nation. The length of the Sunday session was shortened and was focused more on Bible study. All classes and ages were included. Teachers served usually on a voluntary rather than a paid basis. The dominant concern of the Sunday school was for the conversion of its students. The movement was guided by local voluntary societies, largely denominational. In 1816 a New York Sunday School Union Society was formed; the next year the Sunday and Adult School Union was founded in Philadelphia. In 1824 the 2 merged to become the American Sunday School Union, a voluntary, lay-led, nondenominational society that dominated the Sunday school movement for 40 years. It published vast quantities of literature for use in Christian education, especially "Selected Lessons" and "Union Questions." The Union worked for the establishment of Sunday schools on the frontiers of the rapidly expanding nation; its vast "Mississippi Valley enterprise," launched in 1830, led to the organization of some 3,000 new schools. In the later 1830's, however, opposition began to be felt, especially from newly formed denominational Sunday school societies. Vast quantities of literature for the Sunday school poured from church presses, introducing the "Babel era" of Sunday school instruction. By the time of the Civil War, ASSU dominance of the movement was drawing to a close.

Several national conventions of Sunday school leaders had been gathered under Union direction, in 1832 and 1833. In 1859, partly as a result of forces released by the revival of 1857, a 3d national convention in Philadephia planned for its own succession by appointing a lay committee to call another gathering. War delayed it until 1869. Then triennial conventions were planned. The 1872 meeting at Indianapolis invited Canadian participation; thus the 5th convention at Baltimore in 1875 became the 1st International Sunday School Convention. The growth of the movement around the world led to the calling of the World's First Sunday School Convention in 1889 in London. At the 5th world conference at Rome in 1907, British, Continental European, and American leadership precipitated the organization of the World's Sunday School Association as an evangelical and missionary enterprise.

In 1872 another momentous step was taken: it was resolved to produce a system of International Uniform Lessons, by which all ages in Sunday schools would be studying the same Bible passage at the same time. The conventions were guided by a group of able, aggressive laymen under the leadership of a Baptist from Chicago, B. F. Jacobs (1834–1902). These leaders avoided denominational objections by shrewdly treating each convention as a separate enterprise which had to choose its own " new " executive committee to plan for the next gathering. Jacobs worked closely with a Methodist pastor, later bishop, John H. Vincent (1832–1920), who contributed especially to the development of teacher training institutes. The convention period was marked by a vast growth and great popularity of Sunday schools, still dedicated primarily to the winning of converts through Bible study. Tension sometimes developed between congregations and their Sunday schools, which often operated largely independently. State and local Sunday school conventions kept enthusiasm for the movement at a high point, and contributed to the wide acceptance of the International Uniform Lessons system.

Although the domination of the convention and the Uniform Lessons continued into the 20th century, dissatisfaction with the system had arisen in the closing decades of the previous century. Developments in educational theory led to demands for graded, child-centered curricula. In 1884, a National (later International) Primary Union was formed in the interest of graded lessons for younger scholars. In the 1890's, schools of methods advanced the interests of Sunday school reform. Denominations once again began to insist on their right to direct their own Sunday school work, and some published lesson material independently of the Uniform Lessons. Such organizations as the Religious Education Association (founded 1903), which sharply criticized both general and Sunday school education, brought the insights of professional and progressive educators into the field. In 1905 the convention took the name International Sunday School Association. In 1910 the Sunday School Council of the Evangelical Denominations was formed. Beneath the surface of cooperation between Association and Council in a time of continued Sunday school expansion and popularity, the tension between the 2 approaches ran deep. The Association sought to keep

Sunday school lessons focused on Biblical material wholly, whereas the Council felt that additional materials from history, biography, and theology were helpful. The Association stood for united evangelical effort through the use of the Uniform Lessons, whereas the Council promoted the development of pupil-centered, graded curricula and the spread of the multidepartmental Sunday school. The Association wished to maintain nondenominational lay control; the Council sought denominational control of the Sunday schools. The issue was finally compromised by merger in 1922 through the formation of the International Sunday School Council of Religious Education, which in 1924 became the International Council of Religious Education. As the name implies, the Council principle emerged as dominant. In 1950 the ICRE merged with other interdenominational agencies to become the Division of Christian Education of the NCCCUSA. Under Council leadership, the Sunday school movement was led largely by confident professionals, liberal in theology and with life-centered philosophies of education.

In the 1930's and 1940's, the concentration on the Sunday school as the primary agency of religious education began to be questioned; leaders turned hopefully to partnership with the home in the search for greater effectiveness. Neither the evangelical theology that had guided the movement in the union and convention periods nor the liberal theology that had dominated the Council was felt to be fully adequate in a day of theological renewal. The Sunday school movement lost something of its popularity and creativity. Its leaders were seeking new Biblical and theological foundations for Christian education, and finding new ways of fulfilling the educational responsibility of the church.

— *Robert T. Handy*

SUPERINTENDENT, DEPARTMENTAL The departmental superintendent is in a key position. He is in a 2-way channel of administration, helping the teachers have their needs met and helping the divisional chairmen and general superintendent discover the needs of the teachers. In this way the departmental superintendent unlocks the doors for greater service for both teachers and administrators.

The qualifications for the person filling the position of departmental superintendent are demanding. He must be willing to learn, since learning is basic to teaching. He should be alert, have some knowledge of educational philosophy and method, and be willing to stay abreast of always changing educational methods and techniques. He needs to invite the confidence of fellow workmen so that they will feel free to share problems and successful experiences. Being sympathetic to problems (being a good listener) is basic. Of course, punctuality with regard to all appointments and meetings is necessary. All these qualifications need the undergirding of a love for people.

The departmental superintendent has a direct administrative line to the divisional chairman, who has the responsibility for several departments, usually of a similar age grouping. It is through the divisional chairman and the church school superintendent that the needs of the teachers and pupils are made known to the Christian education committee.

The teachers of the department

look to their departmental superintendent to help them become better teachers by arranging for them to have opportunities for training, providing good materials and equipment, and counseling with them in their lesson and session planning. The teachers expect their superintendent to be a friend and co-worker in the mutual task of teaching.

A job description for the departmental superintendent looks quite demanding. The description here is an attempt to list activities for multiple situations; many activities may not apply for some churches. In fact, very small churches may not have departmental superintendents at all, but the work that is done by departmental superintendents still must be done, usually by the general superintendent.

Here are some of the tasks assigned to a departmental superintendent: help develop and correlate the work of the department; recommend materials for use in the department (in line, of course, with the policies of the Christian education committee); help teachers in a supervisory way in the use of materials, planning together with them in actual lesson and session development (in this particular activity the departmental superintendent might provide for supervisory or " helping " teachers to assist the teachers in his department); observe a class, simply to record what is seen as being done in the session (not judgments or opinions of what is done); cooperate in the enlistment and training of teachers for the department; orient new teachers to their tasks and the work of the department; provide teachers with in-service training; arrange for vacations for teachers; provide opportunities for teachers to attend leadership training schools and other training activities.

The departmental superintendent should be able to recommend proper equipment and space, and help teachers make proper use of such. He should construct a budget of askings to the finance committee through the division council, having consulted with his teachers in building the budget so that needs and dreams are reflected in the budget. He should call and preside at departmental conferences. He is responsible for the keeping of accurate records, the encouraging of regular attendance, and the following-up of absentees.

Relations with parents of pupils in the department are important. Arranging for conferences of teachers and parents on an individual family basis can be helpful. Also, parent-teacher meetings, if planned carefully, can be most beneficial to both groups. The departmental superintendent should arrange for and possibly preside at such meetings.

Such a list as this varies as to applicability to churches of different sizes and to different age levels. The departmental superintendent of the nursery department will undertake many activities different from those of the superintendent of the adult department, yet basic functions are similar, regardless of department.

— *D. Allison Holt*

SUPERINTENDENT, GENERAL The general superintendent is the general executive and administrative officer of the church school in a particular church. The best-qualified person available, whether man or woman, ought to be named to this important position.

The method of naming the general superintendent varies from denomination to denomination. He may be elected by the congregation as a whole, appointed by the official board or Christian education committee, or appointed by the minister. The recommended practice is to elect or appoint on an annual basis, subject to reelection or reappointment. The church school superintendent may be the lay administrator for the whole educational program of the church, or he may carry responsibility for the Sunday-morning church school only, but in either case he has similar areas of responsibility.

The general superintendent works in close relation with the committee, board, or commission on Christian education in the local church. He may or may not be a voting member of this policy-making group, depending upon denominational structure, but he is responsible for reporting regularly to the committee, for seeing that the needs of the church school are brought before it, and for carrying out the policies formulated by the committee.

The specific functioning of the general superintendent varies considerably, depending on the organizational structure of the denomination, the size of the church, professional personnel on the staff of the particular church, and the extent to which the church is organized by divisions or departments with superintendents or "lead teachers" subordinate to the general superintendent.

If there is a minister or director of Christian education or an educational assistant on the staff, the general superintendent works closely with him. If there is no such specialist, he needs to assume much greater initiative. In either case, however, he is administratively responsible for the church school program. The professional staff person serves as counselor and guide to help him carry out his responsibilities more effectively but is not expected to perform his job for him.

Although the committee on Christian education has responsibility for securing leadership for the educational program, the superintendent is often expected to make nominations for such leadership. He and the policy-making group together formulate and carry out plans for the adequate training and preparation of leadership, for effective workers' conferences, and for building fellowship and morale among the leaders as well as through the school as a whole.

The superintendent is responsible for the grouping and grading of the church school. In a small church, he may preside over the fellowship and worship for all except the youngest members of the church school, in which case he carries direct program responsibility. In a large church organized into separate departments or into separate grade units that meet independently for an integrated program, he may be primarily a co-ordinator and resource person.

The superintendent assists in making an annual budget and keeps advised on church school income and expenditures. He plans for the best possible use of available space and provides for needed furnishings and equipment. He supervises the ordering and prompt distribution of curriculum materials and the setting up of a system of records and reports. He plans for general observances or coordinates departmental observances of such special days as Christmas and Easter, Christian Education Week, Children's Day, and Christian Family Week. He helps to foster missionary education and stewardship education throughout the church school. The general superintendent is responsible, with the pastor and the Christian education committee, for developing church and home relationships and for reaching the unchurched.

In short, the general superintendent is responsible for having an effectively organized and smoothly running church school. To achieve this, he should be a person of deep Christian experience and personal commitment, understand the educational task of the church and the policies of his own denomination, understand people and how to work with them in a democratic way, and have overall organizational and administrative ability. If the church does not have an actively functioning Christian education committee, the general superintendent must move ahead on his own initiative, always, however, in a close consultative and cooperative relationship with the pastor. — *Eleanor L. Ludy*

SUPERVISION "Supervision" is a term connoting improvement. It has to do ordinarily with improving the effectiveness of educational procedures and increasing the quality of the work being done. Its primary aim has to do with the ultimate outcome, the development of persons, and the enrichment of the experience of all persons involved in education.

Although supervisory procedure is concerned with all aspects of education, it assumes that many things have already taken place, such as the determination of goals, the development of programs, the selection of curricula, the enlistment and training of leaders, the grouping of pupils, and the provision of suitable housing and equipment. Yet all these aspects of education will come under continuous review in the process of supervision. They are fundamental aspects of an effective program. The better they are planned and cared for, the less supervision will be required. The richer the background of training and experience of the persons participating in carrying forward the program, the more readily can supervisory activities bring about improvement.

Supervision is one of the most difficult and advanced procedures in education, yet there is nothing mysterious about it. It calls for analysis, evaluation, and experimental activity. An evaluative attitude must be maintained at all times. It involves breaking down every educational situation into its component parts with a view to discovering those activities which are effective and those which are ineffective. This calls for analysis of every factor involved in the teaching-learning situation. The trained supervisor acquires the ability through experience in human relations, keen observation, evaluation processes, and test forms to lift up for review these various elements. Supervision, in seeking to secure maximum efficiency, is designed, therefore, to enlist all those participating in educational work — pupils, teachers, administrators, boards, counselors, parents, and others.

Supervision has had relatively minor attention in Christian education to date. The major effort has been devoted to such aspects as setting up the organization, outlining the program, providing leadership of some kind, and securing housing and equipment. Very limited leadership and energy have been available to make continuous and serious inquiry into the quality of the work being done. Supervision, serious concern for the effectiveness of the educational program, is the crying need of the hour. Pupils and parents are demanding better work; competition with effective public schools and attractive community activities is being increasingly felt; and the church is realizing afresh the tremendous potential it has in its educational program. Every effort therefore should be made to provide for supervisory leadership.

The procedures used in supervision may be variously stated. They include the development of common understanding of the goals, methods, curricula, program resources, and conditions necessary for effectiveness on the part of all persons giving leadership. Those supervising and those supervised must understand each other and talk the same language, even though they may not agree in all details. Included in procedure is cooperative program-planning and joint evaluation of activities. Involved also is observation of leaders as they work with groups, the study of pupils' responses, and the selection of resources to be used by both pupils and teachers. Demonstration teaching and leading may be a vital part of supervision. Evaluation schedules and teaching report forms will find frequent use. Group meetings of workers to share experiences will be employed. Conferences with individual workers with special problems and needs will engage the time of the supervisor. Committees and boards may engage in short-time or more extensive program-planning and evaluation of the church's educational effort. The continuing provision of teacher training facilities will rank high in the supervisor's plans. Personal counseling of individual students and the use of formal tests and measurements will become part of the procedure

where leadership is trained for this kind of work. Underlying all efforts to improve education will be the constant search on the part of all involved for a better understanding of religion and for the enrichment of their own Christian faith and experience. Workers cannot share what they do not themselves possess, nor can they lead where they themselves have not gone.

Various people may give supervisory leadership. Ideally, persons specially trained and provided with time and opportunity may make this form of activity most effective. Special training and experience, combined with adequate time for this kind of work, are requisites for effective supervision, and usually will be found only among those who are professionally trained. Many ministers now serving as pastors have taken training in seminaries and graduate schools that prepares them to give supervisory leadership if they will do so. A growing number of them now serve in this special capacity in large churches as ministers or directors of religious education. There has been a vast increase in the past quarter century in the number of men and women entering the field of Christian education with professional training. They are working as directors of religious education, directors of children's work, youth leaders, and as adult specialists. Most of these people will naturally be constantly involved in improvement procedures. The growth of this body of workers will undoubtedly increase with the church's growing awareness of the importance of Christian education. The presence of such workers promises much more supervision in Christian education in the future.

Possibly the greatest hope for supervisory leadership in the local church will be found in lay men and women who in increasing numbers are devoting time, energy, and talents in voluntary service in Christian education. Scores of these people are responding to training opportunities represented in laboratory schools, demonstration classes, advanced seminars, and even professional training to equip themselves better for lay service. Such people placed as department and divisional superintendents, resource persons, or helping teachers may render significant service. Since professionally trained people are so few in number compared with the total number of churches, and since the Protestant Church is committed to the use of lay people, these picked lay leaders represent the most hopeful and immediate source of supervisory leadership. Every effort should be made to discover, enlist, and provide special training for those lay people who may become supervisors.

In its simplest form supervision may be exercised by a "helping teacher," a teacher with more training and experience than the average worker. Such a teacher may share insights gained through more training and wider experience, help plan a teaching session, sit through a class period as friendly critic, discuss with the teacher the handling of disciplinary problems, counsel on further training, or do many other things that help a leader with the work at hand. Such supervisory activity may be occurring more often than we have any idea. More workers with such capabilities should give such help.

A form of supervisory leadership that may prove effective in some churches is through the board, committee, or commission on education. Usually the membership of such a group includes many competent people as well as key workers in the program. Such a group can be challenged and trained to study the entire program or certain aspects of it, gather information, make observations, study resources, carry out experiments, and educate the general constituency. It is quite customary for such groups to hold meetings or plan conferences at certain times in the school year to survey the program, draw up plans for improvement, and assign projects of study and development to certain persons or committees. They can often stimulate study on the part of all workers and secure cooperation in forward-looking projects. These efforts may be significant forms of supervision.
— *Frank M. McKibben*

SWEDEN Since education in public schools was made compulsory by Sweden in 1842, every child has received religious instruction. Roman Catholic and Jewish pupils who have their own instruction are exempted, however, from the religious classes in compulsory schools. The total amount of time devoted to such classes has decreased across the years, and later rules prohibit teachers from influencing pupils in any given direction; nevertheless, the instruction is to be offered in such a way as clearly to bring out the seriousness of the matter at hand.

In addition to the school instruction, every denomination gives further instruction. The Church of Sweden stresses confirmation instruction, 86 percent of all youth aged 14 and 15 being confirmed. About 50 to 60 hours of training precede confirmation, the courses usually following Luther's Small Catechism.

Sunday schools exist for the younger children. Since the schools care for formal instruction, the Sunday schools have tended to stress a correlation with worship. The Sunday school often takes the form of a family service, followed by instruction in graded classes. Both the Church of Sweden and the Free Churches have curricula, which differ with regard to certain aspects of age gradation and lesson materials but for the most part are built on the same general principles. Since the school instruction is objective and formal, in the Sunday school an effort is made to help the children acquire Christian attitudes and involvement and to help them become accustomed to the worship services of the church. The Sunday school is occasionally supplemented with weekday gatherings for children. Common Sunday school problems are handled through the Swedish Sunday School Council, in which all denominations are represented.

Every denomination also carries on work among youth and adults through agencies such as Scouting, junior clubs, and youth groups. Adult instruction often is conducted by means of study circles, based on certain plans of study provided by the churches' study councils.

— *Karl Erik Brattgård*

SWITZERLAND   Switzerland, which in 1961 had 5,400,000 inhabitants, of whom approximately 3,000,000 were Protestants, is a union of 24 states called cantons. Every canton is independent and self-governing in church and school affairs, a fact that has produced 24 systems of Christian education. There are pure state churches like that in Zurich, where the pastors are employees of the state. There are other cantons, such as Basel and Geneva, where church and state are completely separated. There are predominantly

Roman Catholic cantons, Protestant cantons, and varieties between the extremes.

Nevertheless, there are sufficient common aspects to permit an overall picture of Christian education in Switzerland to be drawn. The structure in the whole country is that of a people's church. Every inhabitant is considered to be a member of his church, Protestant or Roman Catholic, unless he has declared his nonmembership or has left the church by a legal act. Roman Catholics number approximately 42 percent of the population; Protestants, approximately 55 percent. The Protestant Church holds the Reformed faith, having been established by Zwingli in Zurich (1531) and by Calvin in Geneva (1564). More than 95 percent of the Protestants are members of the Reformed Church.

The Swiss constitution begins with the words, " In the name of God Almighty." This indicates that though it is a secular state technically, Switzerland puts religion into the very 1st range. Education is considered a responsibility of the state. Schools must be open to any citizen and free from denominational pressure, but this does not mean that they must be atheistic or a-religious. Religious education is part of the curriculum. In all grades there are 2 lessons a week on stories from the Bible or (optionally) ethics. In the first 6 grades this subject is normally taught by the regular classroom teacher. The school authorities have supervision of this field of study. Only in matters of curriculum is the church's advice sought. The quality of the teaching depends entirely on the spiritual standards of the teachers. From grade 7 up, religious instruction is usually offered by the ministers, and the program is built into the church's preparation for confirmation.

In the churches, Christian education begins with infant baptism. The Sunday school invites parents to enroll children from ages 4 through 12. The Sunday school is considered as the Sunday worship service of the church's children, with the emphasis being laid on " Sunday " rather than on " school." The Sunday school is conducted by lay people, trained by the minister in a weekly training class. It has become a custom in Switzerland for every child to go to Sunday school, which means that the average enrollment is 90 percent in the country areas and 60 to 70 percent in the cities. The Sunday School Association of Switzerland, a member of the World Council of Christian Education, has as one of its main goals the securing of training facilities for leaders. Two magazines for Sunday school work are published: *Der Weg zum Kinde* for the German-speaking majority, and *Education chrétienne* for the French-speaking.

Around the age of 12, children leave the Sunday school for the department called Kinderlehre. This is a Sunday worship service for the ages 12 to 15, i.e., until confirmation. It is conducted by the minister in the church and has no lay helpers. This service is held before or following the adult service. Attendance is compulsory for all who wish to be confirmed.

Confirmation is the keystone of Christian education. It takes place at 15 or 16 years of age. Confirmation is the summarization of religious instruction and nurture, declaring the children responsible for their own faith and religious actions and giving them admission to the Lord's Table. It also confers social status. Approximately 99 percent of the children are confirmed, all of them having attended 2 to 4 years of religious instruction preparatory to this step. The 1st courses are taught by the ministers in the regular high school curriculum, usually with a concentration in Bible and church history. The last year is conducted as a confirmation class in the church premises, outside school hours. Catechism is taught as a summary of the Christian faith, but no set catechism is used, each minister choosing the way he himself deems best for introducing his class into the faith and life of the church. The average Swiss pastor teaches 10 to 12 hours each week.

Confirmation is regarded as something like graduating from school, with the result that only a few return to the church for further studies. This has led to endless discussions on the improvement of confirmation instruction. Some of the young people attend church regularly, but the majority come only on festival days such as Christmas and Good Friday and for their own wedding ceremonies. The church tries to meet this situation through its youth groups, which are mostly active groups concentrating on Bible study and life problems. Camps, usually 1 week in duration, have proved to be useful instruments of youth work from Sunday school age up to marriage. In spite of these emphases, only about 10 percent of the young people attend youth groups. The youth groups are organized on a national and language basis. The main organizations are Junge Kirche (Young Church), Y.M.C.A., Y.W.C.A., and Blue Cross. They have their individual magazines and are linked in the Swiss Youth Conference.

Adult Christian education is a concern of all churches. There is no general plan for this, nor any central agency, but there is considerable activity by clergy and lay people. The local churches conduct weekly Bible classes, special weeks, men's clubs, women's associations, "weekends," camps for mothers. There are also courses for young couples and schools for parents. There are schools for lay people who are called "working missionaries" (*Werkmissionarskurse*). There are centers of adult work such as Boldern-Männedorf and Crêt Bérard, working somewhat along the lines of the German evangelical academies.

To summarize, Christian education in Switzerland has confirmation as its central pillar, based on baptism and instruction. This is compulsory for anyone who wants to stay with the church, and is generally accepted and legally fixed. Around this central pillar have developed free agencies such as the Sunday schools, youth work, and adult education. This is how the land of Heinrich Pestalozzi sees Christian education today.

— *Emanuel Jung*

SYMBOLISM Symbols are used in everyday life and in almost every sphere of human activity — conversation, sports, mathematics, science, business, government, and religion. The main Christian symbols we wish to survey briefly have to do with God, the cross, apostles, evangelists, the church, the Word of God, the sacraments, symbolic movements, colors, and liturgical vestments.

By way of further introduction, something about the function of symbols and the renewal of interest in the subject may be indicated. Signs, symbols, and monograms in the Christian religion attract attention and create an atmosphere; they can add beauty and balance to the church, and suggest cardinal teachings of the Christian faith, thus stimulating thought as well as devotional and aesthetic feeling. Churches that a few decades ago paid little attention to Christian symbols are discovering that the house of God may be distinctive in appearance and at least as attractive as the house of man.

The danger of idolatry is effectively minimized when the cardinal teachings of Christianity are approached through an understanding of symbols. Symbols can be starting points or object lessons for introducing great Christian themes. Jesus referred to himself as the good shepherd, the door, the light of the world, the true vine. When he wanted to teach his disciples humble service he girded himself with a towel and washed their feet. The Christian church throughout the world well remembers the night when he instituted the Lord's Supper, how he said, when he had taken bread and given thanks, "Take, eat; this is my body." In like manner he also took the cup.

The hand, appearing in various forms, is probably the most outstanding symbol of God the Father, going back to such Biblical bases as Ex. 15:6 and Ps. 48:10.

The good shepherd (John 10:11) and the brazen serpent (John 3:14) refer to our Lord and his sacrifice. Often he is represented by a likeness of himself on the cross. The lamb

(John 1:29) is a well-known symbol of Jesus Christ. Church candles signify Jesus Christ as the Light of the World. In addition to the Alpha and Omega (Rev. 22:13), a monogram visibly linked to Jesus Christ the first and the last, abbreviations for Jesus are IHC or IHS, consisting originally of the capitalized forms of the 1st letters of the Greek word *Iēsous* (Jesus); the chi rho monogram, historically from the Greek word *Christos* (Christ), the rho being put within the chi; the letters of the Greek word *ichthus* (fish), beginning letters of the words forming the phrase "Jesus Christ, Son of God, Savior."

Besides the dove (Mark 1:10), another symbol of the Holy Spirit is the sevenfold flame (Isa. 11:2, to which list piety was added by tradition).

Symbols of the Holy Trinity usually consist of the triangle, the shield of the Trinity, the triquetra, and the interwoven circles.

An object of artistic attention over all the world, the cross may be summarized to signify Christianity itself, God's love and salvation for sinful man and triumphant hope. Specific meanings became attached to some of the forms of the cross, such as suffering to the pointed cross, the worldwide triumph of Christianity to the Latin cross on a glove, and the ultimate in personal victory to the Easter cross with its lilies. The cross and crown is a widely known symbol of being faithful and receiving the reward of life (Rev. 2:10).

Another form of the cross is the Celtic cross, sometimes called the Irish or wheel cross, which has a circle of eternity surrounding its center; the anchor cross refers to a hope both sure and steadfast (Heb. 6:19); some of the better-known elaborate crosses are the budded cross, the cross fleury, the cross patonce, the Jerusalem cross, the Maltese cross, the Trinity cross. The papal cross with its 3 horizontal lines is distinctively Roman Catholic.

All the apostles are represented in symbolism. Peter is represented by the crossed keys (Matt. 16:19; 18:18); Andrew by a cross shaped like the letter X or by 2 fishes crossed to form the same design; James the Greater by 3 scallops, referring to long pilgrimages, or the pilgrim's staff; John by a serpent issuing from the common cup; Philip by a staff surmounted by a cross or 2 loaves of bread on each side of a cross; Bartholomew by 3 flaying knives; Thomas by a carpenter's square and a vertical spear or an arrow; Matthew by 3 moneybags or a purse; James the Less by a saw with handle uppermost or by 3 stones, etc.; Jude by a sailboat; Simon by a fish on a hook; Judas by a blank yellow shield or a moneybag and 30 pieces of silver; Matthias by a double-edged ax in conjunction with a stone or open Bible or a book and sword; Paul by an open Bible with a sword behind it or by crossed swords.

The 4 Evangelists are frequently symbolized, their most common symbols being a winged man for Matthew, indicating the historical importance of the life of our Lord; the winged lion for Mark, indicating our Lord's kingly dignity; the winged ox for Luke, referring to the sacrificial character of our Lord; and the eagle to denote John, whose Gospel, like an eagle soaring to the throne of grace, speaks of the divine character of Jesus.

The church is symbolized by an ark, a ship, the vine and branches, a house or a church on a rock, a city on a hill, wheat and tares. The beehive is a modern symbol of the church, indicating cooperative work on the part of all.

The open book symbolizes the Word of God; the 2 tablets, the Ten Commandments. A baptismal font or baptistry is a symbol of the church's belief in the sacrament of Holy Baptism. The chalice is a symbol of the Lord's Supper.

Among the many symbolic movements and positions in worship, one would mention the standing position as a mark of respect; kneeling as a position of humility; the bowed head a universal act of humble respect and contemplation; laying on of hands conferring a blessing in baptism, confirmation, and ordination; processional marches leading toward the symbols most directly representing God, and recessional marches toward the world of service.

The changing colors on the altar and on pulpit and lectern antependiums point to the significance of festivals and seasons and add variety and warmth. The colors are white, symbolic of light, joy, purity; purple, symbolic of penitence, royalty; red, symbolic of divine zeal on the day of Pentecost and martyrdom; green, symbolic of nature and hope; and black, symbolic of grief and sorrow. Thus the violet or purple is used during Advent, pre-Lent, and Lent — seasons of penitence; white is used on Christmas, Easter, and the Sundays after, denoting joy, purity, light, etc.

The practice of wearing vestments in Protestant churches is becoming more prevalent than in former years. Robes are associated with humility in leading an orderly and dignified worship service; stoles, signifying ordination and the yoke of obedience, are used according to the liturgical colors of the church year; traditional vestments consist of the amice, alb, cincture, maniple, stole, and chasuble.

The broad scope of Christian symbols may be indicated further by merely mentioning numbers, stars, animals, birds, insects, flowers, Old Testament types, etc., which, together with the symbols already referred to, are used in connection with church architecture, paintings, murals, printing, stained glass, stone and wood carvings, embroidery, and a variety of church furnishings.

— *Friedrich Rest*

SYMPOSIUM In the symposium 2 to 4 people with special knowledge of a topic make speeches representing different types of information or points of view. The symposium differs from the panel chiefly in the formality of the opening presentation. The participants are a chairman or moderator, and from 2 to 4 speakers, each of whom talks for a specified time on an assigned phase of the topic. The moderator explains the topic briefly, then introduces the speakers, making clear the part each is to play in the total discussion. At the conclusion the moderator, or someone he selects, may summarize the discussion before inviting audience participation.

Like the panel, the symposium is used either to give the audience pertinent information about the topic or to consider the relative merits of various solutions to a controversial problem. The number of speakers depends on the number of significant sources of information or points of view that should be considered. However, a program with more than 4 speakers usually results in inadequate presentation of any proposal.

As contrasted with the panel, the symposium provides more information, and if the speeches are properly related to one another, a more unified consideration of a topic. Participants are more likely to prepare carefully for a definite assignment; they know the spotlight of attention will be on them while they speak. These same considerations make the symposium more formal than the panel and may restrict the conversational character of the forum period. The symposium is essentially a public-speaking program; the panel discussion is essentially conversational. For this reason the symposium is better adapted to large audiences.

The preparation for the symposium includes: deciding the purpose of the meeting; choosing and framing the topic in such a way as to arouse interest; choosing speakers; choosing a chairman; briefing chairman and speakers on the objectives and procedures.

Speakers should be chosen by a program committee in consultation with the moderator. Unless they are regarded as thoughtful, well-balanced individuals who can speak with some degree of authority, people will not come to hear them. To avoid bias, the committee should choose speakers with about the same degree of prestige, knowledge of the topic, and speaking skill.

The speakers chosen should be willing to spend some time in preparation. Those who attend have a right to expect well-organized speeches, expressed in layman's language. The speakers should remember that there are distinct limits to what an attentive listener can learn in 8 or 10 minutes. Excellence in speaking is, of course, desirable. However, listeners will excuse lack of skill in delivery if they feel the speaker has something he really wants to say and is doing his best to say it effectively.

Whenever possible, the moderator should arrange a briefing session soon after the speakers are chosen. If they cannot meet, the moderator should send them a description of the symposium and the names of their partners. The speakers should understand that their purpose is to help listeners analyze the problem rather than to announce conclusions to them. Each talk is a step in the process of analysis. The briefing should include agreement on time limits of speeches and on procedures during the forum.

Following the briefing session, the moderator should prepare a program, including a statement of the discussion topic, the list of subtopics, the names and qualifications of speakers, time limits and rules on participation in the forum period. This program should be distributed to audience members as they arrive for the meeting. It guides both speakers and listeners, and enables the moderator to get the discussion under way efficiently in 2 or 3 minutes.

The moderator's introductions should focus attention first on the program, then on each speaker's qualifications as an authority. In preparing his introductions, the moderator should avoid two extremes. He should not be content with the general remark that " Mr. X needs no introduction – he is a recognized authority in his field." On the other hand, the introduction need not tell the life story of Mr. X.

Among the limitations of the symposium format are the relatively brief time possible for audience participation, the wordiness of some in the audience and the reticence of others, and the danger of inexpert discussion leadership of the moderator. — *Frank Morgan Smith*

T

TEACHING, ART OF The art of teaching is the art of providing conditions by means of which students can learn and can learn how to learn. Learning is a matter of acquiring or appropriating skills, knowledge, understandings, values, attitudes, and basic orientation. One who can facilitate learning through an intuitive or consciously directed provision of the necessary and desirable conditions for learning in any of these areas is, in that area, a true artist in teaching. Some of the conditions relevant to facilitating learning that contribute to the art of teaching can be specified.

1. Sensitivity to the student and to the factors in his life and experience that affect his learning. Teaching that ignores the condition of the potential learner can expect little success. His previous background, hopes and fears, interests and concerns, anxieties, picture of himself, and level of aspiration — all affect his future learning. These in turn reflect his response to social factors — to the outlook, attitudes, and expectations of his family, class, and peer group, as well as to his own earlier experience in relation to church or secular school and to teachers themselves.

2. Sensitivity to the factors opera-

tive in the social learning situation. The dynamics of group interaction will affect, sometimes in a very decisive manner, both the kind and amount of learning that the teacher is able to facilitate or the student to achieve. The processes going on within a group, often below the surface of the conscious awareness of most members of the group, serve to create the climate of learning that either fosters the learning process or inhibits it.

3. The teacher's mastery of the matter to be learned, its special significance, and its relations to other human concerns. Incompetence or ignorance with respect to what is to be learned never facilitates the learning process, though competence and learning do not themselves guarantee its success, for many learned scholars are unsuccessful teachers. If the art of teaching includes facilitating learning how to learn, then the competence of the teacher must go beyond the limits of the restricted subject matter to basic principles and methods. A continuity of learning can be provided for only by helping the student to learn the method of the area of study and the most basic and underlying structure of what is being learned. Although there is little ap-

parent transfer in terms of formal discipline, there does appear to be significant transfer of general principles and method. It is for the same reason that the teacher needs to understand the larger significance of what is to be learned, to be able to trace its relationships to other human concerns. Such understanding communicated to students may at once increase both motivation and the transfer of what is learned.

4. The teacher's ability to teach in relation to the child's way of viewing things at his given level of experience, interest, and development. A teacher who has mastered the art of teaching takes into account the child's readiness, stage of development, and way of viewing things. Such a conclusion does not necessarily mean putting off to adulthood the most important kinds of learning, but it means the translation of the learning task into a form appropriate to the child's readiness and mode of comprehension.

5. Clarity with respect to short- and long-term goals. Good teaching proceeds out of an awareness of the long-term goals, and of the intermediate goals that need to be achieved step by step if progress is to be made toward the larger ends in view.

6. Use of appropriate methods. There is no single best method for teaching. A teacher must discover which methods are most appropriate considering his own personality, the kinds of students with whom he is working, the factors in the social learning situation, what is to be learned, and the specific long- and short-range goals he is trying to reach. Leaving aside the adaptability of the individual teacher, it is clear that lecture methods, discussion, case methods, projects, learning through vicarious or direct experience, etc., will vary in their appropriateness for fostering one or another kind of learning.

7. Self-criticism and experimentation by the teacher. Nothing will help so much to improve the art of teaching as the teacher's critical reflection on his own and others' teaching experience, if such reflection is combined with a willingness to experiment with new procedures and new sensitivities in response to observation and analysis.

8. The teacher as personal symbol of the art of learning. In spite of the absence of, or relatively poor performance with respect to, the other elements in the art of teaching, teaching may yet facilitate productive learning if the teacher is himself a model by means of which the student can apprehend in personal terms what the relevant learning processes are all about. In this way the teacher may serve as an identification figure, communicating what it means to learn and to be a learner, and indeed perhaps providing something of a lure to achievement.

In varying degrees these 8 aspects of the art of teaching will have a part in the work of every successful teacher. The art of the Christian teacher will in its formal aspects not be at variance with that of a secular teacher. Yet the Christian teacher, wherever he is teaching and at whatever level in and whatever field of study (secular or religious), will approach his task somewhat differently, because he will understand his work within a unique frame of reference and from a unique perspective. Inevitably such understanding will color in various ways his approach to the art of teaching and the kind of impact that his teaching may have.

The Christian faith provides its adherents with a unique way of seeing their world and their fellowmen. It sensitizes them to elements in the human scene that others may neglect, and it provides an interpretation of human experience and of their own vocation not shared by others. Moreover, the Christian faith as radical monotheism judges all human goals and loyalties, and sets a controlling goal for human life that is relevant to teaching and learning as well as to the rest of personal and social life. As a result, teaching for the Christian becomes one of the ministries in Christ's name by means of which God acts for the preservation and redemption of men. God is understood to be present in the teaching-learning process, creating and redeeming, bringing forth new good and overcoming old evil. From a Christian point of view the learning process is holy ground, potent with the possibility of good.

The Christian teacher sees his vocation as a calling from God to minister in and through his teaching — in and through the communication of skills, information, and understanding, or through the forming of attitudes and orientation — to those who are themselves called by God to a fully human life, to authenticity, to becoming centers of freedom and love. Teaching as ministry in this sense does not and cannot mean indoctrination, for indoctrination denies the freedom that is the necessary condition for man to develop into one whose being can be characterized by the love of God and neighbor. Love cannot be coerced. It must be free. Nor can freedom itself be the result of indoctrination or coercion. Rather, the art of Christian teaching implies respect for the integrity and the freedom of those who are taught.

Nor does teaching as ministry threaten the integrity of any area of study. It is, rather, based on the assumption that the truth about man and his world which may be opened to the learner in any field of study can only help the learner see the human predicament and the need for radical healing more clearly if it goes far enough. It can only open the way ultimately for the hearing of the gospel whenever and wherever it is preached, whether in word, symbol, or personal incarnation.

— Perry LeFevre

TEACHING MISSION The Christian Teaching Mission is an 8-day community program, Thursday through Thursday, to help the churches of any community reach and minister to the people. Each church secures a man to serve as a "guest leader." He will help the pastor during the days of the mission. The pastors and the guest leaders attend a daily training seminar where they are instructed by a community director to do the program in their respective churches. The mission is communitywide in scope, but the program itself is carried out by each individual church acting for itself and in harmony with its own beliefs and traditions.

The threefold purpose of the mission is to help each church discover those unchurched persons for whom it may assume responsibility; to set up a plan of fellowship cultivation in each church to interest and to help win these persons; to help each church discover ways and means of making its program adequate to meet its developing opportunities.

There are 4 phases to the Christian Teaching Mission, known in the program as projects: (1) Self-study — representatives from each group in the church attend a session where they evaluate their own group to determine to what extent the resources of the group are being used to reach others. (2) Community census — each church shares in taking a complete religious census. Through this there is no overlooking and no overlapping of responsibility, and each church knows its definite share of the concern for the unconcerned. (3) Fellowship cultivation — the responsibility of each church, as shown by the census, is divided among the groups of the church, and a fellowship cultivation program is launched within the groups to share the concern with those for whom they have taken responsibility. These calls are made on the "listening" basis. The goal is to understand and give support to the needs, spiritual and social, discovered in the lives of the "outsiders." (4) Through the leadership of the guest leader, skillful guidance is given each church in enriching its total program to meet the needs of the least, the last, and the lost.

The Christian Teaching Mission has been adopted and adapted by denominations and councils of churches since its origin in 1946. Now there are many revisions of it. Generally speaking, they are all trying for the same goal, namely, to relate evangelism and education and present the total gospel to the whole man in the entire community.

— *Milton A. Heitzman*

TEAM TEACHING Team teaching is based on a relationship between 2 or more teachers who work cooperatively with a group of pupils. This way of organizing the teaching staff can be employed with any age group, although it is used more frequently in classes of young children.

The relationship between the members of the team is that of a true Christian fellowship. They are united in Christ for the purpose of sharing in a community of learning in which everyone — teachers and pupils — is involved in a creative experience. Ample provision is made for a variety of interests, skills, achievements, aptitudes, and needs within the group. But all these activities contribute to the community of learning so that each person will have maximum opportunity to "increase in wisdom and in stature, and in favor with God and man."

Team teaching is a glorious adventure where the more mature share with the less mature for the good of all and where each member of the group satisfies his own need to participate, to learn, and to grow.

Those who participate in team teaching must do more than plan together. They must respect one another and accept one another as unique individuals. At the same time they must communicate with one another in such a way as to create a harmony of spirit and purpose. They should at all times welcome the opportunity to learn mutually. For example, when the storyteller is sharing a story with the group, he is the teacher for all the leaders as well as for the pupils. In this way all the members of the team, regardless of who is "leading" and who is "listening," become participants in the learning situation. This is one way for all the teachers to learn one another's particular skills. It makes possible both an interchange of function and greater usefulness of each individual teacher.

Careful consideration must be given to securing leaders for a team of teachers. It is not necessary to find a particular person who is adequate to conduct the entire class session alone for the entire period. The teachers can be selected to form a team with a variety of skills and aptitudes. Thus, a team possesses combined skills in music, storytelling, crafts, projects, missions, creative conversation, Bible interpretation, and worship. A battery of leaders skilled in these teaching functions enriches the program of Christian education in a church.

For the purpose of efficient administration it is necessary for a team of skilled teachers to have 1 person serve as the "lead" teacher. This person should be selected carefully, preferably by the committee or board of Christian education. He should possess the ability to work well with others and be thoroughly committed to the team-teaching idea.

If a church is introducing team teaching for the first time, it may be difficult to find just the right lead teacher. If the spirit of team teaching is understood, there will be little difficulty in selecting the coordinator. Future members of the team are much easier to recruit because a person with little teaching experience can be persuaded to be a member of a teaching group where sole responsibility is not required and where opportunity and time to grow in confidence and ability are offered. From within the team there emerges a future lead teacher. This makes for continuity of leadership and high quality of teaching.

How many teachers should constitute a team? This is determined by the number of pupils in the group and by the variety of program offered. A safe guide is to have 1 teacher for every 6 to 10 pupils. In regard to the leadership needs for a well-balanced program, it is well to have a different teacher for each of the following skills: music, storytelling and conversation, creative activities, and worship. It would be ideal if each teacher could be proficient in 2 of these 4 skills. Then the following plan could be used: for a group of 24 pupils there would be 4 teachers. A schedule could be worked out so that only 3 teachers would need to be present at any given session. Each teacher might be free 1 out of 4 sessions or for 1 month out of 4. This plan would eliminate the so-called substitute teacher who just comes in to "pinch-hit," for all teachers would be involved in the planning and would be committed to the carrying out of the same program.

Those who enter into such an experience of working and planning together must remember that this is a demanding type of fellowship. Friendly and good-natured tolerance can hold a team together. But if the relationship is to be a venture in the development of discipleship, it must be based on humility, honesty, commitment, and love. — *Oscar Bollman*

TELEVISION Television is increasingly recognized as an effective educational medium of communication. In its earliest history television was looked upon by those in control, the broadcasters, as primarily an entertainment medium. Anything of an educational nature was thought to "kill" the viewing audience. Today it has become the boast of the broadcasters that large blocks of time are devoted to educational features in addition to programs of an informational nature such as newscasts, recapitulation of great events, serious drama, music appreciation, and "you are there" interpretations of international affairs. Moreover, there is a willingness to concede that whatever is truly educational is interesting and even entertaining.

The highly commercial aspect of television in the U.S.A. is in itself educational and does a great deal to direct the cultural development of our people. Sometimes this direction is good, especially when it coincides with our mores. At other times it is bad. This judgment is varied in terms of the viewer. Although the Governmental agency designated to grant permission for broadcasters to use the airways, the Federal Communications Commission, sets up various codes, only the minimum of control can be exercised because of the sensitivity we have regarding what might become censorship. Television must be free of Governmental censorship, but at the same time the broadcaster must accept responsibility for the public interest and welfare. Many broadcasters are responsible in this regard.

With the designation by the Federal Communications Commission of certain airwave channels for noncommercial educational use, the U.S.A. enjoys an expansion of educational television. It is gratifying to note the expansion of educational television and the willingness on the part of many communities to underwrite the costs. It is even more gratifying to note the widespread use of the medium by viewers to the extent of receiving college credit for courses of study by TV. Many public-school systems in the elementary and secondary classes avail themselves of telecasts that provide greater enrichment and make it possible for larger numbers of students to come in contact with teachers of renown in specialized fields.

Closed-circuit TV used in the training program of industry, the Armed Forces, large school systems, and now in many local churches makes us realize another dimension of this medium of communication.

What makes for real educational experience via TV? In what way is it a teaching medium? In what way is it a learning instrument? If we agree that an experience is educational only when the learner has experienced that which contributes to his own personal development, we can see that TV provides many instances in which someone is trying to provide the viewer with additional information or an experience that will increase his own living. But there must be a complementary act: the viewer must become involved to the point of his accepting the stimulation and making it a part of his own life. In commercial TV the viewer must be motivated to want the product to the extent that he will select it out of all products he sees in the market. In educational TV the viewer must be motivated to further study and experimentation. He must go farther than that in his attempt to prove to the sponsoring institution through the writing of papers and taking of tests that he has been able to absorb the instruction which was telecast. In terms of newscasts, the viewer must be able to absorb the information to the extent of making up his mind about how he shall vote or how he shall participate in domestic and foreign affairs.

There are limitations to the TV medium. In drama it is impossible for the cast to move around in large areas or to establish contact with the audience to the same extent as in the theater. In selling, there is the hazard of time's elapsing between the moment the viewer sees and hears about the product and the time he buys. In educational TV, there is always the chance that the viewer will give up; that he will lose interest; that without the opportunity to ask questions immediately, he will continue his work on the wrong premise. One broadcaster has said that no one ever bought anything on TV. This leads us to believe that TV must have supporting media. TV needs supplementary materials in printed form or in displays at the store or in terms of the salesman.

How do these matters apply to Christian education? In the 1st place, if the gospel is to be communicated, we must use every means and medium available to us in terms of the life experiences of persons today. Television should be added to the tools already understood and used by Christian educators. Yet the telecast by itself is limited in its effectiveness. It must be complemented by planned activities of the local church, skillfully timed to work with the telecast. Such activities include participation in planning, advertising for securing viewers, a follow-up of the telecast with literature and personal contacts, evaluation and learning through mistakes to improve the ministry by television.

Television can enter the experiences of thousands of persons untouched by the Christian fellowship. Television can remind viewers of the need for God, urge them to seek more spiritual development, even, to a great extent, provide them with great enrichment of experience. But the local church must be ready to reach out and make contact with the viewer to bring him into the warmth of the Christian fellowship, providing him with help and guidance.

Christian education TV should allow for the resources of planning, quality in the telecast itself, planned follow-up through local churches, and evaluation for future use of the medium.

Many denominations have joined in such a ministry through the Broadcasting and Film Commission of the National Council of the Churches of Christ in the U.S.A. Networks have contributed greatly through such joint productions as *Frontiers of Faith, Look Up and Live,* and *Directions.* Local churches and church members may secure information on how to team up with the telecasts to make more effective the use of TV in their communities. Local stations have worked with groups of churches in the program called *Talk Back* provided by The Methodist Church through the Broadcasting and Film Commission. Other programs are especially prepared for children. One community offers college credit for Bible study on TV; another provides leadership education for local church workers.

Such programs have the major ingredients for successful Christian education television. They have an aim that is clearly understood — that of telling the gospel story and helping those who view come to know God through Jesus Christ. They are well-produced. They provide means and motivation for church people to work with the telecast in reaching viewers personally. They are continuously evaluated by competent representatives of the churches and through the years have been improved to keep pace with the best in television as we know it today.

The weakest link in Christian education television is the lack of understanding on the part of Christian men and women regarding the way of teaming up with the telecast to bring viewers into the fellowship of believers. — *Pearl Rosser*

TEMPERANCE EDUCATION " Temperance " has been a controversial term in ethics from the time of the Greeks, among whom it meant in general a complete self-control and respect for the gods, in contrast to the self-will and pride of the tragic hero. The traditional definition of temperance, derived from Aristotle and the Scholastics is " moderation in all things." In the 19th century, when the modern temperance movement arose to become a vital part of most of the churches in America, the term was given a more precise meaning as abstinence from the use of alcohol as a beverage, under the by-line of the Woman's Christian Temperance Union: " Moderation in things beneficial and abstinence from things harmful." Actually the 2 definitions are not in conflict because no Scholastic ever advocated the moderate use of things deemed harmful. The decisive question, then, is whether alcohol is ever truly beneficial, and that is a judgment which our generation must make, not on the authority of ancient texts, but on the facts available through scientific study. Through the era of national prohibition, which was not an attempt to legislate morals but to abolish a business, the term " temperance " became identified with abstinence in popular thought. If one wants to talk about " temperate use " and be understood, he should use the term " moderation." He should reckon with the fact that either term has acquired a certain amount of negative emotional connotation in our society.

In the period of the quarterly temperance lesson in Sunday schools (the chief educational program of the temperance movement in the early half of this century) the design was to give an abstinence interpretation to Scripture and to portray social problems such as poverty, crime, and political corruption in the contemporary alcohol culture, together with the benefits of abstinence and prohibition. In the middle decades of this century several new factors have modified temperance education; notably, a more historical interpretation of Scripture, the multiplication of scientific studies on all phases of the alcohol problem, and a new concern for alcoholics and problem drinkers.

Educators must now see this problem as set by the social conditioning in the primary social group and the conflicts that arise as youth moves into the adolescent peer group. The church school program usually reflects and sometimes creates the standards of the primary group, but there is no common agreement on the question of abstinence or moderation. In either case it must cultivate a body of information that should include the nature and classification of alcohol among drugs, the effects on behavior, motivations to drink, the nature of alcoholism, and the principles for ethical evaluation and decision. Objectivity in the sense of accurate use of scientific facts and complete fairness in developing points of view are more and more demanded, especially at mature levels of education. But it must not be assumed that mere knowledge is virtue. Alcohol is a moral problem. It presents every person with a decision of right or wrong, and religious education must not avoid that final responsibility.

The modern temperance movement in America developed amid the utopian idealism of the 19th and 20th centuries. It was integral to the social gospel movement in theology. The idealism which underlay that epoch has received a severe jolt in the failure of national prohibition and the despair that followed 2 world wars. A new realism has arisen in theology. Man's involvement in guilt and anxiety has brought a new sense of sin and the need for Christian faith and forgiveness as the basis for the soul's health and mature development. All this must be assimilated into an adequate temperance education. The success of Alcoholics Anonymous and the new popular interest in the disease concept of alcoholism both indicate the inadequacy of the older idealistic moralizing. Both of these have been questioned on the ground that they remove the problem of drink and drunkenness from the area of sin and moral responsibility. Quite the opposite is the case. For example, the program of Alcoholics Anonymous begins with confession and dependence on God. Most of man's illness, in fact, is connected with his moral responsibility, and especially those diseases derived from his chemical addictions. But both of these have shown that the alcohol problem is too deeply rooted in man's sinful nature and soul struggle to be solved by rational appeal alone. Temperance education must be geared into the redemptive work of the church.

— *Albion Roy King*

THEOLOGICAL EDUCATION Theological education represents in its content the most advanced stage of what the church teaches. A particular aspect of that content includes professionally oriented courses considered necessary for the church's leadership. We shall consider its purposes, for whom and by whom it is provided, its curriculum, its teaching agents, and its frontiers.

Within American Protestantism theological education has had as its primary purpose the provision of a learned ministry. From their early beginnings, Congregationalists, Presbyterians, Episcopalians, and Lutherans have been committed to the idea of a well-educated ministry. Although they arrived at this point somewhat later and with slightly different emphasis, the other major denominational bodies now seek the same for their ministers. Religious bodies with a more recent history also find themselves in the process of providing some form of specialized training for their ministry, which tends to move through the arts or Bible college degree toward the standard B.D., representing 3 years of study beyond the college degree.

The tradition of theological education in Europe that is firmly maintained by some of the most vigorous schools here has as a central purpose continued research in and additions to the science of theology. In this respect theological education stands among the disciplines of the university pursuing its task of constantly validating and adding to its field of knowledge.

The provision of a critically constructive leadership for the church's intellectual worship is a closely related purpose held by many in theological education. Here there is a delicate balance between the right of the church to determine the kind of leadership expected of theological scholars and the necessity for freedom of research and teaching by the scholar.

Theological education is provided for the candidates for the parish ministry of the churches. A large majority of theological students in America become parish ministers. There is, however, deep questioning as to whether the parish system may not be passé and whether ministers are being prepared for a form of church life that is outdated and irrelevant.

Theological education is also provided for various specialized ministries of the church. Christian education, counseling, institutional chaplaincy, industrial chaplaincy, ministry to university students, church social work, religious broadcasting, and church council administration represent specialized ministries by men and women for which preparation is made in various centers of theological education.

We may be moving toward a time when theological education will increasingly be made available to laymen in preparation for their ministry. Even now some centers are reaching out to provide evening classes for laymen. One church for a number of years has succeeded in encouraging a considerable proportion of its potential college faculty to study theology first. This is one of the frontier areas in which the future is not clear.

The earliest approaches to theological education in America were within colleges for which the education of the clergy was a major purpose of their founding, now private universities with a divinity school as an integral part. Other private universities have followed a similar pattern. Faculties in such schools are made up of scholars from many branches of the church.

A small additional part of theological education in America is carried on by schools that are nondenominational and not associated with universities. Such schools have usually been started and are carried on to represent a particular doctrinal emphasis. Faculties here also usually represent many branches of the church.

The largest portion of theological education in America is carried on within seminaries that are more or less directly the agents of the denominations. For the most part such centers are operated by a single denomination although there are some centers that are genuinely interdenominational.

A considerable number of students are securing their theological education in Bible colleges (or institutes) which, although providing terminal education for the ministry at a different level, represent a particular theological emphasis but also are the 1st step toward an educated ministry for some religious groups.

The curriculum traditionally consisted of Old Testament, New Testament, church history, and theology. The peculiarly American and relatively modern addition to this curriculum is pastoral or practical theology, including Christian education and pastoral counseling. Even more recent additions have been Christian social ethics and the study of Christianity and culture.

Constant effort is required to maintain a satisfactory balance between the traditional subjects of the core curriculum of theology and the professional studies that are required for a man to enter into the various forms of ministry. Experimentation is being carried on with various ways of relieving curriculum pressures by teaching the professional subjects by means of field education, internships, special summer institutes, and post-B.D. courses. There is little disagreement that the total curriculum must produce people who are both theologians and professionals.

Theological education at its best uses many resources and agents in the teaching-learning process. Most notable and obvious of such agents is the faculty. Increasingly faculty conceive of themselves as guides whose major purpose is to help students become continuing learners. Greater use is made of seminar and library than formerly, although the well-planned lecture is still used for those purposes for which it is most effective.

The student body who participate in a community of scholars are themselves essential teaching agents. Debate, challenge, encounter, testing of ideas, sharing of insights, cooperation in research — all these are made possible by other students.

The church itself has much responsibility for contributing to the teaching. One director of field education insists that it is the church's responsibility through its own proper agencies for supervising the work of the student so as to make him an authentic minister.

The clinical setting in hospital, court, penal institution, or parish may contribute to the teaching by showing the raw material of theology, by bringing to the fore the right questions, by giving experience in ministering. All these teaching agents should be joined in effective theological education.

Although any aspect of theological education may have developing frontiers for the creative school, at least 2 stand out. (1) There is a great and increasing need for some creative approach to the continuing education of the minister after he has entered into his vocation. (2) There is the relatively unexplored field of the kind of theological education appropriate for the ministry of the laity.

Theological education in North America has found a means of moving ahead cooperatively toward greater excellence through the formation of the American Association of Theological Schools. Composed of most of the theological schools of Canada and the U.S.A., the AATS maintains accrediting operations, provides counsel looking toward greater excellence, sponsors meetings for professors of various disciplines, administers a program of fellowships for faculty members, provides counsel in the relocation or building of new schools, represents the membership to foundations interested in helping theological education, and attempts to provide a clearinghouse of information about theological education.

— *Jesse H. Ziegler*

THEOLOGY AND CHRISTIAN EDUCATION The Christian education movement in American Protestantism has been turning in a new direction for nearly a quarter of a century. Leading theorists and spokesmen within the movement have characterized what is happening in various terms. Sara Little has written about " a changing perspective " and " the emerging new philosophy." James D. Smart likes to put the change in terms of " the redefinition of the goal." D. Campbell Wyckoff has labeled the contemporary period as one of " consolidation and redefinition." Wesner Fallaw sees what has been happening as a shift in orientation from "religious education" to a new and more uniquely Christian focus that he prefers to call "church education."

The new direction is primarily a theological one, as evidenced by the literature produced in the last 2 decades. The stimulus has come, in many respects, from the contemporary renewal of theological and Biblical study that has so profoundly influenced church life since the years immediately prior to World War II. This theological influence has found ready response from leaders in the Christian education movement, particularly those who have deplored the overemphasis on educational and psychological foundations in the movement and the inadequacy of the attention given to theological issues. Some leaders, to be sure, have been fearful and somewhat negative in response to the theological direction of the movement lest the important gains in educational dimensions that have been made since the turn of the century might be lost. In some instances there has been hesitancy about theological influences in the field of Christian education for fear of slavery to rigid theological and doctrinal systems that would result in indoctrination rather than genuine education.

The new theological direction can be traced in recent history within 2 basic categories: (1) statements that have emerged out of conferences and study groups within the structure of cooperative Protestant work in Christian education; (2) writings of individual scholars and theorists who have written their views for publication and general reading.

In 1940 the International Council of Religious Education (forerunner of the current Division of Christian Education of the National Council of the Churches of Christ in the U.S.A.) published a statement of basic philosophy prepared by a committee as the climax of a 3-year study, *Christian Education Today: A Statement of Basic Philosophy*. This statement reflected in many ways the new theological trends. It evidenced some concern for "pressures" that were being exerted on Christian education, and insisted that the movement would not "yield to these extremes." The extremes were, on the one hand, nontheistic humanism, and, on the other hand, the "tendency of those who exalt the absolute otherness of God so as to deny that any way to the knowledge of God can be found." This study committee, however, rejoiced in the fact that "a new life is astir in the Christian churches. . . . The churches are affirming their faith in the Christian gospel with a fresh realization of its meaning and truth."

In less than 4 years a more extensive study of Christian education was authorized by the council. In 1947 this study was fully summarized on behalf of the committee under the title *The Church and Christian Education*, edited by Paul H. Vieth. While seeking to consolidate the educational gains that had been made, the study summary opened up a new era of theological discussion among educators in cooperative Protestantism. Some of its affirmations were significant departures from earlier presuppositions; e.g., in a discussion of the dual nature of man it is affirmed, "His need for deliverance is more real than his need for instruction" (p. 55).

The era of the 1950's brought 2

major studies of objectives of Christian education that have also contributed to the new theological orientation in the Christian education movement. A special committee appointed by the Division of Christian Education of the NCCCUSA produced a study document, *The Objectives of Christian Education.* The committee openly stated that, in part, the need for the restudy was justified because " there have been marked changes in the educational and theological climate in which Christian education takes place." Almost at the same time that this general study was in process leaders in the field of youth work within the Division of Christian Education produced a statement of the objectives of senior high work, *The Objective of Christian Education for Senior High Young People,* which also reflected the theological trend.

During the same period that cooperative committees and study groups were at work, individual theorists also were working. At the threshold of the 1940's, simultaneously with the theological developments within the structure of cooperative Protestantism in Christian education, 2 books emerged that were a revolutionary challenge to the presuppositions of Protestant Christian education. H. Shelton Smith in *Faith and Nurture* charged that " the thought patterns of modern liberal religious nurture have largely exhausted their vitality." He raised the serious question in the midst of his extensive discussion of the theological weaknesses of Protestant religious education, as to whether Protestant nurture would realign its theological foundations with the newer currents of Christian thought or resist the currents and reaffirm its faith in traditional

liberalism. A 2d book, *Can Religious Education Be Christian?* by Harrison S. Elliott, made it clear that some would resist the theological currents and insist on a reaffirmation of the liberal tradition. Elliott argued that the educational process itself was essential as a way of interpretation of the Christian religion, and expressed considerable fear of theological influences upon religious education because " there is not, and has never been, a single authoritative interpretation of the Christian religion " (p. 90).

The 1950's brought ample evidence that the leaders of the movement were ready for a complete and comprehensive formulation of a theory of Christian nurture that would be based on and integral to the historic and normative tradition of the Christian faith. Randolph Crump Miller led the way in many respects with his fresh treatment of theology as the " clue " to Christian education. He wrote in *The Clue to Christian Education* (p. 15): " The clue to Christian education is the rediscovery of a relevant theology which will bridge the gap between content and method, providing the background and perspective of Christian truth by which the best methods and content will be used as tools to bring the learners into the right relationship with the living God who is revealed to us in Jesus Christ, using the guidance of parents and the fellowship of life in the church as the environment in which Christian nurture will take place."

The construction of a complete and comprehensive theory of Christian nurture, while in many respects not as yet fully accomplished in the new theological age, has certainly been approached and carried along rather far. Lewis J. Sherrill developed a sound and basic philosophy of Christian nurture in *The Gift of Power*, which drew on the insights of both theology and psychology and centered on revelation as the essential " given " element in the theory. James D. Smart has written from the standpoint of a Biblical scholar and sought in *The Teaching Ministry of the Church* to clarify the Biblical basis for the teaching ministry; in fact, for the ministry itself. D. Campbell Wyckoff pioneered in *The Gospel and Christian Education* in the development of a theory of Christian education based on the gospel. Iris V. Cully has joined in the reconstructive task, basing her dynamic perspective on the *kērygma*, or the " proclamation of the good news that in Jesus Christ God has entered human existence, seeking and saving men " (*The Dynamics of Christian Education*, p. 9).

Within the general concern to develop a comprehensive theory of Christian nurture in a new theological orientation, several special aspects of theory have been and continue to be studied. Sara Little in *The Role of the Bible in Contemporary Christian Education*, Randolph Crump Miller in *Biblical Theology and Christian Education*, and Iris V. Cully in *Imparting the Word: The Bible in Christian Education* have given special attention to the relevance of the Bible in the emerging theory of contemporary Christian education. Howard Grimes in *The Church Redemptive* and Randolph Crump Miller in *Christian Nurture and the Church* have sought to clarify the nature of the church in relation to Christian nurture. Curriculum theory, in the light of the new theological orientation, has recently been undertaken by D.

Campbell Wyckoff in *Theory and Design of Christian Education Curriculum*. Even before this several major denominations were producing new curriculum materials based on the emerging theological and Biblical emphasis, and this process continues at present and is projected far into the future. Books dealing with age-level Christian education are yet to come in adequate numbers, but in the field of children's work Iris V. Cully has written *Children in the Church*, and David J. Ernsberger has sought to develop a new perspective for adult work in *A Philosophy of Adult Christian Education*.

An estimate and evaluation of what has been happening in Christian education theory might, at present, be premature. The " new perspective " has not yet fully matured and is still coming into its own. It is certain that the modern " religious education " movement, arising in the early 20th century in an era that was predominantly scientific in its methodology and liberal in its theology, has for nearly a quarter of a century been engaged in profound reflection upon its essential nature and task in a new era that is more orthodox in its theology. The result has been that what was once termed religious education is now commonly, and appropriately, termed Christian education. The change represents something far more than that of terminology. It symbolizes, indeed actualizes, a revolutionary change in basic presuppositions and perspectives. — *James Blair Miller*

THOMISM Since Pope Leo issued his important encyclical *Aeterni patris* in 1879 Thomism has been conventionally, although not universally, a kind of official philosophy and theology in the Roman Catholic Church. On the other hand, there have been and still are a not inconsiderable number of Roman Catholic thinkers who are not Thomists. Outside the Roman Church, Thomism has been very influential among some Anglicans, nor has it been completely without support among Protestants in general. Even a certain number of non-Christian thinkers are Thomistic in some aspects of their thought. It would be no exaggeration to say that Thomism in the 20th century has been more influential than ever before. In the 13th century, which saw its birth, Thomism was officially condemned by the church, and although it subsequently wielded great influence, particularly in the 16th and 17th centuries, it has never previously been so highly respected or authoritative as it is today. Thus it would be possible, although not perhaps wholly satisfactory, to write a history of Western philosophy in the 18th and 19th centuries without mentioning Thomas Aquinas, but to omit him from a treatise on philosophy in the 20th century would be quite preposterous.

Thomas was a crisis thinker. The emergence of that great new context for intellectual work and scholarship, the university, more or less coincided in Europe with a recovery of the text of Aristotle. The earlier Middle Ages knew little of Aristotle apart from his logic, and it was influenced to a much greater extent by the kind of Platonism that survived in and was given new life by Augustine. The new enthusiasm for Aristotle threatened to supplant the philosophy and theology of the Augustinians and to produce a new form of skepticism and unbelief. Following in the footsteps of his teacher,

Albertus Magnus, Thomas strove to deal with the intellectual and religious crisis that ensued. It is not necessary to be a Thomist in order to admire the profundity and brilliance with which Thomas handled this delicate situation. Of course, he did not depart from Augustine entirely, any more than Aristotle himself departed entirely from Plato, but we do find in Thomas a new emphasis, a new respect for natural knowledge and the natural conditions of human existence, a healthy belief that all truth is God's truth, and that all particular truths are at least in principle capable of reconciliation with each other.

The Aristotelianism of Thomas was not slavish, and he is never afraid to correct his master. There were, after all, views expressed by Aristotle that were quite incompatible with Christianity. We must notice that whenever Thomas is compelled to choose between Christianity and Aristotle he always prefers Christianity, but he is never content merely to note that at some point or another Aristotle's view is incompatible with Christianity, and to reject it simply on that account. What he does is always to find a good Aristotelian reason for rejecting any Aristotelian opinion that is incompatible with Christian faith. The result is a synthesis of a basically Aristotelian view of nature and man with a basically Biblical view of man and God worked out with such extraordinary analytic power that no man should feel free to reject it until he has first paused sincerely to respect it and to learn from it.

There is something encyclopedic about the scope of Thomas' thought. It includes metaphysics and epistemology, logic and ethics, social philosophy, aesthetics, psychology, theology, and a kind of philosophical physics that at times rather recalls that of our own day. All this was expressed in a medieval Latin style of extraordinary lucidity and, in its own way, of great beauty. The Renaissance view of medieval Latin was far too low. To blame a medieval person for not writing like Cicero is like censoring a modern poet for not writing like Chaucer or Shakespeare. Medieval, or, as it is sometimes called, ecclesiastical Latin was in fact a literary and intellectual instrument of extraordinary subtlety and power, and few mastered its complexities with the genius of Thomas Aquinas.

Indeed, it is a mistake to think of him as merely a cold and remorseless intellectual machine. Thomas was a great saint and a not inconsiderable, if hardly great, devotional poet who in his finest moments can entrance the emotions as well as dazzle the intellect.

We can criticize Thomas from the Augustinian point of view on the general ground that his naturalism sometimes muted and subdued his supernaturalism. Similarly from the point of view of a naturalistic critic his supernaturalism may at times appear to rebel too strongly against his naturalism. Others have criticized him because they would prefer to reject the natural-supernatural dichotomy altogether. But this particular dichotomy in Thomas is never a dualism. For him the very existence of the natural order is a supernatural event, while on the other hand the supernatural always makes itself manifest to us within the context of the natural. The purpose of Christianity is to redeem and not to nullify the fallen natural order that God has created. The intent of these great philosophical and theological distinctions is not to create any kind of dualism but, rather, to enrich our conception of the unity of a universe in which all is from and for God. Some Christian critics, particularly in the Eastern Orthodox Church, have condemned Thomas for his alleged rationalism, but this is a very ambiguous word and it can emphatically be asserted that Thomas was not a rationalist in the bad modern sense. He was a rationalist in a classical and Christian sense, in the belief that all is comprehended by the reason of God, and that the creaturely, human reason has a genuine relationship to the uncreated divine reason that justifies us theologically in pushing the work of reason as far as it will go.

The dialogue and dialectic between natural knowledge and understanding of the world and that spiritual wisdom which derives from understanding of faith continues in every age. It is probably true that every century requires its Thomas; that every age stands in need of such a creative synthesis. In the narrow sense of the term, modern Thomists are presumably people who delight in quoting the letter of Thomas, but the real Thomists are those, rather, who partake of his spirit, who are animated by his robust faith and by his broad sympathy with and understanding of the knowledge of the day and the intellectual tendencies animating the time. Many people have observed that the mere letter of Thomas may destroy the intellectual enterprise, but it is perhaps more important to notice that it is the spirit of Thomas that continually gives it life.

— *J. V. Langmead Casserley*

TIME FOR CHRISTIAN EDUCATION

It is not many years since " time for Christian education " meant to most people merely the time set aside by the church for formal religious instruction in the Sunday school. Although having such a Sunday school hour was itself an advance step, the time came when leaders began to deplore the fact that only " 1 hour a week " was available for Christian nurture. How, they asked, might more time be secured for religious teaching?

During the 20th century the church has been finding various answers to this question, the most significant of which may be mentioned:

1. The vacation church school, originally called the Daily Vacation Bible School, had its beginnings about the turn of the century. Idle church buildings and children with free time were factors that gave appeal to the proposed plan. A 4 weeks' school meeting 5 mornings a week gives as much time as the regular Sunday school for an entire year. During a 10-year period the enrollment curve in the U.S.A. has been almost consistently upward — from 4,399,071 pupils in 1950 to 8,215,-765 in 1959.

2. Bible study for high school credit was a plan that developed in the 2d decade of the century. Under certain conditions, high school credit was given for Bible study under church auspices. In North Dakota, beginning in 1912, this was based on a state examination; in Colorado, beginning the same year, it was based on the accrediting of teachers. The plan spread to many states and the result was more effective Bible study. In recent years, however, the movement has declined.

3. Weekday religious education on released (or dismissed) time had its beginnings in the same decade, the 1st significant experiment being in Gary, Ind., starting in 1914. When conducted without expense to the community, and without using school buildings, the plan has been declared constitutional. Its curve of development has been irregular, with periods of marked growth and periods of decline. In recent years the number of children enrolled has been estimated at about 3,000,000. This has proved an effective means of securing more time for religious education.

4. The extended or expanded session is the Sunday church school meeting for a longer period — 2 to 3 hours instead of 1 hour. It permits longer class periods, more opportunity for creative activities, and an enriched program in other ways. Since at least the 2d or 3d decade of the century churches here and there have experimented in this plan for more adequate time.

5. Summer camps and conferences under church auspices, both denominational and interdenominational, are a significant development of the 20th century. They may be for adults, young people, or boys and girls; family camps or children's day camps; leadership training schools or enrichment experiences. They represent a popular present-day movement.

6. Special weekday classes after school hours or on Saturday mornings, in addition to the Sunday church school, have been found here and there for many years, often under pastoral leadership.

7. The summer session of the Sunday church school, using different leaders from those of the other 9 months and following a freer and more varied program, has proved effective. An attractive summer program encourages a large attendance. In sections of the country where it has been customary to close the Sun-

day school for the summer, adopting a year-round schedule obviously would provide more time.

All 7 of these developments of the present century have increased the amount of time for the church's teaching-learning program.

There is much more, however, to our subject than has been said or implied. Increasingly the church has come to realize that " more time " has to do with more than specific blocks of time set aside for Christian training. Indirect influences may be as significant as those which are direct. Indirect methods that do not bear the Christian education label, but that do have value in Christian nurture, must also be regarded as an integral part of Christian education. It is impossible to mention all the indirect methods or influences that have educational value; but today's leaders are discovering the importance of being alert to new ways of learning and of utilizing ongoing experiences for Christian education purposes.

Youth choirs are examples. They are happy experiences in themselves; they are valuable in cultivating reverence and as training in worship; they bring an appreciation of, and love for, the great hymns of the church; and they have values that inhere in significant group life. A church membership training class is more than an opportunity to consider church membership; it is a chance to open up new understandings and insights, and to help young people to discern what the Christian way of life means. A service project for any age group, when well carried out, has values in the development of Christian attitudes, in better understanding of others, and in the habit of sharing. The family church service tends to unify the family in the

church and to develop the " my church " attitude in even a small child, and at this service the children's sermon or story may have educational values. Religious dramatics, choric speaking, and the rhythmic choir, whether as class activity or in specially organized groups, have real possibilities in the building of Christian character. The minister who has the educational ideal in preaching has expanded the amount of time his church devotes to Christian education. Adult discussion groups on vital subjects are a part of the educational program, regardless of the sponsoring agency. The church that has learned that committee work can be an educational experience has expanded the time for adult Christian education. Service on the finance committee, for example, may mean studying missionary budgets and world needs as well as those of the local church; serving on an art, music, or any other committee, may, if rightly planned, become an educational experience.

The present trend is to recognize that when the educational ideal is entrenched in the life of the church, there is " time for Christian education," not only in " that Sunday morning hour " and other definite blocks of time, but even in ways that are indirect.

The primary place of the home in Christian nurture may be regarded as a rediscovery of the past few decades. In recent years the curricula of many denominations have been including a marked effort to bring parents into responsible participation in the Christian education task. The church, more and more, is helping them to perform their teaching function. There are parents classes, family services at church, family camps and guidance for parents as to

Christian nurture in the home. All of this leads to a growing sense of responsibility on the part of parents. In considering this matter of " time for Christian education," this is a significant trend. For much of this time is in the home or under the supervision of the home. This may have something to do with blocks of time that can be designated or measured; but it has more to do with atmosphere, standards, ideals, family practices, understanding of the Christian faith, commitment to causes — all of which require time, but not time that can easily be measured.

Both church and home are concerned with the question of time for Christian education, but in different ways. The church rightly sets aside specific pieces of time, such as the Sunday-morning church school hour, or its equivalent, or an extension of it. This it must do, just as the public school must have its fixed schedule. But it also plans for activities, influences, and experiences that take time — but not in the same fixed pattern, and often with less formality.

Ideally the home is also concerned about time for Christian education. This may include periods fixed and agreed upon for study, church school projects, or religious practices. But it also includes the living of the Christian life day by day, and the participation of individuals and of families in the experiences of church life, community enterprises, and social activities. — *John Leslie Lobingier*

TIME LINE The time line (time chart, time ladder) is a teaching-learning device using a linear form marked in equal segments to represent a chosen time progression within which important events are chronologically identified and related.

The linear form may be a cord, tape, or string. It may simply be a line drawn on a roll of paper. Depending on the teaching situation, a time line may be long or short, simple or elaborate, and cover centuries or a week. To construct a time line, mark off equal segments on a cord with some material such as tape, tags, buttons, or colored yarn. Next attach at the proper chronological position luggage tags, clothespins, or other markers indicating the names or events under study. These markers may be elaborately illustrated to represent a particular event.

A simple time line on paper may have the names or persons or dates of events marked along a calibrated line. More elaborate time lines may be illustrated like a mural, blending events in a chronological manner. A cord time line may be placed in front of a strip of wallpaper or wrapping paper that has appropriate pictures or symbols at the reference points.

Usually a time line has a reference point of " here and now " so that the pupils can see themselves in relation to historical events. The cord time line is helpful in relating the present to Biblical times, since the intervening centuries not under study can be wound around a stick to conserve space. Occasionally the line can be unwound to show the relationship of the events to the present.

Some variations of the time line are time charts or time ladders. The time chart does not necessarily take linear form, though it must retain equal segments leading from a beginning reference point. A tree with related branches according to certain chronological events is an example. Another is a chart of several lines representing separate but concurrent historical events, and using intersecting lines, indicating interrelatedness. A time ladder would be quite similar, with rungs of the ladder indicating time divisions and the events under study placed chronologically between the rungs.

The time line as a teaching-learning device is valuable in historical study where attention is directed toward chronological development, relatedness of events, gaining a perspective, or summarizing. There is value in the use of the time line as a class project because it involves sharing and working together.

The time line should not be used with small children, since their concept of time has not developed much beyond " a long time ago." The time line becomes a valuable aid to learning, beginning with the 4th grade, where there is a quickening interest in placing people and events in sequence. — *O. Otto Steinhaus*

U

UNDERGRADUATE STUDY IN RE-LIGIOUS EDUCATION Since the Constitution of the U.S.A. separated the church from the state and religion could not be taught in the public schools, the entire responsibility for the Christian nurture of children fell upon the churches. Roman Catholics and some Protestants met the challenge through the parochial school; most Protestants took recourse to the Sunday school. However, the Sunday school did not prove equal to its opportunity; its standards, methods, and leadership were inadequate. For the 1st quarter of this century the pioneers of the religious education movement endeavored to awaken the churches to a greater sense of responsibility toward the religious education of their children, young people, and adults. They also stressed the obvious fact that no satisfactory results could be expected without trained leadership.

By the 2d quarter of the century the churches caught on to the significance of the 1st emphasis, but hardly of the 2d. Special attention was directed to the Sunday school; new educational units were added, and many a church nobly sought to raise standards as outlined by denominational leaders of religious education. However, neither the forward look of the denominational leaders, nor the new curricula, nor the new educational plants achieved the desired ends, for the local churches sadly lagged in educational leadership. Piety and good intentions on the part of loyal church members, eager to help the church school, were not substitutes for trained and consecrated leadership.

Slowly and sometimes reluctantly the churches became conscious of this need, and began looking right and left to secure directors of religious education. They soon discovered that the number of holders of master's degrees in religious education annually produced by theological seminaries and other graduate schools of the country did not begin to meet the need. In despair they turned to college graduates to direct church schools. Well-intentioned and devout Christian young women, who had taken a few courses in religion, but who unfortunately did not possess the ABC's of religious education, were recommended by colleges and engaged by the churches. The consequences were frustrating both to these young women and to the churches.

With the ambition of contributing effectively to the cause of religious education, a number of schools and departments in theological seminaries began to offer a B.S. degree in religious education. These were distinctly professional schools to prepare mostly women for positions of leadership in the educational field of the church. Some of them accepted applicants who had already completed their sophomore year in college. Others offered a combination of 2-year liberal arts courses and 2 years of courses in religious education. Their liberal arts curriculum included most of the traditional courses for freshmen and sophomores in liberal arts colleges. Their 2-year religious education program included such courses as Principles and Methods of Religious Education; Work with Children, Young People, and Adults; the Curriculum, Administration, and Supervision of Religious Education; Worship and Hymnology in the Church School; The Old and New Testaments; The History of the Church; and The Philosophy and Psychology of Religion. In addition there were electives in Audio-Visual Approaches to Religious Education; Weekday Religious Education; Vacation Bible Schools and Camps; The Family and Religious Education; Storytelling and Drama in Religious Education, etc. All students, furthermore, were required to engage in supervised fieldwork in a local church or in a church-related organization. Four years of academic work and of supervised fieldwork provided essential opportunities for the basic training of directors of religious education. To be sure, such people lacked the full liberal arts background, but they acquired a deep insight into the nature of religious education. From the practical point of view these schools have been contributing most significantly, on the undergraduate level, to leadership in the church school.

However, these schools were constantly criticized and often openly attacked by graduate schools of religious education as undermining standards and as offering shortcuts to the profession. Since they were not accredited, their students and graduates met with serious difficulties when they had to transfer to another college or entered graduate work. Graduates of these colleges were not officially recognized as directors of religious education, and were denied full standing in professional organizations. One by one most of these schools have been abandoning their undergraduate programs and seeking affiliation with graduate schools or theological seminaries.

All this does not alter the fact that there is a shortage of directors of religious education, and that graduate schools do not supply the needed numbers. Inevitably churches have to turn to liberal arts colleges for help.

Some denominational colleges saw the opportunity and proceeded to establish majors in religious education. This was (and still continues to be) an emergency step, but it is far superior to that of sending to a church as a leader in religious education someone with a bachelor's degree whose religion work in college was limited to a course in the Bible and another in comparative religion or philosophy of religion. The number of colleges offering such majors are on the increase, and the results are all to the good. Requirements include courses in The Nature of Religious Education, Principles and Methods of Religious Education, Curriculum Materials, The Old and New Testaments, and supervised practical experience in some local church.

The basic difficulty with this plan,

however, is related to the inability of liberal arts colleges to enrich their offerings for majors in religious education. Accrediting agencies insist on certain strictly "liberal arts" requirements for the granting of the bachelor's degree, which automatically exclude additional so-called "professional" courses in religious education. Liberal arts colleges therefore feel that they would jeopardize their accreditation if they included in their religious education program such courses as are being offered by schools of religious education. In other words, what these colleges offer for religious education is hardly adequate. Certain colleges, however, have partly solved this problem by including in their program for majors in religious education courses in education as such, which qualify as liberal arts material.

Accrediting agencies are not concerned about religious education; the churches are. Until such a time as graduate schools can prepare enough young people to fill the vacant positions of directors of religious education in thousands of churches, the churches can lend moral and financial support to schools of religious education now in operation to stabilize their future. They can also encourage all church-related colleges to introduce and maintain majors in religious education. Programs now in use should be scrutinized, enriched, and placed in the hands of competent faculty. Fieldwork should be carefully supervised. Ways also should be found to persuade accrediting agencies that courses in religious education deserve as much recognition as the strictly "liberal arts" courses.

Regardless of all this, however, there still remains a basic problem to attack. Facilities exist in graduate and undergraduate schools for the training of leaders in religious education, but the students are not there in large enough numbers to justify the continuation and enlargement of these programs. The response of young people to the call of religious education has not been heartening. Much therefore has to be done at the home base, i.e., the family and the church, to motivate young people and to inspire them with the desire to enter this type of Christian ministry. Most of them are not conscious of the need for trained leadership in the church school. They are frequently unaware that there is such a profession as religious education work. The local churches have a tremendous responsibility for this, and much at stake.

— *George P. Michaelides*

UNIFORM LESSONS The Uniform Lessons are a series of Biblically centered studies for Sunday school use based on outlines prepared by the Committee on the Uniform Series of the National Council of the Churches of Christ in the U.S.A. They represent a cooperative endeavor among many denominations, and are an illustration of the drive toward ecumenicity that has been characteristic of the churches in this century.

The origin of these lessons, however, extends back into the 19th century, when a Methodist minister, J. H. Vincent, and a Baptist layman, B. F. Jacobs, combined their interests to promote the idea through the National Sunday School Convention.

In 1870 a conference of publishers was called in New York to consider the publication of a uniform series. Unable to reach an agreement, it adjourned. Another conference in 1871 appointed a committee to choose an outline for the following year.

When the National Sunday School Convention met at Indianapolis in 1872, Mr. Jacobs sponsored a resolution that called for a committee of 10 persons to be appointed, 5 to be clergymen and 5 lay persons. They were " to select a course of Bible lessons for a series of years not exceeding seven, which shall, as far as they may decide possible, embrace a general study of the Bible," to be recommended for adoption " by the Sunday schools of the whole country." The resolution was passed and the program set into motion. A succession of committees carried on the work during the following decades.

In 1925 the plan for the outlines that had originally been for all age groups was amended so that it no longer included those below the intermediate (junior high) level. This was because of a growing feeling that the same Scriptural passages that were used for adults were not always suitable for children. The name of the committee was at this time changed to the Committee on Improved Uniform Lessons.

For a number of years, outlines for youth and adults alone were prepared. But in 1945 Uniform Lesson plans were again made available for children below the junior high level, and the committee's name became the Committee on the Uniform Series. As such it continues to serve the participating denominations. Its membership has grown from the original 10 to about 75, representing about 30 denominational groups.

The committee prepares outlines covering a 6-year cycle. Each year is divided into quarters, usually composed of 13 lessons each. The quarterly divisions, frequently called units, mostly treat specific areas of the Bible. Sometimes subjects or themes are selected, and Biblical passages chosen to undergird them. In both instances the Bible is central. New cycles do not simply repeat the previous outlines, although the Scripture passages selected may occasionally overlap.

Individual lesson outlines include an overall title, a selection from the Bible, a specific topic for the age group involved, and a memory passage. Home Bible readings are also chosen to accompany each lesson. These are intended to be used in the devotional life of the family at home.

The outlines of the Committee on the Uniform Series are taken back to the several denominations where they become the basis for fully written lessons. They are usually adapted by the individual denominational groups to their particular needs, interests, and views. Sometimes the lesson description is rewritten on this level, but kept within the subject and Scripture selection of the general committee. In certain instances, denominations use only the adult outlines, preferring to develop their own closely graded curriculum for the other age groupings.

— Charles M. Laymon

UNIT OF STUDY A unit of study is a cluster, group, or chain of related experiences in a specific area, carefully planned and guided to help a person grow as a child of God. A unit extends over a varying number of sessions, the length dependent upon the theme or area to be covered and the needs and interests of the learners. Each session builds on what has gone before and prepares for what is to come until the goal has been reached or the problem solved. All the sessions together achieve a unity or " oneness " in the attempt to fulfill a given purpose.

Basically, units are of 2 types: subject-matter and experience units.

In the subject-matter unit selected materials are expected to be assimilated in order to produce a certain set of understandings, attitudes, or skills. The emphasis is on content and the method frequently used is transmissive in an attempt to assure a set standard of beliefs or particular skills in the use of the materials of the faith (such as the Bible, prayer-book, and catechism).

Experience units emphasize the processes of thinking, appraising, evaluating, and reaching conclusions. The creative group method of instruction is most often relied upon to help the person form habits of Christian thinking in becoming consciously a child of God.

Most units, however, contain elements of both subject matter and experience. The very process of assimilating selected content may be an experience through which the person rediscovers its meaning for him.

In similar fashion an experience unit must rely on content or subject matter for background in the task of developing habits of effective Christian thinking and acting.

A unit of study includes:

1. Specific purposes for both teacher and pupil. These purposes delineate the areas in which it is hoped growth will take place in helping persons think, act, and feel as children of God. The teacher must view these purposes and adapt them in the light of the needs of his own pupils. The teacher needs to know what the group already knows about the area in which the study is to take place, what experiences they have had, and how they feel about the proposed study.

2. Content for background and for the introduction of new experiences. The content may be derived from subject matter or experiences that persons have had in the past at church, or in the home, school, place of business, or from reading. This content is used in the development of new experiences or new materials that will make for a keener awareness, deeper insights, beckoning avenues of exploration, or new appreciations.

3. Activities for growth in specific areas. Most learning takes place through activity that is directed toward a goal when the learner understands the goal and sees some possibility of achieving it. Some activities are engaged in by the entire group. Others absorb the attention of small groups or committees with a common interest. Still others may be engaged in by individuals with specific interests or needs. Three types of activities may be a part of any unit of study: (*a*) Introductory activities. These activities come early in the unit. They stimulate interest in specific areas. They arouse a desire to know more. They provide background for the development of the unit. (*b*) Developmental activities. As background is gained ideas develop, interest is heightened, and thinking increases. The group and individuals within it begin to make choices, evaluate, sort out ideas, re-create and reorganize. Their understandings are deepened, lives enriched, and future experiences made meaningful. (*c*) Culminating activities. The goals are reached, the activity is shared, the work evaluated. Each group that has been engaged in an activity sees how its work has contributed to the larger plans of the whole group. There is preparation on the part of the teach-

er but the activities are planned by pupils and teacher together. The needs and the specialized interests of the group and individuals within the group are taken into consideration. Plans come to life when the unit includes the pupils and their ideas.

The unit of study will allow for a variety of activities. These may include guided study, individual or group research and reports, creative dramatics, role-playing, conversation or discussion, problem-solving, creative writing, picture study, hymn study, reading, painting, drawing, or other work with one's hands and head.

4. Worship, to lift the group above the level of the surroundings and into the presence of God. The culmination of a unit of study or an individual session within the unit with worship gives a sense that what has been done has been done " to the glory of God." As ideas, convictions, and experience are brought together in worship, each person gains perspective, a deeper awareness of himself and his relation to God, and power to meet problems along the way in his " becoming."

5. Resources for guiding and enriching the unit. Each unit of study provides for use of a variety of resources for the fulfillment of its purposes. These resources may be the Bible, denominational curriculum materials, people with special skills, community resources, books (for teachers and pupils), pictures, music, recordings, films and filmstrips, maps, globes, charts, story papers, etc. Their use provides background and content, stimulates ideas for next steps, clarifies ideas, raises important problems, and helps to solve them.

6. Evaluation. No unit of study is complete without evaluation. There may be periodic evaluations as the unit progresses. In these evaluations teachers ask: Are we achieving our purposes? Are we meeting the needs of our pupils in this area? Pupils ask themselves: How well are we doing our work? Is what we are doing contributing to the work of the whole group? What don't we (or I) understand? How can we make our class better? At the conclusion of a unit of study the teachers need to ask themselves: What learnings have taken place in content? What new subject matter has been assimilated? In skills is there greater facility in handling the materials of our faith? In day-to-day living have attitudes, habits of thinking, ways of acting, changed? The leader needs to look back at the purposes to see to what extent the purposes have been realized, what progress was made in helping each individual in his Christian growth, what evidences there are of response to the gospel of love and the will of God, what awarenesses developed of the relevance of the Christian faith to all of life.

The group also must evaluate the unit. Was it a worthwhile study? Why or why not? What was learned? What were the high and low points? Does it make sense in the face of everyday problems?

Such evaluation becomes the foundation of the preparation of a new unit.

Finally, a unit of study takes into consideration the fact that persons develop as children of God in relation to God and to one another. A person finds his deepest satisfactions within a group. His highest potentialities are most often developed within the give-and-take of the group. A unit of study makes provision for the needs of each individual in the group, but is carried on within the framework of the koinonia. — *Carolyn Muller Wolcott*

UNITARIAN UNIVERSALIST ASSOCIATION Religious education in the now merged American Unitarian Association and Universalist Church of America (united as the Unitarian Universalist Association) has roots extending far into the past. The 1st Universalist church school was established in Philadelphia by Benjamin Rush in 1790; the 1st Unitarian church school in Charles Lowell's Boston West Church in 1822.

Three major projects in curriculum building have emerged. The 1st, around the turn of the century, resulted in *The Beacon Series: A Graded Course of Study for the Sunday School*. The 2d, under the direction of Edwin Starbuck, was called *The Beacon Course in Religious Education*. The last, begun in 1936 under the leadership of Sophia Lyon Fahs, is called *The New Beacon Series in Religious Education*, and is subject to constant revision, new books being added each year.

In the Unitarian Universalist Association the published curriculum is looked upon as a library of resource materials from which the local church may select those portions which fit its individual needs. Having no creed to impart, the aim of the series is to help the children develop an adequate philosophy of life, for which it is believed that it is necessary to help them develop sound and adaptable personality structure, and to give them an adequate background of the Judeo-Christian tradition, and a wide view of all the manifestations of religion man has developed, together with a knowledge of where their own denomination fits into this cultural stream.

The nursery curriculum was devised after a careful survey of research in child development as to the interests, problems, and fears of children of the preschool years, and consists of stories calculated to raise these problems for open discussion.

In the primary years the aim is to help the children comprehend certain basic concepts needed for later religious growth: that all people and institutions are different, but to be different is neither good nor bad; that since growth is a process of learning, wrongdoing is primarily an immature way of behaving; that there are 2 basic sources of behavior — instinct, which is primarily the basis of animal behavior and non-adaptable, and learning, which is adaptable and is the primary source of man's behavior; that science offers us a method of thinking that can help children recognize both their place in the universe and the vastness and wonder of that universe; and that man has a long history of attempts to explain the universe and himself, many now discarded; that hence there are no final answers and truth as we see it now may yet change.

In the junior years this whole primary process is continued on a more complex level, with the introduction of myths of the world as related to answers about man's and the world's beginnings, as well as about life and death; the beginning of an attempt to understand the Judeo-Christian and other religious orientations, in the study of men who represent these: Moses, Jesus, Akhenaten. At the same time the curriculum is still presenting the problems of both interpersonal and intrapersonal relations for discussion and solution.

At the junior and senior high school level it then becomes possible, now that the historical time sense is well developed and the young people have achieved the capacity for abtract and logical thinking, to present the full sweep of religious history; this includes both Old and New Testaments, other world religions, the churches of our present environment, and their own unique religious heritage.

Each church works out its own arrangement and sequence of courses, drawing heavily upon *The New Beacon Series in Religious Education,* but also devising and experimenting with materials of its own. Thus the curriculum of any given Unitarian Universalist Association church will be unique, dynamic, and evolving, as is also the published curriculum of the Association as a whole.

In addition to the materials for children, the series contains books presenting the total philosophy for the parents, guides for the use of teachers, worship materials, and a wide assortment of pamphlets dealing with the varied problems of technique, concepts, and personal relations as these affect religious education. During the summer of 1960 the department initiated what is planned as a long-term program of research and evaluation.

— *Dorothy Tilden Spoerl*

UNITED CHRISTIAN ADULT MOVE-MENT

The United Christian Adult Movement was launched officially in the summer of 1936 at Conference Point Camp, Lake Geneva, Wis., when 207 lay and professional delegates of constituent units of the International Council of Religious Education and cooperating agencies gathered to give consideration to the development of plans and a program for such a movement. The move-

ment was launched under the joint sponsorship of the International Council, the Federal Council of Churches, and the agencies representing missionary interests and women's work in the church.

The roots of the movement stretch back through the years to the work done with adults by local churches of the several denominations. Slowly its importance was accepted by the International Council and the denominations. The earliest organized adult work was carried on by the International Sunday School Association whose program consisted primarily of promoting adult Bible classes. During the early years of the Council's history adult work was carried on by the Committee of Adult Work of the Educational Commission and the Adult Professional Advisory Section.

On the basis of their recommendation Harry C. Munro became the 1st director of adult work of the International Council. Three denominational leaders gave the movement great impetus. They were Charles Schofield, Glenn McRae, and Earl F. Zeigler.

Thirty-three professional workers in the adult field met in Chicago in 1930 and worked out an experimental *Program and Study Guide for Adult Work in the Local Church.* This was followed by a bulletin in 1931 entitled *The Religious Education of Adults.* The following February a meeting of the Adult Section of the Council using the theme, " The Religious Growth of Men and Women," enlisted the interest of a large number of pastors.

In 1932 the now-organized Committee on Religious Education of Adults undertook the preparation of courses on 5 units of study. Heretofore there were few adult classes using anything other than International Uniform Lessons. Already the United Christian Adult Movement was getting under way.

The movement gained a great impetus from the findings of E. I. Thorndike's study *Adult Learning*, which showed that effective adult learning never ceases and mature years with their background of experience make for a most effective period of learning.

It took imagination and courage to challenge the traditional view besetting church and society with regard to adult learning. From the Council and denominational leaders down to local churches the whole mental climate toward educating adults changed slowly.

The growing awareness on the part of directors of adult work, pastors, and educators of the limitations of preparing children and youth without comparable preparation of adults who really had the power of ordering society called for a growing emphasis on the education of adults. With support from the Carnegie Foundation, the American Association for Adult Education proposed that a survey of adult Christian education be made. They sought the advice and cooperation of the Council's department of adult work.

Christian education of adults had now become much more than a Bible class of men or women in the church school. The churchwide and communitywide functions of adult Christian education were set forth under 6 heads, suggesting that the church enlist and develop informed adult leadership; organize the total church program on a sound educational basis; educate for parenthood; prepare and organize church manpower to redeem the social order; provide for continuous religious growth of adults; secure commitment of others.

The year 1943 was marked by meetings of area adult groups in Chicago, New York, and the South. The larger Joint Committee on Family and Parent Education with wider representation assumed responsibility previously carried by the Subcommittee on Parent Education. They projected a *Guide to Christian Family Life and Parenthood*. A more comprehensive approach in adult Christian education now led to the council's 1934–1935 emphasis, " Christ the Light of the Home." In addition the 7 objectives in Christian education were increased to 9, one dealing with the home, the other with social ideas and groups. The 1935 section meeting was enlarged by inviting representatives of the Interdenominational Commission on Men's Work to participate.

In 1934 the comprehensive adult Christian education " Learning for Life " program was perfected, and it was launched in 1935 by the issuance of the booklet bearing that title. It became the basic structure for the United Christian Adult Movement. The interests and needs of adults were categorized in 6 areas: the Bible, Christian faith and experience, Christian family life, the church, social relations, and leadership education. Later a 7th was added, world relations. Existing texts suitable for use, along with references, were listed for each area. Four texts were in preparation in 1936 as courses of study in the " Learning for Life " program. *Home and Church Sharing in Christian Education* was published in 1936.

By now the United Christian Adult Movement was fully launched and received the official approval mentioned earlier. To carry the movement forward plans were made in 1937 for a United Christian Education Advance: preaching missions, schools in Christian living, and Christian community and world-building projects.

A 1938 conference and a growing interest in the family resulted in the holding of experimental family camps at Lake Geneva and the issuance of a bulletin on *Planning the Family Camp.*

The United Christian Adult Movement was constantly being broadened. Relations were established with nonchurch community agencies and interchurch cooperation increased. In the early 1940's some 361 denominational and interdenominational representatives and staff members were involved. Following the December, 1938, conference on the family jointly sponsored by the Council, the Federal Council, and the National Council of Church Women, an Inter-Church Committee on Family Life was created. After an initial observance Christian Family Week was made a national observance in 1943, with official endorsement of many mayors, governors, and the President of the U.S.A. This became an interfaith enterprise in 1944. The whole impact of the war years limited activity and turned concern toward conservation of the family in wartime. Family counseling became important. In 1945 the movement concerned itself with returning Armed Service personnel and men and women in industry. A corollary was the developing ecumenical movement.

Young Adults in the Church was rewritten and *Learning for Life* was revised to include 40 new texts and course references. *Pages of Power,* a national family week devotional, received wide use. The White House

Conference on Family Life in May, 1948, gave the movement broader relationships and resulted in new depth. Twenty years from roots to fruits of the United Christian Adult Movement made a real impact on the life of adult Christians.

— *Oscar J. Rumpf*

UNITED CHRISTIAN YOUTH MOVEMENT Affiliated with the National Council of the Churches of Christ in the U.S.A., the United Christian Youth Movement is authorized by the churches as the " official channel for youth cooperation." Its purpose is defined as that of being " an organized expression of the movement of young people and their adult leaders who are joined together in Jesus Christ as divine Lord and Savior, and who are seeking to fulfill their mission in Christ by sharing their convictions, concerns, and experiences, as they face together contemporary problems, making their witness through prayer, study, and action."

As constituted in 1934 by the Christian Youth Council of North America, the movement was characterized by an emphasis on social action. The 1st theme was " Christian Youth Building a New World." Representative councils, composed of youth delegates from Christian churches and youth-serving agencies, attempted to devise a nationwide strategy for the mobilization of Christian youth in study and action projects. The program included a scholarship fund, annual observance of Youth Week, and efforts in behalf of world peace.

The meeting of the World Council of Christian Youth in Oslo, Norway, in 1947, reflected the growth of the faith and order movement. The ensuing theological and ecclesiastical emphasis within the UCYM itself coincided with the organization of the NCCCUSA and resulted in a reformulation of bylaws. Participation and membership in the movement were restricted to youth organizations and agencies of communions clearly professing "Jesus Christ as divine Lord and Savior."

The General Council was established as the governing body of the national UCYM. Representation at the annual meeting was achieved in accordance with the following formula: 4 youths and 1 adult from the interdenominational youth council of each state, 2 youths and 1 adult from each related group, and the officers and staff of the movement. The category "related groups" was defined to include "any youth-serving agency endeavoring to promote a constructive program of cooperative action and service among its youth members and serving some of the youth of the churches holding membership in the UCYM."

Officers of the movement were 3 executive officers and 5 commission chairmen elected by the General Council. The executive secretary of the UCYM and the chairman of the Committee on Youth Work of the NCCCUSA were also named to the executive committee and the cabinet. The commissions, designated earlier with the adoption by the UCYM of the "common commission plan for youth work," were Christian faith, witness, outreach, citizenship, and fellowship. Their functions at General Council included the provision of an opportunity for the sharing of program, projects, and materials; of witnessing to a common faith; and of outlining a program of cooperative study and action to be administered directly by denominations or by the staff of the movement. The

executive staff of the UCYM was the executive staff of the Department of Youth Work of the Commission on General Christian Education of the NCCCUSA. Denominations affiliating with the UCYM contributed to its budget directly through the Division of Christian Education of the National Council.

By 1959 approximately 35 denominations had indicated their intention of continued participation in the movement on the basis of the bylaws.

In 1950 the "Call to United Christian Youth Action" was issued, its goal the commitment of 1,000,-000 youth to united Christian action and the securing of $1,000,000 for youth work around the world during Youth Week, 1952. World Youth Projects, a program of ecumenical aid now administered through the Youth Departments of the World Council of Churches and the World Council of Christian Education, was a direct result. The conference program continued with international affairs seminars, regional training conferences, and, until 1952, the quadrennial Christian Youth Conferences of North America. Work in evangelism focused on the television series *Look Up and Live*, directed at nonchurched youth. Local and state Christian youth councils fulfilled purposes of sharing, planning, serving, training, and witnessing through the observance of Youth Week, weekend and summer work camps, faith and order studies, and examinations of youth culture.

An evaluation begun in 1959 with the 25th anniversary of UCYM, the ecumenical emphasis being provided by the European and North American Ecumenical Youth Assemblies and the New Delhi Assembly of the World Council of Churches, and changing patterns in denominational youth fellowships caused a decisive redirection of the movement. The General Council of 1961 subordinated the functions of cooperative planning and sharing to the purpose of the renewal of the church in its nature and mission, in accordance with an understanding of the " gospel's promises and relevance to, and the nature of, the world for which Christ died." It envisioned the occurrence of ecumenical study and conversation in the general form of representative councils, with the provision that the ongoing tasks of ecumenical and/or interdenominational youth work should be accepted as the direct responsibility of departments of youth work. It affirmed, however, " that youth work is concerned with the total life, mission, and renewal of the church " and should not be subjected to the traditional confines of a Christian education structure. In order to clarify purposes and provide rules of structure and procedure, the Council authorized the UCYM officers and staff to draft a statement of purposes and principles of ecumenical youth work and/or a general plan of organization " providing for the continuation of some channels of ecumenical encounter among the denominational youth leadership of our country."— *Lela Anne Garner*

UNITED CHURCH OF CANADA

The United Church of Canada was formed on June 10, 1925, a union of the Methodist, Presbyterian, and Congregational traditions. Each of the denominational groups brought into the United Church attitudes and practices in Christian education that had much in common.

The heritage of the 3 denominational groups included: (1) A con-cern for the Sunday school as a principal agency for Christian education. (2) Participation in cooperative religious education associations. While these associations, nationally and provincially, consisted mainly of interested persons rather than official representatives, the denominations were interested, supportive, and involved. (3) Highly developed, successful, and significant national church movements for 12- to 17-year-old boys and girls. These movements were not coeducational but provided separate groups for boys and girls. The girls' movement was known as Canadian Girls in Training (CGIT), and the boys' movement was known as Trail Ranger and Tuxis. Although these movements were centered in the local church they derived much strength from rallies, conferences, and camps for boys, girls, and leaders. (4) A varied practice in relation to young people's work. (5) A point of view in Christian education that largely reflected the attitudes of the parent denominations. Some of these concerns were Bible knowledge, Christian commitment, Christian morality, the life situation approach, and the example of Jesus that provided a way of life.

Even before the union of the churches was consummated, plans were being worked out for a national denominational young people's movement that would provide a major responsibility for young people themselves. During the first 10 years of union this national United Church young people's organization grew rapidly, demonstrating the way in which young people and professional workers could work together.

In 1928 there arose a strong concern for denominational graded curriculum. As a result of this, Frank Langford and George A. Little, in cooperation with Christian education secretaries and committees, and the Sunday School Publication editors produced *The Canadian Graded Series of Sunday School Lessons.* These were 1st used in October, 1930.

Another important development of this period was the creation of the Canadian Series of Leadership Training Courses. Charles A. Myers was largely responsible for this development.

One of the major tasks of the Board of Christian Education in cooperation with the Board of Evangelism and Social Service was the formulation of a new Statement of Faith and a United Church Catechism. The 3 churches came into union with doctrinal statements that were contained in a Basis of Union. However, it was felt necessary to prepare a further statement in the language of the day. As a result the Statement of Faith appeared in 1938 and the Catechism in 1944. Both these publications found ready acceptance in the church and brought about extensive study and discussion of theological questions.

During the depression years there grew up in Christian education circles a great concern for a Christian social order, and young people and teen-agers became involved in many social concerns and service projects.

Canada was involved in World War II for a longer period than some other countries, leading to an alarming loss of teachers, leaders, and members of adult classes. During this period the religious education associations gave way to the organization of provincial councils of Christian education and the Religious Education Council of Canada.

These organizations consisted of a larger percentage of members who were officially appointed representatives of the participating denominations.

Although the Board of Christian Education was closely related to the interdenominational developments in Canada, it maintained a strong link with the work of the International Council of Religious Education and participated fully in international committees. Because of this the United Church was fully involved in the international study related to the theological foundations of Christian education. When the final report of this study appeared it was used extensively throughout the church and provided a new concern for the relation of theology and Christian education.

During the period 1925 to 1952 Christian education assumed responsibilities for the age groups. Special functions such as religious education in schools, work with older adults, Christian family life, couples clubs, and church camping were added. There are now nearly 90 campsites related to the work of the United Church across Canada.

The 1950's brought a number of important developments. A Christian Youth Caravan movement developed, enrolling each summer about 140 young people who gave parts of their summer on a volunteer basis to work in vacation church schools, frontier areas, new housing developments, and service projects in institutions. A coeducational movement called Hi-C was developed for high school boys and girls. These groups, meeting for the most part in churches, tended to push the ages of those belonging to youth groups into the age bracket of 18 to 25 years.

The residential Christian Workers' Lay Centers, the 1st of which was initiated at Naramata in 1947, provide long-term residential courses for lay persons, specialized short-term events such as retreats and vocational conferences, and extensive summer programs. Four such centers now exist, 1 each in British Columbia, Saskatchewan, Ontario, and Nova Scotia.

One of the most important developments was the preparation of a new curriculum for the Sunday church school as a result of an action of the General Council in 1952. Christian education secretaries, editors, and publishers have produced *Curriculum Presuppositions* and a curriculum plan. The new cycle-graded curriculum provides 3 annual themes: "God and His Purpose," "Jesus Christ and the Christian Life," and "The Church and the World." The focus of the concern is Christ in relation to persons. It gives attention to 2 factors, the content of the gospel and the necessity for the gospel's affecting the lives of persons here and now in the Christian community. This curriculum will start with adults because of the conviction that effective work with children presupposes informed and committed adults in the church. A preparation period related to the new curriculum emphasizes the need for a supporting community in the church, a knowledge and experience of the Christian message, a sense of call by every church member, and a rebirth of the sense of the koinonia in local churches.

The trends for the future that seem to be taking shape are as follows: further unification of Christian education with men's and women's work so that a total and unified approach may be found in the local church; an increased emphasis on the church itself as the principal teaching agency. — *David I. Forsyth*

UNITED CHURCH OF CHRIST The United Church of Christ is the product of the 1957 union of the Evangelical and Reformed Church and the General Council of the Congregational Christian Churches. The process of union was completed in 1961 when the 3d General Synod adopted the constitution that had prior to that time received approval by the vast majority of synods (Evangelical and Reformed) and local churches (Congregational Christian). Parish educational work of the United Church is the responsibility of the Board for Homeland Ministries, Division of Christian Education. The Division of Higher Education and the American Missionary Association of that Board express the denomination's interests in higher education in cooperation with the Council for Higher Education.

The United Church's heritage is one that demonstrates a persistent concern for a literate laity and clergy. The Pilgrim and Puritan clergymen in the early years of the Plymouth and Massachusetts Bay Colonies were graduates of Oxford and Cambridge. The Congregational concern for learning was expressed in the founding of Harvard in 1636 and in the Massachusetts law of 1647 directing that every town of 50 dwellings should have a primary school and every town of 100 dwellings a grammar school. The former action signified the beginning of university education in America, the latter the development of public elementary and secondary education. The Congregational passion for learning gave birth to Yale, Dartmouth, Williams, Bowdoin, Middlebury, and Amherst. As Congregationalists moved westward, a string of other colleges such as Oberlin, Grinnell, and Doane were founded.

The 1st of several Congregational educational societies, the American Society for the Education of Pious Youth for the Gospel Ministry, was founded and incorporated in 1816. The several societies that developed in subsequent years were brought into one as the Congregational Education Society, founded in 1892. In 1938 the Education Society joined with 6 other independent bodies of Congregationalism in the fields of education, publishing, and home missions to form the Board of Home Missions.

Congregationalists were also pioneers in educating the Negro in America. They founded elementary and secondary schools, academies and colleges, in most Southern states after the Civil War. While most of these schools have become part of the public school system, 6 excellent colleges remain as the symbol of both the South's past and its future.

The Christian Endeavor Society was founded in 1881 by a Congregational minister, Francis E. Clark. It enjoyed wide influence and service in Congregational churches until the development of the Pilgrim Fellowship movement, which since 1934 has been the major youth program of the Congregational Christian Churches.

For those of the Reformed heritage who emigrated from the Palatinate to Pennsylvania, the 1st service of worship was held in 1725 as John Philip Boehm celebrated Holy Communion at Falkner Swamp. In 1746 Michael Schlatter organized these churches into a coetus. A few years later Schlatter founded a church school at First Church, Easton, Pa.

This building and church school have been in continuous service since that time. The Christian education of Reformed churchmen in the early years in America came primarily from the Bible and the Heidelberg Catechism under the guidance of pastors sent to the colonies by the Church of Holland. After the Revolution the Reformed churches became completely free of the Church of Holland.

Franklin College (founded by Benjamin Franklin in 1787 and joined later with Marshall College to form Franklin and Marshall) and Lancaster Seminary (established 1825 in Carlisle, Pa.) were early testimonies to the Reformed emphasis on education.

At the 1st General Synod of the Reformed Church in 1863, a Sunday School Board was organized. Its several successors developed Christian education resources for the Reformed Church until the merger with the Evangelical Synod of North America in 1934.

Evangelical Synod churchmen originated in Germany at the time of the great American migrations westward. They settled along the Mississippi and the Missouri with St. Louis as the center of their activity. Their life reflected Lutheran as well as Reformed influences. Both Luther's Catechism and the Heidelberg Catechism were essentials in the list of possessions they brought with them to America.

In 1840 the Kirchenverein des Westens was formed. It existed 1st as a ministerial association but by 1849 Evangelical congregations were included in its membership. By 1866 it had assumed synodical character. One of its firstfruits was the Evangelical Catechism published in 1847. In 1850, Marthasville, Mo., became the locale for a theological seminary (the present Eden Theological Seminary in Webster Groves, Mo.). Elmhurst College started as a proseminary in 1867 to train teachers for parochial schools of the Evangelical churches and to prepare students for Eden. A Sunday School Board was established by the Evangelical Synod in 1894.

Ministers in each of these traditions served as pastors and teachers to their congregations. Those of the Evangelical and Reformed churches were actually schoolmasters and taught in the parochial schools that the churches maintained before the development of public schools in their areas.

The Congregational Churches united with the Evangelical Protestant Churches in 1925 and in 1931 with the churches of the Christian Connection. The former group consisted mostly of people of German and German Swiss background who settled in Pennsylvania and in the greater Cincinnati area. The Christian group had strength in Vermont, in the eastern Midwest, and in North Carolina and Virginia. The Christian denomination was the 1st indigenous one in America. Its newspaper, *The Herald of Gospel Liberty,* was the 1st American religious newspaper. It was among the first to advocate coeducation and the use of women ministers.

When the Evangelical and Reformed Church was formed in 1934, a Board of Christian Education and Publication was established in which most of the publication and education interests of the 2 parent churches were expressed.

In 1947 the Board of Christian Education and Publication together with the Congregational Christian Division of Christian Education and The Pilgrim Press began cooperative production of curriculum materials. Two curriculum series, identical in most aspects, were developed. *Pilgrim Series* was the Congregational Christian version, *Church and Home Series* that of the Evangelical and Reformed.

When litigation and a court injunction that had delayed the process of union in 1950 were resolved in favor of merger, the 2 educational staffs began the development of a curriculum for the United Church. The 1st meetings were held in 1952 and the 1st materials were off the press in 1960.

The United Church Curriculum takes seriously the emphasis of the United Church Statement of Faith upon the deeds of God. These materials accent the meeting of God with man and of man with man. The church is seen as the context for Christian nurture (the 1st published course intended for nursery age was called *3's in the Christian Community*). Teaching is seen as " one form of proclamation of the gospel " and its task as " the conscious effort to stimulate the learning process."

While taking seriously the developmental task idea, *The United Church Curriculum* lifts up 3 unique Christian tasks as central: to become a whole person; to develop trustful and responsible relations with others; to grow in relation to God (cf. Matt. 22:37-40).

Jesus Christ is represented both as Very God and as very man (though these terms are not used in children's materials). In the materials, God is portrayed as Creator, Sustainer, Judge, and Redeemer. The Holy Spirit is seen to be the educator.

The curriculum is built on a 2-year cycle with two 5-month semesters and a 10-week summer term each year. The 6 semesters rely on 1 of the following unifying themes: "Growing as a Christian"; "Exploring Our Christian Heritage"; "Christian Living with One Another"; "Responding to God's Love"; "Belonging to the Christian Fellowship"; "Living in God's World."

The Bible is central. It is seen as "man's record of God's activity in the world. It declares what God has done, is doing, and eternally stands ready to do. It describes the possibilities of response that are opened up to man, and tells how man has both defied and followed God's will."

The curriculum views Christian education as the invitation into and initiation and nurture within the community of faith in which Christ is remembered, known, and present. It is also participation in the mission of Christ and the church in all the world.

The family is not seen primarily as an extension of the church school but as a nurturing matrix in its own right. Therefore, extensive materials are prepared to help the family interpret its life in Christian terms.

Magazines in the United Church of Christ that support and extend this point of view include *Children's Religion, Church School Worker,* and *Youth.* — *Edward A. Powers*

UNITED CHURCH WOMEN United Church Women (UCW), a general department of the National Council of the Churches of Christ in the U.S.A. brings together in 1 cooperative movement the work of women in the churches eligible to National Council membership. It often describes itself as the "women of the denominations working together." Though an integral part of the struc-

ture of the National Council, it is autonomous in regard to the organizing, programming, and financing of its own work. More than 2,200 local councils are affiliated with UCW; there are state councils in all states and the District of Columbia.

United work among churchwomen is a "movement" as well as an organization. The early dream of uniting across church lines has been dynamic and creative across 60 years, not only increasing women's effectiveness but opening up new concerns, bringing women into close association with the ecumenical movement, and leading them forward toward full participation in the total life of the church, whose leadership, far into the present century, has been traditionally conservative in regard to the place of women.

The work of United Church Women is structured under 6 program committees and a finance committee; it is supported by state and denominational quotas and individual gifts.

Christian World Missions strengthens the interdenominational missionary effort by giving help to local missions institutes and by sponsoring the World Day of Prayer for Missions. The latter is now observed in 145 areas of the world, and offerings on that day support a variety of home and foreign missions projects, such as education for women overseas and work for migrants in this country, in which women pioneered. The 75th anniversary of the World Day of Prayer in March, 1961, was marked in the U.S.A. by an offering of approximately $700,000.

Christian Social Relations promotes a program of study and action in the areas of Christian family life, youth, economics and industrial relations, race relations and civil liberties, and keeps women informed on relevant legislation. Its special spring observance, May Fellowship Day, each year emphasizes some current community problem needing united effort, e.g., " Free Schools in a Free America " (1960).

Christian World Relations, with World Community Day in November, emphasizes the contribution of churchwomen to world peace by a yearly study-discussion program on contemporary issues (" Freedom to Know," 1961), by maintaining an observer at the United Nations, and by projects of material aid. Millions of bundles of food and medical supplies were sent to refugee camps after World War II, and more recently gifts of money have helped make possible self-help projects for women in emerging countries in Africa, the Pacific Islands, and South America.

Leadership Training supplies guidance and materials for developing local leadership, and stimulates the holding of local, regional, and national workshops for this purpose.

Public Relations makes use of all communications media to keep the public and especially churchwomen informed of special events, and helps train local women in the effective use of press, radio, television, films, and visual aids.

The Church Woman (monthly circulation, 38,000), the only interdenominational magazine published by women for women, is a channel of interpretation and information, and an important factor in maintaining unity and common purpose within the movement.

United work grew up around " days of prayer for missions," which date from 1887. Open to women of all churches in a community, these observances engendered a sense of " oneness " that was new and meaningful. In a number of cities, continuing " missionary federations " and " unions " were organized to promote this observance and mission study, and their numbers increased throughout the years before World War I. Sponsored in a general way by local federations of churches, they knew little about one another, however, and had no organized program.

Changes in American life in the postwar 1920's directly affected the lives of women. The advent of women's suffrage, the rapid increase in the employment of women, the coming of motion pictures, the automobile, and the speakeasy wakened women to greater social responsibility. It was not strange that many local mission unions added social problems to their traditional interest in missions, but in these new concerns they could hardly expect guidance from the mission boards.

In December, 1924, the Federal Council of Churches called for a conference at Pittsburgh of representatives of the Council, the Women's Committee of the Board of Foreign Missions, and the Council of Women for Home Missions to discuss the future of such local groups. The St. Louis conference in 1927 expressed a desire for a central organization " through which the work of local interdenominational groups of women may be correlated, systematized, and promoted." In Buffalo, 1928, a National Commission of Protestant Church Women was authorized under the joint auspices of the 3 bodies. Many, however, felt that something more than a " guiding commission " was needed, and at the Boston conference in 1929 after much discussion and some tension the National Council of Federated

Church Women (NCFCW) emerged as an independent organization.

A more difficult time than the depression of 1929 to launch a national organization could scarcely have been found. NCFCW began without funds and without staff, but the devoted work and contributions of women who believed that united work was important kept it alive. The national office was moved to modest quarters in Kansas City (1933) and later to Chicago (1937). Efforts were made to secure the affiliation of existing Day of Prayer groups, to develop a sense of unity and a common program. For most of its work, NCFCW was dependent on cooperative arrangements with other interdenominational bodies. It was a decade in which the women's organization was trying to find itself.

By 1938 a better defined and integrated structure was clearly called for. The pattern for this emerged in 1941, when after long preparation the constitution for a United Council of Church Women was adopted at Atlantic City, Dec., 1941, with a national purpose that has remained unchanged since: "To unite churchwomen in their allegiance to their Lord and Savior, Jesus Christ, through a program leading to their integration in the total life and work of the church and to the building of a world Christian community."

The new organization came into being just as the U.S.A. entered World War II, and a great concern for building lasting peace and for new social issues led to greatly increased activity. Of special concern during this period was the development of local councils and strong volunteer leadership.

Meanwhile, the idea of some overarching body to bring together and correlate the work of the major interdenominational church agencies was growing. UCW was a member of the Committee for Closer Relations Among Inter-Church Agencies from the beginning, but the decision to join such a merger could not be made without a realistic consideration of the present status of women in the churches. Would the effect of such a merger be to facilitate or to hamper the women's program? The answer could not be taken for granted. Yet churchwomen were without question ecumenically minded, and wished above all to be associated with any forward movement in the churches. Careful work on bylaws that would safeguard the continued identity and autonomous nature of the women's program opened the way, and by the overwhelmingly affirmative vote of its Board of Managers, the United Council of Church Women became one of the constituting members of the NCCCUSA at the Cleveland Convention, Dec. 1950, as the General Department of United Church Women.

In the decade since, the wisdom of the decision has not been under question: churchwomen have increasingly participated in the work of every department and committee of the National Council, and at the same time their own program has continued to grow. UCW has been able to speak out effectively on subjects of special concern to women. It has contributed significantly to joint studies in the field of the laity and of employed women, and has exercised effective leadership in church and community, especially in race relations, a field in which its own long interracial experience has enabled it to move forward courageously. — *Gladys G. Calkins*

UNITED PRESBYTERIAN CHURCH IN THE U.S.A., THE The United Presbyterian Church in the United States of America is a communion with Reformed theology and representative government. The word "presbyterian" comes from the Greek word for "elder." In the courts of the Presbyterian Church there is for every minister who has a vote an elder also having a vote. The 1st visit by Presbyterians to America was recorded in 1562 when the French Huguenots went to Florida and South Carolina. Other Presbyterians settled in Virginia and Massachusetts, and by 1706 the 1st presbytery was formed.

The earliest Presbyterian educational concern in America was in the training of ministers. At the beginning, young men were trained by means of personal studies with ministers. Another early concern was the Christian nurture of children. In 1819 a national Board of Education was organized in order that Sunday school material might be prepared. The church took care of the children and young people in local churches by teaching them the faith, but when it came time for their young men and women to secure a higher education, the Presbyterians felt that there needed to be more colleges. As people moved west and settled new land, colleges were formed to train Presbyterian young people in the "knowledge and admonition of the Lord."

Today there are over 3,200,000 adult members. There are 9,222 churches with over 12,000 ministers. The church school enrollment is over 1,900,000.

In the United Presbyterian Church there are 4 governing bodies. The individual congregation is ruled by a session; a group of congregations in a geographical area is ruled by a presbytery; a group of presbyteries form a synod. The national church body is called the General Assembly.

The session is composed of the pastors and the men and/or women elected by the congregation to the position of elder. It has responsibility for the spiritual life of the congregation. This responsibility includes worship, education, evangelism, organizational life, stewardship, and mission.

In the educational thrust of an individual church the session has responsibility for policy, administration, facilities, faculty, leadership training, and finances. Because Christian education is a major work of a congregation, the session often gives the responsibility of these 6 functions to a committee of session called the Christian Education Committee. The session must still review and approve the major decisions of this committee.

A typical educational program of a congregation might be as follows:
1. Church school. Children, youth, and adults are grouped into 7 departments: nursery (birth to 3 years), kindergarten (4 to 5 years), primary (grades 1 to 3), junior (grades 4 to 6), junior high (grades 7 to 9), senior high (grades 10 to 12), and adults. The entire department meets for a period of worship, audio-visuals, and some instruction. Most of the instruction time is spent in classes where each grade has its own teacher. A superintendent is the administrator for each department. Teachers are selected from the congregation, because only those from the community of faith can share faith. Materials are prepared by the

national Board of Christian Education for the pastor's use in training teachers.

2. Women's circle study groups. Most Presbyterian churches today have a women's association. The educational program of the association is carried on through study circles. These groups meet either in the daytime or evening, studying the Bible, mission, and social issues. The women of a local congregation are affiliated with other Presbyterian women in presbyterial, synodical, and national organizations. Study materials are produced nationally for the circle studies.

3. Youth fellowship groups. The typical Presbyterian church has fellowship groups for its junior and senior high young people. These organizations are more than social groups, for they deal with such concerns as social relationships, death, vocation, social ills of the community, alcohol education, preparation for marriage, and theological questions. The young people are given much freedom to decide the direction and curriculum of the group.

4. Church family nights. Many churches are offering families an opportunity to study at church family nights. Usually there is a dinner, followed by age-group classes on a mission or social action theme. These are usually held in the pre-Lenten season and run for 4 to 6 weeks.

5. Special adult education. Many of the larger churches make a special effort to have an adult education program outside the regular church school hours. One pattern is the small Bible study group; another is occasional or regular gatherings by vocation; a 3d is a "lay academy" offering several courses over a period of a few weeks; a 4th pattern is education offered for those who are officers in the church — elders, deacons, trustees, teachers.

The courses of study used in the local churches are prepared in the *Christian Faith and Life* curriculum, published by the Board of Christian Education. This curriculum is written with the understanding that the Bible is the basic textbook; that the curriculum will be theologically consistent with the Reformed faith; that its purpose is to bring people to Jesus Christ; that it will attempt to involve people in committing their life to the mission of the church; that it is church-centered; and that the best Biblical scholarship is used. The curriculum is written with the expectation that the parents of children and youth are teaching in partnership with the church school. To help accomplish this the courses of study are given to the parents in order that they might understand what should be taught in a given period of time. Reading books are provided for each pupil. Three annual themes constitute the curriculum cycle: Jesus Christ, the Bible, and the church.

Forty-eight 4-year colleges and 3 junior colleges are related to the church. On 155 university campuses an educational ministry is being conducted. There is now a program of ongoing education for pastors. All the synods have leadership schools for teachers and other leaders of local churches. Over 50,000 young people attended summer camps and conferences during 1961.

Some of the more recent educational thrusts of this denomination are as follows: All the seminaries involved in curriculum improvements, several of them having group teaching; a renewed interest in the church and participation in cultic events by those in the church's school; training of adults for the mission in the world; training of church leaders; an increase of group teaching in children's departments; church school hours identical with worship hours in larger churches; increased use of audio-visuals; education for mission woven into the regular curriculum; a desire to have young people think through and develop their theological beliefs in junior high and senior high years; an interest in the use of teaching machines; an increased concern with educational opportunities surrounding baptism and confirmation. — *Ellis H. Butler*

UNITY OF THE BRETHREN The roots of the Unity of the Brethren are embedded in the pre-Reformation movement of 15th-century Bohemia. Impetus for its development was the fearless preaching of John Hus. His ringing proclamation and bold application of Scriptural truths to the conditions and needs of his day resulted in great personal popularity and influence, but also contained the seeds of his martyrdom and the subsequent development of the Unity of the Brethren.

Following the condemnation of Hus by the established church and his martyrdom, his followers, in 1457, founded a fellowship, the Unitas Fratrum, or Unity of the Brethren, which was dedicated to fostering the principles for which he lived and died. The growth of this fellowship from the outset was phenomenal. Persecution by the established church, however, ultimately succeeded in declaring the existence of the Unitas Fratrum illegal. Deci-

mation and dispersion of the membership followed. A significant result of the dispersion into Germany is the Moravian Church of today. Those who remained in Bohemia are commonly referred to as "the hidden seed."

Descendants of "the hidden seed" began to migrate to Texas in the mid-19th century. For the most part they arrived either as Lutherans or Reformed, but still harboring the desire to reestablish the ancient Unitas Fratrum. That dream was realized in 1903 when the Evangelical Union of Bohemian-Moravian Brethren united the various individual congregations scattered throughout the state into 1 body. Merger with a body of independent Brethren congregations in 1915 resulted in the official name: The Evangelical Unity of the Czech-Moravian Brethren in North America. In 1959, the name was officially changed to Unity of the Brethren.

Christian life, the only true evidence of doctrinal perfection, has been from the beginning the object of the Unity of the Brethren. Still numerically small and limited in resources, the Unity of the Brethren has no institutions of higher learning. However, the requirement of education at approved seminaries for all ministers in spite of a continuing shortage, the annual 6 to 8 weeks' leadership training course conducted for laymen, and characteristic regular catechetical instruction indicate the recognized importance of Christian education.
— *Daniel J. Marek*

UNIVERSAL BIBLE SUNDAY Variously observed now on the 1st or 2d Sunday in December, Universal Bible Sunday traces its origin to the centennial of the British and Foreign Bible Society, celebrated March 6, 1904. On that date the American Bible Society joined the British and Foreign Bible Society in inviting believers throughout the world to make appropriate recognition of Bible Day. Preparing for its own centennial, the American Bible Society proposed that churches observe Dec. 5, 1915, as Universal Bible Sunday. The Society's 100th anniversary was celebrated with another Universal Bible Sunday on May 7, 1916, in "reverent thanksgiving for the achievements in translation, publication, and circulation of the Scriptures throughout this long and wonderful period." On Dec. 10, 1916, the anniversary year was concluded with still another Universal Bible Sunday.

Meanwhile, the ecclesiastical year had long had a day for worshipers to express gratitude for the written Word as part of their preparation for welcoming the Word incarnate. From 1549, the date of the 1st Prayer Book of King Edward VI, Anglicans had used on the 2d Sunday in Advent the collect by Archbishop Cranmer praying that God who "caused all holy Scriptures to be written for our learning" would enable his people so to "read, mark, learn, and inwardly digest them" that they would be enabled to "hold fast the blessed hope of everlasting life." The epistle for the day is Rom. 15:4-13. Because the civil calendar does not always coincide with the ecclesiastical year, the 2d Sunday in Advent sometimes falls on the 1st, sometimes on the 2d, Sunday in December. Accordingly, Universal Bible Sunday has been expanded to Universal Bible Week, with ministers and congregations urged to emphasize either on the 1st or the 2d Sunday in December "the place of the Scriptures in the life of the nation," with offerings "taken for the circulation of the Scriptures in local communities and throughout the world."

Since 1943 the American Bible Society has made Universal Bible Week a high point of its Worldwide Bible-reading Program, extending each year from Thanksgiving to Christmas. — *J. Carter Swaim*

UNIVERSITY *Universitatis,* as the word was used in the Middle Ages, meant a society. By the end of the 12th century it was being applied to guilds of masters or students. Thus universities, from the start, were social institutions, whether the community was one of learners, as at Bologna, founded in the 12th century, or of scholars, as at Paris and Oxford, established by the early 13th century. Two impulses gave life to these societies. One was the impulse of the individual human mind to seek knowledge, and yet more knowledge, to push the frontiers of the known ever farther; the other, that of the community to pass on its accumulated heritage of knowledge and wisdom to its young, partly for their own enrichment, but partly to train them for the higher functions in society.

Thus in the 12th and 13th centuries scholars hurried through Europe on their quest for knowledge, buzzing round the honeypots of Chartres, then Paris, then Oxford, entering with passion into every philosophical controversy.

Yet already universities were becoming great schools for training the learned professions; e.g., Salerno for medicine, Bologna for law. The uses of higher education in building and maintaining the fabric of society were soon grasped by rulers and governments. Thus many universities founded in the later Middle Ages were created for social or political purposes, whether civic, such as Perugia, Montpellier, Erfurt, or princely, such as Naples, Prague, Heidelberg. Always there has existed a tension between the 2 impulses — between the almost timeless activity of the mind, withdrawn from contemporary pressures and remote from useful skills, and the practical training of a next generation of citizens — yet both have needed the same society in which to flourish. Higher education has never been a solitary process.

The striking feature of these early universities was that the whole enterprise of human learning was developed within a Christian framework. Both the impulses directing the pursuit of knowledge were placed *sub specie aeternitatis*. Knowledge was pursued, not for its own sake, but " to attain to a knowledge of the Creator through a knowledge of the created world "; useful sciences were acquired in order that God might be served through church and state. The Reformation did not radically modify this concept. Thus the Oxford Bidding Prayer continued to place the activities of the university under God's blessing: " And that there may never be wanting a succession of persons duly qualified for the service of God in Church and State, ye shall implore His blessing on all places of religious and useful learning, particularly on our Universities, . . . that here and in all places specially set apart for God's honour and service, true religion and sound learning may for ever flourish." The real break came in the mid-19th century when, in revolt against a framework that had now become a straitjacket, new state and civic universities arose in which theology was barred and service to God in the pursuit of knowledge denied. This coincided with a vast expansion first of the natural sciences, and then of the applied sciences, as activities that belonged to the university. The map of knowledge altered beyond recognition, old disciplines were jostled by new competitors, laboratories came to rank with, and then above, libraries. Above all, the old encyclopedists vanished; scholars became specialists and knowledge increasingly fragmented. By a curious paradox, however, the very fragmentation of knowledge has brought researchers more and more closely together in teamwork and shared enterprises.

Until this century the university, whether in its religious or secular form, remained essentially a product of Western civilization, first in Europe, then in the Americas. The characteristic of the mid-20th century is the phenomenal growth of universities throughout the world, sometimes still under Western influence but often in extremely non-Western soils. Everywhere knowledge is sought, either for its own sake or, increasingly, as useful technical power in the community. Everywhere it is placed in a purely human context. Freedom from any religious obligation, either in the pursuit of knowledge or in the exercise of its power, is claimed as the precious right to " academic freedom," and this claim to freedom is now as characteristic of the older religious foundations as of the new secular ones.

The breakaway from what had become a bondage was salutary and necessary. We now see that the autonomy of the various disciplines of learning is part of the intellectual birthright of man. But to the Christian, nothing can alter the fact that that birthright is given and therefore must be answered for by responsible use. Either of the 2 motives in getting knowledge can become irresponsible if divorced for long from the other; both go rotten at the core if pursued without reference to values beyond themselves. Thus academic purposes that do not strike their roots deep into eternal things produce poisoned fruits. The pursuit of knowledge for its own sake can be corrupted into ivory-tower escapism, into the academic neutrality of those who refuse to enter human commitment, into the idolatry of those who worship the Ph.D. or the scholar's reputation. Or again, learning can be debased into a means to a better job, or enslaved to give power over nature and man, or corrupted into an instrument for conditioning the minds and wills of the next generation.

The final breakdown of the original Christian framework has produced in this mid-20th century a crop of writings examining the nature of the university and its problems. Attention has been focused on the issue of framework or fragmentation. Can or ought there to be a legitimate framework holding all the specialisms together? On the other hand, must there not inevitably be at least a frame of reference in the sense of a set of concealed presuppositions about the "worthness" of this academic enterprise? Are not the academic neutrals blind guides of the young, but are not the "sighted" dangerous guides? Questions of objectivity and subjectivity in one form or another have been much debated. But the fundamental crisis today seems rather to be one of motive. Why do men throughout the globe seek higher knowledge today? For individual experience and self-development, on the one side, and power over things and people on the other. Both are legitimate within limits, but, cut off from a true doctrine of man and society, the one issues in a sterile individualism and the other can lead to totalitarianism. Both can end in the cynicism about the purpose of the pursuit of knowledge, which is prevalent among students today. The whole great enterprise of the *universitatis*, the society of seekers of knowledge, seems in danger either of dwindling to the mere self-satisfaction of academics or of being seized as an instrument of power by the state. The true springs of the motives for seeking knowledge need to be cleared and purified.

Christians affirm that their sources are in God — that the pursuit of knowledge for its own sake is valid only because it is pursued toward the reality of God and that the use of knowledge as power is safe only when earthly loyalties are brought under the scrutiny of a heavenly citizenship. It is not, however, a return to the medieval framework that we need: the freeing of human inquiry, and therefore of the various academic disciplines, from constricting bonds marked an intellectual coming of age from which we could not now retreat. The need is, rather, to bring all the fragmented and autonomous specialisms *sub specie aeternitatis*, to draw out the lines of the intellectual enterprise once more to infinity. The true academic freedoms, both of the individual seeker and the community of learning, find their ultimate safeguard when brought under obedience to God.

— *Marjorie Reeves*

URBAN CHURCH The Christian church began in, and has tended to be identified with, the city. Christian faith in the early centuries was carried from city to city: e.g., Jerusalem, Antioch, Corinth, and Rome. The very term *paganus* (countryman) came to signify non-Christian.

The early settlers of America brought the Christian faith — of the Anglican, dissenting, and Roman Catholic varieties — with them; consequently, since Americans then lived chiefly in small town and rural areas, the numerical strength of the church was found in these places. As the centers of trade and industry became larger, they drew to themselves the more aggressive and frequently the financially more successful. These were also, in the main, churchgoing Christians and, understandably, the church in the city benefited. Through the 19th century the Protestant churches exercised the dominant religious influence in urban America. The flood of immigrants in the latter part of the century, from central, southern, and eastern Europe, were chiefly Roman Catholic, most of them settling in the cities of the North, where jobs in the expanding factories were available. They formed little ethnic colonies in the older and less pleasant parts of the city, from which the earlier residents were eager and able to move.

While Protestantism continued to maintain strong churches in the downtown business district, it had already, by 1900, begun to close some of its weaker churches in what came to be known as the "inner city." Scores of congregations merged or sold their properties, using the assets to build new churches in more propitious environments. Many churches remained in the inner city,

however. Some of these continued their conventional program, often with diminished congregations and part-time ministerial leadership, more intent on serving members who had moved a mile or more away than in discovering and welcoming potential members in the neighborhood.

A minority of churches kept doors open to newcomers regardless of cultural background, actively seeking to minister to their material and spiritual needs and to win them to membership. Before World War I the 7-day-a-week program became the standard pattern for these "institutional churches." Certain of them, such as the Church of All Nations (a popular name) in Boston, New York, and Los Angeles, Erie Chapel and Neighborhood House in Chicago, and, more recently, the East Harlem Protestant Parish, New York, had a spread of activities similar to those found in the social settlements like Hull House, Chicago, and Henry Street Settlement, New York. They organized group activities for boys and girls as well as for adults, mothers clubs, baby clinics; in later years they established counseling centers and rehabilitation ministries for the alcoholic and the drug addict. Unlike the settlements, they maintained a Christian orientation, conserving the elements of a regular church program.

By the middle of the 20th century, the chief strength of Protestantism was either at the very center of the city or, more often the case, in the pleasant residential suburban communities beyond the lower-income, often neglected neighborhoods. Even before 1900 a few leaders perceived how the church might suffer from urban growth and population shifts. This concern was crystallized in the Interchurch World Movement after World War I. One of its principal contributions was the gathering of a vast amount of information through religious censuses, notably in St. Louis, Pittsburgh, and Springfield, Mass. After the movement faded, the impetus for urban religious research was continued through the organization of the Institute of Social and Religious Research, under the leadership of H. Paul Douglass. The institute flourished for a dozen years under Douglass' direction until it ran out of funds at the beginning of the great depression.

With the passage of the years, more sophisticated research procedures were employed in the study of the city from the standpoint of its church needs. Social scientists utilized demographic data in predicting urban development and population movement in order to determine where new churches should be placed. Increased attention was given by a few theological seminaries to study of and research in the urban church.

During the depression decade and World War II relatively little church-building took place. By 1945 the pent-up population pressure in the big cities exploded into the suburban environs and at once there was a struggle on the part of all denominations to establish new congregations in these burgeoning communities with their favorable cultural and financial climates. The comity commissions of the councils of churches, which had the responsibility for preventing either over-churching or underchurching, used all available research resources and called for more.

After 1945 two significant new factors began to reshape the life of Protestantism in the cities, importantly altering the future prospects of the urban church. The 1st of these was the mass movement to the inner-city areas of every great metropolis — and in lesser numbers to smaller cities — of rural whites with a Protestant background, many of them from the South, and also the monumental shift of Negroes from the rural South to the urban North and West. This meant that for the 1st time in a century the major population flow into the central city was Protestant rather than Roman Catholic or Jewish.

The 2d factor was the growing awareness of civic leaders that, since American civilization is tied up with urban life, it would be imperative to rescue the great core of the larger cities from the engulfing deterioration. Public housing projects, begun during the depression to provide decent shelter for some of the poor, became part of a large-scale urban redevelopment program. Since 1950 in cities such as Baltimore, Pittsburgh, and St. Louis, slums have been cleared away from large tracts. Some of the land was designated for industrial and institutional purposes, but generally it was redeveloped for residential use, in some cases by public agencies, in others by private corporations. Older persons whose children were reared and younger middle-income families began to locate in these areas and presented a new opportunity for the Protestant churches.

By 1960 the heads of city missionary organizations were fully aware of the changing situation. Greater interest was being shown in strengthening the ministry of churches remaining in the inner city. Since residential segregation was still

the common pattern, it was difficult to develop interracial churches. Increasingly, membership was open to incoming Negroes and often a Negro minister was placed in charge, but commonly the whites continued to leave and the congregation became entirely Negro. There was much less opposition to the idea of integrated churches than in 1950. In some cases genuinely integrated churches were maintained, a pattern that seemed to become more prevalent.
— *Murray H. Leiffer*

V

VACATION CHURCH SCHOOL

The vacation church school is a short-term, concentrated school that meets during the children's summer vacation from public school. The sessions occupy the entire morning on consecutive days for a term of 2 weeks.

There are, of course, exceptions to this general pattern. Some schools utilize the morning hours for 3 or 4 weeks. A few use both morning and afternoon for 1 week. Occasionally the school is held 2 or 3 mornings a week all summer. Where the public-school system conducts summer schools the churches sometimes hold their sessions in the afternoon.

The flexibility of the school is rooted in its history. It did not begin with just 1 school conceived by 1 person but sprang up in a number of different communities in answer to various felt needs.

During the summer months children often had nothing to do. It was also apparent that they needed a greater knowledge of the Bible. Individuals in widely separated parts of the U.S.A. and Canada put these 2 things together and came up with an answer — the Daily Vacation Bible School, as the 1st schools were called.

The founders of these schools did not know they were making history, and the records are hard to trace. Schools that have received widespread attention were connected with: First Church of Boston, 1866; Royal Arthur (public) School, Montreal, 1877; The Methodist Church of Hopedale, Ill., 1894; and Epiphany Baptist Church, New York City, 1898.

In 1901, Robert G. Boville, executive secretary of the New York Baptist City Mission, saw the need for vacation Bible schools there, plus an additional resource for meeting the need — idle seminary and college students. That summer 5 schools, with a combined enrollment of 1,000 children, were led by students from Union Theological Seminary.

The movement spread quickly to other cities and other denominations. The National Committee on Daily Vacation Bible Schools, organized in 1907, was made up of 100 persons from 15 cities, 8 communions, and 30 colleges. By 1916 the number of schools in Canada necessitated changing the name to the International Association of Daily Vacation Bible Schools.

The success of these schools awakened the denominations to their value. Although many of the schools were interdenominational, frequently sponsored by local councils of churches, they soon had the support of local congregations and general bodies. The Northern Baptist Convention led the way in promoting the schools as an important teaching arm of the church. By the middle of the 1930's most of the major denominations were preparing curriculum materials and actively urging their congregations to take advantage of the teaching opportunities of the summer.

The curriculum of a school always reflects its leaders' views of pupil needs. Dr. Boville's classic statement of the need gives the background against which the 1st curricula were constructed: " Idle children filling the streets. Idle churches darkened and silent. Unemployed students on vacation. Idle vacation days and children's courts." Pupils needed to be kept busy, happy, and out of mischief, and to learn more about the Bible.

The morning was divided into well-defined periods for Bible study and memorization, hymns and songs, handwork and organized games. There was no attempt to coordinate the subjects. Handwork was intended to be fun and to teach certain skills such as sewing and carpentry.

Changes in vacation church school curricula have paralleled those in other schools of the church. In fact, the summertime vacation atmosphere of the church has combined with its youthful flexibility to make it even more responsive than other congregational agencies to changes in Christian education theory.

The growth of the vacation church school had been due both to the peculiar genius of the school itself and to the active promotion of denominational boards. Schools usually are sponsored by individual congregations, groups of congregations of the same denomination, and community councils of churches. The Division of Christian Education of the National Council of the Churches of Christ in the U.S.A. provides promotional help and guidance supplementing the work of individual churches.

Vacation church school is an ideal situation for pupils to study the Scriptures in some depth. The child is encouraged to express and intensify his understanding through activities of many kinds. As he does this he finds himself involved in a network of relationships. His relation to God, to Christian teachers and pupils, the physical world, persons outside the church, are part of the vacation church school experience. He learns through direct experience the meaning of Christian fellowship, or participation in the church. The name " vacation church school," which has been replacing " vacation Bible school," does not minimize the Bible but takes it out of a special subject-matter category and relates it to the total experience of the child in the school.

From the beginning of the movement efforts have been made to secure good leaders and give them special training for this task. Interdenominational and denominational conferences, workshops and institutes, are held early in the spring. Early enlistment and intensive training of teachers is a factor in the successful functioning of the school.

Responsibility for securing and training these teachers lies with the vacation church school committee of the sponsoring organization. Usually this organization will be the governing body of the congregation, through its board or committee on Christian education. The vacation church school committee also appoints a director, provides a meeting place, selects curriculum materials, sets the time of the school, and provides financial help.

Manuals prepared by denominational boards of education and a booklet published by the Division of Christian Education of the NCCCUSA, *The How of Vacation Church School*, provide valuable assistance to the person who is preparing to lead such a school.

— *Margaret A. J. Irvin*

VOCATION Vocation means " calling," from the Latin *vocatio*. The meaning and usage of the word has undergone substantial mutation through the centuries. In English translations of the Bible the word " vocation " rarely appears, though the related word " calling " appears frequently. The literal uses of " call " and " calling " in the Bible refer to God's summons and also to the giving of a name to a thing or person. The giving of a name leads to the idea of a claim set upon a person, his appointment for a special destiny. The action of calling is characteristic of the initiative of God in summoning a people, corporately or individually, for a special task in the world. Vocation bears the image of hearing God's word and responding to it in obedience. The patriarchs and prophets are called to distinctive service within the community. In the Gospels, Jesus calls men and they follow him. In the apostolic writings God calls men to salvation, to eternal life, to be saints, and to his marvelous light. The called people are identified with the chosen or elect (*electoi*) or the " called out " (*ecclesia*, church).

In medieval times the term " vocation " was used to designate the call to the monastic life or to the religious occupations. Luther, Calvin, and other Reformers protested against the narrow use of the word. They preferred to emphasize the calling of every Christian to his everyday task and station, so that the maid in the kitchen was engaged in as worthy a calling as the monk or priest. This emphasis was accompanied by affirmations of the universal priesthood of believers and the denial of all hierarchies of spiritual status in the Christian fellowship. However, the movement was only a partial restoration of the Biblical meaning of vocation.

One of the fruits of modern Biblical and theological studies has been a fresh inquiry into the meaning of vocation. Correlated with this inquiry is the reevaluation of Reformation thought, and the movement to study the place of the laity in the church and world that has found expression particularly in the ecumenical movement. It is conceded that there is 1 vocation common to all Christians, i.e., the calling in Christ. The initiative in the calling process belongs to God, whose word is spoken through the Scriptures and through his servants illumined by the Holy Spirit. Response to the call to repentance and faith brings the person into relation with God and his neighbor in responsible fellowship and service. Thus vocation is a summons to be Christian and to express in faithfulness in all of life the privilege of Christian obedience.

The view is being expressed strongly that vocation and a man's occupation are not identical. In light of the popular contemporary use of the term " vocation " in reference to occupation or profession, it is surprising to notice that nowhere in the Bible do we have a specific reference to "being called" to a job or profession. Paul is called to be an apostle, but there is no suggestion that he is called to be a tentmaker. This does not mean that the Bible treats the fact and necessity of work lightly, but it does mean that it is difficult to identify certain professions or means of earning a living as God-preferred. The Reformers drew the implication that clergy and others engaged in the employment of the church do not possess a superior calling, nor are they to have special religious status.

To affirm that God calls persons to faith and not to jobs in the workaday world is to affirm that the person must confront the human situation as a human being in Christ, making the choice of a job and performing his functions in the world in the light of the best insight available at the given time. The focus of the doctrine of vocation is not in work but in God. The criterion of meaningful work is faithfulness to God, not "work for work's sake."

Turning from the church and its theology relative to vocation, the prevailing use of the term "vocation" in the contemporary scene in the U.S.A. is to refer to an occupation, a career, a profession, or a trade. This usage has no necessary relationship of meaning to Biblical usage.

In the last few decades there has been a phenomenal increase in vocational guidance in schools, colleges, employment agencies, and churches. Guidance is given in assisting a person to choose an occupation, prepare for it, enter upon it, and progress in it. Use is made of educational insights and counseling methods. Aptitude and occupational interest tests are used along with personality inventories to assist the person to plan for the best investment of his time and talents. Information regarding the variety of occupations and their requirements is given to students through books, leaflets, films, and conferences. Teachers and counselors engaged in this type of guidance comprise a sizable new profession in this country.

Vocational guidance should not be confused with vocational education or vocational training. The predominant function of vocational education is in connection with trade and industrial training, including on-the-job learning under supervision; training through special schools provided by the trade, business, or industry; preparation through a system of apprenticeship; learning in shops and schools as a cooperative enterprise; education in technical high schools or in technical departments of secondary schools.

The term "Christian vocation" has come into vogue in more recent years within the church to signify the relationship of God to man within daily work. Emphasis is placed upon the seeking of God's will for the work men do, for guidance in the manner of doing it, and for the situation in which a person's abilities and interests best meet the legitimate needs of God's world.

"Church vocations" has come into usage to suggest the variety of ministries or occupations in the church. The term "ministry" bore the image of preacher, priest, or parson, but was deemed to be an inadequate word to describe the broadening field of occupations in the church. Rarely in Protestantism is vocation used alone to refer to the religious or church-related occupations. It is a common practice, however, to speak

of the "call" to the ministry or other religious occupations. In his book *The Purpose of the Church and Its Ministry* (p. 64), H. Richard Niebuhr suggests 4 facets of the church's meaning of the call to the ministry or a church vocation: (1) the "call to be a Christian"; (2) the "secret call" — the inner persuasion or experience by which a person feels in the deepest sense that this is God's will for him; (3) the "providential call," an assessment of what God has given the person of intellectual, psychological, and moral qualifications — that is, native endowment plus the consciousness of the employment of time and the place of usefulness; (4) the "ecclesiastical call," the acceptance of the ministerial candidate by a particular church and his election to ordination.
— *Marcus J. Priester*

VOLUNTEER PRINCIPLE The volunteer principle may be defined as the practice of using volunteer (unpaid) leadership to carry on most of the educational work of the church, a practice that is in direct contrast with public education where all teachers and administrators are employed on a remunerative basis. This phenomenon has been one of the most striking distinctions in American Christian education. Hardly a church in America could carry on even a small fraction of its present program were it not for the volunteer services of church school teachers and officers, youth group advisers, board and committee members, recreational leaders, and the like.

One of the best indications of the scope of volunteer leadership is the number of persons giving their time as Sunday church school teachers. One million teachers were serving in the U.S.A. by the end of the 1st century of the Sunday school movement, according to reports given at the 1884 International Sunday School Convention. Approximately 1,500,000 teachers were reported at the 1905 Convention. The 2,000,000 mark was achieved in 1926, as noted at the 1930 Convention. The 1961 *Yearbook of American Churches* shows that as of 1958 there were an estimated 3,621,000 teachers in the Sunday church schools of the U.S.A. Recognizing that teachers comprise only a part of the total group of workers in the churches, it is evident that the bulk of work has been done by volunteers.

The teaching ministry of the church has been, in part, the fulfillment of Jesus' command to go into all the world to preach and teach the gospel, but this ministry has always been too great to be placed in the hands of paid workers alone. Volunteer workers in ever-increasing numbers joined the early leaders of the church, starting a practice that continues to the present. Early records of Sunday schools in the U.S.A. show that the volunteer principle was practiced from the beginning. F. G. Lankard reports, e.g., that the Methodist Conference held at Charleston, S.C., on Feb. 17, 1790, arranged for classes for poor children during the early morning and the afternoon hours each Sunday under the direction of unpaid teachers. Reports of the early schools often emphasized the worth of the volunteer principle by calling attention to the many devoted and well-educated people serving without pay as teachers. Such early examples of volunteer service formed the patterns for the future.

The history of the American Sunday school movement is largely the history of the endeavors of countless lay men and women. The occasional opposition and the frequent lack of interest and support of the Sunday school movement on the part of professional religious leaders led to the development of a lay enterprise. Volunteers filled the ranks of teachers, administrators, officers, and national boards. Prominent businessmen gave their time and money to further the Sunday school cause. The enthusiasm of Sunday school workers and leaders influenced others to join the glorious cause, constantly swelling the numbers of those giving their time without pay.

The birth and growth of much of the educational program of the churches came during periods of expansion when the resources of the church were being taxed to the limit. These factors necessitated the use of volunteers to carry on most of the educational work. The early years of the Sunday school movement, e.g., were the years of the birth of foreign missions. Such denominational agencies as the Congregational-sponsored American Board for Foreign Missions (formed 1810), the General Missionary Convention of the Baptist Denomination in the United States for Foreign Missions (1814), and the Board of Foreign Missions of the Presbyterian Church in the U.S.A. (1837), pressed the churches for financial support for the opening of new fields of work around the world. The expansion of home mission work westward brought similar pressures on church finances. Only through the use of volunteers in their own educational program could the churches meet the challenges of such an era of expansion.

The use of volunteers in the educational work of the churches led to the development of a corps of workers who often were not prepared

in any specific way for their tasks. Walter S. Athearn conducted a survey in the State of Indiana in 1920 that secured the following information from 2,072 of the 2,670 teachers in 256 typical Sunday schools: almost none had any professional religious education courses; only a small percentage attended conventions and teachers meetings regularly; only 125 had graduated from leadership schools in the previous 21 years; only 28 of the 256 churches were offering leadership educational classes. The information in the Indiana Survey was considered typical of the country as a whole and in many ways is descriptive of volunteer leadership in later periods — sincerely dedicated to their tasks but often not well prepared.

The church has usually adopted the policy of not expecting too much of volunteer workers and of not directing them to any appreciable degree. The fact that workers have been volunteers has been accepted to mean that they could not be controlled. No one wants to hurt the feelings of a dedicated volunteer. The lack of control over volunteers has also meant that the unsuited person has often been difficult to remove from some position.

It has been very difficult to set educational standards and in-service training requirements when volunteer workers have been involved. As a result, many service positions in the church have been filled by persons whose sole qualification has been a willingness to serve. This has been particularly critical when it is considered that teaching in the church is often more difficult than teaching in public schools because of the lack of proper equipment, the failure to provide adequate space, the lack of sufficient time, and the lapse of a full week between sessions.

Otherwise impossible areas of work of the church have been made possible by the practice of the volunteer principle. Almost every part of the church program beyond the preaching service has resulted from the endeavors of volunteer workers.

The expansion of the work of the church through the use of volunteers has drawn millions of persons into active service. The more responsibility persons have had, the more interest and enthusiasm they have shown. In addition, as larger groups of persons have engaged in the programs of the church, their enthusiasm has been contagious and has affected the total group.

The growth of volunteer service led to the development of formal programs of leadership education by the middle of the 19th century. Such training programs, in turn, have led to an increased supply of workers and to improvement in quality of service. The spread of leadership education has brought a new surge of lay leadership in almost all areas of the work of the church.

Volunteers have needed trained leaders to guide them locally and nationally. The result has been the growth of a new profession, composed mainly of local church directors of Christian education and denominational and interdenominational staff members in Christian education. The ranks of the professional workers have been growing constantly, opening new opportunities of service. Many of those entering the professional groups were motivated to such service by experiences as volunteer workers.

— William H. R. Willkens

WISDOM Wisdom is the ripe fruit of knowledge and experience integrated into the total person, his outlook toward life, his practical dealing with things and his fellowmen, and his understanding of himself and the role of humanity within the natural and divine universe. This means that wisdom, though unattainable without intelligence, is not identical with learning and erudition. These, as many religious leaders have clearly seen, may even prevent it by making a person one-sided, unintegrated, and proud of his segmental achievements.

There is humility in all wisdom, but never servility, for wisdom demands dignity. The wise man will pay due respect to lawful authorities and persons of superior quality because wisdom, as shown especially by the example of Confucius, recognizes the necessity of order in life as a whole. But the wise man will not bow before the mere show of power; least of all, before its abuse. He will prefer kindness and love to harshness and hatred, but he will also know that kindness and love without justice and discipline will defeat themselves. Wisdom is the enemy of sentimentality.

It is one of the characteristics of wisdom that it is recognized to be of universal value. Although wisdom may result from profound speculation and systematic reasoning, in its final formulation it boils complexity down to simplicity. This is one of the reasons why it transcends national and cultural boundaries and builds bridges even between different religions. Just as educated Christians gladly acknowledge the profoundness of the authors of the Upanishads, of Confucius, and of Buddha, so educated men from Asia praise the wisdom of Jesus, though for them he is not " the Christ." Also, the customary barriers between religion and secularism do not hold before the persuasiveness of wisdom. The wisdom in the plays of Shakespeare will not be denied by the pious, and Goethe has often been quoted in the religious literature of Germany, but both belong to the secular tradition.

Furthermore, although wisdom has a moral quality, it is not moralistic. We may even say that, except in regard to historical figures whom a specific culture may revere as divine and therefore sinless (e.g., as Christians revere Jesus Christ), wisdom is impossible of achievement in a life of complete purity. No mortal can become wise who has not gone through severe tensions, who does not know about the tragical and the foolish and even about sin in all human existence, for without these experiences he cannot understand humanity. It is exactly this understanding which we require from a wise person. One must have participated in the human adventure in order to grow above it. *Nihil humani mihi alienum est* may be the excuse of a scoundrel, but it may also be the mark of a superior person.

Here is the reason why many wise men have humor, i.e., a person's quality of looking at himself and the human spectacle with a degree of mellowed irony or a dialectical mood. Without wide and contrasting experience, wisdom would also lack the sense of practicality. No one can give counsel to others in the field of action who does not know the involvement of the acting person in the vicissitudes of human affairs. Just as wisdom itself, so also great action is rarely possible in an atmosphere of complete detachment. The statesman who at the end of his career may be a truly wise person will by necessity have been engaged in deeds that have hurt other persons, often innocent ones, and of which he may not like to think. Is there cruel immorality or realistic wisdom in Plato's *Republic* where it is said that the guardians will be permitted to lie in the interest of the state, whereas the ordinary citizen will be punished when he does so? The wise man, though regretfully, acknowledges somehow the idea of "original sin." He will, therefore, not judge a great statesman for decisions that he would consider criminal if they were made in the statesman's private interest. Wisdom looks with a mood of resignation at the dark abysses in humanity.

Ecclesiastes has these verses:

"And I gave my heart to know wisdom, and to know madness and folly: I perceived that this also is vexation of spirit. For in much wisdom is much vexation, and he that increaseth knowledge increaseth sorrow." (Eccl. 1:17-18, KJV.)

The author of Ecclesiastes would therefore join the many who are suspicious of the mere theoretician and the enthusiastic reformer. Because of lack of mature wisdom and humor, they may create evil with their good intentions. But here is also wisdom's danger. It is the same as the danger of advanced age; the 2 often go together. Wise men tend to become conservative. They know too much to risk the not completely foreseeable. They hesitate to change the old, even though it may be defective, for they know that the change may perhaps repair the old evils but create new ones. Erasmus of Rotterdam, who, according to his own words, "hated discord," is generally regarded as a wise man, but Luther changed the world. As long as Christianity is alive, people will always give different answers to the question: Who was wiser — Erasmus or Luther?

Concerning the meaning of "wisdom" in the Judeo-Christian religion, 3 remarks may be appropriate:

1. There exists the so-called "wisdom" literature. In it we generally count the books of Proverbs, Job, and Ecclesiastes; and in the Apocrypha, the Wisdom of Solomon and Ecclesiasticus. These books, though written relatively late, are part of a long wisdom tradition that started in Egypt in the beginning of the 3d millennium B.C. and can be found in several of the old Asiatic cultures. This kind of literature expresses, often in a mood of sadness about the vanity of life, the ripe experience

of men versed in the affairs of the world. They may know little, if anything, about the Messianic hopes of the prophets and of the promise of the New Testament. Much of this wisdom, e.g., in Ecclesiastes, is heretical. It would not be too bold to compare it with some of the essays in which Montaigne suggests his agnostic stoicism. (The last verses of Ecclesiastes, which recommend the fear of God, are later additions.)

2. If we put, so to speak, the "wisdom" literature into brackets, then we will find that the Bible and the whole Christian tradition distinguish between wisdom that is absolute and eternal because it comes from God (in medieval language, the *ratio divina*) and wisdom that is human (*ratio humana*).

In Isa. 29:14 (KJV) the Lord speaks: "Therefore, behold, I will proceed to do a marvelous work among this people, even a marvelous work and a wonder: for the wisdom of their wise men shall perish, and the understanding of their prudent men shall be hid." And in I Cor. 3:19 (KJV) we find the following: "For the wisdom of this world is foolishness with God: for it is written, He taketh the wise in their own craftiness." For Tertullian and other Christian writers, there exists an *absurdum* far above the logic and wisdom of the empirical world.

3. As a consequence of the Biblical differentiation between divine and "fleshly" wisdom, the Christian tradition reveals a certain split in the attitude toward all knowledge. As the church fathers disputed whether the Greek-Roman intellectual heritage was really wisdom or deception until liberals such as Clement of Alexandria and Origen defeated the intransigent to such a degree that a thousand years later Thomas Aquinas could refer to Aristotle simply as "the teacher," so also Luther and Melanchthon in the early years of the Reformation used harsh words against the heathen Aristotle and medieval Scholasticism for diverting Christians from the simplicity and immediateness of the gospel. But also here the humanist spirit got the upper hand. Melanchthon, at least, retracted his early anti-Aristotelianism. But to a degree the conflict has pervaded the whole Christian culture and especially its education, often with the doubtful result that in the schools for the less privileged wisdom was taught in the form of Christian humility, whereas in the schools for the future leaders the wisdom of the Sermon on the Mount was taught side by side with the wisdom of Cicero and Plutarch. Today we still live in a state of controversy as to where the greater wisdom is — in the Christian heritage or in the humanities and especially in the empirical sciences.

When we turn our attention from the religious tradition to the secular, remaining also here mainly within the framework of Western culture, then the word philosophy (love of wisdom) will immediately come to mind. Indeed, the Greek culture was, and to a degree still is, the source of our secular wisdom. In connection with it many will think of the humble yet so majestically wise figure of Socrates and perhaps also of Plato, who in an attitude of supreme modesty put many of his own insights into the mouth of his teacher. We have here individualism (for were there more stubborn individualists than Socrates and Plato?) combined with complete absorption in the all-transcendent *logos*.

From the Socratic-Platonist and Aristotelian teaching, the concept of *sophia* (wisdom) passed to the schools of the Cynics and the Stoics and was taken over into the Latin realm by men such as Cicero and Seneca, by whom in turn it was transmitted to the Scholastics of the Middle Ages. Thomas Aquinas' definitions of *sapientia* are completely in line with the Greek-Roman heritage. (*Contra Gentiles* I, 94: "Wisdom consists of the understanding of ultimate causes"; and *Summa* I. 1, 6: "A person is wise to the degree to which he orders his human acts according to a moral commitment.")

In spite of all differences in regard to the ultimate source of wisdom (for the Greeks, the *logos;* for the Christians, God — see, however, the interpretation of Logos in John 1:1), it is also a sign of the continuity of profound ideas that for both the Greek and the Christian philosophers wisdom was the source of virtue; in addition, it could be taught. This made it possible that the latter accepted the 4 "cardinal virtues" of the Greeks (wisdom, fortitude, prudence, and justice) and bound them into an inner unity with the specific Christian virtues of faith, love, and hope. In Plato's *Protagoras* they could also find a 5th virtue, piety.

According to this tradition, the wise man is one who will make the 7 cardinal virtues the regulatory principles of his whole thinking and acting. Thus he will achieve the highest possible degree of felicity here on earth, and lasting felicity in the life beyond. — *Robert Ulich*

WITNESS The Greek word for "witness" is *martys* (noun), *martyreō* (verb; cf. English "martyr"). In classical antiquity the word is used 3 ways: in a legal or civic context, to refer to a witness in a trial or a witness to a contract; in a philo-

sophic sense (in Plato and Aristotle and especially among the Stoics) to refer to the wise man as a witness to the truth behind phenomena, accessible to methodical reason; and in a religious sense, the calling of the gods to witness.

Roughly corresponding usages are found in the Bible. The Old Testament contains regulations concerning witnesses in a legal context (Deut. 17:6; 19:15-19) and references to the same are found in the New Testament (II Cor. 13:1; John 8:17; Heb. 10:28). In place of the philosophic witness to abstract truth there is the witness to the commandments and ordinances to God and his will; e.g., the "Tables of the Law" at Sinai are called "tables of witness" (Ex. 31:18; Deut. 4:45; 6:17). Similarly, Jesus is a witness to the truth of God (John 18:37).

The religious meaning is fully developed in the Bible. God is called upon to witness the agreements of men (Jer. 34:15), and it is this which is the deeper or at least later significance of the reference to tangible memorials or ceremonies of witness (Gen. 21:30; 31:48; ch. 52; Josh. 22:10). Further, he is witness of the deeds of the pious and of the wicked and of the work of his servants no less than of the vicissitudes of his people.

The connection between witness and signs (cf. the memorials referred to) and between witness and the Word of God (whether as law or gospel or the Person of Christ) is maintained in those parts of the Bible where the conception is most fully employed. In Second Isaiah (see especially chs. 43:9-13; 44:7-11), Israel is called to be a witness to the Gentiles of the one Creator and Redeemer God and is itself a sign to the nations. So also the witnessing prophet (e.g., Jonah, Isaiah, Ezekiel) is a sign to the men of his generation.

In The Acts of the Apostles there is a virtual pattern according to which the apostolic men give their testimony to (the act of God in) Jesus, and their witness is in turn confirmed by the "signs and wonders" wrought by the Holy Spirit (see Acts 5:32 and 4:30; 5:12; 6:8; 14:3; 15:12). The continuity of their witness with that of their Lord is thereby indicated, for in the same book the deeds of Jesus (cf. especially The Gospel According to Luke) are referred to as "signs and wonders" whereby God attested to (witnessed to) Jesus (Acts 2:22). The work of the Holy Spirit is of course at the same time an attestation to their message (the word of preaching).

The conception of witness plays an equally important role in The Gospel According to John. Witness to Jesus as Son is borne (wittingly or unwittingly) by men: the Baptist, the disciples, Nicodemus, his Jewish opponents, the high priests, Pilate. More important, the signs done, beginning with Cana and culminating in the raising of Lazarus (or the resurrection itself) are the form of the Father's testimony to the Son. Further, the connection between the Word and witness is employed in 2 ways: the Scriptures (i.e., the Old Testament) are said to witness to Christ (John 5:39); and the Holy Spirit will bear witness in relation to Christ as the Word. He will witness to Christ (John 15:26) and he will lead the disciples into all truth by taking the things of Christ and showing them to the disciples (John 16:14).

As to the witness as martyr, the letter to the Hebrews illustrates a difference between the Old and New Testament understandings. The witnesses to faith referred to in Heb., ch. 11, esp. vs. 32-40, like those mentioned in the Old Testament and in II Maccabees, are heroes of faith; the Christians who witness by their suffering, on the other hand, are thereby participants in the sufferings of Christ (so the Pauline letters, Hebrews, Revelation, and probably I Peter, though the intrinsic relation is not there clearly established). It is significant that it is only in relation to his sufferings and his apostleship that Paul speaks of grace given to him.

The primary formulation of the Reformation doctrine of the *testimonium Spiritus sancti internum* (inner witness of the Holy Spirit) was in accord with the Johannine conception as developed in the Gospels and in the epistles. In the 1st Calvinistic confessions, and throughout Luther's writings (so Prenter) the testimony of the Spirit is always given through or in the Word (preaching, the sacraments, and Scripture): the work of the Spirit is to make Christ present. This view is distinct from doctrines of the "inner light" or of the external attestation to Scripture.

Witness is a central conception both for the upbuilding and for the mission of the church. The church is a "witnessing community" (de Dietrich) both as testifying to Christ and as a sign to the nations, and it is a community knit together by the witness borne within it to the life-giving power of the Word.

— *Holt H. Graham*

WOMEN'S WORK The growth and changes that have taken place in the work of women in the churches parallel many of the profound revolutions which have taken place in our society during the past hundred years. Until about the middle of the 19th century, churches in America were largely pioneer ventures, struggling for their existence in new communities across the land. The vast majority of the women members of the churches were wives and mothers, burdened with large families and endless homemaking responsibilities. As new communities were settled and churches established, the women brought to the venture their homemaking skills. The story of hundreds of churches begins with the money raised by women's guilds and sewing societies. The pattern of bake sales, bazaars, and church suppers that paid for the 1st church structures across the land is a thrilling story.

During the latter years of the 19th century, churches were beginning to be well established in most parts of the country, and the great era of missionary outreach began. The interest and enthusiasm of the women, which had come into the building of the churches, began to turn to the mission fields. In almost every Protestant denomination, between 1870 and 1900, women's missionary societies developed. As a rule these started spontaneously in a number of local congregations, and gradually came together in national organizations or fellowships.

The typical program of a women's missionary society in almost any church included 3 activities: missionary education, giving for the spread of missionary work, and sewing for missions. The " sewing " included the making of clothing and other articles for use in mission agencies and hospitals, and the packing of " missionary barrels " with new and used clothing and household goods to help eke out the usually inade-

quate stipend paid to missionaries. The growth and popularity of these missionary societies reflected both the very sincere concern of committed Christian women for the spread of the gospel, and also met a real need of women for fellowship and for personal growth and activity in a day when there were few other activities open to them.

The end of World War I marked the end of an era in much of our common life. Perhaps no more striking changes have taken place than in the lives of women. Emancipation came in many areas. Women had the vote, and were beginning to be looked upon as 1st-class citizens. More and more women were receiving higher education. Jobs and professions of all kinds were opening to women, and the idea of a wife and mother's having a career outside her home began to be accepted. A multitude of organizations for women emerged. Science and technology and the migration from the farm to the city began to lessen greatly the time and energy required of women for homemaking. At the same time, changes were taking place within the churches. There was a growing emphasis on Christian education and social responsibility alongside the traditional interest in missions. With the decline of fundamentalism, some of the feeling of urgency about the missionary task of the church seemed to be dissipated.

In response to these changes, organized women's work in the churches began to be modified. In many denominations, the missionary society became a more general type of organization, with an interest in education, evangelism, and social problems. With a more highly educated constituency, the study programs of churchwomen's groups began to be more wide-ranging and more intellectually advanced. At the same time the competition of non-church activities drew many women away from the churchwomen's societies.

Even greater changes would seem to lie ahead. The current interest in the ministry of the laity is changing many of the older concepts of "church work" and is drawing men and women together in local congregations and in denominations. The rapid increase in the employment of women is forcing changes in meeting times and types of programs. The ecumenical movement is bringing women together across church and national lines, stimulating new questioning and experiments. The fact that many churches still discriminate against women in legislative affairs and in church work is disturbing to many men and women. The fact that active and successful women's organizations may have contributed to an awareness of such discrimination is raising profound questions about the ultimate role of women in the life of the church.

— *Cynthia C. Wedel*

WORDBOOK The term "wordbook" may refer to a volume giving a count of the number of times various words are used in a certain class or level of reading materials, or it may be used to describe a curricular activity whereby students make their own word lists with their own definitions and illustrations in order to build up their vocabularies.

Edward L. Thorndike published his 1st edition of *The Teacher's Word Book* in 1921. This was a basic list of words and their counts. It became a basis for determining the vocabularies to be used in textbooks and graded vocabulary lists for many years. This work was extended to 20,000 words in 1931. Three counts of over 4,500,000 words were used to make the list published in Edward L. Thorndike and Irving Lorge's *The Teacher's Word Book of 30,000 Words* (1944).

For generations teachers have used word lists with pictures to try to teach vocabulary, but in more recent times with the stress on pupil activities there has been an emphasis on helping students or classes to make up their own lists, definitions, and illustrations. Sometimes these are limited to a special geographical area such as a wordbook about "my city." Sometimes these are limited to a subject-matter area such as the home, geography, the Bible, industry of an area.

Usually these activities are planned for children from the 3d to 6th grades. One example in Christian education is the activity "My Church School Word Book," in the *Judson Graded Curriculum* (American Baptist), planned for use throughout primary year 3. Work sheets are provided for each pupil so that as the units of the year are experienced each may make up his own wordbook. Each sheet has the basic term printed, and written in script. Then there are lines under the headings: "What the Word Means" and "Write a Sentence Using the Word." A picture of the object or activity described is included and in some cases a Bible text in which the term is used. The following terms are included: altar, dedicate, dependable, disciple, forgive, gospel, hallowed, responsible, sanctuary, tabernacle, temple, temptation, testament, and worship.

The real value of such a procedure

is that it recognizes that there is a close relation between clear thinking and precise terms. Formerly there was a tendency on the part of many Christian education leaders to shun the use of Biblical and theological terms, many of which others deem alone adequate to convey basic Christian truths. The retreat from Biblical language is sometimes made in an effort to put the Christian message in 20th-century speech. One author of junior high materials wrote, " Of course, with modern youth we shall not use such terms as repentance, inspiration, apocalypse, faith, grace, eschatology, depravity, and so on." There is a basic dishonesty in this advice. It classifies terms necessary to elementary Christianity along with terms even preachers rarely use. The questions arise: Why should not 20th-century youth understand faith, grace, and repentance? Can precise meaning be taught without well-defined terms? The public schools will teach these same youth elementary technical terms for each subject in the curriculum. In mathematics they will be taught numerators, denominators, sums, multiples, dividends, squares, cubes, and formulas. In English they will learn adjectives, adverbs, participles, gerunds, infinitives, superlatives, comparatives, and nominatives. In geography they will discuss continents, latitudes, longitudes, deltas, peninsulas, tributaries, and equatorial winds. Why, then, should we impoverish their minds and vocabularies by failing to teach the elemental terms of Christianity?

The major weakness of such teaching is that many of the words may be learned out of context. Also, rigid meanings may be assigned that will not stand up in other contexts. A 3d

weakness is that since there are no adequate word counts in religious education, the selection of terms tends to be quite arbitrary.

– C. Adrian Heaton

WORKBOOK In public education, " workbook" is a term applied to a variety of types of learning and study books containing exercises and practice material, used especially in the teaching of reading and arithmetic but also adapted to other fields.

In church education a workbook is a similar book or booklet, usually related to a particular unit or course of study and containing many kinds of supplementary teaching-learning materials. These materials may include Bible references, pictorial illustrations, questions for thought and discussion, tests (often involving identification, multiple choice, or sentence completion), outline maps for locating places, assignments for further reading, things to do, suggestions for constructive work, and still other types of guidance for learners to use in the classroom or elsewhere.

For younger children, similar material often takes the form of loose sheets assembled in an envelope. For the older grades, booklets may be titled " Workbook," " Notebook," " Classbook," or something else.

This type of teaching-learning device, in one form or another, came into wide use in the public schools from the 1920's on, and publishers of church school materials for a long time have offered packets of work sheets or booklets with work suggestions as a means of guiding pupil activities. Some of the materials offered for use in Sunday schools have been of questionable value, being little more than devices for keeping children occupied.

The emphasis given to the workbook as an aid to teaching, and the nature of the suggested activities included in it, tend to vary with changing philosophies of Christian education. The better Sunday school leaders saw from the beginning the need of something of this sort, though it often had to be left to the ingenuity of the teacher to provide it. About a century ago Gallaudet's *Picture Defining and Reading Book*, embodying some of the features of the workbook, was popular in the day schools. Writing in 1884, H. Clay Trumbull thought the method equally applicable to Bible teaching in the Sunday school.

Early in this century the emphasis on learning by doing led to greater stress on constructive handwork, clay modeling, " expressional " activities, and the like. Even so, what was then called bookwork, map work, or notebook work was often similar to some of the material found in present-day workbooks.

Educators differ in their estimates of the value of the workbook. There are aspects of Christian education where the checking of facts, the recalling of ideas, and the effort to express meanings in writing or drawing are necessary kinds of learning that the workbook, properly used, may encourage. Proper use would include adequate motivation for the tasks proposed, harmony with the objectives and goals of Christian education, freedom and selectivity in following the suggestions, and the securing of a satisfactory quality of performance.

Our contemporary understanding of the language of relationships and of education as nurturing life in the Christian community does not remove the workbook from among acceptable church school techniques, but it does give it a subordinate place. At the same time, this understanding points up the importance of the social setting in which the workbook is used.

One of the values of the workbook is that it provides for individual, independent work and tests individual achievement. The Christian teacher must, of course, be interested in this kind of learning but he cannot regard it as his main concern in guiding the experience of those who are growing up in the fellowship of the church. Martin Buber, speaking of creative expression, suggests that " individual achievement " is not the whole of the educative process but only its beginning. Solitary accomplishment needs to be made a part of, or lead to, sharing in a common undertaking and " entering into mutuality."

Although the inexperienced teacher may feel the need of precise patterns for the learner's activities, current curriculum trends place the emphasis on resource books and guidance manuals to be used in group planning. — *Wilfred E. Powell*

WORKERS' CONFERENCES Workers' conferences are as essential to a good Christian education program as any of the basic printed materials. In fact, they are more so because at such conferences the staff learn to make good use of materials, understand the children they teach, express their Christian faith, and work together in the fellowship of the church. Accidental planning may occur as staff members see one another in passing on Sunday morning or talk on the telephone, but this will never take the place of regularly scheduled, well-planned conferences.

Although in general Sunday

church school workers are meant, suggestions for their work together may also be applied to groups of youth advisers, weekday or vacation church school workers, and others. By "workers" are meant teachers, secretaries, pianists, substitutes — all who carry responsibility.

The person responsible for the workers' conference is the departmental or divisional superintendent. He must see that meetings are definitely scheduled, preferably at least once a month, and that everyone knows the dates well ahead of time. Attendance should be accepted as a necessary and helpful part of a teaching assignment. Superintendents often underestimate the willingness of their teachers to attend and therefore play down the importance of the meetings.

A half hour at the beginning of a workers' conference could well be spent under a qualified leader discussing the wise use of maps, the place of interest centers in a preschool program, creative dramatics at all ages, basic Christian beliefs, background information integral to the current Bible study, or how to secure active participation in one's class — specific and well-defined topics. The minister, director of Christian education, a local teacher, or an outside resource person can make a brief presentation and/or demonstration and then answer questions. The group, which may have represented more than one department, can divide for consideration of their departmental work.

Three or 4 times a year a thorough look must be taken at the coming quarter's work. This may well consume an entire evening, omitting the possibility of a training period that night. However, at each conference the quarter's theme, the next unit's theme and direction, and the specific materials should all be reviewed. Workers need to see the relation between this quarter's work and that of the last, or between the work on this age level and on another, and especially where their department stands in the whole educational process. Workers in younger departments tend to forget that some facts and concepts are better taught at junior level than at kindergarten. Teachers need to be helped to see why. The study materials need to be reviewed on an adult level of understanding. If the concepts to be taught have no clear meaning for the adult who is teaching, they will have little, if any, for the child.

All churches today have available to them resources of which past generations knew nothing: clear maps of Bible lands; fine filmstrips on many subjects; teaching pictures as well as many others in various publications, which can be mounted and used to great advantage; displays of items from the Holy Land and other countries; and books for all ages, many handsomely published and theologically illuminating. The superintendent should make clear which suggested resources are actually available, and which may be ordered in time to be used. Some can be on display.

Time at a workers' conference must be guarded against frivolous nonessentials. In many matters the superintendent may make and announce decisions. However, when a missionary is to visit the church or a special giving project is ahead, when plans are to be made for Christmas or programs and practices need to be evaluated, then time should be spent in open discussion, probably after the study of the teaching materials.

Underlying training, preview, the sharing of resources, and the planning for special emphases is the worker's own need for a renewed dedication to the task of helping to develop a vital Christian faith in his students. There should be a tone of commitment throughout each meeting. The superintendent's commitment will be obvious as he shows respect for the other members of the staff, listens to their questions, helps them find answers, and allows them to participate fully. If their suggestions and questions are accepted graciously, they in turn will be more likely to accept the contributions of their own pupils without impatience. Individuals on the staff who have special skills to share with the rest or an unusual ability to help others understand difficult concepts should be invited to participate.

A word is in order in favor of the annual " away from the telephone " planning conference at the beginning of the church year. An outside speaker can enrich the lives of all as he shares basic understandings during a morning session, while the departmental previews occupy the afternoon. An informal outdoor environment is conducive to a relaxed sense of fellowship that is hard to achieve in a brief evening session during the year.

— *Barbara A. North*

WORKSHOP The educational workshop is a learning experience in which participants engage in the process of problem-solving through expressing recognized or perceived needs, setting goals, surveying resources, selecting appropriate techniques, and accepting responsibility. Thus the content of a workshop is based on the perceived interest and needs of the participants. Communication is essential in the educative process. The workshop affirms the worth of each individual, implying that his contribution is essential to the effectiveness of the whole and the common good.

Inherent in the philosophy of a workshop are the following assumptions: (1) that persons can change, and that inner growth in terms of attitudes, understandings, and better human relationships can take place; (2) that persons do seek new understandings and can discover these through interaction with other persons and through the use of available resources; (3) that human life is a continuous growth process and therefore individuals seek to perfect their relations with others through communication; (4) that persons respond with the greatest integrity when learning is closely related to the individual's felt or perceived need and his pressing problem; (5) that persons are enriched more by cooperation than by competition.

The workshop purposes to help persons experience a variety of techniques and methods that can be used in other learning situations, and also to help individuals discover processes of evaluation.

A workshop is organized in such a way that individuals get maximum interaction with one another. The 2-way process in communication from the individual to another person and from the leader to a participant and back again is essential for the establishment of a climate of acceptance, basic in workshop philosophy.

Usually the method for organizing the group in a way to get the maximum participation is to begin by having the total group together for large group sessions. In these theory sessions, individuals gain a feeling of a common struggle for understanding of life and work problems. As group members listen to theories that grew out of human experiences, light is thrown on human behavior. In random small groups, individuals spell out, clarify, and identify problems. In small, permanent interest groups, individuals work on defining the problem or the area of concern that the learner seeks to solve. Often if a problem is stated in the form of a question, it is more helpful. In the small, permanent groups the goals are set, resources determined, and techniques and methods applied for problem-solving. It is in the smaller group, through interaction and discussion, that individuals assume responsibility for that part of the goal which they can do best.

The staff serves in 2 major ways: as a guide to group process, and as experienced resource persons contributing information and knowledge.

Three basic educational experiences in a workshop make it unique: planning sessions, work sessions, summary and evaluation sessions.

Planning sessions are essential, in that individuals discover for themselves what it is they plan to do instead of having lecturers "pour in" knowledge. The planning committee is concerned generally with the overall session, which enables the whole workshop to do things together. Morale building frequently is a result of total group sessions because participants discover that they are not alone in their problems. The planning committee usually consists of members from each interest group or from a group of people who are concerned about problems that they would like to

work on in a workshop. Usually a planning committee will meet prior to the general session of the workshop, thereby being able to bring to the total session any decision it has made or would like to have the group make.

Social interaction and evaluation are essential to a good workshop, and these frequently become basic functions of the planning committee. The value to the members of the planning committee is that they develop a sense of responsibility and the feeling of challenge in working, with the able assistance of staff persons, at problems that confront them.

In random groups (sometimes called buzz groups) at the early part of the workshop, individuals, though fearful and hesitant, begin to talk through their surface problems. It is in this process of getting to know one another, warming up, that we begin to list problems. Only after mutual acceptance can the deeper concerns be bared. When many of the problems are identified, it is in small, permanent interest groups, which individuals select on the basis of their own interest and need, that attempts are made at solving the problems of the individuals in each group.

The individual participant discovers that through the interaction of persons he is helped to reshape his attitudes and to examine and discover new methods of relating to others. A participant learns that respect for his own thoughts and opinions is an important part of personal growth. Individuals discover that other persons' experiences throw light on their own problems. Barriers frequently are lowered; through insight, persons become more understanding of the way in which other persons act.

Not uncommon outcomes of a workshop are that individual prejudices are reduced, friendships are formed, new skills are acquired, and a new outlook on meeting life's problems is acquired. Participants gain faith in the group processes as a way of solving problems. In the workshop, persons become goal-directed, evolving plans for problem-solving. A workshop usually is from 2 to 10 days or more in duration.

Conferences planned in advance, leading to outcomes largely predictable, seldom can be called workshops. In a workshop the experiences of all the ingredients are kneaded together in such a way that the content, which is the problems of the participants, rises out of the interaction of the participants.

— *Olivia Pearl Stokes*

WORLD COUNCIL OF CHRISTIAN EDUCATION AND SUNDAY SCHOOL ASSOCIATION The World Council of Christian Education and Sunday School Association (WCCESSA) has this purpose, as stated in its bylaws: "To promote Christian education, including organized Sunday school work, to encourage the study of the Bible, and to participate in the church's task of world evangelization."

This world body is a federation of national and international, interdenominational bodies which carry responsibility for the Christian education programs of the churches of their respective regions. Under certain conditions, membership also is open to autonomous and self-governing denominations.

The member units of the WCCESSA in 1961 numbered 60 in 57 countries. Some are national councils of churches; some are departments of Christian education organized within a national body; others are Sunday school associations. These constituent units, with few exceptions, are responsibly related to churches of their regions.

Beginnings of a world organization came in July, 1889, when the 1st World's Sunday School Convention was held in London. The idea of an international conference of Sunday school workers originated with Benjamin F. Jacobs, of Illinois, and it was approved in 1886 by the Executive Committee of the International Sunday School Association of the U.S.A. and Canada. The program of the world meeting was worked out in correspondence with the London Sunday School Union.

Back of this were a number of contributing developments. One was the instituting of Sunday school unions: American Sunday School Union (1824), India Sunday School Union (1876), and so on. Another was the emergence of a plan for International Uniform Lessons, initiated in 1872. This 1st world convention passed resolutions approving use of the International Uniform Lessons as an aid to unity and cooperation. It also set up a Committee on Sunday School Work Throughout the World, to continue in office until the 2d world convention of Sunday school workers should be held. As a further outcome, a Sunday school missionary to India, James W. Phillips, was employed by the London Sunday School Union.

By 1920, 7 more world conventions had been held — in St. Louis, London, Jerusalem, Rome, Washington, Zurich, and Tokyo. In 1907 the World's Sunday School Association (WSSA) was formed. A resolution stated that "it shall hold conventions and gather information concerning the condition of the Sunday schools throughout the world by correspondence, visitation, etc.," and that "it shall seek to extend the work and increase the efficiency of Sunday schools by cooperation with Sunday school and missionary organizations, especially in those regions of the world most in need of help."

An Executive Committee was elected, with 12 members each from America and Great Britain. There were 2 honorary secretaries, Carey Bonner, of England, and Marion Lawrence, of the U.S.A. Because of travel difficulties, there was a division of responsibilities for work in different parts of the world, the American section taking certain areas for its concern, and the British section, other regions.

In 1917 the World's Sunday School Association was incorporated at Washington. Its constitution provided that "any national or international association might become a section of the World's Sunday School Association, with certain very clearly defined limitations and powers."

This provision marked a movement that came to full development in the period 1924 to 1928. At a meeting of the WSSA Executive Committee in New York in April, 1925, it was agreed that the organization should become a federation of autonomous units, each of which should be represented on the Executive Committee. This reflected understandings arrived at in the world convention held in Glasgow in 1924.

Luther A. Weigle, of Yale University Divinity School, who was Chairman of the WSSA 1928–1958,

reviewed the development in an address given at the 1932 World Convention, held in Rio de Janeiro. He traced 3 stages in the developments to that date: (1) meetings for fellowship, inspiration, and edification; (2) a permanent organization dedicated to the extension of evangelical Sunday schools throughout the world; (3) a world federation of national and international organizations interested in Christian education.

Paid staffs became essential in carrying out work of the 2 administrative committees, 1 in Great Britain, 1 in the U.S.A. Prior to World War II, the WSSA was 1 of the 5 world ecumenical bodies that sponsored the 1st World Conference of Christian Youth, held in Amsterdam in 1939.

In 1947, in a meeting of the Assembly of the World's Sunday School Association in Birmingham, England, it was agreed to change the name to the "World Council of Christian Education," with the proviso that the title would incorporate "World's Sunday School Association." For operating purposes it was agreed in the 1950 meeting of the Assembly to use the title "World Council of Christian Education, and Sunday School Association," though its corporate name is "The World Council of Christian Education."

In 1953 a world office was established to "unify the policy, plans, and budget for the Council and its administrative committees." It was designed for more efficient relations with constituent units of the WCCESSA, and with regions where there are as yet unorganized provisions to meet the needs for Christian nurture. Nelson Chappel became the 1st general secretary of the world office.

Work of the WCCESSA is expressed through the undertakings of its member units as well as by means of the centralized services of the world office. The 2 administrative offices are located in London and in New York, and a staff member has headquarters in the Philippines. Prominent in the programs is concern for children, particularly as these are reached through organized Sunday school movements. One central service in recent years has been making available *Pictures for Children Everywhere* — sets of large and small Bible pictures, and also an illustrated story booklet, *Jesus, Friend of Children Everywhere*, now available in some 60 languages or vernaculars.

A youth department was organized in 1950, with close working relationships with the youth department of the World Council of Churches, 1 committee jointly serving both organizations. Another joint youth work enterprise has been World Youth Projects, through which Christian youth groups anywhere may seek from or proffer to other youth groups financial aid or exchange in 6 areas of youth work.

Audio-Visual Aids (London office) evaluates audio-visual materials with particular reference to the younger churches. A Television Training Center also is conducted.

The development of indigenous curriculum materials is an undertaking involving close relationship among member units of the WCCESSA. Teaching materials are produced for children, youth, adults, and families. Curriculum preparation is actively under way in Latin America, India, the Middle East, Africa south of the Sahara, East and West Pakistan, in the English-speaking Caribbean, and for Chinese in southeast Asia. In each curriculum undertaking, criteria and form are developed by national leaders who work through the cooperative body or bodies of a country or region. The WCCESSA effects interchange of ideas on content and structure of the curriculum and enlists financial assistance.

Related to curriculum are leadership teams, through which a highly trained specialist works with a trained national leader of proved potential, developing leadership training resources for all ages, in cooperation with the churches of a given region.

Attention is also given to helping theological seminaries provide for the preparation of future ministers in matters of Christian nurture.

Financial grants, on a diminishing basis, are made to member units in need, with the aim of aiding each to become self-supporting as well as self-directing.

World fellowship is maintained among those who serve the cause of Christian education in the churches — through world and regional conferences, institutes, and workshops. A quarterly magazine, *World Christian Education*, publishing articles emanating from varied backgrounds of region or communion, has subscribers in over 100 countries.

The 14th World Convention of the WCCESSA was held in Tokyo in August, 1958. World Institutes on Christian Education have been held at Toronto (1950) and Nishinomiya, Japan (1958).

It is significant that the cause of the Sunday school and of Christian nurture was one of the initial occasions for common effort among denominations. Deepening understandings of the theological foundations of Christian education and of the meaning of the church have marked recent developments within the WCCESSA, along with continuing effort to meet on a worldwide scale the immediate needs for Christian nurture for children, youth, and adults, wherever the church has been planted. — *Everett M. Stowe*

WORLD COUNCIL OF CHURCHES

The World Council of Churches is "a fellowship of churches which confess the Lord Jesus Christ as God and Savior according to the Scriptures and therefore seek to fulfill together their common calling to the glory of the one God, Father, Son, and Holy Spirit." The outstanding organizational expression of the ecumenical movement, it comprises some 200 member churches in 60 countries, and represents all major Protestant and Orthodox groups.

The WCC marks the confluence of 3 currents in world Christianity — missionary expansion, interdenominational cooperation, and church unity. A landmark in this development was the world conference in Edinburgh, 1910, under the leadership of John R. Mott and J. H. Oldham. It led in 1921 to the establishment of the International Missionary Council (IMC), which since then has served as the chief cooperative agency in Protestant missions. The Edinburgh conference also gave seminal impulses to 2 other movements. On the initiative of an Episcopal bishop, Charles H. Brent, a movement was formed that, looking beyond practical cooperation, set as its task advancing the cause of a reunited Christendom by engaging the churches in a common exploration of issues of faith and order that have separated them for centuries. World conferences on Faith and Order — held in Lausanne (1927), Edinburgh (1937), Lund (1952),

Montreal (1963) — have been focal points in an ecumenical dialogue, clarifying deep-rooted differences, and registering growing agreements on the church, sacraments, forms of worship, ministry, and goals of unity. Out of World War I grew another movement, organized at Stockholm in 1925 under the leadership of Archbishop Nathan Söderblom of the Church of Sweden. Later known as the Universal Christian Council for Life and Work, it developed an international program of social study, education, and action and in the 1930's, notably through its world conference at Oxford (1937), it became a rallying point in the Christian struggle against the forces of totalitarianism.

In 1937 it was resolved to merge Faith and Order with Life and Work in a World Council of Churches, which held its constituting assembly at Amsterdam (1948). Thereby an epochal step was taken in the development of the ecumenical movement, transforming it from functional associations within the churches into a representative and permanent fellowship of churches with global outreach. Further assemblies were held at Evanston (1954) and New Delhi (1961). On this occasion the recognition of the inseparability of mission and unity was formalized in an integration of WCC and IMC, the latter becoming the WCC Division of World Mission and Evangelism.

The nature and purpose of the WCC are defined in its constitution and have been further articulated in the so-called "Toronto Statement" of 1950. The Council is a fellowship of churches, forming a continuing organ whereby they seek to express and further their unity in all realms of life: witness, teaching, worship, service to the world. It "shall offer counsel and provide opportunity of united action in matters of common interest." Consisting of self-governing church bodies, it possesses no legislative power over these bodies, nor can it speak or act for them except by specific delegation. It is thus no "superchurch." Its authority (in the words of one of its founders, William Temple, Archbishop of Canterbury) "consists in the weight which it carries with the churches by its own wisdom."

The principal authority in the Council is an assembly composed of delegates appointed by the constituent churches. It ordinarily meets every 5 years. Due to its representative galaxy of Christian leaders, the formative influence of its deliberations, and the extensive range of its preparation and follow-up, each such assembly forms a notable event in the life of world Christianity. A central committee of 100 members, meeting once a year, and an executive committee carry responsibility for the execution of the assembly's decisions.

Membership in the Council is open to churches that accept its Trinitarian basis, and in addition fulfill certain requirements concerning autonomy, stability, size, etc. Apart from the basis, membership does not require any conformity in theology or doctrine of the church; this would be contrary to the very nature of the Council. Thus the Council, paradoxically, includes communions that claim to be the one true church, yet have joined with other Christian groups in this fraternal fellowship dedicated to a common cause.

Recalling the message of the constituting assembly, the Evanston assembly declared: "To stay together

is not enough. We must go forward. As we learn more of our unity in Christ, it becomes the more intolerable that we should be divided." The full significance of this intention, and the strains and stresses inherent in the council, become apparent when one considers the heterogeneous character of its membership. It includes churches with the most varied religious, cultural, and political backgrounds, holding contrasting and sometimes irreconcilable beliefs, worshiping in manifold ways, and representing very differing age levels, some shaped by a millenary history, others younger than the Council itself. Many of them have for centuries lived in complete isolation from one another or know about other churches merely through hearsay and caricature. Others carry traumatic memories of bitter fights or religious persecution.

Although Protestant churches in the West form the majority, the members include a rapidly growing number of newly independent churches in Africa, Asia, and Latin America. The participation of 2 Pentecostal churches has suggested a further broadening of the ecumenical spectrum. Major unaffiliated groups are the Southern Baptist Convention and the Lutheran Church — Missouri Synod. The WCC, however, is not a pan-Protestant agency, nor does it allow political and ideological boundaries to limit its religious fellowship. The admission in 1961 of churches in Russia, Poland, Romania, and Bulgaria — joining the ancient patriarchates and other Orthodox charter members — is bound to result in a more forceful and challenging Orthodox contribution. The Roman Catholic Church maintains no official relations with the WCC; but the growth of informal contacts, the creation of a Vatican secretariat for promoting Christian unity, and the presence of official Roman Catholic observers, for the 1st time, at the New Delhi assembly are signs of an improving climate.

Recent years have seen a mounting trend toward regional groupings within the ecumenical community, as instanced by the formation of the East Asia Christian Conference and the All-Africa Conference of Churches. The WCC, moreover, maintains a vast network of cooperative relations with other denominational bodies, such as national Christian councils, world confessional associations, international Christian youth organizations, the World Council of Christian Education, and the United Bible Societies.

The Council's headquarters are located in Geneva, Switzerland, with regional offices in New York and East Asia. Its far-flung program activities are organized in a general secretariat, and these divisions: Studies; Ecumenical Action; Interchurch Aid; Refugee and World Service; World Mission; Evangelism. Each division groups various departmental units and numerous commissions. The Ecumenical Institute at Céligny (Bossey), near Geneva, functions as an international center for advanced ecumenical education and lay leadership training. The Council publishes *The Ecumenical Review* (quarterly), *Ecumenical Press Service* (weekly), and departmental bulletins and reports.

A report of the New Delhi 1961 assembly articulated the evolving consensus in these words: "We believe that the unity which is both God's will and his gift to his church is being made visible as all in each place who are baptized into Jesus Christ and confess him as Lord and Savior are brought by the Holy Spirit into one fully committed fellowship, holding the one apostolic faith, preaching the one gospel, breaking the one bread, joining in common prayer, and having a corporate life reaching out in witness and service to all, and who at the same time are united with the whole Christian fellowship in all places and all ages in such wise that ministry and members are accepted by all, and that all can act and speak together as occasion requires for the tasks to which God calls his people. It is for such a unity that we believe we must pray and work."

— *Nils Ehrenstrom*

WORSHIP The word "worship" is from the Middle English *worschipe*, which in turn derives from the Anglo-Saxon *weorthscipe* (worthship). Thus when one worships God, he is declaring God's worth, our Lord's worthiness to be praised. This is the point of the Shorter Catechism's defining of "the chief end of man": "to glorify God, and enjoy him forever." Worship is to be understood as man's duty and privilege (objective), rather than as a means to his own emotional satisfaction (subjective).

Worship is the only unique function of the Christian community. Public speaking, education, social service, and fellowship all appear in other agencies and institutions. A church that failed to put the worship of God first would be less than a true church.

Of related terms, ritual refers to the words used in worship, and ceremonial to the actions performed. A liturgy is specifically a way of celebration of the Holy Communion.

Thus the only truly "nonliturgical" churches are those which do not celebrate the Communion at all. Nor is it possible for any worshiping group to avoid either ritual or ceremonial. Differences are simply among kinds of observance, which may be classified approximately as "formal" and "informal."

Christian worship has its roots in the practices of Judaism, alike in the Jerusalem Temple, in the synagogues of the scattered Jewish communities of the ancient world, and in the life of the Jewish family. Temple worship was chiefly sacrificial. The synagogue services included praise, prayer, readings from the Scriptures, and instruction (sermons). In the family the father led the worship of the household, especially on the eves of Sabbaths and holy days.

Jesus and his disciples worshiped both at the Temple and in local synagogues. The Last Supper, which marked the beginning of the Christian service of Holy Communion, was a standard religious family meal in which Jesus assumed the role of the father. To the regular usage, however, he added the new meaning: "This is my body. . . . This . . . is the new covenant in my blood."

The Communion service was the principal worship observance of Christianity from the beginnings until the Protestant Reformation. Gradually its procedure became standardized, with regional variations, and as time passed it was greatly elaborated. The continuing use of Latin in Western Catholicism led to a loss of understanding on the part of the laity; and actual congregational participation, whether in the words of the service or in the receiving of the elements, was reduced to a minimum.

The effort of the great Reformers in this realm was not to subordinate worship, but rather to restore it fully to the people. Therefore the services were simplified and translated into the national languages, and congregational singing was reintroduced. Martin Luther in Germany, John Calvin in Geneva, and Thomas Cranmer in England, all regarded the Communion as the principal type of Christian worship, and frequent sharing in it as essential to the Christian life.

More radical rejection of Catholic worship usages occurred among the English Separatists, and reached its extreme in the "silent meetings" of the Society of Friends (Quakers). In Methodism, John Wesley urged weekly Communion, and the use of the Church of England forms of service; but his followers, especially in America, disregarded his advice on both points. Conditions on the American frontier made standardized worship difficult, and the American Revolution contributed to making Church of England practices unpopular.

At the same time the necessity of arguing for Protestant points of view led to a special emphasis upon preaching. The product in most of American Protestantism was the assumption that church services were held for the hearing of sermons. Praise and prayer were continued, but informally and casually, and commonly were thought of as "the preliminaries." Churches were built as auditoriums, focusing on the pulpit and with floors sloped in order to improve visibility. Kneeling dropped out of use, and congregations in general came to listen rather than to participate.

Renewed interest in both the

forms and the meanings of worship has constituted a liturgical revival in our time. Roman Catholics, Anglicans, and Lutherans led the way in a restudy of their own customs, with consequent reforming of many of their practices. In other major denominations there has been, since the beginning of the 20th century, a strong tendency to revive many of the usages that had been discarded after the Protestant Reformation.

The Presbyterian Church in the U.S.A. (now United Presbyterian) issued its *Book of Common Worship* in 1906 (revised editions in 1932 and 1946). The Methodist Church in 1932 restored the "Wesley Sunday Service" (based on the Anglican Morning and Evening Prayer) to official sanction, and in 1945 published *A Book of Worship and Prayer for Church and Home,* currently in process of experimental revision. In 1948 the Congregational Christian Churches (now United Church of Christ) authorized *A Book of Worship for Free Churches.*

All these depend heavily upon the Anglican Book of Common Prayer, and all are designed to encourage standard forms of public worship with greatly increased congregational sharing. They reflect the realization that the old objection to "canned prayers" has deprived the churches of much of the treasury of devotion built up through the centuries, and also that a prayer book is needed if the people are to pray together, just as is a hymnal if they are to sing together.

Fashions in church architecture have been changing concomitantly, in order to place the altar or holy table at the focal point in the sanctuary, with the pulpit moved away from the center. Crosses and candles, once repudiated as being "popish,"

now are generally accepted as meaningful symbols. There has been some disposition to imitate ancient practice without full recognition of meaning, as in the use of Gothic with materials other than stone, and in reproducing the monastic pattern of placement of the choir in the chancel.

Most recently contemporary styles in architecture have gained dominance. These have the dual advantage of being truer to our time and of being much less expensive to construct. The choir often is placed in a rear gallery or in a transept for the reason that its proper function is to support congregational singing rather than to render concert performances.

Another revival of tradition is occurring in the increased use of the historic Christian calendar. Some Protestant extremists attempted at first to refuse recognition even to the festivals of Christmas and Easter, but were not able to secure any large acquiescence. Today the observance of Lent is becoming general, and Whitsuntide (Pentecost) and Advent are widely recognized. The worship books of the major churches all include Biblical "lectionaries," providing for an orderly sequence in reading from the Scriptures, and so for systematic attention to the many varied aspects of Christian history, faith, and life.

Practically all Anglican churches provide at least one celebration of the Holy Communion on Sunday, and another during the week. The standard Lutheran service is of the historic Communion format, and increasingly is being carried through to include the Communion itself. Many of the Presbyterian, Methodist, and Congregational clergy are introducing more frequent Communions, though not yet with enthusiastic support from most of the laity in their churches.

It is not to be expected that any single form of worship will commend itself immediately to all Protestants. What may be hoped for is that with deepened understanding of the meaning of worship in the church, Christian people will learn to worship God more sincerely and more comprehendingly. As they do this, their appreciation of the means of worship in symbolism, music, prayer, and the reading of God's Word may be expected to develop to a significant degree.

— *George Hedley*

WORSHIP, FAMILY A grass-roots movement to encourage parents to bring their children with them to Sunday services started in the Episcopal Church in the 1940's. Clergy dubbed it " the family service " and explained, " You no longer have to taxi your child to and from Sunday school and then rush back to church yourself." This one-trip Sunday made sense, and the family service movement grew. After a generation of disuse the family pew began to be revived. Interest in the family service shortly spread across denominational lines.

The educational importance of this revival was threefold: (1) Children were included in genuine Christian worship. Departmental Sunday school services in children's chapels are " play church " to little children and as such should not be underrated or slighted, but when little ones come into the " big church " with mother and father on special occasions — Christmas or birthdays, e.g. — this is the " real thing." (2) In corporate worship there is a comprehensive and systematic presentation of the Bible's whole story in

the course of every year. This is true to the extent to which the Christian year is faithfully observed. (Cf. William Sydnor, *How and What the Church Teaches* for a fuller treatment of this subject.) (3) Family ties are strengthened. Little children like to do things with their parents, and family participation in regular public worship can be one of the high points of the week because the family does it together. The fact that preschoolers are in church only on special occasions or that those in the early grades leave before the sermon and go to their classes does not dilute the profound significance of the family pew.

In order that a family service be most effective, clergy have to learn to conduct services when the congregation is composed of a cross section of their whole congregation and not just the adult segment of it. They must train parents to worship when children are present.

Mindful of the wide age spectrum among those in church a clergyman is likely to do several things. He gives the page numbers when congregational responses are expected, and he gives time for young participants to find the place. A brief well-prepared sentence or two introducing Scripture readings helps both young and old find them intelligible. Often a short talk (3 to 5 minutes) is addressed especially to the younger worshipers. Finally, the selection of hymns and the way in which prayers are said will also be influenced by the presence of young worshipers.

Parents also need direction. Their children should sit with them and not be made to sit by classes. The service is a family event, not a Sunday school exercise. The pew in which the family sits should be determined by whether the youngest member can see and hear rather than by tradition. Parents need to realize that their example in worship and their assistance to the children in finding page numbers, etc., are more important than any disciplinary authority they may exercise.

These are the kinds of things which go into helping both clergy and parents take part in a service in which children are present. When genuine family worship has begun to be achieved, all worshipers, adults and children alike, begin to gain a real appreciation of what it means to be part of the family of God. — *William Sydnor*

WRITING A kindergarten child hears his teacher ask, " Tell me what you like best about summer." As he replies, he watches her write on a chalkboard some strange-looking marks called " words." Then he hears her reading to him his own answers and those of his classmates. Finally he joins them in saying, " Thank you, God, for all the things that come in summer." This child has been involved in " writing " a prayer of thanksgiving.

A young adult is asked to lead a worship service for members of his study groups. He ponders over the prayer he wants to pray, and begins to write down words and phrases that express the ideas he wants to include. He selects and discards, changes and corrects — and in the end he has written an expression of praise, thanksgiving, confession, and petition. He, too, has been involved in " writing " a prayer.

In both cases, words were chosen and arranged in a form that expressed ideas and feelings. The young child required the helpful skill of the teacher to make of his words a permanent record. The young adult was able to do this for himself. In between these 2 extremes are to be found many ways of making use of words to express and communicate to others facts, feelings, ideas, doubts, and questions.

One definition suggests that " creative activities " are those in which a " work of thought and imagination " is produced. In the area of writing, this may include a wide variety of experiences ranging from the writing of a story as a class project to the preparation of prayers and litanies to be used in group or individual worship. Persons engage in creative writing experiences in order to record ideas, facts, and other findings; express feelings (including doubts and questions); discover new and deeper meanings. In the light of these 3 purposes, the following specific writing experiences can be briefly considered. All these will naturally require a greater degree of teacher guidance for the younger age groups participating. None should be entered upon primarily to produce " works of art " or as areas of competition among pupils, though they should represent the best efforts of their " authors." Rather, they are to provide means of expressing as satisfactorily as possible whatever ideas, feelings, facts, and questions inspired them in the 1st place.

1. Young children enjoy telling an adult a series of facts about some interesting event, and then having those facts written down in simple story form and read back to them over and over. Older children find that writing a story about some fictitious character allows them the freedom to deal in an unselfconscious way with problems, questions,

or puzzling experiences too personal or embarrassing to discuss and admit as their own. Bible stories retold in present-day language help to clarify meaning and often reveal to a teacher or parent many areas of misunderstanding or doubt that otherwise might never be expressed verbally.

2. Simple plays, in which either the persons themselves or some puppets or other stick figures are the actors, are another means of expressing what has been learned about Bible stories or religious teachings. Plays are also a good way of playing out real feelings and attitudes that cannot be described verbally in discussions or during question and answer times.

3. The descriptions and thoughts that even young people put into letter form often are surprising. Letters that say "thank you" for expressions of love and concern, that tell about some activity or experience, that carry on a new friendship, all give many people a chance to talk freely on paper when they are not able to do so face to face.

4. It might be fair to say that not until a person or group attempts to put prayers into words that pass the test of "Does this say what I (we) really mean?" can the liturgy of the church be truly appreciated.

Even young children can suggest and help to arrange prayer thoughts about some particular idea, and to choose 1 simple response such as, "Thank you, God," or "We ask your help, O God," in order to compose a litany for their group.

5. Some children and adults enjoy working with words and expressions in which rhyme and rhythm play a large part. A familiar hymn tune, e.g., can inspire the creation of meaningful new words, growing out of some discussion or class study.

6. In today's world, where so much of what we hear and read is in the form of "digested" facts, many persons feel at home expressing themselves in this way. Reporting incidents that took place long ago, perhaps during Old Testament times or the days when the church was very young, provides an opportunity for interpreting learning about these events in modern-day language.

Creative writing therefore can be construed to include any of the ways in which words are used to express in some meaningful way the ideas, feelings, and discoveries of individuals or groups who are seeking for the meaning of and responses to God's love as it is revealed through Jesus Christ. — *Gertrude Priester*

Y

YOUNG ADULTS Young adults are persons who are beginning to sever their dependency relationship with parents and are assuming the responsibilities of adulthood. This involves earning a living, entering into the marriage relationship, or choosing to remain single. Actually the passage from adolescence to adulthood is not marked clearly. Topological psychology would include that period of life in which a person is leaving home, getting his first full-time job, graduating from college, choosing a life mate or choosing to remain single, and working out a whole series of postmarital adjustments — economic, social, physiological (obtaining and furnishing a home, preparing for parenthood, birth of an infant and infant care, assuming community responsibilities, and beginning to set the children free).

Robert J. Havighurst describes the young adult in terms of the developmental tasks that he must negotiate. These tasks are responses to both inner biological and spiritual needs as well as the social and moral demands that society places upon the individual at this stage of his development.

Psychologists (e.g., Erik Erikson) indicate that young adulthood is the period in which the drives toward intimacy and identity must achieve satisfactory goals. The young adult longs for an authentic affirmation of who he is so that he may say so and mean it. Moreover, the young adult is experiencing others as human beings who have thoughts, feelings, and the right of self-determination. He must relate to them not as a dependent or dominant individual but as person to person.

During young adulthood persons make basic choices that largely determine their development throughout adult life. These choices are their vocations, their life mates, and the standards of values by which they will govern their own lives. The church has a great opportunity to help young adults negotiate all these choices wisely and to build their lives on strong spiritual foundations. Church educational programs that are related to these inner tensions, developmental needs, basic spiritual requirements, and relevant decisions will perform a more adequate ministry than programs unrelated to young adult experiences.

Current social factors influencing the lives of young adults and affecting types of programs and ways of working with them are these: (1) The majority are getting married, establishing homes, and beginning their families before 24 years of age. (2) They are moving from rural regions to the cities, making up a large section of the inner-city population. (3) Job demands in many cases require a high rate of mobility among these persons. (4) The number of persons in the age group of 18 to 30 will more than double during the next decade. (5) The educational level of young adults is high. The median represents persons who are high school graduates. A large proportion of this section of the population have attended college or have availed themselves of post high school educational advantages. (6) Young adults today are not " joiners." They participate in very few community organizations.

Fragmentation is a characteristic of the early young adult years. Many are in the later years of college or graduate school, equipping themselves for a profession. Many, still living at home or living on the campus and having families of their own, feel aimless and rootless or choose to make a career of military life. Another segment of the young adult population are trying to achieve independence and yet meet family responsibilities and maintain primary relationships in their families. Many young adults are living away from home in bachelor apartments within large cities, seeking to overcome loneliness as they make their way in the world on their own. A large segment of the young adult population is made up of young married couples without children. Both may be working in order to accumulate funds for starting a home. Another large segment of the young adult population is made up of young married couples with chil-

dren. They are facing rigorous financial obligations and the responsibilities of rearing children. The factors pulling young adults in different directions are much stronger than those seeking to bring them together. These factors tend to isolate them from the rest of life, to curtail their relationships and limit their participation in community activities. Nonetheless, these young adults need to discover in a personal way their relationship to other adults in the community and to learn in and through the church their responsibilities for the mutual ministry of persons in the Christian community.

These factors have implications for grouping young adults, for the time of meetings, methods of approaches, types of materials used, and the leadership needed.

— *Robert S. Clemmons*

YOUNG MEN'S CHRISTIAN ASSOCIATION

To speak of the Young Men's Christian Association as if there were a central organization with many branches is misleading. In North America, for example, one might properly refer to the National Councils of Y.M.C.A.'s of the U.S.A. or Canada, and with a few exceptions this is the normal pattern in the approximately 80 countries where Y.M.C.A.'s exist. These national movements are bound together in the World Alliance of Young Men's Christian Associations, founded in Paris in 1855. The headquarters of the World Alliance has been in Geneva ever since a secretariat was established in 1878.

Young men's religious societies under various names sprang up in Europe and America during the 1st decades of the 19th century, but the 1st group to call itself a Young Men's

Christian Association was in London in 1844. The 1st Y.M.C.A.'s in North America were established in Montreal and Boston in 1851. The name and the idea spread quickly and within a few years the movement in the U.S.A. was the largest in the world.

One of the driving forces of the Y.M.C.A. movement from the beginning was a desire for greater unity among Christians. At the 1st world conference in Paris 1 of the speakers declared: "It is our deep and earnest conviction that it is the duty of Christians to aim at the restoration of the unity of the church." This unifying goal was seen at first primarily in a Protestant context, but today the constituency of the worldwide Y.M.C.A. movement includes many members of the Orthodox Churches and the Roman Catholic Church. This inclusiveness has sometimes given rise to tensions within the Y.M.C.A. and misunderstandings on the part of church leaders, but it has enabled the Y.M.C.A. to play a pioneering role in the development of the ecumenical movement.

Y.M.C.A.'s differ greatly from country to country in size, program, and organization. Not only are there the familiar city associations with large buildings, but there are also hundreds of groups of young men in towns and villages who meet in small rooms or use the facilities of churches and schools. The Y.M.C.A. is a lay organization not under ecclesiastical control, but there are some situations, particularly in Europe, where Y.M.C.A.'s are closely related to local parishes of the dominant church of the country. In some instances they serve as the youth work of the churches. In those parts of the world where Christians are in a small minority the Y.M.C.A. constituency includes many young men of other faiths. It is characteristic of the Y.M.C.A. to maintain an open door to persons of any faith or none, although the direction remains in the hands of Christians.

Underlying all the variations in emphasis and the diversity of forms around the world there is a statement of purpose that has served in a remarkable way as a bond of unity through more than a century of international conflicts and internal tensions. This is the Paris Basis, formulated by young men at the 1st world conference in 1855. The "fundamental principle" embodied in this statement is the continuing foundation of the work and witness of the World Alliance, and each member must indicate its accord with this Basis: "The Young Men's Christian Associations seek to unite those young men who, regarding Jesus Christ as their God and Savior according to the Holy Scriptures, desire to be his disciples in their faith and in their life, and to associate their efforts for the extension of his Kingdom amongst young men."

Within this world movement the Y.M.C.A.'s of the U.S.A. hold a position of great influence. Their 2,750,000 members comprise more than half of the total world membership. Their 3,800 full-time secretaries are double the number of professional workers in all other national movements combined. Their contribution toward the development of Y.M.C.A.'s in other lands amounts to $1,700,000 or more annually, in addition to occasional campaigns for special projects. Some 50 North American fraternal secretaries are giving assistance to Y.M.C.A. movements in other countries.

Against the background of this

international setting one may define more precisely the characteristics of the Y.M.C.A.'s of the U.S.A. with special reference to their purpose and role in Christian education. What is said here would apply in most respects to the Y.M.C.A.'s of Canada also, since the associations in these 2 neighboring countries have developed over the years in close relationship and with many experiences in common.

1. Y.M.C.A. leaders have reaffirmed repeatedly the Christian character and purpose of this movement. Rarely does one find today in the Y.M.C.A.'s the evangelistic meetings or the regular Bible classes that were a common feature 40 or 50 years ago. Gone is the religious-work department that was associated with the more or less standardized program of earlier years. But Y.M.C.A.'s for the most part have resisted a swing in the opposite direction toward becoming leisure-time social welfare agencies for work with youth scarcely distinguishable from those under secular or governmental auspices. They do not want to be classified simply as a "character-building" agency, nor are they usually content to accept the vague appellation "religious," even though they welcome among their members Jews and persons of other faiths. They hold to a revised national statement of purpose formulated in 1931: "The Young Men's Christian Association we regard as being, in its essential genius, a worldwide fellowship united by a common loyalty to Jesus Christ for the purpose of developing Christian personality and building a Christian society." One of the recommendations of teen-age young people in a recent National Hi-Y Congress (U.S.A.) was that "every person should be drawn into

club membership on the basis of his present interests and contacts, but each should be told that this is a Christian organization and that he is expected to try to live up to its Christian purpose." National leaders are aware of the dangers of superficiality and institutionalism in so large an organization and they are constantly calling for a reexamination of the basic purposes of the Y.M.C.A. as a Christian movement.

2. Y.M.C.A.'s practice a combination of "direct" and "indirect" approaches to Christian education. Fundamental in Y.M.C.A. philosophy is the conviction that Christianity to be vital must be integrally related to all aspects of living. Therefore the association must make provision in its program both for the demonstration of Christianity in practice and for interpretation of what it means to be Christian. Hi-Y Clubs, for example, seek "to create, maintain, and extend throughout the home, school, and community high standards of Christian character," but the induction ceremony of new members, which has explicit Christian content and a period of devotions, is a normal part of club procedure. In Y.M.C.A. summer camps boys learn to pray as a normal part of cabin life and campfire experience. College Y.M.C.A.'s typically have a wide range of activities, including discussion groups, campus service, and recreation, but Bible study and worship have been central elements in their program. To the casual observer the Y.M.C.A. may look simply like a beehive of activity in which young people are having a good time, but one who looks behind the scenes will usually find a group of earnest leaders who are alert to opportunities for relating the Christian purpose of the association to

every activity. Although Christian values are often embodied in a Y.M.C.A. program without direct comment on the part of a leader, it is his responsibility also to look for occasions where there may be an explicit interpretation of Christian standards and an expression of Christian convictions. It is primarily through the impact of persons whose lives and enthusiasms express Christian faith that the Christian purposes of the Y.M.C.A. are achieved. The main emphasis in the Y.M.C.A. is not on religious activities as such but on persons who can communicate Christian insight and knowledge through any type of activity in which young people are interested.

3. Y.M.C.A.'s have many opportunities to develop a Christian concern regarding the great social and international problems of the day. On the whole, Y.M.C.A.'s have not been noted for vigorous pronouncements on controversial issues and they have been wary about getting involved in political action. But many associations have been working quietly at breaking down racial barriers in sports competition, summer camps, and city residence halls. Members of Hi-Y clubs and Student Y.M.C.A.'s have been involved frequently in the sit-in protests in the South. For 25 years groups of high school young people have been going to state capitols under Y.M.C.A. auspices to take part in model legislative sessions; this Y.M.C.A. "Youth and Government" program is now found in 36 states. Probably no other organization sponsors so many conferences where human relations in industry are the chief object of attention. For several years the American Y.M.C.A.'s have sponsored a 2-way exchange between the U.S.A. and the U.S.S.R. for students and experienced secretaries. Education on international affairs is expanding rapidly in Y.M.C.A.'s, along with direct involvement of young people through travel, work camps, and international conferences. All these Y.M.C.A. projects, however short they may fall of meeting fully the needs and opportunities of our day, are to be seen as a significant form of Christian study and action.

4. The Y.M.C.A. as a lay Christian movement supplements the work of the churches at important points. There has been a large measure of friendly cooperation between Y.M.C.A.'s and churches in most countries. Y.M.C.A.'s feel that they must take a share of the responsibility for meeting the spiritual needs of youth, but they can never be a substitute for churches. The Y.M.C.A. is able to reach many young people who are estranged from churches or have never had any vital connection with them. It seeks to meet these young people at the point of individual interest and need and to make Christian faith a reality in daily life. These young people are encouraged to identify themselves actively with a particular church. The Y.M.C.A. is able to provide facilities for weekday activities that can seldom be duplicated by local churches. It can often be more flexible in method and experimental in approach to new situations. It provides a meeting place for young people and adults of all denominations and confessions and has the possibility, not always fully realized, of developing understanding and respect for persons of differing religious backgrounds. It is concerned not only to recruit leaders for the Y.M.C.A. but to equip laymen to carry out their Christian convictions in the sphere of their daily callings and to serve as leaders

in affairs of the community and the nation. Potentially, the Y.M.C.A. is an important form of the Christian lay apostolate. — *Paul M. Limbert*

YOUNG WOMEN'S CHRISTIAN ASSOCIATION The Young Women's Christian Association is a worldwide movement of Christian laywomen, with associations in 65 countries. It endeavors to build a fellowship through which women and girls may come to know more of the love of God as revealed in Jesus Christ for themselves and for all people, and to learn to express that love in responsible action. It believes that unity among Christians is the will of God and desires as a lay movement to make a contribution toward that unity. It recognizes the equal value in God's sight of all human beings without distinction of race, nationality, class, or religion and seeks to promote understanding and cooperation among people of different nations, races, and groups.

When it began more than a century ago, its members were drawn chiefly from among women who were members of Protestant evangelical churches. In 1894, 4 national associations that had grown up in Great Britain, the U.S.A., Norway, and Sweden joined together to form the World Y.W.C.A. As the World Y.W.C.A. grew, leaders and members came from an ever greater number of denominational and confessional groups. As early as 1909, work was started among women who were members of the Greek and other Eastern Orthodox Churches, and by 1911 Y.W.C.A.'s in Eastern Europe included women from Orthodox, Roman Catholic, and Protestant backgrounds. Some national associations joining the World Y.W.C.A. were in countries with 1 dominant

confession and almost all its members from 1 church. Some developed in countries where a great variety of denominations and confessional groups are represented, and others where many belong to a minority church. Y.W.C.A.'s in countries of non-Christian culture brought yet another pattern of work and organization.

The constitution of the World Y.W.C.A., adopted in 1955, expresses for the whole movement the interconfessional basis of the work and the membership: "Article II, Basis: Faith in God the Father Almighty, and in Jesus Christ his only Son our Lord and Savior, and in the Holy Spirit. . . . Article IV, Functions: . . . It brings women and girls of different Christian traditions into a worldwide fellowship in which they may grow as Christians, participating in the life and worship of their church and expressing their faith by word and deed. It includes within its fellowship all women and girls who desire to participate in its program."

The basis of membership in the Y.W.C.A. is personal. No young woman, to whatever branch of the Christian church she belongs, shall be excluded from membership in any national association provided she is in agreement with the Christian basis of the Y.W.C.A. The membership of the Y.W.C.A. represents a cross section of the women of the world. It includes girls working in industry, business and professional women, students, married and single women, young and old women.

As a lay movement the Y.M.C.A. does not assume the functions of a church. It does not attempt to provide a complete religious experience for its members, but endeavors to deepen the participation of each member in the life and worship of the church of her choice and to help non-church-related members to find their place in the fellowship of Christians. When Y.W.C.A. members pray together it is in the form of family prayers, and efforts are made to choose material that may be used by all. Whenever possible those planning family prayers are drawn from all the confessions represented. For over 50 years the World Y.W.C.A. together with the World Alliance of Y.M.C.A.'s has observed a Week of Prayer and World Fellowship. The material for this week is prepared by an international, interconfessional group.

The Y.W.C.A. is founded on prayer, service, faith, and action. It seeks to help its members to discover the relevance of the Christian faith to all life. It does this through a varied program of study and action. The Y.W.C.A. works for international understanding, for improved social and economic conditions, and for basic human rights for all people. The World Y.W.C.A. maintains an active consultative relationship with the United Nations and some of its specialized agencies, and as a Christian movement feels a special responsibility to contribute both thoughts and actions that will help the UN evolve into a truly effective instrument for the maintenance of peace and social justice. It follows closely the work of the Commission on the Status of Women, the Human Rights Commission, and the Economic and Social Council, and keeps national movements informed regarding progress in these areas. As a world movement it has made official pronouncements in regard to certain issues, e.g., Statement of World Y.W.C.A. Policy in Regard to World Peace (1955), World

Y.W.C.A. Resolution on Nuclear Testing (1959), Resolution on Discrimination (1960).

From its earliest days the Y.W.C.A. has sought to combat any form of racial prejudice. The implementation of its policy of racial inclusiveness is considered carefully before a national Y.W.C.A. is accepted for affiliation with the World Y.W.C.A. Some national associations have made special statements of their own interracial policy in order to ensure that local associations grant full rights and privileges, in all programs and services, to all members regardless of race or class (e.g., Y.W.C.A. of U.S.A., 1948).

National Y.W.C.A.'s act in times of emergency to meet special needs, and the World Y.W.C.A. undertakes and sponsors international humanitarian, welfare, and relief work to refugees in accordance with Christian principles, irrespective of religious, social, political, national, or racial differences, when national associations are unable to operate. The long-term nature of the refugee problem in Europe and the Middle East has led the World Y.W.C.A. to continue to serve, in close cooperation with national associations and with intergovernmental and voluntary organizations, in offering special services to refugees in these areas. National associations assist in the permanent settlement of refugees and in the integration of migrants in their countries.

Through the World Y.W.C.A. program of Mutual Service, Y.W.C.A.'s in different parts of the world help one another through sharing financial resources and by the exchange of experience and leadership. Regional conferences and World Y.W.C.A. consultations, seminars, and the 4-yearly World Council meeting provide opportunities for members from different countries to meet, learn from one another, and determine common policy and program.

The program of the Y.W.C.A. is concerned with all that affects the lives of women. Local associations offer a wide variety of educational programs depending on the need: fundamental education, adult education, vocational training. Efforts are made through informal education to bring insight to bear on questions of marriage and family life and to train women as responsible citizens who take their share in working for sound community development. Problems dealt with include city housing, rural improvement, juvenile delinquency, the loneliness of the aged, assimilation of immigrants, combating of racial discrimination. In every case the Y.W.C.A. aims to render the individual social conscience more sensitive and to help each member to carry her responsibility as a citizen of her community, her country, and the world. Much attention is given to leadership training, for it is recognized that without a trained and committed leadership no effective program can be carried out.

In every concern of life, the Y.W.C.A. seeks to lead associations and individual members into a new faithfulness to our common Christian convictions and to teach them how to express in words and in acts the hope and courage that come from faith in God's healing power of peace and reconciliation meant for all men and nations.

— *Katherine S. Strong*

YOUTH GROUPS The youth group in the life of the local church owes much of its present structure to the Christian Endeavor movement, which from 1881 pioneered in Protestant youth work. Specifically, the Christian Endeavor Society functioned on the basis of Sunday-night weekly meetings, the use of recommended program topics, age-group divisions, dependence upon lay adult advisers, an insistence on personal commitment, meetings in the nature of rallies and conventions, and the lusty singing of gospel songs. With the emergence of stronger Christian education departments in several denominations, the Christian Endeavor program was slowly displaced by each denomination's own youth program.

One unfortunate development in the growth of the Christian Endeavor and of the Sunday school movements was that in both cases, the organizations functioned completely apart from each other, and from the local church itself. In an extreme case, there were 3 competing bodies: the church, the Sunday school, and the Christian Endeavor (or denominational youth program).

To correct this error, responsible youth leaders held a series of meetings in the early 1940's and emerged with the youth fellowship concept. It was now understood that the church had 1 blanket responsibility for its young people, under which came the corporate worship of the congregation, the systematic study of the recommended curriculum in the Sunday church school, and the evening fellowship groups for various ages. It was at this point that many denominations included the word "fellowship" as part of the official name for its youth movements: Westminster Fellowship, Pilgrim Fellowship, Methodist Youth Fellowship, Baptist Youth Fellowship, etc.

Then came conversations that sought to correlate the various program emphases being observed by the several denominations participating in the United Christian Youth Movement. In 1951 was adopted the "Plan for Common Commissions in Christian Youth Work" in which all program items were divided into 5 groupings called commissions or program areas. These 5 groupings were identified as Christian faith, witness, world outreach, citizenship, and fellowship. Theoretically, every Christian task and concern could be found in each of these 5 program areas.

To the young people in the local church, the fusion of the denomination's own fellowship program, and some adaptation of the commission (or program area) plan, provided the essential framework for their total program. Prodded by program materials sent from denominational headquarters, exposed to youth rallies and training conferences in the community, and dependent upon the caliber of the adult leadership, the young people carried on their indigenous youth program.

Typically the youth group was the coming together of eager, seeking young people, usually in the age bracket of 14 years to 17 years, numbering about 20 to 25 persons, meeting every Sunday evening at about 7 o'clock at the church. They elected officers, and assigned persons to be responsible for the program of each meeting. A typical meeting opened with a period of worship conducted by 1 of the young people, the program for the evening, and moments of socializing with games or refreshment. A friendship circle usually closed the meeting. The evening program would vary from a film or filmstrip or a special speaker, to some kind of interesting presentation (panel, debate, conversation, roleplay, reports, play-reading, and the

like). There usually was a discussion period following the basic presentation.

In addition to the regular weekly meeting, the exceptional group would be involved in the denomination's missionary concerns, with both study and funds; it would engage in service projects of some kind; it would have an occasional social event. There would be a high level of loyalty to the group and to its programs, and an eager anticipation and excitement would surround its activities. Sometimes it could truly be said that in the youth group, the authentic Christian life was being lived and experienced, that the koinonia existed, that evangelistic outreach and social action concerns were pursued, that honest questions of faith and belief were discussed, that challenges to vocation and mission were present, that high discipleship was evident. In short, this youth group even now expresses the highest hopes of good churchmanship (implying that one need not wait to adulthood to be a churchman).

At the other extreme, and at its worst, the youth group can become the Sunday night social club, gathering young people of the neighborhood without reference to any identification with the morning worship and study of the church. With high priorities for the social aspect of coming together, there are a perfunctory worship period, some attempts at a business meeting to plan for the next money-raising project, and a quick adjournment to allow time for dancing, ping-pong, shuffleboard, or basketball. There is no attempt to be sensitive to the demands of the Christian life, to the relevance of the gospel, to the heritage of the church, and to the expectations of common witness to one another and to the community.

Whether at its best or at its worst, the typical youth group usually involves only a fraction of the potential youth population of the local church. Ideally, there would be 3 age groups: the junior highs, the senior highs, and the post highs. Too often there would be 1 group for the total age span. It was assumed that all these persons would participate in the morning church school classes. In some instances the evening youth group was seen as another church service, a sort of "junior church" service. It was difficult to be frank and pertinent or have soul-searching discussions in a group having the age span of 12 to 24. Inevitably, the hard core of the group settled to the faithful few, probably 15 to 25 persons. The common cry was the difficulty of securing and holding adult advisers, who saw their task as "entertaining" the young people. Success was measured in numbers: high attendance, the amount of money raised, the frequency of socials, etc.

There is renewed interest in reassessing the youth fellowship concept of the youth program. The phrase that best sums up the new vision is the "youth ministry" of the church. Reaffirming the umbrella pattern of the fellowship concept, the new youth ministry insists that there is only 1 ministry which has several manifestations, all related and intertwined in the common task of this objective: "To help persons to be aware of God's self-disclosure and seeking love in Jesus Christ and to respond in faith and love."

"Youth ministry" suggests that young people themselves must participate in the ministry and not be waited upon by the adults. In mutual conversation with adults and with one another, young people can share meaningfully in their own nurture and churchmanship. An adequate and continuing study in the faith and life of the church is assumed. Regular corporate worship is basic. But since they are still teen-agers, these young people need appropriate opportunities for group experience and expressions to help them in their maturing process.

There are valid arguments to provide for separate youth experiences. The high mobility of the population makes for impersonal relationships. The unfortunate cleavage between adults and youth, particularly between parents and children, produces a communication gap that needs to be closed. Rapid social changes require penetrating conversations to accommodate to new responsibilities and to reflect on the eternal values of life. Mostly, teen-age young people need a trusting group where they can ask questions and participate in group discussion in a Christian atmosphere, in the presence of dedicated and interested adult counselors.

The current Christian education program for youth insists less upon the lecture method, and more upon group participation in exploration and discovery. It accents opportunities to delve into the life of the church and the community, glimpses of the worldwide thrust of the church's mission, challenges to give of self in Christian vocation. All these are inherent in the new youth ministry.

The youth group in the local church will no longer put on a series of programs to entertain its members. Instead, it actually becomes several small groups, each numbering about 8 to 10 members, each small group pursuing some specific curriculum study and a 2d subject of its own choosing. It can be a combined church school and youth fellowship group, not necessarily at church on a Sunday morning, but at some other time, such as Tuesday after school, or Thursday evening after homework, in homes. The role of the adult leader is less that of a dominating teacher-director, and more of a counselor-resource person. Each group is encouraged to develop skills and talents in music, drama, recreation, and other group activities. Physical work-service projects are essential tasks; social times are not ignored.

The new youth group will be dual in nature: it insists upon youth's immediate participation in the ongoing life of the congregation as responsible members of that community of faith; it provides for an intimate small group of their own age mates to increase discipleship and church-manship. — *Henry N. Tani*

YOUTH-SERVING AGENCIES If it is to serve youth, the church must cooperate with national, regional, state, and local youth-serving agencies. Youth need a combination of experiences at each stage of their growth. They belong to families, local communities, churches, schools, clubs, and other interest and activity groups. Character and personality are formed in these many activities. The church has a unique function in society. No other institution can substitute for it in carrying out its responsibility for Christian education. However, the church cannot regard an agency group in which its youth are involved as an " outside " organization.

Character-building organizations and agencies for youth are numerous. They are difficult to list because of geographical and cultural factors. Their objectives are usually in harmony with the accepted principles of Christian education. Because church youth are involved in the programs of numerous agencies, the church should know these programs in order to cooperate with them and plan its own programs, activities, and schedules in relation to youth's total experiences.

Among the youth-serving agencies the major ones recognize the role of religion in individual lives and the importance of spiritual values, e.g., Boy and Girl Scouts of America, Camp Fire Girls, Y.M.C.A., Y.W.C.A. These 5 are closely associated with the National Council of the Churches of Christ in the U.S.A. through the Children and Youth Advisory Committee. This committee is composed of representatives from the Committees on Children's and Youth Work of the Division of Christian Education and representatives from each of the 5 agencies. The Committee deals with national policies that become the guiding principles for these agencies and the churches related to them.

The ever-increasing number of activities projected by public and parochial schools, denominations and local churches, and old and new agencies involving the same youth have often led to competition and confusion. The churches and agencies, forgetting that they are allies in a kindred task, have at times become annoyed with one another. When there is full recognition of the role each should play, such conflict is usually resolved and the work of each is strengthened.

Church and agency leaders, concerned about this lack of mutual regard for the purposes and programs of each, have arrived at a consensus of opinion regarding their common and distinctive tasks. Youth need a combination of experiences provided by both the church and character-building agencies. Both agency and church need each other, and to that end a *modus operandi* is being developed. Churches need to learn how to use agency programs and how to provide leadership and equipment needed. Youth programs in the church need to speak to youth where they are. Youth need to understand that even minor decisions can be for or against God's will for them and his world. Thus agency programs should not be regarded as " worldly " but, rather, looked upon as an opportunity to help youth with specific problems that are normal adolescent growth concerns. The church should be concerned with the whole person.

This recognition that the church and the agencies need each other in their common concern for youth is increasing. Furthermore, few churches can afford the types of program offered by the agencies. And many agencies find that churches provide the best setting for the fulfillment of their purposes. Activities conducted outside the church building are more meaningful when participants are rooted in active church relationships.

In selecting the agencies whose groups it wishes to sponsor, a church needs to look at its own goals and then select those agencies which can best help it meet its objectives. The church needs also to understand its obligations to the agency to maintain standards, provide facilities, cooperate in securing and training leaders, and supervise the program. All this must be done within the framework of the agency involved.

Both church and agency must look together at their own community and the needs of their youth. Community planning is necessary to develop a coordinated program.

Parent cooperation is essential to realize fully all the values of any program offered youth. Full cooperation of parents can be secured only as the church and agencies coordinate their activities and draw parents into cooperative planning. This involves more than clearance of schedules. When the church and agencies begin with the home and the needs of youth, and work outward into programs, they come to see clearly that coordination of effort is invaluable.

It is inevitable that problems will arise needing careful study. While the church should be the final arbiter as to what is incorporated in its program, the program elements of an agency are such that if they are modified too greatly the distinctive values inherent in them may be lost. It is essential, therefore, that a church provide a planning or coordinating committee which will look at the needs of youth, at the objectives of the church, and at the types of experience offered by both church and agency. The church should use the programs of the agencies that can best be coordinated with its overall program. This assumes that both the church and agency will have a voice in planning and coordinating the programs, and that the youth themselves will have choices within understandable limits in the selection of activities they wish to pursue.

When a church sponsors an agency program, its committee on Christian education and/or the church's governing body must study the full situation carefully and recommend a policy regarding the program of the sponsored group. Full sponsorship will call for active commitment to cooperative relationships on the part of both groups.

The church committee or other responsible body, after consultation with the agency representatives, should appoint the coordinating committee. The number on this committee will be determined largely by the agency. The personnel of the committee should be drawn from the church membership.

The agency group is related, then, to the total church educational program. Its leader becomes a member of the church's team of workers and is related to the youth department. This representative participates in meetings of the department staff and should be free to make suggestions relative to the planning of the total educational program, as well as report for the agency and receive suggestions relating to the program of the agency. Any matters involving change of policy would, of course, have to be considered and cleared by the church's official and educational boards.

The importance of the selection and training of leaders cannot be overemphasized. The adult leader in the program of the church and of the agency is the key factor in determining the quality of the results to be obtained. This means that whenever an adult is to be enlisted as a leader of youth, he should be examined as to his sincerity, integrity, attitudes, and all the traits that will determine his positive influence upon impressionable youth. It is essential also that specific training be given him by both the church and the agency for the assignment he is to undertake.

Close cooperation is needed in regard to scheduling weekend hikes, cookouts, camping trips, and other activities that are integral to the program of the agencies. Too often it has not been made clear to the agency leaders that the limited time for which the church has its youth must not be further curtailed. Besides, church school curricula include units that must be studied in sequence. Continuity is essential to any process of teaching and learning. When the full year's calendar is projected, church and agency leaders can well designate certain weekend agency activities.

Communitywide planning involving all the churches, schools, and agencies is proving exceedingly valuable, saving youth from the serious results of overexertion and overinvolvement. — *Vartan D. Melconian*

Z

ZWINGLI, HULDREICH Born Jan. 1, 1484, Huldreich Zwingli, the Zurich Reformer, was educated at Wesen, Bern, Vienna, and Basel. He developed humanist interests, a taste for music, and inclinations to theological reform under his final teacher, Wyttenbach. Ordained in 1506, he 1st served at Glarus, where he proved to be a good pastor, preacher, and scholar. As a chaplain with Glarus mercenaries in Italy he earned a papal pension but also came to hate the mercenary system and to suspect medieval developments in the church. In 1516 he moved to the smaller Einsiedeln, a great center of pilgrimage. This gave him wide preaching opportunities, but also leisure for study. He gave himself especially to New Testament study and attained a basic understanding of evangelical doctrine. Not without hierarchical approval, he helped to chase the indulgence salesman, Samson, in 1518.

Called to Zurich in 1518 as people's priest, he began a systematic exposition of Scripture with open Reformation sympathies, although he as yet sought no break with authority. The great plague of 1519, in which he almost died, showed him a good pastor and deepened his convictions. As early as 1521, he won approval from the city council for preaching from Scripture. Rapid action followed (1522–1525) with attacks on fasting and celibacy, the translation of the Bible and services into the vernacular, the opening and final dissolving of convents, liturgical reconstruction, and the reorganizing of the Münster school. Opposition from the orders and older members of the chapter was overcome with the help of the council. The *Sixty-seven Articles* were published in 1523 and the *Commentary on True and False Religion* in 1525. Defying clerical celibacy, Zwingli married Anna Reinhard in 1525, possibly "unofficially" in 1522.

After early successes in Zurich, Zwingli helped to spread the Reformation in other cantons, notably Bern and Basel. He failed, however, in the neighboring Forest Cantons around Lake Lucerne. Unhappy disruption came to Zurich itself with the Anabaptists, who were imprisoned, expelled, or even executed after debates and treatises proved futile. The Eucharistic controversy with the Lutherans also spoiled the period after 1525, and although Zwingli seems to have sought fellowship at the Colloquy of Marburg in 1529, his mainly memorialistic views of the Lord's Supper were unacceptable to Luther. Zwingli thus had to present an independent confession, the *Fidei ratio*, at the Diet of Augsburg in 1530. The isolation of the Reformed cantons at this period caused Zwingli to seek alliances with France and Venice, and also to proceed against the Forest Cantons. In the 1st War of Kappel in 1529 Zurich was successful. Disaster followed on Oct. 11, 1531, however. In that battle Zwingli was killed.

Although Zwingli's comparatively early death resulted in a transfer of Swiss leadership to Calvin and Geneva, already at Zurich the main principles of Reformed faith and order had been established. Zwingli emphasized particularly the authority of Holy Scripture under the living application of the Holy Spirit. He tried conscientiously to reform church services according to a simple New Testament pattern. In relation to the state, he accepted the authority of the city council, but was in a happy position of ascendancy in ecclesiastical questions. He worked strongly for an educated ministry grounded in Greek and Hebrew as well as Latin. The doctrines of divine sovereignty in providence and of predestination played an important part in his theology.

In relation to infant baptism, he laid the early foundation of a strong covenant doctrine. In respect to the Lord's Supper, he was more negative, though the later writings show some movement toward the more positive conception of his successor, Heinrich Bullinger. A good summary of Zwingli's tenets is to be found in the *Exposition of the Faith,* prepared for Francis of France in 1531. Zwingli was a man of open and friendly disposition, a forceful preacher, a good pastor, and a fine scholar who was not too proud finally to master Hebrew in classes in the Münster school in which he also taught. Though there is an intellectual bent in his work, recent research has disclosed both a deeper evangelical perception and a basically theological rather than humanist orientation. His writings are mostly occasional, either polemical or confessional. If they give evidence of hasty composition, they also attest a lively and original mind. The surprising feature of Zwingli is that he accomplished so much in so brief a compass. In spite of the fragmentariness visible at many points, he unquestionably laid down the general lines of Reformed doctrine and order. — *Geoffrey W. Bromiley*

TABLE OF SUBJECT HEADINGS
AND BIBLIOGRAPHICAL REFERENCES

(The numbers after each subject heading refer to the items in the numbered Bibliography on pages 756–797. It is obvious that many other works listed in the total Bibliography are pertinent with regard to the various subject headings.)

Catechetical School: 96, 172, 229, 258, 332, 763

Catechism: 85, 96, 250, 312, 344, 438, 605

Catechumenate: 370, 432, 511, 629

Censorship: 908

Chalkboard: 1220

Chamber Theater: 1198

Character Education: 35, 117, 770, 799, 980, 1081

Character Research Project: 1031, 1032, 1033

Chautauqua Institution: 307

Child Development: 415, 675, 681, 734, 736, 739, 913, 930, 947, 1004, 1005, 1022, 1044, 1086, 1087, 1089, 1090, 1132

Children's Day: 113

China: 218, 260, 283

Choir: 1257

Choir School: 1257

Choric Speech: 902, 1192, 1193, 1198, 1212, 1214, 1215, 1216, 1223

Christian Methodist Episcopal Church: 298

Christian Reformed Church: 280

Church of the Brethren: 210, 233, 290

Church of Christ, Scientist: 236, 308, 334, 383

Church of England: 106, 107, 345

Church of God: 298

Church of Jesus Christ of Latter-day Saints (Mormons): 200, 202, 264

Church of the Nazarene: 298, 313, 336

Church Year: 130, 545, 611, 662

Churches of God in North America (General Eldership): 341, 350, 353

Church-State Relations: 582, 689, 690, 698, 740, 762, 770, 910, 1139

Clay Modeling: 1186, 1188, 1213, 1218, 1235

Clergyman's Role in Christian Education: 49, 52, 72, 97, 132, 148, 159, 162, 327, 382, 530, 571, 572, 587, 618

Coe, George Albert: 29, 30, 39

College, Church-related: 178, 712, 728, 731

Colloquy: 683, 1175

Comenius, John Amos: 33, 34, 337

Comics: 1144

Communication: 395, 443, 446, 530, 537, 557, 567, 568, 595, 664, 908, 1015, 1163

Community Agencies: 77, 967, 977, 1011, 1101, 1107

Conference: 683, 1175

Confession of Sin: 371, 448

Confirmation: 40

Confucianism: 218, 457, 461

Constructive Activities: 78, 79, 153, 729, 1220, 1228, 1244, 1275

Conversation: 995

Conversion: 193, 212, 219, 222, 300, 304, 345, 396, 439, 481, 512, 658, 661, 665, 891, 921, 922, 924, 937, 1001, 1134, 1138, 1154

Cooperative Publication Association: 205

Core Curriculum: 680, 681

Correlation, Principle of: 989

Council of Churches: 205, 208

Counseling: 982, 983, 992, 993, 1073, 1102, 1114, 1148

Couples Club: 70

Covenant: 377, 408, 409, 411, 510, 580, 600

Crafts: 1186, 1209, 1220, 1235, 1241, 1246

Creative Activities: 1197, 1203, 1220, 1228, 1233, 1244

Creed: 286, 402, 413, 434, 449, 521, 616, 617

Culture: 384, 551, 569, 578, 594

Cumberland Presbyterian Church: 214, 294

Curriculum: 7, 12, 172, 192, 205, 282

Dance: 958, 1161, 1184, 1201, 1202, 1234, 1242, 1257

Deaconesses: 1070

Death: 400, 402

Debate: 1207, 1251, 1262

Decision: 519

De la Salle, Jean Baptiste: 198, 199

Democracy: 711, 716, 723, 730, 830, 986, 1130

Demonstration: 1220, 1227

Denmark: 240, 289

Developmental Tasks: 737, 944, 947, 1081, 1211

Devotional Literature: 331, 335

Dewey, John: 203, 225, 262, 442, 716, 717, 718, 722, 767, 827, 828, 837, 840, 842, 939

Didachē: 216, 609

Didache, The: 37, 215, 251, 295, 316, 476, 478

BIBLIOGRAPHY

(In general the Bibliography includes works suggested by the writers of the various articles, along with additional titles. The titles are indicated by their numbers wherever referred to in the preceding Table of Subject Headings and Bibliographical References.)

I. Christian Education

1. Adams, Rachel Swann, *The Small Church and Christian Education*. The Westminster Press, 1961.
2. Anderson, Phoebe M., *Religious Living with Nursery Children*. The Pilgrim Press, 1956.
3. Athearn, Walter S., *The Indiana Survey of Religious Education*, 3 vols. George H. Doran Company, 1923.
4. Avery, Margaret, *Teaching Scripture: A Book on Method*. The Religious Education Press, Wallington, Surrey, 1951.
5. Baxter, Edna M., *Teaching the New Testament*. Christian Education Press, 1960.
6. Bergevin, Paul, and McKinley, John, *Design for Adult Education in the Church*. The Seabury Press, Inc., 1958.
7. Betts, George Herbert, *The Curriculum of Religious Education*. Abingdon Press, 1924.
8. —— *How to Teach Religion*. Abingdon Press, 1910.
9. —— and Hawthorne, Marion O., *Methods in Teaching Religion*. Abingdon Press, 1925.
10. Blankenship, Lois, *Our Church Plans for Children*. Judson Press, 1951.
11. Bowen, C. A., *Child and Church*. Abingdon Press, 1960.
12. Bower, William Clayton, *The Curriculum of Religious Education*. Charles Scribner's Sons, 1925.
13. Bowman, Clarice M., *Ways Youth Learn*. Harper & Brothers, 1952.
14. Bridston, Keith R., *Theological Training in the Modern World*. World's Student Christian Federation, Geneva, 1954.
15. Bushnell, Horace, *Christian Nurture*. Yale University Press, 1947.
16. Butler, J. Donald, *Religious Education: The Foundations and Practice of Nurture*. Harper & Row, Publishers, Inc., 1962.
17. Butt, Elsie Miller, *The Vacation Church School in Christian Education*. Abingdon Press, 1957.
18. Buttrick, George A., *Biblical Thought and the Secular University*. Louisiana State University Press, 1960.
19. Byrne, H. W., *A Christian Approach to Education: A Bibliocentric View*. Zondervan Publishing House, 1961.

20. Cantelon, John, ed., *A Basis for Study: A Theological Prospectus for the Campus Ministry.* Department of Campus Christian Life, Board of Christian Education, The United Presbyterian Church in the U.S.A., 1959.
21. Carter, Gerald Emmett, *The Modern Challenge to Religious Education: God's Message and Our Response.* William H. Sadlier, 1961.
22. Chamberlin, J. Gordon, *Parents and Religion: A Preface to Christian Education.* The Westminister Press, 1961.
23. Chaplin, Dora P., *Children and Religion,* rev. ed. Charles Scribner's Sons, 1961.
24. ——— *The Privilege of Teaching.* Morehouse-Barlow Co., 1962.
25. Chave, Ernest J., *A Functional Approach to Religious Education.* The University of Chicago Press, 1947.
26. Clark, Gordon Haddon, *Christian Philosophy of Education.* Wm. B. Eerdmans Publishing Company, 1946.
27. Clemmons, Robert S., *Dynamics of Christian Adult Education.* Abingdon Press, 1958.
28. ——— *Young Adults in the Church.* Abingdon Press, 1959.
29. Coe, George Albert, *A Social Theory of Religious Education.* Charles Scribner's Sons, 1917.
30. ——— *What Is Christian Education?* Charles Scribner's Sons, 1929.
31. Coleman, John, *The Task of the Christian in the University.* Association Press, 1947.
32. Collins, Joseph B., *Teaching Religion.* The Bruce Publishing Company, 1953.
33. Comenius, John Amos, *The Great Didactic,* tr. by M. W. Keatinge. Adam & Charles Black, Ltd., London, 1896.
34. ——— *The School of Infancy,* ed. by Ernest M. Eller. University of North Carolina Press, 1956.
35. Conover, C. Eugene, *Moral Education in Family, School, and Church.* The Westminster Press, 1962.
36. Cully, Iris V., *Children in the Church.* The Westminster Press, 1960.
37. ——— *The Dynamics of Christian Education.* The Westminster Press, 1958.
38. ——— *Imparting the Word: The Bible in Christian Education.* The Westminster Press, 1963.
39. Cully, Kendig Brubaker, ed., *Basic Writings in Christian Education.* The Westminster Press, 1961.
40. ——— *Confirmation: History, Doctrine, and Practice.* The Seabury Press, Inc., 1962.
41. Culver, Elsie T., *New Church Programs with the Aging.* Association Press, 1961.
42. Cummings, Oliver DeWolf, *Guiding Youth in Christian Growth.* Judson Press, 1954.
43. ——— *The Youth Fellowship.* Judson Press, 1956.
44. *The Curriculum Design for Christian Education,* 6 vols. Lutheran Board of Parish Education, 1960–1962.
45. Dillard, Polly Hargis, *The Church Kindergarten.* Broadman Press, 1958.
46. Eakin, Mildred, and Frank, *The Church School Teacher's Job.* The Macmillan Company, 1949.
47. Ebbut, Arthur James, *The Bible and Christian Education.* The Ryerson Press, Toronto, 1959.
48. Elliott, Harrison S., *Can Religious Education Be Christian?* The Macmillan Company, 1940.
49. Ernsberger, David J., *A Philosophy of Adult Christian Education.* The Westminster Press, 1959.
50. Fahs, Sophia Lyon, *Today's Children and Yesterday's Heritage.* Beacon Press, Inc., 1952.

51. Fairchild, Hoxie N., *Religious Perspectives in College Teaching.* The Ronald Press Company, 1952.
52. Fallaw, Wesner, *Church Education for Tomorrow.* The Westminster Press, 1960.
53. ——— *The Modern Parent and the Teaching Church.* The Macmillan Company, 1946.
54. Fitzpatrick, Edward A., *Exploring a Theology of Education.* The Bruce Publishing Company, 1950.
55. *For Better Teaching.* Orthodox Christian Education Commission, 1957.
56. Fordham, Forrest B., and Alessi, Vincie, *Teaching Older Youth.* Judson Press, 1959.
57. Forsyth, Nathaniel G., ed., *The Minister and Christian Nurture.* Abingdon Press, 1957.
58. Foster, Virgil E., *How a Small Church Can Have Good Christian Education.* Harper & Brothers, 1956.
59. Fox, H. W., *The Child's Approach to Religion.* Harper & Brothers, 1930.
60. Fritz, Dorothy B., *The Spiritual Growth of Children.* The Westminster Press, 1957.
61. Fry, John R., *A Hard Look at Adult Christian Education.* The Westminster Press, 1961.
62. Fuller, Edmund, ed., *The Christian Idea of Education.* Yale University Press, 1957.
63. ——— *Schools and Scholarship: The Christian Idea of Education,* Part II. Yale University Press, 1962.
64. Gable, Lee J., *Christian Nurture Through the Church.* National Council of the Churches of Christ in the U.S.A., 1955.
65. ——— ed., *Encyclopedia for Church Group Leaders.* Association Press, 1959.
66. Gaebelein, Frank E., *Christian Education in a Democracy: The Report of the N.A.E. Committee.* Oxford University Press, Inc., 1951.
67. ——— *The Pattern of God's Truth.* Oxford University Press, Inc., 1954.
68. Gettys, Joseph M., *How to Teach the Bible.* John Knox Press, 1949.
69. ——— *Teaching the Pentateuch.* John Knox Press, 1962.
70. Gleason, George S., *Church Activities for Young Couples.* Association Press, 1949.
71. ——— *Single Young Adults in the Church.* Association Press, 1952.
72. Glen, J. Stanley, *The Recovery of the Teaching Ministry.* The Westminster Press, 1960.
73. Goodykoontz, Harry G., and Betty L., *Training to Teach: A Basic Course in Christian Education.* The Westminster Press, 1962.
74. Griffiths, Louise B., *The Teacher and Young Teens.* The Bethany Press, 1954.
75. ——— *Wide as the World: Junior High and Mission.* Friendship Press, 1957.
76. *Handbuch für evangelische Jugendarbeit.* Verlag Junge Kirche, Zurich, 1948.
77. Harner, Nevin, *The Educational Work of the Church.* Abingdon Press, 1939.
78. Harris, Jane B., *When We Teach Junior Children.* The Westminster Press, 1957.
79. Haynes, Marjorie, *When We Teach Primary Children.* The Westminster Press, 1957.
80. Heim, Ralph D., *Leading a Sunday Church School.* Muhlenberg Press, 1950.
81. Heinz, Mamie W., *Growing and Learning in the Kindergarten.* John Knox Press, 1959.
82. Henderlite, Rachel, *Forgiveness and Hope: Toward a Theology for Protestant Christian Education.* John Knox Press, 1961.
83. Heron, Frances Dunlap, *Kathy Ann, Kindergartner.* Abingdon Press, 1955.
84. Hoag, Victor, *The Ladder of Learning.* The Seabury Press, Inc., 1960.

85. Hofinger, Johannes, S.J., *The Art of Teaching Christian Doctrine: The Good News and Its Proclamation.* University of Notre Dame Press, 1957.
86. Horne, Herman Harrell, *The Philosophy of Christian Education.* Fleming H. Revell Company, 1937.
87. *The How of Vacation Church School*, rev. ed. National Council of the Churches of Christ in the U.S.A., 1960.
88. Hunter, Edith Fisher, *The Questioning Child and Religion.* Starr King Press, 1956.
89. Jaarsma, Cornelius, ed., *Fundamentals in Christian Education.* Wm. B. Eerdmans Publishing Company, 1953.
90. Jeffreys, M. V. C., *Education — Christian or Pagan.* University of London Press, Ltd., London, 1946.
91. Jones, Claude C., *The Teaching Methods of the Master.* The Bethany Press, 1957.
92. Jones, Mary Alice, *Guiding Children in Christian Growth.* Abingdon Press, 1949.
93. Jones, Philip Cowell, *The Church School Superintendent.* Abingdon-Cokesbury Press, 1939.
94. Jung, Emmanuel, *Jugendgottesdienst.* Heinrich Majer, Basel, 1960.
95. —— *Sonntagschule als Kindergottesdienst.* Zwingli Verlag, Zurich, 1942.
96. Jungmann, J. A., *Handing on the Faith: A Manual of Catechetics.* Herder & Herder, Inc., 1959.
97. Kean, Charles D., *The Christian Gospel and the Parish Church.* The Seabury Press, Inc., 1953.
98. Koenig, Robert B., *The Use of the Bible with Adults.* Christian Education Press, 1959.
99. Koulumzin, Sophie, *Lectures in Orthodox Christian Education.* St. Vladimir's Seminary, 1961.
100. Lace, O. Jessie, *Teaching the New Testament.* The Seabury Press, Inc., 1961.
101. —— *Teaching the Old Testament.* The Seabury Press, Inc., 1960.
102. *Leading Young People: A Basic Guide for Adult Leaders of Youth Groups.* The Seabury Press, Inc., 1961.
103. LeBar, Lois E., *Children in the Bible School.* Fleming H. Revell Company, 1952.
104. —— *Education that Is Christian.* Fleming H. Revell Company, 1958.
105. Lee, Florence B., *Primary Children in the Church.* Judson Press, 1961.
106. Leeson, Spencer, *Christian Education.* Longmans, Green & Co., Toronto, 1947.
107. —— *Christian Education Reviewed.* Longmans, Green & Co., Toronto, 1957.
108. LeFevre, Perry D., *The Christian Teacher.* Abingdon Press, 1958.
109. Lewis, Hazel A., *The Primary Church School.* The Bethany Press, 1951.
110. Little, Lawrence C., *Foundations for a Philosophy of Christian Education.* Abingdon Press, 1962.
111. —— ed., *The Future Course of Christian Adult Education.* University of Pittsburgh Press, 1959.
112. Little, Sara, *The Role of the Bible in Contemporary Christian Education.* John Knox Press, 1961.
113. Lobingier, John Leslie, *The Better Church School.* The Pilgrim Press, 1952.
114. —— *If Teaching Is Your Job.* The Pilgrim Press, 1956.
115. *The Local Church Director of Christian Education.* National Council of the Churches of Christ in the U.S.A., 1952.
116. Lotz, Philip Henry, ed., *Orientation in Religious Education.* Abingdon-Cokesbury Press, 1950.
117. —— and Crawford, L. W., eds., *Studies in Religious Education.* Cokesbury Press, 1931.

118. Lowry, Howard, *The Mind's Adventure*. The Westminster Press, 1950.
119. *A Manual for Young Adults*. National Council of the Churches of Christ in the U.S.A., 1960.
120. Manwell, Elizabeth M., and Fahs, Sophia Lyon, *Consider the Children — How They Grow*. Beacon Press, Inc., 1940.
121. Mason, Harold C., *Abiding Values in Christian Education*. Fleming H. Revell Company, 1955.
122. —— *Reclaiming the Sunday School*. Light & Life Press, 1946.
123. McCaughey, J. Davis, *Christian Obedience in the University*. SCM Press Ltd., London, 1958.
124. McCoy, Charles S., and McCarter, Nealy D., *The Gospel on Campus: Rediscovering Evangelism in the Academic Community*. John Knox Press, 1959.
125. McKean, Myra B., *The Church Plans for Kindergarten Children*. The General Board of Education of The Methodist Church, 1958.
126. McKibben, Frank M., *Guiding Workers in Christian Education*. Abingdon Press, 1953.
127. McKinley, John, *Creative Methods for Adult Classes*. The Bethany Press, 1960.
128. McLester, Frances Cole, *Teaching in the Church School*, rev. ed. Abingdon Press, 1961.
129. Miller, Alexander, *Faith and Learning*. Association Press, 1960.
130. Miller, Allen O., *Invitation to Theology*. Christian Education Press, 1958.
131. Miller, Randolph Crump, *Biblical Theology and Christian Education*. Charles Scribner's Sons, 1956.
132. —— *Christian Nurture and the Church*. Charles Scribner's Sons, 1961.
133. ——*The Clue to Christian Education*. Charles Scribner's Sons, 1952.
134. —— *Education for Christian Living*. Prentice-Hall, Inc., 1956.
135. —— *Your Child's Religion*. Doubleday & Company, Inc., 1962.
136. Moberly, Walter, *The Crisis in the University*. SCM Press Ltd., London, 1949.
137. Munro, Harry C., *Protestant Nurture*. Prentice-Hall, Inc., 1956.
138. Murch, James DeForest, *Christian Education and the Local Church*. The Standard Publishing Company, 1943.
139. —— *Cooperation Without Compromise*. Wm. B. Eerdmans Publishing Company, 1956.
140. Murray, A. Victor, *Education Into Religion*. Harper & Brothers, 1954.
141. —— *Teaching the Bible, Especially in Secondary Schools*. Cambridge University Press, 1955.
142. Myers, A. J. William, *Teaching Religion Creatively*. Fleming H. Revell Company, 1932.
143. Newberry, Josephine, *Nursery-Kindergarten Weekday Education in the Church*. John Knox Press, 1960.
144. Niblett, W. R., *Christian Education in a Secular Society*. Oxford University Press, Inc., 1960.
145. *The Objective of Christian Education for Senior High Young People*. National Council of the Churches of Christ in the U.S.A., 1958.
146. Ortmayer, Roger, ed., *Witness to the Campus*. Methodist Student Movement, 1956.
147. Person, Peter P., *An Introduction to Christian Education*. Baker Book House, 1958.
148. —— *The Minister in Christian Education*. Baker Book House, 1960.
149. Reed, William W., *Teaching the Church's Children*. Morehouse-Gorham Co., Inc., 1958.
150. Reinhart, Bruce, *The Institutional Nature of Adult Christian Education*. The Westminster Press, 1962.

151. Rolston, Holmes, *The Bible in Teaching*. John Knox Press, 1962.
152. Roorbach, Rosemary, *Religion in the Kindergarten*. Harper & Brothers, 1949.
153. —— *Teaching Children in the Church*. Abingdon Press, 1959.
154. Schisler, John Q., *Christian Teaching in the Churches*. Abingdon Press, 1954.
155. Schreyer, George M., *Christian Education in Theological Focus*. United Church Press, 1962.
156. Schulz, Florence, *Summer with Nursery Children*. The Pilgrim Press, 1958.
157. Shaver, Erwin L., *The Weekday Church School*. The Pilgrim Press, 1956.
158. Shedd, Clarence P., *The Church Follows Its Students*. Yale University Press, 1938.
159. Sherrill, Lewis Joseph, *The Gift of Power*. The Macmillan Company, 1955.
160. —— *The Opening Doors of Childhood*. The Macmillan Company, 1958.
161. Shinn, Roger L., *The Educational Mission of Our Church*. Christian Education Press, 1962.
162. Smart, James D., *The Teaching Ministry of the Church*. The Westminster Press, 1954.
163. Smith, H. Shelton, *Faith and Nurture*. Charles Scribner's Sons, 1941.
164. Smith, J. W. D., *An Introduction to Scripture Teaching*. Thomas Nelson & Sons, 1949.
165. Smith, Seymour A., *The American College Chaplaincy*. Association Press, 1954.
166. Spaulding, Helen F., ed., *Evaluation and Christian Education*. National Council of the Churches of Christ in the U.S.A., 1961.
167. Strachan, Malcolm, and Beardslee, Alvord M., eds., *The Christian Faith and Youth Today*. The Seabury Press, Inc., 1957.
168. Swearingen, Tilford T., *The Community and Christian Education*. The Bethany Press, 1950.
169. Sydnor, William, *Family Corporate Worship*. The Seabury Press, Inc., 1955.
170. —— *How and What the Church Teaches*. Longmans, Green & Co., Inc., 1960.
171. Tani, Henry N., *Ventures in Youth Work*. Christian Education Press, 1957.
172. Taylor, Marvin J., ed., *Religious Education: A Comprehensive Survey*. Abingdon Press, 1960.
173. Tobey, Kathrene McLandress, *The Church Plans for Kindergarten Children*. The Westminster Press, 1959.
174. —— *When We Teach Kindergarten Children*. The Westminster Press, 1957.
175. Van Dusen, Henry Pitney, *God in Education*. Charles Scribner's Sons, 1951.
176. Vieth, Paul H., ed., *The Church and Christian Education*. The Bethany Press, 1947.
177. —— *The Church School*. Christian Education Press, 1958.
178. von Grueningen, John Paul, ed., *Toward a Christian Philosophy of Higher Education*. The Westminster Press, 1957.
179. Walsh, Chad, *Campus Gods on Trial*. The Macmillan Company, 1953.
180. Waterink, Jan, *Basic Concepts in Christian Pedagogy*. Wm. B. Eerdmans Publishing Company, 1954.
181. Watson, Goodwin B., *Experimentation and Measurement in Religious Education*. Association Press, 1927.
182. Weigle, Luther A., *Jesus and the Educational Method*. Abingdon-Cokesbury Press, 1939.
183. Whitehouse, Elizabeth S., *The Children We Teach*. Judson Press, 1950.
184. Whittemore, Lewis Bliss, *The Church and Secular Education*. The Seabury Press, Inc., 1960.
185. Williams, George A., *The Theological Idea of the University*. National Council of the Churches of Christ in the U.S.A., 1958.

186. Williams, John G., *Worship and the Modern Child.* The Macmillan Company, 1957.
187. Winchester, Benjamin S., *Religious Education and Democracy.* Abingdon Press, 1917.
188. Wyckoff, D. Campbell, *The Gospel and Christian Education.* The Westminster Press, 1959.
189. —— *How to Evaluate Your Christian Education Program.* The Westminster Press, 1962.
190. —— *In One Spirit.* Friendship Press, 1957.
191. —— *The Task of Christian Education.* The Westminster Press, 1955.
192. —— *Theory and Design of Christian Education Curriculum.* The Westminster Press, 1961.
193. Yoder, Gideon, *The Nurture and Evangelism of Children.* Herald Press, 1959.
194. Zeigler, Earl F., *Christian Education of Adults.* The Westminster Press, 1958.

II. BIOGRAPHICAL, DENOMINATIONAL, HISTORICAL, AND REGIONAL

195. Atkins, Gaius Glenn and Fagley, Frederick, *A History of American Congregationalism.* The Pilgrim Press, 1942.
196. Barclay, William, *Train Up a Child: Educational Ideals in the Ancient World.* The Westminster Press, 1960.
197. Barnes, Harry E., ed., *An Introduction to the History of Sociology.* The University of Chicago Press, 1948.
198. Battersby, William John, *De La Salle: A Pioneer of Modern Education.* Longmans, Green & Co., Toronto, 1949.
199. —— *Saint John Baptist De La Salle.* The Macmillan Company, 1957.
200. Bennion, M. Lynn, *Mormonism and Education.* Deseret Book Co., 1939.
201. Benson, Clarence H., *A Popular History of Christian Education.* The Moody Press, 1943.
202. Berrett, William E., *The Restored Church,* 10th ed. Deseret Book Co., 1961.
203. Blewett, John, ed., *John Dewey: His Thought and Influence.* Fordham University Press, 1960.
204. Borgeaud, Charles, *Histoire de l'Université de Genève:* Vol. I, "L'Academie de Calvin, 1559–1798." Georg & Cie., Geneva, 1900.
205. Bower, William Clayton, and Hayward, Percy Roy, *Protestantism Faces Its Educational Task Together.* C. C. Nelson Publishing Company, 1949.
206. Brewer, Clifton H., *History of Religious Education in the Episcopal Church to 1835.* Yale University Press, 1924.
207. Brewer, John M., *et al., History of Vocational Guidance.* Harper & Brothers, 1942.
208. Brown, Arlo A., *A History of Religious Education in Recent Times.* Abingdon Press, 1923.
209. Brown, Willard Dayton, *History of the Reformed Church in America — 1628 to 1928.* Half Moon Press, 1928.
210. Brumbaugh, Martin G., *A History of the German Baptist Brethren in Europe and America.* Brethren Publishing House, 1899.
211. Buckler, Helen, Fiedler, Mary F., and Allen, Martha F., eds., *Wo-He-Lo: The Story of Camp Fire Girls, 1910–1960.* Holt, Rinehart and Winston, Inc., 1961.
212. Bullock, F. W. B., *Evangelical Conversion in Great Britain, 1696–1845.* Budd & Gillat, St. Leonard's-on-Sea, Sussex, England, 1959.
213. Bultmann, Rudolf, *et al., Kerygma and Myth: A Theological Debate,* Vol. I, ed. by Hans Werner Bartsch; tr. by Reginald H. Fuller. S.P.C.K., London; 1953.

214. Campbell, Thomas H., *Studies in Cumberland Presbyterian History*. Cumberland Presbyterian Publishing House, 1944.

215. Carrington, Philip, *The Early Christian Church*, 2 vols. Cambridge University Press, 1957.

216. ———— *The Primitive Christian Catechism*. Cambridge University Press, 1940.

217. Castle, E. B., *Moral Education in Christian Times*. George Allen & Unwin, Ltd., London, 1958.

218. *Christian Education in China: The Report of the China Educational Commission of 1921–1922*. China Educational Commission, 1922.

219. Citron, Bernhard, *New Birth: A Study of the Evangelical Doctrine of Conversion in the Protestant Fathers*. Edinburgh University Press, 1951.

220. Cole, Luella, *A History of Education: Socrates to Montessori*. Rinehart & Company, 1950.

221. Cole, S. G., *A History of Fundamentalism*. Richard R. Smith, 1931.

222. Colquhoun, Frank, *Harringay Story: The Official Record of the Billy Graham Greater London Crusade, 1954*. Hodder & Stoughton, Ltd., London, 1955.

223. Connolly, James, *The Voices of France: A Survey of Contemporary Theology in France*. The Macmillan Company, 1961.

224. Cragg, Gerald Robertson, *The Church and the Age of Reason: 1648–1789* (The Pelican History of the Church). Atheneum Publishers, 1961.

225. Cremin, Lawrence A., *The Transformation of the School: Progressivism in American Education, 1878–1957*. Alfred A. Knopf, Inc., 1961.

226. Cross, Barbara M., *Horace Bushnell: Minister to a Changing America*. The University of Chicago Press, 1958.

227. Cubberley, Ellwood P., ed., *Readings in the History of Education*. Houghton Mifflin Company, 1920.

228. Daly, Lowrie J., *The Medieval University*. Sheed & Ward, Inc., 1961.

229. Danielou, Jean, *Origen*. Sheed & Ward, Inc., 1955.

230. Duckett, Eleanor S., *Alcuin, Friend of Charlemagne*. The Macmillan Company, 1951.

231. Dunn, David, *et al.*, *A History of the Evangelical and Reformed Church*. Christian Education Press, 1961.

232. Dunn, William Kailer, *What Happened to Religious Education?: The Decline of Religious Teaching in the Public Elementary School, 1776–1861*. The Johns Hopkins Press, 1958.

233. Durnbaugh, Donald F., *European Origins of the Brethren*. Brethren Press, 1950.

234. Eby, Frederick, *The Development of Modern Education*, 2d ed. Prentice-Hall, Inc., 1952.

235. ———— *Early Protestant Educators: The Educational Writings of Martin Luther, John Calvin, and Other Leaders of Protestant Thought*. McGraw-Hill Book Company, Inc., 1931.

236. Eddy, Mary Baker, *Science and Health with Key to the Scriptures*. Trustees under the Will of Mary Baker Eddy (many printings).

237. Ellard, Gerald, *Master Alcuin, Liturgist*. Loyola University Press, 1956.

238. *Encyclopedia of Southern Baptists*. Broadman Press, 1958.

239. Erikson, Erik H., *Young Man Luther*. W. W. Norton & Company, Inc., 1958.

240. *Evanston to New Delhi*. World Council of Churches, 1961.

241. *Faith and Practice of the Philadelphia Yearly Meeting of the Religious Society of Friends: A Book of Christian Discipline*. Society of Friends, Philadelphia Yearly Meeting, 1955.

242. Farner, Oskar, *Zwingli the Reformer: His Life and Work*, tr. by D. G. Sear. Philosophical Library, Inc., 1952.

243. Farrell, Allan P., *The Jesuit Code of Liberal Education: Development and Scope of the Ratio Studiorum.* The Bruce Publishing Company, 1938.
244. Fergusson, E. Morris, *Historic Chapters in Christian Education in America.* Fleming H. Revell Company, 1935.
245. Fisher, Miles Mark, *A Short History of the Baptist Denomination.* Sunday School Publishing Board, National Baptist Convention, U.S.A., Inc., 1933.
246. Fitzpatrick, Edward A., ed., *St. Ignatius and the Ratio Studiorum.* McGraw-Hill Book Company, Inc., 1933.
247. Freeman, E. A., *Epoch of Negro Baptist and the Foreign Mission Board.* Central Seminary Press, 1953.
248. Froebel, Friedrich, *Autobiography,* tr. by Emilie Michaelis and H. Keatley Moore. Swan Sonnenschein & Company, London, 1891.
249. Ganss, George E., *St. Ignatius' Idea of a Jesuit University: A Study in the History of Catholic Education.* The Marquette University Press, 1954.
250. Girgensohn, Herbert, *Teaching Luther's Catechism,* tr. by J. W. Doberstein. Muhlenberg Press, 1959.
251. Goguel, Maurice, *The Birth of Christianity,* tr. by H. C. Snape. George Allen & Unwin, Ltd., London, 1953.
252. Gregg, William, *Short History of the Presbyterian Church in Canada.* Knox College, Toronto, 1900.
253. Harbison, E. Harris, *The Christian Scholar in the Age of the Reformation.* Charles Scribner's Sons, 1956.
254. Harmon, Nolan B., *Understanding The Methodist Church.* The Methodist Publishing House, 1955.
255. Harris, J. H., ed., *Robert Raikes: The Man and His Work.* London, 1899.
256. Head, Mabel, *Forward Together: An Historical Sketch of Interdenominational Women's Work and the United Council of Church Women.* United Council of Church Women, 1950.
257. Helmreich, Ernest C., *Religious Education in German Schools.* Harvard University Press, 1959.
258. Hezard, C., *Histoire du catechisme.* Librairie des Catechismes, Paris, 1900.
259. Highet, John, *The Scottish Churches.* Skeffington & Son, Ltd., London, 1960.
260. *Historical Monographs of the Christian Colleges of China.* United Board for Christian Higher Education in China, 1954 ff.
261. Holtom, Daniel Clarence, *The National Faith of Japan: A Study in Modern Shinto.* E. P. Dutton & Co., Inc., 1938.
262. Hook, Sidney, *John Dewey: An Intellectual Portrait.* The John Day Company, 1939.
263. Hughes, Thomas, *Loyola and the Educational System of the Jesuits.* Charles Scribner's Sons, 1892.
264. Hunter, Milton R., *The Mormons and the American Frontier.* Latter Day Saints Department of Education, 1940.
265. Idenburg, P. J., *Survey of the Dutch School System.* Schets van het Nederlandse Schoolwezen, Groningen, 1961.
266. Jaeger, Werner, *Early Christianity and Greek Paideia.* The Belknap Press of Harvard University Press, 1962.
267. ────── *Paideia: Ideals of Greek Culture,* 3 vols. Oxford University Press, Toronto, 1943–1945.
268. Jahsmann, Allan Hart, *What's Lutheran About Education?* Concordia Publishing House, 1960.
269. *Jehovah's Witnesses in the Divine Purpose.* Brooklyn, Watchtower Bible and Tract Society, 1959.
270. *John Amos Comenius, 1592–1670: Selections* (Introduction by Jean Piaget). UNESCO Publications Dept., 1957.

271. Johnson, Albert C., *Advent Christian History*. Advent Christian Publication Society, 1918.
272. Jones, Rufus M., *Spiritual Reformers in the 16th and 17th Centuries*. The Macmillan Company, 1914.
273. Jordan, Lewis G., *Negro Baptist History, U.S.A.* Sunday School Publishing Board, National Baptist Convention, U.S.A., Inc., 1930.
274. Kato, Genchi, *A Study of Shinto: The Religion of the Japanese Nation*. Meiji Japan Society, Tokyo, 1926.
275. Kennedy, Gerald, *The Methodist Way of Life*. Prentice-Hall, Inc., 1958.
276. Kenyon, Sir Frederic George, *Books and Readers in Ancient Greece and Rome*. Oxford University Press, Inc., 1951.
277. Kerwin, Jerome K., *Catholic Viewpoint on Church and State*. Doubleday & Company, Inc., 1960.
278. Kishimoto, Hideo, and Howes, John F., *Japanese Religion in the Meiji Era*. Obunsha, Tokyo, 1956.
279. Kleinclausz, A., *Alcuin*. Société d'édit, Les Belles Lettres, Paris, 1948.
280. Kromminga, J. H., *The Christian Reformed Church*. Baker Book House, 1949.
281. Lange, Frederick Albert, *The History of Materialism*, tr. by E. C. Thomas, 3d ed. The Humanities Press, Inc., 1950.
282. Lankard, Frank Glenn, *A History of the American Sunday School Curriculum*. Abingdon Press, 1927.
283. Latourette, Kenneth Scott, *A History of Christian Missions in China*. The Macmillan Company, 1929.
284. Lee, Umphrey, *Our Fathers and Us: The Heritage of the Methodists*. Southern Methodist University Press, 1958.
285. —— and Sweet, William Warren, *A Short History of Methodism*. Abingdon Press, 1956.
286. Lietzmann, Hans, *The Founding of the Church Universal*, tr. by Bertram Lee Woolf. Charles Scribner's Sons, 1938.
287. Lodge, R. C., *Plato's Theory of Education*. The Humanities Press, Inc., 1958.
288. Macdonald, Alexander B., *Christian Worship in the Primitive Church*. T. & T. Clark, Edinburgh, 1934.
289. Macy, Paul G., *If It Be of God: The Story of the World Council of Churches*. The Bethany Press, 1960.
290. Mallott, Floyd E., *Studies in Brethren History*. Brethren Publishing House, 1954.
291. Manross, William Wilson, *History of the American Episcopal Church*. Morehouse-Gorham Co., Inc., 1950.
292. Mary Janet, S.C., Sister, *Christian Foundation Program in the Catholic Secondary School*. The Catholic University of America Press, 1952.
293. Mayer, Frederick, *A History of Educational Thought*. Charles E. Merrill Books, Inc., 1960.
294. McDonnold, B. W., *History of the Cumberland Presbyterian Church*. Board of Publications of the Cumberland Presbyterian Church, 1888.
295. McGiffert, Arthur Cushman, *A History of Christian Thought*, 2 vols. Charles Scribner's Sons, 1949.
296. McGucken, William J., *The Jesuits and Education*. The Bruce Publishing Company, 1932.
297. McNeill, J. T., *The Presbyterian Church in Canada, 1875–1925*. The General Board, Presbyterian Church, Toronto, 1925.
298. Mead, Frank S., *Handbook of Denominations in the United States*. Abingdon Press, 1961.
299. Mecklin, John Moffatt, *Story of American Dissent*. Harcourt, Brace and Company, 1934.

300. *The Message and Mission of Methodism: Report of the Methodist Conference Committee, 1943.* The Epworth Press, Publishers, London, 1946.
301. Moffatt, James, *The Presbyterian Churches.* Methuen & Co., Ltd., London, 1928.
302. Moore, John Jamison, *History of the A.M.E. Zion Church.* A.M.E. Zion Church, 1884.
303. Neill, Stephen Charles, and Rouse, Ruth, *A History of the Ecumenical Movement, 1517–1948.* The Westminster Press, 1954.
304. Nock, A. D., *Conversion: The Old and the New in Religion from Alexander the Great to Augustine of Hippo.* Clarendon Press, Oxford, 1933.
305. Northcott, Cecil, *For Britain's Children: The Story of the Sunday Schools.* National Sunday School Union, London, 1953.
306. Ohl, J. F., *The Inner Mission.* General Council Publishing House, 1911.
307. Olmstead, Clifton E., *History of Religion in the United States.* Prentice-Hall, Inc., 1960.
308. Peel, Robert, *Christian Science: Its Encounter with American Culture.* Holt, Rinehart and Winston, Inc., 1958.
309. Pelt, Owen D., and Smith, Ralph Lee, *The Story of the National Baptists.* Vantage Press, Inc., 1961.
310. Pestalozzi, Johann Heinrich, *Leonard and Gertrude,* tr. and abridged by Eva Channing. D. C. Heath and Company, 1885.
311. Price, William W., *et al., Quaker Torch Bearers.* Society of Friends, General Conference, 1943.
312. Procter, Francis, and Frere, Walter Howard, *A History of the Book of Common Prayer.* The Macmillan Company, 1902.
313. Redford, M. E., *The Rise of the Church of the Nazarene.* Beacon Hill Press, 1948.
314. Reed, Luther D., *The Lutheran Liturgy.* Muhlenberg Press, 1959.
315. Rice, Edwin W., *The Sunday-School Movement and the American Sunday-School Union,* 2d ed. Union Press, 1927.
316. Richardson, Cyril C., tr. and ed., *Early Christian Fathers* (The Library of Christian Classics, ed. John Baillie, John T. McNeill, and Henry P. Van Dusen, Vol. I). The Westminster Press, 1953.
317. Romig, Edgar F., *The Tercentenary Year — Reformed Church in America: 1628 to 1928.* Half Moon Press, 1929.
318. Rouse, Ruth, *History of the World's Student Christian Federation.* SCM Press Ltd., London, 1948.
319. Rush, Christopher, *A Short Account of the Rise and Progress of the African Methodist Episcopal Church in America.* African Methodist Episcopal Church, 1866.
320. Sacks, Benjamin, *The Religious Issue in the State Schools of England and Wales, 1902–1914: A Nation's Quest for Human Dignity.* University of New Mexico Press, 1961.
321. Sarton, George, *History of Science.* Harvard University Press, 1951.
322. Schneider, Carl E., *The German Church on the American Frontier.* Eden Publishing House, 1939.
323. Scholefield, Harry B., ed., *A Pocket Guide to Unitarianism.* Beacon Press, Inc., 1954.
324. Schwickerath, Robert, *Jesuit Education.* B. Herder Book Company, London, 1904.
325. Shedd, Clarence P., *Two Centuries of Student Christian Movements.* Association Press, 1934.
326. ——— *et al., History of the World's Alliance of Young Men's Christian Associations.* Association Press, 1956.

327. Sherrill, Lewis Joseph, *The Rise of Christian Education*. The Macmillan Company, 1944.
328. Sidgwick, Henry, *Outlines of the History of Ethics*, rev. ed. The Macmillan Company, 1931.
329. Silber, Kate, *Pestalozzi: The Man and His Work*. Routledge & Kegan Paul, Ltd., London, 1960.
330. Simon, Brian, ed., *Psychology in the Soviet Union*. Stanford University Press, 1957.
331. Sloane, William, *Children's Books in England and America in the Seventeenth Century*. King's Crown Press, 1955.
332. Sloyan, Gerard S., ed., *Shaping the Christian Message*. The Macmillan Company, 1958.
333. Smalley, Beryl, *The Study of the Bible in the Middle Ages*, 2d ed. Philosophical Library, Inc., 1952.
334. Smith, Clifford P., *Historical Sketches*. The Christian Science Publishing Society, 1941.
335. Smith, Elva S., *The History of Children's Literature*. American Library Association, 1937.
336. Smith, Timothy L., *History, Church of the Nazarene*. Beacon Hill Press, 1962.
337. Spinka, Matthew, *John Amos Comenius*. The University of Chicago Press, 1943.
338. Stokes, Anson Phelps, *Church and State in the United States*, 3 vols. Harper & Brothers, 1950.
339. Stokes, Mack B., *Major Methodist Beliefs*. The Methodist Publishing House, 1956.
340. Sullivan, John F., *The Externals of the Catholic Church*, 3d ed. P. J. Kenedy & Sons, 1918.
341. *Teachings and Practices of the Churches of God*, rev. ed. Central Publishing House, 1961.
342. Tenrikyo Church Headquarters, *A Short History of Tenrikyo*. The Tenrikyo Printing Office, Tenri, 1958.
343. Thut, I. N., *The Story of Education: Philosophical and Historical Foundations*. McGraw-Hill Book Company, Inc., 1957.
344. Torrance, T. F., ed., *The School of Faith: The Catechisms of the Reformed Church*. James Clarke & Company, Ltd., Publishers, London, 1959.
345. *Towards the Conversion of England: Report of the Archbishops' Committee*, 1945. Press & Publications Board of the Church Assembly, London, 1945.
346. Tyrer, John W., *Historical Survey of Holy Week*. Oxford University Press, Inc., 1932.
347. Ulich, Robert, ed., *Three Centuries of Educational Wisdom*. Harvard University Press, 1947.
348. Wallach, Luitpold, *Alcuin and Charlemagne: Studies in Carolingian History and Literature*. Cornell University Press, 1959.
349. Warnock, Mary, *Ethics Since 1900*. Oxford University Press, Inc., 1960.
350. Winebrenner, John, *A Brief View of the Formation, Government, and Discipline of the Church of God*. Montgomery and Dexter, 1829.
351. Woodson, Carter G., *The History of the Negro Church*. The Associated Publishers, Inc., 1931.
352. Woodward, W. H., *Studies in Education During the Age of the Renaissance, 1400–1600*. Cambridge University Press, 1906.
353. Yahn, Sherman G., *History of the Churches of God in North America*. Central Publishing House, 1926.

III. General Biblical, Religious, and Theological

354. Abel, F. M., *Géographie de la Palestine*. Librairie Lecoffre, J. Gabalda et Cie, Paris, 1933–1938.
355. Aldrich, Donald B., ed., *The Golden Book of Prayer*. Dodd, Mead & Company, Inc., 1941.
356. Ames, Edward Scribner, *Religion*. Henry Holt & Company, Inc., 1935.
357. Anesaki, Masaharu, *History of Japanese Religion*. Kegan Paul, Trench, Trubner & Co., Ltd., London, 1930.
358. —— *Religious Life of the Japanese People: Its Present Status and Historical Background*. The Kokusai Bunka Shinkokai, Tokyo, 1938.
359. Aquinas, Thomas, *Basic Writings of St. Thomas Aquinas*, ed. Anton C. Pegis, 2 vols. Random House, Inc., 1944.
360. —— *On the Truth of the Catholic Faith: Summa contra Gentiles*, tr. by Anton C. Pegis, 5 vols. Doubleday Image Books (Doubleday & Company, Inc.), 1955.
361. —— *Philosophical Texts*, ed. and tr. by Thomas Gilby, O.P. Oxford University Press, Inc., 1951.
362. —— *Summa Theologica*, tr. by Fathers of the English Dominican Province, 3 vols. Benziger Brothers, Inc., 1947.
363. —— *Truth (Quaestiones disputatae de veritate)*, 2. Henry Regnery Company, 1952.
364. Arndt, Elmer J. F., *The Faith We Proclaim*. Christian Education Press, 1960.
365. Aston, W. G., *Shinto, the Way of the Gods*. Longmans, Green & Co., Ltd., London, 1905.
366. Aulen, Gustaf, *The Faith of the Christian Church*, tr. from the 4th Swedish edition by Eric H. Wahlstrom and G. Everett Arden. Muhlenberg Press, 1948.
367. Avi-Yonah, Michael, *The Mababa Mosaic Map*. The Israel Exploration Society, Jerusalem, 1954.
368. Bachman, E. Theodore, *et al.*, *Churches and Social Welfare*, 3 vols. National Council of the Churches of Christ in the U.S.A., 1955.
369. Bader, Jesse M., *Evangelism in a Changing America*. The Bethany Press, 1957.
370. Bailey, Derrick Sherwin, *Sponsors at Baptism and Confirmation*. The Macmillan Company, London, 1950.
371. Baillie, Donald M., *The Theology of the Sacraments*. Charles Scribner's Sons, 1957.
372. —— and Marsh, John, eds., *Intercommunion*. SCM Press Ltd., London, 1952.
373. Baillie, John, *The Idea of Revelation in Recent Thought*. Columbia University Press, 1956.
374. Baly, Denis, *The Geography of the Bible*. Harper & Brothers, 1957.
375. Barnes, Roswell P., *Under Orders: The Churches and Public Affairs*. Doubleday & Company, Inc., 1961.
376. Barth, Karl, *Against the Stream*, ed. by Ronald Gregor Smith. Philosophical Library, Inc., 1954.
377. —— *Church Dogmatics* (successive volumes). T. & T. Clark, Edinburgh, 1936 ff.
378. —— *The Epistle to the Romans*, tr. from the 6th ed. by Edwyn C. Hoskyns. Oxford University Press, Inc., 1933.
379. —— *The Humanity of God*. John Knox Press, 1960.
380. —— *The Knowledge of God and the Service of God*. Hodder & Stoughton, Ltd., London, 1938.

381. —— *The Teaching of the Church Regarding Baptism*, tr. by E. A. Payne. The Macmillan Company, 1948.

382. Baxter, Richard, *The Reformed Pastor*. Sawyer, Ingersoll and Company, 1852.

383. Beasley, Norman, *The Cross and the Crown*. Duell, Sloan & Pearce, Inc., 1952.

384. Bennett, John Coleman, *Christian Ethics and Social Policy*. Charles Scribner's Sons, 1946.

385. —— *Christians and the State*. Charles Scribner's Sons, 1958.

386. Benoit, J. D., *Liturgical Renewal: Studies in Catholic and Protestant Developments on the Continent*. SCM Press Ltd., London, 1958.

387. Berdyaev, Nicolas, *Solitude and Society*. Centenary Press, London, 1938.

388. —— *Spirit and Reality*. Charles Scribner's Sons, 1939.

389. Bethune-Baker, James Franklin, *The Early History of Christian Doctrine*. Methuen & Co., Ltd., London, 1903.

390. Bilheimer, Robert S., *The Quest for Church Unity*. Haddam House, 1952.

391. Bliss, Kathleen, *The Services and Status of Women in the Churches*. SCM Press, Ltd., London, 1952.

392. *A Book of Prayer for Students*. SCM Press, Ltd., London, 1915.

393. Bonhoeffer, Dietrich, *Ethics*, ed. by Eberhard Bethge; tr. by Neville Horton Smith. The Macmillan Company, 1955.

394. Bouyer, Louis, *Liturgical Piety*. University of Notre Dame Press, 1954.

395. Boyd, Malcolm, *Crisis in Communication*. Doubleday & Company, Inc., 1957.

396. Brandon, Owen, *The Battle for the Soul: Aspects of Religious Conversion*. The Westminster Press, 1959.

397. Brightman, Edgar S., *The Problem of God*. Abingdon Press, 1930.

398. Brilioth, Yngve T., *Eucharistic Faith and Practice, Evangelical and Catholic*. S.P.C.K., London, 1930.

399. Brown, William Adams, *Christian Theology in Outline*. Charles Scribner's Sons, 1907.

400. Brunner, Emil, *The Christian Doctrine of God* (*Dogmatics*, Vol. I). The Westminster Press, 1950.

401. —— *The Christian Doctrine of Creation and Redemption* (*Dogmatics*, Vol. II). The Westminster Press, 1952.

402. —— *I Believe in the Living God: Sermons on the Apostles' Creed*, tr. and ed. by John Holden. The Westminster Press, 1961.

403. —— *Man in Revolt*. The Westminster Press, 1947.

404. —— *Revelation and Reason*, tr. by Olive Wyon. The Westminster Press, 1946.

405. —— *The Theology of Crisis*. Charles Scribner's Sons, 1929.

406. Buber, Martin, *Between Man and Man*, tr. by Ronald Gregor Smith. Beacon Press, Inc., 1955.

407. —— *I and Thou*, 2d ed., tr. by Ronald Gregor Smith. Charles Scribner's Sons, 1958.

408. —— *Moses, the Revelation and the Covenant*. Harper Torchbooks (Harper & Brothers), 1958.

409. —— *The Prophetic Faith*. Harper Torchbooks (Harper & Brothers), 1960.

410. Bulgakov, S. N. *The Wisdom of God*. Williams & Norgate, Ltd., London, 1937.

411. Bultmann, Rudolf, *Theology of the New Testament*, tr. by Kendrick Grobel, 2 vols. Charles Scribner's Sons, 1951, 1955.

412. Bunce, William K., *Religions in Japan: Buddhism, Shinto, Christianity*. Charles E. Tuttle Company, 1955.

413. Burn, A. E. *An Introduction to the Creeds and to the Te Deum*. S.P.C.K., London, 1899.

414. Buttrick, George Arthur, *Prayer.* Abingdon-Cokesbury Press, 1942.
415. Cannon, William B., *The Wisdom of the Body.* W. W. Norton & Company, Inc., 1939.
416. Cant, Reginald, *Heart in Pilgrimage.* Harper & Brothers, 1959.
417. Case, Adelaide T., *Liberal Christianity and Religious Education.* The Macmillan Company, 1924.
418. Casteel, John L., *Spiritual Renewal Through Personal Groups.* Association Press, 1937.
419. Cavert, Samuel McCrea, ed., *The New Delhi Assembly: Official Report.* Association Press, 1961.
420. ——— *On the Road to Christian Unity.* Harper & Brothers, 1961.
421. Cheney, Sheldon, *Men Who Have Walked with God.* Alfred A. Knopf, Inc., 1946.
422. Civardi, Luigi, *A Manual of Catholic Action,* tr. by C. C. Martindale. Sheed & Ward, Ltd., London, 1935.
423. Clark, Neville, *An Approach to the Theology of the Sacraments.* Alec R. Allenson, Inc., 1956.
424. Clarke, W. K. Lowther, and Harris, Charles, *Liturgy and Worship.* S.P.C.K., London, 1932.
425. Clarke, William Newton, *An Outline of Christian Theology.* Charles Scribner's Sons, 1926.
426. Cleland, James T., *The True and Lively Word.* Charles Scribner's Sons, 1954.
427. ——— *Wherefore Art Thou Come?: Meditations on the Lord's Supper.* Abingdon Press, 1961.
428. Cochrane, Charles Norris, *Christianity and Classical Culture.* Oxford University Press, Inc., 1944.
429. Come, Arnold B., *Agents of Reconciliation.* The Westminster Press, 1960.
430. Congar, Yves M. J., *Lay People in the Church,* tr. by Donald Attwater. The Newman Press, 1957.
431. Cropper, Margaret, *A Prayer Book for Juniors.* SCM Press Ltd., London, 1958.
432. Cross, F. L., ed., *St. Cyril of Jerusalem's Lectures on the Christian Sacraments.* S.P.C.K., London, 1951.
433. Cullmann, Oscar, *Baptism in the New Testament,* tr. by J. K. S. Reid. Henry Regnery Company, 1951.
434. ——— *The Earliest Christian Confessions.* Lutterworth Press, London, 1949.
435. Cully, Kendig Brubaker, ed., *Prayers for Church Workers.* The Westminster Press, 1961.
436. ——— *Sacraments: A Language of Faith.* Christian Education Press, 1961.
437. Curtis, Muriel Streibert, *The Story of the Bible People.* The Macmillan Company, 1946.
438. Daube, D., *The New Testament and Rabbinic Judaism.* John de Graff, Inc., 1956.
439. De Blank, Joost, *This Is Conversion.* Hodder & Stoughton, Ltd., London, 1957.
440. De La Bedoyère, Michael, *The Layman in the Church.* Henry Regnery Company, 1955.
441. Denzinger, H. J. D., *Enchiridion Symbolorum,* 31st ed. B. Herder Book Company, 1957.
442. Dewey, John, *Reconstruction in Philosophy,* new ed. Beacon Press, Inc., 1949.
443. DeWire, Harry A., *The Christian as Communicator* (Westminster Studies in Christian Communication, ed. by Kendig Brubaker Cully). The Westminster Press, 1960.

444. Diem, H. *Dogmatics*. Oliver & Boyd, Ltd., Edinburgh, 1959.
445. Dillenberger, John, and Welch, Claude, *Protestant Christianity*. Charles Scribner's Sons, 1954.
446. Dillistone, F. W., *Christianity and Communication*. Charles Scribner's Sons, 1956.
447. Dix, Dom Gregory, *The Shape of the Liturgy*. The Dacre Press, London, 1945.
448. Doberstein, John W., *On Wings of Healing*. Muhlenberg Press, 1942.
449. Dodd, C. H., *The Apostolic Preaching and Its Developments*. Harper & Brothers, 1936.
450. Douglass, H. Paul, *Church Unity: Movements in the U.S.A.* Institute of Social and Religious Research Publications, 1929.
451. Duchesne, L., *Christian Worship*. S.P.C.K., London, 1949.
452. Duff, Edward, S.J., *The Social Thought of the World Council of Churches*. Association Press, 1956.
453. Dunkerley, Roderick, ed., *The Ministry and Sacraments*. SCM Press Ltd., London, 1937.
454. Dunkle, William Frederick, Jr., *Values in the Church Year for Evangelical Protestantism*. Abingdon Press, 1959.
455. Edwall, Pehr, Hayman, Eric, and Maxwell, William D., *Ways of Worship*. SCM Press Ltd., London, 1951.
456. Eliade, Mircea, *Patterns in Comparative Religion*, tr. by Rosemary Sheed. Sheed & Ward, Inc., 1958.
457. —— and Kitagawa, Joseph M., eds., *History of Religions: Essays in Methodology*. The University of Chicago Press, 1959.
458. Farmer, Herbert H., *The Servant of the Word*. Charles Scribner's Sons, 1942.
459. —— *Towards Belief in God*. Charles Scribner's Sons, 1943.
460. Farrell, Walter, O.P., *A Companion to the Summa*, 2 vols. Sheed & Ward, Inc., 1952.
461. Ferm, Vergilius, ed., *Encyclopedia of Religion*. Philosophical Library, Inc., 1945.
462. Ferré, Nels F. S., *The Christian Understanding of God*. Harper & Brothers, 1951.
463. Flew, A. G. N., and MacIntyre, Alistair, *New Essays in Philosophical Theology*. The Macmillan Company, 1955.
464. Forsyth, Peter Taylor, *The Church and the Sacraments*. Independent Press, Ltd., London, 1953.
465. Fox, Selina Fitzherbert, *A Chain of Prayer Across the Ages*. John Murray, London, 1913.
466. Frakes, Margaret, *Bridges to Understanding*. Muhlenberg Press, 1960.
467. Frere, Walter Howard, *The Principles of Religious Ceremonial*. A. R. Mowbray & Co., Ltd., London, 1928.
468. *From Paradise Lost to Paradise Regained*. Brooklyn, Watchtower Bible and Tract Society, 1958.
469. Fuller, Reginald H., *What Is Liturgical Preaching?* SCM Press Ltd., London, 1957.
470. *The Fundamentals*. The Testimony Publishing Company, 1909–1915.
471. Garrigou-Lagrange, Reginald, *God, His Existence and His Nature*. B. Herder Book Company, 1939.
472. Gerstner, John H., *The Theology of the Major Sects*. Baker Book House, 1960.
473. Gibbs, Mard, ed., *Meet the Church: The Growth of the Kirchentag Idea in Europe*. World Council of Churches, Geneva, 1959.
474. Gilson, Etienne, ed., *The Church Speaks to the Modern World*. Doubleday Image Books (Doubleday & Company, Inc.), 1954.

475. ——— *God and Philosophy.* Yale University Press, 1941.
476. Goguel, Maurice, *The Birth of Christianity,* tr. by H. C. Snape. George Allen & Unwin, Ltd., London, 1953.
477. Goodall, Norman, *The Ecumenical Movement: What It Is and What It Does.* Oxford University Press, Inc., 1961.
478. Goodspeed, Edgar J., *The Apostolic Fathers: An American Translation.* Harper & Brothers, 1950.
479. ——— *Christianity Goes to Press.* The Macmillan Company, 1940.
480. Grant, John W., *The Ship Under the Cross.* The Ryerson Press, Toronto, 1960.
481. Green, Bryan, *The Practice of Evangelism.* Hodder & Stoughton, Ltd., London, 1959.
482. Grimes, Howard, *The Church Redemptive.* Abingdon Press, 1958.
483. ——— *The Rebirth of the Laity.* Abingdon Press, 1962.
484. Grollenberg, L. H., *Atlas of the Bible.* Thomas Nelson & Sons, 1956.
485. ——— *Shorter Atlas of the Bible.* Thomas Nelson & Sons, 1959.
486. Harbison, E. Harris, *The Christian Scholar in the Age of the Reformation.* Charles Scribner's Sons, 1956.
487. Harkness, Georgia, *The Modern Rivals of Christian Faith.* Abingdon Press, 1952.
488. ——— *Prayer and the Common Life.* Abingdon Press, 1948.
489. Harnack, Adolf, *What Is Christianity?* tr. by T. B. Saunders. Harper & Brothers, 1957.
490. Hartshorne, Charles, *Man's Vision of God.* Willett, Clark & Company, 1941.
491. Hayward, Percy Roy, *Young People's Prayers.* Association Press, 1958.
492. Hebert, Gabriel, *Fundamentalism and the Church.* The Westminster Press, 1957.
493. ——— *Liturgy and Society.* Faber & Faber, Ltd., London, 1935.
494. Hedley, George, *Christian Worship: Some Meanings and Means.* The Macmillan Company, 1953.
495. Heiler, Friedrich, *Prayer: A Study in the History and Psychology of Religion,* tr. and ed. by Samuel McComb and J. E. Park. Oxford University Press, 1932.
496. Heim, Karl, *God Transcendent,* tr. from the 3d German ed. by Edgar P. Dickie. James Nisbet & Co., Ltd., London, 1935.
497. Heim, Ralph D., *Youth's Companion to the Bible.* Muhlenberg Press, 1959.
498. Henry, P., S.M., *The Liturgical Year.* The Bruce Publishing Company, Inc., 1938.
499. Herberg, Will, ed., *Four Existentialist Theologians.* Doubleday & Company, 1958.
500. Heris, C. V., *The Mystery of Christ,* tr. by Denis Fahey. The Newman Press, 1960.
501. Herman, E., *Creative Prayer.* James Clarke & Company, Ltd., Publishers, London, 1921.
502. Hocking, William Ernest, *The Meaning of God in Human Experience.* Yale University Press, 1912.
503. Hogg, W. Richey, *Ecumenical Foundations.* Harper & Brothers, 1952.
504. Holtom, Daniel C., *Modern Japan and Shinto Nationalism,* rev. ed. The University of Chicago Press, 1947.
505. Horton, Walter Marshall, *Christian Theology: An Ecumenical Approach,* rev. ed. Harper & Brothers, 1958.
506. ——— *Contemporary Continental Theology.* Harper & Brothers, 1938.
507. ——— *A Psychological Approach to Theology.* Harper & Brothers, 1931.
508. Howe, Reuel L., *Man's Need and God's Action.* The Seabury Press, Inc., 1955.

509. Huxley, Julian, *Religion Without Revelation*, rev. ed. Harper & Brothers, 1957.
510. Jacobs, Edmond, *Theology of the Old Testament*, Harper & Brothers, 1958.
511. Jeremias, Joachim, *Infant Baptism in the First Four Centuries* (The Library of History and Doctrine). The Westminster Press, 1960.
512. Jones, E. Stanley, *Conversion*. Hodder & Stoughton, Ltd., London, 1960.
513. Jones, Rufus M., *The Flowering of Mysticism*. The Macmillan Company, 1939.
514. —— *New Studies in Mystical Religion*. The Macmillan Company, 1927.
515. —— *Pathways to the Reality of God*. The Macmillan Company, 1931.
516. —— *Studies in Mystical Religion*. The Macmillan Company, London, 1909.
517. Jordan, Louis Henry, *Comparative Religion*. T. & T. Clark, Edinburgh, 1905.
518. Judy, Marvin T., *The Larger Parish and Group Ministry*. Abingdon Press, 1959.
519. Kaufman, Gordon D., *The Content of Decision*. Abingdon Press, 1961.
520. Kelley, Alden D., *Christianity and Political Responsibility* (Westminster Studies in Christian Communication, ed. by Kendig Brubaker Cully). The Westminster Press, 1961.
521. Kelly, J. N. D., *Early Christian Creeds*. Longmans, Green & Co., Inc., 1950.
522. Kierkegaard, Søren, *Fear and Trembling*, tr. by Walter Lowrie. Princeton University Press, 1941.
523. —— *Sickness Unto Death*, tr. by Walter Lowrie. Princeton University Press, 1941.
524. Kirk, Kenneth, *The Vision of God*. Longmans, Green & Co., Inc., 1931.
525. Kittel, Gerhard, ed., *Bible Key Words*, tr. and ed. by John R. Coates. Harper & Brothers, 1951.
526. Knox, John, *The Ethic of Jesus in the Teaching of the Church*. Abingdon Press, 1961.
527. Koenker, Ernest B., *The Liturgical Renaissance in the Roman Catholic Church*. The University of Chicago Press, 1954.
528. Kraeling, Emil G., *Historical Atlas of the Holy Land*. Rand McNally & Company, 1959.
529. —— *Rand McNally Bible Atlas*. Rand McNally & Company, 1956.
530. Kraemer, Hendrik, *The Communication of the Christian Faith*. The Westminster Press, 1956.
531. —— *A Theology of the Laity*. The Westminster Press, 1958.
532. Kuhn, Harold B., ed., *Baker's Dictionary of Theology*. Baker Book House, 1960.
533. Laeuchli, Samuel, *Theology of Faith*. Abingdon Press, 1962.
534. Lamprechut, Sterling P., *Our Religious Traditions*. Harvard University Press, 1950.
535. Littell, Franklin Hamlin, *The German Phoenix*. Doubleday & Company, Inc., 1960.
536. Locke, John, *An Essay Concerning Human Understanding*, collated and annotated by Alexander C. Fraser, 2 vols. Dover Publications, Inc., 1959.
537. Luccock, Halford, *Communicating the Gospel*. Harper & Brothers, 1954.
538. Mackintosh, Hugh Ross, *The Christian Experience of Forgiveness*. Harper & Brothers, 1927.
539. MacLeod, George F., *Only One Way Left*. The Iona Community, 1956.
540. Maritain, Jacques, *Approaches to God*. Harper & Brothers, 1954.
541. Marty, Martin E., *The Improper Opinion: Mass Media and the Christian Faith* (Westminster Studies in Christian Communication, ed. by Kendig Brubaker Cully). The Westminster Press, 1961.

542. Mason, J. W. T., *The Meaning of Shinto*. E. P. Dutton & Company, Inc., 1935.
543. Maury, Phillipe, *Politics and Evangelism*. Doubleday & Company, Inc., 1959.
544. Maxwell, W. D., *An Outline of Christian Worship: Its Development and Forms*. Oxford University Press, Inc., 1936.
545. McArthur, A. Allan, *The Evolution of the Christian Year*. The Seabury Press, Inc., 1953.
546. McCabe, Joseph E., *The Power of God in a Parish Program*. The Westminster Press, 1959.
547. Merton, Thomas, *Seeds of Contemplation*. Dell Publishing Co., Inc., 1953.
548. Micklem, Nathaniel, ed., *Christian Worship*. The Clarendon Press, Oxford, 1936.
549. Mill, John Stuart, *Three Essays on Religion: Nature, the Utility of Religion and Theism*. Henry Holt & Company, Inc., 1874.
550. Miller, Alexander, *Christian Faith and My Job*. Association Press, 1946.
551. ———— *The Renewal of Man*. Doubleday & Company, Inc., 1955.
552. Miller, Samuel M., *The Life of the Soul*. Harper & Brothers, 1951.
553. Minear, Paul S., *Images of the Church in the New Testament*. The Westminster Press, 1960.
554. Moffatt, James, *Grace in the New Testament*. Hodder & Stoughton, Ltd., 1932.
555. Montague, William Pepperell, *Belief Unbound*. Yale University Press, 1930.
556. Montcheuil, Yves de, S.J., *For Men of Action*, tr. by Charles E. Parnell. Fides Publishers Association, n.d.
557. Moreau, Jules Laurence, *Language and Religious Language: A Study in the Dynamics of Translation* (Westminster Studies in Christian Communication, ed. by Kendig Brubaker Cully). The Westminster Press, 1960.
558. Morton, T. Ralph, *The Community of Faith*. Association Press, 1954.
559. Mouroux, Jean, *The Meaning of Man*, tr. by A. H. G. Downes. Sheed & Ward, Ltd., London, 1952.
560. Mozley, J. K., *The Doctrine of God*. S.P.C.K., London, 1928.
561. Murray, John Courtney, *We Hold These Truths: Catholic Reflections on the American Proposition*. Sheed & Ward, Ltd., London, 1960.
562. Nash, Arnold S., ed., *Protestant Thought in the Twentieth Century*. The Macmillan Company, 1951.
563. Nathan, Walter L., *Art and the Message of the Church* (Westminster Studies in Christian Education, ed. by Kendig Brubaker Cully). The Westminster Press, 1961.
564. Neill, Stephen C., *Brothers of the Faith*. Abingdon Press, 1960.
565. Nelson, J. Robert, *One Lord, One Church*. Association Press, 1958.
566. Newman, Jeremiah, *What Is Catholic Action?* The Newman Press, 1956.
567. Nida, Eugene A., *God's World in Man's Language*. Harper & Brothers, 1952.
568. ———— *Message and Mission*. Harper & Brothers, 1960.
569. Niebuhr, H. Richard, *Christ and Culture*. Harper & Brothers, 1951.
570. ———— *The Meaning of Revelation*. The Macmillan Company, 1941.
571. ———— and Williams, Daniel D., *The Ministry in Historical Perspective*. Harper & Brothers, 1956.
572. ———— *The Purpose of the Church and Its Ministry*. Harper & Brothers, 1956.
573. ———— *Radical Monotheism and Western Culture*. Harper & Brothers, 1960.
574. ———— *Social Sources of Denominationalism*. Henry Holt & Company, Inc., 1929.
575. ———— and Williams, Daniel Day, and Gustafson, James M., *The Advancement of Theological Education*. Harper & Brothers, 1957.
576. Niebuhr, Reinhold, *Children of Light and Children of Darkness*. Charles Scribner's Sons, 1944.

577. —— *Christian Realism and Political Problems.* Charles Scribner's Sons, 1953.
578. —— *The Irony of American History.* Charles Scribner's Sons, 1952.
579. —— *The Nature and Destiny of Man.* Charles Scribner's Sons, 1953.
580. Noth, Martin, *The History of Israel.* Harper & Brothers, 1958.
581. Olgiati-Zybura, *Key to the Study of Saint Thomas Aquinas.* B. Herder Book Company, London, 1929.
582. O'Neill, James M., *Religion and Education Under the Constitution.* Harper & Brothers, 1949.
583. Palmer, Albert W., *The Art of Conducting Public Worship.* The Macmillan Company, 1939.
584. Paul, Robert S., *The Atonement and the Sacraments.* Abingdon Press, 1960.
585. Perrin, J. M., *Forward the Layman,* tr. by Katherine Gordon. The Newman Press, 1956.
586. Philips, Gerard, *The Role of the Laity in the Church,* tr. by John R. Gilbert and James W. Moudry. Fides Publishers Association, 1956.
587. Phillips, Godfrey E., *The Transmission of the Faith.* Lutterworth Press, London, 1946.
588. Porter, H. B., *The Day of Light: The Biblical and Liturgical Meaning of Sunday.* The Seabury Press, Inc., 1960.
589. Prestige, G. L., *God in Patristic Thought.* S.P.C.K., London, 1952.
590. Prohl, Russell C., *Woman in the Church.* Wm. B. Eerdmans Publishing Company, 1957.
591. Quick, Oliver Chase, *The Christian Sacraments.* Harper & Brothers, 1927.
592. Raines, Robert, *New Life in the Church.* Harper & Brothers, 1961.
593. Randall, J. H., and Randall, J. H., Jr., *Religion in the Modern World.* Frederick A. Stokes Company, 1929.
594. Rauschenbusch, Walter, *A Theology for the Social Gospel,* new ed. Abingdon Press, 1961.
595. Read, David C., *The Communication of the Gospel.* SCM Press Ltd., London, 1954.
596. Reid, J. K. S., *The Authority of Scripture: A Study of the Reformation and Post-Reformation Understanding of the Bible.* Methuen & Co., Ltd., London, 1957.
597. Reinhold, H. A., *The Dynamics of Liturgy.* The Macmillan Company, 1961.
598. Richardson, Alan, *The Biblical Doctrine of Work.* Alec R. Allenson, Inc., 1954.
599. Robinson, H. Wheeler, ed., *The Bible in Its Ancient and English Versions.* Oxford University Press, London, 1940.
600. —— *The Religious Ideas of the Old Testament.* Gerald Duckworth & Co., Ltd., London, 1956.
601. Ross, G. A. Johnston, *Christian Worship and Its Future.* Abingdon Press, 1927.
602. Rupp, Ernest Gordon, *The Righteousness of God: Luther Studies.* Hodder & Stoughton, Ltd., London, 1953.
603. Santayana, George, *Reason in Religion.* Charles Scribner's Sons, 1922.
604. Sartre, Jean-Paul, *Existentialism,* tr. by Bernard Frechtman. Philosophical Library, Inc., 1957.
605. Schaff, Philip, ed., *Creeds of Christendom,* 4th ed., 3 vols. Harper & Brothers, 1919.
606. Schleiermacher, Friedrich, *The Christian Faith.* T. & T. Clark, Edinburgh, 1928.
607. Sellars, Roy Wood, *Religion Coming of Age.* The Macmillan Company, 1928.
608. Sellers, James E., *The Outsider and the Word of God.* Abingdon Press, 1961.

609. Selwyn, Edward Gordon, *The First Epistle of St. Peter.* The Macmillan Company, London, 1946.
610. Shepherd, Massey H., Jr., ed., *The Liturgical Renewal of the Church.* Oxford University Press, Inc., 1960.
611. —— *The Oxford American Prayer Book Commentary.* Oxford University Press, Inc., 1950.
612. —— *The Paschal Liturgy and the Apocalypse.* John Knox Press, 1960.
613. —— *The Reform of Liturgical Worship: Perspectives and Prospects.* Oxford University Press, Inc., 1961.
614. —— *The Worship of the Church.* The Seabury Press, Inc., 1952.
615. Sherrill, Lewis Joseph, *Guilt and Redemption,* rev. ed. John Knox Press, 1957.
616. Simcox, Carroll E., *Living the Creed.* The Dacre Press, London, 1954.
617. Smart, James D., *The Creed in Christian Teaching.* The Westminster Press, 1962.
618. —— *The Rebirth of Ministry.* The Westminster Press, 1960.
619. Smith, George A., *The Historical Geography of the Holy Land,* 25th ed. Hodder & Stoughton, Ltd., London, 1931.
620. Snaith, Norman Henry, *The Distinctive Ideas of the Old Testament.* The Epworth Press, Publishers, London, 1944.
621. Sperry, Willard L., *Reality in Worship: A Study of Public Worship and Private Religion.* The Macmillan Company, 1925.
622. Spike, Robert W., *In but Not of the World.* Association Press, 1957.
623. Staley, Vernon, *The Liturgical Year.* A. R. Mowbray & Company, London, 1907.
624. Stedman, Joseph F., ed., *My Sunday Missal.* Confraternity of the Precious Blood, 1942.
625. Steere, Douglas V., *Doors Into Life.* Harper & Brothers, 1948.
626. —— *Prayer and Worship.* Association Press, 1938.
627. Stott, John R., *Fundamentalism and Evangelism.* Wm. B. Eerdmans Publishing Company, 1959.
628. Strachan, R. H., *The Authority of Christian Experience: A Study in the Basis of Religious Authority.* Abingdon-Cokesbury Press, 1931.
629. Strawley, J. H., *St. Ambrose on the Sacraments and on the Mysteries.* S.P.C.K., London, 1950.
630. Suhard, Emmanuel Celestin, *The Church Today.* Fides Publishers Association, 1953.
631. —— *Growth or Decline.* Fides Publishers Association, 1948.
632. Swezey, George E., *Effective Evangelism.* Harper & Brothers, 1953.
633. Sydnor, William, *Keeping the Christian Year.* Morehouse-Barlow Co., 1959.
634. Temple, William, *Nature, Man and God.* The Macmillan Company, London, 1934.
635. Tennant, F. R., *Philosophical Theology,* 2 vols. Cambridge University Press, 1930.
636. Terrien, Samuel, *The Golden Bible Atlas.* Golden Press, Inc., 1957.
637. Thils, Gustave, *Christian Attitudes.* Scepter, Dublin, 1959.
638. Thompson, T. K., ed., *Stewardship in Contemporary Theology.* Association Press, 1960.
639. Throckmorton, Burton H., Jr., *The New Testament and Mythology.* The Westminster Press, 1959.
640. Tillich, Paul, *The Courage to Be.* Yale University Press, 1952.
641. —— *The Protestant Era.* The University of Chicago Press, 1948.
642. —— *The Shaking of the Foundations.* Charles Scribner's Sons, 1948.
643. —— *Systematic Theology,* Vols. I and II. The University of Chicago Press, 1951, 1958.

644. —— *Theology of Culture,* ed. by Robert C. Kimball. Oxford University Press, Inc., 1959.
645. Trueblood, Elton, ed., *Doctor Johnson's Prayers.* Harper & Brothers, 1945.
646. Tulga, Chester E., *The Case Against Modernism in Foreign Missions.* Conservative Baptist Fellowship, 1950.
647. Underhill, Evelyn, *The Golden Sequence.* E. P. Dutton & Company, Inc., 1933.
648. —— *Mysticism.* E. P. Dutton & Company, Inc., 1911.
649. —— *Worship.* Harper & Brothers, 1937.
650. Van der Leeuw, Gerardus, *Religion in Essence and Manifestation,* tr. by John Evans Turner. The Macmillan Company, London, 1938.
651. van der Meer, F., and Mohrmann, Christine, *Atlas of the Early Christian World.* Thomas Nelson & Sons, 1958.
652. Visser 't Hooft, W. A., *The Kingship of Christ.* Harper & Brothers, 1948.
653. —— *The Pressure of Our Common Calling.* Doubleday & Company, Inc., 1959.
654. Vogt, Von Ogden, *Art and Religion.* Yale University Press, 1921.
655. von Hügel, Friedrich, *The Life of Prayer.* E. P. Dutton & Company, Inc., 1929.
656. Wach, Joachim, *The Comparative Study of Religions,* ed. by Joseph Kitagawa. Columbia University Press, 1958.
657. —— *Types of Religious Experience.* The University of Chicago Press, 1951.
658. Walker, Alan, *The Whole Gospel for the Whole World.* Marshall, Morgan & Scott, Ltd., London, 1958.
659. Wallace, Ronald S., *Calvin's Doctrine of the Word and Sacrament.* Wm. B. Eerdmans Publishing Company, 1957.
660. Ward, Hiley H., *Creative Giving.* The Macmillan Company, 1958.
661. Warren, Max, *Interpreters: A Study in Contemporary Evangelism.* Highway Press, London, 1936.
662. Watts, Alan W., *Myth and Ritual in Christianity.* Grove Press, Inc., 1960.
663. Webber, George W., *God's Colony in Man's World.* Abingdon Press, 1960.
664. Weber, H. R., *The Communication of the Gospel to Illiterates* (IMC Research Pamphlet No. 4). SCM Press Ltd., London, 1957.
665. Webster, Douglas, *What Is Evangelism?* Highway Press, London, 1959.
666. Whiston, Charles Francis, *Teach Us to Pray.* The Pilgrim Press, 1949.
667. Williams, Daniel Day, *What Present-Day Theologians Are Thinking,* rev. ed. Harper & Brothers, 1959.
668. Winter, Gibson, *The Suburban Captivity of the Churches.* Doubleday & Company, Inc., 1961.
669. Wodehouse, Helen, *One Kind of Religion.* Cambridge University Press, 1944.
670. Wright, G. Ernest, *God Who Acts: Biblical Theology as Recital.* Henry Regnery Company, 1952.
671. —— and Filson, Floyd V., *The Westminster Historical Atlas to the Bible,* rev. ed. The Westminster Press, 1956.
672. Wyker, Mossie A., *Church Women in the Scheme of Things.* The Bethany Press, 1953.
673. Wyon, Olive, *On the Way.* SCM Press Ltd., London, 1958.
674. Yarnold, Greville Dennis, *The Bread Which We Break.* Oxford University Press, Inc., 1960.

IV. GENERAL EDUCATION

675. Association for Supervision and Curriculum Development, *Fostering Mental Health in Our Schools.* National Education Association, 1950.

676. Bailyn, Bernard, *Education in the Forming of American Society*. The University of North Carolina Press, 1960.
677. Baly, Denis, *Academic Illusion*. The Seabury Press, Inc., 1961
678. Baron, Denis, and Bernard, Harold, *Evaluation Techniques for Classroom Teachers*. The Macmillan Company, 1958.
679. Bayles, Ernest E., *Democratic Educational Theory*. Harper & Brothers, 1960.
680. Beck, Robert H., Cooke, Walter W., and Kearney, Nolan C., *Curriculum in the Modern Elementary School*. Prentice-Hall, Inc., 1953.
681. Benne, Kenneth Dean, and Muntyan, Bozidar, *Human Relations in Curriculum Change*. The Dryden Press, Inc., 1951.
682. Bereday, George Z. F., and Lauerys, Joseph A., *Education and Philosophy*. World Book Company, 1957.
683. Bergevin, Paul, and Morris, Dwight, *Group Process for Adult Education*. The Seabury Press, Inc., 1952.
684. Berkson, Isaac Baer, *Education Faces the Future*. Harper & Brothers, 1943.
685. —— *The Ideal and the Community*. Harper & Brothers, 1958.
686. Bernard, Harold W., *Psychology of Learning and Teaching*. McGraw-Hill Book Company, Inc., 1947.
687. Betts, George Herbert, *The Recitation*. Houghton Mifflin Company, 1910.
688. Boles, Donald E., *The Bible, Religion, and the Public Schools*. Iowa State University Press, 1961.
689. Bower, William Clayton, *Church and State in Education*. The University of Chicago Press, 1944.
690. —— *Moral and Spiritual Values in Education*. University of Kentucky Press, 1952.
691. Bradford, James, and Moredock, H. S., *Measurement and Evaluation in Education*. The Macmillan Company, 1957.
692. Brameld, Theodore, *Cultural Foundations of Education*. Harper & Brothers, 1957.
693. —— *Education for the Emerging Age*. Harper & Brothers, 1961.
694. —— *Philosophies of Education in Cultural Perspective*. The Dryden Press, Inc., 1955.
695. —— *Toward a Reconstructed Philosophy of Education*. The Dryden Press, Inc., 1956.
696. Broudy, Harry S., *Building a Philosophy of Education*, 2d ed. Prentice-Hall, Inc., 1961.
697. Brown, K. I., *Not Minds Alone*. Harper & Brothers, 1954.
698. Brown, S. W., *The Secularization of American Education*. Bureau of Publications, Teachers College, Columbia University, 1912.
699. Brubacher, John Seiler, *Eclectic Philosophy of Education: A Book of Readings*. Prentice-Hall, Inc., 1951.
700. —— ed., *Modern Philosophies and Education*. National Society for the Study of Education (54th Yearbook, Part I). The University of Chicago Press, 1955.
701. —— ed., *Modern Philosophies of Education*, 2d ed. McGraw-Hill Book Company, Inc., 1950.
702. —— and Rudy, Willis S., *Higher Education in Transition*. Harper & Brothers, 1958.
703. Butler, J. Donald, *Four Philosophies and Their Practice in Education and Religion*, 2d ed. Harper & Brothers, 1957.
704. Butts, Robert Freeman, *The American Tradition in Religion and Education*. Beacon Press, Inc., 1950.
705. —— and Cremin, Lawrence A., *A History of Education in American Culture*. Henry Holt & Co., Inc., 1953.

706. Cantor, Nathaniel, *The Teaching-Learning Process*. The Dryden Press, Inc., 1958.
707. Childs, John L., *American Pragmatism and Education*. Henry Holt & Co., Inc., 1956.
708. Collier, K. G., *The Social Purposes of Education*. Routledge & Kegan Paul, Ltd., London, 1959.
709. Conant, James B., *The American High School Today*. McGraw-Hill Book Company, Inc., 1959.
710. —— *The Child, the Parent, and the State*. Harvard University Press, 1959.
711. Counts, George S., *Education and the Promise of America*. The Macmillan Company, 1945.
712. Cuninggim, Merrimon, *The College Seeks Religion*. Yale University Press, 1947.
713. Cunningham, William F., *The Pivotal Problems of Education*. The Macmillan Company, 1940.
714. Davies, Rupert E., ed., *An Approach to Christian Education*. The Epworth Press, Publishers, London, 1956.
715. Dawson, Christopher H., *The Crisis of Western Education*. Sheed & Ward, Inc., 1961.
716. Dewey, John, *Democracy and Education*. The Macmillan Company, 1916.
717. —— *Experience and Education*. The Macmillan Company, 1938.
718. —— *The School and Society*, rev. ed. The University of Chicago Press, 1915.
719. —— *Schools of Tomorrow*. E. P. Dutton & Company, Inc., 1915.
720. Ditmanson, Harold, and Hong, Howard, *et al.*, *Christian Faith and the Liberal Arts*. Augsburg Publishing House, 1960.
721. Dubay, Thomas, *Philosophy of the State as Educator*. The Bruce Publishing Company, 1960.
722. Dworkin, Martin S., ed., *Dewey on Education*. Bureau of Publications, Teachers College, Columbia University, 1960.
723. Educational Policies Commission, *Policies for Education in American Democracy*. National Education Association and the American Association of School Administrators, 1946.
724. Ferré, Nels F. S., *Christian Faith and Higher Education*. Harper & Brothers, 1954.
725. Fitzgerald, James, and Patricia A., *Methods and Curricula in Elementary Education*. The Bruce Publishing Company, 1955.
726. Froebel, Friedrich, *Pedagogics of the Kindergarten*, tr. by Josephine Jarvis. D. Appleton & Company, 1895.
727. —— *The Education of Man*, tr. by. W. N. Hailmann. D. Appleton & Company, 1901.
728. Gauss, Christian, *The Teaching of Religion in American Higher Education*. The Ronald Press Company, 1951.
729. Good, Carter V., ed., *Dictionary of Education*. McGraw-Hill Book Company, Inc., 1945.
730. Griswold, Alfred Whitney, *Liberal Education and the Democratic Ideal and Other Essays*. Yale University Press, 1959.
731. Hamill, Robert, *Gods of the Campus*. Abingdon-Cokesbury Press, 1949.
732. Hardie, C. D., *Truth and Fallacy in Educational Theory*. The Macmillan Company, 1942.
733. Harris, Chester W., ed., *Encyclopedia of Educational Research*, 3d ed. The Macmillan Company, 1960.
734. Havighurst, Robert J., *Developmental Tasks and Education*, 2d ed. Longmans, Green & Co., Inc., 1956.

735. ———— *Human Development and Education*. Longmans, Green & Co., Inc., 1953.

736. ———— and Neugarten, Bernice L., *Society and Education*. Allyn and Bacon, Inc., College Division, 1957.

737. ———— and Orr, Betty, *Adult Needs and Adult Education*. Center for the Study of Liberal Education for Adults, The University of Chicago Press, 1956.

738. Heffernan, Helen, ed., *Guiding the Young Child, Kindergarten to Grade Three*, 2d ed. D. C. Heath and Company, 1959.

739. *Helping Teachers Understand Children*. American Council on Education, 1945.

740. Henderson, J. C., *Thomas Jefferson's Views on Education*. G. P. Putnam's Sons, 1890.

741. Herbart, Johann Friedrich, *Outlines of Educational Doctrine*, tr. by Alexis F. Lange. The Macmillan Company, 1913.

742. Highet, Gilbert, *The Art of Teaching*. Vintage Books (Random House, Inc.), 1954.

743. Hoban, Charles F., Charles F., Jr., and Zesman, Samuel B., *Visualizing the Curriculum*. The Cordon Co., Inc., 1937.

744. Hoffmann, R. W., and Plutchik, Robert, *Small-Group Discussion in Orientation and Teaching*. G. P. Putnam's Sons, 1959.

745. Hook, Sidney, *Education for Modern Man*. The Dial Press, Inc., 1946.

746. Hullfish, H. Gordon, and Smith, Phillip G., *Reflective Thinking: The Method of Education*. Dodd, Mead & Company, Inc., 1961.

747. Hutchins, Robert C., *Conflict in Education*. Harper & Brothers, 1953.

748. Imhoff, Myrtle M., *Early Elementary Education*. Appleton-Century-Crofts, Inc., 1959.

749. Jacob, Philip E., *Changing Values in College*. Harper & Brothers, 1957.

750. Jeffreys, M. V. C., *Glaucon: An Inquiry Into the Aims of Education*. Sir Isaac Pitman & Sons, Ltd., London, 1950.

751. Jones, Howard Mumford, *One Great Society: Humane Learning in the United States*. Harcourt, Brace and Company, Inc., 1959.

752. ———— *The Scholar as American*. Harvard University Press, 1960.

753. Judges, A. V., *The Function of Teaching*. Faber & Faber, Ltd., London, 1959.

754. Kilpatrick, William Heard, *Remaking the Curriculum*. Newson & Company, 1936.

755. Kneller, George F., *Existentialism and Education*. Philosophical Library, Inc., 1958.

756. Knowles, Malcolm, *Informal Adult Education*. Association Press, 1950.

757. Lambert, Hazel, *Early Childhood Education*. Allyn and Bacon, Inc., 1960.

758. Langdon, Grace, and Stout, Irving W., *Teaching Moral and Spiritual Values*. The John Day Company, 1962.

759. Leavitt, Jerome E., *Nursery-Kindergarten Education*. McGraw-Hill Book Company, Inc., 1958.

760. Lindgren, Henry C., *Educational Psychology in the Classroom*. John Wiley & Sons, Inc., 1960.

761. Lodge, Rupert C., *Philosophy of Education*. Harper & Brothers, 1947.

762. Mann, Horace, *The Common School Controversy*. Bradley and Company, 1844.

763. Marrou, H. I., *A History of Education in Antiquity*. Sheed & Ward, Inc., 1956.

764. Mason, Robert E., *Educational Ideals in American Society*. Allyn and Bacon, Inc., 1960

765. Mayer, Frederick, *Philosophy of Education for Our Time*. The Odyssey Press, Inc., 1958.
766. Mayer, Martin, *The Schools*. Harper & Brothers, 1961.
767. Mayhew, Katherine Camp, *The Dewey School*. D. Appleton-Century Company, Inc., 1936.
768. McCluskey, Neil G., S.J., *Catholic Viewpoint on Education*. Hanover House, 1959.
769. Mearns, Hughes, *Creative Power*, rev. ed. Dover Publications, Inc., 1958.
770. *Moral and Spiritual Values in the Public Schools*. National Education Association and the American Association of School Administrators, 1951.
771. Morrison, Ida E., and Perry, Ida F., *Kindergarten-Primary Education*. The Ronald Press Company, 1961.
772. Morse, Arthur D., *Schools of Tomorrow — Today!* Doubleday & Company, Inc., 1961.
773. Munro, Thomas, *Art Education: Its Philosophy and Psychology*. Liberal Arts Press, 1960.
774. Nash, Arnold S., *The University in the Modern World*. The Macmillan Company, 1944.
775. National Society for the Study of Education, *The Grouping of Pupils* (35th Yearbook, Part I). Public School Publishing Company, 1936.
776. —— *Learning and Instruction* (49th Yearbook, Part I). The University of Chicago Press, 1950.
777. ——*The Psychology of Learning* (41st Yearbook, Part II). The University of Chicago Press, 1942.
778. Nell, Victor H., *Introduction to Educational Measurement*. Houghton Mifflin Company, 1957.
779. Nietzsche, Friedrich Wilhelm, *On the Future of Our Educational Institutions*, tr. by J. M. Kennedy. The Macmillan Company, 1924.
780. O'Connor, D. J., *Introduction to the Philosophy of Education*. Philosophical Library, Inc., 1957.
781. Park, Joe, ed., *Selected Readings in the Philosophy of Education*. The Macmillan Company, 1958.
782. Peterson, Helen Thomas, *Kindergarten — the Key to Child Growth*. Exposition Press, Inc., 1958.
783. Phenix, Philip H., *Philosophy of Education*. Henry Holt & Co., Inc., 1958.
784. Prescott, Daniel A., *The Child in the Educative Process*. McGraw-Hill Book Company, Inc., 1957.
785. Read, Herbert, *Education Through Art*. Faber & Faber, Ltd., London, 1945.
786. Read, Katherine, *The Nursery School: A Human Relations Laboratory*, W. B. Saunders Company, 1955.
787. Redl, F., and Wattenberg, W. W., *Mental Hygiene and Teaching*. Harcourt, Brace & Co., Inc., 1951.
788. Riesman, David, *Constraint and Variety in American Education*. University of Nebraska Press, 1956.
789. Rivlin, H. N., ed., *Encyclopedia of Modern Education*. Philosophical Library, Inc., 1943.
790. Rusk, Robert R., *The Doctrines of the Great Educators*. St. Martin's Press, Inc., 1954.
791. —— *The Philosophical Bases of Education*. Houghton Mifflin Company, 1956.
792. Scheffler, Israel, *The Language of Education*. Charles C. Thomas, Publisher, 1960.
793. —— *Philosophy and Education*. Allyn and Bacon, Inc., 1958.
794. Schmidt, George P., *The Liberal Arts College*. Rutgers University Press, 1957.

795. Sebaly, A. L., ed., *Teacher Education and Religion*. American Association of Colleges for Teacher Education, 1959.
796. Sheehy, Emma Dickson, *The Fives and Sixes Go to School*. Henry Holt & Co., Inc., 1954.
797. Thayer, V. T., *The Passing of the Recitation*. D. C. Heath and Company, 1928.
798. Trumbull, H. Clay, *Teachers and Teaching*. John D. Wattles & Company, 1884.
799. Tuttle, Harold S., *Character Education by State and Church*. Abingdon Press, 1930.
800. Ulich, Robert, *The Human Career*. Harper & Brothers, 1955.
801. Wahlquist, John T., *The Philosophy of American Education*. The Ronald Press Company, 1942.
802. Walter, Erich A., ed., *Religion and the State University*. University of Michigan Press, 1958.
803. Warner, Ruby H., *The Child and His Elementary School World*. Prentice-Hall, Inc., 1957.
804. Wilder, Amos N., ed., *Liberal Learning and Religion*. Harper & Brothers, 1951.
805. Wiles, Kimball, *Supervision for Better Teaching*. Prentice-Hall, Inc., 1950.
806. Williams, George H., *The Theological Idea of the University*. National Council of the Churches of Christ in the U.S.A., 1958.
807. Williamson, Margaret, *Supervision: New Patterns and Processes*. Association Press, 1961.
808. Wills, Clarice D., and Stegeman, William H., *Living in the Kindergarten*. Follett Publishing Company, 1956.
809. Zeller, Konrad, *Bildungslehre*. Zwingli Verlag, Zurich, 1948.

V. Philosophical and Literary

810. Adkins, Arthur W. H., *Merit and Responsibility: A Study in Greek Values*. Oxford University Press, Inc., 1960.
811. Albertson, Charles Carroll, ed., *Lyra Mystica: An Anthology of Mystical Verse*. The Macmillan Company, 1932.
812. Alexander, Samuel, *Space, Time and Deity*, 2 vols. The Macmillan Company, London, 1927.
813. Aubrey, E. E., *Secularism, A Myth*. Harper & Brothers, 1954.
814. Auer, J. A. C. F., and Hartt, Julian, *Humanism vs. Theism*. The Antioch Press, 1951.
815. Ayer, Alfred Jules, *Language, Truth and Logic*, 2d ed. Dover Publications, Inc., 1952.
816. ———— *The Problem of Knowing*. The Macmillan Company, London, 1955.
817. Bergson, Henri, *Two Sources of Morality and Religion*. Henry Holt & Company, Inc., 1935.
818. Broad, Charlie Dunbar, *Five Types of Ethical Theory*. Harcourt, Brace & Co., Inc., 1930.
819. Buswell, J. O., Jr., *Being and Knowing*. Zondervan Publishing House, 1960.
820. Casserley, J. V. Langmead, *Apologetics and Evangelism* (Westminster Studies in Christian Communication, ed. by Kendig Brubaker Cully). The Westminster Press, 1962.
821. Cassirer, Ernst, *The Problem of Knowledge*. Yale University Press, 1950.
822. Ciardi, John, ed., *Mid-Century American Poets*. Twayne Publishers, Inc., 1950.

823. Cohen, Morris R., *Reason and Nature*. Harcourt, Brace & Company, Inc., 1931.
824. Conant, James B., *Science and Common Sense*. Yale University Press, 1951.
825. Craig, Hardin, *English Religious Drama of the Middle Ages*. Oxford University Press, Inc., 1955.
826. Dennes, William Ray, *Some Dilemmas of Naturalism*. Columbia University Press, 1961.
827. Dewey, John, *Art as Experience*. Minton, Balch & Company, 1934.
828. —— *A Common Faith*. Yale University Press, 1934.
829. —— *Human Nature and Conduct*. Henry Holt & Company, Inc., 1922.
830. —— *Problems of Men*. Philosophical Library, 1946.
831. Donoghue, D., *The Third Voice*. Princeton University Press, 1959.
832. Dooyeweerd, H., *In the Twilight of Western Thought*. Reformed Publishing Company, 1959.
833. Dubos, Rene, *The Dreams of Reason: Science and Utopias*. Columbia University Press, 1961.
834. Elliott, Hugh, *Modern Science and Materialism*. Longmans, Green & Co., Inc., London, 1927.
835. Flew, A. G. N., ed., *Logic and Language* (2d series). Philosophical Library, Inc., 1953.
836. Fowlie, Wallace, *Dionysus in Paris: A Guide to Contemporary French Theater*. Meridian Books (The World Publishing Company), 1960.
837. Frankel, Charles, ed., *The Golden Age of American Philosophy*. George Braziller, Inc., 1960.
838. Ganshof, François Louis, *The Imperial Coronation of Charlemagne*. Jackson, Son & Co., Ltd., Glasgow, 1949.
839. Gardeil, H. D., O.P., *Introduction to the Philosophy of Saint Thomas Aquinas*, tr. by J. D. Otto, 3 vols. B. Herder Book Company, London, 1956.
840. Geiger, George, *John Dewey in Perspective*. Oxford University Press, Inc., 1958.
841. Gillispie, Charles Coulston, *The Edge of Objectivity*. Princeton University Press, 1960.
842. Gutzke, Manford George, *John Dewey's Thought and Its Implications for Christian Education*. King's Crown Press, 1956.
843. Haldane, J. S., *Materialism*. Hodder & Stoughton, Ltd., London, 1932.
844. Hartshorne, Charles, *Beyond Humanism*. Willet, Clark & Company, 1937.
845. —— *Reality as Social Process*. The Free Press of Glencoe, Inc., 1953.
846. Heidegger, Martin, *An Introduction to Metaphysics*, tr. by Ralph Manheim. Yale University Press, 1959.
847. Herz, Richard, *Chance and Symbol*. The University of Chicago Press, 1948.
848. Hicks, G. Dawes, *The Philosophical Bases of Theism*. The Macmillan Company, 1937.
849. Highet, Gilbert, *Man's Unconquerable Mind*. Columbia University Press, 1954.
850. Hill, Caroline Miles, ed., *The World's Great Religious Poetry*. The Macmillan Company, reissued 1954.
851. James, William, *The Meaning of Truth*. Longmans, Green & Co., Inc., 1909.
852. —— *Pragmatism*. Longmans, Green & Co., Inc., 1907.
853. Jaspers, Karl, *The Perennial Scope of Philosophy*, tr. by Ralph Manheim. Routledge & Kegan Paul, Ltd., London, 1950.
854. Kaufmann, Walter, ed., *Existentialism from Dostoevsky to Sartre*. Meridian Books (The World Publishing Company), 1956.
855. Krikorian, Yervant H., ed., *Naturalism and the Human Spirit*. Columbia University Press, 1944.

856. Lamont, Corliss, *Humanism as a Philosophy.* Philosophical Library, Inc., 1949.
857. —— *The Illusion of Immortality,* 2d ed. Philosophical Library, Inc., 1950.
858. Langer, Susanne K., *Philosophy in a New Key.* Harvard University Press, 1942.
859. —— ed., *Reflections on Art: A Source Book of Writings by Artists, Critics, and Philosophers.* The Johns Hopkins Press, 1958.
860. Lippmann, Walter, *A Preface to Morals.* The Macmillan Company, 1929.
861. Marcel, Gabriel, *Man Against Mass Society,* tr. by G. S. Fraser. Henry Regnery Company, 1952.
862. —— *The Mystery of Being.* Henry Regnery Company, 1950.
863. —— *The Philosophy of Existence.* The Harvill Press, Ltd., London, 1948.
864. Maritain, Jacques, *Degrees of Knowledge.* Charles Scribner's Sons, 1958.
865. —— *True Humanism,* tr. by M. R. Adamson, 6th ed. Geoffrey Bles, Ltd., Publishers, London, 1954.
866. Mascall, E. L., *Words and Images.* The Ronald Press Company, 1957.
867. May, Rollo, Angel, Ernest, and Ellenburger, Henri I., eds., *Existence: A New Dimension in Psychiatry and Psychology.* Basic Books, Inc., 1958.
868. Monroe, Harriet, and Henderson, Alice C., eds., *The New Poetry: An Anthology of Twentieth Century Verse in English,* rev. ed. The Macmillan Company, 1947.
869. Moore, Edward C., *American Pragmatism: Peirce, James, and Dewey.* Columbia University Press, 1961.
870. Morris, Van Cleve, *Philosophy and the American School.* Houghton Mifflin Company, 1961.
871. Nagel, Ernest, *Sovereign Reason.* The Free Press of Glencoe, Inc., 1954.
872. Otto, Max Carl, *The Human Enterprise: An Attempt to Relate Philosophy to Daily Life.* F. S. Crofts & Co., 1940.
873. —— *Science and the Moral Life.* The New American Library of World Literature, Inc., 1949.
874. Potter, Charles Francis, *Humanism, a New Religion.* Simon and Schuster, Inc., 1930.
875. Pratt, James Bissett, *Naturalism.* Yale University Press, 1939.
876. Sartre, Jean-Paul, *Existence and Humanism.* Methuen & Co., Ltd., London, 1946.
877. Scott, Nathan, *Modern Literature and the Religious Frontier.* Harper & Brothers, 1958.
878. Sertillanges, A. G., O.P., *Foundations of Thomistic Philosophy,* tr. by Godfrey Anstruther, O.P. B. Herder Book Company, 1931.
879. Spann, J. R., ed., *The Christian Faith and Secularism.* Abingdon-Cokesbury Press, 1948.
880. Steuermann, Walter E., *Logic and Faith: A Study of the Relations Between Science and Religion* (Westminster Studies in Christian Communication, ed. by Kendig Brubaker Cully). The Westminster Press, 1962.
881. Sullivan, J. W. N., *The Limitations of Science.* The New American Library of World Literature, Inc., 1949.
882. Whitehead, Alfred North, *Process and Reality.* The Macmillan Company, 1929.
883. —— *Religion in the Making.* The Macmillan Company, 1926.
884. Wieman, Henry Nelson, *The Source of Human Good.* The University of Chicago Press, 1946.
885. Williams, Oscar, ed., *A Little Treasury of Modern Poetry.* Charles Scribner's Sons, 1946.
886. Wittgenstein, Ludwig, *Philosophical Investigations,* tr. by G. E. M. Anscombe. The Macmillan Company, 1953.

887. ———— *Tractatus Logico-Philosophicus*. Routledge & Kegan Paul, Ltd., London, 1922.

888. Zuurdeeg, Willem E., *An Analytical Philosophy of Religion*. Abingdon Press, 1958.

VI. PSYCHOLOGICAL AND SOCIOLOGICAL

889. Adams, George Sachs, and Torgerson, Theodore, *Measurement and Evaluation*. The Dryden Press, Inc., 1956.

890. Allport, Gordon W., *Becoming*. Yale University Press, 1955.

891. ———— *The Individual and His Religion: A Psychological Interpretation*. The Macmillan Company, 1950.

892. Anderson, Kenneth E., ed., *Research on the Academically Talented Student*. Association Press, 1961.

893. Angyal, András, *Foundations for a Science of Personality*. The Commonwealth Fund, Division of Publications, 1941.

894. Atkinson, John W., *Motives in Fantasy, Action, and Society*. D. Van Nostrand Company, Inc., 1958.

895. Aubrey, Edwin E., *Humanistic Teaching and the Place of Ethical and Religious Values in Higher Education*. University of Pennsylvania Press, 1959.

896. Bailey, Derrick Sherwin, *Sexual Relation in Christian Thought*. Harper & Brothers, 1959.

897. Balint, Alice, *The Early Years of Life*. Basic Books, Inc., 1954.

898. Barron, Milton L., *The Juvenile in Delinquent Society*. Alfred A. Knopf, Inc., 1954.

899. Baruch, Dorothy W., *How to Live with Your Teen-Ager*. McGraw-Hill Book Company, Inc., 1953.

900. ———— *New Ways in Discipline*. McGraw-Hill Book Company, Inc., 1949.

901. Beach, Waldo, *Conscience on Campus*. Association Press, 1958.

902. Becker, Carl L., *Freedom and Responsibility in the American Way of Life*. Alfred A. Knopf, Inc., 1945.

903. Bender, Richard N., ed., *Campus Evangelism in Theory and Practice*. Methodist Student Movement, 1957.

904. Benson, Purnell Handy, *Religion in Contemporary Culture*. Harper & Brothers, 1960.

905. Bindra, Dalbir, *Motivation: A Systematic Reinterpretation*. The Ronald Press Company, 1959.

906. Bloch, Herbert A., and Flynn, Frank T., *Delinquency: The Juvenile Offender in America Today*. Random House, Inc., 1956.

907. Bonner, H., *Group Dynamics*. The Ronald Press Company, 1959.

908. Boyd, Malcolm, *Crisis in Communication*. Doubleday & Company, Inc., 1957.

909. Broom, Leonard, and Selznick, Philip, *Sociology: A Text with Adapted Readings*, 2d ed. Row, Peterson & Company, 1958.

910. Brown, William Adams, *Church and State in Contemporary America*. Charles Scribner's Sons, 1936.

911. Brunner, Edmund de S., *The Growth of a Science*. Harper & Brothers, 1957.

912. Cantor, Nathaniel Freeman, *The Dynamics of Learning*. Foster & Stewart Publishing Corporation, 1946.

913. Carmichael, Leonard, ed., *Manual of Child Psychology*. John Wiley & Sons, Inc., 1946.

914. Carr, Lowell J., *Delinquency Control*, rev. ed. Harper & Brothers, 1950.

915. Carrier, Blanche, *Integrity for Tomorrow's Adults*. Thomas Y. Crowell Company, 1959.

916. Cartwright, Dorwin, and Zander, Alvin, *Group Dynamics: Research and Theory.* Row, Peterson & Company, 1953.
917. Cattell, Raymond B., *Personality and Motivation: Structure and Measurement.* World Book Company, 1957.
918. Cavert, Inez, *Women in American Church Life.* Friendship Press, 1951.
919. Chakerian, Charles G., *The Churches and Social Welfare.* Hartford Seminary Foundation Bulletin, No. 20, 1955.
920. Chase, Stuart, *Roads to Agreement.* Harper & Brothers, 1951.
921. Clark, Elmer T., *The Psychology of Religious Awakening.* The Macmillan Company, 1929.
922. Clark, Walter Houston, *The Psychology of Religion: An Introduction to Religious Experience and Behavior.* The Macmillan Company, 1958.
923. Clinebell, H. J. Jr., *Understanding and Counseling the Alcoholic.* Abingdon Press, 1956.
924. Coe, George Albert, *The Psychology of Religion.* The University of Chicago Press, 1916.
925. Cohen, Frank J., ed., *Youth and Crime — Proceedings of the Law Institute Held at New York University.* International Universities Press, Inc., 1957.
926. Counts, George S., *Dare the School Build a New Social Order?* The John Day Company, 1932.
927. Cronbach, Lee J., *Essentials of Psychological Testing,* 2d ed. Harper & Brothers, 1960.
928. Crook, Roger H., *The Changing American Family: A Study of Family Problems from a Christian Perspective.* The Bethany Press, 1960.
929. Crow, Lester Donald, and A. V., *Educational Psychology,* rev. ed. American Book Company, 1958.
930. Cunningham, Ruth, *et al., Understanding Group Behavior of Boys and Girls.* Bureau of Publications, Teachers College, Columbia University, 1951.
931. Cutts, Norma E., and Moseley, Nicholas, *Bright Children.* G. P. Putnam's Sons, 1953.
932. David, Henry P., and Brengelmann, J. C., *Perspectives in Personality Research.* Springer Publishing Company, Inc., 1960.
933. —— and von Bracken, Helmut, eds., *Perspectives in Personality Theory.* Basic Books, Inc., 1957.
934. Davis, Robert A., *Educational Psychology.* McGraw-Hill Book Company, Inc., 1948.
935. de Grazia, A., and Gurr, T., *American Welfare.* New York University Press, 1961.
936. DeHaan, Robert F., and Havighurst, Robert J., *Educating Gifted Children,* rev. ed. The University of Chicago Press, 1961.
937. De Sanctis, Sante, *Religious Conversion: A Bio-Psychological Study.* Kegan Paul, Trench, Trubner & Co., Ltd., 1927.
938. Deutsch, Albert, *Our Rejected Children.* Little, Brown and Company, 1950.
939. Dewey, John, *How We Think,* rev. ed. D. C. Heath and Company, 1933.
940. —— *Interest and Effort* (Riverside Educational Monographs, ed. by Henry Suzzallo). Houghton Mifflin Company, 1913.
941. Dewhurst, J. Frederic, *et al., America's Needs and Resources: A New Survey.* The Twentieth Century Fund, 1955.
942. Doughty, Mary Alice, *How to Work with Church Groups.* Abingdon Press, 1957.
943. Downe, N. M., *Fundamentals of Measurement: Techniques and Practices.* Oxford University Press, Inc., 1958.
944. Duvall, Evelyn Millis, *Family Development.* J. B. Lippincott Company, 1961.
945. —— and Hill, Reuben L., *Being Married.* Association Press, 1960.

946. Elliott, Harrison S., *The Process of Group Thinking*. Association Press, 1930.
947. Erikson, Erik, *Childhood and Society*. W. W. Norton & Company, Inc., 1950.
948. Fairchild, Roy W., and Wynn, John Charles, *Families in the Church: A Protestant Survey*. Association Press, 1961.
949. Fallaw, Wesner, *Toward Spiritual Security*. The Westminster Press, 1952.
950. Farwell, Gail F., ed., *Guidance Readings for Counselors*. Rand McNally & Company, 1960.
951. Feucht, Oscar, ed., *Helping Families Through the Church*. Concordia Publishing House, 1957.
952. Fichter, Joseph Henry, *Parochial School: A Sociological Study*. University of Notre Dame Press, 1958.
953. —— *Social Relations in the Urban Parish*. The University of Chicago Press, 1954.
954. Fine, Benjamin, *1,000,000 Delinquents*. The World Publishing Company, 1955.
955. Foote, N., and Cottrell, L. S., *Identity and Interpersonal Competence*. The University of Chicago Press, 1956.
956. Forrester, Gertrude, *Occupational Literature: An Annotated Bibliography*. The H. W. Wilson Company, 1958.
957. Frank, Lawrence K., *How to Be a Modern Leader*. Association Press, 1954.
958. Fraser, Ellen D., Bransford, Joan B., and Hastings, Mamie, *The Child and Physical Education*. Prentice-Hall, Inc., 1956.
959. Friedenburg, Edgar Z., *The Vanishing Adolescent*. Beacon Press, Inc., 1959.
960. Friedlander, W. A., *Introduction to Social Welfare*, rev. ed. Prentice-Hall, Inc., 1961.
961. Fromm, Erich, *The Fear of Freedom*. Routledge & Kegan Paul, Ltd., London, 1942.
962. Fullam, Raymond B., ed., *The Popes on Youth*. The American Press, 1956.
963. Gallagher, J. Roswell, and Harris, Herbert I., *Emotional Problems of Adolescents*. Oxford University Press, Inc., 1958.
964. Gerth, H. H., and Mills, C. W., eds., *From Max Weber: Essays in Sociology*. Oxford University Press, Inc., 1946.
965. Gesell, Arnold, Ilg, Frances L., and Ames, Louise B., *Youth: The Years from Ten to Sixteen*. Harper & Brothers, 1956.
966. Getlein, Frank, *Movies, Morals and Art*. Sheed & Ward, Inc., 1961.
967. Ginzberg, Eli, ed., *The Nation's Children: Problems and Prospects*, 3 vols. Columbia University Press, 1960.
968. Gleuck, Sheldon, and Eleanor, *Delinquents in the Making: Paths to Prevention*. Harper & Brothers, 1952.
969. ——*Unraveling Juvenile Delinquency*. The Commonwealth Fund, Division of Publications, 1950.
970. Goodman, Paul, *Growing Up Absurd*. Random House, Inc., 1960.
971. Gordon, Albert I., *Jews in Suburbia*. Beacon Press, Inc., 1959.
972. Gurvitch, George, and Moore, Wilbert E., eds., *Twentieth Century Sociology*. Philosophical Library, Inc., 1945.
973. Haiman, F. S., *Group Leadership and Democratic Action*. Houghton Mifflin Company, 1951.
974. Hall, Calvin S., and Lindzey, Gardner, *Theories of Personality*. John Wiley & Sons, Inc., 1957.
975. Hall, John F., *Psychology of Motivation*. J. B. Lippincott Company, 1961.
976. Hallesby, O., *Temperament and the Christian Faith*. Augsburg Publishing House, 1962.
977. Harper, Ernest B., *Community Organization in Action*. Association Press, 1959.

978. Hartley, Ruth Edith, *The Complete Book of Children's Play.* Thomas Y. Crowell Company, 1957.
979. Hartshorne, Hugh, May, Mark A., and Maller, J., *Studies in Service and Self-control.* The Macmillan Company, 1929.
980. ———— May, Mark A., and Shuttleworth, Frank K., *Studies in the Organization of Character.* The Macmillan Company, 1930.
981. Herbert, W. L., and Jarvis, F. V., *The Art of Marriage Counseling: A Modern Approach.* Emerson Books, Inc., 1960.
982. Hiltner, Seward, *The Counselor in Counseling.* Abingdon Press, 1952.
983. ———— *Pastoral Counseling.* Abingdon Press, 1949.
984. Hollingshead, August B., *Elmtown's Youth: The Impact of Social Classes on Adolescents.* John Wiley & Sons, Inc., 1949.
985. Hopkins, Charles Howard, *The Rise of the Social Gospel in American Protestantism.* Yale University Press, 1940.
986. Hopkins, L. Thomas, *Interaction: The Democratic Process.* D. C. Heath and Company, 1941.
987. Hoveland, Janis, and Kelley, *Communication and Persuasion.* Yale University Press, 1953.
988. Howe, Reuel L., *The Creative Years.* The Seabury Press, Inc., 1959.
989. ———— *Man's Need and God's Action.* The Seabury Press, Inc., 1953.
990. Hughes, Everett, *Men and Their Work.* The Free Press of Glencoe, Inc., 1958.
991. Huizinga, Johan, *Homo Ludens: A Study of the Play Element in Culture.* Roy Publishers, 1950.
992. Hulme, William E., *Counseling and Theology.* Muhlenberg Press, 1956.
993. ———— *How to Start Counseling.* Abingdon Press, 1955.
994. ———— *The Pastoral Care of Families.* Abingdon Press, 1962.
995. Hunter, Edith F., *Conversations with Children.* Beacon Press, Inc., 1961.
996. Hymes, James L., Jr., *A Child Development Point of View.* Prentice-Hall, Inc., 1955.
997. ———— *Understanding Your Child.* Prentice-Hall, Inc., 1952.
998. Jaarsma, Cornelius, *Human Development, Learning and Teaching: A Christian Approach to Educational Psychology.* Wm. B. Eerdmans Publishing Company, 1961.
999. James, William, *Talks to Teachers.* Henry Holt & Co., Inc., 1900.
1000. ———— *The Will to Believe.* Longmans, Green & Co., Inc., 1896.
1001. ———— *The Varieties of Religious Experience,* new ed. Longmans, Green & Co., Inc., 1947.
1002. Jellinek, E. M., *The Disease Concept of Alcoholism.* Hillhouse Press, 1960.
1003. Jenkins, Gladys, Shacter, Helen, and Bauer, William, *These Are Your Children.* Scott, Foresman & Company, 1949.
1004. Jennings, Helen Hall, *Sociometry in Group Relations.* American Council on Education, 1948.
1005. Jersild, Arthur T., *In Search of Self.* Bureau of Publications, Teachers College, Columbia University, 1952.
1006. ———— and Tasch, Ruth, *Children's Interests and What They Suggest for Education.* Bureau of Publications, Teachers College, Columbia University, 1951.
1007. Jones, Marshall R., ed., *Nebraska Symposium on Motivation, 1960.* University of Nebraska Press, 1960.
1008. Kahn, A. J., *Issues in American Social Work.* Columbia University Press, 1959.
1009. Kaplan, M., *Leisure in America: A Social Inquiry.* John Wiley & Sons, Inc., 1960.

1010. Kemp, Charles F., *The Church: The Gifted and Retarded Child.* The Bethany Press, 1957.
1011. —— *The Pastor and Community Resources.* The Bethany Press, 1960.
1012. Kidd, J. R., *How Adults Learn.* Association Press, 1959.
1013. Kincheloe, Samuel Clarence, *The American City and Its Church.* Friendship Press, 1938.
1014. King, Albion Roy, *Basic Information on Alcohol,* rev. ed. Cornell College Press, 1960.
1015. Klapper, Joseph T., *The Effects of Mass Communication.* The Free Press of Glencoe, Inc., 1960.
1016. Kleemeir, R. S., ed., *Aging and Leisure: A Research Perspective Into the Meaningful Use of Time.* Oxford University Press, Inc., 1961.
1017. Kloetzli, Walter, *The City Church, Death or Renewal: A Study of Eight Urban Lutheran Churches.* Muhlenberg Press, 1961.
1018. —— and Hillman, Arthur, *Urban Church Planning.* Muhlenberg Press, 1958.
1019. Knowlton, Daniel C., *History and Other Social Studies.* Charles Scribner's Sons, 1926.
1020. Köhler, Wolfgang, *Gestalt Psychology: An Introduction to New Concepts in Modern Psychology,* rev. ed. Liveright Publishing Corporation, 1947.
1021. Kouch, Jack, and DeHaan, Robert, *Teacher Guidance Handbook.* Science Research Associates, Occupational Information Division, 1950.
1022. Lane, Howard, and Beauchamp, Mary, *Understanding Human Development.* Prentice-Hall, Inc., 1959.
1023. Lazarsfeld, Paul F., *The Academic Mind.* The Free Press of Glencoe, Inc., 1958.
1024. Lee, Irving J., *Customs and Crises in Communication.* Harper & Brothers, 1954.
1025. Lefever, D. Welty, Turrell, Archie M., and Weitzel, Henry I., *Principles and Techniques of Guidance,* rev. ed. The Ronald Press Company, 1950.
1026. Leiffer, Murray H., *The Effective City Church,* 2d rev. ed. Abingdon Press, 1961.
1027. Lewin, Kurt, *A Dynamic Theory of Personality.* McGraw-Hill Book Company, Inc., 1935.
1028. —— *Field Theory in Social Science.* Harper & Brothers, 1951.
1029. Lewis, Clarence Irving, *Our Social Inheritance.* Indiana University Press, 1957.
1030. Lewis, Hazel A., *Knowing Children Better.* The Westminster Press, 1941.
1031. Ligon, Ernest M., *A Greater Generation.* The Macmillan Company, 1948.
1032. —— *Dimensions of Character.* The Macmillan Company, 1956.
1033. —— *Their Future Is Now.* The Macmillan Company, 1930.
1034. Lindquist, E. F., *Educational Measurement.* American Council on Education, 1959.
1035. Lindzey, Gardner, *Assessment of Human Motives.* Rinehart & Company, Inc., 1958.
1036. Linton, Ralph, *The Cultural Background of Personality.* Appleton-Century-Crofts, Inc., 1945.
1037. Little, Sara, *Learning Together in the Christian Fellowship.* John Knox Press, 1956.
1038. Loomis, Earl A., *The Self in Pilgrimage.* Harper & Brothers, 1960.
1039. Lundberg, G., Komarovsky, M., and McInerny, M. A., *Leisure: A Suburban Study.* Columbia University Press, 1934.
1040. Lynch, Kevin, *Image of the City.* Harvard University Press, 1960.
1041. Lynch, William F., *The Image Industries.* Sheed & Ward, Inc., 1959.

1042. MacIver, Robert Morrison, ed., *Dilemmas of Youth: In America Today.* Published for The Institute for Religious and Social Studies, Jewish Theological Seminary of America (Religion and Civilization Series), by Harper & Brothers, 1961.
1043. Mannheim, Karl, *Man and Society in an Age of Reconstruction.* Harcourt, Brace & Co., Inc., 1940.
1044. Martin, William E., and Stendler, Celia Burns, *Child Behavior and Development.* Harcourt, Brace & Co., Inc., 1959.
1045. Maslow, Abraham, *Motivation and Personality.* Harper & Brothers, 1954.
1046. Matthewson, Robert Hendry, *Guidance Policy and Practice.* Harper & Brothers, 1949.
1047. Maves, Paul B., *Understanding Ourselves as Adults.* Abingdon Press, 1959.
1048. ———— and Cedarleaf, J. Lennart, *Older People and the Church.* Abingdon Press, 1949.
1049. May, Henry Farnham, *Protestant Churches and Industrial America.* Harper & Brothers, 1949.
1050. May, Rollo, *Existential Psychology.* Random House, Inc., 1961.
1051. Maynard, Donald M., *Looking Toward Christian Marriage.* Abingdon Press, 1958.
1052. McCann, Richard V., *Delinquency: Sickness or Sin?* Harper & Brothers, 1957.
1053. McCarthy, Raymond G., ed., *Drinking and Intoxication.* The Free Press of Glencoe, Inc., 1959.
1054. McCary, J. L., ed., *Psychology of Personality: Six Modern Approaches.* Grove Press, Inc., 1956.
1055. McClelland, David Clarence, ed., *Studies in Motivation.* Appleton-Century-Crofts, Inc., 1955.
1056. McDonald, Frederick T., *Educational Psychology.* Wadsworth Publishing Company, Inc., 1960.
1057. Merton, Robert King, *Social Theory and Social Structure,* rev. ed. The Free Press of Glencoe, Inc., 1957.
1058. Miles, Matthew B., *Learning to Work in Groups: A Program Guide for Educational Leaders.* Bureau of Publications, Teachers College, Columbia University, 1959.
1059. Miller, Haskell M., *Compassion and Community.* Association Press, 1961.
1060. ———— *Understanding and Preventing Juvenile Delinquency.* Abingdon Press, 1958.
1061. Moreno, Jacob Levy, *Psychodrama,* 2 vols. Beacon House, Inc., 1946, 1959.
1062. ———— ed., *Sociometry and the Science of Man.* Beacon House, Inc., 1956.
1063. Moustakas, Clark E., ed., *The Self: Explorations in Personal Growth.* Harper & Brothers, 1956.
1064. Munroe, Ruth L., *Schools of Psychoanalytic Thought.* The Dryden Press, Inc., 1955.
1065. Mursell, James, *Psychology for Modern Learning.* W. W. Norton & Company, Inc., 1952.
1066. Musselman, G. Paul, *The Church on the Urban Frontier.* Harper & Brothers, 1955.
1067. Mussen, Paul H., ed., *Handbook of Research Methods in Child Development.* John Wiley & Sons, Inc., 1960.
1068. Myers, C. Kilmer, *Light the Dark Streets.* The Seabury Press, Inc., 1957.
1069. Neidhart, Walter, *Psychologie des kirchlichen Unterrichts.* Zwingli Verlag, Zurich, 1960.
1070. Nelson, John Oliver, ed., *Work and Vocation.* Harper & Brothers, 1954.

1071. Neumeyer, Martin H., *Juvenile Delinquency in Modern Society*. D. Van Nostrand Company, Inc., 1955.
1072. Newcomb, T. M., and Hartley, S. L., eds., *Readings in Social Psychology*, rev. ed. Henry Holt & Co., Inc., 1952.
1073. Oates, Wayne, ed., *Introduction to Pastoral Counseling*. Broadman Press, 1959.
1074. Ogburn, William, and Nimkoff, Meyer P., *Sociology*, 2d ed. Houghton Mifflin Company, 1950.
1075. Ohlsen, Merle M., *Guidance: An Introduction*. Harcourt, Brace & Co., Inc., 1955.
1076. Olafson, Frederick Arlan, *Society, Law, and Morality: Readings in Social Philosophy from Classical and Contemporary Sources*. Prentice-Hall, Inc., 1961.
1077. Oraison, Marc, *Love or Constraint: Some Psychological Aspects of Religious Education*. P. J. Kenedy & Sons, 1959.
1078. Ostovsky, Everett S., *Father to the Child*. G. P. Putnam's Sons, 1959.
1079. Overstreet, Harry A., *The Mature Mind*. W. W. Norton & Company, Inc., 1949.
1080. Palmer, Charles E., *The Church and the Exceptional Person*. Abingdon Press, 1961.
1081. Peck, Robert F., Havighurst, Robert J., *et al.*, *The Psychology of Character Development*. John Wiley & Sons, Inc., 1960.
1082. Perloff, Harvey S., ed., *Planning and the Urban Community*. University of Pittsburgh Press, 1961.
1083. Peters, Herman Jacob, *Guidance, a Developmental Approach*. Rand McNally & Company, 1959.
1084. Peters, Richard S., *The Concept of Motivaton*. The Humanities Press, Inc., 1958.
1085. Petersen, Sigurd D., *Retarded Children: God's Children*. The Westminster Press, 1960.
1086. Piaget, Jean, *The Child's Conception of Number*. The Humanities Press, Inc., 1952.
1087. ——— *The Construction of Reality in the Child*. The Humanities Press, Inc., 1954.
1088. ——— *The Moral Judgment of the Child*. The Free Press of Glencoe, Inc., 1960.
1089. ——— *The Origin of Intelligence in the Child*. The Humanities Press, Inc., 1952.
1090. ——— and Inhelder, Barbel, *The Growth of Logical Thinking from Childhood to Adolescence*. Routledge & Kegan Paul, Ltd., London, 1958.
1091. Pieper, Josef, *Leisure the Basis of Culture*. Pantheon Books, Inc., 1952.
1092. Pope, Liston, *Millhands and Preachers*. Oxford University Press, Inc., 1942.
1093. Rasmussen, Albert T., *Christian Social Ethics: Exerting Christian Influence*. Prentice-Hall, Inc., 1956.
1094. Reeves, Marjorie, *Growing Up in a Modern Society*. University of London Press, Ltd., 1946.
1095. Remmers, H. H., and Gage, N. L., *Educational Measurement and Evaluation*, rev. ed. Harper & Brothers, 1955.
1096. ——— and Radler, D. H., *The American Teenager*. The Bobbs-Merrill Company, Inc., 1957.
1097. Ribble, M. A., *The Personality of the Young Child*. Columbia University Press, 1948.
1098. ——— *The Rights of Infants*. Columbia University Press, 1943.
1099. Rich, Mark, *The Rural Church Movement*. Juniper Knoll Press, 1957.

1100. Riesman, David, Glazer, N., and Denney, R., *The Lonely Crowd*. Yale University Press, 1950.
1101. Roberts, Dorothy M., *Partners with Youth*. Association Press, 1956.
1102. Rogers, Carl, *On Becoming a Person: A Therapist's Views of Psychotherapy*. Houghton Mifflin Company, 1961.
1103. Rosenberg, Bernard, and White, David Manning, eds., *Mass Culture*. The Free Press of Glencoe, Inc., 1957.
1104. Ross, Murray G., and Hendry, Charles E., *New Understandings of Leadership*. Association Press, 1957.
1105. Rothney, John W. M., *Guidance Practices and Results*. Harper & Brothers, 1958.
1106. Ruch, Floyd L., *Psychology and Life*. Scott, Foresman & Company, 1953.
1107. Sanders, Irwin T., *The Community*. The Ronald Press Company, 1958.
1108. Sanderson, Ross W., *The Church Serves the Changing City*. Harper & Brothers, 1955.
1109. Schnucker, Calvin, *How to Plan the Rural Church Program*. The Westminster Press, 1954.
1110. Schramm, Wilbur, *Responsibility in Mass Communication*. Harper & Brothers, 1957.
1111. Scudder, Delton L., *Organized Religion and the Older Person* (Institute of Gerontology Series). University of Florida Press, 1958.
1112. Seifert, Harvey, *The Church in Community Action*. Abingdon Press, 1952.
1113. Seldes, Gilbert, *The Public Arts*. Simon and Schuster, Inc., 1956.
1114. Shands, Harley C., *Thinking and Psychotherapy: An Inquiry Into the Process of Communication*. Harvard University Press, 1961.
1115. Sherrill, Lewis Joseph, *The Struggle of the Soul*. The Macmillan Company, 1953.
1116. Shibutoni, T., *Society and Personality*. Prentice-Hall, Inc., 1961.
1117. Shippey, Frederick A., *Church Work in the City*. Abingdon Press, 1952.
1118. Slavson, Samuel Richard, *Creative Group Education*. Association Press, 1948.
1119. Smith, J. W. D., *Psychology and Religion in Early Childhood*. Camelot Press, London, 1953.
1120. Spike, Robert W., *Safe in Bondage*. Friendship Press, 1960.
1121. Spock, Benjamin, *Baby and Child Care*. Pocket Books, Inc., 1946.
1122. Stevens, Stanley Smith, ed., *Handbook of Experimental Psychology*. John Wiley & Sons, Inc., 1951.
1123. Strang, Ruth, *Helping Your Gifted Child*. E. P. Dutton & Company, Inc., 1960.
1124. Strunk, Orlo, Jr., ed., *Readings in the Psychology of Religion*. Abingdon Press, 1959.
1125. —— *Religion: A Psychological Interpretation*. Abingdon Press, 1961.
1126. Sullivan, Dorothea F., ed., *Readings in Group Work*. Association Press, 1952.
1127. Super, Donald E., *The Psychology of Careers*. Harper & Brothers, 1957.
1128. Symonds, Percival M., *Adolescent Fantasy*. Columbia University Press, 1961.
1129. —— and Jensen, Arthur R., *From Adolescent to Adult*. Columbia University Press, 1961.
1130. Tead, Ordway, *Democratic Administration*. Association Press, 1945.
1131. Thelen, Herbert A., *Dynamics of Groups at Work*. The University of Chicago Press, 1954.
1132. Thompson, George E., *Child Psychology: Growth Trends in Psychological Adjustments*. Houghton Mifflin Company, 1952.

1133. —— Gardner, Eric F., and DiVesta, Francis, *Educational Psychology.* Appleton-Century-Crofts, Inc., 1959.
1134. Thouless, Robert H., *An Introduction to the Psychology of Religion.* Cambridge University Press, 1924.
1135. Tilson, Everett, *Should Christians Drink?* Abingdon Press, 1957.
1136. Tournier, Paul, *Guilt and Grace.* Harper & Brothers, 1962.
1137. —— *The Meaning of Persons.* Harper & Brothers, 1957.
1138. Underwood, A. C., *Conversion, Christian and Non-Christian: A Comparative and Psychological Study.* George Allen & Unwin, Ltd., 1925.
1139. Van Dusen, Henry Pitney, *et. al., Church and State in the Modern World.* Harper & Brothers, 1937.
1140. Wach, Joachim, *Sociology of Religion.* The University of Chicago Press, 1944.
1141. Warner, W. Lloyd, *et al., Democracy in Jonesville.* Harper & Brothers, 1949.
1142. —— *The Family of God: A Symbolic Study of Christian Life in America.* Yale University Press, 1961.
1143. Webb, Robert, and Muriel, *The Churches and Juvenile Delinquency.* Association Press, 1957.
1144. Wertham, Frederic, *The Seduction of the Innocent.* Rinehart & Company Incorporated, 1953.
1145. Westberg, Granger, *Premarital Counseling.* National Council of the Churches of Christ in the U.S.A., 1958.
1146. White, Lynn, Jr., ed., *Frontiers of Knowledge in the Study of Man.* Harper & Brothers, 1956.
1147. Wickham, E. R., *Church and People in an Industrial City.* Lutterworth Press, London, 1957.
1148. Wise, Carroll A., *Pastoral Counseling.* Harper & Brothers, 1951.
1149. Wittenberg, R. M., *Adolescence and Discipline.* Association Press, 1959.
1150. Witty, Paul, ed., *The Gifted Child.* D. C. Heath and Company, 1951.
1151. Wrightstone, J. Wayne, Justman, Joseph, and Robbins, Irving, *Evaluation in Modern Education.* American Book Company, 1956.
1152. Wynn, John Charles, *How Christian Parents Face Family Problems.* The Westminster Press, 1955.
1153. —— *Pastoral Ministry to Families.* The Westminster Press, 1957.
1154. Yeaxlee, Basil A., *Religion and the Growing Mind,* 3d ed. The Seabury Press, Inc., 1952.
1155. Yinger, John Milton, *Religion, Society and the Individual.* The Macmillan Company, 1957.
1156. Zerbst, Fritz, *The Office of Woman in the Church,* tr. by A. Merkens. Concordia Publishing House, 1955.
1157. Ziegler, Jesse H., *Psychology and the Teaching Church.* Abingdon Press, 1962.

VII. Special Techniques and Areas

1158. Adair, Thelma, and McCort, Elizabeth, *How to Make Church School Equipment.* The Westminster Press, 1955.
1159. Alexander, Ryllis C., and Goslin, Omar P., *Worship Through Drama.* Harper & Brothers, 1930.
1160. Allstrom, Elizabeth, *Let's Play a Story.* Friendship Press, 1957.
1161. Andrews, Gladys, *Creative Rhythmic Movement for Children.* Prentice-Hall, Inc., 1934.
1162. Atkinson, C. Harry, *Building and Equipping for Christian Education.* National Council of the Churches of Christ in the U.S.A., 1957.

1163. Bachman, John W., *The Church in the World of Radio-Television*. Association Press, 1960.

1164. —— *How to Use Audio-Visual Materials* (Leadership Library). Association Press, 1956.

1165. Bailey, Carolyn S., ed., *The Story-telling Hour*. Dodd, Mead, & Company, Inc., 1934.

1166. Baird, Albert Craig, *Argumentation, Discussion, and Debate*. McGraw-Hill Book Company, Inc., 1950.

1167. —— *Discussion: Principles and Types*. McGraw-Hill Book Company, Inc., 1943.

1168. Balaz, Bela, *Theory of the Film*. Roy Publishers, 1953.

1169. Barbour, Russell, and Ruth, *Religious Ideas for Arts and Crafts*. Christian Education Press, 1959.

1170. Barton, Lucy, *Costuming the Bible Play*. Walter H. Baker Co., 1937.

1171. Baruch, Dorothy W., *New Ways in Sex Education*. McGraw-Hill Book Company, Inc., 1959.

1172. Bate, Esther Willard, *The Art of Producing Pageants*. Walter H. Baker Co., 1925.

1173. Behl, William A., *Discussion and Debate*. The Ronald Press Company, 1953.

1174. Benson, Kenneth, R., and Evelyn H., *Creative Crafts for Children*. Prentice-Hall, Inc., 1958.

1175. Bergevin, Paul, *A Manual for Discussion Leaders*. Community Services in Adult Education, 1954.

1176. Bogardus, LaDonna, *The Church Day Camp*. National Council of the Churches of Christ in the U.S.A., 1955.

1177. —— *Planning the Church Camp*. National Council of the Churches of Christ in the U.S.A., 1955.

1178. Bowman, Clarice M., *Spiritual Values in Camping*. Association Press, 1954.

1179. —— *Worship Ways for Camp*. Association Press, 1955.

1180. Brown, James W., and Lewis, Richard B., *Audio-Visual Instruction Materials and Methods*. McGraw-Hill Book Company, Inc., 1959.

1181. Bryant, Sarah Cone, *How to Tell Stories to Children*. Houghton Mifflin Company, 1905.

1182. *The Cana Manual*. Cana Conference of Chicago, 1961.

1183. Cane, Florence, *Artist in Each of Us*. Pantheon Books, Inc., 1951.

1184. Chujoy, Anatole, ed., *The Dance Encyclopedia*. A. S. Barnes & Co., Inc., 1949.

1185. *Church Camping for Junior Highs* (Cooperative Publication Association). The Westminster Press, 1960.

1186. Cole, Natalie, *The Arts in the Classroom*. The John Day Company, 1940.

1187. Cooper, Austin, *Making a Poster*, rev. ed. (How to Do It Series). Studio Publications, 1945.

1188. Curtis, Edmund deForest, *Pottery: Its Craftsmanship and Its Appreciation*. Harper & Brothers, 1940.

1189. Dale, Edgar, *Audio-Visual Methods in Teaching*, rev. ed. The Dryden Press, Inc., 1954.

1190. —— *Content of Motion Pictures*. The Macmillan Company, 1935.

1191. D'Amico, Victor, *Creative Teaching in Art*, rev. ed. International Textbook Company, 1953.

1192. DeBanke, Cecile, *The Art of Choral Speaking*. Walter H. Baker Co., 1937.

1193. DeWitt, Marguerite E., *et al.*, *Practical Methods in Choral Speaking*. Expression Company, 1936.

1194. Dimock, Hedley S., and Trecker, Harleigh B., *The Supervision of Group Work and Recreation*. Association Press, 1949.

1195. Douglass, Paul F., *The Group Workshop Way in the Church.* Association Press, 1956.
1196. Ehrensperger, Harold, *Conscience on Stage.* Abingdon Press, 1947.
1197. Ellsworth, Maud, and Andrews, Michael F., *Growing with Art.* Benj. H. Sanborn & Co., 1951.
1198. Enfield, Gertrude, *Verse Choir Technique.* Expression Company, 1943.
1199. Ensign, John, and Ruth, *Camping Together as Christians.* John Knox Press, 1958.
1200. Ferguson, George, *Signs and Symbols in Christian Art.* Oxford University Press, Inc., 1954.
1201. Fisk, Margaret Palmer, *The Art of the Rhythmic Choir.* Harper & Brothers, 1950.
1202. —— *Look Up and Live.* Macalester Park Publishing Company, 1953.
1203. Fletcher, Helen Jill, and Deckter, Jack, *The Puppet Book.* Greenberg, Publisher, 1947.
1204. Fritz, Dorothy B., *The Use of Symbolism in Christian Education.* The Westminster Press, 1961.
1205. Gale, Elizabeth Wright, *Have You Tried This?* Judson Press, 1960.
1206. Geldhart, E., *Manual of Church Decoration and Symbolism.* Oxford University Press, London, 1899.
1207. Gilman, Wilbur, Aly, Bower, and Reid, Loren D., *The Fundamentals of Speaking.* The Macmillan Company, 1951.
1208. Gray, Lillian, and Reese, Dora, *Teaching Children to Read.* The Ronald Press Company, 1957.
1209. Griswold, Lester Everett, *Handicraft,* 9th ed. Prentice-Hall, Inc., 1953.
1210. Haas, Kenneth B., and Packer, Harry O., *Preparation and Use of Audio-Visual Aids,* 3d ed. Prentice-Hall, Inc., 1955.
1211. Hamlin, Richard, *Hi-Y Today.* Association Press, 1955.
1212. Hamm, Agnes C., *Choral Speaking Technique,* 3d ed. Tower Press, 1951.
1213. Hartman, Gertrude, and Shumaker, Ann, eds., *Creative Expression.* The John Day Company, 1932.
1214. Heltman, Harry J., and Brown, Helen A., eds., *Choral Readings for Teen-Age Worship and Inspiration.* The Westminster Press, 1959.
1215. —— *Choral Reading for Worship and Inspiration.* The Westminster Press, 1954.
1216. —— *Choral Readings from the Bible.* The Westminster Press, 1955.
1217. Hildreth, Gertrude, *Teaching Reading.* Henry Holt & Co., Inc., 1958.
1218. Honore, York, *Pottery Making from the Ground Up.* The Viking Press, Inc., 1941.
1219. Ickis, Marguerite, and Esh, Reba Selden, *The Book of Arts and Crafts.* Association Press, 1954.
1220. Keiser, Armilda Brome, *Here's How and When.* Friendship Press, 1952.
1221. Kelley, Marjorie, and Roukes, Nicholas, *Let's Make a Mural.* Fearon Publishers, n.d.
1222. Keltner, John William, *Group Discussion Processes.* Longmans, Green & Co., Inc., 1957.
1223. Keppie, Elizabeth, *The Technique of Choric Speech.* Expression Company, 1950.
1224. Klein, Alan F., *How to Use Role Playing Effectively.* Association Press, 1959.
1225. —— *Role Playing in Leadership Training and Group Problem Solving.* Association Press, 1956.
1226. Koos, Leonard V., *The Questionnaire in Education.* The Macmillan Company, 1928.

1227. Leachman, E. W., *The Church's Object Lessons*. Morehouse-Gorham Co., Inc., 1931.

1228. Lobingier, Elizabeth Miller, *Activities in Child Education*. The Pilgrim Press, 1950.

1229. Loney, Glenn Meredith, *Briefing and Conference Techniques*. McGraw-Hill Book Company, Inc., 1959.

1230. Mannino, Philip, *ABC's of Visual Aids*. The Dryden Press, Inc., 1955.

1231. McLeish, Minnie, *Teaching Art to Children*. Studio Publications, 1946.

1232. Mitchell, Viola, and Crawford, I. B., *Camp Counseling*, 2d ed. W. B. Saunders Company, 1955.

1233. *More than Fun*. Arts Cooperative Service, 1950.

1234. Murray, Ruth Lovell, *Dance in Elementary Education*. Harper & Brothers, 1953.

1235. Newkirk, Louis V., *Integrated Handwork for Elementary Schools*. Silver Burdett Company, 1940.

1236. Niebuhr, Hulda, *Ventures in Dramatics*. Charles Scribner's Sons, 1935.

1237. Paine, Irma Littler, *Art Aids for Elementary Teaching*. Burgess Publishing Company, 1959.

1238. Parker, Everett C., *et al.*, *The Television-Radio Audience and Religion*. Harper & Brothers, 1955.

1239. Patterson, Doris T., *Your Family Goes Camping*. Abingdon Press, 1962.

1240. Perkins, Lawrence Bradford, *Work Place for Learning*. Reinhold Publishing Corporation, 1957.

1241. Powers, Margaret, *A Book of Little Crafts*. Manual Arts Press, 1942.

1242. Radir, Ruth Anderson, *Modern Dance for the Youth of America*. A. S. Barnes & Co., Inc., 1944.

1243. Rest, Friedrich, *Our Christian Symbols*. Christian Education Press, 1954.

1244. Rice, Rebecca, *Creative Activities*. The Pilgrim Press, 1947.

1245. Roberts, Dorothy M., *Leadership of Teen-Age Groups*. Association Press, 1950.

1246. Robertson, Seonaid M., *Creative Crafts in Education*. Robert Bentley, Inc., 1953.

1247. Rogers, William L., and Vieth, Paul H., *Visual Aids in the Church*. Christian Education Press, 1946.

1248. Rowe, Kenneth Thorpe, *A Theater in Your Head*. Funk & Wagnalls Company, 1960.

1249. Rumpf, Oscar, *The Use of Audio-Visuals in the Church*. Christian Education Press, 1958.

1250. Sands, Lester B., *Audio-Visual Procedures in Teaching*. The Ronald Press Company, 1956.

1251. Sarett, Lew, Foster, William T., and Sarett, A. J., *Basic Principles of Speech*, 3d ed. Houghton Mifflin Company, 1946.

1252. Seay, Homer H., *Church Posters and Publicity: Graphically Presented*. The Wartburg Press, 1946.

1253. Shaver, Erwin L., *The Project Principle in Religious Education*. The University of Chicago Press, 1924.

1254. Shaw, Ruth Faison, *Finger Painting: A Perfect Medium for Self-expression*. Little, Brown and Company, 1934.

1255. ———— *Finger-Painting and How I Do It*. Leland-Brent Publishing Company, 1947.

1256. Shedlock, Marie L., *The Art of the Story-teller*. D. Appleton-Century Company, Inc., 1936.

1257. Sheehy, Emma D., *Children Discover Music and Dance: A Guide for Parents and Teachers*. Henry Holt & Co., Inc., 1959.

1258. Siks, Geraldine Brain, *Creative Dramatics: An Art for Children*. Harper & Brothers, 1958.
1259. Slade, Peter, *Child Drama*. University of London Press, Ltd., London, 1954.
1260. Spottiswoode, Raymond, *A Grammar of the Film*. University of California Press, 1959.
1261. Strauss, Bertram W., and Frances, *New Ways to Better Meetings*. The Viking Press, Inc., 1951.
1262. Thompson, Wayne N., and Fessenden, Seth A., *Basic Experiences in Speech*. Prentice-Hall, Inc., 1951.
1263. Tooze, Ruth, *Storytelling*. Prentice-Hall, Inc., 1959.
1264. Utterback, William E., *Decision Through Discussion: A Manual for Group Leaders*. Rinehart & Co., Inc., 1946.
1265. Van der Smissen, Betty, *The Church Camp Program*. Faith and Life Press, 1961.
1266. Van Treek, C., and Croft, A., *Symbols of the Church*. The Bruce Publishing Company, 1936.
1267. Venable, Mary, *God at Work in His World*. Abingdon Press, 1955.
1268. Walker, Pamela Prince, *Seven Steps to Creative Children's Dramatics*. Hill & Wang, Inc., Publishers, 1957.
1269. Ward, Winifred, *Drama with and for Children*. U. S. Department of Health, Education and Welfare, Office of Education, 1960.
1270. ———— *Playmaking with Children*, 2d ed. Appleton-Century-Crofts, Inc., 1957.
1271. ———— *Stories to Dramatize*. The Children's Theatre Press, 1952.
1272. Webber, Frederick Roth, *Church Symbolism*, 2d rev. ed. J. H. Jansen, 1938.
1273. Weiser, Francis X., *The Easter Book*. Harcourt, Brace and Company, 1954.
1274. ———— *Handbook of Christian Feasts and Customs*. Harcourt, Brace and Company, 1952.
1275. Wilt, Miriam E., *Creativity in the Elementary School*. Appleton-Century-Crofts, Inc., 1959.
1276. Wittich, Walter Arno, and Schuller, Charles Francis, *Audio-Visual Materials, Their Nature and Use*, 2d ed. Harper & Brothers, 1957.
1277. Yoakam, Gerald, *Basal Reading Instruction*. McGraw-Hill Book Company, Inc., 1955.

CONTRIBUTORS

ABBASS, FRANCIS J., assistant to the director of religious education, Roman Catholic Diocese of Antigonish, N.S., Canada.

ADAMS, CHARLES J., Ph.D., assistant director, Institute of Islamic Studies, McGill University.

AKAISHI, TADASHI, Th.D., associate editor, John Knox Press.

ANDERSON, DALE ANTON, psychodrama interne, St. Elizabeth's Hospital, Washington, D.C.

ANDERSON, PHOEBE N., director of Christian education, Hyde Park Baptist Church, Chicago.

ANDREWS, DOROTHY WESTLAKE, writer of children's materials.

ATKINSON, C. HARRY, editor of the journal *Protestant Church Buildings and Equipment.*

BACHMAN, JOHN W., professor of practical theology and director of the audio-visual program, Union Theological Seminary, New York.

BAILEY, ALBERT ERNEST, instructor in Christian education, Princeton Theological Seminary.

BAILEY, DERRICK SHERWIN, Ph.D., rector of Lyndon with Manton, Rutland, England.

BAILEY, FRANCES E., Ph.D., associate professor of religion, Hobart and William Smith Colleges.

BAINTON, ROLAND H., Ph.D., D.D., Titus Street professor of ecclesiastical history, emeritus, Yale University.

BARBIERI, LOUIS A., JR., Dallas Theological Seminary.

BARCLAY, WILLIAM, D.D. senior lecturer in New Testament language and literature and Hellenistic Greek, University of Glasgow.

BARTH, MARKUS, professor of New Testament, Pittsburgh Theological Seminary.

BARUCH, DOROTHY W., Ph.D., psychologist. *Deceased.*

BATTEN, CHARLES E., professor of pastoral theology, Episcopal Theological School.

BAUS, JOSEPH W., Ed.D., pastor, First Presbyterian Church, Evansville, Ind.

BAXTER, EDNA M., professor of education, emeritus, Hartford Seminary Foundation.

BECKER, EDWIN L., Ph.D., associate professor of applied Christianity, Divinity School, Drake University.

BELFORD, LEE A., Ph.D., chairman, Department of Religious Education, New York University.

BELGUM, DAVID, Ph.D., professor of pastoral theology, Northwestern Lutheran Theological Seminary.

BERGEVIN, PAUL E., director, Bureau of Studies in Adult Education and professor of adult education, Indiana University.

BERRETT, WILLIAM E., vice-administrator in charge of institutes of religion and seminaries, Department of Education, Church of Jesus Christ of Latter-day Saints.

BISHOP, LESLEE J., Ed.D., coordinator of secondary education, Livonia, Mich.

BLISS, KATHLEEN, D.D., general secretary, Church of England Board of Education.

BODLEY, DONALD E., Ph.D., rector, Protestant Episcopal Church, Adrian, Mich.

BOE, JOHN M., organist choirmaster, St. Luke's Episcopal Church, Evanston, Ill.

BOGARDUS, LaDONNA, staff member, Board of Education, The Methodist Church.

BOLES, DONALD E., Ph.D., associate professor of government, Iowa State University.

BOLLMAN, OSCAR, minister of Christian education, First Congregational Church, Elmhurst, Ill.; supervisor of Christian education, Elmhurst College.

BONE, MAURICE D., counselor in campsite development, Board of Christian Education, The United Presbyterian Church in the U.S.A.

BOWER, WILLIAM CLAYTON, D.D., LL.D., professor emeritus, Divinity School, University of Chicago.

BOWMAN, CLARICE M., professor of religious education, Bangor Theological Seminary.

BOWMAN, S. LOREN, D.D., executive secretary, Christian Education Commission, General Brotherhood Board, Church of the Brethren.

BRADLEY, DAVID H., administrative assistant, Christian Education Department, African Methodist Episcopal Zion Church; editor-manager, *African Methodist Episcopal Zion Quarterly Review*.

BRADLEY, WILLIAM L., Ph.D., professor of philosophy of religion, Hartford Seminary Foundation.

BRAMELD, THEODORE, Ph.D., professor of educational philosophy, Boston University.

BRANDON, OWEN RUPERT, tutor, librarian, and lecturer in theology and psychology, London College of Divinity.

BRATTGÅRD, KARL ERIK, executive secretary, Sunday School Board, Church of Sweden.

BRAY, ALLEN F., III, chaplain, Culver Military Academy.

BREEN, ROBERT S., Ph.D., associate professor of speech, Northwestern University.

BREMER, J. STEPHEN, acting dean, Lutheran School of Theology (Maywood).

BRICKMAN, CLARENCE W., executive secretary, Unit of Parish and Preparatory Schools, Department of Christian Education, National Council of the Protestant Episcopal Church; executive secretary, Episcopal School Association.

BROMILEY, GEOFFREY W., Ph.D., Litt.D., D.D., associate professor of church history and historical theology, Fuller Theological Seminary.

BRONKHORST, ALEXANDRE J., Th.D., dean, Protestant Theological Faculty, University of Brussels.

BROWNING, ROBERT W., Ph.D., professor of philosophy, Northwestern University.

BROWN, VAL K., director, General Board of Religious Education, Church of England in Australia.

BRUNNER, EMOD L., Ph.D., headmaster, York School.

BRYANT, MARCUS D., Ph.D., assistant professor of applied Christianity, Divinity School, Drake University.

BURKHART, JOHN E., Ph.D., instructor in systematic theology, McCormick Theological Seminary.

BUTLER, ELLIS H., field director of Christian Education, Presbytery of Chicago, The United Presbyterian Church in the U.S.A.

CALKINS, GLADYS G., United Council of Church Women.

CALVERLEY, EDWIN E., Ph.D., professor emeritus of Arabic and Islamics, Hartford Seminary Foundation; sometime co-editor, *The Moslem World*.

CARLISLE, HELEN HAWK, supervisor of church school music, First Methodist Church, Evanston, Ill.

CARLSON, M. DOSIA, instructor in Christian education, Defiance College.

CASE, WILLIAM F., Ed.D., dean and professor of practical theology, and religious education, St. Paul School of Theology, Methodist.

CASSERLEY, J. V. LANGMEAD, Litt.D., professor of apologetics, Seabury-Western Theological Seminary.

CHAKERIAN, CHARLES G., Ph.D., professor and chairman of the Department of Church and Community, McCormick Theological Seminary.

CHAPLIN, DORA P., S.T.D., assistant professor of practical theology, The General Theological Seminary.

CLAASSEN, WILLARD K., executive secretary, Board of Education and Publication, General Conference, Mennonite Church; editor, *Living Faith Graded Sunday School Series*.

CLARK, WALTER HOUSTON, Ph.D., professor of psychology of religion, Andover-Newton Theological School.

CLARKE, JAMES S., D.D., general secretary, Board of Christian Education, The Presbyterian Church in Canada.

CLELAND, JAMES T., Th.D., D.D., James B. Duke professor of preaching in the Divinity School and dean of the chapel, Duke University.

CLEMMONS, ROBERT S., director, Department of Christian Education of Adults, The Methodist Church.

CLYMER, WAYNE K., Ph.D., dean and professor of pastoral theology, Evangelical Theological Seminary.

COCHRANE, ARTHUR C., Ph.D., professor of systematic theology, Theological Seminary, University of Dubuque.

COFFEY, C. DON, professor of Bible and the ministry, Erskine Theological Seminary.

COHEA, WILLIAM H., JR., pastor, Winnetka Presbyterian Church, Winnetka, Ill.

COLEMAN, C. D., D.D., general secretary, General Board of Christian Education, Christian Methodist Episcopal Church.

COODY, BURT E., Th.D., chairman, Departments of Christian Education and Psychology of Religion, The School of Theology, Anderson College.

CRAIG, FLORENCE, director of Christian education, General Synod, Associate Reformed Presbyterian Church.

CROSS, BARBARA M., Ph.D., assistant professor of English, Barnard College.

CULLY, IRIS V., Ph.D., writer in Christian education.

CULLY, KENDIG BRUBAKER, Ph.D., professor of religious education, Seabury-Western Theological Seminary; general editor, Westminster Studies in Christian Communication.

DAVIS, HAROLD, executive secretary, Board of Publication and Christian Education, Cumberland Presbyterian Church.

DAVIS, WILL B., manager, Committees on Publication, The First Church of Christ, Scientist.

DE CATANZARO CARMINO J., Ph.D., Lydia Hibbard professor of Old Testament literature and languages, Seabury-Western Theological Seminary.

DENBEAUX, FRED, professor of Biblical history, literature, and interpretation, Wellesley College.

DENDY, MARSHALL C., D.D., executive secretary, Board of Christian Education, Presbyterian Church in the U.S.

DeWIRE, HARRY A., Ph.D., Cowden professor of education and psychology, United Theological Seminary.

DeWOLF, L. HAROLD, Ph.D., D.D., professor of systematic theology, Boston University School of Theology.

DIRKS, JOHN EDWARD, Ph.D., Stephen Merrell Clement professor of Christian methods, Divinity School, Yale University; editor, *The Christian Scholar*.

DOBBINS, CHARLES G., staff associate, American Council on Education.

DONOHUE, JOHN W., S.J., Ph.D., assistant professor of history and philosophy of education, School of Education, Fordham University.

DREW, ELWELL M., chairman, Board of Christian Education, Advent Christian Church.

DUBA, ARLO D., Th.D., assistant professor of religion, Westminster Choir College.

DUNSTAN, J. LESLIE, Ph.D., professor of Christian world relations, Andover-Newton Theological School.

EAGAN, MILDRED, church library supervisor, Methodist Publishing House.

EASTMAN, FRANCES, Litt.D., editor, *Children's Religion*.

EDDY, G. NORMAN, Ph.D., chairman, Department of Human Relations, Boston University.

EDICK, HELEN M., Ed.D., professor of education, Hartford Seminary Foundation.

EDWARDS, MARY ALICE DOUTY, Ed.D., associate professor of Christian education, Wesley Theological Seminary.

EHRENSPERGER, HAROLD, professor, Boston University.

EHRENSTROM, NILS, Th.D., professor of ecumenics, Boston University School of Theology; honorary professor, Reformed Theological Academy, Budapest; associate editor, *The Ecumenical Review*.

EISENSTEIN, IRA, Ph.D., D.D., president, Jewish Reconstructionist Foundation.

ELLARD, GERALD B., S.J., Ph.D., professor of liturgical theology, School of Divinity, St. Louis University.

ELLZEY, W. CLARK, head of Department of Marriage and Family, Stephens College.

ELMEN, PAUL H., Ph.D., professor of Christian ethics and moral theology, Seabury-Western Theological Seminary.

ERNSBERGER, DAVID J., pastor, The Greenhills Community Church (United Presbyterian), Cincinnati.

EVENSON, C. RICHARD, Ed.D., executive director, Department of Parish Education, The American Lutheran Church.

FALLAW, WESNER, Ed.D., Howard professor of religious education, Andover-Newton Theological School.

FENN, WILLIAM P., Ph.D., general secretary, United Board for Christian Higher Education in Asia.

FERGUSON, META RUTH, associate secretary, Board on Christian Education, The Five Years Meeting of Friends.

FERRÉ, NELS F. S., Ph.D., D.D., Abbot professor of Christian theology, Andover-Newton Theological School.

FIDLER, FRANK P., D.D., associate secretary, Board of Christian Education, United Church of Canada.

FINEGAN, JACK, LL.D., professor of New Testament, Pacific School of Religion.

FINLAY, PAUL R., Ph.D., associate professor of religious education, Bethel College (Minn.).

FISCHER, ROBERT H., Ph.D., professor of historical theology, Lutheran School of Theology (Maywood).

FISHER, VIRGINIA S., lecturer in Christian education, Lancaster Theological Seminary.

FLOROVSKY, GEORGES, D.D., Th.D., S.T.D., professor of Eastern church history, Divinity School, Harvard University.

FORD, RICHARD S., Ph.D., associate professor of Christian education, Garrett Theological Seminary.

FORD, WILFORD F., director of Christian education, The Methodist Church of New Zealand.

FORELL, GEORGE W., Th.D., professor of Protestant theology, School of Religion, State University of Iowa.

FORSYTH, DAVID I., D.D., secretary, Board of Christian Education, United Church of Canada.

FOSTER, VIRGIL E., D.D., editor, *International Journal of Religious Education.*

FRAKES, MARGARET, associate editor, *The Christian Century.*

FRIEDRICH, JAMES K., president, Cathedral Films.

FRITZ, DOROTHY B., staff member, retired, Board of Christian Education, The United Presbyterian Church in the U.S.A.

FULLER, REGINALD H., S.T.D., professor of New Testament literature and languages, Seabury-Western Theological Seminary.

GABLE, LEE J., D.D., dean and professor of Christian education, Lancaster Theological Seminary.

GAEBELEIN, FRANK E., Litt.D., D.D., LL.D., headmaster emeritus, The Stony Brook School; co-editor, *Christianity Today.*

GARNER, LELA ANNE, chairman, United Christian Youth Movement.

GARRETT, CYRIL D., Ed.D., executive vice-president and dean, Eastern Baptist College.

GIBBONS, RAY, D.D., executive director, Council for Christian Social Action, United Church of Christ.

GILBERT, W. KENT, Ed.D., director, Long-range Program of the Lutheran Boards of Parish Education; editor, *Lutheran Weekday Church School Series.*

GLEASON, JOHN M., national director, Boys Clubs of America.

GOODYKOONTZ, HARRY G., Th.D., professor of Christian education, Louisville Presbyterian Theological Seminary.

GRAHAM, HOLT H., Ph.D., S.T.D., professor of New Testament, The Protestant Episcopal Theological Seminary in Virginia.

GRANT, ROBERT M., Th.D., professor of New Testament, Divinity School, University of Chicago.

GRIMES, HOWARD, Ph.D., professor of Christian education, Perkins School of Theology, Southern Methodist University.

GROENFELDT, JOHN S., D.D., general secretary, Board of Christian Education and Evangelism, Moravian Church, Northern Province; editor, *The Moravian.*

GROFF, WARREN F., Ph.D., dean, Bethany Biblical Seminary.

HALLOWELL, MARGUERITE, formerly field visitor to First-day schools, Philadelphia Yearly Meeting of Friends.

HAM, HOWARD MILLER, Th.D., Ph.D., Bishop W. Earl Ledden professor of religious education, Syracuse University.

HAMMELSBECK, OSKAR, D.D., professor of education, Pedagogical Institute, Wuppertal, Germany.

HAMMILL, RICHARD, Ph.D., associate secretary, Department of Education, General Conference of Seventh-day Adventists.

HANDY, ROBERT T., Ph.D., professor of church history and director of studies, Union Theological Seminary, New York.

HANSEN, CARL A., D.D., executive secretary and minister, Congregational Conference of Minnesota.

HARBOUR, RICHARD L., D.D., executive secretary, Youth Division, Department of Christian Education, National Council of the Protestant Episcopal Church.

HARPER, A. F., Ph.D., D.D., secretary, Board of Education, Church of the Nazarene.

HAUG, CURTIS W., treasurer and acting program director, The Chautauqua Institution.

HAVIGHURST, ROBERT J., Ph.D., professor of education, University of Chicago.

HEATON, C. ADRIAN, Th.D., D.D., president, California Baptist Theological Seminary.

HEDLEY, GEORGE, Th.D, D.D., chaplain, Mills College.

HEIM, RALPH DANIEL, Ph.D., D.D., professor of Christian education and English Bible, Gettysburg Theological Seminary.

HEITZMAN, MILTON A., director of educational evangelism, National Council of the Churches of Christ in the U.S.A.

HELPS, FRED J., editor, Baptist Publications Committee of Canada.

HENDERLITE, RACHEL, Ph.D., L.H.D., director of curriculum development, Board of Christian Education, Presbyterian Church in the U.S.

HENDERSON, W. CLINTON, director, Division of Youth Work and Campus Christian Life, Department of Religious Education, Missouri Association of Christian Churches.

HENKEL, O. V., secretary, Raad voor de zaken van Kerk en School, Nederlandse Hervormde Kerk, Den Haag.

HENRY, CARL F. H., Ph.D., Th.D., editor, *Christianity Today*.

HILL, WILLIAM J., O.P., S.T.D., professor of dogmatic theology, Dominican House of Studies.

HILTNER, SEWARD, Ph.D., D.D., professor of theology and personality, Princeton Theological Seminary.

HOAG, VICTOR, D.D., writer in Christian education.

HOLCOMB, WALTER L., Ed.D., associate professor of religious education, Boston University School of Theology.

HOLT, D. ALLISON, associate executive secretary, Department of Christian Education, United Christian Missionary Society (Disciples of Christ).

HOLTER, DON W., Ph.D., D.D., president, St. Paul School of Theology (Methodist).

HOMRIGHAUSEN, ELMER G., Th.D., D.D., dean and Charles R. Erdman professor of pastoral theology, Princeton Theological Seminary; contributing editor, *Theology Today*.

HORDERN, WILLIAM, Th.D., professor of systematic theology, Garrett Theological Seminary.

HOURTICQ, DENISE, secretary, La Société des Écoles du Dimanche, Paris.

HOWARD, JOHN R., LL.D., president, Lewis and Clark College.

HOWE, REUEL L., S.T.D, D.D., director, Institute for Advanced Pastoral Studies.

HUBBARD, FRANK W., staff associate, National Education Association of the U.S.

HULME, WILLIAM E., Ph.D., professor of pastoral theology and counseling, Wartburg Theological Seminary.

HUMMEL, CHARLES E., field director, Inter-Varsity Christian Fellowship, Chicago.

HUNT, GEORGE LAIRD, D.D., pastor, Fanwood Presbyterian Church, Fanwood, N. J.

HUNTER, DAVID R., Ed.D., D.D., director, Department of Christian Education, National Council of the Protestant Episcopal Church.

HUNTER, EDITH F., writer in Christian education.

IRVIN, MARGARET A. J., editor of vacation school material, Board of Parish Education, Lutheran Church in America.

IRWIN, PAUL B., Ed.D., professor of religious education, Southern California School of Theology.

IVERSON, ALBERT E., D.D., director of Protestant relationships, National Council, Boy Scouts of America.

JAARSMA, CORNELIUS, Ph.D., professor of education, Calvin College.

JACKSON, GORDON E., Ph.D., D.D., dean and professor of pastoral care and counseling, Pittsburgh Theological Seminary.

JENSEN, EJNAR, general secretary, I.M. Børnegudst-jeneste, Roskilde, Denmark.

JEWELL, DAVID W., Ed.D., director of the Schauffler Division of Christian Education and associate professor of Christian education, Graduate School of Theology, Oberlin College.

JOHNSON, CHARLES H., Ed.D., professor of Christian education, Perkins School of Theology, Southern Methodist University.

JONES, TREVOR E., executive secretary, Department of Christian Education, Anglican Church of Canada.

JORDAN, G. RAY, Ph.D., assistant professor, School of Religion, University of Southern California.

JUNG, EMANUEL, pastor, Reformed Church, Zurich.

KELLEY, ALDEN D., S.T.D., professor of Christian apologetics and ethics, Bexley Hall, Kenyon College.

KEMP, CHARLES F., D.D., Distinguished professor of practical ministries, Brite College of the Bible, Texas Christian University.

KENNEDY, WILLIAM BEAN, Ph.D., Robert and Lucy Reynolds Critz associate professor of Christian education, Union Theological Seminary (Richmond).

KHOOBYAR, HELEN, Ed.R.D., associate professor of religious education, Hartford Seminary Foundation.

KING, ALBION ROY, Ph.D., professor of philosophy, Cornell College.

KITAGAWA, JOSEPH M., Ph.D., associate professor of history of religions, Divinity School, University of Chicago.

KLEMME, HUBER F., D.D., associate director, Council for Christian Social Action, United Church of Christ.

KLIPHARDT, DONALD J., sometime director of research and utilization, Department of Audio-Visual and Broadcast Education, National Council of the Churches of Christ in the U.S.A. *Deceased.*

KNAPP, FORREST L., Ph.D., general secretary, Massachusetts Council of Churches.

KNELLER, GEORGE F., Ph.D., professor of education, University of California at Los Angeles.

KNOFF, GERALD E., Ph.D., L.H.D., executive secretary, Division of Christian Education, National Council of the Churches of Christ in the U.S.A.

KNORR, NATHAN H., president, Watchtower Bible and Tract Society of Pennsylvania.

KNOTT, JOHN C., director, Marriage and Family Apostolate, Roman Catholic Archdiocese of Hartford.

KNOWLES, MALCOLM S., Ph.D., associate professor of education, Boston University.

KOENIG, ROBERT E., Ph.D., director of curriculum, Board of Christian Education and Publication, United Church of Christ.

KOSE, ALETHEA S., sometime professor of Christian education, Baptist Missionary Training School.

KOULUMZIN, SOPHIE, executive secretary, Orthodox Christian Education Commission of the Standing Conference of Canonical Orthodox Bishops in the Americas; lecturer in religious education, St. Vladimir's Theological Seminary.

LABERGE, PAUL CLAUDIUS, teacher, Mater Christi High School, Long Island City, N.Y.

LAEUCHLI, SAMUEL, Th.D., professor of history of Christianity, Garrett Theological Seminary.

LANGFORD, NORMAN F., D.D., editor in chief, General Division of Parish Education, Board of Christian Education, The United Presbyterian Church in the U.S.A.

LARGEN, VERA, registrar, Garrett Theological Seminary.

LAURILA, HELEN M., Admissions Department, Hofstra College.

LAYMON, CHARLES M., Th.D., D.D., chairman, Department of Religion, and professor of religion, Florida Southern College.

LeBAR, LOIS E., Ph.D., chairman, Graduate Department of Christian Education, Wheaton College (Ill.).

LeBAR, MARY E., Ph.D., professor of Christian education, Wheaton College (Ill.).

LEE, J. WILLIAM, Ph.D., associate professor of philosophy of religion, Graduate School of Theology, Oberlin College.

LeFEVRE, PERRY, Ph.D., dean of faculty and professor of constructive theology, Chicago Theological Seminary.

LEIFFER, MURRAY H., Ph.D., professor of sociology and social ethics, and director of the Bureau of Social and Religious Research, Garrett Theological Seminary.

LEONARD, DONALD L., Ph.D., executive editor, Board of Christian Education, The United Presbyterian Church in the U.S.A.

LESLIE, ELIZABETH W., director of community relations and associate director, National Public Relations Division, Camp Fire Girls, Inc.

LIBBEY, SCOTT, staff member, Department of Educational Program, Division of Christian Education, United Church of Christ.

LIGON, ERNEST M., Ph.D., LL.D., professor of psychology, Union College; director, Character Research Project.

LIMBERT, PAUL M., Ph.D., LL.D., L.H.D., D.D., sometime general secretary, World Alliance of Young Men's Christian Associations.

LINDBERG, PAUL M., Ph.D., professor of Christian education and pastoral care, Augustana Theological Seminary.

LINDHORST, FRANK A., D.D., professor of Bible and religious education, emeritus, University of the Pacific.

LISTER, RUTH, Ed.D., assistant professor of religious education, Graduate School of Theology, Oberlin College.

LITTLE, SARA, Ph.D., professor of Christian education, Presbyterian School of Christian Education.

LOBB, MARGARET E., associate professor of Christian education, Pacific School of Religion.

LOBINGIER, ELIZABETH MILLER, instructor in painting, Division of Education, Boston Museum of Fine Arts.

LOBINGIER, JOHN LESLIE, D.D., minister emeritus of Christian education, Massachusetts Congregational Christian Conference.

LOOMIS, EARL A., JR., M.D., professor and director of the program in psychiatry and religion, Union Theological Seminary (New York); chief, Division of Child Psychiatry, St. Luke's Hospital, New York.

LOWIE, LUELLA COLE, Ph.D., psychologist and historian of education.

LUDY, ELEANOR L., dean of women and associate professor of Christian education, National College (Mo.).

MAREK, DANIEL J., president, Synodical Committee, Unity of the Brethren.

MARIE CHARLES DOLAN, SISTER, M.H.S.H., conductor of teacher-training courses, Roman Catholic Archdiocese of Detroit.

MARTY, MARTIN E., Ph.D., associate editor, *The Christian Century.*

MASON, MARY ELIZABETH, director of children's leadership and field program, United Christian Missionary Society (Disciples of Christ).

MASTERSON, REGINALD, O. P., superior and rector, St. Rose Priory, Dubuque, Iowa.

MAVES, PAUL B., Ph.D., professor of religious education, Theological School, Drew University.

McARTHUR, HARVEY K., Ph.D., Hosmer professor of New Testament, Hartford Seminary Foundation.

McCORT, ELIZABETH, assistant professor of Christian education, The Theological Seminary, University of Dubuque.

McDOWELL, ELIZABETH TIBBALS, writer of children's books.

McKIBBEN, FRANK M., Ph.D., professor emeritus of religious education, Garrett Theological Seminary; minister of education, Central Methodist Church, Phoenix, Ariz.

McKINLEY, JOHN, Ed.D., assistant professor of adult education, Indiana University.

McNEIL, JESSE JAI, Ed.D., director of publications, Sunday School Publishing Board, National Baptist Convention, U.S.A.

McNEILL, JOHN T., Ph.D., D.D., LL.D., professor emeritus of church history, Union Theological Seminary (New York).

McQUEEN, FRED E., Litt.D., editor of adult material, United Church of Christ.

MELCONIAN, VARTAN D., Ph.D., D.D., professor of practical theology and director of field education, McCormick Theological Seminary.

MESSERLI, JONATHAN, coordinator, International Teacher Development Program, Harvard University.

METZE, MABEL, executive director, Educational Administration Section, Department of Christian Education, United Christian Missionary Society (Disciples of Christ).

MICHAELIDES, GEORGE P., Ph.D., sometime director, Schauffler Division of Christian Education, Graduate School of Theology, Oberlin College. *Deceased.*

MILLEN, NINA L., editor and director, Department of Children's Work, Commission on Missionary Education, National Council of the Churches of Christ in the U.S.A.

MILLER, ALLEN O., Ph.D., professor of systematic theology and philosophy, Eden Theological Seminary.

MILLER, ARTHUR L., Ph.D., executive secretary, Board of Parish Education, Lutheran Church—Missouri Synod.

MILLER, BONNIE, director of Christian education, Covenant Methodist Church, Evanston, Ill.

MILLER, DONALD G., Ph.D., president, Pittsburgh Theological Seminary.

MILLER, HARRIET, assistant professor of Christian education, United Theological Seminary.

MILLER, HASKELL M., Ph.D., professor of sociology and social ethics, Wesley Theological Seminary.

MILLER, JAMES BLAIR, Ed.D., professor of Christian education, Christian Theological Seminary.

MILLER, RANDOLPH CRUMP, Ph.D., D.D., S.T.D., professor of Christian education on the Luther A. Weigle Fund, Divinity School, Yale University; editor, *Religious Education.*

MILLER, T. FRANKLIN, D.D., executive secretary, Board of Christian Education, Church of God; editor, *Christian Leadership.*

MILNER, BENJAMIN CHARLES, JR., instructor in Biblical history, Wellesley College.

MOORE, JESSIE ELEANOR, sometime member of the editorial department, Board of Education, The Methodist Church.

MOREAU, JULES LAURENCE, Ph.D., professor of church history, Seabury-Western Theological School.

MORSCH, VIVIAN SHARP, director of Christian education, Westminster United Presbyterian Church, Piqua, Ohio.

MORTON, MARGARET M., president, Cambridge (Mass.) Council of Churches.

MORTON, NELLE K., associate professor of Christian education, Theological School, Drew University.

MUEDEKING, GEORGE H., D.D., associate professor of functional theology, Pacific Lutheran Theological Seminary.

MULDER, BERNARD J., D.D., executive secretary, Board of Education, Reformed Church in America.

MUNRO, HARRY C., L.H.D., sometime professor of religious education, Brite College of the Bible, Texas Christian University. *Deceased.*

MUNSON, CHARLES R., associate professor of practical theology, Ashland Theological Seminary.

MYERS, A. J. WILLIAM, Ph.D., professor emeritus of religious education, Hartford Seminary Foundation.

NELSON, C. ELLIS, Ph.D., D.D., Skinner and McAlpin professor of practical theology, Union Theological Seminary (New York).

NELSON, JOHN OLIVER, Ph.D., professor of Christian vocation, Divinity School, Yale University.

NELSON, J. ROBERT, Th.D., L.H.D., professor of theology, Graduate School of Theology, Oberlin College.

NEWHALL, JANNETTE E., Ph.D., professor of research methods and librarian, Boston University School of Theology.

NISSIOTIS, NIKOS A., D.D., assistant director, The Ecumenical Institute, Celigny, Switzerland.

NORTH, BARBARA A., director of Christian education, Presbyterian Church, Tenafly, N. J.

NYCE, GERTRUDE S., associate secretary, Department of Ecumenical Personnel, Commission on Ecumenical Mission and Relations, The United Presbyterian Church in the U.S.A.

PAAS, MAURINE V., assistant professor of Christian education, Carroll College.

PARK, JOE E., Ph.D., professor of education, Northwestern University.

PARKER, EVERETT C., D.D., director, Office of Communication, United Church of Christ.

PAUL, ROBERT S., Ph.D., Waldo professor of church history, Hartford Seminary Foundation; editor, *The Hartford Quarterly.*

PEABODY, GEORGE L., coordinator of field services, Department of Christian Education, National Council of the Protestant Episcopal Church.

PEARSE, MAX M., JR., Ed.R.D., associate professor of Christian education, Church Divinity School of the Pacific.

PEARSON, ROY, D.D., dean, Andover-Newton Theological School.

PEREGRINE, RUBY, associate professor of religion, Pacific University.

PERRY, EDMUND, Ph.D., associate professor of history of religions, Northwestern University.

PERSON, PETER P., Ph.D., professor emeritus of psychology and religious education, North Park College.

PIDGEON, HELEN C., publicity representative, Girl Scouts of the U.S.A.

POWELL, WILFRED E., Ph.D., professor of religious education, Graduate Seminary, Phillips University.

POWERS, EDWARD A., executive secretary, Division of Christian Education, Congregational Christian Churches (United Church of Christ).

PRICE, PAUL, D.D., director of administration and leadership (church schools and camps), Evangelical United Brethren Church.

PRIESTER, GERTRUDE, writer of curriculum materials.

PRIESTER, MARCUS J., D.D., professor of Christian education, McCormick Theological Seminary.

RAMPLEY, LESTER C., Th.D., Alexander Hopkins professor of religious education, The College of the Bible (Ky.).

RAYLE, FRED D., D.D., president, Board of Education, General Eldership of Churches of God in North America.

REES, RUSSELL E., executive secretary, Board of Christian Education, Five Years Meeting of Friends.

REEVES, J. DON, Ed.D., assistant professor of religious education, Oklahoma Baptist University.

REEVES, MARJORIE, Ph.D., vice-principal, St. Anne's College, Oxford University.

REST, FRIEDRICH, pastor, St. Paul's United Church of Christ, Evansville, Ind.

RITTER, RICHARD H., pastor emeritus, Wailuku Union Church, Hawaii.

RODENMAYER, BETSY M., liaison officer with the Women of the Church, Department of Ministries, National Council of the Protestant Episcopal Church.

ROOD, WAYNE R., Th.D., professor of Christian education, Pacific School of Religion.

ROORBACH, ROSEMARY K., associate editor of children's publications, The Methodist Church.

ROSE, CAROL C., assistant to the editor in chief of publications, Board of Christian Education, The United Presbyterian Church in the U.S.A.

ROSENQVIST, ARNE, director, Lutherinstituttet Haga, Hoplake, Finland.

ROSSER, PEARL, D.D., staff member, American Baptist Convention.

ROTH, ROBERT PAUL, Ph.D., D.D., professor of systematic theology, Northwestern Lutheran Theological Seminary.

ROUTH, PORTER, LL.D., executive secretary-treasurer, Executive Committee, Southern Baptist Convention.

RUMPF, OSCAR J., professor of Christian education and practical theology, Eden Theological Seminary.

SAHLIN, CLARENCE J., Th.D., associate professor of Christian education, Northern Baptist Theological Seminary.

SANDT, ELEANOR E., editor of curriculum for small church schools, Department of Christian Education, National Council of the Protestant Episcopal Church.

SAUNDERS, ERNEST W., Ph.D., professor of New Testament interpretation, Garrett Theological Seminary.

SCHULZ, FLORENCE, nursery teacher, Winnetka (Ill.) Public Schools.

SCOTFORD, JOHN R., D.D., formerly editor, *Advance* (Congregational Christian Churches).

SCOTT, NATHAN A., JR., Ph.D., associate professor of theology and literature, Divinity School, University of Chicago.

SEIDENSPINNER, CLARENCE, D.D., pastor, First Methodist Church, Racine, Wis.

SEIM, SVERRE, secretary general, Norsk Søndagsckoleforbund, Oslo, Norway.

SEITZ, WILLIAM C., S.T.D., professor of homiletics, religious education, and parish administration, Bexley Hall, Kenyon College.

SELTZER, GEORGE R., Ph.D., professor of liturgics and church art, Lutheran Theological Seminary at Philadelphia; chairman of editorial committee, *Service Book and Hymnal of the Lutheran Church in America, Altar Service Book, The Epistles and Gospels.*

SHELLY, PAUL R., Ph.D., professor of Bible and Christian education, Bluffton College (Ohio).

SHELTON, GENTRY A., Ed.D., professor of religious education, Brite College of the Bible, Texas Christian University.

SHEPHERD, MASSEY H., JR., Ph.D., S.T.D., D.D., Litt.D., professor of liturgics, Church Divinity School of the Pacific.

SHEPPARD, KATHLEEN A. N., head deaconess, Diocese of Melbourne, Church of England in Australia, and senior divinity mistress, Firbank Church of England Girls' Grammar School, Melbourne.

SHINN, ROGER L., Ph.D., William E. Dodge professor of applied Christianity, Union Theological Seminary (New York).

SHIPLEY, DAVID C., Ph.D., professor of theology, Methodist Theological School in Ohio.

SHOCKLEY, GRANT S., Ed.D., professor of Christian education, Garrett Theological Seminary.

SIBLEY, LEONARD A., JR., secretary for research, Board of Parish Education, Lutheran Church in America.

SIE, GEORGIANNA WEI, Ph.D., associate professor of psychology and director of preschool education, Hartford Seminary Foundation.

SILBER, KATE, Ph.D., lecturer in German, University of Edinburgh.

SITTLER, JOSEPH, D.D., L.H.D., LL.D., professor of theology, Divinity School, University of Chicago.

SLADDEN, JULIET E., sometime general secretary, Institute of Christian Education at Home and Overseas, London.

SLATER, ROBERT H. L., Ph.D., D.D., professor of world religions, Divinity School, Harvard University.

SLOYAN, GERARD S., Ph.D., professor of religious education, The Catholic University of America.

SLUSSER, GERALD H., Ph.D., assistant professor of religious education, Hartford Seminary Foundation.

SMITH, FRANK MORGAN, assistant professor of pastoral theology, Bexley Hall, Kenyon College.

SMITH, JAMES W. D., D.D., principal lecturer in religious education, Jordanhill College of Education, Glasgow.

SMITH, ROCKWELL C., Ph.D., D.D., professor of rural church administration and sociology, Garrett Theological Seminary.

SMUCKER, DONOVAN E., Ph.D., chaplain and associate professor of religion, Lake Forest College.

SNYDER, ROSS, professor of religious education, Chicago Theological Seminary.

SPAULDING, HELEN F., director of women's work, United Christian Missionary Society (Disciples of Christ).

SPINKA, MATTHEW, Ph.D., TH.D., D.D., Waldo professor of church history, emeritus, Hartford Seminary Foundation.

SPOERL, DOROTHY TILDEN, Ph.D., director, editorial department, Division of Education, Council of Liberal Churches.

STEINHAUS, O. OTTO, pastor, Immanuel Methodist Church, Canton, Mo.

STEPHENS, EVERETT W., Ed.D., dean of students, Babson Institute of Business Administration.

STEWART, DONALD G., Ed.D., professor of Christian education, San Francisco Theological Seminary.

STOCKLEY, CHRISTINE P., minister to students, United Campus Christian Fellowship, University of New Mexico.

STOKES, OLIVIA PEARL, Ed.D., director, Department of Religious Education, Massachusetts Council of Churches.

STOWE, EVERETT M., Ed.D., associate secretary, World Council of Christian Education and Sunday School Association; editor, *World Christian Education.*

STRANG, RUTH, Ph.D., professor emeritus of education, Teachers College, Columbia University; professor of education and director, Reading Development Center, University of Arizona.

STRENG, WILLIAM D., D.D., professor of Christian education, Wartburg Theological Seminary.

STRONG, KATHERINE S., secretary for research and documentation, World Young Women's Christian Association.

SWAIM, J. CARTER, Ph.D., executive director, Department of English Bible, Division of Christian Education, National Council of the Churches of Christ in the U.S.A.

SWEET, HERMAN J., D.D., field director, Board of Christian Education, Synod of California, Southern Area, The United Presbyterian Church in the U.S.A.

SYDNOR, WILLIAM, rector, Christ Church (Protestant Episcopal), Alexandria, Va.

TANI, HENRY N., LL.D., director of youth work, Board of Christian Education and Publication, United Church of Christ.

TAYLOR, GEORGE OLIVER, D.D., executive secretary, Department of Christian Education, United Christian Missionary Society (Disciples of Christ).

TAYLOR, MARVIN J., Ph.D., associate professor of religious education, St. Paul School of Theology (Methodist).

THEMAN, VIOLA, Ph.D., professor of education, Northwestern University.

THOMPSON, TYLER, Ph.D., professor of philosophy of religion, Garrett Theological Seminary.

THORNTON, W. RANDOLPH, executive director, Department of Administration and Leadership, National Council of the Churches of Christ in the U.S.A.

THROCKMORTON, BURTON H., JR., Ph.D., Hayes professor of New Testament language and literature, Bangor Theological Seminary.

THUT, I. N., Ph.D., professor of education, University of Connecticut.

TOBEY, KATHRENE McLANDRESS, writer of kindergarten materials.

TOOGOOD, MILDRED, librarian, LaGrange (Ill.) Public Library.

TORRANCE, THOMAS F., Th.D., D.D., professor of Christian dogmatics, University of Edinburgh.

TOWER, GRACE STORMS, visiting associate professor of Christian education, Scarritt College.

TRENT, ROBBIE, Litt.D., editor, retired, of children's Sunday school publications, Sunday School Board, Southern Baptist Convention.

ULICH, ROBERT, Ph.D., Litt.D., James Bryant Conant professor of education, emeritus, Harvard University.

VANDENBERGE, PETER N., librarian and lecturer in Christian education, New Brunswick Theological Seminary.

VERNON, WALTER N., administrative associate and editor of general publications, Board of Education, The Methodist Church.

VIETH, PAUL H., Ph.D., L.H.D., Horace Bushnell professor of Christian nurture, Divinity School, Yale University.

VILAKAZI, ABSOLOM, Ph.D., assistant professor of anthropology and African studies, Hartford Seminary Foundation.

VINAY, T. VALDO, D.D., professor of church history and practical theology, Facoltà Valdese di Teologia, Rome.

VOEHRINGER, ERICH T., Ph.D., professor of Christian education, Lutheran Theological Seminary at Philadelphia.

VOELCKER, FRANCIS W., rector, All Saints Church (Protestant Episcopal), Brooklyn, N.Y.

VOSBURGH, ADAH, writer of curriculum materials.

WALZER, WILLIAM C., Ph.D., associate general director, Commission on Missionary Education, National Council of the Churches of Christ in the U.S.A.

WARD, WINIFRED, L.H.D., assistant professor emeritus, School of Speech, Northwestern University.

WATSON, PHILIP S., D.D., Rall professor of systematic theology, Garrett Theological Seminary.

WEDEL, CYNTHIA C., Ph.D., associate general secretary, National Council of the Churches of Christ in the U.S.A.

WEDEL, THEODORE O., Ph.D., D.D., S.T.D., L.H.D., D.C.L., warden emeritus, College of Preachers (Protestant Episcopal), Washington.

WELCH, CLAUDE, Ph.D., Berg professor of religious thought, and chairman, Department of Religious Thought, University of Pennsylvania.

WELKER, EDITH FRANCES, director of Christian education, First Baptist Church, Middletown, Conn.

WENGER, EUGENE B., assistant professor of Christian education, Evangelical Theological Seminary.

WEST, EDWARD N., D.D., Litt.D., Th.D., canon sacrist, Cathedral Church of St. John the Divine (Protestant Episcopal), New York.

WESTERBERG, WESLEY M., D.D., president Kendall College.

WHITAKER, ROBERT H., Ph.D., dean and director of studies, School of Theology, Protestant Episcopal Diocese of Michigan.

WHITE, ANDREW, executive secretary, Division of Christian Education, African Methodist Episcopal Church; editor, *The Journal of Religious Education of the African Methodist Episcopal Church.*

WILLKENS, WILLIAM H. R., professor of Christian education, Crozer Theological Seminary.

WINTER, GIBSON, Ph.D., associate professor of Christian ethics, Divinity School, University of Chicago.

WOLCOTT, CAROLYN MULLER, instructor in religious education, Scarritt College.

WOLCOTT, DOROTHEA K., Ph.D., professor of Christian education and elementary education, Findlay College.

WOLF, H. H., Th.D., director, The Ecumenical Institute, Celigny, Switzerland.

WONDERS, ALICE W., Ed.D., professor of religion, Texas Wesleyan College.

WORLEY, ROBERT C., instructor in Christian education, McCormick Theological Seminary.

WORTH, HOWARD A., Ed.R.D., associate professor of religious education, Iliff School of Theology.

WYCKOFF, D. CAMPBELL, Ph.D., Thomas W. Synnott professor of Christian education, Princeton Theological Seminary.

WYNN, JOHN CHARLES, D.D., associate professor of Christian education, Colgate Rochester Theological Seminary.

WYSHAM, WILLIAM N., D.D., consultant, Near East Christian Council.

WYTON, ALEC, headmaster, Cathedral Choir School and organist choirmaster, Cathedral Church of St. John the Divine (Protestant Episcopal), New York; associate professor, School of Sacred Music, Union Theological Seminary (New York).

YASUMURA, SABROW, D.D., administrative staff member, Inter-Board Field Committee for Christian Work in Japan and Church School Department, National Christian Council in Japan.

ZIEGLER, JESSE H., Ph.D., associate director, American Association of Theological Schools.